Frank Sinc
4 Pump corn,
0207 842 5555

CW01572991

Construction All Risks Insurance

CONSTRUCTION ALL RISKS INSURANCE

Second Edition

SWEET & MAXWELL   THOMSON REUTERS

First Edition 2014
Second Edition 2016

Published in 2016 by Thomson Reuters (Professional) UK Limited trading as
Sweet & Maxwell, Friars House, 160 Blackfriars Road, London, SE1 8EZ
(Registered in England & Wales, Company No.1679046.
Registered Office and address for service: 2nd floor, 1 Mark Square, Leonard
Street, London, EC2A 4EG.).

For further information on our products and services, visit *http://
www.sweetandmaxwell.co.uk*.

Computerset by Sweet & Maxwell.
Printed and bound by CPI Group (UK) Ltd, Croydon, CR0 4YY.
No natural forests were destroyed to make this product: only farmed timber
was used and replanted.
A CIP catalogue record for this book is available from the British Library.

ISBN: 978-0-414-05653-4

AUTHOR'S ACKNOWLEDGMENTS

Contributors

Ebony Alleyne
LLB (Hons)

Thomas Bell
MA (Oxon)

John Beresford
BA (Oxon)

Emily Betts
BSc (Hons), LLM

Brenna Conroy
BA (Oxon)

Sri Carmichael
BSc (Hons)

Jack Dillon
BA (Hons)

Sarah McCann
LLB (Hons), MCIArb

Colm Nugent
BA

Catherine Piercy
BA (Oxon) (Hons), LLM

David Pliener
BSc (Hons)

Charles Raffin
MA (Oxon), MCIArb

Michael Tetstall
LLB (Hons)

Charles Thompson
BA (Oxon)

Jeffrey Thomson
BCom (McGill), LLB
(London),
Maîtrise en droit privé
(Paris I)
Michael Wheater
LLB (Hons), LLM,
MSc, MCIArb
Helena White
BA (Hons) (Oxon)

Principal Researchers

Keifer Conroy
BA (Oxon)

Jasbinder Ghag
LLB (Hons), LLM

FOREWORD TO THE SECOND EDITION

When my colleague Mr Justice Stuart-Smith wrote the Foreword to the first edition of this remarkable book he predicted that it would find its way onto the shelves of all those who have a serious interest in Contractors Risks and insurance generally. His prediction was correct. The first edition has proved to be invaluable, not only for readers in this jurisdiction but also in other parts of the world, particularly the Pacific rim. I endorse everything he said in that foreword.

In this second edition Paul Reed QC has added a valuable chapter on the Insurance Act 2015, which contains a careful and thorough summary of its provisions, together with a helpful analysis of some of the corresponding provisions in the insurance legislation of Australia and New Zealand. The Act has at last replaced the draconian remedy of avoidance for non-disclosure with more proportionate remedies based on the consequences for the insurer and the nature of the insured's conduct. Since the Act came into force two months ago this chapter could not be more timely—and will, I am sure, prove to be of enormous assistance to practitioners who have to advise on its provisions.

This second edition is a worthy successor to the first edition and will be an essential source of reference for those concerned with the insurance of contractors' risks.

The Hon Mr Justice Edwards-Stuart
Judge in Charge, the Technology and Construction Court, 2013–2016
The Rolls Building, London EC4
October 2016

PREFACE TO THE SECOND EDITION

The first edition of *Construction All Risks Insurance* was published in March 2014. Since then there have been substantial changes in the law, including the 2015 Insurance Act which came into force on 12 August 2016. The Act required a new chapter and this permitted the text to be updated. It also allowed a new section to be added on the Wellington Syndicate 2020's Offshore Construction Project Policy ("WELCAR"). The addition of WELCAR to the second edition of the book is important, especially for those who work mainly in maritime construction who need to understand the special risks involved in undertaking marine construction and the specialised nature of CAR insurance available for this type of work.

As ever I would like to express my thanks to those who have provided invaluable assistance in the preparation of the second edition, in particular to my colleagues in chambers and researchers. When I wrote the preface to the first edition I omitted reference to individuals out of concern for those who inadvertently I might miss out. Publication of the second edition has provided a further opportunity to thank a few of those who have over the years helped make the book possible, in particular Daniel Ward, Iain Corbett and John Farrell, although, of course, my thanks go to everyone who helped.

The text is up to date as of the end of August 2016. Any errors or omissions are entirely my responsibility.

Paul Reed
Hardwicke,
New Square, Lincoln's Inn, London
October 2016

TABLE OF CONTENTS

TABLE OF CASES

TABLE OF STATUTES

TABLE OF STATUTORY INSTRUMENTS

CONSTRUCTION ALL RISKS

1.   OVERVIEW

Introduction.   Construction and engineering projects whether: land-based, marine   **1-001**
or aviation, are inherently risky. In order to manage these risks, parties to construction and engineering contracts will usually seek to allocate responsibility for each
different type of risk to a particular party. However, some risks are better managed by insurance[1] rather than by a party; for example, damage caused by fortuitous
events such as fire and flood are often covered only by insurance. Insurance may
be taken out for one party's benefit, or for the benefit of many, if not all of the parties involved in the project. These parties may be named[2] or they may be identified by description in the construction or engineering contract or in the insurance
policy.[3]

Construction insurance.   There are two main categories of construction   **1-002**
insurance: property and liability. The first category, property insurance, covers the
construction and engineering contract works and materials.[4] Property insurance is,
as the title suggests, insurance for the cost of remedying accidental damage caused

---

[1]   In certain jurisdictions, such as Nigeria, insurance is compulsory. In Nigeria, Section 64 of the Insurance Act 2003 (launched on 1 March 2011) by the National Insurance Commission ("NAICOM")
which has been implemented by a number of states provides: "[n]o persons shall cause to be
constructed any building of more than two floors without insuring with a registered insurer his liability in respect of construction risks caused by his negligence or the negligence of his servants,
agents or consultants which may result in bodily injury or loss of life to or damage to property of
any workman on site or any member of the public". See *http://naicom.gov.ng/payload?id=0eba1884-
a033-42eb-ae0d-e988bbea6308* [Accessed 14 April 2016]. In the United Kingdom it is customary
for builders to offer defects insurance, for example, Buildmark for private housing is offered by the
National House-Building Council ("NHBC"). See *http://www.nhbc.co.uk/Warrantiesandcover/
BuildersAndDevelopers//* [Accessed 12 April 2016].
[2]   In *Cooperative Retail Services Ltd v Taylor Young Partnership Ltd* [2002] UKHL 17 at [61] to [65];
[2002] 1 W.L.R. 1419 at 1437–1438; [2002] 1 All E.R. (Comm) 918 at 936–937, the House of Lords
held that where a construction contract stipulates that parties are to be named in an insurance policy,
the risk is also to be shared equally between the parties. Therefore, where the Employer insured the
liability for damage to the project in the joint names of all contractors and sub-contractors, no
contribution could be claimed from any of them for insured losses.
[3]   A contract of insurance is a promise by an insurer to hold a party harmless against a loss, or to make
good the loss suffered by that party: *Yeoman Credit v Latter* [1961] 1 W.L.R. 828 at 831; [1961] 2
All E.R. 294 at 296.
[4]   The terminology in a policy used to describe the types of insurance may not reflect the nature of the
risk covered. Reference should be made to the policy wording and correct classification of the risk
to ascertain the type of cover.

to physical property, but it may be extended to include business-interruption losses resulting from the damage. Property insurance is usually insured by reference to the date when the damage first occurred, which must be within the period of insurance.

1-003   The second main category of insurance is liability insurance. This category includes: (1) insurance for claims by third parties in respect of personal injury and damage caused to their own property—known as Public Liability ("PL") insurance[5]; (2) insurance against the liability of an employer for injury to their employees—known as Employers' Liability ("EL") insurance[6]; and (3) insurance for the liability of construction professionals[7] including architects, engineers and surveyors, whether in contract, the law of tort or under statute. Contractors may also carry professional liability insurance to cover those of their activities that are of a professional nature. A professional liability insurance policy will usually contain a comprehensive definition of what constitutes professional activities.

1-004   Professional liability insurance and public liability insurance are usually written by different markets in the insurance industry, so historically the two types of insurance have been treated as distinct (e.g. a public liability policy will nearly always exclude liability for professional negligence). Professional liability policies are generally written on a "claims made" basis, so that this type of policy will respond to a claim that is first made against the Insured during the period of insurance. Liability policies usually contain a provision by which circumstances likely to give rise to a claim must be reported and, if reported within the period of insurance, will be covered by that policy irrespective of when the claim is finally made.

1-005   Almost all property and liability insurance policies have deductibles and limits (which, in a property policy, may be different for each type of property insured). The policy limit is the amount that the policy or part of the policy will pay, it may be a limit that is applied to each and every claim, or it may be an aggregate limit—so that once the total of all claims under the policy in a given year reaches the limit the policy is effectively exhausted, even if the period of insurance has not expired.

1-006   **Background.**   For almost a hundred years insurers have been prepared to provide insurance against the risk of loss or damage being caused to construction and engineering works, whether those works are of a temporary nature or permanent and for liability for damage caused to third party property.[8] Insurance for damage caused to construction works is known as Construction All Risks ("CAR"),[9] and is also referred to as Contract Works, Project, Engineering All Risks, Erection All Risks ("EAR"),[10] Contractors' All Risks, Builders' Risks and Contractors' Indemnity[11]

---

5   It is also referred to as third party liability insurance.
6   Discussion of this type of insurance is not within the scope of this book.
7   *George Wimpey & Co Ltd v D.V Poole* (1985) 27 B.L.R. 58 at 92, per Webster J.
8   Insurance for the operation of mechanical and electrical plant and equipment after construction is complete is not considered in this textbook.
9   Other forms of all risk insurance include Contractors' Plant and Equipment ("CPE"), Machinery Breakdown ("MB") and Boiler and Pressure Vessel Explosion ("BOIL").
10 In most modern projects there will be civil, mechanical and engineering works. Where the machinery and erection content of the contract is more than 50 per cent of the total contract value then an EAR policy is likely to be issued.
11 M. G. A. Kamal, *Aspects of Contractors' All Risk Insurance: a critical approach* (London: MSc, the City University Business School, September 1978). This is not an exhaustive list; there are many

insurance. The first four titles refer to the type of construction activity that is undertaken. So, for example, EAR insurance provides insurance cover for the risk of loss or damage arising out of the assembly and installation of machinery, plant and steel structures, including physical damage to the contract works, equipment and machinery. The last three titles identify the parties most likely to take out, or have the benefit of the insurance. The range of different descriptions used for this type of insurance has the potential to confuse prospective insureds. It is, therefore, not surprising that the first report of the Insurance Institute of London's advanced study group 208[12] recommended replacing the various different descriptions with: "Construction and Erection Insurance". Despite the obvious good sense in having one unambiguous title for this type of insurance, the insurance market continues to use a wide range of descriptions. In this book the description Construction All Risks, Contractors' All Risk and CAR insurance are used interchangeably.

There are certain risks which a CAR policy will not usually cover. These include: **1-007**
(1) defects caused by negligent design by an architect or engineer—this is better dealt with by professional liability insurance; (2) the cost of correcting defective workmanship—liability for this will usually rest with the Contractor; and (3) employers' liability insurance and other risks expressly excluded. Even where a loss is insured, a party, which will usually be the Contractor or Employer, may still find that they have to bear some of the financial consequences if an insured event occurs. For example, where a claim on the policy exceeds the policy limit, or a deductible is applied, the Contractor will have to pay the difference between the sum paid out under the policy and the amount of the actual loss.

There are, as stated above in para.1-007, some risks that are rarely insured by any **1-008**
form of construction insurance, the most notable of which is defective workman-ship of a contractor that does not result in physical damage. The reason for this is that for an insurer to insure a contractor for defective workmanship would be to treat the insurer as guarantor for the proper performance of the construction works and as a result it would provide the Contractor with no incentive to complete the construction works to the standard required under the construction contract. The better view may be that a contractor is in the best position to assess and manage this particular type of risk.

General overview of a CAR policy. The origin of CAR insurance can be traced **1-009**
back to the expansion of international trade in the nineteenth century and in particular transportation overseas of live cargo by the early steamships.[13] The increase in international trade in the nineteenth century created a demand for insur-ance covering all risks rather than simply for specified perils. It was only in the twentieth century that insurers began to provide land-based CAR insurance and only in the second half of the twentieth century did standard form construction and engineering contracts start to include an option of insurance as a method of allocat-ing risk. For example in the Joint Contracts Tribunal (JCT) 2011 edition, cl.6.5 (previously JCT cl.21.2.1),[14] a contractor is required to take out an insurance policy

---

other alternative names that are used in practice.
[12] Insurance Institute of London, *Construction and Erection Insurance* (London: IIL, 1978).
[13] See further, paras 1-025 to 1-055.
[14] JCT Contracts, *SBC/Q 2011 JCT Standard Form of Building Contract With Quantities 2011* (London: Sweet & Maxwell, 2011), pp.68–69.

in the joint names of the Contractor and the Employer to cover[15] their legal liability for damage to third parties and their property. This type of insurance covers damage to property other than the construction works, including the Employer's own property, adjacent third party property (e.g. existing structures) and the employer's adjoining property. Contract terms making insurance cover available for the construction works are also now routinely included. For example, under the JCT Contract 2011 edition the parties can agree to take out an all-risks insurance policy for the construction works in joint names (respectively Option A and B under the Contract),[16] this may be done either by the Contractor or the Employer. In either case, the insurance will indemnify in respect of the full reinstatement value of the construction works, including professional fees, to be maintained up to the date of the practical completion certificate.

1-010   There is no single overarching CAR policy wording: underwriters have developed their own policy wording over time in response to changing market requirements. In more recent times, brokers have also developed their own wording. Nevertheless, all forms of CAR insurance wording will set out the type of loss and damage that are insured. This will often be defined in the policy as any form of physical loss or damage, but it may be qualified by one or more exceptions depending on the nature of the project. The policy will also define the property that is the subject of the insurance in either the policy's insuring (or operative) clause, in the policy schedule or in one of the "sections" in the policy.[17]

1-011   CAR policies usually share the same basic layout, commencing with the schedule, operative or insuring clause, which is then followed by exclusions and extensions. The later sections of a CAR policy will deal with general conditions, claims and notification. All CAR contract works policies contain some similar types of clauses, in particular with respect to the standard defects exclusion clauses such as the marine *Inchmaree*[18] clauses and the land-based construction and engineering exclusions DE1 to DE5[19] and LEG 1 to LEG 3.[20] Particular care needs to be exercised when interpreting these clauses, as minor variations in wording can result in substantially different meanings and levels of cover.[21]

---

15   JCT Contracts, *SBC/Q 2011 JCT Standard Form of Building Contract With Quantities 2011* (London: Sweet & Maxwell, 2011), pp.68–69, cl.6.5.1. states: "[A]ny expense, liability, loss, claim or proceedings which the Employer may incur or sustain by reason of injury or damage to any property caused by collapse, subsidence, heave, vibration, weakening or removal of support or lowering of ground water arising out of or in the course of or by reason of the carrying out of the Works, excluding injury or damage." Cl.6.5.1.

16   These Insurance Options can be found in Sch.3 to the JCT Standard Building Contract, for which, see JCT Contracts, *SBC/Q 2011 JCT Standard Form of Building Contract With Quantities 2011*, (2011), pp.88-92. The type of project will determine which Option will operate and with which party the obligation to insure will lie. Option A will arise where the project is to build new buildings and the Contractor is obliged to take out a joint names', all risks policy. Option B will arise where the Employer is obliged to take out the joint names', all risks policy. Insurance Option C is for use in the case of alterations to existing property. Option C requires the Employer to take out joint names, all risks insurance for existing structures and their contents. The Option that applies (as agreed between the Contractor and the Employer) will be set out in the Contract Particulars; see JCT Contracts, *SBC/Q 2011 JCT Standard Form of Building Contract With Quantities 2011* (2011), p.93.

17   See Ch.9.

18   See paras 16-024 to 16-028.

19   See paras 16-029 to 16-064.

20   See paras 16-065 to 16-070.

21   See also Ch.13.

"All risks" does not mean all risks. There are two principal requirements for an **1-012** indemnity under a CAR policy: (1) physical "loss of or damage to" property must have occurred during the policy period—this is the insured peril; and (2) the property must be insured. Under a CAR policy, in so far as the cause of loss is concerned, the scope of cover is expressed to be open-ended, albeit not unlimited and as a result the Insured is not required to establish the cause of the loss or damage, to the extent that it was not inevitable. However, the description "all risks" is potentially misleading as CAR insurance only provides cover against all risks of physical loss or damage, not against all losses.[22]

It is implicit in CAR insurance that the insured is relieved of the burden of prov- **1-013** ing the reason for the loss or damage that has been sustained. The underlying principle is that the insurance indemnifies in respect of all events that occur by chance and which are therefore not deliberate. Thus, all risks cover does not generally extend to: (1) loss that is inevitable at the start of the policy; or (2) loss which is brought about by the wilful misconduct of the Insured.[23] In *British & Foreign Marine Insurance Co Ltd v Gaunt*[24] Lord Sumner explained the limits to all risks insurance. He said:

> "There are, of course, limits to 'all risks.' They are risks, and risks insured against. Accordingly, the expression does not cover inherent vice or mere wear and tear ... It covers a risk, not a certainty; it is something, which happens to the subject matter from without, not the natural behaviour of the subject matter, being what it is, in the circumstances under which it is carried. Nor is it a loss which the assured brings about by his own act, for then he has not merely exposed the goods to the chance of injury, he has injured them himself."[25]

The principles of fortuity explained by Lord Sumner apply to any policy in the **1-014** nature of an all risks policy, whether or not the words "all risks" appear in the insuring clause.[26] CAR policies may often also contain express exclusions for non-

---

[22] Marshall said: "There is scarcely any contract which affords a greater number of questions of doubt and difficulty than that of marine insurance. Though the principles of the law applicable to this contract are, in general, well defined; yet the policy being usually of one uniform tenor, and the transactions upon which it is to operate, infinitely various and complicated, the conflicting rights of the parties are often so equally balanced, that it is impossible to decide between them, without resorting to very nice distinctions. It sometimes happens, too, that the real justice of the case, as between the parties, must yield to the strict rules of law: And it seems to be a general subject of complaint, in most commercial countries, that, upon such occasions courts of justice are sometimes tempted to forsake the rules of law, and to lean in favour of the suffering party. It is not to be wondered at, then, if the doctrines delivered from authority ... should be found, in some few instances, to be irreconcilable with the genuine principles of the law of insurance." (V. Dover, *A Handbook to Marine Insurance* 4th edn (London: H.F. & G. Witherby, 1936), p.317).

[23] It is possible to insure against damage which is inevitable, or even against losses that may have already occurred, so long as: (a) words to that effect are used in the policy, and (b) the insured does not actually know that that damage will or has occurred (in which case the policy will be voidable for non-disclosure if entered into prior to 12 August 2016, or, if entered after, voidable as a deliberate qualifying breach under para.2 of Part 1 of Sch.1 to the Insurance Act 2015 (2015 Act)). The 2015 Act came into force on 12 August 2016. It is discussed in detail below in Ch.5.

[24] *British & Foreign Marine Insurance Co Ltd v Gaunt* [1921] 2 A.C. 41; (1921) 7 Ll. L. Rep. 62; 90 L.J.K.B. 801.

[25] *Gaunt* [1921] 2 A.C. 41 at 57; 90 L.J.K.B. 801 at 807.

[26] A contractor's policy headed "All Risks of Physical Loss or Damage", which in the insuring clause indemnified the insured against "all Damage ... of whatsoever nature", was held to require fortuitous loss or damage. *CA Blackwell (Contractors) Ltd v Gerling Allegemeine Verischerungs-AG*; sub nom. *CA Blackwell (Contractors) Ltd v Gerling General Insurance Co* [2007] EWHC 94 (Comm) at [43]; [2007] Lloyd's Rep. I.R. 511 at 519-520; (point was not raised on appeal: [2007] EWCA Civ 1450;

fortuitous occurrences, such as normal action of the sea or repeated flooding, corrosion and fair wear and tear. Accordingly, the insured peril in an all risks insurance policy may be more accurately described as "all risks of accidental physical loss of damage", or "all risks of loss or physical damage, unless excluded by law or by the express wording of the policy".

1-015   Confusion can arise where CAR policies seek to expressly exclude events from cover, which are not insured under the policy. So, for example, there is no cover under a CAR policy for gradual deterioration of the insured property because this type of deterioration is natural and therefore inevitable and accordingly it is not fortuitous or accidental damage, yet in many CAR policies it is excluded expressly.[27] The justification for including a "for the avoidance of doubt" exclusion in a CAR policy is that it makes clear to the reader that the cover provided under the insuring (or operative) clause does not extend to all losses and all damage. If this is the justification for the use of an express exclusion it may be suggested that a more helpful and transparent approach would be to provide an explanatory guidance note[28] describing the cover provided.

1-016   Accordingly, for CAR insurance the identification of accidental damage to insured property occurring during the policy period may be all that is required to satisfy the insurance (or operative) clause which forms the gateway to the cover provided. Identification of the cause of the loss or damage is not relevant for this purpose. This is not to suggest that search for the cause of the loss or damage is not relevant for other purposes, for example identifying the cause of the loss or damage may help establish that the damage was not "caused" accidentally,[29] or that the alleged "damage" is in fact natural deterioration having been "caused" by or resulting from an excluded peril, rather than being insured damage due to accidental accelerated corrosion.

1-017   **Procuring CAR insurance.**   The principles governing the formation of a CAR insurance contract are the same as those that govern the formation of any insurance policy.[30] The position under a CAR policy is different only to the extent that the Employer will usually require a main contractor to maintain insurance in the

---

[2008] 1 All E.R. (Comm) 885; [2008] Lloyd's Rep. I.R. 529); see also, *Insurance Disputes*, edited by J. Mance, I. Goldrein and R. Merkin, 3rd edn (London: Informa, 2012), para.19.15.

[27]   In *Global Process Systems Inc v Syarikat Takaful Malaysia Bhd, The Cendor Mopu*, for example, the court held that an express exclusion for "inherent vice" would be treated as s.55(2)(c) of the Marine Insurance Act 1906 (MIA), and would not exclude damage caused at least in part by a peril of the sea (i.e. fortuitous external occurrence). In this case after analysing the law Lord Mance commented that wear and tear or inherent characteristics are only excluded if there is no external fortuitous accident involved in causing the damage: [2011] UKSC 5 at [81]; [2011] 1 All E.R. 869 at 894; [2011] Bus. L.R. 537 at 561. See further discussion below, para.24-086.

[28]   See for example p.9 of the current NHBC Buildmark policy document called "Buildmark from NHBC" (NHBC: 2015) which applies to newly built, converted or renovated homes registered with NHBC from 1 April 2015, *http://www.nhbc.co.uk/Warrantiesandcover/Buildersanddevelopers/ Privatehousing-Buildmark/Policydetails/* [Accessed 13 April 2016].

[29]   In *C.C.R. Fishing Ltd v British Reserve Insurance Co Ltd* [1990] 1 S.C.R. 814 at 825; (1990) 69 D.L.R. (4th) 112 at 120; [1990] L.R.C. (Comm) 175 at 182–183 (S.C.C.), McLachlin J said: "[I]n determining whether a loss falls within the policy, the cause of the loss should be determined by looking at all the events which gave rise to it and asking whether it is fortuitous in the sense that the accident would not have occurred "but for" or without an act or event which is fortuitous in the sense that it was not to be expected in the ordinary course of things."

[30]   See Ch.4.

joint names of the Employer, subcontractors and other interested parties pursuant to the provisions of its contract with the Employer.[31]

Project or annual CAR insurance.   A contractor who undertakes more than one   **1-018** construction project each year may decide to obtain CAR insurance under either an annual policy, covering all projects to be undertaken by him in the year, or under multiple, project-specific policies. From the perspective of an Employer, a project policy, which is specific to the particular construction or engineering works being undertaken, may be advantageous. For example, a CAR project policy may extend to cover all of the relevant parties to the project and provide additional cover for financial loss; however the premium for this type of policy may be higher than the proportion of the premium paid for the benefit of the Contractor's annual policy; usually the premium will be included within the Contractor's price for the works. If the Contractor undertakes a number of projects in one year, an annual CAR policy will normally be the most economic form of insurance to cover him for the risk of damage to the construction or engineering works.

Types of CAR insurance.   CAR policies usually provide three types of cover: (1)   **1-019** damage to insured property[32]; (2) consequential or "business interruption" losses that may arise as a result of the damage[33]; and (3) legal liability of the insured to third parties (often described as "third party liability" or "public liability insurance").[34] The first type of cover indemnifies in respect of physical loss of or damage to the construction works including temporary structures, construction plant and temporary buildings. The second type of cover relates to particular financial losses suffered by particular insureds as a result of physical damage that has been caused to the construction works. The third type of cover provides an indemnity in respect of the insured's legal liability for loss and damage to third parties' person or property arising as a result of construction activities. Confusion in terminology can arise, because "CAR cover" can sometimes be intended to refer only to the first type of loss, indemnifying the damage to the construction works, but it is also sometimes used to refer to the suite of policies contained within a typical CAR document.

Consequential loss.   Unless expressly stated to be included, consequential losses   **1-020** are not indemnified under the section of the policy that indemnifies for loss or damage to the construction works. In practice most CAR policies also expressly exclude the insurer's liability to indemnify the insured in respect of any consequential loss for this type of damage; that is, those losses which are not directly attributable to restoring the contract works to their former undamaged state. However, insurance in respect of the insured's legal liability to third parties will normally include an indemnity for their financial loss, as well as for the rectification of physical damage to their property.

---

[31]   The principles applied to determine whether or not a particular sub-contractor is insured under a specific CAR policy are discussed in Ch.8.
[32]   The meaning of damage is discussed in Ch.14.
[33]   Insurance for consequential loss is discussed in Ch.17.
[34]   Public liability insurance is discussed in Ch.18.

1-021   **Delay in start-up.**   Delay in start-up ("DSU") insurance[35] is a separate class of insurance that provides cover against the financial consequences of physical damage and it will be contained within its own section of the policy. Cover for this type of insurance will usually be arranged by the Employer in conjunction with the physical loss or damage section of the policy. DSU is an all-risks cover for something that has yet to be completed and provides protection against future costs that may be incurred. This type of insurance, therefore, provides protection to the Employer and Contractor for loss of profits caused by a delay to the programme of works because of an insured peril; the insured peril will usually also trigger the physical damage section of the policy. It is of particular importance to Employers, and is normally taken up by them (as opposed to Contractors) because the financial structuring of modern construction projects is such that any delay usually results in significant economic consequences.

1-022   **Construction liability insurance.**   There are three main types of construction and engineering liability insurance: (1) professional liability insurance; (2) employers' liability insurance; and (3) public liability insurance. The first concerns the legal liability of construction and engineering professionals for the consequences of inadequate advice[36]; the second concerns the legal liability owed by Employers for injury caused to Employees.[37] The third concerns personal injury and the loss of or damage to property incurred by a third party caused by the construction works.[38] A public liability policy provides cover for liability to third parties such as the general public and adjoining owners of properties, who are not party to the construction contract. It normally provides cover for claims in tort or the effect of this liability (i.e. interference with third parties and the type of harm that results as protected by the law of tort), or cover for liability in contract that is co-extensive with duties that arise in tort, but it does not afford (if the words "legally liable" are used) the insured with cover against liability in contract for pure economic loss.[39]

1-023   In the context of construction and engineering works, the principal issue in relation to this type of cover is where damage has been caused by the construction or engineering works to the property after practical completion. In these circumstances a contractor may have far greater insurance cover than if the damage had occurred prior to practical completion. This is because the Contractor will usually be legally liable to the owner for repairing the damage and for consequential financial losses. For example, if after practical completion defective foundations cause damage to the superstructure of a building, the Contractor may be legally liable to the third party owner for rectification of the damage and in respect of the owner's consequential financial loss. The Contractor will be entitled to be indemnified for both types of loss (i.e. repairing the damage and for consequential financial losses) caused by the defective foundation under the public liability section of the CAR policy. This can lead to unusual results, especially in relation to Private Finance

---

[35]   It is also known as "delay in completion insurance" or "advanced loss of profits insurance" ("ALOP").

[36]   This subject is outside the scope of the book.

[37]   This subject is also dealt with in other texts and is outside the scope of the book.

[38]   See Ch.18.

[39]   *Tesco Stores Ltd v Constable* [2008] EWCA Civ 362; [2008] 1 C.L.C. 727; [2008] Lloyd's Rep. I.R. 636.

Initiate ("PFI") contracts where the Contractor, operator and the owner of the building may be subsidiaries of the same parent company.

In practice, a contractor will often try to use the same insurers for his public liability and construction works insurance in order to minimise the risk of disputes as to which policy (and which insurer) should respond.   **1-024**

2.   HISTORICAL CONTEXT

Relevance of historical context.   The development of all-risks insurance provides   **1-025**
perspective and background for the interpretation of standard clauses in CAR policies. In particular, the historical context of particular clauses such as the DE and LEG exclusions and the relationship between clauses, which form part of two suites of well-known alternatives, ought to assist in their interpretation. In *Lloyd's TSB General Insurance Holdings v Lloyd's Bank Group Insurance Co Ltd; Abbey National Plc v Lee*,[40] Lord Hobhouse supported the principle of interpreting particular clauses in the context of established alternatives:

> "[T]here are often well established alternatives open to the parties in the drafting of their agreement. The choice made from among these alternatives represents part of the bargain struck by the parties and must be respected by anyone ... adjudicating upon a dispute arising under the document."

It may be that this approach to interpretation is particularly important in circumstances where there is an internationally accepted suite of defects exclusions providing different levels of insurance cover. It might be thought to be unfortunate that, in relation to the Report of the Insurance Institute of London,[41] which describes the background and market developments and provides a worked example[42] as to the operation of the DE and LEG clauses[43] that Lord Justice Tuckey in the Court of Appeal in England in *CA Blackwell (Contractors) Ltd v Gerling*[44] said, when construing the meaning of the DE3 exclusion, that the Report was:

> "instructive about the purpose of defect exclusion clauses and how they have evolved ... [b]ut... cannot be used as an aid to construction of the clause in question which must be construed according to its terms."[45]

This may be contrasted with the approach adopted by the Court of Appeal for British Columbia in *Acciona Infrastructure Canada Inc.* who construed the meaning of LEG2 in the context of LEG1 and LEG3.[46]

If the view expressed in the Court of Appeal is to be preferred, then the courts will not seek to construe the particular DE or LEG clause in issue in the light of

---

[40]   *Lloyd's TSB General Insurance Holdings Ltd v Lloyd's Bank Group Insurance Co Ltd; Abbey National Plc v Lee* [2003] UKHL 48 at [31]; [2003] 4 All E.R. 43 at 52; [2003] Lloyd's Rep. I.R. 623 at 631.

[41]   Insurance Institute of London, Advanced Study Group Report 208B *Construction Insurance - Report of Advanced Study Group Report 208B* (London: IIL, 1999).

[42]   Insurance Institute of London, Advanced Study Group Report 208B *Construction Insurance – Report of Advanced Study Group Report 208B* (London: IIL, 1999) at paras 8.8.2.3–8.8.2.4.

[43]   See paras 16-039 to 16-042.

[44]   *CA Blackwell (Contractors) Ltd* [2007] EWCA Civ 1450 at [20]; [2008] 1 All E.R. (Comm) 885 at 891; [2008] Lloyd's Rep. I.R. 529 at 533.

[45]   *CA Blackwell (Contractors) Ltd* [2007] EWCA Civ 1450 at [20]; [2008] 1 All E.R. (Comm) 885 at 891; [2008] Lloyd's Rep. I.R. 529 at 533.

[46]   *Acciona Infrastructure Canada Inc. v Allianz Global Risks US Insurance Co* [2015] BCCA 347 at [74].

the others. For example, the fact that DE4 excludes damage to the defective "component part" does not, apparently, assist in interpreting the scope of the phrase "property ... in a defective condition" in DE3. Nor does the fact that the "outright" exclusion in DE1 preserves cover for loss or damage to defective property caused by a peril other than the defect itself assist in determining whether DE5 excludes cover in this situation. This approach may also be thought unfortunate because the clauses were conceived, and have always been understood, as providing different levels of cover. It is therefore possible to criticise the Court of Appeal's hostility towards a comparative approach for being unprincipled: why should the existence of alternative standard clauses, understood throughout the market as standing in a particular relationship to one another, not be considered relevant to the problem of construction?

1-026   **Early historical context.**   The riskiest adventures undertaken by early man were sea voyages; communities sending their goods out to trade in distant countries would have had a mechanism for sharing the risk of the venture, and it is likely that some form of insurance has existed since man's earliest seafaring days. Eighteenth century authors were keen to find classical roots to the modern practice of insurance, and concluded that the first systems of insurance were those of Rhodes,[47] Greece,[48] or Rome,[49] in the first millennium BC. Although there are some classical references to early navigation practice, there are no direct references to insurance itself, and in the nineteenth century the search for a classical pedigree was dismissed as a vogue of the eighteenth century, when "it was felt that nothing could be counted respectable unless its descent were traceable to Rome or Athens".[50]

1-027   It is likely that modern insurance practice emerged amongst the Lombard merchants in the northern Italian states, where other modern commercial practice such as double-entry bookkeeping and the letter of credit developed. The earliest modern European reference to insurance is by a Florentine-named Villani (in the mid-fourteenth century). From Northern Italy, insurance practice flowed outwards and northwards to other European countries. City ordinances and codes regulating insurance were issued in southern European countries in the fifteenth century, and in northern Europe countries in the sixteenth and seventeenth Centuries, culminating in the French "Ordonnance de la Marine" in 1681, a code of such authority that it was included largely unrevised in the Napoleonic "Code de Commerce" of 1801; and the North German Mercantile Code of 1861, which became the German Maritime Code of 1897.

1-028   Although insurance has been practised in England since at least 1189,[51] the earliest extant English insurance policy dates from 1555.[52] It bears marked similarities to the policy laid out in the ordinance of Florence of 1523. In 1601, an act was passed "concerning Matters of Assurances used among Merchants". The Act recites that:

---

[47] J.A. Park, *A System of the Law of Marine Insurances*, 5th edn (London: Butterworths, 1802), p.iii.
[48] Park, *A System of the Law of Marine Insurances* (1802), p.viii.
[49] B.M. Émérigon, *A Treatise on Insurances* (London: Butterworth, 1850) (originally in French, late 18th century: translated from French with an introduction and notes by S. Merideth), p.1.
[50] W. Gow, *Marine Insurance: A Handbook*, 3rd edn (London: Macmillan, 1903) p.2.
[51] Statute of Westminster 1 1275.
[52] W. Gow, *Marine Insurance: A Handbook*, 4th edn (London: Macmillan, 1917), p.4.

"it hath been Time out of Mind an Usage amongst Merchants, both of this Realm and of foreign Nations, when they make any great Adventure, (especially into remote Parts) to give some Consideration of Money to other Persons (which commonly are in no small Number) to have from them Assurance made of their Goods, Merchandizes, Ships and Things adventured, or some Parts thereof, at such Rates and in such Sort as the Parties Assurers and the Parties Assured can agree, which Course of Dealing is commonly termed A Policy of Assurance."[53]

The earliest insurance policies in England are recorded as being written on Lombard Street in London, named after the Lombard merchants who settled there during the reign of Edward I (1239-1307). The standard forms adopted by Lloyd's in the seventeenth century contained the phrase:

1-029

"[A]nd it is agreed by us, the insurers, that this writing or policy of assurance shall be of as much force and effect as the surest writing or policy of assurance heretofore made in Lombard Street, or in the Royal Exchange, or elsewhere in London."

It therefore seems that insurance in England dates back at least to the latter half of the thirteenth century,[54] and arrived with Lombard merchants who settled in London. Indeed, the very word "policy" is said to derive from the Italian *polliza d'assicurazione* (promise of insurance).

Up until the sixteenth century there were very few disputes concerning insurance, possibly because insurers "used to stand so justly and precisely upon their Credits, as few or no Controversies have arisen thereupon".[55] Where disputes did arise, they were heard by a panel appointed by the Lord Mayor of the City of London. That panel consisted of "certain grave and discreet merchants ... Men by reason of their Experience fitted to understand, and speedily to decide those Causes."[56] These informal hearings no longer sufficed as:

1-030

"of late Years that divers Persons have withdrawn themselves from that arbitrary Course, and have sought to draw the Parties assured to seek their monies of every several Assurer, by Suits commenced in her Majesty's Courts, to their great Charges and Delays."[57]

The Act concerning Matters of Assurance used Among Merchants 1601 set up a committee with:

"full Power and Authority to hear, examine, order and decree all and every such Cause and Causes concerning Policies of Assurances in a brief and summary Course, as to their Discretion shall seem meet, without Formalities of Pleadings or Proceedings."[58]

However, this committee was little used, as it was soon decided that a case determined by the committee could still be brought before the Court of Common Pleas.

Lloyd's coffee house probably opened on Lombard Street in the mid-seventeenth century but the first record of its existence dates from 1688. Individual insurers met at Lloyd's and issued insurance by making their mark on a proposal presented to them (known as "scratching the slip").[59] Typically an individual insurer would take only a proportion of the total, with other individuals signing up to remaining

1-031

---

[53] An Act Concerning Matters of Assurance used Among Merchants 1601, c.12.
[54] Statute of Westminster 1 1275.
[55] An Act Concerning Matters of Assurance used Among Merchants 1601, c.12.
[56] An Act Concerning Matters of Assurance used Among Merchants 1601, c.12.
[57] An Act Concerning Matters of Assurance used Among Merchants 1601, c.12.
[58] An Act Concerning Matters of Assurance used Among Merchants 1601, c.12.
[59] See below, para.4-066.

percentages. The internal mechanism by which this occurred is not discussed further here.[60]

1-032   Following the South Sea Bubble financial crisis of 1720, insurance companies were prohibited from writing marine insurance policies, with two exceptions: the Royal Exchange Assurance, and London Assurance. Individual insurance, such as that provided at Lloyd's, was still permitted. At that time it was common for wagers on ships to be placed as marine insurance policies. Someone unconnected with the ship in any way would place a wager that the ship would (or would not) arrive safely at its destination. The point being that the wageror had no interest in the object insured, and therefore would not suffer a loss. Such contracts were prohibited by the Marine Insurance Act of 1745. The 1745 Act also prohibited re-assurance,[61] due to the practice by unscrupulous insurers of taking out a further insurance policy on a ship they knew was already lost. The prohibition on re-assurance was eventually repealed in 1864.[62] In the latter part of the nineteenth century cargo was transported by sail and risks were underwritten on the standard marine "SG policy"[63] (and the common memorandum).[64]

1-033   **Ejusdem generis—all other perils.**   In *Cullen v Butler*,[65] in 1816 the courts first considered general all-perils policy wording which stated:

> "And of all other perils, losses and misfortunes that have or shall come to the hurt, detriment, or damage of the said goods and merchandises and ships, etc. or any thereof."

Whilst this wording may now be construed as excluding every kind of loss or damage not already explicitly specified, the position was different in the first half of the nineteenth century when they were interpreted strictly in accordance with the preceding words, "in this voyage". In *Cullen*,[66] Lord Ellensborough said:

> "The extent and meaning of the general words have not yet been the immediate subject of any judicial construction in our Courts of Law. As they must, however, be considered, as introduced into the policy in furtherance of the objects of marine insurance, and may have the effect of extending a reasonable indemnity to many cases not distinctly covered by the special words, they are entitled to be considered as material and operative words, and to have the due effect assigned to them in the construction of the instrument; and which will be done by allowing them to comprehend and cover other cases of marine damage of the like kind with those which are specially enumerated and occasioned by similar causes."

1-034   By 1876 all risks insurance formed part of the accepted classification of insurance, so for example premiums were quoted on an all risks basis for the transporta-

---

[60] For a full discussion of the history of Lloyd's see P.T. O'Neill and J.W. Wolloneicki, *The Law of Reinsurance in England and Bermuda*, 3rd edn (London: Sweet & Maxwell, 2010), paras 2-001 to 2-007.

[61] With certain exceptions where "the assurer shall be insolvent, become a Bankrupt, or die", fn.63, at iv.

[62] D.M. Holland, *"A Brief History of Reinsurance"* (Society of Actuaries Reinsurance: Special Edition, Reinsurance News, February 2009) 65, p.14. *http://www.soa.org/news-and-publications/ newsletters/reinsurance/reinsurance-detail.aspx* [Accessed 13 April 2016].

[63] See Ch.24, para.24-003, fnn.3 and 7.

[64] The Common Memorandum was first adopted in Lloyd's policies in May 1794. See *Arnould Law of Marine Insurance and Average*, edited by M.J. Mustill and J.C.B Gilman, 16th edn (London: Stevens & Sons, 1981), Vol.2, paras 839-850 and Gow, *Marine Insurance* (1903), pp.171-183.

[65] *Cullen v Butler* (1816) 105 E.R. 1119; (1816) 5 M. & S. 461.

[66] *Cullen* (1816) 105 E.R. 1119 at 1121; (1816) 5 M. & S. 461 at 465.

tion of goods from the United Kingdom and the West Coast of Africa.[67] However, the narrow interpretation of all risks still prevailed. For example, in relation to the shipments of live cattle, which were insured against mortality, the words "and of all other perils, losses, and misfortunes" were interpreted strictly as referring to perils of a like kind with those specified,[68] so that the risks covered were limited to death from natural causes.[69] The justification for a restrictive interpretation of the apparently unlimited words, "all other perils," remained that perils of a dissimilar kind had to be insured against specifically.[70]

The *Inchmaree*. Lord Ellensborough in *Cullen*[71] was quoted by Lord Herschell **1-035** in the *Thames and Mersey Marine Insurance Co Ltd v Hamilton Fraser & Co (Inchmaree)*[72] where the meaning of "all risks" was brought before the House of Lords for the first time. The *Inchmaree* was a test case to determine liability of insurers for damage to ships' machinery insured on an ordinary marine policy. The House of Lords unanimously held that it was impossible to say that the damage was occasioned by a peril *similar* to "perils of the sea". The practical consequence was the immediate introduction of a clause designed to circumvent the House of Lords decision. This clause is the genesis of the modern *Inchmaree*, DE and LEG defects exclusions discussed in Ch.16. The *Inchmaree* clause read as follows:

> "This insurance also specially to cover loss of or damage to hull and machinery through the negligence of the master, mariners, engineers, or pilots, or though explosions, bursting of boilers, breakages of shafts, or through any latent defect in the machinery or hull, provided such loss or damage has not resulted from want of due diligence by the owners of the ship, or any of them, or by the manager."

Accordingly, the principle of interpretation which predated the Marine Insur- **1-036** ance Act 1906 ("MIA"), was that "all risks" was to be construed restrictively so as to include only damage of a kind similar to that identified in the policy and which had been occasioned by a similar cause. With the introduction of the *Inchmaree* clause and other similar clauses and the fact that the principle was not always ap- plied in a restrictive way[73] meant that its significance as a rule of construction reduced over time.

The range of specified perils which were required to be insured continued to **1-037** expand as commerce expanded and insurance developed,[74] so that any distinction between sea and land based perils became less important. Maritime commerce continued to develop with the shipment of live cargo becoming increasingly

---

[67] F. Martin *The History of Lloyd's and of Marine Insurance in Great Britain* (London, Macmillan and Co, 1876), Appendix at 376.

[68] Gow, *Marine Insurance* (1903), p.116.

[69] *St. Paul Fire and Marine Insurance Co v Morice* (1906) 11 Com. Cas. 153; 22 T.L.R. 448.

[70] M.D. Chalmers and D. Owen, *The Marine Insurance Act 1906* (London: William Clowes and Sons Ltd, 1907). *Arnould Law of Marine Insurance and Average*, 6th edn, edited by D. Machlachan (London: Stevens & Sons, 1887), Vol.2 p.789; *Thames and Mersey Marine Insurance Co Ltd v Hamilton Fraser & Co (The Inchmaree)* (1887) 12 App. Cas 484 at 491; 56 L.J.Q.B. 626 at 629.

[71] *Cullen* (1816) 105 E.R. 1119; (1816) 5 M. & S. 461.

[72] *Inchmaree* (1887) 12 App. Cas. 484 at p. 491; 56 L.J.Q.B. 626 at 630-631; 6 Asp. M.L.C. 200 at 204.

[73] *Cullen* (1815) 171 E.R. 92 at 93; (1815) 4 Camp. 289 at 290; (1815) 171 E.R. 426; *Butler v Wild- man* 106 E.R. 708; (1820) 3 B. & Ald. 398; *Phillips v Barker* (1921) 106 E.R. 1151; (1821) 5 B. & Ald. 161 and *Devaux v Jánson* (1839) 5 Bing (NC) 519; 8 L.J.C.P. 284.

[74] Bullion was insured "at and from Boodini to London ... including all risks of every description from the mines by escort to railway station at Raichur ... thence by rail ... to Bombay, thence to London". *Hyderabad (Deccan) Co v Willoughby* (1899) 2 Q.B 530; 68 L.J.Q.B. 862 at 864; 41 Com. Cas. 270.

common. The demand for insurance against mortality and all other risks had to be met, at least initially, by individual polices based upon special wording as this risk was not covered in the common form of policies. The demand for all-risks insurance continued to increase and the move away from insurance for specified perils or even all perils continued. By 1901 there was general acknowledgment, at least in a marine context, of the need for all all risks cover. For example in *Jackson v Mumford*[75] land-based construction was insured in respect of "all risks to completion" which would usually extend to sea trials and acceptance at which stage a marine "all risk" policy would be in force.

1-038   By 1906, the position had been reached where goods were often expressly insured against "all risks by land or by water",[76] in order to ensure that both land and sea risks would be insured under an all risks policy and meet Lord Herschell's restrictive interpretation of the phrase "marine damage" in the *Inchmaree*. The MIA recognised the term "risk" and that it could be used in different senses so, for example, the MIA identified the nature of a peril, such as sea risks which are to be contrasted with land risks and as to whether it is insured against all risks.[77] In the same year, Walton J in *Schloss Brothers v Stevens*,[78] concluded that the words "all risks" covered "all losses by any accidental cause of any kind ... There must be a casualty". Damage, in other words, if it was to be covered by an all-risks policy, must be due to some fortuitous circumstance or casualty. Walton J observed that, "of course, where parties desire to cover all risks of every kind, it can be done simply by saying 'all risks' whatsoever".[79]

1-039   The first set of Institute Cargo Clauses ("ICC") were introduced by the London insurance market on 1 July 1912.[80] These clauses remained largely unaltered until the second half of the twentieth century. There are three alternative forms of the modern ICC clauses: (A), (B) and (C)[81] with cover provided by the (A) clauses being the most analogous to all risks cover. It covers all damage caused by a fortuity unless the cause is excluded. The first set of Institute Clauses for Builders' Risks, which provided insurance for risks that may arise whilst constructing a ship, are believed to have been introduced (although they existed in a different format before this date) on 30 April 1913 (a later version was introduced on 1 November 1918).[82]

1-040   **British & Foreign Marine Insurance Co Ltd v Gaunt.**   The modern law of all-risks insurance was explained by Lord Birkenhead L.C. and Lord Sumner in *Gaunt*.[83] Lord Sumner identified the limits of all risks insurance. He said:

> "[T]he expression does not cover inherent vice or mere wear and tear or British capture. It covers a risk, not a certainty; it is something which happens to the subject-matter being what it is from without, not the natural behaviour of the subject-matter in the circumstances under which it is carried. Nor is

---

75   *Jackson v Mumford* (1902) 19 T.L.R. 18; (1902) 8 Com. Cas. 61; 51 W.R. 91.
76   *Schloss Bros v Stevens* [1906] 2 K.B. 665; 75 L.J.Q.B. 927; 10 Asp. M.L.C. 331.
77   Chalmers and Owen, *The Marine Insurance Act 1906* (1907), p.2.
78   *Schloss Bros* [1906] 2 K.B. 665 at 673.
79   *Schloss Bros* [1906] 2 K.B. 665 at 673.
80   ICC (F.P.A.) (Free of Particular Average) (1/7/12).
81   CL. 382 ICC(A) (1/1/09); CL. 383(B) (1/1/09); and CL. 384 ICC(C) (1/1/09). See below, paras 24-068 to 24-092.
82   See *Marine Insurance Clauses: a Reference Book Containing all Institute of London Underwriters; a Selection of Lloyd's and of General Clauses and Warranties*, 4th edn (London: Witherby & Co, 1921), p.7.
83   *Gaunt* [1921] 2 A.C. 41 at 57; (1921) 7 Ll. L. Rep. 62; 90 L.J.Q.B. 801 at 807.

it a loss which the assured brings about by his own act, for then he has not merely exposed the goods to the chance of injury, he has injured them himself. Finally the description 'all risks' does not alter the general law; only risks are covered which it is lawful to cover, and the onus of proof remains where it would have been on a policy against ordinary sea perils."

Lord Sumner also explained that the "quasi universal" of such cover is to reduce the onus on an insured making a claim:

"[T]he quasi-universality of the description [i.e. "all risks"] does affect the onus of proof in one way. The claimant insured against and averring a loss by fire must prove loss by fire, which involves proving that it is not by something else. When he avers loss by some risk coming within "all risks," as used in this policy, he need only give evidence reasonably showing that the loss was due to a casualty, not to a certainty or to inherent vice or to wear and tear. That is easily done. I do not think he has to go further and pick out one of the multitude of risks covered, so as to show exactly how his loss was caused."[84]

Lord Birkenhead L.C. explained that:

"where all risks are covered by the policy and not merely risks of a specified class or classes, the plaintiff discharges his special onus when he has proved that the loss was caused by some event covered by the general expression, and he is not bound to go further and prove the exact nature of the accident of casualty which, in fact, occasioned his loss."[85]

The earliest construction all-risks policy is recorded as having been written out **1-041** of the companies market in 1929 in relation to the construction of Lambeth Bridge.[86] However, this was unusual as prior to the Second World War, all risks insurance was placed mainly in connection with plant erection and testing risks, and usually written in the marine market and at Lloyd's. During this period there were no standard conditions of construction and engineering contract with a contractor being left to decide which risks he wished to cover. Often contractors would insure only against the risk of fire, the remaining risks being uninsured. In 1930, the first attempts were made to introduce standard form conditions of contract, which resulted in the 1939 edition of the engineering contract conditions. Working out the meaning of loss of cargo and construction all risks insurance through disputes resolved by the courts then followed, so that, for example in 1940 in *Canada Rice Mills Ltd v Union Marine & General Insurance Co Ltd*,[87] a cargo of rice was damaged by overheating, this being due to the closing of ventilators during heavy weather. The practice of insurers had long been to admit condensation damage in such circumstances. However, Wright LJ held:

"The closing of the ventilators is not to be regarded as a separate or independent cause, interposed between the peril, of the sea and the damage, but as being such a mere matter of routine seamanship necessitated by the peril that the damage can be regarded as the direct result of the peril."[88]

Six years later, the 1947 Notes for Guidance of Settling Agents[89] recorded that

---

[84] *Gaunt* [1921] 2 A.C. 41 at 57–58; (1921) 7 Ll. L. Rep. 62; 90 L.J.Q.B. 801 at 807–808.

[85] *Gaunt* [1921] 2 A.C. 41 at 47; (1921) 7 Ll. L. Rep. 62 at 63; 90 L.J.Q.B. 801 at 803-804.

[86] L. Wassmer, "Contractors' All Risk Insurance" (Zurich: Swiss Reinsurance Company, 1998) p.5. *http://ib-apostle.narod.ru/contractorsrisk.Paras.0003.File.pdf* [Accessed 13 April 2016]

[87] *Canada Rice Mills Ltd v Union Marine & General Insurance Co Ltd* [1941] A.C. 55; [1940] 4 All E.R. 169; (1940) 67 Ll. L. Rep. 549.

[88] *Canada Rice Mills Ltd* [1941] A.C. 55 at 70; [1940] 4 All E.R. 169 at 177; (1940) 67 Ll. L. Rep. 549 at 558.

[89] The Institute of London Underwriters *Notes for the Guidance of Settling Agents* (London: ILU, 1947), p.16.

goods are frequently insured against all risks so that almost any damage or loss occurring during the period of the policy, excepting ordinary loss and inherent vice, was covered.

1-042   **Post-war development.**   Whatever may be the genesis of all-risks insurance for construction and engineering projects, the wide cover provided under all risks gained popularity in the period immediately after the Second World War for two reasons; first, it met the requirements of bankers, in particular the International Bank for Reconstruction and Development; and secondly, as a result of the reconstruction work and major projects which had been delayed due to the war. During this period the professional bodies concerned with civil engineering projects pooled their efforts to work out standard conditions of contract and define the obligation of both the contractor and his principal. In 1945, the Institution of Civil Engineers ("ICE") and the Federation of Civil Engineering Contractors ("FCEC") formulated a new model (ICE Conditions of Contract),[90] the second edition of which was published in 1950.[91] Condition 21 of these[92] required the Contractor to insure the contract works on an all-risk basis. It was the introduction of these standard conditions of contract for construction and engineering which contributed to the prevalence of CAR insurance. E.J. Tinson says:

> "[I]t was not until a few years ago that conditions in this country were to a large extent standardised, and today there are the recognised forms of conditions which are to be found in many contracts."[93]

---

[90]   Insititution of Civil Engineers and Federation of Civil Engineering Contractors, *General Conditions of Contract and Forms of Tender Agreement and Bond for use in connection with works of Civil Engineering Construction* (London: FECA, 1945).

[91]   Insititution of Civil Engineers (Great Britain) and Federation of Civil Engineering Contractors, *General Conditions of Contract and Forms of Tender Agreement and Bond for use in connection with works of Civil Engineering Construction Revised*, 2nd edn (London: ICE, 1950).

[92]   "Without limiting his obligations and responsibilities under Clause 20 hereof the contractor shall insure in the joint names of the employer and the contractor against all loss or damage from whatever cause arising (other than the excepted risks) for which he is responsible under the terms of the contract and in such manner that the employer and the contractor are covered during the period of construction of the works and are also covered during the period of maintenance for loss or damage arising from a cause occurring prior to the commencement of the period of maintenance and for any loss or damage occasioned by the contractor in the course of any operations carried out by him for the purpose of complying with his obligations under Clause 49 thereof:

> (a)   The works and the temporary works to the full value of such works executed from time to time.
> (b)   The materials constructional plant and other things brought on to the site by the contractor to the full value of such material constructional plant and other things.

Such insurances shall be effected with an insurer and in terms approved by the employer (which approval shall not be unreasonably withheld) and the contractor shall whenever required produce to the engineer the policy or policies of insurance and the receipts for payment of the current premiums." E.J. Tinsen, *The Insurance Institute of London Contractors' All Risks Insurance* (London: ILL 1955), p.3.

[93]   Tinsen, *The Insurance Institute of London Contractors' All Risks Insurance* (1955), p.2. The Institution of Civil Engineers ("ICE") jointly with the Federation of Civil Engineering Contractors ("FCEC"), and in conjunction with the Association of Consulting Engineers ("ACE") formulated general conditions of contract for use with works of civil engineering construction. Standard conditions were agreed between the Federation of Civil Engineering Contractors and the Association of Consulting Engineers in 1930 but were not widely used. In 1945 revised standard conditions were agreed between those two organisations and in 1950 standard conditions were agreed between all three bodies, the one not being previously mentioned being the Institute of Civil Engineers ("ICE").

Even at this early stage in the development of construction and engineering all **1-043** risks insurance the ambit and applicability of defects exclusions was of concern to the insurance market, with the standard wording stating:

"Loss or damage directly caused by:

(a)   Defective workmanship, material or design ...

Note: The Exclusion of loss or damage caused by (a) ... above shall be limited to the machine structure or work immediately affected and shall not extend to other work or property lost or damaged in consequence of a defect ...

This insurance does not cover consequential loss or damage of any kind or description whatsoever including delay in completing negotiating and loss of contract."[94]

The intention of the exclusion was to emphasise that the cover was to indemnify contractors (and other interested parties) for physical loss or damage to the contract works and other interests covered by the policy. The exclusion of "defective workmanship material or design" was the source of much discussion,[95] partly because hitherto there had been a complete exclusion and because what comprised faulty design was thought to be difficult to decide without resort to the opinion of a non-interested consulting engineer.

In 1954, Advanced Study Group 114 of the Insurance Institute of London was **1-044** formed. It met regularly throughout 1955 and 1956 and in 1957 published a report entitled The Underwriting of Contractors' All Risk Policies.[96] There was no unanimity in the study group on cover for loss arising out of defective design. On the one hand it was argued that the insurance requirements of contracts placed subject to ICE Conditions were already most onerous and that, as the Contractor was not required to insure loss arising from defective design, insurers should not extend voluntarily their polices to provide this cover. Furthermore, loss due to defective design was a professional risk, which could be taken care of by a professional indemnity policy. On the other hand, many members of the group considered that it would be virtually impossible to prove that a loss arose from defective design. The report marked the start of the major role the Insurance Institute of London has played in recent times in explaining and standardising CAR insurance.

Issues regarding the scope and application of all risks cover was not confined to **1-045** the field of construction and engineering; Gorman, commenting on the 1951 Institute Cargo Clauses (All Risks), stated that:

"[t]here will be present in many of the claims reported under the "all risks" form of policy very serious and extremely difficult questions relating to whether an occurrence is fortuitous or natural, what is inherent or extraneous, what is wilful or accidental, and perhaps even what is lawful and unlawful, but these must be decided upon an individual claim basis, using the basic principles herein discussed as a guide."[97]

Problems with the interpretation and application of the defects exclusions **1-046** continued with J.B. Guild writing a paper in 1965 for the Insurance Institute of London[98] reviewing the 1963 Form of Contract (which superseded the 1939 edi-

---

94   Tinsen, *The Insurance Institute of London Contractors' All Risks Insurance* (1955), pp.5 and 9.
95   Tinsen, *The Insurance Institute of London Contractors' All Risks Insurance* (1955), p.9.
96   The Institute of London The Underwriting of Contractors' All Risk Policies: Report of Advanced Study Group 114 London: IIL, 1963).
97   J.P. Gorman "All Risks of Loss v All Loss: An Examination of Broad Form Insurance Coverages" (1959) 34 Notre Dame L. 346, 356.
98   J.B. Guild, *The Insurance Institute of London Claims Under Contractors' All Risks Policies* (London:

tion)[99] that introduced cl.20 A, B and C which allocated the responsibility for insuring the works in respect of all risks between the Employer and the Contractor. The paper records that the insurance policy condition which gave rise to the most difficulty was the exclusion relating to defective materials, workmanship and design.

1-047 As commerce developed new forms of risks were included in policies which required new forms of wording, and there was a demand for new forms of all risk cover including in the field of oil and gas.

The paper also goes on to identify the move to a hierarchy of more restrictive exclusionary wording, examples of which include the following:

"Excluding the cost of making good any portion of the property rendered necessary by defective materials or workmanship but this insurance shall cover destruction or damage to other property which occurs as a result of such defective materials or workmanship",[100]

and a more generous wording which stated:

"Excluding the cost of making good faulty materials, workmanship or design but this exclusion shall not apply to damage to Contract Works resulting from such faulty materials, workmanship or design."[101]

The paper concludes by suggesting that it would be of the greatest service to contractors and their advisers if insurers were to reach some unanimity as to their intentions and agree upon a wording, or a set of wordings which would clearly and unambiguously give effect to these intentions.

1-048 The need for construction and engineering all risks insurance continued to increase with the amount of cover required for projects also increasing. The insurance market responded by sharing risks, for example in 1965 cover of £110 million for the construction of Wylfa power station was shared and there were discussions regarding sharing the risk of the construction of a channel tunnel at an estimated cost of £170 million.

1-049 During the period 1965 to 1969 there was a change in attitude by the underwriters of construction and engineering risks, with ratings increasing as a result of heavy losses from fire damage to buildings, the collapse of cofferdams, bridges and buildings and damage to sea defences. Excesses were increased and a number of insurers declined to provide any cover for wet working.

1-050 The first reference to annual CAR cover was in 1969 in a paper by Smith[102] who suggested that:

"For some years contractors' all risk policies have been issued on an annual blanket basis to cover all work undertaken by the contractor during the year, the usual basis of the insurance being either turnover (that is, value of work done) or the wages paid to employees, and the rate having been set according to claims experience. These annual insurances were originally issued in respect of building work only, where the greatly varying hazards associated with general civil engineering work were not met. They were later issued to cover particular classes of civil engineering work, mainly the construction of roads and/or sewers not exceeding a specified maximum depth. Insurers were feeling their way forward slowly and it once seemed that some insurers would issue blanket policies which would include most types of civil electrical and mechanical engineering work in addition to

IIL, 1965).
99 The predecessor of the JCT Conditions of Contract.
100 Guild, *The Insurance Institute of London Claims Under Contractors' All Risks Policies* (1965), p.12.
101 Guild, *The Insurance Institute of London Claims Under Contractors' All Risks Policies* (1965), p.12.
102 E.S. Smith, "Recent Developments in Contractors' All Risks Insurance" (1969) Chartered Insurance Institute 33, 37–38.

ordinary building work, but with the possible exclusion of work in tidal waters, which presents such varying hazards as always to require individual rating. The adverse experience ... led insurers to check this advance in the issue of annual contractors' all risks policies, and some of them are again restricting blanket annual covers to the types of work they consider the least hazardous, while others require to be specially notified of specified types of work they consider to be hazardous so that these can be separately rated contract by contract within the general framework of the annual policy."

In 1971, the Insurance Institute of London published its second report,[103] express-   **1-051**
ing concern at the "sheer size" of important, new civil engineering projects and the limitations of the world market capacity for insurance during construction, with poor underwriting results and the consequences of insurance company mergers in the United Kingdom having the effect of reducing the available market. How best to describe all-risks construction and engineering insurance still troubled the insurance market with the introduction to the report stating:

"[t]here is a body of opinion which feels that the use of the words 'All Risks' is misleading because of the number of exclusions which appear in the wording. It is, however, generally accepted as an honest attempt by Insurers to describe the maximum coverage obtainable by a Contractor to protect his responsibilities under contract and is much to be preferred to such terms as 'Comprehensive'."[104]

In the same year, a committee was formed by leading insurers in the London   **1-052**
market to promulgate a standard set of defect-exclusion clauses that would adequately define the various "different levels of cover which insurers were prepared to offer"[105] and a suite of standard-form defect-exclusion clauses, was made available to the market. The clauses, labelled "DE1" to "DE5" by the original drafting committee, provide five different levels of cover thought to adequately define the various degrees of cover that insurers were prepared to offer.[106] A similar suite of standard-form defect-exclusion clauses was introduced in 1996 by a consultative group of engineering insurers known as the London Engineering Group ("LEG") for engineering class risk. These clauses are labelled "LEG 1" to "LEG 3".[107] These clauses have been widely adopted in the CAR market,[108] with a revised set of DE clauses published a decade later. The 1995 DE wordings seek to reproduce the levels of cover prescribed by the original clauses, whilst seeking to clarify their meaning in certain respects.[109]

In 1995, the Court of Appeal in *Cementation Piling and Foundations Ltd v Com-*   **1-053**
mercial Union Insurance Plc; sub nom. *Cementation Piling and Foundations Ltd v Aegon Insurance Ltd*[110] considered the application of a defects exclusion. In *Cementation Piling and Foundations Ltd* sand retained by the walls of a newly

---

[103] Insurance Institute of London, The Underwriting of Contractors' All Risks Policies Report of Advanced Study Group No.192 (London: ILL, 1971).

[104] Insurance Institute of London, The Underwriting of Contractors' All Risks Policies Report of Advanced Study Group No.192 (London: ILL, 1971), p.2.

[105] Insurance Institute of London, Construction Insurance - Research Study Group Report 208B (London: IIL, 2010), para.8.8.2.2, p.159.

[106] See Ch.16, para.16-029.

[107] See Ch.16, para.16-065.

[108] Insurance Institute of London, Construction Insurance - Research Study Group Report 208B (London: IIL, 2010), para.8.8.2.4, p.161.

[109] Insurance Institute of London, Construction Insurance - Research Study Group Report 208B (London: IIL, 2010), para.8.8.2.5, p.164.

[110] *Cementation Piling and Foundations Ltd v Commercial Union Insurance Plc*; sub nom *Cementation Piling and Foundations Ltd v Aegon Insurance Ltd* [1995] 1 Lloyd's Rep. 97; (1995) 74 B.L.R. 98; 47 Con. L.R. 14.

constructed dock was found to have escaped into the dock. A claim was made under the project all-risks policy for the removal of the sand and the filling of the voids in the dock walls through which the sand escaped. The policy excluded the cost of remedying defects, "unless the property insured suffers actual loss, destruction or damage as a result of such defect". The clause provided that the:

"additional costs of introducing improvements, betterments or corrections in the rectification of the design, material or workmanship causing such loss or damage shall always be excluded."

The insurers were prepared to pay for the sand clean up, accepting that this constituted damage to the dock, but not for the filling of the gaps in the dock walls, which they regarded as defects in the works, rather than consequential damage. The Court of Appeal held that the insured was entitled to recover the cost of repairing defects in the walls. It held that the insuring clause, which indemnified "in respect of physical damage to the property insured"[111] had to be read in the context provided by the defects exclusion clause.[112]

1-054   By 2002, the position had been reached where changes in working arrangements, advances in technology, failure to assess risk accurately and the failure of standard exclusions to keep abreast of the changes to the standard-form engineering contracts meant that, although there was more capacity in the insurance market, some contractors were having difficulty arranging insurance. During this period, disputes as to the meaning and application of exclusion clauses were coming before the Court of Appeal more frequently. In 2002, in *Skanska Construction Ltd v Egger (Barony) Ltd*,[113] the Court of Appeal, in the context of a particular construction contract, considered the formation of cracks in a defective concrete floor slab was held not to be "loss or damage" under the relevant clause. Mance LJ stated that:

"In this contractual scheme, the mere manifestation of a defect under ordinary usage, which the contractor is anyway obliged to make good under the contractual scheme relating to defects, cannot in my judgment constitute loss or damage to the slab."[114]

Subsequently, in *CA Blackwell (Contractors) Ltd*,[115] the Court of Appeal considered the extent to which property which was in defective condition was excluded under a DE3 exclusion, with the Court of Appeal returning to consider this issue in *Seele Austria GmbH & Co KG v Tokio Marine Europe Insurance Ltd*[116] in 2007. In *Seele Austria GmbH & Co KG* a set of "punched" windows were installed during the construction of the facade of a building. Having been installed, the windows leaked during water testing and had to be replaced, which required the completed stone cladding and internal plaster finishes to be removed to gain access.

---

[111]   *Cementation Piling and Foundations Ltd* [1995] 1 Lloyd's Rep. 97 at 102; (1995) 74 B.L.R. 98 at 105; 47 Con. L.R. 14 at 19, per Sir Ralph Gibson.

[112]   *Cementation Piling and Foundations Ltd* [1995] 1 Lloyd's Rep. 97 at 102; (1995) 74 B.L.R. 98 at 108-109; 47 Con. L.R. 14 at 21-22, per Sir Ralph Gibson.

[113]   *Skanska Construction Ltd v Egger (Barony) Ltd* [2002] EWCA Civ 310; [2002] B.L.R. 236; 83 Con. L.R. 132; [2003] Lloyd's Rep. I.R. 479.

[114]   *Skanska Construction Ltd* [2002] EWCA Civ 310 at [30]; [2002] B.L.R. 236 at 242–243; 83 Con. L.R. 132 at 142–143; [2003] Lloyd's Rep. I.R. 479, per Mance LJ.

[115]   *CA Blackwell (Contractors) Ltd* [2007] EWCA Civ 1450; [2008] 1 All E.R. (Comm) 885; [2008] Lloyd's Rep. I.R. 529.

[116]   *Seele Austria GmbH & Co KG v Tokio Marine Europe Insurance Ltd* [2008] EWCA Civ 441; [2009] 1 All E.R. (Comm) 171; [2008] B.L.R. 337; [2008] Lloyd's Rep. I.R. 739. The primary dispute was over the interpretation of a bespoke additional indemnity for access damage.

The written commentary to the original set of DE clauses included a worked **1-055** example, which was then reproduced by the Insurance Institute of London Advanced Study Group No.208B[117]; this was most recently published in 2010[118] and supplemented in 2013.[119] Exclusions from cover, including the DE and LEG exclusions in all risks polices continue to cause confusion and in a number of instances lead to disputes as to the extent of cover provided. However helpful guidance has now been provided for example, on the interpretation of LEG clauses in the Canadian case of *Acciona Infrastructure Canada Inc.*[120] and in *PCL Constructors Canada Inc* in relation to a similar clause.[121] It is anticipated that disputes will also continue to emerge regarding the circumstances in which a co-insured party is protected from a subrogated claim brought by the insurer in the name of another co-insured under a joint names insurance policy which raise complex questions of law.[122]

Today, the vast majority of CAR insurance comprising works, public liability and delay is purchased together from one insurer and arranged by one broker with only the very largest construction groups having their own captive brokers and insurers. The demand for CAR insurance is likely to rise in line with the increase in the number of major projects across the world,[123] with new products being introduced by insurance companies.[124] An alternative to CAR insurance which has recently received industry and government support is that of the Integrated Project Insurance Model ("IPI") insurance policy and contract,[125] which encourages greater partnership working between parties involved in implementing a building project. This approach is currently being trialled by the government in order to see how effective it is in practice. It is suggested that in the short term this approach is unlikely to be taken up widely by the construction and insurance industries as its success is entirely dependent on the degree to which people trust one another enough to deliver a project, even when things go wrong.

Over the last decade the Law Commission and the Scottish Law Commission **1-056** have consulted extensively on insurance contract law issues. The Law Commissions' overriding aim has been to ensure that there is a better balance of interests

---

[117] Reproduced in: Insurance Institute of London, Construction Insurance - Research Study Group Report 208B (London: IIL, 1999).

[118] Reproduced in: Insurance Institute of London, *Construction Insurance - Research Study Group Report 208B* (London: IIL, 2010), para.8.8.2.3, p.160.

[119] Reproduced in: Insurance Institute of London, *Construction Insurance - A Supplement to Research Study Group Report 208B* (London: IIL, 2012).

[120] *Acciona Infrastructure Canada Inc. v Allianz Global Risks US Insurance Co*, 2014 BCSC 1568. See below, para.9-060 and para.16-067.

[121] *PCL Constructors Canada Inc. v Allianz Global Risks US Insurance Co* [2014] ONSC 7480.

[122] E.g. *Gard Marine & Energy Ltd v China National Chartering Co Ltd; China National Chartering Co Ltd v Daiichii Chuo Kisen Kaisha* [2015] EWCA Civ 16; [2015] 2 All E.R. (Comm) 894; [2015] Lloyd's Rep. I.R. 295. See below, paras 20-040 to 20-052.

[123] E.g. on 27 October 2010 a Construction Erection All Risks Insurance ("CEAR") contract for the largest experimental nuclear fusion facility in the world, called the International Thermonuclear Experimental Reactor ("ITER") facility was signed by the lead insurer Zurich France together with a number of co-insurers. See ITER Newsline 156 "Insurance Contract for ITER Construction Signed" (3 December, 2010) *http://www.iter.org/newsline/156/508* [Accessed 23 June 2016].

[124] E.g. in 2014 Allianz launched an enhanced Construction Project All Risks insurance ("CPAR"), which provides greater third party cover for multiple parties. See *"Allianz Launches Enhanced Construction Project"* (12 March 2014) *http://www.mynewsdesk.com/uk/allianz-insurance/pressreleases/allianz-launches-enhanced-construction-proposition-971701* [Accessed 28 June 2016].

[125] See further below, paras 2-107 to 2-111.

between policy holders and insurers. Their research resulted in the introduction of the Insurance Act 2015 ("the 2015 Act"), which came into force on 12 August 2016. It is the single most important change to have taken place in insurance law over the past century. Although its impact on CAR insurance has yet to be fully understood. In aviation insurance for example, underwriters have already produced some clauses for the market to reflect the 2015 Act.[126] However, in construction insurance the pace of change has, perhaps unsurprisingly, been slower. It is anticipated that in the future some of the CAR policy wordings will change, but that reforming standard market insurance wordings will take time.

1-057   The 2015 Act introduces widespread reforms to the pre-contractual duties of disclosure and misrepresentation owed by the insured with the aim of improving the insurance placement process and protecting policyholders from insurers "underwriting at the claims stage". The draconian remedy of avoidance for any breach of the duty of utmost good faith has been abolished, and instead the insurer will, largely,[127] be confined to proportionate remedies for any breach of the insured's pre-contractual duties based on the ordinary restitutionary principles of contract law.[128] The 2015 Act also introduces new provisions targeting policy terms in order to modify the effect of a breach of warranty[129] and an insurer's capacity to rely on the breach of an irrelevant term in order to deny the indemnity.[130] Finally, the 2015 Act introduces a new statutory remedy for fraudulent claims made by the insured that will, subject to any bespoke terms in the policy, govern the effect of a fraudulent claim on previous or future genuine claims made under the policy and the insurer's right to terminate upon discovery of the fraud.[131] For a detailed analysis of the 2015 Act, see Ch.5.

1-058   The Enterprise Act 2016 ("the 2016 Act") has also come into force. It introduces new provisions into the 2015 Act to allow an insured to claim damages for the late payment of insurance claims. The new provisions operate by introducing an implied term into all insurance policies requiring the insurer to pay claims within a reasonable time, and any breach of this term will entitle the insured to claim damages subject to the usual contractual rules of causation, remoteness and mitigation. For a detailed analysis of the 2016 Act, see Ch.23.

1-059   Notwithstanding the new legislation the construction industry continues to present both challenges and opportunities to the insurance industry, ever more complicated projects being undertaken both on land and at sea. The changing face of construction and the technological advances for example, in the renewables industry mean that the construction professionals and underwriters need to consider carefully the allocation of risks in the construction contract so that they can be suitably managed and mitigated. These will continue to evolve as the legislative landscape and technology evolves.

---

126 Aviation Insurance Clauses Group ("AICG") *http://www.aicg.co.uk/AICG_Web/AICG_Home/AICG_ Web/Home.aspx?hkey=ea855be1-c149-4ed3-96ba-242fc7e49a8c* [Accessed 28 June 2016]. See below, para. 25-014.
127 See below, para.5-073.
128 See below, para.5-080.
129 See below, para.5-090.
130 See below, para.5-103.
131 See below, para.5-116.

Chapter 2

THE ALLOCATION OF RISK IN CONSTRUCTION CONTRACTS

1.   Introduction

(a)   Risk

Introduction.   Construction projects are subject to an array of risks. In the event that any risk materialises, the consequences for the parties involved in the project could be catastrophic; either one or more of the parties involved will lose money or, in the worst case, a project might have to be abandoned because it is not physically possible to complete or because the cost of doing so would be prohibitive. Furthermore, there is the risk that employees or the public at large might suffer injury, damage or loss as a result of implementing the construction project. In every project, some of these risks will be controlled, and some will be beyond the parties' control. It is possible for the parties to evaluate and mitigate those risks that can be identified.   **2-001**

   In order to mitigate relevant risks, the parties to a construction contract should allocate responsibility for each risk to a particular party. As will be seen, the allocation of risk is a process which begins at the very start of a construction project.   **2-002**

(b) Definitions

2-003　**Definitions.**　It is helpful to start by defining some key terms that will assist in understanding what is meant by the allocation of risk in a construction-insurance context.

2-004　**Insurance.**　Insurance is the equitable transfer of risk of a potential loss, from one entity to another, in exchange for a premium. Insurance does not prevent a risk from occurring but merely redistributes the financial losses associated with that risk.

2-005　**Risk.**　The meaning of the word "risk" is multifaceted because it is an expression that can be used in many differing contexts and, thus, it can be a difficult term to define. Risk may simply be described as the possibility of suffering harm or loss. In the context of a construction project, "risk" is best described as a contracting party's exposure to the possibility of suffering harm or loss arising out of an unforeseen event. The parties to a construction contract are primarily concerned with risks that affect productivity, performance, quality and economy of construction.

2-006　**CAR insurance.**　CAR insurance primarily seeks to indemnify against the risk of any physical damage being caused to the Works, whether temporary or permanent Works. This is the main purpose of the policy.

2-007　　There are many risks that a CAR policy may not cover, even if such risks are expressly required to be provided for by the construction contract—these include: damage and defects caused by negligent design, the cost of correcting defective workmanship, employers' liability, gradual pollution caused by the works, inherent defects and damage occurring after the defect liability period has ended, some aspects of maritime and aircraft insurance[1] and motor policies. Some of these exceptions are considered in greater detail below at paras 2-072 to 2-086.

2-008　　A CAR policy will often include additional categories of insurance, including cover for physical damage to types of property other than the Works, such as damage to construction plant, equipment and machinery, materials in transit and for third-party liability[2] and consequential loss.[3] In some cases the construction contract will require that certain of those additional risks are insured to a specific level, including third-party risks and the risk of defective design.

2-009　**Employer.**　The Employer is the party who commissions the construction project. It may be an individual person or organisation, or it could be a conglomerate of venture capitalists. The Employer is desirous of having something built and is responsible for putting the construction project out to tender, or otherwise engaging a principal contractor to complete the Works.

2-010　**Employer's risks.**　A construction contract will usually provide that the Employer will be responsible for the risks that are attributable to his agents, servants or advisors.

2-011　　Employer's risks will usually be specified in the terms of the construction

---

[1]　See further below, Chs 24 and 25.
[2]　See further below, Ch.18.
[3]　See further below, para.17-048.

contract and may include: (i) damage which is an unavoidable result of the construction of the Works in accordance with the Contract, with the exception of damage resulting from the Contractor's methods of working; (ii) defects stemming from the design of the Works, save where the design was provided by the Contractor; and (iii) various risks relating to the location or nature of the site. This last category of risks will generally not be insured, or indeed insurable, under the CAR policy. It includes war,[4] rebellion,[5] riot, strike, commotion[6] and Acts of Government.

2-012 If one of the Employer's risks materialises, it is likely that the Contractor will be allowed more time, more money or both in order to complete the project. The Employer will usually be able to mitigate the risk by arranging specialised insurance, which will usually be obtained in a separate policy or as a "bolt-on" to the CAR policy. For instance, the risk of delay in performance and cost over-run can be dealt with by way of completion risk insurance, while defective design by or on behalf of the Employer can be dealt with by means of professional indemnity insurance and the risk of non-performance can be dealt with by a non-performance surety.[7]

2-013 **Contractor.** The Contractor is the person or group or organisation responsible for implementing the construction project. Where a tender evaluation process is in place, the Contractor will provide a tender for carrying out the construction project. The tender will set out how the Contractor plans to complete the project and it will state the price for which the Contractor is prepared to carry out the construction. In large scale projects the Contractor will usually hire subcontractors to complete specific parts of the construction project.

2-014 **Contractor's risks.** Contractor's risks are those risks that the construction contract allocates to the Contractor. These will include the risks that are attributable to his subcontractors, suppliers and others who are directly connected with his activities. The Contractor will then be responsible for ensuring those risks are properly managed and insured (if indeed they are capable of being insured).

2-015 The Contractor's risks may be specified in the construction contract but it is more likely that the contract will state that the Contractor is deemed to have assumed responsibility for all the risks relating to the construction project that are not stated to be the Employer's risks. The Contractor's risks will include the cost of putting right damage caused to the Works (whether expressed in financial terms or in terms of delay in time).

2-016 As explained above in para.2-007, certain risks borne by the Contractor will be excluded from the CAR policy. An example might be the risk of latent defects in the Works caused by defective workmanship of the Contractor's employees. The Contractor can protect himself against such excluded risks by taking out a decennial insurance[8] or a public liability insurance policy[9] for the project design and can obtain specific cover to insure against the consequences stemming from the use of defective material and workmanship.

---

[4]   See below, paras 15-043 to 15-048.
[5]   See below, paras 15-052 to 15-053.
[6]   See below, paras 15-059 to 15-060.
[7]   See below, para.2-116.
[8]   See below, para.2-017.
[9]   See further below, Ch.18.

2-017   **Decennial insurance.**   Decennial insurance covers any liability of the Contractor for a 10-year period beginning at the date of practical completion of the Works for latent defects in the stability of a structure and for major defects in the weather shield. The 10-year period of cover matches the limitation period for bringing legal action in respect of the stability and major defects in the structure or of important parts of the structure in certain jurisdictions, mostly where the civil code forms the basis of the legal system. Once the 10-year period has passed, then insurance is not necessary because legal action would be barred by the statute of limitations in operation in that jurisdiction. As with a CAR policy, a decennial insurance policy covers the full cost of rebuilding the project. Additional cover can be added to the policy to cover expenses such as the cost of removal of stock and machinery from the premises. The cover does not extend to general wear and tear or maintenance costs and, generally, accidental damage is a prerequisite to indemnity.

2-018   It is possible that some of the risks borne by the Contractor cannot be insured at all, such as the risk: (i) that the Contractor will incur additional cost; or (ii) that the Works will contain patent defects—as opposed to latent defects.

2-019   However, Contractors are willing to take on these risks because if the risks do not eventuate then the Contractor may make additional profit. Therefore, the possibility of non-occurrence of the risk is an incentive for contractors to take on a project.

2-020   **No fault allocation.**   No fault allocation or "Joint Names" insurance covers the insured regardless of which named party to the policy caused the damage and the parties interests will be the same.[10] In the context of insurance for a construction contract, parties are usually regarded as composite insureds; the wrongful act of one joint name will not prejudice the interests of the other party.[11] For example, under a joint names policy if part of a claim brought by one of the parties is fraudulent then that will not invalidate the whole claim, which would otherwise include the claim of the innocent party.

2-021   Under a joint names policy the insurer will usually have no right of subrogation against any other party named as an insured.[12] Thus, where the Contractor makes a claim on the joint names policy for the insurance company to pay out for a loss caused by the fault of the Employer, the insurer cannot then recover damages from the Employer. The position is different under a single name policy. Where, for example, insurance is held by the Contractor only, the insurer would retain a subrogated right to seek to recover losses from the Employer that were caused by the fault of the Employer.

2-022   In *Co-operative Retail Services Ltd v Taylor Young Partnership Ltd (Carillion Construction Ltd, Part 20 Defendants) Co-operative Retail Services Ltd*[13] the House of Lords held that where a construction contract stipulates that parties are to be protected by a joint names insurance policy, there exists an implied term in the construction contract that the risk is also to be shared equally between the parties.[14]

---

[10]   See below, paras 20-030 to 20-037.

[11]   See below, para 20-030.

[12]   See below, para 20-040.

[13]   *Co-operative Retail Services Ltd v Taylor Young Partnership Ltd (Carillion Construction Ltd, Part 20 Defendants) Co-operative Retail Services Ltd* [2002] UKHL 17; [2002] 1 W.L.R. 1419; [2002] 1 All E.R. (Comm) 918.

[14]   *Co-operative Retail Services Ltd* [2002] UKHL 17 at [65]; [2002] 1 W.L.R. 1419 at 1438; [2002] 1

Therefore, where the Employer insured the liability for damage to the project in the joint names of all contractors and subcontractors, no contribution could be claimed from any of them for insured losses.

The court will generally give a strict interpretation to the wording of the underly-   **2-023**
ing clause in the construction contract. For example, in *Tyco Fire & Integrated Solutions (UK) Ltd (formerly Wormald Ansul (UK) Ltd) v Rolls Royce Motor Cars Ltd (formerly Hireus Ltd)*,[15] a mains water pipe burst and caused a flood that damaged the Works and other parts of the plant. On the assumption that the damage had occurred as a result of Tyco's negligence, the issue arose as to whether Tyco, in its capacity as Contractor, was liable to Rolls-Royce in respect of the damage to existing structures. Tyco sought to rely on a clause in the joint names policy that provided protection for both parties relating to the Works. However, the critical clause relating to the existing property provided cover for "others including but not limited to contractors" and did not refer specifically to the Contractor. The court held that an interpretation of the word "others" could not include the Contractor and on that basis the policy could not offer Tyco any protection from a claim for an indemnity.[16]

In spite of the fact that the use of joint names insurance should reduce litigation   **2-024**
by providing a clear and predictable allocation of risk between the relevant parties, that does not necessarily happen in practice, especially because there is no standardised wording used across the market. Therefore, it is crucial for parties to the construction contract to ensure that they are properly covered by the joint names policy.

An example of no-fault allocation of risk can be found in the Joint Contracts   **2-025**
Tribunal ("JCT") Contract 2011 cl.6.5 (previously JCT 21.2.1).[17] This clause requires the Contractor to take out an insurance policy to cover:

> "any expense, liability, loss, claim or proceedings which the Employer may incur or sustain by reason of injury or damage to any property caused by collapse, subsidence, heave, vibration, weakening or removal of support or lowering of ground water arising out of or in the course of or by reason of the carrying out of the Works excluding injury or damage" (except where the damage is caused by a list of excluded causes, which are discussed in more detail in Ch.18)."[18]

This is an insurance clause and not an indemnity clause and requires the Contrac-   **2-026**
tor to arrange insurance in the joint names of the Contractor and the Employer. The insurance will cover any property other than the Works, including the Employer's

---

All E.R. (Comm) 918 at 931, per Lord Hope. His Lordship pointed out that this was not the ratio for the decision in the case, because it had been decided on different facts. However, in the event that the construction contract has no mutual exclusion of liability as between the parties in relation to a particular type of damage then a term would be implied that the parties intended to exclude the right to sue one another, where the insurance had already provided a remedy. This case gave rise to judicial consideration of subrogation and the doctrine of circuity in joint names contracts. For further discussion on this see below, paras 20-032 to 20-034.

[15] *Tyco Fire & Integrated Solutions (UK) Ltd (formerly Wormald Ansul (UK) Ltd) v Rolls Royce Motor Cars Ltd (formerly Hireus Ltd)* [2008] EWCA Civ 286; [2008] 2 All E.R. (Comm) 584; [2008] Lloyd's Rep. I.R. 617.

[16] *Tyco Fire & Integrated Solutions (UK) Ltd* [2008] EWCA Civ 286 at [63]–[65]; [2008] 2 All ER (Comm) 584 at 606 and 607; [2008] Lloyd's Rep. I.R. 617 at 632 and 633, per Rix LJ.

[17] JCT Contracts, SBC/Q 2011 *JCT Standard Form of Building Contract With Quantities 2011* (London: Sweet & Maxwell, 2011), pp.68-69. See further below, paras 18-058 to 18-066.

[18] See below, paras 18-061 to 18-062.

own property, adjacent third-party property (e.g. existing structures) or the employer's adjoining property.

2-027   The clause excludes: (i) damage to the Contract Works, which is usually provided for by alternative insurance options under the contract; (ii) the negligence of the Contractor, his subcontractors and agents—the construction contract will already have provided for the Contractor to indemnify the Employer in respect of loss, injury or damage arising in this way; (iii) negligence of professionals, such as designers, which will be borne by those professionals under their own professional indemnity insurance; and (iv) a further particularised list of exclusions.[19]

2-028   A Contractor will usually use the same insurers for his public liability[20] and cl.6.5 liability in order to avoid disputes as to which policy (and which insurer) should respond. An example of such a dispute might be where the Contractor has separate insurers and there is a dispute between them as to whether or not the relevant damage was in fact caused by the Contractor's negligence. It is also important that the term of the insurance policy coincides with the term of the Contractor's liability under the contract (known as the rectification period/defects liability period).

2-029   Under the JCT contract, it is also possible for the parties to agree to take out an All Risks insurance policy of the Works in Joint Names (respectively Option A and C under the Contract).[21] This will be done either by the Contractor or the Employer. In either case, the insurance must cover the full reinstatement value of the Works, including professional fees, to be maintained up to the date of the practical completion certificate. The onus to notify of any loss or damage remains with the Contractor.[22]

2-030   **Knock-for-knock.**   Knock-for-knock insurance describes cover where the parties agree that they will mutually hold the other harmless for any injury suffered. The parties to the construction contract may write in an indemnity clause whereby they each agree not to hold the other party liable for injury, damage or loss sustained for example in relation to their own employees and property. In other words each party is responsible for injury and damage occurring to its own personnel and property. Again, the purpose behind this type of scheme is to ensure, so far as possible, that such allocation is clear and predictable and will enable disputes to be resolved and that compensation is paid more quickly than would otherwise be the case.

2-031   This is usually achieved by a combination of exclusion clauses and indemnity clauses, as well as mutual insurance obligations. The aim is that insurance will be obtained by each party to cover the losses that that party might suffer and it is

---

[19]   See below, paras 18-061 to 18-062.

[20]   See below, Ch.18.

[21]   These insurance options can be found in Schedule 3 to the JCT Standard Building Contract, for which, see JCT Contracts, *SBC/Q 2011 JCT Standard Form of Building Contract With Quantities 2011* (2011), pp.88–92. The type of project will determine which option will operate and with which party the obligation to insure will lie. Option A will arise where the project is to build new buildings and the Contractor is obliged to take out a joint names, all risks policy. Option B will arise where the Employer is obliged to take out the joint names, all risks policy. Insurance Option C is for use in the case of alterations to existing property. Option C requires the Employer to take out joint names, all risks insurance for existing structures and their contents. The Option that applies (as agreed between the Contractor and the Employer) will be set out in the Contract Particulars; See SBC/Q 2011 p.93.

[22]   See below, paras 21-006 to 21-010 and 21-013 to 21-020.

intended to operate like no fault cover. It is also assumed that the allocated risks will then be covered by insurance.

2. THE PRACTICE OF RISK ALLOCATION

(a) The allocation of risk

Risk allocation. The key principle underpinning risk allocation is that risks should be borne by the party that is best able to evaluate, control, bear the cost of, and benefit from, the assumption of that particular risk. The first stage in the allocation process is to identify the sources and types of risk that are likely to arise in a particular construction project. The next stage is to analyse each risk in order to determine the potential consequences of it eventuating and to assess the likelihood of its occurrence. By doing this, the level of exposure can be established and a value can be placed on the risk. In the case of large construction contracts, risk analysis may require a full technical investigation of the proposed site and all relevant environmental factors relating to the site, such as ground conditions, weather conditions and so forth. These factors are explored in more detail below in paras 2-046 to 2-068.   2-032

The parties will then need to consider what their respective attitudes are to each risk before deciding how to respond. The issues to determine will be, in essence, how the risk can be best managed in practical terms, and whether the risk should be transferred to another party or retained and, if possible, insured or not insured.   2-033

Risk identification. Risk identification can take numerous forms, including using pre-prepared checklists, undertaking site visits and/or technical investigations, analysing prior projects, and even keeping up to date with current socio-political, economic and environmental affairs.   2-034

The aim is to identify all the risks that might prevent, degrade, delay or enhance the progress of the construction project. Although it is likely that unforeseen risks will emerge as the project proceeds, the aim is to identify the foreseeable risks before the project commences so that they can be properly managed. The parties will need to consider the probability of a risk eventuating and the ultimate impact (in terms of cost and delay) if it does materialise.   2-035

The factors that the Employer will be most concerned with are whether: (i) it will be able to obtain and continue to obtain proper funding for the project; (ii) the project will be granted all relevant planning permissions and other approvals, so that the project can commence; (iii) it can be completed within budget; (iv) it can be completed in time; (v) it will meet the end-user requirements and be fit for purpose, meeting all relevant design, construction and performance criteria.   2-036

The Contractor, on the other hand, will be concerned with whether: (i) it will be paid for all the work it does (including contract variations) in accordance with the terms of the contract; (ii) it will be able to achieve its desired margin; (iii) the contract will be—and is capable of being—fairly administered by the contract administrator; and that (iv) it avoids paying any sums to the Employer or third parties as a result of it taking on the construction project.   2-037

The treatment of risks. There are several ways in which a risk, once identified, can be dealt with. These include: (i) risk elimination; (ii) risk reduction; (iii) risk retention; and (iv) risk transference.   2-038

2-039   **Risk elimination.**   The elimination of a risk might entail a decision not to proceed with a particular project or to proceed with only a particular part of it. Alternatively, the parties might decide to proceed with a project in a different way, by for instance using a tried-and-tested method of construction rather than an innovative one.

2-040   **Risk reduction.**   Risk reduction can be achieved by the parties undertaking further investigations into a risk, for instance carrying out tests on ground conditions, studying likely weather conditions or ensuring that there are a sufficient number of workmen on site or that materials and equipment are of a particular quality.

2-041   **Risk retention.**   A party who retains a risk will do so by means of self-insurance (i.e. holding its own reserve), by bearing a large deductible or by the internal management of risks. For instance, an Employer or Contractor might protect himself against a retained risk by obtaining an option to purchase land (where he needs to secure the land to perform the project) or by obtaining detailed advice about cost and duration of the project. These retained risks will generally be accepted, on the basis that they form an acceptable part of the commercial risks which a party must bear in the pursuit of profit.

2-042   **Risk transference.**   Apart from transference by means of insurance, risks can be transferred through the operation of the construction contract, through subcontracting, by modifying contract conditions, or using exclusions, limitations of liability, indemnity clauses, performance bonds and guarantees. These methods of risk transference are described below (see paras 2-112 to 2-116). An in-depth analysis of these methods of risk transference is, however, outside the scope of this book.

2-043   **The misallocation of risk.**   Frequently, risks are allocated by aversion. This will often result in risks being misallocated. Some Employers will be prone to taking every opportunity to shift risk to a principal contractor, who in turn will try to shift that risk onto its subcontractors. The consequence of such misallocation is likely to be that a party is required to assume a risk over which it has little or no control, for which it is not adequately compensated or for which it is not adequately motivated to assume. As a result, an Employer who is conscious to avoid risk may be faced with tender prices inflated to reflect the Contractor's evaluation of the increased risks upon himself (which may even be priced at 100 per cent of the risk). Alternatively, less skilled and experienced contractors will win contracts on the basis that they are more likely to (unknowingly) accept grossly inequitable risk allocation. In those circumstances, it will be a false economy to offload risks onto a Contractor and it is likely to be more cost-effective overall if the Employer, if possible, retains and insures a particular risk itself.

(b)   Risks under the construction contract

2-044   **Risks incorporated into the construction contract.**   Once a construction contract is agreed, the Contractor is obliged to complete the project in accordance with the project specification. Any failure to do so gives rise to a claim in damages (save in very limited circumstances, such as physical or legal impossibility). Construction contracts will also seek to provide very specific remedies in the event of a breach of any one of its terms and conditions and the parties will be afforded specific entitlements should any perceived risks eventuate. This means that nearly every line of a construction contract will allocate a category of risk either to the Contractor or the Employer.

One reason parties are generally content to put such a complex contractual ar- **2-045** rangement in place is that allocating responsibility for certain risks before they eventuate ensures that as few disputes arise as possible as the project proceeds. This is important because such disputes will inevitably disrupt the progress of the project and a clear allocation of risk prior to the commencement of the project will ensure that, when they do arise, disputes can be resolved as efficiently as possible.

Risk in the tender phase.   The Employer will frequently select the main contrac- **2-046** tor for a project by inviting tenders from a number of potential contractors. The contractors will be provided with a specification and other information (i.e. architectural drawings) about the project which the contractor will be required to build. Each contractor will then submit a tender, setting out the price he would expect to be paid for completing the Works.

As part of the pricing process, where a Contractor must bear a particular risk **2-047** under a construction contract, he may include a contingency in the contract bid or price to take account of the cost of assuming that risk. Where a risk is in the Contractor's control, the contingency sum will be small. Where the risk is beyond his control, it might be that the contingency amount reaches the full cost of the occurrence of the risk. In that situation, the Employer has paid for the risk even if it does not eventuate and should it not eventuate then the Contractor will realise more profit. From the Employer's point of view, a contingency is a sum of money paid at the start of a project, in order to avoid having to bear an unpredictable amount of additional cost in the future, should a risk eventuate. Therefore, the Employer might wish to retain some risk, for example, a very expensive but very unlikely risk, in order to obtain a lower bid price.

Risks in the feasibility, planning and design phase.   Where a Contractor is **2-048** required to design the works, he will bear the risk of the design being defective. Where the design has been carried out by a third-party design team, then this team will bear the risk, as it will have, or ought to have, professional indemnity insurance. However, complications arise where designers initially instructed by the Employer are then novated to the Contractor. In this situation, the Contractor will need to define carefully who bears responsibility for the initial design produced whilst the designers are under the Employer's control. Usually, the Contractor will assume responsibility for the risks associated with the defective design, because there will be a presumption that the Contractor will have checked and verified the design. The Contractor will have been able to build into his tendered contract price the risk of taking responsibility of the design, although if the risk is taken on board later on during the course of the construction project this will not necessarily be so.

One important aspect of the planning and feasibility phase of a construction **2-049** project relates to investigations carried out to ensure that the foundations of the Works will be secure and not prone to collapse. A proper investigation into conditions of the ground is essential for this. Borehole testing is carried out and the results will usually be made available to a Contractor by an Employer. Problems are often encountered later on during the construction phase, where an earlier investigation has not been sufficiently thorough or the results have been interpreted incorrectly, or where unexpected subsoil material is found. Differing site conditions fall into two broad categories: (i) subsurface or latent site conditions that differ materially from those indicated in the tender or contract documents (where the failure to discover such conditions is likely to be due to inadequate investigation); and (ii) unforeseeable site conditions that differ materially from those ordinarily encountered in work of the character described in the agreement (which are unlikely to be discovered even on an entirely adequate investigation of the site).

2-050   The Contractor should make clear whether the risk that such investigations turn out to be inadequate is reserved to the Employer or if he is prepared to accept responsibility for them. The effect of the latter is that the Contractor is warranting the accuracy of the investigations. If this position is not reserved then, by accepting the investigations carried out by the Employer, the Contractor is deemed to have approved them. For instance, where the Contractor is invited to tender for a design and build project, the contract will usually provide that the Contractor will be responsible for any information given to him by the Employer in preparation for his tender.

2-051   When the responsibility for the investigations rests with the Employer, in the event problems are encountered as a result of inadequate investigations then the Contractor will be entitled to compensation under the contract, either by being granted more time or money to complete the work. However, the Contractor is unlikely to be entitled to more money or time if that part of the design or planning process that was defective was carried out by the Contractor or responsibility for it was novated to him.

2-052   **Risks during the construction phase.**   One important factor that underpins risk during the construction phase is the fact that this phase of any project will usually be the most expensive. In broad terms, during the construction phase, the main risks with which the parties will be concerned are: (i) whether the project can be completed within the agreed time-scale; (ii) whether the project will be built for the agreed Contract Sum; and (iii) whether the project can be delivered to the requisite quality.

2-053   The Contractor will normally be allocated the risks associated with the technical aspects of the building of the project, on the basis that he is best placed to control and manage such risks. This means that the Contractor will be responsible for defects and deficiencies that arise during construction, including defective design, defective material and workmanship, as well as inadequate site management and defective temporary works. The Contractor will also be responsible for problems that arise without any defect; for instance, perils such as subsidence, corrosion,[23] collapse, ground movement, explosion and fire and the use of dangerous substances. The Contractor will also be expected to bear responsibility for difficulties arising out of the technical complexity of a design or innovation in design requiring new methods of construction.

(c)   Risks inherent in common types of project

(i)   Design and build

2-054   **Design and build.**   Simple design and build projects will be subject to all of the risks considered in this chapter, including the risk of the project going over budget

---

[23] See below paras 15-020 to 15-026.

and over time. The risks that are likely to occur include damage being caused to the Works, damage to third-party property and the occurrence of environmental conditions, such as unexpected weather and ground conditions, which interfere with the ability of the Contractor to implement the programme of works.

Demolition.   The risk posed by the demolition process will depend entirely on the type of project being undertaken. Demolition might be carried out brick by brick or, in the case of large blocks of flats, by controlled explosion. This can be achieved more easily in a remote location than in a built-up area where significant precautions will need to be put in place beforehand. It is likely that the demolition process will have insurance consequences, for instance the need for joint names insurance, such as JCT cl.6.5 protection.[24] If part of an existing structure is to be retained, then damage to this structure may be excluded from the CAR policy and, if so, it will be reflected instead in appropriate public liability insurance.[25]   **2-055**

Foundations in building Works.[26]   Investigation of the ground soil of a site is essential to ensure that the foundations of a building are adequate. Borehole testing is carried out and the results will usually be made available to a Contractor by an Employer. Problems can be encountered during construction where an investigation has not been sufficiently thorough or the results are badly interpreted, or where unexpected subsoil material is found. When borehole testing is undertaken, care needs to be taken to avoid piling into underground services or tunnels.   **2-056**

(ii)   Civil mechanical

Civil mechanical.   Civil mechanical projects include manufacturing plants, power plants (whether thermal, hydroelectric, gas, diesel or nuclear) and refineries. The risks, over and above normal construction and erection risks, are those associated with the breakdown of the plant during testing and other risks associated with testing, such as an increased risk of fire and explosion following the introduction of feedstock into oil refineries and petrochemical plants. In projects involving the construction of functioning process plant, the additional risks associated with plant testing or initiating production processes develop at the end of the construction contract rather than throughout it. The economic value of the Construction Works increases throughout the life of the project due to the Works' incremental development and the addition of materials to build it and to furnish the buildings and so forth. Therefore, the potential for failure in a production process or in the testing phase means that the degree of risk to the Works is higher due to the potential cost of damage, in particular fire damage. Thus, the focus of the construction contract in terms of allocation of risk is likely to be on the lengthy and complex testing and commissioning procedures.   **2-057**

(iii)   Civil engineering

Civil engineering.   Civil engineering projects relate to the design and construction of complicated structures such as tall buildings, dams, bridges, tunnels and   **2-058**

---

[24]   See above, paras 2-020 to 2-029 and below, paras 18-058 to 18-066.
[25]   See further below, Ch.18.
[26]   See above, paras 2-049 to 2-051.

highways. The risks that are likely to eventuate in these sorts of projects are explained in more detail below.

2-059   Airports.   Aside from the separate aviation risks,[27] risks will stem from the fact that such projects can often involve one-off prestige buildings or very large buildings.

2-060   Bridges.   Risks stem from the fact that the bridge's foundations must be appropriate for the ground concerned and must have a sufficient strength for the design. The longer the bridge span, the more important it is to ensure that the subsoil characteristics have been analysed adequately and that the design of the foundations are appropriate. Furthermore, the higher the structure, the more sensitive it will be to the effects of storm and wind during construction. If foundations or piers are in a waterway, there is a greater risk of the Works flooding.

2-061   Tunnels and shafts.   As with foundations, the safe building of tunnels and shafts requires the proper investigation of ground conditions, by means of bore holes and, in larger projects, small test tunnels. The level of risk will depend on the method of construction being used, for example, whether it is a bored tunnel through rock or soft ground, or a cut and cover construction, or immersed tube tunnels constructed on a sea or river bed.

2-062   Dams.   During construction of a dam, rivers will need to be diverted. The most important underwriting consideration will be whether the height of the cofferdam (the watertight area created so the construction works can be carried out) will stand above the highest recorded water level of the river that has accrued during the last decade or more. If overtopping proves impossible to avoid, underwriters will increase the excess levels and restrict the cover by excluding inevitable damage to the cofferdam and main dam.

2-063   Steel-framed buildings.   Such structures are vulnerable to collapse, particularly during storms. The risk can be ameliorated by ensuring that adequate steel bracing and connections (parts that connect the steels together) are in place at all times. Care must also be taken when bolting together the structure because inadequate bolting of even a small section might lead to collapse, if that small section causes strain to the entire structure.

2-064   Tall structures.   There are many risks arising in relation to the construction of tall structures. Such buildings often require complex, deep foundations and materials must be lifted by hoist to their final position, which increases the risk of accidental impact. If built in a congested area, such as a city, materials often have to be stored on the lower floors of the building, which may lead to an increased risk of fire. A fire that starts on the higher elevations of a tall structure will be difficult to extinguish. Where new foundations are laid at a deeper level than those of existing surrounding buildings, there is a risk of cracking and subsidence to third-party properties.

---

[27] See below, para.25-009.

(iv)   Offshore contracts

Offshore contracts.   Construction Works carried out at sea[28] may be very   **2-065**
expensive in part because of the hostility of the environment and the fact that
weather conditions and the condition of the sea are both relatively unpredictable.
Insurers will regard this type of work as presenting a series of high risk operations, from the construction of the platform or other structure (probably at a site at
a significant distance from its final destination), to the float out, the tow to the
offshore position, emplacement and final fit out. Each of these stages will present
its own particular risks, including the significant possibility of total loss whilst out
at sea.

In common with a standard construction project the risk of loss and damage to   **2-066**
the Works will be allocated to the Contractor whilst the Works are under his control.
The exception to that general rule is that if any of the stated Employer's risks occurs (e.g. war,[29] Employer's negligence), this will be borne by the Employer.

The risk of injury to a party's own personnel and its own property is allocated   **2-067**
on a "knock-for-knock" basis.[30] That is to say, the parties agree that they will mutually hold the other harmless for any such injury so that each party is responsible for
injury and damage occurring to its own personnel and property.

The risk of harm to third parties is allocated on a fault basis and consequential   **2-068**
losses are usually mutually excluded. Pollution risk will often be allocated on a
"knock-for-knock" basis with each party assuming the risk of pollution emanating
from its property. Usually, the owner will take responsibility for pollution emanating from a well.

(d)   Risk under the insurance policy/contract

(i)   The CAR policy

The insurance policy/contract.   As discussed above at paras 2-010 to 2-012 and   **2-069**
2-014 to 2-016, the construction contract will allocate to each party the risks and
insurance responsibilities arising out of the construction project. The obligation to
insure does not reduce the likelihood of risks occurring or indeed the responsibility for managing those risks but insurance does transfer the cost of the risks; should
they eventuate the cost will be borne by the insurer. The main contingencies in
construction projects are fire, explosion, storm, flood, burst pipes, vandalism, theft,
impact and accidental damage.

The insurance policy will set out the forms of loss and damage that are to be the   **2-070**
subject of the policy. This will often be defined as any form of physical loss or damage but this may be qualified by one or more exceptions depending on the peculiarities of the project. The policy will also define the property that is the subject of the
insurance and this will usually be defined in either the policy's operative clause, in
the policy schedule or in one of the "sections" in the policy.[31]

As noted below at paras 2-101 to 2-104, some risks are uninsurable whilst other   **2-071**
risks are excluded or are not otherwise the subject of insurance because they fall

---

28   See further below, Ch.24.
29   See below, paras 15-043 to 15-048.
30   See above, paras 2-030 to 2-031.
31   See below, paras 3-023 to 3-025.

under a policy excess or because a party has chosen to self-insure. An insurance policy will define applicable risks not only by listing matters that are covered by the policy but also by listing the matters that are excluded from coverage. So, although the cover provided is described as "all risks" it is, in fact, the exclusion clauses that define the extent of the indemnity provided.

(ii) Excluded risks

2-072 **Excluding risks.**   The purpose of policy exclusions is to allow the underwriter to define the risk that the policy covers as effectively as possible so that the underwriter is not left open to covering risks that he did not contemplate would form part of the Contract Works. Otherwise, the premium charged and the reserve held in respect of a particular project would not be sufficient to cover all possible losses.

2-073   There are several commonly excluded risks, namely war,[32] terrorism,[33] loss due to ionising radioactive contamination[34] or damage caused by pressure waves from aircraft travelling at sonic or supersonic speeds,[35] and damage caused by pollution.[36]

2-074   An insurance policy will not insure against inevitable events or losses and will often define non-fortuitous occurrences (i.e. the occurrence of events that can be readily predicted) in order to provide clarity as to when an event is non-fortuitous and consequently not insurable.[37] Policies will often include express exclusions of non-fortuitous occurrences, such as normal action of the sea[38] or repeated flooding. A number of other exclusions are considered below.

2-075 **Breakdown of plant and motor vehicles.**   Typically a CAR policy will exclude cover for mechanically-propelled vehicles (i.e. motor cars),[39] and constructional plant, where such equipment has been damaged as a result of it breaking down of its own accord. Care must be taken when arranging cover for a Contractor's licensed plant to avoid gaps between the Contract Works, motor and public liability policies. The aim of the policy wording adopted by the insurer will be to avoid losses arising from the Contractor's lack of maintenance procedures of constructional plant by using separate machinery breakdown policies to cover damage of that nature.

2-076 **Marine and aviation risks.**   Marine and aviation risks are better dealt with by a separate and more focused policy and so will be excluded from the CAR policy.[40] Again, the exclusion may be modified so that the CAR policy does in fact cover, for example, waterborne vessels or craft not exceeding a certain length, in order to give realistic cover where work is being carried out on or near water, or where pontoons are being used during bridge, harbour and dock construction projects.

---

32   See below, paras 15-043 to 15-048.
33   See below, para.15-047.
34   See below, paras 15-061 to 15-065.
35   See below, paras 15-066 to 15-067.
36   See below, para.15-039.
37   See below, Ch.10.
38   See below, para.15-040.
39   See below, para.15-094.
40   See below, Chs 24 and 25.

Defective property.[41] The CAR policy will generally exclude work required in   **2-077**
order to repair, replace or rectify property which is defective in material or
workmanship. A policy is also likely to exclude work that is required as part of day-
to-day maintenance and making good. The Contractor must take care to ensure that
the policy will continue to cover damage to parts of the Works that are not
themselves defective, where that damage was caused by defective workmanship or
materials in relation to other parts of the Works. An example might be where a
wall—itself not defective—is damaged by the collapse of a roof defective in its
construction. In this situation, the Contractor would not expect to be covered for
the damage to the roof but may not be covered for the wall either, depending on the
way in which the exclusion clause has been drafted. Accordingly, the Contractor
should check the general exclusion and should seek to modify it to ensure that damage to non-defective parts of the Works is still covered.

Wear and tear, rust, mildew or other deterioration.[42] A clause excluding wear   **2-078**
and tear, deterioration and other such risks must be tailored to suit the requirements of the particular project. For instance, corrosion may not amount to damage
and is something that would usually pose no great concern to the Contractor.
However, in certain types of construction project corrosion may be an important
factor. Corrosion may be caused by two chemical substances mixing together,
perhaps because of an on-site spillage.[43] On the other hand, where construction takes
place on the sea shore or even at sea then corrosion may be a risk that needs to be
mitigated. However, if damage is caused to Works because of chemical corrosion,
then the parties would want the policy to respond to cover the damage caused.
Therefore, the exclusion would have to be worded accordingly to provide the necessary cover for such an eventuality.

**Damage due to fault, defect, error or omission in design, plan or
specification.**[44] Usually, the policy will exclude cover for defective design[45] and   **2-079**
all of its consequences. However, some policies will underwrite the risk of the
consequences of defective work insofar as it causes damage to the Works itself.
Even the widest such cover, however, is not a substitute for a professional indemnity
policy (in respect of the design) because the works cover ceases on practical
completion and only indemnifies the Contractor rather than the design professionals.

Standard market design exclusions. There are some standardised exclusions   **2-080**
used by underwriters that seek to deal with design defects, numbered DE1 to DE5
and LEG 1 to LEG 3.[46] The starting point is an outright design exclusion, whereby
if a building collapses in the course of erection due to a design defect it would not
be insured at all; a position which is commercially unacceptable in most
circumstances. The further exclusions then offer a gradually less restrictive definition of the damage covered (i.e. the policy will respond where there is damage to
property, which is not itself defective but which depended for structural support on

---

41 See below, Ch.16.
42 See below, paras 15-012 to 15-027.
43 See below, para.15-021.
44 See below, Ch.16.
45 See below, Ch.16.
46 See below, paras 16-029 to 16-064 and 16-065 to 16-070.

the defective structure). DE5 contains the most permissive wording and provides comprehensive cover for all damage caused by the defective part of the Works, save that the insurer would not cover the costs of improving the design and any attendant additional works aimed at improving on the original build. This is to ward off a situation where the Contractor wants to attempt to claim the additional cost of improvement under the policy.

2-081   **Existing structures.**   Existing structures will form part of a construction contract where refurbishment, conversion and renovation works are being carried out. The risk of damage to existing structures is often excluded because such structures can be particularly vulnerable to hazards, such as fire (especially in the case of particularly old structures), and because the value of the existing structure is not included in the sum insured under the policy since no premium has been charged for it. It is usual that this will be insured by the Employer under a separate fire and special perils policy.

2-082   **Consequential losses.**   Insurers will want to exclude all losses not flowing directly from the damage to the Works, including those losses that are not directly attributable to restoring the Works to their former state. An example may be the loss of rent revenue following the delay in completion of a project. It should be noted that consequential loss, insofar as it is a legal term of art, refers only to the actual loss of trade or profits[47] and does not include additional costs of rectifying work or costs incurred to avoid further loss or damage. Therefore, losses flowing directly from the occurrence of the insured peril are in fact insured.[48]

2-083   The CAR policy does not usually provide any form of consequential loss cover other than the reasonable costs incurred in connection with repairs or replacements to be indemnified under the contract, such as essential overtime or emergency transport costs. Cover for consequential loss may be included within the policy only by express agreement and all the types of loss under the head of "consequential loss" will be described in detail in the policy.

2-084   **Loss or damage after the completion of the Works.**   Usually, the policy cover will expire at practical completion of the Works and the CAR policy will not respond to loss or damage after completion. There will be a defects liability clause (covering latent defects) in the construction contract, requiring the Contractor to retain some risk for defects in the Works arising after practical completion for a specific period. In the usual circumstances, the risk of loss and damage will pass thereafter to the Employer, who will then be responsible for arranging his own property insurance.[49] Otherwise, the underwriter of the insurance policy would approach his assessment of liability under the policy in a very different way, because he would be open to potential losses for an unlimited period.

2-085   **Excess.**   The excess on a policy is essentially an exclusion against bringing small claims; it is the sum specified as being the insured's liability. The purpose of the excess is to prevent the insurer being troubled by a constant flow of claims for small

---

[47]   See below, para.15-068.
[48]   *Croudace Construction Ltd v Cawoods Concrete Products Ltd* [1978] 2 Lloyd's Rep. 55; 8 B.L.R. 20.
[49]   See below, Ch.26.

losses. The size of the excess will vary according to the nature of the risk involved and the claims history of the insured. For instance, an insured can choose to bear a much higher excess than he would otherwise be required to do, in order to obtain a more economic insurance premium.

Some policies will allow an insured to pay one excess in respect of a number of incidents where those incidents are of a similar nature; for instance, a series of storms which hit the same location over a short period of time, usually 72 hours. In *Mitsubishi Electric UK Ltd v Royal London Insurance (UK) Ltd*[50] for example, 94 individual excesses were sought by the insurer where 94 toilet modules were damaged due to one defect common to each of the 94 modules. The deductible clause provided that a deductible applied "to each loss in respect of any component part which is defective". The Court of Appeal held that only one excess should be deducted from a claim because although there were 94 examples of a defect, this was just one defect that was common to each module. The court also held that this was one composite claim and therefore the deductible could only apply once.[51] **2-086**

(e) Underwriting considerations

As discussed above there are many risks associated with construction projects, which come into existence when a project is conceived and the decision is taken to build. As a project progresses, the risks multiply. Risks may then decrease after the project is completed, but they never disappear completely. Latent defects can appear many years after practical completion. However, one of the risks with the largest capacity to disrupt a project is the risk that damage will be caused to the Works during its construction. **2-087**

As part of the process of assessing risk, the underwriter of the insurance must first decide which risks apply to the project being undertaken. The sorts of risks that should be considered at the start of every project are set out below, although this list is non-exhaustive. The underwriter will need to consider a number of factors, including the type of structure being built, the construction methods that are to be employed and the actual perils that are likely to eventuate as a result of the work being carried out. **2-088**

Design. The underwriter will need to consider whether a design is standard or prototype and whether the Contractor is experienced in implementing a particular sort of design. **2-089**

Structure. Simple buildings such as houses and offices are likely to give rise to relatively common hazards, whereas more complex structures such as power stations and petrochemical works are more likely to require the handling of hazard- **2-090**

---

[50] *Mitsubishi Electric UK Ltd v Royal London Insurance (UK) Ltd* [1994] 2 Lloyd's Rep. 249; [1994] C.L.C. 367; 74 B.L.R. 87.

[51] However, see the judgment of Moore-Bick LJ in *Seele Austria GmbH & Co KG v Tokio Marine Europe Insurance Ltd* [2008] EWCA Civ 441 at [53]–[58]; [2009] 1 All E.R. (Comm) 171 at 188–190; [2008] Lloyd's Rep. I.R. 739 at 752 and 853; [2008] B.L.R. 337 at 350–351, where there was a common defect in numerous windows installed into a building. In that case the Court of Appeal found that the common defect was caused by individual errors of workmanship that had been repeated for each window installed. The court took the view that the errors were separate events and consequently the insureds' retained liability clause had to be interpreted to provide that the insureds were liable for a deductible for each defective window (Waller LJ dissenting).

ous processes and materials. However, even simple structures will be more vulnerable to certain perils. For example, if the Works incorporate an existing structure or there is no division between new and existing structures, then the project is likely to suffer more significantly from the occurrence of a peril such as fire. Similarly, the underwriter would be more concerned about the risk of flood where work is being carried out near water or the risk of explosion where welding work has to be carried out in a chemical plant.

2-091   **Construction methods.**   Most simple structures will be built in the same way; piled foundations, steel portal frames and clad buildings. These will be vulnerable to standard perils, for example collapse, fire or explosion, frost, flood and so on, all of which are described below.[52] Where an innovative or complex method of construction is used, the risk of damage may be greater at certain points in the project. Where the project involves the use of pre-fabricated units or components—bathroom and kitchen units, for example—then the underwriter will have to assess the risk differently. The underwriter will have to assess the risks on the basis that damage to a bathroom or kitchen unit, which contain a lot of pre-fixed electrical wiring, will be significant since the entire unit and not necessarily the component part may have to be replaced.

2-092   **Fire and explosion.**   The consequences of fire and explosion are potentially catastrophic. These risks arise from activities such as use of chemicals, use of heat in confined spaces, blasting or the storage of chemicals. The risks will be greater towards the end of a project when expensive mechanical, electrical and electronic equipment and fitting-out works are installed and tested. For instance, if fire occurs shortly before completion, but before fire prevention measures have been fitted then there is an increased risk that the economic viability of continuing the project will be put in jeopardy or that a project will be destroyed in its entirety. The degree of risk can be reduced if measures are put in place to ensure that hazardous substances are stored and handled safely, activities such as welding in enclosed spaces are carried out with due care, and, more generally, that there are good housekeeping and Health and Safety measures in place in and around the site. Well thought out construction planning will attempt to mitigate fire risk by ensuring that fire prevention aids are installed at the earliest opportunity in the construction phase. For instance, the planners may require that fire hydrants are in place at the outset or that sprinkler systems are introduced at the earliest possible moment. The result might be that underwriters assess the fire risk to a lower degree and this might result in the insured having to pay a lower premium for the insurance of fire risk.

2-093   **Natural perils.**   The occurrence of natural perils will almost entirely be outside the control of the parties. If projects are undertaken in parts of the world where particular natural phenomena are rife, then steps must be taken to minimise the potential adverse effects of those phenomena. Relevant natural perils are discussed below at paras 2-094 to 2-098.

2-094   **Ground movement.**   Ground movement risks arise from triggers including landslip, collapse, underground mining, inadequate support for excavations, inundation by water from within the ground itself and the effect of vibrations or shock

---

[52]   See below, paras 2-092, 2-094, 2-096 and 2-098.

waves. The parties can attempt to manage these risks by undertaking a proper investigation of the ground soil and by producing an adequate design of Temporary Works. An underwriter would be concerned that detailed field assessments and tests in accordance with established civil engineering guidelines are carried out at the project development stage.

Earthquake. The risk of earthquake is mainly a consideration to be taken into account in Asia, America, Africa, Australasia and certain parts of Europe. As with ground movement risks, the parties should ensure that proper investigations have been carried out as to whether there is likely to be any seismic activity during the course of construction so that the project can be planned accordingly. Again, Temporary Works should be designed to withstand shockwaves.   **2-095**

Rain, flood and water peril. Rain and storms might cause rivers and other waterways to flood. There is also a risk of water damage being caused by burst water pipes. This risk can be guarded against by the proper technical assessment of local flood areas. Planning should also take into account the possibility of flash flood, especially in semi-arid areas, and the parties should incorporate sufficient measures into the Works to prevent damage by flooding. Contractors can consider diverting water away from a site but this carries its own potential risk of damage to third-party property and such measures should therefore be approached cautiously.   **2-096**

Wind. Permanent works should be designed to be stable under all types of weather conditions, including hurricane and typhoon. The Works are more at risk of damage whilst in an unfinished state. It may be difficult to take effective precautions against these risks but the parties can monitor weather patterns to obtain an early warning of potential storms in order that the Works can be protected as effectively as possible. This is a risk that bears greater significance for underwriters outside of the United Kingdom, where there is a higher degree of risk of severe weather conditions.   **2-097**

Frost. Frost is only likely to be a problem if there is a failure to take adequate on-site workmanship precautions, for example, by protecting pipework. Therefore, an underwriter is unlikely to be satisfied if these precautions are not in place.   **2-098**

Plant and equipment. Jib and tower cranes, hoists and scaffolding will always be vulnerable to collapse or overbalancing with the possibility that damage may be caused to the Works, third-party property and the risk of injury to employees and others. Underwriters will be keen to see that the parties guard against this risk by ensuring that workers are properly trained in the safe use of such equipment and that such equipment is properly maintained.   **2-099**

Crime risks. The Works will be at risk from people connected or unconnected with the building project who steal materials, equipment or other supplies from the construction site. The risk can be ameliorated by having proper security measures in place at the construction site. It is likely that the deductible will deal with minor pilfering, although there is potential for large scale theft to cause significant disruption to the Works by delaying the project.   **2-100**

2-101   **Uninsured risks.**   Although the following risks will almost always be excluded from the CAR policy, the parties and the underwriter will still want to take steps to manage and mitigate, as far as is possible, the risks listed below at paras 2-102 to 2-104.

2-102   **Riot and civil commotion.**   This risk will generally be excluded from cover if it amounts to a popular uprising. Employing adequate security measures to guard the construction site and all workers is an important way to mitigate this risk. Measures would include perimeter fencing of the site, 24-hour security teams and possibly CCTV. These measures may reduce the premium an underwriter would seek for providing insurance.

2-103   **War risks.**   These risks will also generally be excluded from cover, including damage caused by undiscovered mines.[53]

2-104   **Nuclear risk.**   This risk will be excluded, although the risk of such damage will be insured by pooling agreements between governments.[54]

(f)   How do the construction contract and insurance policy/contract tie together?

2-105   **The relationship between the construction contract and the insurance policy.**   As has been noted in this chapter, the parties should be careful to ensure that the insurance policy or policies they put in place do in fact cover the risks and losses contemplated by the construction contract. The parties must analyse whether the policy wording mirrors the requirements of the parties and, for instance, whether exclusions are tightly worded enough so as to be neither too narrow nor too permissive. As is discussed above, if the parties are content to leave corrosion caused by wear and tear as an uninsured risk, they may nevertheless want the policy to cover chemical corrosion (i.e. corrosion caused by two substances mixing together) and will want the policy to be worded accordingly.

2-106   Even where a loss is insured, a party, usually the Contractor, may still find that they have to bear some of the financial consequences stemming from the eventuation of the risk. For instance, where an insurer under-settles a claim because the value of the claim has been adjusted below the deductible, then the Contractor will have to pay the difference out of his own pocket. This is a possibility that the Contractor must be alive to when assessing the viability of any particular construction project and the insurance that is being offered to him.

(g)   The Integrated Project Insurance ("IPI") Model

2-107   **Integrated Project Insurance ("IPI") Model.**   In 2011 the *Government Construction Strategy* was published.[55] It endorsed in principle the Integrated Project Insurance ("IPI") model, (which had been developed over the previous 10

---

[53]   See below, paras 15-043 to 15-048.
[54]   See below, paras 15-061 to 15-065.
[55]   Cabinet Office, "*Government Construction Strategy*" (Cabinet Office, 2011) *https://www.gov.uk/ government/uploads/system/uploads/attachment_data/file/61152/Government-Construction-Strategy_ 0.pdf* [Accessed 20 June 2016].

years), to be trialled on specific projects. The main aim of the model is to get construction professionals to work together in a more genuinely collaborative way to deliver construction projects than has previously been the case.[56] It is thought that when parties to a construction contract (including the developer) work in a more collaborative way then more can be delivered for less. In July 2011, the Integrated Projects Initiative Ltd was formed which is the delivery arm of the model.

In 2014 guidance on the IPI model was published by the government.[57] It explains how the model should work in practice. At the start of a project an integrated project team (including the contractors and other specialists) is selected. This team then collectively decides where 15 to 20 per cent of project cost savings can be made. The members of the project group then together form a "virtual company" (or enter into an "Alliance Contract", comprising a board,[58] a project manager[59] and a project team[60] amongst others) to implement the project. At the start of the project, members are also required to agree to a "no blame/ no claim" undertaking, which prevents members from initiating proceedings against one another if things go wrong during the project.

2-108

The IPI model is an alternative option that should be considered, when the project risks are such that a risk and reward sharing approach, under a collaborative/ Alliance Contract are considered to be suitable. Presently it is thought that the IPI model is only suitable for projects in the region of £10 to £25 million, given the level of cover available.[61]

The Integrated Project Insurance Alliance Contract. The IPI model is cur- **2-109** rently being trialled through a number of pilot projects which are being conducted under the supervision of Integrated Projects Initiative Ltd. The first IPI public sector pilot commenced on 8 May 2015 under an "Alliance Contract" (which is a non-tiered contract that has been signed by all members of the project team); it concerns the construction of a new advanced technology building in Dudley, which is to be completed in three phases. This project is expected to be completed in March 2017. The "Alliance Contract" adopted has been prepared for use in conjunction with the IPI policy. It is hoped that, by testing and developing of the IPI model, it will result in the "Alliance Contract" becoming the first "New Engineering ('NEC') Alliance Contract".

The Integrated Project Insurance Policy. As part of the IPI model an alterna- **2-110** tive to taking out a CAR policy is the IPI policy. An IPI policy will insure the client and all other "Alliance" members including consultants, construction managers and their supply chains. It is suggested that it also allows the insurer to better

---

[56] Integrated Project Initiatives "*Government Construction Strategy 2011. The Integrated Project Insurance (IPI) Model: Project Procurement and Delivery Guidance*" (Integrated Project Initiatives, 2014), p.3 *https://www.gov.uk/government/uploads/system/uploads/attachment_data/file/326716/20140702_IPI_Guidance_3_July_2014.pdf* [Accessed 20 June 2016].

[57] See fn.55 above.

[58] The Alliance Board is made up of members of practices or firms involved with delivering the project.

[59] The project manager is selected by the "Alliance Board".

[60] The project team comprises of staff from each of the companies or firms which reports to the Alliance Manager and Board.

[61] Integrated Project Initiatives "*Government Construction Strategy 2011. The Integrated Project Insurance (IPI) Model: Project Procurement and Delivery Guidance*" (Integrated Project Initiatives, 2014), p.30 *https://www.gov.uk/government/uploads/system/uploads/attachment_data/file/326716/20140702_IPI_Guidance_3_July_2014.pdf* [Accessed 20 June 2016].

understand the potential risks in implementing a particular project. A single IPI policy will be produced for the project which aims to cover all of the risks associated with the delivery of the project (including providing cover for latent defects for up to 12 years), rather than each party taking out separate cover for particular risks (e.g. professional indemnity insurance and/or public liability insurance) alongside joint cover under a CAR policy. The IPI policy will only be taken out if the design and cost plan agreed by the team for the project has passed independent technical and financial risk assurances. In 2012 the Procurement/Lean Client Task Group Final report stated[62]:

> "This policy would package up all insurances currently held by the client and supply chain members, and would also take the top slice of commercial risks, covering any cost overruns on the project above and beyond a 'pain-share' threshold, split transparently between client, the contracted party and its supply chain."

2-111   The IPI policy therefore covers all overspend on the project up to the liability limit, with the members' liability extending only to the limit of a "pain-share" threshold which is effectively the excess under the financial loss section of the policy. Beyond this the insurers (subject to a maximum indemnity and exclusions) will deal with any overspend, whilst also waiving any rights of subrogation against all of the insured, at every tier. However, if financial exposures exceed the insurer's cap then the client bears responsibility for it. Once the IPI is incepted the project team can then start to implement the project. It is thought that the IPI model will reduce time and costs incurred in delivering construction projects rather than using more traditional project insurance structures. It will be a matter of time, however, before it will be known the extent to which this alternative approach, and its ability to reduce risks during and after construction, has been effective and also whether it will be readily taken up in practice by both the insurance and construction industries.

3.   DEALING WITH RISK OTHERWISE THAN BY INSURANCE

2-112   **Contractual indemnities, bonds and sureties.**   Although this book is about insurance rather than surety, it is appropriate to mention other methods of allocating and managing risk that the parties to a construction contract might adopt. The parties can use contractual indemnities, bonds and sureties.

2-113   **Indemnity.**   The parties can write specific indemnities into the construction contract whereby one party agrees to indemnify and hold another party harmless for all liability for damages arising out of a specific endeavour, which were caused by that party's fault. Invariably, the indemnifying party will obtain insurance so that the insurer promises to take over the task for compensating a wronged party on behalf of the wrongdoer or, in some cases, the reparation of any damages sustained.

2-114   **Bonds and sureties.**   Bonds and sureties both provide ways for the parties to deal with the risk that a party will be unable to fulfil its obligations under the construc-

---

[62] Procurement/Lean Client Task Group "Government Construction Strategy. Final Report to Government by the Procurement/Lean Client Task Group (Procurement/Lean Client Task Group, 2012), p. 16. *https://www.gov.uk/government/uploads/system/uploads/attachment_data/file/61157/Procurement-and-Lean-Client-Group-Final-Report-v2.pdf* [Accessed 20 June 2016].

tion contract. A bond is a security, under which the issuer owes the holder money if the bond is called upon. In the context of a construction contract, parties may put in place a surety bond (called a Performance Bond) issued by an insurance company or a bank to guarantee satisfactory completion of a project by a Contractor.

A bond is not a self-contained contract since it rests on an underlying contractual **2-115** obligation between two parties. The bond remains in force until the contracting party in whose name the bond is issued has completely fulfilled its obligations. There is typically no cancellation clause and no termination date within the performance period.

In a typical scenario in construction, the surety will be a bank or an insurance **2-116** company and it will issue a bond to the Employer in return for a premium. While other forms of surety exist in a common sense, a contract of surety may provide that in the event of non-performance of the contract by the Contractor, the Employer can call upon the surety who will then be obliged to step in and fulfil the Contractor's obligations under the construction contract. The responsibility passes to the surety only if the party in question is unable or unwilling to fulfil his responsibility. An example of this would be where the Contractor has run out of funds to continue the project, perhaps because he has overspent on the project or has become insolvent. The surety will have a right of action against the Contractor for the recovery of his own outlay of resources. Thus, a surety is not a provider of an insurance policy but instead is acting as a guarantor for the performance of the construction project.

4. INTERPRETATION

Interpreting risk. The allocation of risk between parties to a construction project **2-117** will be contentious from the moment a project is conceived and this will continue through implementation and beyond its completion. Having set out how risk is allocated between the parties to a project, whether in the construction contract itself or an insurance policy, the following chapters consider the common features of CAR policies, the clauses within a CAR policy and (where applicable) how they have been understood and interpreted by the courts.

CHAPTER 3

COMMON FEATURES OF CONTRACTORS' ALL RISKS POLICIES

TABLE OF CONTENTS

1. IN GENERAL

No standard wording. There is no single generic CAR policy wording. Underwriters have developed their own policies over time in response to changing market requirements. Matters that will have a bearing on any ultimate policy wording will include the risk to be insured, the number and nature of intended insureds, the scope of cover sought and the quality of cover any given insurer is prepared to provide. Naturally, CAR policies do tend to share some common features. **3-001**

Tripartite cover. Many CAR policies deal with three broad types of cover: (i) damage to insured property; (ii) consequential or "business interruption" losses that might arise;[1] and (iii) liability of the insureds to third parties that might accrue in the course of the construction enterprise (often termed "third-party liability" or "public-liability insurance").[2] **3-002**

In essence, the first type of cover responds to qualifying loss of or damage to (typically) the object of the construction enterprise (be it an office block or otherwise) and the temporary structures assembled to facilitate its construction, together with their constituent materials. Cover is often extended to include Constructional Plant and Temporary Buildings.

The second relates to particular financial losses suffered by particular insureds

---

[1] See below, paras 26-053 to 26-105.
[2] See below, Ch.18.

as caused by qualifying damage to the insured property. The third type of cover responds, typically, to qualifying physical damage to third parties' person or property arising as a result of the material construction activities.

Broadly speaking, a CAR policy will set out terms relevant to all forms of cover provided under the policy and further particularise, in separate sections, key matters such as specific insuring clauses, limits upon liability, defined terms, exclusions and extensions in respect of each.

3-003   **Multiple insureds.**   Almost invariably a CAR policy will provide cover to a number of insureds. Often, the policy will be arranged by one proposed insured on behalf of all. The logic is clear; it is sensible for one party to take out a single policy that covers the whole or a designated part of the risk. This avoids, at best, duplication in administrative effort and at worst, the prospect of "… overlapping claims and cross-claims …" in respect of the same loss or damage.[3]

The insureds will frequently include the Employer, the main Contractor, a project manager, subcontractors, professional advisers[4] and suppliers. The insureds may be identified expressly in the policy by name, or by a general description.[5] The insureds are considered in more detail in Ch.8.

3-004   **Cover under a specific or existing policy.**   CAR cover is generally secured in one of two ways: either by obtaining a policy that addresses the insurance requirements of a particular project (often termed a "single project policy"); or by relying on, or adapting, a current policy that is already held by a party to the construction works (often called an "annual", "open cover" or "floater" policy) that extends cover to other parties to those construction works that the named party might undertake during the relevant indemnity period.

3-005   **Obligations to insure under commonly used construction contracts.**   The parties to construction contracts will frequently agree who is to be responsible for arranging and managing CAR insurance. As the Contractor will usually be responsible for loss and damage to the Contract Works prior to completion, it will often want to ensure it is in a position to manage that risk (by holding an appropriate annual policy or securing apposite single project coverage).[6] Alternatively, an Employer may have greater experience of risk allocation, or closer relationships with relevant insurers and may wish to control the insurance arrangements.[7]

Where the parties to the construction enterprise make use of industry standard terms and conditions, those terms often allocate these responsibilities and dictate what range of cover should be obtained (which may not extend to consequential loss cover).

Standard terms offered by the Joint Contracts Tribunal ("JCT"), Association for

---

[3]   See Lloyd J in *Petrofina (UK) Ltd v Magnaload Ltd* [1984] Q.B. 127 at 136; [1983] 3 All E.R. 35 at 42; [1983] 3 W.L.R. 805 at 813.

[4]   It is useful to note at this stage that a CAR policy does not usually indemnify professional advisors against liability arising from their own professional negligence (in respect of which professional indemnity insurance should be secured).

[5]   For example by reference to a class, such as contractors, subcontractors and suppliers of any tier or to consultants providing professional services in relation to the material project to any otherwise defined insureds.

[6]   See above, paras 2-014 to 2-016.

[7]   See above, paras 2-010 to 2-012.

Consultancy and Engineering ("ACE") and Civil Engineering Contractors Association ("CECA"), and Fédération Internationale des Ingénieurs Conseils ("FIDIC") typically make provision for one or more parties to secure relevant insurance.

An example from the suite of JCT Contracts is the JCT Standard Building Contract,[8] which sets out three insurance options the parties could choose between (at cl.6.7 and in Sch.3 insurance options A–C). In short, these allocate the responsibility to ensure that there is in place (by securing a fresh policy and/or by way of an existing policy held) a level of insurance cover, as dictated by the Contract, to either the Contractor or Employer (depending on the nature of the works that are to be undertaken).[9]

In a similar vein, the Infrastructure Conditions of Contract Measurement Version introduced by ACE and CECA to replace the Institute of Civil Engineers ("ICE") Conditions of Contract[10] contains a number of terms dealing with the arrangement of insurance cover including, at cl.21(1), that the Contractor procures insurance in the joint names of the Contractor and the Employer in respect of (amongst other things) the execution of the Contract Works, together with material plant and equipment; and at cl.23(1) (subject to certain exclusions) liability for death or injury to any person or loss of or damage to any property arising out of performance of the Contract.

Likewise, the Conditions of Contract of Construction for Building and Engineering Works Designed by the Employer[11] provided by FIDIC contain substantial provision (at cl.18.2) for the securing of certain insurance in relation to the Contract

---

[8] Joint Contracts Tribunal. *SBC/Q 2011 JCT Standard Building Contract With Quantities 2011* (London: Sweet & Maxwell, 2011), pp.68, 88–92.

[9] Joint Contracts Tribunal. *SBC/Q 2011 JCT Standard Building Contract With Quantities 2011* (2011). The contract commentary provided by the JCT in respect of all risks insurance should be noted: see p.93; fn.68 states that "Policies issued by insurers are not standardised; the way in which insurance for these risks is expressed varies and in some cases it may not be possible for insurance to be taken out against certain of the risks covered."

[10] Association for Consultancy and Engineering; Civil Engineering Contactors Association; Institute of Civil Engineers (Great Britain). *Infrastructure Conditions of Contract: Measurement Version August 2011 Based on the ICE Conditions of Contract*, 1st edn (London: Association for Consultancy and Engineering, 2011), pp.13–15. The Infrastructure Conditions of Contract Measurement Version replaced the Institute of Civil Engineers Conditions of Contract on the August 1, 2011. The Institute of Civil Engineers, which owned the ICE Conditions of Contract, decided to withdraw the ICE Conditions of Contract and transfer ownership to the Association for Consultancy and Engineering and the Civil Engineering Contractors Association who subsequently decided to rename the ICE Conditions of Contract as the Infrastructure Conditions of Contract.

[11] International Federation of Consulting Engineers (FIDIC). *Conditions of Contract for Construction for Building and Engineering Works Designed by the Employer*, 1st edn (Geneva: International Federation of Consulting Engineers, 1999), pp.54–56. This paperback is more commonly known as the "Red Book". In 2005 FIDIC published a new version of the "Red Book" (more commonly known as the "New Red Book") to deal with projects funded by participating multilateral development banks ("MDBs"). The first version was published in May 2005, the 2nd version published March 2006 and a 3rd version was published in June 2010; e.g. FIDIC *Conditions of Contract for Construction MDB Harmonised Edition for Building and Engineering Works Designed by the Employer. General Conditions, Particular Conditions, Sample Forms*, 3rd edn (Geneva: International Federation of Consulting Engineers, 2010). It is important to note that if projects are not funded by MDBs then the *Conditions of Contract for Construction for Building and Engineering Works Designed by the Employer*, 1st edn (Geneva: International Federation of Consulting Engineers, 1999) must be used. The insurance provisions given in cl.18 of the 1st edn remain unchanged in the "New Red Book".

Works and contractor's equipment; and insurance against injury to persons or damage to property (at cl.18.3).

2. Property

(a) Coverage

3-006 **Property.** The property (or material damage) section of a CAR policy is usually seen as being the key cover provided by the policy. What constitutes the relevant "property" will be defined in the policy. Principally it is the "Contract Works" forming the substance of the construction enterprise in question. Post-completion, insurance for the property itself may be obtained (i.e. all risks property insurance ("ARPI"). ARPI insurance is examined in detail below in Ch.26.

3-007 **Contract works (or the works).** "Contract Works" is usually defined by reference to two other defined terms, "Permanent" and "Temporary Works". Permanent Works is usually defined as the structure(s) that is the envisaged outcome of the construction project, together with materials supplied for incorporation within it. Temporary Works usually comprise structures and their materials that are required to facilitate the construction process. These would include those works necessary for access to or the support of the Permanent Works, which will be removed from the construction site on or before the completion of the project and which will not be re-used again in other construction works. However, non-mechanical equipment such as scaffolding might be classed as either Temporary Works or Constructional Plant. Typically, though, where such equipment is non-reusable on another project, it tends to be classed as Temporary Works.

3-008 **Constructional Plant.** The policy may include coverage in respect of "Constructional Plant" (which is sometimes alternatively defined as "Construction Plant"). Generally, this definition might include tools, tackle, plant, Temporary Buildings[12] and their contents and equipment belonging to the insured (or hired by them). In contrast to materials falling within the definition of Permanent or Temporary Works, Constructional Plant will ordinarily relate to items that are not to form part of the Works and will be reused on other projects (such as scaffolding).

The policy may extend cover for Constructional Plant during not only its use in the execution of the Contract Works, but during its assembly/disassembly off site, and while it is transit and/or storage off-site. Some policies may extend cover to equivalent plant that has been hired by the insured.

3-009 **Materials in transit.** The policy may also cover loss or damage to the Contract Works or Constructional Plant while they are stored off site or while in transit. Exclusions frequently apply serving to limit or exclude cover where transit is to take place by sea or air. Another method by which cover is often limited is in the provision of a time cap for the duration of any off-site storage.

3-010 **Existing property and structures on site.** Ordinarily, property that existed at or around the relevant construction site prior to the commencement of the Contract

---

12 Such as site huts or other temporary accommodation. Some policies employ a separate definition of "Temporary Buildings".

Works will not fall within the definition of "insured property" employed in most CAR policies (and some policies expressly exclude cover for such structures). In the circumstances where the construction project in question involves work around existing structures, an Employer will frequently require the Contractor to take responsibility and to secure specific joint insurance under the CAR policy or otherwise for those retained structures until completion of construction.

(b) Property that is not usually covered by/under CAR policies

Property not usually covered by/under CAR policies. As noted further in Ch.15, CAR policies may exclude cover for loss or damage to property where cover could be obtained elsewhere. These may include the items considered in paras 3-012 to 3-018 below.   **3-011**

Marine and aviation matters. Loss or damage to vessels or craft, to cargo in transit by sea or air and liabilities arising from the use of vessels and craft is ordinarily excluded. Where relevant, specialised and tailored cover is usually available and can be obtained from the marine and aviation insurance markets. Bespoke CAR policies may be available to cover certain marine and aviation risks (see below) in Chs 24 and 25).   **3-012**

Motor vehicles. Loss or damage to, or liability arising out of the ownership, possession or use of mechanically propelled vehicles—or any trailers attached to them—which is required by road traffic legislation to be the subject of compulsory insurance, is also frequently excluded. CAR policy exclusions may contain limitations affording some cover, for example, where such a vehicle is being used as a tool or in respect of the loading or unloading, or the delivery or collection of goods to or from such a vehicle.   **3-013**

Professional indemnity. The liabilities of professionals working on a construction project that might arise out of the execution of their professional duties will usually be excluded. An example might be architects or consulting engineers who are responsible for damage or defects caused by their negligent design or advice. An exception to this will be a circumstance where liability has arisen out of their on-site activities, such as the causing of damage to the Contract Works through negligence. A range of specialised cover against professional indemnity risk is of course widely available and the relevant professionals would ordinarily be expected to have their own indemnity insurance in place. As such, efforts are usually taken to avoid the provision of overlapping cover under the CAR policy.   **3-014**

Performance bonds and guarantees. Liability in respect of loss arising from a failure by a Contractor to fulfil its obligations under a construction Contract, as secured by a bond or guarantee (being a Contract between, typically, the Employer and a third party, providing security against a failure by, usually, the Contractor to comply with its duties arising under the contract) is also normally excluded.   **3-015**

Money. Damage to money and negotiable instruments such as bonds, promissory notes, treasury notes and cash, is likewise commonly excluded.   **3-016**

3-017   **IT equipment.**   Damage that is caused to computers or other items/equipment that process, store or transmit or receive tangible or intangible data by (for example) a computer virus or an attack by computer hackers, is frequently excluded.[13]

3-018   **Latent defects.**   Damage to the construction arising from latent defects existing at the date of completion but which were not discovered or, depending upon the policy wording, that were undiscoverable at the time of completion, is commonly excluded. The topic of insurance for latent defects is considered below in Chs 15 and 16.[14]

3. Consequential loss

3-019   **Consequential loss.**   As a starting point, most CAR policies look to exclude the insurer's liability to indemnify the insureds in respect of any consequential loss. However, as noted in para.3-002, frequently CAR policies will extend cover to certain financial losses suffered by the Employer or principal—and those financing the construction—as a result of loss or damage to the Contract Works. Where such cover is provided, it will usually extend to the consequences of a delay to completion of the project, but the scope of cover may extend to other events giving rise to loss in other ways.[15]

3-020   **Coverage.**   Typical policy coverage might include[16]:

    1.   loss of income from the use, leasing and/or sale of the Permanent Works;
    2.   loss of revenue that would have been enjoyed for services rendered in the course of the operation of the Permanent Works;
    3.   further interest incurred on finance taken out to fund the construction project;
    4.   the costs of steps taken to expedite the Works so as to minimise losses; and
    5.   incidental costs incurred as a result of the delay (such as legal costs).

The insurer will require a range of information (such as the insured's anticipated income or likely revenue from or during the construction project) to appraise the risk, sum to be insured and the premium payable. The policy may make provision for the disclosure of additional information relevant to the estimates provided as time progresses, to allow cover limits and premiums to be adapted during the currency of the policy. This topic (including the calculation and payment of premium) is discussed in more detail in Ch.23.

4. Third-party liability

3-021   **Third-party liability.**   It is not unusual for a CAR policy to provide cover to the insured in respect of liability to third parties for personal injury or death and for damage to third-party property arising from the insured's Construction Works. Typically, a policy will include a separate insuring clause that delineates further the scope of the general insuring clause that is found elsewhere within the policy.

---

[13]   For further discussion about this exclusion in the context of all risks property insurance ("ARPI") see below para.26-119.
[14]   See below, para.15-011 and paras 16-029 to 16-070.
[15]   Such as delay caused by damage to constructional plant.
[16]   Subject to further particular exclusions. See below, paras 3-052 to 3-061 and Ch.15.

Coverage.   Policy coverage might extend to include (subject to further particular   **3-022**
exclusions) any compensation and costs and expenses for which the insured
becomes liable to pay in respect of accidental:

1.   personal injury to any person[17];
2.   damage to material property; and
3.   nuisance, trespass, obstruction, trespass, or interference with any right of
      way, light, air or water.

The policy may also cover certain other costs and expenses of a claimant incurred
by an insured (or other costs or expenses with the insurer's written consent) in connection with the defence of any claim or for the representation of the insured in
related proceedings. Third-party liability is discussed further in Ch.18.

5.   THE STRUCTURE OF CAR POLICIES

Structure of CAR policies.   As noted above in para.3-001, the format of any   **3-023**
given CAR policy will vary in light of, amongst other things, the nature of the
underlying contract or business, the scope of cover provided and the insurer or
broker concerned. However, there are common terms that will arise, which are
discussed next.

(a)   Recitals/preamble

Recitals/preamble.   The recital(s) to the policy—also known as a preamble—is   **3-024**
a clause or series of clauses that will typically record the fact that in return for the
payment of a premium or premiums, the insurer has agreed to indemnify or
otherwise compensate the insured identified in the policy in accordance with its
terms.

There will usually follow an operative or insuring clause. In essence, this records
the fact that subject to the terms of the policy the insurers will indemnify the insured
against qualifying loss or damage. Wording of the insuring agreement will often
vary from policy to policy.

In policies containing multiple sections, there may be an umbrella insuring clause
in a recital, which is later amplified by further insuring clauses relating to individual
types of cover provided in subsequent sections: for instance consequential loss or
third-party liability coverage.

Standard clause wording will contain language to the following effect.

In a policy providing cover in relation to property damage only:

"[t]he insurers will indemnify the Insured in respect of physical loss or damage to the Insured
Property described in the Schedule arising from any cause except as hereafter provided."

In a multi-section policy:

"the Insurers will indemnify or otherwise compensate the Insured named in the Schedule (referred
to as 'the Insured') in accordance with and subject to the terms and conditions of this insurance."

With amplification at the start of various sections, including:

"[l]oss of or damage to the Contract Works described in the Schedule anywhere in the Territorial
Limits occurring during the Period of Insurance."

---

[17]   Liability for injury to employees of the insured is usually excluded.

"The Financial Loss of the Insured resulting from interruption or interference with the Contract Works Programme which causes delay in the scheduled start of commercial operation or sale of the Enterprise during the Indemnity Period in consequence of an Accident."

For discussion of "material loss" and "damage" under a policy, see Ch.14.

Usually, the recital will identify the documentation that is to form part of the contract of insurance (such as the proposal and schedules, exclusions, extensions and conditions of the policy). The recital may also provide guidance as to the construction of the policy and may state, for example, that any word or expression given a specific meaning will have that same meaning wherever it may appear in the policy.

(b) The schedule

3-025   **The schedule.**   The schedule sets out key information upon which the policy operates (such as the identity of the insured; the property insured; and key financial information used in the calculation of both the sum insured and premiums for the coverage provided).

3-026   **Identification of the insured.**   As noted previously, single project policies are usually intended to cover the interests of a number of parties. They frequently cover expressly the Employer, main Contractor and others including financing parties, project manager(s) and suppliers involved. Annual policies are often held in the name of the main Contractor only. Some contain expansive definitions that serve to identify with sufficient particularity the additional parties that are to benefit as "insureds" for construction projects as they arise. Alternatively, the policy may need to be extended expressly to cover those parties (typically, Employers and sometimes associated lenders).

3-027   **Description of key criteria.**   Key matters often found in the schedule to a policy frequently include those discussed below at paras 3-028 to 3-042.

3-028   **Contract/business description.**   Single project policies will describe the material construction project, including the main building contract. In annual policies there is commonly a description of the type of contracts which might fall within the ambit of the policy. Where the policy extends to cover consequential loss, a description of the insured's business is likely to be required (in connection with the definition of the losses covered).

3-029   **Insured property and location.**   The insured property will probably include Contract Works, Constructional Plant and certain materials in transit. Any other property falling under the policy (such as existing structures) would also be identified (and defined in more elaborate terms elsewhere). The location of the insured property will also be set out.

3-030   **Site and territorial limits.**   The schedule will probably identify the material "site", which is likely to include those places defined as a "site" for the purposes of the underlying construction contract(s). It may extend to include off-site storage locations or other specified locations to be used in the course of the construction enterprise. The schedule may also identify any territorial limits within which cover will be provided.

3-031   **Sum insured.**   It is likely that the schedule will set out a limit of the sum(s) insured in respect of the various types of cover afforded under the policy. The limits are likely to be developed further in the body of each material section of the policy wherein each particular type of cover offered is detailed. These limits may be calculated in a number of different ways (see paras 3-032 to 3-033 below).

Estimated value of contract. Single project policies often employ a limit for claims for loss or damage to the Contract Works, which may be in respect of any one loss or in the aggregate. Those limits are formulated by reference to the estimated value of the underlying construction contract(s). Alternatively, limits may be calculated by reference to the reinstatement value of the Permanent Works or by reference to a specified first loss limit (i.e. an estimate of the maximum loss that is likely to occur under the policy). **3-032**

Where cover is provided for Constructional Plant, CAR policies will commonly introduce a per loss or per incident limit or a cap formulated by reference to the market value of relevant material on site at any one time. A common approach adopted in annual policies is to introduce a liability limit calculated by reference to a maximum contract value together with individual limits for each attaching contract and/or to set it at a single sum.

Insured's annual turnover. Where a policy provides indemnification in relation to consequential loss, this may be calculated by reference to an insured's estimated annual turnover (usually for a period following the scheduled completion of the construction enterprise). An alternative basis of calculation might include the insured's anticipated gross revenue and/or the anticipated rent it would have enjoyed in respect of the Permanent Works over such a period. **3-033**

Specified caps on liability. Where the policy extends to third-party liability, the schedule is likely to reflect the limit of indemnity in respect of any one, or series of, qualifying occurrence(s). **3-034**

Escalation in cost.[18] Where the cover is calculated by reference to an underlying contract price, it is common for a policy to provide for the sum insured to be increased automatically—subject to agreed rates—in response to any escalation in the cost of Works during the operation of the Contract. **3-035**

Premium. A considerable number of factors will have been taken into account in formulating the premium appropriate to a policy. Rates are likely to vary between different insurers under the various policies offered. Broadly speaking, premiums in single project policies are often calculated by applying a tailored multiplier to a series of figures, including: the contract price of the Contract Works, the replacement value of material plant and Temporary Buildings and the cost of testing and commissioning. **3-036**

Premium adjustment. Where a premium is calculated by reference to estimates provided at the inception of the policy, a policy will commonly require the insured to provide the insurer with reasonable information to enable the premium charged to be adjusted. Such a provision might provide for a premium to be adjustable on **3-037**

---

[18] Recognising the potential impact of inflationary pressures on the total cost of Contract Works and the cost of any reinstatement works, policies frequently make provision for the adjustment of any estimates provided in connection with securing insurance in line with inflation.

(or shortly prior to) the expiry of the period of cover, to take into account the actual sum from which the provisional premium was determined.

3-038   **Payment of premium.**   Arrangements for the payment of premiums are between the insuring parties. Generally, in projects of a longer duration, a common arrangement is for payment to be made by instalments. In smaller projects, the premium may be payable at the inception of cover.

3-039   **Indemnity period.**   Single project policies typically provide for cover to extend to the expiry of the construction phase. Thereafter, testing and commissioning, defects liability and maintenance periods may follow during which limited indemnification is provided.[19] Given the risk of delay to practical completion, policies frequently make provision for extension in such circumstances (usually subject to additional premiums). Where cover is provided in respect of loss or damage to property, consequential loss and third-party liability, there may well be different indemnity periods in respect of each. As the name would suggest, annual policies ordinarily run for, and are renewed upon, an annual basis. Such cover might be stated to lie for any contracts commenced during the period of coverage, or for the duration of the coverage period only.

3-040   **Deductible/excess.**   The deductible, also known as excess, being the retained liability of the insured in respect of any qualifying claim, is usually set out in the schedule. The draftsmen of policies will frequently go further and set out the particular amount of deductible relevant to each loss and the period of indemnity in question. The policy may contain provision for the automatic adjustment of the deductible in line with inflation and additionally or alternatively, where relevant, in line with fluctuations in exchange rates.

3-041   **Automatic reinstatement.**   It is common for CAR policies to refer to in the schedule (by way of an extension) an automatic reinstatement clause which allows the insured to "reinstate" the limit of liability to its original value after it has been depleted by an insured's claim under the policy. The insured will typically be required to pay a pro rata additional premium to reinstate the limit of the indemnity, which is calculated proportionately to the original premium and the amount of the indemnity being restored. A reinstatement clause therefore provides the insured with a right to obtain further cover under the same policy at the same premium as previously agreed, should the indemnity limit be exhausted before the indemnity period expires.

3-042   **Relevant sections from CAR policies produced by the insurance industry.**   Where an insurer's or broker's standardised policy wording has been employed which sets out a range of different permutations of cover, extensions and/or exclusions, the schedule will normally distil the combination employed in a particular policy.

3-043   **Definitions.**   Frequently occurring words or phrases will be defined within the

---

19   This may be limited to (with further caveats including time limits) loss or damage arising from a defect originating prior to the commencement of these periods or caused by the Contractor in the course of any operations it carries out at the contract site for the purpose of remedying any defects in the Contract Works, or otherwise fulfilling the maintenance obligations under the terms of the contract.

policy. The purpose of this is to allow for greater economy of drafting and to avoid needless repetition in the policy. A general definitional section may be found in the schedule—or separate to it and following it—with further definitions provided in individual sections where necessary.

(c) Delay and third-party liability

Delay in completion.   Where applicable, the CAR policy may contain a section dealing with consequential loss coverage which is likely to include detailed conditions as to coverage, relevant definitions and formulae for the calculation of loss, together with relevant exclusions and extensions. For further discussion, see paras 3-019 to 3-020 above and Ch.17.   **3-044**

Third-party liability.   As with delay in completion, the CAR policy may contain a section dealing with third-party liability which is again likely to set out detailed conditions as to coverage and relevant definitions, together with relevant exclusions and extensions. For further discussion, see para.3-021 above and paras 18-027 to 18-137 below.   **3-045**

(d) Extensions

Extensions to cover.   Property and material damage sections of CAR policies frequently contain a number of clauses that serve to extend cover beyond that set out in the insuring clause. These extensions address the costs incurred by the insured in taking remedial steps to restore insured property following loss or damage for which the insurer accepts liability. The extensions are subject to the terms of the policy, generally. Common extensions, which are usually subject to a liability cap, include those listed in paras 3-047 to 3-051 below.[20]   **3-046**

Professional fees.   The insurer may agree to extend cover to include professional fees incurred in the reinstatement of the Contract Works following qualifying damage for which the insurers have admitted liability. These may include architects, surveyors or consulting engineers' fees.   **3-047**

Debris removal.   A policy will frequently provide that, where qualifying damage has occurred for which the insurer has admitted liability, the insurer will indemnify the insured in respect of reasonable costs incurred in removing debris, or otherwise dismantling or demolishing, shoring up or propping the insured property.   **3-048**

Plans, drawings or other documents.   Cover may be extended to include the cost of materials and labour necessarily incurred to restore plans, drawings and other documents held at the site following qualifying damage.   **3-049**

Expediting expenses.   A policy may include an extension providing for an indemnity in respect of the additional cost of overtime, weekend and shift working payments together with plant-hire charges and delivery costs reasonably incurred by the insured in expediting repair, replacement or rectification following qualifying damage. Such an extension will ordinarily exclude any costs incurred in expediting the ordinary completion of the Contract Works.   **3-050**

---

[20] For further discussion about extensions to cover, see Ch.17.

3-051   **Other common extensions.**   Other common extensions include cover in respect of damage to Contract Works while stored off-site and damage to new and unused machinery forming part of the Contract Works caused by electrical or mechanical breakdown.

(e)   Exclusions: general and specific

3-052   **Exclusions.**   CAR policies are likely to contain both general exclusions—those common to all parts of the policy—and specific exclusions—relevant to specific types of cover provided—that serve to limit the generality of the insuring clause(s) in the policy. A full discussion of frequently encountered policy exclusions may be found in Chs 15 and 16. Common exclusions include liability for the consequences for the items listed in paras 3-053 to 3-061 below.

3-053   **War and kindred risks.**   As might be expected, insurers are reluctant to provide insurance against war related risk (which is by its nature unpredictable).[21] Typically, the definition (and the exclusion) will not apply to all similar risks such as riot and strikes, damage caused by military equipment in peacetime and terrorism.

3-054   **Terrorism.**   Unsurprisingly, insurers tend to adopt a similar position in relation to terrorism and expressly limit or exclude cover for terrorism related risk. Specific top-up cover relating to terrorism risks may, however, be available.

3-055   **Radiation and nuclear.**   Radiation and other nuclear threats (e.g. nuclear materials and nuclear site risks) are typically excluded by insurers. To the extent the material works are to involve working in or around nuclear facilities, parties will normally seek cover from specific bodies that may have been set up to accept risks associated with nuclear projects (such as the United Kingdom Atomic Energy Insurance Committee).[22]

3-056   **Sonic damage.**   In the main, clauses of this nature are directed towards the consequences of sonic bangs caused by pressure waves from aircraft or other aerial devices travelling at sonic or supersonic speeds.[23]

3-057   **Pollution.**   Policies will usually provide extremely limited cover only in relation to the consequences of pollution.[24] An example would be indemnification in respect of the pollution or contamination of insured property caused directly by an occurrence insured under the policy only. Insurers' aversion to accepting risk associated with pollution stems in part from the difficulties frequently encountered in establishing when damage occurred and the possible extent of any damage that might be caused.

3-058   **Defects.**   It is common for a material damage section in a policy to contain an exclusion for some or all loss or damage caused by a defect in design, plan specification, materials or workmanship. As insurers may be prepared to accept liability for some of those risks, policy wording will often make use of one of two

---

[21]   See below, paras 15-043 to 15-060.
[22]   See below, paras 15-061 to 15-065.
[23]   See below, para.15-066 and para.25-040.
[24]   See below, para.15-039.

sets of standard form design defect exclusion clauses: defects exclusion ("DE") clauses and clauses produced by the London Engineering Group ("LEG") defects clauses.[25] Those standard form clauses offer a suite of different wordings that can be tailored to suit the material risk in question. Distinctions between "defects" and "damage" are considered in more detail below in Chs 14 and 16.

Professional advisers. Professional indemnity risks are often excluded. Thus, while the defined insured may include professional advisers such as architects and consulting engineers, the degree of cover they enjoy may be carefully circumscribed so as not to extend the indemnity to professional advisors arising out of breach of professional duty.   3-059

Disappearance or shortage. This exclusion clause is normally provided so as to exclude the insurer from liability in respect of losses caused by the disappearance or shortage of insured property where such loss is only revealed when an inventory is made.   3-060

Normal wear and tear. A CAR policy will frequently exclude liability for the cost of the rectification of wear and tear, erosion, corrosion or other deterioration of the insured property, including the scratching of painted or polished surfaces. However, it will not exclude qualifying damage to insured property caused by such wear and tear. For example, a policy may serve to exclude the cost of replacing a concrete pillar that has deteriorated to the point of collapse (and which has damaged surrounding property), but it will extend cover to the reinstatement costs of the damaged surrounds.   3-061

(f)   Warranties, conditions and due observance clauses

Warranties. The terms "warranty" and "condition" have a particular meaning in the law of insurance, which does not necessarily coincide with that at general contract law. The issue is examined in more detail in Ch.12. In essence, whether a clause is a warranty or condition is a matter of contractual construction. Breach of a qualifying warranty discharges the insurer from liability under the policy on and from the date of breach (on some policy wordings, the discharge of the insurer is automatic upon breach). A CAR policy may include a range of specific warranties alone or together with conditions that reflect particular risks or hazards associated with projects of the type in question and look to limit the insurers' exposure to them. Examples include hot-work warranties, site-security warranties and fire-prevention warranties.   3-062

The 2015 Act has made a number of changes to the effect of a breach of warranty on the insurer's liability to pay out under the policy. For policies and variations entered into after 12 August 2016, a breach of warranty is now capable of being remedied by the insured to restore the insurer's liability as if the breach had never occurred. A breach will also no longer result in the automatic discharge of the insurer's entire liability under the policy. Instead, a breach will only discharge the insurer's liability for losses relevant to the risk that the warranty was intended to mitigate, in order to avoid insurers relying on the breach of an irrelevant warranty to avoid paying out under the policy. This would, for example, prevent an   3-063

---

[25]   See below, paras 16-065 to 16-070.

insurer from relying on a broken burglar alarm to refuse a claim for storm damage. For more on remedying a breach of warranty, see below at paras 5-090 to 5-102. For more on warranties not relevant to the actual loss, see below at paras 5-103 to 5-115.

3-064 **Basis of the contract clauses.** These clauses were historically used by insurers to convert any representations made by the insured on the proposal form into warranties that would discharge the insurer from any liability to pay out under the policy if the representations were later found to be inaccurate or untrue. The wording of these clauses was often ambiguous and obscure, typically requiring the insured to sign a statement that the proposal "shall form the basis of the contract" between insured and insurer without making explicit that the effect of this was to convert every representation into a warranty and allow the insurer to avoid payment after any breach. The use of these clauses has now been abolished by the 2015 Act, and any basis of the contract clauses will cease to have contractual effect if contained within any policy or variation entered into after 12 August 2016. These clauses are examined in more detail below, both pre- and post- the introduction of the 2015 Act at paras 4-024 to 4-026 and para.12-017.

3-065 **Due observance clauses.** In summary, this clause (which is typically a condition) stipulates that the insurer's liability to make payment under the policy will not arise unless the insured complies with the conditions of the policy (which are thereby conditions precedent to liability). See further below para.12-007.

(g) Other clauses

3-066 **Material change of risk clauses.** CAR policies frequently provide that the insured is required to declare any alteration in circumstances that affect the insured risk as soon as the insured becomes aware of them (in essence, where there is a material change in, or addition to, the information provided by the insured with the application for insurance). The reason for the inclusion of such a provision is clear: any changes could significantly alter the insured risk. As such, the insurers require the right to reassess the terms of the cover provided and to consider afresh whether they wish to continue to provide cover.

3-067 **Minimisation of loss clauses.** Under a CAR policy, an insured is often under an obligation to take all reasonable precautions to safeguard the insured property against damage. This may extend to include an obligation to take all reasonable precautions to prevent or minimise other injury or loss. If those steps are taken and material damage occurs, a policy will typically respond. However, if no damage or loss occurs, then the policy will usually not respond: the insured's actions comprising no more than those it should have undertaken in the absence of insurance.

3-068 **Sue and labour.** A CAR policy may contain a clause permitting the insured to recover from the insurer the costs incurred in avoiding or attempting to avert or minimise loss or damage to the insured property, although the policy is likely to contain a liability limit in respect of this. Sue and labour clauses are reviewed further in Ch.17.

3-069 **Waiver of subrogation.** In this context, subrogation is the right enjoyed by the insurer to take over and prosecute in the insured's name any claim that the insured may have against a third party or defend any claim made against the insured by a third party. A waiver of subrogation clause provides in effect that the insurer does not have the right to exercise its rights of subrogation in respect of an insured as against a co-insured (save in certain circumstances). Subrogation and the waiver of subrogation are explored further below.[26]

Claims cooperation. CAR policies typically require the insured to cooperate with   **3-070** the insurer in relation to any claim made by or against the insured. Claims cooperation clauses are examined in more detail in Ch.12.

Typical duties imposed by the policy on the insured include:

1. notifying the insurer of events that might give rise to a claim;
2. providing the insurer with full written details of any claim, as soon as possible;
3. making no admissions as to liability without the written consent of the insurer; and
4. providing the insurer with copies and details of all correspondence and legal documentation related to any claim.

Adjudication. CAR policies often contain provisions requiring the insured to   **3-071** notify the insurers upon the receipt of any notice of intention by another party to refer a dispute to adjudication, or of an intention by the insured to refer a dispute to adjudication—in so far as it relates to material damage which might give rise to a claim under the policy—under the Housing Grants Construction and Regeneration Act 1996 (as amended) or pursuant to material contract terms. Such provisions ordinarily provide, amongst other things, that the insured will cooperate with the insurer in the conduct of the adjudication and will comply with any reasonable request on the part of the insurer to institute legal proceedings or arbitration (if applicable) in accordance with the terms of the original contract in relation to the adjudicator's decision. Claims cooperation and the claims procedure is discussed in more detail in Ch.21.

Fraudulent claims. CAR policies typically provide that the policy shall be forfeit   **3-072** in the event that a claim brought thereunder is fraudulent. Some policies extend the ambit of material fraud to include circumstances where any material damage was caused by the wilful act or wilful neglect of the insured. Fraudulent claims are addressed further in Chs 5, 6, 20 and 21.

Where there is no express term in the policy dealing with fraudulent claims, the courts will look to the common law in order to determine the effect that a fraudulent claim will have on the underlying policy and any previous or subsequent claims that the insured has made under it. For policies and variations entered into after 12 August 2016, the common law position has been codified and clarified by the 2015 Act which now provides the default position in respect of fraudulent claims in the absence of any bespoke contractual arrangements. Under this default regime, an insurer will not be liable to pay the fraudulent claim and they may treat the contract as terminated from the time of the claim, even if the fraud is not discovered until a long time after the claim was made. However, the fraud will not affect any previous valid claims made under the policy. For more on the default position on fraudulent claims, see below at paras 5-116 to 5-132.

---

[26] See below, paras 17-077, 20-042 to 20-052, 20-062 to 20-063 and 20-065.

3-073 **Payment of the limit of the indemnity.** Relating to the third-party liability section of a policy, the effect of such a condition is that the insurer is entitled to pay out at the limit of the indemnity afforded by the policy (and cease thereafter to be liable for further qualifying costs and expenses).

3-074 **Cancellation.** A CAR policy may contain provision for the cancellation of the policy on written notice to the insured's last known address. A cancellation provision will usually provide that where the premium has been paid in full, the insured will be entitled to a proportionate rebate of premium for the unexpired period of insurance. For further consideration of the topic, please see below, para.23-011.

3-075 **Contribution and non-contribution.** As an insured may enjoy coverage in respect of the same loss under more than one policy, CAR policies will frequently contain "contribution" or "non-contribution" clauses, which serve to clarify how the policy will respond in circumstances of multiple insurance. Typically, a contribution clause provides that where other insurance responds to the same loss or damage, the insurers' liability is limited to a specified or calculable amount. Insurers may add a clause to the effect that if the other policy or policies in question contain non-contribution clauses, then the CAR policy will too be subject to a non-contribution provision. A non-contribution clause usually provides that the insurance is not to be called upon and will not respond to any claim in respect of which there is other valid and collectable insurance that will respond to the loss. On the other hand, the clause may stipulate that the current policy will operate in excess of and not contribute with any such insurance.

3-076 **Suspended contracts.** If work ceases and contractors leave a site prematurely, the risk of criminal damage to the Contract Works and other insured materials increases significantly. In these circumstances, CAR policies usually include a clause that unless the insurer agrees to a continuation of cover—which may or may not be at an additional premium and possibly subject to additional terms—insurance is suspended (or even withdrawn) during any period of stoppage.

3-077 **Access and inspection.** CAR policies usually reserve the right on the part of the insurer to inspect the insured property and contract site at any time. The logic behind the reservation is clear as, amongst other things, an insurer may require access to investigate allegations of breach of policy conditions as well as to conduct any loss-adjustment inspections that might have to take place.

3-078 **Law and jurisdiction.** To avoid any potential disputes that may arise where parties and Works may span a number of jurisdictions, CAR policies will typically designate both the governing law and jurisdiction. Provision may be made for the settlement of disputes by court or arbitral proceedings.

THE PLACING AND FORMATION OF THE CONTRACT

1. INTRODUCTION

Introduction. The rules governing the formation of an insurance contract are the same as those which govern the formation of any commercial contract,[1] subject to certain variations created by insurance market practice.[2] The majority of insurance contracts are bilateral contracts formed between the insurer and insured. **4-001**

In relation to procuring insurance under a CAR policy, the main contractor usually takes out the insurance policy in the joint names of the employer, contractor and other interested parties pursuant to the provisions of its contract with the employer.[3] A contractor can obtain insurance under either an annual policy or a project policy[4]; there are advantages and disadvantages to both. Project policies have the advantage of being tailored for the particular works, the one policy covering all the relevant parties. On the other hand, if the contractor is entering into a **4-002**

---

[1] See *Chitty on Contracts*, edited by H.G. Beale, A.S. Burrows et al, 32nd edn (London: Sweet & Maxwell, 2015), Vol.1, paras 2–003 to 8–143.

[2] Such as Lloyd's. See below, para.4-049.

[3] The principles applied to determine whether or not a particular subcontractor is insured under a specific CAR policy are discussed below, in Ch.8.

[4] See below paras 4-008 to 4-013.

large number of projects in a year, it may be an unwelcome burden to negotiate fresh policies for each project in which case an annual policy will be more appropriate.

4-003   The problem facing underwriters in relation to insuring construction projects is that the risks associated with the project are difficult to assess as the works do not exist at the time the insurance is proposed. Most underwriters will therefore use a checklist of essential points when determining whether to underwrite the proposed risk, namely: the type of project; the experience of the contractor; the geographical situation of the project (bearing in mind the probability of natural hazards); local conditions so as to assess the risk of deliberate and wilful third-party damage; the type of construction machinery and equipment to be used; and the method of construction.[5]

4-004   Bearing this in mind, the form of the proposal (that is the request for insurance) advanced by the contractor will depend on the nature of the construction project to be insured. For small-scale construction projects, insurance cover is usually procured by the contractor completing a standard proposal form setting out the material terms of the insurance cover.[6] Contractors involved in large-scale construction projects most often use the services of a specialist construction broker to evaluate and process the insurance contract.[7]

2.   TYPES OF CAR POLICY

4-005   CAR policies have a number of specific features that are not found in other insurance contracts,[8] the most obvious being that such policies invariably include many parties as the named insured. Since it is the contractor who is responsible for protecting the works until completion, it will normally be him who will arrange for the policy to be taken out,[9] though this is not invariably the case.[10] Each named party will be insured for their respective rights and interests.[11]

4-006   Many CAR policies contain standard or near identical clauses, but real care needs to be taken when considering the specific terms of any particular policy because even a minor change in wording can have a significant impact on coverage.

4-007   As highlighted above, the prospective insured has the option of obtaining cover under an annual CAR policy or a project-specific CAR policy. In many cases, the best course for the contractor is to opt for an annual policy to provide cover for smaller contracts and to take out a project policy in respect of the larger contracts carrying higher levels of risk.

---

[5]   See above, Ch.2.

[6]   The material terms include: terms which indicate the parties to the contract; the definition of the risk covered; the commencement and duration of the insurance cover; the amount of the premium (a policy made on the basis that the premium is to be agreed is also valid); the way in which the premium is to be paid; and the amount of insurance payable by the insurer in the event of a loss.

[7]   See below, para.4-049.

[8]   See above, Ch.3.

[9]   The standard contracts make provision for which party is to do this. For example, the JCT Standard Forms provide for a choice: namely insurance options A (the Contractor), B (the Employer) or C (the Employer). See Joint Contracts Tribunal, SBC/Q 2011 *JCT Standard Building Contract With Quantities 2011* (London: Sweet & Maxwell, 2011), pp.88–91. See also below para.8-004 and para.20-061.

[10]   An alternative may be preferable under certain circumstances, such as where an employer has a particular preference for or relationship with an underwriter. See below, para.20-066.

[11]   See below, para.8-007.

(a)   Annual policy

Annual insurance cover.   The annual policy provides cover against losses for a   **4-008**
period of 12 months in respect of all contracts undertaken by the contractor during
this period. This is particularly beneficial to large contractors as it covers activities on a number of different sites at the same time. Cover terminates at the expiry
of the policy, and the insured has to renew the policy in order to obtain cover for
works still in progress. Renewal may be avoided by incorporating a "run-off" clause
in the contract: this provides that the insurance cover continues to operate in respect
of contract works commenced prior to the renewal date until their completion.
However, this has the effect of increasing the insurance premium, which may make
it an uneconomical option for the contractor.

Calculation of the premium.[12]   The premium paid by the contractor is calculated   **4-009**
in relation to his annual contract turnover, excluding any projects insured under a
single-project policy. The average rate of premium charged in respect of all
contracts does not take into account the different level of risks associated with different types of contract. The insured may therefore end up paying more for his
policy than under the single-project policy, which is tailored to each contract. The
contractor is also exposed to the risk of an inflated premium upon renewal of the
annual policy.

This generic approach to assessing rates of premium similarly causes difficulty   **4-010**
in respect of indemnity limits. An insured may require different levels of indemnity
for different contracts depending on the complexity of the construction works
involved. Therefore, an overall limit that provides for all contracts might be one
which the insured pays more for but may never in fact need to be used. Nevertheless, a contractor may choose to obtain insurance under an annual policy because
it is wider in scope than a single project policy, for example most annual policies
include third-party risks,[13] ancillary business activities and legal liabilities and are
also easier to administer, as all contracts are dealt with under one policy.

(b)   Single-project policy

Single-project cover.   The single-project policy allows an employer or contrac-   **4-011**
tor to insure risks in relation to the whole or part of a single project. As the policy
relates to a particular construction contract only, the duration of the policy will be
the period allowed for the contractor to complete the works and may include a
period of maintenance post-completion. The insured benefits from the fact that the
policy provides cover for the specific type of losses, which may emanate from the
project in question and there are no issues with the cover expiring before completion of the project.

Extensions of time.   It is often the case that building projects become delayed and   **4-012**
a contractor will seek an extension of time for completion of the project. In such
circumstances they will also require an extension of their insurance. Sometimes
insurance policies will provide for an automatic extension at an increased premium
or a premium to be arranged. If the insurance contract does not contain such a term,

---

[12]   See below, paras 23-004 and 23-007.
[13]   See below, Ch.18.

the contract will need to be renegotiated with the insurer. In *Jones Construction Co v Alliance Insurance Co Ltd*,[14] delays occurred which led to the date for completion of the project being extended. The claimant claimed that the insurers were bound to extend the insurance policy under a condition stating that they would indemnify the insured

> "for loss arising during the period stated in the Schedule or any subsequent period in respect of which the Insured shall have paid and the Insurers accepted the premium required for this extension of the terms of this Policy."[15]

The court held that the existence of this express term meant that it was impossible to imply a term into the contract that would bind the insurers to extend the period of insurance cover. This was upheld by the Court of Appeal,[16] who affirmed that the terms of the policy could not be used to infer an intention between the parties as relied on by the claimant in circumstances where the express wording of the contract required an acceptance of a premium for an extended period by the insurers.

4-013   **Advantages of a single-project policy.**   There are a number of benefits to an insured in obtaining insurance cover under a single-project policy. These include: (i) cost certainty; the insured does not have to be concerned with inflating premiums, which often occur upon renewal under an annual policy; and (ii) cost effectiveness; the cover is purchased on behalf of all collaborating parties under a particular project. The benefit to the insurer under a single-project policy is that they are provided with full underwriting data and technical information regarding the project; whereas there is a presumption in relation to an annual policy that an insurer will not be provided with such detailed information. Therefore, a single-project policy is likely to lead to an insurer carrying out a more comprehensive and accurate evaluation of risk, although this must be balanced against a more exacting administrative task. This approach does, however, ensure that the premium is set at a more accurate rate.

3.   THE FORM OF PROPOSAL

4-014   In a construction context, the form of the proposal is often related to the scale of the project that the contractor wishes to insure. For simple construction projects, the standard proposal form is usually all that is needed, whereas in relation to a project requiring a more complicated insurance proposal, the proposed insured will often opt to employ a specialist broker to make presentations directly to the insurance company in order to secure the CAR policy. Finally, a third method of formation is utilised when dealing within the Lloyd's insurance market, which requires a Lloyd's broker and uses a slip to complete the agreement.

---

[14]   *Jones Construction Co v Alliance Co Ltd* [1960] 1 Lloyd's Rep. 264.
[15]   [1960] 1 Lloyd's Rep. 264 at 264–265.
[16]   *Jones Construction Co* [1961] 1 Lloyd's Rep. 121.

(a) The use of a standard proposal form in placing the insurance contract

The role of the proposal form.   The standard course of practice for the forma-   **4-015** tion of the majority of low value CAR policies is that an insurer issues a standard proposal form and the offer is made by the contractor when they send their completed proposal to the insurer for consideration. In such circumstances the proposal is the means by which the contractor gives to the insurer the particulars of the risk that he wishes them to underwrite, which may induce the insurer to enter into a binding contract. The contract is formed where the offer is accepted by the insurer on terms that do not differ from those in the offer and there are no major terms to be agreed.[17]

Suitability for smaller construction projects.   The standard proposal form is of-   **4-016** fered by most insurance companies for small-scale construction work as the decision to insure such projects, by their nature, requires a less comprehensive analysis of the project than is entailed by a large complex construction project. The form is therefore tailored to be as expedient as possible, by requesting all of the information necessary, which constitutes the proposer's offer to take out a policy. The form asks for information on matters relevant to the proposed risk, in particular: proposal policy holder details; the overall estimated contract value and split values of major works; a description of the contract work; construction site location including details of significant physical and environmental features; the construction, testing and maintenance periods required to be insured; the interest to be covered; additional coverage; and the duration of cover. This information is in most cases enough for the insurance company to decide whether to insure.

Documents provided with the proposal form.   A proposer is generally expected   **4-017** to enclose relevant documentation with the proposal form including details of other insurances in place, the underlying contract (if any) and a relevant claims history. Upon receipt of the proposal, the underwriters assess the technical information along with the project risk information to decide whether the level of risk is one that is feasible for them to cover.

(i) The proposal form as the offer

Material terms.   The material terms that need to be agreed in order for a standard   **4-018** insurance contract to gain legal effect are: the terms which identify the parties to the contract; the definition of the risk covered; the commencement and duration of the insurance cover[18]; the amount of the premium[19]; the way in which the premium is to be paid; and the amount of insurance payable by the insurer in the event of a loss. The proposal form requests all of this information meaning that the form is in itself enough to constitute an offer to contract capable of being legally binding

---

[17]   The contract can have no effect in law unless all material terms are agreed, see *Allis-Chalmers Co v Maryland Fidelity and Deposit Co* (1916) 114 L.T. 433; 32 T.L.R. 263.

[18]   Though this may be capable of being inferred from a course of dealing between the insured and insurer, see *Winne v Niagara Fire Ins Co* (1883) 46 Sickels 185; 91 NY 185.

[19]   A policy made on the basis that the premium is to be agreed may also be valid: *F Gliksten & Son Ltd v State Assurance Co* (1922) 10 Ll. L. Rep. 604.

upon acceptance; the formation of a CAR insurance contract requires only the proposal form and the insurance company's acceptance of that form.

4-019   **Standard terms.**   An insured is deemed to have applied for and agreed to the insurer's usual terms and conditions; if the insurer has accepted the offer on those terms, they form the terms of the insurance contract. In *Rust v Abbey Life Insurance*,[20] Brandon LJ stated:

> "It is clear that in ordinary insurance cases a policy may become a binding contract between an insured and insurers even though the insured has not seen or expressly assented to all the detailed terms of the policy, provided always that such terms are the usual terms of the insurers."[21]

The absence of such a presumption would require all offers to come from the insurance company themselves in order to secure the inclusion of the standard terms, adding a needless arbitrary step that would unduly complicate the process.[22]

4-020   **Knowledge.**   The presumption operates at law by assuming the insured has knowledge of the insurer's standard terms and conditions. Whilst the prospective insured need not have actual knowledge of the standard terms,[23] the terms must be available for examination by the prospective insured so that he is deemed to have the means of knowledge.[24] In the case of *Thompson v London Midland & Scottish*

---

20   *Rust v Abbey Life Insurance Co Ltd* [1979] 2 Lloyd's Rep. 334.

21   [1979] 2 Lloyd's Rep. 334 at 339.

22   See *Adie & Sons v Insurances Corp Ltd* (1898) 14 T.L.R. 554 and *General Accident Insurance Corp v Cronk* (1901) 17 T.L.R. 233; 45 Sol Jo 261. In the latter case the defendant submitted a proposal that did not contain all of the terms subsequently set out in the policy. The defendant argued that the policy amounted to a counter-offer and no contract had been formed. This was rejected by the court, which ruled that a person making a proposal must be taken to have applied for the ordinary form of policy issued by the company. This presumption is followed in other jurisdictions. In *Eames v Home Insurance Co* (1872) 94 U.S. 621 at 629; 4 Otto 621; 24 L.Ed. 298, the Supreme Court of the United States observed: "[i]f no preliminary contract would be valid unless it specified minutely the terms to be contained in the policy to be issued, no such contract could ever be made or would ever be of any use. The very reason for sustaining such contracts is that the parties may have the benefit of them during that incipient period when the papers are being perfected and transmitted. It is sufficient if one party proposes to be insured, and the other party agrees to insure, and the subject, the period, the amount and the rate of insurance is ascertained or understood, and the premium paid if demanded. It will be presumed that they contemplate such form of policy, containing such conditions and limitations as are usual in such cases, or have been used before between the parties. This is the sense and reason of the thing, and any contrary requirement should be expressly notified to the party to be affected by it."

23   See *Watkins v Rymill* (1883) 10 Q.B.D. 178 where the court held that if a document in a common form is delivered to a contracting party, stating the terms by which the party delivering it will enter into the proposed contract, it is binding on the offeree upon acceptance whether he reads the document or otherwise informs himself of the contents or not. Stephen J at 188–189 set out a number of exceptions to this rule, for instance, where the offeree reasonably supposes the document is a mere acknowledgement of an agreement and in cases of fraud or misrepresentation.

24   In *Dickens v St Paul Fire & Marine Insurance Co (UK) Ltd* (1936) 6 Beeler 403; 170 Tenn. 403; 95 SW 2d 910 at 913, the court stated that the insured must have a "reasonable opportunity to ascertain the contents of the policy before mere acceptance can amount to a representation of the contents [of the policy]."

Railway Co,[25] Lord Hanworth M.R.[26] cited the judgment of Chief Baron Pollock in *Stewart v The London and North Western Railway Co*[27] who said:

"There is a rule in the English law that every man must be taken to know that which he has the means of knowing, whether he has availed himself of those means or not."[28]

Course of dealing. Where, over a previous course of dealing, a party has conducted itself in a manner that has led the other contracting party reasonably to believe that the former has accepted its terms and conditions, then those terms may be held to be incorporated into the present contract.[29] Much will depend on whether such terms have previously been reasonably drawn to the party's attention,[30] though it is not necessary that the terms had themselves been expressly stated in the contract.[31] For instance, it might be sufficient that a letter of correspondence

4-021

---

25 *Thompson v London Midland & Scottish Railway Co* [1930] 1 K.B. 41; 98 L.J.K.B. 615; [1929] All E.R. Rep 474.
26 *Thompson* [1930] 1 K.B. 41 at [48]; 98 L.J.K.B. 615 at 619; [1929] All E.R. Rep. 474 at 479.
27 *Stewart v The London and Northern Western Railway Co* 3 Hurl. & C. 135; 33 L.J. (Ex.) 199; (1864) 10 Jur NS 805.
28 *Stewart* 33 L.J. (Ex.) 199 at 200; (1864) 3 Hurl. & C. 135 at 138. In the second report cited, the quote is nuanced slightly, though there is no material difference in its meaning. The principle set out in the case, however, may explain the decision of *Allis-Chalmers Co* (1916) 114 L.T. 433; 32 T.L.R. 263, in which it was held that there was no binding contract until the applicant had seen and accepted the bond prepared by the company. Whilst this seems to imply that the proposer must have actual knowledge of the standard terms of the insurer—at law, the proposer was deemed to have no knowledge until it was literally presented to and accepted by him—in this case the terms of the proposed contract had never been stated so there was in effect no means by which the proposer was capable of having knowledge. See *MacGillivray on Insurance Law*, edited by J. Birds, B. Lynch and S. Milnes, 13th edn (London: Sweet & Maxwell, 2015), para.2–010, where the editors state that it is difficult to reconcile the reasoning in this case with the authorities cited in favour of the principle that the proposer need not have actual knowledge, unless it is interpreted as meaning that there was no evidence that the company had standard or usual terms, and if so, what these were. In *Rust* [1979] 2 Lloyd's Rep. 334, the court held that there was a binding contract despite the fact that the contract came into existence before the applicant was able to study the prepared policy. However, this case can be distinguished on the basis that the proposer had the basic terms of the insurance explained to her prior to the formation of the contract.
29 *Henry Kendall & Sons v William Lillico and Sons Ltd; Holland Colombo Trading Society Ltd v Grimsdale & Sons Ltd; Grimsdale & Sons Ltd v Suffolk Agricultural Poultry Producers Association;* [Appeals from *Hardwick Game Farm v Suffolk Agricultural and Poultry Producers Association Ltd*] [1969] 2 A.C. 31 at 113; [1968] 3 W.L.R. 110 at 164; [1968] 2 All E.R. 444 at 481–482, per Lord Pearce. In the Court of Appeal in *Hardwick Game Farm v Suffolk Agricultural and Poultry Producers Association Ltd; William Lillico & Son Ltd v Grimsdale & Sons Ltd; Henry Kendall & Sons v Holland Colombo Trading Society Ltd* [1966] 1 W.L.R. 287 at 339; [1966] 1 All E.R. 309 at 344–345; [1966] 1 Lloyd's Rep. 197 at 241, per Diplock LJ; *Johnson Matthey Bankers Ltd v The State Trading Corp of India Ltd* [1984] 1 Lloyd's Rep. 427 at 433, per Staughton LJ, *SIAT di del Ferro v Tradax Overseas SA* [1978] 2 Lloyd's Rep. 470 at 490, per Donaldson J. It is not a necessary requirement for incorporating the term that the party had actual knowledge of the terms incorporated in the previous course of dealings. It had previously been stated by Lord Devlin, obiter, in *McCutcheon v David MacBrayne Ltd* [1964] 1 W.L.R. 125 at 134; [1964] 1 All E.R. 430 at 437; [1964] 1 Lloyd's Rep. 16 at 25, that only actual knowledge would suffice. This has been challenged on the basis that incorporation is determined from what it can objectively be ascertained that the parties are agreeing to, based on an expectation created by a long course of dealing or a knowledge of the industry standard. See *Hardwick Game Farm; William Lillico & Son Ltd; Henry Kendall & Sons* [1966] 1 W.L.R. 287 at 308, 316 and 339; [1966] 1 All E.R. 309 at 322, 328 and 345; [1966] 1 Lloyd's Rep. 197 at 220, 226 and 241, per Pearce, Reid and Diplock LJJ.
30 *Keeton Sons & Co Ltd v Carl Prior Ltd* [1986] B.T.L.C. 30 at 32, per Ackner LJ.
31 *Circle Freight International Ltd v Medeast Gulf Exports Ltd* [1988] 2 Lloyd's Rep. 427 at 433; *Thornton v Shoe Lane Parking* [1971] 2 Q.B. 163 at 172; [1971] 2 W.L.R. 585 at 591; [1971] 1 All

between the parties states at its foot, "[all] business [transacted in accordance with] standard trading conditions of the company"[32] or, an invoice that states that standard terms and conditions apply and are "available on request".[33] This rule on incorporation of terms can also apply to contracts formed orally.[34] Where, however, it can be shown that previous transactions were sporadic then this may not amount to a course of dealing and the terms may not be incorporated.[35] Where the form of dealing in question departs from the previous course of dealing as between the parties then, again, the term may not be incorporated.[36]

4-022   **The effect of the presumption.**   Where the standard terms and conditions have been incorporated through one of the above methods, they will be deemed to form part of the offer contained within the proposal form. It is, therefore, not open to the insured to argue that there is no binding contract due to the alleged acceptance being in fact a counter-offer containing the standard terms and conditions, which did not form part of the offer made in the proposal form. Similarly, the insured cannot argue that there is a binding contract but that those standard terms were not incorporated.

4-023   **Rebuttal of the presumption.**   The presumption that the insured and insurer have contracted on the insurer's standard terms can, however, be rebutted if there are no standard terms for the risk proposed or the insurer indicates, prior to the formation of the contract that the standard terms do not apply. Terms other than the insurer's standard terms may also be incorporated if the proposal expressly refers to those other terms or if the insurer advances a policy on terms different to its standard terms. In the latter case, the insurer's response would amount to a counter offer. In *South-East Lancashire Insurance Co Ltd v Croisdale*,[37] the insured was entitled to reject an insurance policy on the basis that the rebate term in the policy had been deleted. MacNaghten J stated:

> "The question is, was he bound to accept the policies? I do not think he was ... Even if nothing had been said about rebate when the proposal form was signed, I think under the terms of the proposal form he was entitled to a policy in the ordinary form issued by the company, and on the evidence before me and the policy itself it is clear that the rebate clause is part of the ordinary policy of the company."[38]

E.R. 686 at 692, per Megaw LJ. Compare *Interfoto Picture Library Ltd v Stiletto Visual Programmes Ltd* [1989] Q.B. 433 at 445; [1988] 2 W.L.R. 615 at 626; [1988] 1 All E.R. 348 at 357, per Bingham LJ, where there exists a more stringent requirement to bring onerous terms and conditions to the attention of the other party.

[32] *Keeton Sons & Co Ltd* [1986] B.T.L.C. 30 at 33. Ackner LJ held that this was a reasonable attempt to bring the terms to the attention of the party.

[33] *Circle Freight International Ltd* [1988] 2 Lloyd's Rep. 427 at 429 and 433–434; *Eastman Chemical International AG v NMT Trading and Eagle Transport* [1972] 2 Lloyd's Rep. 25 at 31.

[34] *Henry Kendall & Sons; Holland Colombo Trading Society Ltd; Grimsdale & Sons Ltd*; [Appeals from *Hardwick Game*] [1969] 2 A.C. 31; [1968] 3 W.L.R. 110; [1968] 2 All E.R. 444; *Circle Freight International Ltd* [1988] 2 Lloyd's Rep. 427.

[35] *Hollier v Rambler Motors (AMC) Ltd* [1972] 2 Q.B. 71 at 76; [1972] 2 W.L.R. 401 at 404; [1972] 1 All E.R. 399 at 402, per Salmon LJ, where it was stated, obiter, that three or four transactions in five years could not amount to a course of dealing.

[36] *McCutcheon* [1964] 1 W.L.R. 125 at 128 and 138; [1964] 1 All E.R. 430 at 432, 439–440; [1964] 1 Lloyd's Rep. 16 at 21 and 27, per Reid and Pearce LJJ.

[37] *South-East Lancashire Insurance Co Ltd v Croisdale* (1931) 40 Ll. L. Rep. 22.

[38] (1931) 40 Ll. L. Rep. 22 at 24.

The presumption is also rebutted if a higher degree of notice is required, as under the common law rule, for particularly onerous terms or terms that are unusual as compared to the market's standard terms.[39]

Basis of contract clauses. A proposal may contain a clause that states that the   **4-024**
prospective insured warrants that the answers contained in the proposal form are true and will "form the basis of the contract" between the insured and insurer. If the proposal contains such a "basis of contract" clause, the pre-contractual representations on the proposal form are converted into contractual warranties.[40] This means that if any statement given in the proposal is incorrect, the insurer may refuse all claims, even if the mistake is unimportant. Such clauses therefore allow insurers to use a form of words that extend the protections otherwise available in respect of misrepresentation or material non-disclosure to cover answers that are not material to the risk, or are made without fraud or negligence. The use of basis of contract clauses has now been abolished by the Insurance Act 2015 ("the 2015 Act") rendering any such clause on the proposal form ineffective for policies incepted after 12 August 2016. However, for policies incepted before the 2015 Act comes into force, basis of contract clauses will continue to have contractual effect.

Basis of contract clauses were considered recently by Mr Justice Akenhead in   **4-025**
Genesis Housing Association v Liberty Syndicate Management Ltd,[41] which concerned a policy of latent defects insurance. The proposal form submitted by the prospective insured contained a basis of contract clause. The judge determined that the effect of this clause was to create a warranty as to the accuracy of the answers given. Mr Justice Akenhead held that in the present case there was a breach of the warranty given on the proposal form as the claimant had failed to identify the contractor correctly in the proposal. As the warranty given was a "basis of contract" clause, the breach rendered the policy void from inception. The insurer did not need to prove the misrepresentation was material or that it induced the underwriter to write the risk.

In giving his judgment, Mr Justice Akenhead set out a number of propositions   **4-026**
regarding basis of contract clauses derived from the authorities.[42] He said:

"(a)   It is well established that in principle 'basis of contract' clauses and warranties in relation to insurance are enforceable in law and not contrary to law or public policy at least yet. This will change in the case of consumer contracts of insurance when the new Act comes into force.
(b)   The enforceability will generally come about either by such clauses or warranties

---

[39]   *Interfoto Picture Library Ltd v Stiletto Visual Programmes Ltd* [1989] Q.B. 433; [1988] 2 W.L.R. 615; [1988] 1 All E.R. 348, *US Trading Ltd v Axa Insurance Co Ltd* [2010] Lloyd's Rep. I.R. 505 at 515, per H.H.J Simon Brown QC.
[40]   See below, para.12-017.
[41]   *Genesis Housing Association Ltd v Liberty Syndicate Management Ltd* [2012] EWHC 3105 (TCC); [2013] B.L.R. 28.
[42]   *Dawsons Ltd v Bonnin* [1922] 2 A.C. 413; (1922) 12 Ll. L. Rep. 237; *Condogianis v Guardian Assurance Co Ltd* [1921] 2 A.C. 125; (1920) 3 Ll. L. Rep. 40; (1921) 7 Ll. L. Rep. 155; *Holmes v Scottish Legal Life Assurance Society* (1932) T.L.R. 306; *Rozanes v Bowen* (1928) 32 Ll. L. Rep 98; *Bank of Nova Scotia v Hellenic Mutual War Risk Association (Bermuda) Ltd (The Good Luck)* [1992] 1 A.C. 233 at 262–263; [1991] 2 W.L.R. 1279 at 1294–1295; [1991] 3 All E.R. at 14–15; *Unipac (Scotland) Ltd v Aegon Insurance Co (UK) Ltd* 1996 S.L.T. 1197; [1996] C.L.C. 918; *Kumar v AGF Insurance Ltd* [1999] 1 W.L.R. 1747; [1998] 4 All E.R. 788; [1999] Lloyd's Rep. I.R. 147; *Economides v Commercial Union Assurance Co Plc* [1998] Q.B. 587; [1997] 3 W.L.R. 1066; [1997] 3 All E.R. 636; *Zeller v British Caymanian Insurance Co Ltd* [2008] Lloyd's Rep. I.R. 545.

being incorporated within the contract of insurance or as a stand-alone warranty by the insured given to the insurer through the proposal form or other document in which the 'basis of contract' expression or declaration is given.

(c) If the insured has innocently or otherwise signed a document, usually the proposal, as the basis of the insurance contract entered or to be entered into, which confirms (either to the best of the insured's knowledge or belief or absolutely) as true the contents of that document, the insurance contract will be void or unenforceable if the contents are untrue.

(d) The contract of insurance, whether contained in the policy itself or any other documents such as the quotation or a certificate of insurance, may as a matter of construction modify, amend or even render of no or limited effect the 'basis of contract' declaration or warranty. The ordinary principles of contractual interpretation apply to this exercise.

(e) Declarations said to be true or correct to the best knowledge or belief of the declarer will often be in the case of an individual person reviewable by reference to the honesty of that person in making the declaration. Thus Mr Zeller and Mr Economides in their respective cases honestly believed that what they were declaring was true in the sense it was to their best knowledge and belief. However, in determining particularly whether a corporate organisation making a declaration as to various statements being true to the best of its knowledge and belief is wrongful, the court must determine what it corporately is likely to have known when it made the declaration. There does not have to be dishonesty as such on the part of the organisation but, if that organisation actually knows that something said to be true on the declaration is in fact wrong, then it is making a statement which is not true to the best of its knowledge or belief."[43]

The Court of Appeal upheld that decision[44] and concluded that:

"The principle which emerges from these authorities is that where a proposal form contains a 'basis of contract' clause, (i) the proposal form has contractual effect even if the policy contains no reference to the proposal form; (ii) all statements in the proposal from constitute warranties on which the insurance contract is based. They cannot therefore be treated as immaterial."[45]

Intriguingly, Jackson LJ commented that the insured may have been correct in asserting that the first of those principles had been accepted without proper argument in the reported decisions, but he noted that the principle was not open to challenge at the Court of Appeal level. The principle would still apply if the policy made no mention of the proposal form and even if, as in this case, the policy listed the contractual documents and omitted reference to the proposal form, unless the contract used clear and unequivocal language.[46]

(ii) Circumstances in which the proposal form does not constitute an offer.

4-027 **Offer from the insurer.** In certain circumstances, the offer will be deemed to have come from the insurer rather than by the advancement of a proposal form. If the insurer has introduced new terms or conditions into the policy before return-

---

[43] *Genesis Housing Association Ltd* [2012] EWHC 3105 (TCC) at [38]; [2013] B.L.R. 28 at 41.

[44] *Genesis Housing Association Ltd v Liberty Syndicate Management Ltd* [2013] EWCA Civ 1173; [2013] C.I.L.L. 3417; [2013] 42 E.G. 124 (C.S.).

[45] *Genesis Housing Association Ltd* [2013] EWCA Civ 1173; [2013] C.I.L.L. 3417; [2013] 42 E.G. 124 (C.S.).

[46] *Genesis Housing Association Ltd* [2013] EWCA Civ 1173; [2013] C.I.L.L. 3417; [2013] 42 E.G. 124 (C.S.).

ing it to the insured, the insurer is held to have made a counter-offer for the insured to then accept or decline.[47] An insurer may also have directly approached a prospective insured stating that the insurance is available; in such circumstances, the offer will be deemed to have been made by the insurer and not the prospective insured. A renewal notice may also amount to an offer by the insurer to grant a further policy on the same risk.[48]

Negotiations. Agreement of the essential terms of the contract may be achieved   **4-028**
at once, simply by the insurer accepting the policy form completed by the prospective insured. However, it may be that a lengthy period of negotiation ensues; this is common in the case of large commercial risks. If a dispute arises as to the formation of the contract and its requisite terms, it is necessary to view the whole course of negotiations to see if there was a full agreement of the material terms of the contract at any stage of the negotiations.

Contracting through electronic communication.   The Electronic Commerce   **4-029**
(EC Directive) Regulations 2002 (SI 2002/2013)[49] apply to any insurance cover negotiated through electronic communication by which the insurer conveys its terms and conditions to the proposed insured. The insurer, as a service provider, must provide the following information: the technical steps involved in placing an order; the name of the service provider, its email address and a geographic address; the company's registration number and place of registration; membership details; a clear price, stating whether tax or shipping costs are included; and acknowledgement of the order by electronic means and information on how to amend input errors made during the order process.[50] The insurer must also provide the terms and conditions under which the contract is made. The 2002 Regulations specify that the terms must be provided by the insurer in a manner in which they can be stored and reproduced.[51]

(iii)   Acceptance of the offer contained in the proposal form

The legal requirements for acceptance of the offer.   The general rules of   **4-030**
contract formation apply so that an insurance contract will only be concluded where the offeree accepts the offer unconditionally,[52] unequivocally and communicates that

---

[47]   *South-East Lancashire Insurance Co Ltd* (1931) 40 Ll. L. Rep. 22 at 23.
[48]   A renewal notice may be construed as a conditional offer to renew or an invitation to treat requiring the insured to make a fresh offer because of the insured's duty of utmost good faith, which requires disclosure of material facts upon renewal. See below, para.4-048.
[49]   The Electronic Commerce (EC Directive) Regulations 2002 (SI 2002/2013) (the "2002 Regulations") incorporates into English law Directive 2000/31/EC of the European Parliament and of Council of 8 June 2000 on certain legal aspects of information society services, in particular electronic commerce, in the Internal Market ("Directive on electronic-commerce") [2000] OJ L178/ 1–16.
[50]   Regulation 6 of The Electronic Commerce (EC Directive) Regulations 2002 (SI 2002/2013) provides that such information must be "in a form and manner which is easily, directly and permanently accessible".
[51]   See reg.9(3) of the 2002 Regulations.
[52]   As with general common law rules regarding formation of the contract, there must be correspondence between offer and acceptance so that the insurer can be said to have unconditionally accepted the offer on terms that do not differ from those proposed by the prospective insured.

acceptance to the offeror.[53] If an inconsistency is established, the offeree's response is not capable of amounting to an acceptance of the offer at law. The response may amount to a counter offer to contract on new terms, which extinguishes the original offer.[54] An insurer is not obliged to accept an offer from a prospective insured, nor must an insurer renew a policy upon termination of the period of cover.

4-031   **Form of acceptance.**   In an insurance context, no particular form of acceptance is required,[55] although it is usually implied from the execution of the policy[56] or a demand or acceptance of premium by the insurer. Therefore, in *Pearl Life Assurance Co v Johnson*; *Pearl Life Assurance Co v Greenhalgh*[57] the insurance company was estopped from contending that there was no contract concluded with the insured on the basis that the company had issued the insurance policy and was in receipt of the premiums.[58]

4-032   However, delivery of the policy or payment of the premium is not a prerequisite for the establishment of a binding contract,[59] unless such a condition is stipulated in the terms of the agreement.[60] Therefore, acceptance may be expressed in words, writing or conduct as with a normal commercial contract, so long as the acceptance is unequivocal. General common law rules on contract formation stipulate that

---

[53]   Subject to clauses delaying the formation of a binding contract as discussed below, at para.4-038.

[54]   See *South-East Lancashire Insurance Co Ltd* (1931) 40 Ll. L. Rep. 22 at 23.

[55]   The exception in English law being a contract of marine insurance, which must be embodied in a policy and cannot be enforced otherwise, for which see s.22 of the Marine Insurance Act ("MIA") 1906. However, the Law Commissions propose to abolish s.22 as part of its reform of the MIA. See Law Commission and the Scottish Law Commission *Insurance Contract Law: Post Contract Duties and Other Issues, A Joint Consultation Paper*, Ch.4 Pt 15, 16 and para.17.5; Law Commission and the Scottish Law Commission, *Insurance Contract Law Summary of Responses to Issues Paper 9 The Requirement for a Formal Marine Policy: Should Section 22 be Repealed?* (Law Commission, Scottish Law Commission, 2011); Law Commission and the Scottish Law Commission *Insurance Contract Law: Business Disclosure; Warranties; Insurer's Remedies for Fraudulent Claims and Late Payment*, paras 15.16 to 15.19 (HMSO, 2014) *http://www.lawcom.gov.uk/wp-content/uploads/2015/11/Report-Insurance-contract-law.pdf* [Accessed 23 June 2016].The Law Commission was expected to publish a final report covering issues (such as on s.22 of the MIA 1906) that were not addressed by the Insurance Act 2015 but were previously considered by it in 2015. However, as at the date of writing it still has not been produced.

[56]   *Roberts v Security Co Ltd* [1897] 1 Q.B. 111. Although it is worth noting that under the Financial Services and Markets Act 2000 (FSMA 2000) there is no general requirement for insurers to issue a policy document. See further *Colinvaux's Law of Insurance*, edited by R. Merkin, 10th edn (London: Sweet & Maxwell, 2014), paras 1-023 and 13-023.

[57]   *Pearl Life Assurance Co v Johnson* [1909] 2 K.B. 288; 73 J.P. 216; 78 L.J.K.B. 777.

[58]   See Lord Alverstone C.J.'s judgment in *Pearl Life Assurance Co* [1909] 2 K.B. 288 at 295; 73 J.P. 216 at 218; 78 L.J.K.B. 777 at 780.

[59]   *Wooding v Monmouthshire and South Wales Mutual Indemnity Society Ltd*; James v Monmouthshire and South Wales Indemnity Society Ltd; Hawkins v Monmouthshire and South Wales Indemnity Society Ltd [1939] 4 All E.R. 570 at 594; 162 L.T. 98; 56 T.L.R. 292. Once the terms of the insurance contract have been agreed between the insurer and the insured, at law there is a binding contract. In such circumstances, the delivery of the policy and payment of the premium are properly identified as obligations placed on the parties as per the terms of the insurance contract.

[60]   Another example is where the offeror has stipulated a particular mode of acceptance; under general common law rules, the offeree may accept using that method or any equally expeditious method unless that mode of acceptance is stipulated as being exclusive. See *Manchester Diocesan Council for Education v Commercial & General Investments Ltd* [1970] 1 W.L.R. 241; [1969] 3 All E.R. 1593; (1970) 21 P. & C.R. 38.

acceptance must be communicated to the offeror and so silence or ambivalent conduct is not usually sufficient.[61]

Silence as acceptance. The issue of silence constituting acceptance is significant in an insurance contract as the insurer may fail to act on a proposal or neglect to notify the applicant of its acceptance of the proposal. It may be that silence will amount to acceptance if the insurer undertakes an obligation to notify the prospective insured within a given period if he wishes to reject the proposal.[62] In the absence of such an obligation, the general contractual principles apply.   **4-033**

Exceptions. There are, however, exceptions to the rule that acceptance must be communicated to the offeror. In *Roberts*[63] it was held that where an insurer signs a policy in the form of a deed, a binding contract is made even if the policy is not delivered to the prospective insured who therefore has no notification of such acceptance. Furthermore, the requirement for communication may also be waived if acceptance is made in a manner expressly prescribed by the terms of the offer or in the course of business.   **4-034**

(iv) Acceptance by the insured

Acceptance by the insured. Where an offer is made by the insurer, there will equally be a binding contract as soon as the prospective insured has notified his unconditional acceptance. One issue that arises in the insurance contract is the extent to which notification is required from the insured so as to amount to acceptance at law. Reliance by the insured on the policy is generally all that is required.   **4-035**

As stated above in para.4-027, a renewal notice of insurance may be held to be an offer made by the insurer. In *Taylor v Allon*,[64] the court held that an insured who relies on a renewal notice as if he considered himself insured by it, may be deemed to have accepted the offer through his conduct. In that case the defendant had been charged with driving without valid insurance. The court found that the defendant was unaware that his original insurer had provided him with a temporary cover note for motor insurance; that he did not use his car in reliance on it, and so held that there had not been a valid acceptance of the offer by him.[65] In *Rust*,[66] the applicant's failure to object to a policy issued by the insurer within a reasonable time was construed as acceptance of the contract.   **4-036**

Refusal of the policy by the insured. Whether or not the prospective insured is entitled to refuse the policy issued by the insurer depends on the course of dealing between the parties. As stated above in para.4-031, issuing the policy may amount to an acceptance of the applicant's proposal, at which time the contract has already come into existence. Such a refusal would therefore amount to a proposed variation of the contract, which the insurer is free to accept or reject. If, however, no   **4-037**

---

[61] *Felthouse v Bindley* (1863) 1 New Rep 401; 11 W.R. 429; 7 L.T. 835.
[62] See *Colinvaux's Law of Insurance*, edited by R. Merkin, 10th edn (London: Sweet & Maxwell, 2014), para.1-047.
[63] *Roberts* [1897] 1 Q.B. 111; this may be distinguished on the basis that it was a contract under seal. See also s.68 Law of Property Act 1925 (LPA 1925).
[64] *Taylor v Allon* [1966] 1 Q.B. 304; [1965] 2 W.L.R. 598; [1965] 1 All E.R. 557.
[65] See Lord Parker's judgment at *Taylor* [1966] 1 Q.B. 304 at 311–312; [1965] 2 W.L.R. 598 at 603–604; [1965] 1 All E.R. 557 at 559–560. See also below, paras 7-026 to 7-029.
[66] *Rust* [1978] 2 Lloyd's Rep. 386 at 393–394.

contract already exists (for example if the policy does not correspond to the proposal), then the prospective insured is entitled to reject the policy; the issue of the policy on terms inconsistent with the terms of the proposal represents a counter-offer which the applicant is not obliged to accept.

(v)   Delaying commencement of the contract or risk

4-038   The insurer may impose conditions that must be satisfied by the insured before the insurance will operate, such as payment of the premium or the issue of a policy. This is because once there is a binding contract the insurer must deliver the policy and the insured must pay the premium, and the insurer may wish to guard against becoming bound to insure before they have secured payment. Clauses that stipulate such conditions may operate by delaying the actual agreement or delaying cover of the risk. Whether it is the agreement or the risk that is suspended remains a matter of construction.

4-039   Whether or not a clause suspends an agreement or suspends a contract is important to determine because it is crucial to ascertaining whether the insured is covered for a loss occurring before the condition has been fulfilled. If the condition suspends the actual agreement, then there is no binding contract under which an insurer can be liable for losses suffered and the insurer is not bound to accept a premium after the loss occurs. In *The Sickness and Accident Assurance Association, Ltd v The General Accident Assurance Corporation, Ltd*,[67] the insurance contract was to become binding only once the premium had been paid, and so the insurers had no duty to indemnify a loss that occurred after the proposed date of the commencement for the coverage had passed but before that premium had passed into their hands. Lord Adam stated that the rationale behind this principle was that the offer was to indemnify against the risk of an accident happening, and not the actual consequences of one that had happened. Thus if the clause is construed as suspending the agreement, it not only suspends cover until the receipt of a premium but also discharges the insurers from all liability in the event of a loss prior to payment.[68]

4-040   **Delaying commencement of the contract.**   An example of a condition suspending the agreement was discussed in *Canning v Farquhar*.[69] In that case the proposal was made to an insurance company upon the terms that no insurance should take effect until the premium was paid. The court held that the contract commenced at the time when the premium was offered and that

> "[t]here is no insurance before that, but only a contract to the effect, '[i]f you will offer the premium we will insure."[70]

4-041   Similarly, the courts have held that if the basis of the insurance contract and the risk covered is dependent upon the continuation of a material fact, if that material fact changes between offer and acceptance, the insurance company will not be

---

[67]   *The Sickness and Accident Assurance Association, Ltd v The General Accident Assurance Corporation, Ltd* (1892) 19 R. 977; 29 S.L.R. 836.
[68]   *The Sickness and Accident Assurance Association, Ltd* (1892) 19 R. 977 at 986; 29 S.L.R. 836 at 840, applying the authority of *Canning v Farquhar* (1886) 16 Q.B.D. 727; 55 L.J.Q.B. 225; 34 W.R. 423.
[69]   *Canning* (1886) 16 Q.B.D. 727; 55 L.J.Q.B. 225; 34 W.R. 423.
[70]   *Canning* (1886) 16 Q.B.D. 727 at 731; 55 L.J.Q.B. 225 at 226; 34 W.R. 423 at 424–425.

bound. Thus in *Looker v Law Union & Rock Insurance Co Ltd*[71] the insurance company escaped liability on the basis that the proposer was no longer free from disease at the time of acceptance, contrary to what he had represented in his proposal. The condition going to the root of the contract, namely that the proposer had a clean bill of health, had not been fulfilled.

A clause stating that the issue of the policy is a condition precedent to the forma-   **4-042**
tion of the contract has the effect of rendering the acceptance of a proposal (such as words or conduct) of no legal significance. The effect of the clause is to make it clear that the parties did not intend to make a binding contract when the insurers approved the proposed terms. The proposer may therefore recover any premium paid prior to the delivery of the policy.

It may be worthy to note that the cases in which the courts have been willing to   **4-043**
construe clauses as suspending the existence of a contract unless the condition has been fulfilled are life assurance cases. In cases involving insurance policies other than life assurances, the courts may be less lenient, especially if the type of insurance offers temporary cover. In the case of Lloyd's insurance, the slip constitutes a binding contract upon being signed, irrespective of the payment of the premium.[72]

Delaying commencement of risk.   The general rule is that the risk runs from the   **4-044**
date of issue of the policy, unless an alternative date is specified.[73] The alternative date may fall before or after the policy is issued, if for example the contract specifies that risk runs from the date of acceptance of the offer or payment of the premium.[74]

If the condition operates to suspend only the risk and not the agreement, then the   **4-045**
ability of the insured to recover depends on the nature of the condition to be fulfilled. If the risk is attached to a date or event, and the loss occurs before the date or event in question, then the insured cannot recover. Similarly, if the insured has yet to pay the premium as a condition to risk attaching, then it is likely that an insured will be unable to recover losses suffered before payment of the premium, unless the insurer is deemed to have waived the condition.[75] If, however, the risk is stated to commence upon issue of the policy and the insurer has accepted the premium without issuing the policy, then it is likely that the insurer would be estopped from arguing that there is not a binding contract in place.[76]

Termination of cover.   The period of risk covered by the insurance contract usu-   **4-046**
ally continues until the precise time specified in the policy for its expiration, unless the policy is determined at an earlier date by the insurer[77] or the insured[78] or cancelled by both parties in favour of executing a new contract. The insurance

---

[71]   *Looker v Law Union & Rock Insurance Co Ltd* [1928] 1 K.B. 554.
[72]   *General Reinsurance Corp v Forsakringsaktiebolaget Fennia Patria* [1983] Q.B. 856; [1983] 3 W.L.R. 318; [1983] 2 Lloyd's Rep. 287. See below, paras 4-064 to 4-067.
[73]   *McMaster v New York Life Insurance Co* (1901) 183 U.S. 25; 22 S.C.T 10.
[74]   There is no principle of law that obliges an insurer to assume risk at any particular date.
[75]   For example, by issuing the policy despite not receiving the premium. See *Colinvaux's Law of Insurance*, edited by R. Merkin (2014), para.1-053. The point has not been tested in court; compare *Roberts* [1897] 1 Q.B. 111; 66 L.J.Q.B. 119; 45 W.R. 214, where a waiver was contained in the recital of a policy affixed with a seal.
[76]   See *Pearl Life Assurance Co; Pearl Life Assurance Co v Greenhalgh* [1909] 2 K.B. 288; 73 J.P. 216; 78 L.J.K.B. 777. See also *Colinvaux's Law of Insurance*, edited by R. Merkin (2014), para.1-053.
[77]   For example, if there has been a breach of duty of utmost good faith by the insured.
[78]   For example, the insured under a life insurance contract may have the right to cancel the contract under statute.

contract may contain a clause enabling either party to terminate the contract in specific circumstances. If the insurance contract places a cap on liability for losses after a particular sum is reached, the insurer's liability will be discharged upon reaching that sum, which has the effect of bringing the policy to an end.

(vi)   Contract renewal

4-047   The renewal of an insurance policy amounts to the formation of a new insurance contract, and is therefore governed by the normal legal rules on formation.[79] The renewal contract is usually to insure the same risk and on the same terms as the insured is entitled to assume,[80] but subject to slight changes in the premium to be paid by the insured. Insurers are not obliged to renew existing insurance contracts upon expiry,[81] nor is it permissible for an insured to challenge the insurer's motives for refusing to renew an existing contract.

4-048   **The renewal notice.**   The insurer will usually send a renewal notice to the insured. If the insurer intends the renewal to be on new terms, he must give clear notice of the terms. The renewal notice amounts to an offer of cover to either be accepted or rejected by the insured. The notice usually states a period in which the offer must be accepted by the insured, after which the offer of cover lapses.[82] Sending a letter with the renewal notice that explains the changes in the contract, thereby giving the insured notice of the new terms, has been deemed sufficient notice for the purpose of incorporation of the new terms.

(b)   The use of a specialist broker in placing the insurance contract

4-049   Contractors involved in large-scale construction projects most often use the services of a specialist construction broker to evaluate and process the insurance contract. This is because many of these projects depend upon a sound understanding of business procedures and technical matters to enable the risk for which cover is sought to be properly assessed. In these cases, the associated risks are often spread across several participating insurance companies and/or Lloyd's syndicates[83] and the broker is in a position to offer a proportion of the risk to several underwriters unless the risk has very unusual characteristics, in which case a larger number of underwriters will be approached.

(i)   The role of the broker

4-050   The role of the broker in the formation of the insurance contract can be separated into two stages. The first stage is where the contractor approaches the broker with

---

[79]   It is important to distinguish a "renewal" from a "variation" of the insurance contract in that it relates to the duty of disclosure owed by the insured upon renewal of a policy, upon which the insured is treated as if he is contracting the insurance for the first time.

[80]   See *Great North Eastern Railway Ltd v Avon Insurance Plc* [2001] EWCA Civ 780; [2001] 2 All E.R. (Comm) 526; [2001] 2 Lloyd's Rep. 649, in which the Court of Appeal held that a fax entitled "renewal of policy" could only refer to the previous year's terms.

[81]   With the exception of life insurance.

[82]   However, the insurer may be deemed to have waived the right to acceptance on issuing a renewal notice so that an insured who responds to the renewal notice as if he considered himself insured may be deemed to have accepted the offer through his conduct. See *Taylor* [1966] 1 Q.B. 304; [1965] 2 W.L.R. 598; 1 All E.R. 557 and above, para.4-036.

[83]   Although Lloyd's does not normally specialise in construction insurance and so there are only a few syndicates that underwrite this type of risk.

information regarding the risk which needs to be covered. The second stage is where the broker puts forward a policy or presentation containing all the placing information for the contractor. The broker therefore plays a dual role in placing the insurance for the underwriter's consideration. First, he obtains the relevant information from the contractor in order to provide advice in selecting the appropriate form of insurance and relevant insurers for the risk. He then procures the contract by preparing the policy, slip or presentation in such a manner that the insurers have an accurate indication of the insured's project and the nature of the risk involved.

The broker will discuss the development project with the contractor and may also **4-051** involve his own estimator and engineer to further elucidate and verify matters concerning the assessment of risk and the contractor's insurance requirements. On the basis of the information provided by the contractor, the broker will compile a summary of the proposed insurance contract in the form of a proposal or slip. This will be provided to the insurer along with "placing information" presented in support of the broker's arguments.

Placing information. The placing information usually consists of proposal forms, **4-052** details of the insured, intermediary details, the duration of the cover required, the insured's claims history (usually backdated five years), general details including the location of the project and information regarding criminal record or insurance history of directors, partners or family members of the contractor, and the type of cover required including asset protection, revenue protection, legal liabilities or employee benefits. In the case of contract works, it will also consist of information regarding estimated turnovers for annual policies or contract details for project policies and surveys of the insured's risk management techniques. It may also include any background information and any other information likely to be material to the insurer's assessment of the risk, such as the contracts and specification.

Presentation. Rather than provide a proposal or a slip, a broker may work closely **4-053** with the contractor's risk manager in order to put forward a presentation of risk to the insurers. A presentation is often used when the project is particularly complex, involving a more thorough assessment of risk by the insurer; in such circumstances, a highly detailed presentation providing comprehensive information of the risk to be insured is required. It follows that in these cases there is no need for a proposal from the insurer. The quality of the presentation of risk information is crucial to the insured obtaining the most competitive terms from insurers.[84]

(ii) Legal status and duties of the broker

Duties of the broker. As with any intermediary holding himself out as an agent **4-054** of the principal, a broker must exercise due care and skill in the execution of his

---

[84] According to research commissioned by Bowring Marsh of Marsh 2010 undertaken on its behalf by an independent research firm called "FWD", who surveyed underwriting decision-makers in Bermuda, Dublin, London, Miami, Sao Paulo, Singapore and Zurich and asked them to identify their most important considerations when deciding whether to quote for a risk: almost half of those surveyed said that the quality of a broker's presentation of risk was most important; 30 per cent said that the most important factor was the client's approach to risk, whilst 21 per cent cited the underwriter's relationship with the broker as being the key determining factor. See Bowring Marsh, *"Marsh Stresses Importance of 'High Quality Risk Information' Presentations"* (2010). (Insurance Journal, 18 May 2010) *http://www.insurancejournal.com/news/international/2010/05/18/109936.htm* [Accessed 21 March 2013].

responsibilities, must never place himself in a position of conflict of interest with the principal and must act in accordance with the principal's instructions. There is no implication that the broker has to guarantee that all needs of the insured, whether disclosed or not, are met by the policy; it is merely a duty to act according to the standards that could be expected from a prudent broker in the market at that time.

4-055 **Agency relationship.** The legal relationship between the broker and the contractor or other proposed insured is a relationship of agency between principal and agent. The status of the broker in construction insurance will therefore, prima facie, be as agent of the insured. Lloyd's brokers almost invariably will be agents for the insured.[85] The result of this relationship is that any mistakes or errors made by the broker during the ordinary course of business will bind the contractor as against third parties. The contractor's recourse will be to sue the broker. Also, knowledge gained by the broker whilst acting within the ordinary course of business will be imputed to the contractor. The broker will also have its own duty of disclosure to the insurer or underwriter.

4-056 **Dual agency.** It has been suggested that at times a broker can also act as agent of the insurer so long as there is no conflict of interest[86] or the broker has the informed consent of the insured.[87] In *HIH Casualty & General Insurance Ltd v JLT Risk Solutions Ltd*,[88] Auld LJ discussed the concept of dual agency and said that

> "[i]n its simplest form, the negotiation of insurance, the broker acts as agent for the insured, but normally receives his remuneration from the insurer in the form of commission; he may, in certain circumstances, act for both. Where there is reinsurance of an insured risk, the same broker may act on behalf of the insured in placing the insurance and on behalf of the insurer in placing the reinsurance."[89]

Therefore, the practicalities of the insurance market make it very difficult to associate the role of a broker exclusively with the insured because

> "a broker carrying out instructions on behalf of an intending assured may have to undertake obligations to others in order to perform his mandate."[90]

4-057 It follows that in some cases a broker may be called a "common agent" acting for both parties.[91] Whether the broker is acting as an agent for the insured or for the insurer in a given situation will depend on which party's instructions the broker is acting on. This may have implications for the formation of the insurance contract for at least two reasons. First, the broker has power to bind its principal to the consequences of its own actions when forming the contract, but where the broker

---

85 *Rozanes* (1928) 32 Ll. L. Rep. 98.

86 *Pryke v Gibbs Hartley Cooper Ltd* [1991] 1 Lloyd's Rep. 602.

87 *Excess Life Insurance Co Ltd v Fireman's Insurance Co of Newark New Jersey* [1982] 2 Lloyd's Rep. 599.

88 *HIH Casualty & General Insurance Ltd v JLT Risk Solutions Ltd (formerly Lloyd Thompson Ltd)* [2007] EWCA Civ 710; [2007] 2 All E.R. (Comm) 1106; [2008] Bus. L. R. 180.

89 *HIH Casualty & General Insurance Ltd* [2007] EWCA Civ 710 at [60]; 2 All E.R. (Comm) 1106 at 1122; [2008] Bus. L. R. 180 at 198.

90 Saville LJ in *Societe Anonyme d'Intermediaries Luxembourgeois (SAIL) v Farex Gie* [1995] L.R.L.R. 116 at 156; [1994] C.L.C. 1094 at 1119. This view was approved by Rix LJ in *Goshawk Dedicated Ltd v Tyser & Co Ltd* [2006] EWCA Civ 54 at [65]; [2006] 1 All E.R. (Comm) 501 at 518; [2006] 1 Lloyd's Rep. 566 at 577.

91 *Heath Lambert Ltd v Sociedad de Corretaje de Seguros* [2004] EWCA Civ 792 at [22]; [2004] 1 W.L.R. 2820 at 2828; [2004] 2 All E.R. (Comm) 656 at 663.

is acting beyond the scope of its actual or apparent authority the power to bind may be lost, which might adversely impact either or both of the parties for whom it is purporting to act . Secondly, the agent is under duties to disclose information about its principal as well as information it gains during the course of acting for its principal. The status of the agent will determine to whom its knowledge is imputed and when its own knowledge is acquired in the ordinary course of business. Again, where the agent is acting beyond the scope of its authority, adverse consequences can arise for either or both the parties it is working for.[92] This second scenario is likely to be relevant to misrepresentation and non-disclosure prior to the formation of the contract of insurance and to breaches of warranty once the contract is formed.[93]

Disclosure. The broker must warn the insured of their duty to disclose all material facts so as to ensure that all relevant facts are included in the presentation to the insurer and accompanying placement information.[94] After the coming into force of the 2015 Act, the broker is now also under a duty to ensure, in a broad sense, that the insured is aware of the requirements imposed by the 2015 Act, including the duty upon the insured to provide a fair presentation of risk.[95] Even before the 2015 Act, in *Jones v Environcom Ltd; MS PLC t/a Miles Smith Insurance Brokers, third party;* sub nom. *Woodbrook v Environcom Ltd*,[96] the High Court ruled that an insurance broker must satisfy himself that the duty of disclosure is fully understood by the client. It was insufficient for an insurance broker to rely on written standard form explanations that had been provided to the insured. The High Court's decision was upheld by the Court of Appeal.[97] **4-058**

The decision of David Steel J in *Jones*[98] caused some consternation since it suggested that, even where the insured is not a consumer, brokers should follow up any conversations about the duty of disclosure with a note of their advice and the insured's response to it, ideally asking the insured to confirm in writing that they have understood the advice given. In *Synergy Health (UK) Ltd v CGU Insurance Plc (t/a Norwich Union)*,[99] Flaux J said that *Jones*[100] did not make it an immutable requirement that brokers should have given oral advice about disclosure and he said that evidence to this effect from Synergy's broker expert was too inflexible. He went on to say: **4-059**

> "Whilst it may be advisable to give such oral advice in a particular case, whether it is necessary to do so and whether the failure to do so is a breach of duty, will depend upon the circumstances. In

---

[92] See further, *Bowstead and Reynolds on Agency*, edited by P. Watts and F.M.B Reynolds, 20th edn (London: Sweet & Maxwell, 2014), paras 8-207 to 8-215.

[93] See below, Chs 5, 6 and 11.

[94] *Gunns v Par Insurance Brokers* [1997] 1 Lloyd's Rep. 173.

[95] For a detailed analysis of the requirements of a "fair presentation of risk" see below, Ch.5.

[96] *Jones v Environcom Ltd; MS Plc t/a Miles Smith Insurance Brokers, third party*; sub nom. *Woodbrook v Environcom Ltd* [2010] EWHC 759 (Comm); [2010] Lloyd's Rep. I.R. 676; [2010] All E.R. (D) 76 (Apr)

[97] *Jones; sub nom. Woodbrook* [2011] EWCA Civ 1152; [2012] Lloyd's Rep. I.R. 277; [2011] All E.R. (D) 116 (Oct).

[98] *Jones* [2010] EWHC 759 (Comm); [2010] Lloyd's Rep. I.R. 676; [2010] All E.R. (D) 76 (Apr).

[99] *Synergy Health (UK) Ltd v CGU Insurance Plc (t/a Norwich Union)* [2010] EWHC 2583 (Comm); [2011] Lloyd's Rep. I.R. 500.

[100] *Jones* [2010] EWHC 759 (Comm); [2010] Lloyd's Rep. I.R. 676; [2010] All E.R. (D) 76 (Apr).

the present case, there had been a long history of dealings with this client and the Risk Register sent to the client spelt out the duty of disclosure in clear terms."[101]

It had been hoped that these two potentially conflicting first instance decisions would be reviewed by the Court of Appeal in *Jones*[102] and clearer guidance given about brokers' duties. This issue was not touched on at all by the Court of Appeal, so the position remains uncertain.

4-060   **Enquiries.** The broker is also under a duty to make proper enquires of the insured, which would involve questioning the insured to determine whether he falls within the category of persons whom the insurer will cover,[103] as well as ascertaining whether the insured's likely needs will fall within the scope of the cover.[104] The obligation to make reasonable inquiries also requires asking the type of questions that the broker would expect the underwriters to ask or raise concerns about. A broker who decides to refrain from asking certain questions that actually appear on the proposal form will be liable to the insured if it is established that asking those questions would have disclosed material facts,[105] though this is only applicable where the insured is fully reliant on the broker's assistance and is not involved in perusing the completed form themselves.[106]

4-061   The obligation to make reasonable enquiries does not require the broker to undertake a fishing expedition in order to unmask the truth; where the insured deliberately withholds facts from the broker, the insured will not be able to hold the broker liable if the policy is subsequently avoided by the insurers. In most cases, the broker is also entitled to expect the insured to demonstrate some common sense in respect of what material ought to be disclosed.[107] The broker must, however, endeavour to ask the right questions in the right way by taking into account the level of sophistication that can be expected from the insured in question. In *Sharp v Sphere Drake Insurance (The Moonacre)*; sub nom. *Sharp and Roarer Investments Ltd v Sphere Drake Insurance Plc, Minster Insurance Co Ltd and E C Parker*

---

[101]   *Synergy Health (UK) Ltd* [2010] EWHC 2583 (Comm) at [213]; [2011] Lloyd's Rep. I.R. 500 at 532.

[102]   *Jones* [2011] EWCA Civ 1152; [2012] Lloyd's Rep. I.R. 277; [2011] All E.R. (D) 116 (Oct).

[103]   In *McNealy v Pennine Insurance Co Ltd* [1978] 2 Lloyd's Rep. 18; [1978] R.T.R. 285; (1978) 122 S.J. 229, the broker failed to make reasonable enquiries that would have revealed that apart from being a property repairer, the claimant was also a part-time musician, which meant that he fell within the excluded category of persons under the policy. It was held that given the broker's knowledge of the existence of a list of excluded professions and the low premiums indicative of the restricted availability of cover, the broker was under a duty to probe further and inform the insured of the list to discern whether he fell within any of those categories.

[104]   *Sharp v Sphere Drake Insurance (The Moonacre)*; sub nom. *Sharp and Roarer Investments Ltd v Sphere Drake Insurance Plc, Minster Insurance Co Ltd and E C Parker & Co Ltd (The Moonacre)* [1992] 2 Lloyd's Rep. 501.

[105]   *Warren v Henry Sutton & Co* [1976] 2 Lloyd's Rep. 276.

[106]   In *O'Connor v BDB Kirby & Co* [1972] 1 Q.B. 90; [1971] 2 W.L.R. 1233; [1971] 2 All E.R. 1415, the broker gave the completed proposal form back to the insured for checking who only took a cursory glance at the papers and signed it without spotting the error that was made by the broker in answering a question. No recovery was allowed against the broker when the claim by the insured failed owing to the error made by the broker. See also *Kapur v JW Francis & Co (No.2)* [2000] Lloyd's Rep. I.R. 361; [1999] Lloyd's Rep. P.N. 834, where it was held that although the form was completed with the broker's assistance who was negligent, since the insured had noticed the omission in the form and decided not to amend it, the insured was the sole and effective cause of the loss.

[107]   See *Fanhaven Pty Ltd v Bain Dawes Northern Pty Ltd* [1982] 2 N.S.W.L.R. 57; (1982) 2 ANZ Ins Co 60–480 where it was held that there was no liability for the broker where the insured failed to disclose the criminal record of directors because the insured was a reputable company and the brokers could not therefore be expected to suspect the existence of such records.

& Co Ltd (The Moonacre),[108] the broker made an attempt to simplify the questions on the proposal form for the benefit of the insured, a successful—now retired—businessman, by enquiring whether the insured was intending to live on the boat during winter time. The actual question on the form asked whether the yacht was to be used as a houseboat. The insured replied to the broker's question in the negative and did not inform the broker that a single crewman lived on board in order to work on the vessel and provide security when she was laid up. It was held that the broker ought to have put the question to the insured as it was on the proposal form rather than attempting to paraphrase it in a manner that failed to convey the essence of the insurers query.

Disclosure to the insurer. A broker is under a duty to disclose material facts that are within their possession. This is particularly important because often the insured relies on brokers for keeping and maintaining records,[109] given that brokers are expected to adopt a focused and organised strategy to handling the insured's affairs. This was summarised by Mr David Mackie Q.C. succinctly in *Alexander Forbes Europe Ltd (formerly Nelson Hurst UK Ltd) v SJB Ltd*.[110] He said: **4-062**

"Brokers owe duties going beyond those of a post box. It was for the brokers to get a grip on the proposed notification, to appraise it and to ensure that the information was relayed to the right place in the correct form. As the expert put it they need a strategy for handling claims."[111]

A situation may arise where the broker has obtained information from the insured but decided not to pass it on to the insurer on the basis that it is not material to the consideration of the risk involved. In such a case, the broker's decision to withhold information is judged on the basis of whether a broker acting with reasonable skill and care would have taken that view regarding the information in question.[112] Where a broker is in doubt as to whether a fact is material or not, it is advisable to disclose it. **4-063**

(iii)   The use of a slip in placing the insurance contract

The practice of using a slip in placing an insurance contract has evolved primarily within the Lloyd's insurance market, and the rules of formation are very different to general legal principles governing commercial contracts. In general only a Lloyd's broker is allowed to approach Lloyd's underwriters, as specified in the Lloyd's Act 1982.[113] A prospective insured—the proposer—must therefore appoint an intermediary who is responsible for preparing the slip, which is a sheet of paper recording the essentials of the risk proposed. The broker takes the slip and **4-064**

---

[108] *Sharp* [1992] 2 Lloyd's Rep. 501.

[109] *Alfred James Dunbar v A&B Painters Ltd and Economic Insurance Co Ltd and Whitehouse & Co* [1985] 2 Lloyd's Rep. 616.

[110] *Alexander Forbes Europe Ltd (formerly Nelson Hurst UK Ltd) v SJB Ltd* [2002] EWHC 3121 (Comm); [2003] Lloyd's Rep. I.R. 432; [2003] Lloyd's Rep. P.N. 137.

[111] *Alexander Forbes Europe Ltd* [2002] EWHC 3121 (Comm) at [36]; [2003] Lloyd's Rep. I.R. 432 at 441; [2003] Lloyd's Rep. P.N. 137 at 444.

[112] *Aiken v Stewart Wrightson Members Agency Ltd* [1995] 1 W.L.R. 1281; [1995] 3 All E.R. 449; [1995] 2 Lloyd's Rep. 618.

[113] The Lloyd's Act 1982 was amended on 18 November 2008 by the Legislative Reform (Lloyd's) Order 2008 (SI 2008/3001) and since 12 January 2009 syndicates' managing agents can accept business from individuals other than Lloyd's brokers under Lloyd's byelaws, which will specify the conditions under which such agents can act.

placing information to appropriate syndicates in the Lloyd's market, seeking subscriptions to the risk as offered in the slip. The broker will approach a representative underwriter from each carefully chosen syndicate and each representative has the authority to bind the members of his syndicate to the specified risks.

4-065 **Contract formation.** If the representative underwriter accepts the proposer's offer, he will stamp the slip with the name of his syndicate, initial it and state the amount of liability that is to be underwritten. This is known as "scratching" the slip. The slip will then be presented to other representative underwriters from other syndicates by the broker until 100 per cent subscription is obtained. It is often beneficial for a broker to obtain more than 100 per cent subscription as this makes it easier for the broker to obtain further cover if needed.[114]

4-066 In the context of Lloyd's insurance, the act of the broker presenting the slip on behalf of the prospective insured constitutes an offer, which the underwriter accepts when he initials the slip.[115] This construction accords with the intention of the Lloyd's market. Each initialling of the slip represents a separate contract between the insured and each individual underwriter.[116]

4-067 The slip may then be presented to an authorised insurer, who issues a single policy containing the terms and conditions on the slip, on behalf of all the contributing underwriters.[117] Whilst the contract of insurance is contained in the slip, once a policy is issued this becomes the document containing the terms of the contract.[118] There is a line of authorities that have established a rule that the policy cannot be construed by reference to the slip,[119] though this position has since been qualified by the Court of Appeal[120] and it appears that use of the slip as an aid to construc-

---

[114] For example, if construction costs increase or the cover is needed for a longer period.

[115] *General Reinsurance Corp* [1983] Q.B. 856 at 866–867; [1983] 3 W.L.R. 318 at 324; [1983] 2 Lloyd's Rep. 287 at 290–291.

[116] *Touche Ross & Co v Baker (Colin)* [1992] 2 Lloyd's Rep. 207; (1992) 89(28) L.S.G. 31; (1992) 136 S.J.L.B. 190. It is a fundamental principle that individual underwriters have several and not joint liability to an insurance slip. See *Touche* [1992] 2 Lloyd's Rep. 207 at 209–210. See also, s.8 of The Lloyd's Act 1982.

[117] Since 1 May 2001 the issue of a policy on the terms of a slip has been carried out by "Xchanging Ins-sure Services" ("XIS"). The services formerly offered by the Lloyd's Policy Signing Office ("LPSO") were transferred to XIS. In addition to this, XIS also acts for Lloyd's syndicates, members of the International Underwriting Association ("IUA") and for any other company authorising it.

[118] It has been argued that there is a rebuttable presumption that the policy will supersede the slip. See *HIH Casualty & General Insurance Ltd v New Hampshire Insurance Co* [2001] EWCA Civ 735 at [93]; [2001] 2 All E.R. (Comm) 39 at 65; [2001] 2 Lloyd's Rep. 161 at 181.

[119] *Youell v Bland Welch & Co Ltd (No.1)* [1990] 2 Lloyd's Rep. 423 at 428–429; *Ionides v Pacific Fire & Marine Insurance Co* (1870–71) L.R. 6 Q.B. 674 at 685; 41 L.J.Q.B. 33 at 40; 1 Asp. M.L.C. 141 at 146–147; affirmed (1871–72) L.R. 7 Q.B. 517 at 526; 41 L.J.Q.B. 190 at 200; 1 Asp. M.L.C. 330 at 335; *Punjab National Bank v De Boinville* [1992] 1 Lloyd's Rep. 7 at 12; Financial Times, February 1, 1991; *St Paul Fire & Marine Insurance Co (UK) Ltd v McConnell Dowell Constructors Ltd* [1993] 2 Lloyd's Rep. 503 at 516–517; 67 B.L.R. 72 at 100–101; 37 Con. L.R. 96 at 119–120; *New Hampshire Insurance Co Ltd v MGN Ltd; Maxwell Communication Corp Plc (In Administration) v New Hampshire Insurance Co Ltd* [1997] L.R.L.R. 24 at 53, 54; [1996] C.L.C. 1728 at 1732; *Wimpey Construction (UK) Ltd v Poole (DV)* [1984] 2 Lloyd's Rep. 499 at 513; 27 B.L.R. 58 at 90–91, per Webster J. These cases cite the operation of the parol evidence rule as a rule of law precluding the use of the slip as an aid to construction, except for the purposes of rectification, identifying mistake or fraud.

[120] *HIH Casualty and General Insurance Ltd* [2001] EWCA Civ 735 at [83]; [2001] 2 All E.R. (Comm) 39 at 59–66; [2001] 2 Lloyd's Rep. 161 at 178; and see generally [2001] EWCA Civ 735 at [69]–[97]; [2001] 2 All E.R. (Comm) 39 at 59–66; [2001] 2 Lloyd's Rep. 161 at 176–181. Whether or

tion may be permitted by the courts.[121] The issue of a policy is not a condition of the formation or validity of the insurance and in many cases a policy is not issued at all.

Partial subscription. Given that the market practice at Lloyd's involves obtain-   **4-068**
ing subscriptions to risk, specified as a percentage or portion of the overall cover sought by the proposer, a situation may arise whereby the broker fails to obtain contracts for insurance that cover 100 per cent of the risk. In *General Reinsurance Corp*,[122] it was argued that there was a custom of the Lloyd's market that meant that the insured had an option to rescind the contracts already agreed before the risk had been fully subscribed. Whilst trade custom is capable of overriding non-mandatory rules of law, this argument was rejected on appeal[123] on the basis that the court was unable to accept that such a custom did in fact exist in the Lloyd's market. At Lloyd's, in the absence of an established custom, if the broker only gets a partial subscription to the risk, he can persuade prior subscribers to accept cancellation though cannot compel them to do so.[124]

4. TEMPORARY COVER

Temporary cover. An insurer will usually take some time in considering the   **4-069**
proposal form advanced by the proposer before accepting or rejecting the offer for insurance cover. Insurers may provide temporary cover during this interim period in exchange for payment of a premium, the purpose of which is to provide immediate cover until the time at which the proposal is accepted or declined.[125]

The cover note. The interim cover is often recorded in a cover note, although   **4-070**
interim insurance can be made in any form. The cover note is usually issued by the

---

not the slip can be admissible as an aid to construction may depend on whether the parties had intended the policy to supersede the slip; for where it is not agreed that the policy will supersede the slip, the slip may be admitted in order to establish what the true construction of the contract should be. See in particular *HIH Casualty and General Insurance Ltd* [2001] EWCA Civ 735 at [81]–[84]; [2001] 2 All E.R. (Comm) 39 at 62–63; [2001] 2 Lloyd's Rep. 161 at 178–179. The point made by Rix LJ was that circumstances arise where previous contracts may be used as an aid to construction and by analogy so could a slip. He goes on to point out that in a situation where the loss occurs prior to the issue of the policy, the slip will be the only contract in existence at the time of the loss: *HIH Casualty and General Insurance Ltd* [2001] EWCA Civ 735 at [91]; [2001] 2 All E.R. (Comm) 39 at 65; [2001] 2 Lloyd's Rep. 161 at 180.

[121] See the judgment of Tomlinson J in *Standard Life Assurance Ltd v Oak Dedicated Ltd* [2008] EWHC 222 (Comm) at [91]; [2008] 2 All E.R. (Comm) 916 at 949–950; [2008] Lloyd's Rep. I.R. 552 at 576, in particular where he says "It is counter intuitive to regard words which appear in the excess provision on the face of the slip as not being part of the substantive words descriptive of underwriters' obligations... [T]o ignore the slip in this case is to deprive oneself of a valuable aid to the proper approach to construction of the policy. That will not always be so, but it is here." He goes on to say that "[t]he slip plays a pivotal role in the making of a contract of insurance such as this, and it would in this case be a triumph of form over substance if the court were to be denied such assistance as it may give in elucidating the terms of the bargain struck"; *Standard Life Assurance Ltd* [2008] EWHC 222 (Comm) at [92]; [2008] 2 All E.R. (Comm) 916 at 950; [2008] Lloyd's Rep. I.R. 552 at 576

[122] *General Reinsurance Corp* [1982] Q.B. 1022; [1982] 2 WLR 518; [1982] 1 Lloyd's Rep. 87.

[123] *General Reinsurance Corp* [1983] Q.B. 856; [1983] 3 W.L.R. 318; [1983] 2 Lloyd's Rep. 287.

[124] *General Reinsurance Corp* [1983] Q.B. 856 at 872–874; [1983] 3 W.L.R. 318 at 329–331; [1983] 2 Lloyd's Rep. 287 at 294–295, per Kerr LJ.

[125] This practice is particularly common to Lloyd's underwriters where insurers require time to assess the risk and to decide whether to offer cover over a longer period. See below, Ch.7.

insurer or its agents[126] and sets out the agreement, which is a contract of temporary insurance. Whether or not a document evidences the terms of the interim contract or whether it is a mere receipt for a premium paid is a matter of construction.[127]

4-071 Any loss claimed during this period is covered by the terms of the interim cover and the formation of the interim contract is subject to the same rules as the permanent insurance contract. It therefore requires agreement to be reached on all material terms[128] and the same duties apply to the prospective insured.[129] General principles apply so that the interim insurance contract may be subject to policy terms not set out in the note itself, subject to the rules of actual or constructive notice. The rules governing commencement of the interim insurance are similar to those governing the commencement of the main policy and may be affected by the same conditions delaying commencement discussed above at para.4-038.

4-072 **Termination of temporary cover.** If the interim insurance cover is provided for a specified period, the cover provided by the interim insurance will terminate in accordance with the terms of the insurance contract. If there is no period of cover specified, the interim insurance cover will end if the insurer accepts or rejects the main policy proposal.[130] However, if the insurer accepts the main proposal and the policy terms in the main proposal differ from those governing the interim period of insurance, the issuing of the policy does not terminate the interim insurance contract. The interim insurance contract remains in force until termination upon some other ground, for example if the terms of the insurer's counter offer are not acceptable to the prospective insured; this may be taken as an explicit termination of the interim cover.

---

[126] The agent must have authority from the insurer to grant such insurance; this can be actual authority, express, implied, or apparent authority.

[127] See below, Ch.7. See also *MacGillivray on Insurance Law*, edited by Birds, Lynch and Milnes (2015), paras 4-003 to 4-005.

[128] That is, the parties, subject matter, risk, duration of cover, premium to be paid and amount of cover. See above, para.4-018.

[129] For discussion see below, Ch.8.

[130] If the main proposal is accepted, interim insurance cover ends when the insurer issues the main policy.

CHAPTER 5

THE INSURANCE ACT 2015

1. INTRODUCTION

Statutory reform. The enactment of the Insurance Act 2015 ("the 2015 Act")   **5-001**
introduces the most substantial reforms to the United Kingdom's law of insurance
since the Marine Insurance Act 1906 ("MIA") was passed over a century ago. The
2015 Act arrives after a long and detailed consultation process that started with the

Law Reform Committee Report in 1957,[1] that was pronounced "too long delayed" by the Law Commission Review in 1980[2] and that finally emerged into statute decades later following the extensive 2006 Law Commission project that spanned over seven years of research and culminated in the July 2014 Report.[3] The 2015 Act was preceded by similar reforms to insurance law made in New Zealand with the Insurance Law Reform Act 1977 and Australia with the Insurance Contracts Act 1984, and the 2015 Act is informed by both Acts' successes and missteps.[4] The new reforms are targeted to directly impact market practice and will require an immediate recognition of new obligations. The remit of the 2015 Act encompasses all sizes of business and all fields of insurance, and provides the new default regime for pre-contractual disclosure, breach of warranties (and other terms) and an insurer's remedy for fraudulent claims made under the policy.

5-002 **Non-consumer insurance.** The changes introduced by the 2015 Act are intended, in respect of matters within that Act's remit, as a default regime for all non-consumer insurance contracts that will strike a fair balance between the rights of the insurer and the insured in the majority of foreseeable circumstances. Changes in relation to consumer insurance contracts were affected by the Consumer Insurance (Disclosure and Representations) Act 2012 ("CIDRA") following the aforementioned consultation process, and the 2015 Act is therefore targeted to regulate business insurance contracts rather than adopting the widespread approach taken by the Australian and New Zealand reforms. Nevertheless, the ambit of the 2015 Act will encompass policies placed by an array of insureds with varying levels of size and sophistication, from the smallest of microbusinesses to the largest of multinational corporate bodies. The provisions of the 2015 Act are designed to offer a standard level of policyholder protection for those businesses that are unlikely to have any degree of bargaining power during the placement process, with the intention that larger, more sophisticated policyholders will be able to contract out of the default provisions and substitute more suitable bespoke arrangements.

5-003 **Enactment.** In recognition that the new legislation will require a substantial departure from current insurance market contracting practice, the 2015 Act allowed a period of 18 months for insurers to adapt insurance placement processes and the content of their policies in order to comply with the new provisions. The 2015 Act came into force on 12 August 2016,[5] and governs all policies entered into after that date. For policies entered into before 12 August but subsequently varied after the 2015 Act came into force, the provisions relating to breach of warranties

[1] Fifth Report of the Law Reform Committee (1957) Cmnd 62.
[2] Law Commission "*Insurance law: Non-disclosure and Breach of Warranty*", (Law Commission, 1980) at para.1.21.
[3] Law Commission "*Insurance Contract Law: Business Disclosure; Warranties; Insurers' Remedies for Fraudulent Claims; and Late Payment*", (Law Commission, 2014). *http://www.lawcom.gov.uk/wp-content/uploads/2015/03/lc353_insurance-contract-law.pdf* [Accessed 24 June 2016]. This report was the result of a joint project between the Law Commission of England and Wales and the Scottish Law Commission.
[4] See below, paras 5-103 to 5-109.
[5] Section 23(2) of the 2015 Act. Section 23(2) provides: "[t]his Act (apart from Part 6 and this section) comes into force at the end of the period of 18 months beginning with the day on which it is passed".

and similar terms will not apply to the underlying insurance policy but the new duty of fair presentation must be complied with in relation to the variation.[6]

Statutory interpretation. The provisions of the 2015 Act were first formulated in the draft Bill upended to the 2014 Law Commission Report, with the body of the report elucidating the purpose and intent behind each provision. The report is therefore a critical tool for the courts to interpret the provisions of the 2015 Act, and is admissible in evidence in any dispute arising under the new provisions.[7]   **5-004**

2. DUTY OF FAIR PRESENTATION

Introductory. Part 2 of the 2015 Act introduces a single duty of fair presentation to replace the current duties regarding disclosure and misrepresentation contained in ss.17–20 of the MIA. The law of disclosure for consumer insurance is now contained in CIDRA, leaving the 2015 Act to codify the new default regime for pre-contractual disclosure that will apply to all non-consumer insurance contracts.   **5-005**

Background. The new duty of fair presentation promotes disclosure as a cooperative exercise between insured and insurer. The insured will know the specific facts of how the business is run, and the insurer will know which of those facts will be relevant to the assessment of risk. Changes to the way businesses are directed and the information available to both insured and insurer have had a dramatic impact on how the underwriting decision is made since the enactment of the MIA over 100 years ago, and the information revolution has transformed the volume and scope of material available to both parties. A large corporate insured may now hold thousands of files and records which could be material to the risk in question, whilst the prospective insurer may have access to sophisticated risk models which require highly detailed information to make a realistic analysis of the risk. It no longer follows commercial sense to allow the insurer to watch a presentation without asking questions and making enquiries about those matters which are significant to the risk, and their guidance will often be crucial to the insured when placing a policy to cover an unusual risk or one which requires unusually extensive disclosure. Similarly, the insured must be able to ascertain what needs to be disclosed out of the thousands of documents and records they may hold in order to comply with their duty and to do so in good faith. Insurers' best practice and a string of recent court decisions[8] have already done some of the groundwork to move insurance law towards the requirements of the modern insurance market, and the 2015 Act invigorates this process by redrawing the lines around what must be disclosed in a way which promotes the intended collaborative approach between the parties. Although the Law Commission described the new duty of fair presentation as a rebalancing exercise[9] for insurance law, it is important to understand that the 2015 Act reflects   **5-006**

---

[6] Section 22 of the 2015 Act.

[7] See *Bennion on Statutory Interpretation*, edited by Oliver Jones, 6th edn (London: LexisNexis, 2013), Section 214.

[8] See below, para.6-030.

[9] Law Commission "*Insurance Contract Law: Business Disclosure; Warranties; Insurers' Remedies for Fraudulent Claims; and Late Payment*", (Law Commission, 2014). *http://www.lawcom.gov.uk/wp-content/uploads/2015/03/lc353_insurance-contract-law.pdf* [Accessed 24 June 2016] at para.5.63.

a substantial amount of the previous case law on disclosure[10] and contains provisions which merely codify what many insurers had already regarded as best practice for the insurance market.[11]

5-007 The new duty of fair presentation arrives as the result of increasing dissatisfaction with the disclosure duties contained in the MIA. As originally enacted, the MIA was designed to suit a fledgling insurance market at a time when the insured had all the knowledge about the risk and the insurer was entirely reliant on their disclosure in order to make an accurate assessment. Sections 17–20 of the MIA were enacted in recognition of the weaker position of the insurer, and provided them with an aggressive legal toolset in order to safeguard against the high potential for abuse or fraud. Such is evidenced by the draconian remedy of avoidance for non-disclosure, regardless of whether the non-disclosure was mistaken or intentional, and regardless of whether the insurer would have merely accepted the risk at a slightly higher premium if the disclosure had been made.[12] This position was found to be unacceptable by the Law Commission because allowing the unmeritorious refusals of claims under a policy ran the risk of bringing the entire UK insurance market into disrepute.[13] Despite indications that best practice had moved away from insurers utilising such technical arguments, the Law Commission expressed dissatisfaction that the current law would give insurers an excessively strong bargaining position from which to negotiate lower payments by threatening to deprive the insured of the entire payment if they did not agree to a lower settlement figure.[14] The new provisions were designed to address these issues and bring insurance law back in touch with the modern realities of the market.

5-008 **Overview of changes.** The new duty of fair presentation is designed as a default regime to be effective for all businesses, whatever size or sophistication, and for all insurance markets, including marine and reinsurance. As with all other parts of the 2015 Act, the parties are free to contract out of these provisions and substitute more stringent obligations on the insured, provided that any changes made are in accordance with the transparency requirements.[15] Whilst more bespoke arrangements are expected to become the norm in sophisticated industries such as marine,[16] it may be some time before the market adjusts to the requirements of the new legislation and these arrangements become commonplace. In a similar vein, the Law Commission anticipate guidance protocols being issued for many of the major insurance markets and industries to provide greater clarity for what the insured must disclose, though it remains to be seen whether the market takes up the challenge

---

[10] See, for example, paras 5-021 and 5-061.

[11] Law Commission *"Insurance Contract Law: Business Disclosure; Warranties; Insurers' Remedies for Fraudulent Claims; and Late Payment"*, (Law Commission, 2014). *http://www.lawcom.gov.uk/wp-content/uploads/2015/03/lc353_insurance-contract-law.pdf* [Accessed 24 June 2016] at paras 5.49 to 5.54.

[12] See below, para.6-004.

[13] Law Commission *"Insurance Contract Law: Business Disclosure; Warranties; Insurers' Remedies for Fraudulent Claims; and Late Payment"*, (Law Commission, 2014). *http://www.lawcom.gov.uk/wp-content/uploads/2015/03/lc353_insurance-contract-law.pdf* [Accessed 24 June2016] at para.1.26.

[14] See fn.13 above at para.5.42.

[15] See below, para.5-135.

[16] Law Commission *"Insurance Contract Law: Business Disclosure; Warranties; Insurers' Remedies for Fraudulent Claims; and Late Payment"*, (Law Commission, 2014). *http://www.lawcom.gov.uk/wp-content/uploads/2015/03/lc353_insurance-contract-law.pdf* [Accessed 24 June 2016] at para.6.23.

of providing these protocols and whether such protocols will have any significant legal impact.[17]

Where the parties do not contract, the basic provisions of the 2015 Act will apply. **5-009** The statutory duty of fair presentation includes both a positive and a negative constituent element: the insured must disclose all material circumstances within their knowledge, and they must not make any misrepresentations to the insurer. Significantly, the duty now defines not just the content that must be disclosed, but also the form that the disclosure must take—if a presentation is particularly substantial, it must be adequately signposted to enable the insurer to appreciate the significant details of the risk. The Law Commission's intention behind the provision was to prevent a large insured from concealing key elements of a risk amidst a raft of documents by "data dumping" the insurer with a large volume of unsorted information,[18] but the provision also marks some of the conceptual movement that has taken place behind the new duty of fair presentation. The 2015 Act has moved away from requiring a minute disclosure of every material circumstance relating to the risk in question, likely due to such a requirement being unworkable in certain cases and out of touch with the modern realities of the market in others.[19] Without the disclosure test operating as a formalistic exercise in which the insured must tick every last box in order to discharge their duty, the 2015 Act has had to qualify the circumstances in which an incomplete disclosure will be sufficient by adding new controls which discriminate between an adequate and an inadequate presentation without relying on the technical completeness of the disclosure. The clarity requirements are just one example of how the 2015 Act achieves this, but similar controls can be seen with the retention of good faith as an interpretative principle[20] and the requirement that the insured must conduct a reasonable search of the information at their disposal.[21]

For those familiar with the disclosure duties under the MIA, the 2015 Act utilises **5-010** many of the same principles but substantially alters their content and application. This can be most clearly observed from the changes to the insured's knowledge, which will now encompass all of the material that would reasonably have been revealed by a reasonable search of the information available to the insured rather than just including actual and "blind eye" knowledge. More subtle changes have been worked into the attribution of knowledge to the insured where the insured is an artificial legal personality, and in particular the attribution of fraudulent knowledge has been refined and clarified to distinguish between frauds that will be attributed to the insured and frauds that will not. In contrast to the changes to the insured's knowledge, the concept of materiality has not undergone nearly so radical a surgery under the 2015 Act and the new provisions can best be seen as setting out on the face of the statute what would already have been deemed material to the underwriting decision under the MIA. Instead, the 2015 Act attempts to clarify for the insured the information that will be deemed material and provides a mechanism through which industry stakeholders can establish protocols listing

---

17 See below, para.5-024.
18 Explanatory Notes to the Insurance Act 2015, para.46.
19 Law Commission *"Insurance Contract Law: Business Disclosure; Warranties; Insurers' Remedies for Fraudulent Claims; and Late Payment"*, (Law Commission, 2014). *http://www.lawcom.gov.uk/wp-content/uploads/2015/03/lc353_insurance-contract-law.pdf* [Accessed 24 June 2016] at para.7.35.
20 See below, paras 5-141 to 5-142.
21 See below, paras 5-036 to 5-039.

material information for particular sectors and industries which are likely to have legal force.

The 2015 Act also replaces the draconian remedy of avoidance with proportionate remedies based on the detriment suffered by the insurer and the nature of the insured's mistake. If the insured has made a deliberate or reckless breach of their duty of fair presentation, the insurer will be entitled to avoid the contract and refuse payment of all claims. This was seen by the Law Commission as a penalty commensurate with a dishonest breach of duty because such breaches undermine the insurance contract as one made in good faith.[22] Where the breach was not deliberate and was not reckless, the remedy will instead put the insurer in the position they would have been in had the insured fulfilled its duties. Consequently, the remedy will depend upon what the insurer would have done if the proper disclosure had been made: if the insurer would not have entered into the contract at all, the policy will be avoided; if the insurer would have merely entered on different terms, the contract will be treated as having included those terms; and if the insurer would have opted to charge a higher premium than was agreed, the insurer may reduce proportionately the payment for the insured's claim. This effectively brings insurance law into line with the general remedial principles of contract law, save for those circumstances in which the insured has deliberately or recklessly disregarded the principle that an insurance contract must be made in good faith.

5-011 **Good Faith.** The principle that insurance is based on the utmost good faith persists in s.17 of the MIA, and the 2015 Act does not attempt to recast or replicate the provision. Instead, s.14(1) of the 2015 Act abolishes the remedy of avoidance for breach of the duty, leaving the scope and effect of the remaining principle uncertain. The Law Commission suggest that the 2015 Act retains the duty of good faith as an interpretative principle,[23] though they do not seek to substantiate much of what the principle is to be used to interpret. Some guidance is provided in relation to how the principle of good faith will affect the duty of fair presentation in that good faith is intended to influence the way in which courts determine the adequacy of a presentation. Accordingly, an insured would be in breach of the duty of good faith if they sought to satisfy the technical minimum necessary for disclosure by abusing the "sufficient information to put a prudent insurer on notice"[24] standard to conceal material elements of the risk.[25] It seems likely that the courts will extend the remit of the principle to cover other situations in which a presentation may be technically adequate and yet conceal or fail to disclose material circumstances regarding the risk. For instance, the courts may utilise the principle where an insured has provided a very voluminous disclosure to the insurer that meets the requirements of signposting and clarity but does not attempt to provide a summary or abstract that gives an overall impression of the risk. Where there are particularly unusual or significant elements about the risk that are contained within that presentation, a court might find that the insured has breached

---

[22] Law Commission "*Insurance Contract Law: Business Disclosure; Warranties; Insurers' Remedies for Fraudulent Claims; and Late Payment*", (Law Commission, 2014). *http://www.lawcom.gov.uk/wp-content/uploads/2015/03/lc353_insurance-contract-law.pdf* [Accessed 24 June 2016] at para.11.36.

[23] See below, para.5-141.

[24] See below, para.5-061.

[25] Law Commission "*Insurance Contract Law: Business Disclosure; Warranties; Insurers' Remedies for Fraudulent Claims; and Late Payment*", (Law Commission, 2014). *http://www.lawcom.gov.uk/wp-content/uploads/2015/03/lc353_insurance-contract-law.pdf* [Accessed 24 June 2016] at para.30.23.

the duty of good faith by not seeking to draw the insurer's attention to those elements despite the presentation being clearly set out and adequately indexed.[26] The principle may also be used to interpret s.4(6) of the 2015 Act, which provides that the insured must make a reasonable search of the material available to them in order to fulfil its disclosure duties. Since the 2015 Act does not define what is meant by a "reasonable search" and the Law Commission's guidance is only concerned with identifying information repositories that could potentially be available to a prospective insured for searching,[27] it is possible that the courts will use the concept of good faith as an aid to discriminate between an adequate and an inadequate search of available information.

(a) Before the contract is entered into

Introductory. Section 3(1) of the 2015 Act provides that the duty of fair presentation must be complied with by the prospective insured "before the insurance contract is entered into", replicating the effect of s.18(1) of the MIA with updated wording.[28] If the insured opts to obtain cover under an annual CAR policy, the policy will fall due for renewal each year and each renewal will amount to the formation of a new insurance contract.[29] Accordingly, the duty must be complied with by the insured in relation to the entire risk before each renewal, though the disclosure requirements will be tempered to reflect the fact that a contractor-insured often will not have information about every project planned to be undertaken that year, and will be unlikely to know at that stage which of its tenders will be accepted for that year. The position is simpler if the prospective insured obtains cover under a single-project policy, as the insured will usually be able to provide the insurer with the technical information regarding the project in order to allow an accurate underwriting decision to be made.

5-012

Variations. The scope of the duty in relation to variations is set out in s.2(2) of the 2015 Act. Duplicating the previous position under the MIA, the insured is only required to disclose material circumstances relating to "changes in the risk relevant to the proposed variation"[30] and so the insured does not need to present the entire risk again. Accordingly, if there have been any significant changes to the risk covered in the underlying contract then there is no duty to disclose these changes to the insurer before agreeing the variation and there will be no penalty on the insured for failing to do so, unless the changes are material to the variation. If the insured breaches the duty of fair presentation in respect of the agreed variations, then the remedies available to the insurer will affect only the variations and not the underlying contract.[31]

5-013

---

[26] See below, para.5-064.

[27] See below, para.5-037.

[28] Law Commission "*Insurance Contract Law: Business Disclosure; Warranties; Insurers' Remedies for Fraudulent Claims; and Late Payment*", (Law Commission, 2014). *http://www.lawcom.gov.uk/wp-content/uploads/2015/03/lc353_insurance-contract-law.pdf* [Accessed 24 June 2016] at para.7.9.

[29] See above, para.4-047.

[30] Section 2(2)(a) of the 2015 Act. Section 2(2)(a) provides that "references to the risk are to be read as references to changes in the risk relevant to the proposed variation".

[31] See below, para.5-088.

(b) The insured

5-014 **The Insured.**   The insured is defined under s.1 of the 2015 Act as "the party to a contract of insurance who is the insured under the contract, or would be if the contract were entered into." The individuals or corporate entities that fall under this definition must generally be identified before the contract is entered into if there is a group insurance scheme or similar multi-insured arrangement in place, principally because the scope of the disclosure required to fulfil the duty of fair presentation may include information attributed from other insureds or information discoverable through a reasonable search of the materials held by other insureds.[32]

5-015   The second limb of the definition includes the party who "would be" the insured under the contract if it were entered into. This limb is included to impose the duty on the prospective insured before the contract is entered into, though no legal consequences for breach will crystallise unless the contract is concluded. Once the contract has been agreed, any previous breaches of the disclosure duty will provide the insurer with the right to exercise the remedies set out in s.8 of the 2015 Act, which may result in the avoidance of the contract, changes to the terms of the contract or a reduction of the indemnity for the insured's claim under the policy.

5-016 **Co-insurance.**   The 2015 Act does not seek to specifically define who "the insured" will be under arrangements involving multiple named assureds, leaving the previous case law on the subject to apply as a gloss over the statutory definition.

      The legal identity of a policy covering a number of co-insureds can have an important effect on both the required disclosure under the duty of fair presentation and the consequences for its breach, in particular where one of the co-insureds has perpetrated a fraud against the insurer. The courts will look at the true construction of the policy to determine whether the co-insurance is joint or composite, representing either a single policy covering all of the insureds or a bundle of separate policies arranged on behalf of each insured. Although the same disclosure will need to be made under both policies, breach under a composite policy will usually affect only that party's own individual contract, whereas a breach under a joint policy will affect the contract covering all of the insureds.[33] It is important to note that the form of the disclosure presentation is unlikely to affect the construction of the policy as either joint or composite, as a single presentation can equally be made on behalf of all insureds to satisfy their joint duty of disclosure or their separate duties under separate contracts.

5-017 **CAR policy.**   It is now settled that, subject to express wording to the contrary, a CAR policy will be deemed to be composite rather than joint and therefore represents a bundle of separate insurance policies agreed between each insured and the insurer. For more on co-insurance and the consequences that flow from such an arrangement, see Ch.20.

---

[32] See below, para.5-028.

[33] Law Commission *"Insurance Contract Law: Business Disclosure; Warranties; Insurers' Remedies for Fraudulent Claims; and Late Payment"*, (Law Commission, 2014). *http://www.lawcom.gov.uk/ wp-content/uploads/2015/03/lc353_insurance-contract-law.pdf* [Accessed 24 June 2016] at para.7.15.

(c) Fair presentation of risk

There are three requirements that must be met in order for the insured to make a **5-018** fair presentation of risk, as provided by s.3(3) of the 2015 Act:

"(3) A fair presentation of the risk is one—
    (a) which makes the disclosure required by subsection (4),
    (b) which makes that disclosure in a manner which would be reasonably clear and accessible to a prudent insurer, and
    (c) in which every material representation as to a matter of fact is substantially correct, and every material representation as to a matter of expectation or belief is made in good faith."

Each subsection sets out a different requisite element of a fair presentation: s.3(3)(a) incorporates s.3(4) of the 2015 Act which defines the scope of the information that must be disclosed; s.3(3)(b) defines the form that the disclosure must take; and s.3(3)(c) brings the rules of misrepresentation previously contained in s.20(1) of the MIA under the umbrella of the overarching duty of fair presentation.

(i) Makes disclosure required

General. Section 3(4) of the 2015 Act provides two alternative limbs that the **5-019** insured may satisfy in order to discharge their duty of disclosure:

"(4) The disclosure required is as follows, except as provided in subsection (5)—
    (a) disclosure of every material circumstance which the insured knows or ought to know, or
    (b) failing that, disclosure which gives the insurer sufficient information to put a prudent insurer on notice that it needs to make further enquiries for the purpose of revealing those material circumstances."

The first limb of the new test directly incorporates the concepts employed by s.18(1) of the MIA by requiring the disclosure of every material circumstance[34] that the insured knows or ought to know.[35] Alternatively, s.(4)(b) also embodies recent case law[36] on disclosure which has marked a movement away from the technical disclosure of every material circumstance towards the newer concept of requiring a fair presentation of the risk in which:

"In this regard a minute disclosure of every material circumstance is not required; the assured complies with the rule if he discloses sufficient to call the attention of the underwriter to the matter in such a way that, if he desires further information, he can ask for it; accordingly a presentation will be fair and accurate if it would enable a prudent insurer to form a proper judgement, either on the presentation alone, or by asking questions if he was sufficiently put upon enquiry and wanted to know further details."[37]

---

[34] See below, para.6-033.
[35] See below, para.6-011.
[36] See *Iron Trades Mutual Insurance Co Ltd v Companhia de Seguros Imperio* [1991] 1 Re LR 213; *Garnat Trading & Shipping (Singapore) Pte Ltd v Baominh Insurance Corporation* [2010] EWHC 2578 (Comm), [2011] 1 Lloyd's Rep 366 at [135]; and *AXA Versicherung AG v ARAB Insurance Group (B.S.C.)* [2015] EWHC 1939 (Comm).
[37] *AXA Versicherung AG v ARAB Insurance Group (B.S.C.)* [2015] EWHC 1939 (Comm), per Males J at 113.

Section 3(4)(b) does not mark a radical departure from the existing law, but instead reinforces the need for insurer involvement at the underwriting stage to balance the insured's difficult task of trying to detail every circumstance the insurer may have an interest in. It is thought by the Law Commission that codifying this position in statute will prevent the trend of insurers remaining silent during a presentation and later "underwriting at the claims stage" in circumstances where the insured had provided sufficient signposts to alert the prudent insurer that further enquiries needed to be made during a presentation.[38] The section will also enable the insured to make a fair presentation of risk where they hold a particularly large quantity of information that may be material or where the risk is one for which adequate disclosure would not be possible without heavy insurer involvement and guidance.[39]

(ii) Materiality

5-020 **Every material circumstance.**   In order to satisfy the disclosure duty, the insured must first understand the concept of materiality which acts as a partition between the information that will be relevant to the risk in question and all of the other documents and data that they or their company may possess. Section 7(3) of the 2015 Act defines a material circumstance in the following manner:

> "(3) A circumstance or representation is material if it would influence the judgement of a prudent insurer in determining whether to take the risk and, if so, on what terms."[40]

The task of determining what would influence the judgment of a prudent insurer has traditionally proved to be difficult for the insured as it requires them to place themselves in the insurer's position and evaluate which circumstances will be relevant to the underwriting decision. Materiality was retained by the Law Commission because it was seen to be one of the key strengths of the UK insurance market that allowed for the underwriting of risks considered uninsurable in other jurisdictions.[41] Nevertheless, the 2015 Act makes a number of changes aimed at improving an insured's understanding of this requirement by providing greater clarity with regard to the general categories of information that will be material to the risk in question and hence require disclosure. Accordingly, s.7(4) of the 2015 Act lists some usual circumstances that the insured will need to disclose, largely taken from recent case law on non-disclosure:

> "(4) Examples of things which may be material circumstances are—
>> (a) special or unusual facts relating to the risk,
>> (b) any particular concerns which led the insured to seek insurance cover for the risk,
>> (c) anything which those concerned with the class of insurance and field of activity in question would generally understand as being something that should be dealt with in a fair presentation of risks of the type in question."

---

[38] Law Commission "*Insurance Contract Law: Business Disclosure; Warranties; Insurers' Remedies for Fraudulent Claims; and Late Payment*", (Law Commission, 2014). *http://www.lawcom.gov.uk/wp-content/uploads/2015/03/lc353_insurance-contract-law.pdf* [Accessed June 24, 2016], at para.7.38.

[39] See fn.38 above, at para.7.39.

[40] This reflects the previous common law position in *Pan Atlantic Insurance Co Ltd v Pine Top Insurance Co Ltd* [1995] 1 A.C. 501; [1994] 3 W.L.R. 677; [1994] 3 All E.R. 581.

[41] Law Commission "*Insurance Contract Law: Business Disclosure; Warranties; Insurers' Remedies for Fraudulent Claims; and Late Payment*", (Law Commission, 2014). *http://www.lawcom.gov.uk/wp-content/uploads/2015/03/lc353_insurance-contract-law.pdf* [Accessed 24 June 2016] at para.5.70.

Special or unusual facts relating to risk. The first category of material **5-021** circumstances referred to by the 2015 Act directs the insured to any factor which is sufficiently unusual or special to make it obvious that it should be disclosed, rendering any presentation of risk absent of such disclosure fatally distorted. This requirement is illustrated by the case of *Container Transport International Inc v Oceanus Mutual Underwriting Association (Bermuda) Ltd*[42] which concerned all risks insurance for the business of leasing out containers. The pertinent non-disclosure was in relation to a summary which the insured had prepared detailing the loss ratio on gross premiums for the period of October 1971 to June 1974, but leaving out the figures thereafter. Kerr LJ considered that the dramatic deterioration in the loss ratio over the following months was a fact obviously requiring disclosure because it would have "radically altered the picture conveyed by those figures which were in fact disclosed."[43] As a result of this, it could not be said that the insurer had been put on enquiry about the figures for the months after June 1974 simply by being told the figures for the preceding months, and so they had not waived that disclosure by failing to make those enquiries as:

"The doctrine of waiver cannot be applied to undisclosed facts which are unusual or special, so that their non-disclosure distorts the presentation of the risk. In such cases, the underwriter is not put on enquiry about the existence of such facts."[44]

The Law Commission gave a number of further examples of what might be **5-022** considered to be unusual or specific facts relating to the risk which a policyholder should realise would be material to the insurer. They noted:

"In taking out life insurance, one should normally disclose a death threat and we would expect the same principle to apply, for example, where a business received an arson threat. Again, a business would be expected to mention that it had recently acquired an explosives factory; or that (in product liability insurance) its products were used in nuclear power plants."[45]

The examples given suggest that the provision is primarily one intended as a clarifying measure rather than representing any substantive change to the concept of materiality.

Particular concerns which led the insured to seek insurance cover for the risk. A decision to take out insurance or to take out a policy providing more **5-023** coverage than previously held can often be motivated by the insured perceiving a loss event approaching on the horizon. The 2015 Act provides that any particular concerns which led to the prospective insured taking out cover must be raised before the contract is entered into in order for the disclosure duty to be discharged.

This requirement was drawn from the case of *Aiken v Stewart Wrightson Members Agency Ltd*,[46] which concerned a material non-disclosure made by Lloyd's

---

[42] *Container Transport International Inc v Oceanus Mutual Underwriting Association (Bermuda) Ltd* [1984] 1 Lloyd's Rep. 476.

[43] *Container Transport International Inc v Oceanus Mutual Underwriting Association (Bermuda) Ltd (No.1)* [1984] 1 Lloyd's Rep. 476 at 498.

[44] See fn.43 above.

[45] Law Commission "*Insurance Contract Law: The Business Insured's Duty of Disclosure and the Law of Warranties*", (Law Commission, 2012). *http://www.lawcom.gov.uk/wp-content/uploads/2015/11/Consultation-Paper-The-business-insureds-duty-of-disclosure-and-the-law-of-warranties-consultation-paper.pdf* [Accessed 24 June 2016] at para.5.33.

[46] *Aiken v Stewart Wrightson Members Agency Ltd* [1995] 1 W.L.R. 1281.

underwriters when placing run-off reinsurance. The underwriters had failed to disclose to the reinsurer that the reason they had opted to take out the cover was that there were growing concerns in the US market about the possible escalation of claims for asbestosis, which at the time depended on pending decisions in cases that were currently being litigated in the US courts. Potter J considered that it was abundantly clear such circumstances should have been disclosed to the reinsurers because:

"This duty applied especially to the matters which were giving Pulbrook concern and were arguably, if not obviously, material to the prudent reinsurer, in particular the mounting claims for asbestosis and DES which were the reason why the reinsurance was sought in the first place."[47]

Although a relatively obvious identifier of information that may be material to the risk, the intention of s.7(4)(b) of the 2015 Act is presumably to shift the enquiry towards one which the insured will find far easier to comply with. Rather than attempting to probe the factors which the insurer may have an interest in to identify information requiring disclosure, the insured is instead directed towards its own motivations for purchasing the cover which will often be far easier to identify.

5-024   **Class of insurance and field of activity in question.**   This category of material circumstances is a new creation of the Law Commission which is intended to allow particular industries to develop their own protocols outlining what needs to be disclosed to insurers underwriting a risk in their field. The intent is that prospective insureds will utilise these protocols as guidance for what needs to be disclosed, and in turn the courts will interpret the insured's disclosure duties in line with the requirements of the protocol. This may turn out to be one of the key mechanisms of the 2015 Act which enables it to be effective for all sizes of business and fields of insurance, as it provides a route through which the law on disclosure can be tailored to suit the needs of each industry under one unified wording in the statute. The Law Commission expressed the following rationale behind the provision, stating:

"Of these three categories, we think (c) has the most potential for development by the market. It is intended to recognise that the type of information which should be disclosed may vary significantly depending on the 'class' of insurance being purchased (for example, professional indemnity, employer's liability, property) and the 'field of activity' in which the insured operates (for example, heavy industries, shipping, financial auditing)."[48]

By defining the required disclosure in accordance with industry protocols in place before the insured takes out the policy, the 2015 Act makes an insured's duty clear from the outset and therefore takes another step towards shifting insurers away from "underwriting at the claims stage" and encouraging active involvement before the policy is concluded. It makes sense that for a disclosure test defined by what the prudent insurer would consider to be material to the underwriting decision, insurers should be encouraged to participate in the creation of these protocols which set out the factors that would influence their appreciation of the risk in question. It would likely be the case under the new law that where an insured's disclosure was

---

[47] See above, fn.46 at 1313.
[48] Law Commission "*Insurance Contract Law: Business Disclosure; Warranties; Insurers' Remedies for Fraudulent Claims; and Late Payment*", (Law Commission, 2014). *http://www.lawcom.gov.uk/wp-content/uploads/2015/03/lc353_insurance-contract-law.pdf* [Accessed 24 June 2016] at para.7.29.

in accordance with the applicable protocol and the insurer also failed to make enquiries about a particular aspect of the risk, it would be much harder for that insurer to rely on a material non-disclosure as the insured would then have two bases to show that they had made a good, honest attempt to disclose all that they considered would be relevant to the insurer. Where a particular industry, like construction, is one in which technological advancements can create a degree of uncertainty over what might be material to the risk in question or how likely a new method of works or new construction materials might be to fail and cause damage, it would also appear that the requirement to develop protocols will help to entrench the disclosure requirements upon established market understanding at the time the policy was entered into rather than what might subsequently be found out to increase the risk or danger by the time a claim is made under the policy.

Guidance and protocols for the construction industry. The creation of these new protocols will be particularly useful to the construction industry where the practice of taking out annual rather than project specific cover can lead to a degree of uncertainty over what needs to be disclosed. For instance, when a contractor is renewing annual cover he may still be uncertain of how many projects he will be involved in that year, which of his tenders will be accepted by prospective employers and the identities of all the parties who will subsequently fall to be covered under his policy. These protocols will help to shift the burden onto the insurer to argue that a protocol-compliant disclosure was nevertheless inadequate, which may prove to be a particularly useful tool where the industry practice is to accept a more speculative risk at a higher premium, as where the insurer is fully aware that disclosure will necessarily be more limited than the detailed presentation that could be provided for a project specific policy. **5-025**

Contracting out. As with all other parts of the 2015 Act, the parties are free to contract out of the default disclosure requirements in favour of more demanding requirements for the prospective insured provided that such changes are made in accordance with the transparency requirements, discussed below at para.5-135. This may be desirable for larger companies where there is material knowledge available to them that would not be cost effective to sort through and disclose, in which case the policy may specifically provide for information that will be exempt from the duty of fair presentation. **5-026**

(iii) Knowledge

General. Adopting the same approach as the MIA, the 2015 Act utilises the concept of an insured's knowledge alongside the concept of materiality in order to determine the content of the disclosure required to give a fair presentation of risk. Out of all of the information and records which might be available to the prospective insured, it is only what is both material and within their knowledge or deemed knowledge that has to be disclosed to the insurer. Under the new provisions, the knowledge of a number of people may be relevant to the scope of disclosure required in order for the insured to discharge their duty: where the insured is an individual, they will be attributed with the knowledge of any broker or individual who arranges their insurance; they may have constructive knowledge of information held by other individuals to whom enquiries should have been made under the duty to conduct a reasonable search; and they will not need to disclose anything that **5-027**

is already known to the insurer. Similarly, where the insured is a non-individual such as a corporate entity, the insured will be attributed with the knowledge of its senior management and persons responsible for arranging the insurance; the insured may have constructive knowledge of information held by other individuals (whether employees or not) under the requirement to conduct a reasonable search; and, again, the insured will not need to disclose anything already within the knowledge of the insurer. The 2015 Act can best be understood as employing a general definition of "knowledge" for the purposes of the insured's disclosure duties which is then tailored to determine how it will specifically apply to an individual insured, a non-individual insured, an insurance broker and an insurer. There are therefore principles which will apply more generally to all knowledge which is pertinent to an insured's disclosure under the 2015 Act, such as the *Hampshire Land*[49] principle and Nelsonian or "blind eye" knowledge, and there are also more specific provisions which tailor the scope of that knowledge depending on whether the relevant circumstances are known to the insured, the broker, or the insurer. This section considers the basic principles which will apply to all knowledge that is relevant to disclosure.

It is also useful to appreciate the difficulties that arose under the previous case law concerning knowledge in order to understand the specific issues that the new provisions were intended to address. The Law Commission identified the most problematic and uncertain areas of the case law under the MIA as the issue of attribution of knowledge and the issue of constructive knowledge, particularly as they apply to a non-individual or "corporate insured". The Law Commission considered that the area had become difficult primarily because of the uncertainty introduced by the case law on the subject:

"The current law on these issues is malleable and driven by the facts of individual cases. The various issues are often considered together, which obfuscates the true meaning of section 18(1) of the 1906 Act."[50]

The new provisions of the 2015 Act were therefore designed as "a restatement of the law, which will draw on the best principles in the current case law to clarify both whose knowledge is relevant, and what enquiries need to be made."[51] Whilst the courts may still use the previous case law as a starting point to determine how the new provisions should operate, the 2015 Act has substantially reformed and clarified the law concerning constructive and attributed knowledge and can therefore be seen as overtaking the common law and providing a new, clearer test for what will be held to be within an individual's or a corporate entity's knowledge.

5-028   **Attributed and constructive knowledge.**   There are two distinct mechanisms under the 2015 Act which are used to determine the knowledge of the insured: the attribution of knowledge held by relevant individuals and constructive knowledge determined through the requirement to conduct a reasonable search. Where the

---

49   See below, fn.64.
50   Law Commission "*Insurance Contract Law: Business Disclosure; Warranties; Insurers' Remedies for Fraudulent Claims; and Late Payment*", (Law Commission, 2014). *http://www.lawcom.gov.uk/wp-content/uploads/2015/03/lc353_insurance-contract-law.pdf* [Accessed 24 June 2016] at para.8.21.
51   Law Commission "*Insurance Contract Law: The Business Insured's Duty of Disclosure and the Law of Warranties*", (Law Commission, 2012). *http://www.lawcom.gov.uk/wp-content/uploads/2015/11/Consultation-Paper-The-business-insureds-duty-of-disclosure-and-the-law-of-warranties-consultation-paper.pdf* [Accessed 24 June 2016] at para.6.73.

insured is an individual, they will possess the attributed knowledge of any broker or agent used to place the insurance policy and they will also have constructive knowledge of all of those matters they *ought* to have found out after conducting a reasonable search.[52] Where the insured is a non-individual such as a company, it will be attributed with the knowledge of all of its senior management and employees responsible for the placement of the insurance policy (as the "directing mind and will" of the company), and it will be deemed to have the constructive knowledge of everything that company *ought* to have known after conducting a reasonable search. Some conceptual confusion may arise in the case of a non-individual insured where the material information is held by a company employee, for example an individual working in the underwriting department, that may have its knowledge captured both constructively and by attribution. For other company employees, it will be crucial to determine whether information held by them is captured constructively or by attribution as the mechanism employed can have a radical effect on the content of information transposed onto the company. The Law Commission envisage the paradigm example of this as the case of an individual fraudulently withholding information from the insurer and the insured company, with very different consequences depending on whether that person's knowledge is caught constructively or by attribution. Where their knowledge is directly attributed onto the insured company then it will of course include all of the details of the fraud being perpetrated against the insurer, whereas the knowledge artificially ascribed to the company through the duty to make enquiries of that person will not include the fraudulent knowledge as the fraudster is unlikely to disclose the details of that fraud in response to any enquiries.[53] A fraudster's knowledge is therefore capable of being caught by attribution but not constructively. A similar scenario would arise where a particular individual is aware of material knowledge to the risk but is not aware of its relevance to the enquiries made as part of the duty to conduct a reasonable search. If that individual's knowledge is attributed to the company, then it will of course include all of their knowledge whether that person knows it to be relevant or not, whereas it would be difficult to argue that the knowledge should have been unlocked constructively through the requirement to conduct a reasonable search when the person would not have volunteered that information in response to enquiries. Where material information has not been disclosed to the insurer, it will therefore be a matter of some importance to determine the individuals which held that knowledge and whether their knowledge is caught constructively or by attribution.

The knowledge provisions contained under ss.18(1) and 19(1) of the MIA employed both attributed and constructive knowledge to determine the extent of the insured's disclosure obligations,[54] but there remained a degree of uncertainty regarding the exact remit of an insured's constructive knowledge and the individuals whose knowledge would be attributed to a company or other legal entity. The 2015 Act therefore seeks to provide clarity by setting out, on the face of the statute, the full range of the individuals whose knowledge will be attributed to the insured and

---

[52] See below, paras 5-036 to 5-038.

[53] Law Commission "*Insurance Contract Law: The Business Insured's Duty of Disclosure and the Law of Warranties*", (Law Commission, 2012). *http://www.lawcom.gov.uk/wp-content/uploads/2015/11/Consultation-Paper-The-business-insureds-duty-of-disclosure-and-the-law-of-warranties-consultation-paper.pdf* [Accessed 24 June 2016] at para.6.53.

[54] See below, para.6-011.

a more exact mechanism for determining the scope of the insured's constructive knowledge. Although the insured's attributed knowledge has not undergone any substantial change beyond clarification, the 2015 Act entirely rewrites the test for an insured's constructive knowledge. The reasonable search requirement has supplanted the previous test of what an insured ought to know in the ordinary course of business, with the aim of directing the insured to conduct a search before entering into the insurance policy in order to encourage a more effective placement process. The Law Commission was conscious of the need to resolve the following ambiguities inherent under the constructive knowledge test contained in s.18(1) of the MIA: first, whether the insured's constructive knowledge went beyond Nelsonian knowledge[55]; secondly, whether the test was objective or subjective[56]; and thirdly, whether it also extended to a duty on the insured to make positive enquiries.[57] As well as resolving these uncertainties, what should also be noted about the provisions of the 2015 Act is that they adopt a narrow test for attributed knowledge and widen the scope of constructive knowledge with the intention that most of the knowledge will be caught by a reasonable search rather than by direct imputation of knowledge which could not reasonably have been discovered. The Law Commission expressed the clear intention to limit the circumstances in which a fraudster's knowledge is attributed to the insured in circumstances where the principal could never reasonably have discovered that fraud, which in many cases offends common sense. They noted:

"Further, an insured party cannot exercise control over all of its employees and agents. From a policy perspective, protecting itself against the fraud and negligence of employees may be one of an insured's reasons for purchasing insurance. We think that a limited number of people should have their knowledge attributed to an insured in a disclosure context. Instead, insureds should be under a clear duty to carry out a reasonable search."[58]

The 2015 Act can therefore be understood as setting out a more rigorously defined (and in many cases expanded) set of tests to determine what is within the insured's constructive and attributed knowledge, with the aim of bringing more certainty and clarity to the law in an area which had been left confused by scattershot decisions made in cases determined on their own facts.

5-029   **Blind eye knowledge.**   The 2015 Act preserves the common law principle that an insured will be deemed to know knowledge that he has "turned a blind eye to" and deliberately refrained from finding out. Section 6(1) of the 2015 Act provides that:

"For the purposes of sections 3 to 5, references to an individual's knowledge include not only actual knowledge, but also matters which the individual suspected, and of which the individual would have had knowledge but for deliberately refraining from confirming them or enquiring about them."

---

[55]   Law Commission "*Insurance Contract Law: Business Disclosure; Warranties; Insurers' Remedies for Fraudulent Claims; and Late Payment*", (Law Commission, 2014). *http://www.lawcom.gov.uk/ wp-content/uploads/2015/03/lc353_insurance-contract-law.pdf* [Accessed 24 June 016] at para.8.25.
[56]   See above, fn.55 at para.8.26.
[57]   See above, fn.55 at para.8.25.
[58]   Law Commission "*Insurance Contract Law: Business Disclosure; Warranties; Insurers' Remedies for Fraudulent Claims; and Late Payment*", (Law Commission, 2014). *http://www.lawcom.gov.uk/ wp-content/uploads/2015/03/lc353_insurance-contract-law.pdf* [Accessed 24 June 2016] at para.8.35.

The case law on "blind eye" knowledge under the MIA, which will continue to apply under the 2015 Act, is discussed in more detail below at para.6-011. For the purposes of the 2015 Act, the concept of "blind eye" knowledge is applied in ss.3, 4 and 5, namely the provisions defining an insured's knowledge, the knowledge attributed to the insured from his insurance broker[59] and matters within an insurer's knowledge for which no disclosure is required.[60]

For the purposes of the new legislation, it is useful to consider the scope of "blind eye" knowledge and where it is intended to fit alongside the requirement that the insured conduct a reasonable search. It might be questioned why the Law Commission decided that it was necessary to retain the "blind eye" principle at all when knowledge that an insured has deliberately "turned a blind eye to" would almost certainly have been discovered by a reasonable search of the information available to the insured. There are two potential answers which address why the principle was included. The first is that it applies to define what the insurer as well as the insured knows, and therefore if the insurer has "turned a blind eye" towards any information that is easily discoverable about the insured before taking out the policy then the insured will not need to disclose that information. The insurer is, of course, under no duty to conduct a reasonable search itself before arranging the policy, so this requirement may be seen as another measure encouraging active insurer engagement during the presentation of risk and the placement process. If this were the only remaining scope for the "blind eye" principle under the 2015 Act, then one could rightly question why s.6(1) specifically includes reference to s.3 of the 2015 Act which defines the knowledge of the insured. One can presumably infer that the principle has been retained in order to capture information of which the insured would not have constructive knowledge merely by undertaking a reasonable search. The difference between the two tests can be understood by reference to the cases the Law Commission drew from to inform the wording of the new provision.

The Law Commission quoted with approval Lord Scott's statement of the law on blind eye knowledge in *The Star Sea*,[61] in which he said:

"It is, I think, common ground—and if it is not, it should be—that an imputation of blind-eye knowledge requires an amalgam of suspicion that certain facts may exist and a decision to refrain from taking any step to confirm their existence."

The issues in *The Star Sea* arose out of the non-disclosure of the unseaworthiness of the *Star Sea* to the insurers before entering the policy and shortly before the total loss of the vessel. The question was whether the insured had any "blind eye" knowledge of the vessel's unseaworthiness which would enable the insurers to avoid the policy as a breach of the duty of utmost good faith. Lord Scott (and the Law Commission)[62] considered that the key element of "blind eye" knowledge was that it was far more blameworthy than mere negligence, and so there had to be a clear line drawn between the two states of mind. Accordingly, rather than the insured failing to discover information through mere carelessness, what was

---

[59] See below, para 5-041 onwards.
[60] See below, para.5-051 onwards.
[61] *Manifest Shipping Co Ltd v Uni-Polaris Insurance Co Ltd (The Star Sea)* [2001] UKHL 1; [2003] 1 A.C. 469; [2001] 2 W.L.R. 170.
[62] Law Commission "*Insurance Contract Law: Business Disclosure; Warranties; Insurers' Remedies for Fraudulent Claims; and Late Payment*", (Law Commission, 2014). *http://www.lawcom.gov.uk/wp-content/uploads/2015/03/lc353_insurance-contract-law.pdf* [Accessed 24 June 2016] at para.8.23.

required for "blind eye" knowledge was that the insured had a strong suspicion and deliberately decided not to look in order to avoid confirming that suspicion. Lord Scott concluded:

> "In summary, blind-eye knowledge requires, in my opinion, a suspicion that the relevant facts do exist and a deliberate decision to avoid confirming that they exist. But a warning should be sounded. Suspicion is a word that can be used to describe a state-of-mind that may, at one extreme, be no more than a vague feeling of unease and, at the other extreme, reflect a firm belief in the existence of the relevant facts. In my opinion, in order for there to be blind-eye knowledge, the suspicion must be firmly grounded and targeted on specific facts. The deliberate decision must be a decision to avoid obtaining confirmation of facts in whose existence the individual has good reason to believe. To allow blind-eye knowledge to be constituted by a decision not to enquire into an untargeted or speculative suspicion would be to allow negligence, albeit gross, to be the basis of a finding of privity. That, in my opinion, is not warranted by section 39(5)."

The "blind eye" test is therefore inherently subjective, requiring the judge to make a finding of a "deliberate decision" not to look which must be predicated on a firmly grounded suspicion that certain facts exist. In contrast, the requirement that the insured conduct a reasonable search of the materials available to it is applied objectively: thus, for example the required scope of the search will be judged objectively, by reference to the standard of a reasonable, prudent insured in that class.[63] It may, accordingly, be possible for information which escapes the requirement of a reasonable search to be imputed to the insured through the "blind eye" principle.

5-030 **Fraudulent knowledge.** The *Hampshire Land*[64] principle that fraudulent knowledge will not generally be attributed from a fraudster to its principal is preserved by s.6(2) of the 2015 Act, which provides that:

> "(2) Nothing in this Part affects the operation of any rule of law according to which knowledge of a fraud perpetrated by an individual ('F') either on the insured or on the insurer is not to be attributed to the insured or to the insurer (respectively), where—
>   (a) if the fraud is on the insured, F is any of the individuals mentioned in section 4(2)(b) or (3), or
>   (b) if the fraud is on the insurer, F is any of the individuals mentioned in section 5(1)."

The effect of the provision is that even where knowledge would be attributed to the insured from a fraudster under the provisions of the 2015 Act, the *Hampshire Land* principle may still operate to prevent that attribution of knowledge. Section 6(2)(a) and (b) make clear that this will be the case whether the knowledge is attributed to an individual insured from its agent or broker, to a non-individual insured from its senior management or those responsible for its insurance, or to the insurer from its employees participating in the underwriting decision. The body of case law that has arisen in respect of the *Hampshire Land* principle will therefore continue to apply under the 2015 Act, and it will be up to the courts to develop the principle to operate effectively alongside the new provisions.[65] Nevertheless, the Law Commission

---

[63] See below, para.5-037.
[64] From *Re Hampshire Land Company* [1896] 2 Ch. 743.
[65] Law Commission "*Insurance Contract Law: Business Disclosure; Warranties; Insurers' Remedies for Fraudulent Claims; and Late Payment*", (Law Commission, 2014). *http://www.lawcom.gov.uk/wp-content/uploads/2015/03/lc353_insurance-contract-law.pdf* [Accessed 24 June 2016] at para.8.75.

did express its opinion as to how the courts should resolve some of the ambiguities inherent in the principle's current incarnation, and this may prove to be persuasive to the courts when the matter arises under the 2015 Act. The key uncertainty under *Hampshire Land* relates to whether it only prevents the attribution of knowledge to the insured where the fraud is being perpetrated *against that insured*, or whether it would also prevent the attribution of fraudulent knowledge concerning a fraud perpetrated *against the insurer but outside the awareness of the insured*. Formulated another way, the uncertainty is whether the insured has to be the primary victim of the fraud in order to avoid being attributed with the fraudulent knowledge, or whether it could also avoid attribution of the knowledge if it is only a secondary victim to the real fraud being perpetrated against the insurer. The Law Commission noted the variety of judicial opinion apparent from even the (then) most recent House of Lords decision on the subject,[66] and felt it necessary to offer some recommendation as to how the principle would operate under the 2015 Act. The Law Commission ultimately considered that the principle should be kept within narrow bounds, such that *Hampshire Land* would only prevent the attribution of knowledge where the insured was the primary victim of the fraud. It stated:

"To some extent, our knowledge proposals are intentionally designed so that the fraud of certain individuals is attributed to their principal. For example, where senior managers of a company fraudulently misrepresent the extent of the risks in their business practices to obtain cheaper insurance, we think that this should be attributed to the company so that the insurer is entitled to avoid the policy. Therefore, we do not think that the wider interpretation of the Hampshire Land principle should be applied to limit our knowledge provisions.

However, we see a policy argument in favour of the Hampshire Land principle in its more restricted sense, where the insured company is the direct victim of the fraud perpetrated by an individual or individuals who should be representing its interests. The rationale is that it is contrary to common sense and justice to attribute to a principal knowledge of something that their agent would be anxious to conceal from them."[67]

(iv)   The insured's knowledge

Insured is an individual.   The content of an insured's knowledge is generally the   **5-031** most straightforward when that insured is an individual rather than a legal person such as a company or charity. Determining what an individual knows is simply a matter of fact and evidence, which is quite distinct from the issues of which individuals' knowledge will be attributed to an artificial legal entity that must be addressed when the insured is a non-individual. The 2015 Act therefore contains separate provisions defining the scope of the knowledge held by an insured "who is an individual" in s.4(2) of the 2015 Act and an insured "who is not an individual" in s.4(3) of the 2015 Act. Section 4(2) provides that:

"(2)   An insured who is an individual knows only—
     (a)   what is known to the individual, and

---

[66]   *Moore Stephens v Stone & Rolls Ltd* [2009] UKHL 39; [2009] 1 A.C. 1391, as discussed in the Law Commission's report "*Insurance Contract Law: Business Disclosure; Warranties; Insurers' Remedies for Fraudulent Claims; and Late Payment*", (Law Commission, 2014). *http://www.lawcom.gov.uk/ wp-content/uploads/2015/03/lc353_insurance-contract-law.pdf* [Accessed 24 June 2016] at para.8.68. See now *Jetivia SA v Bilta (UK) Ltd (In Liquidation)* [2015] UKSC 23; [2015] 2 W.L.R. 1168.

[67]   Law Commission "*Insurance Contract Law: Business Disclosure; Warranties; Insurers' Remedies for Fraudulent Claims; and Late Payment*", (Law Commission, 2014). *http://www.lawcom.gov.uk/ wp-content/uploads/2015/03/lc353_insurance-contract-law.pdf* [Accessed 24 June 2016] at paras 8.70 to 8.71.

(b) what is known to one or more of the individuals who are responsible for the insured's insurance."

Alongside the individual's actual knowledge, an individual insured will be attributed with the knowledge of those "responsible for the insured's insurance" subject to any exclusion under the *Hampshire Land* principle discussed above at para.5-030. This would apply to the knowledge of the insured's broker or agent, although such knowledge is subject to a number of more nuanced rules regarding the types of information which will and will not be imputed onto the insured from its broker, discussed below at paras 5-041 to 5-050. An individual insured may also be held to have constructive knowledge of information held by other people under the requirement to conduct a reasonable search, discussed below at paras 5-036 to 5-038.

5-032   **Insured is a non-individual.**   Whilst the knowledge held by an individual is simply a matter of fact and evidence, there are difficult questions surrounding the knowledge that will be attributed to a corporation or other artificial legal personality. The problem has traditionally arisen in the field of corporate regulation, where it is often necessary to distinguish between the actions of low-level employees that are primarily attributed to the individual and the actions of those directors and managers who are the embodiment of the "directing mind and will" of the company such that they can be said to be actions of the company itself rather than just actions of the individual. Lord Denning's statement of the law in *HL Bolton (Engineering) Co Ltd v TJ Graham & Sons Ltd*[68] makes this distinction clear, as he held:

"Some of the people in the company are mere servants and agents who are nothing more than hands to do the work and cannot be said to represent the mind or will. Others are directors and managers who represent the directing mind and will of the company and control what it does. The state of mind of those managers is the state of mind of the company and is treated by the law as such."[69]

Beyond just the "directing mind and will" of the company, more recent case law has recognised that there may be other individuals whose actions will need to be attributed to the company in order for particular corporate offences to be properly regulated. The Law Commission used the example of a supermarket clerk selling a video classified as "18" to a 14-year-old, where it is clearly the actions and knowledge of the sales clerk that would be pertinent to the offence rather than those of the managers or the company board. Whether these actions can be attributed to the company will be determined by the interpretation of the regulatory provision in question and a consideration of whether a wider test for attribution would further the purposes of those regulations, which can introduce a degree of uncertainty about how the provision will operate before it first appears before the courts. Lord Hoffman in *Meridian Global Funds Management Asia Ltd v Securities Commission*[70] considered that such determinations would need be made individually for each provision and on the basis of a purposive interpretation of the statute in question. He outlined the enquiry as follows:

---

[68]   *HL Bolton Engineering Co Ltd v TJ Graham & Sons Ltd* [1957] 1 Q.B. 159; [1956] 3 W.L.R. 804.
[69]   See above, fn.68 at 172.
[70]   *Meridian Global Funds Management Asia Ltd v Securities Commission* [1995] 2 A.C. 500 at 507; [1995] 3 W.L.R. 413; [1995] 3 All E.R. 918.

"Whose act (or knowledge, or state of mind) was for this purpose intended to count as the act etc of the company? One finds the answer to the question by applying the usual canons of interpretation, taking into account the language of the rule (if it is a statute) and its content and policy."

Though the Law Commission was persuaded that this approach to attribution was clearly the correct one, it was less enamoured with the uncertainty that would be created in circumstances where it was up to the courts to determine the width of the attribution test based on their reading of a particular statutory instrument.[71] The new provisions were designed to clarify the disclosure duties on a prospective insured and it would be undesirable if such a vital element of a corporate insured's deemed knowledge fell to be determined only retrospectively in the courtroom. The Law Commission therefore stepped away from including the "directing mind and will" test within the statute in favour of clearer provisions identifying both the high level directors and managers who represent the more narrow embodiment of the "directing mind and will" of the company and the specific individuals whose knowledge will be attributed to the company for the purposes of the fair presentation requirements. Those other individuals were identified under s.18 of the MIA in *PCW syndicates v PCW reinsurers*[72] as the "employees whose business it was to arrange insurance for the company", and the Law Commission adopted this approach. Section 4(3) of the 2015 Act therefore provides that the knowledge attributed to a non-individual insured will be both the knowledge of that insured's senior management and the knowledge of any individuals who are directly involved with the placement of the insurance. It states:

"(3) An insured who is not an individual knows only what is known to one or more of the individuals who are—
(a) part of the insured's senior management, or
(b) responsible for the insured's insurance."

Whilst the knowledge held by other individuals within the corporation may be relevant under the requirement to conduct a reasonable search, it is important to distinguish between the constructive knowledge of the corporation and the attributed knowledge of the corporation in circumstances where a particular employee is intending to defraud the insurer and it must be determined whether the company would be imputed with the fraudulent knowledge and would thus be guilty of non-disclosure. Where the individual's knowledge is caught only constructively under the obligation to conduct a reasonable search, it is clear that the fraudulent knowledge will not normally be imputed to the corporation as the corporation could not have discovered the details of the fraud by making reasonable enquiries of the fraudster. The position is more complicated where the individual's knowledge will be attributed to the corporation, and whether the fraudulent knowledge is similarly attributed will depend on the operation of the *Hampshire Land* principle discussed above at para.5-030.

Senior management. As discussed above, the Law Commission utilised the concept of "senior management" for the purposes of a corporate insured's   **5-033**

---

[71] Law Commission "*Insurance Contract Law: Business Disclosure; Warranties; Insurers' Remedies for Fraudulent Claims; and Late Payment*", (Law Commission, 2014). *http://www.lawcom.gov.uk/wp-content/uploads/2015/03/lc353_insurance-contract-law.pdf* [Accessed 24 June 2016] at para.8.14.
[72] *PCW syndicates v PCW reinsurers* [1996] 1 W.L.R. 1136 at 1142; [1996] 1 All E.R. 774; [1996] 1 Lloyd's Rep. 241.

knowledge rather than relying on the common law test of the corporation's "directing mind and will." The intention was to replicate the effect of the common law test without including its wider applications and so:

"The definition would include (and be more or less limited to) board members or their equivalent in a non-corporate organisation. It is not generally intended to capture, for example, regional or middle managers. It replicates the common law 'directing mind and will' test, but without its broader extensions."[73]

The senior management of a corporation is defined by s.4(8)(c) of the 2015 Act in the following manner:

"(c) "senior management" means those individuals who play significant roles in the making of decisions about how the insured's activities are to be managed or organised."

As there is a diverse range of legal entities, other than companies, who may wish to procure an insurance policy, the test refers to those individuals who manage the affairs of the entity and play a significant role in decision making rather than relying upon job title or a particular ranking in the corporate hierarchy. The Law Commission helpfully set out the individuals they consider to be caught by this definition for various different types of entity that may wish to procure insurance in the following passage:

"We appreciate that legal persons includes a diverse range of entities beyond registered companies. This has implications for the approach to identifying the highest level of management of the entity. It might be helpful to consider who we think would be the 'senior management' in different situations.

(1)   Limited liability partnership (LLP) – normally, an LLP would have a board. We expect that the board would constitute the 'senior management'.
(2)   National company – the board would constitute the senior management.
(3)   Multinational or global corporation with subsidiaries – this will depend on how the particular insurance policy is structured. As we have discussed, we think that this type of policy would usually be construed as a number of separate composite contracts of insurance. On this basis, each entity would be an 'insured' with fair presentation obligations and the knowledge of the board of the relevant insured would be attributed to it.
(4)   Local authority – the Executive (or equivalent) would constitute the senior management.
(5)   Charitable Incorporated Organisation (CIO) or Scottish Charitable Incorporated Organisation (SCIO) – the charity trustees would constitute the senior management." [74]

Though the courts will be free to depart from these recommendations to suit the needs of a particular case, such recommendations may prove to be persuasive or, in the context of multinational corporations and local authorities, at the very least frame the enquiry the courts are likely to undergo in order to identify the individuals who constitute "senior management."

5-034   **Responsible for the insured's insurance.**   The second limb of an insured's attributed knowledge captures the knowledge held by all individuals who are responsible for the insured's insurance. If the insured is an individual, those "responsible for the insured's insurance" will typically be the insured's broker or agent and the scope of the knowledge imputed from that broker will be determined

---

[73] Law Commission "*Insurance Contract Law: Business Disclosure; Warranties; Insurers' Remedies for Fraudulent Claims; and Late Payment*", (Law Commission, 2014). *http://www.lawcom.gov.uk/wp-content/uploads/2015/03/lc353_insurance-contract-law.pdf* [Accessed 24 June 2016] at para.8.55.
[74] See above, fn.73 at para.8.54.

by the specific rules introduced to cover the attribution of knowledge from a broker, discussed in greater detail below at paras 5-041 to 5-050.

The position is slightly more complex where the insured is a non-individual. Whilst those "responsible for the insured's insurance" can similarly include external brokers or contractors, the wording of the statute is also intended to capture the knowledge of those working in the insurance department of the corporation itself such as risk managers and others who are involved in the insurance procurement process. Whilst the knowledge of external brokers or contractors will be subject to the same limitations applicable to brokers generally, internal risk managers are treated as part of the "directing mind and will" of the company and will therefore have all their knowledge (subject to the *Hampshire Land* principle) attributed to the corporation.[75] Accordingly, s.4(8)(b) of the 2015 Act is worded to capture both external brokers and internal employees. It states:

> "(b)   an individual is responsible for the insured's insurance if the individual participates on behalf of the insured in the process of procuring the insured's insurance (whether the individual does so as the insured's employee or agent, as an employee of the insured's agent or in any other capacity)."

There are two important points to note about this definition. The first is that it applies to "an individual" who is responsible for the insured's insurance, not a corporation or other legal entity. As such, it will only be the knowledge of a particular broker rather than the knowledge held by his entire brokerage firm that will be attributed to the insured. The second point to note is that the Law Commission have drafted this provision to be intentionally wide, catching any individual who participates in any stage of the placement process of the policy. This would include individuals involved in "collating information about the risk for the purposes of the disclosure obligation, negotiating with insurers or brokers, giving instructions to brokers on behalf of the insured or approving tenders."[76] Finally, it is clear that a prospective insured will not be able to escape the attribution of knowledge from those who arrange their insurance by splitting the procurement process into different stages that will be handled between different teams. The Law Commission notes:

> "Such people may be risk managers or a more general procurement officer or team, for example. They may also be external contractors. The individuals concerned may well be quite junior (particularly in some small and medium sized companies). If the final purchasing decision is escalated, we think the knowledge of both the people who compiled the information and the people making the final purchase decision should be attributed to the insured."[77]

This definition may prove to have surprising consequences in the context of CAR insurance. Where the employer takes out a policy on behalf of the contractor and any subcontractors, the policy is treated as "composite insurance" that represents a bundle of separate insurance policies agreed between each party to the building contract and the insurer. The effect of this legal fiction is that the employer is ef-

---

[75]   The inclusion of employees responsible for the placement of the insurance policy within the "directing mind and will" of the company for the purposes of placement was taken from the case of *PCW Syndicates v PCW Reinsurers*, as discussed above at para.5-032. The *Hampshire Land* principle is discussed above at para.5-030.

[76]   Law Commission "*Insurance Contract Law: Business Disclosure; Warranties; Insurers' Remedies for Fraudulent Claims; and Late Payment*", (Law Commission, 2014). *http://www.lawcom.gov.uk/ wp-content/uploads/2015/03/lc353_insurance-contract-law.pdf* [Accessed 24 June 2016] at para.8.63.

[77]   See above, fn.76 at para.8.64.

fectively made responsible for placing the insurance policy on behalf of the contractor and any subcontractors, and would therefore appear to be subject to the same rules of attribution of knowledge as those applying to a normal insurance broker or outside agent who places a policy on behalf of an insured. Although the employer's knowledge would, generally, be treated as the constructive knowledge of the contractor and any subcontractors under the requirement to conduct a reasonable search, the re-qualification of the employer as the individual responsible for the insurance of their contractors may lead to a surprising result where the employer conducts a fraud against the insurer. As the employer's knowledge is directly attributed to the contractor and subcontractors, the fraudulent knowledge would also be attributed and every policy under the "composite bundle" would be tainted by the fraud. This position can be contrasted against that where the employer takes out the CAR policy but it is the contractor that defrauds the insurer, in which case the contractor's knowledge would not be attributed to the employer as the contractor is not the employer's agent, and fraudulent knowledge cannot be caught constructively.

The second limb of an insured's knowledge may appear to operate most unfairly in relation to CAR insurance because there can often be a large number of parties insured who have no connection with each other aside from through the construction contracts. This position is to be contrasted with that in relation to post-contractual fraudulent claims, in which the fraudulent party's policy will be the only one affected by by its fraud.[78]

5-035   **Contracting out.**   As with all other areas of the 2015 Act, the parties are free to contract out of the default regime in favour of imposing bespoke obligations on the insured so long as those arrangements comply with the transparency requirements.[79] It may be desirable for the parties to define more broadly whose knowledge will be attributed to the insured rather than relying on the reasonable search requirement, which may be "particularly appropriate if there is an employee or other agent of the insured whose knowledge will be particularly relevant to the insured risk."[80] Similarly, the parties may wish to exclude the knowledge of particular people from the knowledge that would be attributed to the insured. The Law Commission give the example of a group professional indemnity policy purchased for the benefit of the directors of the company, where it would clearly defeat the purposes of the policy if the knowledge of one fraudulent director would be attributed to all of the directors and hence taint all of the policies.[81]

(v)   The insured's constructive knowledge

5-036   **Reasonable search duty.**   By far the most radical reform to the insured's duty of fair presentation under the 2015 Act is the requirement that the insured conduct a reasonable search of the information and materials available to it before entering the policy. Under the MIA, there was some uncertainty regarding the extent of an insured's constructive knowledge and particularly as to whether the insured ought

---

[78]   See below, para.5-132.
[79]   See below, para.5-135.
[80]   Law Commission "*Insurance Contract Law: Business Disclosure; Warranties; Insurers' Remedies for Fraudulent Claims; and Late Payment*", (Law Commission, 2014). *http://www.lawcom.gov.uk/wp-content/uploads/2015/03/lc353_insurance-contract-law.pdf* [Accessed 24 June 2016] at para.8.93.
[81]   See above, fn.80 at para.8.94.

to know only what they had "turned a blind eye" to or whether this extended to a duty to make reasonable enquiries.[82] Beyond mere clarification of the scope of the law, the Law Commission considered that it was crucial to include a positive search obligation on the insured in order to encourage the reciprocal exchange of information that was necessary to promote an effective insurance placement process. It noted:

> "Conducting a reasonable search of information available to the insured is part of a good insurance placement process. The insurer is entitled to expect that the insured knows more about its operations than that which the directing mind and will or senior management happen to know, particularly in large, potentially multinational companies where the board members or equivalent could not generally be expected to have more than a high level, strategic overview."[83]

The Law Commission's intention was that the reasonable search requirement should capture most of the information necessary for the fair presentation of risk, with far narrower provisions for knowledge that would be directly attributed to the insured. The "reasonable search" is therefore defined widely by s.4(6) of the 2015 Act which states:

> "(6) Whether an individual or not, an insured ought to know what should reasonably have been revealed by a reasonable search of information available to the insured (whether the search is conducted by making enquiries or by any other means)."

There are three key elements which determine the scope of the required search by the insured: first, what constitutes a "reasonable search"; secondly, what "should reasonably have been revealed"; and thirdly, what is "available" to the insured. A further layer of complexity is added to the interpretation of these requirements as there is the potential for confusion surrounding the extent to which each requirement is subjective or objective, or perhaps a blend of the two. An illustrative example would be that of a negligently run and disorganised company, as one could rightly question whether a reasonable search of that negligent company under the 2015 Act would be judged against the standards of what a reasonable search would have revealed in a reasonably organised and well-run company, or whether the required search would only be judged by reference to a hypothe- tical reasonable search of the insured company as it actually was. The Law Commission give guidance as to how each element of the reasonable search test is expected to operate.

Reasonable search.   The scope of the search necessary to satisfy the require-   **5-037**
ment of reasonableness "will depend on the size, nature and complexity of the business" and will be judged objectively "by reference to a reasonable, prudent insured in that class."[84] Because the wording of the statute encompasses searches conducted by making enquiries "or by any other means", it is able to capture information held by individuals, data contained within electronic or physical records and may potentially include any other data so long as it would have been reasonable for a prospective insured in that industry and size of business to have included it within their search. Although this may appear to raise questions about whether the provision could capture information that could be obtained, for example, by conducting a new groundwork survey of the construction site, such information may not meet the requirement of availability and would not be included within the ambit of the

---

[82]   See below, para.6-011.
[83]   See above, fn.80 at para.8.78.
[84]   See above, fn.80 at para.8.83.

required search.[85] Where there is any uncertainty surrounding the extent of the necessary search in the context of larger companies arranging more complex or extensive cover, the Law Commission considered that the requirements of the search could be negotiated and clarified by the parties themselves rather than relying on the basic statutory provisions. The Law Commission stated:

"For large insurance contracts, we hope that the parties will discuss and reach agreement on the nature of the search to be undertaken. This process would be made much easier by the development of industry-produced protocols on the types of search which are expected."[86]

Although the industry protocols are primarily expected to introduce guidance to help the insured determine the information that would be "material" to the underwriting decision,[87] it would therefore appear that the Law Commission expect such protocols to also detail the requirements of a reasonable search for a participant within a particular industry. Should such protocols become a reality of the insurance market, then it is likely that the reasonable search duty will be judged primarily against the requirements of the protocol with the statutory provisions playing a secondary role to cover more exceptional or unexpected circumstances.

5-038   **Matters which should reasonably have been revealed.**   The insured is required to disclose all matters which should reasonably have been revealed by undertaking a reasonable search, as judged against the parameters of the search that would have been conducted by the reasonable, prudent insured in that class. Since a reasonable search or enquiry is unlikely to uncover an individual's fraudulent or negligent withholding of information, this requirement is the principal cause of the delineation of an insured's constructive knowledge from the knowledge imputed to it by attribution.[88] Indeed, the Law Commission note that the wording is principally targeted at excluding an individual's fraudulent or negligent withholding of information, stating:

"We recommend that the insured ought to know only what should reasonably have been revealed by the reasonable search. The insured should not be taken to have constructive knowledge of information which could not reasonably have been discovered, such as information which would have been withheld through negligence or fraud."[89]

What remains partially unclear is whether the test of what should reasonably have been revealed is entirely subjective or also contains an objective element. An insured should not expect an employee to admit to its own negligence, but where the insured's entire organisation suffers from negligent or inadequate record keeping it is uncertain whether the information that would have been in those records had the company been well run would also be caught as matters which should reasonably have been revealed. For example, a prudent contractor placing a project specific policy to cover the construction of a power plant would presumably search through its records of previous similar projects and its corresponding claims his-

---

85   See below, para.5-039.

86   Law Commission *"Insurance Contract Law: Business Disclosure; Warranties; Insurers' Remedies for Fraudulent Claims; and Late Payment"*, (Law Commission, 2014). *http://www.lawcom.gov.uk/wp-content/uploads/2015/03/lc353_insurance-contract-law.pdf* [Accessed 24 June 2016] at para.8.85.

87   See above, para.5-024.

88   See above, para.5-028.

89   Law Commission *"Insurance Contract Law: Business Disclosure; Warranties; Insurers' Remedies for Fraudulent Claims; and Late Payment"*, (Law Commission, 2014). *http://www.lawcom.gov.uk/wp-content/uploads/2015/03/lc353_insurance-contract-law.pdf* [Accessed 24 June 2016] at para.8.86.

tory before making the presentation of risk to the insurer. If the contractor company fails to keep adequate records of that claims history, then the objective "reasonable search" would include a search through all of the records that the company does possess but the search could not "reasonably have revealed" records which were never in fact in existence. It would appear from the wording of the statute that the scope of the required search is judged objectively but the content uncovered by the search can only be judged subjectively, although it is unfortunate that neither the Law Commission report nor the explanatory notes to the 2015 Act spell out the exact position.

Available to the insured.   The information and materials that will be held to be   **5-039**
available to the insured are "necessarily a matter of fact in the circumstances of a particular case."[90] Since the requirement to conduct a reasonable search could potentially be used to impose a breadth of knowledge on the insured that would be particularly wide or uncertain, the Law Commission sought to narrow the scope of the search by limiting it to only those materials, records and individuals which are "available" to the insured. The intention from the Law Commission appears to be that those matters which are available would include anything held within the company, as it stated:

> "We would generally expect it to include information held within the insured's organisation, including in computer records and known to employees (within reason). We think that how far an insured must go to question individual employees will vary widely depending on how many there are. It might be, for example, that all managers of a certain level should be consulted."[91]

Further clarity is given by s.4(7) of the 2015 Act, which provides that the information that could be discovered through the search is not just limited to information held internally. Whilst it does not demarcate the exact parameters around the scope of the required external search, the provision does provide specific examples of which external information would be caught:

> "(7)   In subsection (6) 'information' includes information held within the insured's organisation or by any other person (such as the insured's agent or a person for whom cover is provided by the contract of insurance)."

In the context of CAR insurance, it would therefore appear to be the case that each party sharing the benefit of the cover, or identified as a prospective insured at the time of placement, would be required to disclose all of the material information that could have reasonably been revealed through a search of information held by all other such parties.

Contracting out.   As with all other areas of the 2015 Act, the parties are free to   **5-040**
contract out of the default regime in favour of imposing bespoke terms which delineate the exact pre-contractual search required of the insured. Given that there are a number of potential uncertainties regarding the application of the reasonable search provisions to larger companies and multinational corporate entities, this may prove to be desirable where the scope of the required search is more indeterminate and the insured is keen to ensure that the policy will respond as anticipated.

---

[90]   See above, fn.89 at para.8.88.
[91]   See above, fn.89 at para.8.89.

(vi)   The broker's knowledge

5-041   **Introduction.**   It is common practice for employers and contractors involved in large-scale construction projects to engage the services of a specialist construction insurance broker in order to arrange the placement of the CAR policy. Where this practice is adopted, the knowledge of the broker can have a substantial impact on the insured's disclosure duties and this is equally as true under the provisions of the 2015 Act as it was under the MIA.[92] One of the primary purposes of the 2015 Act was to promote an effective reciprocal exchange of information by the parties before the placement of the policy, and the Law Commission recognised that information held by the broker could provide a critical fund of knowledge to the insurer that was essential for an effective underwriting decision to be made and for the premium to be set at an adequate level. This information could include detailed historical knowledge accrued over the course of a long-standing business relationship between the agent and the prospective insured, as well as more generic risk data about a particular type of risk or field of insurance obtained by the broker over the course of acting for hundreds of clients in a variety of capacities. Whilst the Law Commission recognised that an insurer would be keen to benefit from both aspects of the broker's knowledge, there was also a danger that if the disclosure duties were drafted too widely then the broker would be required to disclose confidential information relating to a number of other clients which would place it in a position of conflicting interests. The 2015 Act therefore strikes a careful balance between the useful information held by the broker that will form part of the insured's disclosure duties, and all other sensitive information that the broker will not be required to disclose.

5-042   **Extension of insured's duty to disclose.**   Previously there was some confusion under the provisions of the MIA as to whether the duty to disclose knowledge held by the broker attached to the broker himself or whether this was a mere extension of the insured's own disclosure duties. Although s.19 of the MIA appeared to place this duty onto the broker, the effect of any non-disclosure was to give insurers the right to avoid the policy and so the duty could best be understood as one placed onto the insured. The Law Commission considered that this position was somewhat opaque under the MIA[93] and so the 2015 Act makes clear that the broker's knowledge forms part and parcel of the insured's knowledge that will need to be disclosed.[94]

5-043   **Individual broker.**   Section 4(2)(b) and 4(3)(b) of the 2015 Act attribute the insured with the knowledge held by *individuals* responsible for the insured's insurance. The insured will therefore only be attributed with the knowledge of that specific broker engaged to arrange the insurance policy, rather than the knowledge of their entire brokerage firm.

5-044   **Multiple agents or brokers.**   The 2015 Act provides the following definition of an individual responsible for the insured's insurance under s.4(8)(b):

---

[92]   See below, para.6-020.

[93]   Law Commission "*Insurance Contract Law: Business Disclosure; Warranties; Insurers' Remedies for Fraudulent Claims; and Late Payment*", (Law Commission, 2014). *http://www.lawcom.gov.uk/ wp-content/uploads/2015/03/lc353_insurance-contract-law.pdf* [Accessed 24 June 2016] at para.9.1.

[94]   See above, para.5-034.

"(b) an individual is responsible for the insured's insurance if the individual participates on behalf of the insured in the process of procuring the insured's insurance (whether the individual does so as the insured's employee or agent, as an employee of the insured's agent or in any other capacity)."

An individual responsible for the insured's insurance will therefore include any individual who participates in any stage of the procurement process, and will accordingly apply to each broker or agent where the insurance is arranged by a chain of brokers. When considering the disclosure obligations of the insured in relation to external agents, it is also worth remembering that individuals whose knowledge is not attributed to the insured may still have that knowledge caught under the requirement to conduct a reasonable search. In relation to this point, the Law Commission notes:

"The knowledge of other agents, such as technical advisors and lawyers, would not be caught by the provision unless they take an active role in the insurance-buying process (perhaps, for example, if a surveyor is asked to report on a building for the purposes of obtaining insurance for it). Instead, information held by other agents may be captured by the obligation to make a reasonable search."[95]

Confidential information. Section 4(4)(b) of the 2015 Act places an important limitation on the knowledge attributed from the broker in order to prevent a conflict of interest arising under the new provisions, as it states: **5-045**

"(4) An insured is not by virtue of subsection (2)(b) or (3)(b) taken to know confidential information known to an individual if—
  (a)   the individual is, or is an employee of, the insured's agent; and
  (b)   the information was acquired by the insured's agent (or by an employee of that agent) through a business relationship with a person who is not connected with the contract of insurance."

The provision is notable in its approach to the scope of attributed knowledge that will need to be disclosed to the insurer. Rather than carving out that small portion of the broker's knowledge which is directly relevant to a particular insured, the provision instead potentially captures all knowledge held by the broker save for anything which is confidential to other clients. The provision is therefore able to capture generic risk information learned whilst acting for a number of other clients, save for any specific details that are held by the broker in confidence. Section 4(4)(b) also serves to ensure that any knowledge held by the broker from previous dealings with the prospective insured will not be carved out of the disclosure duties despite being "confidential".

This position also raises an interesting question about the way in which the confidential information obtained by the broker over the course of acting for many clients can become general or generic enough to require disclosure, and where the line will be drawn between the two. The Law Commission discussed the problem in the following extract, and considered that the broker's confidentiality duties must be given primacy in order to avoid placing him in a conflict of interest:

"However, when brokers receive information about risks or possible claims facing particular clients, matters become less easy when that information could potentially be relevant to the risks which other clients are seeking to insure. Take a case where a broker acts for E, which manufactures medical

---

[95] Law Commission "*Insurance Contract Law: Business Disclosure; Warranties; Insurers' Remedies for Fraudulent Claims; and Late Payment*", (Law Commission, 2014). *http://www.lawcom.gov.uk/wp-content/uploads/2015/03/lc353_insurance-contract-law.pdf* [Accessed 24 June 2016] at para.9.32.

implants. If the broker is told of risks associated with the implants this information may be relevant not only to E's insurer but also to an insurer providing liability cover to a clinic using the implant, for whom the broker also acts. Again, if the broker acts for a motor manufacturer, F, and receives information suggesting problems with the brakes on its trucks, this may influence the insurer of a haulier using those trucks. However, we do not think that the knowledge of the broker should be attributed to the clinic, or the haulier, for the purposes of the duty of fair presentation if the broker has a duty of confidentiality not to reveal that information."[96]

Where the precise line is to be drawn between confidential and non-confidential information will therefore be left for the courts to interpret, though it would seem likely that judges will err on the side of caution in order to avoid inadvertently placing brokers or agents in a position where there is a real risk that they will be in a conflict of interests and unable to fulfil their professional duties.

5-046   **Fraudulent knowledge.**   As the broker's knowledge is caught by attribution rather than just through the requirement to conduct a reasonable search, it is possible for fraudulent knowledge to be imputed to the insured in circumstances where a broker intends to commit a fraud. The imputation of knowledge and the consequences for the insured are discussed in more detail above at para.5-030, but the general position is likely to be that a fraudulent or negligent withholding by the broker will be directly attributed to the insured unless that insured is the primary target of the broker's fraud.

5-047   **Blind eye knowledge.**   As discussed above at para.5-029, the broker's or agent's knowledge will be subject to the same general provisions that apply to all knowledge under s.6 of the 2015 Act. The broker will therefore be imputed with any knowledge that he has deliberately turned a blind eye to.

5-048   **Reasonable search.**   Alongside the direct attribution of the broker's knowledge to the insured, knowledge held by the broker or agent can also be caught under the requirement that the insured conduct a reasonable search before entering into the policy. This is evident from s.4(7) of the 2015 Act, which provides that the information that can be captured by the reasonable search can include:

"(7) In subsection (6) "information" includes information held within the insured's organisation or by any other person (such as the insured's agent or a person for whom cover is provided by the contract of insurance)."

The first point to note about this definition is that it purports to capture a much wider array of the insured's agents than just those involved in the placement of the policy, such as external lawyers or technical advisors who may hold information which is material to the risk in question. Whether the knowledge of such agents will be included within the reasonable search requirement will be an evaluative question, dependent on the facts and circumstances of the case, and in any case largely determined by the type of cover being sought by the insured. By way of example, the Law Commission note that the reasonable search requirement could extend to the insured's solicitor when placing a professional indemnity policy but is far less likely to extend to that solicitor when taking out a building and contents policy.[97]

The second point to note from the provision is that unlike the broker's attributed knowledge, the information uncovered through a reasonable search is not

---

[96]   See above, fn.95 at para.9.45.
[97]   See above, fn.95 at para.9.38.

limited to information held by any particular individuals and can therefore incorporate knowledge held across a brokerage firm rather than just the single broker. Whilst this may seem to be an unduly wide array of information that the insured will need to obtain and consider before an adequate presentation of risk can be made, the Law Commission considered that the requirement for the information to be "available to the insured" limits the scope of such constructive knowledge to within reasonable boundaries. It noted:

> "Furthermore, information caught by the reasonable search requirement will potentially cover all information held by the agent's organisation, rather than just information known to the individual agent acting for the insured. However, the information which will be caught is limited by the fact that the information must be *available to the insured*. The insured cannot be regarded as having unlimited access to its agents' records. In particular, it will not have access to confidential information held by its agents on behalf of other clients."[98]

The final point to note regarding the insured's constructive knowledge of information held by its agents is that the requirement to carry out the search rests on the insured and not on the agent. Although the agent will frequently be the individual that actually carries out the search, it is still a duty on the insured and so will still be limited by what is available to *that insured* rather than what is available to that agent. As such, it is difficult to imagine how information held by the brokerage firm that does not relate to that particular client could ever form part of the information unlocked through the reasonable search requirement, as such information would never have been "available" to the insured in the first place.

CAR policy. The rules relating to agency and the attribution of knowledge may lead to some unexpected results in the context of CAR insurance. The CAR policy itself is treated as a "composite policy" comprising a bundle of separate policies between each insured and the insurer. This has the potential to cause a number of peculiarities concerning the effect of a non-disclosure by the employer or the contractor on the cover provided to the other insureds. The first point to note is that each insured, identifiable as such at the time of placement of the policy (an "identified insured"), will be required to conduct its own reasonable search of the information and materials available to it before entering the policy, which will normally include information held by the other identified insureds. However, as the CAR policy is treated as a bundle of separate insurance policies, the party that takes out the policy on behalf of all insureds (identified or not) is, under the provisions of the 2015 Act, an agent responsible for arranging their insurance. For example, where the employer takes out the CAR policy for the building project it will be acting as agent for the contractor and any subcontractors and so they will be attributed with the knowledge held by the employer which they must also disclose. This creates an obvious disparity in the disclosure obligations owed by each party, as the employer will only have to disclose what could have been uncovered through a reasonable search of information available to the identified contractor and subcontractors, whilst the identified contractor and subcontractors would have to disclose both the information uncovered by a reasonable search as well as all of the information imputed to them from the employer. If the employer perpetrates a fraud against the insurers, it would therefore be possible that the fraudulent knowledge would be attributed to every other named insured and would therefore taint the entire bundle of insurance contracts, whereas a fraud perpetrated by the contractor or subcontrac-

5-049

---

98 See above, fn.95 at para.9.39.

tor would only taint their own individual policy. Another unusual quirk of this analysis is that the information attributed from an agent is only that individual's own knowledge rather than the knowledge of the entire company. Thus, the contractor and subcontractors would be attributed with the knowledge of the risk managers within the employer's underwriting department who actually placed the CAR policy but would not be attributed with the rest of the knowledge held by that employer.

In reality these issues are unlikely to be of importance. It is often the case that the employer takes out the policy before the contractor and any subcontractors have even been selected for the project, and so the possibility of such points arising before the courts is small. Equally, where the insured takes out annual rather than project specific cover it will, similarly, be unable to conduct a reasonable search of parties that have not yet been identified and may not be until many months after the placement of the policy.

5-050   **Contracting out.**   As with all other parts of the 2015 Act, the parties are free to contract out of the provisions concerning the broker's knowledge and its relevance to the insured's disclosure obligations so long as any changes are made in accordance with the transparency requirements, discussed below at para.5-135.

(vii)   The insurer's knowledge

5-051   **Counterweight to disclosure.**   Replicating the previous position under s.18(3)(b) of the MIA, the 2015 Act provides that the insured will not be required to disclose those matters which are already within the insurer's knowledge in presenting the proposed risk. It is a cornerstone of the insurance placement process that an insured is entitled to expect an insurer to have a general understanding of matters relevant to the field of insurance in question, and the insured will not therefore be required to disclose those general matters before taking out the policy. Equally, if the insured has a longstanding business relationship with a particular insurer then it may be reasonable for the insured to rely on the insurer's knowledge and records relating to the insured's previous claims rather than having to disclose each of them again. The insurer's knowledge therefore forms an important counterweight to the disclosure obligations of the insured, and where an insurer alleges that there has been a qualifying breach of the insured's disclosure duties it may be open to the insured to argue that the matter complained of was one which the insurer should already have had knowledge of, subject to the insured being able to prove this on the balance of probabilities.

Although the substance of this exception has not substantially changed from that under the MIA, the 2015 Act introduces a number of reforms aimed at clarifying the scope of the knowledge that the insurer will be held to possess. The new provisions are also intended to reflect the modern realities of electronic record keeping that can leave the insurer with a significant repository of material information at its fingertips, and the Law Commission noted that:

> "The insurance (and reinsurance) market has evolved significantly since the 1906 Act and the cases that preceded it. Modern communication, particularly the internet, has led to a modern professional insurer being able actively to inform himself about a risk in a way that his predecessors, with access to far less information in times when communications were far slower, could not."[99]

---

[99]   See above, fn.95 at para.10.29.

Accordingly, s.3(5) of the 2015 Act lists the following three exceptions to an insured's disclosure duties. It provides:

"(5) In the absence of enquiry, subsection (4) does not require the insured to disclose a circumstance if—...
   (b) the insurer knows it,
   (c) the insurer ought to know it,
   (d) the insurer is presumed to know it."

The ambit of each of these exceptions is clarified under s.5 of the 2015 Act.

What the insurer knows.   Since the majority of insurers operating within the   **5-052** industry will be companies rather than individuals,[100] the determining insurer's knowledge is subject to the same conceptual challenges encountered when attributing knowledge to any artificial legal entity.[101] Although the common law test for attribution to a company will looks primarily look for its "directing mind and will" in order to which individuals' actions and knowledge represent the embodied will of that company, the 2015 Act does not replicate this test for the insurer's knowledge and similarly does not employ the definition of "senior management" used for the attribution to a non-individual insured. The Law Commission considered that the knowledge held by the board of directors of an insurance company would in fact be of little relevance to the assessment of risk, as those directors would not normally have any input in the underwriting decision or the fixing of the premium and would not normally hold any information relevant to the specific risk or the specific insured.[102] Instead, it is the knowledge held by the individual underwriter that will be material and so the 2015 Act replicates the wider applications of the "directing mind and will" test to catch those who participate in the insurance placement process, but does not also target those at the top of the corporate hierarchy. Section 5(1) of the 2015 Act therefore provides:

"(1) For the purposes of section 3(5)(b), an insurer knows something only if it is known to one or more of the individuals who participate on behalf of the insurer in the decision whether to take the risk, and if so on what terms (whether the individual does so as the insurer's employee or agent, as an employee of the insurer's agent or in any other capacity)."

Beyond just the individual that makes the final underwriting decision, this provision will capture the knowledge of any individuals that participate in the setting of the premium or the inclusion of particular policy terms when accepting the specified risk. The Law Commission gave the following examples of the types of individuals that would be included under the provision:

"The definition is intended to catch any persons who play a meaningful role in the underwriting decision. If a team has been working on a big contract then we think the knowledge residing in that team and each individual member should be caught. If a risk is escalated to the underwriter's manager to be signed off, the manager is the person who makes the final underwriting decision but the original underwriter's knowledge is also attributed to the insurer. If the decision is made by a junior

---

[100] With some notable exceptions, for example any remaining individual Lloyd's Names.
[101] See above, para.5-032.
[102] Law Commission "*Insurance Contract Law: Business Disclosure; Warranties; Insurers' Remedies for Fraudulent Claims; and Late Payment*", (Law Commission, 2014). *http://www.lawcom.gov.uk/wp-content/uploads/2015/03/lc353_insurance-contract-law.pdf* [Accessed 24 June 2016] at para.10.38.

underwriter with a manager having ultimate responsibility for that decision, they would both be covered."[103]

The Law Commission also considered how the provision would operate where the insured purchases off-the-shelf insurance online by inputting data into a computer program which makes the decision electronically. In this instance, it will be the individuals "who signed off on the pricing structure and the risk weightings on which the program is based"[104] that have made the underwriting decision, and so their knowledge about the general risk would be attributed to the insured.

5-053 **Blind eye and fraudulent knowledge.** The generic provisions contained in s.6 of the 2015 Act that apply to all knowledge relevant to the presentation of risk will similarly apply to the insurer's knowledge. The insurer will therefore be held to know anything that it has "turned a blind eye" to and deliberately refrained from finding out, as discussed in greater detail above at para.5-029.

An insurer will not be attributed with the knowledge of any fraud being committed by its employee against the insurer, possibly in conjunction with the insured. The attribution of fraudulent knowledge is discussed in more detail above at para.5-030.

5-054 **What the insurer ought to know.** Although it is only the knowledge held by the specific underwriters who accept the risk that will be attributed to the insurer, the insurer may be held to have constructive knowledge of information held by other employees or agents and information contained within the insurer's records or files. Section 5(2) of the 2015 Act provides:

> "(2) For the purposes of section 3(5)(c), an insurer ought to know something only if—
>
> (a) an employee or agent of the insurer knows it, and ought reasonably to have passed on the relevant information to an individual mentioned in subsection (1), or
>
> (b) the relevant information is held by the insurer and is readily available to an individual mentioned in subsection (1)."

These provisions are noticeably different from those governing the constructive knowledge of the insured, which are based on the insured conducting a reasonable search of the information available to it before entering the policy. Although the 2015 Act is designed to discourage insurer passivity at the underwriting stage, there are limits to what an insurer can reasonably be expected to do before making the underwriting decision and it is the prospective insured who must present all of the information material to the risk, with there generally being only a limited exception covering matters already within the insurer's knowledge. Instead of the insurer having to conduct a search through the information held by its employees, agents, and physical or electronic records, the insurer's constructive knowledge will only consist of information held by the insurer's employees or agents who ought reasonably to have passed it on to the individual underwriter and those electronic or physical records which the underwriter has at its fingertips.

5-055 **An employee or agent knows it and ought reasonably to have passed it on.** The first portion of the insurer's constructive knowledge will consist of information known by employees or agents who do not participate in the decision

---

[103] See above, fn.102 at para.10.40.
[104] See above, fn.102 at para.10.41.

to underwrite the risk in question, but who nevertheless ought to have passed that information on to those who do. If the individual works in the underwriting department and is merely involved in an earlier stage of the placement process rather than the final decision, a court may construe that information as part of what ought to have been passed on to the underwriter. More difficult questions arise where the information is known to an agent or employee of the insurer who does not specifically work in the underwriting department, such as a surveyor asked to report on a prospective building site or a loss adjuster making a site visit on a previous unrelated claim. Whilst one would generally expect an agent hired to investigate matters pertaining to a particular insurance policy to pass that knowledge on to the underwriter in question, the more remote the employee or agent is from the underwriting decision and the policy, the less ready the courts are likely to be to make that assertion. In this regard, the Law Commission stated:

"A more difficult question arises where the information has been gathered in relation to a claim on a different policy. During our limited consultation on the draft clauses, DAC Beachcroft gave an example of the insurer's loss adjuster making a site visit in connection with such a claim. If the loss adjuster notices something unusual about the insured property (such as a thatched roof), ought it reasonably to have passed this back to the underwriter? We think that a loss adjuster is unlikely to have any relationship with the underwriter and would not be expected to pass information to them. Unlike a surveyor instructed by the underwriter to assess a risk, the loss adjuster's relationship is with the claims department and concerns a historic loss. However, if the loss adjuster includes information in a report to the claims department, this may be available to the underwriter under limb (b)."[105]

Although what ought to have been passed on to the underwriter in question will ultimately be a matter for the courts to assess in each case, it would seem likely that the insurer will not have the constructive knowledge of individuals entirely unconnected with a particular policy unless that information has been entered into the insurer's records and files.

Held by the insurer and readily available to the underwriter. The second portion of the insurer's constructive knowledge is derived from the physical and electronic records which are within the insurer's organisation and readily available to the underwriter. The Law Commission recognised that "historic data about policyholders will become an increasingly important source of data,"[106] and insurers should not be encouraged to ignore such a vital fund of information by keeping that data as part of the insured's disclosure obligations. However, any positive obligation on the insurer would need to be kept within a sensible remit in order to avoid placing too strong an obligation on them that could sterilise the efficiency of the insurance placement process. Section 5(2)(b) of the 2015 Act is therefore intended to "balance the competing interests of insured and insurer"[107] by only including information that is both "held by the insurer" and "readily available to the relevant insurers."

5-056

What is "readily available to the underwriter" is a subjective requirement based on the arrangement of the insurance firm and the capacity of the underwriter to consult records. The Law Commission considered that the key factors to determine whether claims information is available to the underwriter would be whether, in practice, the underwriting department had convenient access to that information in

---

[105] See above, fn.102 at para.10.48.
[106] See above, fn.102 at para.10.53.
[107] See above, fn.102 at para.10.52.

the insurers' systems. On this, the Law Commission comments:

> "However, insurers have been wary of accepting any positive obligation to search their records, particularly because claims information may not be available to the underwriting department. Further, insurers may hold information on a variety of outdated 'legacy' systems which cannot be searched by all staff ... Where the underwriter genuinely does not have electronic access to the claims department's records, the information contained there may not be 'readily available' to the underwriter."[108]

Rather than providing the insurer with an incentive to update its legacy records and supply information from the claims department to the underwriting department, the 2015 Act ostensibly encourages insurers to keep historical data out of reach of its underwriting department in order to reduce the amount of information that will be carved out of the insured's disclosure requirements. Nevertheless, one can reasonably expect that an insurer would be unlikely to forego the benefits of electronic record keeping simply to restrict the constructive knowledge of its underwriters, so the point is unlikely to bear any practical significance.

5-057   **What the insurer is presumed to know.**   Along with the insurer's actual and constructive knowledge, the 2015 Act also affixes the insurer with the knowledge that a prospective insured is entitled to expect a competent underwriter in a particular field to possess. Just as an insurer cannot remain passive during a presentation of risk without making enquiries when put on notice, an insurer similarly cannot rely on their own naivety in order to increase the breadth of the insured's disclosure obligations. Section 5(3) of the 2015 Act therefore provides:

> "(3) For the purposes of section 3(5)(d), an insurer is presumed to know—
> (a)   things which are common knowledge, and
> (b)   things which an insurer offering insurance of the class in question to insureds in the field of activity in question would reasonably be expected to know in the ordinary course of business."

As the provision is a mere restatement of the law under the MIA, the case law under s.18(3)(b) will continue to apply and "common knowledge" will be construed objectively according to those matters which a generally well-informed person might fairly be expected to know.[109] The Law Commission considered that the provision could be interpreted broadly to include information that is widely publicised on the internet and on social media, illustrated in the following example:

> "X, a well-known entertainer, is regularly rumoured in the mainstream media to have a drug problem and has not commenced libel proceedings against those making the allegations. When cancellation of event cover is sought for X's next tour, we think these rumours would be found to be matters of common knowledge that need not be disclosed to the underwriter."[110]

The circumstances an insurer would reasonably be expected to know in the ordinary course of business will vary considerably depending on the class of insurance and field of activity in question. In the context of CAR insurance, one could expect, for example, that an employer procuring a policy to cover an extension to an existing

---

[108] See above, fn.102 at paras 10.51 to 10.52.
[109] See below, para.6-027.
[110] Law Commission *"Insurance Contract Law: Business Disclosure; Warranties; Insurers' Remedies for Fraudulent Claims; and Late Payment"*, (Law Commission, 2014). *http://www.lawcom.gov.uk/wp-content/uploads/2015/03/lc353_insurance-contract-law.pdf* [Accessed 24 June 2016] at para.10.59.

structure would not need to explain to the insurer that the construction works may run the risk of upsetting the foundations of the original building and thereby causing subsidence or collapse. Similarly, an employer would not have to disclose to the insurer that it is the usual practice for rights of subrogation to be excluded by the building contract before taking out the policy. The degree of understanding that the insurer should be expected to have will depend on the industry in question, and insurers will usually be expected to "understand a broad outline of the risks."[111]

Contracting out.   As with all other parts of the 2015 Act, the parties are free to contract out of the default provisions in favour of adopting a more expansive or restrictive remit for the insurer's knowledge. This may be desirable if the prospective insured has used the same insurer for a number of consecutive years and wishes to ensure that it is not required to disclosure the entire claims history before taking out a policy, in case the insurer's records are contained within an outdated legacy system or are not available to the underwriting department. If any part of the policy reduces the knowledge attributed to the insurer and thereby increases the required disclosure from the insured, the insured will have been placed in a worse position than they would otherwise have been in under the 2015 Act and the changes must be made in accordance with the transparency requirements discussed below at para.5-135.

5-058

(viii)   Other exceptions

Diminishes the risk.   Section 3(5)(a) of the 2015 Act provides that a prospective insured need not disclose anything which diminishes the risk in question. This exception replicates s.18(3)(a) of the MIA with identical effect, and so the previous case law will continue to apply under the 2015 Act. This is discussed below at para.6-025.

5-059

Waiver.   Section 3(5)(e) of the 2015 Act provides that the insured will not need to disclose any information to which the insurer has waived the right to be told. Although this exception had a significant role to play under the MIA by limiting the insured's disclosure requirements when an insurer remained passive during the presentation of risk,[112] under the 2015 Act these concerns are instead mitigated under s.3(4)(b).[113] The remaining scope for the waiver exception to apply will therefore be diminished, though it can of course still be relied on, and established applications of the exception should remain, e.g. the implied waiver by an insurer of information beyond the scope of limited questions on the proposal form.[114]

5-060

(ix)   Sufficient information to put a prudent insurer on notice

Alternative to disclosure requirement.   The 2015 Act provides two alternative ways in which an insured may discharge its disclosure duties, the first by disclosing all information that is both material to the risk and within the insured's knowledge, and the second by providing an honest but not entirely comprehensive

5-061

---

[111]   See above, fn.110 at para.10.63.
[112]   See below, para.6-030.
[113]   See below, para.5-061.
[114]   See below, para.6-030.

disclosure which nevertheless puts the insurer on notice that further enquiries need to be made. Section 3(4) of the 2015 Act therefore provides:

"(4) The disclosure required is as follows, except as provided in subsection (5)—
(a) disclosure of every material circumstance which the insured knows or ought to know, or
(b) failing that, disclosure which gives the insurer sufficient information to put a prudent insurer on notice that it needs to make further enquiries for the purpose of revealing those material circumstances."

The alternative disclosure requirement contained in s.3(4)(b) is largely drawn from the previous case law on implied waiver of information by the insurer under s.18(3)(c) of the MIA.[115] Although the 2015 Act presents both limbs as alternative routes by which the insured may discharge its disclosure duties, it is clear that the bulk of the disclosure must be made in accordance with s.3(4)(a) with s.3(4)(b) expected to constitute only a narrow exception to the rule.[116] Accordingly, the Law Commission considered that "the courts would treat clause 3(4)(b) as an alternative only where the insured has tried but failed to comply with clause 3(4)(a) and shows that it has given the insurer a good base on which to make its enquiries."[117] Indeed, while s.3(4)(b) this might appear at first sight to allow the insured to justify material non-disclosures if it can link back every undisclosed fact to something disclosed within the presentation of risk that might have suggested more information was available, the retention of good faith as an interpretive principle[118] and the materiality provisions[119] suggest such an approach will not be effective.

5-062   **Sufficient signposts.**   Whether the insured has provided "sufficient information" to put the prudent insurer on notice during the presentation of risk will be determined by the presence of sufficient "signposts" to alert the insurer that further information is available, should appropriate enquiries be made.[120] An example of such a "signpost" would be where a prospective insured represents to the insurer that it plans to adopt a new mining technique without also disclosing that the technique tends to increase the risk of a collapse,[121] as a prudent insurer would have been put on notice to enquire about the new methods employed and the increased risks associated with those methods. The sufficiency of a signpost will in part be determined by the scope of what is left undisclosed and the extent to which the undisclosed information would affect an insurer's perception of the risk; if a non-disclosure is particularly significant or surprising, a court may find itself far less ready to infer that the insurer had been put "on notice" of the undisclosed information. The Law Commission demonstrated the difference with the example of an insured taking out product liability insurance and describing itself as the maker

---

[115] See above, fn.114.
[116] Law Commission *"Insurance Contract Law: Business Disclosure; Warranties; Insurers' Remedies for Fraudulent Claims; and Late Payment"*, (Law Commission, 2014). *http://www.lawcom.gov.uk/wp-content/uploads/2015/03/lc353_insurance-contract-law.pdf* [Accessed 24 June 2016] at paras 5.66 to 5.69.
[117] See above, fn.116 at para.7.39.
[118] See below, para.5-141.
[119] See above, para.5-020.
[120] Law Commission *"Insurance Contract Law: Business Disclosure; Warranties; Insurers' Remedies for Fraudulent Claims; and Late Payment"*, (Law Commission, 2014). *http://www.lawcom.gov.uk/wp-content/uploads/2015/03/lc353_insurance-contract-law.pdf* [Accessed 24 June 2016] at para.7.37.
[121] See below, para.6-030.

of "valves", without disclosing that the valves are in fact used in the petrochemical industry and bear the risk of explosion. In this example, the Law Commission were of the mind that:

> "We think that the mere mention of 'valves' is not sufficient. It is too vague to attract any attention or put the insurer 'on notice'. If X Co had described itself as making 'specialist' valves, the position might be less clear. There is certainly an argument that the mention of 'specialist' valves would lead a prudent underwriter to question the meaning of this term. Certainly, if X Co had listed its three principal clients (all in the petrochemical industry), we think it would have met the fair presentation standard. A prudent insurer would be aware of the need for further enquiries about the possible risks should a valve fail."[122]

The sufficiency of any signposting will be determined on the facts of a particular case, and a truthful but minimal representation is likely to only be sufficient where the insured is not deliberately evading the disclosure of a particularly significant material fact about the risk.

(x) A manner reasonably clear and accessible to a prudent insurer

The need to structure, index and signpost information. The new duty of fair **5-063** presentation under the 2015 Act includes requirements that go to the form of the presentation rather than just the completeness of the disclosure, as a means of encouraging the effective pre-contractual exchange of information. Section 3(3)(b) of the 2015 Act therefore provides:

> "(3) A fair presentation of the risk is one—...
>   (b) which makes that disclosure in a manner which would be reasonably clear and accessible to a prudent insurer."

Although the provision is principally aimed at preventing "data dumping" by the insured to conceal material elements of the risk, the Law Commission considered that this requirement would not just be activated where the quantity of information supplied to the insurer was exceptionally broad or extensive. By nature, some industries and fields of insurance would require the provision of a wide array of information to the insurer for an accurate assessment of risk to be made, and so it would be undesirable for compliance with s.3(3)(b) to turn on simply the volume of the disclosed information. Indeed, the Law Commission noted that:

> "We anticipate that whether this requirement has been breached will be highly fact specific: an underwriter's 'data dump' may be an insured's 'detailed risk information'. We do not see this duty as relating to the amount of information. Instead it is about the need to structure, index and signpost the information which is given."[123]

However, a prospective insured will clearly have to do more to ensure that the presentation is reasonably clear and accessible when providing highly comprehensive and extensive risk information to the insurer. What is "reasonably clear and accessible" to the insurer will necessarily be determined by the facts and circumstances of the case and the particular type of risk that is being underwritten, but the provision does contain the objective element that the presentation must be reason-

---

[122] Law Commission "*Insurance Contract Law: Business Disclosure; Warranties; Insurers' Remedies for Fraudulent Claims; and Late Payment*", (Law Commission, 2014). *http://www.lawcom.gov.uk/wp-content/uploads/2015/03/lc353_insurance-contract-law.pdf* [Accessed 24 June 2016] at para.7.38.
[123] See above, fn.122 at para.7.43.

ably clear to a "prudent insurer". This has the consequence that the adequacy of the presentation will be determined without regard to whether a particular underwriter fully appreciated all of the material elements of the risk before making the underwriting decision, as instead the court will look at the presentation itself to see if the salient factors were reasonably comprehensible and clear. Expert evidence may become necessary where it is the practice of a particular class of insurance for insurers to receive and digest a very large quantity of information before making the underwriting decision, particularly where insuring a particular industry involves the disclosure of technical or scientific information which may well be incomprehensible to an underwriter writing risks in a different field.

5-064 **Summaries.**   Where a presentation of risk is particularly long and detailed, it may be harder for the insured to provide the information in a "reasonably clear and accessible" manner without also providing a summary or overview of the salient facts about the risk. Following the case of *CTI v Oceanus*,[124] a summary must not omit any fact or circumstance which would significantly alter an underwriter's appreciation of the risk in question or else the summary itself will constitute a breach of the insured's disclosure obligations despite the material information appearing elsewhere in the presentation.[125] The task of preparing a summary is therefore a more difficult one for the insured to perform as it will require the exercise of judgment regarding the most important information relating to the risk in question, rather than just the adequate signposting and indexing necessary to lubricate the insurer's navigation of the documents provided. The 2015 Act and the Law Commission are both silent on the question of whether a detailed risk information that has not been provided with an accompanying summary but is thoroughly indexed and carefully arranged would be s.3(3)(b) compliant, and it may be that the courts will not readily impose such a requirement upon the insured where it is not expressly required by the statute. An insured may therefore find it undesirable to open itself up to an allegation that a summary was inaccurate or unfair and, rather than prepare one, may instead rely on sufficient indexing and signposting to satisfy the "reasonably clear and accessible" requirement.

(xi)   Misrepresentation

5-065 **General.**   The 2015 Act brings the law of misrepresentation previously contained under s.20 of the MIA within the overarching duty of fair presentation. Accordingly, s.3(3)(c) of the 2015 Act provides:

"(3) A fair presentation of the risk is one—...
(c)   in which every material representation as to a matter of fact is substantially correct, and every material representation as to a matter of expectation or belief is made in good faith."

This new arrangement acknowledges that insurers frequently plead misrepresentation alongside non-disclosure on the basis of the same withheld information and for the same remedy, with little practical difference between the two actions.[126] For

---

[124]   *CTI v Oceanus Mutual Underwriting Association (Bermuda) Ltd* [1984] 1 Lloyd's Rep. 476.
[125]   See above, para.5-021.
[126]   Law Commission "*Insurance Contract Law: Business Disclosure; Warranties; Insurers' Remedies for Fraudulent Claims; and Late Payment*", (Law Commission, 2014). *http://www.lawcom.gov.uk/*

example, an insurer may plead that a contractor made a material misrepresentation that it did not carry out tunnelling works on railway lines which were active, whilst also pleading in the alternative that the contractor failed to disclose that a railway line had been active during those tunnelling works.[127] Where the insurer does raise both defences, misrepresentation will frequently play the subordinate role to allegations of non-disclosure because the broad width of an insured's disclosure duties will only require the insurer to identify a material fact that was not disclosed rather than the more onerous task of trying to find a statement that is demonstrably incorrect or made in bad faith.[128]

The new provisions do not make any substantive change to the law on misrepresentation and so the previous case law under the MIA will continue to apply under the 2015 Act. For a misrepresentation to be actionable for the insurer, the insurer is required to prove, on the balance of probabilities, that there was a material representation of fact that was not substantially correct, or a material representation of expectation or belief that was not made in good faith.

Representations of fact and belief. The 2015 Act retains the division of representations under the MIA between representations of fact and representations of expectation or belief. Every material representation as to a matter of fact must be substantially correct, and every material representation of expectation or belief must be made in good faith. The question of whether a particular representation is one of fact or one of belief is a matter of construction and will often be determined by the respective knowledge held by the insured and the insured's agents when making the representation rather than the specific words used. In *Kamidian v Wareham Holt*,[129] the court had to construe an implied representation from the insured that a particular antique was a genuine Fabergé egg clock. Tomlinson J considered that it would be an unlikely result if this was held to be a representation of fact, since the insured would not have wished to warrant the authenticity of the piece when the provenance of the clock was incapable of proof by direct evidence and could only be established on the weight of informed opinion. Neither would the representation be one of the insured's belief that the clock was genuine, as it would have been an implausible and uncommercial result if the insurer had been held to adopt as the basis for its insurance the belief of one individual for which there might be no reasonable grounds in the context of a "fine arts" policy. Instead, the commercially sensible result was that the representation was a more limited representation of fact that there was a general acceptance in the art world that the piece was an authentic Fabergé egg clock, which would require only proof that the opinion was held rather than requiring a determination of the veracity of that opinion or whether it was reasonable.[130]

Accordingly, even a representation by the insured which is preceded by the words "it is our belief that" or "we have been informed that" may be held to be a statement of fact, and a clear statement of fact about something the insured would not

5-066

---

wp-content/uploads/2015/03/lc353_insurance-contract-law.pdf [Accessed 24 June 2016] at para.7.47.

[127] *Brit UW Ltd v F&R Trenchless Solutions Ltd* [2015] EWHC 2237 (Comm); [2016] Lloyd's Rep. I.R. 69.

[128] Law Commission *"Insurance Contract Law: Business Disclosure; Warranties; Insurers' Remedies for Fraudulent Claims; and Late Payment"*, (Law Commission, 2014). *http://www.lawcom.gov.uk/wp-content/uploads/2015/03/lc353_insurance-contract-law.pdf* [Accessed 24 June 2016] at para.4.42.

[129] *Kamidian v Wareham Holt* [2008] EWHC 1483 (Comm); [2009] Lloyd's Rep. I.R. 242.

[130] See above, fn.129 at [92].

be expected to know about may be held to be a matter of expectation or belief. This may have significance in the context of CAR insurance, for example, where a contractor represents to the insurer that a particular construction site is suitable for the planned building works when the site is in fact contaminated by asbestos. In such circumstances, the courts may construe such a representation as a statement of the contractor's belief that the site was suitable, or alternatively as a representation of the fact that the contractor believed that groundwork surveys already conducted on the site had not uncovered anything suggesting it was unsuitable.

Where the insurer has asked a specific question in a way which invites a representation of belief, it is likely that the courts will consider that any answer given is a representation of belief rather than one of fact despite clear words being used. This will be the case where the questions on the proposal form are preceded by the words "to the best of your knowledge", which will have the effect of converting every representation made on the proposal form into one of expectation or belief.

5-067   **Material representations.**   A misrepresentation by the insured must be material in order to be actionable by the insurer. The test for materiality for the purposes of misrepresentation is the same as for the insured's disclosure duties, as set out in s.7(3) of the 2015 Act, which provides:

> "(3) A circumstance or representation is material if it would influence the judgement of a prudent insurer in determining whether to take the risk and, if so, on what terms."

An insurer will therefore be unable to rely on a trivial misrepresentation that made no difference to the risk in question or the level at which the premium was set. Although under the MIA an insured would have been astute to submit that a representation was not material in order to escape the draconian remedy of avoidance, it is likely that the new regime for remedies under the 2015 Act would obviate much of the need for any emphasis to be placed on the materiality requirement. Rather than adopting the all or nothing approach prescribed by the MIA, the court is now better placed to consider the weight of the representation made by the insured and provide a remedy which is proportionate to the detriment suffered by the insurer in reliance on that representation. One would therefore expect that the breadth of information considered to be material under the new provisions would be wider than that under the MIA.

5-068   **Substantially correct.**   Where a representation is determined to be one of fact rather than one of expectation or belief, the burden will be on the insurer to show that the representation was not substantially correct. "Substantially correct" is defined under s.7(5) of the 2015 Act in the following manner:

> "(5) A material representation is substantially correct if a prudent insurer would not consider the difference between what is represented and what is actually correct to be material."

The provision therefore determines the veracity of a representation by applying the test of materiality to any difference between what was represented and what was actually correct, rather than relying on the objective truth of the statement as might be established in court.

5-069   **In good faith.**   Where a representation is of expectation or belief, the insurer will be required to prove that the representation was not made in good faith in order for the misrepresentation to be actionable. This raises the question whether the requirement that a representation be made "in good faith" is an entirely subjective one requiring only the honesty of the representor, or whether it includes an objective element that the belief must have been based on reasonable grounds. The test was construed subjectively by the Court of Appeal in *Economides v Commercial Assurance Co Plc*[131] as requiring only the insured's honesty, and this position will continue to apply under the provisions of the 2015 Act.

Withdrawing a representation. Replicating the effect of s.20(6) of the MIA, a **5-070** prospective insured may withdraw a representation before the policy is concluded and that representation will cease to have legal effect. Section 7(6) of the 2015 Act provides:

> "(6) A representation may be withdrawn or corrected before the contract of insurance is entered into."

Contracting out. The parties are free to contract out of the default position **5-071** contained in the 2015 Act in favour of imposing more or less onerous obligations upon the insured in relation to its representations of fact and belief. This may be desirable in circumstances where the parties do not wish to place an obligation on the insured to check the veracity of information given beyond the requirement that representations are made in good faith, particularly in circumstances where there is a risk that, contrary to the intention of the parties, and despite the express words used, a court may construe a representation as one of fact (rather than of expectation or belief) .[132] If any substituted provisions place the insured in a less advantageous position than they would otherwise have been in under the 2015 Act, the changes must be made in accordance with the transparency requirements discussed below at para.5-135.

(d) Remedies

General. The 2015 Act replaces the previous system of remedies for breaches of **5-072** the insured's disclosure duties and for misrepresentation. The sole remedy of avoidance under the MIA was condemned as an "overly harsh" remedy that failed to recognise the full array of circumstances in which a breach of disclosure duties could arise, particularly in cases where a breach was accidental or the detriment suffered by the insurer as a result of the breach was minimal.[133] The Law Commission considered that this position was out of touch with commercial reality because:

> "Avoidance is an inflexible remedy which can over-compensate the insurer. It fails to reflect normal compensatory principles and commercial reality. Very few consultees defended it."[134]

In abandoning avoidance as the sole remedy for material non-disclosure or misrepresentation, the 2015 Act is intended to align insurance law with the general compensatory and restitutionary principles of contract law. Save for where a breach

---

[131] *Economides v Commercial Assurance Co Plc* [1997] 3 W.L.R. 1066.
[132] See, for example, Law Commission *"Insurance Contract Law: Business Disclosure; Warranties; Insurers' Remedies for Fraudulent Claims; and Late Payment"*, (Law Commission, 2014). *http://www.lawcom.gov.uk/wp-content/uploads/2015/03/lc353_insurance-contract-law.pdf* [Accessed 24 June 2016] at para.8.93.
[133] See above, fn.132 at para.11.14.
[134] See above, fn.132 at para.11.31.

of duty is committed intentionally or recklessly, the remedies are accordingly aimed to restore the insurer to the position they would have been in had the insured fulfilled its duty of fair presentation. These proportionate remedies will apply to any failure by the insured to meet its obligations contained within Part 2 of the 2015 Act, whether occasioned by non-disclosure, misrepresentation or by the provision of an insufficiently clear, structured and signposted presentation of risk.

5-073   **A dual system of remedies.**   The 2015 Act contains a dual system of remedies, one punitive for those circumstances in which a breach of the duty of fair presentation was occasioned intentionally or recklessly, and one compensatory for those circumstances in which the breach was not intentional and was not reckless. Deliberate or reckless breaches will give rise to a right for insurers to avoid the policy and retain the premium, discussed in more detail below at para.5-078.

For breaches of the duty of fair presentation which are not committed intentionally or recklessly, the new system of remedies under the 2015 Act is based on compensatory principles that aim to put the insurer in the position it would have been in if it had received a fair presentation of risk, so far as is practicable. The precise remedy available to the insurer will therefore depend on considerations of how the insurer would have acted had it received a fair presentation of risk from the insured, and the 2015 Act identifies three different possible scenarios that may be pleaded in combination:

1.   where the insurer would not have entered the policy on any terms, the remedy will be avoidance but the insurer will have to return the premiums to the insured[135];

2.   where the insurer would have agreed to the policy but with the inclusion of additional terms, the policy will be treated as including those terms[136]; and

3.   where the insurer would have charged a higher premium, the insurer is entitled to reduce the payment on all claims by the percentage difference between the actual premium on the policy and the premium that would have been charged had the insurer been in receipt of all the material facts.[137]

5-074   **Inducement test.**   For a breach of the duty of fair presentation to be actionable, the insurer must show on the balance of probabilities that it would have acted differently had the breach not occurred. This is the case whether the breach was intentional or reckless, or neither intentional nor reckless. The requirement to establish inducement can be seen to complement the requirement of materiality in order for a non-disclosure or misrepresentation to provide insurers with a defence: to be material, the non-disclosure or misrepresentation must affect the judgment of a prudent insurer; and to have induced the contract, the non-disclosure or misrepresentation must have also affected the judgment of the actual underwriter when arranging the policy. Section 8(1) of the 2015 Act accordingly provides:

"**Remedies for breach**
   8.(1)   The insurer has a remedy against the insured for a breach of the duty of fair presentation only if the insurer shows that, but for the breach, the insurer—
      (a)   would not have entered into the contract of insurance at all, or
      (b)   would have done so only on different terms."

---

[135] See below, para.5-081.
[136] See below, para.5-082.
[137] See below, para.5-083.

Without the remedy of avoidance for any kind of breach, it seems likely that the question of inducement will often be subsumed within the question of what remedy the insurer is entitled to because both questions will be answered by the same enquiry—what would the insurer have done had the proper presentation been made? The issue of inducement may, however, have some part to play in relation to deliberate or reckless breaches, where the insurer may be able to establish that the relevant underwriter was induced to enter into the policy by the non-disclosure or misrepresentation, but not that the underwriter would not have written the policy on any terms at all in their absence: in such a case, proof of inducement will nevertheless afford insurers with a right to avoid.

Once the insurer has established on the balance of probabilities that the non-disclosure or misrepresentation did induce them to enter the contract on particular terms, the insured's breach of the duty of fair presentation will constitute a "qualifying breach", as provided by s.8(3) of the 2015 Act:

> "(3) A breach for which the insurer has a remedy against the insured is referred to in this
> Act as a 'qualifying breach'."

Deliberate breach. Where the insured's breach of the duty of fair presentation **5-075** is deliberate, the 2015 Act entitles the insurer to avoid the policy, refuse all claims made under it and retain any premiums paid pursuant to it. The punitive remedy of avoidance was considered to be commensurate with a dishonest breach of duty because such breaches undermine the nature of the insurance contract as one made in good faith, and should therefore be treated with apposite harshness.[138] Although a deliberate breach of the duty of fair presentation essentially denotes that the insured has committed a fraud against the insurer, such breaches are described as "deliberate" in order to avoid imposing the higher standard of proof required to establish fraud. In this regard the Law Commission stated:

> "In IP1 we described dishonest disclosures and misrepresentations as 'fraudulent'. However, many
> insurers associated that term with criminal standards of proof, and thought that they would only very
> rarely be in a position to prove that an insured had acted fraudulently in preparing its presentation.
> It is not our intention that the insurer's task of proving that a breach of the duty of fair presentation
> was made deliberately or recklessly should be unduly onerous, or require an exceptionally high
> standard of proof."[139]

Pre-contractual fraud will therefore be considered as a "deliberate or reckless" breaches of the duty of fair presentation. The 2015 Act contains separate rules in relation to fraudulent claims made after the policy is concluded, discussed below at para.5-116.

The definition of a deliberate breach of duty is provided by s.8(5)(a) of the 2015 Act, which states:

> "(5) A qualifying breach is deliberate or reckless if the insured—
> (a) knew that it was in breach of the duty of fair presentation."

In one sense, any breach of the duty of fair presentation that involves a conscious choice by the insured will be "deliberate" because the insured will have made a decision as to which information and documents will be disclosed to the insurer and

---

[138] Law Commission "*Insurance Contract Law: Business Disclosure; Warranties; Insurers' Remedies for Fraudulent Claims; and Late Payment*", (Law Commission, 2014). *http://www.lawcom.gov.uk/wp-content/uploads/2015/03/lc353_insurance-contract-law.pdf* [Accessed 24 June 2016] at para.11.36.
[139] See above, fn.138 at para.11.37.

in what manner. However, s.8(5)(a) makes clear that the concept of deliberate breach is not intended to discriminate between an honest but mistaken decision not to disclose, to disclose in an unclear or inaccessible manner, or to make a misrepresentation, on the one hand, and an inadvertent or negligent failure to do so on the other. Instead, "deliberate" is used to connote an intentional failure to make a fair presentation to the insurer where the insured knows the presentation is unfair. The section may raise issues concerning the exact mental state required to constitute a deliberate unfair presentation. Given the wording of s.8(5)(a), one might question whether the insured is required to know how the provisions of the 2015 Act operate in order to commit a deliberate breach: how else is an insured to know its presentation is unfair as defined in the Act? However, it would make little sense in practice if an insured was able to rely on its ignorance of the details of the 2015 Act in circumstances where it was fully aware, for example, that it possessed information that was pertinent to the risk in question, but deliberately chose not to pass it on to the insurer. It is suggested that , in this example, a non-disclosure will be found to have been deliberate under s.8(5)(a) where the insured was aware that it possessed material that should have been disclosed to the insurer because it was patently obvious that it was something the insurer would need to know. More borderline breaches should fall to be considered under "reckless" breaches of the duty.

The Law Commission set out the following list of possible ways an insured may deliberately breach the duty of fair presentation, which may provide further guidance:

"We think a deliberate breach of the duty of fair presentation could involve intentionally:

(1)   refraining from disclosing a circumstance which the insured knows to be material;
(2)   making a data dump or otherwise presenting risk in a particular way in order to conceal certain information (as in the case where a summary is very misleading); or
(3)   intentionally lying about a material representation, either in the initial presentation or by knowingly giving a false response to an insurer enquiry." [140]

It is therefore clear that an insured can deliberately breach any of its obligations to provide a fair presentation of risk, whether by a deliberate non-disclosure of material information a deliberate misrepresentation, or a deliberate breach of the clarity requirements. Where the breach is in terms commensurate with example (1), an insurer may quite readily be able to prove that the insured knew it was in breach of the duty of fair presentation as the court will presumably be willing to infer this where the non-disclosed circumstance was obviously one which was highly material and yet the insured failed to disclose it. It may be a more challenging task for an insurer to prove that a data dump or insufficiently structured and indexed presentation was made deliberately with the knowledge that the resulting presentation was unfair as it may often be difficult to distinguish such a presentation from one that was prepared negligently or without much thought to clarity and form. Deliberate breach of the clarity requirements will be easier to establish in circumstances where the summary provided is quite clearly misleading, or perhaps where an obviously crucial fact is hidden in a mass of documents. In some cases, an insurer may find it easier to establish a defence by arguing that a poorly structured presentation of risk was made recklessly, see below para.5-076.

---

[140]   See above, fn.138 at para.11.43.

Reckless breach.   A reckless breach is defined by s.8(5)(b) of the 2015 Act as a   **5-076**
breach of the duty of fair presentation that is committed by an insured who "did not
care whether or not it was in breach of that duty." The 2015 Act therefore adopts
the definition of recklessness used by the House of Lords in *Derry v Peek*[141] where
a statement was held to be fraudulent if made without the maker caring whether it
was true or false, to be distinguished from a mere careless or negligent
misrepresentation. The Law Commission considered that the concept of a reckless
breach would have significance in the context of breaches occasioned by provision of an unclear or insufficiently signposted presentation of risk, perhaps recognising that it may be difficult to prove a deliberate breach of those requirements:

> "We think that recklessness might be particularly salient in the data dump context, where an insured
> does not care whether the insurer will be able to make sense of the information provided, with the
> result that obviously important information may well be missed. It may also be shown by answer-
> ing a question with no attempt to check the facts."[142]

Although a reckless statement can quite readily be distinguished from a negligent
one, this distinction may be harder to elucidate in relation to breaches of the clarity requirements under the 2015 Act. There may be many situations where an ill-
structured presentation of risk that has been prepared negligently will justify the
inference that the insured was in fact wholly unconcerned as to whether the insurer
will be able to make sense of the material provided. It is suggested that if the courts
utilise the concept of recklessness to target breaches of the clarity requirements in
the way suggested by the Law Commission, then in a high proportion of such cases
there may be little scope for the insured to argue that it was merely negligent.

Burden of proof.   In accordance with normal legal principles, s.8(6) of the 2015   **5-077**
Act provides that the burden will be on the insurer to prove that the breach was accompanied by a deliberate or reckless disregard for the duty of fair presentation.
The Law Commission deliberately avoided use of the common law notion of fraud
in defining deliberate or reckless breaches, and so the insurer must prove that the
insured acted deliberately or recklessly on the balance of probabilities, rather than
any higher standard.[143]

Remedy for a deliberate or reckless breach.   Rather than a proportionate remedy   **5-078**
designed to place the insurer in the position they would have been in had a fair
presentation of risk been made, a deliberate or reckless breach of duty is treated as
a matter contrary to the concept of the insurance contract as one based on good
faith, and so the insurer is entitled to the remedy of avoidance. This measure is punitive to the insured, entitling the insurer to refuse all claims under the policy and
retain all premiums. Schedule 1 to the 2015 Act provides the remedies for an
insured's breach of duty, of which para.2 sets out the remedy for a deliberate or
reckless breach:

> **"2.**   If a qualifying breach was deliberate or reckless, the insurer—
>   (a)   may avoid the contract and refuse all claims, and

---

[141] *Derry v Peek* (1889) 14 App. Cas. 337.
[142] Law Commission "*Insurance Contract Law: Business Disclosure; Warranties; Insurers' Remedies
for Fraudulent Claims; and Late Payment*", (Law Commission, 2014). *http://www.lawcom.gov.uk/
wp-content/uploads/2015/03/lc353_insurance-contract-law.pdf* [Accessed 24 June 2016] at para.11.46.
[143] See above, fn.142 at paras 11.37 and 11.48.

(b)   need not return any of the premiums paid."

5-079   **Retention of premium.**   The previous position under the MIA was that avoidance of the policy would require restitution, so that the parties would be placed back in the position they would have been in had the contract never been made. This would entitle the insured to the return of any premiums paid pursuant to the policy, but there was an exception contained in s.84(3)(a) that the premium would only be returned "provided there has been no fraud or illegality on the part of the assured."[144] In a number of respects, the concept of a "deliberate and reckless" breach of duty contained within the 2015 Act is markedly different from cases of fraud. The insured can, for example, commit a reckless breach of the duty to arrange the presentation in a clear and accessible manner: such a breach bears little resemblance to a fraudulent misrepresentation, and yet the effect of the 2015 Act is that an insured who collects all of the salient data but then makes no attempt to provide any structure for the insurer should be subjected to the same consequences as an insured who answers an insurer's questions without any attempt to check the veracity of its statements. Whilst in the former case the insured will have certainly been unhelpful to the insurer, it is at least possible that their conduct does not contain the same degree of dishonesty as the latter case, so as to justify depriving the insured of their premium (e.g. where the production of an unclear and inaccessible presentation was deliberate, but not motivated by an intention to conceal any particular information). Nevertheless, it is worth emphasising that the provision is intended as a deterrent.

5-080   **Proportionate remedies.**   Where the insured has committed a breach of the duty of fair presentation that was not deliberate and was not reckless, the insurer will be entitled to a proportionate remedy designed to place it in the position it would have been in had a fair presentation of risk been made. The remedy that the insurer is entitled to will therefore depend upon what the insurer would have done had the correct presentation been made.

5-081   **The insurer would not have contracted on any terms.**   Despite being entitled to only a proportionate remedy, an insurer may still be able to avoid the policy if it can show that it would not have contracted on any terms had the proper presentation of risk been made. However, in such circumstances the insurer will not be entitled to the retention of the premium because the insured's conduct has not been dishonest in the sense of deliberately or recklessly breaching the requirements of the 2015 Act. Paragraph 4 of Schedule 1 to the 2015 Act therefore provides:

> "**4.**   If, in the absence of the qualifying breach, the insurer would not have entered into the contract on any terms, the insurer may avoid the contract and refuse all claims, but must in that event return the premiums paid."

5-082   **The insurer would have included additional terms.**   Where the insurer would have included additional terms in the policy had the duty of fair presentation been properly discharged by the insured, the insurer will be entitled to treat the policy as if it had been concluded on those terms. Paragraph 5 of Schedule 1 to the 2015 Act therefore provides:

---

[144] See below, para.6-051.

"**5.** If the insurer would have entered into the contract, but on different terms (other than terms relating to the premium), the contract is to be treated as if it had been entered into on those different terms if the insurer so requires."

Although at first sight this might appear contrary to ordinary contract law principles as it allows the courts a much stronger power to rectify a defective policy than they might otherwise have had (i.e. rather than limiting the available remedies to damages), the terms imported into the policy will typically be exclusions or other terms delimiting the scope of the risk accepted by the insurer. As such, the result of a circuitous action whereby the insurer who pays a claim that would otherwise have been excluded under the additional terms of the policy, would claim back the payment as the damages resulting from the insured's breach of duty. The Law Commission considered that the remedy could accommodate any type of term that the insurer would have imposed (save for those relating to the premium), but that the principal terms insurers will seek to impose would be the following:

"(1) Exclusions: if a fair presentation had been made, the insurer might have excluded liability for certain types of loss. If so, the validity of a claim will depend upon whether it falls within the terms of the exclusion.

(2) Warranties and other terms designed to reduce particular risks: knowing the full facts, an insurer might have required the insured to warrant that it would act in a certain way. If the insured's actions have put it in breach of that warranty, the insurer's liability will be suspended either entirely or in respect of the particular type of loss to which the warranty is relevant.

(3) Excesses: the insurer might have imposed an excess. The excess may cover the whole policy or particular types of loss. If the claim falls within the terms of the excess it will be reduced by the amount of the excess."[145]

The insurer would have charged a higher premium. The remedy for the insurer   **5-083**
that is likely to be most controversial applies where the insurer can prove that they would have charged a higher premium if they had been in full receipt of all of the material circumstances of the risk. Rather than an entitlement to treat the policy as having been concluded with the higher premium or an entitlement to damages, the insurer is instead entitled to reduce proportionately the amount to be paid under each claim. Paragraph 6 of Schedule 1 to the 2015 Act accordingly provides:

"**6.**(1) In addition, if the insurer would have entered into the contract (whether the terms relating to matters other than the premium would have been the same or different), but would have charged a higher premium, the insurer may reduce proportionately the amount to be paid on a claim.

(2) In sub-paragraph (1), 'reduce proportionately' means that the insurer need pay on the claim only X% of what it would otherwise have been under an obligation to pay under the terms of the contract (or, if applicable, under the different terms provided for by virtue of paragraph 5), where—

$$X = \frac{\text{Premium actually charged}}{\text{Higher premium}} \quad x100"$$

[145] Law Commission "*Insurance Contract Law: Business Disclosure; Warranties; Insurers' Remedies for Fraudulent Claims; and Late Payment*", (Law Commission, 2014). *http://www.lawcom.gov.uk/wp-content/uploads/2015/03/lc353_insurance-contract-law.pdf* [Accessed 24 June 2016] at para.11.67.

This can be demonstrated through a worked example:

1. An employer takes out a project specific CAR policy to cover the construction of a power plant before the project has been released for tender.

2. During the presentation of risk, the employer provides a mistaken estimation to the insurer that the value of the completed works will be £180 million. It later transpires that the value is £250 million.

3. After the commencement of the project, subsidence causes the collapse of the building works and the employer makes a claim under the policy for £40 million.

4. The insurer defends the claim on the basis that they would have charged a premium of £1.25 million calculated in relation to the £250 million value of the works instead of the £1 million actually charged.

5. The insurer is therefore entitled to reduce the employer's claim and any future claims made under the policy by 20%.

6. The insurer would therefore only have to pay out £32 million, which saves the insurer £8 million compared with the extra premium they would have charged at only £250,000 (but is more favourable to the insured, by £32 million, than the remedy the insurers might have had under the MIA, avoidance). This is therefore a statutory appl to the common law principle of "average".

7. If there is no term in the policy for a proportionate increase in the premium to take account of the increased build cost, as is usual in CAR policies, the employer would have to negotiate in order to restore full coverage for any future claims under the policy, or else would have to take out additional coverage elsewhere.

In some circumstances, on one view, this remedy may appear to over-compensate the insurer, and it might be questioned why the Law Commission determined that this mechanism should be chosen as the one which would put the insurer in the position they would have been in had the proper presentation of risk been made. Although the ex post facto modification of the premium charged under the insurance policy would effectively put the insured in breach of their obligation to pay the higher premium and could therefore have the effect of suspending cover if there is a premium payment warranty within the policy, one might question why the Law Commission did not just treat this as an ordinary breach of contract requiring the insured to pay damages calculated as the difference between the actual premium the insurer charged and the higher premium they would have charged. The rationale advanced by the Law Commission was that they considered such a measure would under-compensate the insurer because the effect of the non-disclosure was to deprive them of the information required to accurately assess the risk, and so the better option was to reduce proportionately the payment of claims. They stated:

> "Insureds are not given a right to pay the extra premium that the insurer would have charged in order to retain cover. This would under-compensate the insurer, who would thereby be forced to cover the risk after it had materialised, despite not having been given sufficient information to gauge accurately the degree of likelihood of it materialising or its extent. It would be open to insurers to decide to accept the higher premium as part of a commercial settlement."[146]

This reasoning recognises that to limit the insurer's remedy to an ex post facto increase in premium would be to disregard a factor of central importance, namely that by the time the remedy is awarded the risk has been run and the insurer has lost.

---

[146] See above, fn.145 at para.11.72.

To borrow a stock-market analogy: if an investor means to buy 200 shares from another person on Monday, but mistakenly enters an order for 100 shares instead, and by the end of the week they have doubled in value, Monday's seller is unlikely to be willing on Friday to sell 100 more shares to the buyer at Monday's price: and it would be unfair to the seller to compel him to do so. It might be added that, by hypothesis, had a fair presentation of the risk been made prior to the occurrence of any loss, the insurer would have set a higher premium, which the insured may or may not have accepted. Accordingly, it can be seen with hindsight that, by reason of the insured's breach of duty, the insurer has lost a chance to avoid being on risk at the time of the casualty that in fact occurred. Solely to increase the premium, ex post facto, does not compensate the insurer for this. Moreover, allowing the insured to recover on their claim, at the cost of an increase in premium (which, in general, will be small in relation to the size of the claim), diminishes the insured's incentive to make a fair and accurate presentation of the risk prior to inception. Avoidance may have been too extreme a consequence, for these purposes: but solely to increase the premium could have been perceived by the insurance market as providing too little protection.

Clearly, where failure to make a fair presentation leads underwriters to set an inadequate premium, and the breach is not discovered until after a loss, the choice of a remedy that sets a fair balance between insurers and insureds presents difficulties. The proportionate reduction of the claim is a compromise between avoidance ab initio and increasing the premium ex post, which from one case to the next may be perceived as unsatisfactory by either party to the policy, or by both.

Combination of remedies. The insurer is entitled to apply any combination of **5-084** remedies in respect of the breach of the duty of fair presentation, so long as they are able to establish that they would have included additional terms and would have also varied the premium.[147]

Proving how the insurer would have acted. The insurer's entitlement to the **5-085** proportionate remedies contained in the 2015 Act will be dependent on whether it can satisfy the courts as to the way it would have acted if it had been in receipt of fair presentation of the risk. This may be a simple matter if the insurer can rely on pricing tariffs or other comparable policies concluded within the same timeframe, but where the insurance is bespoke and the risk is an unusual one it may be far more difficult to satisfy the courts that the insurer would have responded in a particular way to a particular piece of information. Although this may create difficulties for the insurer in a number of circumstances, the Law Commission considered that this was the inevitable result of including proportionate remedies for breach[148] which in any event would involve a similar enquiry to that which the courts routinely undertake in relation to issues of materiality and inducement.[149] Ultimately, the issue will be resolved as a matter of evidence, and this:

"Evidence of how the insurer would have acted may be derived from a number of sources, including pricing manuals and models, contemporaneous policies and oral evidence from the individual underwriter or expert witnesses. There may also be commercial reasons for similar risks being writ-

---

[147] See above, fn.145 at para.11.73.
[148] See above, fn.145 at para.11.75.
[149] See above, fn.145 at para.11.78.

ten on different terms for different policyholders. This would also be a matter of evidence in the circumstances."[150]

The Law Commission also anticipated that there may be difficulties in circumstances where the insurer could have chosen one of a number of options, for example accepting the risk for a high premium or at a lower premium with an exclusion or warranty. This would also be a matter for the court to determine based on which offer the insurer would most likely have put to the insured.[151]

5-086 **The limits on considering what would have happened.** The Law Commission emphasised that there should be limits placed on the parties' hypothetical scenarios regarding how the insured and the insurer would have acted if the duty of fair presentation had been complied with. However, the 2015 Act makes no provision for any such issues and it remains to be seen whether the courts will adopt the Law Commission's suggestions. The Law Commission suggests that the insurer's counter-factual case should be limited to the hypothetical content of the policy, noting that:

> "We do not think that the enquiry should extend to whether the insurer would have reinsured the risk or acted differently in accepting subsequent risks (for example, in relation to capacity limits in group life cover). This is necessary to prevent complicated evidential arguments arising about how the insurer would have conducted itself and the terms on which it could have obtained reinsurance cover."[152]

Similarly, the insured should not be heard to speculate as to what would have happened if the parties had negotiated on a different basis, for example by suggesting that they would have obtained insurance at a lower premium elsewhere[153] or they would have complied with any exclusion or warranty the insurer would have included within the policy.[154] Although these suggestions would curtail the ability of the courts to truly place the insurer in the position they would have been in had the duty of fair presentation been properly discharged, the Law Commission considered that the position was satisfactory for a default regime which the parties could contract out of if they considered it to be inappropriate for their particular arrangements.[155]

5-087 **A right to cancel.** When considering the scope of the proposed reforms, the Law Commission questioned whether there should be a statutory right to cancel the policy exercisable by both the insured and the insurer following a breach of the duty of fair presentation. Although contractual cancellation rights are already the market norm, the Law Commission voiced concerns that a statutory right might be desirable since the new reforms could potentially leave an insured with a policy that would no longer meet their needs (e.g. if every future claim payment would be reduced proportionately) or leave an insurer covering a different risk on different terms than they had originally agreed to.[156] The Law Commission were clearly in

---

[150] See above, fn.145 at para.11.76.
[151] See above, fn.145 at para.11.77.
[152] See above, fn.145 at para.11.83.
[153] See above, fn.145 at para.11.81.
[154] See above, fn.145 at para.11.82.
[155] See above, fn.145 at para.11.84.
[156] See above, fn.145 at para.11.85.

favour of a right to cancel,[157] but eventually determined that this was best left as a matter for the parties to address in their contract.[158]

Variations. Part 2 of Schedule 1 to the 2015 Act provides remedies for the insurer **5-088** in circumstances where the insured has committed a qualifying breach of the duty of fair presentation in relation to a variation rather than the underlying policy. The remedies available are the same as those for a breach in relation to the underlying policy, which should prove simple to apply where the insurer can prove that it would not have accepted the variation on any terms or would have included additional terms within the variation. The matter will prove more complicated if the insurer would have increased the premium by more than it did, or would not have reduced the premium as much as it did when agreeing to the variation if it had been in receipt of a fair presentation of the risk. Here, the "proportionate reduction" for any claims made under the policy will be calculated as follows (where Y is the % reduction):

$$X = \frac{\text{Premium actually charged}}{\text{Higher premium}} \times 100"$$

The value of P will change depending on whether the premium was reduced or increased as a result of the variation. Where the premium was increased but the insurer would have increased the premium even further, then the value of P will be the total premium they would have charged.[159] Where the premium was decreased but the insurer would have decreased it by less, would have kept the premium the same or would have increased the premium when agreeing to the variation, then the value of P will be the higher premium that they would have charged.[160] Where the insurer would not have varied the premium, the value of P will be the original premium.[161]

Contracting out. As with all other parts of the 2015 Act, the parties are free to **5-089** contract out of the default provisions and substitute their own system of remedies so long as any changes are made in accordance with the transparency requirements.[162] This may prove to be particularly desirable where the policy provides cover for a bespoke or unusual risk, as it may be difficult to establish one's case under the system of proportionate remedies without any contemporaneous policies on similar risks to refer to as evidence regarding how the insurrer would have acted had the duty of fair presentation been discharged.

3. WARRANTIES

Introductory. The 2015 Act substantially reforms the law of insurance warran- **5-090** ties with the aim of restoring coherence to an area of the law that has been described

---

[157] See above, fn.145 at para.11.87.
[158] See above, fn.145 at para.11.89.
[159] Paragraph 11(3)(c) of Schedule 1 to the 2015 Act.
[160] Paragraph 11(3)(c) of Schedule 1 to the 2015 Act.
[161] Paragraph 11(3)(b) of Schedule 1 to the 2015 Act.
[162] See below, para.5-135.

as "anomalous and unexpected",[163] "unjust"[164] and out of touch with prudent commercial practice.[165] The new provisions are designed to afford a better balance between the interests of the insured and the insurer and allow the policy to respond as anticipated by both, rather than entitling the insurer to pursue technical arguments that have the effect of depriving the insured of its cover under the policy. These objectives were seen as vital to the Law Commission in order to avoid letting the UK insurance market fall into disrepute, a danger at risk of emerging if the law continued to favour the interests of the insurer over those of the insured. To that end, the effect of a breach of warranty on the policy between the parties is now governed by s.10 of the 2015 Act, which provides that cover will merely be suspended until the breach is remedied rather than being extinguished completely. There are also additional controls under s.11 of the 2015 Act, limiting the effect of terms designed to prevent a particular type of loss, which can also be applied to warranties, discussed in greater detail below at para.5-103.

5-091   **Background.**   Unlike the position in the general law of contract where a breach of warranty will only entitle the aggrieved party to damages, a warranty in an insurance policy is treated as one of the key terms defining the scope of the risk the insurer has agreed to cover. Accordingly, the provisions of the MIA provided that any breach of warranty by the insured would automatically discharge the insurer from all liability for losses arising after the date of breach,[166] which has led some judges to describe warranties as conditions precedent to liability attaching on the insurer.[167] Under the previous law, warranties required exact compliance by the insured or else the insurer would be discharged from liability, whether the breach of warranty was related to the loss or not, whether the breach was only very minor and whether the insured had remedied the breach before the loss was caused. A breach of warranty was treated even more seriously than a misrepresentation or non-disclosure by the insured under the MIA, as there was no requirement to establish materiality in order for the insurer to avoid liability.[168]

The law of insurance warranties has long been recognised as overly harsh and capable of abuse by insurers advancing technical arguments to avoid payment in circumstances where the deprivation of cover is wholly unreasonable to the insured.[169] The Law Commission considered that the harshness of the law was doubly undesirable as it had also led to inconsistencies with the way in which courts had approached the issue of how to identify warranties in the policy in order to do justice in individual cases.[170] This was because the identification of warranties was naturally a matter of contractual construction, and over the years the courts had taken the opportunity to utilise the principles of interpretation to ameliorate some

---

163 Law Commission "*Insurance Contract Law: Business Disclosure; Warranties; Insurers' Remedies for Fraudulent Claims; and Late Payment*", (Law Commission, 2014). *http://www.lawcom.gov.uk/ wp-content/uploads/2015/03/lc353_insurance-contract-law.pdf* [Accessed 24 June 2016] at para.14.2.
164 See above, fn.163 at para.14.1.
165 See above, fn.163 at para.14.4.
166 See below, para.12-020.
167 *Bank of Nova Scotia Appellants v Hellenic Mutual War Risks Association (Bermuda) Ltd. Respondents* [1991] 2 W.L.R. 1279.
168 See below, para.12-022.
169 Law Commission "*Insurance Contract Law: Business Disclosure; Warranties; Insurers' Remedies for Fraudulent Claims; and Late Payment*", (Law Commission, 2014). *http://www.lawcom.gov.uk/ wp-content/uploads/2015/03/lc353_insurance-contract-law.pdf* [Accessed 24 June 2016] at para.14.29.
170 See above, fn.169 at para.13.5.

of the harshness of the law.[171] The Law Commission were of the opinion that the courts' inconsistent approach to the identification of warranties within insurance policies was symptomatic of an inadequate and unfair set of rules that the courts did not appear to want to apply in a consistent and technical manner.[172] They therefore identified four main concerns with the law on warranties as enacted under the MIA:

> "(1) An insurer may refuse a claim for a trivial mistake which has no bearing on the risk.
> (2) The insured cannot use the defence that the breach has been remedied.
> (3) The breach of warranty discharges the insurer from all liability, not just liability for the type of loss in question. For example, a failure to install the right sort of burglar alarm would discharge the insurer from liability for a flood claim.
> (4) A statement may be converted into a warranty using obscure words that few policyholders understand. For example, if a policyholder signs a statement on a proposal form that their answers form the 'basis of the contract', this can have draconian consequences."[173]

Sections 9–11 of the 2015 Act are directed to these issues, and they radically transform the effect of a breach of warranty on the subsisting policy between the parties. Section 9 of the 2015 Act abolishes basis of the contract clauses, discussed below at para.5-092. Section 10 of the 2015 Act reforms the insurer's remedies for breach of warranty, discussed below from paras 5-093 to 5-102. Section 11 of the 2015 Act prevents insurers relying on trivial or unrelated mistakes by the insured to avoid payment, discussed below from paras 5-103 to 5-115.

Although the reforms are targeted at the remedies available to the insurer for a breach of warranty and do not make any explicit changes to the identification of warranties within the policy, the judicial approach to identification of warranties is almost certain to be affected. There will now be no practical difference between the operation of warranties and suspensory provisions, and therefore no need to distinguish between them.[174] Nor will there be any need to emphasise, in relation to combined policies, that the separate sections each provide a different kind of insurance cover, so as to contend that a breach of warranty should only allow the insurer to avoid liability for claims arising under a particular section.[175] Finally, the approach of the courts is likely to establish a more coherent body of law governing the identification of warranties.

(a) Basis of the contract clauses

General. Basis of the contract clauses were traditionally used by insurers as a   **5-092** mechanism to convert answers given by the insured on the proposal form into warranties, for which any breach would automatically discharge the insurer from liability. The device used to accomplish this would typically be a cryptic statement on the proposal form declaring that the answers given would form "the basis of the contract" between the insured and insurer, without necessarily explaining that the effect of the declaration was to convert the insured's representations into warranties. The Law Commission noted that there had been widespread criticism of basis of the contract clauses as they could be used as "traps" for the insured

---

[171] See above, fn.169 at para.13.24.
[172] See above, fn.169 at para.14.29.
[173] See above, fn.169 at para.12.4.
[174] See below, para.12-014.
[175] See below, para.12-023.

which would allow the insurer to refuse payment based on any error or mistake, with no requirement for the insurer to establish that the mistake was material as would be necessary for misrepresentation or non-disclosure.[176] The use of these clauses has therefore been abolished by s.9(2) of the 2015 Act, and basis of the contract clauses will cease to have contractual effect. Section 9 provides:

> "*Warranties and representations*
>
> (1) This section applies to representations made by the insured in connection with—
>   (a) a proposed non-consumer insurance contract, or
>   (b) a proposed variation to a non-consumer insurance contract.
> (2) Such a representation is not capable of being converted into a warranty by means of any provision of the non-consumer insurance contract (or of the terms of the variation), or of any other contract (and whether by declaring the representation to form the basis of the contract or otherwise)."

The provision prevents an insurer from using any mechanism or device within the policy, whether basis of the contract clause or otherwise, which purports to convert an insured's representations into warranties. Although s.16(1) of the 2015 Act specifically prevents the insurer contracting out of this provision, an insurer who would nevertheless like to ensure the veracity of a particular representation from the insured is free to do so by including specific warranties relating to the same information given on the proposal form within the body of the policy. Indeed, if a particular representation is so important to the insurer that it is their practice not to agree to cover risks where a particular answer is given on the proposal form, it will make little difference whether the insurer includes that answer as a warranty within the policy as any misrepresentation by the insured is likely to entitle the insurer to avoid the policy.[177]

(b) Breach of warranty

5-093   **Identifying the breach.** Once a term has been identified as a warranty, the insured must comply strictly with the term whether material to the risk or not in order to avoid the suspension of liability. The 2015 Act changes the consequences of a breach of warranty but does not alter the identification of the breach, which will remain a matter of the proper construction of the obligations placed on the insured.[178] Section 10(1) and (2) of the 2015 Act repeal the consequences for a breach of warranty under the MIA and instate the new remedy of suspension of liability rather than extinction:

> "*Breach of warranty*
>
> (1) Any rule of law that breach of a warranty (express or implied) in a contract of insurance results in the discharge of the insurer's liability under the contract is abolished.
> (2) An insurer has no liability under a contract of insurance in respect of any loss occurring, or attributable to something happening, after a warranty (express or implied) in the contract has been breached but before the breach has been remedied."

---

[176] Law Commission "*Insurance Contract Law: Business Disclosure; Warranties; Insurers' Remedies for Fraudulent Claims; and Late Payment*", (Law Commission, 2014). *http://www.lawcom.gov.uk/wp-content/uploads/2015/03/lc353_insurance-contract-law.pdf* [Accessed 24 June 2016] at para.13.9.
[177] See above, para.5-088.
[178] See below, para.12-021.

Determining the time of breach will continue to be of vital importance under the 2015 Act in order to establish the time from which the insurer's liability for loss is suspended. Once the period of suspension has been identified, s.10(4) of the 2015 Act provides that the insurer's liability will continue for losses that occur before the warranty has been breached or after the breach has been remedied, so long as the loss is not attributable to something that happened during the period of breach:

> "(4) Subsection (2) does not affect the liability of the insurer in respect of losses occurring, or attributable to something happening—
> (a)   before the breach of warranty, or
> (b)   if the breach can be remedied, after it has been remedied."

Losses attributable to something happening during the period of suspension.   Whilst the insurer will be put back on risk as soon as the insured's breach of warranty has been remedied, there may still be losses that accrue after the date of remedy but which are attributable to something that happened during the period of suspension. Where such losses occur, s.10(4) of the 2015 Act provides that the insurer will not be liable for them. The effect of this can be illustrated with an example. A CAR policy may contain a warranty along the following terms:

5-094

> "The insured undertakes to comply with The Joint Code of Fire Practice on the Protection from Fire of Construction Sites and Buildings Undergoing Renovation 9th edition hereinafter referred to as the Joint Fire Code."

A contractor may be in breach of the Joint Fire Code for a number of reasons relating to the safety of the site and the likelihood of fire, such as by using flammable materials as a cover for scaffolding or the improper use or storage of acetylene. Section 12.8 of the 9th edition requires the insured to ensure that the construction site is monitored by 24-hour onsite security, a provision it will be in breach of if there is any period in which onsite security is suspended. If an arsonist were able to enter the site during a lapse in the onsite security, but only started a fire once the security guard had returned to site, then the loss would have occurred after the date of remedy but would still be attributable to something that happened during the period of suspension. As such, the insurer would still escape liability.

The exact test for what losses will be "attributable" to something that happened during the period of suspension will likely be a matter for the courts to elucidate and interpret to meet the requirements of particular cases. However, the Law Commission indicate that the test of attribution requires something stronger than just "but for" causation. For instance, if an insured vessel was able to shave two days off of a journey by taking a shortcut through a war zone that the insured had warranted not to traverse, the mere fact that the vessel was caught in a storm which otherwise would have been avoided if the vessel had arrived two days later would not be enough for the storm damage to be attributable to the insured's breach of warranty.[179]

---

[179] Law Commission "*Insurance Contract Law: Business Disclosure; Warranties; Insurers' Remedies for Fraudulent Claims; and Late Payment*", (Law Commission, 2014). *http://www.lawcom.gov.uk/wp-content/uploads/2015/03/lc353_insurance-contract-law.pdf* [Accessed 24 June 2016] at para.17.35.

(c) Remedying the breach

5-095 **Remedying the breach of a "general" warranty.** To some, the concept of "remedying" a breach of warranty might raise concerns over the extent to which an insurer can realistically be put back into a position as if the breach of warranty had never occurred. Particularly where the insured warrants that a piece of information is accurate or warrants to do something by a specified time, the insured's non-compliance with that term may be logically incapable of being fixed, leaving the concept of "remedying" the breach an inapt descriptor for the requisite actions needed to bring the insurer back on risk. There will be clear situations where a warranty is not capable of being remedied at all, for example where an insured warrants that it has no previous convictions for any driving related offences before taking out a policy. For warranties that are capable of being remedied, s.10(5) of the 2015 Act defines the requisite actions the insured must undertake in order to bring the insurer back on risk in the following manner:

> "(5) For the purposes of this section, a breach of warranty is to be taken as remedied—
>
> (a) in a case falling within subsection (6), if the risk to which the warranty relates later becomes essentially the same as that originally contemplated by the parties,
>
> (b) in any other case, if the insured ceases to be in breach of the warranty."

Section 10(5)(a) concerns time specific warranties and is discussed in greater detail below.[180] Section 10(5)(b) will operate for the majority of general warranties and provides that the insurer's liability reattaches as soon as the insured ceases to be in breach, rather than engaging more nebulous and conceptually uncertain approaches such as remedying the detriment suffered by the insurer. This position is subject to an important proviso that an insured will not be able to rely on overly technical arguments to assert that a breach had been remedied at the precise moment a loss occurred if the loss was still incidental to the breach of warranty. The Law Commission use the example of a car insured for personal use under a policy that contained a corresponding warranty that the car was not to be used for hire purposes, in circumstances where the insured went on to use the car predominantly for hire purposes.[181] Even if the car was later destroyed whilst parked overnight in a garage, and was therefore destroyed at a time when the insured had technically ceased to be in breach of the hire warranty, the fact that the overnight parking was "incidental" to the breach of warranty would be sufficient for the insurer to avoid liability. This was considered necessary in order to prevent policyholders "playing the system" by purchasing the incorrect type of cover.[182]

5-096 **Remedying the breach of a time specific warranty.** Section 10(5)(a) of the 2015 Act provides that a time specific warranty may be remedied where the risk becomes essentially the same as that originally contemplated by the parties. The provision was included to prevent an insurer from rendering warranties incapable of remedy

---

180 See below, para.5-081.

181 These facts were taken from the case of *Murray v Scottish Automobile & General Insurance Co Ltd* 1929 S.C. 48; 1929 S.L.T. 114.

182 Law Commission *"Insurance Contract Law: Business Disclosure; Warranties; Insurers' Remedies for Fraudulent Claims; and Late Payment"*, (Law Commission, 2014). *http://www.lawcom.gov.uk/wp-content/uploads/2015/03/lc353_insurance-contract-law.pdf* [Accessed 24 June 2016] at para.17.39.

simply by applying a deadline or other contingency to a term that would prevent an insured, on a literal interpretation, from ever ceasing to be in breach. The warranties caught by s.10(5)(b) are defined in s.10(6) as comprising the following:

"(6) A case falls within this subsection if—
   (a) the warranty in question requires that by an ascertainable time something is to be done (or not done), or a condition is to be fulfilled, or something is (or is not) to be the case, and
   (b) that requirement is not complied with."

A clear example of a time specific warranty that would be capable of remedy in accordance with s.10(5)(b) would be where the policy requires the insured to warrant that a scaffolding burglar alarm will be inspected once every 30 days. If the burglar alarm is in fact not inspected for a period of 40 days, on a literal reading the insured would still be in breach of that warranty as there has been a lapse of time greater than 30 days in which the alarm was not inspected. However, once the alarm has been inspected on the 40th day, the risk has returned to what was originally contemplated by the parties because the scaffolding would now be fitted with an alarm that had been inspected within the past 30 days. Accordingly, for losses sustained between the 30th and 40th days since the last inspection, the insurer would not be liable but liability would reattach as soon as the insured inspected the burglar alarm.

In other cases, the question of whether a risk has become essentially the same as that originally contemplated by the parties will be more difficult to resolve. The Law Commission used the example of a warranty covering wine storage in order to illustrate those circumstances in which a risk cannot be restored to that originally contemplated by the parties.[183] In their example, the insurance policy included a warranty that the insured would store the wine horizontally in a cool cellar within one month of receipt of the bottles, but in fact the insured did not move the wine bottles into the cellar until four months after receipt. During the time before storage, irreversible damage was caused to the corks which meant that the wine later spoiled despite being stored in the correct orientation and at the correct temperature at the time the losses occurred. Whilst it is clear that the risk had not become essentially the same as that originally contemplated by the parties when the wine bottles were eventually moved into the cellar, it is suggested that this particular example is unhelpful because the losses were attributable to something that happened during the breach and so the insurer would be able to avoid liability regardless of whether the breach could later be said to have been remedied.[184] Perhaps a more cogent example would be that of a car insured for private use under a policy containing a warranty that required the insured not to put the vehicle to any commercial use during the entire period of cover. If the owner went on to use the vehicle for his taxi business during the first few months of the policy but thereafter returned the car to private use, it might be possible to argue that even after the commercial usage ended the risk would not have returned to that originally contemplated by the parties. This is because the warranty in question would typically be utilised by the insurer as a control mechanism to prevent exposure to a whole swath of risks that the vehicle might encounter during commercial usage, which are simply never factored into a vehicle insurance policy that is provided for private use. Because

---

[183] See above, fn.182 at para.17.46.
[184] See above, para.5-094.

the commercial usage had fundamentally altered the type of risk into one which had never been anticipated by the insurer and was entirely outside the remit of the policy provided, it might be possible to argue that the breach was incapable of remedy because the risk could not be returned to that originally contemplated by the parties. Indeed, the Law Commission express that the purpose of the warranty can be a key factor used to determine whether the risk is capable of being returned to what was originally contemplated by the parties, stating:

> "We think that the correct approach to take when considering whether a time-specific warranty has been remedied is to look at the purpose for which the warranty was inserted in the contract and ask whether that purpose has been frustrated or whether, due to the actions taken to remedy the breach of warranty, the purpose is still in substance fulfilled and the risk profile is restored to that which the insurer accepted. As above, if warranties are risk control measures, then we see no reason why an insurer should have no liability if the risk is effectively that which it agreed to accept."[185]

5-097   **Breaches incapable of remedy.**   Section 10(4)(b) of the 2015 Act explicitly recognises that some breaches of warranty will not be capable of being remedied by any means. The most common warranties that will be incapable of remedy will be those where the insured is effectively warranting the existence of a past or present fact where the fact is later found to be inaccurate, such as where an insured warrants that a house is constructed from bricks and mortar when it is actually made of wood.[186] The Law Commission also use the example of a breach of a warranty relating to a confidentiality duty, which can never be remedied once compromised.[187]

5-098   **Liability for premium in suspension.**   The 2015 Act makes no changes to an insured's liability for the premium after a breach of warranty, with the intention that it will continue to be governed by the precise terms of the policy.[188] An insured must be particularly careful to keep up the payment of premium instalments during the period of suspension where the policy allows the insurer to terminate the contract if premium instalments are missed,[189] in order to preserve the effectiveness of the cover once the breach has been remedied.

5-099   **A right to cancel.**   There is no statutory right to cancel the insurance policy for either the insured or insurer after a breach of warranty, and so this will continue to be determined by whatever termination provisions are included in the terms of the policy.

5-100   **Other exclusions.**   The 2015 Act also provides for circumstances in which an insured will be exempt from compliance with a particular warranty, mirroring the effect of s.34 of the MIA.[190] Accordingly, s.10(3) of the 2015 Act provides that a breach of warranty will not suspend the insurer's liability where:

---

[185] Law Commission *"Insurance Contract Law: Business Disclosure; Warranties; Insurers' Remedies for Fraudulent Claims; and Late Payment"*, (Law Commission, 2014). *http://www.lawcom.gov.uk/wp-content/uploads/2015/03/lc353_insurance-contract-law.pdf* [Accessed 24 June 2016] at para.17.48.
[186] See above, fn.185 at para.17.49.
[187] See above, fn.185 at para.17.49.
[188] See above, fn.185 at para.17.58.
[189] See above, fn.185 at para.17.59.
[190] See below, paras 12-029 to 12-032.

"(a) because of a change of circumstances, the warranty ceases to be applicable to the circumstances of the contract,

(b) compliance with the warranty is rendered unlawful by any subsequent law, or

(c) the insurer waives the breach of warranty."

Of these exceptions, (c) will continue to have the most relevance. Although under the previous law it was only possible for an insurer to waive a breach of warranty by estoppel,[191] the Law Commission anticipate[192] that the new provisions would allow waiver by election because the effect of a breach of warranty is now to suspend liability rather than to bring the insurance policy to an end. As such, a waiver by the insurer will no longer have to operate by "waiving a dead contract back to life". Waiver of breach of warranty could thus, in appropriate cases, be based either on election or estoppel, under the 2015 Act.

Contracting out.   As with all other areas of the 2015 Act, the parties are free to contract out of the default regime of remedies for breach of warranty in lieu of imposing more onerous consequences on the insured. Any contracting out which places the insured in a worse position than they would have been in under the provisions of the 2015 Act must meet the transparency requirements in order to have contractual effect,[193] and in the context of warranties a particular emphasis will be placed on the requirement that a term must be unambiguous as to its effect. If a warranty is particularly crucial to the risk in question, an insurer would be advised to draft a clearly worded term within the policy which sets out the exact consequences of a breach by the insured in order to ensure that the courts give the term its desired contractual effect.   **5-101**

Identification of warranties under the policy.   Section 10 of the 2015 Act does not seek to define what is meant by the term "warranty" and the Law Commission expressed the intention that warranties would continue to be identified in accordance with the statutory definition under s.33 of the MIA and the case law that has arisen on the subject.[194] Nevertheless, it is clear that the new provisions will have a profound impact on the courts' treatment of policy terms and the way that particular obligations on the insured will be construed in the event of breach. The first point to note is that much of the previous case law on the identification of warranties will now largely be redundant on the matter, as the relevant cases predominantly required judges to distinguish "warranties" from "suspensory conditions" which, under the provisions of the MIA, carried far less severe consequences for the insured.[195] Now that there is no useful distinction to be made between terms which are warranties and terms which are suspensory conditions, a more important distinction under the 2015 Act will be between warranties and more onerous terms, such as conditions precedent.   **5-102**

This point merits some further discussion. In their treatment of contracting out

---

[191] See below, para.12-031.

[192] Law Commission *"Insurance Contract Law: Business Disclosure; Warranties; Insurers' Remedies for Fraudulent Claims; and Late Payment"*, (Law Commission, 2014). *http://www.lawcom.gov.uk/wp-content/uploads/2015/03/lc353_insurance-contract-law.pdf* [Accessed 24 June 2016] at para.17.68.

[193] See below, para.5-135.

[194] Law Commission "Insurance Contract Law: Business Disclosure; Warranties; Insurers' Remedies for Fraudulent Claims; and Late Payment", (Law Commission, 2014). *http://www.lawcom.gov.uk/wp-content/uploads/2015/03/lc353_insurance-contract-law.pdf* [Accessed 24 June 2016], at paras 15.13 to 15.15.

[195] See below, para.12-014.

of the default regime applicable to warranties under the 2015 Act, the Law Commission addressed the issue of other terms suspending, excluding or extinguishing liability. They acknowledged that the parties remained free to provide for severe consequences, including discharging the insurer from liability, in the event that a particular term was breached. However, the Law Commission also suggested that in construing "onerous terms" under the 2015 Act, the courts should now be inclined, at least where some ambiguity of meaning is present, to treat such terms as warranties, with the result that the insured-favourable provisions of s.10 of the 2015 Act should apply. They stated:

> "However, even under the current law, the courts are reluctant to give effect to a term that purports to discharge liability without it being very clear that that is what the parties intended. We would anticipate this interpretative attitude persisting under our recommendations. As we have seen, courts have re-categorised terms which appear to be 'warranties' in order to avoid the harsh consequences. *If our recommendations are enacted, courts might well start to find that onerous terms are warranties in order to reach the conclusion that liability is suspended rather than completely extinguished. Although it would be possible for an insurer to write a clearly worded term which would result in discharge of liability if breached* (or which would prevent liability attaching if not complied with by a certain time), *where there is ambiguity we would anticipate the term being treated in this way.*"[196] (emphasis supplied)

Were the courts to adopt the Law Commission's suggestion to, all else being equal, incline to construe onerous terms as warranties, subject to s.10 of the 2015 Act, it could transpire in practice that most terms purporting to extinguish the insurer's liability as a consequence of breach, rather than merely suspending that liability, would be ineffective, unless drafted in accordance with the 2015 Act's transparency requirements. Whether or not such an outcome should be desired, it is suggested that for the courts to adopt the Law Commission's suggestion would be wrong. Contrary to the Law Commission's view, the mode of reasoning they refer to—which, before the 2015 Act, led courts to construe terms purporting to be warranties as less onerous terms—does not support their suggested judicial inclination to construe terms as warranties under the 2015 Act. In the absence of the support of this mode of reasoning, their suggestion would represent an interference with the parties' contractual freedom for which there is no justification in the 2015 Act itself.

To explain further: under the 2015 Act, as before, a warranty should be identified, and distinguished from other types of terms, on the basis of the wording of the particular term, by reference to the broad definition in s.33(1) of the MIA and relevant case law. As noted by the Law Commission, the courts, even in the face of terms purporting in relatively clear language to be warranties, have in some cases allowed themselves to take into account, inter alia, the severe consequences for the insured of so construing the term. In those cases, the courts have reasoned that the unlikelihood that the parties would have intended such severe consequences is a factor in favour of construing the term in question as something other than a warranty (often as a suspensory condition). This mode of reasoning remains open to the courts today.

What should be the effect of the 2015 Act on the courts' approach to identifying a warranty? A term may, in this regard, be subject to at least two types of ambiguity: one, as to whether the parties intended to make a warranty, or something

[196] Law Commission "Insurance Contract Law: Business Disclosure; Warranties; Insurers' Remedies for Fraudulent Claims; and Late Payment", (Law Commission, 2014). *http://www.lawcom.gov.uk/wp-content/uploads/2015/03/lc353_insurance-contract-law.pdf* [Accessed 24 June 2016], at para.17.74.

else; and a second, as to whether or not the parties intended to provide for consequences more severe than those applicable under s.10 of the 2015 Act, in the event of breach. The Law Commission's suggestion conflates these two issues in circumstances where a consideration of both types of ambiguity would better aid the courts' interpretation of the policy term. In this regard, a number of possible scenarios may arise.

First, where it is clear the parties intended to make a warranty, but there is ambiguity as to whether the language purports to attach more severe consequences to breach than those set out in s.10, then s.10 will apply, and application of the transparency requirements provided for under ss.16(2) and 17 should mean that no more severe consequences will apply. Resolution of the ambiguity in relation to the second issue should be unnecessary.

Secondly, where it is clear the parties intended to make a non-warranty, but the intended severity of the consequences of breach is unclear, s.10 should not apply: by hypothesis, as the term is clearly not a warranty, there is no room for the Law Commission's suggested judicial inclination, to construe the term as a warranty, to apply. The ambiguity regarding the severity of the consequences of breach will be resolved as a matter of construction, as it would have been before the 2015 Act.

Thirdly, where it is clear that the parties intended to provide for consequences of breach that are more severe than those provided for under s.10, but it is ambiguous whether the term was intended to be a warranty, then all else being equal—and contrary to the Law Commission's suggestion—there is reason to argue that the courts should incline against construing the term as a warranty. This is because it would seem contradictory for the parties both to intend for their term to be a warranty subject to s.10, and also for breach of that term to attract consequences more severe than those applicable under s.10. In addition, to conclude that the parties intended to create a warranty with more onerous consequences of breach than under s.10, would be to attribute to the parties an (unlikely) intention to submit the effectiveness of their term to being controlled by reference to the transparency requirements set out in s.17. It is submitted that, where it is clear that the parties intended to create a term more onerous than a warranty subject to s.10, this should be taken as an indication that the term was not intended to be a warranty, and this indication should be into account in resolving any ambiguity regarding the classification of the term.

Fourthly, where it is clear that the parties intended to provide for consequences of breach of lesser or equal severity to those applicable under s.10, but it is not clear whether the term was intended to be a warranty or not, the ambiguity is immaterial: the term should apply with its intended severity. Further, in such a case, under the 2015 Act there would seem to be no reason for the courts to consider either construction—warranty or non-warranty—to be more likely than the other.

Finally, where there is ambiguity both as to whether the intended consequences of breach were to be more severe than under s.10, and as to whether or not the term was intended to be a warranty, then, all else being equal, the courts may incline towards resolving the ambiguity as to the intended severity of the clause in favour of the insured, with the result that this scenario is in effect the same as the fourth.

Accordingly, where there is any ambiguity about whether a term is intended to be a warranty under the 2015 Act, then all else being equal, there is no reason to expect the courts to tend one way or the other: save in a case where it is clear that the intended consequences of breach are to be more severe than those applicable under s.10, in which case there is reason to suggest that the courts should incline against finding that the term is a warranty.

4. TERMS RELEVANT TO PARTICULAR DESCRIPTIONS OF LOSS

5-103 **Reliance by insurers on irrelevant warranties.** The provisions contained within s.11 of the 2015 Act bear a pedigree that can be traced back through the insurance law reforms enacted by New Zealand under s.11 of the Insurance Law Reform Act 1977 ("ILRA") and Australia under s.54 of the Insurance Contracts Act 1984 ("ICA"). Both provisions have attracted a degree of notoriety around the extent to which they are perceived disproportionately to favour the insured against (what would appear to be) the explicit terms and requirements of the policy, and one can safely assume that s.11 of the 2015 Act will attract similar scrutiny from the insurance world. Some of the challenges encountered under the Australian and New Zealand provisions illuminate the difficulties which s.11 of the 2015 Act has been drafted to avoid, and may therefore be of use when interpreting and applying the provisions.

In essence, s.11 of the 2015 Act can be understood as targeting a very specific mischief caused when insurers rely on an irrelevant breach of warranty to avoid liability for a claim. A paradigm example of this mischief would be where an insurer relies on the absence of a fire alarm in order to escape payment of a claim for flood damage under a policy which covers both perils. The broad effect of s.11 will be to act as a control over particular terms within the policy that would otherwise allow the insurer to avoid liability, and if a particular term falls within the scope of s.11 then that term will only afford insurers with a defence to a claim where the breach of the term was relevant to the loss.

Reform in this area has faced difficulties because s.11 had to be drafted in a way which cuts across the insurer's arrangement of the policy so as to identify all of the terms intended to be restricted by the new controls. If s.11 had been drafted to only effect "warranties", an insurer could quite easily escape all of the effects of s.11 by re-casting the terms, previously drafted as warranties, as conditions precedent or exclusions, which would unacceptably sterilise the operation of the provision. On the other hand, there are certain policy terms which are clearly intended to delimit the scope of cover rather than just manage risks, and these terms should operate unimpeded by s.11 to extinguish or suspend the entire cover under the policy. The first difficulty faced by s.11 is therefore the way in which it will discriminate between the policy terms which should be caught by the new controls and the terms which are more generally descriptive of the risk the insurer has agreed to cover. In this respect, the 2015 Act differs from the laws of Australia and New Zealand because it only targets terms which tend to reduce the risk of losses of a particular type or at a particular time or place, and it will not be applied to terms defining the risk as a whole. In contrast, s.11 of the ILRA will not apply to terms which specify a kind of loss or quantum of loss not indemnified, and s.54 of the ICA will only apply to a term limiting coverage in response to some act or omission by the insured, unless that act was the omission to obtain wider cover. As there is nothing within the 2015 Act that purports to determine how to identify a term defining the risk as a whole, the approach taken in other jurisdictions may inform the UK courts' approach to the issue of identifying policy terms which should be exempt from the provisions of s.11.

5-104 **Causation.** Once a term has been found to fall within the ambit of s.11, there is the further question of the necessary degree of connection between the breach of the warranty and the loss that occurred in order to allow the insurer to avoid liability. Expressed another way, it is the question of when a breach of policy term will be "relevant" to the loss such that there is no mischief in allowing the insurer to rely on it. Both s.11 of the ILRA and s.54 of the ICA employ a test of causation under which an insured can restore cover if it can prove a loss was not caused or contributed to by the breach. However, s.11 of the 2015 Act adopts the looser test of whether the non-compliance with the term of the policy could not have increased the risk of the loss which actually occurred in the circumstances in which it occurred. Thus, for example, a breach of any term relating to the risk of fire will suspend cover in respect of fire damage, even if the breach did not contribute to the actual loss.

(a)   The Australian law

An act or omission by the insured or some other person.   Section 54 of the ICA   **5-105** has attracted widespread scrutiny over the scope of terms which have been found to engage the provision. This is primarily due to the broad drafting of s.54, which will apply where:

> "(1) ... the effect of a contract of insurance would, but for this section, be that the insurer may refuse to pay a claim, either in whole or in part, *by reason of some act of the insured or of some other person*, being an act that occurred after the contract was entered into. [emphasis supplied]
>
> ...
>
> (6) A reference in this section to an act includes a reference to:
>   (a)   omission;"

The provision therefore requires the courts to entirely disregard the form of terms within the policy and simply identify an act or omission by the insured or some other person which the policy responds to in a way that allows the insurer to deny the indemnity. The High Court of Australia confirmed that the form of the terms and the legal character of the insurer's reason for refusal were irrelevant to the question of whether a term is caught under s.54 in *Antico v Heath Fielding Australia Pty Ltd*[197] when holding that:

> "Sub-section (1) of s 54 focuses not on the legal character of a reason which entitles an insurer to refuse to pay a claim – falling outside a covered risk, coming within an exclusion or non-compliance with a condition – but on the actual conduct of the insured, that is, on some act which the insured does or omits to do. The legal classification of the act or omission is immaterial."

The drafting of s.54 is exceptionally wide and could potentially restore cover in a number of situations for which the policy was worded specifically to exclude. As a result, the courts were divided over the application of s.54 and the question of whether there were any types of acts or omissions which should not bring the provisions into play. The starting point from *Antico* was that the wording of s.54 was broad enough to encapsulate an omission by the insured to exercise its rights under the policy:

> "The legislation is expressed in broad terms and, on its face, there is no reason why the omission of the insured may not be a failure to exercise a right, choice or liberty which the insured enjoys under the contract of insurance."

---

[197] *Antico v Heath Fielding Australia Pty* [1997] HCA 35.

This position caused anxiety amongst insurers where the underlying cover was provided by a "claims made" rather than "occurrence based" policy, such as under professional indemnity cover. There was cause for concern that an interpretation of s.54 along the lines suggested by *Antico* would eradicate the main benefit of a claims made policy, which is that it prevents the "long tail" liability that can attach to an insurer if a claim is brought a number of years after the conclusion of the policy against the insured for negligent conduct during the period of cover. Under the explicit wording of s.54 of the ICA, the failure of the third party to bring a claim against the insured during the currency of the policy could constitute an "omission" by some other person that would allow the insurer to refuse cover, and would therefore be caught by the provisions. Because the insurer would be unable to identify any prejudice suffered as a result of the third party's omission to bring a claim before the policy expired, the insurer would be unable to refuse cover and the policy would have to respond. This position would have had the effect of rendering a claims made policy no different from an occurrence based policy, and would therefore have been destructive to the availability of claims made policies throughout Australia.

Some limit to the types of acts and omissions capable of falling within s.54 was therefore required, and a number of different controls were postulated by the judiciary in different cases. In *Greentree v FAI General Insurance Co Ltd*[198] the Court of Appeal sought to distinguish between an "omission" and a "non-event", the latter of which was said to involve conduct "wholly external" to the policy that would therefore not be caught by the s.54 controls.[199] Using this reasoning, the Court of Appeal considered that the making of a claim against the insured by a third party would be "wholly external" to events falling under the policy, and so s.54 would not operate to restore cover in those circumstances. However, this position was short lived as the High Court overruled it in *FAI General Insurance Co Ltd v Australian Hospital Care Pty Ltd*[200] after the majority concluded that:

> "The difficulty with referring to events as 'wholly external to the policy' is that no question about the effect of a contract of insurance can ever be asked in isolation from external facts and circumstances. The question is inevitably about the application of the contract in the light of certain real or hypothesised facts and circumstances. Those facts and circumstances will always be wholly 'external' to the policy."[201]

Such a distinction, they argued, would break down in circumstances where it was a person who had failed to do something rather than an event that had failed to happen because it was impossible to draw the line between omissions by a person which would be caught under the s.54 controls and omissions by a person which would instead be classed as "non-events" unsuitable for control by s.54.[202] Whilst the majority therefore determined that s.54 was broad enough to include most acts or omissions, they determined that s.54 would not apply where the omission was to obtain the more ample insurance cover:

> "Applying a commonsense approach, and accepting that s 54(1) of the Act is not limited to a sole or unique cause of the entitlement to refuse payment, such entitlement is not related to a third person's

---

[198] *Greentree v FAI General Insurance Co Ltd* (1998) 44 NSWLR 706.
[199] See above, fn.198 at 710.
[200] *FAI General Insurance Co Ltd v Australian Hospital Care Pty Ltd* [2001] HCA 38.
[201] See above, fn.200 at para.[37].
[202] See above, fn.200 at para.[38].

'omission'. It is no more 'by reason of' such 'omission' [viz. to bring a claim against the insured within the policy period], in the sense that s 54(1) contemplates, than it would be 'by reason of' an omission on the part of the insured itself to secure a better, larger or more ample policy of insurance. Similarly, the 'omission' of the insured to take steps, prior to a loss, to elect an expanded form of cover, would not be an 'omission' of the kind which would attract relief under s 54(1) of the Act. In such a case, the 'reason' for the insurer's refusal to pay would be classified by the law as the absence of relevant cover between the insurer and the insured, not the 'omission' of the insured to obtain a cover that was more ample."[203]

Although this would appear capable of constricting the application of s.54 to contain it within a more sensible remit, the facts of *FAI General Insurance Co Ltd* reveal that this exception was far narrower than might first have appeared. The insurance policy in question was a "discovery" policy which differed from a "claims made" policy in the important respect that, in addition to the insurer providing cover against third party claims made against the insured during the currency of the policy, the insurer would also cover claims where the insured notified the insurer of an "occurrence which may subsequently give rise to a claim against [the insured] for breach of professional duty" before the policy had expired. The policy therefore provided a mechanism for the insured to extend cover to claims that were brought after expiration, provided that the insured notified the insurer of a relevant occurrence. In the circumstances of the case, Australian Hospital Care Pty Ltd was made aware of a potential claim against one of its doctors which the policy would have indemnified had the proper notification procedures been followed. However, the hospital had failed to make a notification of the claim to FAI because it appeared that the claim would not go ahead against the doctor. The policy expired and the claim was brought shortly thereafter, and the High Court had to determine whether the failure of the insured to adopt the proper notification procedure for the claim was an omission capable of engaging s.54 of the ICA or whether the claim fell entirely outside of the scope of cover provided. Somewhat problematically, the High Court did not consider that this would be a case where the insured's omission was a failure to obtain more ample cover. Instead, Kirby J considered that s.54 would be engaged as:

"The real 'reason' for the rejection of a claim, otherwise fully viable and to which, had there been notification, the policy of insurance would undoubtedly have responded, will be classified as the 'omission' on the insured's part to notify the claim."[204]

In support of this position, Kirby J relied on a distinction first drawn in the earlier case of *East End Real Estate Pty Ltd v CE Heath Casualty & General Insurance Ltd*[205] between circumstances in which the claim made was simply not within the cover provided and circumstances where it was *by reason of* an act of the insured that the claim fell outside the scope of cover. Accordingly, because the failure to notify FAI of the possibly pending claim was the sole reason the claim fell outside of the policy, s.54 would be engaged and the insurer was liable to cover the loss. This division between a simple absence of cover and an act of the insured rendering a claim outside of the scope of cover is problematic in a number of respects.

First, applying this distinction to the facts of the case, it is not easy to see how the courts would have distinguished between claims not covered *by reason of* the

---

[203] See above, fn.200 at para.[84].
[204] See above, fn.200 at para.[85].
[205] *East End Real Estate Pty Ltd v CE Heath Casualty & General Insurance Ltd* (1991) 25 NSWLR 400 at 407.

insured's failure to notify, and all other "long tail" claims that could presumably be brought under the policy. The only discernible difference would appear to be that the insured had been made aware of the occurrence giving rise to the existence of the possible claim in *FAI General Insurance Co Ltd*, and so in those circumstances the reason that the cover failed to respond could appropriately be characterised as the insured's failure to notify rather than the third party's failure to bring a claim. However, it is not easy to see how such a distinction would ever work in practice – would it be sufficient for a claim to be brought within the ambit of s.54 simply because the doctor in question had suspicions that it may have acted negligently during a surgery, with nothing else to suggest that a claim might later be brought? The application of the distinction in such a case would clearly lead to difficult questions as to whether the insured had acquired sufficient information to give notice of an occurrence prior to expiry of the policy period. More generally, the effect of Kirby J's distinction would seem to have been to create an unpalatable uncertainty for the insurer for many years after the policy has expired. This would also undermine the key advantage of a discovery policy, which is that upon expiry, the insurer should be aware of the full measure of liability accrued under the policy and all possible future claims which it may still be required to indemnify.

Secondly, the distinction between an absence of cover caused by an act of the insured and an absence of cover that necessarily results from the nature and extent of the policy provided is not, it is suggested, a sensible line to be drawn between refusals s.54 will control and refusals to pay claims it will not. The effect of such a distinction would be to prevent insurers defining the scope of the insurance cover by reference to any type of act by the insured or any use made of the insured property, as any such definitions would inevitably bring s.54 into play as soon as the insurer sought to rely on them to refuse cover. This would mean that, for example, a car insurance policy covering personal use would still be capable of responding if the car were used commercially, and contents cover for a home would be capable of responding if the home were also used as a business. Although the detriment suffered by insurers in such circumstances will often be mitigated by the operation of the rest of s.54, it is undesirable that an insurer should be unable to define the scope of cover provided along such lines without furnishing the courts with the power to modify the policy and recast the insurer's obligations in a manner contrary to the policy's express terms.

The latter criticism was implicitly recognised in the Supreme Court case of *Rae Johnson v Triple C Furniture & Electrical Pty Ltd*.[206] In *Rae Johnson*, the insurers had provided aviation insurance to the insured which carried the requirement that the pilot operating the plane had satisfactorily undertaken a flight review within the previous two years. There was a crash, and the court was able to conclude that the pilot was in breach of this requirement. However, the court did not consider that this would be an omission by the insured which would be caught by s.54 on the basis that:

> "the policy did not offer indemnity in circumstances where the aircraft was flown by a pilot who had not satisfactorily completed a flight review within two years previous to the loss."[207]

---

[206] *Rae Johnson v Triple C Furniture & Electrical Pty Ltd* [2010] QCA 282.
[207] See above, fn.206 at para.77.

Rae Johnson therefore reached the opposite conclusion to the High Court in *FAI General Insurance Co Ltd* as it allowed the insurer to define the scope of cover provided by reference to an omission by the insured without bringing s.54 into play. However, the issue came before the High Court once again in *Maxwell v Highway Hauliers Pty Ltd*[208] in what is now leading authority on the application of s.54 of the ICA. The insurance policy was provided by Lloyd's Underwriters against loss or damage to a fleet of vehicles, and included a term which stated:

> "No indemnity is provided under this policy of Insurance when Your Vehicle/s are being operated by drivers of B Doubles ... unless the driver:
> ...
> Has a PAQS driver profile score of at least 36, or an equivalent program approved by Us."

Two of the insured's vehicles were damaged in separate accidents whilst being driven by a driver who had not undertaken the requisite PAQS test, and the court had to determine whether this would be an omission capable of activating s.54 despite the policy stating that the indemnity was only provided in respect of properly qualified drivers. The High Court found that s.54 was engaged:

> "Here the fact that each vehicle was being operated at the time of the accident by an untested driver is properly characterised as having been by reason of an 'act' that occurred after the contract of insurance was entered into. There was an omission of the Insured to ensure that each vehicle was operated by a driver who had undertaken a PAQS test or an equivalent program approved by the Insurers. That omission occurred during the Period of Insurance.
> The Insured having made claims seeking indemnity under the Policy in relation to accidents which occurred during the Period of Insurance, it is sufficient to engage s 54(1) that the effect of the Policy is that the Insurers may refuse to pay those claims by reason only of acts which occurred after the contract was entered into. Precisely how the Policy produced that effect is not to the point. The conclusion of the Court of Appeal in the present case was correct."[209]

The High Court therefore reinforced the decision in *FAI General Insurance Co Ltd* and explicitly overruled *Rae Johnson*.[210] The position under the ICA remains that an insurer is unable to define the scope of cover by reference to any act or use of the insured property by the insured without activating s.54, a position which threatens the effectiveness of terms which can properly be construed as descriptive of the scope of cover. The failure of the ICA to provide an appropriate mechanism to distinguish between terms which should be subject to judicial regulation and terms which should not has crucially informed the Law Commissions' own recommendations in respect of UK law.[211]

Act did not cause the loss.   Once a policy term has been found to fall within s.54   **5-106**
of the ICA, the effect on the insurer's liability for the claim will depend upon whether the act by the insured or other person was capable of causing or contributing to the loss that occurred. Where the act was so capable, s.54(2) provides that the insurer may refuse to pay the entirety of the claim:

> "(2) Subject to the succeeding provisions of this section, where the act could reasonably be regarded as being capable of causing or contributing to a loss in respect of which insurance cover is provided by the contract, the insurer may refuse to pay the claim."

---

[208] *Maxwell v Highway Hauliers Pty Ltd* [2014] HCA 33.
[209] See above, fn.208 at paras 26 to 27.
[210] See above, fn.208 at para.28.
[211] See below, para.5-110.

However, the insured will still be allowed its claim if it can prove that no part of the loss was in fact caused by the relevant act, or a specific part of the loss was not caused by it. Thus, s.5(3) and (4) provide:

"(3) Where the insured proves that no part of the loss that gave rise to the claim was caused by the act, the insurer may not refuse to pay the claim by reason only of the act.

(4) Where the insured proves that some part of the loss that gave rise to the claim was not caused by the act, the insurer may not refuse to pay the claim, so far as it concerns that part of the loss, by reason only of the act."

Using the example of building cover which includes fire as a specified peril, an insurer may be able to avoid liability for fire damage to the building where the insured failed to comply with a warranty to inspect a fire alarm every 30 days as this could reasonably be regarded as being capable of contributing to the fire damage. However, the insured would have a defence if it could prove that the circumstances of the fire were such that, even if the alarm had been operational, it would not have made a difference to the losses that occurred, for example because the fire brigade would not have reached the building in time to prevent the losses in any event. The provisions therefore employ a test of causation, but the burden is on the insured to prove that its breach of policy term, whilst capable of contributing to a particular type of loss, did not in fact cause the losses in the circumstances of the case.

5-107 **Insurer prejudiced by act not reasonably capable of causing or contributing to a loss.** Where the act itself is not one that could reasonably be regarded as being capable of causing or contributing to a loss in respect of which insurance cover is provided, the consequences of the act will be determined under s.54(1) of the ICA which provides:

"(1) Subject to this section, where the effect of a contract of insurance would, but for this section, be that the insurer may refuse to pay a claim, either in whole or in part, by reason of some act of the insured or of some other person, being an act that occurred after the contract was entered into but not being an act in respect of which subsection (2) applies, the insurer may not refuse to pay the claim by reason only of that act but the insurer's liability in respect of the claim is reduced by the amount that fairly represents the extent to which the insurer's interests were prejudiced as a result of that act."

The insurer must therefore cover the insured's losses fully save for where it can show that it has suffered some prejudice as a result of the insured's act. There may be cases where the extent of the insurer's "prejudice" may operate to allow a claim to be reduced to nil. This was the case in *Ferrcom Pty Ltd v Commercial Union Assurance Company of Australia Ltd*,[212] where the insurer was able to show that the prejudice it had suffered from the insured registering a crane to be driven on public roads was the chance it would otherwise have had to cancel the policy or provide alternative cover with an exclusion for the type of loss which actually occurred. However, it may be impossible for the insurer to show that it suffered any prejudice at all, and this would render them liable for the entire claim despite the insured breaching the terms of the policy and operating outside of the scope of cover provided. This was the result in both *FAI General Insurance Co Ltd* and *Maxwell*,

---

[212] *Ferrcom Pty Ltd v Commercial Union Assurance Company of Australia Ltd* (1993) 111 ALR 339.

where the insurer did not suffer any identifiable prejudice from the insured failing to notify the insurer of a potential claim or of the drivers failing to undertake the PAQS test, respectively. It is undesirable that terms which quite clearly delineate the scope of the cover provided as a whole could be rendered entirely ineffective because the insurer is unable to establish any prejudice suffered as a result of their being breached. This has undoubtedly influenced the provisions of the 2015 Act.[213]

(b) The New Zealand law

Events or circumstances likely to increase the risk of such loss occurring. The controls employed under the New Zealand ILRA are drafted more narrowly than the Australian reforms, but have attracted a similar degree of scrutiny over the wide range of policy terms that the courts initially found were within the ambit of Section 11. Rather than being engaged by any act or omission of the insured, s.11 of the ILRA will operate to control any terms which exclude or limit the insurer's liability based on the happening of certain events or the existence of certain circumstances which are likely to increase the risk of the type of loss the cover is provided for. Accordingly, s.11 provides: **5-108**

> *"Certain exclusions forbidden*
> Where—
>
> (a) by the provisions of a contract of insurance the circumstances in which the insurer is bound to indemnify the insured against loss are so defined as to exclude or limit the liability of the insurer to indemnify the insured on the happening of certain events or on the existence of certain circumstances; and
> (b) in the view of the court or arbitrator determining the claim of the insured the liability of the insurer has been so defined because the happening of such events or the existence of such circumstances was in the view of the insurer likely to increase the risk of such loss occurring,—
>
> the insured shall not be disentitled to be indemnified by the insurer by reason only of such provisions of the contract of insurance if the insured proves on the balance of probability that the loss in respect of which the insured seeks to be indemnified was not caused or contributed to by the happening of such events or the existence of such circumstances."

The ILRA therefore designates a two-stage enquiry to determine whether an insured can rely on s.11 to prevent an insurer refusing liability on the basis of a particular policy term: first, the term must meet the requirements of s.11(a) and (b) to be caught by the provision, and second, the insured must prove that the loss was not caused or contributed to by events or circumstances falling within that term. The first stage of the enquiry requires the courts to interrogate the purpose behind the inclusion of a particular policy term, and if the court considers that the term was intended to mitigate the risk posed by particular events or particular circumstances then the term will be caught and subjected to the causation test. However, the courts' application of s.11 initially cast the net too wide, and was used to attack policy terms which really went to the heart of the risk profile the insurer had agreed to accept.

Terms specifying a kind of loss or quantum of loss not indemnified. The tension encountered by the courts when operating s.11 of the ILRA arose in relation to policy terms which could, on the one hand, be construed as delineating the scope **5-109**

---

[213] See below, para.5-110.

of the cover provided to the insured, but could also, on the other, be construed as terms preventing exposure to a whole swathe of risks that the insurer wished to mitigate. For example, a policy term requiring that the insured will not operate an insured vehicle for commercial use is one which clearly defines the scope of cover provided, but it is also a term that could be construed as preventing exposure to all of the risks a commercially operated vehicle would encounter that are not factored in to a policy provided for private usage. Some distinction was needed to prevent such terms falling within the remit of s.11, and in *Barnaby v The South British Insurance Co Ltd*[214] the High Court of New Zealand determined that s.11 would not capture terms specifying a kind of loss or quantum of loss not indemnified:

> "the section is designed to deal with those kinds of exclusion clauses which provide for circumstances likely to increase the risk of a loss which the policy actually covers. The most common examples are found in the field of motor vehicle insurance, such as driving a motor vehicle whilst under the influence of alcohol, or driving a motor vehicle which is in an unsafe condition. The section is not designed to deal with exclusion clauses which specify the kind of loss or the quantum of loss to which the cover does not apply at all."

Whilst this approach was an eminently sensible one, the courts in later decisions failed to draw the distinction between terms specifying the scope of cover and terms that merely manage risks. Thus, in *Sun Alliance Insurance Ltd v Travel the Earth Ltd*,[215] the District Court of Auckland found that an employment exclusion in a travel insurance policy would engage the provisions of s.11 of the ILRA on the basis that the employment exclusion had clearly been intended to reduce the risks that the individual would be exposed to during the period of cover:

> "However, it is not difficult sensibly to recognise that for one to work as well as to play when travelling can widen the field of exposure to include a number of additional, in some cases possibly quite serious, risks. Work can involve the use of dangerous plant or equipment. Work can involve more time on the road or in the air than would otherwise be the case …
>
> I feel comfortable with the conclusion that this provision *was* designed to confine risks, to avoid their increase from the ordinary, and in that respect find it a perfectly legitimate limitation."

There were widespread concerns that the courts had interpreted the ambit of s.11 in a way which was too wide, and this anxiety was recognised in the New Zealand Law Commission report produced in 1998[216] which voiced concerns that s.11 had been applied to terms which were clearly those delimiting the risk the insurer had agreed to accept. The issue was considered again in the case of *Hall v FP North Ltd (in Liquidation)*,[217] which concerned a professional indemnity policy that contained two exclusions, the first for "claims relating directly or indirectly, attributable to or in consequence of the insolvency of any financial institution or fund manager" and the second for claims "alleging, arising out of, based upon … depreciation, or failure to appreciate in value, of any investments." FP North had been engaged by the claimant trustees to recommend a conservative investment portfolio, but had negligently recommended that the claimants invest $658,000 in fixed interest securities offered by ten companies, all of which had since gone into receivership or had

---

[214] *Barnaby v The South British Insurance Co Ltd* (1980) 1 ANZ Insurance Cases 60-401.

[215] *Sun Alliance Insurance Ltd v Travel the Earth Ltd* [1997] DCR 331.

[216] New Zealand Law Commission *"Some Insurance Law Problems"*, (New Zealand Law Commission, 1998) NZLC R46. *http://www.nzlii.org/nz/other/nzlc/report/R46/R46-3.html* [Accessed 24 June 2016] at para [43].

[217] *Hall v FP North Ltd (in Liquidation)* HC NEP CIV-2008-443-324.

moratoria placed on invested deposits. The claimants lost $300,000 from the investment, and after FP North went into liquidation, they brought an action directly against FP North's insurers by virtue of s.9(4) of the Law Reform Act 1936. To obtain leave to commence proceedings under s.9(4), the claimants had to show an arguable case that the insurer was liable to pay under the policy.

Abbott J determined that there were two reasons the exclusions would not fall within the controls of s.11. The first was that, properly construed, the two exclusions could not be considered as terms which reduced the risk of losses occurring:

"The insolvency of a financial institution or a fund manager, or depreciation in value in investments made as a result of FP North's advice, are not matters which are likely to increase the risk of FP North's liability ... They do not increase the risk that FP North will act in a way that will increase its liability."

Abbott J was also addressed on whether, following *Barnaby*, the two exclusions were actually terms which specified a kind of loss or quantum of loss not indemnified. Interestingly, the claimants sought to argue that the scope of cover provided should be interpreted in relation to only the insuring clause and extensions, rather than by considering the entire policy. Abbott J was unreceptive to such arguments. The exclusions were clearly intended to limit the scope of cover to circumstances where the losses were not related to insolvency or the depreciation of investments, as these were intended to fall outside of the remit of the cover provided:

"Counsel ... argued, in effect, that the loss covered by the policy should be decided only by reference to the insuring clause (civil liability) and automatic extension (breach of contract) of the policy. However, the endorsements are as much a part of the insurance contract as the policy terms and schedule ... The scope of the policy is determined by reading all together. In my opinion, when one reads it all together, it is apparent that the two clauses specify kinds of loss that are not covered by the policy, namely loss related to insolvency or [sic] financial institutions or fund managers, and loss related to depreciation in investment."

Accordingly, the claimants had not established an arguable case that the insurer would be liable to pay under the policy, and so the claim was dismissed.

This approach was followed in *Nelson Forests Ltd v Three Tuis Ltd*[218] in relation to a "Provider Farm Policy" that contained a clause excluding cover for personal liability in relation to "any business activity whether for profit or not". The relevant losses had been caused by the insured's failure to dispose of ashes properly in relation to a side business of letting out two tourist cabins on the property, with the result that a forest fire was started and the insured was personally liable for it. The question for the courts to determine was whether s.11 would apply to this exclusion, and Osborne J answered it with a resounding "no" on the basis that s.11 "does not operate to give the defendant cover for a business which Tower Insurance had not agreed to cover.

The New Zealand insurance reforms therefore serve to demonstrate some of the dangers that can be encountered when the statutory tools are inapt to properly discriminate between terms delineating the scope of cover provided and terms which merely manage risk. Under the New Zealand reforms, the judiciary were left with the task of creating a mechanism which would determine the scope of terms

---

[218] *Nelson Forests Ltd v Three Tuis Ltd* [2010] NZHC 2178.

to which s.11 should apply, and the cases following *Barnaby* elucidate some of the issues that may face the UK courts' application of s.11 of the 2015 Act.

(c) The UK approach

5-110 **General.** The UK provisions differ from those adopted in the Australian and New Zealand reforms in both the mechanisms used to distinguish between terms that will and will not be caught under the controls of s.11 of the 2015 Act, and the degree of connection required between the term and the loss necessary for the term to be effective. The Law Commission identified two categories of term that should not be caught by the provisions, and these exceptions are included on the face of the statute:

> "Not all warranties, conditions precedent or similar terms are about particular risks. As we said in CP3, some address more general issues, for example those relating to a policyholder's criminal record. Some define the whole contract, such as terms restricting use of a vehicle or property to private rather than commercial use. These terms should not be affected by these recommended reforms. Nor should the recommendations affect terms which have no bearing on the risk of a loss, such as premium payment warranties."[219]

The first exclusion from the ambit of s.11 is provided for terms that have no bearing on the risk of a loss at all, such as premium payment warranties and terms requiring the insured to adopt formalities during the claims procedure, the effectiveness of which s.11 was never intended to restrict. In that sense, the UK position is far narrower than that in Australia and will not have any impact on the operation of claims-made and discovery policies. This seems sensible as s.11 is aimed at the regulation of a very specific mischief and should not be used unduly to restrict the capacity of insurers to provide policies with particular modes of operation. The UK position is also brought into alignment with the New Zealand provisions in targeting those terms included by the insurer to prevent circumstances and events that increase the risk of losses, although the wording of the UK law emphasises the objective nature of the enquiry which must steer away from the subjective intentions of the actual insurer when deciding to include a particular term.[220]

The second exclusion from s.11 of the 2015 Act relates to terms which define the risk as a whole, though the statute does not provide any substantive definition for such terms. The 2015 Act therefore adopts the position taken by the courts of New Zealand in *Barnaby* that the provision should not be used to attack terms specifying the scope of cover provided under the policy.

5-111 **Compliance would "tend to reduce the risk".** Section 11(1) of the 2015 Act provides that the section will only be engaged by terms which would tend to reduce the risk of losses of a particular kind, at a particular location or at a particular time:

> "(1) This section applies to a term (express or implied) of a contract of insurance, other than a term defining the risk as a whole, if compliance with it would tend to reduce the risk of one or more of the following—
> (a) loss of a particular kind,
> (b) loss at a particular location,

---

[219] Law Commission "*Insurance Contract Law: Business Disclosure; Warranties; Insurers' Remedies for Fraudulent Claims; and Late Payment*", (Law Commission, 2014). *http://www.lawcom.gov.uk/wp-content/uploads/2015/03/lc353_insurance-contract-law.pdf* [Accessed 24 June 2016] at para.16.3.
[220] See below, para.5-111.

(c)   loss at a particular time."

The requirement that compliance with a term should "tend to reduce the risk" of a particular loss before being caught by the provision can be seen to be similar to the New Zealand reforms, which target terms that the insurer has specifically included for the purpose of mitigating risks. However, the test under s.11(1) of the 2015 Act is looser than the wording of the New Zealand statute because it employs objective criteria rather than requiring an investigation of why the particular insurer in the particular circumstances introduced the term. The Law Commission considered that this would appropriately reflect the fact that insurance policies are often in standard form and it is unlikely that evidence could be heard from the individual drafter to substantiate the purpose behind a particular policy term.[221] Part of the rationale behind the choice of an objective test was also to shift the enquiry that the courts were required to undertake away from issues concerning any causal connection between the term and the losses that occurred, in favour of a more basic enquiry about what a particular term would tend to achieve. The Law Commission remarks that:

> "The consciously objective element is intended to allow the court to look at what the effect of compliance might generally be. Importantly, it does not introduce a causal element about whether compliance would have prevented the loss, or whether the breach caused or contributed to it. It is simply whether compliance might usually be thought to reduce the chances of the particular type of loss being suffered."[222]

Accordingly, the provision requires the courts to look at the policy term itself and determine whether it is one which is generally capable of reducing particular risks.

Kind, location, time.   Section 11(1) of the 2015 Act specifies that the section will **5-112** only be engaged by terms which limit the risk of losses of a particular kind, at a particular location, or at a particular time. This is intended as the primary mechanism which will distinguish between terms which are used to manage risks and terms which delimit the scope of cover more generally.[223] For example, a term specifying that a vehicle is insured for private use[224] or a requirement in a marine policy that a ship is of a particular class[225] could not be said to reduce the risk of losses of a particular kind, at a particular location or at a particular time. The provision would also prevent Section 11 being applied to more general policy terms which are unconnected to the risk of loss, such as premium payment warranties or terms which identify the policy as "claims made" rather than "occurrence based". The 2015 Act therefore provides, on the face of the statute, clear limits to the courts' powers to interfere with policy terms under s.11 in order to avoid the difficulties encountered from the judicial interpretations of the Australian and New Zealand reforms.

---

[221] Law Commission "*Insurance Contract Law: Business Disclosure; Warranties; Insurers' Remedies for Fraudulent Claims; and Late Payment*", (Law Commission, 2014). *http://www.lawcom.gov.uk/wp-content/uploads/2015/03/lc353_insurance-contract-law.pdf* [Accessed 24 June 2016] at para.18.12.
[222] See above, fn.221 at para.18.16.
[223] See above, fn.221 at para.18.18.
[224] See above, fn.221 at para.18.22.
[225] See above, fn.221 at para.18.24.

5-113 **Could not have increased the risk of the loss which actually occurred in the circumstances in which it occurred.** Section 11(2) and (3) of the 2015 Act provide that an insurer will not be able to rely on a term that falls within the controls of the section if the insured can satisfy the courts that the breach of term could not have increased the risk of the loss which actually occurred in the circumstances in which it occurred:

> "(2) If a loss occurs, and the term has not been complied with, the insurer may not rely on the non-compliance to exclude, limit or discharge its liability under the contract for the loss if the insured satisfies subsection (3).
>
> (3) The insured satisfies this subsection if it shows that the non-compliance with the term could not have increased the risk of the loss which actually occurred in the circumstances in which it occurred."

Rather than employing a test of causation, the provisions require, more broadly, the insured to establish that the breached policy term was unconnected to the risk of the loss. Accordingly, the Law Commission considered that an insured would be able to satisfy this section by demonstrating that the "type of loss" which was actually suffered was outside of the ambit of what compliance with a particular term would "tend to achieve."[226] For example, a warranty requiring the insured to hire a watchman to guard the construction site at night would tend to reduce the risk of loss during the night, and so a breach of that warranty could not be used by the insurer to refuse liability for a burglary during the day. The application of s.11(2) and (3) will therefore depend on what the courts identify as the type of loss the risk of which the term would tend to reduce, and the more broadly the courts interpret the losses targeted by a clause, the more likely an insurer will be able to rely on it to avoid payment of the claim.

It is important to emphasise the differences between the test under s.11(2) and (3) and the test of causation employed under the Australian and New Zealand reforms. Using the example of the night watchman above, if the burglary occurred during the night it is undoubtedly the case s.11 would not prevent the insurer from relying on the breach of warranty regardless of whether the absence of the watchmen had any causal connection to the losses or not. However, the application of s.11(2) and (3) may involve some uncertainty in particular cases as to whether compliance with a term is relevant to the type of losses sustained by the insured. For example, if the warranty required that the insured use a scaffolding burglar alarm, then the courts could decide that this, too, would be a term that would tend to reduce the risk of burglary, with the effect that the absence of the alarm would take the insurer off risk for all burglary related losses. However, the courts may instead decide that the term would only tend to reduce the risk of burglary *from the scaffolding*, with the effect that any burglaries from other parts of the construction site would still be covered under the policy in the absence of the alarm. The more restrictively the courts decide to interpret the losses the risk of which would be reduced by compliance with the terms of the insurance policy, the closer the UK approach will become in practice to the causation provisions brought in by the Australian and New Zealand reforms.

5-114 **Warranties, conditions precedent, definitions of risk, exclusion clauses.** Because the controls under s.11 of the 2015 Act will apply to a term regardless of how it is identified within the policy, the provisions are capable of ap-

---

[226] See above, fn.221 at para.18.38.

plying to warranties, conditions precedent, definitions of risk and exclusion clauses. The key test will be for the courts to look at the content of the policy term and determine whether, despite being framed as a term defining the risk insured, an exclusion clause or a condition precedent, the general effect of the term will be to reduce the risk of losses of a particular kind, at a particular time or at a particular location. However, the legal nature of the policy term will affect how the provisions of s.11 operate to restrict the insurer's reliance on such a term. Where the term is a warranty, exclusion or definition of risk, the provisions of s.11 will have the effect that cover is only suspended or excluded in relation to connected losses. Where the term is a condition precedent to liability attaching under the policy, the effect of s.11 will instead be that liability will attach for all unconnected losses despite the insured's breach of the term.

Contracting out.   As with all other parts of the 2015 Act, the parties are free to contract out of the provisions of s.11 in favour of including policy terms which suspend the entire cover under the policy rather than just suspending cover for losses connected to that term. This may be desirable where particular terms are considered to be fundamental conditions of the policy which should suspend the entirety of the insurer's cover, rather than less important terms which are primarily included to manage risk. Any terms which place the insured in a worse position than they would be by virtue of s.11 of the 2015 Act must be drafted in accordance with the transparency requirements.[227]   **5-115**

5.   FRAUD

One statutory remedy.   The 2015 Act creates a new statutory remedy for fraudulent claims that will apply in the absence of any bespoke terms under the policy which stipulate a specific remedy for the insured's fraud. In the insurance context, "fraud" can be invoked in relation to both the pre-contractual duties of fair presentation and disclosure and at the post-contractual stage in relation to fraudulent claims; the 2015 Act distinguishes between the obligations owed by the insured at each stage, and the provisions relating to fraud are aimed solely at fraudulent claims. Any pre-contractual fraud by the insured at the disclosure and presentation stages of placement will instead attract liability as a deliberate or reckless breach of the duty of fair presentation under s.8(5) of the 2015 Act.[228]   **5-116**

The implementation of a statutory remedy for fraudulent claims was necessitated by a small area of uncertainty concerning the effect of a fraudulent claim on the underlying insurance policy. The confusion had previously arisen regarding the potential for the insurer to choose between dual remedies—one for forfeiture of the fraudulent claim under common law, and one for avoidance of the policy arising out of the insured's breach of the duty of good faith under the MIA. In relation to the former remedy raised a number of questions remained in doubt as to the effect that the fraudulent claim would have on honest claims made subsequent to the fraudulent claim but before discovery of the fraud, and as to whether a fraud automatically terminated the policy or whether, instead, it was a repudiatory breach that had to be accepted. The remedy of avoidance seemed an overly harsh and punitive remedy that went against the core value of finality in UK law (viz. the finality

---

[227]   See below, para.5-135.
[228]   See above, paras 5-073 to 5-079.

of claims agreed and paid prior to the fraud.[229] The Law Commission therefore determined that a single remedy should be established for all fraudulent claims where the terms of the policy do not themselves specify the consequences for the insured's fraud. The Law Commission also noted a clear need for the statutory remedy to include a punitive dimension in order to act as a deterrent to the insured, and stated:

> "It is important for the law to set out clear sanctions to deter policyholders from acting fraudulently. Although insurance fraud is a criminal offence, prosecutions are relatively rare, meaning that the civil law has an important part to play in deterring fraud. It should also grant remedies to insurers which are principled, proportionate and reliable."[230]

Although the inclusion of a punitive or deterrent aspect to a civil remedy is an unusual imposition and one which attracted persuasive criticism during the consultation process,[231] the Law Commission ultimately justified the remedy on the basis that the reforms were aimed to benefit *all* policyholders, particularly the honest policyholders that have to bear the burden of increased premiums as a result of losses suffered by insurers for fraudulent claims and the costs of investigating and detecting fraud.[232]

5-117 **Frauds perpetrated by the insured.** The statutory remedy for fraudulent claims will only apply as against a claim made by "the insured", defined under s.1 of the 2015 Act as "the party to a contract of insurance who is the insured under the contract, or would be if the contract were entered into." Where a person other than the insured commits a fraud, the legal consequences will depend on the position of the fraudster and the circumstances in which the fraud was committed, but in general the 2015 Act will only govern fraud committed by the insured under the insurance policy. For all other cases of fraud, the general common law principles will apply in lieu of any specific provisions under the 2015 Act.

5-118 **Third Parties (Rights Against Insurers) Act 2010.** The Third Parties (Rights Against Insurers) Act 2010 ("the 2010 Act") came into force on 1 August 2016. Its provisions allow a third party creditor of the insured to claim losses directly from an insurer without first having to establish the liability of the insured by settlement with or in court or arbitral proceedings against the latter.[233] The insurer's remedies for fraudulent claims under s.12 will apply equally to a claim made by a third party who has been vested with the rights of the insured under the 2010 Act, because the third party cannot be placed in a better position than the insured would have been in under the 2015 Act.

5-119 **Contracting out.** It is common practice for insurance policies to include bespoke contractual terms which set out the insurer's remedy for an insured's fraudulent claim under the policy. If the policy term places the insured in a worse position than they would be under the 2015 Act, for example by requiring the return of any sums

---

[229] Law Commission "*Insurance Contract Law: Business Disclosure; Warranties; Insurers' Remedies for Fraudulent Claims; and Late Payment*", (Law Commission, 2014). *http://www.lawcom.gov.uk/wp-content/uploads/2015/03/lc353_insurance-contract-law.pdf* [Accessed 24 June 2016] at para.20.10.

[230] See above, fn.229 at para.19.3.

[231] See above, fn.229 at para.21.16.

[232] See above, fn.229 at para.19.2.

[233] As was previously required under Third Parties (Rights against Insurers) Act 1930.

paid out under previous genuine claims, then any such term must comply with the transparency requirements.[234]

(a) Remedy for the insurer

A clear deterrent. The Law Commission emphasised the need for the statutory remedies in the event of a fraudulent claim to include a punitive element in order to act as a deterrent to the insured.[235] The position under the 2015 Act was contrasted with the position at common law in the case of third party fraud, such as that committed by an individual exaggerating their personal injury claims. Whilst in the latter case the individual would only be deprived of the fraudulent exaggeration to an otherwise honest claim, the remedies under the 2015 Act place the insured in a far worse position in a number of important respects:

5-120

1. the entire fraudulent claim is forfeited, even where the fraud is a minor exaggeration in comparison to the total value of the claim;
2. an insurer may elect to terminate the cover at the time of discovery, and the termination will take effect retrospectively from the date of the fraudulent claim;
3. if an insurer does elect to terminate the cover from the time of the fraudulent act, they may recover any genuine claims made after the date of the fraud but before the date of discovery;
4. the insurer is also entitled to keep the premiums paid by the insured during that period.

Forfeiture of the fraudulent claim. The principal remedy for a fraudulent claim made by the insured under the policy is the forfeiture of the entire claim. Section 12(1) of the 2015 Act accordingly provides:

5-121

"(1) If the insured makes a fraudulent claim under a contract of insurance—
    (a) the insurer is not liable to pay the claim,
    (b) the insurer may recover from the insured any sums paid by the insurer to the insured in respect of the claim, and
    (c) in addition, the insurer may by notice to the insured treat the contract as having been terminated with effect from the time of the fraudulent act."

As the remedy of avoidance for breach of the duty of good faith has been abolished by the 2015 Act,[236] forfeiture of the fraudulent claim and the option to treat the policy as terminated are now the sole remedies available to the insurer, subject to any bespoke terms within the insurance policy that set out a different remedy. What constituted "the fraudulent claim" was a matter left for the courts to interpret and develop after the 2015 Act came into force, and as such the Law Commission did not form a definitive opinion on the matter.[237] However, the Supreme Court has recently reconsidered the fraudulent claims rule and has delivered judgment on its

---

[234] See below, para.5-135.
[235] Law Commission *"Insurance Contract Law: Business Disclosure; Warranties; Insurers' Remedies for Fraudulent Claims; and Late Payment"*, (Law Commission, 2014). *http://www.lawcom.gov.uk/wp-content/uploads/2015/03/lc353_insurance-contract-law.pdf* [Accessed 24 June 2016] at para.19.3.
[236] See below, para.5-141.
[237] Law Commission "Insurance Contract Law: Business Disclosure; Warranties; Insurers' Remedies for Fraudulent Claims; and Late Payment", (Law Commission, 2014). *http://www.lawcom.gov.uk/wp-content/uploads/2015/03/lc353_insurance-contract-law.pdf* [Accessed 24 June 2016], at para.23.17.

operation under both the MIA and the 2015 Act.[238]

In *Versloot Dredging BV v HDI Gerling Industrie Versicherung AG*,[239] issues surrounding the application of the fraudulent claims rule arose in relation to losses sustained by a vessel after an ingress of water caused damage to the ship's engine room. During the investigation of the claim, the insured had recklessly made a false representation that the bilge alarm had activated in order to accelerate payment from the insurer, but the lie later turned out to be irrelevant to the recoverability of the substantive claim.

The case fell to be determined under the pre-2015 Act law. The issue for the Supreme Court to determine was, squarely, "what constitutes a fraudulent claim": this was said "a controversial question at common law, which the Act of 2015 does not resolve."[240] More specifically, the issue was whether a collateral lie would fall under the fraudulent claims rule and defeat the insured's otherwise genuine claim under the policy.

The Court regarded it as settled that an insured who advances a fabricated or fraudulently embellished claim forfeits the right to recover the entirety of that claim, including any genuine losses alongside the fraudulent embellishment. However, it was not clear that those same policy reasons that permitted the forfeiture of the entire claim in instances of fraudulent exaggeration would apply equally to collateral lies which merely "gilded the lily" regarding the merits of an entirely justified claim. Delivering the leading judgment of the Supreme Court, Lord Sumption JSC considered the critical point to be that the insured was claiming no more than the law regarded as his entitlement and would gain nothing from the lie to which he did not already have the legal right:

> "The position is different where the insured is trying to obtain no more than the law regards as his entitlement and the lie is irrelevant to the existence or amount of that entitlement. In this case the lie is dishonest, but the claim is not. The immateriality of the lie to the claim makes it not just possible but appropriate to distinguish between them. I do not accept that a policy of deterrence justifies the application of the fraudulent claim rule in this situation."[241]

The Supreme Court therefore declined to extend the fraudulent claims rule to cover collateral lies which are immaterial to the recoverability of the insured's substantive claim. Lord Sumption JSC gave further guidance as to how a collateral lie would be distinguished from one that was material to the claim and would therefore fall under the fraudulent claims rule, a matter left in some doubt following the earlier Court of Appeal decision in *Versloot Dredging BV*.[242] Although a test of materiality based on the degree to which the lie had yielded an improvement in the insured's prospects of success prior to a final determination of the parties' rights had been initially proposed by Mance LJ (as he then was) in *Agapitos v Agnew (The Aegeon) (No.1)*,[243] Lord Sumption JSC considered that such a test was not rational

---

[238] For further discussion of the legal basis and operation of the fraudulent claims rule as applied under the MIA, see below, para.6-049. For discussion of the fraudulent claims rule in relation to claims procedure, see below, para.21-045.

[239] *Versloot Dredging BV v HDI Gerling Industrie Versicherung AG* [2016] UKSC 45; [2016] 3 W.L.R. 543; [2016] Lloyd's Rep. I.R. 468.

[240] See above, fn.3, per Lord Sumption JSC at [1].

[241] See above, fn.3 at [26].

[242] *Versloot Dredging BV v HDI Gerling Industrie Versicherung AG* [2014] EWCA Civ 1349 at [165]; [2015] Q.B. 608; [2015] 2 W.L.R. 1063.

[243] *Agapitos v Agnew (The Aegeon) (No.1)* [2002] EWCA Civ 247 at [38]; [2003] Q.B. 556; [2002] 3

when the full measure of the insurer's liability had already crystallised from the moment the loss had occurred. He considered:

> "[W]hen deciding whether to accept a claim under an existing contract, the insurer's position is very different. He has no discretion, because he is already bound. The only question properly before him is whether to acknowledge a liability that if it exists at all exists already, whether or not he realises it. Ultimately, his assessment is simply an attempt to predict what a court would decide. In that context, the only rational test of the materiality of a lie must be based on its relevance to a court which is in a position to find the relevant facts.
>
> For this reason, although a lie uttered in support of a claim need not have any adverse impact on the insurer, I consider that it must at least go to the recoverability of the claim on the true facts."[244]

Accordingly, a collateral lie told by the insured that has induced the insurer into any form of action or is capable of prompting a faster settlement of a justified claim than would otherwise have been achieved is not a fraudulent claim. In order to fall within the fraudulent claims rule, the lie must go to the recoverability of the claim as determined with hindsight, by reference to the facts and merits of the claim as they truly were.

Recovery of sums already paid.   Where the fraud is not discovered by the insurer   **5-122**
until after sums have already been paid in respect of the fraudulent claim, Section 12(1)(b) of the 2015 Act empowers the insurer to recover any such sums from the insured. Should the money paid out under the fraudulent claim end up in the hands of an innocent third party, the insurer's rights to the recovery of those sums will be determined in accordance with common law remedies (e.g. tracing).[245]

(b)   Option to treat the contract as terminated from the time of the fraudulent act

Optional remedy.   Absent any bespoke terms within the policy which determine   **5-123**
the consequences of a fraudulent claim on the underlying agreement, s.12(1)(c) of the 2015 Act grants the insurer the statutory right to terminate the policy upon the discovery of the fraudulent claim. This optional remedy will apply in addition to the automatic forfeiture of the fraudulent claim.

Retrospective effect.   Part of the punitive dimension to the insurer's remedy is   **5-124**
provided by the termination being given retrospective effect from the time of the fraudulent act rather than taking effect after discovery. Accordingly, s.12(2) of the 2015 Act provides:

> "(2) If the insurer does treat the contract as having been terminated—
>
>   (a)   it may refuse all liability to the insured under the contract in respect of a relevant event occurring after the time of the fraudulent act, and
>
>   (b)   it need not return any of the premiums paid under the contract."

Section 12(2)(a) would therefore appear to allow the insurer to refute liability for genuine claims paid after the fraudulent act but before discovery of the fraud, a position discussed in more detail below.[246] Assuming this position is correct, where the

---

W.L.R. 616.

[244] See above, fn.3 at [35]–[36].

[245] See above, fn.238 at para.23.20.

[246] See below, para.5-130.

fraud is discovered quite quickly after the fraudulent act then the impact on the insured will be much less severe as the insured will be aware of the need to obtain new cover before the occurrence of any subsequent loss events. The provision will be far more punishing where there is any substantial period of time between the fraudulent act itself and the insurers' discovery of that fraud, particularly where the insured has made a number of genuine claims on the policy within that intervening period. Not only will the insured be obliged to repay what may be very substantial claims, but the insured may not have been aware that the policy was ineffective during that intervening period and would therefore have been denied the chance to obtain further cover elsewhere. Although the harshness of this position may be somewhat mitigated where it is standard practice to take out a new policy every year, as this will in practice limit the number of claims for which coverage may be denied by reason of any one fraudulent act, there will no doubt be cases where the insured suffers a considerable detriment as a result of a relatively minor fraudulent exaggeration.

5-125   **Exercisable at the point the fraud is discovered.**   The insurer may exercise its right of election to treat the contract as terminated once it has discovered the fraud. The Law Commission envisaged that there would need to be a balance struck between the insurer having to make a decision in a timeous fashion in order to allow the insured to seek cover elsewhere if required, and the insurer's need to obtain sufficient proof of the fraud before committing itself to a course of action.[247] Although there is no statutory requirement to elect shortly after the point of discovery, the Law Commission considered that there were two potential controls to prevent an insurer acting unreasonably to disadvantage the insured: first, the doctrine of waiver would apply where the insurer did not make any attempt to confirm its suspicions until a later genuine claim arose, and second, the requirement of good faith may prevent an insurer from relying on the remedy in an unfair way.[248]

5-126   **The "fraudulent act".**   Under s.12(2)(a) of the 2015 Act, termination because of a fraudulent claim will take effect from the time of the "fraudulent act" rather than the time of the fraudulent claim. Although the 2015 Act does not provide a definition for what will constitute the fraudulent act, it is quite clear that the timing will refer to the fraudulent element itself, and so, for example, where a genuine claim for fire damage is made in January and the insured only later fraudulently claims in March for additional contents allegedly lost in that fire, the "fraudulent act" will have been committed in March and any genuine claims made under the policy in February will be recoverable.[249] The Law Commission describe the fraudulent act as "the behaviour which makes a claim fraudulent",[250] and set out the following examples of how the concept would operate for the five classes of fraud identified by Mance LJ in *Agapitos v Agnew*[251]:

---

[247] Law Commission "*Insurance Contract Law: Business Disclosure; Warranties; Insurers' Remedies for Fraudulent Claims; and Late Payment*", (Law Commission, 2014). *http://www.lawcom.gov.uk/ wp-content/uploads/2015/03/lc353_insurance-contract-law.pdf* [Accessed 24 June 2016] at para.23.39.

[248] See above, fn.241 at para.23.40.

[249] See above, fn.241 at para.23.57.

[250] See above, fn.241 at para.23.33.

[251] *Agapitos v Agnew (The Aegeon) (No.1)* [2002] EWCA Civ 247; [2003] Q.B. 556; [2002] 3 W.L.R.

"(1) The insured suffered no genuine loss at all or the loss was caused by the deliberate act of the insured with fraudulent intent. In these cases, the date of the fraudulent act is the submission of the claim (in the latter case, together with the failure to admit the cause of the loss). Although it may be a step towards the fraudulent claim, the commission of a deliberate act, such as setting fire to property, is not in itself fraudulent.

(2) The insured suffered some loss but exaggerates that loss (for example, overvaluation of property or adding additional items to the list of property genuinely lost). Here, the fraudulent act would be when the exaggerated element is communicated to the insurer. This could be at the initial submission of the claim or a later date.

(3) The insured, having apparently sustained a loss, subsequently discovers that there is no loss or loss of a smaller amount but continues to press for the original claim. We think the fraudulent act only occurs when the party has failed to advise the insurer of the new information within a reasonable time. What is a reasonable time would be for the courts to decide in the circumstances.

(4) The insured makes a claim against the insurers knowing that the insurers have a defence and fails to advise the insurers of that. It has been queried whether it is really the case that an insured has to draw a defence to the insurers' attention if the insurers could have discovered it based upon the facts known to them. If so, the fraudulent act is the failure to disclose the defence. If the defence is known at the point of submission of the claim, the fraudulent act is at that point. If the defence is only discovered later, the fraudulent act is as in (3) above."[252]

The exact timing of the fraudulent act will therefore be a matter for the courts to determine using a common sense approach to the facts and circumstances of each particular case.

No liability for losses suffered after fraudulent act.   Once the policy has been **5-127** retrospectively terminated by the insurer, there may be some confusion as to whether this will affect a genuine claim that was not submitted to the insurer until after the fraudulent act, but was made in respect of losses which arose beforehand. Section 12(3) and (4) of the 2015 Act provide that this will depend on the nature of the insurance policy itself and, for example, whether it is an "occurrence" policy or a "claims made" policy:

"(3) Treating a contract as having been terminated under this section does not affect the rights and obligations of the parties to the contract with respect to a relevant event occurring before the time of the fraudulent act.

(4) In subsections (2)(a) and (3), 'relevant event' refers to whatever gives rise to the insurer's liability under the contract (and includes, for example, the occurrence of a loss, the making of a claim, or the notification of a potential claim, depending on how the contract is written)."

So long as the event or action which triggers the insurer's liability occurs before the fraudulent act, the insurer will be liable to cover the genuine claim.

Need not return premiums paid before right is exercised.   Section 12(2)(b) of **5-128** the 2015 Act provides that the insurer need not repay any premiums to the insured whether paid before or after the fraudulent act. This is in line with the insurer's

---

616.

[252] Law Commission "*Insurance Contract Law: Business Disclosure; Warranties; Insurers' Remedies for Fraudulent Claims; and Late Payment*", (Law Commission, 2014). *http://www.lawcom.gov.uk/wp-content/uploads/2015/03/lc353_insurance-contract-law.pdf* [Accessed 24 June 2016] at para.23.36.

remedies for a deliberate or reckless breach of the duty of fair presentation, where the premium may similarly be retained.[253]

5-129 **Subsequent or separate contracts.** The fraudulent act will not taint any subsequent or separate insurance policies under the remedies provided by the 2015 Act. Thus, the termination will not affect a subsequently renewed insurance policy[254] or a different insurer's liability for the same loss where no fraud was perpetrated against that insurer.[255]

5-130 **Payments made for genuine claims subsequent to fraudulent act.** The exact position of the 2015 Act in relation to payments made for genuine claims subsequent to the fraudulent act is at this point uncertain. The starting point is that the remedy is clearly one with retrospective effect, so the termination itself will be deemed to have occurred at the time the fraudulent act was perpetrated by the insured. This was justified by the Law Commission on the basis that there was likely to be a lag time between the fraud and its discovery, and fraudsters must expect that insurers would not wish to continue to have dealings with them.[256] The wording of s.12(2)(a) of the 2015 Act also provides that the insurer may refuse all liability for relevant events subsequent to the fraudulent act, which would appear to permit them recovery of sums paid out that they were not liable for. However, the Law Commission state that this does not give insurers a statutory right to recovery of those sums, only a non-liability for them.[257] The Law Commission considered that there were other legal and policy considerations in relation to sums paid on later genuine claims, and any such right to repayment would arise as a result of the law of unjust enrichment:

> "Consider, for example, whether the insurer's payment is valid and irreversible because it was made in accordance with a subsisting contract, or is reversible because it was made in mistake or error or because the purpose for which it was made came to an end. If it is reversible in principle, there may also be a question about whether and to what extent an insured's change of position may provide a defence to recovery. We are not aware of any such use of enrichment law in practice by insurers, however.
>
> Because of the vast range of circumstances which could engage these issues and the different considerations which are at play, we do not think it is appropriate to try to formulate a statutory rule where there is common law jurisprudence which affords the necessary flexibility of response. This is consistent with our policy on fair presentation."[258]

Despite the Law Commission's failure to arrive at any definitive stance on the matter, a few salient points can be observed about their approach to the issue which may explain their reticence. It is clear that the Law Commission wanted to permit recovery of the sums paid out after the making of the fraudulent claim, but also wanted to ensure that the insurer was given the option to not continue with the relationship if it so desired. It made logical sense for the right to recover fraudulent monies to be tied in with the right to termination, as the right to exercise both remedies arises as soon as the fraudulent act is perpetrated by the insured. It is sug-

---

[253] See above, para.5-079.
[254] Law Commission "*Insurance Contract Law: Business Disclosure; Warranties; Insurers' Remedies for Fraudulent Claims; and Late Payment*", (Law Commission, 2014). *http://www.lawcom.gov.uk/wp-content/uploads/2015/03/lc353_insurance-contract-law.pdf* [Accessed 24 June 2016] at para.23.31.
[255] See above, fn.248 at para.23.32.
[256] See above, fn.248 at para.23.26.
[257] See above, fn.248 at para.23.48.
[258] See above, fn.248 at paras 23.50 to 23.51.

gested that it is for this reason that the Law Commission insisted on a retrospective remedy for termination, but without engaging fully with the most significant consequence that a retrospective remedy would have for the parties, i.e. the effect on any genuine claims made after the fraud but before its discovery. The position can therefore be summarised as follows—under the 2015 Act, where the contract is terminated this will take effect from the date of the fraudulent act, which may be prior to subsequent genuine claims, in which case the insurer will have no liability for those claims even if it has paid out on them. The insurer therefore is treated as never having had any obligation to pay those claims, and will likely be able to recover them under the law of unjust enrichment.

(c) Fraud by a member of a group insurance scheme

Same penalty for fraudulent beneficiary. Section 13 of the 2015 Act sets out **5-131** the remedies available to the insurer where a beneficiary of a group insurance scheme submits a fraudulent claim under the policy. The typical example of such an insurance scheme is where an employer takes out health or life insurance for employees, who will all be covered by the group policy but will not be policyholders or parties to the contract themselves. The 2015 Act establishes that a fraudulent claim under such a policy will only be capable of affecting the insurance cover provided for that one beneficiary, and the insurer will possess the same remedies against that beneficiary as it would against a fraudulent insured—the forfeiture of the fraudulent claim and the option to treat the cover as provided to the fraudulent beneficiary as terminated from the time of the fraud. Section 13(2) provides that the exercise of these remedies will be incapable of affecting the cover provided in respect of the other beneficiaries:

> "(2) Section 12 applies in relation to the claim as if the cover provided for [the fraudulent beneficiary] were provided under an individual insurance contract between the insurer and [the fraudulent beneficiary] as the insured; and, accordingly—
>> (a) the insurer's rights under section 12 are exercisable only in relation to the cover provided for [the fraudulent beneficiary], and
>> (b) the exercise of any of those rights does not affect the cover provided under the contract for anyone else."

Section 13(3)(a) of the 2015 Act similarly makes the position clear that insurance monies paid out in respect of the fraudulent claim will be recoverable whether they are being held by the policy holder or the fraudulent beneficiary.

CAR policy. A CAR policy is not treated as group insurance taken out by the **5-132** employer or contractor with every party to the construction works being a beneficiary. Instead, the CAR policy is treated as composite insurance, comprising of a bundle of separate policies agreed between each insured and the insurer rather than one contract covering every insured. Where a fraudulent claim is made by one party to the construction contract in respect of damage to the works, the insurer will be entitled to refuse the fraudulent claim and treat the policy with that one party as terminated. However, this will not affect the cover provided in respect of the other parties to the construction works, who will also be able to claim for those same losses under their own cover. This position is to be contrasted with the effect of a pre-contractual fraud perpetrated against the insurer by the party taking out the CAR policy on behalf of all other named insureds, which appears to be capable of tainting the policies held by each insured. This position is discussed in greater detail above at para.5-034.

6. CONTRACTING OUT

5-133   **A default regime for non-consumer insurance.** The provisions of the 2015 Act are intended as a default regime for all non-consumer insurance contracts, whatever the size of the insured's undertaking and whatever the complexity of the field of insurance. Although as a default position the 2015 Act is intended to strike a fair balance between the interests of the insurer and the insured, it would be impossible for one statute to provide an appropriate set of remedies in respect of every business operating in every field, particularly given the UK insurance market's reputation for offering a wide variety of insurance products and its capacity for the insurance of risks considered uninsurable elsewhere. Attempts by the Law Commission to distinguish between separate categories of policyholder failed.[259] During the consultation process, insurers at the high-value end of the market were sceptical of any provisions purporting to limit their freedom of contract and impose restrictions on what they could put in their policies.[260] At the opposite end of the scale, the Law Commission were concerned that many micro businesses would have little to no bargaining power to negotiate terms with the insurer and would often have a very poor understanding of how insurance terms may operate, particularly where those terms were ambiguously worded. Accordingly, it would not be overstating the point to suggest that the effectiveness of the contracting-out mechanism, subject to the transparency requirements, in allowing the balancing of competing interests for the full range of participants in the insurance market is of critical importance for the success of the 2015 Act in regulating all sizes of business and fields of insurance.

Several important points should be noted about the contracting out provisions of the 2015 Act. The first is that "contracting out" is given the specific definition under s.16(2) of the 2015 Act as applying wherever an insurer includes a term "which would put the insured in a worse position" than they would be under the default provisions of the 2015 Act. Thus, an insurer would be contracting out of the 2015 Act to a policy which was otherwise entirely consistent merely by adding a further condition precedent to the insurer's liability in addition to the provisions of the 2015 Act. Any such condition precedent would have to meet the transparency requirements in order to be effective. The second point to note is that the transparency requirements will have subjective application depending on the sophistication of the insured, and so where contracting out of particular provisions of the 2015 Act becomes the norm in particularly complex markets in which bespoke arrangements are fundamental to the insurer's capacity to cover a certain risk, the transparency requirements will be met by the barest acknowledgement that the insured is being placed in a more onerous position than that under the 2015 Act.[261] In this way, the transparency requirements will not become an unduly burdensome procedural hurdle for sophisticated market participants who may habitually substitute a different apportionment of risk for that provided by the 2015 Act.

---

[259] See above, fn.248 at para.29.26.
[260] See above, fn.248 at para.29.27.
[261] See below, para.5-136.

No restriction on the extent of contracting out. The transparency require- **5-134** ments are designed as a procedural control on the way in which the parties are able to contract out of the default provisions, rather than offering any substantive control on the extent to which the parties can contract out. The 2015 Act therefore gives primacy to the parties' freedom of contract, but seeks to establish controls which will help balance the position between the insurer and insured in circumstances where the insurer has far greater bargaining power and the insured has little understanding of how the terms of an insurance policy may operate harshly against them, for instance where the insured is a microbusiness purchasing off-the-shelf insurance online. Although the Law Commission were unwilling to place any substantive controls on the extent of contracting out of the 2015 Act beyond disal- lowing basis of the contract clauses and similar provisions,[262] there was nothing to prevent the imposition of requirements that the insurer clarifies the effect of any disadvantageous terms included in the contract to the insured before the policy is concluded. Whilst this would not resolve the problems created by the insured's lack of bargaining power when contracting on an insurer's standard terms and condi- tions, the provisions would at least allow the insured to understand exactly the policy they were agreeing to and would therefore ensure that, if nothing else, the policy would respond in the way the insured would expect. The careful balance that needed to be struck was acknowledged by the Law Commission in order to achieve the following aims:

"The requirements proposed are intended to balance those interests and achieve the following aims:

(1) To encourage insurers to consider whether opting out of the default regime is necessary or appropriate in the circumstances.
(2) To enable policyholders to make an informed decision (with or without the aid of a broker) about whether to agree to the alternative position, to negotiate for the default position or to seek an alternative insurance provider.
(3) To ensure that the contracting out provisions are not so onerous as to interfere with the smooth running of the insurance market, particularly at the more bespoke and sophisticated end of the market.
(4) To give the courts room to differentiate between different scenarios, from well-advised, commercially aware insurance buyers to smaller insureds buying 'off the shelf' and, increas- ingly, online." [263]

The extent to which aim (1) will be achieved by the 2015 Act will depend upon the reaction of insurers to the new provisions and whether it becomes standard practice to include boilerplate clauses within their policies that meet the transparency requirements. Aims (2), (3) and (4) rely on the subjective application of the transpar- ency requirements to impose only minor procedural hurdles in sophisticated markets, whilst imposing much more onerous obligations where the insured is a smaller business with far less bargaining power and understanding of general insur- ance law.

The transparency requirements. Section 16(2) of the 2015 Act establishes that **5-135** any term:

---

[262] Law Commission "*Insurance Contract Law: Business Disclosure; Warranties; Insurers' Remedies for Fraudulent Claims; and Late Payment*", (Law Commission, 2014). *http://www.lawcom.gov.uk/ wp-content/uploads/2015/03/lc353_insurance-contract-law.pdf* [Accessed 24 June 2016] at para.29.18.
[263] See above, fn.256 at para.29.29.

"which would put the insured in a worse position as respects any of the other matters provided for in Part 2, 3 or 4 of this Act than the insured would be in by virtue of the provisions of those Parts (so far as relating to non-consumer insurance contracts) is to that extent of no effect, unless the requirements of section 17 have been satisfied in relation to the term."

The process of applying the transparency requirements to the insurance policy will therefore involve looking at the policy terms in order to determine which specific terms place the insured in a worse position than under the 2015 Act, and any terms so identified must meet both of the transparency requirements contained in s.17 in order to have contractual effect. The transparency requirements themselves are set out under s.17(2) and (3) of the 2015 Act, and must be met by each identified disadvantageous term:

"(2)   The insurer must take sufficient steps to draw the disadvantageous term to the insured's attention before the contract is entered into or the variation agreed.
(3)   The disadvantageous term must be clear and unambiguous as to its effect."

Section 17(3) requires there to be no ambiguity as to a term's *effect*. It will not be sufficient for the insurer to use clear and precise wording in lieu of obscure legal jargon where the consequences of the term are nevertheless disguised or ambiguous. The example given by the Law Commission is a term stating that, for example, "Section 11 of the Insurance Act 2015 does not apply to this policy", which uses clear and precise wording but does not spell out that the effect would be to allow the insurer to rely on the breach of a warranty or other term that was irrelevant to the actual loss in order to discharge their liability under the policy.[264] The Law Commission were also keen to express that this provision would be stronger than the *contra proferentem* rule[265] as it would apply to all disadvantageous terms and not merely those containing ambiguity.[266]

Section 17(2) takes the position further and requires that the insurer must take sufficient steps to draw each disadvantageous term to the insured's attention, rather than just being able to satisfy the transparency requirements with clear and precise drafting. The presumed intention behind the provision is that it will be used by the courts to diminish the effectiveness of boilerplate clauses that are expressed using clear language but not explained to the insured prior to agreement, in circumstances where the insured is a micro business or other small corporate entity not being assisted by a broker. Presumably the Law Commission were of the opinion that the more difficult the 2015 Act made it for insurers to opt out of the default provisions as a matter of routine, at least when contracting with smaller businesses, the more likely the insurers would be to consider whether the contracting out was necessary before including it as standard within their policies.

5-136   **Subjective application.**   The subjective application of the transparency requirements to insureds of different sizes and sophistication is in many ways at the core of the transparency requirements, and will certainly be an aspect most likely to receive significant judicial attention. The Law Commission recognised the need for the 2015 Act to strike a balance between requirements which are sufficiently potent to offer protection to small businesses with little or no bargaining power, but do not

---

[264] See above, fn.256 at para.29.50.
[265] See below, para.13-060.
[266] Law Commission "*Insurance Contract Law: Business Disclosure; Warranties; Insurers' Remedies for Fraudulent Claims; and Late Payment*", (Law Commission, 2014). *http://www.lawcom.gov.uk/wp-content/uploads/2015/03/lc353_insurance-contract-law.pdf* [Accessed 24 June 2016] at para.29.49.

impose undue procedural hurdles to commercially aware insureds or require insurers to behave artificially.[267] Section 17(4) of the 2015 Act provides that the transparency requirements will be applied subjectively based on the characteristics of the insured and the circumstances of the transaction:

"(4) In determining whether the requirements of subsections (2) and (3) have been met, the characteristics of insured persons of the kind in question, and the circumstances of the transaction, are to be taken into account."

How the transparency requirements will be applied to different cases is therefore ultimately left for the courts to determine, and could vary significantly from case to case. What will be sufficient to draw a term to the attention of an insured will partially depend on the size and sophistication of the insured, with factors such as whether the insured has used a broker to arrange the policy affecting the required steps the insurer must take to draw attention to a disadvantageous term.[268] Although not contained explicitly within the 2015 Act, as a matter of the general law of agency an insurer should only need to take sufficient steps to draw a term to the attention of a broker and should be able to rely on the broker passing that information on to the insured. What must also be noted about the wording of the provision is that it applies to an insured person "of the kind in question" which incorporates an objective element into the test—a large company containing a poorly run and negligent underwriting department might not be able to escape the effectiveness of the disadvantageous term on the basis that their own careless employees did not appreciate the effect of a particular term or condition.

The Law Commission provided a number of examples of what they considered would be sufficient to meet the transparency requirements in particular circumstances and insurance markets, and these examples may provide some illustration of how the courts are likely to alter their application of the transparency requirements to fit particular circumstances:

1. An owner of a small business purchasing insurance online will not be put on notice of a disadvantageous term contained within the insurer's standard terms and conditions if the agreement requires the owner to tick a box stating that he agrees to those conditions with a link to open them in a new window.[269] However, if the disadvantageous term appeared in a box containing the "key terms" of the policy, then it is likely the transparency requirements would be met.[270]

2. A medium sized enterprise using a regional broker to place the insurance would be put on notice of a disadvantageous term contained within the insurer's standard terms and conditions where the insurer states to the broker that the policy will be on the insurer's standard terms and conditions, emails the broker a copy of them, includes an asterisk next to the disadvantageous term and then asks the broker whether he has had a chance to go through those terms and conditions.[271] In the same scenario where the medium sized enterprise does not use a broker, the transparency requirements would not

---

[267] See above, fn.260 at para.29.36.
[268] See above, fn.260 at para.29.41.
[269] See above, fn.260 at para.29.62.
[270] See above, fn.260 at para.29.63.
[271] See above, fn.260 at para.29.64.

be met as the insurer cannot expect that the enterprise will go through their standard terms and conditions.[272]

3.   Where a sophisticated insurance buyer is purchasing cover through Lloyd's, it will be sufficient to note codes such as LC1 or LC2 on the slip which apply standard wordings routinely used to disapply the 2015 Act's reforms on warranties.[273] However, this would depend on the extent to which such codes are known by brokers generally and a court may find such codes ineffective if it would not be reasonably obvious to a broker that the code has the effect of incorporating a particular disadvantageous term.[274]

Although the provision is likely to receive judicial attention, the subjective application of the transparency requirements to particular sizes of business may operate to prevent the courts from building a reliable body of case law upon which to base a set of standard insurance terms and conditions which will be found to meet the transparency requirements in every case. Nevertheless, the courts will likely be able to set clear precedents for more sophisticated markets where less emphasis will be placed on the requirement to draw a particular term to the insured's attention.

5-137   **Insured's knowledge of the disadvantageous term.**   Where the insured has actual knowledge of the disadvantageous term, it is quite clear that it should be unable to argue that the disadvantageous term is nevertheless ineffective because of some failure by the insurer to satisfy the objective requirements set out under s.17(4) of the 2015 Act. Accordingly, s.17(5) of the 2015 Act provides:

> "(5)   The insured may not rely on any failure on the part of the insurer to meet the requirements of subsection (2) if the insured (or its agent) had actual knowledge of the disadvantageous term when the contract was entered into or the variation agreed."

The Law Commission considered that the provision may apply where the insurance broker is aware of the disadvantageous term but the insured is not, on the basis of the normal laws of agency.[275] This would likely also apply to an employer or contractor taking out the CAR policy to cover the project: the policy is treated as composite insurance comprising of a bundle of separate insurance contracts agreed between the insurer and each named insured, where the employer or contractor is therefore treated as the agent arranging the insurance on behalf of the other named insureds. For further analysis of co-insurance and the position of the parties under a CAR policy, see below Ch.20.

5-138   **Basis of the contract clauses.**   The one limit imposed on the extent to which parties are capable of contracting out of the provisions of the 2015 Act is that any term purporting to convert an insured's representations into warranties will be of no contractual effect, as provided by s.16(1).[276]

5-139   **Settlement agreements.**   The transparency requirements will also have no effect on settlement agreements between the parties, as provided by s.16(4) of the 2015 Act. It would clearly be undesirable for the courts to be able to interfere with settlement agreements purely on the basis that they may place the insured in a less

---

[272]   See above, fn.260 at para.29.65.
[273]   See above, fn.260 at para.29.66.
[274]   See above, fn.260 at para.29.67.
[275]   See above, fn.260 at para.29.46.
[276]   See above, para.5-092.

favourable position than a court would have awarded following a trial of the underlying claim under the policy.

Cancellation rights.   Although not contained within the explicit provisions of the 2015 Act, the Law Commission were of the opinion that an insurer's cancellation rights contained within the policy would not place the insured in a worse position than under the 2015 Act because they operate prospectively and are usually tied to an obligation to return premiums pro rata.[277]   **5-140**

7.   GOOD FAITH

Removal of remedy for breach.   One of the question marks hanging over the 2015 Act rests above the principle of good faith and the role that it will play after the new provisions come into force. Section 14 of the 2015 Act removes the remedy of avoidance for the breach of the duty but leaves the underlying duty untouched, which will continue to apply as an "interpretative principle"[278] to guide judicial interpretation of insurance contracts generally and as a tool to help interpret the provisions of the 2015 Act. Although the Law Commission list a number of circumstances in which the duty of good faith may come into play in conjunction with the new provisions,[279] it seems likely that the principle will play a subordinate role in the new legislation, perhaps mainly being relied upon in particularly harsh or difficult cases.   **5-141**

An interpretative principle.   After the provisions of the 2015 Act come into force, s.17 of the MIA will simply state that "a contract of marine insurance is a contract based upon the utmost good faith." The principle of good faith will therefore continue to percolate throughout insurance law as an interpretative principle that may find application in particularly difficult circumstances which the courts do not feel are adequately provided for by the explicit provisions of the 2015 Act. The Law Commission envisage the following three roles for the principle: **5-142**

"(1)   To interpret the duty of fair presentation. Both parties are expected to act in good faith in exchanging information. For example, if a court were to find that an insured had intentionally disclosed only the bare minimum of information, hoping that the insurer would fail to make further enquiries to reveal the full picture, the insured would not have acted in good faith and would therefore be in breach of the duty of fair presentation.

(2)   To inform the need to imply contractual terms into the policy under the traditional 'business efficacy' test. Good faith provides a background when considering whether it is necessary to imply a particular term.

(3)   To leave some room for judicial flexibility. It is possible that the principle of a mutual duty of good faith could provide a solution to an especially hard case or emergent difficulty. Although we think such cases would be extremely rare, it is possible that the courts could develop the concept to prevent an insurer from relying on a right to deny a claim where it would be manifestly unfair to do so."[280]

Fair presentation.   Many of the changes introduced to the insured's pre-   **5-143**

---

[277] Law Commission "*Insurance Contract Law: Business Disclosure; Warranties; Insurers' Remedies for Fraudulent Claims; and Late Payment*", (Law Commission, 2014). *http://www.lawcom.gov.uk/ wp-content/uploads/2015/03/lc353_insurance-contract-law.pdf* [Accessed 24 June 2016] at para.29.60.

[278] See above, fn.271 at para.30.5.

[279] See below, para.5-142.

[280] Law Commission "*Insurance Contract Law: Business Disclosure; Warranties; Insurers' Remedies*

contractual disclosure duties are designed to encourage active insurer engagement at the underwriting stage and promote the reciprocal exchange of information necessary to furnish an effective insurance policy that is appropriately tailored to suit the circumstances of the insured. The primary device used by the 2015 Act to accomplish this purpose is a two-limbed test of fair presentation of the risk[281] under which an insured can discharge their obligations either by making a full disclosure of every material circumstance within their knowledge, or making a partial disclosure that puts an insurer on notice that more information would be available were they to request it. Such a provision is capable of abuse by a prospective insured who may intentionally use it as a means to provide the most minimal disclosure possible, with the intention of misleading the insurer about material elements of the risk. In such circumstances, the Law Commission considered that the principle of good faith would be relied upon to support the conclusion that the insured had nevertheless breached its disclosure requirements despite complying with the strict letter of the provisions.[282]

5-144 **Implied terms for business efficacy.** The principle of good faith is also used in considering the needs of "business efficacy" for the implication of terms within the insurance policy, and this will remain unchanged by the provisions of the 2015 Act.[283] The principle is likely to operate in relation to a party's exercise of a discretion conferred under the terms of the policy, such as the right to terminate, which would therefore be subject to an obligation to exercise the discretion in good faith. The Law Commission note that the imposition of implied terms based on good faith has historically been used to impose both positive rights and restrictions.[284]

5-145 **Judicial flexibility.** The Law Commission were unable to suggest any particular circumstances in which judicial resort to the principle of good faith would be needed in order to avoid manifest injustice, save by making a broad reference to an especially hard case where the courts may wish to prevent an insurer from denying a claim where this would be manifestly unfair. As such, the use of good faith as a tool to permit judicial creativity should probably be seen as a matter of last resort, unlikely to find use unless circumstances arise which were beyond the contemplation of the Law Commission during the consultation process and are not adequately provided for under the statutory provisions.

---

for Fraudulent Claims; and Late Payment", (Law Commission, 2014). *http://www.lawcom.gov.uk/ wp-content/uploads/2015/03/lc353_insurance-contract-law.pdf* [Accessed 24 June 2016] at para.30.23.

[281] See above, para.5-019.

[282] See above, para.5-011.

[283] Law Commission "*Insurance Contract Law: Business Disclosure; Warranties; Insurers' Remedies for Fraudulent Claims; and Late Payment*", (Law Commission, 2014). *http://www.lawcom.gov.uk/ wp-content/uploads/2015/03/lc353_insurance-contract-law.pdf* [Accessed 24 June 2016] at para.30.61.

[284] See above, fn.277 at para.30.60.

Chapter 6

MISREPRESENTATION, FRAUD AND THE DUTY OF UTMOST GOOD FAITH

Introduction.   The duty of good faith and the remedy of avoidance have been **6-001** central features of insurance law for centuries. The duty of good faith relates to two similar but different concepts: misrepresentations and disclosure. For many years these concepts have been provided for by statute and slowly developed by the common law. Owing to recent legislative changes, practitioners now need to be familiar with two different statutes: the Marine Insurance Act 1906 ("MIA") and the Insurance Act 2015 ("the 2015 Act").

Sections 17 to 20 of the MIA and case law under those sections set out the previous law on the duty of good faith relating to non-consumer insurance. Those provisions were in force from 1 January 1907, but have since been repealed with effect from 12 August 2016. The MIA will continue to be relevant for practitioners as it applies to any non-consumer policy incepted up to 11 August 2016 for the full term of that policy, until claims under the policy become statute barred. It is also likely that some case law under the MIA regime will remain relevant under the new regime.

Part 2 of the 2015 Act introduces a new default statutory regime for non-consumer insurance contracts incepted on or after 12 August 2016. The 2015 Act marks the culmination of a particularly long and drawn out legislative process and is the most substantial reform to insurance law in England and Wales since the introduction of the MIA over a century ago. The central reform, for this chapter, is the introduction of a statutory duty of fair presentation of risk. The duty of fair presentation partially repeals, overlaps with, clarifies and develops the duty of good faith.

This chapter is divided unequally into two parts. The first and most substantial part deals with the law on the duty of good faith under the MIA. Where relevant, brief commentary regarding changes brought about by the 2015 Act has been inserted. The second part is an introduction to the duty of fair presentation under the 2015 Act which covers the major points of interest and the important features of the statutory regime. This introduction is not, and is not intended to be, comprehensive. A comprehensive introduction to the 2015 Act is provided above at Ch.5.

This chapter covers non-consumer insurance law and does not deal with consumer insurance. The law in relation to consumer insurance is now contained separately in the Consumer Insurance (Disclosure and Representations) Act 2012, in force since early 2013 and which arose from the same reform and consultative processes as the 2015 Act. The reforms aim to make the law of insurance simpler for consumers and businesses to understand, to codify existing best practices and to protect consumers by providing proportionate remedies to insurers for inadvertent breaches of the duty of disclosure and for misrepresentation.

1. UBERRIMAE FIDES—THE DUTY OF UTMOST GOOD FAITH

6-002 **Origin of the duty of the utmost good faith.** Insurance contracts are a type of contract traditionally described as uberrimae fides, i.e. of utmost good faith. The duty of utmost good faith developed with the growth of marine insurance; the mechanism of proposal in marine insurance, whereby the proposer presents information to the insurer who accepts that information at face value and as being complete, necessitated a duty on the parties to act in good faith towards each other.[1] The duty does not arise out of the contract but is a separate common law duty.[2] The rationale of the duty was set out by Lord Mansfield in 1776 in *Carter v Boehm*. He said:

> "[I]nsurance is a contract upon speculation. The special facts, upon which the contingent chance is to be computed, lie most commonly in the knowledge of the *insured* only: the under-writer trusts to his representation, and proceeds upon confidence that he does not keep back any circumstance in his knowledge, to mislead the under-writer into a belief that the circumstance does not exist. ... The keeping back such circumstance is a *fraud*, and therefore the policy is *void*. Although the suppression should happen through *mistake*, without any fraudulent intention; yet still the under-writer is *deceived*, and the policy is *void*; because the risque run is really different from the risque understood and intended to be run, at the time of the agreement. The policy would equally be void, against the *under-writer*, if *he* concealed ... Good faith forbids either party by concealing what he privately knows, to draw the other into a bargain, from his ignorance of that fact, and his believing the contrary."[3]

---

[1] See below, para.6-012. In *Banque Keyser Ullmann SA v Skandia (UK) Insurance Co* [1990] 1 Q.B. 665 at 769; [1989] 3 W.L.R. 25 at 78; [1989] 2 All E.R. 952 at 989, Slade, Lloyd and Gibson LJJ stated, in respect of contracts of good faith: "[t]he common features of contracts which are classified by the law as contracts uberrimae fidei is that by their very nature one party is likely to have the command of means of knowledge not available to the other".

[2] On this point Lord Atkin said in *Bell v Lever Brothers Ltd* [1932] A.C. 161 at 227; [1931] All E.R. Rep. 1 at 32; 101 L.J.K.B. 129 at 160: "[t]here are certain contracts expressed by the law to be contracts of the utmost good faith, where material facts must be disclosed; if not, the contract is voidable. Apart from special fiduciary relationships, contracts for partnership and contracts of insurance are the leading instances. In such cases the duty does not arise out of contract; the duty of a person proposing an insurance arises before a contract is made, so of an intending partner". See also Lord Hobhouse in *Manifest Shipping Co Ltd v Uni-Polaris Shipping Co Ltd (The Star Sea)* [2001] UKHL 1 at [46]; [2003] 1 A.C. 469 at 493; [2001] 2 W.L.R. 170 at 185–186.

[3] *Carter v Boehm* (1766) 3 Burr. 1905 at [1909]–[1910]; 97 E.R. 1162 at 1164.

This remains an accurate definition of the duty as it developed under the MIA, with the exception that an insurance policy entered into on the basis of misleading information is voidable under the MIA, rather than void. The emphasis of Lord Mansfield's judgment in *Carter* is on the existence of a duty of disclosure and the onus on the insured to disclose, as it is the insured that possesses knowledge of the facts relevant to the insurance requested by it and the insurer must rely on the accuracy and integrity of the facts communicated to it by the insured when agreeing to provide the insurance. Lord Mansfield's judgment makes it clear that both the insured and the insurer have a duty of the utmost good faith towards each other, which includes duties of disclosure and truthful representation.

Codifying the duty of utmost good faith.   The duty of utmost good faith as first   **6-003**
explained by Lord Mansfield was codified in ss.17–20 of the MIA,[4] although the duty had developed in the common law over the century between his judgment and the implementation of the MIA. In particular, the scope of that which the insured was required to disclose became more accurately defined in the case law.[5]

The MIA reflects the common law position and ss.17–20 have been held to apply to both marine and non-marine insurance. In *Pan Atlantic Insurance Co Ltd v Pine Top Insurance Co Ltd*, Lord Mustill said:

"[I]n relevant respects the common law relating to the two types of insurance is the same, and … the Act embodies a partial codification of the common law."[6]

It can be said that the MIA is an accurate representation of the common law of insurance including the duty of utmost good faith, though some common law principles and rules which remain outside the scope of the MIA will still apply to insurance contracts under that regime. Section 91(2) of the MIA provides:

"The rules of the common law including the law merchant save in so far as they are inconsistent with the express provisions of this Act, shall continue to apply to contracts of marine insurance."

Decisions since 1906 have interpreted the law as it is set out in the MIA and have had the effect of aligning the common law with the MIA.[7] For example, the law on non-disclosure now requires inducement of the actual underwriter, the effect of which is to bring the MIA into line with the common law position on misrepresentation, which requires inducement.[8] The MIA provides that the insurer can only avoid an insurance policy where non-disclosure is material to the risk, but the authori-

---

[4]   Marine Insurance Act 1906 ("MIA").
[5]   The MIA is described in the headnote of the legislation as "An Act to codify the Law relating to Marine Insurance". For an overview of the historical development of the duty of good faith, includ ing changes in nomenclature, see Lord Hobhouse in *Manifest Shipping Co Ltd* [2001] UKHL 1 at [40]–[45]; [2003] 1 A.C. 469 at 491–492; [2001] 2 W.L.R. 170 at 184–185.
[6]   *Pan Atlantic Insurance Co Ltd v Pine Top Insurance Co Ltd* [1995] 1 A.C. 501 at 518; [1994] 3 W.L.R. 677 at 683; [1994] 3 All E.R. 581 at 588. Similarly, Longmore LJ in *K/S Merc–Scandia XXXXII v Lloyd's Underwriters (The Mercandian Continent)* [2001] EWCA Civ 1275 at [21]; [2001] 2 Lloyd's Rep. 563 at 570; [2001] C.L.C. 1836 at 1843 referring to the MIA said: "[t]he law as there stated is, in general, no different from that for other forms of insurance in so far as the duties in rela tion to good faith, disclosure and representations are concerned".
[7]   See *Banque Keyser Ullmann SA* [1990] 1 Q.B. 665 at 779–780; [1989] 3 W.L.R. 25 at 87–88; [1989] 2 All E.R. 952 at 996, which decided that damages were not available for breach of the duty of utmost good faith.
[8]   A consequence of the decision in *Pan Atlantic Insurance Co Ltd* [1995] 1 A.C. 501; [1994] 3 W.L.R. 677; [1994] 3 All E.R. 581. See below, paras 6-037 to 6-038.

ties follow the common law position on fraudulent non-disclosure where an insurer can avoid a policy even though the non-disclosure is not material.[9]

The 2015 Act marks a significant development for the duty of good faith, and the new provisions have in many respects overtaken the role of good faith under the MIA by introducing new duties and remedies which are intended to strike a more appropriate balance between the interests of the insurer and the insured in the majority of foreseeable circumstances. Whereas the duty of utmost good faith was a central tenet of the insurance policy under the MIA, the provisions of the 2015 Act instead aim to provide a complete statutory regime. The new regime aims to allow the courts to discriminate between an adequate and inadequate presentation of risk without recourse to the principle of good faith, which in certain cases held the potential to introduce uncertainty regarding its application. The approach taken under the 2015 Act is intended to be advantageous for the insurer and insured and provide greater certainty in relation to the court's approach to the insured's compliance with disclosure duties. It is hoped that it will reduce litigation. Nevertheless, the 2015 Act does not repeal the duty of good faith entirely and instead removes the remedy of avoidance for its breach. The duty therefore remains on a statutory footing as an interpretative principle. But at present it is uncertain whether the courts will continue to apply good faith in relation to the insured's pre-contractual disclosure duties and, if so, how the principle will sit alongside the new duty of fair presentation.[10]

6-004 **Breach of the duty of good faith.** The contract of insurance is based upon reciprocal duties of utmost good faith and applies both pre- and post-contract.[11] Section 17 of the MIA provides:

> "A contract of marine insurance is a contract based upon the utmost good faith, and, if the utmost good faith be not observed by either party, the contract may be avoided by the other party."[12]

Under the MIA, if one party does not act with the utmost good faith, the contract may be avoided by the other party. The contract is not void but is voidable ab initio at the election of the other party. The injured party has the right to elect to waive the breach and continue with the contract. The decision to avoid a policy will be effective immediately upon communication to the other party or declaratory relief by the courts. Ab initio avoidance has the same effect as the rescission of a contract, where both parties are returned to the position each was in prior to entering into the contract. But conceptually the two are distinct: a rescission is not available for a breach of duty that occurred before a contract has been entered into. A post-

---

9 Provided that the fraud induced the insurer to enter into the contract. See *The Bedouin* [1894] P. 1 at 12, per Lord Esher M.R. In *HIH Casualty & General Insurance Ltd v Chase Manhattan Bank* [2003] UKHL 6 at [70]–[75]; [2003] 1 All E.R. (Comm) 349 at 371–372; [2003] 2 Lloyd's Rep. 61 at 77–78, Lord Hoffmann accepted the existence of the concept of fraudulent non-disclosure.

10 See above, Ch.5.

11 *Manifest Shipping Co Ltd* [2001] UKHL 1 at [48]–[49]; [2003] 1 A.C. 469 at 493–494; [2001] 2 W.L.R. 170 at 186; *K/S Merc-Scandia XXXXII* [2001] EWCA Civ 1275; [2001] 2 Lloyd's Rep. 563; [2001] C.L.C. 1836.

12 In *Manifest Shipping Co Ltd* [2001] UKHL 1 at [48]; [2003] 1 A.C. 469 at 493–494; [2001] 2 W.L.R. 170 at 186, Lord Hobhouse stated, considering the legal issues surrounding s.17: "In his book upon the Act published in 1907, Sir Mackenzie Chalmers added this note to s.17: 'Note: The general principle is stated in this section because the special sections which follow are not exhaustive.' (*The Marine Insurance Act 1906*, 1st edn (1907), p.25)."

contractual breach of duty, that is, a breach occurring after the formation of the insurance contract, would only give the party not in breach the right to avoid the contract in limited circumstances under the MIA.[13] The insured's duties of disclosure and truthful representation under the MIA are contained in ss.18–20. The insurer's duties are not set out in the MIA but remain embodied in the common law.[14]

In the case of CAR insurance, where there can be multiple insureds, each insured's interest and liabilities are individually insured and the policy is considered to be composite. The actions or omissions of one party may have no effect on the rights of the others. Generally speaking a vitiating act by one insured will not prejudice another. It is not considered that this will change under the 2015 Act, although it remains a possibility under the wording of the statute.[15]

The 2015 Act introduces a single duty of fair presentation of risk to replace the duties under the MIA. The remedy for breach is not only one of avoidance. There is a dual system of remedies for, first, deliberate or reckless breaches and, secondly, other breaches.

2. MISREPRESENTATION AND THE MIA

Good faith and the insured's duty of truthful representation. The insurance contract is based on information supplied by the insured to the insurer that relates to the risk. This is so that the insurer can provide appropriate insurance cover for the insured and so it can impose terms and set a premium that it considers to be appropriate for the risk that it may have to indemnify the insured for. Due to the distinctive nature of contracts for insurance, the law of insurance places the insured under an obligation to make representations, whereas in the law of contract the parties are not usually under such obligation.[16]

6-005

Under the MIA, these representations must be true; if they are not the insurer may avoid the contract. Section 20(1) provides:

"Every material representation made by the assured or his agent to the insurer during the negotiations for the contract, and before the contract is concluded, must be true. If it be untrue the insurer may avoid the contract."

---

[13] Indeed, the existence of a remedy of avoidance for a post-contractual breach of good faith was brought into question by the case of *AXA General Insurance Ltd v Gottlieb* [2005] EWCA Civ 112; [2005] 1 All E.R. (Comm) 445; [2005] Lloyd's Rep. I.R. 369.

[14] See below, paras 6-040 to 6-043.

[15] For a background on co-insurance and discussion of the issues that can flow from it, see above, Ch.20 generally.

[16] In *St Paul Fire & Marine Insurance Co (UK) Ltd v McConnell Dowell Constructors Ltd* [1996] 1 All E.R. 96 at 103; [1995] 2 Lloyd's Rep. 116 at 121–122; [1995] C.L.C. 818 at 824, Evans LJ said: "The right of an insurer to avoid the contract of insurance in the event of material misrepresentation made to him is no different from the law of contract generally. There is a difference in relation to non-disclosure, because there is no general obligation upon a contracting party to disclose even material facts to the other party (provided the nondisclosure does not make any positive representations misleading) whereas contracts of insurance being of the utmost good faith (s.17 of the Act) do give rise to such a duty". The same point was also made earlier in *Bell v Lever Brothers Ltd* [1932] A.C. 161 at 227; [1931] All E.R. Rep. 1 at 32; 101 L.J.K.B. 129 at 160 by Lord Atkin who said: "Ordinarily the failure to disclose a material fact which might influence the mind of a prudent contractor does not give the right to avoid the contract. The principle of caveat emptor applies beyond contracts of sale."

6-006   **Categories of representation.**   Insurance law differs from normal contract law in recognising representations of opinion, for statements of opinion generally will not be held to amount to representations for the purposes of the law of misrepresentation.[17] However, in relation to insurance contracts, s.20(3) of the MIA provides that "[a] representation may be either a representation as to a matter of fact, or as to a matter of expectation or belief." Each kind of representation has its own test of veracity. A representation of fact is considered to be true if the difference between the representation and the actual truth would not affect the judgment of a prudent underwriter.[18] A representation of expectation or belief is true if it is made in good faith.[19] Representations that are corrected or withdrawn will have no further effect.[20]

6-007   **Representations of fact.**   A misrepresentation is defined in the law of contract as a false statement of fact by party A (or its agent) that induces party B to enter into a contract with party A. Certain de minimis statements are regarded as "puffs" and are not classed as actionable misrepresentations. Representations of fact are given the same treatment in insurance law under the MIA as they are in contract law[21] except that in insurance law there is a requirement of materiality as well as the normal requirement of inducement.[22]

6-008   **Representation of expectation or belief.**   A representation as to a matter of expectation or belief is true if it has been made in good faith. The test for whether a representation is made in good faith is not laid out in the MIA, but it was considered by the Court of Appeal in *Economides v Commercial Union Assurance Co Plc*.[23] The question for the court was whether an insured, in order to make a representation of belief in good faith, needed to have objectively reasonable grounds for his belief, or whether it was sufficient that the insured genuinely considered it to be reasonably held (a subjective standard). In *Economides* the insured had a household contents policy valued at £12,000. During the course of the policy the insured's parents came to live with him bringing additional valuables. On the advice of his father, the insured increased the contents cover by £4,000; the flat was subsequently burgled and the loss transpired to be £30,970. The claim that followed was rejected by the insurers on the basis of misrepresentation. The Court of

---

17   Though where the opinion was intended to mislead, it may be a representation of fact of the state of mind of the representor: *Bisset v Wilkinson* [1927] A.C. 177; see, for example, the judgment of Nugee J (appealed unsuccessfully on a different point) in *Barnsley v Noble* [2014] EWHC 2657 (Ch) at [208] and [209].

18   Section 20(4) of the MIA provides that "[a] representation as to a matter of fact is true, if it be substantially correct, that is to say, if the difference between what is represented and what is actually correct would not be considered material by a prudent insurer."

19   Section 20(5) of the MIA provides that "[a] representation as to a matter of expectation or belief is true if it be made in good faith."

20   Section 20(6) of the MIA provides that "[a] representation may be withdrawn or corrected before the contract is concluded."

21   See further *Chitty on Contracts* (2015) Vol.1, Ch.7.

22   See below, paras 6-037 to 6-039.

23   *Economides v Commercial Union Assurance Co Plc* [1998] Q.B. 587; [1997] 3 W.L.R. 1066; [1997] 3 All E.R. 636. Applied in *Zeller v British Caymanian Insurance Co Ltd* [2008] UKPC 4; [2008] Lloyd's Rep. I.R. 545. Both were distinguished in *Genesis Housing Association Ltd v Liberty Syndicate Management Ltd* [2013] EWCA Civ 1173 at [68] and [69]; [2013] Bus LR 1399 at 1410.

Appeal, allowing the appeal (Sir Iain Glidewell dissenting),[24] held that there was no requirement of objectively reasonable grounds for a belief, and that a subjective honest belief by Mr Economides was sufficient for a representation to have been made in good faith, thus satisfying s.20(5) of the MIA. There must, however, be some basis for holding the belief, for an objective assessment of such a belief may show that it was not held in good faith.[25] A statement expressed as an opinion can be held to be a statement of fact; for example, the insertion of "we have been informed that" at the front of a statement that fire hydrants were installed in a building did not mean the statement was one of opinion.[26]

Misrepresentation under the 2015 Act   By default under the 2015 Act, the   **6-009**
insured is under a duty to make a fair presentation of risk. This duty includes both positive and negative elements. The negative element relates to misrepresentations. Section 3(3)(c) of the 2015 Act provides that

> "A fair presentation of the risk is one … in which every material representation as to a matter of fact is substantially correct, and every material representation as to a matter of expectation is made in good faith."

Accordingly, the 2015 Act retains the division between representations of fact and of opinion and provides for similar, if slightly diluted, tests in both cases. The concepts of materiality and inducement are retained. As with the MIA, a misrepresentation can be withdrawn or corrected before inception of a policy.[27]

These changes do not significantly change what constitutes misrepresentation. It therefore seems likely that case law, or at least judicial reasoning, under the MIA will continue to be relevant. The significant change under the 2015 Act relates to remedies to insurers where an insured's misrepresentation has breached the duty of fair presentation.

3.   DISCLOSURE AND THE MIA

Good faith and the insured's duty of disclosure.   The law of contract does not   **6-010**
generally impose on contracting parties any duty to make disclosure to each other before reaching a bargain. Contracts of insurance are an exception; the duty of good faith requires more and so the proposer is under a duty to disclose certain matters.

Under the MIA, the duty is to disclose to the insurer material circumstances of which he has knowledge before the contract is completed. Section 18(1) of the MIA provides:

> "[T]he assured must disclose to the insurer, before the contract is concluded, every material circumstance which is known to the assured, and the assured is deemed to know every circumstance which, in the ordinary course of business, ought to be known by him. If the assured fails to make such disclosure, the insurer may avoid the contract."

---

24 *Economides* [1998] Q.B. 587 at 600 and 606; [1997] 3 W.L.R. 1066 at 1076, 1082–1083; [1997] 3 All E.R. 636 at 646, 652–653, per Brown and Gibson LJJ. At [1998] Q.B. 587 at 609; [1997] 3 W.L.R. 1066 at 1085; [1997] 3 All E.R. 636 at 655, Sir Iain Glidewell proposed an objective test.
25 *Economides* [1998] Q.B. 587 at 599 and 606; [1997] 3 W.L.R. 1066 at 1076, 1082–1083; [1997] 3 All E.R. 636 at 646, 652–653, per Brown and Gibson LJJ.
26 *Sirius International Insurance Corp v Oriental Assurance Corp* [1999] 1 All E.R. (Comm) 699; [1999] Lloyd's Rep. I.R. 343.
27 Section 7(6) of the 2015 Insurance Act (the "2015 Act") provides that "A representation may be withdrawn or corrected before the contract of insurance is entered into."

6-011   **Knowledge.**   Under the MIA, the duty to disclose extends, in the first instance, to any material circumstance "known to the assured."[28] These circumstances include both the actual knowledge of the insured and constructive knowledge; the latter means those facts which the insurer would be expected to know in the usual course of business. An agent's knowledge can be attributed to a principal. The insured will further be deemed to have so-called "blind eye" knowledge, which describes the situation where the insured has a suspicion that relevant facts do exist and takes "a deliberate decision to avoid confirming that they exist."[29] In *London General Insurance Co Ltd v General Marine Underwriters Association Ltd*,[30] insurance cover was already in place on a ship, and the insurers wished to reinsure their risk. The decision by the proposers to insure the risk with the insurers was taken on 24 September, the proposal was dated 25 September, and the insurance was effected at 4pm on the same day. However, on the morning of 25 September information had reached the proposer in the form of a Lloyd's "casualty list" that the ship had been partially damaged by fire. The casualty list was placed in a desk drawer and not looked at until after the insurance had been affected at 4pm. The Court of Appeal held that the proposer was already "upon the risk" (i.e. aware) of the ship and ought, in the ordinary course of their business, to have checked the casualty slip, whereupon they would have discovered that the ship was partially damaged. They should then have then disclosed that information to the reinsurer before the insurance was affected. As such, there had been a non-disclosure of a material circumstance, and the reinsurer was entitled to avoid the policy.

Non-disclosure of information that a reasonable insured did not believe to exist will not entitle the insurer to avoid the policy. In *Decorum Investments Ltd v Atkin ("The Elena G")*[31] insurers sought to avoid an insurance policy providing an indemnity for loss and fire damage to a yacht. The yacht *Elena G* was registered to a company, which was in turn controlled by a holding company. The holding company's majority shareholder was a Russian businessman and political activist at risk of attack and possible assassination. The insured company did not disclose any details of the Russian businessman, nor was it aware of any threats to him. It was held that the insured had not failed to comply with its duty of disclosure.[32]

Knowledge is one of the areas in which the 2015 Act makes substantial reforms. The 2015 Act was drafted with an intention to clarify the law on knowledge and to reduce existing uncertainties. Under the 2015 Act, distinct tests are provided for the knowledge of individual and non-individual insureds; in the latter case a non-individual insured's knowledge is defined by reference to the insured's senior management. "Blind eye" knowledge remains. A test for constructive knowledge has been provided by the introduction of what would have been revealed by a

---

28   Section18(1) of the MIA.
29   *Manifest Shipping Co Ltd* [2001] UKHL 1 at [116]; [2003] 1 A.C. 469 at 517; [2001] 2 W.L.R. 170 at 209, per Lord Scott. The same point was also made in *Economides* [1998] Q.B. 587 at 608; [1997] 3 W.L.R. 1066 at 1084; [1997] 3 All E.R. 636 at 654, where Glidewell LJ said that: "...'knowledge' means actual knowledge, subject only to the qualification that an insured cannot be heard to say that he does not know a fact when he has wilfully and deliberately shut his eyes to evidence of that fact".
30   *London General Insurance Co Ltd v General Marine Underwriters Association Ltd* [1921] 1 K.B. 104; (1920) 3 Ll. L. Rep. 199.
31   *Decorum Investments Ltd v Atkin (The Elena G)* [2001] 2 Lloyd's Rep. 378; [2002] Lloyd's Rep. I.R. 450.
32   See also *Norwich Union Insurance Ltd v Meisels* [2006] EWHC 2811 (QB); [2007] 1 All E.R. (Comm) 1138; [2007] Lloyd's Rep. I.R. 69.

reasonable search of the information available to the insured. Clarification has been given as to when knowledge of a fraud on the part of an agent will and will not be attributed to its principal.[33]

Disclosure in the proposal form. The insured must check the accuracy of oral answers given to an insurer's agent who is helping to fill out a proposal form. In *Newsholme Bros v Road Transport & General Insurance Co Ltd* the insurer's agent erroneously filled out a proposal on behalf of the proposed insured, even though the insured had given correct answers to all questions asked orally. The broker had not been instructed to fill out proposal forms by its employer and thus the court held that the responsibility lay with the insured to check that the content had correctly been filled out, which it failed to do.[34] In that case the agent was held to be de facto agent of the insured since it was effectively acting as amanuensis for the insured.[35] **6-012**

In the case of CAR insurance, the proposal usually requires details of the insured, intermediary details, the duration of cover required, the insured's claims history (usually backdated five years), general details including the location of the project and information regarding the criminal record or insurance history of directors.[36]

Correction. Under the MIA, where a misrepresentation has been made or there has been a material non-disclosure, provided that the insured corrects the misstatement or the non-disclosure prior to the completion of the contract with the insurer, the breach of duty cannot then be relied upon by the insurer at a later date.[37] It has been held that "the correction has to be fairly made to the insurer, such that the corrected picture is presented fairly to the insurer, and comes to his knowledge."[38] **6-013**

Disclosure under the 2015 Act. Under the 2015 Act, the insured is under a default duty to make a fair presentation of risk. This duty includes both positive and negative elements. The positive element relates to disclosure. Section 3(3)(a) and (b) provide that **6-014**

"A fair presentation of the risk is one (a) which makes the disclosure required by subsection (4) [and] (b) which makes that disclosure in a manner which would be reasonably clear and accessible to a prudent insurer".

Section 3(4)(a) and (b) outlines the content required to be disclosed:

"(a) disclosure of every material circumstance which the insured knows or ought to know, or (b) failing that, disclosure which gives the insurer sufficient information to put a prudent insurer on notice that it needs to make further enquiries for the purpose of revealing those material circumstances."

---

[33] For a comprehensive discussion of knowledge under the 2015 Act, see above paras 5-027 to 5-058.
[34] *Newsholme Bros v Road Transport & General Insurance Co Ltd* [1929] 2 K.B. 356; (1929) 34 Ll. L. Rep. 247.
[35] *Newsholme Bros* [1929] 2 K.B. 356 at 364, per Scrutton LJ.
[36] See above, Ch.4.
[37] *Assicurazioni Generali SpA v Arab Insurance Group (BSC)* [2002] EWCA Civ 1642 at [63]–[64]; [2003] 1 All E.R. (Comm) 140 at 158–159; [2003] Lloyd's Rep. I.R. 131 at 149. cf. *Peekay Intermark Ltd v Australia & New Zealand Banking Group Ltd* [2006] EWCA Civ 386; [2006] 2 Lloyd's Rep. 511, where it was held that the contract terms were clear, unambiguous and not hidden in small print and the plaintiff's signature of the terms was enough to show he had not relied on the representation.
[38] *Western Trading Ltd v Great Lakes Reinsurance (UK) Plc* [2015] EWHC 103 (QB) at [63].

There are exceptions, similar to those under the MIA.[39] Accordingly, the new provisions incorporate both the concepts of s.18(1) of the MIA and the trend of the recent case law under that section, which developed the courts approach from a technical analysis towards an analysis more focused on fair presentation of risk.[40]

4. KNOWLEDGE, AGENTS AND UTMOST GOOD FAITH

6-015   **Origin of the agents' duty of disclosure.** The duty of disclosure imposed on the insured also extends to its agents under the MIA. The origin of this duty is to be found in two related cases: *Blackburn Low & Co v Haslam*[41] and *Blackburn Low & Co v Vigors*[42] both of which concerned the ship *The State of Florida*. The plaintiff insurers sought to effect reinsurance of the vessel which was on passage from New York to Glasgow. In *Haslam*, the brokers acting on behalf of the plaintiffs became aware that the ship had been lost during the voyage but nevertheless proceeded to obtain reinsurance through their own broker without informing the plaintiffs of the loss. The court held that the reinsurer was entitled to avoid the policy because the broker had not disclosed to the reinsurer this information, which was both important and material. However, in *Vigors* the same plaintiff secured reinsurance of the ship through a different broker and was able to recover on that reinsurance policy because neither they nor the broker were aware of the loss of the ship.

The principle explained in *Vigors* and *Haslam* is that the agent of the insured is under a separate duty to the insurer to disclose all material circumstances known to it even if not known to the insured[43] and the result of a failure to do so will provide the insurer the right against the insured to avoid the policy.[44] A different principle also considered in *Vigors* was that the knowledge that ought to be disclosed by the agent is imputed to the principal, though the approach is now not preferred by the courts.[45]

This section, for the most part, discusses the way in which the current regime under the MIA deals with the knowledge of the insured's agent. This is an area of

---

39   These are set out in s.3(5) of the 2015 Act.
40   See *Iron Trades Mutual Insurance Co Ltd v Companhia de Seguros Imperio* [1991] 1 Re LR 213; *Garnat Trading & Shipping (Singapore) Pte Ltd v Baominh Insurance Corporation* [20101] EWHC 2578 (Comm), [2011] 1 L.R. 366 at [135]; *AXA Verischerung AG v ARAB Insurance Group (BSC)* [2015] EWHC 1939 (Comm) at [113]. See above, Ch.5 fn.36.
41   *Blackburn Low & Co v Haslam* (1888) 21 Q.B.D. 144.
42   *Blackburn Low & Co v Vigors* (1887) 12 App. Cas. 531.
43   *Vigors* (1887) 12 App. Cas. 531 at 543, per Lord Macnagthen. Approved in *PCW Syndicates v PCW Reinsurers* [1996] 1 W.L.R. 1136 at 1145; [1996] 1 All E.R. 774 at 783; [1996] 1 Lloyd's Rep. 241 at 255, per Staughton LJ, *HIH Casualty & General Insurance Ltd* [2003] UKHL 6 at [42] and [87]; [2003] 1 All E.R. (Comm) 349 at 364 and 374; [2003] 2 Lloyd's Rep. 61 at 72 and 79, per Lords Hoffmann and Hobhouse.
44   See *PCW Syndicates v PCW Reinsurers* [1996] 1 W.L.R. 1136 at 1145; [1996] 1 All E.R. 774 at 783; [1996] 1 Lloyd's Rep. 241 at 255, per Staughton LJ.
45   *Vigors* (1887) 12 App. Cas. 531. Unlike Lord Macnaghten, Lord Halsbury L.C. and Lords Watson and Fitzgerald adopted the imputation principle. If attribution or imputation of knowledge was the correct mechanism then such attribution of the broker's knowledge in *Haslam* would have led to the position where the plaintiff would have the requisite knowledge in *Vigors*. In *Societe Anonyme d'intermediaries Luxembourgeois (SAIL) v Farex Gie* [1995] L.R.L.R. 116 at 150; [1994] C.L.C. 1094 at 1111, Hoffmann LJ approved of Lord Macnaghten's principle and pointed out that imputation makes s.19 MIA redundant since s.18 MIA already provides for imputation of agent's knowledge. Imputation of material circumstances will become relevant where the agent is not an agent to insure. See below, para.6-022.

the law that has been substantially reformed by the introduction of the 2015 Act. For a comprehensive discussion of the reformed position, see Ch.5.

Agent's disclosure under statute. The principle established by those two cases   **6-016**
is currently to be found in s.19 of the MIA,[46] which provides that

> "[W]here insurance is effected for the insured by an agent, the agent must disclose to the insurer–
>
> (a)   Every material circumstance which is known to himself, and an agent to insure is deemed to know every circumstance which in the ordinary course of business ought to be known by, or to have been communicated to, him; and
>
> (b)   Every material circumstance which the assured is bound to disclose, unless it come to his knowledge too late to communicate it to the agent."

Section 19 requires disclosure of knowledge of material circumstances in three situations: (i) where there are material circumstances known to the agent, whether or not they are known to the insured; (ii) where the agent ought to have known of the material circumstances in the course of his business; and (iii) where there are material circumstances which the insured is bound to disclose. It is therefore possible that s.19(a) could give rise to a situation in which the insurer is entitled to avoid a policy where the insured does not know and could not be expected to know of the material information and where the agent does not know, but ought to know. It is suggested that s.19(b) does not add anything beyond that which is already provided by s.18(1), since under that provision the requirement that the insured discloses every material circumstance known or ought to be known to it necessarily means the insured has the knowledge which its agents have, or ought to have.[47]

For policies incepted on or after 12 August 2016, the regime under the 2015 Act governs non-consumer insurance rather than the MIA, save for those parties that contract out of its provisions. The disclosure obligations which fall on the insured as part of the wider duty of fair presentation under the 2015 Act provide for how to treat the insured's agent's knowledge. For a comprehensive discussion of the new regime, see Ch.5.

Type of agent.   Section 19 of the MIA states that the duty to disclose material facts   **6-017**
to the insurer applies to an "agent to insure." It is therefore necessary to identify the agent to insure and to consider other types of insured's agent. A broker who is responsible for placing the proposal directly with the underwriting market and securing the contract for insurance or reinsurance with the underwriter is often called the placing broker.[48] A broker whose role is to put forward a proposal or presentation to a placing broker is known as a "producing broker." The producing broker is likely to be a separate commercial insurance broking firm, which specialises in obtaining bespoke insurance. An intermediate broker is a broker who may become involved in procuring insurance at an earlier stage in the process by

---

[46]   The MIA applies both to marine and non-marine insurance policies. See *PCW Syndicates* [1996] 1 W.L.R. 1136 at 1140; [1996] 1 All E.R. 774 at 779; [1996] 1 Lloyd's Rep. 241 at 252, per Staughton LJ *Societe Anonyme d'intermediaries Luxembourgeois* [1995] L.R.L.R. 116 at 141; [1994] C.L.C. 1094 at 1100, per Dillon LJ.

[47]   See, for example, the Law Commission and the Scottish Law Commission, *Insurance Contract Law: Business Disclosure; Warranties; Insurer's Remedies for Fraudluent Claims; and Late Payment* (HMSO, 2014) at 9.10.

[48]   See above, Ch.4.

negotiating with the producing or placing broker over the insurance cover and price, though there is not always a clear distinction between the intermediate broker and the producing broker.[49]

6-018   **Agent to insure.**   It has been held that the term "agent to insure," in s.19 of the MIA, only refers to placing brokers. In *PCW Syndicates*[50] the producing brokers of an insurer were responsible for obtaining reinsurance of the insurer's liability, which they did through their own agent, a placing broker. The producing brokers had also been fraudulently misusing money from premium receipts they were collecting on behalf of the insurer. Upon being informed of the fraud the reinsurer sought to avoid its reinsurance policy with the insurer. The Court of Appeal held that the term "agent to insure" only encompasses "those agents who actually deal with the insurers concerned and make the contract in question"[51] and that would extend only to a placing broker, so that PCW's producing broker would not come under the duty in s.19. This decision appears to conflict with the decision in *Haslam*,[52] since in that case the broker who knew that the ship had been lost was a producing broker who obtained the insurance through his own placing agent. The decision in *Haslam*[53] is explained by Saville LJ in *PCW*.[54] He concluded that the s.19 duty does accord with the *Haslam*[55] decision because in that case the producing brokers should have communicated the knowledge of the lost ship to the placing broker, meaning that it was knowledge that the placing broker ought to have had communicated to it in its ordinary course of business, therefore giving rise to the placing broker's duty to disclose. The distinction between *Haslam*[56] and *PCW*[57] was that in the latter case the knowledge in question was knowledge of fraud and it could not be said that the placing broker ought to have known about it in the ordinary course of business.[58]

6-019   The decision in *PCW* has been questioned in two cases and so it is possible that the duty is not restricted to the placing agent.[59] In *ERC Frankona Reinsurance v American National Insurance Co*,[60] a case of non-disclosure by an intermediate broker of a previous conviction for securities fraud, Andrew Smith J acknowledged the decision in *PCW* had been "forcefully criticised"[61] but accepted that he was bound by the Court of Appeal's decision. Further, no reference was made in *PCW* to an earlier case, *GMA v Uni Storebrand International Insurance AS*,[62] in which

---

49   Duty of disclosure of "other agents" of the insured is discussed below at para.6-022.
50   *PCW Syndicates* [1996] 1 W.L.R. 1136; [1996] 1 All E.R. 774; [1996] 1 Lloyd's Rep. 241.
51   *PCW Syndicates* [1996] 1 W.L.R. 1136 at 1148; [1996] 1 All E.R. 774 at 786; [1996] 1 Lloyd's Rep. 241 at 257, per Rose LJ.
52   *Haslam* (1888) 21 Q.B.D. 144.
53   *Haslam* (1888) 21 Q.B.D. 144.
54   *PCW Syndicates* [1996] 1 W.L.R. 1136 at 1151; [1996] 1 All E.R. 774 at 789; [1996] 1 Lloyd's Rep. 241 at 259.
55   *Haslam* (1888) 21 Q.B.D. 144.
56   *Haslam* (1888) 21 Q.B.D. 144.
57   *PCW Syndicates* [1996] 1 W.L.R. 1136; [1996] 1 All E.R. 774; [1996] 1 Lloyd's Rep. 241.
58   Disclosure of an agent's own fraud is discussed below at para.6-024.
59   *ERC Frankona Reinsurance v American National Insurance Co* [2005] EWHC 1381 (Comm); [2006] Lloyd's Rep. I.R. 157; *Baker v Lombard Continental Insurance Plc* Unreported April 22, 1996 Q.B.D. (Comm).
60   *ERC Frankona Reinsurance* [2005] EWHC 1381 (Comm); [2006] Lloyd's Rep. I.R.
61   *ERC Frankona Reinsurance* [2005] EWHC 1381 (Comm) at [124]; [2006] Lloyd's Rep. I.R. 157 at 182.
62   *GMA v Uni Storebrand International Insurance AS* [1995] L.R.L.R. 333.

Rix J held that an intermediate broker with knowledge of the insured's portfolio was under a duty of disclosure.

In *PCW* the House of Lords declined to hear an appeal from the Court of Appeal on the s.19 question; the reasons for so doing are not known. Accordingly, it is not possible to reach a conclusion as to whether the House of Lords did not consider that there was merit in the proposed appeal. It is suggested the most authoritative statement of the position is that of Saville LJ in *PCW*.

Specialist construction brokers. Construction companies often rely upon 6-020 independent specialist insurance brokers to assist in the preparation of a proposal, to obtain a quotation and to place the insurance with underwriters. This may involve a number of separate intermediate, producing and placing brokers, all engaged in securing the insurance for the insured and each of whom may have knowledge of material circumstances required to be disclosed. It is suggested that there will be limited circumstances where this type of material information will not have to be disclosed under the MIA by an intermediate broker or producing broker. Applying Saville LJ's logic in *PCW*,[63] where material information is not disclosed further up the chain, but ought to have been disclosed, it works its way down the chain through each agent because they will all be under a duty to disclose knowledge of material circumstances and will be deemed to know that which they ought to know.[64] The s.19 duty is also subject to two further principles, which are discussed below.[65]

Scope of agent's duty under the MIA. Whether a duty of disclosure under s.19 6-021 of the MIA applies to agents will depend on the source of the material knowledge and how it was obtained. In many cases, insurance brokers of insured parties will acquire information concerning their principals though their commercial relationships, though it may be that the information does not come to the attention of the agent during its ordinary course of business.

When information is acquired from dealing with other clients or from sources unrelated to the insurance industry, the question arises as to which categories or types of material knowledge are required to be disclosed by the broker. It is well established that knowledge acquired by the broker in its capacity as agent of the insured will be disclosable.[66] The position as regards knowledge acquired by an agent from its business dealings other than with the insured or acquired from sources unrelated to the broker's business has been subject to judicial consideration. In *SAIL v Farex Gie*,[67] Farex—the reinsurer—entered into a reinsurance agreement with SAIL, which had been brokered by Heath Fielding acting in its capacity for SAIL. Farex stipulated that it would only reinsure SAIL if its own reinsurance was protected by a retrocession, which Heath Fielding subsequently arranged

---

[63] *PCW Syndicates* [1996] 1 W.L.R. 1136 at 1151; [1996] 1 All E.R. 774 at 789; [1996] 1 Lloyd's Rep. 241 at 259.

[64] The position may be different where the construction company has an in-house insurance department or a separate subsidiary company that is responsible for obtaining insurance, for the individual or organisation with the knowledge will not be an agent to insure: s.18 MIA is likely to apply instead See above, para.6-023.

[65] Below, at para.6-021 and the fraud exception, at para.6-024.

[66] *Vigors* (1887) 12 App. Cas. 531; *PCW Syndicates* [1996] 1 W.L.R. 1136; [1996] 1 All E.R. 774; [1996] 1 Lloyd's Rep. 241; *HIH Casualty and General Insurance Ltd* [2003] UKHL 6; [2003] 1 All E.R. (Comm) 349; [2003] 2 Lloyd's Rep. 61, unless there has been fraud by the agent.

[67] *Societe Anonyme d'intermediaries Luxembourgeois* [1995] L.R.L.R. 116; [1994] C.L.C. 1094.

with St. Paul, a retrocessionary. However, St. Paul later repudiated its retrocession of Farex on the ground that its own employee had no authority to enter into the agreement with Farex. Farex then sought to avoid its reinsurance of SAIL on the ground that Heath Fielding had been the broker of SAIL and had a duty to disclose under s.19. It was held by the Court of Appeal that Heath Fielding obtained the knowledge in its capacity as agent for Farex and not in its capacity acting for SAIL, which meant it was not obliged to disclose the knowledge and thus Farex could not avoid its reinsurance policy.[68] *SAIL v Farex Gie*[69] confirms that it is only information acquired in the course of acting for the insured that must be disclosed. Hoffmann LJ stated that the courts could not impose an obligation to "disclose matters relevant only to the interest of the insurer under a different contract to which the insured is not a party."[70] However, he added that agents were under a duty to disclose knowledge of material circumstances "irrespective of the way in which that knowledge was acquired."[71] According to Saville LJ the "correct assertion" was that the duty of disclosure on the agent "is not confined to knowledge acquired from the assured but extends to knowledge otherwise acquired."[72]

These two comments support the assertion that knowledge acquired by the agent otherwise than in the course of working for the principal will be required to be disclosed under s.19. However, in *PCW*,[73] after reviewing the authorities including *SAIL*,[74] Staughton L held that he did not

"find in the authorities any decision that an agent to insure is required by section 19 to disclose information which he has received otherwise than in the character of agent for the assured."[75]

Despite the inconsistency in the reasoning of the Court of Appeal, it is suggested that the current position is that an agent to insure is not required by s.19 to disclose information that he has received otherwise than in his capacity as agent for the insured. Nevertheless, it would be of assistance if the courts clarified the position under the MIA, in particular as to whether information received by an agent prior to the commencement of its business relationship with the insured must be disclosed.

6-022 **Knowledge of other agents.** Under the MIA, knowledge of circumstances material to a risk may also come to agents of the insured in circumstances where that agent has no involvement with the insured's activities in obtaining insurance: that

---

68   The position may have been different had SAIL given Heath Fielding instructions or authority to arrange retrocession for the reinsurer if it would help in securing the reinsurance.

69   *Societe Anonyme d'intermediaries Luxembourgeois* [1995] L.R.L.R. 116; [1994] C.L.C. 1094.

70   *Societe Anonyme d'intermediaries Luxembourgeois* [1995] L.R.L.R. 116 at 150; [1994] C.L.C. 1094 at 1111. The same view was expressed by Dillon LJ at [1995] L.R.L.R. 116 at 143; [1994] C.L.C. 1094 at 1102 who said: "I cannot for my part see that s.19 can be invoked by Farex, to the detriment of SAIL, so as to require disclosure from Heath Fielding in its capacity of agent for SAIL of information which Heath Fielding, in its capacity of agent for Farex, was already under a direct obligation to disclose to Farex, and which was not SAIL's concern."

71   *Societe Anonyme d'intermediaries Luxembourgeois* [1995] L.R.L.R. 116 at 150; [1994] C.L.C. 1094 at 1111.

72   *Societe Anonyme d'intermediaries Luxembourgeois* [1995] L.R.L.R. 116 at 157; [1994] C.L.C. 1094 at 1120, per Saville LJ.

73   *PCW Syndicates* [1996] 1 W.L.R. 1136; [1996] 1 All E.R. 774; [1996] 1 Lloyd's Rep. 241.

74   *Societe Anonyme d'Intermediaries Luxembourgeois* [1995] L.R.L.R. 116; [1994] C.L.C. 1094.

75   *PCW Syndicates* [1996] 1 W.L.R. 1136 at 1147; [1996] 1 All E.R. 774 at 785; [1996] 1 Lloyd's Rep. 241 at 257.

is to say, the agent is not an "agent to insure" under s.19 of the MIA. Under s.18 the insured has to disclose all material circumstances known to it and is deemed to know the circumstances that it ought to know in the course of business including knowledge of its agents. This means that an agent's knowledge is attributed—or imputed—to the insured.[76] In such circumstances a duty of disclosure arises where the agent is an "agent to know"—that is, an agent who is responsible for communicating material information to the insured.

In the construction industry, a contractor who is required to obtain insurance for a construction project will often subcontract parts of the work to other companies. The subcontractor by virtue of this relationship may possess or obtain knowledge of circumstances material to the insurance of the project. For example, an electrical subcontractor may know that the use of certain building materials for cladding may heighten the risk of electrical fire. Whether knowledge of the electrical subcontractor is imputed to the insured contractor will depend on whether the subcontractor falls within the definition of an "agent to know" and/or is a named insured under the policy.

The leading case of *Simner v New India Assurance*[77] concerned purported avoidance of reinsurance on the basis of non-disclosure by the insured of material circumstances, which would have affected the decision of the reinsurer to reinsure. HHJ Diamond QC held that a duty of disclosure of an insured's agent to know exists in two situations: (i) where the insured is reliant upon the agent for information concerning the risk[78] (in which case a failure of the agent to communicate the knowledge will result in the knowledge being imputed to the insured); and (ii) where the agent holds a predominant position in relation to the insured.[79] The first situation arose in *Australia & New Zealand Bank Ltd v Colonial & Eagle Wharves Ltd*[80] where insurers of a wharfingers' business sought to avoid the policy based on information from an employee of the wharfingers who was aware that the business was not run efficiently and that losses of goods were occurring frequently. It was held that his position did not require him to monitor and report to the directors on efficiency levels or problems with goods and thus such information could not be imputed to the owner. An example of the second situation can be found in the case of *Regina Fur Co Ltd v Bossom*[81] in which a previous conviction of one of the two company directors was attributed to the company because of his predominant position within the company and the fact that he was "sufficiently concerned with the company's insurance transactions."[82] Accordingly, if neither of the situations identified in *Simner*[83] are satisfied then the knowledge of the agent is not required to be disclosed.

---

[76] The imputation principle, which was rejected as being the principle of s.19 of the MIA, is of direct application under s.18.
[77] *Simner v New India Assurance Co Ltd* [1995] L.R.L.R. 240; *Times,* July 21, 1994.
[78] *Simner* [1995] L.R.L.R. 240 at 254; *Fitzherbert v Mather* 99 E.R. 944; (1785) 1 Term Rep. 12; *Gladstone v King* 105 E.R. 13; (1813) 1 M. & S. 35; *Proudfoot v Montefiore* (1867–67) L.R. 2 Q.B. 511; *Vigors* (1887) 12 App. Cas. 531.
[79] *Simner* [1995] L.R.L.R. 240 at 255; *Vigors* (1887) 12 App. Cas. 531; *Regina Fur Co v Bossom* [1957] 2 Lloyd's Rep. 466.
[80] *Australia & New Zealand Bank Ltd v Colonial & Eagle Wharves Ltd* [1960] 2 Lloyd's Rep. 241.
[81] *Regina Fur Co* [1957] 2 Lloyd's Rep. 466.
[82] *Regina Fur Co* [1957] 2 Lloyd's Rep. 466 at 484.
[83] *Simner* [1995] L.R.L.R. 240.

6-023 **Knowledge within the company.** The *Regina Fur* case[84] illustrates the proposition that under the MIA an employee may be viewed by the court as the *alter ego*[85] of a company and that the knowledge he or she may possess may be imputed to the company. That case concerned a company with only two directors, which made the task of finding that one of the directors had a predominant position easier. Where the company is a large organisation the issue is more difficult as the question arises of whom within the organisation may possess knowledge attributable to the company.

The courts have applied the concept of the *alter ego* broadly and consider the size of the organisation and the role of the individual within the organisation in determining the question whether such knowledge should be attributed to the company or its directing mind.[86] In *Meridian Global Funds Management Asia Ltd v Securities Commission*[87] Lord Hoffmann found that it was a "matter of interpretation" in each case

> "given that it [knowledge] was intended to apply to a company, how was it intended to apply? Whose act (or knowledge, or state of mind) was *for this purpose* intended to count as the act etc. of the company?"[88]

It has been held that knowledge of a company under s.18 of the MIA should not be restricted to what is known at a high level but also to

> "knowledge held by employees whose business it was to arrange insurance for the company ... and perhaps also the knowledge of some other employees."[89]

The ruling of Lord Hoffmann in *Meridian Global*[90] may result in a wide net being cast in the construction context. It seems inevitable that the knowledge of an employee engaged in the contractor's business of arranging insurance may need to be disclosed and it is suggested that *Meridian Global*[91] leaves open the possibility that material knowledge of senior employees in subcontracting companies may fall within the scope of s.18 and be subject to disclosure. Further, where a construction company has an internal department or a subsidiary company which it uses to procure insurance, then if such a department or subsidiary cannot be classed as "agent to insure" under s.19, they may be treated as an "agent to know" under s.18

---

[84]   *Regina Fur Co* [1957] 2 Lloyd's Rep. 466.

[85]   A term used by Lord Watson in *Vigors* (1887) 12 App. Cas. 531 at 540.

[86]   A term used to describe those natural persons defined in the articles of association as controlling the company, i.e. the board members and managing director. See *Lennard's Carrying Co Ltd v Asiatic Petroleum Co Ltd* [1915] A.C. 705 at 713; [1914-15] All E.R. Rep. 280 at 283, per Viscount Haldane LC ("active and directing will ... directing mind"); *HL Bolton Engineering Co Ltd v T J Graham & Sons Ltd* [1956] 3 All E.R. 624 at 630, [1957] 1 Q.B. 159 at 172, per Denning LJ; *Tesco Supermarkets Ltd v Nattrass* [1971] 2 All E.R. 127 at 131, [1972] A.C. 153 at 171, per Lord Reid; and *Bilta (UK) Ltd (in liquidation) v Nazir (No. 2)* [2015] UKSC 23 at [65] to [70]; [2016] A.C. 1 at 27 to 29; [2015] 2 W.L.R. 1168 at 1189 to 1192.

[87]   *Meridian Global Funds Management Asia Ltd v Securities Commission* [1995] 2 A.C. 500; [1995] 3 W.L.R. 413; [1995] 3 All E.R. 918.

[88]   *Meridian Global Funds Management Asia Ltd* [1995] 2 A.C. 500 at 507; [1995] 3 W.L.R. 413 at 419; 3 All E.R. 918 at 924, per Lord Hoffmann.

[89]   *PCW Syndicates* [1996] 1 W.L.R. 1136; [1996] 1 All E.R. 774 at 780; [1996] 1 Lloyd's Rep. 241, per Staughton LJ.

[90]   *Meridian Global Funds Management Asia Ltd* [1995] 2 A.C. 500; [1995] 3 W.L.R. 413; [1995] 3 All E.R. 918.

[91]   *Meridian Global Funds Management Asia Ltd* [1995] 2 A.C. 500; [1995] 3 W.L.R. 413; [1995] 3 All E.R. 918.

or possibly come within the *alter ego* category for the company employees and agents.

The current position under the MIA can be contrasted with the new concept of a non-individual insured's senior management in the regime provided for under the 2015 Act. For a comprehensive discussion of the latter, see above at paras 5-032 to 5-033.

Knowledge of fraud. An agent engaged in defrauding his principal is not under a duty to disclose to an insurer its own knowledge of the fraud.[92] By its nature an agent's fraud involves concealment of material circumstances that it cannot be said the insured ought to know about in the ordinary course of business. Thus knowledge cannot be imputed to the insured under s.18 of the MIA. The agent cannot be required to disclose the information of his own fraud under s.19 because the agent does not obtain knowledge of that information in his capacity as agent of the insured. It cannot be said that in defrauding the insured the agent is acting as agent. Consequently, an insurer will not be able to avoid an insurance policy due to non-disclosure by an agent of its own fraud. In *PCW*[93] the fraud was held not to be required to be disclosed either under statute or under the *Re Hampshire Land* principle.[94] This principle is retained in the new default regime under the 2015 Act. **6-024**

5. MATTERS NOT REQUIRING DISCLOSURE

Matters which need not be disclosed. Under the MIA, certain circumstances, which are by definition material, currently need not be disclosed to the insurer in the absence of inquiry.[95] Those circumstances are set out in s.18(3) of the MIA: **6-025**

"In the absence of inquiry the following circumstances need not be disclosed, namely:—

(a) Any circumstance which diminishes the risk;

(b) Any circumstance which is known or presumed to be known to the insurer. The insurer is presumed to know matters of common notoriety or knowledge, and matters which an insurer in the ordinary course of his business, as such, ought to know;

(c) Any circumstance as to which information is waived by the insurer;

(d) Any circumstance which it is superfluous to disclose by reason of any express or implied warranty."

The exceptions created by the MIA are replicated and updated by s.3(5) of the 2015 Act in the new default regime for non-consumer insurance contracts. The central change is to the definition of an insurer's knowledge. For a comprehensive discussion, see Ch.5.

Circumstances which diminish the risk. The insured does not need to disclose circumstances that diminish the risk. The rationale is that if the insured pays a **6-026**

---

[92] *PCW Syndicates* [1996] 1 W.L.R. 1136; [1996] 1 All E.R. 774 at 780; [1996] 1 Lloyd's Rep. 241; *Group Josi Re Co SA v Walbrook Insurance Co Ltd* [1996] 1 W.L.R. 1152; [1996] 1 All E.R. 791; [1996] 1 Lloyd's Rep. 345.

[93] *PCW Syndicates* [1996] 1 W.L.R. 1136 at 1145; [1996] 1 All E.R. 774 at 783–784; [1996] 1 Lloyd's Rep. 241 at 255–256.

[94] Named after *Re Hampshire Land Co (No.2)* [1896] 2 Ch. 743.

[95] *St Paul Fire & Marine Insurance Co (UK) Ltd* [1996] 1 All E.R. 96 at 107; [1995] 2 Lloyd's Rep. 116 at 124; [1995] C.L.C. 818 at 827, per Evans LJ: "If the circumstance was not material, it would be unnecessary to provide that it should not be disclosed."

premium appropriate to a certain level of risk, he takes insurance up to and including that level of risk; if the risk in fact turns out to be lower than that for which he has paid, the overpayment is his business alone. Lord Mansfield stated the principle in *Carter*[96] from the standpoint of the insurer, saying:

> "If he insures for three years, he needs not be told any circumstance to shew it may be over in two: or if he insures a voyage, with liberty of deviation, he needs not be told what tends to shew there will be no deviation."[97]

The wording of the 2015 Act is materially identical and so it appears likely that the existing case law will continue to be relevant under the new regime.[98]

6-027   **Circumstances known by the insurer.**   Under the MIA, the insured need not disclose circumstances that are known or presumed to be known by the insurer, either as a matter of common notoriety or as a matter that he ought to know in the ordinary course of his business.[99] Section 18(3)(b) makes it clear that the insurer is presumed to know both circumstances specific to the type of interest being insured and a more general level of common knowledge. In construction, the insurer may be presumed to possess specific knowledge, for an "underwriter is presumed to be acquainted with the practice of the trade he insures [and] if he does not know, he ought to know."[100] For instance, an underwriter of construction insurance may be presumed to know the issues that surround building on certain terrain, or the dangers and risks associated with specific construction techniques. More generally, the insurer will be presumed to know of political risks, economic risks and other items of common knowledge including threats of criminal activity or risks of using dangerous substances.[101]

However, the insurer is not under a duty to make enquiries that would in effect relieve the insured of his duty of disclosure, for it is the insured that has the burden of making a fair representation of the risk.[102] For instance, in the *London General Insurance Co v General Marine Underwriters Association Ltd* case,[103] the Court of Appeal, having already decided that the insured ought to have been aware of the damage to the ship *The Vigo* by virtue of having received a Lloyd's "casualty list", then considered whether the insurers, who had also received the list before the insurance was effected, were deemed to have knowledge of the casualty in the course of their business. If so then the insured would be relieved of its duty of disclosure. The Court of Appeal held that at the time the insurer received the casualty list it was not aware and had no knowledge of the ship in question. It therefore had no interest in the ship and would have no reason to take note of that particular name among several on the casualty list. It would be unreasonable to expect an insurer to keep

---

96   *Carter* (1766) 3 Burr. 1905; 97 E.R. 1162.

97   *Carter* (1766) 3 Burr. 1905 at [1911]; 97 E.R. 1162 at 1165.

98   See above, para.5-059.

99   MIA 1906 s.18(3)(b).

100   *Noble v Kennaway* (1780) 2 Doug. K.B. 511 at 513; 99 E.R. 326 at 327. For example, in *Margate Theatre Royal Trust Ltd v Patrick White* [2005] EWHC 2171 (TCC) at [34], HHJ Peter Coulson QC found that an insurer was "deemed to know what work was necessary for and incidental to ground work and pipe moleing, whether or not it was all spelled out in the policy."

101   *Carter* (1766) 3 Burr 1905 at [1910]; 97 E.R. 1162 at 1165.

102   *Kingscroft Insurance Co Ltd v Nissan Fire and Marine Insurance Co Ltd (No.2)* [2000] 1 All E.R. (Comm) 272; [1999] C.L.C. 1875; [1999] Lloyd's Rep. I.R. 603.

103   *London General Insurance Co Ltd v General Marine Underwriters Association Ltd* [1921] 1 K.B. 104; (1920) 4 Ll. L Rep. 382; 89 L.J.K.B. 1245.

what was, to him, irrelevant information at the forefront of his mind when considering proposals. The determining factor is whether an insurer was "upon the risk,"
i.e. had an interest in the thing to be insured.[104]

In another, recent example, *Sea Glory Maritime Co v Al Sagr National Insurance Co ("The Nancy")*[105] the insured did not disclose a history of detentions. At
trial the insured relied upon the availability of the information online and the market
practice for insurers to access such information at renewal. It accordingly contended
that the insurer was presumed to know about the history of detentions under
s.18(3)(b) MIA. The contention was rejected. Blair J held that the question was:

> "whether there has been a fair presentation of the risk in all the circumstances ... Whilst the
> circumstances may include the availability of on-line information, whether the insurer should be
> treated as having knowledge of it is something which has to be judged on the particular facts."[106]

The 2015 Act substantially reforms, develops and clarifies the definition of the
insurer's knowledge. For a comprehensive discussion, see above at paras 5-051 to
5-058.

Circumstances waived by the insurer.   Under s.18(3)(c) of the MIA, the insured   **6-028**
is not obliged to disclose circumstances waived by the insurer or the insurer's agent.
Waiver can be both express or implied, and the cases in which the courts have found
an insurer to have waived the right to be told information are discussed below. This
exception continues under the provisions of the 2015 Act,[107] but it is expected to
play a reduced role; the 2015 Act has recast the insured's disclosure duties, and a
disclosure will now be sufficient if the insured has made a disclosure "which gives
the insurer sufficient information to put a prudent insurer on notice that it needs to
make further enquiries."[108] As discussed in para.6-030 below, the courts had previously used the waiver exception to temper the insured's disclosure duties in
circumstances where the insurer had remained silent during the risk presentation and
failed to make enquiries about those matters to which the insured had signposted
the availability of further information. Accordingly, many of the cases previously
falling under the waiver exception will now be dealt with directly as cases in which
the insured had satisfied the second limb of its disclosure duties. The change is
intended to acknowledge the importance of the insurer's involvement during the risk
presentation and prevent the trend of insurers failing to participate during the
presentation and instead "underwriting at the claims stage".[109]

Express waiver.   An express waiver may take the form of a "truth of statement"   **6-029**
clause contained in the insurance policy.[110] The purpose of a truth of statement
clause is to exclude the insurer's rights of avoidance of the policy and thereby
protect the insured from misrepresentations made and non-disclosure, which would

---

[104] *London General Insurance Co Ltd* [1921] 1 K.B. 104 at 110–111; (1920) 4 Ll. L. Rep. 382 at 383;
89 L.J.K.B. 1245 at 1247–1248, per Lord Sterndale M.R.

[105] [2013] EWHC 2116 (Comm); [2013] 2 All E.R. (Comm) 913.

[106] *Sea Glory Maritime Co v Al Sagr National Insurance Co ("The Nancy")* [2013] EWHC 2116
(Comm) at [175]; [2013] 2 All E.R. (Comm) 913.

[107] Section 3(5)(e) of the 2015 Act.

[108] Section 3(4)(b) of the 2015 Act.

[109] For further discussion of the second limb of an insured's disclosure duties under the 2015 Act, see
above, paras 5-061 to 5-062.

[110] *Chase Manhattan Bank* [2003] UKHL 6; [2003] 1 All E.R. (Comm) 349; [2003] 2 Lloyd's Rep. 61.

ordinarily give rise to the right of avoidance. One reason for having such a clause is to redistribute the responsibility to the insurer or to agents for the ultimate understanding of material circumstances and risk, for it is possible that the insured is not necessarily in a better position than the insurer or broker to estimate the risk. The clause may extend to protect the insured from non-disclosure or misrepresentations of its agents or brokers, provided the wording of the clause leaves no doubt as to its true construction.[111] It may also be possible to exclude avoidance for the fraudulent misrepresentation or non-disclosure of an agent or broker, though a clause would only survive if expressed in the clearest terms.[112]

6-030   **Implied waiver.** The insurer may also be subject to an implied waiver.[113] The waiver can arise where the scope of a particular question in a proposal form is limited. For example, an insurer that poses a question about losses in the last three years may be taken to have waived information about losses more than three years old.[114] Where such a narrow question is also ambiguous then it may be construed against an insurer who asserts that the answer given did not provide the disclosure required.[115] However, the insured cannot rely on the specificity of a question to avoid disclosing material information, because his "independent obligation to disclose"[116] remains. For example, when a proposal asked if there had been any claims on a business premises in the last five years and there had not been, a truthful answer was defeated because of non-disclosure of three attempts at armed robbery on the premises in that time, none of which had resulted in a claim.[117]

A waiver can also arise where the insured has provided a truthful but minimal answer to a question put by the insurer that puts the insurer on notice of the existence of the circumstance. If the insurer fails to request further information, that he later seeks to rely on in avoiding the policy for non-disclosure, he will be taken to have impliedly waived the need to disclose it.[118] In *Scottish Coal Co Ltd v Royal and Sun Alliance Insurance Plc*[119] the claimants, owners of a colliery, planned to

---

[111] *Chase Manhattan Bank* [2003] UKHL 6 at [15]; [2003] 1 All E.R. (Comm) 349; [2003] 2 Lloyd's Rep. 61, per Lord Bingham.

[112] *Chase Manhattan Bank* [2003] UKHL 6 at [16] and [124]–[128]; [2003] 1 All E.R. (Comm) 349 at 358, 383–384; [2003] 2 Lloyd's Rep. 61 at 68, 85–86.

[113] *Laing v Union Marine Insurance Co* (1895) 1 Com. Cas. 11.

[114] *Revell v London General Insurance Co Ltd* [1934] All E.R. Rep. 744; (1934) 50 Ll. L. Rep. 114; *Taylor v Eagle Star Insurance Co Ltd* (1940) 67 Ll. L. Rep. 136.

[115] The contra proferentum principle, see *R&R Developments Ltd v AXA Insurance UK Plc* [2009] EWHC 2429 (Ch); [2010] 2 All E.R. (Comm) 527; [2010] Lloyd's Rep. I.R. 521. Leggatt J justified the application of the contra preferentem rule to proposal forms on the basis that "the questions asked in a proposal form are the unilateral choice of the insurer" in *Involnert Management Inc v Aprilgrange Ltd* [2015] EWHC 2225 (Comm) at [194].

[116] *MacGillivray on Insurance Law*, edited by J. Birds, B. Lynch and S. Milnes, 13th edn (London: Sweet & Maxwell, 2015), para.17–018.

[117] *Noblebright Ltd v Sirius International Corp* [2007] Lloyd's Rep. I.R. 584.

[118] *Asfar & Co v Blundell* [1896] 1 Q.B. 123 at 129; 65 L.J.Q.B. 138 at 141; 12 T.L.R. 29 at 30, per Lord Esher M.R.: "...[I]t is not necessary to disclose minutely every material fact; assuming that there is a material fact which he is bound to disclose, the rule is satisfied if he discloses sufficient to call the attention of the underwriters in such a manner that they can see that if they require further information they ought to ask for it." (the last two reports do not contain transcript of the judgment). See also *George Cohen Sons & Co v Standard Marine Insurance Ltd* (1925) 21 Ll. L. Rep. 30; *Synergy Health (UK) Ltd v CGU Insurance Plc (t/a Norwich Union)* [2010] EWHC 2583 (Comm); [2011] Lloyd's Rep I.R. 500.

[119] *Scottish Coal Co Ltd v Royal and Sun Alliance Insurance Plc* [2008] EWHC 880 (Comm); [2008]

adopt a new mining technique, which they disclosed to the insurer. The fact the new technique tended to increase the risk of a collapse was not disclosed. It was held that the claimant's disclosure of the plan was sufficient to put the insurers on enquiry as to the use of the technique and in the absence of enquiry the insurers were taken not to be concerned with the consequences of such use.[120] Also, in *Pan Atlantic Insurance Co Ltd v Pine Top Insurance Co Ltd*,[121] brokers managed to disclose poor claims records of the insured in a surreptitious manner, which meant the material information evaded the attention of the insurers. The court held that the insurers' failure to make enquiries by looking at the disclosed material amounted to a waiver. In *Sea Glory Maritime Co v Al Sagr National Insurance co ("The Nancy")* the insured unsuccessfully attempted to rely on the availability of online information relating to undisclosed detentions as a matter giving rise to waiver.[122]

Waiver by insurer's agent.   Assuming the broker is an employee or contractor of the insurance company and is instructed or paid by the insurer to canvass and procure proposals for them, as the case may be,[123] he will be the agent of the insurer. It has been held that where the broker has actual or apparent authority to fill out a proposal form on behalf of the insured and fills it out erroneously despite the insured giving correct oral answers to questions posed, then the broker impliedly waives the insured's duty of disclosure[124]; the broker's knowledge of the correct oral answers will be imputed to the insurer.[125]

    6-031

Conversely, if the broker has not been instructed to record the insured's answers on the proposal form but proceeds to do so then he has exceeded his authority. By doing so the broker was acting in breach of duty of skill and care to the insurer. A broker may do this fraudulently, in order to heighten the chance of securing the insurance and thus increase his own commission, or simply through negligence. In either event, the broker will not be acting in the ordinary course of business and consequently his knowledge of the correct oral answers cannot be imputed to the insurer.[126] Therefore the insured is placed under an obligation to check that the answers are correct before signing the proposal form.

Circumstances rendered superfluous by warranty.   Under s.18(3)(d) of the MIA, where the insured warrants a circumstance he is relieved of his duty of disclosure concerning that circumstance. The insured chooses to hold himself to the higher standard of a warranty, making it a condition of the contract that the circumstance is as warranted.[127] In such a situation it is not necessary, nor commercially expedient, to give disclosure.

    6-032

Lloyd's Rep. I.R. 718.
[120] *Scottish Coal Co Ltd* [2008] EWHC 880 (Comm) at [79]; [2008] Lloyd's Rep. I.R. 718 at 731.
[121] *Pan Atlantic Insurance Co Ltd* [1995] 1 A.C. 501 at 550–551; [1994] 3 W.L.R. 677 at 713; [1994] 3 All E.R. 581 at 618.
[122] See above, para.6-027.
[123] *Newsholme Bros* [1929] 2 K.B. 356 at 362; [1929] All E.R. Rep 442 at 444.
[124] *Stone v Reliance Mutual Insurance Society Ltd* [1972] 1 Lloyd's Rep. 469.
[125] *Stone* [1972] 1 Lloyd's Rep. 469.
[126] *Newsholme Bros* [1929] 2 K.B. 356 at 374; [1929] All E.R. Rep. 442.
[127] See below, Ch.12.

6. MATERIALITY AND INDUCEMENT

(a) Materiality

6-033 **Materiality—the judgment of a prudent insurer.** Section 18(2) of the MIA provides that:

> "Every circumstance is material which would influence the judgment of a prudent insurer in fixing the premium, or determining whether he will take the risk."[128]

In *Pan Atlantic Insurance Co Ltd v Pine Top Insurance Co Ltd*,[129] the House of Lords considered the correct test to be applied in deciding whether a circumstance would influence the judgment of a prudent insurer and legitimately allow "for avoidance by an insurer of a contract of insurance or reinsurance on the ground of non-disclosure"[130] (though the test applies equally to misrepresentations as non-disclosure). Previously in *Container Transport International Inc v Oceanus Mutual Underwriting Association (Bermuda) Ltd (No.1)*[131] and in *Pan Atlantic* it had been argued that s.18(2) of the Act required that disclosure of the material circumstance must have a "decisive influence" on the judgment of a prudent underwriter to entitle the insurer to avoid the policy; that is, that

> "full and accurate disclosure would have led the prudent insurer either to reject the risk or at least to have accepted it on more onerous terms."[132]

In *Pan Atlantic* it was held (Lord Lloyd dissenting)[133] that the circumstance need only be something that would be taken into account by the prudent insurer when assessing the risk, and that a natural, ordinary, and sensible[134] meaning should be given to the words used in the Act. Lord Goff said

> "the words in section 18(2) 'would influence the judgment of a prudent insurer in determining whether he will take the risk' denote no more than an effect on the mind of the insurer in weighing up the risk. The subsection does not require that the circumstance in question should have a decisive influence on the judgment of the insurer; and I, for my part, can see no basis for reading this requirement into the subsection."[135]

---

128 MIA 1906 s.20(2).
129 *Pan Atlantic Insurance Co Ltd* [1995] 1 A.C. 501; [1994] 3 W.L.R. 677; [1994] 3 All E.R. 581.
130 *Pan Atlantic Insurance Co Ltd* [1995] 1 A.C. 501 at 553; [1994] 3 W.L.R. 677 at 716; [1994] 3 All E.R. 581 at 621, per Lord Lloyd.
131 *Container Transport International Inc v Oceanus Mutual Underwriting Association (Bermuda) Ltd (No.1)* [1984] 1 Lloyd's Rep. 476.
132 *Pan Atlantic Insurance Co Ltd* [1995] 1 A.C. 501 at 516; [1994] 3 W.L.R. 677 at 681; [1994] 3 All E.R. 581 at 586, per Lord Goff.
133 In *Pan Atlantic Insurance Co Ltd* [1995] 1 A.C. 501 at 559; [1994] 3 W.L.R. 677 at 721; [1994] 3 All E.R. 581 at 626, Lord Lloyd preferred an "increased risk theory of materiality" theory, i.e. disclosure is only material if it would have increased the risk and potentially altered the premium.
134 *Pan Atlantic Insurance Co Ltd* [1995] 1 A.C. 501 at 518; [1994] 3 W.L.R. 677 at 683; [1994] 3 All E.R. 581 at 588, per Lord Goff.
135 *Pan Atlantic Insurance Co Ltd* [1995] 1 A.C. 501 at 516–517; [1994] 3 W.L.R. 677 at 682; [1994] 3 All E.R. 581 at 587.

On this point Lord Mustill also said:

> "A circumstance may be material even though a full and accurate disclosure of it would not in itself have had a decisive effect on the prudent underwriter's decision whether to accept the risk and if so at what premium."[136]

The question of the materiality of a circumstance is to be determined objectively from the perspective of a hypothetical prudent insurer and the reason for the non-disclosure (or, presumably, misrepresentation) is immaterial.[137] It is a question of fact resting on the court's "appraisal of the relevance of the disputed fact to the subject-matter of insurance" and "not something which is settled automatically by current practice or by the opinion of insurers."[138] The court must make a "value judgment."[139] Authority has no status as precedent, although it can be relevant in providing a sanity test.[140]

Following *Pan Atlantic*, information is regarded as material if the insurer can show that he was merely interested in knowing it. The insurer does not have to show that the information would have been decisive in the decision whether to insure at all or on what terms.[141] An example is the case of *Locker & Woolf Ltd v Western Australian Insurance Co Ltd*[142] where the insured submitted a proposal for fire insurance and did not disclose that it had been declined a policy for motor insurance on the basis of non-disclosure and misrepresentations. It was held that the non-disclosure was considered to be a material fact that could affect the judgment of the insurer in terms of determining whether it would be prepared to take the risk. On that basis it was deemed that the insurance company was entitled to avoid the policy. It was also held that questions asked by an insurer to a proposer as to whether insurance proposals have been declined by any other insurance companies relate to "any" type of insurance and not only to the "type" proposed to be insured, e.g. fire or motor insurance. In *Involnert Management Inc v Aprilgrange Ltd* Leggatt J held that the fact of an insured yacht being marketed for sale at the time of the placing of the risk was not material, but the fact that the yacht was being marketing with an asking price of £8m when the insured was seeking to insure it for £13m was material.[143]

A further example is *AXA Versicherung AG v Arab Insurance Group*, in which Males J accepted that past loss statistics relating to insurance written by a proposed reinsured will generally be material.[144] He emphasised that this was a common sense proposition of fact rather than law.[145] The reinsured contended that the non-disclosure and/or misrepresentation was immaterial because energy constructions risks are each unique and that a radically new and more rigorous underwriting policy had been adopted. This was rejected because

---

[136] *Pan Atlantic Insurance Co Ltd* [1995] 1 A.C. 501 at 550; [1994] 3 W.L.R. 677 at 713; [1994] 3 All E.R. 581 at 618.
[137] *Brit UW Ltd v F&B Trenchless Solutions Ltd* [2015] EWHC 2237 (Comm) at [105].
[138] *Brit UW Ltd v F&B Trenchless Solutions Ltd* [2015] EWHC 2237 (Comm) at [102].
[139] *Involnert Management Inc v Aprilgrange Ltd* [2015] EWHC 2225 (Comm) at [98].
[140] *Involnert Management Inc v Aprilgrange Ltd* [2015] EWHC 2225 (Comm) at [97].
[141] This part of the decision in *Pan Atlantic* was affirmed in *St Paul Fire & Marine Insurance Co (UK) Ltd* [1996] 1 All E.R. 96; [1995] 2 Lloyd's Rep. 116; [1995] C.L.C. 818.
[142] *Locker & Woolf Ltd v Western Australian Insurance Co Ltd* [1936] 1 K.B. 408.
[143] *Involnert Management Inc v Aprilgrange Ltd* [2015] EWHC 2225 (Comm) at [128].
[144] *AXA Versicherung AG v Arab Insurance Group* [2015] EWHC 1939 (Comm) at [131].
[145] *AXA Versicherung AG v Arab Insurance Group* [2015] EWHC 1939 (Comm) at [131].

"it would not be consistent with the duty of utmost good faith for the reinsured to conceal from the reinsurer the existence of poor or disastrous loss records on the grounds that the underwriter or the strategy had changed, even if that is true. To conclude otherwise would go a long way to deprive the insurer of the protection of a fair presentation to which it is entitled and which, in the case of reinsurance ... is the only protection which he has."[146]

6-034 **Timing of materiality.** Under the MIA, materiality is considered as at the time that the insurance contract is concluded.[147] After the contract is concluded, the duties of disclosure and representation do not apply. Renewal and variation of a policy are treated as pre-contractual and therefore the duties contained in ss.18–20 apply.[148]

6-035 **No connection between materiality and subsequent truth.** The failure to disclose a material circumstance is not mitigated under the MIA by later developments concerning that circumstance. In *Brotherton v Aseguradora Colseguros SA*[149] allegations of misconduct against the insured (which later proved to be unfounded) were not disclosed and the insurer subsequently avoided the policy. The Court of Appeal held that it did not matter that the allegations were later shown to be false; what mattered was the non-disclosure of material circumstances at the time that the contract was concluded

"and whether, if the claimants had known of the reports at that time, such knowledge would have induced all or any of them to act differently."[150]

The alternative view – that the insurers would have lost nothing because there was in fact no difference between the actual risk and the risk as they understood it – was rejected unanimously by the Court of Appeal. Buxton LJ stated the insurer "... lost the opportunity to take an informed decision at the time of placement."[151] Depriving the insurer of the opportunity to take an informed decision is a breach of the insured's duty of good faith.[152]

This position was confirmed in *North Star Shipping Ltd v Sphere Drake Insurance Plc*,[153] in which the insured had failed to disclose allegations of criminality. The insurer held the policy void for non-disclosure, though the allegations later transpired to be false. The Court of Appeal found that the insurer was entitled to avoid the policy for non-disclosure; Waller and Longmore LJJ both considered that such an outcome was harsh and suggested that this might be an area for reform.[154]

---

[146] *AXA Versicherung AG v Arab Insurance Group* [2015] EWHC 1939 (Comm) at [138].

[147] See, for example, *Brotherton v Aseguradora Colseguros SA (No.2)* [2003] EWCA Civ 705 at [18]; [2003] 2 All E.R. (Comm) 298 at 307. Section 18(1) MIA requires disclosure by an assured "before the contract is concluded." Section 20(1) MIA is similarly concerned with the period "during the negotiations for the contract, and before the contract is concluded."

[148] See *K/S Merc-Scandia XXXXII* [2001] EWCA Civ 1275; [2001] 2 Lloyd's Rep. 563; [2001] C.L.C. 1836; ERC Frankona Reinsurance [2006] Lloyd's Rep. I.R. 157.

[149] *Brotherton* [2003] EWCA Civ 705; [2003] 2 All E.R. (Comm) 298; [2003] Lloyd's Rep. I.R. 746.

[150] *Brotherton* [2003] EWCA Civ 705 at [9]; [2003] 2 All E.R. (Comm) 298 at 302; [2003] Lloyd's Rep. I.R. 746 at 751.

[151] *Brotherton* [2003] EWCA Civ 705 at [40]; [2003] 2 All E.R. (Comm) 298 at 315; [2003] Lloyd's Rep. I.R. 746 at 759. See also *Pan Atlantic Insurance Co Ltd* [1995] 1 A.C. 501 at 528; [1994] 3 W.L.R. 677 at 692–693; [1994] 3 All E.R. 581 at 597, per Lord Mustill.

[152] Though where the insurer turns a blind eye to material circumstances it knows to exist, which had not been disclosed by the insured, it may lose its right to avoid the policy. See above, para.6-011.

[153] *North Star Shipping Ltd v Sphere Drake Insurance Plc* [2006] EWCA Civ 378; [2006] 2 All E.R. (Comm) 65; [2006] 2 Lloyd's Rep. 183.

[154] *North Star Shipping Ltd* [2006] EWCA Civ 378 at [20] and [53]–[54]; [2006] 2 All E.R. (Comm)

Materiality and the 2015 Act   Materiality was considered by the Law Commis-   **6-036**
sions to be one of the strengths of existing insurance law, albeit that it placed an
onerous burden on the insured to put itself in the position of an insurer in order to
determine the information that would be material to the underwriting decision. The
2015 Act was intended to retain and to clarify the concept of materiality in order
to provide the insured with greater certainty as to what has to be disclosed to the
insurer during the presentation of risk. This may remain a difficult task for an
insured attempting to underwrite an unusual risk or one for which there is very little industry guidance on what information requires disclosure. Accordingly, s.18(2)
of the MIA is largely reproduced by s.7(3) of the 2015 Act. The definition of
materiality set out in *Pan Atlantic* is put onto a statutory footing. Further, s.7(4) of
the 2015 Act provides a non-exhaustive list of typical material circumstances. For
a comprehensive discussion of the new provisions, see above, paras 5-020 and
5-067.

(b)   Inducement

In *Pan Atlantic Insurance Co Ltd v Pine Top Insurance Co Ltd*,[155] the House of   **6-037**
Lords held that under the MIA an undisclosed circumstance or misrepresentation,
in addition to being material, must also induce the actual underwriter to enter into
the contract in order for the insurer to avoid the policy. The requirement of inducement applies equally to misrepresentations and to non-disclosure and "must be
regarded as an implied qualification of the right to avoid the contract under the
[Marine Insurance] Act."[156] There is no requirement that the inducement be the sole
inducement affecting the insurer, but the insurer must demonstrate that " but for the
relevant non-disclosure or misrepresentation he would not have entered into the
contract on those terms."[157] The decision in *Pan Atlantic*[158] realigned insurance law
with the general law of contract where misrepresentation requires actual inducement[159] and now the insurer has to establish on the balance of probabilities that he
was induced.[160] Evidence must usually be adduced by the insurer at trial to sup-

---

65 at 73, 79–80; [2006] 2 Lloyd's Rep. 183 at 189 and 193.
[155] *Pan Atlantic Insurance Co Ltd* [1995] 1 A.C. 501; [1994] 3 W.L.R. 677; [1994] 3 All E.R. 581.
[156] *St Paul Fire & Marine Insurance Co (UK) Ltd* [1996] 1 All E.R. 96 at 103; [1995] 2 Lloyd's Rep.
116 at 122; [1995] C.L.C. 818 at 824, per Evans LJ, referring to the judgment of Lord Mustill in
Pan Atlantic Insurance Co Ltd [1995] 1 A.C. 501 at 549; [1994] 3 W.L.R. 677 at 712; [1994] 3 All
E.R. 581 at 617, where Lord Mustill said: "I conclude that there is to be implied in the Act of 1906
a qualification that a material misrepresentation will not entitle the underwriter to avoid the policy
unless the misrepresentation induced the making of the contract, using 'induced' in the sense in
which it is used in the general law of contract."
[157] *Assicurazioni Generali SpA* [2002] EWCA Civ 1642 at [62]; [2003] 1 All E.R. (Comm) 140 at 158;
[2003] Lloyd's Rep. I.R. 131 at 149, per Clarke LJ.
[158] *Pan Atlantic Insurance Co Ltd* [1995] 1 A.C. 501; [1994] 3 W.L.R. 677; [1994] 3 All E.R. 581.
[159] The previous law was set out it in *Container Transport International Inc and Reliance Group Inc*
[1984] 1 Lloyd's Rep. 476, where it was held that actual inducement was not required and instead
a decisive influence on the judgment of a prudent underwriter was required. For a detailed explanation of why that case was in effect overruled, see the judgment of Lord Goff in *Pan Atlantic Insurance Co Ltd* [1995] 1 A.C. 501 at 517; [1994] 3 W.L.R. 677 at 682; [1994] 3 All E.R. 581 at 587
and Lord Mustill at [1995] 1 A.C. 501 at 549–550; [1994] 3 W.L.R. 677 at 711–712; [1994] 3 All
E.R. 581 at 617.
[160] *Assicurazioni Generali SpA* [2002] EWCA Civ 1642 at [62]; [2003] 1 All E.R. (Comm) 140 at 158;
[2003] Lloyd's Rep. I.R. 131 at 149.

port his averment that he was induced.[161] The position in *Pan Atlantic*[162] has arguably been altered by the subsequent decision of the Court of Appeal in *Assicurazione Generali SpA*[163] where it was held that the inducement must be an effective cause of entering into the contract and on those particular terms offered by the underwriter.[164] Sir Christopher Staughton (with whom Clarke LJ concurred) stated:

"A misrepresentation or non-disclosure which did not make any difference, in the sense that the underwriter would have agreed to the same contract on the same terms if it had never been made, cannot be an inducement."[165]

Clarke LJ stated that in order to determine whether the underwriter was induced there was a need for the non-disclosure to be a "real and substantial" cause of the insurer entering into the contract.[166] However, Ward LJ sounded a note of caution on setting a test that required a search for an effective cause when he said "[w]e must be careful not to be led back into the error that the cause has to be a decisive cause." He did accept, however, that there was a requirement for some causative effect but did not then go on to define what a causative effect was.[167]

The issue of inducement was considered again in the *Brotherton case*,[168] where Mance LJ said:

"Whether a material non-disclosure induced the actual underwriter to act to his prejudice depends likewise upon whether the circumstances withheld would, if known, have caused him to act differently, either by not writing the insurance at all or by only writing it on different terms."[169]

It appears that the current state of the law is that, while there is no requirement of decisive influence for the purposes of materiality, there is something akin to decisive influence required for actual inducement. The re-introduction of this requirement brings additional protection to the insured in that it limits the scope of the insurer's ability to avoid the policy.

It is commonly stated that the principles which apply to inducement are the same for non-disclosure and misrepresentation cases. But Leggatt J's comments in *Involnert Management Inc v Aprilgrange Ltd*[170] explain that there are differences because:

"there is still in the insurance context a conceptual distinction between a claim based on non-disclosure and a claim based on misrepresentation. The former is governed by the section 18 of the Act and the latter by section 20. The relevant principles, although similar, are not the same. Plainly,

---

[161] *Berger and Light Diffusers Pty Ltd v Pollock* [1973] 2 Lloyd's Rep. 442 at 463.

[162] *Pan Atlantic Insurance Co Ltd* [1995] 1 A.C. 501; [1994] 3 W.L.R. 677; [1994] 3 All E.R. 581.

[163] *Assicurazioni Generali SpA* [2002] EWCA Civ 1642; [2003] 1 All E.R. (Comm) 140; [2003] Lloyd's Rep. I.R. 131.

[164] *Assicurazioni Generali SpA* [2002] EWCA Civ 1642 at [78]; [2003] 1 All E.R. (Comm) 140 at 162; [2003] Lloyd's Rep. I.R. 131 at 151, per Clarke LJ.

[165] *Assicurazioni Generali SpA* [2002] EWCA Civ 1642 at [187]; [2003] 1 All E.R. (Comm) 140 at 189; [2003] Lloyd's Rep. I.R. 131 at 170, per Staughton LJ.

[166] *Assicurazioni Generali SpA* [2002] EWCA Civ 1642 at [78]; [2003] 1 All E.R. (Comm) 140 at 162; [2003] Lloyd's Rep. I.R. 131 at 151, per Clarke LJ.

[167] *Assicurazioni Generali SpA* [2002] EWCA Civ 1642 at [218]; [2003] 1 All E.R. (Comm) 140 at 196; [2003] Lloyd's Rep. I.R. 131 at 175, per Ward LJ.

[168] *Brotherton* [2003] EWCA Civ 705; [2003] 2 All E.R. (Comm) 298; [2003] 2 C.L.C. 629.

[169] *Brotherton* [2003] EWCA Civ 705 at [18]; [2003] 2 All E.R. (Comm) 298 at 307; [2003] 2 C.L.C. 629 at 648.

[170] *Involnert Management Inc v Aprilgrange Ltd* [2015] EWHC 2225 (Comm) at [214].

where the claim is based on non-disclosure of a material fact, the relevant question when considering inducement is what the insurer would have done if told that fact. In so far, however, as the claim is based on a misrepresentation, then in the insurance context just as in any other context it is what was actually said to the insurer – rather than what was not said – which is the foundation of the claim, and the relevant test is therefore what the insurer would have done in the absence of the representation."

Determining whether the insurer was induced is a question of fact. The court will generally make its determination after hearing evidence given by underwriters who are experts in insurance markets. The burden of proof will be on the insurer to show that it was induced. There may be evidential difficulties where the insurance was placed with numerous underwriters. It may also be difficult for an underwriter to say what he would have done hypothetically if the non-disclosure had not occurred, a problem acknowledged by Colman J in *North Star Shipping* as leading to "exaggeration and embellishment, requiring the evidence to be rigorously tested by independent evidence."[171] In another recent example, *AXA Versicherung AG v Arab Insurance Group*, the reinsurer failed to demonstrate that it was more likely than not that it would have refused to write a certain treaty if it had seen certain material loss statistics.[172]

Inference of inducement. Where there is no direct evidence of actual inducement, it may be possible to rely on an inference of inducement.[173] This is an inference of fact, not a presumption of law,[174] and is a prima facie inference that is capable of being rebutted by evidence. In *St Paul Fire & Marine Insurance Co (UK) Ltd*,[175] three out of four underwriters had given evidence of inducement, and the fourth had not. The Court of Appeal found that the exceptional circumstances of the case[176] were sufficient to raise an inference of inducement for the fourth underwriter (which was not rebutted on the facts), entitling him to avoid the policy for non-

6-038

---

[171] *North Star Shipping Ltd* [2005] EWHC 665 (Comm) at [254]; [2005] 2 Lloyd's Rep. 76 at 127; see also *Lewis v Norwich Union Healthcare Ltd* [2010] Lloyd's Rep. I.R. 198.

[172] *AXA Versicherung AG v Arab Insurance Group* [2015] EWHC 1939 (Comm) at [179]. See also *Brit UW Ltd v F&B Trenchless Solutions Ltd* [2015] EWHC 2237 (Comm) at [148]. See too *Involnert Management Inc v Aprilgrange Ltd* [2015] EWHC 2225 (Comm) at [220].

[173] *Brit UW Ltd v F&B Trenchless Solutions Ltd* [2015] EWHC 2237 (Comm) at [114].

[174] *Pan Atlantic Insurance Co Ltd* [1995] 1 A.C. 501 at 551; [1994] 3 W.L.R. 677 at 714; [1994] 3 All E.R. 581 at 619, per Lord Mustill: "There is ample material both in the general law and in the specialist works on insurance to suggest that there is a presumption in favour of a causative effect." However, Lord Lloyd in *Pan Atlantic* considered the "ample material" to be the judgment of Jessell M.R. in *Redgrave v Hurd* (1881) 20 Ch. D. 1 at 21, (where it is said that inducement can be inferred from proven materiality, as a matter of law) and said: "Despite receiving the 'embarrassing imprimatur' of so eminent a judge ... this heresy has long since been exploded by, among others, per Lord Blackburn in *Smith v Chadwick* (1884) 9 App. Cas. 187, 196.": *Pan Atlantic Insurance Co Ltd* [1995] 1 A.C. 501 at 570; [1994] 3 W.L.R. 677 at 731; [1994] 3 All E.R. 581 at 637, per Lord Lloyd. In *St Paul Fire & Marine Insurance Co (UK) Ltd* [1996] 1 All E.R. 96; [1995] 2 Lloyd's Rep. 116; [1995] C.L.C. 818, the apparent contradiction was settled by holding that the presumption is in fact only an inference of fact, and that the correct course is for the actual underwriter to give evidence of inducement.

[175] *St Paul Fire & Marine Insurance Co (UK) Ltd* [1996] 1 All E.R. 96; [1995] 2 Lloyd's Rep. 116; [1995] C.L.C. 818.

[176] The reason that the 4th underwriter did not give evidence was that the first instance hearing of *St Paul Fire & Marine Insurance Co Ltd* took place prior to the House of Lords decision in *Pan Atlantic* requiring actual inducement. See *St Paul Fire & Marine Insurance Co Ltd* [1996] 1 All E.R. 96 at 111–112; [1995] 2 Lloyd's Rep. 116 at 127; [1995] C.L.C. 818 at 830.

disclosure. In practice it is always preferable to call the actual underwriter to give evidence of inducement.[177]

6-039   **Changes under the 2015 Act.**   Under the default regime brought in by the 2015 Act, a breach of the duty of fair presentation by the insurer is not actionable without inducement. The 2015 Act has repealed the remedy of avoidance for a breach of the duty of good faith, introducing a dual system of remedies: a punitive remedy for intentional or reckless breaches of the duty of fair presentation and a compensatory remedy for other breaches. For both aspects of the new system, it remains necessary for an insurer to show that the insured's breach of the fair presentation of risk induced the insurer to enter the contract of insurance. The requirement is set out in s.8(1) of the 2015 Act. It appears likely that case law under the MIA will continue to be relevant to inducement under the 2015 Act.

7. INSURER'S DUTY OF THE UTMOST GOOD FAITH

6-040   **Origin of the duty.**   The historic common law and current statutory duty of utmost good faith under the MIA applies equally to insurer and to insured. The existence of a duty upon the insurer is clear from the wording of s.17 of the MIA,[178] but the question of what that duty comprises is not. An early example of the duty of disclosure upon an insurer was given by Lord Mansfield in the case of *Carter*[179]:

> "The policy would equally be void, against the underwriter, if he concealed; as, if he insured a ship on her voyage, which he privately knew to be arrived: and an action would lie to recover the premium."[180]

The 2015 Act leaves intact the wording in s.17 of the MIA that imposes the duty of utmost good faith upon insurance contracts but it repeals the remedy of avoidance for breach of the duty. It is therefore not clear what role the duty of utmost good faith will play under the 2015 Act, particularly given that the new provisions do not attempt to codify the insurer's duties in relation to good faith, save for the requirement to pay insurance claims within a reasonable time.[181] Although there were only a few cases under the MIA in which the content of an insurer's obligations pursuant to the duty of good faith were considered, it appears that none of the identified duties are placed on statutory footing by the new provisions. Accordingly, whilst the matters discussed below remain relevant to policies governed by the provisions of the MIA, it is likely that an insured will be left without any remedy should similar circumstances arise under the 2015 Act.

6-041   **Scope.**   The question concerning the scope of the insurer's duty of disclosure had not arisen in the courts for over 200 years since Lord Mansfield's judgment – an indication that there are very limited circumstances where the insurer will be under

---

[177] *Berger and Light Diffusers Pty Ltd* [1973] 2 Lloyd's Rep. 442 at 463, and see above, fn.174.

[178] Section 17 of the MIA provides that "A contract of marine insurance is a contract based upon the utmost good faith, and, if the utmost good faith be not observed by either party, the contract may be avoided by the other party".

[179] *Carter* (1766) 3 Burr. 1905; 97 E.R. 1162.

[180] *Carter* (1766) 3 Burr. 1905 at 1909; 97 E.R. 1162 at 1164.

[181] See below, Ch.23.

a duty to disclose material facts. Clarification of the duty was provided in *Banque Financiere de la Cite SA*[182]:

> "The duty extends to the insurer as well as to the insured: *Carter v. Boehm* (1766) 3 Burr. 1905. The duty is, however, limited to facts which are material to the risk insured, that is to say, facts which would influence ... a prudent insured in entering into the contract on the terms proposed by the insurer. Thus ... any facts known to the insurer but not to the insured, which would reduce the risk, should be disclosed by the insurer."[183]

The duty is divided into two categories: first, to disclose facts material to the nature of the risk and, secondly, to disclose facts which are material to the recoverability of a claim under the policy.[184] The test of materiality is whether the fact would be one that

> "a prudent insured would take into account in deciding whether or not to place the risk for which he seeks cover with that insurer."[185]

Level of risk. The first category of information the insurer is required to disclose is material knowledge concerning the level of risk itself. Logically, where the risk abates or ceases this will affect the decision of the insured as to whether it will obtain the insurance at the given premium or at all. Conversely, the insured's decision whether to obtain insurance at a given premium will not be affected where the risk has increased (it is more likely he will wish to obtain the insurance at that price). Thus, the duty on the insurer so far as risk is concerned is only to disclose facts that would reduce the risk and thereby decrease the premium.[186] The duty does not extend to informing the insured that another underwriter would write the same risk at a lower premium,[187] or on different terms, nor does the duty require the insurer to inform the insured of the adequacy of the insurance cover the insured requested. The nature and level of risk inherent in construction is considered in Ch.2.

6-042

Recoverability of a claim. The duty of disclosure of material facts relating to the recoverability of a claim on the policy is not well defined, for it is not clear what is meant by the term "recoverability of a claim." Non-disclosure of material facts relating to the recoverability of a claim was pleaded in the case of *Banque Financiere de la Cite SA*,[188] which concerned agent's fraud. A consortium of banks

6-043

---

[182] *Banque Financiere de la Cite SA* [1991] 2 A.C. 249; [1990] 3 W.L.R. 364; [1990] 2 All E.R. 947.

[183] *Banque Financiere de la Cite SA* [1991] 2 A.C. 249 at 281-282; [1990] 3 W.L.R. 364 at 381; [1990] 2 All E.R. 947 at 960.

[184] *Banque Financiere de la Cite SA* [1990] 1 Q.B. 665 at 772; [1989] 3 W.L.R. 25 at 80-81; [1989] 2 All E.R. 952 at 990, per Slade LJ. This point was approved in the House of Lords by Lord Bridge [1991] 2 A.C. 249 at 268; [1990] 3 W.L.R. 364 at 369; [1990] 2 All E.R. 947 at 950.

[185] *Banque Financiere de la Cite SA* [1990] 1 Q.B. 665 at 772; [1989] 3 W.L.R. 25 at 81; [1989] 2 All E.R. 952 at 990.

[186] Just as the insured is relieved of his duty to disclose information that might decrease the risk, so the insurer is relieved of the duty to disclose information that might increase the risk. See Lord Jauncey in *Banque Financiere de la Cite SA*; sub nom. *Banque Keyser Ullmann SA* [1991] 2 A.C. 249 at 281-282; [1990] 3 W.L.R. 364 at 381-382; [1990] 2 All E.R. 947 at 960.

[187] *Banque Financiere de la Cite SA* [1990] 1 Q.B. 665 at 772; [1989] 3 W.L.R. 25 at 80; [1989] 2 All E.R. 952 at 990. On this point, Slade LJ said: "In our judgment the mere existence of the relationship of insurers and insured would not place upon them the duty to inform the insured of this fact."

[188] *Banque Financiere de la Cite SA*; sub nom. *Banque Keyser Ullmann SA* [1991] 2 A.C. 249; [1990] 3 W.L.R 364; [1990] 2 All E.R. 947.

instructed a broker to arrange insurance for loans they were prepared to issue to various companies under the control of one businessman. The broker sought the insurance required, but provided fraudulent cover notes of insurance to the banks, receipt of which induced the banks to release the loan capital to the companies, though this fraud subsequently became obsolete when the full insurance agreements were finalised. The lead insurer, through one of its employees, had knowledge of the fraud but did not reveal the facts to the banks. After the businessman perpetrated a fraud of his own by embezzling the loan monies and fleeing, the banks were unsuccessful in claiming on the insurance policies due to a clause in the contract of insurance providing that the insurers would not be liable for any claims caused by fraud. The banks then brought an action for damages against the insurers for non-disclosure of the broker's fraud, of which the insurer had knowledge through its employee. The banks contended that the information concerned the banks' ability to recover under the policy since if the insurer could have repudiated liability on the grounds of its broker's fraud then the banks would have been left without a valid policy of insurance on which to claim.

Lord Bridge held that while the duty exists, facts would only have been material under the "recoverability of claim" branch of the duty if they would entitle the insurer to repudiate liability,[189] and that the insurer could not have repudiated liability since the fraud of the broker was not of the type in the fraud exclusion clause, which set out the insurers entitlement to repudiate. Since the insurer could not repudiate liability to the insured, the insured had not lost its ability to recover for a claim under the policy. Consequently, the insurer was under no obligation to disclose the information, it being immaterial. Lord Jauncey did not refer to the recoverability of claim branch of the duty and stated that the broker's "dishonesty neither increased nor decreased the risk,"[190] was therefore irrelevant, and as such was not required to be disclosed. Lord Jauncey's analysis is consistent with the first branch of the duty of disclosure: that disclosure by the insurer is only required when the facts are material to the risk. There is some support for the view that facts relating to the recoverability of a claim do come within the duty of disclosure.[191] However, the existence of this branch of the duty has been doubted and, if it does exist, its ambit has not been discussed in case law.[192]

It is clear that the scope of materiality and therefore disclosure is narrower for an insurer than for an insured. The insured must disclose any matter that might affect the judgment of a prudent underwriter, whereas the insurer's duty of disclosure is limited to information of material circumstances that would reduce the premium to be paid and to information regarding the insured's ability to recover on the policy.

---

[189] *Banque Financiere de la Cite SA* [1991] 2 A.C. 249 at 268–269; [1990] 3 W.L.R. 364 at 369; [1990] 2 All E.R. 947 at 950. On this point, Lord Bridge said: "But an obligation on Mr Dungate to disclose what he knew of Mr Lee's first fraud could only fall within the ambit of the duty as 'material ... to the recoverability of a claim under the policy' if Mr Lee's frauds were such as would entitle the insurer to repudiate liability."

[190] *Banque Financiere de la Cite SA* [1991] 2 A.C. 249 at 282; [1990] 3 W.L.R. 364 at 382; [1990] 2 All E.R. 947 at 960.

[191] See *Norwich Union Life Insurance Co Ltd v Qureshi* [1999] 2 All E.R. (Comm) 707 at 716; [1999] C.L.C. 1963 at 1970; [2000] Lloyd's Rep. I.R. 1 at 7.

[192] Lord Bridge in *Banque Financiere de la Cite SA* accepted that the recoverability of claim category existed but did not give any explanation at [1991] 2 A.C. 249 at 268; [1990] 3 W.L.R. 364 at 369; [1990] 2 All E.R. 947 at 950. For further criticism, see *Colinvaux's Law of Insurance*, edited by R. Merkin, 10th edn (London: Sweet & Maxwell, 2014), para.6–123.

This is reflective of the fact the onus is largely on the insured to fully provide accurate and relevant information about the risk since it is the insurer that is vulnerable to fraudulent requests for insurance and therefore requires protection of the law. Case law is silent on whether inducement of the insured is required, though given that the duty of utmost good faith is reciprocal, it would be surprising if the law concerning the insurer's duty did not also require inducement.

8. POST-CONTRACTUAL GOOD FAITH UNDER THE MIA

Introduction. Once the contract of insurance has been entered into, the duties of disclosure and truthful representation referred to in ss.18–20 of the MIA no longer apply.[193] Those provisions expressly refer to the period prior to formation of the contract and, in theory, all information material to the insurer should have been disclosed. As a consequence, any subsequent increase in risk is not required to be disclosed since it is not material to fixing the premium at the time the contract was formed, though it is not unusual for the terms of the policy to require further post-contract disclosure of changes to the risk which occur after the inception of the policy. The insured may even be able to increase the risk, provided that is not in contravention of warranties contained within the policy.[194] For example, in *Mitchell Conveyor & Transporter Co v Pulbrook*[195] contractors engaged in laying foundations for a construction project decided to adopt a new kind of concrete mix with granite chippings, which proved to be unsatisfactory. The underwriter agreed to provide insurance for design defects without coming to agreement on the proportions for the concrete mix. The new kind of concrete mix was held to be a type of design and, therefore, the insurer had not excluded the use of a riskier technique from the cover it provided.

6-044

Renewals, variations and "held covered" clauses. The duties expressed in ss.18–20 of the MIA will apply to a renewal, a variation or an extension of an existing insurance policy, since each in effect is a fresh agreement and therefore pre-contractual in nature.[196] As a result, a breach of duty relating to the renewal, variation or extension will mean that part of the contract is voidable but it will not cause the original contract to be voidable as well.[197] This principle also applies to "held covered" clauses.[198] Such a clause is contained in the original contract of insurance and operates to provide cover to the insured in the event that it innocently misrepresented material circumstances prior to the inception of the contract. The insurer in effect agrees in the original contract that he will hold the insured covered for events not previously covered, provided the insured makes payment of an ad-

6-045

---

[193] *Manifest Shipping Co Ltd* [2001] UKHL 1 at [48]–[49]; 2003 1 A.C. 469 at 493–494; [2001] 2 W.L.R. 170 at 186.

[194] *Toulmin v Inglis* 170 E.R. 1007; (1808) 1 Camp. 421.

[195] *Mitchell Conveyor & Transporter Co Ltd v Pulbrook* (1933) 45 Ll. L. Rep. 239.

[196] *Lambert v Cooperative Insurance Society Ltd* [1975] 2 Lloyd's Rep. 485 at 487; *K/S Merc-Scandia XXXXII* [2001] EWCA Civ 1275 at [31]; [2001] 2 Lloyd's Rep. 563 at 574; [2001] C.L.C. 1836 at 1848.

[197] *K/S Merc-Scandia XXXXII* [2001] EWCA Civ 1275 at [22]; [2001] 2 Lloyd's Rep. 563 at 571–572; [2001] C.L.C. 1836 at 1844–1845; *Lishman v Northern Maritime Insurance Co* (1874–75) L.R. 10 C.P. 179.

[198] See *Fraser Shipping Ltd v Colton* [1997] 1 Lloyd's Rep. 586 at 597; *K/S Merc-Scandia XXXXII* [2001] EWCA Civ 1275 at [22]; [2001] 2 Lloyd's Rep. 563 at 571–572; [2001] C.L.C. 1836 at 1844–1845.

ditional premium. Although the right to be held covered is expressed in the original contract, the payment of an additional premium signifies that it is in effect a new agreement, to which a new duty of disclosure attaches.[199]

6-046 **Scope of the duty.** The courts have accepted that there is a post-contractual duty of utmost good faith.[200] For example, s.17 of the MIA, which provides a reciprocal duty of good faith, is not expressed in terms that restrict the duty to the pre-contractual period in the same way that ss.18–20 are.[201] The scope of the post-contractual duty has been discussed in three recent cases[202] and the final analysis, which came in *The Mercandian Continent*,[203] would appear to be that the duty only has application in limited circumstances since the court should look first to the contract itself to resolve a dispute.[204] Having recognised that renewals, variations and extensions were governed by the pre-contractual duty rules, Longmore LJ considered that only two separate instances of a standalone post-contractual duty of good faith exist.[205] The first is where the contract provides that the insurer has a right to information, in which case there exists a duty of good faith on the insured to provide such information. The second is where the insurer exercises a right to take over the insured's defence, in which case the two parties will owe duties of good faith towards each other. For example, the insured will owe a duty of disclosure and the insurer will owe a duty to settle the dispute in a proper manner by taking account of the interests of the insured. It is suggested that the judgment of Longmore LJ is the most accurate reflection of the present state of the scope of the duty, although it has not been confirmed or rejected by the Supreme Court. In light of the decision in *The Mercandian Continent*, it appears there are very few circumstances in which a post-contractual duty of good faith on the insured will arise.

Avoidance as a remedy for post-contractual breach of duty of good
6-047 **faith.** Because s.17 of the MIA provides for ab initio avoidance of the contract, the courts are reluctant to allow a party, usually the insurer, to invoke s.17 for an insured's post-contractual breach of good faith. Avoidance of a contract for post-contractual breaches of good faith could in theory enable an insurer to escape liability for valid claims made by the insured under the policy. Indeed, it has been said the application of that remedy post-contractually is "wholly one-sided" and "disproportionate" for it is unlikely that the insured will ever want to avoid an insur-

---

199 cf. *K/S Merc-Scandia XXXXII* [2001] EWCA Civ 1275 at [22]; [2001] 2 Lloyd's Rep. 563 at 571–572; [2001] C.L.C. 1836 at 1844–1845, where Longmore LJ described it as "puzzling" that a new duty of disclosure applied to rights already contained within an existing contract.

200 *Black King Shipping Corp v Massie (The Litsion Pride)* [1985] 1 Lloyd's Rep. 437; (1984) 134 N.L.J. 887; *Bank of Nova Scotia v Hellenic Mutual War Risk Association (Bermuda) Ltd (The Good Luck)* [1990] 1 Q.B. 818 at 888; [1990] 2 W.L.R. 547 at 591; [1989] 3 All E.R. 628 at 660.

201 Indeed, this was noted by the draftsman, Sir Mackenzie Chalmers. See above, fn.12.

202 *Black King Shipping Corp* [1985] 1 Lloyd's Rep. 437; (1984) 134 N.L.J. 887; *Manifest Shipping Co Ltd* [2001] UKHL 1; [2003] 1 A.C. 469; [2001] 2 W.L.R. 170; *K/S Merc-Scandia XXXXII* [2001] EWCA Civ 1275; [2001] 2 Lloyd's Rep. 563; [2001] C.L.C. 1836.

203 *K/S Merc-Scandia XXXXII* [2001] EWCA Civ 1275; [2001] 2 Lloyd's Rep. 563; [2001] All E.R. (D) 459.

204 *K/S Merc-Scandia XXXXII* [2001] EWCA Civ 1275 at [9]; [2001] 2 Lloyd's Rep. 563 at 568; [2001] C.L.C. 1836 at 1840, per Longmore LJ.

205 *K/S Merc-Scandia XXXXII* [2001] EWCA Civ 1275 at [22]; [2001] 2 Lloyd's Rep. 563 at 571–572; [2001] C.L.C. 1836 at 1844–1845, per Longmore LJ.

ance policy after inception.[206] The insurer on the other hand would wish to avoid the policy if possible.

In *The Mercandian Continent*, Longmore LJ made clear that avoidance for a breach of a post-contractual duty of utmost good faith should only be possible if the breach had "at least the same quality of conduct as would justify the insurer in accepting the insured's conduct as a repudiation of the contract".[207] He went on to hold that for the policy to be validly avoided, a breach of duty would have to amount to a material fraud "in the sense that it would have an effect on underwriters' ultimate liability", which would have enabled the underwriter to terminate for breach of contract.[208] In light of the decision, few circumstances will give the insurer the right to avoid the policy ab initio and, in light of the fraud requirement seemingly set out in the test of Longmore LJ, the appropriate remedy may not be ab inito avoidance but may be analogous with the remedy of forfeiture for fraudulent claims, which is discussed further below.[209]

Litigation.   The post-contractual duty of good faith does not extend into all   **6-048**
litigation. In the *Manifest Shipping Co Ltd* case[210] the defendants argued that the claimant's conduct of the litigation, particularly relating to disclosure, was itself a breach of the duty of utmost good faith entitling the defendants to avoid the policy. This argument was rejected by the House of Lords. Lord Hobhouse said that the post-contractual duty of utmost good faith is "exhausted or at the least superseded by the rules of litigation".[211] He also said:

> "I am therefore strongly of the view that once the parties are in litigation it is the procedural rules which govern the extent of the disclosure which should be given in the litigation, not s.17 as such, though s.17 may influence the court in the exercise of its discretion."[212]

Fraudulent claims as part of the post-contractual duty of good faith.   There   **6-049**
is a rule dating from the early nineteenth century, specific to insurance law, that an insured who makes a fraudulent or dishonestly exaggerated claim forfeits the right to recover under the policy, even where the insured could also make an honest, smaller claim ("the fraudulent claims rule"). This rule is discussed both under the MIA and in the context of the 2015 Act above at para.5-021[213] and below at paras 21-027 to 21-047. This section discusses the specific question whether or not the rule derives from the duty of utmost good faith. This has been an important question, though its importance may have diminished with the recent legislative

---

[206] *Manifest Shipping Co Ltd* [2001] UKHL 1 at [57]; 2003 1 A.C. 469 at 496–497; [2001] 2 W.L.R. 170 at 189; *Drake Insurance Plc v Providence Insurance Plc* [2003] EWCA Civ 1834 at [177]; [2004] Q.B. 601 at 649-650.

[207] *K/S Merc-Scandia XXXXII* [2001] EWCA Civ 1275 at [26]; [2001] 2 Lloyd's Rep. 563 at 573; [2001] C.L.C. 1836 at 1846–1847, per Longmore LJ.

[208] *K/S Merc-Scandia XXXXII* [2001] EWCA Civ 1275 at [35]; [2001] 2 Lloyd's Rep. 563 at 575; [2001] C.L.C. 1836 at 1849–1850, per Longmore LJ.

[209] See below, para.6-049.

[210] *Manifest Shipping Co Ltd* [2001] UKHL 1; [2003] 1 A.C. 469; [2001] 2 W.L.R. 170.

[211] *Manifest Shipping Co Ltd* [2001] UKHL 1 at [76]; [2003] 1 A.C. 469 at 505; [2001] 2 W.L.R. 170 at 197, per Lord Hobhouse. However, see the comments of LJ Mance relating to cases not involving fraudulents claims or devices in *Agapitos v Agnew* [2002] EWCA Civ 247 at [51]; [2003] Q.B. 556 at 557.

[212] *Manifest Shipping Co Ltd* [2001] UKHL 1 at [77]; [2003] 1 A.C. 469 at 505; [2001] 2 W.L.R. 170 at 197–198, per Lord Hobhouse.

[213] See also above, paras 5-116 to 5-130 for discussion of the 2015 Act's provision for fraudulent claims.

reforms—the 2015 Act provides for the consequences of fraudulent claims expressly. Previously however, if the fraudulent claims rule were to be considered an aspect of the duty of good faith then the remedy for breach would be avoidance ab initio. If avoidance ab initio were the remedy then an insurer would theoretically be able to invoke the rule not just in defence of a fraudulent claim but additionally to void the policy and perhaps reclaim any payments already made under the same policy but in respect of separate, unimpeachable claims. This discussion does not apply to the 2015 Act.

The relationship between the fraudulent claims rule and the duty of utmost good faith was the subject of debate for some time but remained undecided. In *Britton v Royal Insurance Co*, an early case decided during the development of the rule, the fraudulent claims rule was explained to the jury by Willes J on the basis that contracts of insurance were "of perfect good faith".[214] It was not necessary to decide the point in the *Manifest Shipping Co Ltd* case,[215] although obiter dicta supported the position that the fraudulent claims rule is a special rule of the common law.[216] In *Agapitos v Agnew (No.1) ("The Aegeon")*, Mance LJ's "tentative view" was that the rule against fraudulent claims fell outside the scope of the duty of utmost good faith.[217] When the question came before Mance LJ again in *Axa General Insurance Ltd v Gottlieb*, sub nom. *Gottlieb v Axa General Insurance Ltd*, he held, with Keene and Pill LJJ, agreeing with him, that the "rule relating to fraudulent insurance claims is accordingly a special common law rule" and that the proper scope of the rule

"is to forfeit the whole of the claim to which the fraud relates, with the effect that the consideration for any interim payments made on that claim fails and they are recoverable."[218]

The fraudulent claims rule came before the Supreme Court recently in the landmark case *Versloot Dredging BV v HDI Gerling Industrie Verischerung AG (the DC Merwestone)*[219] The question for determination was whether or not a fraudulent device (also referred to as a collateral lie) deployed by an insured, in seeking an indemnity to which the insured was entitled under an insurance policy, would also lead to the forfeiture of an otherwise genuine claim in its entirety. Lords Sumption and Hughes JJSC (with whom Lords Clarke and Toulson JJSC agreed) held that it would not; the rule against fraudulent claims does not apply to a lie used to embellish a genuine claim which the true facts, once admitted or ascertained, showed to be immaterial to the validity of the claim and to the insured's right to recover.[220]

---

214 *Britton v Royal Insurance Co* (1866) 4 F. & F. 905 at 908; 176 E.R. 843 at 844. See also *Orapko v Barclays Insurance Services Co Ltd* [1995] L.R.L.R. 443; [1994] C.L.C. 373 and *Galloway v Guardian Royal Exchange (UK)* [1999] Lloyd's Rep. I.R. 209. These three cases all involved fraudulently exaggerated claims.

215 *Manifest Shipping Co Ltd* [2001] UKHL 1 at [110]; [2003] 1 A.C. 469 at 514–515; [2001] 2 W.L.R. 170 at 207.

216 See Lord Hobhouse in *Manifest Shipping Co Ltd* [2001] UKHL 1 at [62]; [2003] 1 A.C. 469 at 499; [2001] 2 W.L.R. 170 at 191 who endorsed the notion that the rule against fraudulent claims derived from the common law rather than the uberimmae fidei nature of a contract of insurance.

217 *Agapitos v Agnew (No.1) ("The Aegeon")* [2002] EWCA Civ 247 at [45]; [2003] Q.B. 556 at 575; [2002] 3 W.L.R. 616 at 633–634.

218 *Axa General Insurance Ltd v Gottlieb* [2005] EWCA Civ 112 at [31]–[32]; [2005] 1 All E.R. (Comm) 445 at 458–459; [2005] Lloyd's Rep. I.R. 369 at 378.

219 *Versloot Dredging BV v HDI Gerling Industrie Verischerung AG (the DC Merwestone)* [2016] UKSC 45; [2016] 3 W.L.R. 543.

220 *Versloot Dredging BV* [2016] UKSC 45 at [23]–[26], [29]–[30], [32]–[36], [39], [46]–[47], [50],

Lord Mance JSC dissented. His view was that materiality had to be judged by reference to the position at the time when the fraudulent device was deployed.[221] He proposed an updated version of the materiality threshold he had set out in *The Aegeon*: whether the fraudulent device

"would, if believed, have tended, objectively but prior to any final determination at trial of the parties' rights, to yield a [significant] improvement in the insured's prospects — whether they be prospects of obtaining a settlement, or a better settlement, or of winning at trial."[222]

Lord Mance JSC also differed from the rest of their Lordships in relation to whether public policy aimed at deterring insurance fraud justified the extension of the fraudulent claims rule to fraudulent devices. He emphasised the lack of any qualitative difference between the types of dishonest conduct covered by the rule—in particular, exaggerated claims—and fraudulent devices, which the majority held were beyond the scope of the rule.

It was, regrettably, not necessary for the Supreme Court to decide whether the fraudulent claims rule was an aspect of the duty of utmost good faith, because the insurers were seeking only to avoid the claim, rather than the contract. Accordingly, the discussion and analysis mainly focussed on the rationale of the rule – to discourage fraud – and the proportionality of the remedy. However there are useful obiter dicta at various levels of appellate court. For example, Christopher Clarke LJ, in the Court of Appeal, favoured the view of Willes J in *Britton*'s case, i.e. that the fraudulent claims rule is an aspect of the duty of utmost good faith.[223]

In the Supreme Court Lord Sumption J.S.C., giving the leading judgment, held that the fraudulent claims rule is

"peculiar to contracts of insurance, and there can be little doubt that historically it is because they are contracts of utmost good faith that they have this unique characteristic. But I am inclined to agree with the view expressed by Lord Hobhouse of Woodborough in *The 'STAR SEA'* (paras 50, 61–62) that once the contract is made, the content of the duty of good faith and the consequences of its breach must be accommodated within the general principles of the law of contract. On that view of the matter, the fraudulent claims rule must be regarded as a term implied or inferred by law, or at any rate an incident of the contract."[224]

Lord Hughes J.S.C. took the view that the fraudulent claims rule is a

"rule of law, imposed by the courts ... It seems more realistic to acknowledge it as having achieved the status of a rule of common law, grounded in sound policy, rather than depending on an implied term in the contract."[225]

He based this conclusion partly on the basis that the content of the duty of utmost good faith "differs significantly from the pre-contract rule both as to the obligation which it imposes and as to the remedy for breach" compared to the duty of

---

[90]–[93], [100] and [104]; [2016] 3 W.L.R. 543 at 557–562, 564–565, 576–577 and 579–580.

[221] *Versloot Dredging BV* [2016] UKSC 45 at [111] and [125] to [130]; [2016] 3 W.L.R. 543 at 582, 586–588.

[222] *Agapitos* [2002] EWCA Civ 247 at [38]; [2003] Q.B. 556 at 572; [2002] 3 W.L.R. 616 at 631. Mance LJ's original formulation was "not insignificant," but he amended this to "significant," [2016] UKSC 45 at [113]; [2016] 3 W.L.R. 543 at 583.

[223] *Versloot Dredging BV v HDI Gerling Industrie Verischerung AG (The DC Merwestone)* [2014] EWCA Civ 1349 at [76]–[77]; [2015] Q.B. 608 at 630–631; [2015] 2 W.L.R. 1063 at 1084.

[224] *Versloot Dredging BV* [2016] UKSC 45 at [8]; [2016] 3 W.L.R. 543 at 548.

[225] *Versloot Dredging BV* [2016] UKSC 45 at [55]; [2016] 3 W.L.R. 543 at 566.

good faith post-contract as found by the House of Lords in *The Star Sea*.[226] Lord Mance, in his dissenting opinion, stated the fraudulent claims principle to be a rule of law

> "albeit, one may add, a rule of law no doubt deriving from the foundation of good faith on which insurance rests …, but tailored to the post-contractual position."[227]

The dicta set out above are obiter and the true basis for the fraudulent claims rule remains undetermined; it may either be explained as a rule of the common law or as a contractual term or "incident" implied at law. However, the opinions of the judgment of the Supreme Court in *Versloot Dredging BV*[228] appear to confirm that the fraudulent claims rule is not an aspect of the duty of utmost good faith, though both the rule and the duty derive from and respond to the same legal policy concerns.

9. REMEDIES FOR NON-DISCLOSURE AND MISREPRESENTATION

6-050   **Avoidance.** The remedy under the MIA for both non-disclosure and misrepresentation is avoidance of the policy.[229] It has been held that a clear inference of the MIA is that:

> "Parliament did not contemplate that a breach of the obligation would give rise to a claim for damages in the case of such contracts. Otherwise it would surely have said so."[230]

6-051   **Election to avoid.** Where the contract is rendered voidable under the MIA as a result of a breach by one party of the duty of utmost good faith, the innocent party (almost always the insurer) may elect to hold the contract void, which would result in the contract being void ab initio.[231] If the decision is made to avoid the policy, then the policy will be held void immediately upon communication of the decision to the party in breach or declaratory relief by the court.

The consequence of holding the policy void ab initio is that the contract is treated as if it had never existed. Both parties are therefore entitled in restitution to a return of all money that changed hands under the contract.[232] This includes the premium and any payments made for losses under s.84(1) of the MIA, though it is possible for the policy terms to exclude the return of premiums already paid. However,

---

226 *Versloot Dredging BV* [2016] UKSC 45 at [67]–[68]; [2016] 3 W.L.R. 543 at 569–570.

227 *Versloot Dredging BV* [2016] UKSC 45 at [119]; [2016] 3 W.L.R. 543 at 585.

228 *Versloot Dredging BV* [2016] UKSC 45; [2016] 3 W.L.R. 543.

229 MIA 1906 ss.18(1) and 20(1).

230 See Slade LJ (in a combined judgment of the Court of Appeal) in *Banque Financiere de la Cite SA* [1990] 1 Q.B. 665 at 781; [1989] 3 W.L.R. 25 at 88–89; [1989] 2 All E.R. 952 at 997. The point was affirmed in the House of Lords in the same case by Lord Templeman: [1991] 2 A.C. 249 at 280; [1990] 3 W.L.R. 364; [1990] 2 All E.R. 947 at 959, where he said that "a breach of the obligation does not sound in damages. The only remedy open to the insured is to rescind the policy and recover the premium. The authorities cited and the cogent reasons advanced by Slade LJ are to be found in the report of the proceedings in the Court of Appeal [1990] 1 Q.B. 665, 777–781".

231 *Pan Atlantic Insurance Co Ltd* [1995] 1 A.C. 501 at 544; [1994] 3 W.L.R. 677 at 707–708; [1994] 3 All E.R. 581 at 612–613, per Lord Mustill; *Strive Shipping Corp* [2002] EWHC 203 at [271] (Comm); [2002] 2 All E.R. (Comm) 213 at 270; [2002] Lloyd's Rep. I.R. 669 at 716.

232 In *Manifest Shipping Co Ltd* [2001] UKHL 1 at [51]; [2003] 1 A.C. 469 at 494; [2001] 2 W.L.R. 170 at 187, Lord Hobhouse said: "If any adjustment of the parties' financial positions is to take place, it is done under the law of restitution not under the law of contract."

where the misrepresentation or non-disclosure was fraudulent on the part of an insured, there will be no repayment of the premium.[233]

Successful avoidance of the policy will not affect jurisdiction or arbitration clauses, both of which are regarded as separate contracts and which remain unaffected by avoidance of the main contract of insurance.[234] It is almost always the insurer rather than the insured who seeks to avoid an insurance contract. If the insurer successfully avoids the contract he will not have to pay the claim but must return the premium. It is suggested that there are few circumstances where avoidance will be a useful remedy to the insured following an insurer's breach.[235] An example of such a circumstance would be where an insured has already arranged alternative insurance elsewhere and seeks to recoup his premium. The following paragraphs assume that it will be the insurer who seeks to avoid the policy, although the principles apply equally to the insured.

The insurer may also lose its right to elect by affirmation. The burden is on the insured to show that the insurer has unequivocally elected by words or conduct to keep the policy in force having full knowledge of its right (as a matter of both fact and of law)[236] to avoid the policy for misrepresentation or non-disclosure.[237]

Loss of right to avoid. Avoidance ab initio is an equitable remedy and therefore the insurer is under a duty to act in good faith when avoiding an insurance policy; otherwise expressed, the insurer must act with clean hands. Accordingly, the insurer can lose its right to avoid if, for example, it has not clearly communicated its avoidance to the insured, or if it had knowledge of material circumstances that had not been disclosed by the insured but entered into the contract notwithstanding, or if it turned a blind eye to material facts not disclosed by the insured. In such types of circumstances, then it may be inequitable to avoid the policy.[238]

6-052

Delay. Once the insurer is aware of circumstances entitling him to avoid the policy, he may elect to either avoid or affirm the contract. Election, once taken, is final and binding.[239] Unless a decision to affirm the contract is clearly communicated to the insured, the right to avoid remains open.[240] Failing to make an election within a reasonable time does not automatically mean that the election is no

6-053

---

[233] *Marshall on the Law of Marine Insurance, Bottomry and Respondentia*, edited by W. Shee, 4th edn (London: Shaw & Sons, 1861), p.525; *Biggar v Rock Life Assurance Co* [1902] 1 K.B. 516 at 526; cf. *Joel v Law Union & Crown Insurance Co* [1908] 2 K.B. 431 at 440.

[234] See s.7 of the Arbitration Act 1996 and *Mackender v Feldia AG* [1967] 2 Q.B. 590 at 598; [1967] 2 W.L.R. 119; [1966] 3 All E.R. 847.

[235] In *Manifest Shipping Co Ltd* [2001] UKHL 1 at [57]; [2003] 1 A.C. 469 at 497; [2001] 2 W.L.R. 170 at 189, Lord Hobhouse said. "An inevitable consequence in the post-contract situation is that the remedy of avoidance of the contract is in practical terms wholly one-sided." See the comments of Pill LJ in *Drake* [2003] EWCA Civ 1834 at [177]; [2004] Q.B. 601 at 649–650; [2004] 2 W.L.R. 530, regarding the consequences of the one-sidedness of the remedy for the duty of utmost good faith as it relates to the insurer.

[236] See judicial criticism of the need for knowledge of the legal right by Leggatt J in *Involnert Management Inc v Aprilgrange Ltd* [2015] EWHC 2225 (Comm) at [160].

[237] *Brit UW Ltd v F&R Trenchless Solutions Ltd* [2015] EWHC 2237 (Comm) at [115].

[238] *Drake Insurance Plc (In Provisional Liquidation) v Provident Insurance Plc* [2003] EWCA Civ 1834 at [87], [144] and [177]; [2004] Q.B. 601 at 628, 642–643 and 649–650; [2004] 2 W.L.R. 530.

[239] *Scarf v Jardine* (1881–82) L.R. 7 App. Cas. 345 at 360; [1881–85] All E.R. Rep. 651 at 658, per Lord Blackburn.

[240] *Motor Oil Hellas (Corinth) Refineries SA v Shipping Corp of India (The Kanchenjunga)* [1990] 1 Lloyd's Rep. 391 at 398, per Lord Goff.

longer available, but a significant delay may be considered by the court in deciding whether an insurer has either affirmed or is estopped from avoiding a policy. If
the insurer acts "in a manner which is consistent only with his having chosen one
of the two alternative and inconsistent courses then open to him,"[241] he will be held
to have made his election accordingly.[242]

6-054   **Damages.**   *Banque Financiere de la Cite SA* confirmed that damages are not available for non-disclosure under the MIA.[243] Damages may, however, be available for
fraudulent or negligent misrepresentation under s.2(1) of the Misrepresentation Act
1967 ("the 1967 Act"),[244] although it would be unusual for an insurer to seek damages for misrepresentation or non-disclosure rather than avoid the policy. The
burden is on the insurer to prove that a representation was made, that it was false,
and that it induced the insurer to enter the policy. It is sometimes possible for
misrepresentation and non-disclosure to be pleaded in the alternative; in practice
it is common to plead both. It is possible that a material non-disclosure could be
pleaded as an implied misrepresentation, though it is more likely that a positive
representation will be required since s.2(1) does not apply to non-disclosure. It
would also be contrary to the established principle that avoidance is the only remedy
for a breach of the duty of utmost good faith.

Under s.2(2) of the 1967 Act,[245] where there has been an innocent misrepresentation the court could, at least in theory, declare the contract subsisting and award
damages in lieu of rescission if it considers it equitable to do so. This seeming
contradiction between s.2(2) of the 1967 Act and s.20(1) of the MIA—which
provides that the remedy for material misrepresentation is avoidance—was addressed in *Highlands Insurance Co v Continental Insurance Co*.[246] The court held
that, in cases involving commercial contracts of insurance, it would be inequitable
for the courts to grant relief from avoidance under s.2(2). In particular, the court
considered that avoidance would "fulfil an important 'policing' function"[247] and thus
a greater disincentive to non-disclosure. While the point remains undecided, it is

---

[241] *Motor Oil Hellas (Corinth) Refineries SA v Shipping Corp of India (The Kanchenjunga)* [1990] 1
Lloyd's Rep. 391 at 398, per Lord Goff.

[242] In *Drake Insurance Plc* [2003] EWCA Civ 1834; [2004] Q.B. 601; [2004] 2 W.L.R. 530 where the
insurer accepted a premium, it was held to have affirmed the contract.

[243] *Banque Financiere de la Cite SA* [1991] 2 A.C. 249 at 280; [1990] 3 W.L.R. 364 at 380; [1990] 2
All E.R. 947 at 959, per Lord Templeman.

[244] Misrepresentation Act 1967, s.2(1) provides: "Where a person has entered into a contract after a
misrepresentation has been made to him by another party thereto and as a result thereof he has suffered loss, then, if the person making the misrepresentation would be liable to damages in respect
thereof had the misrepresentation been made fraudulently, that person shall be so liable notwithstanding that the misrepresentation was not made fraudulently, unless he proves that he had reasonable
ground to believe and did believe up to the time the contract was made the facts represented were
true."

[245] Misrepresentation Act 1967, s.2(2) provides: "Where a person has entered into a contract after a
misrepresentation has been made to him otherwise than fraudulently, and he would be entitled, by
reason of the misrepresentation, to rescind the contract, then, if it is claimed, in any proceedings arising out of the contract, that the contract ought to be or has been rescinded, the court or arbitrator
may declare the contract subsisting and award damages in lieu of rescission, if of opinion that it
would be equitable to do so, having regard to the nature of the misrepresentation and the loss that
would be caused by it if the contract were upheld, as well as to the loss that rescission would cause
to the other party."

[246] *Highlands Insurance Co v Continental Insurance Co* [1987] 1 Lloyd's Rep. 109.

[247] *Highlands Insurance Co* [1987] 1 Lloyd's Rep. 109 at 118.

suggested that, were the court to consider whether to exercise its discretion under s.2(2) of the 1967 Act, the remedy of avoidance for non-disclosure would take precedence.[248]

Remedies under the 2015 Act.   One of the criticisms of the MIA was that the draconian remedy of avoidance was available to insurers even where the insured was guilty only of the most trivial breach—accordingly the remedy was viewed by many as inflexible and often disproportionate. One of the aims of the reform process behind the introduction of the 2015 Act was to introduce a system of remedies that aligned insurance law with the relief available under contract law. It was thought that such a system would be fairer for the insured because less powerful remedies are left in the hands of the insurer. Rather than providing for a single remedy in respect of any breach, as under the MIA, the 2015 Act provides for a dual system of remedies responding to the seriousness of the breach. This dual system comprises: a punitive element in which an insurer is entitled to avoid the policy and to retain the premium for deliberate or reckless breaches of the duty of fair presentation[249]; and a proportionate remedy for any other breach in which the insurer's remedy depends upon what the insurer would have done if a fair presentation of risk had been made.[250]

6-055

10.   THE INSURANCE ACT 2015

Reform.   Following a lengthy reform process, the 2015 Act received royal assent on 12 February 2015 and became law on 12 August 2016.[251] The 2015 Act creates a default statutory regime for non-consumer insurance law that will replace the MIA almost entirely.[252] The reforms are intended to change the insurance market and the way that insurance is sought and placed by creating a more flexible regime to encourage a cooperative and engaged relationship between insurer and insured.

6-056

The consequences of reform are likely to be far reaching; the market was permitted a relatively long time to anticipate and adjust to the likely effects of the reforms before they became law. Nonetheless it appears likely that the reforms will create a degree of uncertainty and that the insurance market, including the CAR market, will need to go through a period of adjustment. While it is likely that there will be significant litigation relating to various aspects of the new regime, it is anticipated that the reforms, once bedded in, will reduce the number of disputes between insurer and insured.

---

[248] For a fuller discussion of these points, see *Arnould's Law of Marine Insurance and Average*, edited by J. Gilman et al, 17th edn (London: Sweet & Maxwell, 2008), paras 17-104 to 17-113; *Arnould Law of Marine Insurance and Average First Supplement to the Seventeenth Edition* (London: Sweet & Maxwell, 2010) para.17-112.

[249] Arguably this is a harsher remedy than that under the MIA, which provided for the return of the premium paid under a voided policy except where there was fraud by the insured.

[250] For a comprehensive discussion of relief under the 2015 Act see above, paras 5-072 to 5-089.

[251] Readers interested in the reform process should consult the previous edition of this work, at paras 5-050 to 5-060, and Ch.5 above generally.

[252] The duty of good faith itself, provided for by s.17 of the MIA, will continue in force but the remedy of avoidance for breach in the same section is repealed. It is unclear what effect s.17 of the MIA will have under the 2015 Act but it has been suggested that it will continue to have an interpretative effect. See above, para.5-141.

6-057 **Duty of fair presentation of risk.** The duty of fair presentation of risk is imposed on the insured by Part 2 of the 2015 Act and replaces the duties currently contained in ss.18 to 20 of the MIA. It is a duty that applies both before inception and variation of insurance policies. The regime is intended for all non-consumer insureds of all size and complexities and so it will apply to all non-consumer insurance contracts. Part 2 of the 2015 Act is a default regime and so parties are free to contract out of its provisions, subject to compliance with the statutory transparency requirements, and so bespoke arrangements can be expected to materialise in due course. The English and Scottish Law Commissions anticipate that many major insurance markets will issue protocols further defining what is expected of insureds in making a fair presentation.

The duty of fair presentation is a single duty encompassing various aspects. There are positive and negative elements of the duty: a duty to give appropriate disclosure to an insurer in a certain manner and a duty not to make misrepresentations to the insurer. The wording of the new duty of fair presentation replicates and updates some parts of the MIA and clarifies and develops others. Compliance with the duty will increase the burden associated with obtaining insurance on an insured but redresses the balance of insurance law back towards the insured and provides a fairer and more flexible choice of remedy.

The duty of fair presentation is set out in s.3(3) to (5) of the 2015 Act. It states:

> "(3) A fair presentation of the risk is one—
>
> > (a) which makes the disclosure required by subsection (4),
> > (b) which makes that disclosure in a manner which would be reasonably clear and accessible to a prudent insurer, and
> > (c) in which every material representation as to a matter of fact is substantially correct, and every material representation as to a matter of expectation or belief is made in good faith.
>
> (4) The disclosure required is as follows, except as provided in subsection (5)—
>
> > (a) disclosure of every material circumstance which the insured knows or ought to know, or
> > (b) failing that, disclosure which gives the insurer sufficient information to put a prudent insurer on notice that it needs to make further enquiries for the purpose of revealing those material circumstances.
>
> (5) In the absence of enquiry, subsection (4) does not require the insured to disclose a circumstance if—
>
> > (a) it diminishes the risk,
> > (b) the insurer knows it,
> > (c) the insurer ought to know it,
> > (d) the insurer is presumed to know it, or
> > (e) it is something as to which the insurer waives information."

6-058 **Disclosure and the fair presentation of risk.** The disclosure aspect of the duty of fair presentation under the 2015 Act provides a more nuanced approach to cooperation between the parties. The duty has two limbs,[253] which are considered below.

6-059 **What must be disclosed.** The first limb requires disclosure by the insured of every material circumstance which the insured knows or ought to know. Therefore much of the current duty under s.18(1) of the MIA is retained. The key develop-

---

[253] The first limb is s.3(3)(4)(a), the second is s.3(3)(4)(b) of the 2015 Act.

ment is the reform to the definition of what the insured ought to know, which is discussed below. Even if the insured does not comply with the first limb, then the insured can nonetheless still fairly present the risk under the second limb by giving disclosure which gives the insurer sufficient information to put a prudent insurer on notice that it needs to make further enquiries. The second limb incorporates principles explained in recent case law.[254] This is a significant change. Under the MIA, an insurer who was put on notice but failed to make further enquires might have waived its right to avoid. Under the 2015 Act, the insurer is required to go further than previously if it is to have a remedy.

Materiality continues to underpin what must be disclosed under the 2015 Act. The test under the 2015 Act for material non-disclosure puts the current *Pan Atlantic Insurance Co Ltd*[255] test onto a statutory footing.[256] Furthermore, a non-exhaustive illustrative list of material circumstances has been provided to clarify the meaning of materiality: special or unusual facts relating to the risk; particular concerns which led the insured to seek insurance cover; and anything which those concerned with the class of insurance and field of activity in question would generally understand as being something that should be dealt with in a fair presentation.[257] The third of these categories is considered likely to lead to protocols being issued in specific markets, such as CAR insurance. Insurance protocols in the CAR market are likely to present their own unique challenges reflecting the size and international reach of construction companies and the often complex contractual relationships that development around constructions projects.

Knowledge. Knowledge has always presented a difficult problem for insurance law. In particular, when an insured does not have actual knowledge of a material circumstance and so has not disclosed that circumstance, when will the insured be deemed—by the mechanisms of constructive or attributed knowledge—to have the knowledge such that the non-disclosure amounts to a breach? The concept of knowledge has been significantly clarified by s.4 of the 2015 Act and distinct tests are introduced for individual and non-individual insureds.[258] Old concepts are retained, such as so-called "blind eye" knowledge,[259] and new concepts are introduced, such as: the new test for an insured's constructive knowledge— whether it should reasonably have been revealed by a reasonable search of information available to the insured[260]; the attribution to the insured of knowledge held by individuals responsible for the insured's insurance[261]; and the notion of the senior management of a non-individual insured.[262] The new test for constructive knowledge may well be the most significant change to be brought in by the 2015 Act and puts insureds under a greater burden when obtaining insurance cover. There

6-060

---

[254] See above, Ch.5, fn.36.

[255] *Pan Atlantic Insurance Co Ltd* [1995] 1 A.C. 501; [1994] 3 W.L.R. 677; [1994] 3 All E.R. 581.

[256] Section 7(3) of the 2015 Act provides that "A circumstance or representation is material if it would influence the judgement of a prudent insurer in determining whether to take the risk and, if so, on what terms."

[257] Section 7(3) and (4) of the 2015 Act.

[258] Section 4(2) and (3) of the 2015 Act respectively. See above, paras 5-031 and 5-032.

[259] Section 6(1) of the 2015 Act. See above, para.5-029.

[260] Section 4(1) and (6) of the 2015 Act. For further discussion see above, paras 5-036 to 5-040.

[261] Section 4(2)(b), (3)(b) and (8)(b) of the 2015 Act. For further discussion see above, para.5-034 and paras 5-041 to 5-050.

[262] Section 4(3)(a) and (8)(c) of the 2015 Act.

has also been clarification of the circumstances in which frauds will and will not be attributed to an insured.[263] The 2015 Act also reforms and clarifies the approach to the insurer's knowledge, as it relates to the exceptions to the disclosure aspect of the duty of fair presentation of risk.[264] This concept is developed as a counterweight and increases the obligations and burden on an insurer in providing cover.

6-061   **How disclosure must be given.**   The 2015 Act requires an insured to present the risk fairly, not only by making sufficient disclosure but also by making that disclosure in a manner which would be reasonably clear and accessible to a prudent insurer. This obligation ought to help an insurer process the insured's disclosure, which on occasion, and in relation to CAR insureds, can be particularly extensive. In part, this reform responds to changes in the insurance industry and to businesses generally, which all now store vastly increased amounts of, mostly electronic, data. It is also an attempt to discourage attempts to hide small pieces of damaging information in much larger rafts of innocuous disclosure—a practice known as "data dumping". The reforms put significant new burdens on an insured seeking to obtain insurance cover. On the other hand, insurers are encouraged to play a more cooperative role under the new regime and to engage in the disclosure process. An insured must also take action when put on notice of the need to make inquiries.

6-062   **Misrepresentation.**   The 2015 Act brings misrepresentation within the overarching duty of fair presentation of risk but incorporates many of the principles existing under the current MIA regime. Every material representation made by an insured as to a matter of fact must be substantially correct and every representation as to a matter of expectation or belief must be made in good faith.[265]

It would appear that much of the existing case law under s.20 of the MIA will continue to be relevant. For example, the division between representation as to fact and as to expectation or belief is retained. Materiality and inducement remain necessary pre-conditions to relief. One significant change is that the 2015 Act only requires a representation of fact to be substantially correct rather than true, which is a dilution of the test under s.20 of the MIA. A new statutory test is used to determine whether a representation is substantially correct by reference to the notional prudent insurer.[266] The test set out by the Court of Appeal in *Economides v Commercial Union Assurance Co Plc* for whether a representation as to a matter of expectation or belief was made in good faith has been put on a statutory footing.

6-063   **Remedies for breach of the duty of fair presentation.**   The single remedy under the MIA of avoidance for any breach of the duties in ss.17 to 20 has been reformed. In its place, the 2015 Act introduces a dual system of remedies. The first requirement is that the breach has induced the insurer to insure the risk on the terms that it did.[267] Inducement therefore remains an important concept under the new regime.

Under the dual system, the nature of the remedy depends on the nature of the breach, specifically whether or not the insured deliberately or recklessly breached

---

[263] Section 6(2) of the 2015 Act. See above, para.5-030.
[264] Sections 3(5)(b) and (c) and 5 of the 2015 Act.
[265] Section 3(3)(c) of the 2015 Act.
[266] Section 7(5) of the 2015 Act.
[267] Section 8(1) of the 2015 Act.

the duty of fair presentation. A breach will be deliberate or reckless if the insured knew that it was in breach of the duty of fair presentation or did not care whether or not it was in breach.[268] The burden of proof falls on the insurer.[269] Where the breach was deliberate or reckless, the insurer will be entitled to elect to avoid the policy and to retain the premium. In all other cases, the insured is entitled to a remedy to put it into the position it would have been if a fair presentation of risk had been made. Three situations arise. First, where the insurer would not have insured the risk at all if faced with a fair presentation, then the remedy of avoidance is still available subject to the insurer returning the policy.[270] Secondly, where the insurer would have insured the risk, but on different terms, then the policy will be treated as having been made on those terms.[271] Examples of such terms include exclusions, warranties and excesses. Thirdly, where the insurer would have insured the risk on the same terms but charged a higher premium, then the insurer may proportionately reduce the payment of the insured's claim. This remedy still favours the insured because the difference between the notional higher premium and the actual premium will likely be significantly smaller than any reduction to the payment of the insured's claim.

The reforms are intended to introduce a fairer system of remedies. One unwanted consequence may be increased litigation as parties argue about what the insurer hypothetically would have done if faced with a fair presentation, particularly in cases involving bespoke policies.

For a comprehensive discussion of the matters introduced above, see Ch.5.

---

[268] Section 8(5) of the 2015 Act.
[269] Section 8(6) of the 2015 Act.
[270] Paragraph 4 of Sch.1 to the 2015 Act.
[271] Paragraph 5 of Sch.1 to the 2015 Act.

INTERIM INSURANCE

1. PRELIMINARY

Introduction. It is almost always the case that there will be a period of time   **7-001**
between the submission of a proposal for insurance and a final decision by the
insurer to accept or reject that proposal. Absent any other mechanism, a proposer
would be without cover during that period. Many proposers, however, require some
form of cover to commence immediately upon proposal and to continue in force
until the proposal is accepted or rejected. This form of cover is often referred to as
interim or temporary insurance.[1]

Most of us are familiar with the concept of interim insurance in relation to mo-   **7-002**
tor, travel and home contents policies; but it is now commonplace for insurers and
Lloyd's underwriters to issue or authorise the issue of interim insurance across many
different types of policy.

Interim insurance is a binding contract of insurance that stands separate from any   **7-003**
subsequent policy issued. Its purpose is to provide immediate cover during the
period prior to a decision being made on the proposal and it is effective until either
a proposal is accepted, the period of cover lapses or notification is given that the

---

[1]   In the United States this type of insurance is called a "binder".

insurer has declined the proposal.[2] Agreements to provide interim insurance are usually evidenced in memoranda, commonly referred to as "cover notes".[3]

7-004   There is a surprising lack of English authority on interim insurance and our thinking is therefore guided by a number of authorities from the United States and Canada, and to a lesser extent from other common law jurisdictions. Furthermore, the interface between the interim insurance and the full policy has often been the subject of muddled thinking and many of the authorities in this area should be treated with caution.

2.   INTERIM INSURANCE

(a)   Relevance to the construction industry

7-005   **Interim insurance in the construction industry.**   The majority of project policies and main contractors' annual policies are underwritten following a presentation,[4] rather than a proposal. Further whilst some larger and more unusual policies are placed through the Lloyd's market, the majority are not.

7-006   In relation to project policies, the terms of cover will usually have been negotiated in advance of the commencement of works, in accordance with the requirements of the underlying construction contract. Evidence that such insurance is in place is usually a condition precedent to commencement and many funding arrangements. The policy will normally come into force upon the site being handed over to the contractor and, therefore, it is rare that interim insurance is required in relation to project policies. It arises more frequently in relation to lower value developments, particularly smaller residential developments, where policies are more frequently written following a proposal and are all too often arranged late in the day, thus requiring interim cover in order to preserve commencement dates.

7-007   In relation to the majority of larger contractors' annual policies, the key issue is renewal. Whilst at the inception of the initial policy, a presentation would usually be required, contractors' annual policies are often renewed on the basis of the existing terms of cover and against the background of a known and disclosed claims history. In those circumstances, there will often be no requirement for a contractor to make a further proposal or presentation even where the contractor proposes to change insurer. Smaller contractors and subcontractors are sometimes required to re-present or propose when changing insurer. In addition, some annual policies provide for interim cover in relation to individual contracts exceeding the policy limit, thereby allowing the insurer to assess the additional risk and pending agreement as to any enhanced premium.

---

[2]   *Citizens Insurance Co of Canada v Parsons; Queen Insurance Co v Parsons* (1881) 7 App. Cas. 96 at 124–125; (1881) 8 CRAC 406 at 440–441; (1881) 1 Cart BNA 265 at 298.

[3]   There is no prescribed format for a cover note. Cover may be agreed verbally or be included within other documents, such as receipts for policy premiums and renewal notices. In this chapter the description "cover note" is used to describe all contracts of interim insurance.

[4]   See above, para.4-053.

(b)   Nature of interim insurance

Interim insurance defined.   The defining feature of interim insurance is that it **7-008**
is a contract of insurance separate to any policy that might subsequently be written following acceptance of the proposal.[5] In *Stockton*,[6] Lord Diplock said:

> "The essential nature of the contract of interim insurance is that it is for a temporary period, gener-
> ally a maximum of 30 days or so, but is terminable by notice by the insurer at any time during that
> period."[7]

Interim insurance distinguished.   Interim insurance attracts its own premium[8] **7-009**
and is governed by its own terms (usually set out in the cover note); the terms of
the final contract of insurance are separate and will be governed by the policy itself.[9]
Claims made during the period of interim cover will be governed by the terms of
the interim insurance, even if the proposal is subsequently accepted and the main
policy written. Further, interim insurance will be effective during the period of
interim cover even if the underlying proposal is subsequently rejected by insurers,
or if no decision is made during the interim period to enter into a full policy.

Cover note does not normally bind the insurer to provide full cover.   A true **7-010**
contract of interim insurance will not bind the insurer to issue the full policy
proposed; rather the purpose of the interim insurance is to cover the proposer for a
finite period in order to allow the insurer to decide on the proposal. There is,
however, a group of Canadian cases illustrating the need for caution in settling the
terms of a cover note.[10] There is little doubt that, in those cases, the insurers' intention was to issue temporary cover notes of finite duration; however, in each case
the cover note was drafted so as to bind the insurer to provide the full cover unless
the insurer declined cover within a specified time.

In *Patterson*,[11] a cover note was issued by the insurer's agent in the following **7-011**
terms:

> "[Received of proposer the sum of $ ....], 'being the premium of insurance upon property for
> twelve months and for which a policy will be issued by the [insurers] within sixty days if approved
> by the manager in Toronto, otherwise, this receipt will be cancelled and the amount of unearned
> premium refunded,"

The agent failed to inform the Toronto manager and therefore no approval was
given. Nevertheless, the court held that the cover note bound the insurer until it was
rejected and that as it was not rejected within 60 days, the proposer was entitled to
12 months' cover.

---

5   *Neil v South-East Lancashire Insurance Co Ltd* 1932 S.C. 35; 1932 S.L.T. 29.
6   *Stockton v Mason* [1978] 2 Lloyd's Rep. 430; [1979] R.T.R. 130.
7   *Stockton* [1978] 2 Lloyd's Rep. 430 at 431; [1979] R.T.R. 130 at 133.
8   *Taylor v Allon* [1966] 1 Q.B. 304; [1965] 2 W.L.R. 598; [1965] 1 All E.R. 557. See below, paras
    7-032 to 7-034 for further discussion.
9   This distinction is of particular importance where the conditions of the main policy are more oner-
    ous than those of the interim insurance. For further discussion, see below, paras 7-059 to 7-070.
10 *Patterson v The Royal Insurance Co* (1867) 14 Gr. 169; *Hawke v Niagra District Mutual Fire Insur-
    ance Co* (1876) 23 Gr. 139; *Barnes v Dominion Grange Mutual Fire Insurance Association* (1895)
    22 OAR 68.
11 *Patterson* (1867) 14 Gr. 169.

7-012   Similarly in *Hawke*[12] the cover note issued by the insurer's agent read:

"Received from [proposer] the sum of $ ... , being the premium for an insurance ... for the term of one year as described in application; and also on the conditions only therein expressed, ... subject to the approval of the Board of Directors ... and to the clauses and conditions of the policy when issued. The said party and property to be considered insured until otherwise notified ... within one month from the date hereof, when, if declined, this receipt shall become void and be surrendered.

Note—Should applicant not receive a policy in conformity with his application within twenty days from the date hereof, he must communicate with the Secretary direct, as after one month from this date, the receipt becomes void."

Having heard nothing within 20 days, the proposer repeatedly contacted the agent, who informed him that delays were not unusual and issued further cover notes on the same terms. The agent never passed the risk to the insurer. The proposer made a claim for a loss suffered outside the first month. Insurers argued that there was no cover and that the agent had no authority to issue further cover notes. Proudfoot V.C. held that the subsequent cover notes were irrelevant because on a proper construction, the proposer was insured under the original cover note "until otherwise notified" and that the one-month time limit referred not to a period of separate interim cover but was instead the time in which the insurer could decline cover. In other words, the insurance was binding on the insurer for a year unless it chose to repudiate the risk within a month.

7-013   Finally in *Barnes*,[13] the court considered the following cover note in respect of a four-year policy of fire insurance. It read:

"Received from [proposer] ... the sum of $ ...., being the premium for an insurance to the extent of fifteen hundred dollars, on the property described in his application of this date numbered 16. Subject, however, to the approval of the board of directors, who shall have power to cancel this contract at any time within fifty days from this date, by causing a notice to that effect to be mailed to the applicant at [the specified address]. And it is hereby mutually agreed that until this receipt be followed by a policy within the said fifty days from this date, the contract of insurance shall wholly cease and determine, and all liability on the part of the association shall be at an end.

The non-receipt by the applicant of a policy within the time specified is to be taken with or without notice as absolute and incontrovertible evidence of the rejection of this contract of insurance by the said board of directors."

The proposer heard nothing within the 50 days. Around a month later, possibly due to a clerical error, the insurer sought payment of the premium. A notice that the policy had been rejected was posted the next day. The proposer's property was damaged by fire six days later. At first instance,[14] Falconbridge J dismissed the proposer's claim and declined to submit it to a jury; however, the proposer was able to persuade the court to direct a new trial. The insurers appealed that decision. On appeal, the court comprising of four judges was equally divided in opinion. Hagarty C.J.O. and Maclennan J.A. held that the cover note bound the insurer to provide four years' cover and that the fifty-day provision was merely an insurer's right of cancellation that had not been exercised; whilst Burton and Osler JJ.A. held that the cover note provided for only 50 days' cover and had come to an end due to the effluxion of time.

---

12   *Hawke v Niagra District Mutual Fire Insurance Co* (1876) 23 Gr. 139.
13   *Barnes* (1895) 22 OAR 68.
14   See *Barnes* (1895) 25 O.R. 100 at 104.

Retrospective cover. Interim insurance must also be distinguished from an of- **7-014**
fer for retrospective insurance, whereby the insurer agrees, in the event of accepting the proposal, to indemnify from a date earlier than the date of acceptance.[15] If
such insurance is written, there is no separate contract for insurance during the
proposal period; the main policy simply applies retrospectively. Furthermore, if the
insurer declines the proposal, the proposer is left uninsured for losses incurred during the proposal period.

In the event of a loss occurring during the proposal period, there is nothing to **7-015**
prevent the insurer electing to underwrite the insurance in any event. Such a policy
is referred to as an agreement to insure "lost or not lost" and the policy terms should
make clear that the policy is intended to indemnify the insured against past losses.[16]
Furthermore, if both the insured and the insurer are unaware of the loss during the
proposal period, the policy can still be accepted and the insurer bound to indemnify
retrospectively.[17] It seems clear, however, that the proposer remains bound by the
duty of utmost good faith and is required to disclose any loss occurring during the
proposal period.[18] Underwriters deciding whether to accept the proposal will, of
course, take this into account. Thus an offer for retrospective insurance leaves the
proposer in a much less secure position.

The mere fact that proposed cover is retrospective does not prevent the insurer **7-016**
from offering interim insurance. In *Re Coleman's Depositories Ltd and Life &
Health Assurance Association's Arbitration*[19] the insurer issued a cover note pending its decision, despite the fact that the policy sought was to be retrospective to the
date of the proposal.[20]

Cover notes distinguished from other instruments. Cover notes can be **7-017**
described in many ways. Terms such as "Receipt",[21] "Agent's Provisional
Receipt",[22] "Memorandum of Deposit"[23] and "Protection Note"[24] are commonplace.
It is also clear that specific nomenclature used by the insurer or an intermediary is
immaterial; the court will look to the substance of the document in order to
determine whether it is in fact a cover note. That said, there are a number of common instruments[25] used in the insurance industry, which should be distinguished
from cover notes.

Lloyd's slips.[26] When insurance is placed at Lloyd's, a broker will prepare a **7-018**
presentation document known as a "slip".[27] The slip will invariably describe the

---

[15] Usually—but not necessarily—the date of the proposal.
[16] There is no magic in the words "lost or not lost" and a policy can apply retrospectively provided
that clear words are used.
[17] *Mead v Davison* (1835) 3 Ad. & El. 303; 111 E.R. 428; *Bradford v Symondson* (1881) 7 Q.B.D 456.
[18] There is no authority on this point in relation to retrospective insurance; however, the general
principle applies as the duty of good faith is binding up to the conclusion of the insurance.
[19] *Re Coleman's Depositories Ltd and Life & Health Assurance Association's Arbitration* [1907] 2. K.B.
798; [1907] L.J.K.B. 865; [1904-7] All E.R. Rep. 383.
[20] *Coleman's Depositories Ltd* [1907] 2 K.B. 798; [1907] L.J.K.B. 865; [1904-7] All E.R. Rep. 383.
[21] *Hawke* (1876) 23 Gr. 139.
[22] *Patterson* (1867) 14 Gr. 169.
[23] *Mackie v The European Assurance Society* (1869) 17 W.R. 987; (1869) 21 L.T. 102.
[24] *Roberts v Security Co Ltd* [1897] 1 Q.B. 111.
[25] E.g. Lloyd's slips; broker's notes; Lloyd's cover-holders and receipts.
[26] See above, paras 4-064 to 4-067.
[27] It is possible for there to be agreement on Lloyd's insurance prior to the preparation of the slip and

proposer, the subject matter of the insurance, the financial and temporal limits of cover sought and the perils to be insured against. The slip will usually specify the terms on which cover is to be provided, whether by reference to Lloyd's or other standard terms. The slip is then taken to the market, usually to an established and respected underwriter in the relevant sector (the lead underwriter). If the terms of the slip are acceptable, the lead will stamp the slip on behalf of his syndicate and initial or sign the slip; he will also indicate the percentage or financial limit of the risk, which the underwriter accepts; this is known as "scratching" the slip. The slip will then be circulated to underwriters in the market (known as the following market) who will also scratch the slip for their portion until the required level of subscription has been obtained.

7-019 Whilst a slip may be superseded by a formal policy document, the slip is not a form of interim insurance. The slip is an offer, which the underwriter accepts when he scratches the slip. A slip creates a series of individual contracts of insurance with each scratch binding the underwriter to his portion for the full period of insurance,[28] regardless of whether a formal policy is later issued.[29]

7-020 **Brokers' notes.** Often, once the subscription has been taken up, a broker will issue a memorandum to the insured describing the level of cover obtained and the identities and portions of the lead insurer and following market. Unhelpfully, this document is often referred to as a "cover note" or "broker's slip". A broker's note in this context is not a cover note and has no relevance to the incidence of temporary cover, nor is it a slip.

7-021 **Lloyd's cover-holders.** Lloyd's "cover-holders" have been given authority by underwriters representing various syndicates to issue cover notes for interim insurance. As such, cover-holders' notes are evidence of a binding contract of interim insurance.[30] The evolution of Lloyd's cover-holders was intended to apply to motor insurance in order to allow Lloyd's to offer interim insurance in the same

---

circulation to the market (see for example *Assicuriazioni Generali SpA v Arab Insurance Group (BSC)* [2002] EWCA Civ 1642; [2003] 1 W.L.R. 577; [2003] 1 All E.R. (Comm) 140) but such situations are rare.

28 Care must be taken when examining older authorities on the status of the slip. Some cases suggest that the slip is a form of temporary insurance to take effect pending the issue of a policy: *Thompson v Adams* (1889) 23 Q.B.D. 361; *Grover & Grover Ltd v Mathews* [1910] 2 K.B. 401. The position was clarified by the Court of Appeal in *General Reinsurance Corp v Forsakringsaktiebolaget Fennia Patria* [1983] Q.B. 856; [1983] 3 W.L.R. 318, where it was held that the slip itself is a binding contract of insurance. Further, the slip will be immediately binding unless expressed to be conditional: *Eagle Star Insurance Co Ltd v Spratt* [1971] 2 Lloyd's Rep. 116.

29 Where the slip is inconsistent with the policy, the insured may seek rectification of the policy to bring it in line with the slip: see for example *Eagle Star & British Dominions Insurance Co Ltd v Reiner* (1927) 27 Ll. L. Rep. 173. Whether the insurer is entitled to seek rectification is more problematic given the intervention of the Lloyd's Policy Signing Office (now called Xchanging Ins-sure Services) signing policies on behalf of the underwriters; see *Eagle Star Insurance Co Ltd* [1971] 2 Lloyd's Rep. 116. It is, however, clear that the slip can be used as an aid to construction of the subsequent policy: *HIH Casualty & General Insurance Ltd v New Hampshire Insurance Co* [2001] EWCA Civ 735; [2001] 2 All E.R. (Comm) 39; [2001] 2 Lloyd's Rep. 161; [2001] Lloyd's Rep. I.R. 596; *Standard Life Assurance Ltd v Oak Dedicated Ltd* [2008] EWHC 222 (Comm); [2008] 2 All E.R. (Comm) 916; [2008] Lloyd's Rep. I.R. 552; *Mopani Copper Mines Plc v Millennium Underwriting Ltd* [2008] EWHC 1331 (Comm); [2008] 2 All E.R. (Comm) 976; [2009] Lloyd's Rep. I.R. 158.

30 See *Praet (Julien) et Cie S/A v HG Poland Ltd* [1960] 1 Lloyd's Rep. 416.

way as other insurers. Accordingly, the use of cover-holders outside the motor insurance arena is not common.

Receipts.   When interim insurance is sought it is usual for the proposer to pay the premium or part of it together with the proposal. As a result, the cover note will often record receipt of that part of the proposal and cover notes have often been referred to as "receipts". Again, this terminology is unhelpful as a mere receipt of premium does not, without more, imply an agreement to insure.[31]

7-022

(c)   Formation of interim insurance

Formation of interim insurance.[32]   A contract of interim insurance is governed by the same rules as any other contract of insurance. Thus the normal rules of contract formation apply, as do the fundamental requirements of contracts of insurance. There are no prescribed formalities for contracts of interim insurance, although the insurer's offer is normally recorded in a cover note.

7-023

Offer.   It is usually obvious if an insurer is offering interim insurance as it will normally have been requested and the terms of the offer will usually be clear, particularly if it is recorded in a cover note. Ultimately, however, the effect of an insurer's offer is a matter of construction. In *Patterson*,[33] a proposer received a receipt for the premium, from the insurer's agent, entitled "Agent's Provisional Receipt".[34]

7-024

On its face, the receipt did not purport to provide interim insurance cover, rather it referred to receipt of the premium and the time in which an underwriting decision would be made. However, the words "unearned premium" clearly meant that some part of the premium would be earned during the interim period and would not be returned. This was construed as consistent with an intention to insure during the interim period. Further, the word "cancelled" was also consistent with an intention to insure. It was held that the true construction of the receipt was to evidence an agreement to provide interim insurance and was therefore held to be a cover note.

7-025

Acceptance.   The question of acceptance is somewhat more difficult. More often than not, acceptance of an offer of interim insurance will manifest itself by the insured carrying on activity in reliance on the existence of the cover. This conduct may or may not come to the attention of the insurer. In *Taylor*[35] for example, a motorist's insurance lapsed on 5 April 1964. Insurers sent a cover note starting on 6 April 1964 for a period of 15 days. That cover note was expressed as follows:

7-026

> "Temporary cover note. Insurance is hereby granted in terms of the policy referred to in this notice for a period of fifteen days commencing from and including the due date referred to in this notice, ... subject otherwise to the terms, exceptions and conditions of the said policy, and in accordance with the particulars of the certificate of motor insurance relating to the said policy up to the said due date, and provided that an insurance covering the aforesaid liability has not been effected with any other authorised insurer."

---

[31]   *Linford v Provincial Horse & Cattle Insurance Co* (1864) 34 Beav. 291; 55 E.R. 647.
[32]   For more detailed commentary on the formation of insurance policies generally see above, Ch.4.
[33]   *Patterson* (1867) 14 Gr. 169.
[34]   The text of the receipt is set out above at para.7-011.
[35]   *Taylor* [1966] 1 Q.B. 304; [1965] 2 W.L.R. 598; [1965] 1 All E.R. 557.

7-027   At some point, the motorist decided to obtain quotes from alternative insurers and he received a cover note from a new insurer due to commence on 16 April 1964. The motorist was stopped by the police on 15 April 1964 and was later found guilty of driving without a valid certificate of insurance.

7-028   It was held that a valid certificate of insurance could include a cover note provided that the cover note amounted to an enforceable contract of insurance. However, Parker CJ considered that the motorist had not accepted the offer of temporary cover for the following reasons: (i) he had not produced the cover note at first instance; (ii) he had not given evidence at his trial and had not therefore stated that he relied upon the interim cover; and (iii) when stopped by the police his evidence was that he had not realised that his insurance had ended. However, inconsistently, he accepted that he had been negotiating for new insurance.

7-029   The *Taylor* case has been cited as authority for the proposition that there is no reliance on a cover note if the insured, "having received an offer of cover, seeks insurance elsewhere".[36] However, the decision must be treated with caution. It cannot be the case that whenever a party seeks alternative quotes, he has rejected an offer of interim insurance. It is easy to envisage circumstances where a proposer, who has found satisfactory cover and obtained interim insurance pending approval, nevertheless seeks further quotes in order to get a better deal, all the time relying on the existence of the interim cover. Thus negotiation with a second insurer may not automatically result in the rejection of an offer of interim insurance.[37]

(d)   Construction of the cover note

7-030   **Evidence admissible on construction.**   Some cover notes are issued together with full written terms and conditions setting out the rights and obligations of the parties. Such cover notes are rare but where they do exist and it can truly be said that the agreement for interim insurance has been reduced to writing, the normal rules of construction apply and evidence of negotiations or oral agreements will be inadmissible as aids to the construction of the written document.[38]

7-031   The majority of cover notes, however, do not express the full terms of the interim insurance; rather a cover note is a memorandum outlining the agreement to provide interim cover. They are often issued after or at the same time as an oral agreement to provide interim cover has been concluded. In such circumstances the parol evidence rule does not apply and parties are entitled to adduce evidence of precontractual negotiations in order to establish that the cover note is not a true or complete reflection of the agreement that was in fact reached.

(e)   Consideration

7-032   **Consideration and premium.**   It has been suggested that there is often difficulty in identifying the consideration passing from the proposer in situations of interim insurance. A cover note will usually record that the proposer has tendered

---

[36] See *Colinvaux's Law of Insurance*, edited by R. Merkin, 10th edn (London: Sweet & Maxwell, 2014), para.1-048.

[37] *Mackie* (1869) 17 W.R. 987; (1869) 21 L.T. 102. See also *Survey Research Co Ltd v Sentry Insurance Co Ltd*, Unreported 9 December 1985 Supreme Court of Hong Kong High Court but available on Westlaw [1986] HKEC 11.

[38] For more detailed commentary on the rules of construction, see below, Ch.13.

the first premium or the first instalment of the premium. The majority of cover notes provide that if the policy is declined, the insurer will return the premium less the premium for the interim period. It must therefore be the case that the premium payable by the proposer includes an element intended to cover the interim period; it is this element of the premium that amounts to the proposer's consideration for the interim insurance. In *Henry v The Agricultural Mutual Assurance Association*,[39] the proposer provided the insurer's agent with a promissory note, which could be called on by the insurer on demand in such proportions as might be required to cover either the period of the policy or the period of any interim cover.

In the *Taylor* case[40] however, the court considered that even if the premium has **7-033** not been paid at the date of the cover note, acceptance of the interim insurance provided by the cover note carries with it the implied promise, by the insured, to pay the premium either for the policy if issued or at least for the period of interimcover if the proposal is declined.[41] The theory of implied promise has support in the United States where authorities have determined that in the absence of any agreement, the premium for interim cover can be determined on the basis of a reasonable premium based on the market and the circumstances of the case.[42]

Alternatively, it has been suggested that the proposer's consideration for the cover **7-034** note is his making an application to that particular insurer for the full cover sought.[43] Whilst Colinvaux suggests that this analysis is rather artificial, it is not clear why that is the case. Insurers only offer interim insurance to those who apply for insurance with them. The business case for such arrangements is easily seen; the insurer gains time to investigate the proposal and increases the insurer's prospects of securing that business, whilst also retaining the option to decline full cover on unattractive proposals. Ultimately, the concept of consideration flowing from the application might assist the court in rare cases where the implied promise argument may not succeed.

3. UTMOST GOOD FAITH AND INTERIM INSURANCE

The duty of utmost good faith. Despite the fact that there is no English author- **7-035** ity as to whether the insured owes a duty of utmost good faith prior to the inception of interim insurance, it is considered that the duty does apply. That conclusion flows simply from the fact that a contract for interim insurance is nevertheless a contract of insurance and such contracts are contracts of utmost good faith.[44] The potential difficulty in applying such reasoning to interim insurance is clear if one considers the seminal words of Lord Mansfield in *Carter v Boehm*[45]:

"Insurance is a contract upon speculation. The special facts, upon which the contingent chance is to be computed, lie most commonly in the knowledge of the *insured* only; the under-writer trusts to his representation, and proceeds upon confidence that he does not keep back any circumstance in his knowledge, to mislead the under-writer into a belief that the circumstance does not exist, and to

---

[39] *Henry v The Agricultural Mutual Assurance Association* (1865) 11 Gr. 125.
[40] *Taylor* [1966] 1 Q.B. 304; [1965] 2 W.L.R. 598; [1965] 1 All E.R. 557. See above, paras 7-026 to 7-029.
[41] *Taylor* [1966] 1 Q.B. 304 at 311; [1965] 2 W.L.R. 598 at 603; [1965] 1 All E.R. 557 at 559.
[42] See *Preferred Risk Fire Insurance Co v Neet* 262 Ky. 257 (Ky. Dec 17, 1935), 90 SW 2d 39 (Ky. Dec 17, 1935); *Cummings v New England Insurance Co* 266 F 2d 888 (5 Cir, 1959).
[43] *Colinvaux's Law of Insurance*, edited by R. Merkin, (2014), para.1-084.
[44] For detailed commentary on the duty of utmost good faith and disclosure see above, Ch.6.
[45] *Carter v Boehm* (1766) 3 Burr. 1905; 97 E.R. 1162.

induce him to estimate the risque, as if it did not exist ... Good faith forbids either party by conceal-ing what he privately knows, to draw the other into a bargain, from his ignorance of that fact and his believing the contrary ... The question must therefore always be whether there was, under all the circumstances at the time the policy was under-written, a *fair representation; or a concealment*; fraudulent, if *designed*; or, though not designed, *varying materially the object* of the policy and *changing the risque* understood to be run."[46]

7-036   In interim insurance, the underwriter rarely undertakes a computation of the risk in the manner envisaged by Lord Mansfield; rather the point of interim insurance is to allow the insurer time to consider the proposal in order to undertake the computation of the risk. The practical reality of interim insurance is that insurers have many years of experience of certain markets and have satisfied themselves that the benefits of taking time to consider a proposal and the benefits of offering interim insurance to the marketplace outweigh the risk of a loss occurring during the interim period. They are therefore willing to provide such cover without any detailed consideration of a proposal and without carrying out the same enquiries that are inherent in making the main underwriting decision.

7-037   In the vast majority of cases therefore, the insurer will not have considered the proposal at the point that the cover note is issued; in fact, the proposer may not even have submitted the proposal at the date the cover note is issued. Cover is often confirmed by insurers and their intermediaries orally by telephone and the proposer is not asked to recount all information that will be included on the proposal form and often has little opportunity to do so.[47] Furthermore, it is possible to question how failure to disclose certain information can be considered "material" in circumstances where the underwriter is prepared to offer cover without considera-tion of any information.

7-038   **The duty to disclose.**   Notwithstanding the above, two leading authorities at present suggest that a proposer is under the full duty of utmost good faith for the purposes of interim cover as he is for the full policy. In *Mayne Nickless Ltd*,[48] the proposer purchased a car from a garage; the garage contacted insurers and ar-ranged for interim cover. A cover note was issued on 3 June 1968. That cover note was said to be provided subject to receipt of a "satisfactory" proposal by the insurer. On 4 June 1968, the proposer's wife completed a proposal form, in which she failed to disclose the fact that the proposer had been involved in an accident earlier that year. On 5 June 1968, the proposer was involved in a car accident and suffered injuries from which he died.

7-039   The court held that the cover note was subject to an unfulfilled condition precedent and that cover had never been engaged.[49] The court went on however, to consider, obiter, the issue of good faith. The court concluded that, despite the fact that a proposal form may not have been completed nor any questions raised, a contract of interim insurance is nevertheless a contract of insurance and the insured is under the same duty of good faith as any other insured; in other words there is a duty to disclose all facts that a reasonable prudent insurer would take into account in fixing the premium or determining whether to accept the risk. Consequently, the

---

[46]   *Carter* (1766) 3 Burr. 1905 at [1909]-[1911]; 97 E.R. 1162 at 1164–1165 (emphasis added).
[47]   It would be absurd if the proposer was required to recount the full contents of the proposal in order for the insurer to decide whether to provide interim cover or not; such an approach would defeat the whole object of interim cover.
[48]   *Mayne Nickless Ltd v Pegler* [1974] 1 NSWLR 228.
[49]   This aspect of the decision is discussed below at para.7-045.

court held that the cover note would have been voidable on the basis of material non-disclosure.

In *Marene Knitting Mills Pty*,[50] the Privy Council considered a case where a cover note was issued for fire on 14 August 1973, following a conversation between the insurer and the proposer's broker but prior to any proposal being completed. A fire erupted on 15 August 1973, causing damage. For reasons that are not entirely clear, the insurer continued to require the proposer to complete proposal forms and those proposals were completed on 4 September 1973. The proposal forms did not mention, (despite the fact that the proposer was aware of this fact) that the business had experienced two fires in the previous 10 years and the same was not disclosed to the insurer prior to the cover note being issued. **7-040**

At first instance, Yeldham J[51] applied *Mayne Nickless Ltd*[52] and held that the failure to mention the previous fires was a failure to disclose material facts. Lord Fraser, giving the judgment of the Privy Council agreed.[53] Unfortunately the Privy Council did not consider whether it was appropriate to hold an interim insured to the same standards of disclosure as an insured; instead Lord Fraser simply subscribed to the view that the duty of disclosure summarised in *Mayne Nickless Ltd* was **7-041**

"substantially in accordance with that which has been applied in many previous cases and their Lordships are satisfied that it was the appropriate test for the present case."[54]

Those cases therefore suggest that the proposer is under a full duty to disclose all material facts, prior to the grant of interim insurance, even if the cover note is issued before any enquiries have been undertaken or any information sought from the proposer. With respect to the learned judges in those cases, it is suggested that they have conflated the factors to be taken into account when granting interim cover with those that are material to underwriting decision of the main policy. For the reasons set out above, it is suggested that such thinking is unsound, in that the insurer usually authorises the grant of interim insurance before considering the proposal and often before the proposal has been completed. The proposal itself contains material information relevant to the underwriting decision but the insurer nevertheless elects to issue interim insurance without regard to that information. **7-042**

If a full duty of good faith is deemed to apply to contracts of interim insurance, that requirement may substantially deprive cover notes of any purpose. It places an almost insurmountable burden on proposers, namely: to envisage and disclose any and all material facts that might have a bearing on the insurer's underwriting decision (which may include answers to questions on a proposal form they have not completed and may not even have seen). The proposer who obtains a cover note following a brief telephone conversation with the insurer or his intermediary clearly illustrates the absurdity of that position. Such an approach might allow insurers to avoid cover in a huge number of cases thus rendering cover notes valueless. **7-043**

Finally, it is useful to consider the case of *Neil*,[55] in which a proposal form was **7-044**

[50] *Marene Knitting Mills Pty v Greater Pacific General Insurance* [1976] 11 A.L.R. 167; [1976] 2 Lloyd's Rep. 631.
[51] See *Marene Knitting Mills Pty* [1976] 11 A.L.R. 167; [1976] 2 Lloyd's Rep. 637–639.
[52] *Mayne Nickless Ltd* [1974] 1 NSWLR 228.
[53] *Marene Knitting Mills Pty* [1976] 11 A.L.R. 167; [1976] 2 Lloyd's Rep. 631.
[54] *Marene Knitting Mills Pty* [1976] 11 A.L.R. 167 at 172; [1976] 2 Lloyd's Rep. 631 at 642.
[55] *Neil* 1932 S.C. 35; 1932 S.L.T. 29.

completed nine days after a cover note had been issued. It transpired that an answer on that proposal form was incorrect. The central issue in the case was not whether the interim cover could be avoided for failure to disclose but instead whether the cover note incorporated the warranties contained in the proposal form.[56] On this point Lord Mackay said:

> "[O]n principle I fail to see how such an interim protection can in accordance with either equity or justice be avoided because of something which happened later. This is all the more clear when that something is not a fraud on the insurance company or a dishonest concealment, but is ... a very innocent inaccuracy. That question had not been asked in writing at the date when the risk accrued. ... the cover note would have been good for this risk even though no policy had resulted, it would seem ridiculous that it should be bad for this risk because in point of fact an apparent policy resulted which was itself void on account of an inaccuracy occurring in the interim period."[57]

7-045   An alternative approach, not considered in the authorities to date, is that the insurer should take the risk of issuing interim insurance if it chooses to grant cover notes without making any enquiries. Given that the proposal form seeks to elicit the information that the insurer considers to be material to underwriting that type of risk, it is at least arguable that if the insurer grants cover without regard to that proposal, it has waived the requirement to disclose that information for the purposes of the interim cover. It is suggested that in the absence of fraud or misleading information requested of him and provided specifically in advance of and in relation to the interim cover, an insured should not be liable for failing to disclose any further information.[58] Nevertheless, until the courts determine these particular issues, the current position must be that the full test of good faith remains the relevant standard in respect of the duty to disclose for the purposes of interim cover.

7-046   Due to the introduction of the Insurance Act 2015 ("the 2015 Act"), the duty of the proposer is now to make a fair presentation of the risk before obtaining interim insurance rather than to comply with the disclosure duties enshrined in ss.17–20 of the MIA.[59] It is suggested that the introduction of the 2015 Act is likely to have little impact on the proposer's disclosure duties prior to obtaining interim insurance, as the application of the new provisions would lead to the same conceptual difficulties faced when applying the disclosure provisions of the MIA to interim cover.

4. CONDITIONS PRECEDENT

7-047   **Conditions precedent.**   As with any form of insurance, a cover note may be expressed so as to render the provision of interim insurance conditional. In *Mayne Nickless Ltd*[60] a cover note was expressed to be "[s]ubject to the conditions of this Company's ... [standard policy terms] and a satisfactory proposal for your insurance." It was held that this was a condition precedent to the provision of

---

[56] Due to the introduction of the Insurance Act 2015 this issue no longer arises as s.9 of the 2015 Act abolishes "basis of contract" clauses and prevents representations made by a non-consumer insured from being converted into warranties by the operation of any other provision of a policy. See further above, para.5-092.

[57] *Neil* 1932 S.C. 35 at 38; 1932 S.L.T. 29 at 31.

[58] For a case where a cover note was avoided on the grounds that it had been obtained by fraud and misrepresentation, see *General Accident Fire and Life Assurance Corp Ltd v Shuttleworth* (1938) 60 Ll. L. Rep. 301.

[59] See above, paras 5-005 to 5-089.

[60] *Mayne Nickless Ltd* [1974] 1 NSWLR 228.

interim cover and that the provision of a proposal containing inaccurate information was not "satisfactory" and that therefore cover was not engaged.[61]

Whilst *Mayne Nickless Ltd* stands as authority for the proposition that interim insurance can be granted conditionally, the courts will generally seek to construe interim contracts so as to avoid that conclusion. In *Goodfellow*,[62] a cover note stated:　　**7-048**

"[Agents] [r]eceived from [proposer], the sum of $14 being the premium for an insurance ... on property described in the order of this date, *subject to the approval of the board at Kingston*, the said party to be considered insured for twenty-one days from the above date, within which time the determination of the board will be notified."

The court construed the words "subject to the approval of the board at Kingston" as applying to the main policy only; the interim cover was not conditional but could be brought to an end by notice of the board's decision within the 21 days. The rationale for this approach is obvious. The purpose of interim insurance is to provide immediate cover pending approval of the proposal; if interim cover is commonly held to be conditional, it would often render the cover worthless.　　**7-049**

5. AUTHORITY

Authority to issue cover notes. It is almost invariably the case that the insurer is the party who accepts or declines a proposal for insurance.[63] However, authority to grant interim insurance is often vested in insurance intermediaries acting as agent for the insurer. In such cases, the normal rules of agency apply[64] and the insurer will be bound by the actions of an agent acting within the scope of his actual or apparent authority.　　**7-050**

In relation to brokers, the general position is that a broker appointed by the proposer acts on behalf of the proposer. However, many brokers are also authorised to act as intermediaries by insurers. It is well established that, provided the principals consent and there is no conflict of interests between them, a broker may act with dual authority and may be permitted to issue interim cover notes on behalf of the insurer.[65]　　**7-051**

Actual authority. In many areas of insurance business, it is commonplace for intermediaries to be given express authority to bind insurers to contracts of interim　　**7-052**

---

[61] The decision in *Mayne Nickless Ltd* has been the subject of much criticism; see for example John Birds, "What is a cover note worth?" (1977) 40 (Jan) M.L.R. 79. The court does not appear to have considered the possibility that the cover note was in fact agreed orally by telephone and that the subsequent memorandum sought to introduce a new unenforceable condition (see *Re Coleman's Depositories Ltd* [1907] 2. K.B. 798; [1907] L.J.K.B. 865; [1904–7] All E.R. Rep. 383 and the commentary below at paras 7-065 to 7-070). Further the court seems to have made no attempt to construe the cover note contra proferentem, thereby going against the court's usual practice of seeking to construe interim cover as unconditional.

[62] *Goodfellow v The Times and Beacon Assurance Co* (1859) 17 U.C.R. 411.

[63] An agent does not normally have such authority, see *Linford* (1864) 34 Beav. 291; 55 E.R. 647; *Levy v Scottish Employers' Insurance Co* (1901) 17 T.L.R. 229.

[64] See above paras 4-055 to 4-063 and *MacGillivray on Insurance Law* edited by J. Birds, B. Lynch, S. Milnes, 13th edn (London: Sweet & Maxwell, 2015), paras 38–056 to 38–072; *Colinvaux's Law of Insurance*, edited by R. Merkin, (2014), paras 15-001 to 15-021; P. Watts and F.M.B. Reynolds, *Bowstead and Reynolds on Agency*, 20th edn (London: Sweet & Maxwell, 2014).

[65] *Stockton* [1978] 2 Lloyd's Rep. 430; [1979] R.T.R. 130.

insurance.[66] Furthermore, an agent will have implied actual authority to enter into such contracts on behalf of his principal as would usually be made by an agent in that role[67] unless there is some limitation on the agent's authority of which the proposer has notice.[68] When assessing what falls within the usual scope of an agent's duties, it is necessary to consider the customs of the particular insurance market in which the agent operates.[69]

7-053 **Apparent authority.**   If an intermediary does not have actual authority to issue cover notes, the insurer may, nevertheless, act in such a way as to hold out the intermediary as having apparent authority to conclude contracts of interim insurance on his behalf. In *Mackie*,[70] the fact that the insurer had provided the intermediary with blank cover notes was held to be sufficient.

7-054   In *Murfitt v Royal Insurance Co*[71] (a case concerning an alleged oral cover note) the court considered evidence that the insured was known to be an authorised agent of the insurer and had issued oral cover notes regularly for a period of years without objection from the insurer. In those circumstances, the court upheld the validity of the oral cover note and held that the particular facts of the case permitted a finding of apparent authority.

7-055   In *Dicks*,[72] Miller J considered the following statement, regarding who was deemed to have authority to issue interim insurance (as stated in the then current edition of Halsbury's Laws of England),[73] to be too wide. The relevant extract said:

"[T]he issue of such interim insurance falls within the authority of an insurance agent unless he is excluded, expressly or impliedly, by the terms of his authority from committing his principal in that way."[74]

He considered the nature of the holding out in *Mackie* and concluded that Mc-Cardie J had expressly qualified his judgment in *Murfitt* by referring to the special facts of that case. Against that background Miller J concluded that for an agent to have apparent authority to give oral cover notes there would have to be a holding out similar to that in *Mackie*, whether by the provision of blank cover notes or otherwise.

---

[66] That authority can extend to the instruction of sub-agents to carry out certain functions: see *Rossiter v The Trafalgar Life Assurance* (1859) 27 Beav. 377; 54 E.R. 148.

[67] *Hely-Hutchinson v Brayhead Ltd* [1968] 1 Q.B. 549 at 583; [1967] 3 W.L.R. 1408 at 1415–1416; [1967] 3 All E.R. 98 at 102, per Denning MR.

[68] In *Levy* (1901) 17 T.L.R. 229, the proposal made clear that "The proposed insurance shall not be binding on the Company until a policy shall be issued in respect thereof," thus the agent had no authority to represent that cover would commence immediately. See also *Henry* (1865) 11 Gr. 125, where similar representations by the agent were held to be ineffective as the cover note provided that the issue of a policy was "subject to approval of the Board of Directors".

[69] *Graves v Legg*; sub nom. *Greaves v Legg* (1857) 2 Hurl. & N. 210; 157 E.R. 88; *Dicks v South African Mutual Fire and General Insurance Co* (1963) 4 S.A. 501 (NPD) at 505. Previous decisions should be treated with caution, since what constitutes normal market practice will change over time.

[70] *Mackie* (1869) 17 W.R. 987; (1869) 21 L.T. 102.

[71] *Murfitt v Royal Insurance Co* (1922) 10 Ll. L. Rep. 191; (1922) 38 T.L.R. 334.

[72] *Dicks* (1963) 4 S.A. 501 (NPD) at 505.

[73] *Halsbury's Laws of England*, 3rd edn (London: Butterworth & Co (Publishers) Ltd, 1958), para.391.

[74] *Dicks* (1963) 4 S.A. 501 (NPD) at 505.

Brokers: a special case?   In Stockton,[75] Lord Diplock made the dramatic and   **7-056**
sweeping suggestion that

> "[a] broker in non-marine insurance has implied authority to issue on behalf of the insurer or enter
> into as agent for the insurer contracts of interim insurance, which are normally recorded in cover
> notes."[76]

It has been suggested that this is a radical departure from the usual rules in rela-   **7-057**
tion to intermediaries.[77] Further, as *Stockton*[78] purports to be a case of implied actual
authority, it suggests that it will always be within the function of non-marine brokers
to issue cover notes. However, Lord Diplock's judgment concerned the principles
of brokers' agency on behalf of the insurer and considered the tripartite nature of
the relationship between insurer, broker and insured. Whilst it is not at all clear from
the judgment, it is suggested that the broker's implied actual authority arises only
in relation to insurers for whom the broker is authorised to act as agent and in
contrast does not apply to all insurers with whom an insured's broker seeks to place
a policy.[79]

Further, while Lord Diplock's judgment suggests general market practice is for   **7-058**
insurers' brokers to be invariably authorised to issue cover notes, the position may
be different in relation to certain species of insurance, such as contractor's all risk
insurance, where interim insurance is not an invariable practise. It is suggested in
these circumstances a broker may not have implied actual authority to issue cover
notes.

6.   THE TERMS OF INTERIM COVER

Terms of interim cover.   One of the most fundamental issues when dealing with   **7-059**
interim insurance is to determine the terms of the insurance during the interim
period. If a written cover note is issued at all it will usually be a much less
comprehensive document than a full policy of insurance. It may or may not refer
to the proposal; it may or may not refer to the insurer's policy conditions.
Furthermore, having considered a proposal, the insurer may require special conditions when issuing the main policy. In terms of disputes, it is often crucial to
determine whether the insurer's provisions relating to claims notification are
incorporated into the interim insurance.

(a)   Incorporation of terms into cover note by reference

Incorporation by reference.   Insurers will often seek to ensure that any period   **7-060**
of interim insurance is governed by the insurer's standard terms for such policies.
It is well established that an insurer may incorporate such terms by reference[80] and

---

[75] *Stockton* [1978] 2 Lloyd's Rep. 430; [1979] R.T.R. 130.
[76] *Stockton* [1978] 2 Lloyd's Rep. 430 at 431; [1979] R.T.R. 130 at 133.
[77] *MacGillivray on Insurance Law*, edited by J. Birds, B. Lynch, S. Milnes (2015), para.4-026.
[78] *Stockton* [1978] 2 Lloyd's Rep. 430; [1979] R.T.R. 130.
[79] It is said that this decision reflects the general market practice whereby insurers' brokers are invariably authorised.
[80] See for example: *Citizens Insurance Co of Canada; Queen Insurance Co* (1881) 7 App. Cas. 96;
   (1881) 8 CRAC 406; (1881) 1 Cart BNA 265; *Taylor* [1966] 1 Q.B. 304; [1965] 2 W.L.R. 598;
   [1965] 1 All E.R. 557.

that terms may be incorporated via reference to a proposal form, which is itself subject to the insurer's usual terms and conditions.[81]

7-061   In *Wyndham Rather Ltd*,[82] a cover note against fire damage was expressed to be subject to a proposal form; the proposal form was expressed to be subject to the usual conditions of the company's policy. The issue was whether an agreement to arbitrate, contained in the terms and conditions, was incorporated into the cover note. Atkin J held:

> "The cover note is subject to the usual terms of the company's policy, and as one of those terms is an arbitration clause the [cover note] ... is, to my mind a contract which contains a submission to arbitration."[83]

Sargant LJ added:

> "[I]t cannot be properly supposed that the insurers are giving the assured in that interval a protection upon greater or other conditions than those which are to be embodied in the ultimate policy."[84]

One of the issues, however, in the *Wyndham Rather Ltd* case, which was not considered in the judgment on appeal, was the fact that after the proposal the insurer carried out a survey of the premises and required the insured to take additional precautions. At first instance it was held that the additional requirement was a condition precedent to the main policy but was not incorporated into the cover note.[85]

7-062   The case of *Stockton*[86] concerned the transfer of a motor vehicle policy. The insured held insurance himself and for named drivers for one vehicle; he then contacted brokers to transfer that insurance to another vehicle. An oral cover note was granted but 10 days later insurers issued a notice that further information was required in relation to the named drivers and that in the meantime only the insured would be covered. The court held that the cover note was made at the time of the telephone call and did not incorporate the qualification later required.[87]

7-063   In the case of *Neil*,[88] insurers sought to avoid a cover note on the basis of incorrect answers given in the proposal. The proposal post-dated the cover note but was expressed to be "subject to the usual terms and conditions of the Company's policy". Insurers argued that this provision enabled them to avoid cover on the basis of answers in the proposal, which would have become incorporated into their policy. Clerk LJ gave this argument short shrift and held:

> "[I]f that was intended or desired by the [insurer], a more clumsy and ... more ineffective way of bringing about that result it is impossible to conceive ... But the language is general, not particular. The reference is not to a special policy and its contents, but to the [insurer's] general form of policy. In that general form of policy one finds a variety of conditions set forth, which sufficiently satisfy the words in the cover note ... It is more reasonable, in my view, and more consonant with the limit-

---

[81] *Wyndham Rather Ltd v Eagle Star & British Dominions Insurance Co Ltd* (1925) 21 Ll. L. Rep. 214; *Hawke* (1876) 23 Gr. 139, 147–148.

[82] *Wyndham Rather Ltd* (1925) 21 Ll. L. Rep. 214.

[83] *Wyndham Rather Ltd* (1925) 21 Ll. L. Rep. 214 at 215.

[84] *Wyndham Rather Ltd* (1925) 21 Ll. L. Rep. 214 at 215.

[85] *Wyndham Rather Ltd* (1925) 21 Ll. L. Rep. 214 at 215.

[86] *Stockton* [1978] 2 Lloyd's Rep. 430; [1979] R.T.R. 130.

[87] *Stockton* [1978] 2 Lloyd's Rep. 430; [1979] R.T.R. 130. The case illustrates the importance of identifying when a contract of interim insurance is formed. Further it also confirms the fact that cover notes can be made in the most informal language. In the case, the words "Yes that will be alright. We will see to that" from the broker were held to be sufficient to provide interim cover following the request to transfer the insurance to another.

[88] *Neil* 1932 S.C. 35; 1932 S.L.T. 29.

ing words contained in the cover note, to hold that they refer to these existing conditions than to hold that they refer to an event which had not then taken place, and to a document that was not then in existence."[89]

(b) No express reference to terms and conditions in the cover note

No express reference. When there is no express reference to terms and condi-   **7-064**
tions in the cover note, there is a tension between the general rule that a proposer
is deemed to apply for insurance on the insurer's standard terms[90] and the fact that
those terms may never have been brought to his attention. In *Hawke*,[91] Proudfoot
VC suggested that a cover note should be held to incorporate the ordinary conditions of the policy and said:

> "[I]t is proper that it should be so on the plain principles of justice. It would be unreasonable to hold
> that by giving such a receipt the company meant to insure a larger liability than they were subject to
> on a policy; they must be understood as contracting for an insurance of the ordinary kind. The plaintiff
> asks for the completion of the contract by the issuing of a policy, and he does not pretend that he is
> entitled to any other than the ordinary policy: he cannot therefore be in any better condition than if
> he had the policy in his possession."[92]

Proudfoot V.C. also cited the American case of *The Eureka Insurance Co*[93] where
Strong J held that

> "[t]here having been no policy issued, and nothing more than the memorandum above quoted ... the
> contract is to be regarded as made upon the terms and subject to the conditions contained in the
> ordinary form of policies used by the company at the time."[94]

An alternative approach has, however, been voiced in two cases, which are not   **7-065**
easy to follow and do not make clear why they appear to depart from the general
rule. In *Re Coleman's Depositories Ltd*,[95] a proposer completed a proposal form on
28 December 1904 and received a cover note the same day. The cover note did not
refer to any conditions. An accident occurred on 2 January 1905. On 3 January 1905
insurers sealed a policy (which was expressed to be in force from 1 January 1905)
and on 9 January 1905 the proposer received the policy document. The proposer
did not notify the accident until 14 March 1905; insurers sought to deny cover on
the basis that the policy contained an immediate notification provision.

An unusual feature of the case is that, for some reason, the claim was brought   **7-066**
under the policy rather than the cover note. Such a claim should have been doomed
to fail as the policy had not been issued and, although expressed to be retrospective, was not of the "lost or not lost" variety.[96] Furthermore, the proposer's claim

---

[89] *Neil* 1932 S.C. 35 at 41, 1932 S.L.T. 29 at 33. A similar sentiment was expressed in *Symington &
Co v Union Insurance Society of Canton Ltd* (1928) 32 Ll. L. Rep. 287 which, although concerned
with slips rather than cover notes, held that the principle of implied incorporation did not extend to
a marginal condition in the insurer's standard policy wording limiting the scope of cover in a manner that was not usual for policies of this type.

[90] *General Accident Insurance Corp v Cronk* (1901) 17 T.L.R. 233; (1901) 45 Sol. Jo. 261.

[91] *Hawke* (1876) 23 Gr. 139.

[92] *Hawke* (1876) 23 Gr. 139 at 148.

[93] *Eureka Insurance Co v Robinson Rea & Co* 56 Pa 256 (Sup. Ct. 1867); 94 Am. Dec. 65 (1867); 6.
P.F. Smith 256 (Pa. 1867).

[94] *Eureka Insurance Co* 56 Pa 256 at 264 (1867).

[95] *Re Coleman's Depositories Ltd* [1907] 2 K.B. 798; [1907] L.J.K.B. 865; [1904–7] All E.R. Rep. 383.

[96] *Re Coleman's Depositories Ltd* [1907] 2.K.B. 798 at 810–811; [1907] L.J.K.B. 865 at 871–873;
[1904–7] All E.R. Rep. 383 at 388–389. A point made robustly in the dissenting judgment of Fletcher

was brought under the policy and had initially been referred to arbitration by the proposer in reliance on the arbitration provisions of the policy; it is unattractive, then, for the proposer to argue that it was not bound by the notification provisions of the policy. The majority of the Court of Appeal disagreed[97] and held that in the absence of any evidence that the proposer knew of, or had the opportunity of knowing of, the existence of the condition at the date of the accident, then either: (i) the condition was not incorporated[98]; or (ii) it was impossible to perform.[99]

7-067   Whilst one may sympathise with the proposer in the case *Re Coleman's Depositories Ltd*,[100] the rationale underlying the majority judgment is not easy to understand. The court did not refer to the *General Accident Insurance Corp* case,[101] nor did it consider the general rule that a proposer is deemed to apply for insurance on the insurer's standard terms. Further, Fletcher Moulton LJ gave little credence to the impossibility argument saying:

> "[I] see nothing to prevent an adequate performance of the conditions precedent at the date when, so far as the Court is aware, the policy might have been obtained by the employer if he had chosen to ask for it."[102]

7-068   The decision in *Re Coleman's Depositories Ltd*[103] cannot extend to the insurer's standard terms relating to the scope of cover; the weight of authorities already discussed shows that insurers are not required to give greater protection on the interim cover than they would provide under the standard terms of their main policy. Perhaps, then, the rationale of this case is that because the proposer knows the limits of the cover that he is applying for but does not know the conditions that the insurer will require in order to provide that cover, the court should intervene to offer protection. If that is indeed the rationale, then the legal basis for it has not been explained in the authorities.

7-069   The decision in *Re Coleman's Depositories Ltd* was followed in the Scottish case *Parker & Co (Sandbank) Ltd*.[104] The case concerned an oral cover note. The reasoning adopted by the court was that the oral cover note was subject to no conditions but if the insurers had delivered a cover note referring to conditions then they would take effect from the point of delivery. The reasoning is not easy to explain; if the court accepted that a contract of insurance had been concluded orally with no conditions, it is unclear how post-contract unilateral notice of additional conditions would suffice to incorporate them. Again, the case did not address the general rule.

7-070   Whilst the decision in *Re Coleman's Depositories Ltd*[105] has never been expressly overruled, it is suggested that if the issue were reconsidered by the Court of Appeal, the decision may not stand. In practical terms, however, the majority of cover

---

Moulton LJ. See above para.7-016.
97   Per Vaughan Williams and Buckley LJJ.
98   *Re Coleman's Depositories Ltd* [1907] 2 K.B. 798 at 804, per Vaughan Williams LJ; [1907] L.J.K.B. 865 at 869; [1904–7] All E.R. Rep. 383 at 385.
99   *Re Coleman's Depositories Ltd* [1907] 2 K.B. 798 at 812, per Buckley L.J; [1907] L.J.K.B. 865 at 873; [1904–7] All E.R. Rep. 383 at 389.
100 *Re Coleman's Depositories Ltd* [1907] 2 K.B. 798; [1907] L.J.K.B. 865; [1904–7] All E.R. Rep. 383.
101 *General Accident Insurance Corp* (1901) 17 T.L.R. 233; (1901) 45 Sol. Jo. 261.
102 *Re Coleman's Depositories Ltd* [1907] 2 K.B. 798 at 811; [1907] L.J.K.B. 865 at 872; [1904–7] All E.R. Rep. 383 at 389.
103 *Re Coleman's Depositories Ltd* [1907] 2 K.B. 798; [1907] L.J.K.B. 865; [1904–7] All E.R. Rep. 383.
104 *Parker & Co (Sandbank) Ltd v Western Insurance Co* (1925) 21 Ll. L. Rep. 52; 1925 S.L.T. 131 at 134, per Lord Constable.
105 *Re Coleman's Depositories Ltd* [1907] 2 K.B. 798; [1907] L.J.K.B. 865; [1904–7] All E.R. Rep. 383.

notes make clear that policy terms are incorporated and thus they will be deemed to apply regardless of whether the proposer has seen them or had an opportunity to consider them.[106] Furthermore, it is suggested that the advent of the internet may render the case of *Re Coleman's Depositories Ltd* redundant. Both Buckley and Vaughan Williams LJJ referred to the fact that the proposer had no way of knowing the terms of the insurer's standard policy; the position in 1907 may be considered to be different from today, where conditions are usually available on the internet and thus are readily accessible to the vast majority of people.

7. DURATION OF INTERIM COVER

Duration of interim cover.   Interim insurance is almost always provided for a set period of days or weeks or linked to a specific event, usually the issue of the main policy or the rejection of the proposal. It will be rare that an agreement to provide interim insurance will not include an express agreement as to duration. In the absence of an express provision, it is suggested that the court may imply a term that the cover will subsist for a reasonable time. A Californian case suggests that a reasonable duration of interim insurance will be until the proposal is accepted or rejected.[107]   **7-071**

Once the specified period has expired, cover lapses unless the cover note is worded so as to compel cover until notification.[108] It is important to construe cover notes carefully in order to determine when cover in fact lapses. For example in the *Cartwright* case,[109] a 15-day cover note recorded the date and time of issue as 11.45 on 2 December 1959. The proposer was involved in an accident at 17.45 on 17 December 1959. The cover note contained the following provisions: **7-072**

"This cover note is only valid for 15 days from the commencement date of risk."

"Under no circumstances is the time and date of commencement of risk to be prior to the actual time of issue of this cover note."

"In any event the duration of this cover note shall not be more than FIFTEEN DAYS from the date of commencement of insurance stated herein."

Both of the clauses specifying the duration of the cover referred only to the date of the cover whereas only the clause referring to the commencement of risk referred to the time. Accordingly, the court construed the duration by reference to date alone and, by the normal rules for the computation of time, the cover was held to be effective for 15 days from midnight on 2 December 1959.

8. TERMINATION BY THE INSURER

Termination by the insurer.   The insurer is entitled to terminate the contract of interim insurance at any time during the period of interim cover if it has reserved   **7-073**

---

[106] *McQueen v The Phoenix Mutual Fire Insurance Co* (1879) 29 UCCP 511 at 521, per Wilson CJ.
[107] *Parlier Fruit Co v Fireman's Fund Insurance Co* 151 Cal.App.2d 6 (May 15, 1957); 311 P 2d 62 (May 15, 1957).
[108] *Patterson* (1867) 14 Gr. 169; *Hawke* (1876) 23 Gr. 139.
[109] *Cartwright v MacCormack* [1963] 1 W.L.R. 18; [1963] 1 All E.R. 11; [1962] 2 Lloyd's Rep. 328.

that right.[110] If that right has not been reserved, it is debateable whether the insurer may terminate before the expiry of the interim cover.[111]

7-074   In order to terminate interim insurance, notice of revocation must be given to the proposer or an agent authorised to receive notice on his behalf.[112] The general rule is that the proposer must actually receive the notice but if the proposer specifies a method of communication then it is the proposer's obligation to check that method. In *Henry*,[113] the proposer specified a local post office as his address for mail. Notice declining cover had been sent to that address within the time stipulated in the cover note and it had remained there unchecked for some six weeks or more. The court held that even though the notice had not in fact come to the attention of the proposer, this was due to "very great negligence"[114] on his behalf and so the notice was therefore effective.

7-075   **Supersession by issue of the formal policy.**   The purpose of a cover note is to embody the agreement between the insurer and the proposer up to the date that the proposal is either accepted or rejected. Once the main policy is incepted, the main policy supersedes the cover provided by the interim insurance.[115] The policy takes over from the date that it is issued and not before. Even where a policy is expressed to be retrospective, unless it is a "lost or not lost"[116] policy, losses arising during the period of interim cover will be dealt with under the cover note.[117]

7-076   **Termination by the proposer.**   The proposer retains the right to terminate the interim cover at any time during the period of cover.[118] Some authorities such as *Taylor*,[119] have, for example, held that seeking alternative insurance during the interim period amounts to a rejection of the offer of interim cover; however, such cases will be fact dependent and it is suggested that the mere fact that the proposer seeks alternative insurance, and nothing more, will not normally be sufficient to amount to rejection of the interim cover.[120]

9.   INTERIM COVER PENDING POLICY RENEWAL

7-077   **Interim cover pending policy renewal.**   Unless expressly agreed, policies are not renewable beyond their original term and will lapse upon expiry of the cover period.[121] Renewal of a policy of insurance amounts to the creation of a new

---

[110] *Mackie* (1869) 17 W.R. 987; (1869) 21 L.T. 102; *Stockton* [1978] 2 Lloyd's Rep. 430; [1979] R.T.R. 130.

[111] *Smith v National Mutual Fire Insurance Co Ltd* [1974] 1 NZLR 278.

[112] *Goodfellow* (1859) 17 U.C.R. 411; *Rossiter* (1859) 27 Beav. 377; *Mackie* (1869) 17 W.R. 987; (1869) 21 L.T. 102.

[113] *Henry* (1865) 11 Gr. 125.

[114] *Henry* (1865) 11 Gr. 125 at 131.

[115] This is particularly important as this is the time from which any additional or specific policy conditions over and above the "usual" terms of cover take effect.

[116] See above para.7-015.

[117] See *Neil* 1932 S.C. 35; 1932 S.L.T. 29. The decision in *Re Coleman's Depositories Ltd* [1907] 2 K.B. 798; [1907] L.J.K.B. 865; [1904–7] All E.R. Rep. 383 must be seen as anomalous in this regard.

[118] *Mackie* (1869) 17 W.R. 987; (1869) 21 L.T. 102.

[119] *Taylor* [1966] 1 Q.B. 304; [1965] 2 W.L.R. 598; [1965] 1 All E.R. 557.

[120] See discussion above at para.7-029 and fn.37.

[121] See above paras 4-046 to 4-048.

contract of insurance. Thus it must always be remembered that the duty of utmost good faith and disclosure is re-engaged at each renewal.

In the construction industry, project policies are often expressed to be of longer **7-078** duration and the period of cover will normally be linked to the anticipated practical completion of the works. Moreover, many project policies often include an additional period of cover during any defects liability or maintenance period. Further, in order to reflect the terms of the underlying construction contracts, most project policies will have provisions to extend the period of cover in order to accommodate for any delays or disruption to the underlying programme of works.

Contractors' policies, on the other hand, will be annual policies requiring an- **7-079** nual renewal. Those policies will either provide cover for all projects commenced during the period or will cover works actually undertaken during the annual period. In the latter case, cover will terminate in relation to all projects at the expiry of the annual period. This can be a major issue for parties to a development, particularly if the contractor is unable to secure continuing insurance on the same terms.

Many insurers issue renewal notices at the end of the period of cover in order to **7-080** encourage insureds to renew their policies with them. The policy and/or the renewal notice will usually allow "days of grace" whereby they allow a short period after the term of the policy for the insured to tender and for the insurer to accept the renewal premium without voiding the underlying policy. It should be noted, however, that the indulgence provided during the days of grace does not, of itself, provide interim cover. In order to provide interim cover, the insurer must offer the same by way of a cover note.

Where a cover note is issued, it has been held that it is an offer by the insurer to **7-081** provide interim cover; the key issue will be acceptance by the insured.[122] The insured must be able to show that he has accepted the offer, either expressly or by acting in reliance on it. If the insured seeks alternative cover during the period of the cover note, that conduct may be used as evidence that the interim cover was not accepted.[123]

---

[122] *Taylor* [1966] 1 Q.B. 304; [1965] 2 W.L.R. 598; [1965] 1 All E.R. 557.
[123] See further above para.7-029.

CHAPTER 8

THE INSURED

TABLE OF CONTENTS

1. INTRODUCTION

Introduction. In a construction insurance contract, an insured with an insurable   **8-001**
interest in the contract works is entitled to be indemnified by the insurer following
loss or damage to insured property. A particular hallmark of CAR policies is the appearance of multiple parties as named insureds under one policy. The parties
involved with any given project may include the employer, funders, the main
contractor, contractors or subcontractors with specific areas of responsibility, professional consultants for their on-site activities, suppliers of materials, and then parties such as sub-suppliers or manufacturers who sit a further "tier" or "tiers"
removed from the works taking place on site. The actions of any one of them may
result in property damage connected with the construction project and when that
occurs, the question arises as to whether damage caused by a particular party is
insured under the CAR policy.

This chapter considers the typical parties insured under a CAR policy, the man-   **8-002**
ner in which the courts have defined and interpreted the facets of the term "The
Insured", and the scope of the cover enjoyed by the insured, including reference to
the issues that can arise over the insurable interest of parties whose activities are
to varying extents distanced from the central project of construction. There is a full
discussion of the concept and practical operation of the insurable interest doctrine
in Ch.9.

The question of co-assurance. The decided authorities[1] are considered in this   **8-003**
chapter in order to understand who the insured is and to demonstrate the complexities that can arise where claims are made under policies for projects involving a
broad category of insureds. Unsurprisingly, insurers commonly seek to limit the
number of parties covered under the policy in order to limit their risk and in some
instances to maximise the scope for the exercise of their rights of subrogation by
avoiding the potential problems of claiming against a co-insured. In contrast,
interested parties will seek to bring themselves within the terms of the policy, to
obtain cover and also to take the corresponding potential advantages of being a co-
insured with other insured parties. The meaning, scope and effect of joint names

---

[1] The cases discussed in this chapter are also considered in Chs 9 and 20, but from different
perspectives.

insurance is considered in full in Ch.20; the cases considered in this chapter are discussed only in the context of identifying whether a party is an insured, rather than considering further whether they are a co-insured and of the consequences that flow from that status.

2.   PARTIES TO THE CAR POLICY

8-004   **Parties to a CAR policy.**   The majority of CAR policies are either taken out by the employer or the contractor responsible for completing single project works.[2] For example, the Joint Contracts Tribunal ("JCT") Standard Form of Building Contract[3] provides an option for either the contractor[4] or the employer[5] to take out a joint-names[6] all-risks policy for the contract works. However, under the Infrastructure Conditions of Contract Measurement Version ("ICC")[7] (previously called the Institute of Civil Engineers (ICE) Conditions of Contract) form, the contractor is obliged to obtain cover in the joint names of himself and the employer in respect of all risks of loss or damage arising under the project.[8]

8-005   **Becoming an insured party.**   The name of the "all risks" policy suggests that it provides cover for risks emanating from the work of all the participants in the construction project. In fact, in order to be an insured party under the CAR policy, a party will need to demonstrate that the contractual rights contained in the policy have been conferred upon them. Establishing that one party is insured requires the CAR policy to be construed to ascertain the intentions of the executing parties as to the further parties they wish to be covered by it. In practice, there are three key routes for an interested party to show that they are insured:

  1.   the party must be actually named in the policy as an insured;

---

[2]   For ease of reference, in this chapter it is assumed that the employer is obtaining the cover unless specifically stated otherwise.

[3]   Joint Contracts Tribunal, *SBC/Q 2011 JCT Standard Building Contract With Quantities 2011* (London: Sweet & Maxwell, 2011).

[4]   Joint Contracts Tribunal, *SBC/Q 2011 JCT Standard Building Contract With Quantities 2011* (London: Sweet & Maxwell, 2011), pp.88-89; Sch.3, Insurance Option A.

[5]   Joint Contracts Tribunal, *SBC/Q 2011 JCT Standard Building Contract With Quantities 2011* (London: Sweet & Maxwell, 2011), p.90; Sch.3, Insurance Option B.

[6]   Joint Contracts Tribunal, *SBC/Q 2011 JCT Standard Building Contract With Quantities 2011* (London: Sweet & Maxwell, 2011), p.91. Sch.3, Insurance Option C. The term "joint names" is simply a convenient term for a policy that names more than one person as a co-insured—it does not indicate that the rights of the parties are "joint" rather than "composite". For a full discussion of co-insurance, please see Ch.20 below. The point is made clear under the *SBC/Q 2011 JCT Standard Building Contract With Quantities 2011* at p.70, which defines a "Joint Names Policy" in cl.6.8 as "a policy of insurance which includes the Employer and the Contractor as a composite insured".

[7]   Association for Consultancy and Engineering; Civil Engineering Contractors Association; Institute of Civil Engineers (Great Britain), *Infrastructure Conditions of Contract: Measurement Version August 2011 Based on the ICE Conditions of Contract*, 1st edn (London: Association for Consultancy and Engineering: Civil Engineering Contractors Association, 2011).

[8]   Association for Consultancy and Engineering; Civil Engineering Contractors Association; Institute of Civil Engineers (Great Britain), *Infrastructure Conditions of Contract: Measurement Version August 2011 Based on the ICE Conditions of Contract*, 1st edn (London: Association for Consultancy and Engineering: Civil Engineering Contractors Association, 2011), cl.21. For further details on Joint Contracts Tribunal (JCT) and the new Infrastructure Conditions of Contract relating to co-insureds, see below paras 20-067 to 20-071.

2. it must be a member of an identified class of insured parties referred to in the policy; or
3. it must have the benefit of an obligation by the main insured to provide it with cover under the policy.

An exercise of construction. Each of these different enquiries involves a question of construction of the policy: that of ascertaining the objective meaning to be ascribed to the policy's wording when considered against the relevant factual matrix of the insurance contract, and then considering, in the light of that meaning, whether any given party is an insured.[9] However, as discussed below,[10] the nature of the exercise adopted in constructing the policy differs according to the route by which a party asserts that it is an insured. **8-006**

Named insureds. For parties expressly named in the contract of insurance, the position is generally straightforward. Those commonly identified in this way will include the employer, who is often the owner of the construction site and is responsible for hiring the main contractor, who is responsible for completing the building project. These parties may well be referred to by their individual names ("A N Example Co Limited"). The question of construction is in effect limited to ascertaining that the claiming party is the same party as the person or body named in the policy. **8-007**

Parties named by definitive description. Parties might also be referred to in the policy by way of a definitive description to which only they correspond; for example, "the Employer" or "the M & E Contractor". The policy itself may elsewhere define who the "Employer" or the "M & E Contractor" is. Failing this, in most cases the construction contract between the contractor and the employer will define terms such as "Employer" or "Contractor" and may therefore resolve many of the simpler definitional questions over the scope of the parties covered under the policy. For this reason, the construction contract is frequently the first point of reference for the parties, as well as for courts considering disputes regarding which party has the benefit of the insurance. **8-008**

Members of a class. A party who is not identified or identifiable in either of these ways may still be an insured if he is a member of a class of insureds referred to in the policy. Typically CAR policies include a number of such classes, such as "Subcontractors" or "Suppliers of any tier". Once again the construction contract will often be an important feature of the "factual matrix" against which such terms in the policy fall to be construed, as it will commonly define which parties are within terms like "subcontractor" or "supplier". **8-009**

However, as soon as a party is not specifically identified by name or by a definitive description, there may be an issue as to whether it was intended that the policy should embrace them. Classes identified in the policy will most commonly be predicated on function: "Subcontractors" or "Engineers". The assessment therefore shifts to focus upon whether the functions or activities performed by an interested **8-010**

---

[9] *Investors Compensation Scheme Ltd v West Bromwich Building Society; Investors Compensation Scheme Ltd v Hopkin & Sons (A Firm); Alford v West Bromwich Building Society, Armitage v West Bromwich Building Society* [1998] 1 W.L.R. 896; [1998] 1 All E.R. 98; [1998] 1 B.C.L.C. 531 HL. See below, Ch.13, for further discussion of this point.
[10] Below, paras 8-007 to 8-010.

party in connection with the project are such as to constitute them a subcontractor or engineer within the meaning of such terms in the policy. Function-based terms have a potentially broad ambit and questions have arisen as to their scope and proper interpretation.

8-011 **"Contractors".** The question of whether a particular party is a "contractor" has often come before the courts. *Hopewell Project Management Ltd v Ewbank Preece Ltd*[11] suggests that only those engaged in the core work of construction will be considered to be covered by this phrase. In that case, the main contractor, Hopewell, entered into a construction contract with the National Power Corporation for the Philippines to build, operate and hand over a power station at Navotas. The defendant, Ewbank Preece Ltd ("EPL"), was a professional advisor that agreed to provide certain engineering services to Hopewell. Hopewell then made insurance arrangements pursuant to the construction contract and entered into separate CAR and Advance Loss of Profit ("ALOP") policies with Sun Alliance. The CAR policy originally named various identified parties including the main contractor and the employer, but then also insured "and/or subcontractors".[12] By a later endorsement the definition was extended to cover "all contractors and subcontractors".[13]

8-012 Damage occurred during the commissioning of turbines at the site. Hopewell's insurers subrogated to a claim against EPL alleging that the damage was due to EPL's negligence. EPL contended that it was an insured and that accordingly the claim could not be maintained against them by the insurers standing in the shoes of a co-insured. Mr Recorder Jackson QC (as then known) first had to consider whether EPL was a "contractor" or "subcontractor" within those definitions set out in the policy.

8-013 **"Contractor" distinct from professional services.** Mr Recorder Jackson QC held that the terms "contractor" or "subcontractor" were invariably used to refer to parties who carried out physical works of construction and not just anyone who entered into a contractual relationship with the developer or main contractor. Accordingly, when the terms "contractor" or "subcontractor" appeared in a CAR policy it was held that they would not normally embrace a firm providing services of a professional nature, such as EPL's engineering services. He said:

> "I am bound to say that in my experience the terms 'contractor' and 'subcontractor' are invariably used to refer to persons, firms or companies who carry out physical works of construction. Sometimes such persons, firms or companies also carry out professional work. For example, some building contractors offer a design service as well. Moreover, it is commonplace for specialist subcontractors to offer a design service within the area of their specialisation. Nevertheless, in all these instances, design services are offered as an adjunct to construction work. It is not normal practice to describe a professional firm as a contractor or a subcontractor, even though that firm enters into contracts with its clients ... [I] find that it would be most unusual for the term 'contractor' or 'subcontractor', appearing in a contractors' all risk policy, to mean or to include within its meaning a firm providing professional services."[14]

8-014 Mr Recorder Jackson QC supported his view by reference to previous domestic

---

[11] *Hopewell Project Management Ltd v Ewbank Preece Ltd* [1998] 1 Lloyd's Rep. 448 QBD.
[12] *Hopewell Project Management Ltd* [1998] 1 Lloyd's Rep. 448 QBD at 454.
[13] *Hopewell Project Management Ltd* [1998] 1 Lloyd's Rep. 448 QBD at 454. The Advance Loss of Profit ("ALOP") policy defined the insured in identical terms and was subject to an identical variation.
[14] *Hopewell Project Management Ltd* [1998] 1 Lloyd's Rep. (448 QBD) at 455.

and international authority. He noted that in *Pool Construction Ltd v Guardian Insurance; Rogers Pass Construction Co Ltd, Third Parties*[15] the Trial Division of the Alberta Supreme Court had construed the term "contractors' equipment" by reference to the *Websters' Third International Dictionary* "Unabridged" definition, which states that a contractor was someone who contracts

"on predetermined terms to provide labour and materials and to be responsible for the performance of a construction job in accordance with established specifications or plans."[16]

Similarly, in *Canadian Pacific Ltd v Base-fort Security Services (BC) Ltd*,[17] it had been held that security guards were not contractors, as the definition of "contractors" "refers to those persons without whose contribution the project could not even get off the ground, much less be completed" or those "within the mainstream of the construction activities".[18] Accordingly in *Hopewell*,[19] the professional advisers EPL were held not to be a contractor.[20]

Labour or materials as an adjunct to professional service. A professional may   **8-015** also provide materials and labour as an adjunct to his professional services. Is such a party generally to be regarded as a "contractor" or "subcontractor" in respect of those additional activities? There is no direct authority on the point, but by extension of the reasoning adopted in Mr Recorder Jackson's judgment in *Hopewell*[21] and by application of his analogous reasoning in the Court of Appeal in *Robinson v PE Jones (Contractors) Ltd*[22] concerning the definition of contractors, it is suggested not. Without a clear express statement that such a party is to be treated as a party who provides physical works, the essence of their service would remain professional in nature, and be removed from the "mainstream" construction activities. Similar reasoning may be applied, for example, in respect of consultant engineers who are hired for the purpose of approving a project design. Such a party would not, it is suggested, fall within the category of "contractors and subcontractors" because their main activity does not relate to the actual physical works.

Professional activities causing damage. As a general proposition in respect of   **8-016** professional services, the more natural vehicle for seeking redress through insurance may be a claim upon the service provider's professional indemnity policy. However, the relationship between professional indemnity and CAR insurance is complex. Even where a professional is not to be regarded as a contractor (or subcontractor) for the purposes of defining "the Insured" within the project insurance policy, there may nonetheless be cover available under it in respect of damage occurring as a result of their services.

Defect exclusion clauses. An example of this is in relation to defects and   **8-017**

---

[15] *Pool Construction Ltd v Guardian Insurance; Rogers Pass Construction Co Ltd, Third Parties* [1977] I.L.R. 1-879; 4 A.R. 417.
[16] *Hopewell Project Management Ltd* [1998] 1 Lloyd's Rep. 448 QBD at 455.
[17] *Canadian Pacific Ltd v Base-fort Security Services (B.C.) Ltd* (1991) 77 D.L.R. (4th) 178; (1990) 52 B.C.L.R. (2d) 393.
[18] *Canadian Pacific Ltd* (1991) 77 D.L.R. (4th) 178 at 185; (1990) 52 B.C.L.R. (2d) 393 at 400.
[19] *Hopewell Project Management Ltd* [1998] 1 Lloyd's Rep. 448 QBD.
[20] This conclusion was noted without disapproval by H.H. Judge Seymour QC in *Yarm Road Ltd (formerly Kvaerner Cleveland Bridge UK Ltd) Hewden Tower Cranes Ltd* [2002] EWHC 2265 (TCC), at [75]; 85 Con. L.R. 142 [2002] at 174; [2002] All E.R. (D) 23 (Nov) at 31.
[21] *Hopewell Project Management Ltd* [1998] 1 Lloyd's Rep. 448 QBD.
[22] *Robinson v PE Jones (Contractors) Ltd* [2011] EWCA Civ 9; [2012] Q.B. 44; [2011] 3 W.L.R. 815.

consequential damage flowing from them. Although there are two prominent "suites" of standard form clauses—namely the defects exclusion ("DE") clauses and the London Engineering Group ("LEG") clauses (known as the "DE1" to "DE5" and "LEG 1" to "LEG 3" clauses respectively) excluding cover in relation to loss or damage connected with defects,[23] the scope of these exclusions varies significantly according to which of the options is used in a CAR policy; further significant modifications to the exclusion may also result from relatively minor amendments to the wording of the individual clauses.[24] In particular, under clauses DE5 and LEG 3 (the "Design Improvement Exclusion")[25] cover is excluded only in relation to the cost of replacing, repairing or rectifying insured property that is defective in design, plan, specification, materials or workmanship, and loss or damage caused so as to enable such replacement (or repairs/rectification) to be carried out. In respect of other damage consequential upon the defect, cover is excluded only to the extent of "the costs of additional work resulting from the additional costs of improvement to the original design, plan, specification, materials or workmanship".

8-018 **Design defects.** Thus, in a situation where either clause DE5 or LEG 2[26] appears in the CAR policy, cover would be available[27] to an insured (by way of example) for damage consequent upon the provision of a defectively designed component by a professional participant in the project or in respect of damage consequent upon the professional's own negligent actions in designing a defective aspect of the works, even though the professional is not an insured.

8-019 **Multi-step analysis.** The central point illustrated by the above discussion of professional consultants and contractors is that a consideration of whether any particular damage is covered under a CAR policy is a multi-step analysis, of which establishing whether any given party falls within the definition of "the Insured" is a first step. It remains necessary to focus carefully upon the specific nature of the activity from which the relevant damage arose and to consider the terms of the policy that address the scope of cover both provided and excluded.[28]

8-020 **Professionals for their on-site activities.** Professionals may be included in a CAR policy as a class of insured for their "on-site activities". The object or purpose is to provide an indemnity to professionals for physical damage caused to the works whilst they are on site. The most common example of this type of damage is accidental physical damage. Including professionals as a class of insured for their on-site activities does not provide insurance cover overlapping or co-extensive with professional liability insurance. Therefore professionals will not be covered under

---

23 Defects exclusion (DE) clauses. Clauses "DE1" to "DE5", promulgated by the Insurance Institute of London Advanced Study Group No.208B in its report called *Construction Insurance report of Advanced Study Group 208B*. (London: IIL, 1999). See below, paras 16-029 to 16-064. Similarly in 1996 a consultative group of engineers called the London Engineering Group (LEG) produced defects exclusions wordings to cover engineering risks (i.e. LEG 1 to LEG 3, with the last one being revised in 2006). See below, paras 16-017 to 16-018 and paras 16-065 to 16-070.

24 The scope and operation of the DE clauses is complex and is discussed in detail below in Ch.16.

25 i.e. the 1995 revision of DE5 (modified exclusion) and the 2006 version of LEG 3. See below, paras 16-044 to 16-061 and paras 16-069 to 16-070.

26 The 1995 revision of DE5 (modified exclusion); the 1996 version of LEG 2. See below, paras 16-044 to 16-061 and paras 16-067 to 16-068 respectively.

27 Subject always to the further terms of the policy.

28 See below, Chs 15 and 16.

a CAR policy for activities that they would usually undertake off-site but which they in fact carry out on-site; accordingly the provision of design information and professional advice that happens to have been given on-site is not indemnified. The rationale behind this approach may be that information supplied on-site by a professional will most often result in a defect being incorporated into the works as part of the design, specification or by validating workmanship. The correction of the defect would only be indemnified under professional liability insurance unless damage also occurs. Professional liability insurance would indemnify the cost of remedying the defect and consequential damage. The position is potentially more problematic in relation to activities that are only undertaken on-site. These include decisions taken by resident engineers, site architects and clerks of works. It is suggested that such activities are also not indemnified if they are of a type that is covered by professional liability insurance; this includes the provision of on-site information and decisions that require professional judgment and skill. In this regard, the position is no different from that of a design-and-build contractor, who will have professional indemnity insurance for all matters associated with the exercise of professional judgment and skill on-site.

Relevance of commercial reality. The insured clause should also be construed against the realities of the commercial background in which it was drafted and entered into. In *Petrofina (UK) Ltd v Magnaload Ltd*,[29] the court was asked to consider the meaning of "subcontractors" in a CAR policy. The relevant project involved an extension to an oil refinery in Humberside. The main contractors, Foster Wheeler Ltd, subcontracted the heavy lifting operation to Greenham (Plant Hire) Limited, who then sub-subcontracted the lifting of the heaviest components to a Dutch company, Mammoet Stoof B.V. As the lifting equipment was being dismantled the gantry to which the hoist was fixed became detached, causing serious damage to the works in progress and killing two workers. The main contractors had taken out a CAR policy worth £92 million which insured certain named parties as well as "Contractors and/or Subcontractors."[30] As in *Hopewell*,[31] the insurers settled the refinery owner's claim and subrogated to a recovery from (amongst others) the defendant sub-subcontractors Mammoet Stoof B.V. Mammoet Stoof B.V argued that they came within the term "subcontractors" and were therefore a co-insured under the CAR policy, against whom no claim could be maintained. Lloyd J construed the clause and held that they were an insured subcontractor. He said:

8-021

> "It frequently happens that businessmen do not tie up their contracts in ways which seem satisfactory to lawyers; particularly where the parties are companies which, though not members of the same group in the strict sense, are nevertheless as closely associated as these were."[32]

Main insured's intention or obligation to procure cover for unidentified insureds. Parties who are neither named nor members of an identifying class based on function (such as "Engineers" or "Suppliers") will have to have recourse to a residual provision, such as being an "Other Assured with an insurable interest in the project" or an "Additional Assured". In identifying the parameters of such terms, the central feature of the construction exercise is not the nature of the party's

8-022

---

[29] *Petrofina (UK) Ltd v Magnaload Ltd* [1984] Q.B. 127; [1983] 3 W.L.R. 805; [1983] 3 All E.R. 35 QBD.
[30] *Petrofina (UK) Ltd* [1984] Q.B. 127 at 131; [1983] 3 W.L.R. 805 at 808; [1983] 3 All E.R. 35 at 38.
[31] *Hopewell Project Management Ltd* [1998] 1 Lloyd's Rep. 448 QBD.
[32] *Petrofina (UK) Ltd* [1984] Q.B. 127 at 133; [1983] 3 W.L.R. 805 at 810; [1983] 3 All E.R. 35 at 40.

activities, but the obligations and intentions of the principal parties actually executing the policy, to extend or not extend its cover to third parties who are often not specifically contemplated at the time of taking out the insurance. Thus in *National Oilwell (UK) Ltd v Davy Offshore Ltd*[33] it was held that the "other" insureds not specifically named in the policy could only have the benefit of the relevant insurance if their own contract with the principal insured required the latter to take out insurance for their benefit and then only to the extent of the obligation.

8-023   In *National Oilwell (UK) Ltd*[34] the main contractors, Davy Offshore Ltd ("DOL"), engaged the subcontractor, National Oilwell (UK) Ltd ("NOL"), to supply various equipment in support of a significant offshore construction project. DOL's insurers paid claims said to have been caused by NOL's late delivery and supply of defective goods. In the insurers' claim against them, NOL asserted their status was of a co-insured, an argument that depended upon their falling within the residual definition of an "other assured" in the policy taken out by DOL.

8-024   Colman J upheld NOL's contention. The basis for the decision in this regard was an application of the doctrine of agency for an undisclosed principal.[35] If the main insured and the "other" party have between themselves agreed an entitlement on the part of that other to take the benefit of the CAR insurance, then when the main insured obtains the CAR policy he is fixed with an intention to also be arranging cover for the "other party". The insurer is taken to have expressed itself content to extend cover to parties who were unspecified at the time of entering the policy, by agreeing to a form of words covering "other parties" or "other assureds". In contrast, if the main insured had no contractual obligation in this regard, then neither the main insured nor insurers are taken to have intended to extend cover to such other parties.

8-025   Colman J applied his own decision in *National Oilwell (UK) Ltd*[36] in *BP Exploration Operating Co Ltd v Kvaerner Oilfield Products Ltd*,[37] saying:

> "Since *National Oilwell v Davy Offshore*, supra, it is settled law and was when the CAR policy was underwritten that in order for a contractor not identified as a principal co-assured in a CAR policy to be entitled to the benefit of cover as an other assured under such policy, the insured operator must have assumed a contractual obligation to such contractor to procure the benefit of cover from him. A mere intention to do so in the future is insufficient. Consequently, when an underwriter insures under a CAR policy a Principal Assured and an unidentified Other Assured the cover to which he agrees extends only to that which is given by the policy to the Principal Assured and to those Other Assured with whom the Principal [Assured] has contracted and will contract to procure cover and only to the extent to which such cover is by the terms of the contract to be procured."[38]

8-026   **Other interested parties insured: suppliers of any tier.**   Many CAR policies include "suppliers of any tier" in their list of insureds. If this is interpreted literally, it would imply that the suppliers of components of every description, class and size would be included in the cover provided by the policy. The key consideration must be the intentions of the main insured and insurers as to whether, objectively considered, they can really have wanted a particular party to be covered. In this

---

[33] *National Oilwell (UK) Ltd v Davy Offshore Ltd* [1993] 2 Lloyd's Rep. 582; [1994] C.L.Y. 4086 QBD.
[34] *National Oilwell (UK) Ltd* [1993] 2 Lloyd's Rep. 582; [1994] C.L.Y. 4086 QBD.
[35] See below paras 20-014 to 20-016.
[36] *National Oilwell (UK) Ltd* [1993] 2 Lloyd's Rep. 582; [1994] C.L.Y. 4086 QBD.
[37] *BP Exploration Operating Co Ltd v Kvaerner Oilfield Products Ltd* [2004] EWHC 999 (Comm); [2004] 2 All E.R. (Comm) 266; [2005] 1 Lloyd's Rep. 307 at 322.
[38] *BP Exploration Operating Co Ltd* [2004] EWHC 999 (Comm) at [99]; [2004] 2 All E.R. (Comm) 266 at 288; [2005] 1 Lloyd's Rep. 307 at 322.

respect it is helpful to distinguish in the first instance between suppliers who provide a complete, composite item on site from those "sub-suppliers" who merely supply some part of the product to be supplied.

A project insurer may typically insure the supplier of the complete product, but **8-027** without more should not be taken as insuring each one of the sub-suppliers of the many components supplied to that supplier and included in the production of that product. To argue otherwise would involve an excessively literal interpretation of a provision such as "supplier of any tier", and would fail to appreciate the differences between contractors and suppliers. In particular, whereas both the provision of skilled or unskilled labour for a construction process, or the supply of a product, are reasonably capable of being monitored, the quality of manufacture of parts is generally a matter outside the sphere of control of the insurer and main contractor and, because of this, is not capable of being monitored or influenced in the same or even a similar way. It is unlikely that the parties to a CAR policy will generally intend to provide cover against the risk of failings in processes so far removed from their control. This may be contrasted with the position of subcontractors on site, whose activities are within the sphere of the insurer's or main contractor's influence.

Other interested parties: funders.   Most construction projects are funded by a   **8-028** financial organisation such as a bank. Given that the bank would surely have an interest in having the project completed so that it could recover its investment, it is commonplace for construction contracts to give the bank an express "step-in" right. A "step-in" right allows the bank to take over the project and complete the building process upon the contractor becoming insolvent during the currency of the project. It is important to note that this is not a contractual right, as the bank is not privy to the contract when it is concluded between the developer and the contractor. It is, therefore, a third-party right. Furthermore, where the bank has been included in the list of insureds in the CAR policy, the "step-in" rights give the bank an insurable interest in the contract works. Therefore, the bank would be able to enjoy the benefits of the policy and take its share from the proceeds under it.

Noted in the policy.   In other cases, the bank may be "noted" as a party in the   **8-029** policy. Having the interest of the bank noted in the policy, as opposed to being included in the list of insureds, appears to have limited legal effect. When a developer becomes insolvent, the bank would seek to enforce its "step-in" right either pursuant to the construction contract or as a third party under the Contract (Rights of Third Parties) Act 1999 (the "1999 Act"). It is unlikely that the bank would be able to assume a contractual position as it is not a contracting party in the construction contract and having an express contractual right would render the operation of the 1999 Act irrelevant. Therefore, it is unclear whether the bank would be able to derive any benefit under the insurance policy or take a share in the proceeds where it is not named as an insured. The only practical consequence of having the bank's interest noted is to make the insurers conscious of the fact that the bank is an investor in the project and that they should notify the bank where the contractor has fallen behind with premium payments. This is because the bank may want to continue the payment of premiums in order to maintain the insurance.

3.   Scope of cover

Scope of cover provided.   As noted above at para.8-019, establishing the identity   **8-030** of the party or parties insured is one step in a multi-stage analysis of whether the project insurance policy provides cover for the loss or damage that has occurred.[39] A further important consideration is the scope of the cover enjoyed by any particular party to the construction project. Once such a party has demonstrated that as a matter of the policy wording they are an insured, it will still be necessary to establish the cover they enjoy.

8-031   **Ascertaining insurable interest.**   Each party insured under the policy is usually insured to the extent of their respective interest. However, where this severance of liability is not indicated through the policy terms, the main contractor and other subcontractors may be insured in respect of the entire works. In the former case, only the party whose specific interest is affected would be able to pursue a claim against the insurer, whereas in the case of the latter, any of the "insureds" would be entitled to seek indemnity following loss or damage to insured property. By corollary, where the entitlement extends to the entire contract works, the insurer would also not be able to able to pursue a subrogated action against any co-insureds because of the implied term barring a subrogated claim in cases of co-insurance.[40] For this reason it is imperative that the insurers are able to identify the different categories of insureds for the project in question, and the extent of their respective insured interests. The law governing the role of a party's insurable interest is in an uncertain state and has been the subject of proposals for reform by the English and Scottish Law Commissions since 2006.[41] For further discussion about the current position of the Law Commissions proposals for reform in this area see below at para.9-040.

8-032   **Scope of insurable interest influenced by rights enjoyed.**   An employer is able to establish his insurable interest by virtue of his possessory or proprietary interest in the project site. A contractor's insurable interest derives from the fact that the property is effectively at his "risk".[42] Parties occupying less central roles in the project may possess limited rights over the entire contract works, and unless the insured damage relates to the works undertaken by them, it is more difficult to identify their insurable interest and its scope. This point frequently arises in the defence of subrogated claims.[43]

---

[39]   See below, Chs 9 to 17.

[40]   See *Hopewell Project Management Ltd* [1998] 1 Ll Rep 448 at 458; *Co-operative Retail Services Ltd v Taylor Young Partnership* [2002] UKHL 17 at [63]-[65]; [2002] 1 W.L.R. 1419 at 1438; [2002] 1 All E.R. (Comm) 918 at 936-937; and *Rathbone Bros Plc v Novae Corporate Underwriting Ltd* [2014] EWCA Civ 1464 at [84]-[85]; [2014] 2 C.L.C. 818 at 841; [2015] Lloyd's Rep. I.R. 95 at 109. These cases were considered and approved in the recent case of *Gard Marine & Energy Ltd v China National Chartering Co Ltd; China National Chartering Co Ltd v Daiichii Chuo Kisen Kaisha Ocean Victory, The* [2015] EWCA Civ 16; [2015] 2 All E.R. (Comm) 894; [2015] Lloyd's Rep. I.R. 295. At the time of writing the Appeal for this case is still outstanding. See further below, paras 20-040 to 20-063.

[41]   See the Law Commission and the Scottish Law Commission *Insurance Contract Law: Post Contract Duties and Other Issues*, A Joint Consultation Paper, Ch.3 (Law Commission, Scottish Law Commission, 2012). Law Commission and the Scottish Law Commission *Insurance Contract Law: Summary of Responses to Issues Paper 10: Insurable Interest* (Law Commission, Scottish Law Commission, 2016) *http://www.lawcom.gov.uk/wp-content/uploads/2016/04/insurable_interest_responses.pdf* [Accessed 27 June 2016].

[42]   For a detailed discussion on insurable interest, see below, paras 9-005 to 9-055.

[43]   See below, paras 20-053 to 20-061.

Scope of insurable interest influenced by proximate relationship to insured property and attendant risk of liability.[44] Subcontractors typify the potential argument surrounding establishment and scope of the insurable interest in the contract works. **8-033**

In 1977, the Supreme Court of Canada in *Commonwealth Construction Co Ltd v Imperial Oil Ltd*[45] stated that subcontractors have a "pervasive interest" in the entire contract works.[46] This exposed them to potential liability for causing damage to any part of the contract works and this was held sufficient to constitute an insurable interest in the entire works.[47] Applying this principle, it would seem to follow that a subcontractor employed, for example, to install and commission windows in a block of flats will be able to insure himself for damage to the entire works irrespective of his limited interest in the project and the works, thereby entitling him to be able to claim on the policy for loss to works that are neither his property nor at his risk.[48] **8-034**

In the United Kingdom, the courts have not been consistent in their approach to the question being considered. In *Petrofina (UK) Ltd*[49] Lloyd J followed the approach of *Commonwealth Construction Co Ltd*[50] and found the sub-subcontractor's insurable interest by reference to the potential that they could damage any part of the contract works, giving rise to liability. The then Mr Recorder Jackson in *Hopewell*[51] described this approach as having "obvious good sense ... from a commercial point of view".[52] In *National Oilwell (UK) Ltd*[53] Colman J followed *Petrofina (UK) Ltd*[54] on this point and held that a supplier of equipment who takes no part in construction at the project nonetheless has an insurable interest in the works, rooted in the: **8-035**

"[P]otential liability arising from the existence of a contract between the assured and the owner of property or from the assured's proximate physical relationship to the property in question."[55]

The analyses in *Petrofina*,[56] *National Oilwell (UK) Ltd*[57] and the reasoning of **8-036**

---

[44] See below, Chs 9 and 20.
[45] *Commonwealth Construction Co Ltd v Imperial Oil Ltd* [1978] 1 S.C.R. 317; (1977) 69 D.L.R. (3d) 558; [1976] 6 W.W.R. 219 (Can SC).
[46] *Commonwealth Construction Co Ltd* [1978] 1 S.C.R. 317 at 320; (1977) 69 D.L.R. (3d) 558 at 560; [1976] 6 W.W.R. 219 at 221 (Can SC).
[47] *Commonwealth Construction Co Ltd* [1978] 1 S.C.R. 317 at 322–324; (1977) 69 D.L.R. (3d) 558 at 562; [1976] 6 W.W.R. 219 at 223–224 (Can SC). This view was also affirmed by Colman J in *National Oilwell (UK) Ltd* [1993] 2 Lloyd's Rep. 582 at 611–612; [1994] C.L.Y. 4086 QBD at [4086].
[48] *Petrofina (UK) Ltd* [1984] Q.B. 127 at 136; [1983] 3 W.L.R. 805 at 813; [1983] 3 All E.R. 35 at 42 QBD. Lloyd J held that any amount recovered in excess of the subcontractor's interest would be held on trust for the other insured parties.
[49] *Petrofina (UK) Ltd* [1984] Q.B. 127; [1983] 3 W.L.R. 805; [1983] 3 All E.R. 35 QBD.
[50] *Commonwealth Construction Co Ltd* [1978] 1 S.C.R. 317; (1977) 69 D.L.R. (3d) 558; [1976] 6 W.W.R. 219 (Can SC).
[51] *Hopewell Project Management Ltd* [1998] 1 Lloyd's Rep. 448 QBD.
[52] *Hopewell Project Management Ltd* [1998] 1 Lloyd's Rep. 448 QBD at 456.
[53] *National Oilwell (UK) Ltd* [1993] 2 Lloyd's Rep. 582 at 611–612; [1994] C.L.Y. 4086 QBD.
[54] *Petrofina (UK) Ltd* [1984] Q.B. 127; [1983] 3 W.L.R. 805; [1983] 3 All E.R. 35 QBD.
[55] *National Oilwell (UK) Ltd* [1993] 2 Lloyd's Rep. 582 at 611; [1994] C.L.Y. 4086 QBD. This decision was also referred to with apparent approval in *Hopewell Project Management Ltd* [1998] 1 Lloyd's Rep. 448 QBD at 465.
[56] *Petrofina (UK) Ltd* [1984] Q.B. 127; [1983] 3 W.L.R. 805; [1983] 3 All E.R. 35 QBD.
[57] *National Oilwell (UK) Ltd* [1993] 2 Lloyd's Rep. 582; [1994] C.L.Y. 4086 QBD.

Stone Vickers Ltd v Appledore Ferguson Shipbuilders Ltd[58] are therefore to the effect that the subcontractor's insurable interest in the work or plant as a whole derives from the risk of liability arising out the close relationship of its labour or activity to the insured property. All three decisions were approved on this issue in the judgment of Brooke LJ in *Co-operative Retail Services Ltd v Taylor Young Partnership Ltd.*[59]

8-037 **Conflicting authority.** However, the Court of Appeal in the case of *Deepak Fertilisers and Petrochemicals Corp v Davy McKee (London) Ltd*[60] took a different view, holding that the mere risk of being held liable for causing damage to the contract works could not of itself create an insurable interest, and that the subcontractor would need to show a legal or equitable right in the subject matter insured, or a legal or equitable right that was dependent upon the continued existence of the subject matter. Thus, on the facts, a subcontractor whose right to remuneration for the work carried out by him was dependent on the completion of the project had an insurable interest in the whole contract works.

8-038 The decision in *Deepak*[61] was subject to analysis by the Court of Appeal in *Feasey v Sun Life Assurance Corp of Canada; Steamship Mutual Underwriting Association (Bermuda) Ltd v Feasey.*[62] Noting the differences in approach between this decision and the first instance rulings referred to above,[63] it was observed the true answer may be[64]

> "that the risk of being held liable for causing damage to property, will not *by itself* create an insurable interest in the property, but if there is a further legal link that interest may also be embraced within the subject of the insurance. I suggest that the question truly is one of construction. It may be more usual to cover liability with liability insurance. But there is no hard and fast rule and where the subject of insurance is intended to be and can properly be construed as embracing the insurable interest in relation to liability, there is no reason not to so construe it."[65]

8-039 The tension between *Deepak*[66] and the first instance decisions in *Petrofina (UK) Ltd,*[67] *National Oilwell (UK) Ltd,*[68] and *Stone Vickers Ltd*[69] therefore remains. It is

---

58 *Stone Vickers Ltd v Appledore Ferguson Shipbuilders Ltd* [1992] 2 Lloyd's Rep. 578.

59 *Co-operative Retail Services Ltd v Taylor Young Partnership Ltd; (Carillion Construction Ltd (formerly Tarmac Construction (Contracts) Ltd, third party); (Genergy Plc (formerly Dale Power Systems Plc), fourth party) (Flue-Stox Engineering Ltd, fifth party)* [2000] 2 All E.R. (Comm) 865; 74 Con LR 12; [2000] B.L.R. 461; (2001) 3 T.C.L.R. CA approved by the House of Lords in this respect at [2002] UKHL 17; [2002] 1 W.L.R. 1419; [2002] 1 All E.R. (Comm) 918.

60 *Deepak Fertilisers and Petrochemicals Corp v Davy McKee (London) Ltd* [1999] 1 All E.R. (Comm.) 69; [1999] 1 Lloyd's Rep. 387; [1999] B.L.R. 41 CA.

61 *Deepak Fertilisers and Petrochemicals Corp* [1999] 1 All ER (Comm) 69; [1999] 1 Lloyd's Rep. 387; [1999] B.L.R. 41 CA.

62 *Feasey v Sun Life Assurance Corp of Canada; Steamship Mutual Underwriting Association (Bermuda) Ltd v Feasey* [2003] EWCA Civ 885; [2003] 2 All E.R. (Comm) 587; [2004] 1 C.L.C. 237; [2003] Lloyd's Rep. I.R. 637. See below, paras 9-051 to 9-054.

63 *Petrofina (UK) Ltd* [1984] Q.B. 127; [1983] 3 W.L.R. 805; [1983] 3 All E.R. 35 QBD; *National Oilwell (UK) Ltd* [1993] 2 Lloyd's Rep. 582; [1994] C.L.Y. 4086 QBD; and *Stone Vickers Ltd* [1992] 2 Lloyd's Rep. 578. See above, paras 8-034 to 8-036 and below, paras 9-043 to 9-055.

64 *Feasey* [2003] EWCA Civ 885; [2003] 2 All E.R. (Comm) 587; [2004] 1 C.L.C. 237; [2003] Lloyd's Rep. I.R. 637.

65 *Feasey* [2003] EWCA Civ 885 at [95]; [2003] 2 All E.R. (Comm) 587 at 613; [2004] 1 C.L.C. 237 [95] at 269; [2003] Lloyd's Rep. I.R. 637 at 659, per Waller LJ.

66 *Deepak Fertilisers and Petrochemicals Corp* [1999] 1 All ER (Comm) 69; [1999] 1 Lloyd's Rep. 387; [1999] B.L.R. 41 CA.

67 *Petrofina (UK) Ltd* [1984] Q.B. 127; [1983] 3 W.L.R. 805; [1983] 3 All E.R. 35 QBD.

suggested that by reason of its precedence, the ruling in *Deepak*[70] is to be taken as reflecting the correct position, such that the risk of being held liable for causing damage to the contract works does not of itself create an insurable interest. In light of the dicta in *Feasey*[71] this position may be the subject of further consideration by the Court of Appeal or the Supreme Court.

4. PARTICULAR POLICY TERMS

The scope of the policy. Particular terms of the policy will obviously also affect the scope of the cover enjoyed by any particular insured. The most critical terms affecting the breadth of the cover provided are discussed in full in later chapters of this work.[72] The remaining paragraphs of this chapter are an introduction to some of these issues, focusing in particular upon what the party who becomes "an Insured" actually becomes entitled to.

8-040

The works, extensions and existing structures. In the ordinary course, the insureds under a policy are only able to enforce the contract provided the loss or damage relates to the contract works. Cover can also be obtained in relation to work in or extensions to existing structures, but this must be specifically selected and contracted for.[73]

8-041

Damage from defects. It is important to note that CAR policies commonly exclude (as a minimum) the cost of rectifying design or product defects, unless, possibly, defect exclusion clause DE5 and/or LEG 3 are selected.[74] However, the scope of the cover provided in respect of the consequences of such defects varies significantly according to the manner in which indemnity for these losses is excluded or preserved.[75]

8-042

---

[68] *National Oilwell (UK) Ltd* [1993] 2 Lloyd's Rep. 582; [1994] C.L.Y. 4086 QBD [1993] 2 Lloyd's Rep 582; [1994] CLY 4086.

[69] *Stone Vickers Ltd* [1992] 2 Lloyd's Rep. 578.

[70] *Deepak Fertilisers and Petrochemicals Corp* [1999] 1 All ER (Comm) 69; [1999] 1 Lloyd's Rep. 387; [1999] B.L.R. 41 CA.

[71] *Feasey* [2003] EWCA Civ 885; [2003] 2 All E.R. (Comm) 587; [2004] 1 C.L.C. 237; [2003] Lloyd's Rep. I.R. 637. See further below paras 9-051 to 9-054.

[72] See below, Ch.15 (exclusions), Ch.16, (defects and defect exclusions), Ch.17, (extensions to cover), and Ch.18, (public liability).

[73] Joint Contracts Tribunal, *SBC/Q2011 JCT Standard Building Contract With Quantities 2011* (London: Sweet & Maxwell, 2011), p.91; Sch.3, Insurance Option C.

[74] See above, para.8-017, and below, Ch.16.

[75] Pursuant to the suite of standard form DE clauses; see Ch.16 below for a full discussion.

8-043 **Public liability.** CAR polices may also contain a "public liability" section,[76] which entitles an insured to claim indemnity for any sums it is liable to pay as a result of a liability imposed upon the insured by law. Typical formulations of the public liability insuring clause may define the liability as

> "[c]ompensation which the insured shall become legally liable to pay for (inter alia) accidental damage to property happening in the course of the [construction of the works]"

or "costs and expenses of litigation".[77] The insurers' key concern with such a clause is likely to be minimising its exposure to liability arising pursuant to the insured's contractual obligations. In the Canadian decision of *Dominion Bridge Co Ltd v Toronto General Insurance Co*[78] the clause in the public liability section indemnified the insured in respect of

> "all sums which the [Insured] shall become obligated to pay by reason of the liability imposed upon the [Insured] by law for damages because of injury to or destruction of property caused by accident ... [except] liability assumed by the [Insured] under any contract."[79]

8-044 **Concurrent contractual liability.** In the *Dominion Bridge Co Ltd*[80] case, the insured party (the contractors) entered into a contract with the Bridging Authority to erect the steelwork for a bridge in British Columbia. Owing to their negligence, the steelwork collapsed causing further damage to the structure, which the insured had to rectify as per its contractual obligations with the Bridging Authority. When the insured contractors sought to recover the costs of repairs from the insurers, the insurers denied liability contending that the insured's liability rested on a contractual premise that was excluded under the policy and that the current situation was not one where the insured was seeking indemnity for "liability imposed by the law". The insured argued that, as it would have been liable to the Bridging Authority in tort irrespective of its contractual obligations, the exclusion did not operate and the costs incurred fell within the ambit of the public liability insurance. It was held that this was not a liability imposed by law and the insurers were able to deny liability under the policy to the insured by relying on the exclusion clause. It was immaterial that a co-existent tortious liability may have existed. The liability imposed by law and the liability assumed under the contract were for one and the same loss.

8-045 It is suggested that a similar approach would be adopted in the case of a policy clause that excluded liability that "may arise", rather than which is assumed, under a contract concurrently with a tortious claim. It is not entirely clear whether in such cases the starting point for the courts would be to assume liability in tort as if there is no binding contract between the parties, or to treat the scenario as one where the liability is co-extensive in both contract and tort. It is likely that the courts would approve the former approach because the purpose behind constructing the clause

---

[76] See below, Ch.18.

[77] Derived from *Howard Farrow Ltd v Ocean Accident & Guarantee Corp Ltd* (1940) 67 Ll. L. Rep. 27; [1940] 84 Sol Jo 466; [1939-1940] 56 T.L.R. 622 and cited in *MacGillivray on Insurance Law*, edited by J. Birds, B. Lynch, S. Milnes, 13th edn (London: Sweet & Maxwell, 2015), para.34-017.

[78] *Dominion Bridge Co Ltd v Toronto General Insurance Co* [1964] 1 Lloyd's Rep. 194 at 196; [1963] 40 D.L.R. (2d) 840 (Can SC).

[79] *Dominion Bridge Co Ltd* [1964] 1 Lloyd's Rep. 194; [1963] 40 D.L.R. (2d) 840 at 841–842 (Can SC).

[80] *Dominion Bridge Co Ltd* [1964] 1 Lloyd's Rep. 194; [1963] 40 D.L.R. (2d) 840 (Can SC).

in this manner would be to absolve an insurer from liability that arises from a contractual premise.[81]

In *Tesco Stores Ltd v Constable*,[82] Tesco claimed an indemnity from its public **8-046** liability insurers in respect of Chiltern's claim by relying on the general insuring clause and a "contractual liability" extension. It was held that Tesco could not recover its pure economic loss under the public liability policy, which provided indemnity only in respect of liability arising in tort. In this particular case, the wording of the policy was such that it could be interpreted to cover contractual liability, which was co-extensive with liability in tort, but not to cover a liability in contract arising solely under a contract of indemnity. The court was conscious of the "ordinary and traditional notions"[83] of public liability insurance and observed that any contrary decision in the case would alter the fundamental nature of such policies. To evince an intention to indemnify the insured against liability for a type of economic loss that is regarded as falling outside the scope of tortuous liability, clear words would have to be used.

---

[81] *MacGillivray on Insurance Law*, J. Birds, B. Lynch, S. Milnes (eds) (2015), para.34-018.
[82] *Tesco Stores Ltd v Constable* [2008] EWCA Civ 362; [2008] 1 C.L.C. 727; [2008] Lloyd's Rep. I.R. 636; [2008] C.I.L.L. 2593.
[83] *Tesco Stores Ltd* [2008] EWCA Civ 362; [2008] Lloyd's Rep I.R. 636; [2008] C.I.L.L. 2593 at 14 and 18, as applied recently in the case of *AXA Insurance UK Plc v Thermonex Ltd (in liquidation)* [2012] EWHC B10 (Mercantile) at [63]–[65]; [2013] Lloyd's Rep. I.R. 323 at 334–335; [2013] T.C.L.R 3 at T42.

INSURED PROPERTY

1. INTRODUCTION

Introduction. The exact wording of the insuring clause in the Material Damage **9-001** section of a CAR Policy in respect of insured property will vary from policy to policy. However, as a minimum, they will all set out that the insured is indemnified in respect of "loss of or damage to the Insured Property" or contain words with equivalent effect.

This chapter considers what is typically included within and excluded from the **9-002** term "Insured Property" in such a policy. Sometimes the insuring clause itself will include more guidance, such as where it refers directly to "Insured Property as described in the Schedule". Alternatively, the answer may need to be sought in the "Definitions" or "Exclusions" sections of the policy. In addition to this, what is and what is not Insured Property may also depend upon where the property is located, how it is being used and when the damage occurs. All of these matters need to be carefully considered in detail and are considered later on in this chapter.[1]

Understanding the scope of the definition is important for two reasons. First, and **9-003** most obviously, it identifies the property for which, if damaged, the insured can claim their indemnity. Secondly, and less obviously, it identifies items that are not Insured Property and which, if damaged, may need to be considered under the third party/public liability section of the policy,[2] often subject to different limits and exceptions.

However, the starting point for understanding the meaning of Insured Property **9-004** in a CAR policy is an understanding of the requirement, in a construction context, for the insured to have an "insurable interest" in the Insured Property. As will become evident, this is a complicated issue and as such most of this chapter is devoted to considering the rationale and meaning of this requirement. The third section considers what is meant by the words "insured property" within a CAR policy.

---

[1] See below, paras 9-056 to 9-077.
[2] See below Ch.18.

2. INSURABLE INTEREST AND THE INDEMNITY PRINCIPLE

(a) Insurable interest

9-005 **What is an insurable interest?** It is often stated that an insurance contract can only insure something in which the insured has an "insurable interest". However, Parliament and the courts have done little to assist with a clear understanding of what is meant by an "insurable interest". As explained below, it may well be that in some circumstances this is no longer a requirement, and that the matter is better understood and governed by the indemnity principle.[3] The law on insurable interest is in a state of confusion and flux and ripe for reform. The scope of such reform has been the subject of debate within the industry for some time and has formed a key element of the Law Commissions programme of work on insurance contract law.[4]

9-006 **Defining insurable interest.** Any understanding of what is meant by an insurable interest invariably starts with the House of Lords decision in *Lucena v Craufurd*.[5] In that case Lord Eldon explained that an insurable interest was

> "a right in the property, or a right derivable out of some contract about the property, which in either case may be lost upon some contingency affecting the possession or enjoyment of the party."[6]

9-007 As was sometimes the procedure at the time, in advance of handing down judgment, the Law Lords invited other judges to provide their views. One of those judges was Lawrence J. His suggested definition, which was provided as an advice to the court and is not strictly speaking part of the judgment, was wider than that outlined by Lord Eldon. Instead of requiring a proprietary or contractual right, which was the basis of Lord Eldon's definition, he considered it would suffice if a party had an "interest" in the property that would be prejudiced by the contingency affecting the property, even if the interest was something less than a legal right. Lawrence J said:

> "A man is interested in a thing to whom advantage may arise or prejudice happen from the circumstances which may attend it; ... [a]nd whom it importeth that its condition as to safety or other quality should continue: interest does not necessarily imply a right to the whole, or a part of the thing, nor necessarily and exclusively that which may be the subject of privation, but the having some relation to, or concern in the subject of the insurance, which relation or concern by the happening of the perils insured against may be so affected as to produce a damage, detriment or prejudice to the person insuring: and where a man is so circumstanced with respect to ... advantage or benefit, but for those risks or dangers he may be said to be interested in the safety of the thing. To be interested in the preservation of a thing is to be so circumstanced with respect to it as to have the benefit from its existence, prejudice from its destruction. The property of a thing and the interest deviseable from it may be very different: of the first the price is generally the measure, but by interest in a thing, every benefit and advantage arising out of or depending on such a thing may be considered as being comprehended."[7]

9-008 Much of the development of the law from that date onwards is made up of shifts

---

[3] See below, paras 9-037 to 9-040.
[4] See further, below para.9-040.
[5] *Lucena v Craufurd* 127 E.R. 630; (1806) 2 Bos. & P. N.R. 269.
[6] *Lucena* 127 E.R. 630; (1806) 2 Bos. & P. N.R. 269 at 321.
[7] *Lucena* 127 E.R. 630; (1806) 2 Bos. & P. N.R. 269 at 302–303.

from Lord Eldon's narrower view of the meaning of an insurable interest towards the wider interpretation of Lawrence J.

The narrow definition. Initially, it was Lord Eldon's view that prevailed. Section 5(2) of the Marine Insurance Act 1906 ("MIA") provided that: **9-009**

> "In particular a person is interested in a marine adventure where he stands in any legal or equitable relation to the adventure or to any insurable property at risk therein, in consequence of which he may benefit by the safety or due arrival of insurable property, or may be prejudiced by its loss, or by damage thereto, or by the detention thereof, or may incur liability in respect thereof."

Whilst this definition does adopt some of the language used by Lawrence J in relation to the concept of prejudice, it is clear that there must be a legal or equitable right in the first place to the property in question. This approach was followed in the (non-marine) case of *Macaura v Northern Assurance Co Ltd*.[8] Mr Macaura owned a plot of land and sold the timber from that land to a company of which he or his nominees were the sole shareholders. The timber remained insured under a policy taken out by Mr Macaura in person and not by the company. A fire destroyed most of the timber stock and Mr Macaura claimed on his insurance policy. **9-010**

The House of Lords held that Mr Macaura could not recover any sums under his policy. He had no insurable interest in the timber, which was owned by the company. Their Lordships reached this decision even though **9-011**

> "at first sight the facts suggest that there really was no person other than the plaintiff who was interested in the preservation of the timber. It is true that the timber was owned by the company, but practically the whole interest in the company was owned by the appellant. He would receive the benefit of any profit and on him would fall the burden of any loss."[9]

Their Lordships stressed the need for a legal or equitable interest in the property in question. Mr Macaura's only legal or equitable interest was in the company's shares or as a creditor. As Lord Sumner put it: **9-012**

> "He owned almost all the shares in the company, and the company owed him a good deal of money, but, neither as creditor nor as shareholder, could he insure the company's assets. The debt was not exposed to fire, nor were the shares, and the fact that he was virtually the company's only creditor, while the timber was its only asset, seems to me to make no difference. He stood in no 'legal or equitable relation to' the timber at all. He had no 'concern in' the subject insured. His relation was to the company, not to its goods, and after the fire he was directly prejudiced by the paucity of the company's assets, not by the fire."[10]

The broad definition. However, more recent cases have moved away from this narrow approach and have looked more to the definition of Lawrence J. In *Mark Rowlands Ltd v Berni Inns Ltd*,[11] Kerr LJ referred to Lawrence J's view as "the classic definition of insurable interest",[12] as did Neil LJ in *Glengate-KG Properties Ltd* **9-013**

---

[8] *Macaura v Northern Assurance Co Ltd* [1925] A.C. 619; [1925] All E.R. Rep. 51.

[9] *Macaura* [1925] A.C. 619 at 625; [1925] All E.R. Rep. 51 at 53, per Lord Buckmaster.

[10] *Macaura* [1925] A.C. 619 at 630; [1925] All E.R. Rep 51 at 55.

[11] *Mark Rowlands Ltd v Berni Inns Ltd* [1986] 1 Q.B. 211; [1985] 3 W.L.R. 964; [1985] 3 All E.R. 473 CA.

[12] *Mark Rowlands Ltd* [1986] 1 Q.B. 211 at 228; [1985] 3 W.L.R. 964 at 975; [1985] 3 All E.R. 473 at 481 CA.

v Norwich Union Fire Insurance Society Ltd.[13] Noticeably, neither case made reference to Lord Eldon's narrower view.

9-014 The courts have been openly reluctant to allow a plea of no insurable interest to defeat an otherwise meritorious claim. As long ago as the late 19th century, the Court of Appeal made the point that

> "it is the duty of a court always to lean in favour of an insurable interest, if possible, for it seems to me that after underwriters have received the premium, the objection that there was no insurable interest is often, as nearly as possible, a technical objection, and one which has no real merit, certainly not as between the assured and the insurer. Of course we must not assume facts which do not exist, nor stretch the law beyond its proper limits, but we ought, I think, to consider the question with a mind, if the facts and the law will allow it, to find in favour of an insurable interest."[14]

9-015 That approach has continued into more modern times. Mance J took the view in *The Capricorn*[15] that if insurers

> "make a contract in deliberate terms which covers their assured in respect of a specific situation, a Court is likely to hesitate before accepting a defence of lack of insurable interest."[16]

9-016 **Feasey v Sun Life Assurance.** The latest leading case to grapple with these issues is *Feasey v Sun Life Assurance Co of Canada*.[17] The lead judgment was given by Waller LJ who noted that any definition of "insurable interest" needed to be looked at in the context of the terms of the particular policy and the nature of the risk being insured; a definition derived from a property context might not be appropriate for a life insurance context and vice versa. He explained that:

> "the court is concerned to analyse by reference to the terms of the policy what is the subject of the insurance; to analyse what insurable interest a person has in the subject of the policy; and to consider whether the subject 'embraces that [insurable] interest'."[18]

9-017 On that basis, he identified four categories of cases where the courts had identified an insurable interest[19]:

1. "Group 1"[20] is where the subject matter of the policy is an item of property and the insurance is to recover the value of that property. In those cases there must be a real or equitable interest in the property. This included cases such as *Lucena v Craufurd*[21] and *Macaura*.[22]

2. "Group 2"[23] is where the subject matter is a life and the claim is for a sum

---

13 *Glengate-KG Properties Ltd v Norwich Union Fire Insurance Society Ltd* [1996] 2 All E.R. 487 at 496; [1996] 1 Lloyd's Rep. 614 at 621; [1996] C.L.C. 676 at 684.

14 *Stock v Inglis* (1884) 12 Q.B.D 564 CA at 571, per Brett M.R.

15 *Cepheus Shipping Corp v Guardian Royal Exchange Assurance Plc (The Capricorn)* [1995] 1 Lloyd's Rep. 622 QBD.

16 *The Capricorn* [1995] 1 Lloyd's Rep. 622 at 641 QBD.

17 *Feasey v Sun Life Assurance Co of Canada* [2003] EWCA Civ 885; [2003] All E.R. (Comm) 587; [2003] Lloyd's Rep. I.R. 637 CA.

18 *Feasey* [2003] EWCA Civ 885 at [80]; [2003] All E.R. (Comm) 587 at 607; [2003] Lloyd's Rep. I.R. 637 at 655.

19 *Feasey* [2003] EWCA Civ 885 at [81]–[91]; [2003] All E.R. (Comm) 587 at 607–611; [2003] Lloyd's Rep. I.R. 637 at 655–658.

20 *Feasey* [2003] EWCA Civ 885 at [81]; [2003] All E.R. (Comm) 587 at 607; [2003] Lloyd's Rep. I.R. 637 at 655–656.

21 *Lucena* (1806) 127 E.R. 630; (1806) 2 Bos. & P. N.R. 269.

22 *Macaura* [1925] A.C. 619; [1925] All E.R. Rep 51.

23 *Feasey* [2003] EWCA Civ 885 at [82]–[86]; [2003] All E.R. (Comm) 587 at 608; [2003] Lloyd's

payable upon death. The cases confirm the requirement for the insured to have a pecuniary interest in the life insured, where there is no interest on the grounds of natural affection.[24]

3. "Group 3"[25] covers situations where, although the subject matter appears to be a particular property, in fact, properly construed, the policy covers "such insurable interest as the insured has". Waller LJ referred to the "important decision" of *Wilson v Jones*,[26] in which a shareholder took out insurance on the laying of a telegraph cable between Ireland and Newfoundland. The precise wording was that the insurance was to cover "every risk and contingency attending the conveyance and successful laying of the cable". The court took the view that the subject matter of the insurance was wider than the property in the cable, in which, as a shareholder, the insured had no interest, and allowed the claim.

4. "Group 4"[27] stretches to situations where the interests are "not even strictly pecuniary" and are "something less" than a legal or equitable interest. Waller LJ referred to the case of *The Moonacre*[28] where, on similar facts to *Macaura*[29] the court was able to identify an insurable interest as a result of two powers of attorney granted by the company to the insured for the use of the property (in this case, a boat).

Waller LJ concluded that: **9-018**

"[i]t is not a requirement of property insurance that the insured must have a 'legal or equitable' interest in the property as those terms might normally be understood. It is sufficient for a subcontractor to have a contract that relates to the property and a potential liability for damage to the property to have an insurable interest in the property."[30]

Continued uncertainty. However, the position remains unsatisfactory and   **9-019**
unclear. Notwithstanding *Feasey*[31] and *Mark Rowlands Ltd*,[32] the requirement for a legal and equitable interest as a necessary element of an insurable interest remains the latest, albeit historic, stance of the House of Lords as reflected in both *Lucena*[33] and *Macaura*.[34] It is difficult to see how *Mark Rowlands Ltd*[35] or *Glengate-KG*[36]

Rep. I.R. 637 at 656.

[24] *Richard Halford v Kymer* 109 E.R. 619; (1830) 10 B. & C. 724; *Law v The London Indisputable Life Policy Co* 69 E.R. 439; (1855) 1 Kay & J. 223; *Harse v Pearl Life Assurance Co* [1903] 2 K.B. 92.

[25] *Feasey* [2003] EWCA Civ 885 at [87]–[89]; [2003] All E.R. (Comm) 587 at 608–610; [2003] Lloyd's Rep. I.R. 637 at 656–657.

[26] *Wilson v Jones* (1866-1867) L.R. 2 Ex. 139.

[27] *Feasey* [2003] EWCA Civ 885 at [90]–[91]; [2003] All E.R. (Comm) 587 at 610–611; [2003] Lloyd's Rep. I.R. 637 at 657–658.

[28] *Sharp v Sphere Drake Insurance (The Moonacre)* [1992] 2 Lloyd's Rep. 501.

[29] *Macaura* [1925] A.C. 619; [1925] All E.R. Rep 51.

[30] *Feasey* [2003] EWCA Civ 885 at [97]; [2003] All E.R. (Comm) 587 at 614; [2003] Lloyd's Rep. I.R. 637 at 660.

[31] *Feasey* [2003] EWCA Civ 885; [2003] All E.R. (Comm) 587; [2003] Lloyd's Rep. I.R. 637.

[32] *Mark Rowlands Ltd* [1986] 1 Q.B. 211; [1985] 3 W.L.R. 964; [1985] 3 All E.R. 473.

[33] *Lucena* (1806) 127 E.R. 630; (1806) 2 Bos. & P. N.R. 269.

[34] *Macaura* [1925] A.C. 619; [1925] All E.R. Rep 51. It was these decisions which forced Ward LJ.to dissent in *Feasey*, despite expressly seeking to find a way to find against the insurer: see *Feasey* [2003] EWCA Civ 885 at [191]–[192]; [2003] All E.R. (Comm) 587 at 639; [2003] Lloyd's Rep. I.R. 637 at 676.

[35] *Mark Rowlands Ltd* [1986] 1 Q.B. 211; [1985] 3 W.L.R. 964; [1985] 3 All E.R. 473.

[36] *Glengate-KG Properties Ltd* [1996] 2 All E.R. 487; [1996] 1 Lloyd's Rep. 614; [1996] C.L.C. 676.

could be taken to have moved the law away from the *Lucena*[37] orthodoxy in circumstances where both courts relied upon the advice of Lawrence J and made no mention of the judgment of Lord Eldon. Also, Waller LJ's "Group 4" in *Feasey*[38] relies upon facts such as in *The Moonacre*[39] as being part of a category of situations where an insurable interest was found despite there being no legal or equitable interest. Such an approach is not supported by the decision in *The Moonacre*.[40] As Ward LJ pointed out,[41] *The Moonacre* is actually a case that applies *Macaura*,[42] because it identified the powers of attorney as creating the necessary legal interest.

9-020   The category of cases identified by Waller LJ in *Feasey* as "Group 3"[43] is a more promising area for legal development. It allows for the subject matter of policies to be construed widely, beyond the property in question to the overall venture and seeks to identify the relevant interest in that wider venture. On that basis, one could seek to distinguish both Lord Eldon in *Lucena*[44] and the decision in *Macaura*[45] as being confined to pure property/goods insurance. Such an approach has the benefit of policing the jurisdiction by reference to the particular policy wording agreed by the parties. This idea is developed below when looking at the concept of insurable interest in a construction context.[46]

9-021   The position is further complicated by the fact that it is now unclear whether the law still requires there to be an insurable interest at all.[47]

9-022   **Background—statutory intervention.**   The most obvious objection to allowing an insured to insure something in which he has no interest and nothing to lose is that it may facilitate a fraud. If the destruction of the property will cause the insured no loss, insuring it becomes a "one-way bet", as the insured's only interest is in the destruction of the property.

9-023   A perhaps less obvious concern arose out of increasingly stern attitudes to gambling in the late 18th and early 19th centuries. Both gambling contracts and insurance contracts involve agreements for one party to pay out money upon the fortuitous happening of an event. An insurance contract, bereft of an insurable interest, is in reality no more than a wager unless there is an expectation of future benefit from the insured property.

9-024   The approach of the common law to such contracts, prior to statutory intervention, is a matter of some uncertainty and, potentially, of some importance now that on one view the statutory restrictions have been relaxed.

9-025   MacGillivray,[48] Colinvaux[49] and the Law Commissions[50] take the view that although some earlier decisions had cancelled policies for a lack of insurable inter-

---

37   *Lucena* (1806) 127 E.R. 630; (1806) 2 Bos. & P. N.R. 269.
38   See above, para.9-017 and fn.27.
39   *The Moonacre* [1992] 2 Lloyd's Rep. 501.
40   *The Moonacre* [1992] 2 Lloyd's Rep. 501.
41   *Feasey* [2003] EWCA Civ 885 at [184]; [2003] All E.R. (Comm) 587 at 636; [2003] Lloyd's Rep. I.R. 637 at 674.
42   *Macaura* [1925] A.C. 619; [1925] All E.R. Rep 51.
43   See above, para.9-017.
44   *Lucena* (1806) 127 E.R. 630; (1806) 2 Bos. & P. N.R. 269.
45   *Macaura* [1925] A.C. 619; [1925] All E.R. Rep 51.
46   See below, paras 9-041 to 9-054.
47   See below, paras 9-033 to 9-034.
48   *MacGillivray on Insurance Law*, J. Birds, B. Lynch and S. Milnes (eds), 13th edn (London: Sweet & Maxwell, 2015), paras 1-021 to 1-022.
49   *Colinvaux's Law of Insurance* edited by R. Merkin, 10th edn (London: Sweet & Maxwell, 2014), para.4-003.

est, by the early 1700s the difficulty was being outflanked by parties expressly agreeing that the contract was to be "interest or no interest". In other words, as long as the parties made clear that they intended to gamble and not to provide an indemnity, the courts would enforce their agreement. It was the increasing use of such contracts in the face of rising distaste for gambling that led to Parliament's involvement. On that basis, but for the intervention of Parliament, the courts would have continued to allow insurance policies to be taken out without the need to show an insurable interest.

However, prior to Parliament's involvement, the courts' position regarding the requirement of an insurable interest was not clear. Contrary to the view expressed by MacGillivray, Colinvaux and the Law Commissions,[51] Lord Hardwicke stated in *The Sadlers Company v Badcock*[52]: **9-026**

"I am of opinion, it is necessary the party insured, should have an interest or property at the time of the insuring, and at the time the fire happens."[53]

He recognised that the practice had developed in marine insurance for this principle to be outflanked by "interest or no interest" policies. He commented that **9-027**

"[t]he common law leant strongly against these policies for some time, but being found beneficial to merchants, they winked at it."[54]

More recently, in responding to the Law Commissions 2008 paper,[55] which tentatively recommended the removal of the requirement for an insurable interest, at least in relation to indemnity insurance, the City of London Law Society[56] referred to this and other cases[57] to conclude that the proper position at common law was that: **9-028**

"Before 1745 contracts of insurance did require that the insured have an insurable interest, but the courts began to wink where marine contracts expressly stated that proof of the interest was not required. The 1745 Act brought an end to that."[58]

In any event, whether it was for this reason or not, Parliamentary intervention **9-029**

---

[50] Law Commission and the Scottish Law Commission "*Insurance Contract Law: Insurable Interest*", Insurance Contract Law Issues Paper 4, p.6, (Law Commission, Scottish Law Commission, 2008) *http://www.scotlawcom.gov.uk/files/1812/7981/4030/cpinsurance_issue4.pdf* [Accessed 1 July 2016].

[51] See above, para.9-025.

[52] *The Sadlers Company v Badcock* 26 E.R. 733; (1743) 2 Atk. 554.

[53] *The Sadlers Company* 26 E.R. 733; (1743) 2 Atk. 554 at 555.

[54] *The Sadlers Company* 26 E.R. 733; (1743) 2 Atk. 554 at 556. Curiously this case makes reference to the fact, when referring to the marine "interest or no interest" policies, that "such insurances are rendered void by stat. 19 Geo. 2, c.37", which is the Marine Insurance Act 1745.

[55] Law Commission and the Scottish Law Commission "*Insurance Contract Law: Insurable Interest*", Insurance Contract Law Issues Paper 4 (Law Commission, Scottish Law Commission, 2008) *http://www.scotlawcom.gov.uk/files/1812/7981/4030/cpinsurance_issue4.pdf* [Accessed 1 July 2016].

[56] City of London Law Society, Insurance Law Committee "Response to the English and Scottish Law Commissions' Issues Paper 4 on Insurance Contract Law—Insurable Interest", (City of London Law Society, 2008) *http://www.citysolicitors.org.uk/index.php?option=com_content&view=category&id=135&Itemid=469* [Accessed 1 July 2016].

[57] See City of London Law Society, Insurance Law Committee "Response to the English and Scottish Law Commissions' Issues Paper 4 on Insurance Contract Law—Insurable Interest", pp.16–17 (City of London Law Society, 2008) *http://www.citysolicitors.org.uk/FileServer.aspx?oID=338&lID=0* [Accessed 1 July 2016].

[58] See City of London Law Society, Insurance Law Committee "Response to the English and Scottish Law Commissions' Issues Paper 4 on Insurance Contract Law—Insurable Interest", pp.16–17 (City of London Law Society, 2008) *http://www.citysolicitors.org.uk/FileServer.aspx?oID=338&lID=0*

began with the Marine Insurance Act 1745 ("MIA 1745"), which rendered marine insurance policies void unless there was an insurable interest and prohibited "interest or no interest" policies. This was followed up by the Life Assurance Act 1774, which took effect in relation to lives and "other events", but excluded goods, merchandises and ships.[59]

9-030   The Marine Insurance Act 1788 ("MIA 1788"), amongst other matters, required the names of those with an insurable interest to be named in the policy. It is unclear whether the MIA 1788 also extended the requirement for an insurable interest beyond marine insurance. The MIA 1788 refers to "goods, merchandises, effects or other property whatsoever"[60] but is worded so as to refer to "consignors" and "consignees" and so is thought to cover only marine matters.

9-031   Section 18 of the Gaming Act 1845 then rendered void "All contracts or agreements ... by way of gaming or wagering".[61] This had the effect of requiring an insurable interest in all other insurance contracts so as to avoid falling foul of the prohibition against gaming (unless, of course, the common law already required the same, as discussed above).[62]

9-032   The MIA 1906 later replaced the MIA 1745 and, in relation to marine insurance, the MIA 1788. Additionally, the Marine Insurance (Gambling Policies) Act 1909 made it a criminal offence to take out marine insurance without an insurable interest.

9-033   **The Gambling Act 2005.**   There matters stood until the Gambling Act 2005 repealed s.18 of the Gaming Act 1845 and declared gambling contracts enforceable from 1 September 2007. The unintended consequence of that piece of legislation has been to confuse the position as to the requirement for an insurable interest. The current situation may be summarised as follows:

1.   In relation to marine insurance, it is unclear whether the Gambling Act 2005 was intended to repeal the Marine Insurance Act 1906 and thereby remove the requirement for an insurable interest. This text is not concerned with marine insurance, save insofar as it informs the law on CAR policies, and it suffices for present purposes to note that most commentators have concluded that the Gambling Act 2005 has left unchanged the law in relation to marine insurance.[63]

2.   Life Policies continue to be governed by the Life Assurance Act 1774, which requires there to be an insurable interest at the commencement of the policy.

3.   As a result of the Gambling Act 2005, the prohibition contained in s.18 of the Gaming Act 1845 no longer has effect. Unless the common law itself requires it, indemnity insurance (including policies covering goods, build-

[Accessed 1 July 2016]
59   The Life Assurance Act 1774 Act does not apply to indemnity policies: *Mark Rowlands Ltd* [1986] 1 Q.B. 211 at 227; [1985] 3 W.L.R. 964 at 974; [1985] 3 All E.R. 473 at 480, or to liability policies: *Siu Yin Kwan v Eastern Insurance Co Ltd* [1994] 2 A.C. 199 at 211; [1994] 2 W.L.R. 370 at 379–380; [1994] 1 All E.R. 213 at 222–223.
60   Marine Insurance Act 1788 (28 Geo 3, c.56).
61   Gaming Act 1845.
62   See above, paras 9-024 to 9-028.
63   The editors of MacGillivray are clear that this is the position (see *MacGillivray on Insurance Law*, Birds, Lynch and Milnes (eds) (2015), para.1-039). Professor Robert Merkin, however, disagrees (see R. Merkin, "Insurable interest, the repeal of the prohibition on gambling" (2005) *Insurance Law Monthly*, pp.4–5).

ings or land) and liability policies probably no longer require any insurable interest. That statement is subject to the confusion identified above as to whether the MIA 1788 applies to non-marine policies,[64] as well as some continued uncertainty concerning whether the Life Assurance Act 1774 applied to land and buildings despite the decision in *Mark Rowlands Ltd*.[65]

4. On the other hand, if, as discussed above, the common law position does require an insurable interest,[66] then the Gambling Act 2005 has no practical effect upon indemnity or liability policies. As the City of London Law Society point out:

> "The 1845 [Gaming] Act does not mention insurance ... The 2005 Act s.335 does not mention insurance ... It is almost inconceivable that it was the intent of the legislature to abolish 250 years of law without mention of this aspect in the 2005 Act or discussion during the Bill's progress (Hansard has nothing on this section)."[67]

On this basis, there remains a requirement for an insurable interest in respect of indemnity and liability policies.

It is clearly unsatisfactory for the law on insurable interest to remain so confused and fragmentary. The lack of a holistic approach is no better demonstrated than by the fact that the Gambling Act 2005 may have reversed a hundred years of law by accident.   **9-034**

At what point is an insurable interest required?   The position is clear in rela-   **9-035**
tion to marine insurance because s.6 of the MIA states that:

> "[t]he assured must be interested in the subject matter insured at the time of the loss though he need not be interested when the insurance is effected."[68]

It is generally understood that non-marine indemnity insurance, like marine insurance, requires the insurable interest to be established at the time of the loss, otherwise there would be no loss to indemnify. The law is less clear about whether, in the context of non-marine indemnity insurance, anything more is required. Clarke takes the view that it is also necessary that "at the time of making the contract of insurance the person making it ... had a reasonable expectation of acquiring an interest".[69] Life insurance, by contrast, requires the interest at the time of contract alone, unless it is on its construction a policy of indemnity.[70]

Other jurisdictions.   There is little consistency in how other jurisdictions deal   **9-036**
with the issue of insurable interest. Section 3401 of the 2012 New York

---

64 See above, para.9-030.
65 *Mark Rowlands Ltd* [1986] 1 Q.B. 211; [1985] 3 W.L.R. 964; [1985] 3 All E.R. 473.
66 See above, paras 9-024 to 9-028.
67 City of London Law Society, Insurance Law Committee "Response to the English and Scottish Law Commissions' Issues Paper 4 on Insurance Contract Law—Insurable Interest", p.24 (City of London Law Society, 2008) *http://www.citysolicitors.org.uk/FileServer.aspx?oID=338&lID=0* [Accessed 1 July 2016].
68 MIA 1906, s.6.
69 M. Clarke, *The Law of Insurance Contracts*, (London: Informa), Vol.1, para.4-4.
70 *Dalby v India and London Life Assurance Co* [1843-60] All E.R. Rep 1040; 139 E.R. 465; (1854) 15 C.B. 365.

Consolidated Laws[71] requires an insurable interest to be established for any enforceable insurance property contract. Similarly, Canadian Law, under s.7 of the Marine Insurance Act 1993 ("MIA 1993") requires an insurable interest for all indemnity policies. Spain requires an insurable interest at the time of entering into the contract in relation to indemnity policies (art.4 of the Insurance Contract Act Law Number 50/1980). However, Australian law abandoned the requirement for an insurable interest in indemnity policies in 1984.[72]

(b)   The indemnity principle

9-037   **The indemnity principle.**   Even if it is the case that the law no longer requires a party to show an insurable interest in any property in order to recover under a policy, it certainly remains the case that the party can still only recover that which it has lost and no more.[73] This "indemnity principle" will often lead to the same result as would the requirement to show an insurable interest. For example, if a person insures property in which he has no interest, when it is damaged his claim could be rejected on both grounds.

9-038   **The indemnity principle and insurable interest compared.**   Although the indemnity principle and the requirement to show an insurable interest may often lead to the same result, the two principles are distinct and are not necessarily co-extensive. The first key difference between the two concepts is in their source. The requirement for an insurable interest either arose by virtue of statute (until recently) or by virtue of common law policy. By contrast, the indemnity principle derives from an implied term of the contract. Consequently, as with any implied term, the parties can amend or waive it by express agreement. A second significant difference is that there is nothing inherent in the indemnity principle that would limit the kind of losses recoverable to only those where an insured has a legal or equitable interest. An insured could suffer losses as a result of damage to a property in which they have no legal or equitable interest at all, such as where a souvenir shop next to a tourist attraction suffers losses if that attraction is damaged and shut down.[74]

9-039   Despite the differences identified between the two concepts, the Law Commissions view in 2008 was that:

---

71   "§ 3401. Insurable interest in property. No contract or policy of insurance on property made or issued in this state, or made or issued upon any property in this state, shall be enforceable except for the benefit of some person having an insurable interest in the property insured. In this article, 'insurable interest' shall include any lawful and substantial economic interest in the safety or preservation of property from loss, destruction or pecuniary damage."

72   The Insurance Contracts Act 1984.

73   Life policies and Valued policies are the recognised "exceptions". The value of a life is not measurable by any conventional means and so the parties contract for a given sum to be paid out. Similarly, the parties can agree to a stipulated payout in the event of a casualty, even if that sum is different from the true value. Since the indemnity principle is a creature of contract, neither of these are truly "exceptions" but rather a means by which the parties can agree the level of the indemnity in advance.

74   This was the example given by the City of London Law Society, Insurance Law Committee "*Response to the English and Scottish Law Commissions' Issues Paper 4 on Insurance Contract Law—Insurable Interest*", pp.25-26 (City of London Law Society, 2008) *http://www.citysolicitors.org.uk/FileServer.aspx?oID=338&lID=0* [Accessed 1 July 2016].

"In indemnity insurance it is difficult to see what a statutory requirement of insurable interest added to the common law indemnity principle, certainly if insurable interest was only demanded at the time of loss."[75]

Consequently, the view of the Law Commissions in 2008[76] was that the position is adequately policed by the indemnity principle. Indeed, as outlined above,[77] this is the approach of a number of other jurisdictions without any insurmountable difficulties being experienced. However, responses to the Law Commissions suggestions were not uniformly positive and in their 2011 consultation paper,[78] the Law Commissions changed their stance. It recognised the arguments in favour of retaining the need for an insurable interest and proposed, instead of removing the requirement, to regulate it. They suggested that the law on insurable interest should be clarified and codified into one statute and should be imposed by that statute alone, removing the confusion of the overlapping statutory and common law provisions.[79] In March 2015 they published an issues paper[80] (seeking views) in which they retained this recommendation and suggested that a new statute should provide a definition of insurable interest and set out a non-exhaustive list of examples. In April 2016 the Law Commissions produced a draft Bill for consultation, which clarified the need for an insurable interest, but used a wide definition to include anyone who would suffer economic loss if the insured event occurs. That consultation has now ended, and, at the time of writing, it is anticipated that the Law Commissions will provide a final report later in 2016, with a view to drafting a potential Bill thereafter.[81]

9-040

(c)   The construction context

Insurable interest in a construction policy.   The issues surrounding the requirement for an insurable interest are a particular and recurring problem for construction policies. This is because contractors and subcontractors of any tier will invariably want to insure themselves against damage to property that is not theirs and over which they have no obvious legal or equitable interest. This is an unavoidable

9-041

---

[75]   Law Commission, Scottish Law Commission "*Insurance Contract Law: Insurable Interest*", Insurance Contract Law Issues Paper 4 (Law Commission, Scottish Law Commission, 2008) p.56 *http://www.scotlawcom.gov.uk/files/1812/7981/4030/cpinsurance_issue4.pdf* [Accessed 1 July 2016].

[76]   Law Commission and the Scottish Law Commission *Insurance Contract Law: Insurable Interest*, Insurance Contract Law Issues Paper 4 (Law Commission, Scottish Law Commission, 2008) p.57 *http://lawcommission.justice.gov.uk/consultations/insurable-interest.htm* [Accessed 1 July 2016].

[77]   See above, para.9-036.

[78]   Law Commission and the Scottish Law Commission *Insurance Contract Law: Post Contract Duties and Other Issues, A Joint Consultation Paper*, Ch.3: Insurable Interest (Law Commission, Scottish Law Commission, 2012) *http://www.lawcom.gov.uk/wp-content/uploads/2015/03/cp201_ICL_post_contract_duties.pdf* [Accessed 1 July 2016].

[79]   Law Commission and the Scottish Law Commission *Insurance Contract Law: Post Contract Duties and Other Issues, A Joint Consultation Paper*, Ch.3: Insurable Interest (Law Commission, Scottish Law Commission, 2012) *http://www.lawcom.gov.uk/wp-content/uploads/2015/03/cp201_ICL_post_contract_duties.pdf* [Accessed 1 July 2016].

[80]   Law Commission and the Scottish Law Commission *Reforming Insurance Contract Law, Issues Paper 10; Insurable Interest: Updated Proposals* (Law Commission, Scottish Law Commission, 2015) *http://www.lawcom.gov.uk/wp-content/uploads/2015/06/ICL10_insurable_interest_issues.pdf* [Accessed 1 July 2016].

[81]   Law Commission and the Scottish Law Commission "*Draft Insurable Interest Bill*" (Law Commission, Scottish Law Commission, 2016) *http://www.lawcom.gov.uk/wp-content/uploads/2016/04/draft_Insurable_Interest_Bill_April_2016.pdf* [Accessed 1 July 2016]. The Law Commissions first published its draft Insurable Interest Bill on 19 April 2016.

consequence of the nature of most construction projects. A contractor has no obvious legal or equitable interest in pre-existing property on site. A subcontractor has no obvious legal or equitable interest in the property in most of the contract works. Both risk being significantly prejudiced by damage to such property. It is this interdependence that both complicates and, as set out below,[82] provides the means of resolving the difficulty in identifying an insurable interest in property that is not owned or controlled by one of the parties.

9-042   Before considering the existing law in the area, it is important to note that it was developed in advance of the disputed impact of the Gambling Act 2005. Consequently, it was not a permissible answer for the court to simply apply the indemnity principle, which may well have been a less strained approach. If it is the case that the Gambling Act 2005 has removed the requirement for an insurable interest in property and liability policies, it may be that these cases lose much of their relevance. For the purpose of exploring the law as it has developed, this section of the chapter presumes that the law still requires an insurable interest to be established. Also, the run of cases that discuss insurable interest in the construction context are also often those that, unsurprisingly, outline the concept of joint names insurance. The meaning, scope and effect of joint names insurance is considered in Ch.20 and insofar as is practical the cases are considered here only in the context of an insurable interest.[83]

9-043   **The Petrofina approach.**   In England the starting point is the first instance decision of *Petrofina (UK) Ltd v Magnaload Ltd*,[84] which adopted the reasoning of the Canadian Supreme Court case of *Commonwealth Construction Co Ltd v Imperial Oil Ltd*.[85] In *Petrofina (UK) Ltd*,[86] as part of extension works to an oil refinery, the gantry came loose, fell to the ground and damaged the works. The matter came before the court because the insurer had paid out to the main contractor and then brought a subrogated claim against the subcontractors, who had been carrying out the works to the gantry. The subcontractors defended the claim on the basis that they were insured for loss and damage to the entirety of the works, not just their own works, and therefore could take advantage of a joint names defence.[87]

9-044   Lloyd J considered whether a contractor or subcontractor had an insurable interest in all the contract works including such property as was not in their control and to which they had no property rights. He relied upon the well-established rule that a bailee could insure for the full value of the goods, even though their interest in the goods was limited,[88] although of course a bailee has a legal right over all the goods, whereas a subcontractor does not. As a matter of principle he took the view that it was plainly more convenient and commercially sensible for the law to al-

---

[82]   See below, paras 9-043 to 9-054.

[83]   See also below, Ch.8, where many of the same cases are considered in order to determine who the insured is.

[84]   *Petrofina (UK) Ltd v Magnaload Ltd* [1984] Q.B. 127; [1983] 3 W.L.R. 805; [1983] 3 All E.R. 35.

[85]   *Commonwealth Construction Co Ltd v Imperial Oil Ltd* [1978] 1 S.C.R. 317; [1977] 69 D.L.R. (3rd) 558.

[86]   *Petrofina (UK) Ltd* [1984] Q.B. 127; [1983] 3 W.L.R. 805; [1983] 3 All E.R. 35.

[87]   See above, para.8-021.

[88]   *Waters v Monarch Fire and Life Assurance Co* [1834-60] All E.R. Rep 654; 119 E.R. 705; (1856) 5 El. & Bl. 870; *A. Tomlinson (Hauliers) Ltd v Hepburn* [1966] A.C. 451; [1966] 2 W.L.R. 453; [1966] 1 All E.R. 418.

low such cover and that *Commonwealth Construction Co Ltd*[89] provided highly persuasive authority that he was right.

In *Commonwealth Construction Co Ltd*,[90] the Supreme Court of Canada decided   **9-045** that the contractor and subcontractors each had a "pervasive interest" in all the works because "there is ever present the possibility of damage by one tradesman to the property of another and to the construction as a whole"[91] and, consequently, that they each had "such a relationship with the entire works that their potential liability therefore constituted an insurable interest in the whole".[92]

Petrofina (UK) Ltd[93] was referred to with approval by the Court of Appeal in   **9-046** *Mark Rowlands*,[94] but was not directly on point. The *Petrofina*[95] principle was then relied upon by Colman J in a series of decisions in the early 1990s. In *Stone Vickers Ltd*,[96] the then Mr Anthony Colman QC adopted the *Petrofina*[97] approach and set out the test as being:

> "...whether the supplier of a part to be installed into the vessel or contract works under construction might be materially adversely affected by loss of or damage to the vessel or other works by reason of the incidence of any of the perils insured against by the policy in question. If the answer to that question is in the affirmative there is no reason in principle why such a sub–contractor should not also have sufficient interest in the whole contract works to be included as co-assured under the protection of the head contractor's policy."[98]

Colman J then returned to the issue in *National Oilwell (UK) Ltd v Davy Offshore*   **9-047** *Ltd*.[99] He explained that in the *Commonwealth Construction Co Ltd*[100] case:

> "The fundamental point being made by the Supreme Court was thus that the subcontractor, by reason of the terms of the subcontract stood in that relationship to all the property insured that loss of or damage to such property caused by that subcontractor's fault could give rise to liability on his part to the owners of the property. He therefore had sufficient relationship to the property to found an insurable interest in the subject matter of that property insurance policy."[101]

Relying in part on his own analysis in *The Moonacre*[102] he went on to state that: **9-048**

> "[t]he suggestion that there cannot as a matter of law be an insurable interest based merely on potential liability arising from the existence of a contract between the assured and the owner of property or from the assured's proximate physical relationship to the property in question, is in my judgement, to confine far too narrowly the requirements of insurable interest."[103]

That line of cases has not gone unchallenged.

---

89 *Commonwealth Construction Co Ltd* [1978] 1 S.C.R. 317; [1977] 69 D.L.R. (3rd) 558.
90 *Commonwealth Construction Co Ltd* [1978] 1 S.C.R. 317; [1977] 69 D.L.R. (3rd) 558.
91 *Commonwealth Construction Co Ltd* [1978] 1 S.C.R. 317 at 323; [1977] 69 D.L.R. (3rd) 558 at 562.
92 *Commonwealth Construction Co Ltd* [1978] 1 S.C.R. 317 at 322; [1977] 69 D.L.R. (3rd) 558 at 562.
93 *Petrofina (UK) Ltd* [1984] Q.B. 127; [1983] 3 W.L.R. 805; [1983] 3 All E.R. 35.
94 *Mark Rowlands* [1986] 1 Q.B. 211; [1985] 3 W.L.R. 964; [1985] 3 All E.R. 473.
95 *Petrofina (UK) Ltd* [1984] Q.B. 127; [1983] 3 W.L.R. 805; [1983] 3 All E.R. 35.
96 *Stone Vickers Ltd v Appledore Ferguson Shipbuilders Ltd* [1991] 2 Lloyd's Rep. 288.
97 *Petrofina (UK) Ltd* [1984] Q.B. 127; [1983] 3 W.L.R. 805; [1983] 3 All E.R. 35.
98 *Stone Vickers Ltd* [1991] 2 Lloyd's Rep. 288 at 301. The decision was reversed by the Court of Appeal, but on different grounds: [1992] 2 Lloyd's Rep. 578. At p.585, the Court of Appeal expressly declined to comment upon the arguments based on *Commonwealth Construction Co Ltd* [1978] 1 S.C.R. 317; [1977] 69 D.L.R. (3rd) 558 and *Petrofina (UK) Ltd* [1984] Q.B. 127; [1983] 3 W.L.R. 805; [1983] 3 All E.R. 35.
99 *National Oilwell (UK) Ltd v Davy Offshore Ltd* [1993] 2 Lloyd's Rep. 582.
100 *Commonwealth Construction Co Ltd* [1978] 1 S.C.R. 317; [1977] 69 D.L.R. (3rd) 558.
101 *National Oilwell (UK) Ltd* [1993] 2 Lloyd's Rep. 582.
102 *The Moonacre* [1992] 2 Lloyd's Rep. 501.
103 *National Oilwell (UK) Ltd* [1993] 2 Lloyd's Rep. 582.

9-049 **Deepak Fertilisers and Petrochemical Co.**   In *Deepak Fertilisers and Petrochemical Co v Davy Mckee (London) Ltd*,[104] the defendant contractor was responsible for designing and supervising the construction of a power plant, which exploded after the plant began operating. An action was brought in the name of the employers against the defendant for negligence. It was argued that the claimant employers were contractually obliged to procure joint insurance naming the defendants and that an action brought in the name of the employers was therefore excluded. The claimants accepted that the claim would fail inasmuch as they were obliged to procure insurance that would cover the loss, but denied that the defendants had any relevant insurable interest at the time of the explosion. Overruling the decision of the judge on this point, the Court of Appeal[105] held that the defendant would have had no insurable interest after the works were completed:

> "In our judgment Davy undoubtedly had an insurable interest in the plant under construction and on which they were working because they might lose the opportunity to do the work and to be remunerated for it if the property or structure were damaged or destroyed by any of the 'all risks', such as fire or flood. Thereafter Davy would only suffer disadvantage if the damage to or destruction of the property or structure was the result of their breach of contract or duty of care. In order to protect the contractor and subcontractors against the risk of disadvantage by reason of damage or destruction of the property or structure resulting from their breach of contract or duty they would, in accordance with normal practice, take out liability insurance or, in the case of architects, professional indemnity insurance."[106]

9-050 **Petrofina and Deepak approaches compared.**   This analysis of what constitutes an insurable interest in *Deepak*[107] is plainly at odds with the reasoning in *Petrofina (UK) Ltd*[108] and *National Oilwell (UK) Ltd*[109]: in the earlier cases, the pervasive interest of the subcontractor was justified on the basis of the subcontractors' "potential liability" for damaging the works, not merely that they might lose the opportunity to complete the contract if the subject matter was destroyed. Indeed, in *National Oilwell (UK) Ltd*[110] the losses were sustained after delivery by the subcontractor of the items it had contracted to supply and yet the judge found that the subcontractor had an insurable interest.[111] It is unfortunate that the Court of Appeal in *Deepak*[112] did not, apparently, even notice this marked departure from the earlier authorities.

9-051 However, the inconsistency was noted by the Court of Appeal in *Feasey v Sun Life Assurance Co of Canada*,[113] where there was a difference of opinion as to the

---

104 *Deepak Fertilisers and Petrochemical Co v Davy Mckee (London) Ltd* [1999] 1 All E.R. (Comm) 69; [1999] 1 Lloyd's Rep. 387; (1999) 1 T.C.L.R. 200.
105 *Deepak* [1999] 1 All E.R. (Comm) 69; [1999] 1 Lloyd's Rep. 387; (1999) 1 T.C.L.R. 200.
106 *Deepak* [1999] 1 All E.R. (Comm) 69 at 103; [1999] 1 Lloyd's Rep. 387 at 399; (1999) 1 T.C.L.R. 200 at 222.
107 *Deepak* [1999] 1 All E.R. (Comm) 69; [1999] 1 Lloyd's Rep. 387; (1999) 1 T.C.L.R. 200.
108 *Petrofina (UK) Ltd* [1984] Q.B. 127; [1983] 3 W.L.R. 805; [1983] 3 All E.R. 35.
109 *National Oilwell (UK) Ltd* [1993] 2 Lloyd's Rep. 582.
110 *National Oilwell (UK) Ltd* [1993] 2 Lloyd's Rep. 582.
111 *National Oilwell (UK) Ltd* [1993] 2 Lloyd's Rep. 582 at 608–612.
112 *Deepak* [1999] 1 All E.R. (Comm) 69; [1999] 1 Lloyd's Rep. 387; (1999) 1 T.C.L.R. 200.
113 *Feasey* [2003] EWCA Civ 885; [2003] All E.R. (Comm) 587; [2003] Lloyd's Rep. I.R. 637. The court's observations on the pervasive interest doctrine in CAR insurance were obiter inasmuch as the case was concerned with insurable interest in the very different context of a quasi-reinsurance policy, which paid fixed benefits to a protection and indemnity (P&I) insurer triggered by the occurrence of personal injuries to the employees of its members. Also, see above, paras 9-016 to 9-018.

proper approach. Ward LJ, in a minority, approved the approach in *Deepak*[114] and rejected the *Petrofina*[115] approach. He emphasised that

> "there has to be some legal or equitable interest between the insured and the subject matter of the insurance, expectation of harm or benefit not being enough."[116]

Although *Deepak*[117] itself clearly went beyond this, in finding that a subcontractor has an interest in the pre-completion works based on his expectation of remuneration for the job, this was a return to the high orthodoxy of Lord Eldon in *Lucena*[118] and the decision in *Macaura*.[119]

Dyson LJ, on the other hand, sharply criticised the distinction drawn in *Deepak*[120] between a contractors' interest pre- and post-completion. He considered that: **9-052**

> "the subcontractor's commercial interest in the plant as a whole during the construction and commissioning stage lies at least as much in his potential liability for damage caused to the plant by his breach of contract and duty as in his interest in not losing the opportunity to do the work and be remunerated for it if the plant is damaged or destroyed by any of the risks covered by an all risks policy."[121]

There is force in this point. Surely one either takes the view that an insured under   **9-053**
a property policy suffers no relevant loss unless he has a proprietary interest in the thing that has been damaged, or otherwise one accepts that a person can have a pervasive interest entitling him to the benefit of insurance on property based on potential detriment to him or loss of benefit if the property is harmed? Either way, there seems to be no reason for drawing the line at the subcontractors' interest in the opportunity of completing the works. In that regard it cannot be said, as did the court in *Deepak*,[122] that an interest in avoiding liability in respect of the property should be insured via liability insurance; by the same logic, the subcontractors' economic interest in protecting his remuneration should the works be destroyed must be protected by insurance that responds to loss of profit.

By contrast, Waller LJ was strongly supportive of the *Petrofina*[123] line of cases.[124]   **9-054**
He pointed out that they were considered in detail and approved of by the Court of Appeal in *Co-operative Retail Services Ltd v Taylor Young Partnership Ltd*[125] and that the Court of Appeal decision was approved by the House of Lords.[126] Whilst neither court directly addressed the insurable interest point (they were concerned with the joint names defence), had any of the judges considered *Petrofina (UK)*

---

[114] *Deepak* [1999] 1 All E.R. (Comm) 69; [1999] 1 Lloyd's Rep. 387; (1999) 1 T.C.L.R. 200.

[115] *Petrofina (UK) Ltd* [1984] Q.B. 127; [1983] 3 W.L.R. 805; [1983] 3 All E.R. 35.

[116] *Feasey* [2003] EWCA Civ 885 at [188]; [2003] All E.R. (Comm) 587 at 638; [2003] Lloyd's Rep. I.R. 637 at 675, per Ward LJ.

[117] *Deepak* [1999] 1 All E.R. (Comm) 69; [1999] 1 Lloyd's Rep. 387; (1999) 1 T.C.L.R. 200.

[118] *Lucena* 127 E.R. 630; (1806) 2 Bos. & P. N.R. 269.

[119] *Macaura* [1925] A.C. 619; [1925] All E.R. Rep 51.

[120] *Deepak* [1999] 1 All E.R. (Comm) 69; [1999] 1 Lloyd's Rep. 387; (1999) 1 T.C.L.R. 200.

[121] *Feasey* [2003] EWCA Civ 885 at [122]; [2003] All E.R. (Comm) 587 at 619; [2003] Lloyd's Rep. I.R. 637 at 663, per Dyson LJ.

[122] *Deepak* [1999] 1 All E.R. (Comm) 69; [1999] 1 Lloyd's Rep. 387; (1999) 1 T.C.L.R. 200.

[123] *Petrofina (UK) Ltd* [1984] Q.B. 127; [1983] 3 W.L.R. 805; [1983] 3 All E.R. 35.

[124] *Feasey* [2003] EWCA Civ 885 at [94]; [2003] All E.R. (Comm) 587 at 612–613; [2003] Lloyd's Rep. I.R. 637 at 659, per Waller LJ.

[125] *Co-operative Retail Services Ltd v Taylor Young Partnership Ltd* [2000] 2 All E.R. (Comm) 865; [2000] B.L.R. 461; (2001) 3 T.C.L.R. 4 CA.

[126] *Co-operative Retail Services Ltd* [2002] UKHL 17; [2002] 1 W.L.R. 1419; [2002] 1 All E.R. (Comm) 918.

Ltd[127] and the other cases to be heresy, one might have expected them to make this clear.

(d) Summary

9-055   **Summary.**   It is unsatisfactory that the courts have collectively failed to provide a coherent explanation as to why Lord Eldon in *Lucena*[128] and the decision in *Macaura*[129] were wrong. Of course, this analysis is all predicated on the need to establish an insurable interest, which, as set out above, may now be an anachronism.[130] Whilst the scope of the "pervasive interest" doctrine remains in need of clarification, it is clear that the firm current trend, overtly in the Court of Appeal and impliedly in the House of Lords, is to endorse the *Petrofina*[131] approach. It is suggested that this is a sensible, commercial approach, which recognises the practical realities of how construction projects are progressed and does not suffer from some of the wider concerns with the wholesale abolition of the need for an insurable interest. The benefits of the approach were outlined by Lloyd J in *Petrofina (UK) Ltd* where he considered:

> "In the case of a building or engineering contract, where numerous different subcontractors may be engaged, there can be no doubt about the convenience from everybody's point of view, including, I would think, the insurers, of allowing the head contractor to take out a single policy covering the whole risk, that is to say covering all contractors and subcontractors in respect of loss of or damage to the entire contract works. Otherwise each subcontractor would be compelled to take out his own separate policy. This would mean, at the very least, extra paperwork; at worst it could lead to overlapping claims and cross-claims in the event of an accident. Furthermore, as Mr. Wignall pointed out in the course of his evidence, the cost of insuring his liability might, in the case of a small subcontractor, be uneconomic. The premium might be out of all proportion to the value of the subcontract. If the subcontractor had to insure his liability in respect of the entire works, he might well have to decline the contract."[132]

3.   WHAT IS MEANT BY INSURED PROPERTY?

9-056   **The meaning of Insured Property.**   Once any difficulties with insurable interest are overcome, the question of what is meant by "Insured Property" within the CAR policy becomes primarily one of construction.[133]

(a)   Interpretation

9-057   **Construction of terms.**   There is ample case law addressing how the courts should go about the task of construing a particular term in a contract. In *Rainy Sky v Kookmin Bank*,[134] Lord Clarke said that:

---

127 *Petrofina (UK) Ltd* [1984] Q.B. 127; [1983] 3 W.L.R. 805; [1983] 3 All E.R. 35.
128 *Lucena* 127 E.R. 630; (1806) 2 Bos. & P. N.R. 269.
129 *Macaura* [1925] A.C. 619; [1925] All E.R. Rep 51.
130 See above, paras 9-022 to 9-034.
131 *Petrofina (UK) Ltd* [1984] Q.B. 127; [1983] 3 W.L.R. 805; [1983] 3 All E.R. 35.
132 *Petrofina (UK) Ltd* [1984] Q.B. 127 at 136; [1983] 3 W.L.R. 805 at 813; [1983] 3 All E.R. 35 at 42.
133 See below, Ch.13.
134 *Rainy Sky SA v Kookmin Bank* [2011] UKSC 50; [2011] 1 W.L.R. 2900; [2012] 1 All E.R. 1137.

"[T]hose cases show that the ultimate aim of interpreting a provision in a contract, especially a commercial contract, is to determine what the parties meant by the language used, which involves ascertaining what a reasonable person would have understood the parties to have meant."[135]

Background information as an aid to interpretation. In considering what a reasonable person would have understood the parties to mean, one can look beyond the strict literal meaning of the words and consider business common sense, the knowledge, expertise and experience of the parties at the time of the contract, as well as the other terms of the contract.[136] Where there is a genuine ambiguity in what a reasonable person would have understood the parties to have meant, the court is likely to prefer the construction that is more consistent with business common sense.[137] However, unless there is a claim for rectification, one cannot seek to construe the contract by reference to the pre-contractual negotiations.[138] That aside, the relevant background information, which can be taken into account to inform what the parties objectively must have meant, can include:

9-058

"Subject to the requirement that it should have been reasonably available to the parties ... absolutely anything which would have affected the way in which the language of the document would have been understood by a reasonable man."[139]

Evidence as to industry practice as an aid to interpretation. Whilst many policies will adopt very similar wording, the precise wording of each policy will vary and each must be considered on its merits. Indeed, the courts have been reluctant to admit evidence as to industry practice as an aid to construction. In *CA Blackwell (Contractors) Ltd v Gerling Allegemeine Verischerungs-AG*[140] the Court of Appeal had to construe the meaning of a standard Defects Exclusion clause (DE3), which formed one of a suite of clauses (DE1 through to DE5) commonly used in the industry.[141] The insurers argued that the cover sought by the insured would have been provided under the more generous DE4, but that the insured had selected the more limited cover provided by DE3, with no doubt a consequent saving in cost. The Court of Appeal did not agree. As Tuckey LJ explained, referring to the

9-059

---

135 *Rainy Sky SA* [2011] UKSC 50 at [14]; [2011] 1 W.L.R. 2900 at 2907; [2012] 1 All E.R. 1137 at 1144; adopting the comments of Lord Neuberger M.R. in *Pink Floyd Music Ltd v EMI Records Ltd* [2010] EWCA Civ 1429 at [17]; [2011] 1 W.L.R. 770; and Lord Hoffmann in *Mannai Investment Co Ltd v Eagle Star Life Assurance Co Ltd* [1997] A.C. 749; [1997] 2 W.L.R. 945; [1997] 3 All E.R. 352; and in *Investors Compensation Scheme Ltd v West Bromwich Building Society* [1998] 1 W.L.R. 896 at 912–913; [1998] 1 All E.R. 98 at 114–115; [1997] C.L.C. 1243 at 1257–1258. This approach was approved by the Supreme Court in *Arnold v Britton* [2015] UKSC 36; [2015] A.C. 1619; [2015] 2 W.L.R. 1593.
136 *Pink Floyd Music Ltd* [2010] EWCA Civ 1429 at [18]; [2011] 1 W.L.R. 770.
137 *Rainy Sky SA* [2011] UKSC 50 at [21]; [2011] 1 W.L.R. 2900 at 2908; [2012] 1 All E.R. 1137 at 1146. The Supreme Court in *Arnold v Britton* [2015] UKSC 36; [2015] A.C. 1619; [2015] 2 W.L.R. 1593, emphasised that a court should be very slow to reject the natural meaning of the words in favour of a more commercially prudent meaning. See below, para.13-010.
138 *Chartbrook Ltd v Persimmon Homes Ltd* [2009] UKHL 38; [2009] 1 A.C. 1101; [2009] 3 W.L.R. 267. This follows from Lord Hoffmann's statement in *Investors Compensation Scheme Ltd* that "[t]he law excludes from the admissible background the previous negotiations of the parties and their declarations of subjective intent. They are admissible only in an action for rectification": [1998] 1 W.L.R. 896 at 914; [1998] 1 All E.R. 98 at 114; [1997] C.L.C. 1243 at 1258.
139 *Investors Compensation Scheme Ltd* [1998] 1 W.L.R. 896 at 913; [1998] 1 All E.R. 98 at 114; [1997] C.L.C. 1243 at 1258, per Lord Hoffmann.
140 *CA Blackwell (Contractors) Ltd v Gerling Allegemeine Verischerungs-AG* [2007] EWCA Civ 1450; [2008] 1 All E.R. (Comm) 885; [2008] Lloyd's Rep. I.R. 529.
141 See below, paras 16-036 to 16-042.

Advanced Study Group Report of the Institute of Insurance[142] which sets out the history and workings of the DE clauses:

> "This report is instructive about the purpose of defect exclusion clauses and how they have evolved. But it cannot be used as an aid to construction of the clause in question which must be construed according to its terms. The intention of those who drafted it and other similar clauses is not relevant or admissible."[143]

9-060   It is not clear how that conclusion is consistent with the principles set out by Lord Hoffmann in *Investors Compensation Scheme Ltd*.[144] The background information that can be taken into account includes "absolutely anything"[145] that would have affected the "way in which the language of the document would have been understood by"[146] the parties. If both parties were experienced in construction insurance, there would surely be an argument that the use and standard application of the DE clauses would be relevant and admissible.[147] Indeed, evidence of industry practice has recently been admitted as an aid to the interpretation of defects exclusions in another jurisdiction, in respect of LEG 2/96 in the case of *Acciona Infrastructure Canada Inc. v Allianz Global Risks US Insurance Co*.[148]

(b) Policy wording

9-061   **Typical wording.**   Whilst each form of policy wording will vary, a typical insuring clause would expressly include within "Insured Property" both "Permanent" and "Temporary Works" as well as the "Contractor's Plant".

9-062   **Permanent Works and Temporary Works.**   The Insured Property will almost always be defined as including, amongst other matters, "the Contract Works", which will typically be subdivided into the Permanent and Temporary Works. In general terms the Permanent Works are the structures being built pursuant to the construction contract, and the Temporary Works include anything that is designed or constructed so as to build the Permanent Works.[149] Policies will invariably include the materials that have been or are to be incorporated into those Works.

9-063   **Permanent Works.**   What comprises the Permanent Works will usually be straightforward, either as a matter of common sense, as set out in the construction contract or in a schedule to the policy. However, more difficult questions can arise in seeking to distinguish between the Permanent Works and the pre-existing site. These distinctions can be crucial, because damage to the pre-existing site will not usually be covered by the policy.

9-064   Where the building project is a new build on virgin ground, no issues arise as to

---

[142]   Insurance Institute of London. Advanced Study Group No.208B. *Construction Insurance/report of Advanced Study Group Report 208B* (London: IIL, 1999).

[143]   *CA Blackwell (Contractors) Ltd* [2007] EWCA Civ 1450 at [20]; [2008] 1 All E.R. (Comm) 885 at 891; [2008] Lloyd's Rep. I.R. 529 at 533.

[144]   *Investors Compensation Scheme Ltd* [1998] 1 W.L.R. 896 at 913; [1998] 1 All E.R. 98 at 114; [1997] C.L.C. 1243 at 1258, per Lord Hoffmann.

[145]   *Investors Compensation Scheme Ltd* [1998] 1 W.L.R. 896 at 913; [1998] 1 All E.R. 98 at 114; [1997] C.L.C. 1243 at 1258, per Lord Hoffmann.

[146]   *Investors Compensation Scheme Ltd* [1998] 1 W.L.R. 896 at 913; [1998] 1 All E.R. 98 at 114; [1997] C.L.C. 1243 at 1258, per Lord Hoffmann.

[147]   See below, Ch.16.

[148]   2014 BCSC 1568 at [164]–[167]; 71 B.C.L.R. (Stn) 64 at 99–100.

[149]   See above, para.3-007.

the status of any existing property. However, even in those circumstances there will be a pre-existing site with land and vegetation. In the absence of additional cover, the policy will not respond to damage caused to that pre-existing land site. There would be cover if, say, there was a land-slip on part of the site, which damaged the Permanent or Temporary Works, but the cover would be limited to the cost of repair to the Works and would not extend to the cost of replacing or moving the earth. Once excavation works have commenced on the virgin land, that land becomes part of the contract works and damage to it would therefore be covered by the policy.

Matters can become more difficult where the works involve a refurbishment or **9-065** the demolition of an existing property. Unless additional cover is granted, which it often will be, the existing structure will not be Insured Property and damage to it will not be covered, even if the works involve demolition of or integration with the existing structure. One way of addressing this problem that is commonly adopted (and required under many of the standard form construction contracts) is for the Employer and Contractor to take out joint insurance of any of the retained structure being worked on as part of the project. This additional cover could be included as part of the policy, but is typically on a "specified peril" rather on an "all risks" basis. In such circumstances, the Employer would also have to consider how such insurance tallies with any existing annual property insurance.

Another complication can arise where the works themselves involve or require **9-066** the temporary removal of part of the existing structure, such as a roof detail, which is later to be reinstated in the same condition. Most policies will deal with such a situation by including within the definition of Insured Property a category for what is known as "Free Issue Materials". These are materials supplied by the Employer, for which the Contractor is responsible and for which a value has been declared in the policy.

Temporary Works. Temporary Works are those structures erected for the purpose **9-067** of building the Permanent Works but that will not form part of the final build. For example, on a road-construction project, temporary drainage structures that will not be incorporated into the final drainage scheme would constitute Temporary Works. The definition would also typically include any structures necessary for access to or for the support of the Permanent Works, or that are required in their construction.

There can be some confusion and potential overlap between items that might be **9-068** considered either Temporary Works or part of the Contractor's Plant. One such example is scaffolding. On one view it is something constructed in order to build the Works but that will not form part of the final build and should therefore be considered Temporary Works. On another view, it is part of the Contractor's Plant, akin to a crane, that is used on successive projects. A sensible distinction would be that anything that is intended to be reused would more readily be considered as Contractor's Plant. It is clearly preferable to clarify the position in the policy and some policies will specify that Temporary Works are only those that will be removed from site after the work is finished and will not normally be used again on other contracts. Normally, such a distinction will not matter, as both will be included in the definition of Insured Property but that will depend upon the wording and whether or not the two categories are both subject to the same terms and coverage levels.[150]

Contractor's Plant. Insured Property will also invariably include the Contrac- **9-069**

---

[150] See above, paras 3-007 to 3-008.

tor's Plant, machinery, apparatus, tools, equipment and temporary buildings, offices and site huts such as are necessary for the construction of the Works. The definition will usually expressly extend to include all such plant that is owned by or in the control or custody of the Contractor, or for which they are otherwise responsible. There will often be provision for the inclusion of employee's tools and effects, albeit usually subject to a more modest policy limit.

9-070 **Location.** Single-project policies will normally limit the cover for damage to Insured Property to solely damage or loss suffered whilst at the specified location. In addition, most policies will provide cover for Insured Property while in transit to and from the contract site, as well as for incidental storage as part of that transit. Both of these matters can be tailored as required. For example, the transit cover is often limited to within the United Kingdom, but this may not be appropriate in some projects. Off-site storage cover could be limited to short, defined periods in order to facilitate the transit but, if the parties agree, will sometimes extend to cover storage at the contractor's depot or elsewhere. Such agreements are common where materials are ordered in advance of construction and are stored off-site. The Contractor will wish to be paid for the purchase of the materials and the Employer will acquire ownership and require the materials to be insured. This is achieved by extending the definition of Insured Property to include off-site materials or by including an extension to the cover provided.[151] An annual policy of course cannot define the contract site in the same way and will often refer to "any contract site in the UK", but this definition may not be adequate to cover materials stored away from the contract site.

9-071 **Period.** On a single project policy the period of insurance will normally be the construction period set out in the construction contract, ending at either practical or substantial completion. That can either be done by reference to the construction contract or by specified dates in the policy. However, construction policies rarely run to schedule and the parties need to agree how the insurance policy will deal with changes in the specified period of insurance. One option is to include an automatic provision which extends the policy in line with any contract extensions to the construction contract, at agreed premium rates. That has the benefit of certainty for both sides, but can be unattractive to insurers who may well wish to reconsider the risk profile of the project in light of what might be very considerable delays. Consequently, the more usual approach is to include a term in the policy that defines the Period of Insurance as extending to "any subsequent period for which the insurer accepts payment".

9-072 In *Jones Construction Co v Alliance Assurance Co*,[152] the insured sought to argue that the insurer was under an obligation to extend the period of cover on the basis of a term that read:

"[O]r any subsequent period in respect of which the Insured shall have paid and the Insurers accepted the premium required for this extension."[153]

The insured argued that this must have been what the parties intended as no contractor would ever agree to a policy that might leave them uninsured in the event of any prolongation of the works. Neither the Judge at first instance nor the Court of Appeal was willing to construe the clear express terms in that manner.

---

[151] See below, para.17-024.
[152] *Jones Construction Co v Alliance Assurance Co* [1961] 1 Lloyd's Rep. 121.
[153] *Jones Construction Co* [1961] 1 Lloyd's Rep. 121 at 128.

Alteration in the risk. There can also be difficulties where the construction works **9-073** come to an early end because, for example, the Employer's funds have run out. Just such a problem was encountered in *Swiss Reinsurance v United India Insurance Co Ltd*[154] in relation to a policy covering Phase II of the construction of two generating plants and a liquefied natural gas facility. In that case there was a specific clause that provided that the cover would continue if work was stopped for six months without additional premium, after which any further extension would need to be by agreement. The dispute concerned a claim for the return of part of the premium, but in answering that question Morison J analysed what the position would have been without such a clause. In his view, absent the clause, the policy would lapse on the cessation of work due to there being a material alteration in the risk. He said:

> "The Insurance was directed to cover a substantial building project, with its attendant risks. When a project is abandoned by the contractors, then the nature of the risk alters. The site is no longer an active building site; rather it becomes a warehouse or repository for the various equipment and installations which were more or less completed at the time of abandonment. The nature of the hazards has changed. Instead of there being risks associated with a building project with a contractors' all risks cover, the emphasis is now on the dangers of fire, deterioration owing to climate and damage due to inclement weather. The site is passive and not active. What was insurance in relation to a substantial building project has become an insurance resembling property insurance."[155]

This approach was endorsed by Christopher Clarke J in *Mopani Copper Mines* **9-074** *Plc v Millennium Underwriting Ltd*[156] who commented that:

> "As Morison J.'s judgment makes clear, CAR risks are essentially different from property insurance and insureds may find themselves without cover if, in the events which have happened, there is no longer any construction going on, even though the period of the policy has not expired."[157]

This raises interesting questions as to whether any suspension of work might end **9-075** the policy cover and, if not, what would be required in order to do so. In order to amount to a sufficiently material alteration in the risk it is necessary to show that the alteration was not within the contemplation of the parties as being within the cover at the time they entered into the contract.[158] The new situation would need to be "something which, on the true construction of the policy, they had not agreed to cover".[159] It is likely that a brief suspension would be within the contemplation of the parties and would not materially alter the risk, in contrast to a complete abandonment of the project. It may, however, be difficult at the time to identify the precise moment at which the one evolves into the other.

At the other end of the timescale, there can be a need to bring forward the period **9-076** of insurance to works carried out before the construction works commence. Many larger projects will involve procurement work, ground investigations and other

---

[154] *Swiss Reinsurance v United India Insurance Co Ltd* [2005] EWHC 237 (Comm); [2005] 2 All E.R. (Comm) 367; [2005] 1 C.L.C. 203 QBD.

[155] *Swiss Reinsurance* [2005] EWHC 237 (Comm) at [32]; [2005] 2 All E.R. (Comm) 367 at 376; [2005] 1 C.L.C. 203 at 216. Morison J took the law on material change of risk from *Kausar v EagleStar Insurance Co Ltd* [1997] C.L.C. 129; [2000] Lloyd's Rep. I.R. 154 and *Law Guarantee Trust and Accident Society v Munich Reinsurance Co* [1912] 1 Ch. 138.

[156] *Mopani Copper Mines Plc v Millennium Underwriting Ltd* [2008] EWHC 1331 (Comm); [2008] 2 All E.R. (Comm) 976; [2008] 1 C.L.C. 992.

[157] *Mopani Copper Mines Plc* [2008] EWHC 1331 (Comm) at [64]; [2008] 2 All E.R. (Comm) 976 at 991; [2008] 1 C.L.C. 992 at 1011.

[158] *Law Guarantee Trust and Accident Society v Munich Reinsurance Co* [1912] 1 Ch. 138 at 153-154, per Warrington J.

[159] *Kausar* [1997] C.L.C. 129 at 131; [2000] Lloyd's Rep. I.R. 154 at 156, per Saville LJ.

preparatory design steps, which the parties may wish to incorporate into the policy, but they will need to do so with clear express terms.

9-077   Even where the construction works are completed within the intended period, there will often be a subsequent maintenance/testing or defects liability period during which the contractor may need to return to site and carry out further works. That work can be covered by the CAR policy but will require express inclusion. Otherwise, any damage caused during that work will need to be covered by a different form of insurance. Typically, insurers will want to ensure that any such extension to cover is dealt with separately to the main insuring obligation, not least because the risks involved at that stage are different to those that existed during the construction phase.

FORTUITY

TABLE OF CONTENTS

1. INTRODUCTION

Introduction. All risks insurance provides cover against all risks of loss, not **10-001** against all losses. Insurance is essentially a matter of indemnifying against chance, uncertain or accidental events. This means that all risks cover does not generally extend to: (i) loss which was inevitable at the start of the policy; nor (ii) loss that is brought about by the wilful misconduct of the insured.

Insurance lawyers sometimes use the word "fortuitous" in its literal sense of **10-002** "happening by chance". However, it is just as often used as an umbrella label for an event which, as well as being non-inevitable, is not caused by the inherent vice of the subject matter, nor by ordinary wear and tear, nor through wilful misconduct. This terminology is well-established, but is not particularly apt. Loss can occur due to an inherent vice and yet still be a fortuitous occurrence.[1] As for wilful misconduct, the objection to cover is not based on the loss being predestined to happen, but on its being deliberate and non-accidental. The overarching idea connecting these concepts is that insurance is designed to provide cover for *accidental* events—the term accidental implying an event that occurs by chance and is non-deliberate, as well as implying to some extent an external, rather than an internal, cause.

The principles of fortuity apply to any policy in the nature of an "all risks" policy **10-003** whether or not the words "all risks" appear in the insuring clause. A contractor's policy headed "All Risks of Physical Loss or Damage", which in the insuring clause indemnified the insured against "all Damage ... of whatsoever nature", was held to require fortuitous loss or damage.[2]

2. INEVITABLE LOSS

Rationale. It is seen as inherent in the concept of "risk", and perhaps also in the **10-004** notion of "insurance",[3] that "all risks" insurance "covers a risk, not a certainty".[4]

---

[1] See below, para.10-014.

[2] *CA Blackwell (Contractors) Ltd v Gerling Allegemeine Verischerungs-AG* [2007] EWHC 94 (Comm) at [43]; [2007] Lloyd's Rep I.R. 511 at 519–520; (point was not raised on appeal: [2007] EWCA Civ 1450; [2008] 1 All E.R. (Comm) 885; [2008] Lloyd's Rep I.R. 529); see also J. Mance, I. Goldrein and R. Merkin, *Insurance Disputes*, 3rd edn (London: Informa, 2011), para.19.15.

[3] In *Hutchins Bros v Royal Exchange Assurance Corp* [1911] 2 K.B. 398 at 411, Fletcher Moulton LJ said: "To hold that the clause covers it [an existing defect] would be to make the underwriters

Thus inevitable loss is impliedly excluded from all risks cover. It is important to appreciate that this implied exclusion for inevitable loss is ultimately a matter of contractual construction. So it is possible to insure against damage that is inevitable, or even against losses that may have already occurred, so long as: (a) words to that effect are used in the policy; and (b) the insured does not actually know that that damage will or has occurred (in which case the policy will be voidable for non-disclosure). This position contrasts with some US jurisdictions, which have treated fortuity as a rule of public policy rather than a rule of construction.[5]

10-005 Degree of inevitability. It is clear that the fortuity principle does not mean that the event causing the loss or damage has to be extraordinarily unusual or calamitous: it is enough that the event was non-inevitable.[6] In the leading House of Lords authority, *British & Foreign Marine Insurance Co Ltd v Gaunt*,[7] a cargo of wool bales was damaged by exposure to water during transit to its port of shipment. This was held to be sufficiently fortuitous in that such damage "could not be expected to occur in the course of a normal transit."[8] There did not have to be an "extraordinary or unusually heavy fall of rain"[9]; instead it was enough that due to some "accidental circumstances the goods were left uncovered when rain was falling."[10] Fortuity cannot be equated with unforeseeability. In *The Miss Jay Jay*,[11] the insured yacht was damaged during a voyage across the English Channel in conditions that were worse than average but such that a person navigating in the area "could have anticipated that he might find, but would hope that he would not".[12] The cause of the loss was held to fall within the covered peril of "external accidental means".[13] The Court of Appeal affirmed this ruling, and stated that

---

not insurers, but guarantors, and to turn the clause into a warranty that the hull and machinery are free from latent defects ... There are no words in the clause which warrant such an interpretation. The fact that it begins with the word "insurance" negatives, in my opinion, the possibility of its being so interpreted."

4 *British and Foreign Marine Insurance Co Ltd v Gaunt* [1921] 2 A.C. 41 at 57; [1921] All E.R. Rep 447 at 455, per Lord Sumner. In *Schloss Brothers v Stevens* [1906] 2 K.B. 665 at 673, Walton J concluded that the words "all risks" covered "all losses by any accidental cause of any kind ... There must be a casualty". Also, as per Lord Herschell in *Thomas Wilson Sons & Co v Owners of Cargo of the Xantho (The Xantho)* (1887) 12 App. Cas. 503 (H.L.) he stated at [509]; 56 LJP 116 at 118; 6 Asp. M.L.C. 207 at 209 that: "The purpose of the policy is to secure an indemnity against accidents which may happen, not against events which must happen."

5 In *Underwriters Subscribing to Lloyd's Insurance v Magi* 790 F.Supp. 1043 (1991) at 1047 District Judge Van Sickle cites the case of *Intermetal Mexicana, S.A. v Insurance Co of North America* , 866 F.2d 71, 75 (3d Cir.1989) which in turn cites "(...Cozen & Bennett, *Fortuity: The Unnamed Exclusion*, XX Forum 222, 222 (Winter 1985)) (emphasis in original)." who said the following: "The exclusion exists as a matter of public policy, because "it would encourage fraud to allow recovery on an insurance loss which is certain to occur."

6 *Gaunt* [1921] 2 A.C. 41 at 47, 52 and 58; [1921] All E.R. Rep. 447 at 450, 452 and 455.

7 *Gaunt* [1921] 2 A.C. 41; [1921] All E.R. Rep 447; (1921) 7 Ll. L. Rep. 62.

8 *Gaunt* [1921] 2 A.C. 41 at 47; [1921] All E.R. Rep. 447 at 450; (1921) 7 Ll. L. Rep. 62 at 63, per Lord Birkenhead L.C.

9 *Gaunt* [1921] 2 A.C. 41 at 52; [1921] All E.R. Rep. 447 at 452, per Viscount Finlay.

10 *Gaunt* [1921] 2 A.C. 41 at 52; [1921] All E.R. Rep. 447 at 452, per Viscount Finlay.

11 *JJ Lloyd Instruments v Northern Star Insurance Co (The Miss Jay Jay)* [1985] 1 Lloyd's Rep. 264, affirmed [1987] 1 Lloyd's Rep. 32.

12 *The Miss Jay Jay* [1985] 1 Lloyd's Rep. 264 at 270, per Mustill J.

13 *The Miss Jay Jay* [1985] 1 Lloyd's Rep. 264 at 265.

"[e]ven if the occurrence of a particular unwanted event, which may or may not occur, is a readily foreseeable risk, the event may still be properly regarded as accidental when it does in fact occur."[14]

Must the event be completely inevitable, before the loss is excluded for lack of **10-006** fortuity? It has been argued that a commercial approach to inevitability is appropriate, as opposed to a requirement of an absolute scientific or "statistical" certainty. So that if the parties to the contract would readily view the event as something that was going to happen, it should not be regarded as fortuitous. In *CA Blackwell (Contractors) Ltd v Gerling Allegemeine Verischerungs-AG*,[15] the insured claimed an indemnity for the cost of restoring motorway earthworks washed away during rainfall that, the evidence suggested, was "not exceptional" for the Manchester area. The point was made by the insurer that such rainfall was practically inevitable at some stage during the policy, and that the insured subcontractor had even attributed, during the tender process, part of the contract price to "weather risk". Nonetheless, it was held that the damage was not inevitable on the facts.[16] The judge appeared to reject the proposition that rain in Manchester lacked fortuity,[17] although another and probably better explanation of the decision on this point would be that the interaction of the rainfall and the vagaries of what happened on site could be considered fortuitous.[18] The decision may be justified on its facts, but can it really be correct that in order for the principle of fortuity to apply, there has to be an absolute statistical certainty of the event? To put it another way, surely the insured cannot defeat the contention that an event lacked fortuity by posing a scientifically possible, but nevertheless fanciful, chance of the event not happening? The underlying principle is that insureds seek insurance for—and insurers are prepared to underwrite—a set of risks. It is suggested that something that the parties would fully expect to happen in the normal course of events ought not to be viewed as a risk in this, the relevant, sense of the word.

Inevitability within period of cover. Another related point of contention between **10-007** the parties in *CA Blackwell (Contractors) Ltd*[19]—whether the defence of inevitability requires that the peril would inevitably occur at the particular time that it did in fact occur, or whether it is enough that the event would be inevitable at *some point* in the duration of the policy—was not expressly dealt with by the judge. The insurer argued that insofar as it was inevitable that it would rain heavily at some point during the 12 months of the policy, there was no fortuity; the insured, on the other hand, contended that the element of chance was supplied by the uncertainty as to whether

---

[14] *The Miss Jay Jay* [1987] 1 Lloyd's Rep. 32 at 39, per Slade LJ.

[15] *CA Blackwell (Contractors) Ltd* [2007] EWHC 94 (Comm); [2007] Lloyd's Rep. I.R. 511.

[16] *CA Blackwell (Contractors) Ltd* [2007] EWHC 94 (Comm) at [48]; [2007] Lloyd's Rep. I.R. 511 at 521.

[17] The comment at *CA Blackwell (Contractors) Ltd* [2007] EWHC 94 (Comm) at [48]; [2007] Lloyd's Rep. I.R. 511 at 521; that the insured's case "does not require rainfall to be exceptionally heavy", was presumably intended to echo the words of Viscount Finlay in *Gaunt* [1921] 2 A.C. 41 at 52; [1921] All E.R. Rep. 447 at 452: that it was not necessary to "establish that there was an extraordinary or unusually heavy fall of rain." However, that speech goes on: "It would be quite enough if owing to some accidental circumstances the goods were left uncovered when rain was falling.": [1921] 2 A.C. 41 at 52; [1921] All E.R. Rep. 447 at 452. Taken as a whole, this dictum rather stands against the proposition that rainfall is fortuitous in and of itself.

[18] Essentially this was the contention of the insured: *CA Blackwell (Contractors) Ltd* [2007] EWHC 94 (Comm) at [45]; [2007] Lloyd's Rep. I.R. 511 at 520.

[19] *CA Blackwell (Contractors) Ltd* [2007] EWHC 94 (Comm); [2007] Lloyd's Rep. I.R. 511.

it would rain on a given day. It is suggested the better view is that fortuity is assessed by reference to the whole insurance period. The essential question is whether the insurer is bound to pay out under the policy, thereby making the cover a one-way bet for the insured—and the answer to this question may depend on the period of cover. This principle works both ways. In some cases, what may on the face of the evidence be a complete certainty of damage is not necessarily inevitable—and so perfectly insurable—within the limits of the period of cover. In *Insurance Co of North America Inc v US Gypsum Co Inc*,[20] the evidence was that there is a certainty of subsidence from the moment that mining operations begin at any given location. The court held that the subsidence that occurred was fortuitous; "the fact that it is known that subsidence will occur does not mean that it will occur during the policy period."[21]

10-008 Knowledge—proper standpoint for assessing inevitability. The certainty or risk of loss has to be assessed prospectively from the time the policy is taken out: the issue is whether the event was, at that time, inevitable. In assessing risk, one cannot simply adopt everything one knows about the sequence of events leading up to the loss, because this approach inexorably leads to the conclusion that whatever happened was inevitable. Chance is a function of what one does not know. But this being so, what information *can* be used to determine whether the event was either certain or fortuitous? Is the matter approached objectively, so that one takes account of everything one can discover about the circumstances pertaining at the start of the policy, whether or not all of those facts were practically available to the insured, or is it approached subjectively so that inevitability is assessed using only that information that was available to the insured at the time?[22]

10-009 In the shipping context, insurance is commonly secured by merchants who have acquired title to the cargo through a documentary purchase and would have no practical way of ascertaining the condition of the goods at the time of shipment. Assuming that the policy covers loss due to inherent vice,[23] is there sufficient fortuity

---

[20] *Insurance Co of North America Inc v US Gypsum Co Inc* (1989) 870 F. 2d 148.

[21] *Insurance Co of North America Inc* (1989) 870 F. 2d 148 at 152.

[22] Clarke frames the question differently: should the element of risk be assessed "with the benefit of omniscience" or "with the knowledge of the parties"? (M. Clarke, *The Law of Insurance Contracts*, (London: Informa), Vol.2 para.17-3A2.) However, "omniscience" implies one should take account of not just the known facts, but also (notionally) matters, which could not be discovered even using the best available tests. Inasmuch as the physical world is deterministic the concept of "chance" is a function simply of what we do not know, and so to notionally assume complete "omniscience" would, in the context of assessing inevitability, simply be to say that any and every outcome which occurs is inevitable (see H. Reece, "Losses of Chances in the Law" (1996) 59 M.L.R. 188). So "with the benefit of omniscience" cannot be the right starting point; a more plausible version of an objective approach would be, as suggested above in para.10-008, to ask whether the event was inevitable taking into account of what we do in fact know, albeit with the benefit of hindsight, about the circumstances pertaining at the start of the policy. At the other end of the scale, assessing risk with the actual knowledge of the parties cannot, with respect, be the right approach either: on that view an event would be inevitable only when the insured actually knew that it would occur, in which case the policy would anyway be voidable for non-disclosure. Instead, the most plausible version of the subjective test would be—as suggested above, in para.10-008—whether the certainty of the event could practically have been discovered by the insured: "a certainty which is, or should be, known at least to the assured": *Soya GmbH Mainz KG v White* [1982] 1 Lloyd's Rep. 136 at 150, per Donaldson LJ.

[23] The Court of Appeal determined in *Soya GmbH Mainz KG* [1982] 1 Lloyd's Rep. 136 that a cargo can suffer from inherent vice without loss being inevitable; the two matters must be considered

if due to some quality of the goods unknown, and, in practice unknowable, to the insured they will inevitably deteriorate during the voyage? In *Soya GmbH v White*,[24] the expert evidence was that a cargo of soya beans shipped with a moisture content of between 12 and 14 per cent had a risk of heating (deterioration), whereas beans shipped with a moisture content of greater than 14 per cent would inevitably suffer heating; beans shipped with a moisture content of under 12 per cent would not be exposed to any risk of heating. The judge found that the insured cargo had been shipped with a moisture content of just under 13 per cent, so there was a risk rather than an inevitability of the cargo being damaged; accordingly the loss was fortuitous. The Court of Appeal[25] went on to address the position on the counterfactual assumption that the moisture content upon shipment exceeded 14 per cent. They were in no doubt that damage suffered in those circumstances would be outside cover for lack of fortuity.[26] This would seem to be support for the proposition that fortuity is assessed objectively, that is, not taking into account whether the information establishing inevitability was available to the insured, given that neither the Netherlands-based importers who arranged cover nor the German buyers who had the benefit of the policy would be in a position, practically, to ascertain the moisture content of a consignment of beans upon their shipment from Indonesia. However, there are dicta in the speech of Donaldson LJ that are inconsistent with an objective approach, and indeed (it is suggested) inconsistent with his own conclusion that the loss would lack fortuity if the actual moisture content of the beans upon shipment had made their deterioration biologically inevitable. He said:

"In a sense the use of the term 'inevitability' misleads. In practical terms there is as much a risk if the inevitability of a loss is not known as if the loss itself may or may not occur. Overdue ships and cargo can be insured, notwithstanding that ... their loss may not only be inevitable, but already have occurred. I would therefore prefer to use the term 'known certainty' instead of 'inevitability.'"[27]

Later, Donaldson LJ is even more explicit in stating that the defence of certainty of loss is "subject to the qualification that it must be a certainty which is, or should be, known at least to the assured".[28] Yet if Donaldson LJ thought (contrary to Lord Diplock's understanding of the facts)[29] that the insured consignee knew or could be expected to ascertain the moisture content of the beans upon shipment, he did not give his reasons. On appeal to the House of Lords,[30] Lord Diplock, with whom the other Lordships agreed,[31] declined to consider whether there would be lack of fortuity if the moisture content, unknown to the insured, had been high enough to make heating inevitable, that issue being obiter on the facts.[32]

So the question of which assumptions one must make in respect of inevitability **10-010** has not been adequately resolved. However, in the case of certain insured perils it is clear that a subjective approach must apply to the extent that fortuity is required at all. Under marine "lost or not lost" cover, the fact that the subject matter was,

---

separately: see below, paras 10-013 to 10-014.

[24] *Soya GmbH Mainz KG* [1982] 1 Lloyd's Rep. 136, affirmed [1983] 1 Lloyd's Rep. 122.
[25] *Soya GmbH Mainz KG* [1982] 1 Lloyd's Rep. 136.
[26] *Soya GmbH Mainz KG* [1982] 1 Lloyd's Rep. 136 at 140–141, per Waller LJ.
[27] *Soya GmbH Mainz KG* [1982] 1 Lloyd's Rep. 136 at 149, per Donaldson LJ.
[28] *Soya GmbH Mainz KG* [1982] 1 Lloyd's Rep. 136 at 150, per Donaldson LJ.
[29] *Soya GmbH Mainz KG* [1983] 1 Lloyd's Rep. 122 at 125, per Lord Diplock.
[30] *Soya GmbH Mainz KG* [1983] 1 Lloyd's Rep 122.
[31] Per Lord Keith of Kinkel, Lord Scarman, Lord Roskill and Lord Templeman.
[32] *Soya GmbH Mainz KG* [1983] 1 Lloyd's Rep. 122 at 126, per Lord Diplock.

unknown to the parties, lost before the insured acquired an interest will not defeat a claim.[33] As regards cover for damage consequent on a latent defect (in "DE" clauses and "Inchmaree" clauses),[34] it is clear that a form of the subjective test applies. So long as it is possible to identify unintentional damage over and above the defect itself,[35] it will not avail the insurer to argue that the design flaw in question meant that it was mechanically inevitable that the structure would, due to its defective condition, collapse or explode, etc. In *The Nukila*,[36] Hobhouse LJ said:

> "The presence or absence of a latent defect in the hull or machinery of a vessel is, by definition, unknown to the assured and whether or not there is such a defect and whether or not it will during a given period of time or maritime adventure have an impact or cause any damage is fortuitous from the point of view of the insured. As is demonstrated by the Inchmaree clause and other similar clauses which have been introduced into policies ... there is both a market need for such cover and a willingness to provide it."[37]

10-011   Where the insured has obtained cover specifically for consequences stemming from some inherent quality of the subject matter of which, *ex hypothesi*, he is unaware, it makes good sense for the law to refrain from stigmatising loss so caused as the inevitable consequence of that quality (although, as discussed above, the Court of Appeal was apparently prepared to do so in *Soya GmbH Mainz KG*).[38] However, where there is no cover for inherent vice (which is the default position under an all risks policy), there is perhaps less justification for treating inevitability as a function of what the insured knew or could be expected to know, as an objective approach might be expected to promote commercial certainty.[39]

10-012   **Ordinary wear and tear.**[40]   Deterioration of the subject matter due to ordinary wear and tear is implicitly excluded from all risks cover: "such damage as is inevitable from ordinary wear and tear and inevitable depreciation is not within the policies."[41] Ordinary wear and tear is usually treated as an aspect of inevitability. This analysis holds well in most instances, such as rusting of metal and rotting of food, but the principle is wider than this. It may be correct to state that every component in a car will one day wear out, but it is not necessarily inevitable that the windscreen wipers, say, will stop working during the period of cover as opposed to at a later date—nonetheless this would be treated as an instance of ordinary

---

33   H. Bennett, *The Law of Marine Insurance*, 2nd edn (Oxford: OUP, 2006), para.3.13.
34   See below, Ch.16.
35   See below, paras 14-016 to 14-021.
36   *Promet Engineering (Singapore) Pte Ltd v Sturge (The Nukila)* [1997] 2 Lloyd's Rep. 146; [1997] C.L.C. 966.
37   *The Nukila* [1997] 2 Lloyd's Rep. 146 at 151; [1997] C.L.C. 966 at 971.
38   *Soya GmbH Mainz KG* [1982] 1 Lloyd's Rep. 136.
39   However, it could well be argued that it is often forensically easier (and less expensive) to come to a view about whether the parties knew or could reasonably be expected to know that the loss was inevitable, than to carry out testing of the subject matter and have experts interpret the results to determine whether the loss was "scientifically" inevitable. *Soya GmbH Mainz KG* [1982] 1 Lloyd's Rep. 136, affirmed [1983] 1 Lloyd's Rep. 122 is a case in point.
40   See below, paras 15-014 to 15-019.
41   *Gaunt* [1921] 2 A.C. 41 at 46, 52, 56-57; [1921] All E.R. Rep. 447 at 449, 452, 454-455; (1921) 7 Ll. L. Rep. 62 at 63. Similarly, "perils of the seas" covers only "fortuitous accidents or casualties of the seas. It does not include the ordinary action of the winds and waves": r.7 in Sch.1 to the Marine Insurance Act 1906. A loss is not caused by a peril of the sea if the vessel sinks because it is "so weak as to give way from the mere pressure of the water on her port, without anything more": *Dudgeon v Pembroke* (1873–74) L.R. 9 Q.B. 581 at 597.

wear and tear. Instead, it seems that ordinary wear and tear is outside of the cover because it does not have the necessary aspect of an "accident" or "casualty". All risks insurance is not an indemnity against the ordinary action of the elements. Yet where the subject matter has deteriorated due to exposure to the weather, that element of an accident *can* be supplied by evidence or the inference that those employed to keep it protected, neglected their duty,[42] that exposure was aggravated by a significant delay in transit,[43] or that the damage was due to a flaw in the system of weather-protection adopted by the contractor.[44] In the same way, in the common scenario where damage results from a combination of: (i) a defect in the way the property is designed; and (ii) the effects of ordinary usage of that property, the implied exclusion for ordinary wear and tear is not engaged[45]; the unforeseen consequences of the design defect supply the element of fortuity. The key distinction appears to be between those cases where the casualty was caused by an inherent weakness as opposed to those where there has been some external fortuitous event.[46]

Inherent vice. An "inherent vice" is an internal quality of the insured property **10-013** tending to its loss, damage or destruction.[47] Examples include the tendency of food to rot and iron to rust. Loss or damage due to inherent vice is implicitly excluded from all risks cover.[48] In the context of marine insurance, s.55(2)(c) of the Marine Insurance Act 1906 ("MIA") confirms this principle by providing that:

"Unless the policy otherwise provides, the insurer is not liable for ordinary wear and tear, ordinary leakage and breakage, inherent vice or nature of the subject-matter insured."

The presumption against cover for inherent vice can be rebutted by express words or necessary implication,[49] such as by the inclusion of perils that are apt to describe the consequences of particular kinds of inherent vice.[50] So long as the included peril is "commonly" caused by inherent vice, the presumption is displaced, notwithstanding that the risk might sometimes arise from some external agency.[51] Outside of the

---

[42] *Gaunt* [1921] 2 A.C. 41; [1921] All E.R. Rep. 447; (1921) 7 Ll. L. Rep. 62.

[43] *Schloss Bros v Stevens* [1906] 2 K.B. 665.

[44] *CA Blackwell (Contractors) Ltd* [2007] EWHC 94 (Comm) at [45]; [2007] Lloyd's Rep. I.R. 511 at 520.

[45] *Prudent Tankers SA v Dominion Insurance Co (The Caribbean Sea)* [1980] 1 Lloyd's Rep. 338 at 347; *The Miss Jay Jay* [1985] 1 Lloyd's Rep. 264, affirmed [1987] 1 Lloyd's Rep. 32.

[46] *Versloot Dredging BV v HDI Gerling Industrie Versicherung AG ("The DC Merwestone")* [2012] EWHC 1666 (Comm) at [57]; [2013] 2 All E.R. (Comm) 465 at 483–484; [2013] 2 Lloyd's Rep. I.R. 131 at 147 (on a point not forming part of the appeal to the Court of Appeal, who affirmed the decision (*Versloot Dredging BV* [2014] EWCA Civ 1349; [2015] Q.B. 608; [2015] 2 W.L.R. 1063), nor as part of the appeal to the Supreme Court which reversed the decision [2016] UKSC 45; [2016] 3 W.L.R. 543.

[47] M. Clarke, *The Law of Insurance Contracts* (London: Informa), Vol.2, para.17-3A1. Although a latent defect in the subject-matter is a case of inherent vice, the concept is not confined to this. For instance, the tendency of fruit to rot sooner or later is an example of inherent vice, whether or not the fruit was in good condition when it was acquired.

[48] *Gaunt* [1921] 2 A.C. 41 at 57-58; [1921] All E.R. Rep. 447 at 455, per Lord Sumner.

[49] *Soya GmbH Mainz KG* [1983] 1 Lloyd's Rep. 122 at 126, per Lord Diplock.

[50] In *Soya GmbH Mainz KG*, there was cover against "heat, sweat and spontaneous combustion" (known as an "HSSC" policy). This was held to displace the presumption against inherent vice to the extent that the damage was due to the tendency of the cargo to become hot, to sweat or to combust spontaneously: [1983] 1 Lloyd's Rep. 122.

[51] *Soya GmbH Mainz KG* [1983] 1 Lloyd's Rep. 122 at 126, per Lord Diplock.

MIA, the presumption against cover for inherent vice is, again, a matter of construction, and it can be rebutted in the same way. An insurer cannot defeat a contractor's claim under a policy that expressly covers the cost of replacing defectively designed works, by arguing that the damage was a result of inherent vice in the works or materials.[52] This is because if the policy covers the cost of repairing a latent defect, or of damage consequent on a latent defect, the presumption against cover for inherent vice is rebutted to that extent. Where the only fortuity operating on works or materials comes from the works or materials themselves, the proximate cause of the loss will be the inherent vice or nature of the subject matter insured. However, inherent vice of the works or materials will not be established by showing that the subject matter in question was not capable of withstanding the normal incidents of weather or other insured perils.[53]

10-014   Just as with ordinary wear and tear, inherent vice was treated in the early authorities as part of the concept of certainty of loss.[54] However, it is now clear that damage can be a consequence of inherent vice without it being inevitable.[55] This means that if damage to the subject-matter is due to some internal process that occurs unpredictably, i.e. in some cases but not others, the loss may still be implicitly excluded from all risks cover. Arnould for instance notes: "[d]amage from inherent vice may be just as capricious in its incidence as damage caused by perils of the seas".[56] In *TM Noten BV v Harding*,[57] which was considered in *Global Process Systems Inc v Syarikat Takaful Malaysia Bhd (The Cendor Mopu)*,[58] it was unsuccessfully argued that as the insured cargo—leather gloves, which had been damaged by damp during shipment—was one of a number of similar consignments in which damage had occurred sometimes but not other times, the damage was not inevitable and hence not a case of inherent vice. This was rejected on the basis that damage "may be caused by inherent vice without being inevitable"[59] and on the facts because, as Bingham LJ pointed out, there was no untoward or unusual event of any kind.[60] Conversely, if there is express cover for loss caused by a form of inherent vice—thereby rebutting the presumption against such cover—it is still necessary to determine whether the loss was fortuitous,[61] albeit that a subjective test of inevitability arguably applies.[62]

10-015   What is the position where there are two or more effective causes, one of which

---

52   *Mitchell Conveyor & Transporter Co Ltd v Pulbrook* (1933) 45 Ll. L. Rep. 239 at 241–243, per Roche J.
53   *Global Process Systems Inc v Syarikat Takaful Malaysia Bhd (The Cendor Mopu)* [2011] UKSC 5; [2011] Bus. L.R. 537; [2011] 1 All E.R. 869.
54   In *Gaunt* [1921] 2 A.C. 41, e.g. at 57; [1921] All E.R. Rep. 447, e.g. at 455 Lord Sumner said: "the expression does not cover inherent vice or mere wear and tear ... It covers a risk, not a certainty; it is something, which happens to the subject matter from without, not the natural behaviour of that subject matter, being what it is".
55   *Soya GmbH Mainz KG* [1982] 1 Lloyd's Rep. 136 at 149 and 150, per Donaldson L.J; *TM Noten BV v Harding* [1990] 2 Lloyd's Rep. 283 at 289, per Bingham LJ.
56   *Arnould's Law of Marine Insurance and Average*, edited by J. Gilman et al., 18th edn (London: Sweet & Maxwell, 2013), para.22-25.
57   *TM Noten BV* [1990] 2 Lloyd's Rep. 283.
58   *The Cendor Mopu* [2011] UKSC 5; [2011] Bus. L.R. 537; [2011] 1 All E.R. 869 at [28].
59   *T M Noten BV* [1990] 2 Lloyd's Rep. 283 at 289, per Bingham LJ.
60   *T M Noten BV* [1990] 2 Lloyd's Rep. 283 at 289.
61   *Soya GmbH Mainz KG* [1982] 1 Lloyd's Rep. 136, affirmed [1983] 1 Lloyd's Rep. 122.
62   *The Nukila* [1997] 2 Lloyd's Rep. 146 at 151; [1997] C.L.C. 966 at 971, per Hobhouse LJ (see above, para.10-010); cf. *Soya GmbH Mainz KG* [1983] 1 Lloyd's Rep. 122 where the Court of Appeal came, obiter, to the opposite conclusion (criticised above at paras 10-009 and 10-011).

is an insured peril and one an inherent characteristic of the insured property? In *The Cendor Mopu*[63] an oil rig being carried on a barge from the United States to Malaysia was damaged as a result of the action of waves, which were no worse than could reasonably have been expected. The Insurers' defence to the claim for indemnity was that the damage was as a result of inherent vice because the legs of the oil rig were unable to withstand reasonably foreseeable weather conditions. The Supreme Court considered the position where there are two proximate causes of the damage, one of which is a pre-existing susceptibility in the insured property and the other a fortuitous event. Although the fortuitous event was able to cause damage to the insured property because of its impact upon or interaction with its pre-existing characteristics, it was the insured peril that was the proximate cause. Inability of insured property to withstand foreseeable fortuitous events does not prevent the loss being caused by an insured peril. Lord Diplock in *Soya*[64] was approved in *The Cendor Mopu* as correctly stating the law:

> "[Inherent vice] means the risk of deterioration of the goods shipped as a result of their natural behaviour in the ordinary course of the contemplated voyage without the intervention of any fortuitous external accident or casualty."[65]

3. INTENTIONAL DAMAGE AND WILFUL MISCONDUCT

Wilful misconduct. There is no cover under an all risks policy for loss or damage caused by the "wilful misconduct" of the insured.[66] This implied exclusion can be seen as a reflection of the general rule of public policy that an insured cannot recover for loss and damage he has deliberately brought about. However, the concept of "wilful misconduct" is wider than the deliberate sabotage of the subject matter by the insured: it extends to the reckless running of risks. At the same time, the rule against cover for intentionally caused loss is not limited to circumstances where the insured's conduct is blameworthy: if the insured consciously albeit reasonably damages the insured property, the principle that the damage must be accidental, excludes recovery. **10-016**

Loss brought about by the wilful misconduct of third parties is, by contrast, fortuitous: if a third party steals or converts the insured property, the loss will be covered by an all risks policy.[67] **10-017**

Intentional damage. If the insured has deliberately damaged or abandoned the subject matter in full knowledge that loss or damage will result, there will be no recovery under an all risks insuring clause even if there were perfectly good reasons for this course of action, because the loss will not be accidental.[68] However, par- **10-018**

---

[63] *The Cendor Mopu* [2011] UKSC 5; [2011] Bus. L.R. 537; [2011] 1 All ER. 869. For a full discussion of the facts of this case, see below, para.24-086.

[64] *Soya GmbH Mainz KG* [1983] 1 Lloyd's Rep. 122.

[65] Soya GmbH Mainz KG [1983] 1 Lloyd's Rep. 122 at 126.

[66] *Gaunt* [1921] 2 A.C. 41 at 52, (per Viscount Finlay); at 57 (per Lord Sumner); [1921] All E.R. Rep. 447 at 452 (per Viscount Finlay); at 455 (per Lord Sumner). Section 55(2)(a) of the MIA provides that: "The insurer is not liable for any loss attributable to the wilful misconduct of the assured, but, unless the policy otherwise provides, he is liable for any loss proximately caused by a peril insured against, even though the loss would not have happened but for the misconduct or negligence of the master or crew."

[67] *London & Provincial Leather Processes Ltd v Hudson* [1939] 2 K.B. 724; [1939] 3 All E.R. 857.

[68] Inasmuch as the insured is acting for reasonable, non-fraudulent reasons, it seems perverse to call

ties are free to insert within an all risks policy a specific indemnity for "intentional damage" to cover, for example, the cost of damaging or dismantling works in order to gain access to dangerous or defective works.[69]

10-019 **Recklessness.** Obviously, if the insured deliberately destroys the insured property without good reason this will amount to wilful misconduct. The rule against cover for the consequences of wilful misconduct is not, however, limited to the situation where the insured actually intends to bring about the loss or damage that occurs. Recklessness is sufficient[70] and in this context recklessness means either: (i) actual awareness by the insured that his conduct will increase the risk of loss or damage; or (ii) not caring whether there is a risk or not, i.e. "reckless indifference". In *Patrick v Royal London Mutual Insurance Society Ltd*,[71] the claimant brought proceedings against the liability insurer of an 11-year-old boy who set fire to some pallets in the corner of a mill, starting a blaze that damaged the claimant's stock. The child had intended only to set fire to the pallets and did not think that the mill would be burned down. On the issue of whether this conduct fell within an express exclusion in the policy for "wilful ... acts", the judge at first instance, namely HHJ Seymour QC, considered that damage arising from a wilful act is damage both deliberately caused and consciously intended. He considered that if the phrase simply meant a "deliberate" act, this would exclude most cases of negligence. He also said that

"[a] car driven into a wall is being driven consciously, and thus deliberately, even if it was not intended to drive into the wall."[72]

On appeal,[73] Tuckey LJ agreed that something more than deliberate activity is required—there had to be some awareness of the consequences—but recklessness was enough. He said:

"[I]f the insured is aware that what he is about to do risks damage of the kind which gives rise to the claim or does not care whether there is such a risk or not, he will act recklessly if he goes ahead and does it."[74]

---

such conduct "wilful misconduct"; rather one reaches the conclusion that the loss is not covered by applying the principle that all risks insurance requires accidental, unintentional damage. But in *National Oilwell (UK) Ltd v Davy Offshore Ltd* [1993] 2 Lloyd's Rep. 582 at 622, Colman J suggested that whilst deliberately sinking a ship because it was not economical to run would not be wilful misconduct; that conduct would become misconduct if a claim in respect of the loss of the ship were presented. This is a somewhat circular way of explaining the point.

69 *Seele Austria GmbH & Co KG v Tokio Marine Europe Insurance Ltd* [2008] EWCA Civ 441; [2009] 1 All E.R. (Comm) 171. The issue that divided the Court of Appeal in the case was whether on a proper construction of the particular policy wording an extension of cover for intentional access damage was conditional, on there being fortuitous damage or, instead, a stand-alone indemnity.

70 *Patrick v Royal London Mutual Insurance Society Ltd* [2006] EWCA Civ 421; [2006] 2 All E.R. (Comm) 344; [2006] 1 C.L.C. 576; *CA Blackwell (Contractors) Ltd* [2007] EWHC 94 (Comm) at [49]; [2007] Lloyd's Rep. I.R. 511 at 521.

71 *Patrick* [2006] EWCA Civ 421; [2006] 2 All E.R. (Comm) 344; [2006] 1 C.L.C. 576.

72 *Patrick* [2005] EWHC 1767 (QB) at [23]; [2005] 2 All E.R. (Comm) 453 at 463, affirmed [2006] EWCA Civ 421; [2006] 2 All E.R. (Comm) 344; [2006] 1 C.L.C. 576. *Harris v Poland* [1941] 1 K.B. 462; [1941] 1 All E.R. 204 provides an illustration of this point. An insured homeowner stashed jewellery and money inside her fireplace, and later, forgetting that she had done so, lit a fire destroying the hidden items. The insurers contended that there was no "damage by fire" where property was damaged by fire intentionally lighted and burning quite properly. This defence was rejected by the judge, who held that the policy responded to the ignition of something not intended to be ignited.

73 *Patrick* [2006] EWCA Civ 421; [2006] 2 All E.R. (Comm) 344; [2006] 1 C.L.C. 576.

74 *Patrick* [2006] EWCA Civ 421 at [16]; [2006] 2 All E.R. (Comm) 344 at 360; [2006] 1 C.L.C. 576

Nonetheless, the Court of Appeal, in applying this test, upheld the decision of the judge that the child's conduct was not wilful: it might have been "stupid" conduct, but inasmuch as the child was unaware of the risk that he might burn down the mill. Given that the evidence did not show that he was careless as to whether he might have done so or not, it was held he had not been reckless.

There is a potential tension between the principle that insurance is presumed to **10-020** cover the negligence of the insured,[75] and a rule that excludes cover where the insured runs a known risk of damage. Suppose a contractor, in order to avoid paying liquidated damages for late completion, rushes the construction of the foundations and the quality of the work suffers. If the building subsequently collapses, this could no doubt be characterised as the result of negligence. But inasmuch as the contractor was aware that hurrying the works would increase the risk of their failure, would a claim under an insurance policy be excluded for wilful misconduct?

In practice, direct evidence of the state of mind of the contractor may be hard to **10-021** obtain and courts may be unwilling to make the inference that a contractor deliberately and wrongly ran an increased risk of causing loss or damage. Part of the reason for this is undoubtedly that courts are careful to avoid eroding the principle that an insured's negligence is covered. Moreover, it is recognised that there is always an element of risk inherent in complex construction projects. This being so, it would be unattractive to stigmatise a novel and/or more efficient methodology as wrongful simply because it might be more risky in one respect. In *CA Blackwell (Contractors) Ltd*,[76] the insurer argued that the insured earthworks contractor had acted recklessly by continuing to work through the winter months after it had seen, in the autumn, that its temporary drainage works were inadequate.[77] The insurer also contended that the use of capping material of a type known to degrade and turn into slurry in wet conditions, necessitated additional protective measures and that it was reckless for the insured contractor not to take these measures. The judge held that there was no wilful misconduct. The insurer's contentions "read more like allegations of negligence than of recklessness".[78] He stressed that there was no sign that the fellow professionals on site sensed that the insured was deliberately running a risk, nor was there evidence of the contractor having a previous record for rushing jobs.[79] Those two aspects emphasised by the judge but found to be missing on the facts of the case (i.e.: (i) external warnings from other professionals or inspectors; and (ii) a previous record for rushing works) might therefore be factors that could be important in establishing a claim of wilful misconduct in this type of situation.

Corporate knowledge. Since the defence of wilful misconduct depends on the **10-022** insured having actual awareness that a risk of loss or damage is being run (or indifference to the fact), in the case of an insured company the normal principles for

---

at 580.
[75] See, e.g. M. Clarke, *The Law of Insurance Contracts* (London: Informa), Vol.2, para.19-2A.
[76] *CA Blackwell (Contractors) Ltd* [2007] EWHC 94 (Comm); [2007] Lloyd's Rep. I.R. 511, affirmed [2007] EWCA Civ 1450; [2008] 1 All E.R. (Comm) 885; [2008] Lloyd's Rep. I.R. 529
[77] *CA Blackwell (Contractors) Ltd* [2007] EWHC 94 (Comm) at [50]; [2007] Lloyd's Rep. I.R. 511 at 521.
[78] *CA Blackwell (Contractors) Ltd* [2007] EWHC 94 (Comm) at [52]; [2007] Lloyd's Rep. I.R. 511 at 521, per HHJ Mackie QC.
[79] *CA Blackwell (Contractors) Ltd* [2007] EWHC 94 (Comm) at [52]; [2007] Lloyd's Rep. I.R. 511 at 521, per H.H.J Mackie QC.

determining corporate knowledge apply.[80] This involves identifying the director or manager who would have the responsibility of taking decisions, without reference back to the board, in the area of the company's activities as to which the company is said to have been in wilful default.[81]

10-023 **Ordinary trading consequences of voluntary conduct.** In *Ikerigi Compania Naviera SA v Palmer (The Wondrous)*,[82] the insured's vessel was detained in port pending the discharge of its liabilities to the port authority. Hobhouse J held that this period of detention could not be characterised as fortuitous because it was simply the consequence of the insured's choice not to pay the port dues:

> "It did not happen by chance but by the choice of the assured. Put another way, it would be in the ordinary course that, if the owners of the vessel do not pay the port dues for which they are liable to the port authority ... the vessel will not be cleared. For the purposes of the law of insurance, in the absence of an express agreement to the contrary, a policy should not be construed as covering the ordinary consequences of voluntary conduct of the assured arising out of the ordinary incidents of trading; it is not a risk."[83]

10-024 The reference to "the ordinary consequences of voluntary conduct" should not be treated as weakening or contradicting the requirement that the insured actually foresee the risk of loss or damage. It was self-evident on the facts of *The Wondrous*[84] that the insured ship-owner would have understood that as a consequence of failing to discharge the port liabilities the vessel would not be cleared; hence the description of the detention as the "choice" of the insured.

10-025 It has been held in the United States that where insured property is seized by creditors of the insured, the loss is not fortuitous.[85] This must be correct: in running up unpaid debts the insured assumes the risk inherent in the concept of debt that the creditor will resort to action against the debtor's assets to achieve satisfaction. In contrast, if the seizure is by the creditor of a third party to whom the insured property has been entrusted, the loss is covered.[86]

10-026 **Misconduct of co-insured.** Where one of two or more co-insureds is guilty of wilful misconduct, the question of whether the innocent party is fixed with this misconduct depends on whether the policy is construed as joint (insurance of a common interest) or composite (insurance of several interests).[87] But even if the innocent co-insured is not tainted with the misconduct of the other, can the insurer still maintain that because the loss was deliberately brought about by one of the insureds the loss lacks fortuity? The answer to this question was held to be "no",

---

[80] *National Oilwell (UK) Ltd* [1993] 2 Lloyd's Rep 582 at 620, per Colman J. See more generally: *Lennard's Carrying Co Ltd v Asiatic Petroleum Co Ltd* [1915] A.C. 705 at 713; [1914–15] All E.R. Rep. 280 at 283; *HL Bolton Engineering Co Ltd v TJ Graham & Sons Ltd* [1957] 1 Q.B. 159 at 172; [1956] 3 All E.R. 624 at 630; *Arthur Guinness, Son & Co (Dublin) Ltd v Owners of the Motor Vessel Freshfield (The Lady Gwendolen)* [1965] 3 W.L.R. 91 at 105–107; [1965] 2 All E.R. 283 at 294–295; [1965] P. 294 at 343–345.

[81] *National Oilwell (UK) Ltd* [1993] 2 Lloyd's Rep. 582 at 620.

[82] *Ikerigi Compania Naviera SA v Palmer (The Wondrous)* [1991] 1 Lloyd's Rep. 400, affirmed on other grounds [1992] 2 Lloyd's Rep. 566.

[83] *The Wondrous* [1991] 1 Lloyd's Rep. 400 at 416.

[84] *The Wondrous* [1991] 1 Lloyd's Rep. 400, affirmed [1992] 2 Lloyd's Rep. 566.

[85] *Intermetal Mexicana SA v INA* 866 F. 2d 71 (3rd Cir 1989).

[86] *London & Provincial Leather* [1939] 2 K.B. 724; [1939] 3 All E.R. 857.

[87] See below, paras 20-030 to 20-037.

so far as all risks insurance is concerned, by Rix J in *State of the Netherlands v Youell*.[88] This must be correct: as the interests of the co-insureds are divisible for the purposes of the defence of wilful misconduct, the innocent party should logically be in the same position as where the subject matter is deliberately damaged by a third party—the loss should be regarded as fortuitous and non-deliberate from the non-defaulting party's perspective.

---

[88] *Netherlands v Youell* [1997] 2 Lloyd's Rep. 440 at 454; [1997] C.L.C. 938 at 956–957. The judge there distinguished the decision in *P Samuel & Co Ltd v Dumas* [1924] A.C. 431; (1924) 18 Ll. L. Rep. 211, where it was held that the deliberate scuttling of a ship is not a "peril of the sea", on the basis that the definition of "perils of the sea" is idiosyncratic; the general rule is that deliberate misconduct by someone other than the claimant insured does constitute a "risk". (Point was not raised on appeal: [1998] 1 Lloyd's Rep. 236; [1998] C.L.C. 44.)

THE INDEMNITY

1.   Introduction

Introduction.   The principles governing indemnity are of central importance to   **11-001**
the parties to an insurance contract. These principles developed by the courts in relation to the apportionment of subrogated recoveries between the insured and insurers and limitations placed on the insured's recoverable losses are also considered.

Meaning of loss and damage.   The meaning of loss and damage is considered in   **11-002**
Ch.14 and the distinction between damage and defects which cause damage is
considered in Ch.16, to which reference should be made for detailed discussion.
This chapter assumes that, for the purposes of a claim on a CAR policy, physical
loss or damage comprising an adverse change in the physical condition of the
insured property exists.

Rectification by third party.   Where there is damage that would be indemnified   **11-003**
under the policy, an insured may still not be able to claim an indemnity where the
damage has been remedied or rectified by a third party without payment from the
insured, prior to payment by the insurers. The exception to this principle is where
the contractual obligations between the insured and the third party state the manner in which the insurance monies are to be used or impose a duty to account for
those monies leaving the insured under-indemnified.[1]

2.   Measure of indemnity

Valued policy.   A valued policy is one in which the agreed value of the property   **11-004**
is identified in the policy. This form of policy is to be contrasted with an unvalued
policy where the policy identifies the insurer's maximum liability. Valued polices
are not common in CAR insurance, although there are occasions where the parties
may choose to agree the value of a particular item, such as an item that has artistic
value and which may not be capable of direct replacement. Under a valued policy
the total loss will be the agreed value of the property.

---

[1]   *Lonsdale & Thompson Ltd v Black Arrow Group Plc* [1993] Ch. 361; [1993] 2 W.L.R. 815; [1993]
3 All E.R. 648.

11-005 **Partial loss.** Under a valued policy, partial loss is paid as a fraction of the agreed value calculated as a proportion of the damage that has been suffered. In most situations this is a simple calculation, at least in theory, representing the percentage reduction in value of the property multiplied by the agreed value of the item in the policy. In a case of overvaluation, the proportion is calculated by reference to the true reduction in value of the subject matter rather than by reference to the agreed value, this proportion is then applied to the agreed value.[2] In *Elcock v Thomson* it was suggested that under a valued policy the insurer may be able or compelled to pay the cost of repair in a case of partial loss that is over or undervalued, where this is considered to be more appropriate compensation.[3]

11-006 **Unvalued policy.** A CAR policy will usually be unvalued and the measure of indemnity will be defined as the "sum insured" in respect of the insured peril. The principle of indemnity provides that an insured party has the right to be indemnified in respect of his insured loss or damage, subject to the policy terms concerning deductibles and policy limits. A typical policy term relating to the sum insured reads as follows:

> "£X each occurrence unlimited as to the number of occurrences during the Period of Insurance".

The clause illustrates that the phrase "sum insured" does not amount to an agreed valuation but fixes a ceiling of liability.[4] This type of policy is classified as an "unvalued" policy. In the example term cited above, a fresh limit would apply to each claim on the policy provided it is in respect of a sufficiently distinct event. If the sum insured is simply given as a figure without such qualification, however, it represents a global maximum amount for which the insurers can be liable under the policy: a pot that can be exhausted by a series of claims, even if they are unrelated. A CAR project policy will usually identify the estimated contract value as the basis for calculating the sum insured; sometimes a proportionally higher figure (e.g. "130 per cent of Estimated Contract Value") will be obtained if the insureds wish to be protected in the event of variations and/or increased costs of rebuilding following damage. Where a policy is unvalued and the insured party is underinsured, the insured will not be able to recover more than the policy indemnity limit, but it may be reduced proportionately; this situation is considered below, in para.11-019.

11-007 **Reinstatement.** Where there is no clause in the policy requiring reinstatement, the insurer cannot require the works to be reinstated. In relation to existing structures there is likely to be an element of betterment that is inherent in reinstatement, as the old structure is being replaced with a new structure; in new build projects there is unlikely to be any appreciable betterment. Where there are multiple insurers of the same subject-matter, they are entitled to reinstate jointly, this will usually be cheaper than the combined cost of indemnifying under the individual policies.

---

[2] *Elcock v Thomson* [1949] 2 K.B. 755; [1949] 2 All E.R. 381; (1948-49) 82 Ll. L. Rep. 892. This calculation is set out as an equation in D. Jess, *The Insurance of Commercial Risks: Law and Practice*, 4th edn (London: Sweet & Maxwell, 2011), para.19-06.

[3] *Elcock* [1949] 2 K.B. 755 at 764; [1949] 2 All E.R. 381 at 387-388; (1948–49) 82 Ll. L. Rep. 892 at 902.

[4] *Quorum A/S v Schramm (Damage)* [2001] EWHC 494 (Comm) at [71]-[72]; [2002] 2 All E.R. (Comm) 147 at 163-164; [2002] Lloyd's Rep I.R. 292 at [71]-[72].

A clause in a CAR policy that provides an insurer with an election to reinstate **11-008** or repair may be in the following terms:

"If the Insurer elects or becomes bound to reinstate or replace any property insured, then the Insured shall at its own expense provide all plans, documents and information as the Insurer may reasonably require. The Insurer shall not be bound to reinstate exactly or completely but only as circumstances permit and in a reasonably sufficient manner and it shall not be bound to expend more than the sum insured."

Section 83 of the Fires Prevention (Metropolis) Act 1774. Section 83 of the **11-009** Fires Prevention (Metropolis) Act 1774 was introduced to deter insureds from setting fire to property. It operates to allow an interested third party, such as a mortgagee, to request that the sum claimed under the indemnity be directed to reinstatement instead. Detailed explanation of the effect of s.83 of the 1774 Act is set out below in para.26-008. It is noted that the 1774 Act has been subject to consideration by the Law Commission.[5]

Cost of reinstatement. A policy of indemnity against physical damage to the **11-010** construction works is concerned only with financial compensation representing the cost of remedying damage to property. Nevertheless, there may be circumstances where property that has been damaged has some special characteristic that justifies spending whatever is required to put it back into its pre-damage condition. A common example is a rare vintage car that, by its nature, is more than merely a form of conveyance. However, where one is concerned with business property, the primary purpose of which is to enable its owner to conduct a business and to make profits, considerations of reasonableness may become relevant:

"Where business premises are concerned, the need to carry on the business and to mitigate the loss of earnings is an important factor."[6]

So although the starting point is always likely to be the financial cost of reinstatement, the insured may not be justified in insisting on full and precise reinstatement of the works to its pre-damaged state if it would be unreasonable or eccentric to do so.[7] The degree and cost of the reinstatement that can be justified will depend upon the objective that needs to be achieved.

Date for calculation. Where a CAR policy indemnifies against physical loss or **11-011** damage, the starting point is to establish when that loss or damage occurred since it may be appropriate to calculate the amount of the indemnity as at that date. The date of damage is most likely to be appropriate if the indemnity is going to be calculated by reference to the diminution in value caused by the damage. Where, however, the indemnity is calculated by reference to the cost of repairs, the indemnity will normally be calculated by reference to the cost of the repairs when they are carried out, since the adoption of any other basis is likely to be hypothetical and to lead to either over or under-indemnification. If an insured fails to carry

---

[5] The majority of responses to the Law Commission favoured its retention. See Law Commission, *Law Commission: Review of Insurance Contract Law. Section 83 Summary of Responses* (February 2010), *http://www.lawcom.gov.uk/wp-content/uploads/2015/03/ICL_s83_Fires_Prevention_Act_ responses.pdf* [Accessed 1 July 2016].

[6] *Dominion Mosaics & Tile Co v Trafalgar Trucking Co* [1990] 2 All E.R. 246 at 249, per Taylor LJ.

[7] *Reynolds v Phoenix Assurance Co Ltd* [1978] 2 Lloyd's Rep. 440 at 453, per Forbes J.

out necessary repairs for no good reason and the cost or content of the repairs is thereby increased, it is open to insurers to maintain that the increased cost or content is attributable to the unwarranted delay rather than to initial damage.

11-012 **Total loss.** The insured is indemnified for either the cost of repairing the property that has been damaged or for the diminution in value in the case of goods and chattels intended for resale. The measure of the indemnity is fixed by reference to the condition of the insured subject matter immediately prior to the occurrence of the damage. However, some marine policies give insurers the option to reinstate insured property by treating it as totally lost. The sum payable in respect of a total loss is the market value of the subject matter at the time of the loss, even if the value has increased or decreased since the loss. Market value refers to the price at which goods are available, not that at which they would have been sold, so it does not account for loss of profits. The doctrine of constructive total loss does not apply to conventional land-based CAR insurance.

11-013 **Partial loss.** In CAR insurance the insured is indemnified for partial loss as well as for total loss. This reflects the fact that the property may only be damaged and not totally destroyed. There are two possible bases for calculating the indemnity: the cost of repairing damage to the property and the diminution in value of the property as a result of the damage. In some cases it will cost more to repair the property that has been damaged than the sum by which the property's value has diminished as a result of the damage. In this situation an insured's intention to undertake repairs may be important in deciding the appropriate basis for the indemnity.[8] In *Reynolds v Phoenix Assurance Co Ltd*,[9] Forbes J acknowledged this point. He said:

> "The question of the proper measure of indemnity thus becomes a matter of fact and degree to be decided on the circumstances of each case."

The cost of repair will be awarded where there is an intention to repair property even if this measure is substantially higher than diminution in value, so long as the intention is not a mere eccentricity.[10]

11-014 **Consequential loss.** Consequential loss is, prima facie, not indemnified under a CAR policy as this type of policy indemnifies only in respect of physical loss and damage. However, a CAR policy will often include an express extension for specific forms of consequential loss, such as loss of profit. Extensions to cover for consequential loss are considered below in Ch.17.[11]

11-015 **Assessors.** Assessor clauses are not common in CAR insurance, as insurers prefer to appoint specialist loss adjusters who provide reports to the insurer regarding the amount of the indemnity and a CAR insurer may authorise a loss adjuster to agree with the insured the amount of the indemnity due to the insured. Where a complex

---

[8] *Leppard v Excess Insurance Co Ltd* [1979] 1 W.L.R. 512; [1979] 2 All E.R. 668; [1979] 2 Lloyd's Rep. 91.
[9] *Reynolds* [1978] 2 Lloyd's Rep. 440 at 451.
[10] *Reynolds* [1978] 2 Lloyd's Rep. 440 at 453.
[11] Consequential loss is also considered in the context of all risks property insurance ("ARPI"). See below, Ch.26.

mathematical calculation is required, e.g. when calculating the period of delay caused by damage, a policy may provide for an assessor to be appointed whose decisions will be binding.

Betterment. The general rule in an insurance policy that indemnifies an insured **11-016** for the cost of repairing damage to contract works is that no deduction will be made even though the repaired structure may be superior to the original, unless the insured will be placed in a position where he will be making a profit.[12] In the case of marine insurance an insured is required to give a customary allowance of one-third in respect of the cost of repairing damage to a ship.[13] In land-based CAR insurance the position is less clear, although guidance provided by the courts in tort law may be relevant. This lack of clarity is less important in CAR insurance than for other forms of property insurance, because damage to the contract works usually occurs during construction or shortly thereafter and the repaired contract works are unlikely to be superior to the original works. There are occasions when a structure must be rebuilt or repaired in a different manner or in a different location and CAR insurance may also indemnify damage caused to existing structures. In respect of repair and reinstatement of these categories of damage, betterment may be relevant. This is illustrated by the case of *Reynolds*,[14] where the policy contained a pay, reinstate or replace clause. A fire almost totally destroyed what was an obsolete building. Whilst the insured was successful in his claim to be indemnified for reinstatement, a deduction for betterment was made, although it was modest because the insured intended to use second-hand and inferior materials. Forbes J stated:

"Now the principle of betterment is too well established in the law of insurance to be departed from at this stage even though it may sometimes work hardship on the insured. It is simply that an allowance must be made because the assured is getting something new for something old."[15]

The court's approach in *Reynolds*[16] may be contrasted with the approach in **11-017** *Exchange Theatre Ltd v Iron Trades Mutual Insurance Co Ltd*,[17] where the court declined to award the cost of reinstating a Victorian hall used for playing bingo and awarded the cost of a modern equivalent instead. A different approach was also adopted in *Leppard v Excess Insurance Co Ltd*,[18] where the insured's house was destroyed by fire with the agreed cost of replacement after deduction for betterment being £8,694. The insured accepted that he would have sold the house for £4,500 before the fire. The judge at first instance made a deduction for betterment but the Court of Appeal dealt with it differently by holding that the sum payable under the policy was £3,000, that being £4,500 less the value of the land of £1,500.

CAR policies may contain a DE5 or LEG 3 defects exclusion clause, which **11-018** provides that the cost of remedying defective and damaged works is indemnified but excludes the additional cost of improvement, this is considered below in Ch.16.

---

[12] Some CAR policies expressly exclude betterment. A typical clause will state: "The cost of any alterations, additions and/or improvements which may be undertaken as a result of any loss or damage shall not be recoverable hereunder. The insurers may at their option repair replace reinstate or pay cash in lieu of repairs."
[13] That being the "customary deduction" referred to in s.69(1) of the Marine Insurance Act 1906.
[14] *Reynolds* [1978] 2 Lloyd's Rep. 440.
[15] *Reynolds* [1978] 2 Lloyd's Rep. 440 at 453.
[16] *Reynolds* [1978] 2 Lloyd's Rep. 440.
[17] *Exchange Theatre Ltd v Iron Trades Mutual Insurance Co Ltd* [1983] 1 Lloyd's Rep. 674.
[18] *Leppard* [1979] 1 W.L.R. 512; [1979] 2 All E.R. 668; [1979] 2 Lloyd's Rep. 91.

It is to be noted, however, that an improvement in design may occur where the insured has elected to change the original design or where he had no reasonable choice about the improvement. In both situations the DE5 and LEG 3 exclusions make clear that the additional cost will not be indemnified.

11-019 **Average.** By means of an average clause, it is common for insurance policies to provide that the insured will be paid the proportion of the loss and damage he suffers relative to the size of the risk that was made known to the insurer. The principle underpinning average is that the insured is his own insurer for the difference between the sum insured and the true value of the subject matter and is liable for a proportionate amount of the loss. Where there is no average clause in a policy the insured will be entitled to be paid the full sum insured, except in the case of marine insurance where an average clause is implied.

11-020 CAR insurance differs from the usual position for property insurance to the extent that the insurer will be expected to know the extent of the risk associated with a particular project, as the contract sum is stated in the building contract and the policy will contain a formula for increasing the premium if the cost of the works increases. Annual CAR policies may specify a maximum contract value[19] and therefore they may contain average clauses or a formula whereby the premium payable is increased if the maximum contract value is exceeded.

11-021 **Late Payment.** Under English law, the present position is that normal breach of contract rules do not apply to insurance and damages are not payable by an insurer for late payment of sums due under a policy. There is no implied term that an insurer will negotiate and pay sums due with reasonable diligence and due expedition.[20] The insured is entitled to claim interest and his legal costs once legal proceedings have been issued under the High Court's power to award interest pursuant to s.35A of the Senior Courts Act 1981 and in Arbitration under s.69 of the Arbitration Act 1996. The reason why damages are not recoverable for late payment is based on the legal fiction that the insurer has promised to keep the insured safe from harm. If harm does occur, the insurer has breached that promise and is liable to pay the amount of the claim as unliquidated damages. This means that, if the insurer rejects a valid claim or pays it late and the insured suffers additional loss as a result, he cannot claim additional compensation from the insurer because English law does not permit a claim for "damages on damages". In *Sprung v Royal Insurance (UK) Ltd*,[21] plant and machinery at Mr Sprung's factory were vandalised and his insurers disputed the claim. Mr Sprung could not afford to carry out the repairs himself or get a loan and his business collapsed. Four years later, the court found the insurance claim should have been paid within a few months and awarded him an indemnity for the damage to his property, plus interest and costs. The Court of Appeal said he could not be compensated for losing the opportunity to sell the business, a loss estimated at £75,000 because, under English law, there can be no award of damages for the late payment of damages. The courts have also, on occasion,

---

19 An average clause may provide that "if after the occurrence of loss or damage it is found that the maximum contract value is less than the maximum value of the contracts undertaken by the Insured, then the amount recoverable shall be reduced in the same proportion as the amount of the agreed maximum contract value bears to the actual maximum contract value undertaken".

20 *Insurance Corp of the Channel Islands Ltd v McHugh* [1997] L.R.L.R. 94 at 136–137.

21 *Sprung v Royal Insurance (UK) Ltd* [1997] C.L.C. 70; [1999] 1 Lloyd's Rep. I.R. 111.

found that interest accrues from the date the insurers are notified of the claim, or from a date that allows for a reasonable investigation to have been conducted.[22]

On 4 May 2017 the position changes, with the introduction of a term implied into **11-022** all contracts of insurance that insurers must pay any sums due to the insured within a "reasonable time."[23] Section 13A of the Insurance Act 2015 ("the 2015 Act") provides a non-exhaustive list of matters which may be taken into consideration when determining what is a reasonable time for payment in the particular circumstances of the case, and states that a reasonable time will always include time to investigate and assess the claim. Section 13A(3) identifies three circumstances, two of which are of particular relevance to construction insurance, these are: (a) the type of insurance; and (b) the size and complexity of the claim. CAR insurance will usually provide an indemnity for the cost of reinstatement and in this situation it may be reasonable for the insurer to wait until the remedial works and their cost have been identified before paying any sums. There may also be occasions where it will be reasonable for an insurer to wait until costs have been incurred before making payment.

Reinstatement and remedial works can often be complex and substantial and in relation to CAR policy claims it may be unreasonable to expect an insurer to pay a claim without having undertaken a detailed investigation into the cause of the damage and the extent and cost of such works. Delay in start-up insurance ("DSU") claims[24] often require remedial works to be completed and the project to be finished before the extent of delay will be known. DSU is considered below in Ch.17.

An insurer does not breach the implied term if it is able to show that there were **11-023** reasonable grounds for disputing the claim (whether as to the amount of any sum payable, or as to whether anything at all is payable). However, the conduct of the insurer in handling the claim may be a relevant factor in deciding whether that term is breached and, if so, when. Insurers' criteria for claims management, instructions to Loss Adjusters and communications with the insured may be relevant in deciding whether the handling of a claim is reasonable. Remedies (for example, damages) are available for breach of the implied term are in addition to and distinct from any right to enforce payment of the sums due, and any right to interest on those sums.

Contracting out is permitted in the case of non-consumer insurance, provided that **11-024** the insurer satisfies the transparency requirements in the 2015 Act. However, an insurer is unable to contract out of the implied term as respects deliberate or reckless breaches and any term purporting to allow the insurer to do so will have no contractual effect. The 2016 Act is considered below at paras 23-013 to 23-021.

3. LIMITS TO RECOVERY

Excesses. An excess—also sometimes referred to as a deductible—is a sum **11-025** required by the policy to be borne by the insured as the first part of his loss. Losses

---

[22] *McClean Enterprises v Ecclesiastical Insurance Office* [1986] 2 Lloyd's Rep. 416 at 427–428. See also *Seele Austria GmbH & Co KG v Tokio Marine Europe Insurance Ltd* [2009] EWHC 2066 (TCC) at [50]; [2009] B.L.R. 481 at 490; [2010] Lloyd's Rep I.R. 490 at 499, where the date on which a cause of action accrues was considered.

[23] Sections 13A and 16A of the 2015 Act were introduced by ss.29 and 30 of the Enterprise Act 2016 ("the 2016 Act").

[24] See further below, paras 17-051 to 17-077.

above the excess, up to the relevant limit of the policy, are recoverable. The excess is treated as a first or bottom layer of cover, for which the insured is his own insurer, with the insurance itself treated as a second layer of cover.[25] This affects the way the proceeds of subrogated claims are allocated between insurer and insured. A "retained liability"[26] is treated as the insured's loss, the consequence being that a claim on the policy will not be capable of being made until the loss exceeds the retained liability.

11-026   Excess clauses have several functions. By excluding trivial claims the costs of administering the policy will be reduced. Moreover, whereas only large losses will pierce a high layer of cover (say, £150,000 to £200,000), all losses, both large and small, will pass through the lowest layer of cover of the same width (zero to £50,000). Thus, even with a level distribution of large and small losses, increasing the level of excess cumulatively brings more losses out of the cover as well as reducing the insurer's liability on all claims, whereas reducing the liability ceiling only has an effect at the margins (i.e. on higher value claims). The fact that smaller losses are more frequent aggravates this effect. At the same time, it is generally thought that an excess clause imposes an incentive on the insured to look after the property and take measures to avoid damage being sustained.

11-027   **Aggregation of losses.**   Excess clauses usually provide for multiple deductibles, which apply on a loss-by-loss basis as opposed to creating a single excess in respect of any loss claimed within the period of the policy. Similarly, whilst the "sum insured" can be worded as a per-policy limit, it will take effect as a per-loss/event limit if qualified by the words "each loss" or "each event".[27] The purpose of aggregation wording is to enable

> "two or more separate losses covered by the policy to be treated as a single loss ... when they are linked by a unifying factor of some kind."[28]

Aggregation has the opposite effect, so far as the interests of the parties are concerned, depending on whether losses are being aggregated for the purpose of applying a deductible or a limit. In the case of a deductible, the insured will wish to group together as much of the damage as possible before an excess is applied; in the case of a limit, the insurer will want to aggregate as many items of damage as possible so that the largest possible amount of loss exceeds the financial limit of the policy or section of the policy.

---

[25] *Lord Napier and Ettrick v RF Kershaw Ltd (No.1)* [1993] A.C. 713; [1993] 2 W.L.R. 42; [1993] 1 All E.R. 385.

[26] The phrase "retained liability" makes sense in a liability insurance policy, but is not particularly appropriate in the context of first party loss insurance given that the assured is not "liable" for his own loss; "retained loss" would be more accurate. However, CAR policies often refer expressly to retained liabilities, e.g. *Seele Austria GmbH & Co KG* [2009] EWHC 2066 (TCC) at [8]; [2009] B.L.R. 481 at 484; [2010] Lloyd's Rep I.R. 490 at 492, per Clarke J.

[27] See below, para.11-028.

[28] *Lloyds TSB General Insurance Holdings Ltd v Lloyds Bank Group Insurance Co Ltd; Abbey National Plc v Lee* [2001] 1 All E.R. (Comm) 13 at 24; [2001] Lloyd's Rep. I.R. 237 at 245, affirmed [2003] UKHL 48 at [14]; [2003] All E.R. 43 at 48; [2003] Lloyd's Rep. I.R. 623 at 629. Considered and approved in *AIG Europe Ltd v OC320301 LLP (formerly the International Law Partnership LLP)* [2016] EWCA Civ 367; [2016] Lloyd's Rep. I.R. 289, there must be some intrinsic rather than remote connection between transactions for them to be "related".

"Loss" or "event".   The policy may be structured so that words of aggregation   **11-028**
are contained in a policy-wide definition of "loss" or "event" (an "aggregation
clause"). In other cases, the relevant language is part of the deductible or liability
limit clause itself: e.g. "£5,000 per occurrence of damage arising out of any one
event". If there is no express policy provision to the effect that losses must be aggregated, however, none will be implied.[29] Nor is there any presumption that the
parties intend to apply the same test of aggregation to deductibles as to the limit of
the insurer's liability.[30] Where the deductible/limit applies simply to "each loss" the
problem remains: how should one divide up the damage that has occurred for these
purposes?[31] If an office block collapsed due to an earthquake, most people would
describe "the loss" as the destruction of the block. Yet if instead only the roof fell
in, damaging equipment below, one might plausibly argue (perhaps paradoxically
given the previous example) that the roof and the equipment are separate losses. It
is difficult to identify the scope of a discrete "loss" without referring to unifying factors—such as timing and causation—that aggregation wording speaks to; an
advantage of such wording is that it is more expressive as to how these concepts
are to be applied.

Search for a unifying factor.   The more general the description of the unifying   **11-029**
factor prescribed by the aggregation wording, the wider the scope of the clause.[32]
The most common aggregation wordings are "series of related acts or omissions",
"arising from one event" and "arising from [or "attributable to"] one original [or
"originating"] cause". The latter two phrases have different meanings. An event is
"something which happens at a particular time, at a particular place, in a particular
way"; it is a narrower concept than a "cause", in that the latter can embrace a state
of affairs or an omission to act.[33] Often, the occurrence of the peril that brought
about the entire damage—the fire, the flood or hurricane, etc.—will undoubtedly
qualify as an event. However, where pervasive damage has occurred as a result of
defective design or build in the case of CAR, or inherent vice in relation to cargo
insurance, it may be more difficult to link all the items of damage to a single event.
This will be an issue where a series of repeated or similar workmanship errors
produces a cascade of damage to various parts of the property.

---

[29]   *Mabey & Johnson Ltd v Ecclesiastical Insurance Office Plc* [2003] EWHC 1523 (Comm) at [3];
[2004] Lloyd's Rep. I.R. 10 at 11. In the decision there referred to, the insurer's liability under a
professional indemnity policy was limited to £2 million "for a single claim". It was held that no aggregation language (such as "all claims arising out of the same act of negligence") had been agreed
and none could properly be implied. One has to be careful here, however: if a particular figure is
stated to be the "sum insured" without any further qualification, that figure applies as a global limit
which can be reached by the aggregation of *all* losses under the policy (see above, para.11-006)—
not because aggregation wording must be implied, but because there is no reason to imply multiple
limits. The point recognised in *Mabey & Johnson Ltd* is simply that inasmuch as a limit or deductible operates on a multiple (i.e. per claim or per loss) basis, no aggregation will be implied.

[30]   *Countrywide Assured Group Plc v Marshall* [2002] EWHC 2082 (Comm); [2003] 1 All E.R.
(Comm) 237; [2003] Lloyd's Rep. I.R. 195.

[31]   The problem of interpreting the phrase "for a single claim" in the context of professional indemnity
insurance was discussed in *Mabey & Johnson Ltd* [2003] EWHC 1523; [2004] Lloyd's Rep. I.R. 10.

[32]   *Lloyds TSB General Insurance Holdings Ltd; Abbey National Plc* [2003] UKHL 48 at [15]; [2003]
All E.R. 43 at 48; [2003] Lloyd's Rep. I.R. 623 at 629.

[33]   *AXA Reinsurance (UK) Ltd v Field* [1996] 1 W.L.R. 1026 at 1035; [1996] 3 All E.R. 517 at 526;
[1996] 2 Lloyd's Rep. 233 at 239, per Lord Mustill.

11-030 **"Series of related acts or omissions"** In *AIG Europe Ltd*,[34] OC320301 LLP was engaged to advise on international property law aspects of two transactions. Their policy terms were subject to cl.2.5 of the Solicitors' Minimum Terms, namely "… [a]ll Claims against any one or more Insured arising from: … (ii) one series of related acts or omissions".[35] Longmore LJ concluded that—on a linguistic analysis—the wording of the clause required that there should be some sort of connection between the transactions for them to be related. He went on to conclude that the connection had to be intrinsic rather than remote—for example, transactions which took place in contemplation of each other might be connected. The Court of Appeal rejected the idea that *any* degree of relatedness would suffice, concluding that this would result in an impossibly wide construction of the clause.

11-031 **"Arising out of any one event".** In *Seele Austria GmbH & Co KG*,[36] a subcontractor installed a number of window units in the building, which were found to leak due to defective sealing. Having decided that those costs were recoverable under the relevant clause,[37] the question arose whether a deductible for the first £10,000 of the cost of "each and every occurrence or series of occurrences arising out of any one event" applied in respect of each window, or whether it applied to the totality of the damage caused by the defects in the whole set of windows. Moore-Bick LJ reasoned that, since repeated instances of poor workmanship were to blame for the defective sealing, it could not be said that the series of defective installations arose out of one event.[38] This view accords with authorities in the context of professional indemnity insurance to the effect that where an underwriter has negligently entered into a series of transactions it is not possible to treat his propensity to act negligently, or his failure to carry out sufficient research, as a single event for these purposes.[39] The result might have been different if the windows had suffered from a common defect in design or manufacture or if the mistakes

> "were attributable to a single event, such as giving the workmen wrong instructions which they then conscientiously followed so as to produce a series of similar defects."[40]

11-032 **"Each and every loss in respect of any component".** In *Mitsubishi Electric UK Ltd v Royal London Insurance (UK) Ltd*[41] the insured was engaged under a subcontract to carry out the design, manufacture and installation of 94 toilet modules.

---

[34] *AIG Europe Ltd v OC320301 LLP* [2016] EWCA Civ 367.

[35] *AIG Europe Ltd v OC320301 LLP* [2016] EWCA Civ 367 at [8].

[36] *Seele Austria GmbH & Co KG* [2008] EWCA Civ 441; [2009] 1 All E.R. (Comm) 171; [2008] Lloyd's Rep. I.R. 739.

[37] See below, Ch.16.

[38] *Seele Austria GmbH & Co KG* [2008] EWCA Civ 441 at [55]-[57]; [2009] 1 All E.R. (Comm) 171 at 188-189; [2008] Lloyd's Rep. I.R. 739 at 752-753.

[39] *Caudle v Sharp* [1995] C.L.C. 642; [1995] L.R.L.R. 433; *AXA Reinsurance (UK) Plc* [1996] 1 W.L.R. 1026; [1996] 3 All E.R. 517; [1996] 2 Lloyd's Rep. 233.

[40] *Seele Austria GmbH & Co KG* [2008] EWCA Civ 441 at [56]; [2009] 1 All E.R. (Comm) 171 at 189; [2008] Lloyd's Rep. I.R. 739 at 753, per Moore-Bick LJ. Similarly, in *Dawson's Field Arbitration Award*, March 29, 1972 (set out in *Kuwait Airways Corp v Kuwait Insurance Co SAK* [1996] 1 Lloyd's Rep. 664 at 685) Mr M. Kerr QC held that where three aircraft had been blown up by hijackers as the result of a single decision or order to blow up the aircraft, the carrying out of that decision or order was one event: [1996] 1 Lloyd's Rep. 664 at 686.

[41] *Mitsubishi Electric UK Ltd v Royal London Insurance (UK) Ltd* [1994] 2 Lloyd's Rep. 249; [1994] C.L.C. 367; 74 B.L.R. 87.

Several months after installation, it was found that the walls of the modules were bowing and the tiles were cracking. The insured sought to recover the costs of the remedial work. The CAR works policy included a clause that provided that the insured was to pay the first £250,000

> "of each and every loss in respect of any component part which is defective in design plan specification materials or workmanship…"

The insurer argued that the deductible was payable for each of the 94 modules. The insured argued that the claim arose from one defective component part—that is to say the cement board; or alternatively, the claim comprised a single loss relating to all of the damaged toilet modules, so that only one excess was payable. The Court of Appeal agreed with the insured. The correct question (according to Sir Thomas Bingham MR) was whether the defective board gave rise to one claim or multiple claims. It was held that the insured was alleging a single, albeit composite, head of loss and there was no basis for applying the deductible more than once, "it must on a common sense view be regarded as one defective component or component part, not 94".[42] This approach can be contrasted with the approach taken by the Court of Appeal in *Seele Austria GmbH & Co KG*.[43]

"Originating cause".   In *AXA Reinsurance (UK) Plc v Field*,[44] Lord Mustill held   **11-033** that the expression "arising from one originating cause" was materially wider than the expression "arising out of any one event":

> "[A]n event is something which happens at a particular time, at a particular place, in a particular way. … A cause is to my mind something altogether less constricted. It can be a continuing state of affairs; it can be the absence of something happening. Equally, the word 'originating' was in my view consciously chosen to open up the widest possible search for a unifying factor in the history of the losses which it is sought to aggregate. To my mind the one expression has a much wider connotation than the other."[45]

This construction was applied in *Municipal Mutual Insurance Ltd v Sea Insurance Co Ltd*,[46] in which a number of instances of theft and vandalism of machinery left on the dockside taking place over a period of 18 months could be aggregated as having "one source or original cause" in the port's failure to guard and protect the machinery from pilferage and vandalism. It is suggested that if the aggregation wording in *Seele Austria GmbH & Co KG*[47] had been framed in similar terms, the subcontractor may have been able to contend that the deductible applied to the totality of the damage: the deficiencies in workmanship, if sufficiently similar in each case, could be viewed as a common cause.

Allocation of subrogated recoveries.   The proceeds of a claim against a third   **11-034** party in respect of the loss paid under the policy will be treated differently depend-

---

[42] *Mitsubishi Electric UK Ltd* [1994] 2 Lloyd's Rep. 249 at 253; [1994] C.L.C. 367 at 371; 74 B.L.R. 87 at 89.

[43] *Seele Austria GmbH & Co KG* [2008] EWCA Civ 441; [2009] 1 All E.R. (Comm) 171; [2008] Lloyd's Rep. I.R. 739.

[44] *AXA Reinsurance (UK) Plc* [1996] 1 W.L.R. 1026; [1996] 3 All E.R. 517; [1996] 2 Lloyd's Rep. 233.

[45] *AXA Reinsurance (UK) Plc* [1996] 1 W.L.R. 1026 at 1035; [1996] 3 All E.R. 517 at 526-527; [1996] 2 Lloyd's Rep. 233 at 239.

[46] *Municipal Mutual Insurance Ltd v Sea Insurance Co Ltd* [1998] EWCA Civ 546; [1998] C.L.C. 957; [1998] Lloyd's Rep. I.R. 421.

[47] See above, para.11-027.

ing on whether the loss is "uninsured", e.g. loss in excess of the policy limit or losses represented by the excess. The principle is that the sums are to be applied to the highest layer of insurance first. In *Lord Napier and Ettrick v RF Kershaw Ltd (No.1)*,[48] the House of Lords held that the portion of loss above the policy limit was, in effect, to be treated as a top layer of insurance and that part of the loss represented by the excess was to be treated as a bottom layer of cover. The principle was analysed by reference to a hypothetical example, whereby the insured suffers a loss of £160,000 covered by a policy with an excess of £25,000, and a liability limit of £100,000. The insured recovers £130,000 in damages having received £100,000 under the policy. The judge at first instance considered that the insured would be entitled to keep £60,000 (i.e. up to a full indemnity for the loss), and would pay the insurer £70,000.

The House of Lords held that this analysis ignored the fact that the insured had agreed to bear the first £25,000 of the loss. Lord Templeman explained that one should imagine that the insured had insured the first £25,000 of any loss (corresponding to the excess) under a first policy, insured the £100,000 (covered by the policy in the original example) under a second policy and insured any loss over the £125,000 (corresponding the uninsured loss) with a third policy. A loss of £160,000 would be paid in the sum of £25,000 by the first insurer, £100,000 by the second and £35,000 by the third. Of the £130,000 damages, the third insurer would be entitled to recover his £35,000; the second insurer would then be subrogated to the balance of £95,000, which would exhaust the damages and leave nothing for the first insurer. An insured who agreed to bear an excess was not entitled to be in a better position than he would be if he had taken out those three insurances.

11-035 **Excess/uninsured losses.** The differing treatment of losses within the excess and uninsured losses can be seen by comparing two examples with the same cover and hence the same initial recovery under the policy. The insured's loss is £120,000 and damages of £75,000 have been recovered from the third party responsible:

Example 1
The excess under the policy is £50,000. The insurer is liable for losses between £50,000 and £100,000. Accordingly, the policy pays out £50,000. Of the damages of £75,000:

- the insured receives £20,000 in respect of his uninsured loss (£120,000 less the £50,000 recovery under the policy and the £50,000 excess);
- the insurer receives £50,000 in respect of the indemnity provided under the insurance; and
- the insured then receives £5,000, in respect of his retained losses (or the excess), which exhausts the damages.

Therefore, in the final account:

- the insured has £75,000 (the £50,000 paid under the policy plus a £25,000 share of the damages), or £45,000 short of a full indemnity; and
- the insurer is fully reimbursed.

---

[48] *Lord Napier and Ettrick* [1993] A.C. 713; [1993] 2 W.L.R. 42; [1993] 1 All E.R. 385.

Example 2

The excess is now zero, whilst the insurer is liable for losses between £0 and £50,000. Accordingly, the pay-out under the policy is still £50,000. Of the damages of £75,000:

- the insured receives £70,000 in respect of the uninsured loss (£120,000 less the £50,000 recovered under the policy); and
- the insurer then receives £5,000, which exhausts the fund of damages.

Therefore, in the final account:

- the insured has £120,000, i.e. a full indemnity; and
- The insurer has made a net payment of £45,000.

Distribution of unallocated recoveries between insured and uninsured events. The *Lord Napier and Ettrick*[49] does not provide guidance on the alloca- **11-036** tion of undivided proceeds of a claim against a third party in respect of losses paid under a CAR policy and a loss suffered by the insured which is not a deductible or excess. In *Affiliated FM Insurance Co v Quintette Coal Ltd*[50] the Court of Appeal of British Columbia considered thus issue the question being posed:

> "If an insured with insured and uninsured claims against a wrongdoer recovers an unallocated lump sum from the wrongdoer, admittedly less than the full amount of the claims, does the insurer who has paid according to the policy on the insured claim have any right to any part of the recovery?"[51]

Madam Justice Southin with whom the rest of the Court agreed, concluded that:

> "There is a maxim of equity that 'equality is equity'. Like all equitable maxims, it can only apply if there is not some good reason in law and equity why it ought not to apply.
> As it is explained in Lord Hailsham, ed., *Halsbury's Laws of England*, 4th edn, (London: Butterworths, 1992), Vol.16, para.747:
>
> > The maxim that equality is equity expresses in a general way the object both of law and equity, namely to effect a distribution of property and losses proportionate to the several claims or to the several liabilities of the persons concerned. Equality in this connection does not necessarily mean literal equality, but may mean proportionate equality...
>
> Proportionate equality can be achieved in this case by assuming that the proportion of recovery of the belt claim is the same as the proportion of recovery of all the claims, insured and uninsured."[52]

The case may be seen as a pragmatic response to a relatively simple question of how to distribute an unallocated recovery between insured and uninsured claims.

Claims for an indemnity by an insured in relation to a loss that has been crystal- **11-037** lised by a settlement with a third party, the effect of a global settlement on an indemnity claim and an insurer's right to equitable contribution are considered in Ch.21.

---

[49] *Lord Napier and Ettrick* [1993] A C. 713; [1993] 2 W.L.R. 42; [1993] 1 All E.R. 385.
[50] *Affiliated FM Insurance Co v Quintette Coal Ltd* 156 DLR (4th) 307 at [49]; [1998] 8 WWR 139 at 150; 48 BCLR (3d) at 20.
[51] *Affiliated FM Insurance Co v Quintette Coal Ltd* 156 DLR (4th) 307 at [52]–[54]; [1998] 8 WWR 139 at 151; 48 BCLR (3d) at 20.
[52] *Affiliated FM Insurance Co v Quintette Coal Ltd* 156 DLR (4th) 307; [1998] 8 WWR 139; 48 BCLR (3d) 8; 102 BCAC 286.

4. COSTS AND SETTLEMENT

11-038 **Insured's cost of preparing his/her claim.** Unless a CAR policy states that the costs of the insured in preparing its claim under the policy are indemnified, they will not be recoverable from the insurer. However, the costs of preparing and pursuing legal proceedings may be recoverable from an insurer if the insured succeeds. Indemnity costs can be awarded against either the insurer[53] or the insured[54] for unreasonable conduct.[55]

11-039 **Interim payment.** Settlements are considered below in Ch.21 on Claims Procedures and Ch.23 on Payment. Unless a CAR policy expressly provides that there is a right to interim payments an insurer is not obliged to make an interim payment to the insured. However, insurers will often consider it to be in their interests to make interim payments as they may ensure that damage is repaired economically without additional delay and as a result reduce delay losses, which it may also insure. If the works are located overseas and the insurance market is widely spread, the insurers may decide to establish an escrow account from which interim payments can be made upon recommendation by a loss adjuster who is located on site.

11-040 **Incorrect payment.** If payment is made to a broker who is acting as the agent of the insured, the insurer may reclaim money paid to him under a mistake, if the broker is still in possession of the payment, but not if the funds have been paid to the insured. Since a CAR policy is one of indemnity, the insurer will have a restitutionary remedy against the insured. Where a part payment is made by the insurer, but subsequently it is discovered that the insured does not have a valid claim under the policy, the insurer will have a restitutionary remedy against the insured. If the full sum has been paid to the insured the position is less clear, but it is suggested that under a CAR policy the insured may still be required to repay the money. Finally, if similar policies of insurance respond to precisely the same loss, the insurer who has paid out will have an equitable right to contribution from the other insurer.

---

[53] *Wailes v Stapleton Construction and Commercial Services* [1997] 2 Lloyd's Rep. 112; *Martini Investments v McGuin* [2000] 2 Lloyd's Rep. 313 at 317.

[54] *Cepheus Shipping Corp v Guardian Royal Exchange Assurance Plc (Costs)* [1995] 1 Lloyd's Rep. 647; *NLA Group Ltd v Bowers* [1999] 1 Lloyd's Rep. 109.

[55] After 4 May 2017 an insured may claim damages for an insurer's unreasonable delay in making payment. See ss.13A and 16A of the 2015 Act introduced by ss.29 and 30 of the Enterprise Act 2016. See above, para.11-021 and Ch.23.

CHAPTER 12

WARRANTIES AND OTHER TYPES OF INSURANCE POLICY TERMS

TABLE OF CONTENTS

1. PRELIMINARY

Introduction. An insurance policy, including the documents that may be **12-001** incorporated into it by reference, consists of a hierarchy of different types of terms, the breach of which will have consequences of varying severity for the insurer and the insured depending upon the importance of the term and its arrangement within the policy. The classification of terms under the policy has attracted a substantial amount of judicial attention. In many cases the construction of a policy term is the critical factor that determines whether the insurer is on risk at the time of the loss or whether the insured's breach of a term prevents the policy from responding. Because it is an area of the law that can significantly alter the rights of both parties to the policy, the effect of particular policy terms has received recent legislative attention under the Insurance Act 2015 ("2015 Act"), which has reformed an insurer's remedies for breach of warranty and imposed new restrictions on the capacity of insurers to include policy terms which suspend or extinguish cover under the policy.

A warranty is one of the most important policy terms because it is used to define the scope of cover provided to the insured as well as mitigate particular risks by reducing the chance that they will eventuate. A breach of warranty will therefore carry severe consequences for the insured, and it will have the effect of suspending or extinguishing cover under the policy rather than only providing the insurer with a right to damages. For that reason, a warranty in the context of an insurance policy has a markedly different meaning to that in general contract law where it is considered to be a minor term, the breach of which entitles a party to claim damages rather than to avoid liability. Prior to the 2015 Act, a breach of a warranty had the effect of automatically discharging an insurer from all liability under the policy as from the date of breach; this was regardless of whether the warranty breached was material to the loss suffered by the insured. For policies incepted after the 2015 Act comes into force, the position has been fundamentally altered. Section 10 of the 2015 Act provides that so long as the breach of warranty is remedied prior to loss, the cover will remain in place and the insurer's liability will be resurrected as at the date of remedy. Section 11 of the 2015 Act applies to prevent insurers from avoiding policies in circumstances where the breach of warranty has no connection to the loss suffered by the insured. In addition to these changes, s.9 of the 2015 Act has rendered ineffective basis of contract clauses.[1] For a comprehensive discussion of the reforms introduced by the 2015 Act, see Ch.5 above.

If a term in an insurance policy is held to be an ancillary term or condition rather than a warranty, a breach of it will not discharge the insurer from liability under the policy but will only entitle the insurer to recover damages if it can establish loss caused by the breach. It is not always easy to distinguish a warranty from other types of terms within an insurance policy, because parties and the courts have often used condition and warranty terminology interchangeably or incorrectly.[2] In determining whether a particular clause is a warranty and, if so, the ambit of that warranty, the court applies the general principles of contractual construction as discussed in Ch.13. The courts have taken the opportunity to stress on a number of occasions that if the insurer wishes to impose a warranty (or a condition precedent that, as discussed below, may have the same effect as a warranty), that must be expressed in clear, unambiguous language because of what has been described as the "draconian" effects of breach. While the consequences of breach are now less draconian under the 2015 Act, the court's approach is unlikely to change.

While the 2015 Act has fundamentally reformed this area of law, the pre-2015 Act law remains important because: (1) it applies to those policies entered into before 12 August 2016; (2) in business contracts, the parties may contract out of the provisions of the 2015 Act, save for in respect of the abolition of basis of contract clauses provided for by s.9[3]; (3) the reforms introduced by the 2015 Act do not affect the way in which the courts will classify the different types of terms incorporated into a policy.

12-002 **Application to CAR policies.** A CAR insurance policy will contain warranties and other terms that may be signposted in a table of contents and then allocated to the categories of insured risk; typically, the construction works, delay in start-up/ business interruption, public/third-party liability and possibly cover for damage to plant and materials. Each category will have conditions and warranties attached to it that relate directly to those types of cover. The CAR policy will also contain more general terms, which are overarching in their reach; that is, not merely applicable to the individual category of insured risk, but to the overall management of the policy. Such general terms will include terms relating to the payment of the premium, claims notification provisions, the insured's obligation to take precautionary measures, mitigate its risk and to deliver progress reports on the project to the insurer. Whether or not such terms take effect as warranties or ancillary conditions will depend on their true construction.

It may be said that it is easier to identify and categorise the types of term in operation in a single project CAR policy than in annual CAR policies or consumer insurance policies, which tend to be more generic in coverage and in style of draftsmanship. Single project CAR policies for large construction projects will be bespoke, insomuch as they are tailored to the individual construction project tak-

---

[1] See below, para.12-017.
[2] See, for example, *W&J Lane v Spratt* [1970] 2 Q.B. 480 at 486–487; [1969] 3 W.L.R. 950 at 955–956; [1970] 1 All E.R. 162 at 166–167, per Roskill J.
[3] See paras 5-133 to 5-140 above for a discussion of contracting out of the Insurance Act 2015 ("2015 Act").

ing place. It is likely that each term, or at least the key terms, will be negotiated over and thus will be worded with a degree of clarity not found in an annual policy covering the more general activities of smaller contractors or subcontractors. Nevertheless, there will inevitably be scope with a CAR policy for a contractor to apply an interpretation to an individual term that conflicts with the interpretation preferred by the insurer, which will consequently lead to disputes and litigation.

2. Conditions precedent

Conditions precedent. A condition precedent is a condition that must be complied with before the insurer will be liable. Conditions precedent can fall into two categories: (1) conditions precedent to the existence of the policy or inception or continuation of the risk; or (2) conditions precedent to the insurer's liability to indemnify the insured on a claim or claims. **12-003**

Conditions precedent to risk. If there is a condition precedent to risk in the policy the consequence of it not being complied with is that the insurer never goes on risk and the policy is essentially void ab initio.[4] A common example of this first category of condition precedent is a requirement to pay the premium, which will often be phrased in consumer insurance policies or generic annual CAR policies as a condition precedent to risk.[5] Another example would be a clause providing that **12-004**

> "it is a condition precedent to this policy that the construction is to be designed and built to standard building regulation requirements".

A clause stating that "it is a condition precedent to risk that the insured remains solvent throughout the course of the construction" is an example of a condition precedent to the continuation rather than the inception of the risk. Should the insured become insolvent, the policy will come to an end. This last example could also be construed as a warranty, and highlights the potential confusion caused by the use of language by the draftsman.

Under the 2015 Act, a condition precedent to risk may fall within the ambit of the s.11 controls on policy terms if its effect is to reduce the risk of losses of a particular kind, at a particular time or at a particular location. If a condition precedent does fall within s.11 and is not complied with by the insured, the effect will be that the insurer will still be on risk for "unconnected" losses from the inception of the policy but will only go on risk for those losses which are connected to the condition precedent once the condition has been complied with.[6]

There is also a possibility that the courts will apply the s.10 controls on warranties under the 2015 Act to conditions precedent to risk under the policy. This will depend upon the willingness of the courts to treat a term purporting to impose a more onerous consequence for an insured's breach than a suspension of liability as

---

[4]   For cases concerning such conditions precedent see *Canning v Farquhar* (1886) 16 Q.B.D. 727; *Harrington v Pearl Life Assurance Co Ltd* (1914) 30 T.L.R. 613 and *Looker v Law Union & Rock Insurance Co Ltd* [1928] 1 K.B. 554. See also ss.84(1) and 84(3)(a) of the Marine Insurance Act 1906 ("MIA"), which set out the general principle.

[5]   It is more likely in a single project CAR policy that a failure to pay the premium will result in the insurer not being liable for losses or damage occurring before the premium is paid rather than being a condition precedent to risk attaching at all, i.e. a condition precedent to liability rather than risk.

[6]   For further discussion of this point, see above, para.5-114.

a "warranty" that is contracting out of the remedial regime imposed under the 2015 Act. For example, a condition precedent may require an insured to pay the entirety of the premium by a specified date, or else the insurer will not go on risk under the policy at all. If the insured fails to pay the premium, the effect ought to be that the insurer does not go on risk as the policy is treated as void ab initio by reason of the insured's breach of condition precedent to risk. However, there is some suggestion by the English and Scottish Law Commissions that such a term would be treated as a warranty (and therefore would only be capable of suspending the insurer's liability) if it fails to comply with the transparency requirements for contracting out of the effects of s.10.[7] Accordingly, the insured would be entitled to revive the cover by paying the premium to the insurer at any point after the original date for payment had passed, notwithstanding the insured's critical failure to satisfy the condition precedent by the time required under the express terms of the policy. If the courts decide to treat s.10 as applying to conditions precedent to risk, the effect would be that the insurer would not be able to affix extinguishment of all liability under the policy as a consequence for the insured's breach of the condition precedent without also complying with the transparency requirements; instead, the insurer's liability would only be suspended until the point at which the insured remedied the breach, despite this being inconsistent with the established legal understanding of a condition precedent to risk. This example serves to highlight the difficulties that surround the application of s.10. One might also question whether it is permissible for a condition precedent to risk to be treated in this way: if a policy term is drafted in such a way that the effect of non-compliance is that the policy is void ab initio, then it follows that there is no "warranty" for s.10 to bite into at all as the policy never came into existence in the first place.

12-005 **Conditions precedent to liability.** This type of condition precedent normally relates to the actions that an insured must take after a loss has occurred. For instance, the insurer may expressly provide that compliance with certain types of claims conditions (for example, notification, claims co-operation and claims-control conditions)[8] is a condition precedent to the insurer being liable to indemnify the insured.[9] Another common condition precedent is that the insured must exercise reasonable precautions against or otherwise mitigate its loss. Subject to the precise wording of the condition precedent, breach of this second type of condition precedent will prevent a claim or claims being made or paid out under the policy.[10]

12-006 **Comparison to warranties.** Although the position has now been changed by the provisions of the 2015 Act, under the MIA a breach of a condition precedent would generally have had the same effect as a breach of a warranty in that the insurer would automatically be discharged from liability for a breach of both terms.[11]

---

[7]   For further discussion of this point, see above para.5-102.
[8]   For example of a claims notification condition precedent, see *Ted Baker Plc v Axa Insurance UK Plc* [2014] EWHC 3548 (Comm); [2015] Lloyd's Rep. I.R. 325 (under appeal).
[9]   The labelling of a term as a condition precedent or warranty is not determinative of the construction which will be placed on the term by the courts but will be influential, see below, para.13-067.
[10] The precise wording is crucial because the wording may be such that non-compliance does not operate as an absolute bar to recovery but only prevents one particular type of claim or part of a claim being recovered.
[11] See Bowen LJ in *Barnard v Faber* [1893] 1 Q.B. 340 at 343–344; 62 L.J.Q.B. 159 at 162; 4 R. 201 at 205–206 and Lord Goff of Chievely in *Bank of Nova Scotia v Hellenic Mutual War Risks Associa-*

Indeed, the terms "warranty" and "condition precedent" were often used interchangeably in the authorities. However, whilst the effect may have been the same where the condition is a precedent to risk attaching in the first place (i.e. those in the first category above), the effect is not strictly the same where the condition is a precedent to a claim or claims being indemnified (i.e. those in the second category). Non-fulfilment of the second type of condition will generally, subject to its precise wording, only bar that particular claim and not any future claim. By contrast, as is discussed below at para.12-020, prior to the 2015 Act, a breach of warranty discharged the insurer from any liability from the date of the breach and therefore no future liability could arise on the part of the insurer.

Due observance clauses. A due observance clause will invariably be included as **12-007** a standard term of the insurance contract in an attempt to bolster protection for the insurer. Such a clause will typically state:

"The liability of the insurer shall be conditional on the observance by the insured of the terms, provisions, conditions and endorsements of this policy."

It is well-established that such a clause may make compliance with those terms a condition precedent to liability.[12] However, the courts have often sought to protect the parties from the draconian effect of such a clause. For instance, in *Aspen Insurance UK Ltd v Pectel Ltd*,[13] Teare J refused to construe a due observance clause as rendering compliance with all clauses a condition precedent because that literal interpretation was not required to achieve the objective purpose of the clause in question and the clause could sensibly be construed without such draconian consequences by applying a purposive construction.

Requirement of prejudice. In the past it was considered that in order to rely upon **12-008** a condition precedent the insurer had to show that it had been prejudiced by the breach. This approach was adopted by Lord Denning M.R. in the case of *Barrett Bros (Taxis) Ltd v Davies*; sub nom. *Lickiss v Milestone Motor Policies at Lloyds*,[14] which concerned breach of a notification condition precedent. Lord Denning M.R. stated:

"This condition 1 was inserted in the policy so as to afford a protection to the insurers so they should know in good time about the accident and any proceedings consequent on it. If they obtained all the material knowledge from another source so that they are not prejudiced at all by the failure of the insured himself to tell him [sic], then they cannot rely on the condition to defeat the claim."[15]

tion (Bermuda) Ltd (The Good Luck) [1992] 1 A.C. 233 at 262; [1991] 2 W.L.R. 1279 at 1294–1295; [1991] 3 All E.R. 1 at 16 citing Lord Blackburn in *Thomson v Weems* (1884) 9 App. Cas. 671 at 684; (1884) 11 R. (H.L.) 48 at 51.
12 See *London Guarantie Co v Fearnley* (1880) 5 App. Cas. 911 at 915–916 and 918.
13 *Aspen Insurance UK Ltd v Pectel Ltd* [2008] EWHC 2804 (Comm); [2009] 2 All E.R. (Comm) 873; [2009] Lloyd's Rep. I.R. 440.
14 *Barrett Bros (Taxis) Ltd v Davies*; sub nom. *Lickiss v Milestone Motor Policies at Lloyds* [1966] 1 W.L.R. 1334; [1966] 2 All E.R. 972; [1966] 2 Lloyd's Rep. 1.
15 *Barrett Bros (Taxis) Ltd*; sub nom.*Lickiss* [1966] 1 W.L.R. 1334 at 1340; [1966] 2 All E.R. 972 at 976; [1966] 2 Lloyd's Rep. 1 at 5.

This was referred to as a "surprising proposition" by MacKenna J at first instance in *Farrell v Federated Employers' Insurance Association Ltd*,[16] although he considered that prejudice had occurred in that case in any event as the insurers had had no opportunity to defend a claim leading to judgment in default against the insured. It was assumed for the purpose of the appeal of that decision[17] that *Barrett Bros (Taxis) Ltd*[18] was authority for the proposition that prejudice was required, because the Court of Appeal was also of the view that there was undoubtedly prejudice suffered by the insurer.

It has now been clearly established that no prejudice is required in order to rely upon non-fulfilment of a condition precedent as discharging liability. This was made clear by Bingham J in *Pioneer Concrete (UK) Ltd v National Employers Mutual General Insurance Association Ltd*.[19] In that case, machinery owned by the claimants was damaged as a result of being negligently erected by contractors 10 months earlier. The contractors' insurance policy required the contractors to give written notice of "any accident or claim or proceedings immediately the same shall have come to the knowledge of the Insured or his representative." The third party, Pioneer Concrete, informed the insurers of the accident and their intention to claim and then issued a claim against the contractors, who were in liquidation. The insurers were never notified of the proceedings. Pioneer Concrete brought an action against the insurers under s.1 of the Third Parties (Rights Against Insurers) Act 1930, claiming the sum due from the contractors and saying that the insurers had to show that they had been prejudiced by the breach. The notification condition was a condition precedent to liability in the policy. It was held that the insurers were entitled to rely on the failure to notify even if they had not been prejudiced, because the term was a clear condition precedent to the insurers' liability to pay under the policy.[20]

3. ANCILLARY CONDITIONS AND INNOMINATE TERMS

12-009 **Fundamental versus ancillary conditions.** In general contract law a condition is a term that is fundamental, in that it goes to the root of the contract. In theory, there may be terms in an insurance policy that are conditions in this sense. However, this situation must be considered to be exceptional in the context of insurance where even a term requiring payment of a premium has been held not to be fundamental unless it is stipulated that time for payment is of the essence,[21] or the insured has demonstrated that as a result of its insolvency it is unable or unwilling to make any payment of the premium.[22] A CAR policy may include a notice clause stating: "this

---

16   *Farrell v Federated Employers' Insurance Association Ltd* [1970] 1 W.L.R. 498 at 502; [1970] 1 All E.R. 360 at 363; [1970] 1 Lloyd's Rep. 129 at 135.

17   *Farrell* [1970] 1 W.L.R. 1400; [1970] 3 All E.R. 632; [1970] 2 Lloyd's Rep. 170.

18   *Barrett Bros (Taxis) Ltd v Davies*; sub nom. *Lickiss v Milestone Motor Policies at Lloyds* [1966] 1 W.L.R. 1334; [1966] 2 All E.R. 972; [1966] 2 Lloyd's Rep. 1.

19   *Pioneer Concrete (UK) Ltd v National Employers Mutual General Insurance Association Ltd* [1985] 2 All E.R. 395; [1985] 1 Lloyd's Rep. 274; [1985] Fin. L.R. 251.

20   For a further example see *Kier Construction v Royal Insurance (UK)* 30 Con. L.R. 45, which followed *Pioneer Concrete (UK) Ltd* [1985] 2 All E.R. 395; [1985] 1 Lloyd's Rep. 274; [1985] Fin. L.R. 251.

21   *Fenton Insurance Co v Gothaer Versicherungsbank VVaG* [1991] 1 Lloyd's Rep. 172 at 180; *Pacific & General Insurance Co Ltd v Hazell* [1997] L.R.L.R. 65; [1997] B.C.C. 400; [1997] 6 Re. L.R. 157 and *Figre Ltd v Mander* [1999] Lloyd's Rep. I.R. 193 citing both of those cases.

22   As was the position in *Pacific & General Insurance Co Ltd* [1997] L.R.L.R. 65; [1997] B.C.C. 400; [1997] 6 Re. L.R. 157.

policy shall not be invalidated for failure to pay any premium due without the insurer first giving not less than 14 days written notice". The initial obligation to pay is not a fundamental condition but once notice has been given time for compliance becomes "of the essence" and a failure to pay would signal the insured's intention to repudiate the contract, which the insurer may then accept.

The majority of terms in insurance contracts that are not clearly defined as conditions precedent by virtue of due observance clauses or otherwise will be either "ancillary conditions" or "innominate terms". An ancillary condition is minor in nature and consequently its breach will only permit the insurer to claim damages for the insured's breach (provided it can establish it has suffered a quantifiable loss as a result of that breach).[23]

For instance, it has been held consistently since *Alfred McAlpine Plc v BAI (Run-Off) Ltd*[24] that notification clauses are not fundamental terms but are ancillary or innominate.[25] Mance LJ stated in *Friends Provident Life & Pensions Ltd v Sirius International Insurance Corp* that he agreed with Waller LJ in *Alfred McAlpine Plc*

> "that it is not easy to conceive of a breach of such an ancillary term in an insurance like the present as going to the root of the whole contract".[26]

Other claims conditions, such as claims co-operation and claims control clauses, have also been held to be ancillary or innominate terms and it is difficult to see how any claims condition could be considered otherwise.[27]

Innominate terms. Innominate terms are those terms that are not classified as either a condition or a warranty as defined in the general law of contract. Innominate terms is the phrase used to describe terms that can be breached, resulting in adverse consequences to the non-breaching party, but where the adverse consequences may be of a differing degree of severity on a given occasion. The classic definition of innominate terms stems from the case of *Hong Kong Fir Shipping Co Ltd v Kawasaki Kisen Kaisha Ltd (The Hongkong Fir)*[28] where Diplock LJ stated: **12-010**

> "[S]ome breaches will and others will not give rise to an event which will deprive the party not in default of substantially the whole benefit which it was intended that he should obtain from the

---

[23] For some of the difficulties in proving and assessing damages see *Friends Provident Life & Pensions Ltd v Sirius International Insurance Corp* [2005] EWCA Civ 601; [2005] 2 All E.R. (Comm) 145; [2005] 2 Lloyd's Rep. 517; *Hussain v Brown (No. 2)* Unreported 1996; and *Porter v Zurich Insurance Co* [2009] EWHC 376 (QB); [2009] 2 All E.R. (Comm) 658; [2010] Lloyd's Rep. I.R. 373.

[24] *Alfred McAlpine Plc v BAI (Run-Off) Ltd* [2000] 1 All E.R. (Comm) 545; [2000] 1 Lloyd's Rep. 437; [2000] C.L.C 812. This case has been doubted as discussed below, at para.12-011 but not on this point.

[25] For example, *Friends Provident Life & Pensions Ltd* [2005] EWCA Civ 601; [2005] 2 All E.R. (Comm) 145; [2005] 2 Lloyd's Rep. 517. The decision in *Taylor v Builders Accident Insurance Ltd* [1997] P.I.Q.R P247 holding otherwise must now be considered to be wrong.

[26] *Friends Provident Life & Pensions Ltd* [2005] EWCA Civ 601 at [29]; [2005] 2 All E.R. (Comm) 145 at 160; [2005] 2 Lloyd's Rep. 517 at 529.

[27] As stated by the majority in *Friends Provident Life & Pensions Ltd* although Waller LJ dissenting considered [2005] EWCA Civ 601 at [42]; [2005] 2 All E.R. (Comm) 145 at 164; [2005] 2 Lloyd's Rep. 517 at 532, that breach of a claims condition could be repudiatory "in extreme circumstances of consistent breach over a number of claims."

[28] *Hong Kong Fir Shipping Co Ltd v Kawasaki Kisen Kaisha Ltd (The Hongkong Fir)* [1962] 2 Q.B. 26; [1962] 2 W.L.R. 474; [1962] 1 All E.R. 474.

contract; and the legal consequences of a breach of such an undertaking, unless provided for expressly in the contract, depend upon the nature of the event to which the breach gives rise and do not follow automatically from a prior classification of the undertaking as a 'condition' or a 'warranty'."[29]

Therefore, in general contract law, innominate terms are terms that are neither conditions nor warranties but are terms, a breach of which will entitle the innocent party to treat the contract as at an end if the consequences of the breach are so serious that they deprive the parties of substantially the whole benefit, which it was the parties' intention they should have. If that is not the case, an innocent party is only entitled to claim damages. This is the approach that has been adopted in the context of insurance, in that the insurer may repudiate the policy only if it has suffered prejudice from the breach going to the root of the contract; otherwise its remedy lies only in damages. On the decided cases though, it seems that an innominate term will rarely give rise to a right to repudiate the policy.[30]

4. TERM ENTITLING REPUDIATION OF A CLAIM

12-011 **Terms entitling repudiation of a claim.** For a period recently, it appeared as if there may also be a fourth category of term in addition to conditions, warranties and innominate terms, namely

> "a term ... a breach of which was so serious for underwriters that it would give them a right to reject the claim without having to accept the breach of contract as being a repudiation of the contract as a whole".[31]

In other words, that there could be a repudiation of the claim rather than of the contract. This stemmed from the decision of the Court of Appeal in *Alfred McAlpine Plc*.[32] The case concerned a notification clause requiring the insured to provide notification of a claim as soon as possible. It was argued by the insurer that a breach of such a term could become a repudiatory breach if it was able to show that it had thereby suffered prejudice. Although not a pleaded issue before the court, it held that that was an innominate term as defined in *The Hong Kong Fir*[33] and that, although it was unlikely that the breach of such a term could ever amount to a repudiation of the insurance contract itself, a breach that evinced an intention not to proceed with a claim or that had serious consequences for the insurer would entitle the insurer to reject the claim under consideration, rather than accepting a repudiation of the entire contract. Waller LJ, delivering the court's judgment, considered that support for this finding could be derived from the judgment of Giles J in the Australian case of *Trans-Pacific Insurance Co (Australia) Ltd v Grand Union Insurance Co Ltd*.[34] The finding on the facts in the *Alfred McAlpine Plc*[35] case

---

[29] *Hong Kong Fir Shipping Co Ltd* [1962] 2 Q.B. 26 at 70; [1962] 2 W.L.R. 474 at 493–494; [1962] 1 All E.R. 474 at 487.

[30] See *Alfred McAlpine Plc* [2000] 1 All E.R. (Comm) 545; [2000] 1 Lloyd's Rep. 437; [2000] C.L.C. 812; *K/S Merc-Scandia XXXXII v Lloyd's Underwriters (The Mercandian Continent)* [2001] EWCA Civ 1275; [2001] 2 Lloyd's Rep. 563; [2001] C.L.C. 1836; and *Friends Provident Life & Pensions Ltd* [2005] EWCA Civ 601; [2005] 2 All E.R. (Comm) 145; [2005] 2 Lloyd's Rep. 517.

[31] Longmore LJ in *The Mercandian Continent* [2001] EWCA Civ 1275 at [14]; [2001] 2 Lloyd's Rep. 563 at 569; [2001] C.L.C. 1836 at 1842 commenting on the Court of Appeal's decision in *Alfred McAlpine Plc* [2000] 1 All E.R. (Comm) 545; [2000] 1 Lloyd's Rep. 437; [2000] C.L.C. 812.

[32] *Alfred McAlpine Plc* [2000] 1 All E.R. (Comm) 545; [2001] 1 Lloyd's Rep. 437; [2000] C.L.C. 812.

[33] *Hong Kong Fir Shipping Co Ltd* [1962] 2 Q.B. 26; [1962] 2 W.L.R. 474; [1962] 1 All E.R. 474.

[34] *Trans-Pacific Insurance Co (Australia) Ltd v Grand Union Insurance Co Ltd* (1989) 18 N.S.W.L.R.

was that the insurer had not been entitled to reject the claim because it had been provided with sufficient details to investigate the claim despite the insured's breach of the notification term and, at that time, it had not suffered irremediable prejudice. The dicta of Waller LJ was referred to by the Court of Appeal in subsequent cases,[36] but only one first instance case, *Bankers Insurance Co Ltd v Patrick South*[37] applied the reasoning of Waller LJ to enable insurers to avoid liability for one particular claim only.[38]

The death knell was sounded for this new type of clause and the concept of repudiation of a claim by the majority of the Court of Appeal in *Friends Provident Life & Pensions Ltd*.[39] The majority of the court rejected the argument put forward by Waller LJ in *Alfred McAlpine Plc*[40] that a serious breach of contractual obligations would defeat only a particular claim and not lead to termination of the policy. In endorsing the classical view, Mance LJ, with whom Sir William Aldous agreed, stated that there was no authority in insurance law to support Waller LJ's "new doctrine of partial repudiatory breach" whereby

"a party to a contract may be relieved from a particular obligation under a composite contract such as the present, by reason of a serious breach with serious consequences relating to an ancillary obligation, absent some express or implied condition precedent or other provision to that effect".[41]

Unsurprisingly, Waller LJ, who was also sitting in *Friends Provident Life & Pensions Ltd*,[42] dissented in respect of this part and attempted to support his view in *Alfred McAlpine Plc*[43] by citing the example of instalment contracts and stating that it is

"not unknown to the law of contract that in relation to severable obligations a failure in some respect may give rise to a right to 'reject' simply and only the particular counterpart of the severable obligation".[44]

---

675 at 702–703.

[35] *Alfred McAlpine Plc* [2000] 1 All E.R. (Comm) 545; [2000] 1 Lloyd's Rep. 437; [2000] C.L.C. 812.

[36] See *The Mercandian Continent* [2001] EWCA Civ 1275; [2001] 2 Lloyd's Rep. 563; [2001] C.L.C. 1836; *George Hunt Cranes Ltd v Scottish Boiler & General Insurance Co Ltd* [2001] EWCA Civ 1964; [2002] 1 All E.R. (Comm) 366; [2003] 1 C.L.C. 1; *Glencore International AG v Ryan (The Beursgracht) (No.1)* [2001] EWCA Civ 2051; [2002] 1 Lloyd's Rep. 574; [2002] C.L.C. 547 and *Pilkington United Kingdom Ltd v CGU Insurance Plc* [2004] EWCA Civ 23; [2005] 1 All E.R. (Comm) 283; [2004] 1 C.L.C. 1059.

[37] *Bankers Insurance Co Ltd v Patrick South* [2003] EWHC 380 (QB); [2004] Lloyd's Rep. I.R. 1; [2003] P.I.Q.R. P28.

[38] Certainly, that was the only case referred to the Court of Appeal in *Friends Provident Life & Pensions Ltd* [2005] EWCA Civ 601; [2005] 2 All E.R. (Comm) 145; [2005] 2 Lloyd's Rep. 517 where the reasoning of *Alfred McAlpine Plc* [2000] 1 All E.R. (Comm) 545; [2000] 1 Lloyd's Rep. 437; [2000] C.L.C. 812 had been applied for that purpose.

[39] *Friends Provident Life & Pensions Ltd* [2005] EWCA Civ 601; [2005] 2 All E.R. (Comm) 145; [2005] 2 Lloyd's Rep.517.

[40] *Alfred McAlpine Plc* [2000] 1 All E.R. (Comm) 545; [2000] 1 Lloyd's Rep. 437; [2000] C.L.C. 812.

[41] *Friends Provident Life & Pensions Ltd* [2005] EWCA Civ 601 at [31]; [2005] 2 All E.R. (Comm) 145 at 161–162; [2005] 2 Lloyd's Rep. 517 at 530.

[42] *Friends Provident Life & Pensions Ltd* [2005] EWCA Civ 601; [2005] 2 All E.R. (Comm) 145; [2005] 2 Lloyd's Rep. 517.

[43] *Alfred McAlpine Plc* [2000] 1 All E.R. (Comm) 545; [2000] 1 Lloyd's Rep. 437; [2000] C.L.C. 812.

[44] *Friends Provident Life & Pensions Ltd* [2005] EWCA Civ 601 at [43]; [2005] 2 All E.R. (Comm) 145 at 164; [2005] 2 Lloyd's Rep. 517 at 532.

Nevertheless, the Court of Appeal was not bound by Waller LJ's views in *Alfred McAlpine Plc*[45] because his remarks were technically obiter. Waller LJ's views were not followed in the subsequent case of *Ronson International Ltd v Patrick*; sub nom. *Patrick v Royal London Mutual Insurance Society Ltd*,[46] where HHJ Seymour Q. felt bound by the decision of Mance LJ in *Friends Provident Life & Pensions Ltd*,[47] stating:

> "[W]hat the case decided was that it was not permissible in law, by any mechanism, to achieve the result considered by Waller L.J. in *Alfred McAlpine plc v BAI (Run-Off) Ltd*. Not only did Mance L.J. and Sir William Aldous hold that there was no rule of law to the effect considered by Waller L.J., they also held that there was no warrant for construing a term as to notification which was not a condition precedent in an insurance contract, in the absence of express words, as producing that conclusion and no basis in law upon which to imply a term to that effect. I reject the submission ... that both Mance L.J. and Sir William Aldous envisaged that in an appropriate case a term to the effect that a serious breach of a notification requirement which produced serious consequences for an insurer should entitle the insurer to reject liability for the particular claim affected could be implied."[48]

The partial repudiation doctrine that Waller LJ attempted to introduce has not therefore found favour with the courts.

5. CLAUSES DESCRIBING, DELIMITING OR SUSPENDING RISK

12-012 Descriptive, delimiting or suspensive conditions. Certain clauses of the insurance policy may be descriptive of the risk in the sense that whilst they are not being complied with by the insured, the insurer will be under no liability to indemnify the insured but that liability resumes upon compliance. These clauses are termed in the case law as descriptive, delimiting or suspensive conditions or warranties although they are not in fact warranties within the real meaning of that term in insurance law (at least prior to the passing of the 2015 Act). The distinction between clauses describing, delimiting or suspending risk and warranties has been rendered redundant for insurance policies entered into after 12 August 2016 by reason of s.10 of the 2015 Act which has transformed all warranties into suspensive conditions (whereby an insurer will only be able to avoid liability if the insured was in breach of the warranty at the time of loss). As such, going forward, the courts will no longer need to draw a distinction between warranties and suspensive conditions in respect of those policies to which the 2015 Act applies.

For those policies to which the 2015 Act does not apply, the case law does not set out a specific test for determining whether a clause is to be construed as a condition of this type rather than a warranty. The matter will fall to be determined by reference to the general principles of construction and, in particular, whether the court is persuaded that the parties intended breach of the clause in question to have the draconian effect it will have if held to be a warranty, i.e. that any breach will automatically determine the insurer's liability from the date of breach as discussed below at para.12-020.

---

45 *Alfred McAlpine Plc* [2000] 1 All E.R. (Comm) 545; [2000] 1 Lloyd's Rep. 437; [2000] C.L.C. 812.
46 *Patrick v Royal London Mutual Insurance Society Ltd* [2005] EWHC 1767 (QB); [2005] 2 All E.R. (Comm) 453; [2006] Lloyd's Rep. I.R. 194 affirmed on other grounds at [2006] EWCA Civ 421; [2006] 2 All E.R. (Comm) 344.
47 *Friends Provident Life & Pensions Ltd* [2005] EWCA Civ 601; [2005] 2 All E.R. (Comm) 145; [2005] 2 Lloyd's Rep. 517.
48 *Patrick* [2005] EWHC 1767 (QB) at [41]; [2005] 2 All E.R. (Comm) 453 at 471; [2006] Lloyd's Rep. I.R. 194 at 206.

Clauses descriptive of the risk. An early example of when the court had to **12-013** consider whether a clause was a warranty or only descriptive of the risk is the case of *Farr v Motor Traders Mutual Insurance Society Ltd.*[49] In that case the insured stated in the proposal form that the two taxis he was seeking to insure were each driven in one shift per 24 hours. There was a basis of the contract clause causing that statement to be incorporated as a term of the policy.[50] After the policy had been incepted, there was a very short period during August when one of the taxis was driven in two shifts per 24 hours. In the following November, when the taxis were being driven again in one shift per 24 hours, one of the taxis was damaged in an accident. The insurers refused to indemnify the insured citing the use of the taxi for two shifts per 24 hours in August as an alleged breach of warranty, which had the effect of discharging their liability at that date. The Court of Appeal held that the statement in the proposal was not a warranty but was merely descriptive of the risk, indicating that the taxi, whilst being driven in more than one shift per 24 hours would cease to be covered by the policy, but would be covered whilst bring driven in one shift. Accordingly, the defendant insurers were held liable to indemnify the insured.[51]

The case of *Farr*[52] was referred to by the Court of Appeal in *Roberts v Anglo-Saxon Insurance Association Ltd,*[53] in which it was also held that a description as to the use to which a vehicle was to be put was descriptive of the character of the risk rather than a warranty that that particular use was the exclusive one to which the vehicles would be put. Shortly afterwards, in *Provincial Insurance Co Ltd v Morgan & Foxon,*[54] the House of Lords had to consider a term in the proposal form where the owners of a lorry declared that the lorry was to be used for carrying coal. The lorry was then used for a delivery of both coal and timber and was involved in a collision. At the time of the collision the lorry was carrying coal, though earlier in the day it had been carrying timber for the Forestry Commission. The House of Lords held that the clause was no more than descriptive of the risk and thus at the time of the collision the insurer was on risk. Lord Russell of Killowen stated:

"If it had really been the intention of the insurance company that the carrying of goods other than coal at any time should free them from liability in respect of an accident happening subsequently, it was incumbent on them to make that abundantly clear to the proposers."[55]

---

[49] *Farr v Motor Traders Mutual Insurance Society Ltd* [1920] 3 K.B. 669.
[50] See below, para.12-017.
[51] For further examples of cases where clauses have been held to be clauses delimiting the risk rather than warranties see *Hussain v Brown* [1966] 1 Lloyd's Rep. 627; *Times,* December 15, 1995; Lloyd's List, February 13, 1996; *De Maurier (Jewels) Ltd v Bastion Insurance Co Ltd and Coronet Insurance Co Ltd* [1967] 2 Lloyd's Rep. 550; (1967) 117 N.L.J. 1112; *CTN. Cash and Carry Ltd v General Accident Fire and Life Assurance Corp Plc* [1989] 1 Lloyd's Rep. 299; *Kler Knitwear Ltd v Lombard General Insurance Co Ltd* [2000] Lloyd's Rep. I.R. 47 and the obiter comments of Gross J in *GE Frankona Reinsurance Ltd v CMM Trust No. 1400 (The Newfoundland Explorer)* [2006] EWHC 429 (Admlty); [2006] 1 All E.R. (Comm) 665; [2008] 1 C.L.C. 500. For an example of a case where such an argument failed see *Palatine Insurance Co Ltd v Gregory* [1926] A.C. 90; (1925) 23 Ll. L. Rep. 12.
[52] *Farr* [1920] 3 K.B. 669; 90 L.J.K.B. 215; 123 L.T. 765.
[53] *Roberts v Anglo-Saxon Insurance Association Ltd* (1927) 27 Ll. L. Rep. 313.
[54] *Provincial Insurance Co Ltd v Morgan & Foxon* [1933] A.C. 240; (1932) 44 Ll. L. Rep. 275; 102 L.J.K.B. 164.
[55] *Provincial Insurance Co Ltd* [1933] A.C. 240 at 249; (1932) 44 Ll. L. Rep. 275 at 278; 102 L.J.K.B. 164 at 167.

Lord Buckmaster expressed the principle in these terms:

"[T]he question that arises is, were these words intended to mean that the use of the vehicle was to be exclusively confined to that of carrying coal, so that any temporary, trivial, and incidental use would completely defeat the policy, or was it not? I wish again to repeat that it is perfectly open to people to make such a bargain, and when made it is useless to complain that the bargain is harsh. But it is at least essential that the bargain should be plain in order that it may be clear that a man has contracted on the faith of something which may rob the insurance of the greater part of its value ... To state in full the purposes for which the vehicle is to be used is not the same thing as to state in full the purposes for which the vehicle will be exclusively used, and as a general description of the use of the vehicle it is not suggested that the answer was inaccurate."[56]

12-014 Suspensory conditions. It has been said that it may be easier to construe a term as a suspensory condition where the obligation on the insured is to comply with some deadline as opposed to where there is a warranty as to a state of affairs.[57] For instance, in *Kler Knitwear Ltd v Lombard General Insurance Co Ltd*,[58] one of the warranties upon renewal of a policy provided that the sprinkler installations at the insured's factory had to be inspected within 30 days of renewal with all necessary rectification work commissioned within 14 days of the inspection report being received. The sprinkler installations were not inspected as prescribed within 30 days of renewal; they were inspected 60 days late with no rectification work determined to be necessary. Subsequently, the property was damaged due to adverse weather conditions and the insured brought a claim under the policy. The insurer denied liability for property and business interruption loss following the storm damage to the factory on the ground that there was a breach of warranty by the insured in respect of the sprinkler installations. After setting out the principles and guidelines upon which the court had to approach the question of construction, Morland J held that there was no authority suggesting that a clause containing a once and for all obligation is indicative of a warranty rather than of a suspensive condition and had no hesitation in concluding that the clause was a suspensive condition and not a warranty.[59] The effect of that clause left the insurer without a defence of breach of warranty and the insured was able to recover under the policy since the eventual inspection of the sprinkler system put the insurer back on risk.

The case of *Kler Knitwear*[60] was considered by Burton J in *Sugar Hut Group Ltd v Great Lakes Reinsurance (UK) Plc*.[61] A fire had occurred at the insured's nightclub and the issues for consideration by the court were whether the insurer was entitled to rely on breaches of warranty relating to: (1) frying and cooking equipment, which was to be cleaned regularly and maintained and checked at least once every six months; and (2) that a particular burglar alarm system was installed and would be upgraded by a particular date. Burton J said that he would be persuaded that the obligation to carry out six-monthly inspections could be interpreted as being a suspensive condition but, unlike in the case of *Kler Knitwear Ltd*,[62] the inspection had not occurred late but had not occurred at all at the time of the fire; therefore,

---

[56] *Provincial Insurance Co Ltd* [1933] A.C. 240 at 247; (1932) 44 Ll. L. Rep. 275 at 277–278; 102 L.J.K.B. 164 at 166.
[57] Burton J in *Sugar Hut Group Ltd v Great Lakes Reinsurance (UK) Plc* [2010] EWHC 2636 (Comm) at [41]; [2011] Lloyd's Rep. I.R. 198 at 208.
[58] *Kler Knitwear Ltd* [2000] Lloyd's Rep. I.R. 47.
[59] *Kler Knitwear Ltd* [2000] Lloyd's Rep. I.R. 47.
[60] *Kler Knitwear Ltd* [2000] Lloyd's Rep. I.R. 47.
[61] *Sugar Hut Group Ltd* [2010] EWHC 2636 (Comm); [2011] Lloyd's Rep. I.R. 198.
[62] *Kler Knitwear Ltd* [2000] Lloyd's Rep. I.R. 47.

the suspensive nature of the condition was still operative and consequently would not assist the insured.[63] In the case of the burglar alarm warranty, the judge was satisfied:

> "for a number of reasons that compliance with the Risk Improvement Notice and Contract Endorsement 8 [containing the requirement to upgrade the system] by the extended deadline of August 21, 2009 constituted a suspensory condition and not a *true warranty*."[64]

The judge went on to dismiss the insured's argument that the insurer had waived the breach but in so doing stated:

> "[A]lthough the original *true warranty* was not therefore, in my judgment, waived by the requirements of the Risk Improvement Notice, there was plainly a time extension until August 21 for work to the burglar alarm. It is inconceivable that there can be construed to have been running in parallel a *true warranty*, breach of which automatically discharged insurers from liability, and a suspensive condition/extension of time ... However, unlike the position in *Kler*, where the sprinkler installation was in fact complied with, but after the expiry of the deadline, so that, in fact by the time of the storm damage, insurance was found to be back in place, in this case the upgrade work never was carried out, and the Central Station Monitoring never was instituted, so that the suspensive condition continued in effect, and there was no insurance in place at the date of the fire."[65]

A typical clause in a CAR policy is to compel the insured to comply with the Joint Code of Practice for Fire Prevention on construction sites including that any breaches of the Code be remedied. The policy may then provide, for example:

> "Under the terms of this notice the Insurers may suspend or cancel all cover under the Policy from the date named in the notice not being a date earlier than the date named for completion of the Remedial Measures it being understood that upon suspension such cover shall be reinstated when the Insurers are satisfied that the Remedial Measures have been completed."

Although this is often found in the section detailing the cover of the construction works, it might be difficult for an insured to argue that such a clause does not have the effect of suspending cover of risks in relation to other sections of the policy, such as third party or business interruption liability, because of its reference to "all cover". The wording also provides that the insurer may "suspend" or "cancel" the cover, which leaves open the difficulty of construction of the true meaning of the clause, since it suggests that the insurer may elect either to suspend in which case it must reinstate, or that it may cancel and not reinstate the cover.

6.   WARRANTIES

Definition.   The 2015 Act has not explicitly changed the definition of a warranty   **12-015** which will continue to be determined in accordance with the pre-existing law.[66] The term "warranty" for the purpose of any type of insurance policy is to be found in s.33(1) of the MIA 1906, which defines a "promissory warranty" as:

---

[63]   *Sugar Hut Group Ltd* [2010] EWHC 2636 (Comm) at [46]; [2011] Lloyd's Rep. I.R. 198 at 209, per Burton J.

[64]   *Sugar Hut Group Ltd* [2010] EWHC 2636 (Comm) at [52]; [2011] Lloyd's Rep. I.R. 198 at 210, per Burton J.

[65]   *Sugar Hut Group Ltd* [2010] EWHC 2636 (Comm) at [54]; [2011] Lloyd's Rep. I.R. 198 at 210, per Burton J.

[66]   See above, para.5-091.

"[A] warranty by which the assured undertakes that some particular thing shall or shall not be done, or that some condition shall be fulfilled, or whereby he affirms or negatives the existence of a particular state of affairs".

12-016 Creation of warranties. A warranty must be a term of the contract that exists between the insurer and the insured; this is one of the characteristics that differentiate it from a mere representation. Section 33(2) of the MIA 1906 provides that a warranty may be an express or implied term. There are certain statutory terms implied into marine insurance contracts by virtue of the provisions of the MIA 1906,[67] however, they do not extend to non-marine insurance contracts. Whilst, in theory, a warranty could arise by implication, in the case of non-marine insurance the courts have held that the test for implication is, as a matter of policy, not satisfied because as stated in *Euro-Diam Ltd v Bathurst*[68]:

"No implication of a warranty by statute can ... arise. Nor is there any basis for the implication of such a warranty at common law. In the field of insurance a warranty is a term whose breach discharges the insurer from liability ... I can see no basis for holding that any such draconian implication is necessary from the point of view of business efficacy."

A further point of distinction between marine and non-marine insurance in this regard is that by s.35(2) of the MIA 1906 an express warranty

"must be included in, or written upon, the policy, and must be contained in some document incorporated by reference into the policy".

In the non-marine context, however, warranties can be created even where they are not contained in the policy or in a document referred to in the policy.[69] As a general rule, however, where an alleged warranty is not properly reflected in the contractual documentation, usually on the face of the policy itself, it will be unlikely to be considered a warranty.[70]

12-017 Basis of contract clauses. Prior to the 2015 Act taking effect, where a policy was incepted following the submission of a proposal form, other than including a warranty in the body of the policy itself,[71] a common way of creating warranties was to include a basis of contract clause in the proposal form whereby the proposer warranted that the statements contained therein were true and that they would form the basis of the contract between it and the insurer.[72] The effect of basis of contract clauses is to convert the statements in the proposal form into warranties.[73] A common basis of contract clause may read as follows:

---

67 Sections 36–41 of the MIA 1906.
68 *Euro-Diam Ltd v Bathurst* [1990] 1 Q.B. 1 at 40–41; [1988] 2 W.L.R. 517 at 531; [1988] 2 All E.R. 23 at 32.
69 See *Anglo-Californian Bank Ltd v London and Provincial Marine and General Insurance Co Ltd* (1904) 10 Com. Cas 1; 20 T.L.R. 665; *Condogianis v Guardian Assurance Co Ltd* [1921] 2 A.C. 125; (1921) 7 Ll. L. Rep. 155; and *Rozanes v Bowen* (1928) 32 Ll. L. Rep. 98.
70 See *ERC Frakona Reinsurance v American National Insurance Co* [2005] EWHC 1381 (Comm) at [193]; [2006] Lloyd's Rep. I.R. 157 at 191.
71 Older authorities held that it made no difference to the validity of the term as a warranty whether it was at the top, bottom, or even the margin of the policy, *Blackhurst v Cockell* (1789) 3 Term Rep. 360; 100 E.R. 620; *Bean v Stupart* (1778) 1 Doug. K.B. 11; 99 E.R. 9; and *Kenyon v Berthon* (1778) 1 Doug. K.B. 12n.
72 Basis of contract clauses are discussed in detail above at para.5-092 and the issues arising on construction where the terms of the proposal are inconsistent with the policy below at para.13-045.
73 *Condongianis* [1921] 2 A.C. 125 at 129; (1921) 7 Ll. L. Rep. 155.

"This proposal is the basis of the contract and is to be taken as part of the policy and (if accepted) the particulars are to be deemed express and continuing warranties furnished by or on behalf of the proponent; and any questions remaining unanswered will be deemed to be replied to in the negative."

Ordinarily, a misrepresentation or non-disclosure would not entitle the insurer to avoid liability because of the safeguards that the misrepresentation or non-disclosure in question must be material and must have induced the insurer to enter into the policy in order for it to be avoided. However, if the basis of contract clause turns the representations into warranties, any breach of them, however immaterial, will discharge the insurer from any liability from the date of that breach.[74]

To address what could often be the draconian effect of basis of contract clauses, they were rendered ineffective in non-consumer insurance contracts by s.9 of the 2015 Act. This followed s.6 of the Consumer Insurance (Disclosure and Representations) Act 2012 which abolished basis of contract clauses in respect of consumer insurance contracts. It is not possible to contract out of the application of s.9 of the 2015.[75]

Construction of the clause.   Although expressing clauses in the policy as "warranties" and/or specifying that a breach of the term will have consequences consistent with a breach of a warranty may assist in establishing that the term is a warranty, it must be remembered that it is a question of construction in each case. In determining whether a clause is a warranty, the courts have most recently found assistance from the comments of Rix LJ in *HIH Casualty & General Insurance Ltd v New Hampshire Insurance Co*[76] where he stated that it   **12-018**

"is a question of construction, and the presence or absence of the word 'warranty' or 'warranted' is not conclusive. One test is whether it is a term which goes to the root of the transaction; a second, whether it is descriptive of or bears materially on the risk of loss; a third, whether damages would be an unsatisfactory or inadequate remedy. As Bowen L.J. said in *Barnard v Faber*, [1893] 1 KB 340 at 344: 'A term as regards the risk must be a condition.' Otherwise the insurer is merely left to a cross-claim in a matter which goes to the risk itself, which is unbusinesslike".[77]

That case concerned insurance agreements for the provision of collateral in order to secure funds to make six films, with the insurers to receive a portion of the revenues generated by the films once the films had broken even. In the event, not all six films were made, with the effect that the revenue expected was not achieved. The relevant clause, namely that six films would be made, was held to satisfy each of the three possible tests. This paragraph of Rix LJ has been cited and applied in subsequent cases[78] including by Burton J in *Sugar Hut Group Ltd*.[79] It is likely that

---

[74]   If the parties intend to deprive of contractual effect a proposal form which purports to be the basis of their contract, they must have done so by clear and unequivocal language in the policy: *Genesis Housing Association Ltd v Liberty Syndicate Management Ltd* [2013] EWCA Civ 1173 at [62]; [2013] Bus. L.R. 1399 at 1409; [2013] 2 C.L.C. 444 at 457, per Jackson LJ.

[75]   Section 16 of the 2015 Act. See below, paras 5-133 to 5-140 for a general discussion of contracting out of the provisions of the 2015 Act.

[76]   *HIH Casualty & General Insurance Ltd v New Hampshire Insurance Co* [2001] EWCA Civ 735; [2001] 2 All E.R. (Comm) 39; [2001] 2 Lloyd's Rep 161

[77]   *HIH Casualty & General Insurance Ltd* [2001] EWCA Civ 735 at [101]; [2001] 2 All E.R. (Comm) 39 at 67; [2001] 2 Lloyd's Rep. 161 at 182.

[78]   See *GE Reinsurance Corp (formerly Kemper Reinsurance Co) v New Hampshire Insurance Co; GE Reinsurance Corp v Willis Ltd* [2003] EWHC 302 (Comm) at [48] and [60]; [2004] Lloyd's Rep. I.R. 404 at 413 and *Toomey v Banco Vitalico de Espana SA de Seguros y Reaseguros* [2003] EWHC 1102 (Comm) at [93]; [2004] Lloyd's Rep. I.R. 354 at 371.

his three tests will continue to be used as three tests, which, whilst separate tests, must all be satisfied for a term to be construed as a warranty.

It is important to note that much of the previous case law on the identification of warranties involved the courts distinguishing warranties from suspensive conditions. Given that the 2015 Act has rendered defunct this distinction, going forward, the earlier authorities will be of little utility in assisting with the identification of warranties.[80]

12-019 Present or continuing warranty.   The broad definition contained in s.33(1) of the MIA 1906 permits a warranty to take a number of different forms. For instance, an insured may warrant that a particular fact exists or does not exist, a condition has or has not been fulfilled, or that it holds a particular belief or intention. It is clear that such a warranty can be limited to a promise of a state of affairs as at a particular point in time despite the lack of specific reference to that in s.33(1) of the MIA 1906; such a clause is a present warranty. Alternatively, the insured may warrant that it is not just the position as at the date the warranty is made (or other specified date) but that it will remain so throughout the currency of the policy. This is known as a continuing warranty. A warranty may therefore be a present or continuing warranty and as stated by Morland J in *Kler Knitwear Ltd*[81]:

> "A warranty in a proposal form that statements of existing facts are true and accurate is a world apart from a warranty which in effect is a promise as to future conduct. The former is clearly crucial to the assessment of risk and the level of premium. The latter too may affect the assessment of risk and the level of premium because a proposed insured who is willing to give an obligation as to his future conduct may be giving an indication of his reliability and business efficiency. Still unbroken or unfulfilled promises as to the future conduct as opposed to the future existence of a state of affairs are of a very different character to breaches of warranties as to existing facts."

Many of the cases before the courts have involved construing whether a warranty has the element of futurity required to render it a continuing warranty. In the context of warranties relating to an insured's state of mind or intention such warranties are more likely to be considered present warranties. So, for instance, in *Kirkbride v Donner*[82] the insured warranted by the proposal that she did not intend that any person under the age of 25, other than herself, should drive the insured car. It was held that that was limited to a warranty as to her intention at that time and not to a continuing warranty that that would be her intention.[83] The courts have had more difficulties when considering warranties as to facts.

In relation to an insured's responses in the proposal form, the question whether the warranty has the quality of futurity will again turn upon the proper construction of the term, a point expressed by the Court of Appeal in *Hussain v Brown*[84] where Saville LJ stated:

> "[T]here is no special principle of insurance law requiring answers in proposal forms to be read prima facie or otherwise, as importing promises as to the future. Whether or not they do depends upon ordinary rules of construction, namely consideration of the words the parties have used in the light

---

[79] *Sugar Hut Group* [2010] EWHC 2636 (Comm) at [41]; [2011] Lloyd's Rep. I.R. 198 at 208.
[80] See above, para.5-102 for a fuller discussion of the issues that may arise in respect of identifying warranties under the 2015 Act.
[81] *Kler Knitwear Ltd* [2000] Lloyd's Rep. I.R. 47 at 49.
[82] *Kirkbride v Donner* [1974] 1 Lloyd's Rep. 549.
[83] See also *Benham v The United Guarantie and Life Assurance Company* (1852) 7 Ex. 744.
[84] *Hussain* [1996] 1 Lloyd's Rep. 627 at 629.

of the context in which they have used them and (where the words admit of more than one meaning) selection of that meaning which seems more closely to correspond with the presumed intention of the parties."

In *Hussain*,[85] the Court of Appeal had to consider a warranty arising out of a question in the proposal form which asked:

"Are the premises fitted with any system of intruder alarm? If YES, give name of installing company (Please provide a copy alarm specification if applicable)."

The insured answered "Yes" and "See specification", a copy of which was sent to the insurer's agents with the proposal form. The insurer argued that this was a continuing warranty that the premises were fitted with an intruder alarm, that the alarm was operational and/or would be habitually set by the insured when the premises were unattended. The insurer relied upon the case of *Hales v Reliance Fire and Accident Insurance Corp Ltd*,[86] in which an insured had responded to a question in the proposal form for a fire policy whether any inflammable oils or goods were used or kept on the premises with the answer "lighter fuel" and this was held to be a continuing warranty. However, Saville LJ in *Hussain*[87] doubted the persuasive strength of the decision in *Hales*[88] because McNair J had not been referred in that case to the earlier cases of *Weber v Employers Liability Assurance Corp*[89] and *Woolfall & Rimmer Ltd v Moyle*[90] and had approved a passage of *MacGillivray on Insurance Law*,[91] which had been superseded by the time of *Hussain*.[92] In both of the earlier cases the court had construed questions in proposal forms using the present tense as only amounting to present warranties; that too was held to be the position in *Hussain*.[93]

A useful review of the authorities is contained in the Scottish case of *Forfar Weavers Ltd v MSF Pritchard Syndicate*,[94] in which the court held that a warranty that "all stock is stored on racks, pallets or stillages at least 10cm above floor level" concerned the customary or habitual storage of stock at the time the warranty was given and was not a future or continuing warranty.[95] The judge stated that had it

---

85 *Hussain* [1996] 1 Lloyd's Rep. 627; *Times,* December 15, 1995; Lloyd's List, February 13, 1996.
86 *Hales v Reliance Fire and Accident Insurance Corp Ltd* [1960] 2 Lloyd's Rep. 391; *Times,* November 30, 1960.
87 *Hussain* [1996] 1 Lloyd's Rep. 627; *Times,* December 15, 1995; Lloyd's List, February 13, 1996.
88 *Hales* [1960] 2 Lloyd's Rep. 391; *Times,* November 30, 1960.
89 *Weber v Employers Liability Assurance Corp* (1926) 24 Ll. L. Rep. 321.
90 *Woolfall & Rimmer Ltd v Moyle* [1942] 1 K.B. 66; [1941] 3 All E.R. 304; (1941) 71 Ll. L. Rep. 15.
91 E.J MacGillivray and D. Browne, *MacGillivray on Insurance Law*, 4th edn (London: Sweet & Maxwell, 1953), para.903.
92 Saville LJ in *Hussain* [1996] 1 Lloyd's Rep. 627 at 629; *Times,* December 15, 1995 at 677 678.
93 *Hussain* [1996] 1 Lloyd's Rep. 627; *Times,* December 15, 1995; Lloyd's List February 13, 1996.
94 *Forfar Weavers Ltd v MSF Pritchard Syndicate* (2006) S.L.T. (Sh Ct) 19; 2006 G.W.D. 6–111.
95 *Hales* [1960] 2 Lloyd's Rep. 391; *Times,* November 30, 1960. cf. *Palatine Insurance Co Ltd* [1926] A.C. 90; [1925] 23 Ll. L. Rep. 12 at 13 where the insured warranted that a "continuous clear space of 50 feet shall hereafter be maintained between the timber hereby insured and any sawmill ..." where, although the clause was held to be inoperative as not expressed in the manner required by New Brunswick legislation, the Privy Council was satisfied that it was a continuing warranty. For other examples of continuing warranties see *Dawsons Ltd v Bonnin* [1922] 2 A.C. 413; (1922) 12 Ll. L Rep. 237; 1922 S.C (H.L) 156; *Beauchamp v National Mutual Indemnity Insurance Co* [1937] 3 All E.R. 19; (1937) 57 Ll. L Rep. 272; *Vaughan Motors and Sheldon Motor Services Ltd v Scottish General Insurance Co Ltd* [1960] 1 Lloyd's Rep. 479; *Agapitos v Agnew (The Aegeon) (No. 2)*; sub nom. *Agapitos v Laiki Bank (Hellas) SA* [2002] EWHC 1558 (Comm); [2003] Lloyd's Rep. I.R. 54.

been intended that the stock should never, at any time "not even for one transitory moment"[96] be stored otherwise then the stillage warranty should have said so but "[a]s framed, the nature, extent and character of the warranty [were] ... bereft of any futurity".[97] The judge also emphasised that a continuing warranty was to be distinguished from a present warranty which continued in force during the policy term for the policy contained a clause which purported to give effect to the other warranties in the contract. General condition 4 read as follows:

"Every warranty shall from the time that the warranty attaches apply and continue to be enforced during the whole currency of this Insurance and non-compliance with any such warrant whether it increases the risk or not shall be a bar to any claim."[98]

It was the insurer's defence to the claim that this condition provided the futurity necessary for the clause concerning stillages to have continuing effect. However, the judge held that condition 4 only operated to facilitate the insurer's continuing ability to enforce the present warranties in the policy and could not alter the intrinsic nature of the other warranties to give them the quality of futurity.

More recently, in the case of *AC Ward & Son Ltd v Catlin (Five) Ltd*[99] the Court of Appeal has considered the position, again in the context of burglar alarm and protection maintenance warranties. The court held that a warranty stemming from the proposal form in relation to the security devices or protections at the insured premises only related to the maintenance of the protections, which were in place at the time. Further, reference to the burglar alarm system on the proposal was construed as a reference only to the system in place at the insured property at the time of the inception of the insurance.

Notwithstanding the assistance, which may be derived from some of the previous authorities[100] as to the court's likely interpretation of a clause, the courts have continually made it abundantly clear that the question is always no more than one of construction. As expressed by the judge in the *Forfar Weavers Ltd* case

"ample authority exists for the proposition that where insurers or underwriters seek a particular level of protection then they must make the necessary provision in clear terms within the policy documentation".[101]

Therefore, those seeking the protection of a continuing warranty should ensure that it is expressly stated in unambiguous terms in the policy terms in order to be guaranteed the benefit of the same.

7. BREACH OF WARRANTY

12-020   The consequences that follow from an insured's breach of a warranty have been fundamentally reformed by the 2015 Act. Previously, a breach of a warranty had the effect of automatically discharging an insurer from all liability under the policy as from the date of breach; this was regardless of whether the warranty breached

---

[96] *Forfar Weavers Ltd* (2006) S.L.T. (Sh Ct) 19 at 22.
[97] *Forfar Weavers Ltd* (2006) S.L.T. (Sh Ct) 19 at 22.
[98] *Forfar Weavers Ltd* (2006) S.L.T. (Sh Ct) 19.
[99] *AC Ward & Son Ltd v Catlin (Five) Ltd* [2009] EWCA Civ 1098; [2010] Lloyd's Rep. I.R. 301.
[100] For another example of a case where a warranty was held to be present rather than continuing see *Hearts of Oak Permanent Building Society v Law Union & Rock Insurance Co Ltd* [1936] 2 All E.R. 619; (1936) 55 Ll. L. Rep. 153.
[101] *Forfar Weavers Ltd* 2006 S.L.T. (Sh Ct) 19 at 23.

was material to the loss suffered by the insured. This position was provided for by s.33(3) of the MIA 1906:

> "[a] warranty, as above defined, is a condition which must be exactly complied with, whether it be material to the risk or not. If it be not so complied with, then, subject to any express provision in the policy, the insurer is discharged from liability as from the date of the breach of warranty, but without prejudice to any liability incurred by him before that date".

Section 33(3) of the MIA 1906 no longer applies in respect of insurance contracts entered into after 12 August 2016,[102] however, its effect has been preserved in respect of those insurance contracts entered into before this date (including variations to these contracts made after 12 August 2016) or where the provisions of the 2015 Act have ben contracted out of by the parties.[103]

For those insurance contracts entered into after 12 August 2016, ss.10 and 11 of the 2015 Act apply. Section 10 of the 2015 Act provides that so long as the breach of warranty is remedied prior to loss, the cover will remain in place and the insurer's liability will be resumed as at the date of remedy. Section 11 of the 2015 Act applies to prevent insurers from avoiding policies in circumstances where the breach of warranty has no connection to the loss suffered by the insured. The effect of these provisions is discussed in further detail below. For a more comprehensive discussion of these reforms, see above at paras 5-090 to 5-115.

Breach as a matter of construction. Whether the insured has failed to comply   **12-021** exactly with the warranty will be determined on a proper construction of the obligations imposed by the warranty in each case. For instance, those warranties that relate to an insured's opinion will be complied with if the insured has honestly stated his opinion or intention at the time, unless on an objective test the insured could not possibly have held such an opinion.[104] In relation to warranties generally, the principles of construction can militate against the draconian effects of a warranty not being strictly complied with because the insured is not required to do anything more than is clearly required by the warranty. The classic early example is that of *Hide v Bruce*,[105] where a warranty that a ship had 20 guns was held not to be breached by the fact there were only 25 men aboard the ship, when in order for the 20 guns to be operated 60 men were required. There are other decided cases where it might be suggested that the courts have placed emphasis on the consequences of non-compliance when applying the canons of construction to the warranty when arriving at their decision.

Once the ambit of the warranty has been determined, it must be strictly complied with.[106] The circumstances in which the breach has come about or whether there is any fault on the part of the insured is irrelevant. Further, no defence is afforded to

---

[102] See s.10(7)(a) of the 2015 Act.

[103] See s.22(2) of the 2015 Act.

[104] See *Arab Bank Plc v Zurich Insurance Co; Banque Bruxelles Lambert SA v Zurich Insurance Co* [1999] 1 Lloyd's Rep. 262; [1998] C.L.C. 1351; and *Gerling Konzern General Insurance Co v Polygram Holdings Inc; Copenhagen Reinsurance Co (UK) Ltd v Polygram Holdings Inc* [1998] 2 Lloyd's Rep. 544.

[105] *Hide* (1783) 3 Doug. K.B. 213.

[106] For an early and clear example of this principle see *Worsley v Wood, Assignees of Lockyer and Bream, Brankrupts; in Error* (1796) 6 Term Rep. 710; 101 E.R. 785. The burden of proving that it has not been rests upon the insurer, *Stebbing v Liverpool & London & Globe Insurance Co* [1917] 2 K.B. 433 at 438; [1916–17] All E.R. Rep 248 at 252–253; 86 L.J.K.B. 1155 at 1159–1160; and *Bond Air Services v Hill* [1955] 2 Q.B. 417; [1955] 2 W.L.R. 1194; [1955] 2 All E.R. 476.

the insured where it is unaware of the breach, where compliance was a matter for third parties, or where the breach was in some other way not the fault of the insured. The extreme nature of this can be seen from the case of *International Management Group (UK) Ltd v Simmonds*,[107] which concerned a policy insuring against the cancellation of a cricket tournament between India and Pakistan, containing a warranty that the insured would "ensure that all necessary licences, visas and permits were obtained within sufficient time prior to the insured event."[108] It was found by Cooke J that approval or permission of the Indian Government was "necessary" within the meaning of the warranty and represented a "necessary visa, licence or permit."[109] The Indian Government's refusal to allow its national team to participate amounted to a breach of warranty on the part of the insured even though it was a matter that was obviously outside of its control.

12-022 **The materiality of risk to loss** Long before the MIA 1906 it was recognised by the courts that it was:

> "a matter of indifference whether the thing warranted be or be not material; but it must be literally complied with; and if it be so, that is sufficient".[110]

While a representation may be equitably and substantially answered,[111] a warranty must be strictly complied with.[112] This rule was placed on statutory footing by s.33(3) of the MIA 1906, which provides that:

> "[a] warranty, as above defined, is a condition which must be exactly complied with, whether it be material to the risk or not. If it be not so complied with, then, subject to any express provision in the policy, the insurer is discharged from liability as from the date of the breach of warranty, but without prejudice to any liability incurred by him before that date".

Thus, under the MIA 1906, whether the warranty is material to the risk or in any other way material is irrelevant, save to the extent that the presence or lack of materiality may assist the court in determining whether a term is a warranty in accordance with one of the tests postulated by Rix LJ in *HIH Casualty and General Insurance Ltd*,[113] when there is any dispute on the point.[114] The position is substantially different under s.11 of the 2015 Act which provides that:

> "(1) This section applies to a term (express or implied) of a contract of insurance, other than a term defining the risk as a whole, if compliance with it would tend to reduce the risk of one or more of the following—
>   (a) loss of a particular kind
>   (b) loss at a particular location,
>   (c) loss at a particular time.
> (2) If a loss occurs, and the term has not been complied with, the insurer may not rely

---

107 *International Management Group (UK) Ltd v Simmonds* [2003] EWHC 177 (Comm); [2004] Lloyd's Rep. I.R. 247.
108 *Simmonds* [2003] EWHC 177 (Comm) at [79]; [2004] Lloyd's Rep. I.R. 247 at 248.
109 *Simmonds* [2003] EWHC 177 (Comm) at [115]; [2004] Lloyd's Rep. I.R. 247 at 269.
110 Buller J in *Blackhurst* (1789) 3 Term Rep. 360. See also *De Hahn v Hartley* (1786) 1 Term Rep. 343.
111 *De Hahn* (1786) 1 Term Rep. 343.
112 For cases dealing with the distinction between a representation and a warranty see *Pawson v Watson* (1778) 2 Cowp. 785; *Hide v Bruce* (1783) 3 Doug. K.B. 213; *De Hahn* (1786) 1 Term Rep. 343; and *Weems* (1884) 9 App. Cas. 671; (1884) 11 R. (H.L.) 48.
113 *HIH Casualty and General Insurance Ltd* [2001] EWCA Civ 735; [2001] 2 All E.R. (Comm) 39; [2001] 2 Lloyd's Rep. 161.
114 The test is set out above, in para.12-018.

on the non-compliance to exclude, limit or discharge its liability under the contract for the loss if the insured satisfies subsection (3).

(3) The insured satisfies this subsection if it shows that the non-compliance with the term could not have increased the risk of the loss which actually occurred in the circumstances in which it occurred.

(4) This section may apply in addition to section 10."

This provision introduces a test of relevance between the breach of warranty and the losses sustained by the insured in order to determine whether an insurer can rely upon the breach to avoid liability under the policy. If a warranty would have the general effect of reducing losses of a particular kind, at a particular location or at a particular time, then a breach of that warranty will not allow the insurer to avoid liability where the insured is able to satisfy the courts that the non-compliance with the warranty could not have increased the risk of the losses that occurred in the circumstances in which they occurred. In effect, the provision will therefore target "risk mitigation" warranties and will "lock in" those warranties to a particular type of cover or a particular category of losses. This can best be illustrated through an example: if a policy covers the specified perils of storm, flood and fire, it will commonly include a number of "risk mitigation" warranties such as one requiring the insured to keep a working fire alarm within the covered building. Such a warranty will generally have the effect of reducing the risk of fire, and so will be caught by s.11(1)(a) of the 2015 Act as a term that would generally reduce the risk of losses of a particular kind. If storm damage occurs to the building whilst the fire alarm is broken, under the previous law the insurer would have been off risk for the entire cover under the policy as from the date that the warranty was first breached. However, s.11(3) of the 2015 Act will allow the insured to put the insurer back on risk if it can show that the breach of warranty could not have increased the risk of storm damage in the circumstances in which that damage occurred. As the broken fire alarm will have had no bearing on the risk of storm damage, the insurer will not be able to rely on the breach to avoid liability under the policy. The general effect of s.11 can therefore be understood as "locking in" risk mitigation warranties to only suspend cover for the risks they are designed to mitigate. For a comprehensive discussion of the operation of this provision, see paras 5-110 to 5-114 above.

Divisibility of the policy under the MIA 1906. As a general rule, under the MIA 1906, a breach of warranty will discharge an insurer from liability under the whole policy. However, it was recognised by the Court of Appeal in *Printpak v AGF Insurance Ltd*[115] that that may not always be the case. That case concerned a commercial inclusive insurance policy with separate schedules, each concerned with a different type of risk and with different section endorsements in the same fashion as a typical CAR policy. The policy provided insurance under Section A to cover damage to stock resulting from fire. Section B of the policy provided cover for theft and attached to Section B was an endorsement including a warranty that the burglar alarms would be fully operational when the insured's premises was closed for business. The insured suffered a fire at the insured factory and the insurer refused the insured's claim on the ground that the fire started while the burglar alarm was turned off during building work and that there was therefore a breach of warranty. At first instance it was held as a preliminary issue that the breach of warranty did

12-023

---

[115] *Printpak v AGF Insurance Ltd* [1999] 1 All E.R. (Comm.) 466; [1999] Lloyd's Rep. I.R. 542; *Times*, February 3, 1999.

not invalidate cover under the policy. The insurer appealed, arguing that the policy was a single contract and therefore it followed automatically that the breach of the warranty entitled it not to indemnify the insured by virtue of s.33(3) of the MIA 1906. The Court of Appeal accepted that the policy was a single contract but nevertheless dismissed the insurer's appeal because the endorsements were described as "section endorsements" and "operative only as stated in the policy schedule".[116] The court considered that those words explicitly tied the warranties to the individual sections so that a breach of warranty in one section did not invalidate cover under the other sections. Hirst LJ, delivering the court's main judgment, said that the relevant words writing the warranty only into the theft section of the policy were an "express provision" for the purposes of s.33(3), to which the automatic discharge of the insurer under the policy was therefore subject.[117] Therefore, if an insured can establish on the proper construction of the policy that the relevant warranty only relates to part of the policy, it may be able to argue successfully that cover should only cease under that part of the policy. Such an argument may be of use to an insured in the context of a CAR policy because most CAR insurance policies adopt a similar structure to that in the *Printpak*[118] case. It may also be possible to argue, subject to the precise wording of the warranty, that if the insurance is for construction taking place at multiple sites, a breach of warranty in relation to one site will not discharge the insurer from liability in respect of the other sites. As a note of caution, however, the decision in *Printpak* that the warranty could be divisible and not impact the entire policy appears to have turned on the inclusion in each section schedule of the "Commercial Inclusive Endorsements, operative only as stated in the policy schedules".[119] These inclusions persuaded the court that the insurer had intended that the warranties were only to apply to each section. Without such a clause the task of successfully pleading divisibility may be harder.

12-024 **Discharge from liability.** Under the MIA 1906, where there has been a breach of warranty, s.33(3) provides that:

> "[S]ubject to any express provision in the policy, the insurer is discharged from liability as from the date of the breach of warranty, but without prejudice to any liability incurred by him before that date."

Section 34(2) of the MIA 1906 expressly provides that it is no defence to a breach of warranty that the breach has been remedied prior to the loss.[120]

The position is very different under s.10 of the 2015 Act which provides that:

> "(1) Any rule of law that breach of a warranty (express or implied) in a contract of insurance results in the discharge of the insurer's liability under the contract is abolished.
>
> (2) An insurer has no liability under a contract of insurance in respect of any loss occurring, or attributable to something happening, after a warranty (express or implied) in the contract has been breached but before the breach has been remedied."

---

[116] *Printpak* [1999] 1 All E.R. (Comm.) 466 at 471; [1999] Lloyd's Rep. I.R. 542; *Times*, February 3, 1999.

[117] *Printpak* [1999] 1 All E.R. (Comm.) 466 at 470; [1999] Lloyd's Rep. I.R. 542 at 545.

[118] *Printpak* [1999] 1 All E.R. (Comm.) 466; [1999] Lloyd's Rep. I.R. 542; *Times*, February 3, 1999.

[119] *Printpak* [1999] 1 All E.R. (Comm.) 466 at 468; [1999] Lloyd's Rep. I.R. 542 at 544; *Times*, February 3, 1999.

[120] By reason of s.10(7), s.33(4) of the MIA 1906 does not apply in respect of insurance contracts entered into after 12 August 2016. However, by reason of s.22(3) of the 2015 Act, its effect has been preserved in respect of insurance contracts entered into prior to this date.

Therefore, for those policies entered into after 12 August 2016, the insurer is only discharged from liability where there the insured is in breach of the warranty at the time of loss (or the loss is attributable to an earlier breach of warranty that has since been remedied). The effect of this provision is to transform all warranties into suspensive conditions,[121] where the insurer's liability under the policy will resume upon the breach of warranty being remedied. For a comprehensive discussion of the effect of s.10 of the 2015 Act, see paras 5-090 to 5-102 above.

Notwithstanding the clarity of s.33(3), over the years, the courts often referred to an insurer having a right to treat the contract as repudiated to affirm it.[122] This was finally resolved by the House of Lords in *The Good Luck*[123] where Lord Goff of Chieveley, delivering the lead judgment with which their Lordships agreed, stated:

"So it is laid down in section 33(3) that, subject to any express provision in the policy, the insurer is discharged from liability as from the date of the breach of warranty. Those words are clear. They show that discharge of the insurer from liability is automatic and is not dependent upon any decision by the insurer to treat the contract or the insurance as at an end; though, under section 34(3), the insurer may waive the breach of warranty."

Citing Lord Blackburn in Weems,[124] Lord Goff went on to say that it was

"readily understandable that, if a promissory warranty is not complied with, the insurer is discharged from liability as from the date of the breach of warranty, for the simple reason that fulfilment of the warranty is a condition precedent to the liability of the insurer."[125]

It was stressed by Lord Goff that the texts were wrong to talk of the insurer being entitled to avoid the policy or to repudiate it because the insurer was simply discharged from liability as from the date of the breach. Moreover, Lord Goff stated that s.33(3):

"does not have the effect of avoiding the contract ab initio. Nor, strictly speaking, does it have the effect of bringing the contract to an end. It is possible that there may be obligations of the assured under the contract which will survive the discharge of the insurer from liability, as for example a continuing liability to pay a premium".[126]

De minimis breaches of warranty.   It has been suggested that there may be a "de   **12-025** minimis" defence for a breach of warranty. This was argued in *Sugar Hut Group Ltd*,[127] where there was an area of some 15 square metres of ducting which the insured had warranted would be kept free from contact with combustible materials and there was an area of contact which was only 114cm or so. Part of the insured's case was that the breach should in those circumstances be treated as "de minimis" and excused. Counsel for the insurer accepted that there were obiter refer-

---

[121] See above, para.12-014.

[122] For example see *West v National Motor and Accident Insurance Union* [1955] 1 W.L.R. 343; [1955] 1 All E.R. 800; [1955] 1 Lloyd's Rep. 207; *Mint Security Ltd v Blair, Miller (Thomas R) & Son (Home) and Darwin Clayton (E C) and Co* [1982] 1 Lloyd's Rep. 188; *Hadenfayre v British National Insurance Society; Trident General Insurance Co v Lombard Elizabethan Insurance Co* [1984] 2 Lloyd's Rep. 393; (1984) 134 N.L.J. 1017; and *Iron Trades Mutual Insurance Co Ltd v Companhia De Seguros Imperio* [1992] Re. I.R. 213.

[123] *The Good Luck* [1992] 1 A.C. 233 at 262; [1991] 2 W.L.R. 1279 at 1294; [1991] 3 All E.R. 1 at 13.

[124] *Weems* (1884) 9 App. Cas. 671 at 684; (1884) 11 R. (H.L.) 48 at 51–52.

[125] *The Good Luck* [1992] 1 A.C. 233 at 262–263; [1991] 2 W.L.R. 1279 at 1295; [1991] 3 All E.R. 1 at 13.

[126] *The Good Luck* [1992] 1 A.C. 233 at 263; [1991] 2 W.L.R. 1279 at 1295; [1991] 3 All E.R. 1 at 13.

[127] *Sugar Hut Group Ltd* [2010] EWHC 2636 (Comm); [2011] Lloyd's Rep. I.R. 198.

ences to the possibility of "de minimis" in the insurance field in the cases of *Overseas Commodities Ltd v Style*[128] and *Bennett (t/a Soho Pizzeria) v Axa Insurance Plc*[129] but it was stressed that there is no decision which has in fact found the concept to apply so as to excuse a breach of an insurance warranty. Burton J in *Sugar Hut Group Ltd* was in any event "entirely satisfied that, even if the concept could be applicable" it could not apply on the facts of that case.[130] Such a "de minimis" exception would be wholly contrary to the express wording of s.33(3) of the MIA 1906; it must therefore be correct that it has no place in the context of insurance warranties save to the extent that any particular warranty permits of that qualification on its proper construction in accordance with general principles of construction.

12-026 **Relevance of date of breach.** For the reasons stated above, the effect of the breach will depend upon when it occurs. If the breach is of a warranty, which was offered at the time of the proposal and the breach can be established as existing as at that date, the consequence of the insurer being discharged from liability as at the date of breach is that they would never have gone on risk. As a result, any premiums paid by the insured to the insurer must be repaid to the insured, on the basis that there has been a total failure of consideration,[131] and the insurer is entitled to be reimbursed for any sums paid out under the policy during its term. If the breach occurs during the term of the policy then the insured will not be entitled to any return of the premium on the basis that in the usual case a premium is an entire premium. As stated by Lord Mansfield in *Tyrie v Fletcher*[132]:

> "[I]f the risk of a contract of indemnity has once commenced, there shall be no apportionment or return of premium afterwards. For though the premium is estimated, and the risk depends upon the nature and length of the voyage, yet, if it has commenced, though it be only for twenty-four hours or less, the risk is run; the contract is for the whole entire risk, and no part of the consideration shall be returned; and yet, it is as easy to apportion for the length of the voyage, as it is for the time."

In *JA Chapman & Co Ltd v Kadirga Denizcilik ve Ticaret AS*,[133] the Court of Appeal considered the position where the premium was payable by four instalments. It held that although the payment of premium clause provided for payment in those terms, it was clear from the wording of the policy that there remained only one single premium. They considered that the judge at first instance had erred, inter alia, by failing to recognise that the premium was being paid "for ... the entire risk accepted by insurers under the policy"[134] and that, therefore, the insured remained liable to pay the instalments that had not yet become due at the date of the breach of warranty. It will therefore only be where the risk itself is divisible between the payment dates, expressed in *JA Chapman & Co Ltd (In Liquidation)* as "a series of

---

[128] *Overseas Commodities Ltd v Style* [1958] 1 Lloyd's Rep. 546 at 557, per McNair J.
[129] *Bennett (t/a Soho Pizzeria) v Axa Insurance Plc* [2003] EWHC 86 (Comm) at [20]; [2004] Lloyd's Rep. I.R. 615 at 620, per Tomlinson J.
[130] *Sugar Hut Group Ltd* [2010] EWHC 2636 (Comm) at [44]; [2011] Lloyd's Rep. I.R. 198 at 209.
[131] See ss.84(1)(a) and (3)(a) of the MIA 1906.
[132] *Tyrie v Fletcher* (1777) 2 Cowp. 666 at 668.
[133] *JA Chapman & Co Ltd (In Liquidation) v Kadirga Denizcilik ve Ticaret AS* [1998] C.L.C. 860; [1998] Lloyd's Rep. I.R. 377; *Times,* March 19, 1988.
[134] *JA Chapman & Co Ltd (In Liquidation)* [1998] C.L.C. 860 at 869; [1998] Lloyd's Rep. I.R. 377, per Sir Brian Neill.

premiums payable in respect of risks during successive periods"[135] where the insured may be discharged from future instalments; that will be exceptional in practice.

Determining the date of breach will be of vital importance under the 2015 Act in order to establish the time from which the insurer's liability is suspended. Once the period of suspension has been identified, s.10(4) of the 2015 Act provides that the insurer's liability will continue for losses that occur before the warranty has been breached or after the breach has been remedied, so long as the loss is not attributable to something that happened during the period of breach.

Divisibility between co-insureds. A question may arise where there is a breach **12-027** of warranty by one insured whether the automatic discharge of the insurer's liability applies as against the innocent co-insured(s). That question was addressed by Rix J in *Arab Bank Plc; Banque Bruxelles Lambert SA*.[136] The court had to consider preliminary issues in actions brought by banks against the professional liability insurers of negligent valuers. The managing director of the valuer company prepared fraudulent valuations in the name of the company for the claimant banks and the insurer sought to avoid the insurance on the ground of that fraud. The managing director had signed the proposal form for the insurance, which warranted that the statements therein were true to the best of each of the insured's knowledge.[137] On the assumed facts, aside from the managing director and one other, the remaining directors were unaware that the statements were not true. After holding that the insurance was composite insurance of a type under which there were several insureds (the company and the directors) with separate interests and the policy was to be treated as a bundle of separate contracts, Rix J went on to consider the nature of the warranty in the proposal. He considered that:

> "reliance on Mr Browne's [the managing director's] warranty goes no further than reliance on his misrepresentations and non-disclosures. It would have been otherwise if the warranty had been purely as to the truth of the statements. Then ignorance [of the other insureds] would have been no defence, and I am prepared to assume that the terms of the proposal, incorporated into the policy by means of the "basis of the contract" provision, would have taken precedence over the other provisions of the policy".[138]

Rix J was influenced by other terms of the policy, which he said were designed to fit with the qualification of the warranty such that an innocent insured would not be in breach and they would continue to benefit from cover. It would seem that where a warranty relates to an insured's state of knowledge or belief, as in *Arab Bank Plc*,[139] a breach by one insured will not affect another insured under a composite policy but the position will be different where the warranty is in absolute terms.[140] For instance, had the basis of contract clause been worded without reference to the knowledge of each insured but just as to the truth of the statements generally, or had the warranty related to the description of the risk, a breach by one

---

[135] *JA Chapman & Co Ltd (In Liquidation)* [1998] C.L.C. 860 at 868; [1998] Lloyd's Rep. I.R. 377 at 380, per Sir Brian Neill.

[136] *Arab Bank Plc* [1999] 1 Lloyd's Rep. 262; [1998] C.L.C. 1351.

[137] Basis of contract clauses have since been abolished by s.9 of the 2015 Act. See above, para.12-017.

[138] *Arab Bank Plc* [1999] 1 Lloyd's Rep. 262 at 283; [1998] C.L.C. 1351 at 1377.

[139] *Arab Bank Plc* [1999] 1 Lloyd's Rep. 262; [1998] C.L.C. 1351.

[140] *Arab Bank Plc* [1999] 1 Lloyd's Rep. 262; [1998] C.L.C. 1351 has been doubted by the Court of Appeal in *Stone & Rolls Ltd (In Liquidation) v Moore Stephens (A Firm)* [2008] EWCA Civ 644; [2008] 3 W.L.R. 1146; [2008] 2 Lloyd's Rep. 319 but not on this point.

insured would have affected the cover of all of the insureds.

CAR policies may well provide for divisibility of liability as between co-insureds, particularly where it is envisaged that there will be numerous parties to the construction project. Such a clause might be worded in the following way:

> "The rights and indemnity of any of the parties who are not guilty of any fraud, misrepresentation, non-disclosure or breach of condition shall not be prejudiced or affected by any fraud, misrepresentation, non-disclosure or breach of condition by any of the other parties comprising the Insured."

This would protect an innocent insured from the consequences of a breach of warranty by its co-insured(s).[141]

12-028   **Term contrary to automatic discharge.** As evidenced by the decision in *Printpak*[142] discussed above in para.12-023, the effect of s.33(3) of the MIA 1906 may be limited by any express term in the policy. A common such term in practice to avoid the draconian effects of a breach of warranty is that the insurer will only rely upon breach of warranty where that breach increases the risk of damage and/or has in some way or materially caused or contributed to the insurer's loss. Such a term restricts the effect of s.33(3) that there is no need for a causal connection between the breach of warranty and the loss and that the insurer is automatically discharged from liability at the date of breach, regardless of whether or not the breach of warranty caused or contributed to the loss or was in any other way material. Recently in *Seashell of Lisson Grove Ltd v Aviva Insurance Ltd*,[143] the court considered such a term, which provided that a failure to comply with any warranty in a fire policy:

> "shall invalidate any claim for loss destruction damage or liability which is wholly or partly due to or affected by such failure to comply".

By way of preliminary issue, Teare J determined that the clause limited the common law rule as to the effect of a breach of warranty by introducing a causal connection between the breach and the loss, destruction, damage or liability claimed. The court held that the clause did not mean that so long as there was a link between the breach of warranty and at least some of the loss, then the breach discharged the insurer from liability. Instead, loss that was not wholly or partly due to or affected by the breach could be claimed notwithstanding the breach of warranty.[144]

8. DEFENCES

12-029   **Defences.** There are limited defences available to an insured where it has been found to be in breach of a warranty upon its proper construction.

For those policies entered into before 12 August 2016, s.34(1) and (3) of the MIA 1906 provide two defences to the insured. These defences have been replicated by s.10(3) of the 2015 Act in respect of those policies entered into after 12 August

---

141   Joint insurance is dealt with in more detail above in Ch.8 and below, in Ch.20.

142   *Printpak* [1999] 1 All E.R. (Comm.) 466; [1999] Lloyd's Rep. I.R. 542; *Times,* February 3, 1999.

143   *Seashell of Lisson Grove Ltd v Aviva Insurance Ltd* [2011] EWHC 1761 (Comm) at [3]; [2012] 1 All E.R. (Comm.) 754; [2011] 2 C.L.C. 831.

144   *Seashell of Lisson Grove Ltd* [2011] EWHC 1761 (Comm) at [8]–[12]; [2012] 1 All E.R. (Comm) 754 at 758; [2011] 2 C.L.C. 831 at 834–835. For an earlier example of the treatment of causal connection clauses, see *Bennett (t/a Soho Pizzeria)* [2003] EWHC 86 (Comm); [2004] Lloyd's Rep. I.R. 615.

2016. As such, the defences discussed below apply to all CAR policies, regardless of the date of inception.

Change of circumstances.   Section 34(1) of the MIA 1906 excuses non-compliance with a warranty where   **12-030**

"by reason of a change of circumstances, the warranty ceases to be applicable to the circumstances of the contract, or when compliance with the warranty is rendered unlawful by any subsequent law."

The same is provided for by s.10(3)(a) and (b) of the 2015 Act.

This is not an argument that is often raised before the courts but was in the two cases of *Agapitos v Agnew (The Aegeon) (No.2)*; sub nom. *Agapitos v Laiki Bank (Hellas) SA*[145] and *Sugar Hut Group Ltd.*[146] In *The Aegeon,*[147] a ship became a total loss following a fire on board when it was moored at Drapetsona undergoing conversion from a roll-on, roll-off car ferry to a passenger cruise ship. The fire was caused by sparks from hot works being carried out on board. The insurers argued that the owners had breached one or more of the policy warranties, one relating to London Salvage Association ("LSA") approval of location, firefighting and mooring arrangements and compliance with the LSA's recommendations; and the other that no hot works were to be commenced until LSA approval was received. The vessel was subsequently moved under tow from Drapetsona to the lay-up anchorage at Eleusis and there were various further endorsements containing warranties also alleged to have been breached. In respect of the original warranties it was submitted that the shipowners' decision to move the ship to Eleusis brought about a change in circumstances, as a result of which those warranties ceased to be applicable within s.34(1) pending her removal from *Drapetsona*, and that any breach of warranty during that period was excused. Moore-Bick J rejected that argument on the basis that: (1) it was not clear that the owners' decision to move the vessel had been taken by the relevant time but, perhaps more importantly; (2) even if it had, the circumstances to which the warranties were directed remained unchanged throughout the period during which the vessel remained at *Drapetsona* and therefore they did not cease to be applicable in any sense because the location of the vessel had been irrelevant.[148] There was some attempt to argue in *Sugar Hut Group Ltd*[149] that the kitchen of the insured property being closed and no longer in use at the time of the fire would excuse non-compliance with the warranty relating to the kitchen equipment. However, on the evidence, it was plainly not the case that the kitchen was not being used. The judge made no observation as to whether that argument would otherwise have succeeded.[150]

Waiver.   Section 34(3) of the MIA 1906 provides that "[a] breach of warranty may   **12-031**
be waived by the insurer". Similarly, s.10(3)(c) of the 2015 Act excuses non-compliance where "the insurer waives the breach of the warranty".

There are two circumstances in English contract law in which a party may rely on waiver as a defence to a repudiatory breach, namely where: (1) the performance

---

[145] *The Aegeon* [2002] EWHC 1558 (Comm); [2003] Lloyd's Rep I R 54
[146] *Sugar Hut Group Ltd* [2010] EWHC 2636 (Comm); [2011] Lloyd's Rep. I.R. 198.
[147] *The Aegeon* [2002] EWHC 1558 (Comm); [2003] Lloyd's Rep. I.R. 54.
[148] *The Aegeon* [2002] EWHC 1558 (Comm) at [59]; [2003] Lloyd's Rep. I.R. 54 at 65.
[149] *Sugar Hut Group Ltd* [2010] EWHC 2636 (Comm); [2011] Lloyd's Rep. I.R. 198.
[150] *The Aegeon* [2002] EWHC 1558 (Comm) at [42]; [2003] Lloyd's Rep. I.R. 54 at 62–63, per Burton J.

of the warranty is waived prior to the breach of it occurring; or (2) the right to rely on any such breach to repudiate the contract is waived, either before or after breach. In general contract law, both such waivers may arise by express or implied agreement between the parties, by election or by estoppel. The classic statement on the difference between waiver by election and waiver by estoppel[151] is that of Lord Diplock in *Kammins Ballrooms Co Ltd v Zenith Investments (Torquay) Ltd*:

> "'Waiver' is a word sometimes used loosely to describe a number of different legal grounds on which a person may be debarred from asserting a substantive right which he once possessed or from raising a particular defence to a claim against him which would otherwise be available to him ... If he has knowledge of the facts which give rise in law to these alternative rights and acts in a manner which is consistent only with his having chosen to rely on one of them, the law holds him to his choice even though he was unaware that this would be the legal consequence of what he did ... He is sometimes said to have 'waived' the alternative right, as for instance a right to forfeit a lease or to rescind a contract of sale for wrongful repudiation or breach of condition; but this is better categorised as 'election' rather than as 'waiver' ... The second type of waiver which debars a person from raising a particular defence to a claim against him, arises when he either agrees with the claimant not to raise that particular defence or so conducts himself as to be estopped from raising it ... The ordinary principles of estoppel apply to it."[152]

However, in respect of those policies entered into before 12 August 2016 there can be no waiver by election because it is not possible for the insurer to waive a breach of warranty and continue with the policy, since s.33(3) of the MIA 1906 provides that a breach automatically brings the policy to an end. This was confirmed in *The Good Luck*,[153] which held that there is no scope for waiver by election in insurance contracts and that breach of warranty may only be waived in the circumstances that give rise to an estoppel. This was considered to be the position by the first instance courts after *The Good Luck*[154] in a number of cases.[155] The Court of Appeal subsequently confirmed the fact that waiver must be waiver by estoppel, rather than by election in *Kosmar Villa Holdings Plc v Trustees of Syndicate 1243*.[156] In *Lexington Insurance Co v Multinacional de Seguros SA*,[157] the court held that logically there is also no place for waiver by election of a future breach after a breach

---

151 See below, para.12-032 for the requirements of waiver by estoppel.
152 *Kammins Ballrooms Co Ltd v Zenith Investments (Torquay) Ltd* [1971] AC 850 at 882/883, [1970] 3 W.L.R. 287, (1971) 22 P. & C.R. 74 at 104.
153 *The Good Luck* [1992] 1 A.C. 233; [1991] 2 W.L.R. 1279; [1991] 3 All E.R. 1.
154 *The Good Luck* [1992] 1 A.C. 233; [1991] 2 W.L.R. 1279; [1991] 3 All E.R. 1.
155 The point was conceded in *Kirkaldy & Sons Ltd v Walker* [1999] 1 All E.R. (Comm.) 334; [1999] C.L.C. 722; [1999] Lloyd's Rep. I.R. 410; *Brownsville Holdings Ltd v Adamjee Insurance Co Ltd (The Milasan)* [2000] 2 All E.R. (Comm) 803; [2000] 2 Lloyd's Rep. 458 and *The Aegeon* [2002] EWHC 1558 (Comm) at [70]; [2003] Lloyd's Rep. I.R. 54 at 66. In *HIH Casualty and General Insurance Ltd* [2002] Lloyd's Rep. I.R. 325 at 330–331 it was argued at first instance that *Kirkaldy* [1999] 1 All E.R. (Comm.) 334; [1999] C.L.C. 722; [1999] Lloyd's Rep. I.R. 410 was wrongly decided but was followed by the judge, waiver by election was not pursued by the insurer on the appeal of *HIH Casualty & General Insurance Ltd* [2003] EWCA Civ 1253; [2002] 2 All E.R. (Comm) 1053; [2003] Lloyd's Rep. I.R. 1, although Tuckey LJ appeared to endorse the principle that there is no scope for waiver by election [2003] EWCA Civ 1253 at [7]; [2002] 2 All E.R. (Comm) 1053 at 1057; [2003] Lloyd's Rep. I.R. 1 at 5.
156 *Kosmar Villa Holidays Plc v Trustees of Syndicate 1243* [2008] EWCA Civ 147; [2008] 2 All E.R. (Comm) 14; [2008] Lloyd's Rep. I.R. 489.
157 *Lexington Insurance Co v Multinacional de Seguros SA* [2008] EWHC 1170 (Comm); [2009] 1 All E.R. (Comm) 35; [2009] Lloyd's Rep. I.R. 1.

of warranty has already occurred because of the automatic discharge of liability at the point of the original breach.[158]

For those policies to which the 2015 Act applies, given that breach of a warranty no longer automatically discharges an insurer from liability, the difficulties discussed above do not by necessity arise and as such, a breach of warranty may be waived by election or estoppel.[159]

Waiver by estoppel. After reviewing the classic statement of the difference between waiver by election and waiver by estoppel of Lord Diplock in *Kammins Ballrooms Co Ltd v Zenith Investments (Torquay) Ltd (No.1)*,[160] as discussed by Lord Goff in *Motor Oil Hellas (Corinth) Refineries SA v Shipping Corp of India (The Kachenjunga)*,[161] in *Kosmar Villa Holdings Plc* Rix LJ articulated the requirements to set up an estoppel:

12-032

> "Estoppel ... is a promise, supported not by consideration but by reliance. It is a promise not to rely upon a defence (per Lord Diplock) or a right (per Lord Goff). It requires a representation, in words or conduct, which must be unequivocal and must have been relied upon in circumstances where it would be inequitable for the promise to be withdrawn. The need for such unfairness probably means that the reliance of the representee has to constitute a detriment, but even the detriment has, I would think, to be such as to make it inequitable for the promise to be withdrawn. For these reasons, the estoppel may not be irrevocable, but may be suspensory only. An unequivocal representation without the necessary reliance, and the reliance without the necessary unequivocal representation, are each insufficient."[162]

The ingredients of a waiver by estoppel are as set out by Rix LJ, save that it is also necessary for the insurer to be aware of the breach that it is alleged to be waiving.

Although many of the cases prior to *The Good Luck*[163] and *Kosmar Villa Holdings Plc*[164] talk, incorrectly, in terms of affirmation of the contract, on a proper examination of those cases the facts would support findings of waiver by estoppel. For instance, in *Compagnia Tirrena Di Assicurazioni SpA v Grand Union Insurance Co Ltd*,[165] it was held that where an insurer was fully aware of the insured's breaches of warranty and its own rights and yet made subsequent demands of

---

[158] In *Diab v Regent Insurance Co Ltd* [2006] UKPC 29; [2007] 1 W.L.R. 797; [2006] 2 All E.R. (Comm) 704 the Privy Council held that there could be waiver by an insurer of a procedural obligation on the insured by conduct either before or after the insured was in breach of its obligation. However, Rix LJ in *Kosmar Villa Holdings Plc* [2008] EWCA Civ 147 at [46]; [2008] 2 All E.R. (Comm) 14 at 30; [2008] Lloyd's Rep. I.R. 489 at 501 considered that there was nothing of real value from that case on the issue of waiver by election as distinct from waiver by estoppel. See also *HIH Casualty and General Insurance Ltd* [2003] EWCA Civ 1253; [2002] 2 All E.R. (Comm) 1053; [2003] Lloyd's Rep. I.R. 1.

[159] This is the view taken by the Law Commission and the Scottish Law Commission in *"Insurance Contract Law: Business Disclosure; Warranties; Insurers' Remedies for Fraudulent Claims; and Late Payment"*, (HMSO, 2014). *http://www.lawcom.gov.uk/wp-content/uploads/2015/03/lc353_insurance-contract-law.pdf* [Accessed 24 June 2016], at para.17.68.

[160] *Kammins Ballrooms Co Ltd v Zenith Investments (Torquay) Ltd (No.1)* [1971] A.C. 850 at 883; [1970] 3 W.L.R. 287 at 312–313; [1970] 2 All E.R. 871 at 894–895.

[161] *Motor Oil Hellas (Corinth) Refineries SA v Shipping Corp of India (The Kachenjunga)* [1990] 1 Lloyd's Rep. 391 at 398–399; *Times,* February 19, 1990.

[162] *Kosmar Villa Holdings Plc* [2008] EWCA Civ 147 at [38]; [2008] 2 All E.R. (Comm) 14 at 26; [2008] Lloyd's Rep. I.R. 489 at 499.

[163] *The Good Luck* [1992] 1 A.C. 233; [1991] 2 W.L.R. 1279; [1991] 3 All E.R. 1.

[164] *Kosmar Villa Holdings Plc* [2008] EWCA Civ 147; [2008] 2 All E.R. (Comm) 14; [2008] Lloyd's Rep. I.R. 489.

[165] *Compagnia Tirrena Di Assicurazioni SpA v Grand Union Insurance Co Ltd* [1991] 2 Lloyd's Rep. 143.

premiums from the insured that was an unequivocal act only consistent with an intention to continue with the contracts and they had thus affirmed the contract. Such factual circumstances could equally support a plea of estoppel if it could be shown that the insured relied to its detriment on that demand as a representation by the insurer that it was honouring the contract and had waived the breach. It is worth comparing this to the case of *The Milasan*,[166] where no particulars of reliance were pleaded by the insured and there was nothing in the evidence to show any reliance by the insured on a demand for the second instalment of the premium as a representation that the insurer was waiving compliance with the warranty. In that case, the breach of warranty was also not relied upon by the insurer until some five years after it knew of the breach and there was no evidence that the insured regarded the failure to take the warranty point as a representation that the insurer waived compliance with the warranty or that the insured relied upon that failure. Aikens J held in any event that even if that had been pleaded it was very difficult to see what reliance there could have been.

12-033 **Non-invalidation clauses.** There may be a term in the policy stating that the insurer will not avoid liability upon certain broadly specified grounds. Where that is the case, the term in question will have to be carefully examined to ascertain whether the breach of warranty falls within one of those grounds. For instance, in *Kumar v AGF Insurance Ltd*,[167] the policy stated that the insurer would not seek to "avoid, repudiate or rescind this insurance upon any ground whatsoever, including in particular non-disclosure or misrepresentation". On the basis of the decision in *The Good Luck*,[168] it was argued by the insurer that avoidance, repudiation and rescission are all terms that are not applicable to a breach of warranty and as such the insured could not rely on the non-invalidation clause to nullify the insurer's defence of the insured's breach of warranty. Thomas J accepted that this was the correct legal position as stated in *The Good Luck*,[169] but nevertheless held that the clause was sufficient to extend to a breach of warranty so that it prevented the automatic discharge of the insurer's liability. The judge's reasoning was that the clause had to be construed as against the commercial background in place at the time and, at the time the proposal was drafted and in use, the House of Lords had not given its decision in *The Good Luck*[170]:

> "and the precise consequence and precise analysis of the consequences of a breach of warranty, had not been as fully elucidated then as it was by that decision".[171]

A similar decision was reached in *Arab Bank Plc*,[172] where the court considered that:

> "the language of avoidance reflects the (albeit erroneous) understanding of the law relating to warranties as it was at the time of the proposal and the policy and prior to the reversal of the Court of Appeal in *The Good Luck* by the House of Lords in May 1991".

---

[166] *The Milasan* [2000] 2 All E.R. (Comm) 803; [2000] 2 Lloyd's Rep. 458.
[167] *Kumar v AGF Insurance Ltd* [1999] 1 W.L.R. 1747; [1998] 4 All E.R. 788 at 793.
[168] *The Good Luck* [1992] 1 A.C. 233; [1991] 2 W.L.R. 1279; [1991] 3 All E.R. 1.
[169] *The Good Luck* [1992] 1 A.C. 233; [1991] 2 W.L.R. 1279; [1991] 3 All E.R. 1.
[170] *The Good Luck* [1992] 1 A.C. 233; [1991] 2 W.L.R. 1279; [1991] 3 All E.R. 1.
[171] *Kumar* [1999] 1 W.L.R. 1747 at 1754; [1998] 4 All E.R. 788 at 796; [1999] Lloyd's Rep. I.R. 147 at 153.
[172] *Arab Bank Plc* [1999] 1 Lloyd's Rep. 262 at 283; [1998] C.L.C. 1351 at 1377.

Therefore, where the policy was incepted prior to 1991 it would still be possible for language such as that in the clause considered in *Kumar*[173] to provide a defence to a breach of warranty claim. However, the courts have not taken the same approach to policies incepted after that time. For instance, in *HIH Casualty and General Insurance Ltd*,[174] the Court of Appeal had to decide whether the following clause was capable of operating to waive an insurer's right of automatic discharge from a policy for an insured's breach of warranty:

"To the fullest extent permissible by applicable law, the Insurer hereby agrees that it will not seek to or be entitled to avoid or rescind this Policy or reject any claim hereunder or be entitled to seek any remedy or redress on the grounds of invalidity or unenforceability of any of its arrangements with [Company] Ltd or any other person (or of any arrangements between [Company] Ltd and the Purchaser) or non-disclosure or misrepresentation by any person or any other similar grounds. The Insurer irrevocably agrees not to assert and waives any and all defences and rights of set-off and/or counterclaim (including without limitation any such rights acquired by assignment or otherwise) which it may have against the Assured or which may be available so as to deny payment of any amount due hereunder in accordance with the express terms hereof."

The court held that the expression "to the fullest extent permissible by applicable law" did not mean that a warranty was necessarily included within the ambit of the clause simply because a breach of warranty created a remedy under the applicable law.[175] Further, the subject matters of the clause, namely non-disclosure, misrepresentation and invalidity or unenforceablility of arrangements, were all considered by the court to be "extra-contractual".[176] As warranties are contractual they did not constitute "similar grounds" and were therefore not within the scope of the clause.[177] The court also noted that the phrase "so as to deny payment of any amount due hereunder in accordance with the express terms hereof" recognises the continuance of the policy post breach by the insured.[178] This inclusion would not have been necessary had the clause intended to refer to warranties, since post breach of warranty there is no continuing contract and thus the insured would have no claim that was capable of being set-off or counterclaimed against.[179]

In *Seashell of Lisson Grove Ltd*,[180] a non-invalidation clause was also considered, which stated that the insurance would not be invalidated by "any act, omission or alteration" either unknown to the insured or beyond its control, which increases the risk of damage.[181] On the question of construction, it was held that the words "any act or omission" could not reasonably be understood as meaning any act or omission except breaches of warranty and the clause was intended to apply to breaches

---

[173] *Kumar* [1999] 1 W.L.R. 1747; [1988] 4 All E.R. 788; [1999] Lloyd's Rep. I.R. 147.

[174] *HIH Casualty and General Insurance Ltd* [2001] EWCA Civ 735 at 35; [2001] 2 All E.R. (Comm) 39 at 51; [2001] 2 Lloyd's Rep. 161 at 170–171.

[175] *HIH Casualty and General Insurance Ltd* [2001] EWCA Civ 735 at [119]; [2001] 2 All E.R. (Comm) 39 at 71; [2001] 2 Lloyd's Rep. 161 at 184.

[176] *HIH Casualty and General Insurance Ltd* [2001] EWCA Civ 735 at [118]; [2001] 2 All E.R. (Comm) 39 at 70–71; [2001] 2 Lloyd's Rep. 161 at 184.

[177] *HIH Casualty and General Insurance Ltd* [2001] EWCA Civ 735 at [118]; [2001] 2 All E.R. (Comm) 39 at 70–71; [2001] 2 Lloyd's Rep. 161 at 184.

[178] *HIH Casualty and General Insurance Ltd* [2001] EWCA Civ 735 at 121; [2001] 2 All E.R. (Comm) 39 at 71; [2001] 2 Lloyd's Rep. 161 at 184.

[179] See *HIH Casualty and General Insurance Ltd* [2001] EWCA Civ 735 at [112]–[125]; [2001] 2 All E.R. (Comm) 39 at 69–72; [2001] 2 Lloyd's Rep. 161 at 183–185 of the judgment.

[180] *Seashell of Lisson Grove Ltd* [2011] EWHC 1761 (Comm); [2012] 1 All E.R. (Comm) 754; [2011] 2 C.L.C. 831.9

[181] *Seashell of Lisson Grove Ltd* [2011] EWHC 1761 (Comm) at [22]–[23]; [2012] 1 All E.R. (Comm) 754 at 760; [2011] 2 C.L.C. 831 at 837.

of warranty.[182] Moreover, the court held that the clause in question operated in cases where damage had in fact already occurred and since a breach of warranty would usually increase the risk of damage, effect was given to the words "which increase the risk of damage."[183]

These cases illustrate the complexity of the task of draftsmanship in relation to non-invalidation clauses and how it might become difficult to find the true construction of such clauses.

---

[182] *Seashell of Lisson Grove Ltd* [2011] EWHC 1761 (Comm) at [26]; [2012] 1 All E.R. (Comm) 754 at 760; [2011] 2 C.L.C. 831 at 838.

[183] *Seashell of Lisson Grove Ltd* [2011] EWHC 1761 (Comm) at [27]; [2012] 1 All ER (Comm) 754 at 760; [2011] 2 C.L.C. 831 at 838.

CHAPTER 13

PRINCIPLES OF CONSTRUCTION AND RECTIFICATION

TABLE OF CONTENTS

1. INTRODUCTION

Introduction. Jean-Paul Sartre once said "words are loaded pistols"; nowhere is **13-001** this more evident than in disputes about the interpretation of contracts. The difficulty is that contracts are reduced to words and, as Lord Hoffmann has pointed out, "the meaning of words is so sensitive to syntax and context, the natural meaning of words in one sentence may be quite unnatural in another".[1] Put simply, the purpose of interpretation is to ascertain the meaning and legal effect of the words that the parties have used in their agreement. In order to achieve that aim, the courts have established various principles that can be deployed when interpreting a contract. Policies of insurance are no different, in this respect, from other instruments and they fall to be interpreted under the same principles.[2]

2. PRINCIPLES OF CONSTRUCTION

(a) Fundamental principles

The starting point. There are many hundreds of cases dealing with the interpreta- **13-002** tion of contracts, from which numerous principles have been created in order to deal with new challenges of interpretation as they have arisen. However, it is generally accepted that the starting point when dealing with issues of interpretation is found in the speech of Lord Hoffmann in *Investors Compensation Scheme Ltd v West Bromwich Building Society; Same v Hopkin & Sons (a firm),*[3] where he explained the framework of contractual interpretation in five principles:

---

[1] *Charter Reinsurance Co Ltd (In Liquidation) v Fagan* [1997] A.C. 313 at 391; [1996] 2 W.L.R. 726 at 762; [1996] 3 All E.R. 46 at 57 HL.
[2] See, for example, *Robertson v French* 102 E.R. 779 at 781; (1803) 4 East 130 at 135; [1803-13] All E.R. Rep. 350 at 353 KB, per Lord Ellenborough CJ. For a recent application in the construction context, see *Cementation Piling & Foundations Ltd v Aegon Insurance Co Ltd* [1995] 1 Lloyd's Rep. 97 at 101; 74 B.L.R. 98; (1994) 47 Con. L.R. 14 CA.
[3] *Investors Compensation Scheme Ltd v West Bromwich Building Society; Same v Hopkin & Sons (a*

"(1) Interpretation is the ascertainment of the meaning which the document would convey to a reasonable person having all the knowledge which would reasonably have been available to the parties in the situation in which they were at the time of the contract.

(2) The background was famously referred to by Lord Wilberforce as the 'matrix of fact',[4] ... Subject to the requirement that it should have been reasonably available to the parties and to the exception to be mentioned next, it includes absolutely anything which would have affected the way in which the language of the document would have been understood by a reasonable man.

(3) The law excludes from the admissible background the previous negotiations of the parties and their declarations of subjective intent. They are admissible only in an action for rectification ...

(4) The meaning which a document (or any other utterance) would convey to a reasonable man is not the same thing as the meaning of its words. The meaning of words is a matter for dictionaries and grammars; the meaning of the document is what the parties using those words against the relevant background would reasonably have been understood to mean. The background may not merely enable the reasonable man to choose between the possible meanings of words which are ambiguous but even (as occasionally happens in ordinary life) to conclude that the parties must, for whatever reason, have used the wrong words or syntax (see *Mannai Investment Co Ltd v Eagle Star Life Assurance Co Ltd*).[5]

(5) The 'rule' that words should be given their 'natural and ordinary meaning' reflects the common sense proposition that we do not easily accept that people have made linguistic mistakes, particularly in formal documents. On the other hand, if one would nevertheless conclude from the background that something must have gone wrong with the language, the law does not require judges to attribute to the parties an intention which they plainly could not have had.[6]"

13-003 Objective intention of the parties. In English Law, as in many other common law jurisdictions, the purpose of interpretation is often expressed as an investigation of the common intention of the parties. However, such language should be treated with caution because the courts are not concerned with discerning the actual subjective intentions of the parties.[7] The basic presumption is that the parties meant to use the words that they in fact used[8] and therefore the courts seek to assess the objective meaning that those words would convey to a reasonable man.[9] In *Deutsche Genossenschaftsbank v Burnhope*, Lord Steyn explained that:

[ ] *firm*) [1998] 1 W.L.R. 896 at 912–913; [1998] 1 All E.R. 98 at 114–115; [1998] 1 B.C.L.C. 493 at 547–548 Ch.

[4] *Prenn v Simmonds* [1971] 1 W.L.R. 1381; [1971] 3 All E.R. 237; (1971) 115 S.J. 654 HL.

[5] *Mannai Investment Co Ltd v Eagle Star Life Assurance Co Ltd* [1997] A.C. 749; 2 W.L.R. 945; [1997] 3 All E.R. 352 HL.

[6] A strong case is required to persuade the court that something must have gone wrong with the language: *Chartbrook Ltd v Persimmon Homes Ltd* [2009] UKHL 38 at [15]; [2009] 1 A.C. 1101 at 1112D; [2009] 3 W.L.R. 267 at 274; [2009] 4 All E.R. 677 at 686 HL, per Lord Hoffmann. See also *Bank of Credit and Commerce International SA (In Liquidation) v Ali* [2001] UKHL 8 at [39]; [2002] 1 A.C. 251 at 269; [2001] 2 W.L.R. 735 at 749 and *Kirin-Amgen Inc v Hoechst Marion Roussel Ltd; Hoechst Marion Roussel Ltd v Kirin-Amgen Inc*; sub nom. *Kirin-Amgen Inc v Transkaryotic Therapies Inc (No.2) or Kirin-Amgen Inc's European Patent (No. 148605) (No.2)* [2004] UKHL 46 at [35]; [2005] 1 All E.R. 667 at 681–682; [2005] R.P.C. 169 at 186–187.

[7] Earlier authorities suggesting a more subjective approach (such as *Borradaile v Hunter* (1843) 5 Man. & G. 639 and *Polpen Shipping Co Ltd v Commercial Union Assurance Co Ltd* [1943] K.B. 161; [1943] 1 All E.R. 162; (1942) 74 Ll. L. Rep. 157 KB) have not been followed.

[8] *British Movietonews Ltd v London & District Cinemas Ltd* [1952] A.C. 166; [1951] 2 All E.R. 617; [1951] 2 T.L.R. 571 HL.

[9] *Smith v Hughes* (1871) L.R. 6; Q.B. 597 at 607; 40 L.J.Q.B. 221 at 227; 19 W.R. 1059 at 1062; *Man-*

"the objective of the construction is to give effect to the intention of the parties. But our law of construction is based on an objective theory. The methodology is not to probe the real intentions of the parties but to ascertain the contextual meaning of the relevant contractual language. Intention is determined by reference to expressed rather than actual intention ... It is therefore wrong to speculate about the actual intention of the parties."[10]

His Lordship revisited this subject in *Sirius International Insurance Co (Publ) v FAI General Insurance Ltd*[11] when he said:

"The inquiry is objective: the question is what a reasonable person circumstanced as the actual parties were, would have understood the parties to have meant by the use of specific language."

The Supreme Court has recently reaffirmed this approach as follows:

"[T]he ultimate aim of interpreting a provision in a contract, especially a commercial contract, is to determine what the parties meant by the language used, which involves ascertaining what a reasonable person would have understood the parties to have meant. As Lord Hoffmann made clear in the first of the principles he summarised in the *Investors Compensation Scheme* case at p 912H, the relevant reasonable person is one who has all the background knowledge which would reasonably have been available to the parties in the situation in which they were at the time of the contract."[12]

The ordinary meaning of words. The starting point for any exercise of **13-004** interpretation is to consider the words that the parties have used in their agreement. The parties have control over the language they use in their contracts and, save in particularly unusual circumstances, the parties must be taken to have been focusing on the issues covered by the language they have used and the issues related to the clauses they negotiated. Accordingly, save in an unusual case, the objective meaning of the clauses is most obviously to be gleaned from the words the parties have used.[13]

The basic presumption in English law is that the words the parties have used should be interpreted in line with their natural and ordinary meaning; policies of insurance are no different[14] and the words should be interpreted in line with their

---

nai *Investment Co Ltd* [1997] A.C. 749 at 767, 775 and 782; [1997] 2 W.L.R. 945 at 961, 968–969 and 974–975; [1997] 3 All E.R. 352 at 369, 376 and 382–383; *Investors Compensation Scheme* [1998] 1 W.L.R. 896 at 912–913; [1998] 1 All E.R. 98 at 114; [1998] 1 B.C.L.C. 493 at 547; *Equitable Life Assurance Society v Hyman* [2002] 1 A.C. 408 at 457–458; [2000] 3 W.L.R. 529 at 537–538; [2000] 3 All E.R. 961 at 969 HL; *Inntrepreneur Pub Co Ltd v East Crown Ltd* [2000] 2 Lloyd's Rep. 611 at [10]; [2000] 3 E.G.L.R. 31 at 33; [2000] 41 E.G. 209 at 212 Ch; *Chartbrook Ltd* [2009] UKHL 38 at [21]–[26]; [2009] 1 A.C. 1101, 1113–1115; [2009] 3 W.L.R. 267 at 275–277; [2009] 4 All E.R. 677 at 688–689; *Attorney General of Belize v Belize Telecom Ltd* [2009] UKPC 10 at [20]–[24]; [2009] 1 W.L.R. 1988 at 1994; [2009] 2 All E.R. 1127 at 1133–1134; *Pink Floyd Music Ltd v EMI Records Ltd* [2010] EWCA Civ 1429 at [17]; [2011] 1 W.L.R. 770; *Stena Line Ltd v Merchant Navy Ratings Pension Fund Trustees Ltd P & O Ferries Ltd* [2011] EWCA Civ 543 at [41]; [2011] Pens. L.R. 223 at 233; *Wood v Sureterm Direct Ltd & Capita Insurance Services Ltd* [2015] EWCA Civ 839; *Arnold v Britton* [2015] UKSC 36; [2015] A.C. 1619; [2016] 1 All E.R. 1.

10 *Deutsche Genossenschaftsbank v Burnhope* [1995] 1 W.L.R. 1580 at 1587; [1995] 4 All E.R. 717 at 724; [1996] 1 Lloyd's Rep. 113 at 122.

11 *Sirius International Insurance Co (Publ) v FAI General Insurance Ltd* [2004] UKHL 54 at [18]; [2004] 1 W.L.R. 3251 at 3257; [2005] 1 All E.R. 191 at 200.

12 *Rainy Sky SA v Kookmin Bank* [2011] UKSC 50 at [14]; [2011] 1 W.L.R. 2900 at 2907; [2012] 1 All E.R. 1137 at 1144.

13 *Arnold v Britton* [2015] UKSC 36 at [17]; [2015] A.C. 1619; [2016] 1 All E.R. 1, per Lord Neuberger.

14 *John Cory & Sons v Burr* (1883) 8 App. Cas. 393 at 405 HL; [1881-5] All E.R. Rep 414 at 421; 52 L.J.Q.B. 657 at 664; *Sun Fire Office v Hart* (1889) 14 App. Cas. 98 at 104; 53 J.P. 548 at 549; (1889)

"plain, ordinary, and popular sense".[15] However, the natural meaning of words is heavily influenced by context and thus cannot be discerned without consideration of the factual circumstances in which they were used.[16] As Lord Hoffmann explained in *Mannai Investment Co Ltd v Eagle Star Life Assurance Co Ltd*[17]:

> "the law is not concerned with the speaker's subjective intentions. But the notion that the law's concern is therefore with the 'meaning of his words' conceals an important ambiguity. The ambiguity lies in a failure to distinguish between the meanings of words and the question of what would be understood as the meaning of a person who uses words. The meaning of words, as they would appear in a dictionary, and the effect of their syntactical arrangement, as it would appear in a grammar, is part of the material which we use to understand a speaker's utterance. But it is only a part; another part is our knowledge of the background against which the utterance was made. It is that background which enables us, not only to choose the intended meaning when a word has more than one dictionary meaning but also … to understand a speaker's meaning, often without ambiguity, when he has used the wrong words."

13-005   Thus whilst the law presumes that reasonable men intend to use language in its ordinary context, it is accepted that against the specific background of the parties' relationship and dealings, apparently clear words may have an entirely different meaning. Thus, whilst "the inquiry will start, and usually finish, by asking what is the ordinary meaning of the words used",[18] it is permissible to adduce evidence that the parties intended their words to have a scientific or technical meaning,[19] or that the use of certain words has developed a meaning by virtue of trade custom.[20]

13-006   **The importance of context.**   The task of interpretation is to ascertain the meaning and effect of those words within the context of the parties' circumstances as at the date of the contract. Put another way

> "the question to be answered always is, 'What is the meaning of what the parties have said?' not, 'What did the parties mean to say?' … it being a presumption … that the parties intended to say that which they have said."[21]

13-007   The context in which a particular word or phrase is used is central to its

---

58 L.J.P.C. 69 at 72–73; *Re United London and Scottish Insurance Co Ltd* [1915] 2 Ch. 167 at 172; 84 L.J. Ch. 620 at 623.

[15]   *Robertson v French* [1803-13] All E.R. Rep 350 at 353; 4 East 130 at 135; 102 E.R. 779 at 781; *Smith v The Accident Insurance Co* (1870) L.R. 5 Exch. 302 at 307; 39 L.J. Ex 211 at 214–215; 18 W.R. 1107 at 1108, where it said that a court will also avoid any violent interference with the words used; *Margate Theatre Royal Trust Ltd v White (t/a A1 Moleing Services) (AXA Insurance UK Plc, Part 20 defendant)*; sub nom. *White v AXA Insurance UK Plc* [2005] EWHC 2171 (TCC) at [27]–[32]; 106 Con. L.R. 1 at 7–9; [2006] Lloyd's Rep. I.R. 93 at 98; *GE Frankona Reinsurance Ltd v CMM Trust No. 1400 (The Newfoundland Explorer)* [2006] EWHC 429 (Admlty) at [14]–[16]; [2006] 1 All E.R. (Comm) 665; [2006] Lloyd's Rep. I.R. 704.

[16]   *Charter Reinsurance Co Ltd (In Liquidation) v Fagan* [1997] A.C. 313 at 391; [1996] 2 W.L.R. 726 at 761–762; [1996] 3 All E.R. 46 at 56–57.

[17]   *Mannai Investment Co Ltd* [1997] A.C. 749 at 775; [1997] 2 W.L.R. 945 at 968; [1997] 3 All E.R. 352 at 376. See also Lord Hoffmann's similar comments in *Investors Compensation Scheme Ltd* [1998] 1 W.L.R. 896 at 912–13; [1998] 1 All E.R. 98 at 114; [1998] 1 B.C.L.C. 493 at 547; and also *Sirius International Insurance (Publ)* [2004] UKHL 54, [2004] 1 W.L.R. 3251; *Canmer International Inc v UK Mutual Steamship Assurance Assn (Bermuda) Ltd (The Rays)* [2005] EWHC 1694 (Comm); [2005] 2 Lloyd's Rep. 479.

[18]   *Charter Reinsurance Co Ltd* [1997] A.C. 313 at 384; [1996] 2 W.L.R. 726 at 755; [1996] 3 All E.R. 46 at 50.

[19]   See below, para.13-015.

[20]   See below, para.13-019.

[21]   Per Lord Simon in *L Schuler AG v Wickman Machine Tool Sales Ltd* [1974] A.C. 235 at 263; [1973] 2 W.L.R. 683 at 700; [1973] 2 All E.R. 39 at 55, citing this summary from R.F. Norton, assisted by R.H. Bunn and Digby L.F. Koe, in *A Treatise on Deeds* (London: Sweet & Maxwell, 1906), p.43 as

interpretation.[22] In *Tektrol Ltd v International Insurance Co of Hanover Ltd* it was said:

> "The construction of the disputed clauses in this policy ... turn not on the meaning of particular words, in respect of which issues of ambiguity might potentially arise, but on the context in which the disputed words are used, and the purpose that is to be drawn from that context."[23]

The context in which a phrase is used will always be relevant; parties to an agreement are unlikely to intend that a term be defined by a different set of circumstances other than their own and the reasonable man would therefore interpret the parties' agreement against that same background. It is also common sense to interpret contracts in the context against which they are made.[24] It can thus be seen that whilst the court's objective is to ascertain the objective meaning of the words used by the parties, the court is not confined to an isolated syntactical analysis of the words themselves; indeed the recent trend of the courts is to admit more rather than less evidence as part of the factual matrix.[25] **13-008**

Further the historical context in which clauses developed may be relevant. CAR clauses such as the defects exclusion ("DE") and London Engineering Group clauses ("LEG"), form part of a hierarchy of well-known exclusion clauses whose history and development should not be divorced from their interpretation.[26] Furthermore, the suite of DE and LEG clauses are established alternative exclusion clauses each with a different nuance and the context of the suite as a whole ought to assist in interpreting the meaning of each individual exclusion.

In *Lloyd's TSB General Insurance Holdings Ltd v Lloyd's Bank Group Insurance Co Ltd*[27] Lord Hobhouse supported the principle of interpreting particular clauses in the context of established alternatives; he said:

> "[T]here are often well established alternatives open to the parties in the drafting of their agreement. The choice made from among these alternatives represents part of the bargain struck by the parties and must be respected by anyone ... adjudicating upon a dispute arising under the document."

"most pungently" expressing the general principle.

[22] In *Charter Reinsurance Co Ltd* [1997] A.C. 313 at 386, 392 and 395; [1996] 2 W.L.R. 726 at 757–758, 762–763, and 765; [1966] 3 All E.R. 46 at 52–53, 57–58, and 60 the ordinary meaning of "actually paid" was rejected in preference of the contextual meaning.

[23] *Tektrol Ltd v International Insurance Co of Hanover Ltd* [2005] EWCA Civ 845 at [7]; [2006] 1 All E.R. (Comm) 780 at 784; [2005] 2 Lloyd's Rep. 701 at 704. See also *British-American Insurance (Kenya) Ltd v Matelec SAL* [2013] EWHC 3278 Comm at [47], per Walker J; and *Cape Distribution Ltd v Cape Intermediate Holdings Ltd* [2016] EWHC 1119 (QB) at [6], per Picken J when he said: "In a commercial contract, it is certainly right that a tribunal should know the commercial purpose of the contract. This presupposes knowledge of the genesis of the contract, the background, the context and the market to which the parties are operating".

[24] See for example *Kearney v General Accident Fire and Life Assurance Corp Ltd* [1968] 2 Lloyd's Rep. 240 (a employer's liability policy had to be construed against the background of an employment relationship); *Charlton v Fisher*; sub nom. *Churchill Insurance v Charlton* [2001] EWCA Civ 112; [2002] Q.B. 578; [2001] 3 W.L.R. 1435 (the word "accident" in a motor insurance policy had to be construed in the context of the use of motor vehicles).

[25] See below, para.13-076.

[26] For a more detailed commentary on the development, effect and interpretation of the DE and LEG clauses see above, Ch.1 and below, Ch.16 generally.

[27] *Lloyd's TSB General Insurance Holdings Ltd v Lloyd's Bank Group Insurance Co Ltd* [2003] UKHL 48 at [31]; [2003] All E.R. 43 at 52; [2003] Lloyd's Rep. I.R. 623 at 631.

However, in relation to the Report by the Advanced Study Group No.208B of the Insurance Institute of London,[28] which describes the background and market developments as to the operation of the DE and LEG clauses,[29] Lord Justice Tuckey in the Court of Appeal in *CA Blackwell (Contractors) Ltd v Gerling Allegemeine Verischerungs-AG*; sub nom. *CA Blackwell (Contractors) Ltd v Gerling General Insurance Co*[30] said, that the report was:

"instructive about the purpose of defect exclusion clauses and how they have evolved ... [b]ut ... cannot be used as an aid to construction of the clause in question which must be construed according to its terms."[31]

This may be contrasted with the approach adopted by the Court of Appeal for British Columbia in *Acciona Infrastructure Canada Inc.* who construed the meaning of LEG2 in the context of LEG1 and LEG3.[32] If the view expressed in the Court of Appeal is to be preferred then the courts will not seek to construe a particular DE or LEG clause in the context of the others.

13-009 **Commercial common sense.** Whenever the courts consider the interpretation of commercial documents, they strive to give effect to the commercial intent behind those documents.[33] Lord Diplock in *Antaios Compania Naviera SA v Salen Rederierna AB (The Antaious)* famously stated:

"[I]f detailed semantic and syntactical analysis of words in a commercial contract is going to lead to a conclusion that flouts business common sense, it must be made to yield to business common sense."[34]

13-010 It is now widely accepted that in construing a commercial document it should be construed in a way that has good business or commercial sense.[35] The Supreme Court has reaffirmed this approach in *Rainy Sky SA v Kookmin Bank* where Lord

---

[28] Advanced Study Group No.208B *Construction Insurance/report of Advanced Study Group 208B* (London: Insurance Institute of London, 1999).

[29] Discussed below, in Ch.16.

[30] *CA Blackwell (Contractors) Ltd v Gerling Allegemeine Verischerungs-AG*; sub nom. *CA Blackwell (Contractors) Ltd v Gerling General Insurance Co* [2007] EWCA Civ 1450 at [20]; [2008] 1 All E.R. (Comm) 885 at 891; [2008] Lloyd's Rep. I.R. 529 at 533.

[31] *CA Blackwell (Contractors) Ltd* [2007] EWCA Civ 1450 at [20]; [2008] 1 All E.R. (Comm) 885 at 891; [2008] Lloyd's Rep. I.R. 529 at 533.

[32] *Acciona Infrastructure Canada Inc. v Allianz Global Risks US Insurance Co* [2015] BCCA 347 at [74].

[33] *Bank of Credit and Commerce International SA v Ali* [2001] UKHL 8 at [47]; [2002] 1 A.C. 251 at 271; [2001] 2 W.L.R. 735 at 751.

[34] *Antaios Compania Naviera SA v Salen Rederierna AB (The Antaious)* [1985] A.C. 191 at 201; [1984] 3 W.L.R. 592 at 598; [1984] 3 All E.R. 229 at 233 HL.

[35] See, for example: *Clift v Schwabe* 136 E.R. 175; (1846) 3 C.B. 437 at 455–456 and 458; *Pearson v Commercial Union Assurance Co* (1876) 1 App. Cas. 498; *Glynn v Margetson & Co* [1893] A.C. 351 at 359; 62 L.J.Q.B. 466 at 470–471; 7 Asp. M.L.C. 366 at 359; *Hydarnes Steamship Co v Indemnity Mutual Marine Insurance Co* [1895] 1 Q.B. 500 at 504; 64 L.J.QB. 353 at 356; 7 Asp. M.L.C. 553 at 555; *Lowenstein (J) & Co Ltd v Poplar Motor Transport Ltd (Lymm) Ltd (Gooda, third party)* [1968] 2 Lloyd's Rep. 233 QB; *Mitsui Construction Co Ltd v Attorney-General of Hong Kong* (1986) 33 B.L.R. 1 at 3, 14; (1986) 10 Con. L.R. 1 at 41; [1986] L.R.C. (Comm) 245 at 253; *International Fina Services AG v Katrina Shipping Ltd and Tonen Tanker Kabushiki Kaisha (The Fina Samco)* [1995] 2 Lloyd's Rep. 344 at 350; [1995] C.L.C. 1335 at 1341 CA; *Yorkshire Water Services Ltd v Sun Alliance & London Insurance Plc (No 1)* [1997] 2 Lloyd's Rep. 21 at 28; [1997] C.L.C. 213 at 221; *Mannai Investment Co Ltd* [1997] A.C. 749 at 771; [1997] 2 W.L.R. 945 at 964–965; [1997] 3 All E.R.352 at 372; *Society of Lloyd's v Robinson*; sub nom. *Lord Napier and Ettrick v RF Kershaw Ltd (No.2); Society of Lloyd's v Woodward* [1999] 1 W.L.R. 756 at 763; [1999] 1 All

Clarke confirmed that the resolution of a question of construction is an iterative process that involves checking rival meanings against the other provisions of the contract and investigating the commercial consequences of each meaning,[36] and said:

"If there are two possible constructions, the court is entitled to prefer the construction which is consistent with business common sense and to reject the other."[37]

However, business common sense has its limits[38] and, as Patten LJ pointed out in the Court of Appeal:

"[T]he circumstances in which the court can confidently declare that one or other possible meaning of the words used is uncommercial needs to be defined with some care. In a commercial contract (like any other contract) the parties have chosen to define the limits of the obligations which they have undertaken by the language they have used."[39]

Those limits of commercial common sense have recently been emphasised in *Arnold v Britton*[40] where Lord Neuberger confirmed the proper approach in a series of principles[41] which can be summarised as follows:

1. Commercial common sense should not be allowed to displace the importance of the language the parties have used. The clearer the language of the contract, the more difficult it is to justify departing from it.

2. The court should not carry search for "drafting infelicities in order to facilitate a departure from the natural meaning" of the words used.

3. Commercial common sense should not be invoked because, in hindsight, an agreement has "worked out badly, or even disastrously, for one of the parties". Commercial common sense must be assessed prospectively at the time that the parties entered into the contract.

4. Further, even if the court considers that the natural meaning of a provision was a particularly imprudent term for one of the parties to agree, the court should be very slow to reject the natural meaning. It is not for the court to

E.R. (Comm) 545 at 551; [1999] C.L.C. 987 at 992; *Bank of Credit and Commerce International SA* [2001] UKHL 8 at [8]; [2002] 1 A.C. 251 at 259; [2001] 2 W.L.R. 735 at 739; *Hombourg Houtimport BV v Agrosin Private Ltd (The Starsin); Hunter Timber Ltd v Agrosin Private Ltd*; sub nom. *Owners of Cargo Lately Laden on Board The Starsin v Owners of The Starsin* [2003] UKHL 12 at [10]; [2004] 1 A.C. 715 at 737; [2003] 2 W.L.R. 711 at 718; *Harper v Interchange Group Ltd* [2007] EWHC 1834 (Comm) at [85]; [2007] All E.R. (D) 169 (Aug) at 15–16.

36 *Rainy Sky SA* [2011] UKSC 50 at [28]; see also *Gan Insurance Co Ltd v Tai Ping Insurance Co Ltd (No.2)* [2001] 1 All ER (Comm) 299 at [16], per Mance LJ.

37 *Rainy Sky SA* [2011] UKSC 50 at [21]; [2011] 1 W.L.R. 2900 at 2908; [2012] 1 All E.R. 1137 at 1146. See also *British-American Insurance Kenya Ltd v Matelec SAL* [2013] EWHC 3278 (Comm) at [48], per Walker J.; and *Ted Baker Plc v Axa Insurance UK plc* [2012] EWHC 1406 (Comm), where Eder J confirmed, at [81], that business common sense should only be taken into account where a term of a contract is truly open to more than one interpretation. In *Anzen Ltd v Hermes One Ltd* [2016] UKPC 1, the Privy Council endorsed that where there was more than one (non-fanciful) alternative meaning, the Court was not bound to the interpretation most in line with the ordinary meaning of the words and could elect to adopt the interpretation which accorded most with business common sense.

38 For example, the court may be more prepared to depart from the ordinary meaning of words in a badly drafted contract than in a carefully drafted one; see, for example, *Mitsui Construction Co Ltd* (1986) 33 B.L.R. 1 at 14; (1986) 10 Con. L.R. 1 at 41; [1986] L.R.C. (Comm) 245 at 253.

39 *Rainy Sky SA* [2010] EWCA Civ 582 at [36]; [2011] 1 All E.R. (Comm) 18 at 28; [2011] 1 Lloyd's Rep. 233 at 240.

40 *Arnold v Britton* [2015] UKSC 36; [2015] A.C. 1619; [2016] 1 All E.R. 1.

41 [2015] UKSC 36; [2015] A.C. 1619; [2016] 1 All E.R. 1 at [16]–[22].

re-write the parties' bargain and the court must ascertain what the parties have in fact agreed and not what the court thinks they should have agreed.[42]

13-011 **The confines of the parties' language.** Accordingly, whilst the courts will strive to give an agreement a common sense interpretation, they can only do so within the confines of the words that the parties have used. In *Trollope & Colls v North West Metropolitan Regional Hospital Board*, Lord Pearson made clear that[43]:

> "If the express terms are perfectly clear and free from ambiguity, there is no choice to be made between different possible meanings: the clear terms must be applied even if the court thinks some other terms would have been more suitable. An unexpressed term can be implied if and only if the court finds that the parties must have intended that term to form part of their contract: it is not enough for the court to find that such a term would have been adopted by the parties as reasonable men if it had been suggested to them: it must have been a term that went without saying, a term *necessary* to give business efficacy to the contract, a term which, though tacit, formed part of the contract which the parties made for themselves."

This is particularly important in the insurance context and, as Hobhouse J noted in *M/S Aswan v Iron Trades Mutual Insurance Co Ltd*[44]:

> "This principle is reinforced where it is an insurance company that is seeking to reject the ordinary meaning and where the document is, as it is here, a standard form document produced by the insurance company itself."

13-012 It is not for the court to re-write the parties' bargain to impose a reasonable contract in the place of the actual agreement.[45] In *Chartbrook Ltd v Persimmon Homes Ltd*,[46] Lord Hoffmann confirmed that

> "the fact that a contract may appear to be unduly favourable to one of the parties is not a sufficient reason for supposing that it does not mean what it says. The reasonable addressee of the instrument has not been privy to the negotiations and cannot tell whether a provision favourable to one side was not in exchange for some concession elsewhere or simply a bad bargain."

That does not, however, preclude the court from expressing its conclusion as to the appropriate construction of a clause in very different language to that used by the parties:

> "When the language used in an instrument gives rise to difficulties of construction, the process of interpretation does not require one to formulate some alternative form of words which approximates as closely as possible to that of the parties. It is to decide what a reasonable person would

---

[42] See also *Mutual Energy Ltd v Starr Underwriting Agents Ltd* [2016] EWHC 590 (TCC) where Coulson J noted, at [30]: "Businessmen sometimes make bad or poor bargains for a number of different reasons such as weak negotiating position, poor negotiating or drafting skills, inadequate advice or inadvertence. If they do so, it is not the function of the court to improve their bargain or make it more reasonable by a process of interpretation which amounts to rewriting".

[43] *Trollope & Colls Ltd v North West Metropolitan Regional Hospital Board* [1973] 1 W.L.R. 601 at 609; [1973] 2 All E.R. 260 at 268; 9 B.L.R. 60 at 61 HL; see also *Charter Reinsurance Co Ltd* [1997] A.C. 313; [1996] 2 W.L.R. 726; [1996] 3 All E.R. 46; *Sinochem International Oil (London) Co Ltd v Mobil Sales and Supply Corp* [2000] 1 All E.R. (Comm) 474; [2000] 1 Lloyd's Rep. 339; [2000] C.L.C. 878; *HSBC Bank Plc v Liberty Mutual Insurance Co (UK) Ltd* (2001), *Times,* 11 June, 2001; *BP Exploration Operating Co Ltd v Dolphin Drilling Ltd, The Byford Dolphin* [2009] EWHC 3119 (Comm); [2010] 2 Lloyd's Rep. 192; [2009] All E.R. (D) 48 (Dec).

[44] *M/S Aswan v Iron Trades Mutual Insurance Co Ltd* [1989] 1 Lloyd's Rep. 289 at 293.

[45] *Re George and Goldsmiths' and General Burglary Ins Ass Ltd's Arbitration* [1899] 1 Q.B. 595; 68 L.J.Q.B. 365; 47 W.R. 474; *Jason v British Traders' Ins Co*; sub nom. *Jason v Batten* (1930) Ltd [1969] 1 Lloyd's Rep. 281; (1969) 119 N.L.J. 697 QB.

[46] *Chartbrook Ltd* [2009] UKHL 38 at [20]; [2009] 1 A.C. 1101 at 1113; [2009] 4 All E.R. 677 at 687.

have understood the parties to have meant by using the language which they did. The fact that the court might have to express that language quite different from that used by the parties... is no reason for not giving effect to what they appear to have meant."[47]

(b)   The meaning of words

Types of meaning.   When seeking to ascertain the meaning of words, courts tend   **13-013**
to analyse words within three categories of meaning: (i) the ordinary or natural meaning of the words; (ii) any technical, customary or special meaning of the words; and (iii) the "judicial" meaning of the words; in other words whether the meaning of words or phrases has been determined in binding authority.

The ordinary meaning.   The basic presumption is that words should be given   **13-014**
their plain, natural and ordinary meaning. It is, however, clear that the ordinary meaning of words depends on the context in which they are used. Whilst the principal approach to construction has historically been to start from the literal meaning of the words and only to displace that meaning where there is clear reason to do so, the more modern approach has been to shift away from the literal methods of interpretation and to view contracts with a more commercial or technically sensitive eye.[48] That shifting approach is illustrated in *Arbuthnott v Fagan*, where Bingham M.R. stated that:

"construction is a composite exercise, neither uncompromisingly literal nor unswervingly purposive: the instrument must speak for itself, but it must do so in situ and not be transported to the laboratory for microscopic analysis."[49]

Scientific/technical meaning.   Some words are inherently scientific or technical   **13-015**
in nature. In such cases, the court will normally presume that the parties meant to use the words in their scientific or technical way.[50] Where there is dispute as to how scientific terms are to be interpreted, expert evidence can be adduced to prove the meaning of the term but that evidence must not stray into an opinion of the meaning of the clause to be construed.[51]

A more interesting challenge arises where an ordinary word shares a scientific   **13-016**
or technical meaning. In such cases, the court will start from the presumption that the ordinary meaning was intended[52]; however that presumption is not to be rigidly applied and it will be rebutted if the factual matrix makes clear that the technical

---

[47]   *Chartbrook Ltd* [2009] UKHL 38 at [21]; [2009] 1 A.C. 1101 at 1113–1114; [2009] 4 All E.R. 677 at 688, per Lord Hoffmann.

[48]   *Sirius International Insurance Co (Publ)* [2004] UKHL 54 at [19]; [2004] 1 W.L.R. 3251 at 3257–3258; [2005] 1 All E.R. (Comm) 117 at 125, per Lord Hoffmann.

[49]   *Arbuthnott v Fagan* [1996] L.R.L.R.; [1995] C.L.C. 1396 at 1400. 135 at 139; *Independent*, October 1, 1993.

[50]   In *Holt & Co v Collyer* (1881) 16 Ch. D. 718 at 720; 45 J.P. 456; 50 L.J. Ch. 311 at 312, Fry, J said: "If it is a word which is of a technical and scientific character, then it must be construed according to that which is its primary meaning, namely, its technical and scientific meaning." See also Jessel, M.R. in *Laird v Briggs* (1881) 19 Ch. D. 22 at 34; 45 L.T. 238 at 240.

[51]   *Shore v Wilson, Lady Hewley's Charities* 8 E.R. 450; (1842) 9 Cl. & Fin. 355; *Encia Remediation Ltd v Canopius Managing Agents Ltd* [2007] EWHC 916 (Comm) at [173]; [2007] 2 All E.R. (Comm) 947 at 982; [2007] 1 C.L.C. 818 at 861–862.

[52]   *Borys v Canadian Pacific Railway Co* [1953] A.C. 217 at 223; [1953] 2 W.L.R. 224 at 229–230; [1953] 1 All E.R. 451 at 454–455 (Can PC).

meaning was intended.[53] Examples of this approach include cases involving the words "gas",[54] "iron",[55] "sober and temperate"[56] and "under the influence of intoxicating liquor".[57]

13-017   A further problem area is where scientific or technical terms are misused. The misuse of technical terms requires a careful consideration of the instrument to determine whether from the document as a whole a particular interpretation may be obtained. In *Graham v Ewart*, the correct approach was described as follows:

> "[W]hen it is clear from the context of an instrument in what sense words are used in that instrument, the sound rule of construction is to attribute to them that meaning even though the words be technical and have technically a different meaning."[58]

13-018   Special meaning.   There may be circumstances where it can be shown that certain words, which would otherwise have an obvious ordinary meaning, have been given a particular meaning by the parties.[59] In these situations the court will apply the special meaning. In each case the assessment of whether there is a special meaning attached to the words will depend upon the evaluation of the factual matrix.[60]

13-019   Custom and practice.   Words can also attract a special meaning through their customary usage in a particular area or industry. The construction and insurance industries are no exception; indeed, both are notorious for their jargon. Where a party contends that a word has a particular customary meaning, evidence of that meaning is generally admissible[61] and where a customary meaning is established the court will give effect to it.[62] The threshold for establishing a customary meaning is relatively high. For example in *Nelson v Dahl*[63] it was said that:

---

53   *Earl of Lonsdale v Attorney General* [1982] 1 W.L.R. 887; [1982] 3 All E.R. 579; (1983) 45 P. & C.R. 1 in relation to "minerals".

54   *Stanley v The Western Insurance Co* (1867-1868) L.R. 3 Exch. 71 at 72–73; 37 L.J. Ex 73-75; 16 W.R. 369 at 370–371, where the term "gas" was interpreted in its "ordinary and popular sense" and did not include "vapour" produced from the extraction of oil from shoddy, which set fire to the premises in which it was being produced. See also: "explosion" in *Aegis Electrical and Gas International Services Co Ltd v Continental Casualty Co* [2007] EWHC 1762 (Comm) at [72], [76] and [78]; [2008] Lloyd's Rep I.R. 17 at 28; [2007] All E.R. (D) 382 (Jul), where the technical meaning of the word was not used.

55   Per Lord Esher in *Hart v Standard Marine Insurance Co Ltd* (1889) 22 Q.B.D 499 at 501; 58 L.J.Q.B. 284 at 285–286; 6 Asp. M.L.C. 368 at 369–370, the term "iron" in the circumstances included "steel" for the purposes of marine insurance.

56   *Yorke v Yorkshire Insurance Co Ltd* [1918] 1 K.B. 662 at 666; [1918-19] All E.R. Rep 877 at 878 and 879; 87 LJKB 881 at 883, McCardie J.; the term "sober and temperate" referred to alcohol and not drugs.

57   *Mair (Administratrix) v Railway Passengers Assurance Co Ltd* (1877) 37 L.T. 356 at 358, under the influence of intoxicating liquor means so that it "disturbs the balance of a man's mind".

58   *Graham v Ewart* 156 E.R. 1320; (1856) 1 Hurl. & N. 550 at 562–563.

59   *Shore v Wilson* (1842) 9 Cl. & Fin. 355; *Perrin v Morgan* [1943] A.C. 399; [1943] 1 All E.R. 187; 112 L.J. Ch. 81; *Zeus Tradition Marine Ltd v Bell, (The Zeus V)* [1999] 1 Lloyd's Rep. 703; [1999] C.L.C. 391; [1998] All E.R. (D) 525 QB.

60   See for example: *Rowlinson Construction Ltd v Insurance Co of North America (UK) Ltd* [1981] 1 Lloyd's Rep. 332 at 335 QB.

61   *Crofts v Marshall* 173 E.R. 262; (1836) 7 Car. & P. 597.

62   *Pike v Ongley* (1887) 18 Q.B.D. 708; 56 L.J.Q.B. 373; 35 W.R. 534 CA; *EE & Brian Smith (1928) Ltd v Wheatsheaf Mills Ltd* [1939] 2 K.B. 302; [1939] 2 All E.R. 251; (1939) 63 Ll. L. Rep. 237.

63   *Nelson v Dahl* (1879) 12 Ch. D 568; 41 L.T. 365; 28 W.R. 57.

"like all other customs, it must be strictly proved. It must be so notorious that everybody in the trade enters into a contract with that usage as an implied term. It must be uniform as well as reasonable, and it must have quite as much certainty as the written contract itself."[64]

The later case of *Strathlorne Steamship Co Ltd v Hugh Baird & Sons Ltd* explained the standard as follows:

"In order that a custom or, to use a more exact phrase, a commercial usage, may be binding upon parties to a contract, it is essential that it should be certain, that it should be uniform, that it should be reasonable, and that it should be notorious."[65]

The requirement for notoriety is a reference to the industry in which the term is **13-020** used; it is not necessary that both parties are aware of the customary meaning. In such circumstances, the ignorant party may be deemed cognisant of the practice.[66] Obviously this may have significant impact in CAR and other technical forms of insurance, where technical terms used in a presentation or proposal may be well understood in the construction industry to have a specific meaning that is unknown to the underwriter that has a material impact on the proposed risk.[67]

In more recent times, there may have been a retreat from the strict requirements in relation to trade custom and practice. In particular, the court is entitled to hear evidence of market practice falling short of trade usage or custom as part of its assessment of the factual matrix.[68] Evidence of such market practice is not confined to expert evidence and, in the insurance sector, evidence of market practice can be given by other witnesses such as brokers or underwriters experienced in the particular sector.[69] However, declarations of the subjective understanding of such witnesses are of no assistance to the exercise of construction.[70]

Imprecise words. Parties are often forced to use words that are incapable of **13-021** precise definition. Such words are often used to describe classes of things and the boundaries that apply to definitions. When the court encounters imprecise words, it is required to decide, as a matter of fact, whether the particular thing in dispute falls inside or outside the meaning of the word used. Perhaps the most apt exposition of this difficulty in construction circles is the definition of the word "building" examined by Byles J in *Stevens v Gourley*,[71] where he said:

"The imperfection of human language renders it not only difficult but absolutely impossible to define the word 'building' with any approach to accuracy. One may say of this or that structure, this or that is not a building; but no general definition can be given; and our lexicographers do not attempt it."[72]

Legal terms of art. Legal terms of art are another form of words with a techni- **13-022**

---

[64] *Dahl* (1879) 12 Ch. D 568 at 575. Later affirmed in the House of Lords, *Dahl* (1881) 6 App. Cas. 38; 50 L.J. Ch. 411; 4 Asp M.L.C. 392.

[65] *Strathlorne Steamship Co Ltd v Hugh Baird & Sons Ltd* 1916 S.C. (H.L.) 134 at 135–136; (1916) 53 S.L.R. 293 at 294; (1916) 1 S.L.T. 221 at 222.

[66] *Sutton v Tatham* 113 E.R. 11; (1839) 10 Ad. & El. 27 at 29; 8 L.J.Q.B. 210 at 211.

[67] Albeit in practice, construction underwriters tend to be highly specialist and well versed in the relevant terms of art and technical issues; nevertheless experts are often consulted by underwriters when underwriting higher value and more technical projects.

[68] See for example *Crema v Cenkos Securities Plc* [2011] 1 W.L.R. 2066 (CA) at 2078 and 2079, per Aikens LJ; *Cape Distribution Ltd v Cape Intermediate Holdings Ltd* [2016] EWHC 1119 (QB) at [7], per Picken J.

[69] *Gard Marine & Energy Ltd v Tunnicliffe* [2011] EWHC 1658 at [38]–[39] and [44].

[70] *Ted Baker plc v Axa Insurance UK Plc* [2012] EWHC 1406 (Comm) at [88] to [90], per Eder J.

[71] *Stevens v Gourley* 141 E.R. 752; (1859) 7 C.B. N.S. 99; 8 W.R. 85; 1 L.T. 33.

[72] *Stevens* 141 E.R. 752; (1859) 7 C.B. N.S. 99 at 112.

cal or special meaning. Accordingly, where legal terms of art are used, the court will normally presume that the legal meaning is intended unless it is clear from the factual matrix that the reasonable man would construe the word some other way. The key distinction, however, between legal and technical terms is that legal terms will often have acquired their meaning as a result of judicial determination and will have been deployed precisely because they have been held to have that meaning.[73] Therefore, the presumption that a legal term is intended to have its legal rather than ordinary meaning is a strong one and will require robust evidence to rebut.[74]

13-023 Judicial meaning. The interpretation of a document will involve issues of both fact and law. This principle was best explained by Lindley LJ in *Chatenay v The Brazilian Submarine Telegraph Co Ltd* when he said:

> "The expression 'construction', as applied to a document, at all events as used by English lawyers, includes two things: first, the meaning of the words; and secondly their legal effect, or the effect which is to be given to them. The meaning of the words I take to be a question of fact in all cases, whether we are dealing with a poem or a legal document. The effect of the words is a question of law."[75]

It is not only the ordinary meaning of words that will fall to be determined as a question of fact[76]; but also technical meanings,[77] customary meanings[78] and meanings of words within the parties' own lexicon.[79]

13-024 Once the meaning of the words has been determined, the court will rule on the legal effect of those words. Accordingly, a corpus of authority has accumulated in which the court has considered and determined the effect of various words and phrases in the context of various contracts and policies. Given that the effect of words is a question of law then, in theory, lower courts are bound to follow decisions of superior courts that have dealt with the clause under consideration.[80]

13-025 The impact of authority on interpretation is particularly relevant in industries such

---

73 *Sydall v Castings Ltd* [1967] 1 Q.B. 302; [1966] 3 W.L.R. 1126; [1966] 3 All E.R. 770 CA; *Infiniteland Ltd v Artisan Contracting Ltd* [2005] EWCA Civ 758; [2006] B.C.L.C. 632; [2005] All E.R. (D) 236 (Jun); *Durham v BAI (Run Off) Ltd (In Scheme of Arrangement); Re Employers' Liability Policy 'Trigger' Litigation*; sub nom. *Fleming v Independent Insurance Co Ltd; Edwards v Excess Insurance Co Ltd Thomas Bates & Son Ltd v BAI (Run Off) Ltd; Akzo Nobel UK Ltd v Excess Insurance Co Ltd; Municipal Mutual Insurance Ltd v Zurich Insurance Co* [2010] EWCA Civ 1096; [2011] 1 All E.R. 605; [2011] 1 All E.R. (Comm) 811; [2011] Lloyd's Rep. I.R. 1.

74 *Inland Revenue Commissioners v Williams* [1969] 1 W.L.R. 1197; [1969] 3 All E.R. 614; [1969] T.R. 153 Ch; *Re: Kaupthing Singer & Friedlander Ltd (In Administration)* [2010] EWHC 316 (Ch); [2010] All E.R. (D) 35 (Jun). The standard may, however, be lower where it is clear that the document was not drafted by a lawyer (see *Sydall* [1967] 1 Q.B. 302; [1966] 3 W.L.R. 1126; [1966] 3 All E.R. 770).

75 *Chatenay v The Brazilian Submarine Telegraph Co Ltd* [1891] 1 Q.B. 79 at 85; 60 L.J.Q.B. 295 at 298; 39 W.R. 65 at 66 CA. The quote in the last two reports is nuanced slightly differently but the point being made is the same. See also discussion by Roskill LJ in *Cehave NV v Bremer Handels GmbH (The Hansa Nord)*; sub nom. *Cehave N.V. v Bremer Handelsgesellschaft M.B.H. (The Hansa Nord)* [1976] Q.B. 44 at 74; [1975] 3 W.L.R. 447 at 468; [1975] 3 All E.R. 739 at 758 CA.

76 *Cozens v Brutus* [1973] A.C. 854 at 861; [1972] 3 W.L.R. 521 at 525; [1972] 2 All E.R. 1297 at 1299; *Commonwealth Smelting Ltd v Guardian Royal Exchange Assurance Ltd*; sub nom. *Commonwealth Smelting Ltd and AM & S Europe Ltd v Guardian Royal Exchange Assurance Ltd* [1986] 1 Lloyd's Rep. 121 at 122 and 125–126; *Norwich Union Life Insurance Society v P&O Property Holdings Ltd* [1993] 1 E.G.L.R. 164 at 168; [1993] 13 E.G. 108 at 111–112; [1993] N.P.C. 1 at 2.

77 *Hill v Evans* 45 E.R. 1195; (1862) 4 De G.F. & J. 288 at 293–295; 31 L.J. Ch. 457 at 460–461; 8 Jur. N.S. 525 at 527 QB.

78 See above, para.13-019.

79 See above, para.13-018 (special meanings).

80 *Clift v Schwabe* 136 E.R. 175; (1846) 3 C.B. 437 at 470.

as the construction industry, where the majority of projects are let on standard-form contracts and many policies of insurance are written on insurers' standard terms; many more policies are written incorporating terms that have become standard clauses in the industry, for example the DE and LEG clauses in CAR policies.[81]

It should, however, always be remembered that every contract is a consensual ar-   **13-026** rangement between parties against the particular factual matrix of their own transaction. Thus the matters to be taken into account on interpretation will be different in every case. It is suggested, therefore, that a lower court will strictly be bound by a previous decision on interpretation only in cases where the wording and the factual matrix under consideration is identical or extremely similar to those considered in that previous case.[82]

That is not to say that previous decisions have no relevance. Where the construc-   **13-027** tion of a word or phrase has been decided by the Courts, that decision may have a strong persuasive influence on later courts to apply a similar construction. In *Enterprise Inns Plc v The Forest Hill Tavern Public House Ltd*, Morrit C. explained:

> "Plainly [a previous decision on a similar clause] cannot be conclusive as to the interpretation of other contracts made at different times, between different parties and in different circumstances, even though both are questions of law. But a decision on the interpretation of a contract may be persuasive as to the interpretation of another contract using similar language by parties involved in a similar trade and in similar circumstances, particularly where knowledge of the previous decision may be imputed to the parties."[83]

Further, the courts have acknowledged that some decisions are so well known,   **13-028** or are supported by sufficient following authority, that commercial men should reasonably be aware of those decisions and must reasonably expect their contracts to be interpreted in accordance with them.[84] To that end, the courts are often slow to interfere in the established meaning of certain clauses.[85] For example, in *Ramco (UK) Ltd v International Insurance Co of Hannover*,[86] the Court of Appeal upheld an interpretation of long standing and renown despite expressing doubts as to the intellectual integrity of that interpretation. Waller LJ, delivering the judgment of the

---

[81] See below, Ch.16.
[82] *Fraser v BN Furman (Productions) Ltd (Miller Smith & Partners, third parties)* [1967] 1 W.L.R. 898; [1967] 3 All E.R. 57; [1967] 2 Lloyd's Rep. 1 CA.
[83] *Enterprise Inns Plc v The Forest Hill Tavern Public House Ltd; Albrecht v Unique Pub Properties Ltd* [2010] EWHC 2368 (Ch) at [22]; [2010] N.P.C. 104.
[84] *Re National Coffee Palace Co Ex Parte Panmure* (1883) 24 Ch. D. 367 at 370; 53 L.J. Ch. 57 at 58; 32 W.R. 236 at 237 CA; *Toomey* [1994] 1 Lloyd's Rep. 516 at 520 CA; *British Sugar Plc v NEI Power Projects Ltd* 87 B.L.R. 42; [1997-98] Info. T.L.R. 353; [1998] I.T.C.L.R. 125 CA; *Starmark Enterprises Ltd v CPL Distribution Ltd* [2001] EWCA Civ 1252; [2002] Ch. 306, [2002] 2 W.L.R. 1009; *KG Blominflot Bunkergellesellschaft fur Mineraloele GmbH & Co v Petroplus Marketing AG (The Mercini Lady)* [2010] EWCA Civ 1145; [2011] 2 All E.R. (Comm) 522 CA.
[85] *Dunlop & Sons v Balfour Williamson & Co* [1892] 1 Q.B. 507; 61 L.J.Q.B. 354; 7 Asp. M.L.C. 181 CA; *Re Hooley Hill Rubber & Chemical Co Ltd and Royal Insurance Co Ltd's Arbitration* [1920] 1 K.B. 257; (1919) 1 Ll. L. Rep. 25; 89 L.J.K.B. 179 CA; sub nom. *Atlantic Shipping & Trading Co v Louis Dreyfus & Co (The Quantock)* [1922] 2 A.C. 250 at 257; 10 Ll. L. Rep. 707 HL; *The Annefield: Owners of the Ship Annefield v Owners of the Cargo Lately Laden on Board the Ship Annefield* [1971] P. 168; [1971] 2 W.L.R. 320; [1971] All E.R. 394 CA; *Excess Insurance Co Ltd v Mander* [1997] 2 Lloyd's Rep. 119; [1995] L.R.L.R. 358; [1995] C.L.C. 838; *British Sugar Plc* 87 B.L.R. 42 at 50; [1997-98] Info. T.L.R. 353 at 360; *Henry Boot Construction Ltd v Alstom Combined Cycles Ltd* [2005] EWCA Civ 814; [2005] 1 W.L.R. 3850; [2005] 3 All E.R. 832.
[86] *Ramco (UK) Ltd v International Insurance Co of Hannover* [2004] EWCA Civ 675; [2004] 2 All E.R. (Comm) 866; [2004] 2 Lloyd's Rep. 595.

court, said:

> "If a form of words has been in use for 80 years which describes one sort of insurance rather than the other, it would be meddlesome for this court to decide that the selected form of words do not achieve their intended purpose, unless there was some real reason for supposing that the form of words is unsatisfactory in practice. The fact that the form of words is the subject-matter of a previous decision of this court is a compelling reason why the courts should not depart from that settled meaning."[87]

13-029   In construction insurance, a high proportion of larger contractors' annual policies and project policies are bespoke and tend to contain amendments from the strict wording of standard clauses[88]; in such circumstances, the court is entitled to consider historic interpretations of standard forms when considering the latest evolution of a particular form or clause or a bespoke amendment to the same. The rationale behind this approach was explained in relation to construction contracts as follows:

> "It is also important to have regard to the course of earlier judicial authority and practice on the construction of similar contracts. The evolution of standard forms is often the result of interaction between the draftsmen and the courts and the efforts of the draftsmen cannot be properly understood without reference to the meaning which the judges have given to the language used by his predecessors."[89]

13-030   The influence of foreign authorities.   Foreign authorities are frequently cited in the English courts, perhaps more so in insurance than in any other area of law. This is simply because the business of insurance has been transnational in its scope and the commercial world has great interest in principles of insurance being applied consistently. Indeed, as Kirby J stated in the Australian case of *Johnson v American Home Assurance*:

> "[I]nsurance is commonly offered on standard form policies which have a national or international provenance ... the consequence that risks may be assessed, and re-insurance procured, on the footing that settled interpretations of commonly used language will not be disturbed without good reason."[90]

13-031   It must, however, always be borne in mind that foreign authorities have no more than persuasive authority. English policies will, therefore, be interpreted on the basis of English law where an English court is highly unlikely to follow an overseas decision in preference to an English authority. Scrutton LJ once famously said:

> "I am not impressed by the fact that a different view has been taken by American Courts on American policies. Those courts frequently differ from ours on the construction of mercantile documents. English Courts construe documents by the light of English decisions."[91]

---

[87] *Ramco (UK) Ltd* [2004] EWCA Civ 675 at [32]; [2004] 2 All E.R. (Comm) 866 at 878; [2004] 2 Lloyd's Rep. 595 at 603.

[88] See for example, the discussion of the DE and LEG clauses below in Ch.15 and the discussion as to the different approaches in *Cementation Piling and Foundations Ltd* [1995] 1 Lloyd's Rep. 97; (1994) 74 B.L.R. 102; 47 Con. L.R. 14 and the approach in *Seele Austria GMBH & Co KG v Tokio Marine Europe Insurance Ltd* [2008] EWCA Civ 441; [2009] 1 All E.R. (Comm) 171; [2008] Lloyd's Rep. I.R. 739.

[89] *Beaufort Developments (N.I.) Ltd v Gilbert-Ash (N.I.) Ltd* [1999] A.C. 266; [1998] 2 W.L.R. 860; [1998] 2 All E.R. 778.

[90] *Johnson v American Home Assurance Co* (1998) 192 C.L.R. 266 at 272–273; (1998) 152 A.L.R. 162 at 167; 72 A.L.J.R. 610 at 612.

[91] *Re Hooley Hill Rubber* [1920] 1 K.B. 257 at 272 CA.

Similarly, where parties have adopted a foreign standard form of policy but agreed that English law will apply, it is not relevant that the policy would usually be interpreted under foreign law. In *Astrazeneca Insurance Company Ltd v XL Insurance (Bermuda) Ltd*[92] the policy was based on XL004, a "Bermuda Form" liability insurance. Under an unamended Bermuda Form, disputes would usually be resolved in London by a panel of arbitrators but New York law governed the contract. In Astrazeneca, the Bermuda Form was amended so that the policy was governed by the law of England and Wales. The Court rejected the suggestion that it should treat the New York approach to the Bermuda Form as relevant, indeed "it would be quite wrong to construe the contract in any respect by reference to New York law".[93]

(c) Rules of interpretation

Rules of interpretation. In order to assist the court in ascertaining the meaning   **13-032** of the words used, various rules and principles of construction, sometimes referred to as "canons" of construction, have emerged. Traditionally the court applied these rules within a particularly rigid framework[94]; however, it is now appreciated that

> "[r]ules of construction are not rules of law; they are merely guidelines to the presumed intention of the parties in the light of the events which have occurred."[95]

The court has become much more flexible in its approach to construction and acknowledges that the various rules should be applied holistically and should not be allowed to compartmentalise the process of interpretation. In *Bank of Credit and Commerce International SA v Ali*, Lord Clyde made clear that:

> "[s]uch guides to construction as have been identified in the past should not be allowed to constrain an approach to construction which looks to commercial reality or common sense. If they are elevated to anything approaching the status of rules they would deservedly be regarded as *impedimenta* in the task of construction. But they may be seen as reflections upon the way in which people may ordinarily be expected to express themselves."[96]

Construing the contract as a whole. One of the oldest principles in English   **13-033** contract law is that every contract is to be interpreted by reference to all of its terms.[97] It does not matter that only one clause, sub-clause or phrase is in dispute.[98] This principle is as relevant today as it ever was and Sir Anthony Clarke M.R. recently reaffirmed that

---

[92]   *Astrazeneca Insurance Company Ltd v XL Insurance (Bermuda) Ltd* [2013] EWHC 349 (Comm).

[93]   [2013] EWHC 349 (Comm) at [19], per Flaux J. That decision was upheld by the Court of Appeal [2013] EWCA Civ 1660, where Clarke LJ, at [24] described the proposition that the English Court, construing an English Law policy should be guided by the principles of New York law was "heretical".

[94]   For this reason, some earlier authorities should be treated with caution as the application of one canon of construction rather than another could lead to drastically different results.

[95]   *Mitchell (George) (Chesterhall) Ltd v Finney Lock Seeds Ltd* [1983] Q.B. 284 at 310; [1982] 3 W.L.R. 1036 at 1055; [1983] 1 All E.R. 108 at 123.

[96]   *Bank of Credit and Commerce International SA* [2001] UKHL 8 at [79]; [2002] 1 A.C. 251 at 282; [2001] 2 W.L.R. 735 at 762; see also *Investors Compensation Scheme Ltd* [1998] 1 W.L.R. 896 at 912; [1998] 1 All E.R. 98 at 114; [1998] 1 B.C.L.C. 493 at 547, per Lord Hoffmann; *Don King Productions Inc v Warren* [1998] 2 All E.R. 608 at 624; [1998] 2 Lloyd's Rep. 176 at 188; [1998] 2 B.C.L.C. 132 at 149–150, per Lightman J.; *KPMG LLP v Network Rail Infrastructure Ltd* [2007] EWCA Civ 363 at [50]; [2007] Bus. L.R. 1336 at 1351; [2008] 1 P. & C.R. 11 187 at 204, per Carnwarth LJ.

[97]   *Throgmorton v Tracey*; sub nom. *Throckmerton v Tracey* (1556) 1 Plowd 145 at 161; *Reid v*

"the primary source for understanding what the parties meant is their language interpreted in accordance with conventional usage. Of course, the particular provision must be construed in the context of the clause as a whole, and the clause itself must be construed in the context of the contract as a whole, which must in turn be considered in its factual matrix or against the circumstances surrounding it."[99]

Similarly in the mesothelioma trigger litigation, the Supreme Court emphasised that "it is necessary to avoid over-concentration on the meaning of single words or phrases viewed in isolation" and that it was necessary to consider the policies more broadly.[100]

However, where the document has not been drafted "as a coherent whole", the court may be more likely to reject a term or parts of the document for one of the reasons set out below.[101]

13-034 Avoidance of redundancy. It follows from the presumption that the parties intended to use the language they did and that a contract should be construed as a whole that, in general, words used in a contract are not intended to be redundant. The courts therefore strive to avoid a conclusion that a clause within a contract is redundant and should be disregarded.[102] The seminal statement of this principle flows from *Re Strand Music Hall Co Ltd, Ex p European and American Finance Co Ltd* where it was said that

"[t]he proper mode of construing any written instrument is to give effect to every part of it, if this be possible, and not to strike out or nullify one clause in a deed, unless it be impossible to reconcile it with another and more express clause in the same deed."[103]

13-035 However, the presumption against redundant language is applied with differing degrees of rigour dependent on the type of contract being interpreted. Some contracts are renowned for their impenetrable language and the fact that provisions are often retained due to an abundance of caution on the part of the draftsman rather than through any need for the specific words used. In relation to the interpretation of leases, Hoffmann J once said:

"I have never found the presumption against superfluous language particularly useful in the construction of leases. The draftsmen traditionally employ linguistic overkill and try to obliterate the conceptual target by using a number of phrases expressing more or less the same idea."[104]

13-036 In construction insurance, a sensible approach to the rule against redundancy is

---

Fairbanks; sub nom. *Read v Fairbanks* 138 E.R. 1371; (1853) 13 C.B. 692 at 730; *Miller v Borner & Co* [1900] 1 Q.B. 691; 69 L.J.Q.B. 429; 9 Asp. M.L.C. 3.

[98] *Glynn* [1893] A.C. 351; 62 L.J.Q.B. 466; 7 Asp. M.L.C. 366; *Cornish v The Accident Insurance Co Ltd* (1889) 23 Q.B.D 453; 54 J.P. 262; 58 L.J.Q.B. 591; *Cementation Piling & Foundations Ltd* [1995] 1 Lloyd's Rep. 97 at 101; 74 B.L.R. 98 at 108; 47 Con. L.R. 14 at 21.

[99] *Cosmos Holidays Plc v Dhanjal Investments Ltd* [2009] EWCA Civ 316 at [17].

[100] *BAI (Runn-off) Ltd v Durham* [2012] UKSC 14 at [19], per Lord Mance; see also *Oakapple Homes (Glossop) Ltd v DTR* (2009) Ltd [2013] EWHC 2394 (TCC) at [24], per Ramsey J.

[101] *Yien Yieh Commercial Bank Ltd v Kwai Ching Cold Storage Ltd* [1989] 2 HKLR 639, PC, per Lord Goff; *British-American Insurance (Kenya) Ltd v Matelec SAL* [2013] EWHC 3278 (Comm) at [50], per Walker J.

[102] See for example, *Cornish* (1889) 23 Q.B.D. 453; 54 J.P. 262; 58 L.J.Q.B. 591.

[103] *Re Strand Music Hall Co Ltd, Ex p European and American Finance Co Ltd* 55 E.R.853; (1865) 35 Beav. 153 at 159 Ch.

[104] *Tea Trade Properties Ltd v CIN Properties Ltd* [1990] 1 E.G.L.R. 155 at 158; [1990] 22 E.G. 67 at 71 Ch; see also similar sentiments expressed by Staughton LJ in *Total Transport Corp v Arcadia Petroleum Ltd, The Eurus* [1998] 1 Lloyd's Rep. 351 at 357; [1998] C.L.C. 90 at 97 CA; *Jani-King (GB) Ltd v Pula Enterprises Ltd* [2007] EWHC 2433 (QB); [2008] 1 All E.R. (Comm) 451; [2007]

necessary. Both insurance contracts[105] and construction contracts[106] have been criticised for their use of superfluous words as draftsmen attempt to close-off as many eventualities as possible in relation to complex projects and complex risks. Ultimately, where there is no sensible way in which a certain term in a contract may be carried out then it is possible to eliminate the conflicting term. In *Stone v The Mayor, Alderman, and Burgesses of Yeovil*; sub nom. *Stone v Yeovil Corp*[107] it was said:

> "[I]f there be a word or a phrase therein to which no sensible meaning can be given, it must be eliminated."

For example in *Baring Bros & Co v The Marine Insurance Co*,[108] a policy of **13-037** insurance was taken out to cover carriage of goods by land; however, the policy used was a form appropriate for carriage of goods by sea. In this instance the court was able to ignore clauses and words that could only apply to carriage by sea and apply it to the contract in front of them. Similarly, in *Stewart & Co v Merchants Marine Insurance Co Ltd*[109] a policy of marine insurance was based on a form normally used for cargo; the court was able to disregard any clauses that obviously did not apply to the insurance of the vessel.

Preserving the agreement. Where there are two interpretations of a document, **13-038** one leading to a valid instrument and the other leading to an invalid one, the court should try to give effect to the former construction.[110] However, there are limits to how far the court can go in giving effect to an agreement. In *Hillas & Co Ltd v Arcos Ltd; WN Hillas & Co Ltd v Arcos Ltd (Quantum)*, Lord Wright stated that:

> "[b]usiness men often record the most important agreements in crude and summary fashion; modes of expression sufficient and clear to them in the course of their business may appear to those unfamiliar with the business far from complete or precise. It is, accordingly, the duty of the court to construe such documents fairly and broadly, without being too astute or subtle in finding defects ... That maxim, however, does not mean that the court is to make a contract for the parties, or to go outside the words they have used, except insofar as there are appropriate implications."[111]

All E.R. (D) 355 (Oct); *Whitsea Shipping and Trading Corp v El Paso Rio Clara Ltda (The Marielle Bolten)* [2009] EWHC 2552 (Comm); [2010] 1 Lloyd's Rep. 648; [2009] 2 C.L.C. 596.

[105] *Arbuthnott v Fagan*; sub nom. *Deeny v Gooda Walker Ltd* [1996] L.R.L.R. 135; [1995] C.L.C. 1396 CA; *Independent*, October 1, 1993; *Tektrol Ltd* [2005] EWCA Civ 845; [2006] 1 All E.R. (Comm) 780; [2005] 2 Lloyd's Rep. 701; *Milton Furniture Ltd v Brit Insurance Ltd* [2014] EWHC 965 (QB) (upheld on appeal [2015] EWCA Civ 671).

[106] *Beaufort Developments (NI) Ltd* [1999] 1 A.C. 266 at 273–274; [1998] 2 W.L.R. 860; [1998] 2 All E.R. 778.

[107] *Stone v The Mayor, Alderman, and Burgesses of Yeovil* (1876) 1 C.P.D. 691 at 701.

[108] *Baring Bros & Co v The Marine Insurance Co* (1894) 10 T.L.R. 276.

[109] *Stewart & Co v Merchants Marine Insurance Co Ltd* (1885) 16 Q.B.D. 619.

[110] See for example: *Mills v Dunham* [1891] 1 Ch. 576 at 590 where it was said: "it is also a settled canon of construction that where a clause is ambiguous a construction which will make it valid is to be preferred to one which will make it void". See also: *Kingscroft Insurance Co Ltd v Nissan Fire and Marine Insurance Co Ltd* [2000] 1 All E.R. (Comm) 272; [1999] C.L.C. 1875; [1999] Lloyd's Rep. I.R. 603.

[111] *Hillas & Co Ltd v Arcos Ltd; WN Hillas & Co Ltd v Arcos Ltd (Quantum)* (1932) 38 Com. Cas. 23 at 36–37; 43 Ll. L. Rep. 359 at 367; 147 L.T. 503 at 514; [1932] All E.R. Rep. 494 at 503.

More definitively, in *G Scammell and Nephew Ltd v HC & JG Ouston*,[112] the court held that:

> "If these words, considered however broadly and untechnically and with due regard to all the just implications, fail to evince any definite meaning on which the court can safely act, the court has no choice but to say that there is no contract."

13-039 **Terms operating to destroy the main purpose of the contract.** Similarly, where a clause would defeat the fundamental purpose of the contract, those clauses should be rejected.[113] In *Glynn*, Lord Halsbury said that:

> "Looking at the whole of the instrument, and seeing what one must regard, for a reason which I will give in a moment, as its main purpose, one must reject words, indeed whole provisions, if they are inconsistent with what one assumes to be the main purpose of the contract."[114]

13-040 **Avoidance of absurdity.** Similarly, where more than one interpretation of a clause is possible, a construction that leads to an absurd result will be rejected in favour of a construction that produces a more reasonable result.[115] Whilst the law seeks to ascertain the objective intention of the parties based on the words they have chosen, "the law does not require judges to attribute to the parties an intention which they plainly could not have had.[116] In *L Schuler AG* Lord Reid summarised the position thus:

> "The fact that a particular construction leads to a very unreasonable result must be a relevant consideration. The more unreasonable the result the more unlikely it is that the parties can have intended it, and if they do intend it the more necessary it is that they shall make that intention abundantly clear."[117]

However, Lord Reid's comments must now be read subject to the observations of Lord Neuberger in *Arnold v Britton* when he said:

> "... The mere fact that a contractual arrangement, if interpreted according to its natural language, has worked out badly, or even disastrously, for one of the parties is not a reason for departing from the natural language. Commercial common sense is only relevant to the extent of how matters would or could have been perceived by the parties, or by reasonable people in the position of the parties, as at the date that the contract was made. Judicial observations such as those of Lord Reid in *Wickman Machine Tools Sales Ltd v L Schuler AG* [1974] A.C. 235, 251 and Lord Diplock in *Antaios Cia Naviera SA v Salen Rederierna AB (The Antaios)* [1985] A.C. 191, 201, quoted by Lord Carnwath JSC at para 110, have to be read and applied bearing that important point in mind.
> ... while commercial common sense is a very important factor to take into account when interpreting a contract, a court should be very slow to reject the natural meaning of a provision as correct simply because it appears to be a very imprudent term for one of the parties to have agreed, even ignoring the benefit of wisdom of hindsight. The purpose of interpretation is to identify what the parties have agreed, not what the court thinks that they should have agreed. Experience shows that it is by no means unknown for people to enter into arrangements which are ill-advised, even ignoring the

---

112 *G Scammell and Nephew Ltd v HC & JG Ouston* [1941] A.C. 251 at 268; [1941] 1 All E.R. 14 at 25–26; 110 L.J.K.B. 197 at 205.
113 *Mark Taylor v Rive Droite Music Ltd* [2005] EWCA Civ 1300; [2006] E.M.L.R. 4; [2005] All E.R. (D) 72 (Nov).
114 *Glynn* [1893] A.C. 351 at 357; 62 L.J.Q.B. 466 at 469; 7 Asp. M.L.C. 366 at 367.
115 Stuart-Smith LJ said in *Yorkshire Water Services Ltd (No 1)* [1997] C.L.C. 213 at 221; [1997] 2 Lloyd's Rep. 21 at 28: "a literal construction that leads to an absurd result or one otherwise manifestly contrary to the real intention of the parties should be rejected, if an alternative more reasonable construction can be adopted without doing violence to the language used".
116 *Investors Compensation Scheme Ltd* [1998] 1 W.L.R. 896 at 913; [1998] 1 All E.R. 98 at 115; [1998] 1 B.C.L.C. 493 at 548.
117 *L Schuler AG* [1974] A.C. 235 at 251; [1973] 2 W.L.R. 683 at 689; [1973] 2 All E.R. 39 at 45.

benefit of wisdom of hindsight, and it is not the function of a court when interpreting an agreement to relieve a party from the consequences of his imprudence or poor advice. Accordingly, when interpreting a contract a judge should avoid re-writing it in an attempt to assist an unwise party or to penalise an astute party."[118]

Priority of terms. In contracts where there is a mix of standard terms and bespoke terms, where there is a conflict between them, priority is given to the bespoke terms.[119] Similarly where there are pre-printed written terms and additional handwritten terms, the handwritten terms will prevail. It should go without saying that the court will endeavour to avoid inconsistency[120] and that if the provisions can sensibly be reconciled there is no need to consider which has overriding force.[121] In *Homburg Houtimport BV v Agrosin Private Ltd (The Starsin)* Lord Bingham made clear that: **13-041**

> "it is common sense that greater weight should attach to terms which the particular contracting parties have chosen to include in the contract than to pre-printed terms probably devised to cover very many situations to which the particular contracting parties have never addressed their minds."[122]

Similarly, where a contract contains general clauses and special clauses relating to specific circumstances, the special provisions will usually take precedence over the general.[123] The leading exposition of this principle is in the judgment of Fry LJ in *Glynn*:   **13-042**

> "This principle is applicable wherever specific words are used to express the main object and intent of the instrument, and in some other parts general words are used which in their utmost generality would be inconsistent with and destructive of the main object of the contract. When the Court in dealing with a contract or document of that kind finds that difficulty, it always, so far as I know, follows this principle that the general words must be limited so that they shall be consistent with and shall not defeat the main object of the contracting parties."[124]

Again, this principle applies only where the general and specific clauses are truly in conflict and cannot be reconciled.[125]

Inconsistency between terms. If a policy contains two or more provisions that   **13-043**

---

[118] *Arnold v Britton* [2015] UKSC 36 at [19]–[20]; [2015] A.C. 1619; [2016] 1 All E.R. 1.
[119] *Robertson v French* 102 E.R. 779; (1803) 4 East 130; *The Mercantile Marine Insurance Co Ltd v Titherington* 122 E.R. 1015; (1864) 5 B. & S. 765 KB; *Dudgeon v Pembroke* (1877) 2 App. Cas. 284; 46 L.J.Q.B. 409; 3 Asp. M.L.C. 393 HL; *Adamastos Shipping Co Ltd v Anglo-Saxon Petroleum Co Ltd* [1959] A.C. 133; [1958] 2 W.L.R. 688; [1958] 1 All E.R. 725 HL; *Eagle Star Insurance Co Ltd v J N Cresswell* [2004] EWCA Civ 602; [2004] 2 All E.R. (Comm) 244; *Cubitt Building and Interiors Ltd v Richardson Roofing (Industrial) Ltd* [2008] EWHC 1020 (TCC); [2008] B.L.R. 354; (2008) 119 Con. L.R. 137; *Bovis Lend Lease Ltd v Cofely Engineering Services* [2009] EWHC 1120 (TCC); [2009] All E.R. (D) 23 (Sep).
[120] *Yorkshire Insurance Co Ltd v Campbell* [1917] A.C. 218; 85 L.J.P.C. 85; 115 L.T. 644; *Farmers' Co-operative Ltd v National Benefit Assurance Co Ltd; Argonaut Marine Insurance Co Ltd; Importers' & Exporters' Marine Insurance Co and National Marine & Fire Insurance Co Ltd* (1922) 13 Lloyd's Rep. 417.
[121] *Bayoil SA v Seaward Tankers Corp (The Leonidas)* [2001] 1 All E.R. (Comm) 392; [2001] 1 Lloyd's Rep. 533; [2001] C.L.C. 1800; *Alchemy Estates Ltd v Astor* [2008] EWHC 2675 (Ch); [2009] 1 W.L.R. 940; [2009] 2 P. & C.R. 5.
[122] *The Starsin* [2003] UKHL 12 at [11]; [2004] 1 A.C. 715 at 737; [2003] 2 W.L.R. 711 at 718.
[123] Embodied in the Latin maxim "*generalia specialibus non derogant*": the general should not derogate from the particular.
[124] *Glynn* [1892] 1 Q.B. 337 at 344; 61 L.J.Q.B. 186 at 190; 66 L.T. 142 The quote in the last two reports is slightly different but the same point is made.
[125] *Petroleum Oil and Gas Corp of South Africa (Pty) Ltd v FR8 Singapore PTE Ltd (The Eternity)* [2008] EWHC 2480 (Comm); [2009] 1 All E.R. (Comm) 556; [2009] 1 Lloyd's Rep. 107.

appear to be inconsistent with each other, the court will try to adopt a construction which resolves that inconsistency provided that such a construction can be conscientiously and fairly done.[126]

13-044 **Inconsistency between policy sections.** Where different sections of a policy are inconsistent the courts will strive to give effect to the contract as a whole. Normally, different sections of the policy apply to different types of cover and it is often possible to construe the sections separately or to construe a later section as qualifying an earlier one.

13-045 **Inconsistency between the policy and the proposal.** Where there is a conflict between a policy and a proposal it is usual that the policy takes precedence. In *Izzard v Universal Insurance Co Ltd* the court held that

> "the warranties and conditions expressed in the proposal are declared to be basic conditions of the policy, that must be subject to their being overridden by any express terms to the contrary effect in the actual policy. No doubt the proposal conditions and the express conditions of the policy must be read together, and, as far as may be, reconciled, so that every part of the contract may receive effect."[127]

13-046 **Inconsistency between the policy and the slip.** Similarly, where there is a conflict between the policy and the slip, the policy will usually prevail. In *Youell v Bland Welch & Co Ltd (No.1)*, Lord Justice Beldam stated:

> "Although the slip initialled by underwriters records the original agreement between the parties, if it contains words showing an intention that the terms will subsequently be incorporated into a policy form, when the policy has been issued it is the policy and not the slip which constitutes the contract or agreement between the parties."[128]

Although where there is a conflict between the slip and the policy it may be possible to bring a claim to rectify the policy.[129]

13-047 **Expressio unius.**[130] Where a clause expressly mentions a specific thing or things, the court will often be able to infer that anything not mentioned was deliberately omitted.

The rationale for this approach is simple: where the parties have expressly delineated their rights and obligations by mentioning one or more particular things, it tends to suggest that they did not intend to include other things that they have not mentioned and it is not desirable for the court to extend the parties' agreement.

Unlike the approaches discussed above which concentrate on the interplay between different parts of the agreement, this maxim is the first of a series seeking to derive assistance in determining meaning and context from the way that individual clauses are drafted. Indeed, Lord Diplock considers these maxims as

---

[126] *Pagnan SpA v Tradax Ocean Transportation SA* [1986] 2 Lloyd's Rep. 646 at 635, per Steyn J; approved in the Court of Appeal [1987] 2 Lloyd's Rep 342 at 350, per Bingham LJ. See also *British-American Insurance (Kenya) Ltd v Matelec SAL* [2013] EWHC 3278 (Comm) at [49], per Walker J.

[127] *Izzard v Universal Insurance Co Ltd* [1937] A.C. 773 at 779–780; [1937] 3 All E.R. 79 at 81–82; 58 Ll. L. Rep 121 at 125. See also: *Thor Navigation Inc v Ingosstrakh Insurance Co Ltd, Schwarzmeer Und Ostee Versicherungs-Aktiengesellschaft* [2005] EWHC 19 (Comm); [2005] 1 Lloyd's Rep. 547; [2005] 1 C.L.C. 12.

[128] *Youell v Bland Welch & Co Ltd (No.1)* [1992] 2 Lloyd's Rep. 127 at 141 CA.

[129] See below, paras 13-087 to 13-101.

[130] *"Expressio unius est exclusio alterius"*: the expression of one thing is the exclusion of others.

"general rules of composition which any writer seeking clarity of expression is likely to follow".[131]

This maxim is of particular importance in an insurance context where cover may **13-048** be expressed to engage in specific circumstances and exclusions from cover are likely to be particularised; anything not expressly listed is apt to be treated as if its omission was deliberate. For example, in *Hooley Hill Rubber & Chemical Co Ltd*,[132] the policy contained an exclusion for "loss or damage [caused] by explosion, except loss or damage caused by explosion of illuminating gas". Bankes LJ considered the exclusion and held that:

> "[t]he exception of one particular kind of explosion from the general exclusion of explosions shows that the parties intended to exclude from the risks covered by the policy all kinds of explosion other than the one expressly excepted."[133]

The *expressio unius* approach to construction is often misapplied and has often **13-049** been criticised. For example in *Colquhoun v Brooks*,[134] Wills J explained that the rule should be treated carefully because

> "[t]he failure to make the 'expressio' complete very often arises from accident, very often from the fact that it never struck the draftsman that the thing supposed to be excluded required specific mention of any kind."

Nevertheless, the maxim is still frequently deployed and has formed part of the **13-050** reasoning in a series of recent Court of Appeal decisions, culminating in *Colour Quest Ltd v Total Downstream UK Plc; Total UK Ltd v Chevron Ltd*; sub nom. *Shell UK Ltd v Total UK Ltd*,[135] in which the court considered whether an indemnity clause extended to include negligence. Waller LJ stated that[136]:

> "we are not inclined unless driven to it to contemplate that where detailed agreements are drawn up, one will have been tacitly extended or by implication extended. We suggest that where the parties have drawn up a series of detailed agreements and the draftsmen have expressly dealt with negligence, a more significant canon of construction is that which would suggest that where it has not been expressly referred to that would be likely to be a deliberate decision by the draftsman to exclude negligence."

Ejusdem generis. This maxim is concerned with the meaning of general words. **13-051** Ejusdem generis means "of the same kind as" and the essence of this maxim is that where there is an enumerated list of several words, clauses or terms that share common characteristics and those terms are followed by general words, such as "or otherwise", the general words will be interpreted as if they were limited to the same class of things as the preceding words. This canon of construction was most clearly defined in the case of *Sun Fire Office* by Lord Watson where he said:

---

[131] *Prestcold (Central) Ltd v Minister of Labour* [1969] 1 W.L.R. 89 at 96; [1969] 1 All E.R. 69 at 75; 47 A.T.C. 331 at 336.

[132] *Hooley Hill Rubber & Chemical Co Ltd* [1920] 1 K.B. 257 at 269; (1919) 1 Ll. L. Rep 25 at 3; 89 L.J.K.B. 179 at 182.

[133] *Hooley Hill Rubber & Chemical Co Ltd* [1920] 1 K.B. 257 at 269.

[134] *Colquhoun v Brooks* [1887] L.R. 19 Q.B.D 400 at 406; 57 L.J.Q.B. 70 at 73.

[135] *Colour Quest Ltd v Total Downstream UK Plc; Total UK Ltd v Chevron Ltd*; sub nom. *Shell UK Ltd v Total UK Ltd* [2010] EWCA Civ 180; [2011] Q.B. 86; [2010] 3 W.L.R. 1192; see also *Port of Tilbury (London) Ltd v Stora Enso Transport & Distribution Ltd* [2009] EWCA Civ 16; [2009] 1 Lloyd's Rep. 391; [2009] 1 C.L.C. 35 and *Chinnock v Hocaoglu* [2008] EWCA Civ 1175; [2009] 1 W.L.R. 765; [2009] 2 P. & C.R. 18.

[136] *Colour Quest Ltd; Total UK Ltd* [2010] EWCA Civ 180 at [15]; [2010] 3 All E.R. 793 at 798; [2010] 2 Lloyd's Rep. 467 at 472; [2010] 1 C.L.C. 343 at 350.

"It is a well known canon of construction, that where a particular enumeration is followed by such words as 'or other', the latter expression ought, if not enlarged by the context, to be limited to matters ejusdem generis with those specially enumerated."[137]

13-052 To that extent, the ejusdem generis rule seeks to limit the natural and ordinary meaning of the general words. Kennedy LJ described this as follows:

"The doctrine of 'ejusdem generis' is that you treat general words which might under certain circumstances have a wider meaning as being restricted because, according to the true construction of the immediately preceding expression, you find it to designate things which may properly be described as belonging to the same genus."[138]

13-053 For example, in *Lambourn v McLellan*[139] a tenant was required to yield up the demised premises at the end of the term together with:

"all doors, locks, keys, bolts, bars, staples, hinges, iron pins, wainscots, hearths, stoves, marble and other chimney-pieces, slabs, shutters, fastenings, partitions, pipes, pumps, sinks, gutters of lead, posts, pales, rails, dressers, shelves, and all other erections, buildings, improvements, fixtures, and things which are ... fixed, fastened, or belong to the ... premises or any part thereof."[140]

The court held that the words "all other ... fixtures and things" should be interpreted as meaning fixtures and things of the same genus as the preceding list and was not therefore apt to include the tenant's machinery even though he had fixed the machinery to the premises.

13-054 The logic behind the maxim is that where words with a common characteristic are followed by general words, it is more likely that the general words were intended to encompass other things of the same type that may have been omitted from the specific list rather than being intended to expand the scope of the clause dramatically. The use of general words in this context has been referred to as "sweeping up what had been overlooked".[141]

13-055 The maxim is particularly relevant in the insurance context where specific risks are often enumerated in an insuring clause followed by general words insuring against other risks. In such circumstances, the general words will often be restricted to encompass other risks of the same kind as those specifically enumerated. For example, in *Thames and Mersey Marine Insurance Co Ltd v Hamilton Fraser & Co*,[142] the perils covered by a policy of marine insurance included:

"perils which the capital stock and funds of the said company are made liable unto by this insur-

---

[137] *Sun Fire Office* (1889) 14 App. Cas. 98 at 103–104; 53 J.P. 548 at 549; 58 L.J.P.C. 69 at 72.

[138] *Tillmanns & Co v SS Knutsford Ltd* [1908] 2 K.B. 385 at 408; 77 L.J.K.B. 778 at 790; 13 Com. Cas. 244 at 261 CA (in the last report the quote is worded slightly differently but the same point is made); however there are some rare cases where the principle has been applied even where the court has not been able strictly to identify a common genus. See for example *Foscolo Mango & Co Ltd v Stag Line Ltd*; sub nom. *Stag Line Ltd v Foscolo Mango & Co Ltd or Foscolo Mango & Co Ltd and HC Vivian Ltd v Stag Line Ltd* [1931] 2 K.B. 48; (1931) 39 Ll. L. Rep. 101; 100 L.J.K.B. 421 and *Chandris v Isbrandtsen-Moller Co Inc* [1951] 1 K.B. 240; [1950] 2 All E.R. 618; 84 Ll. L. Rep. 347.

[139] *Lambourn v McLellan* [1903] 2 Ch. 268; 72 L.J. Ch. 617; 51 W.R. 594 CA.

[140] *Lambourn* [1903] 2 Ch. 268 at 269; 72 L.J. Ch. 617 at 618; 51 W.R. 594 at 595 CA.

[141] *Crompton v Jarratt* (1885) 30 Ch. D. 298 at 317; 54 L.J. Ch. 1109 at 1120; 33 W.R. 913 at 915, per Lindley LJ it has been suggested that the maxim cannot operate in reverse, i.e. where the general words precede the enumerated provisions (see for example *Ambatielos v Anton Jurgens Margarine Works* [1922] 2 K.B. 185 at 194; (1922) 10 Ll. L. Rep. 781 at 782–783; 91 L.J.K.B. 703 at 706; upheld [1923] A.C. 175 at 183; (1922) 13 Ll. L. Rep. 357 at 359; 92 L.J. Ch. 306 at 308–309) the reasoning of such a view is difficult to understand. If the draftsman has enumerated specific examples of what was meant by a specific phrase that must surely be an appropriate guide to interpretation.

[142] *Thames and Mersey Marine Insurance Co Ltd v Hamilton Fraser & Co* (1887) 12 App. Cas. 484; 56 L.J.Q.B. 626; 6 Asp. M.L.C. 200 see also *Stott (Baltic) Steamers Ltd v Marten* [1916] 1 A.C. 304;

ance, they are, of the seas, men-of-war, fire, enemies, pirates, rovers, thieves, jettisons, letters of mart and countermart, surprisals, takings at sea, arrests, restraints and detainments of all kings, princes, and people of what nation, condition, or quality so ever, barratry of the master and mariners, and of all other perils, losses, and misfortunes that have or shall come to the hurt, detriment, or damage of the aforesaid subject-matter of this insurance, or any part thereof."[143]

The vessel was damaged while a pump was being used for the purpose of filling the vessel's boilers. The claimant argued that the damage came within the definition of "all other perils, losses and misfortunes".[144] Whilst the court held that it was certain that a loss or misfortune had occurred, it held that the loss was not covered because the general words "other perils" must be construed ejusdem generis with the preceding words, which were all perils of the sea.[145]

It is, however, possible to avoid the consequences of the rule by making plain **13-056** in the drafting that the general words were intended to have general effect. In *Chandris v Isbrandtsen-Moller Co Inc*, Devlin J explained that[146]:

"[l]egal draftsmen are all familiar with the existence of the rule, and familiar too with the proper signals to hoist if they do not want it to apply. Phrases such as 'whether or not similar to the foregoing' and 'without prejudice to the generality of the foregoing' are often employed in legal draftsmanship; and if the draftsman has read the report of *Larsen v Sylvester & Co*,[147] he will know that the addition of 'whatsoever' generally serves the same purpose."

Noscitur a sociis.[148]   Sometimes a word can be construed in the context of the **13-057** words used around it. For example, in *Tektrol Ltd*[149] the court considered a clause in a business interruption policy excluding cover for loss arising from:

"erasure loss distortion or corruption of information on computer systems or other records programmes or software caused deliberately by rioters strikers locked-out workers persons taking part in labour disturbances or civil commotion or malicious persons."

The court held that the word "loss" in this context could not extend to information on computer systems lost through a burglary because the context of the surrounding words made clear that the "loss" contemplated by the clause was loss through electronic means such as "erasure" and the "distortion or corruption of

---

85 L.J.K.B. 97; 13 Asp. M.L.C. 200 HL. For an example of a case where the principle did not apply, see *Reilly v National Insurance & Guarantee Corp Ltd* [2008] EWHC 722 (Comm) at [6]; [2008] 2 All E.R. (Comm) 612 at 616; [2008] Lloyd's Rep. I.R. 695 at 698 where a policy excluding the failure of "any fire or intruder alarm, switch gear, control panel or machinery to perform its intended function" was considered. The court held that "machinery" was independent of the words "fire or intruder alarm".

[143] *Thames and Mersey Marine Insurance Co Ltd* (1887) 12 App. Cas. 484 at 485.

[144] *Thames and Mersey Marine Insurance Co Ltd* (1887) 12 App. Cas. 484 at 492; 56 L.J.Q.B. 626 at 629; 6 Asp. M.L.C. 200 at 203.

[145] See also *Tillmanns & Co* [1908] 2 K.B. 385 at 395, 406 and 408; 77 L.J.K.B. 778 at 782–783, 788 and 790; 13 Com. Cas. 244 at 247, 259 and 261–262 upheld on appeal [1908] A.C. 406 at 408 and 410; 77 L.J.K.B. 977 at 782–783; 11 Asp. M.L.C. 105 at 114 whereby a clause including the words "should the entry and discharge at a port be deemed by the master unsafe in consequence of war, disturbance or any other cause" was construed so that "any other cause" was read ejusdem generis with "war or disturbance".

[146] *Chandris v Isbrandtsen-Moller Co Inc* [1951] 1 K.B. 240 at 245; [1950] 2 All E.R. 618 at 772.

[147] *Larsen v Sylvester & Co* [1908] A.C. 295; 77 L.J.K.B. 993; 11 Asp. M.L.C. 78; but see *BOC Group Plc v Centeon LLC* [1999] 1 All E.R. (Comm) 970 at 979; 63 Con. L.R. 104 at 130 where Evans LJ suggested that it may in some circumstances be possible to construe the word "whatsoever" ejusdem generis by reference to the context in which it is used.

[148] It is known from its associates.

[149] *Tektrol Ltd* [2005] EWCA Civ 845 at [5]; [2006] 1 All E.R. (Comm) 780 at 783; [2005] 2 Lloyd's Rep. 701.

information".[150]

13-058 This maxim can only go so far and it will not allow the court to construe a word with a distinct meaning as being consistent with the words around it if to do so would obviously distort the language. Buckley J made the following observation that:

> "the principle of *noscitur a sociis* does not in my judgment entitle one to overlook self-evident facts. If you meet seven men with black hair and one with red hair, you are not entitled to say that here are eight men with black hair."[151]

13-059 **Expressum facit.**[152] This approach provides that where a contract expressly deals with an issue, there is no room to imply terms that extend those obligations. This is based on the theory that if the parties have chosen to express themselves in a particular way, it is unlikely that they intended to be bound in a manner that goes beyond their agreement. Further, the canon of *expressum facit* is reflective of the more general rule that implied terms cannot be inconsistent with the express terms of the contract.[153] In *Aspdin v Austin*, the position was expressed as follows:

> "Where parties have entered into written engagements with expressed stipulations, it is manifestly not desirable to extend them by any implications: the presumption is that, having expressed some, they have expressed all the conditions by which they intend to be bound under that instrument."[154]

13-060 **The contra proferentem rule.**[155] This maxim applies where clauses are ambiguous and it requires that where a clause is capable of multiple meanings, the meaning most disadvantageous to the drafting party should be adopted.[156] The rationale behind the rule is that the party that proposes a term is best placed to draft it so as

---

[150] *Tektrol Ltd* [2005] EWCA Civ 845 at [29]; [2006] 1 All E.R. (Comm) 780 at 788; [2005] 2 Lloyd's Rep. 701 at 706, per Sir Martin Nourse.

[151] *Re Jenkins's Will Trusts; Public Trustee v British Union for the Abolition of Vivisection* [1966] Ch. 249 at 256; [1966] 2 W.L.R. 615 at 620; [1966] 1 All E.R. 926 at 929.

[152] *Expressum facit cessare tacitum* (the expression of one thing in an instrument may exclude another thing in an instrument and render what is implied silent).

[153] *Equitable Life Assurance Society v Hyman* [2002] 1 A.C. 408; [2000] 3 W.L.R. 529; [2000] 3 All E.R. 961; *Persimmon Homes (South Coast) Ltd v Hall Aggregates (South Coast) Ltd* [2008] EWHC 2379 (TCC); [2008] All E.R. (D) 114 (Oct); *Anders & Kern UK Ltd (t/a Anders & Kern Presentation Systems) v CGU Insurance Plc (t/a Norwich Union Insurance)* [2007] EWCA Civ 1481; [2008] 2 All E.R. (Comm) 1185; [2008] Lloyd's Rep. I.R. 460; *Autoclenz Ltd v Belcher* [2009] EWCA Civ 1046; [2010] I.R.L.R. 70; (2009) *Times*, 16 October (approved by the Supreme Court at [2011] UKSC 41; [2011] 4 All E.R. 745; [2011] I.C.R. 1157).

[154] *Aspdin v Austin* 114 E.R. 1402; (1844) 5 Q.B. 671 at 684; 1 Dav. & Mer. 515 at 522 QB. See also *Greig v Insole; World Series Cricket Pty Ltd v Insole* [1978] 1 W.L.R. 302; [1978] 3 All E.R. 449; 122 S.J. 163.

[155] *Verba chartarum fortius accipiuntur contra proferentem*: the words of deeds are to be interpreted most strongly against him who uses them.

[156] *Throgmorton v Tracey* (1556) 1 Plowd 145; *Tarleton v Staniforth* (1794) 5 T.R. 695; *Borradaile v Hunter* (1843) 5 Man. & G. 639; *Anderson v Fitzgerald* 10 E.R. 551; (1853) 4 H.L. Cas. 484; *Birrell v Dryer* (1884) 9 App. Cas. 345; 5 Asp. M.L.C. 267; 51 L.T. 130; *Smith v Accident Insurance Co* (1870) L.R. 5 Ex 302; 39 L.J. Ex 211; 18 W.R. 1107; *Cornish* (1889) 23 Q.B.D 453; 54 J.P. 262; 58 L.J.Q.B.; 38 W.R. 139; *London & Lancashire Fire Insurance Co Ltd v Bolands Ltd* [1924] A.C. 836; 19 Ll. L. Rep. 1; 93 L.J.P.C. 230; *Lake v Simmons* [1927] A.C. 487; 27 Ll. L. Rep. 153, 377; 96 L.J.K.B. 621; *Houghton v Trafalgar Insurance Co Ltd* [1954] 1 Q.B. 247; [1953] W.L.R. 985; [1953] 2 All E.R. 1409; *Taylor v National Insurance & Guarantee Corp* [1989] C.L.Y. 2059; *Zeus Tradition Marine Ltd v Bell, The Zeus V* [1999] 1 Lloyd's Rep. 703; [1999] C.L.C. 391; [1998] All E.R. (D) 525; *Royal & Sun Alliance Insurance Plc v Dornoch Ltd* [2005] EWCA Civ 238; [2005] 1 All E.R. (Comm) 590; [2005] 1 C.L.C. 466; *Tektrol Ltd* [2005] EWCA Civ 845; [2006] 1 All E.R. (Comm) 780; [2005] 2 Lloyd's Rep. 701; *Durham* [2008] EWHC 2692 (QB); [2009] 2 All E.R. 26;

to protect himself and therefore should not be able to take the benefit of any ambiguity.[157]

Ironically the maxim itself is ambiguous as it could apply equally to the person who prepares the contract as a whole and to the person who proposes the individual ambiguous clause. In the context of insurance it will usually be the insurer who has prepared the relevant policy wording and thus it is for them to ensure that the policy is sufficiently clear and precise. In some circumstances, however, where sections of a proposal or presentation prepared by the insured are incorporated into the policy the situation may be reversed.[158] In *Youell*,[159] the Court of Appeal stated that an application of the *contra proferentem* rule should be done with consideration to two factors. First, "wording in a contract is to be construed against a party who seeks to rely on it"[160]; and secondly, "wording is to be construed against the party who proposed it for inclusion in the contract".[161]

The rule only applies if there is some genuine ambiguity as to the interpretation of a clause.[162] That means that the court must exhaust other methods of construction before concluding that a clause is ambiguous[163]; the maxim is therefore one of "if not last, very late resort".[164] A clause is not rendered ambiguous because the clear construction of the clause is unattractive[165]; nor will a clause be considered ambiguous if its meaning is rendered clear when read in conjunction with the policy as a whole.[166]   **13-061**

(d) Admissible evidence

The contract. It should be apparent from the preceding discussion that the principal evidence of the parties' agreement is the contract itself, together with any documents incorporated into it.   **13-062**

[2009] Lloyd's Rep. I.R. 295.

[157] *Houghton* [1954] 1 Q.B. 247; [1953] W.L.R. 985; [1953] 2 All E.R. 1409; *Tektrol Ltd* [2005] EWCA Civ 845; [2006] 1 All E.R. (Comm) 780; [2005] 2 Lloyd's Rep. 701.

[158] *Birrell* (1884) 9 App. Cas. 345; 5 Asp. M.L.C. 267; 51 L.T. 130. See also cases where the ambiguity is caused by the insured's broker where ambiguity is resolved in favour of the insurer: *Denby v English & Scottish Maritime Insurance Co Ltd; Yasuda Fire & Marine Insurance Co of Europe Ltd v Lloyd's Underwriting Syndicate No.229*; sub nom. *Denby v MJ Marchant* [1998] C.L.C. 870; [1998] Lloyd's Rep. I.R. 343; [1998] All E.R. (D) 88 CA; *Eurodale Manufacturing Ltd (t/a Connekt Cellular Communications) v Ecclesiastical Insurance Office Plc* [2003] EWCA Civ 203; [2003] Lloyd's Rep. I.R. 444; [2003] 13 L.S. Gaz. R. 26.

[159] *Youell* [1992] 2 Lloyd's Rep. 127.

[160] *Youell* [1992] 2 Lloyd's Rep. 127 at 134.

[161] *Youell* [1992] 2 Lloyd's Rep. 127 at 134.

[162] *Drinkwater v London Assurance Corp*; sub nom. *John Drinkwater v The Royal Exchange Assurance Co* 95 E.R. 863; (1767) 2 Wils 363; *Birrell* (1884) 9 App. Cas. 345; 5 Asp. M.L.C. 267; 51 L.T. 130; *Cornish* (1889) 23 Q.B.D. 453; 54 J.P. 262; 58 L.J.Q.B. 591; *Cole v Accident Insurance Co Ltd* (1889) 5 T.L.R. 736; (1889) 23 Q.B.D. 453; *Denby* [1998] C.L.C. 870; [1998] Lloyd's Rep. I.R. 343; [1998] All E.R. (D) 88.

[163] *Bolands* (1936) 54 Lloyd's Rep. 92; 80 S.J. 167; 154 L.T. 258; *Direct Travel Insurance v McGeown* [2003] EWCA Civ 1606; [2004] 1 All E.R. (Comm) 609; [2004] Lloyd's Rep. I.R. 599.

[164] *Lakeport Navigation Co Panama SA v Anonima Petroli Italiana SpA (The Olympic Brilliance)* [1982] 2 Lloyd's Rep. 205 at 206; [1982] Com L.R. 162, per Eveleigh LJ.

[165] *Smith v The Accident Insurance Co* (1870) L.R. 5 Exch. 302; 39 L.J. Ex 211; 18 W.R. 1107; *Nittan (UK) Ltd v Solent Steel Fabrication Ltd (t/a Sargrove Automation) and Cornhill Insurance Co Ltd* [1981] 1 Lloyd's Rep. 633; *Times,* October 24, 1980.

[166] *Young v Sun Alliance and London Insurance Ltd* [1977] 1 W.L.R. 104; [1976] 3 All E.R. 561; [1976] 2 Lloyd's Rep. 189.

13-063   **Contract documents.**   As with other contracts, when construing a policy of insurance, it is the entire policy that is considered.[167] The requirement to construe the policy as a whole ensures that where terms of an agreement are embodied across multiple documents then all of those documents must be considered. Documents other than the policy conditions and schedule are often incorporated into the agreement. Sometimes, documents such as the slip will be physically attached to the policy.[168] Documents such as the proposal[169] can also be incorporated into the policy by reference.[170]

13-064   **Priority of documents.**   All too frequently, however, contracts make no provision or no adequate provision for the hierarchy of the documents in the event of conflict. Where a contract comprises more than one document, more weight should be afforded to bespoke documents as opposed to standard printed terms.[171] Further, greater weight should normally be afforded to the most recent document on the basis that where there is a change contained within a later document it was clear that the later document came to represent a change in the will of the parties.[172]

13-065   **Previous contracts and slips.**   It has been held that previous concluded contracts can be admissible for the purposes of interpreting current contracts. In *HIH Casualty & General Insurance Ltd v New Hampshire Insurance Co*[173] it was said:

> "In my judgment, there is nothing in these citations which binds this court to rule that where a prior contract has been followed by a further contract, or where in an insurance context a slip contract has been followed by a policy, there is a rule of law which makes it inadmissible to consider the terms of the prior contract, or that the parol evidence rule has the same effect ... In principle, it would seem to me that it is always admissible to look at a prior contract as part of the matrix or surrounding circumstances of a later contract. I do not see how the parol evidence rule can exclude prior contracts, as distinct from mere negotiations."

13-066   In an insurance context, it would therefore be permissible to consider previous policies of insurance over the same subject matter and to consider the impact of any slip on the construction of the policy.[174]

13-067   **Recitals, headings, labels and marginal notes.**   Unless the contract provides otherwise, if the words within a policy are unclear, recitals can be used to establish the intentions of the parties.[175] However, if the operative term under consideration

---

[167]   *Re George and Goldsmiths' and General Burglary Ins Ass Ltd's Arbitration* [1899] 1 Q.B. 595 at 605; 68 L.J.Q.B. 365; 47 W.R. 474.

[168]   In *Thomas Cheshire & Co v Vaughan Bros & Co* [1920] 3 K.B. 240 at 257; 84 J.P. 233 at 236; 89 L.J.K.B. 1168 at 1177. Atkin LJ at 257 said: "I think the intention of the parties was, and must be taken to have been, in view of the fact that they attached the slip to the written document and signed the document with the slip attached, to include in the contract the terms contained in the slip."

[169]   The proposal or any presentation or declaration by the insured will usually be incorporated into the policy by reference. However, express words of incorporation are needed in the policy or in the proposal itself; mere mention of the proposal in the policy may not be sufficient.

[170]   *Worsley v Wood* 101 E.R. 785(1796) 6 Term Rep. 710.

[171]   See above, para.13-041.

[172]   *Williams v Agius* [1914] A.C. 510; 83 L.J.K.B. 715; 19 Com. Cas HL.

[173]   *HIH Casualty & General Insurance Ltd v New Hampshire Insurance Co* [2001] EWCA Civ 735 at [81] and [83]; [2001] 2 All E.R. (Comm) 39 at 62–63; [2001] 2 Lloyd's Rep. 161 at 178–179.

[174]   Where there is inconsistency between the slip and the policy it may be possible to seek rectification of the policy, see above, paras 13-044 to 13-046 and below, paras 13-087 to 13-101.

[175]   *Walsh v Trevanion* (1850) 15 Q.B. 733; 19 L.J.Q.B. 458; 14 Jur 1134; *Re Michell's Trusts* (1878) 9

is clear and unambiguous, it will not be overridden or qualified by information set out in the recitals.[176]

In relation to headings and marginal notes, again the general rule is that they can be taken into account as an aid to construction unless the contract expressly provides otherwise.[177] The description of a term will be of some influence, although the fact that a term is labelled "warranty" or "condition precedent" does not necessarily make it so; the court will look to the substance of the clause to determine its effect.[178] That said, the courts have traditionally given headings and marginal notes less weight than recitals.[179]

Where a contract provides expressly that headings, marginal notes or recitals **13-068** should not be used as an aid to interpretation, opinion is divided as to the efficacy of such clauses. The strict—and probably correct—view is that the court should uphold the parties' agreement and should not consider the prohibited material[180]; however, there are conflicting authorities on the point.[181]

Deletions and strike-throughs. It is common in many standard form contracts **13-069** for the parties to delete words or phrases. The court is now permitted to consider deletions on the face of a document in order to construe the remaining clauses.[182] Further, the suggestion that the court could only consider deletions in standard form

---

Ch. D. 5; 48 L.J. Ch. 50; 26 W.R. 762; *Leggott v Barrett*; sub nom. *Leggett v Barratt* (1880) L.R. 15 Ch. D. 306; 51 L.J. Ch. 90; 28 W.R. 962; *Orr v Mitchell* [1893] A.C. 238; 1 R 147; 9 T.L.R. 356; *Crouch v Crouch* [1912] 1 K.B. 378; 81 L.J.K.B. 275; 56 S.J. 188; *Blascheck v Russell* (1916) 33 T.L.R. 74; *Square Mile Partnership Ltd v Fitzmaurice McCall Ltd* [2006] EWCA Civ 1690; [2007] 2 B.C.L.C. 23; [2006] All E.R. (D) 262 (Dec); *GB Gas Holdings Ltd v Accenture (UK) Ltd* [2010] EWCA Civ 912; [2010] All E.R. (D) 341 (Jul).

[176] *Holliday v Overton* 51 E.R. 366; (1852) 14 Beav 467; *Leggott v Barrett* (1880) L.R. 15 Ch. D. 306; 51 L.J. Ch. 90; 28 W.R. 962; *Mackenzie v Duke of Devonshire*; sub nom. *Duke of Devonshire, Special Case; Lady Constance Mackenzie v Countess of Cromartie; Special Case for the Duke of Devonshire* [1896] A.C. 400; (1896) 23 R. (H.L.) 32; (1896) 4 S.L.T. 12; *Royal Insurance Co Ltd v G&S Assured Investment Co Ltd and Growth and Secured Life Assurance Society Ltd* [1972] 1 Lloyd's Rep. 267 Ch; *Rutter (Inspector of Taxes) v Charles Sharpe & Co Ltd* [1979] 1 W.L.R. 1429; [1979] S.T.C. 711; 53 T.C. 163 Ch; *Brookfield Construction (UK) Ltd v Foster & Partners Ltd*; sub nom. *Brookfield Construction (UK) Ltd v Foster* [2009] EWHC 307 (TCC); [2009] B.L.R. 246; 123 Con. L.R. 47.

[177] *Farstad Supply AS v Enviroco Ltd; The Far Service* [2011] UKSC 16; [2011] 1 W.L.R. 921; [2011] 3 All E.R. 451.

[178] See for example *Barnard v Faber* [1893] 1 Q.B. 340; 62 L.J.Q.B. 159; 4 R 201; *Cresswell* [2004] EWCA Civ 602; [2004] 2 All E.R. (Comm) 244; [2004] Lloyd's Rep. I.R. 537. See also above, Ch.12 for further discussion of warranties, conditions, conditions precedent and innominate terms.

[179] *National Farmers' Union Mutual Insurance Society Ltd v Dawson* [1941] 2 K.B. 424; 70 Ll. L. Rep. 167; 111 L.J.K.B. 38; *Navrom v Callitsis Ship Management SA (The Radauti)* [1987] 2 Lloyd's Rep. 276 QB and on appeal at [1988] 2 Lloyd's Rep. 416 CA.

[180] *Gregory Projects (Halifax) Ltd v Tenpin (Halifax) Ltd* [2009] EWHC 2639 (Ch); [2010] 2 All E.R. (Comm) 646; [2009] N.P.C. 122; *Bank of New York Mellon v GV Films Ltd* [2009] EWHC 3315 (Comm); [2010] 2 All E.R. (Comm) 285; [2010] 1 Lloyd's Rep. 425.

[181] See for example *SBJ Stephenson Ltd v Mandy* [2000] I.R.L.R. 233 at 237; [2000] F.S.R. 286 at 297 where the court held that "although ... the agreement provides that clause headings are inserted for convenience only and shall not affect the construction of the agreement, it seems to me that the convenience which they provide is to tell the reader what the clause is all about". Similar reasoning was applied in *Doughty Hanson & Co Ltd v Roe* [2007] EWHC 2212 (Ch); [2009] B.C.C. 126; [2008] 1 B.C.L.C. 404.

[182] The orthodox, absolutist view that deleted words ceased to exist at the point of deletion and could not be considered (see *A & J Inglis v Buttery & Co* (1878) 3 App. Cas. 552; (1878) 5 R (H.L.) 87; 15 S.L.R. 462) has been softened in recent years; see for example *City and Westminster Properties (1934) Ltd v Mudd* [1959] Ch. 129; [1958] 3 W.L.R. 312; [1958] All E.R. 733; *Wates Construction (London) Ltd v Franthom Property Ltd* (1991) 53 B.L.R. 23; (1991) 7 Const. L.J. 243 CA.

documents[183] appears now to be doubted.[184] Further, it is a truism that the consideration of deleted clauses is more useful in determining what the parties did not intend as opposed to what they did intend[185]; however, that can be of particular importance and use when considering whether terms should be implied into a contract should it be necessary.[186]

13-070 **Explanatory notes.** It is debateable whether explanatory notes to contracts will be admissible. It has been suggested that at the very least they might inform the factual matrix and thus what the reasonable observer would have understood the contract to mean.[187] However, there are conflicting authorities as to whether the guidance notes issued together with construction contracts ought to be considered.[188]

Other general guidance is not admissible; accordingly in *CA Blackwell (Contractors) Ltd v Gerling Allegemeine Verischerungs AG*,[189] the court declined to take account of a report by the Advanced Study Group No.208B of the Insurance Institute of London[190] when construing the meaning and effect of the DE clauses.[191] Further, the courts have made clear that notes prepared by the parties themselves are likely to be treated as inadmissible statements of their subjective opinion as to the meaning of the contract.[192]

13-071 **The parol evidence rule.** The extent to which parties may rely on extrinsic evidence in order to establish the meaning of a contract are severely curtailed by the parol evidence rule. In short the rule does not permit parties to adduce any extrinsic evidence to qualify the written words used or to evince the intentions of

---

183 See for example *Dreyfus (Louis) et Cie v Parnaso Cia Naviera SA, The Dominator* [1959] 1 Q.B. 498 at 513; [1959] 2 W.L.R. 405 at 412; [1959] 1 All E.R. 502 at 506–507, per Diplock J and *Timber Shipping Co SA v London & Overseas Freighters Ltd* [1972] A.C. 1 at 15; [1971] 2 W.L.R. 1360 at 1366; [1971] 2 All E.R. 599 at 603, per Lord Reid.

184 See for example *Bovis Lend Lease Ltd v Cofely Engineering Services* [2009] EWHC 1120 (TCC); [2009] All E.R. (D) 23 (Sep); *Mopani Copper Mines Plc v Millenium Underwriting Ltd* [2008] EWHC 1331 (Comm); [2008] 2 All E.R. (Comm) 976; [2008] 1 C.L.C. 992; *Ted Baker plc v Axa Insurance UK Plc* [2012] EWHC 1406 (Comm) at [83]–[84], per Eder J.

185 *City and Westminster Properties (1934) Ltd v Mudd* [1959] 1 Ch. 129; [1958] 3 W.L.R. 312; [1958] All E.R. 733 Ch; *Punjab National Bank v De Boinville* [1992] 1 W.L.R. 1138; [1992] 3 All E.R. 104; [1992] 1 Lloyd's Rep. 7 CA.

186 See for example *Team Services Plc v Kier Management & Design Ltd* (1993) 63 B.L.R. 76; (1993) 36 Con. L.R. 32, where the court rejected a suggested implied term that would have been inconsistent with a clear deletion from the contract.

187 *Investors Compensation Scheme Ltd* [1998] 1 W.L.R. 896; [1998] 1 All E.R. 98; [1998] 1 B.C.L.C. 493.

188 In *Hall Ortech (Matthew) Ltd v Tarmac Roadstone Ltd* (1997) 87 B.L.R. 96 QB, the court considered that it could have regard to the guidance notes in relation to the Institute of Chemical Engineers, *Model Form of Conditions of Contract for Process Plants: Suitable for Lump Sum Contracts in the United Kingdom*, 2nd edn (Rugby: Institute of Chemical Engineers, 1981); whereas in *TFW Printers Ltd v Interserve Project Services Ltd* [2006] EWCA Civ 875; [2006] 2 C.L.C. 106; [2006] B.L.R. 299 the Court of Appeal was less convinced that it should consider the guidance notes to the JCT, *Joint Contracts Tribunal Agreement for Minor Building Works* (London: RIBA Publications, 1993).

189 *CA Blackwell (Contractors) Ltd* [2007] EWCA Civ 1450; [2008] 1 All E.R. (Comm) 885; [2008] Lloyd's Rep. I.R. 529.

190 Advanced Study Group No. 208B. *Construction Insurance/report of Advanced Study Group 208B.* (London: IIL, 1999).

191 See below, Ch.16.

192 See for example *Young v Brooks* [2008] EWCA Civ 816 at [10] and [12]; [2008] 3 E.G.L.R. 27 at 29; [2008] 37 E.G. 148 at 150–151, per Rimer L.J.

the parties.[193] Despite the nomenclature, parol evidence extends to any evidence whether oral or written.[194] The rule is fundamental to the concept that contracts must be interpreted objectively and that the parties' evidence of their subjective intentions is irrelevant. As Lord Hobhouse said:

> "The rule that other evidence may not be adduced to contradict the provisions of a contract contained in a written document is fundamental to the mercantile law of this country; the bargain is the document; the certainty of the contract depends on it."[195]

Pre-contractual negotiations and draft contracts. The key exclusion from the   **13-072** matters that the court may take into account when construing a document is evidence of the parties' pre-contractual negotiations.[196] This exclusion was expressly preserved by Lord Hoffmann in *Investors Compensation Scheme Ltd*[197] and is rooted in public policy. Indeed, it has been said "in this respect only, legal interpretation differs from the way we would interpret utterances in ordinary life".[198]

In *Prenn v Simmonds* it was said: **13-073**

> "The reason for not admitting evidence of these exchanges is not a technical one or even mainly one of convenience … It is simply that such evidence is unhelpful. By the nature of things, where negotiations are difficult, the parties' positions, with each passing letter, are changing and until the final agreement, though converging, still divergent. It is only the final document which records a consensus. If the previous documents use different expressions, how does construction of those expressions, itself a doubtful process, help on the construction of the contractual words? If the same expressions are used, nothing is gained by looking back: indeed, something may be lost since the relevant surrounding circumstances may be different. And at this stage there is no consensus of the parties to appeal to. It may be said that previous documents may be looked at to explain the aims of the parties. In a limited sense this is true: the commercial, or business object, of the transaction, objectively ascertained, may be a surrounding fact."[199]

A similar approach has been adopted in relation to draft documents. In *National*   **13-074**
Bank of Australasia Ltd v J Falkingham & Sons[200] Lord Lindley made clear that

---

[193] *Gillespie Bros & Co v Cheney, Eggar & Co* [1896] 2 Q.B. 59; 65 L.J.Q.B. 552; 1 Com. Cas. 373; *Burges v Wickham* 122 E.R. 251; (1863) 3 B. & S. 669 at 696; *Blackett v The Royal Exchange Assurance Co* 149 E.R. 106; (1832) 2 Cr. & J. 244 at 251; *Reliance Marine Insurance Co v Duder* [1913] 1 K.B. 265 at 273; 81 L.J.K.B. 870; 12 Asp. M.L.C. 223.

[194] *Miller v Travers* 131 E.R. 395; (1832) 8 Bing. 244.

[195] *Shogun Finance Ltd v Hudson* [2003] UKHL 62 at [49]; [2004] 1 A.C. 919 at 944; [2003] 3 W.L.R. 1371 at 1385–1387.

[196] Brett LJ. In *Leggott* (1880) L.R. 15 Ch. D. 306 at 311; 51 L.J. Ch. 90 at 93; 28 W.R. 962 at 963; *Henderson v Arthur* [1907] 1 K.B. 10 at 13; 76 L.J.K.B. 22 at 24; 51 S.J. 65.

[197] *Investors Compensation Scheme Ltd* [1998] 1 W.L.R. 896 at 912–913; [1998] 1 All E.R. 98 at 114 115; [1998] 1 B.C.L.C. 493 at 547–548. The rationale for the exclusion was discussed in detail in *Chartbrook Ltd* [2009] UKHL 38 at [28]–[29]; [2009] A.C. 1101 at 1102 and 1115–1122; [2009] 4 All E.R. 677 at 689–690. See also *Ted Baker Plc v Axa Insurance UK Plc* [2012] EWHC 1406 (Comm) at [87], per Eder J.

[198] *Investors Compensation Scheme Ltd* [1998] 1 W.L.R. 896 at 913; [1998] 1 All E.R. 98 at 114; [1998] 1 B.C.L.C. 493 at 547.

[199] *Prenn* [1971] 1 W.L.R. 1381 at 1384 1385; [1971] 3 All E.R. 237 at 240.

[200] *National Bank of Australasia Ltd v J Falkingham & Sons* [1902] A.C. 585 at 591; 71 L.J.PC. 105 at 106; 18 T.L.R. 737 at 738; see also *Leggott* (1880) L.R. 15 Ch. D. 306; 51 L.J. Ch. 90; 28 W.R. 962; *Mercantile Bank of Sydney v Taylor* [1893] A.C. 317; 57 J.P. 741; 1 R. 371; *Lee v Alexander* (1883) 8 App. Cas. 853; 10 R. (H.L.) 91; 20 S.L.R. 877; *British Equitable Assurance Co Ltd v Baily* [1906] A.C. 35; 75 L.J. Ch. 73; 13 Mans 13; *City and Westminster Properties (1934) Ltd v Mudd* [1959] Ch. 129; [1958] 3 W.L.R. 312; [1958] All E.R. 733.

drafts, as with previous negotiations, are generally inadmissible; however, a signed draft may be admissible when the final copies did not reflect that agreement.[201]

13-075   It follows from the rule that pre-contractual negotiations are inadmissible that evidence that clauses were specifically deleted from earlier drafts is not admissible in relation to the interpretation of the final concluded agreement. However, it is arguable that evidence of previous drafts may be admitted as part of the investigation of the factual matrix to prove that a fact was known to the parties. In *Chartbrook Ltd*, Lord Hoffmann said:

> "The [parol evidence] rule excludes evidence of what was said or done during the course of negotiating the agreement for the purpose of drawing inferences about what the contract meant. It does not exclude the use of such evidence for other purposes: for example, to establish that a fact which may be relevant as background was known to the parties, or to support a claim for rectification or estoppel. These are not exceptions to the rule, they operate outside it."[202]

13-076 The factual matrix.   The court may consider extrinsic evidence in order to determine the background knowledge that would reasonably have been available to the parties at the time of the contract. In *Reardon Smith Line Ltd v Hansen-Tangen (The Diana Prosperity)* Lord Wilberforce stated that

> "what the court must do must be to place itself in thought in the same factual matrix as that in which the parties were. All of these opinions seem to me implicitly to recognise that, in the search for the relevant background, there may be facts which form part of the circumstances in which the parties contract in which one, or both, may take no particular interest, their minds being addressed to or concentrated on other facts so that if asked they would assert that they did not have these facts in the forefront of their mind, but that will not prevent those facts from forming part of an objective setting in which the contract is to be construed."[203]

13-077   This factual matrix includes:

> "absolutely anything which would have affected the way in which the language of the document would have been understood by a reasonable man,"[204]

subject to the proviso that the information would reasonably have been available to the parties at the time of, or before the contract was entered into.[205] It ought to have gone without saying but the House of Lords has also confirmed that the factual

---

[201] *Ingleby v Slack* (1890) 6 T.L.R. 284.

[202] *Chartbrook Ltd* [2009] UKHL 38 at [42]; [2009] 1 A.C. 1101 at 1121; [2009] 4 All E.R. 677 at 695 see also *Governor and Co of the Bank of Scotland v Dunedin Property Investment Co Ltd* 1998 S.C. 657; S.L.T. 470; 1998 S.C.L.R. 531.

[203] *Reardon Smith Line Ltd v Yngvar Hansen-Tangen (t/a H.E. Hansen-Tangen); Yngvar Hansen-Tangen (t/a H.E. Hansen-Tangen) v Sanko Steamship Co*; sub nom. *Reardon Smith Line Ltd v Hansen-Tangen (The Diana Prosperity); Hansen-Tangen v Sanko Steamship Co Ltd, The Diana Prosperity* [1976] 1 W.L.R. 989 at 997; [1976] 3 All E.R. 570 at 575; [1976] 2 Lloyd's Rep. 621 at 625–626.

[204] *Investors Compensation Scheme* [1998] 1 W.L.R. 896 at 913; [1998] 1 All E.R. 98 at 114; [1998] 1 B.C.L.C. 493 at 494, per Lord Hoffmann. The factual matrix includes the statutory context and the relevant law at the time the contract was entered into; *Doleman v Shaw* [2009] EWCA Civ 279; [2009] Bus LR 1175 at [35], per Mummery LJ and at [56], per Elias LJ.

[205] *Prenn* [1971] 1 W.L.R. 1381 at 1385; [1971] 3 All E.R. 237 at 240–241; *Investors Compensation Scheme* [1998] 1 W.L.R. 896 at 912–913; [1998] 1 All E.R. 98 at 114–115; [1998] 1 B.C.L.C. 493 at 547–548, per Lord Hoffmann; *Arnold v Britton* [2015] UKSC 36 at [21]; [2015] A.C. 1619; [2016] 1 All E.R. 1, per Lord Neuberger who emphasised that: "When interpreting a contractual provision, one can only take into account facts or circumstances which existed at the time that the contract was made, and which were known or reasonably available to both parties. Given that a contract is a bilateral, or synallagmatic, arrangement involving both parties, it cannot be right, when interpreting a contractual provision, to take into account a fact or circumstance known only to one of the

matrix only includes matters that a reasonable person would have regarded as relevant.[206]

Other admissible extrinsic evidence. Despite the impact of the parol evidence **13-078** rule, extrinsic evidence still plays a major part in disputes as to the meaning and effect of contracts. It is apparent from the preceding discussions that there are in fact a number of circumstances in which the court is permitted to consider extrinsic evidence and it is probably fair to say that the parol evidence rule is probably easier defined by its exclusions. In particular, extrinsic evidence may be admissible:

1. in order to establish whether a contract has come into existence at all because the parties were never ad idem,[207] or because there was no consideration[208];
2. in order to establish which party proffered a term for the purposes of the *contra proferentem* rule[209];
3. where a contract is part written and part oral or where it can be demonstrated that the policy documents were not intended to be a complete record of the contract[210];
4. where the court must determine disputes over words with specialist, technical or customary meanings and to determine the meanings given by the parties to words in their own lexicon[211];
5. where a party alleges that the document does not embody the true agreement between the parties[212];
6. in order to cure uncertainty or patent or latent ambiguity in a written instrument[213];
7. where the court is required to consider alleged variations,[214] waivers and questions of estoppel[215];
8. where there are allegations as to the existence of a collateral agreement inconsistent or different to the agreement being construed;

---

parties".
[206] *Bank of Credit and Commerce International SA* [2001] UKHL 8; [2002] 1 A.C. 251; [2001] 2 W.L.R. 735.
[207] See for example *Pattle v Hornibrook* [1897] 1 Ch. 25; 66 L.J. Ch. 144; 45 W.R. 123; *Scriven Bros & Co v Hindley & Co* [1913] 3 K.B. 564; 83 LJKB 40; 109 L.T. 526; *Orion Insurance Co Plc v Sphere Drake Insurance Plc* [1992] 1 Lloyd's Rep. 239.
[208] *Equitable Fire and Accident Office Ltd v Ching Wo Hong* [1907] A.C. 96; 76 L.J.P.C. 31; 96 L.T. 1.
[209] *Denby* [1998] C.L.C. 870; [1998] Lloyd's Rep. I.R. 343; [1998] All E.R. (D) 88.
[210] See *Gillespie Bros & Co* [1896] 2 Q.B. 59; 65 L.J.Q.B. 552; 1 Com. Cas. 373 where Lord Russell CJ explained that although the reduction of an agreement to writing created a strong presumption that the agreement embodied the parties' agreement, that presumption can be rebutted and parties should be allowed to adduce evidence in order to do so. See also *City and Westminster Properties* (1934) Ltd [1959] 1 Ch. 129; [1958] 3 W.L.R. 312; [1958] All E.R. 733. That presumption is even stronger in relation to insurance policies; *Wheelton v Hardisty* (1858) 8 El. & Bl. 285.
[211] See above paras 13-015 to 13-019.
[212] *Guardian Ocean Cargoes Ltd v Banco do Brasil SA (The Golden Med)*; sub nom. *Guardian Ocean Cargoes Ltd, Transorient Ship Cargoes Ltd, Middle East Agents SAL and Med Lines SA v Banco do Brasil SA* [1991] 2 Lloyd's Rep. 68.
[213] See discussion above at para.13-044.
[214] *Goss v Lord Nugent* [1824] All E.R. Rep. 305; (1833) 5 B. & Ad. 58.
[215] *Stuart v Freeman* [1903] 1 K.B. 47; 72 L.J.K.B. 1; 51 W.R. 211; *Davies v National Fire and Marine Insurance Co of New Zealand* [1891] A.C. 485; 60 L.J.P.C. 73; 65 L.T. 560.

9. where there are allegations that the contract is void or voidable on the basis of duress,[216] fraud or misrepresentation,[217] or illegality[218];
10. where the relief sought is an equitable remedy such as rectification, rescission or specific performance.

13-079 Post-contract events. The meaning of a contract will be construed as at the time that it was entered into.[219] Events that occur after a contract is entered into can have no bearing on its meaning; accordingly evidence of post-contract events will be inadmissible for the purpose of interpretation.[220] The rationale for this approach is obvious; should subsequent conduct be taken into account, it could mean that an agreement meant one thing the day it was signed but something completely different at some point in the future.[221]

13-080 However evidence of post-contract events may be admissible in a limited number of circumstances, principally:

1. in order to determine the terms of a contract that were part-written and part-oral[222]; and
2. where it is alleged that there has been a variation, waiver or estoppel by convention.[223]

13-081 In some cases, if a subsequent event occurs that, on the basis of the language used in the contract, was neither intended nor contemplated by the parties, the Court is entitled to consider how such events can be dealt with under the contract. If it is clear from the language used by the parties and from the context of the contract as a whole what the parties would have intended, the Court may give effect to that intention.

---

[216] *Williams v Bayley* (1866) L.R. 1 H.L. 200; 30 JP 500; 35 L.J. Ch. 717.

[217] *Pickering v Dowson* 128 E.R. 537; (1813) 4 Taunt. 779; *Dobell v Stevens* 107 E.R. 864; (1825) 3 B. & C. 623; *Pennsylvania Shipping Co v Compagnie National de Navigation* [1936] 2 All E.R. 1167; 55 Ll. L. Rep. 271; 42 Com. Cas. 45; *Curtis v Chemical Cleaning and Dyeing Co* [1951] 1 K.B. 805; [1951] 1 All E.R. 631; [1951] 1 T.L.R. 452 CA.

[218] *Madell v Thomas & Co* [1891] 1 Q.B. 230; 60 L.J.Q.B. 227; 39 W.R. 280; *Morris v Baron & Co* [1918] A.C. 1; 87 L.J.K.B. 145; 118 L.T. 34.

[219] *James Miller & Partners v Whitworth Street Estates (Manchester) Ltd* [1970] A.C. 583; [1970] 2 W.L.R. 728; [1970] 1 All E.R. 796; *L Schuler AG* [1974] A.C. 235; [1973] 2 W.L.R. 683; [1973] 2 All E.R. 39.

[220] *Union Insurance Society of Canton Ltd v George Willis & Co* [1916] 1 A.C. 281; 85 L.J.C. 82, 13 Asp. M.L.C. 233; *Absalom (on behalf of Lloyd's Syndicate 957) v TCRU Ltd; Absalom v TCRU Ltd (formerly Monument Insurance Brokers Ltd)* [2005] EWCA Civ 1586; [2006] 1 All E.R. (Comm) 375; [2006] 2 Lloyd's Rep. 129.

[221] Compare *Amalgamated Investment and Property Co Ltd (In Liquidation) v Texas Commerce International Bank Ltd* [1982] Q.B. 84 at 120; [1981] 3 W.L.R. 565 at 573; [1981] 3 All E.R. 577 at 584 where Lord Denning accepted the state of the current law but questioned its application when interpreting ambiguous clauses.

[222] In *Maggs (t/a BM Builders) v Marsh* [2006] EWCA Civ 1058; [2006] B.L.R. 395; [2006] C.I.L.L. 2369, Smith LJ explained that where oral terms were contended for, the court's task was to assess the accuracy of the parties' recollections as to what was agreed; their conduct in reliance on that agreement was admissible evidence as to whose recollection was more likely. See also, *Kellogg Brown & Root Inc v Concordia Maritime AG* [2006] EWHC 3358 (Comm); *Great North Eastern Railway Ltd v Avon Insurance Plc* [2001] EWCA Civ 780; [2001] 2 All E.R. (Comm) 526; [2001] 2 Lloyd's Rep. 649; *ED&F Man Commodity Advisers Ltd v Fluxo-Cane Overseas Ltd* [2009] EWCA Civ 406; *Kier Regional Ltd (t/a Wallis) v City & General (Holborn) Ltd* [2008] EWHC 2454 (TCC); [2009] B.L.R. 90; (2009) 25 Const. L.J. 36.

[223] *James Miller & Partners Ltd* [1970] A.C. 583 at 611; [1970] 2 W.L.R. 728 at 739–740; [1970] 1 All E.R. 796 at 805; *Amalgamated Investment and Property Co Ltd (In Liquidation)* [1982] Q.B. 84; [1981] 3 W.L.R. 565; [1981] 3 All E.R. 577.

In *Aberdeen City Council v Stewart Milne Group Ltd*,[224] the Supreme Court considered a contract for the sale of development land which provided for the vendor to receive an uplift on the purchase price based on a specified percentage of the "estimated profit" (defined by reference to "open market value") or "the gross sale proceeds" upon disposal of the land by the purchaser. The purchaser sold the land at an undervalue to an associated company. Lord Clarke appreciated that:

"... unlike *Rainy Sky*, this is not a case in where there are two alternative available constructions of the language used. It is rather a case in which, notwithstanding the language used, the parties must have intended that, in the event of an on sale, the appellants would pay the respondents the appropriate share of the proceeds of sale on the assumption that the on sale was at a market price."

Lord Clarke resolved the question in *Aberdeen City Council* by holding that there was an implied term that, in the event of a sale which was not at arm's length in the open market, an open market valuation should be used. However, the Supreme Court in *Arnold v Britton* considered that this could equally be a question of construction. Approving the approach in *Aberdeen City Council*, Lord Neuberger (with whom Lord Sumption and Lord Hughes agreed) said:

"... in some cases, an event subsequently occurs which was plainly not intended or contemplated by the parties, judging from the language of their contract. In such a case, if it is clear what the parties would have intended, the court will give effect to that intention. An example of such a case is *Aberdeen City Council v Stewart Milne Group Ltd* [2011] UKSC 56, 2012 SCLR 114, where the court concluded that 'any ... approach' other than that which was adopted 'would defeat the parties' clear objectives', but the conclusion was based on what the parties 'had in mind when they entered into' the contract (see paras 17 and 22)."[225]

3. RECTIFICATION AND THE CORRECTION OF MISTAKES

Correction of mistakes. The construction principles referred to demonstrate that the courts have developed various techniques for construing words in a way that is commercially sensible and that the court will strive, where possible, to give effect to the intention of the parties. There may, however, be situations in which the disconnect between the parties' actual agreement and the words they have used to record it is so great that the record itself must be modified in order to reflect the parties' intentions. In English law there are two primary routes by which such corrections can be made. First, the court may use the techniques of construction discussed above in order to correct obvious mistakes. Secondly, the equitable remedy of rectification is available where the document recording the parties' agreement does not accord with their common intention. **13-082**

Correction by construction. Where there are obvious errors in a policy that mean the policy does not accurately reflect the true agreement between the parties and where the required correction is also clear, the court may correct the mistake without recourse to the equitable remedy of rectification.[226] In *East v Pantiles (Plant Hire) Ltd* it was said that: **13-083**

---

[224] *Aberdeen City Council v Stewart Milne Group Ltd* [2011] UKSC 576; 2012 SCLR 114.

[225] *Arnold v Britton* at [22]. See also Lord Hodge at [71] who considered *Aberdeen City Council* as an example of a case where "the internal context of the contract pointed towards the commercially sensible interpretation" and Lord Carnwath, who in his dissenting judgment, also noted that the decision in *Aberdeen City Council* could be considered a case of correction by interpretation (see below, paras.13-083 to 13-086).

[226] This technique is sometimes referred to as "common law rectification"; however such nomenclature

"a mistake in a written instrument can, in limited circumstances, be corrected as a matter of construction without obtaining a decree in an action for rectification. Two conditions must be satisfied: first, there must be a clear mistake on the face of the instrument; secondly, it must be clear what correction ought to be made in order to cure the mistake. If those conditions are satisfied, then the correction is made as a matter of construction. If they are not satisfied, then either the claimant must pursue an action for rectification or he must leave it to a court of construction to reach what answer it can on the basis that the uncorrected wording represents the manner in which the parties decided to express their intention."[227]

13-084   That approach has been cited with approval by the House of Lords in *Chartbrook Ltd*,[228] subject to the two qualifications set down by Carnwarth LJ in *KPMG LLP v Network Rail Infrastructure Ltd*, which are:

1.   correction by construction is merely part of the process of construing a document and should not be considered a separate exercise or some form of summary rectification procedure[229]; and
2.   whilst the mistake must be evident on the "face of the instrument", in determining whether such a mistake exists, the court is entitled to consider the same evidence of the factual matrix as it could consider on any other exercise of interpretation.[230]

13-085   The limits of correction by construction are presently unclear but it is apparent that the courts will take a broad approach. In *G & S Brough Ltd v Salvage Wharf Ltd* Jackson LJ said:

"Where a written agreement as drafted is a nonsense and it is clear what the parties were trying to say the court will, as a matter of construction, give effect to the obvious intentions of the parties."[231]

Further, Lord Hoffmann made clear in *Chartbrook Ltd* that

"there is not, so to speak, a limit to the amount of red ink or verbal rearrangement or correction which the court is allowed. All that is required is that it should be clear ... what a reasonable person would have understood the parties to have meant."[232]

13-086   For example, in *Mourmand v Le Clair*, the court was able to insert a unit of payment by construction where the underlying agreement was silent.[233] Whilst in

---

is misleading. Correction by construction remains bound by the normal rules of construction and the strictures of admissible evidence: see *Chartbrook Ltd* [2009] UKHL 38; [2009] 1 A.C. 1101; [2009] 4 All E.R. 677.

[227] *East v Pantiles (Plant Hire) Ltd* [1982] 2 E.G.L.R. 111 at 112; 263 E.G. 61; see also *City Alliance Ltd v Oxford Forecasting Services Ltd* [2001] 1 All E.R. (Comm) 233; [2000] All E.R. (D) 1865.

[228] *Chartbrook Ltd* [2009] UKHL 38 at [23]–[25]; [2009] 1 A.C. 1101 at 1114; [2009] 4 All E.R. 677 at 688–699.

[229] *KPMG LLP v Network Rail Infrastructure Ltd* [2007] EWCA Civ 363 at [47]–[50]; [2007] Bus L.R. 1336 at 1350 and 1351; [2008] 1 P. & C.R. 11 187 at 203–204.

[230] *KPMG LLP* [2007] EWCA Civ 363 at [46]–[50]; [2007] Bus L.R. 1336 at 1350–1351; [2008] 1 P. & C.R. 11 187 at 202–204. See also *Holding & Barnes Plc v Hill House Hammond Ltd* [2001] EWCA Civ 1334; [2002] 2 P. & C.R. 11 145; *The Starsin* [2003] UKHL 12; [2004] 1 A.C. 715; [2003] 2 W.L.R. 711.

[231] *G & S Brough Ltd v Salvage Wharf Ltd* [2009] EWCA Civ 21 at [80]; [2010] Ch. 11 at 29; [2009] 3 W.L.R. 990 at 1006.

[232] *Chartbrook Ltd* [2009] UKHL 38 at [25]; [2009] 1 A.C. 1101 at 1114; [2009] 4 All E.R. 677 at 688–689.

[233] *Mourmand v Le Clair* [1903] 2 K.B. 216; 72 L.J.K.B. 496; 10 Mans. 261 K.B. The contract provided for repayments of "seven" per month. The court was able to construe the clause as seven pounds on the basis that seven shillings or seven pence would be absurd.

another case the court was able to read the words "actually paid" as meaning "actually payable" in the context of a reinsurance policy.[234]

Rectification. Where a policy does not reflect the parties' intentions and cannot   **13-087**
be corrected by construction (perhaps because it is not obvious in the language that there is a mistake or because the correction required in order to reflect the parties' intentions is not readily apparent) either party has the right to seek rectification of the policy.[235] It is important to note that the remedy of rectification is not there to rewrite the parties' bargain it is only used to rewrite the written expression of that bargain where it is clear that the writing does not reflect the true agreement.[236] As Mustill J stated in *Etablissements Georges et Paul Levy*:

> "Rectification may be granted in two situations: (a) where there is a mistake common to both parties, the mistake being that the document accurately records the transaction. (The fact that the mistake must be shared does not necessarily mean that it must arise in the same way on each side. Very often the mistake of one party occurs in the writing and of the other in the signing of the document, but the mistaken belief is common to both.); (b) where one party is mistaken as to the compliance of the document with the transaction and the other party knows of this mistaken belief but does nothing to correct it. The person seeking rectification in this situation must, in effect, establish that his opponent was guilty of sharp practice."[237]

Mutual mistake. The most common claim for rectification of insurance poli-   **13-088**
cies is based on the notion of mutual mistake; in other words the idea that both parties had reached a prior understanding that was not accurately reflected in the agreement. The label "mutual mistake" has been criticised as confusing the element of mutuality, which requires a mutual common intention, with the element of mistake, which can be an error committed by any party that results in the agreement as drafted failing to reflect the mutual common intention.[238] The requirements of a claim for rectification on the basis of mutual mistake have been authoritatively and helpfully stated by Gibson LJ in *Swainland Builders Ltd v Freehold Properties Ltd* as follows:

> "The party seeking rectification must show that: (1) the parties had a common continuing intention, whether or not amounting to an agreement, in respect of a particular matter in the instrument to be rectified; (2) there was an outward expression of accord; (3) the intention continued at the same time

---

[234] *Charter Reinsurance Co Ltd v Fagan* [1997] A.C. 313; [1996] 2 W.L.R. 726; [1996] 3 All E.R. 46 HL.

[235] See for example *Motteux v The Governor & Co of London Assurance* 26 E.R. 343; (1739) 1 Atk 545; *Henkle v Royal Exchange Assurance Co* 27 E.R. 1055; (1749) 1 Ves. Sen. 317; *Collett v Morrison* 68 E.R. 458; (1851) 9 Hare 162; *Burroughes v Abbott* [1922] 1 Ch. 86; 91 L.J. Ch. 157; [1921] All E.R. Rep. 709 Ch; *Jervis v Howle and Talke Colliery Co Ltd* [1937] Ch. 67; [1936] 3 All E.R. 193; 106 L.J. Ch. 34; *Sun Life Assurance Co of Canada v Jervis* [1943] 2 All E.R. 425.

[236] *Etablissements Levy (Georges et Paul) v Adderley Navigation Co Panama SA (The Olympic Pride)* [1980] 2 Lloyd's Rep. 67 QB; *Agip SpA v Navigazione Alta Italia SpA (The Nai Genova and Nai Superba)* [1984] 1 Lloyd's Rep. 353; *Youell* [1992] 2 Lloyd's Rep. 127.

[237] *Establissements Levy (Georges et Paul)* [1980] 2 Lloyd's Rep. 67 at 72 QB.

[238] For further discussion see the commentary in *MacGillivray on Insurance Law*, edited by J. Birds, B. Lynch, S. Milnes, 13th edn (London: Sweet & Maxwell, 2015), paras 12-007 to 12-009. One of the most common "mistakes" is clerical error either by a broker or by clerical staff of the insurer In either instance it is impossible to say that the "mistake" was mutual; however rectification is available if the mistake renders the policy different to the parties' common intention (see *Alliance Aeroplane Co Ltd v Union Insurance Society of Canton Ltd* (1920) 5 Lloyd's Reports 341; *Sun Life Assurance Co of Canada* [1943] 2 All E.R. 425). For general purposes the parenthetical comments from Mustill J in a passage from *Establissements Levy (Georges et Paul)* [1980] 2 Lloyd's Rep. 67, set out above in para.13-087, serve as an excellent guide to keeping the two concepts separate.

of the execution of the instrument sought to be rectified; (4) by mistake, the instrument did not reflect that common intention."[239]

13-089 Common intention. Some older authorities suggested that the remedy of rectification was only available in circumstances where the claimant could prove that there had been a concluded antecedent agreement inconsistent with the written record.[240] That is no longer the case; and it is sufficient to prove that there was an existing common intention evidenced by an outward expression of accord,[241] even if that expression of accord was not sufficient to create a contract.[242] However, it is necessary for the party claiming rectification to be able to express the common intention with precision; uncertainty may be fatal to a claim in rectification.[243]

13-090 Objective common intention. When assessing whether there was a common intention, again, the court adopts an objective test, indeed

> "it would be anomalous if the 'common continuing intention' were to be an objective fact if it amounted to an enforceable contract but a subjective belief if it did not."[244]

Perhaps the best exposition of this principle is the statement by Denning LJ in *Frederick E Rose (London) Ltd v William H Pim Junior & Co Ltd*:

> "Rectification is concerned with contracts and documents, not with intentions. In order to get rectification it is necessary to show that the parties were in complete agreement on the terms of their contract, but by an error wrote them down wrongly; and in this regard, in order to ascertain the terms of the contract, you do not look into the inner minds of the parties—into their intentions—any more than you do in the formation of any other contract. You look at their outward acts, that is, at what they said or wrote to one another in coming to their agreement, and then compare it with the document which they have signed. If you can predicate with certainty what their contract was, and that it is, by a common mistake, wrongly expressed in the document, then you rectify the document; but nothing less will suffice."[245]

13-091 In *Daventry District Council v Daventry & District Housing Association*,

---

[239] *Swainland Builders Ltd v Freehold Properties Ltd* [2002] EWCA Civ 560 at [33]; [2002] 2 E.G.L.R. 71 at 74; [2002] 23 E.G. 123 at 126. This formulation was cited with approval by the Court of Appeal in *Daventry District Council v Daventry & District Housing Association Ltd* [2011] EWCA Civ 1153; [2012] 1 W.L.R. 1333; [2012] 2 All E.R. (Comm) 142. See also the similar formulation proposed by Slade LJ in *Agip SpA* [1984] 1 Lloyd's Rep. 353 at 359 as approved in *Kiriacoulis Lines SA v Compagnie d'Assurances Maritime Aeriennes et Terrestres (CAMAT) (The Demetra K)* [2002] EWCA Civ 1070; [2002] 2 Lloyd's Rep. 581; [2002] Lloyd's I.R. 795; *Dunlop Haywards (DHL) Ltd v Erinaceous Insurance Services Ltd* [2009] EWCA Civ 354; [2009] Lloyd's Rep. I.R. 464.
[240] See for example *Lovell & Christmas Ltd v Wall* (1911) 104 L.T. 85; 27 T.L.R. 236; [1911-13] All E.R. Rep. Ext 1630.
[241] Some authorities suggested that the requirement for an outward expression of accord was more of an evidential matter than a strict part of the legal test (see for example *Munt v Beasley* [2006] EWCA Civ 370; [2006] All E.R. (D) 29 (Apr)); however, *Chartbrook Ltd* [2009] UKHL 38; [2009] 1 A.C. 1101; [2009] 4 All E.R. 677 has now reconfirmed that it is part of the legal requirement for rectification.
[242] *Alliance Aeroplane Co Ltd* (1920) 5 Lloyd's Rep. 341; *Joscelyne v Nissen* [1970] 2 Q.B. 86; [1970] 2 W.L.R. 509; [1970] 1 All E.R. 1213 approved by the supreme Court in *Chartbrook Ltd* [2009] UKHL 38 at [57]–[61]; [2009] 1 A.C. 1101 at 1125–1126; [2009] 4 All E.R. 677 at 699–700.
[243] *C H Pearce & Sons Ltd v Stonechester Ltd*, (Unreported) *Times*, 17 November 1983.
[244] *Chartbrook Ltd* [2009] UKHL 38 at [60]; [2009] 1 A.C. 1101 at 1126; [2009] 4 All E.R. 677 at 700, per Lord Hoffmann.
[245] *Frederick E Rose (London) Ltd v William H Pim Junior & Co Ltd* [1953] 2 Q.B. 450 at 461; [1953] 3 W.L.R. 497 at 504–505; [1953] 2 All E.R. 739 at 747 CA; see also *George Cohen Sons & Co Ltd v Docks and Inland Waterways Executive* (1950) 84 Lloyd's Rep. 97; 155 E.G. 290; *Etablissements Levy (Georges et Paul)* [1980] 2 Lloyd's Rep. 67.

Etherton LJ categorised four scenarios that arise from the objective analysis of common intention[246]:

1. first, where parties both subjectively and objectively share a common intention, which is not reflected in the written agreement, the document should normally be rectified (subject to any equitable defences);

2. secondly, where the parties were not subjectively *ad idem* but the contemporaneous communications objectively showed that there was a common intention, a claim in rectification should be refused even though that would bind one or both parties to an intention they did not subjectively possess;

3. thirdly, where there was objectively a common intention, but one of the parties subjectively changed its mind prior to the execution of the contract and did not objectively communicate that change of mind to the other party, then if the document as executed reflects the original common intention, it should not be rectified; whereas if the document as executed reflects the subjective change of mind, it should be rectified to give effect to the objective prior understanding;

4. fourthly, where there was objectively a common intention and one of the parties changed its mind and objectively communicated the same to the other party, then (saving any questions of unilateral mistake) if the document reflects the change of mind, rectification should be refused.

Continuing common intention. In order to advance a claim for rectification it **13-092** is not enough to show that the parties had reached an understanding or accord at some time prior to the execution of the contract; it will often be the case that matters are agreed during negotiations and then deliberately departed from later. It is necessary therefore to show that the common intention continued to subsist at the date of the agreement itself.[247]

Antecedent agreements and slips. Whilst it is no longer a strict requirement to **13-093** prove a binding antecedent agreement in order to establish a claim for rectification, if it can be shown that an antecedent agreement was reached then that will give additional support to a claim in rectification.[248] In the insurance context, this will often arise where there is a discrepancy between the slip and the policy. Where a slip is relied upon it will not matter as to the degree that a slip is incorporated if it shows the intentions of the parties, nor does it matter whether it is a Lloyd's slip, which is enforceable as its own document, or whether it is evidence of an agree-

---

[246] *Daventry District Council* [2011] EWCA Civ 1153 at [85]–[88]; [2012] 1 W.L.R. 1333 at 1355–1356; [2012] 2 All E.R. (Comm) 142 at 164–165. Etherton LJ gave a powerful dissenting judgment but his analysis of the law was accepted by Lord Neuberger MR. See [2011] EWCA Civ 1153 at [227]; [2012] 1 W.L.R. 1333 at 1388; [2012] 2 All E.R. (Comm) 142 at 196.

[247] *Agip SpA* [1984] 1 Lloyd's Rep. 353; *Kiriacoulis Lines SA* [2002] EWCA Civ 1070; [2002] 2 Lloyd's Rep. 581; [2003] 1 C.L.C. 579; *Swainland Builders Ltd v Freehold Properties Ltd* [2002] EWCA Civ 560; [2002] 2 E.G.L.R. 71; [2002] 23 E.G. 123; *Chartbrook Ltd* [2009] UKHL 38; [2009] 1 A.C. 1101, [2009] 4 All E.R. 677; *Dunlop Haywards (DHL) Ltd v Erinaceous Insurance Services Ltd* [2009] EWCA Civ 354; [2009] Lloyd's Rep. I.R. 464; *Dunlop Haywards (DHL) Ltd v Barbon Insurance Group Ltd* [2009] EWHC 2900 (Comm); [2010] Lloyd's Rep. I.R. 149; [2009] All E.R. (D) 254 (Nov); *Daventry District Council* [2011] EWCA Civ 1153; [2012] 1 W.L.R. 1333; [2012] 2 All E.R. (Comm) 142.

[248] Alternatively, if there was a binding antecedent agreement it may be possible for the insured simply to sue on the earlier agreement.

ment to be concluded later[249] it will be evidence of an intention between the parties, which the court may act upon. Further, where the slip itself does not conform with the intention of the parties the slip may be rectified.[250]

13-094 Standard of proof for rectification. Claims for rectification are not treated lightly[251]; whilst the standard of proof is the normal civil standard of proof on the balance of probabilities,[252] a party seeking rectification must adduce "convincing proof"[253] in order to "counteract the cogent evidence of the parties' intention contained in the written contract".[254] The party seeking rectification must prove not only that the policy does not reflect the true agreement between the parties but also that the proposed wording does reflect that intention.[255]

13-095 Whilst a claim for rectification may be proved on the basis of oral evidence,[256] rectification will rarely be granted on one party's say-so.[257] Indeed, a firm contention from a defendant that the policy as drafted does reflect the true agreement will often have substantial force. Strong contemporaneous evidence showing the actual

---

[249] *The Aikshaw* (1893) 9 T.L.R. 605; *Spalding v Crocker*; sub nom. *Crocker v Sturge* [1897] 1 Q.B. 330; (1897) 2 Com. Cas. 189; 13 T.L.R. 396; *Letts v Excess Insurance Co* (1916) 32 T.L.R. 361; *Alliance Aeroplane Co Ltd* (1920) 5 Ll. L. Rep. 341; *Gagniere & Co Ltd v Eastern Co of Warehouses Insurance and Transport of Goods with Advances Ltd* (1921) 8 Ll. L. Rep. 365; *Re London County Commercial Reinsurance Office Ltd* [1922] 2 Ch. 67; 10 Ll. L. Rep. 100, 370; 91 L.J. Ch. 337; *Eagle Star and British Dominions Insurance Co Ltd v Reiner* (1927) 27 Ll. L. Rep. 173; 71 S.J. 176, 43 T.L.R. 259; *American Employers Insurance Co v St Paul Fire and Marine Insurance Co Ltd* 436 F. Supp. 873; 1977 A.M.C. 2127; [1978] 1 Lloyd's Rep. 417; *Commercial Union Assurance Co Plc v Sun Alliance Insurance Group Plc and Guardian Royal Exchange Plc* [1992] 1 Lloyd's Rep. 475; *Kiriacoulis Lines SA* [2002] EWCA Civ 1070; [2002] 2 Lloyd's Rep. 581; [2003] 1 C.L.C. 579.
[250] *Crocker* [1897] 1 Q.B. 330; (1897) 2 Com. Cas. 189; 13 T.L.R. 396.
[251] In *Whiteside v Whiteside* [1950] Ch. 65 at 71; [1949] 2 All E.R. 913 at 915; 66 (Pt 1) T.L.R. 126 at 128 it was said that the remedy of rectification "must be cautiously watched and jealously exercised". See also *Pasquali & Co v Traders' and General Insurance Association* (1921) 9 Ll. L. Rep. 514.
[252] The suggestion that different civil causes of action carried with them different standards of proof has been roundly rejected (see *Re: B (Children) (Sexual Abuse: Standard of Proof)*; sub nom. *Local Authority X v B* [2008] UKHL 35; [2009] 1 A.C. 11; [2008] 3 W.L.R. 1 and *Re S-B (Children) (Perpetrator: Non-Accidental Injury)*; sub nom. *S-B (Children) (Care Proceedings: Standard of Proof); Re S-B (Children) (Non-Accidental Injury); Re S-B (Identification of Perpetrator)* [2009] UKSC 17; [2010] 1 A.C. 678; [2010] 2 W.L.R. 238). However, it is equally true to say that where an allegation is particularly onerous, serious or unusual, it may require more evidence in order to prove that on the balance of probabilities that the allegation is correct.
[253] *Joscelyne v Nissen* [1970] 2 Q.B. 86; [1970] 2 W.L.R. 509; [1970] 1 All E.R. 1213; see also *Parsons v Bignold* (1846) 15 L.J. Ch. 379; *Allom v Property Insurance Co*, (Unreported) *Times,* February 10, 1911; *Crane v Hegeman-Harris Co Inc* [1971] 1 W.L.R. 1390; [1939] 1 All E.R. 662; 83 S.J. 315; *American Airlines Inc v Hope*; sub nom. *Banque Sabbag SAL v Hope* [1974] 2 Lloyd's Rep. 301; *Agip SpA* [1984] 1 Lloyd's Rep. 353; *Commercial Union Assurance Co Plc* [1992] 1 Lloyd's Rep. 475; *Kiriacoulis Lines SA* [2002] EWCA Civ 1070; [2002] 2 Lloyd's Rep. 581; [2003] 1 C.L.C. 579. Some cases suggest that the burden of proof is the criminal standard (see for example *Gagniere & Co Ltd* (1921) 8 Ll. L. Rep. 365; *Atlantic Maritime Transport Corp v Coscol Petroleum Corp (The Pina)* [1991] 1 Lloyd's Rep. 246) but such authorities are in the minority and are not generally followed.
[254] *Thor Navigation Inc* [2005] EWHC 19 (Comm) at [51]; [2005] 1 Lloyd's Rep. 547 at 560; [2005] 1 C.L.C. 12 at 32.
[255] *Constantinidi v Ralli* [1935] Ch. 427; 104 L.J. Ch. 249; 79 S.J. 195.
[256] *Aetna Life Ins v Brodie* (1880) 5 S.C.R. 1.
[257] See for example *Parsons* (1846) 15 L.J. Ch. 379 where insufficient evidence of particular conversations was given and despite the agent admitting there may have been an error it was held that there was insufficient proof to permit rectification.

accord will usually be required.[258] One of the key reasons for bringing a claim for rectification is to avoid the exclusionary operation of the parol evidence rule because extrinsic evidence will always be admissible, where relevant, in support of a claim for rectification.[259] In reality, this also blurs the boundaries or permissible evidence on matters of strict construction.

Claims for rectification.   Whilst a claim for rectification may be brought as a stand-alone claim in order to clarify the rights and obligations of the parties, it is rare for such claims to be brought.[260] It is far more common for a claim for rectification to be combined with a claim on the policy or to be raised as a counterclaim together with the defence of such a claim.[261] Insureds should be cautious when bringing claims for rectification; a court may conclude, having heard the evidence, that the parties had never in fact reached agreement and order that the policy never took effect and that premiums should be returned.[262]   **13-096**

Unilateral mistake.   The leading case on rectification for unilateral mistake is *Thomas Bates & Son Ltd v Wyndham's (Lingerie) Ltd*, which stated: **13-097**

> "Of course if a document is executed in circumstances in which one party realises that in some respect it does not accurately reflect what down to that moment had been the common intention of the parties, it cannot be said that the document is executed under a common mistake, because the party who has realised the mistake is no longer labouring under the mistake."[263]

The conditions for rectification in a case of unilateral mistake were set out in the judgment and it stated the following: **13-098**

> "[I]t must be shown: first, that one party A erroneously believed that the document sought to be rectified contained a particular term or provision, or possibly did not contain a particular term or provision which, mistakenly, it did contain; secondly, that the other party B was aware of the omission or the inclusion and that it was due to a mistake on the part of A; thirdly, that B has omitted to draw the mistake to the notice of A. And I think there must be a fourth element involved, namely, that the mistake must be one calculated to benefit B. if these requirements are satisfied, the court may regard it as inequitable to allow B to resist rectification to give effect to A's intention on the ground that the mistake was not, at the time of execution of the document, a mutual mistake."[264]

Knowledge of mistake.   Claims for rectification on this ground are based on the notion of "sharp practice" on the part of one of the negotiating parties.[265] The "guilty" party must know that the innocent party is labouring under a mistaken ap-   **13-099**

---

[258] *Snamprogetti Ltd v Phillips Petroleum Co (UK) Ltd* [2001] EWCA Civ 889.

[259] For discussion of the admissibility of extrinsic evidence generally see above para.13-087 but it is clear that evidence of both pre- and post-contract events are admissible (see *Kiriacoulis Lines SA* [2002] EWCA Civ 1070; [2002] 2 Lloyd's Rep. 581, [2003] 1 C.L.C. 579; *Swainland Builders Ltd* [2002] EWCA Civ 560; [2002] 2 EGLR 71; [2002] 23 EG 123).

[260] In general there must be some kind of "live" issue between the parties; the court is entitled to refuse a claim for rectification if there is no issue between the parties and no practical purpose to the claim: *Etablissements Levy (Georges et Paul)* [1980] 2 Lloyd's Rep. 67.

[261] See for example *Letts* (1916) 32 T.L.R. 361.

[262] *Fowler v The Scottish Equitable Life Assurance Society and Ritchie* (1858) 28 L.J. Ch. 225; 4 Jur 1169; 7 W.R. 5.

[263] *Thomas Bates & Son Ltd v Wyndham's (Lingerie) Ltd* [1981] 1 W.L.R. 505 at 515; [1981] 1 All E.R. 1077 at 1085; (1981) 41 P. & C.R. 345 at 353.

[264] *Thomas Bates & Son Ltd* [1981] 1 W.L.R. 505 at 516; [1981] 1 All E.R. 1077 at 1086; (1981) 41 P. & C.R. 345 at 354.

[265] *Riverlate Properties Ltd v Paul* [1975] Ch. 133; [1974] 3 W.L.R. 564; [1974] 2 All E.R. 656; whilst some authorities have doubted the use of phrases such as "sharp practice", Millet J in *Agip (Africa)*

prehension as to the meaning of the document.[266] For these purposes, "knowledge" means one of the first three categories of knowledge described by Gibson J in *Baden v Societe Generale pour Favouriser le Developpement du Commerce et de l'Industrie en France SA*; sub nom. *Baden Delvaux & Lecuit v Societe Generale pour Favoriser le Development du Commerce Baden v Societe Generale*,[267] namely: (i) actual knowledge; (ii) wilfully shutting one's eyes to the obvious; and (iii) wilfully and recklessly failing to make such inquiries as an honest and reasonable man would make.

13-100 **Losing the right to rectification.** It should not be forgotten that rectification is an equitable remedy and is available at the discretion of the court.[268] Accordingly, there may be some instance where the right to rectification is lost. Where, for example, a party discovers an error in the agreement, but then seeks to enforce the contract without seeking to rectify the error, he will often be deemed to have adopted the contract as drafted.[269]

13-101 It is also possible to lose the right to claim rectification through delay. Whilst delay in and of itself does not preclude a claim in rectification, delay once a party has knowledge of the mistake may do. As Blackburne J put it:

> "That merely leaves the laches defence. As to this, it is well established that the doctrine does not come into play before the person against whom it is raised as a defence has discovered the material facts, in this case the mistake. It must be shown that the subsequent delay in pursuing the claim renders it "practically unjust to give a remedy, either because the party has, by his conduct, done that which might fairly be regarded as a waiver of it, or where by his conduct and neglect he has, though perhaps not waiving that remedy, yet put the other party in a situation in which it would not be reasonable to place him if the remedy were otherwise to be asserted."

See *Lindsay Petroleum Co v Hurd*.[270] As Lord Selborne went on (at 240) to observe:

> "Two circumstances, always important in such cases, are the length of the delay and the nature of the acts done during the interval, which might affect either party and cause a balance of justice or injustice in taking one course or the other, so far as relates to the remedy."[271]

4. ESTOPPEL BY CONVENTION

13-102 **Estoppel by convention.** Where two parties share a common understanding or belief and both are aware that their negotiations have proceeded on the basis of that

---

Ltd v Jackson [1990] Ch. 265 at 293; [1989] 3 W.L.R. 1367 at 1390; [1992] 4 All E.R. 385 at 405 stated that "[t]he true distinction is between honesty and dishonesty" and in *George Wimpey UK Ltd v VIC Construction Ltd* [2005] EWCA Civ 77 at [65]; [2005] B.L.R. 135 at 147; 103 Con. L.R. 67 at 85, Sedley LJ stated that "sharp practice has no defined boundary", a concept with which Toulson LJ agreed in *Daventry District Council* [2011] EWCA Civ 1153 at [184]; [2012] 1 W.L.R. 1333 at 1378; [2012] 2 All E.R. (Comm) 142 at 186.

[266] Unilateral mistake should not be confused with misrepresentation.

[267] *Baden v Societe Generale pour Favouriser le Developpement du Commerce et de l'Industrie en France SA*; sub nom. *Baden Delvaux & Lecuit v Societe Generale pour Favoriser le Development du Commerce* [1993] 1 W.L.R. 509; [1992] 4 All E.R. 161; [1983] B.C.L.C. 325 Ch; applied in *Commission for New Towns v Cooper (Great Britain) Ltd*; sub nom. *Milton Keynes Development Corp v Cooper (Great Britain) Ltd* [1995] Ch. 259; [1995] 2 W.L.R. 677; [1995] 2 All E.R. 929; *George Wimpey UK Ltd* [2005] EWCA Civ 77; [2005] B.L.R. 135; 103 Con. L.R. 67.

[268] *KPMG LLP* [2006] EWHC 67 (Ch); [2006] 2 P. & C.R. 109; [2006] 6 E.G. 171 (C.S.).

[269] *Caird v Moss* (1886) 33 Ch. D. 22; 55 L.J. Ch. 854; 35 W.R. 52; *Baker v Yorkshire Fire and Life Assurance Co* [1892] 1 Q.B. 44; 61 L.J.Q.B. 838; 66 L.T. 161.

[270] *Lindsay Petroleum Co v Hurd* (1873) 5 App. Cas. 221 at 239, per Lord Selborne.

[271] *KPMG LLP* [2006] EWHC 67 (Ch) at [197]; [2006] 2 P & CR 109 at 163; see also *Cape Plc v Iron Trades Employers Insurance Association Ltd* [2004] Lloyd's Rep. I.R. 75; [1999] P.I.Q.R. Q212 QB.

common understanding or belief, there are some circumstances where the parties are bound by that common understanding, or, more accurately, are estopped from departing from it. The doctrine has been described as follows:

"This form of estoppel is founded, not on a representation of fact made by a representor and believed by a representee, but on an agreed statement of facts the truth of which has been assumed, by the convention of the parties, as the basis of a transaction into which they are about to enter. When the parties have acted in their transaction upon the agreed assumption that a given statement of facts is to be accepted between them as true, then as regards that transaction each will be estopped as against the other from questioning the truth of the statement of facts so assumed."[272]

That summary is subject to three provisos[273]:   **13-103**

1.   the agreed assumption need not be of fact, it can be of law;
2.   the parties do not need to be on the cusp of a transaction when they acquire the common assumption; it can precede or post-date the contract: "[what] is important for an estoppel by convention is that there should have been a common assumption which has been acted upon"[274]; and
3.   estoppel by convention will only be permitted where departure from the common assumption would be unconscionable.

Lord Denning in *Amalgamated Investment and Property Co Ltd (In Liquida-*   **13-104**
tion) v Texas Commerce International Bank Ltd put the matter thus:

"The doctrine of estoppel is one of the most flexible and useful in the armoury of the law. But it has become overloaded with cases ... All these can now be seen to merge into one general principle shorn of limitations. When the parties to a transaction proceed on the basis of an underlying assumption—either of fact or of law—whether due to misrepresentation or mistake makes no difference—on which they have conducted the dealings between them—neither of them will be allowed to go back on that assumption when it would be unfair or unjust to allow him to do so. If one of them does seek to go back on it, the courts will give the other such remedy as the equity of the case demands."[275]

In order for the doctrine to be engaged, there must be a clear communication of   **13-105**
the assumption between the parties.[276] In other words, the principle cannot survive where parties have not expressed their assumption and have subjectively applied their own meaning to the situation. In *K Lokumal & Sons (London) Ltd v Lotte Shipping Co Pte Ltd (The August Leonhardt)*, Kerr LJ stated that there had to be "some

[272]   *The Law Relating to Estoppel by Representation/the original text by George Spencer Bower*, edited by Sir Alexander Kingcome Turner, 3rd edn (London: Boston Butterworths, 1997), p.157 cited with approval in *Amalgamated Investment and Property Co Ltd (In Liquidation)* [1982] Q.B. 84 at 130–131; [1981] 3 W.L.R. 565 at 583; [1981] 3 All E.R. 577 at 591.

[273]   *Hamel-Smith v Pycroft* (Unreported) 5 February 1987, Gibson LJ, cited with approval in *Norwegian American Cruises A/S (formerly Norwegian American Lines A/S) v Paul Mundy Ltd, The Vistafjord* [1988] 2 Lloyd's Rep. 343; *Times,* April 22, 1988.

[274]   *Norwegian American Cruises A/S (formerly Norwegian American Lines A/S)* [1988] 2 Lloyd's Rep. 343 at 351–352.

[275]   *Amalgamated Investment and Property Co Ltd (In Liquidation)* [1982] Q.B. 84 at 122; [1981] 3 W.L.R. 565 at 575; [1981] 3 All E.R. 577 at 584 cited in: *Hiscox v Outhwaite* [1992] 1 A.C. 562 at 574—575; [1991] 3 W.L.R. 297; and *London Borough of Hillingdon v ARC Ltd*; sub nom. *Hillingdon LBC v ARC Ltd* [2001] C.P, Rep. 33; [2000] 3 E.G.L.R. 97; [2000] R.V.R. 283.

[276]   *K Lokumal & Sons (London) Ltd v Lotte Shipping Co Pte Ltd (The August Leonhardt)* [1985] 2 Lloyd's Rep. 28 CA; *Financial Times,* April 23, 1985; *Norwegian American Cruises A/S (formerly Norwegian American Lines A/S)* [1988] 2 Lloyd's Rep. 343; *Times,* April 22, 1988; *Glencore Grain Ltd v Flacker Shipping Ltd (The Happy Day)* [2002] EWCA Civ 1068; [2002] 2 All E.R. (Comm) 896; [2002] 2 Lloyd's Rep. 487. See also: *London Borough of Hillingdon* [2001] C.P. Rep. 33; [2000] 3 E.G.L.R. 97; [2000] RVR 283, where there was no estoppel by convention because the assumption was not communicated.

manifest representation which crosses the line between representor and representee, either by statement or conduct".[277]

13-106   Further, there can be no estoppel unless it can be shown that the parties have acted on their common intention.[278] In *London Borough of Hillingdon v Arc Ltd*; sub nom. *Hillingdon LBC v ARC Ltd* it was said:

> "In a convention estoppel case, the assumption arises by inference or implication rather than from anything said expressly, and this presents difficulties when it comes to showing that the party seeking to rely on the estoppel took some course on the faith of the assumption as communicated to him by the party to be estopped."[279]

13-107 **Deploying the doctrine.**   In common with other forms of estoppel, estoppel by convention is a shield and not a sword; it cannot be used to found a cause of action[280] but may be prayed in aid of a defence or as the basis of a claim for declaratory relief.[281] Similar to a claim of rectification, extrinsic evidence is admissible in order to establish a communicated common understanding.

---

277 *K Lokumal & Sons (London) Ltd* [1985] 2 Lloyd's Rep. 28 at 34; Financial Times, April 23, 1985.
278 *K Lokumal & Sons (London) Ltd* [1985] 2 Lloyd's Rep. 28; Financial Times, April 23, 1985.
279 *London Borough of Hillingdon* [2001] C.P, Rep. 33 at [68]; [2000] 3 E.G.L.R. 97 at 105; [2000] RVR 283 at 292.
280 *Baird Textiles Holdings Ltd v Marks & Spencer Plc*; sub nom. *Baird Textiles Holdings Ltd v Marks & Spencer Plc* [2001] EWCA Civ 274; [2002] 1 All E.R. (Comm) 737; [2001] C.L.C. 999; *Tesco Stores Ltd v Costain Construction Ltd* [2003] EWHC 1487 (TCC); [2003] All E.R. (D) 394 (Jul).
281 *John v George* (1996) 71 P. & C.R. 375; [1996] 1 E.G.L.R. 7; [1996] 08 E.G. 140.

LOSS AND DAMAGE

1. INTRODUCTION

Introduction. There are three dimensions to the scope of cover under an insur- **14-001** ance policy[1]: (i) the event affecting the insured: in the case of an all risks policy, the occurrence of "loss or damage to" the property insured; (ii) the identity of the insured property; and (iii) the cause of loss—the particular peril (or set of perils) insured under the policy.

Under an all risks policy, so far as the cause of loss (point (iii) above) is **14-002** concerned, the scope of cover is open-ended, albeit not unlimited. Given the wide range of risks insured, mapping the precise contours of what constitutes "loss or damage" is important in delimiting the scope of cover. If the policy is for a specific insured peril, the nature of the risk may answer the question of what is required for the way of loss or damage: fire insurance plainly does not cover the disassembly of the subject matter or its fracturing due to internal stresses, whereas these matters may constitute "damage" under an all risks policy. Moreover, all risks policies are often litigated in light of high-technology engineering diagnostic techniques, which have raised difficult conceptual issues, such as whether submolecular changes constitute damage.

2. LOSS

The meaning of "loss" under an all risks policy. A policy which covers "all **14-003** risks of loss of or damage to" the insured property responds only to physical loss of, or damage to, the property. "Loss" thus means physical deprivation. In *Coven SpA v Hong Kong Chinese Insurance Co*,[2] a consignment of broad beans was insured under a marine policy covering "All Risks ... including shortage." The quantity of beans delivered to port was less than the tonnage stated on the bill of lading. The judge dismissed a claim brought by the insured, finding that the quantity

---

[1] M. Clarke, *The Law of Insurance Contracts*, (London: Informa), Vol.1, para.16–1. One could include the period of cover (or the timing of loss) as a fourth dimension.

[2] *Coven SpA v Hong Kong Chinese Insurance Co* [1999] C.L.C. 223; [1999] Lloyd's Rep. I.R. 565. See also *Outokumpu Stainless Ltd v AXA Global Risks (UK) Ltd* [2007] EWHC 2555 (Comm) at [23]–[28]; [2008] Lloyd's Rep. I.R. 147 at 155–157, in which it was held that the phrase "loss destruction or damage" in an extension of cover for radioactive contamination did not include economic loss sustained by the insured due to the necessity of arranging safe disposal of (already worthless) by-products, which had been contaminated.

of beans shipped was the same as the quantity discharged and that the reason for the discrepancy was measurement error; this was not a loss within cover. It was confirmed, on the insured's appeal, that a policy for all risks of loss and damage required *physical* loss or damage to the goods.[3] In the context of the claim, there had to be a shortage in weight as against the weight which the goods had when the voyage began. A mere "paper loss" due to mismeasurement was not within the cover.[4] If the claimant's contentions were correct, insurers would, in effect, be guaranteeing the accuracy of the figures declared to them by the insured.[5] Similarly, where the insured contracts to purchase oil shipped in drums that upon opening turn out to be full of water there is no loss within the meaning of an all risks cargo policy where the evidence fails to establish that the drums contained anything other than water upon shipment.[6]

14-004 **Need for loss within the period of cover.** In the case of non-marine insurance, if there is no actual, materialised loss during the cover period, there is no right to recovery, unless the policy indicates otherwise, even if loss seems likely.[7] As financial loss is not included as "loss and damage" under an all risks policy, the insured has to point to actual loss of or physical damage to the insured property, as opposed to a trading or commercial loss, within the period of the policy. In *Moore v Evans*,[8] London jewellers insured pearls on a non-marine policy for a year from 8 January 1914. The pearls were sent to trade customers in Germany and Belgium on a sale or return basis.[9] It became impossible for the jewellers to recover possession of the pearls due to the outbreak of war between Britain and Germany. It was held that in the absence of evidence that the pearls had been confiscated by the German authorities or had otherwise left the possession of the consignees (or the bank vault where some of the pearls had been deposited), it could not be said that there had been "loss ... damage or misfortune"[10] in relation to the goods. The fact that the insured jewellers had been deprived of the commercial use of the pearls during the currency of the policy was insufficient to amount to "loss": one should not "confound loss of the goods with the loss of the market for them."[11] Lord Atkinson disavowed the idea that the concept of constructive total loss under the Marine Insurance Act 1906 ("MIA"),[12] or some analogous principle, should apply outside the marine context.[13]

---

[3] *Coven SpA* [1999] C.L.C. 223 at 225; [1999] Lloyd's Rep. I.R. 565 at 568.
[4] *Coven SpA* [1999] C.L.C. 223 at 226–227; [1999] Lloyd's Rep. I.R. 565 at 569.
[5] *Coven SpA* [1999] C.L.C. 223 at 226; [1999] Lloyd's Rep. I.R. 565 at 568.
[6] *Fuerst Day Lawson Ltd v Orion Insurance Co Ltd* [1980] 1 Lloyd's Rep. 656.
[7] *Moore v Evans* [1918] A.C. 185.
[8] *Moore* [1918] A.C. 185.
[9] That is, the jewellers retained ownership of the pearls.
[10] *Moore* [1918] A.C. 185 at 191, per Lord Atkinson.
[11] *Moore* [1918] A.C. 185 at 193, per Lord Atkinson.
[12] See below, para.14-005.
[13] *Moore* [1918] A.C. 185 at 194, 196. In *Mitsui v Mumford* [1915] 2 K.B. 27 at 31 and 33, Bailhache J suggested that there might be loss where temporary deprivation was such that there was "loss in a commercial sense", e.g. if the costs of warehousing were likely to exceed the value of the goods (at 31), while confirming that the mere loss of the ability to market goods was not "loss" for the purposes of a non-marine property policy (at 33). The correctness of this view, which appeared to apply the principles of constructive total loss "in effect, though not in name", was doubted in *Moore* [1918] A.C. 185 at 195–196. *Moore* was followed by Staunton J in *ICI Fibres v Mat Transport Ltd* [1987] 1 Lloyd's Rep. 354; [1987] 1 F.T.L.R. 145 in that it was held that the principles of constructive total

Constructive total loss. For the purposes of marine insurance, the definition of **14-005** loss is extended by the MIA to include constructive total loss ("CTL").[14] Constructive total loss occurs when the subject matter is reasonably abandoned, either: (i) on account of its actual total loss "appearing to be unavoidable"; or (ii) because the subject matter could only be preserved by incurring an expenditure greater than its value.[15] The MIA provides that "in particular", there is constructive total loss:

(i) where the assured is deprived of the possession of his ship or goods: and
    (a) it is unlikely that he can recover the ship or goods; or
    (b) the cost of recovering the ship or goods would exceed their value when repaired; or
(ii) in the case of damage to a ship, where damage is so great that the cost of repair would exceed the value of the ship when repaired.[16]

The insured has a choice of treating the loss as partial loss or of abandoning the subject matter to the insurer in which case he may treat it as actual total loss. If he chooses abandonment, he must give notice to the insurer.[17]

Temporary deprivation. It follows from the decision in *Moore*[18] that temporary **14-006** deprivation of the subject matter is not loss. If there is no reason to believe that the insured will not get the subject matter back, albeit it cannot be said *when*, he has failed to prove loss. However, the law does not require the insured to prove to a certainty that he will never get the thing back.[19] In the context of seizure of aircraft, the courts have drawn a distinction between a hijacking, where the aircraft may or may not be returned—in which case there is no "loss"—and a situation analogous to a marine "capture":

> "[W]here it can be inferred that there was a clear intention at the time of dispossession permanently to deprive the owner of possession and ownership"

in which case loss of the property will be established.[20]

3. DAMAGE

The basic definition of "damage". Damage is an adverse change in physical **14-007** condition.[21] There are three elements to this. First, damage is concerned with the *physical condition* of the subject matter. Secondly, damage requires a *change* to that

---

loss did not apply to the *Convention on the Contract for the International Carriage of Goods by Road* (CMR) (1956) UNTS Vol.399 p.189 (given effect by the Carriage of Goods by Road Act 1965 and contained in Sch.1): *ICI Fibres* [1987] 1 Lloyd's Rep. 354 at 358–359.

[14] Marine Insurance Act 1906 s.56(2) provides: "A total loss may be either an actual total loss, or a constructive total loss."
[15] MIA s.60(1).
[16] MIA s.60(2).
[17] MIA s.62(1). There is no need to give notice if there would be no possibility of benefit to the insurer if notice were given: MIA s.62(7).
[18] *Moore* [1917] 1 K.B. 458, affirmed [1918] A.C. 185; see above, para.14-004.
[19] *Moore* [1917] 1 K.B. 458 at 471, per Bankes LJ.
[20] *Kuwait Airways Corp v Kuwait Insurance Co SAK (No.1)* [1996] 1 Lloyd's Rep. 664 at 689.
[21] *Ranicar v Frigmobile Pty Ltd; Ranicar v Royal Insurance Pty Ltd* [1983] Tas. R. 113 at 116: "the phrase 'damage to' when used in relation to goods, is a physical alteration or change, not necessarily permanent or irreparable, which impairs the usefulness of the things said to be damaged"; *Promet Engineering (Singapore) Pte v Sturge (The Nukila)* [1997] 2 Lloyd's Rep. 146 at 151; [1997] C.L.C. 966 at 971: "some change in the physical state of the vessel"; *Hunter v Canary Wharf Ltd; Hunter*

physical condition occurring within the period of cover. This aspect is crucial to understanding the distinction between damage and a latent defect.[22] Thirdly, the change must, obviously, be for the worse—it must *impair the use or worth* of the item. The basic definition raises a number of issues: does the adverse change have to be permanent? Does the very composition of the subject matter have to be altered, or is it enough that it is rendered less useful, e.g. by being mixed with another substance? Does a latent design defect qualify as damage?

14-008　**Physical condition of the subject matter must be affected.** The requirement that the physical condition of the subject matter be affected means that the mere fact that something is rendered less valuable or useful does not in itself constitute damage. If someone builds a brick wall all the way around a person's land just outside the boundary, denying any access, this will affect the utility of the land, but will not count as damage. But where the subject matter is added to, defaced or contaminated by some other substance, it is a matter of degree whether this will be regarded as affecting the physical condition of the property. The plugging-up of the feed-pipe of a steam engine so that it was rendered useless[23] and the dumping of 30 lorry-loads of rubbish onto a building site have both been held to be damage.[24] Similarly, where radioactive particles intermingled with soil on the claimant's land this amounted to damage.[25] In *Hunter v Canary Wharf Ltd*,[26] it was acknowledged that whilst dust was an "inevitable incident of urban life", "excessive deposits" of dust such as would lessen the value of a carpet into which it was trodden, or would require professional cleaning, would constitute damage.[27] In *Losinjska*,[28] the spillage of hydrochloric acid onto a vessel, requiring decontamination, was held to be damage, even on the assumption that the cleaning operation that was carried out prevented any corrosion from occurring.

14-009　However, the New South Wales Court of Appeal rejected an argument that the blockage of a grain silo by grain constituted damage.[29] In another context, the mere presence of alpha-emitting radionuclides within the claimant's house where there

---

v *London Docklands Development Corp* [1996] 2 W.L.R. 348 at 366; [1996] 1 All E.R. 482 at 498; [1996] C.L.C. 197 at 210 (reversed on other grounds [1997] A.C. 655; [1997] 2 W.L.R. 684; [1997] 2 All E.R. 426): "physical change which renders the article less useful or less valuable"; *Pilkington United Kingdom Ltd v CGU Insurance Plc* [2004] EWCA Civ 23 at [51]; [2005] 1 All E.R. (Comm) 283 at 298; [2004] 1 C.L.C. 1059 at 1077: "some altered state, the relevant alteration being harmful in the commercial context."

22　See below, para.14-014.

23　*R. v Fisher (William)* (1865–1872) L.R. 1 C.C.R. 7 (i.e. in this case it was deemed to be criminal damage).

24　*R v Henderson and Batley* Unreported November 29, 1984 CA (Crim Div). Although a criminal damage case, *Henderson* was cited with approval in *Losinjska Plovidba v Transco Overseas Ltd (The Orjula)* [1995] 2 Lloyd's Rep. 395 at 398–399; [1995] C.L.C. 1325 at 1328–1329, where Mance J held that the criminal test was relevant in a civil context.

25　*Blue Circle Industries Plc v Ministry of Defence* [1999] Ch 289; [1999] 2 W.L.R. 295; [1998] 3 All E.R. 385 (negligence). In *Outokumpu Stainless Ltd v AXA Global Risks (UK) Ltd* [2007] EWHC 2555; [2008] Lloyd's Rep. I.R. 147, insurers conceded that "slagpots" contaminated with radioactive waste requiring their decontamination were to be regarded as having suffered physical damage.

26　*Hunter* [1996] 2 W.L.R. 348; [1996] 1 All E.R. 482; [1996] C.L.C. 197 (nuisance).

27　*Hunter* [1996] 2 W.L.R. 348 at 366; [1996] 1 All E.R. 482 at 498; [1996] C.L.C. 197 at 210, per Pill LJ.

28　*Losinjska Plovidba* [1995] 2 Lloyd's Rep. 395; [1995] C.L.C. 1325 (negligence).

29　*Transfield Constructions Pty Ltd v GIO Australia Holdings Pty Ltd* (1996) 9 ANZ Ins Cas 61-336.

had been no alteration in the physical fabric of the house was held not to be "damage to ... property" for the purpose of the Nuclear Installations Act 1965 s.7(1).[30]

Incorporation of a defect in the process of manufacture is not damage. The **14-010** cases cited above[31] establish that "contamination" of the subject matter by another, unwanted substance is capable of constituting damage. One situation, however, where the introduction of undesired material to the insured property will not apparently amount to damage is where Material A is intentionally combined with Material B to produce a finished product, and Material B is discovered to be harmful or otherwise defective. In *Bacardi-Martini Beverages Ltd v Thomas Hardy Packaging Ltd*,[32] carbon dioxide supplied by the defendant was added to the claimant's alcoholic beverages as part of the manufacturing process. It transpired that the carbon dioxide was contaminated with benzene, which, due to its carcinogenic properties in higher doses, necessitated a recall of the finished drinks. The claimant brought a claim alleging that the defendant had caused damage to the finished drinks, or alternatively to the alcoholic concentrate supplied by the claimant. The judge rejected the claim on this basis and his decision was upheld on appeal.[33] Since the manufacturers actually intended to introduce the carbon dioxide into the drinks, the complaint was essentially that one of the components was defective, i.e. it was contaminated with benzene, and that "a defective product resulted".[34] A similar analysis was adopted by the Court of Appeal in *Pilkington v CGU Insurance*,[35] in response to the suggestion that "the incorporation of a potentially dangerous and defective product into the physical structure of a building" amounted to damage to the building.[36] The insured was responsible for installing glass panels in the construction of the Eurostar Terminal at Waterloo; the main contractor brought a claim against the insured for installing defective panels, which fractured. Since cover for defective works under the insured's liability policy was limited to damage caused to property not belonging to the insured, the insured needed to argue that the terminal building was damaged by the installation in it of the defective panels. The Court of Appeal rejected that argument, saying that

> "generally speaking, damage requires some altered state, the relevant alteration being harmful in the commercial context. This plainly covers a situation where there is a poisoning or contaminating effect upon the property of a third party as a result of the introduction or intermixture of the product supplied ... However, it will not extend to a position where the commodity supplied is installed in or juxtaposed with the property of the third party in circumstances where it does no physical harm and the harmful effect of any later defect or deterioration is contained within it."[37]

Damage need not be permanent. The adverse change in physical condition does **14-011**

---

[30] *Merlin v British Nuclear Fuels Plc* [1990] 2 Q.B. 557; [1990] 3 W.L.R. 383; [1990] 3 All E.R. 711.

[31] See above, para.14-008.

[32] *Bacardi-Martini Beverages Ltd v Thomas Hardy Packaging Ltd*; sub nom. *Messer UK Ltd v Thomas Hardy Packaging Ltd*; sub nom. *Messer UK Ltd v Bacardi-Martini Beverages Ltd* [2002] EWCA Civ 549; [2002] 2 All E.R. (Comm) 335; [2002] 2 Lloyd's Rep. 379.

[33] *Bacardi-Martini Beverages Ltd* [2002] 1 Lloyd's Rep. 62, affirmed [2002] EWCA Civ 549; [2002] 2 All E.R. (Comm) 335; [2002] 2 Lloyd's Rep. 379.

[34] *Bacardi-Martini Beverages Ltd* [2002] EWCA Civ 549 at [11]; [2002] 2 All E.R. (Comm) 335 at 342; [2002] 2 Lloyd's Rep. 379 at 384.

[35] *Pilkington* [2004] EWCA Civ 23; [2005] 1 All E.R. (Comm) 283; [2004] 1 C.L.C. 1059.

[36] *Pilkington* [2004] EWCA Civ 23 at [22]; [2005] 1 All E.R. (Comm) 283 at 290; [2004] 1 C.L.C. 1059 at 1068.

[37] *Pilkington* [2004] EWCA Civ 23 at [51]; [2005] 1 All E.R. (Comm) 283 at 298; [2004] 1 C.L.C. 1059 at 1077, per Lord Justice Potter; see also *Seele Austria GmbH & Co v Tokio Marine Europe Insurance Ltd* [2008] EWCA Civ 441 at [51]; [2009] 1 All E.R. (Comm) 171 at 187 (where defects

not have to be permanent to constitute damage.[38] There can be damage even if the condition of the property can be restored without great cost, e.g. by the cleaning away of dust or debris.[39] So the careful dismantling of individual stones from a work of stone cladding constitutes damage to the overall stonework, notwithstanding that the stones can later be reassembled.[40]

14-012 **Whether change is adverse is assessed by reference to intended use.** So long as there is a change in physical condition of the subject matter, then in assessing whether this has rendered the property less useful or valuable, considerations extraneous to the property itself—especially the intended use—can be relevant. In one case,[41] scallops that were perfectly fit for immediate consumption were raised to a temperature that shortened their shelf-life so that they could no longer be exported for sale in a foreign market. This was held to be damage: it involved a physical change to the scallops, which rendered them less valuable to the insured.[42] Similarly, where a defective titanium dioxide pigment caused discolouration to uPVC products, the unwanted change of colour in the uPVC was a physical change, which impaired the value of the product and was damage within the meaning of the policy.[43] Conversely, the Court of Appeal has recognised that there can theoretically be damage even without a drop in the market value of the property. For example, in one case it was stated that:

> "If a lump of concrete is dropped on X's car, property damage has been inflicted even if someone can persuade an avant garde gallery curator that the resultant object is a work of art worth more than X paid for the car."[44]

14-013 In novel cases of putative "damage" establishing impairment of use or value is unproblematic. Any difficulty in establishing that there is damage, lies in establishing that the *physical* condition of the subject matter is affected, or in establishing that there has been a *change* in the condition of the subject matter within the lifetime of the policy rather than the mere uncovering of a latent defect.

14-014 **Discovery of an existing defect does not amount to damage.** The term "damage" does not include the diminution in value represented by a pre-existing defect in the subject matter nor the cost of remedying it.[45] There are two ways of explaining this. First, the terms "defect" and "damage" bear different meanings. Something

---

in window panels installed in the walls of a building were "not themselves damage and did not cause damage to other parts of the works").

[38] Note that this contrasts with the position regarding "loss", which does not embrace temporary deprivation: see above, para.14-006.

[39] *Hunter* [1996] 2 W.L.R. 348; [1996] 1 All E.R. 482; [1996] C.L.C. 197.

[40] *Seele Austria GmbH & Co* [2007] EWHC 1411 at [36]; [2007] 1 C.L.C. 972 at 984, point affirmed on appeal: [2008] EWCA Civ 441 at [51]; [2009] 1 All E.R. (Comm) 171 at 187.

[41] *Ranicar v Frigmobile Pty Ltd* [1983] Tas. R. 114.

[42] *Ranicar* [1983] Tas. R. 113 at 116. See also *Quorum A/S v Schramm* [2001] EWHC 494 (Comm); [2002] 2 All E.R. (Comm) 147; [2002] 1 Lloyd's Rep. 249, in which submolecular change to a Degas pastel painting sustained by its being in proximity to a fire, even though invisible to the viewer, constituted damage as this increased the risk of future deterioration and shortened the life of the painting.

[43] *Tioxide Europe Ltd v CGU International Insurance Plc* [2004] EWHC 2116 (Comm); [2005] Lloyd's Rep. I.R. 114. See also *Blue Circle Industries Plc v Ministry of Defence* [1999] Ch 289; [1999] 2 W.L.R. 295; [1998] 3 All E.R. 385 (contamination of land by radioactive material).

[44] *Jan De Nul (UK) Ltd v AXA Royale Belge SA (formerly NV Royale Belge)* [2002] EWCA Civ 209 at [92]; [2002] 1 All E.R. (Comm) 767 at 785; [2002] 1 Lloyd's Rep. 583 at 595.

[45] *Oceanic Steamship Co v Faber* (1906) 11 Com. Cas. 179 at 188; affirmed (1907) 13 Com. Cas. 28.

will be defective if it does not function as it should.[46] This is a static concept: to talk about the occurrence of a defect is to say that a defect exists but not that it has developed just now or at any particular time. Indeed, something can be defective from the moment it was designed and constructed—hence the term "design defect". By contrast, to say that property has sustained "damage" is to imply that the item has suffered some event, or process, which has changed its physical condition.[47] Secondly, there is a lack of fortuity in the manifestation of a defect pre-dating the period of cover:

"To hold that the clause covers it [the cost of repairing a defective frame] would be to make the underwriters not insurers, but guarantors, and to turn the clause into a warranty that the hull and machinery are free from latent defects, and, consequently, to make all such defects repairable at the expense of the underwriters ... The fact that it begins with the word 'insurance' negatives, in my opinion, the possibility of its being so interpreted."[48]

The point being made is that if the insurers were liable to indemnify against the cost of making good existing defects in the subject matter, they would be warranting that the subject matter was in good working condition. The contract would then be one of guarantee rather than of insurance. In *Promet Engineering (Singapore) Pte v Sturge (The Nukila)*,[49] Hobhouse LJ said:

"Insurance covers fortuities, not losses which have occurred through the ordinary incidents of the operation of the vessel ... A policy of insurance does not cover matters which already exist at the date when the policy attaches. The assured if he is to recover an indemnity has to show that some loss or damage has occurred during the period covered by the policy."[50]

However, the principle that losses must be fortuitous has to be treated with cau- **14-015** tion when dealing with a policy that specifically covers loss or damage caused by a defect.[51] In such cases, so long as it is possible to identify unintentional damage over and above the defect itself occurring within the period of cover, it will not avail the insurer to argue that the design flaw in question meant that it was inevitable that the structure would, due to its defective condition, collapse, etc.[52] Indeed, appropri-

---

[46] See below, Ch.16.
[47] In the Insurance Institute of London's *Construction Insurance/Report of Research Study Group 208B* (London: IIL, 2010), p.158, para.8.8.2.1, this distinction is explained "[b]y normal usage of the terms, 'defect' is a *condition* not an *occurrence*".
[48] *Hutchins Brothers v Royal Exchange Assurance Corp* [1911] 2 K.B. 398 at 411, per Fletcher Moulton LJ.
[49] *The Nukila* [1997] 2 Lloyd's Rep. 146; [1997] C.L.C. 966.
[50] *The Nukila* [1997] 2 Lloyd's Rep. 146 at 151; [1997] C.L.C. 966 at 971.
[51] In marine insurance, the *Inchmaree* clause: see below, paras 16-024 to 16-028.
[52] e.g. In *The Nukila* [1997] 2 Lloyd's Rep. 146 at 151; [1997] C.L.C. 966 at 971, Hobhouse LJ said: "the presence or absence of a latent defect in the hull or machinery of a vessel is, by definition, unknown to the assured and whether or not there is such a defect and whether or not it will during a given period of time or maritime adventure have an impact or cause any damage is fortuitous from the point of view of the assured. As is demonstrated by the Inchmaree clause and other similar clauses which have been introduced into policies ... there is both a market need for such cover and a willingness to provide it". Similarly, the presumption against cover for the consequences of inherent vice (as found in s.52(2)(c) of the MIA) has no application where there is express cover for the cost of replacing defective works: *Mitchell Conveyor & Transporter Co Ltd v Pulbrook* (1933) 45 Ll. L. Rep. 239 (contractors' policy); *Prudent Tankers Ltd SA v Dominion Insurance Co Ltd (The Caribbean Sea)* [1980] 1 Lloyd's Rep. 338 at 347. See further above, Ch.10 and below, Ch.24.

ate wording may even cover replacement of the defective yet undamaged part that caused the damage.[53]

Consequential deterioration in condition due to a defect constitutes
14-016 **damage.** If a latent design flaw actually produces an adverse change in physical condition in the property during the period of cover, it will be possible to identify "damage". To take a clear example, where flammable paint is inappropriately applied to the interior of a manufacturing plant and later catches fire destroying the plant, there is clearly damage by the fire. At the other end of the scale is the mere discovery of a defect. Thus in a case where the repainting of a vessel revealed that its frame had been defectively cast so as to cause shrinkage cracks requiring its replacement, there was no "damage": this was a straightforward matter of a latent defect revealing itself.[54]

14-017   In other circumstances it may be conceptually difficult to distinguish the latent defect itself from consequential damage. In the leading case on this issue, *The Nukila*,[55] Ward LJ said:

> "If one is considering whether there is damage to the hull and whether such damage is caused by a latent defect in the hull, it follows that the damage must be something different from ... and incrementally greater than the latent defect itself. Where the line is to be drawn is a matter of fact and degree."[56]

14-018   In *The Nukila*, the legs of an offshore platform were susceptible to excessive metal fatigue stress as a result of defective welding in their construction. The evidence was that this defect had initiated tiny undetectable fatigue cracks by the time the owners took out the policy, but that larger and visible fractures had occurred during the period of cover, which necessitated repairs.[57] The owners made a claim under the *Inchmaree* clause (extending cover to "damage to the subject matter insured caused by ... any latent defect in the machinery or hull") as well as under an Additional Perils Clause, which provided cover for the cost of repairing or replacing "[a]ny defective part which has caused loss or damage to the vessel".[58] The underwriters denied liability. They argued that there was no consequential "damage"—all that occurred was that the latent defect in each leg had manifested itself. The trial judge found for the defendants, ruling that there had to be damage to some "part" of the vessel other than the defective part for there to be damage "caused by" the defect, and that here the relevant part was each leg of the platform, including the welding. Since the cracking that occurred was *within* the legs, it did not amount to damage. That decision was reversed by the Court of Appeal.[59] The court considered that there was nothing in the wording of the relevant clauses, nor inherent in the concept of "damage", that required the damage to be in a different part of the subject matter to the part that is identified as defective.[60] That being so,

---

53   *Cementation Piling and Foundations Ltd v Commercial Union Insurance Co Plc* [1995] 1 Lloyd's Rep. 97; (1995) 74 B.L.R. 98; see below, para.14-022.
54   *Hutchins Brothers* [1911] 2 K.B. 398.
55   *The Nukila* [1997] 2 Lloyd's Rep. 146; [1997] C.L.C. 966.
56   *The Nukila* [1997] 2 Lloyd's Rep. 146 at 157; [1997] C.L.C. 966 at 980.
57   *The Nukila* [1997] 2 Lloyd's Rep. 146 at 150; [1997] C.L.C. 966 at 969.
58   *The Nukila* [1997] 2 Lloyd's Rep. 146 at 149; [1997] C.L.C. 966 at 969.
59   *The Nukila* [1996] 1 Lloyd's Rep. 85, reversed [1997] 2 Lloyd's Rep. 146; [1997] C.L.C. 966.
60   *The Nukila* [1997] 2 Lloyd's Rep. 146 at 156; [1997] C.L.C. 966 at 978–979.

"on any ordinary use of language" there was damage to the legs of the platform.[61] Hobhouse LJ recognised that there was

> "potentially a factual problem involved in distinguishing between an embryonic fatigue crack as a latent defect and a system of cracking of such magnitude and severity that it significantly weakens the integrity or tensile or shear strength of the structure of the vessel."[62]

This must "at least in part, be a question of degree".[63]

Damage to the defective part itself capable of constituting damage. Is an **14-019** adverse change in the condition of a defective part or component itself damage? In the light of the decision in *The Nukila*,[64] the answer is undoubtedly "yes". The Court of Appeal was very clear in rejecting the argument that damage caused by a defect in the insured property meant damage to some "other" component or part of the property distinct from the defective part.[65] The test, instead, is simply whether there is some damage over and above the existing defect, whatever the location of this damage.[66]

However, where the alleged damage is essentially a progressive deterioration in **14-020** the condition of the property—such as through the deepening and spreading of cracks—the evidence will need to establish that deterioration has occurred within the period of cover, and probably that it is more than de minimis: this seems to be implicit in the dicta that the distinction is a "question of degree".[67] There will be no recoverable loss if the component in question was already worthless at the start of the period of cover.[68]

In practice, CAR policies frequently include defects exclusions which specifi- **14-021**

---

[61] *The Nukila* [1997] 2 Lloyd's Rep. 146 at 156; [1997] C.L.C. 966 at 978.

[62] *The Nukila* [1997] 2 Lloyd's Rep. 146 at 156; [1997] C.L.C. 966 at 978.

[63] *The Nukila* [1997] 2 Lloyd's Rep. 146 at 156; [1997] C.L.C. 966 at 978, and see the dicta of Ward LJ set out above in para.13-017.

[64] *The Nukila* [1997] 2 Lloyd's Rep. 146; [1997] C.L.C. 966.

[65] See commentary above in para.14-018.

[66] In this respect, the correct approach to "damage to property" for the purposes of interpreting insurance contracts is sharply different to the approach that applies in tort liability. In negligence, one starts from the proposition that in order to recover against the manufacturer of a defective product or building for costs occasioned by a latent defect, the owner must show damage to other property: *East River Steamship Corp v Transamerica Delaval Inc* (1986) 476 U.S 858; 106 S. Ct. 2295; 1986 A.M.C. 2027; *Murphy v Brentwood DC* [1991] 1 A.C. 469; [1990] 3 W.L.R. 414; [1990] 2 All E.R. 908. Damage caused by the product to the product itself is viewed as economic loss. It is not possible to argue that the spreading of a crack in the foundations of a building is damage to "other property" so as to found an action in negligence: "once the first cracks appear, the structure as a whole is seen to be defective and the nature of the defect is known": [1991] 1 A.C. 469 at 478; [1990] 3 W.L.R. 414 at 439; [1990] 2 All E.R. 908 at 927, per Lord Bridge. So if in *The Nukila* [1997] 2 Lloyd's Rep. 146; [1997] C.L.C. 966, The Nukila had been re-purchased before the condition of the legs was discovered, the purchasers would not be able to maintain an action in tort against the engineers even if negligence in design or construction was established because there would be no relevant damage to property. Conversely, following *The Nukila*, an insurer cannot argue that since a structure was susceptible to cracking at the start of the policy the insured's loss is purely economic.

[67] *The Nukila* [1997] 2 Lloyd's Rep. 146 at 156 (per Hobhouse L.J.), 157 (per Ward LJ); [1997] C.L.C. 966 at 978 (per Hobhouse L.J.), 980 (per Ward L.J.). It is not fatal to a claim under a latent defects clause that ordinary wear and tear, or the "ordinary working of the ship", has contributed to an accident in combination with the way the subject matter was designed: *Prudent Tankers SA v The Dominion Insurance Co (The Caribbean Sea)* [1980] 1 Lloyd's Rep. 338 at 347.

[68] *Scindia Steamships (London) Ltd v The London Assurance Co Ltd* [1937] 1 K.B. 639; [1937] 3 All E.R. 895. In that case a latent defect in the tail end shaft of the vessel caused it to break in two as it was being drawn from the vessel during routine repairs. Before breaking, the shaft had already been in a condition that required it to be condemned. The judge held there was no damage within the

cally distinguish between damage to the defective part itself (excluded) as distinct from damage caused by the defect to the rest of the property (covered).[69] Alternatively, cover in respect of damage caused by a defect may be limited to property "other than property of the insured". Otherwise, however, there is nothing inherent in the concept of damage that requires the division of the insured property into notional parts.

14-022 **Cover for repair or replacement of defect.** Although the discovery of a latent defect in the insured property will not constitute "damage", an all risks policy may nonetheless cover the cost of remedying a defect if that is the proper construction of the policy read in the context of its particular extensions and exclusions. A clause that excludes the cost of rectifying defects in design, materials or workmanship "unless the property insured suffers actual loss, destruction or damage as a result of such a defect" (in effect, defects exclusion clause DE5 wording) will, despite being framed as an exception to the insuring clause, bring the costs of rectifying pre-existing defects that cause physical damage within the scope of cover.[70] On that wording it is still necessary to show, as the trigger to an indemnity, that some damage has occurred beyond the mere discovery of a defect on the *Nukila*[71] principles.

14-023 **The phrase "mere materialisation of defect" is unhelpful.** When dealing with all risks policies, it is dangerous, it is suggested, to use the phrase "mere materialisation of a defect" in contradistinction to "damage". This is because in other areas the line between "defect" and "damage" is drawn in different places,[72] and the phrase "mere materialisation of a defect" has been equated elsewhere with precisely the kind of adverse physical change consequent on a defect that is regarded as damage following *The Nukila*.[73] For example, in the context of a particular construction contract, the formation of cracks in a defective concrete floor slab was held not to be "loss or damage" under the relevant clause:

> "In this contractual scheme, the mere manifestation of a defect under ordinary usage, which the contractor is anyway obliged to make good under the contractual scheme relating to defects, cannot in my judgment constitute loss or damage to the slab."[74]

---

meaning of the policy. The decision was considered to be correct on its facts in *The Nukila*: [1997] 2 Lloyd's Rep. 146 at 156; [1997] C.L.C. 966 at 977–978. In *Outokumpu Stainless Ltd v AXA Global Risks (UK) Ltd* [2007] EWHC 2555 at [5]; [2008] Lloyd's Rep. I.R. 147 at 149 slag produced in the production of stainless steel became contaminated with radioactive material; no claim was made for the value of the contaminated slag, which would have anyway been worthless.

69 The standard defect exclusion clauses (DE clauses) serve this function and are considered below in Ch.16. DE2, DE3 and DE4 exclude damage to the defective part itself (defined progressively narrowly in each version of the clause). DE1, on the other hand, excludes all loss of or damage to the insured property due to defective design, workmanship etc., whereas DE5 does not exclude damage to the defective part so long as the defect does cause some unintended damage.

70 *Cementation Piling and Foundations Ltd* [1995] 1 Lloyd's Rep. 97; (1995) 74 B.L.R. 98. See below, paras 16-059 to 16-064 for a full discussion of this issue.

71 *The Nukila* [1997] 2 Lloyd's Rep. 146; [1997] C.L.C. 966.

72 See above, fn.67.

73 *The Nukila* [1997] 2 Lloyd's Rep. 146; [1997] C.L.C. 966.

74 *Skanska Construction Ltd v Egger (Barony) Ltd* [2002] EWCA Civ 310 at [30]; [2002] B.L.R. 236 at 242–243; [2003] Lloyd's Rep. I.R. 479 at 486. Mance LJ has stated (wrongly it is suggested) that this dictum casts doubt on the proposition that consequential cracking or other deterioration to a structure due to a latent defect constitutes "damage". The issue in the case was whether a clause requiring the employer to obtain insurance cover for the benefit of the contractor in respect of "all loss or damage from whatever cause arising for which the Contractor is responsible under the terms

Yet there can be no doubt that the cracking of the floor slab would constitute "loss and damage" for the purposes of an all risks policy,[75] as long as the policy did not expressly exclude damage to the defective part itself. The better way of expressing the relevant distinction is to contrast a latent defect becoming patent (or being "uncovered") with damage over and above the defect itself.

Cover for sudden and unforeseen damage. The requirement for damage to be **14-024** sudden and unforeseen is most commonly to be found in operational policies or policies for the installation of plant and machinery; it is less often to be found in policies covering civil engineering works, although the International Association of Engineering Insurers ("IMIA") standard wording requires damage to be "sudden" and it is also in the Munich Re standard form CAR wording. In the United Kingdom and to a lesser extent in the Middle East and North America insuring clauses in All Risks (or Builders) policies for civil engineering risks are less likely to include the words "sudden and unforeseen" than clauses in "Pacific rim" project policies.

In *Burts & Harvey Ltd*[76] a consequential loss (breakdown) policy, which covered **14-025** "sudden and accidental damage" by any fortuitous cause excluded from cover loss or damage resulting from: "wear and tear, corrosion, erosion, failure of any part or parts the nature or functions of which necessitate their regular replacement."[77] A claim was made for business interruption arising out of damage caused by the build-up of high pressure within the plant. The breakdown was due to a crack in the tube in the heat exchanger which had allowed water to mix with gaseous maleic anhydride and caused corrosive maleic acid. It was this corrosive material that had caused damage. Insurers contended that the damage was, amongst other reasons, due to gradual deterioration. Lawton J held that the splitting of the tube was sudden and accidental. He said:

---

of the Contract" referred: (i) only to loss and damage sustained due to mishap during the carrying out of works; or (ii) extended also to loss and damage caused by the defective quality of the works ([2002] EWCA Civ 310 at [17]–[18]; [2003] Lloyd's Rep. I.R. 479 at 484; [2002] B.L.R. 236 at 241). The Court of Appeal held that interpretation (i) was the correct one, and accordingly that the employer did not breach the clause by obtaining cover under a policy with a DE3 exclusion (i.e. excluding the cost of damage to the defective part). The matter for which the contractor sought an indemnity was the cracking of a defective floor slab. The particular interpretation of "loss and damage" articulated by Mance LJ (under "this contractual scheme") was clearly not intended to be of general application to all insurance which requires there to be "damage"—not least because, if it were, the contractor's complaint that a more generous defects exclusion should have been obtained would be entirely moot (see below, fn.76). In any event, *The Nukila* [1997] 2 Lloyd's Rep. 146; [1997] C.L.C. 966 line of authority was not cited or referred to, so the decision is *per incuriam* to the extent that it is inconsistent with the case law on the meaning of "loss and damage" under insurance contracts.

[75] If it were otherwise, the whole point in issue in *Skanska Construction Ltd* [2002] EWCA Civ 310; [2003] Lloyd's Rep. I.R. 479; [2002] B.L.R. 236—whether the employer was obliged under the contract to obtain insurance with a more generous "DE5" exclusion—would be moot. The short answer to the contractor's complaint would be that a policy with a less strict defects exclusion would have been of no benefit: the cracking of the slab could not (if the dicta of Mance LJ were of general application) constitute "loss or damage" under the insuring clause.

[76] *Burts & Harvey Ltd v Vulcan Boiler and General Insurance Co*; sub nom. *Alchemy Ltd v Vulcan Boiler and General Insurance Co Ltd* [1966] 1 Lloyd's Rep. 161; 116 N.L.J. 639.

[77] *Burts & Harvey Ltd* [1966] 1 Lloyd's Rep. 161

"... I need not deal with this matter on the basis of any burden of proof, because I am quite satisfied that this split in the tube occurred not gradually but quite dramatically, in the sense that it occurred between 7p.m. and 11p.m. on June 4, 1961."[78]

Citation of examples of the meaning of a particular word or phrase in a CAR policy can be of limited assistance where the range of insured subject matter is diverse. For example in relation to a mining project policy, the word "sudden" may be assessed using a geological timescale, which may relate to an event which takes hundreds if not millions of years to occur, or it may be assessed in seconds if an aquifer has been breached. The emphasis in the cases, is on the need for a dramatic change to have occurred during a relatively short period of time. In *African Products (Pty) Ltd*[79] the South African Supreme Court of Appeal approved synonyms such as "abrupt" or "taking place all at once" for the word sudden.

14-026   The Australian case of *Vee H Aviation Products (Pty) Ltd*[80] was referred to in the *African Products (Pty) Ltd* case which confirmed that the test is objective. Mpati P. stated:

"An objective perspective seems to me to be in accordance with sound commercial principles and good business sense. I say this because if the unforeseen physical damage occurs suddenly, viewed objectively, the insurer will become liable. If, on the other hand, it is not sudden from an objective perspective no liability will attach. It would otherwise be difficult, if not impossible, to dislodge an assertion by a claimant that, viewed subjectively, physical damage was sudden even though such damage may be shown to have been gradual and to have occurred over a long period. In my view, this could never have been the intention of the parties."[81]

Sudden change is distinguishable from the process of gradual deterioration (or gradual change). In *Amec Civil Engineering Ltd*[82] concrete blocks to install a sea wall failed to meet the minimum standard required to cover the internal reinforcement. The CAR insurer declined to indemnify on the basis that the damage resulted from defective workmanship or alternatively from rust, which fell within gradual deterioration of the property. In respect of gradual deterioration, it was held that this meant "... a deterioration which is progressive by degrees, as opposed to sudden and catastrophic."[83]

The Singapore authority of *Pacific Chemicals Pte Ltd*[84] emphasises that it is the damage and not its cause that must be sudden. In the Australian case of *Vee H Aviation (Pty) Ltd*[85] the defendant indemnified the plaintiff for the costs of rectification arising from a "breakdown" of the plaintiff's aircraft engine with breakdown being defined as "sudden and unforeseen damage resulting from".[86] Consistent with the reasoning in *Burts & Harvey Ltd*,[87] the Supreme Court of the Australian Capital Territory held that it is the damage that must be sudden:

---

[78]   *Burts & Harvey Ltd* [1966] 1 Lloyd's Rep. 161 at 171; 116 N.L.J. 639.
[79]   *African Products (Pty) Ltd v AIG South Africa Ltd* [2009] ZASCA 27 at [22]; 2009 (3) SA 473 (SCA); [2009] 4 All SA 99 (SCA) (27 March 2009).
[80]   *Vee H Aviation (Pty) Ltd v Australian Aviation Underwriting Pool (Pty) Ltd* [1996] ACTSC 123.
[81]   *African Products (Pty) Ltd v AIG South Africa Ltd* [2009] ZASCA 27 at [22]; 2009 (3) SA 473 (SCA) at 482.
[82]   *Amec Civil Engineering Ltd v Norwich Union Fire Insurance Society Ltd* [2003] EWHC 1341 (TCC).
[83]   [2003] EWHC 1341 (TCC) at [75].
[84]   *Pacific Chemicals Pte Ltd v MSIG Insurance (Singapore) Pte Ltd* [2013] 11 SLR 324 at 331; [2012] SGHC 198 at [8]; [2013] Lloyd's Rep. I.R. 389 at 393.
[85]   *Vee H Aviation (Pty) Ltd* [1996] ACTSC 123.
[86]   *Vee H Aviation (Pty) Ltd* [1996] ACTSC 123 at [4].
[87]   *Burts & Harvey Ltd* [1966] 1 Lloyd's Rep. 161; 116 N.L.J. 639.

"The definition clearly contemplates that the cause of the damage may be something that has been taking place over a period of time, such as the wearing out or loosening of a part, or fatigue ... The definition of Breakdown used in this particular policy required that the damage, as distinct from the cause of it, should be both sudden and unforeseen."[88]

The policy identified the physical parts indemnified and the type of damage, for example "[b]reaking seizing or burning out of Aircraft Engine parts".[89] Thus, the breaking, seizing or burning of the parts must be sudden to be indemnified even if it is caused by an event occurring over a much longer period, for example by loss of oil or poor maintenance.

In *Bina Puri Sdn Bhd v MUI Continental Insurance Bhd (formerly known as MUI Continental Insurance Sdn Bhd)*; sub nom. *Bina Puri v MUI Continental Insurance*[90] the plaintiff, who had a CAR policy with the defendant insurers, was a main contractor. In early 1996, cracks appeared in buildings and drains near the work site. The policy covered damage to the contract works for "any unforeseen and sudden physical loss or damage from any cause, other than those specifically excluded ...". The court posed the question "[w]as it 'sudden'?"[91] and answered the question as follows:

"... The events as set out in the background facts reveal that the deflections of the wall were progressive over a period of several months between [January] 1996 and April 1996, although cracks near the site and around it, appeared earlier in January. It is evident that the deflections to the wall were progressive. In fact remedial measures were taken to try and stop the damage to the retaining wall as well as the third party property. In these circumstances can it be said that the damage was 'sudden'? The nature of the deflections and the period over which they occurred suggest that the damage to the wall was not sudden ... In these circumstances, given the progressive nature of the failure and the manner in which it occurred, it appears to this court that the damage is not sudden."[92]

A requirement that damage must be unforeseen is subjective and is to be evalu- **14-027**
ated prior to the damage occurring. Thus, even though damage may have been foreseeable and the cause of the damage may have been foreseen, if the damage was not actually foreseen by the insured, then it will be indemnified.

---

88 *Vee H Aviation (Pty) Ltd* [1996] ACTSC 123 at [29] and [34].
89 *Vee H Aviation (Pty) Ltd* [1996] ACTSC 123 at [4]
90 *Bina Puri Sdn Bhd* [2010] 1 M.L.J. 347.
91 *Bina Puri Sdn Bhd* [2010] 1 M.L.J. 347 at [90]
92 *Bina Puri Sdn Bhd* [2010] 1 M.L.J. 347 at [91].

CHAPTER 15

EXCLUSIONS

1. INTRODUCTION

Introduction. A key characteristic of CAR policies is that, in contrast to other **15-001** types of insurance, the insuring clause is not limited by specified perils—instead it covers all risks of damage unless it is excluded (either expressly or by implication). Therefore exclusion clauses[1] are significant because they may define the extent of cover provided. The proper interpretation of exclusion clauses is important to the operation of the policy.

As explained below in Ch.22, the burden is on the insurer to prove that the loss falls within one of the exclusions. To determine whether the loss is excluded, the court will start from the premise that all risks are covered save for where they are clearly and unambiguously excluded.[2] Where there is any ambiguity over the meaning of the clause, it will be construed against the insurer, pursuant to the rule of contra proferentum.[3] As a result, a number of standard exclusions have developed and commonly appear in a variety of insurance policies whose purpose is to try to reduce the risk of ambiguity in such clauses and, therefore, reduce the need to apply the contra proferentum rule.

In a further effort to avoid uncertainty, some CAR policies also expressly exclude matters which may, in any event, have been impliedly excluded as a matter of law, for example wear and tear and inherent vice. The advantage of this is that where the loss results from two concurrent events and only one of these falls within a specific exclusion to cover, it is settled law that an express exclusion will prevail over the insuring clause and the loss will not be recoverable under the policy. It also

---

[1] In insurance law, exclusions may also be referred to as exceptions, "terms delimiting risk, conditions, ... temporal exclusions,... or limitations of risk". See further M. Clarke, *The Law of Insurance Contracts*, (London: Informa Law), Vol.2, para.19–1A.
[2] See, for example *Tektrol Ltd (formerly Atto Power Controls Ltd) v International Insurance Co of Hanover Ltd* [2005] EWCA Civ 845 at [20]; [2006] 1 All E.R. (Comm) 780 at 786–787; [2005] 2 Lloyd's Rep. 701 at 705–706, per Carnwath LJ; [2005] 2 C.L.C. 339; [2006] Lloyd's Rep. I.R. 38.
[3] See above, paras 13-060 to 13-061.

makes it clear to the insured that the policy is not, in fact, covering any and all risks that may arise and assists in identifying those matters which are excluded.

15-002 Stages of interpretation of clauses.   The first step when approaching a claim under a CAR policy, whether acting for the insured or the insurer, is to examine the structure of that policy. As described above in Ch.2, typically a CAR policy will contain at least two distinct sections: a section dealing with the insurance of the works undertaken ("the Works Section") and a section dealing with the contractor's potential public liability ("the PL Section"). The first stage of interpreting any particular policy is to determine whether the event which you wish to claim is covered under the first or second (or both) of these sections.

Once it has been determined under which section of the policy the claim falls, it is necessary to examine the actual operative clause, together with the definitions, to see if it responds to the property insured. If it does, it is then necessary to consider any exclusion clauses.

In a CAR policy a standard opening phrase such as "[t]he indemnity provided by this section shall not apply to or include" will apply to all of the exclusions listed in the exclusions to the material damage section of the policy coupled with a phrase that concerns each particular exclusion. The standard opening phrase is not repeated in relation to each exclusion clause. Both of the phrases are important in terms of interpreting the meaning of the exclusion clause as a whole and, as such, both clauses will always follow the wording of the insuring clause as near as possible.

15-003 Outline.   This chapter is divided into two main areas:

1.   General exclusions. These are general exclusion clauses which are common to insurance policies, irrespective of whether they are CAR policies.
2.   Construction exclusions. These specifically relate to construction (and CAR policies). These exclusions are normally included in the section of the policy called "general exclusions to section 1".

In addition to the above, CAR policies may be combined with (but must be distinguished from) public liability exclusions (if selected by the insured) which are normally contained in a separate section of a CAR policy. Public liability exclusions are examined further below at paras 18-076 to 18-137.

2.   GENERAL EXCLUSIONS

15-004 General exclusions.   There are several exclusions which are common to most "all risks" policies and CAR policies. The common characteristic of these exclusions is that they deal with risks which are not specific to a construction context. Instead, they cover situations and risks which are either uninsurable or for which the insured would need to pay a premium. Six particular forms of general exclusion (including a general condition which can also be considered as an exclusion) are explained below: "non-risk" events exclusions; exclusions relating to natural events; conflicts exclusion; nuclear material exclusion; consequential loss exclusion and the requirement to take reasonable precautions (also referred to as a restrictive/general condition).

(a) "Non-risk" events

Non-risk events. The exclusions considered in this section are categorised according to whether the event is deemed to be a "non-risk" event or not. Known non-risk events normally found in construction policies include: inherent vice, latent defect, wear and tear, corrosion or erosion, gradual deterioration and the excess/deductible. The question of risk and how contracts apportion risk is discussed in further detail in Ch.2.[4]   **15-005**

Inherent vice. An inherent vice is an internal quality of the subject matter of the insurance tending to its loss, damage or destruction. The term "inherent vice" will not be expressly stated in an exclusion clause as such. As set out above in Ch.10, inherent vice is impliedly excluded from insurance policies as a result of the general principle that insurance is to cover risks and not certainties. However, the implied term can be rebutted by the express language of the policy or where excluding inherent vice would defeat the intention of the parties.   **15-006**

For example, in *Soya GmBH Mainz Kommanditgesellschaft v White*[5] the heating of a cargo of soya beans during the voyage resulted in the condition of the beans deteriorating. The insurers denied liability on the basis that the proximate cause of the damage was inherent vice and relied on s.55(2)(c) of the Marine Insurance Act ("MIA") 1906 to deny liability. Lord Diplock defined inherent vice in this case as

> "the risk of deterioration of the goods shipped as a result of their natural behaviour in the ordinary course of the contemplated voyage without the intervention of any fortuitous external accident or casualty".[6]

There was, however, a specific provision in the policy which provided cover for "heat sweat and spontaneous combustion" which rebutted the exclusion of liability in s.55(2)(c). As a result, the House of Lords found that such perils were covered, even if they arose from an inherent vice.

By contrast, where there was no express provision in the policy to cover such damage, the insurers were permitted to rely on the inherent vice exception. In *T M Noten BV v Harding*,[7] the Court of Appeal held that the leather gloves insured had deteriorated and become damaged as a result of their natural behaviour in the ordinary course of the particular voyage, without the intervention of any fortuitous external accident or casualty. Essentially, the goods were damaged because they were shipped wet. The fact that the moisture from the gloves had evaporated and then condensed back on to the cargo did not prevent the insurers relying on the exclusion as there had been no fortuitous event. Bingham LJ specifically referred to the fact that the insurers had never undertaken to insure against the occurrence of hot and humid weather.[8]   **15-007**

This decision has been followed by the British Columbia Court of Appeal in rela-

---

[4]   See in particular paras 2-005, 2-044 to 2-045.
[5]   *Soya GmBH Mainz KG v White* [1983] 1 Lloyd's Rep. 122; [1983] Com. L.R. 46; (1983) 133 N.L.J. 64.
[6]   *Soya GmBH Mainz KG* [1983] 1 Lloyd's Rep. 122 at 126; [1983] Com. L.R. 46; (1983) 133 N.L.J. 64.
[7]   *TM Noten BV v Harding* [1990] 2 Lloyd's Rep. 283.
[8]   *TM Noten BV* [1990] 2 Lloyd's Rep. 283 at 289.

tion to moisture damage to shipments of laminated truck flooring.[9] The court found that there was no fortuitous external occurrence which caused the flooring to deteriorate, but the damage was attributable to the nature of the subject matter of the insurance and was not, therefore, covered by the policy.

15-008   As can be seen, many of the cases considering the circumstances in which an insurer can rely on this exclusion arise in the context of marine insurance, largely as a result of s.55(2)(c) of the MIA 1906 which specifically provides that the insurer is not liable for inherent vice. However, the development of the law on inherent vice was not exclusive to marine insurance, as the case of *Blower v Great Western Railway* Co[10] demonstrates. The claimant delivered a bullock to the defendant to be carried by train to Nottingham pursuant to the terms of a consignment-note. The defendant carrier was to be liable for its own negligence during the carriage of the animal, but would also attract liability as an insurer for other damage that was caused during the conveyance. Although the animal had been properly secured, it managed to escape during the journey and was killed. The judge made a finding that there had been no negligence on the defendant's part and so its liability could only arise qua insurer, unless the loss had been caused by inherent vice. It was held that the defendant was not responsible for the consequences of an inherent vice in the thing, in this case the animal, being carried, which results in its destruction without any negligence on its part. Willies J considered that inherent vice referred to:

> "that sort of vice which by its internal development tends to the destruction or the injury of the animal or thing to be carried, and which is likely to lead to such a result."[11]

The bullock had managed to escape as a result of its own character and determination to do so. There was no external element which caused or contributed to the damage, but the damage was caused by the bullock's reaction to being confined to an enclosed space and its inherent motivation to escape. For that reason, the defendant could not be found liable for the death of the bullock.

15-009   The Supreme Court has emphasised the ingredient of fortuity in its recent decision in *Global Process Systems Inc v Syarikat Takaful Malaysia Bhd (The Cendor Mopu)*.[12] The subject matter of the insurance claim was three tubular legs of an oil rig (made of steel), which had broken off and fallen into the sea whilst being transported on a barge. Each of the legs weighed 404 tons. It was held that the loss resulted from metal fatigue in the three legs, which arose out of the effect of waves on the legs, due to their position on—and the motion of—the barge. The trial judge found that the legs were not capable of withstanding the normal incidents of the insured voyage, which meant that the cause of the loss was inherent vice. The Court of Appeal, however, concluded that the proximate cause of the loss was the occurrence of a "leg breaking wave", which resulted in increased strain on the remaining legs, causing them to break off. Therefore, the exclusion for inherent vice did not apply. The Supreme Court agreed, finding that the loss did not arise from inherent vice, or indeed wear and tear or the ordinary action of the wind and waves, but

---

[9]   *Nelson Marketing International Inc v Royal & Sun Alliance Insurance Co of Canada* 228 B.C.A.C 194; 57 BCLR (4th) 27; 40 C.C.L.I (4th) 36.

[10]   *Blower v Great Western Railway* (1871-72) L.R. 7 C.P. 655.

[11]   *Blower* (1871-72) L.R. 7 C.P. 655 at 662–663.

[12]   *Global Process Systems Inc v Syarikat Takaful Malaysia Bhd (The Cendor Mopu)* [2011] UKSC 5; [2011] 1 All E.R. 869; [2012] 1 All E.R. (Comm) 111; [2011] Bus. L.R. 537; [2011] 1 Lloyd's Rep. 560; [2011] 1 C.L.C. 1; [2011] Lloyd's Rep. I.R. 302; 2011 A.M.C. 305; *Times,* February 9, 2011. This case is also discussed above in para.10-014.

as a result of an external fortuitous accident or casualty of the seas in the form of rolling and pitching of the barge, which caught the first leg at just the right moment to produce stresses sufficient to cause it to break, leading to the breakage of the other two legs. This was, therefore, a fortuitous event. Mance LJ stated that the defence of inherent vice would be available to insurers where:

"the loss or damage could be said to be due to ... inherent characteristics of the hull or cargo not involving any fortuitous external accident or casualty".[13]

He also made clear that inevitability of loss or damage is not a crucial ingredient, stating:

"Inevitability is not the test of inherent vice, just as the lack of inevitability is no proof of a fortuitous external accident or casualty."[14]

This echoes the excerpt from *Arnould Law of Marine Insurance and Average* **15-010** which was quoted with approval by Lord Bingham in *T M Noten BV*[15] and also approved by Clarke LJ in *Global Process Systems Inc*, which says:

"The suggestion has sometimes been made that inherent vice means the same thing as damage that must inevitably happen, but this is not so. The distinction is between damage caused by any external occurrence, and damage resulting solely from the nature of the thing itself."[16]

This statement makes clear that inevitability is not a crucial part of proving that damage was caused as a result of inherent vice and that what must be considered is the cause of the damage and whether this was as a result of an inherent characteristic of the subject matter of the insurance or as a result of some external occurrence.

Latent defect.   The term "latent" is defined as: "[of a quality or state] existing but **15-011** not yet developed or manifest; hidden or concealed".[17] When coupled with the term "defect", it signifies something that is hidden or concealed—a flaw in the works that remains undiscovered for some time, even after an item has been reasonably inspected.[18] In practice, a latent defect may be difficult to distinguish from an inherent vice or wear and tear; all three exclusions describe an inherent quality of the subject matter that may cause premature failure of the part, sometimes in advance of its anticipated lifespan. This may be a matter of some significance where the policy contains exclusions for wear and tear and inherent vice, but expressly covers latent defects such as in a marine policy that incorporates the *Inchmaree* clause. However, a defect can be distinguished from the other exclusions as it is created by a positive act of human agency, usually a fault in the manufacture, design or materials within a part. It is a condition causing premature failure which was either present on construction or installation, or has resulted from the way the part was

---

13   *Global Process Systems Inc* [2011] UKSC 5 at [81]; [2011] 1 All E.R. 869 at 894; [2011] 1 Lloyd's Rep. 560 at 576.
14   *Global Process Systems Inc* [2011] UKSC 5 at [51]; [2011] 1 All E.R. 869 at 881; [2011] 1 Lloyd's Rep. 560 at 568.
15   See above, para.15-007.
16   *Arnould Law of Marine Insurance and Average*, edited by M.J. Mustill, and J.C.B. Gilman, 16th edn (London: Stevens & Sons, 1981), Vol.2, para.782.
17   *Oxford Dictionaries*, "latent" (Oxford Dictionaries Online, 2016), *http://oxforddictionaries.com/definition/english/latent* [Accessed 24 June 2016].
18   *Triple Five Corp v Simcoe & Erie Group* (1994) 159 A.R. 1; 29 CCLI 2 (d) 219; 1994 Carswell Alta 45; appeal dismissed [1997] A.J. No.248 (AltaCA); 145 DLR (4th) 236; [1997] 5 WWR 1.

designed or constructed or installed. It is a defect in the internal quality of the subject matter which manifests as a failure that cannot be attributed to the ordinary characteristics of the part operating within the expected tolerances and under the anticipated environmental forces.

Latent defects differ from patent defects in that a patent defect can be discovered after reasonable inspection. When a latent defect becomes manifest, it ceases to be latent defect and, instead, becomes a patent defect. There is generally no cover merely because a latent defect has become patent; some independent damage is required.[19]

15-012   **Wear and tear, corrosion or erosion and gradual deterioration.**   Wear and tear is impliedly excluded from cover unless there is some provision to the contrary. The aim of excluding wear and tear is to exclude cover where the proximate cause of the loss is the result of the processes of nature or the ordinary use or exposure of the subject matter of the insurance. An exclusion clause to the material damage section of the policy may include a provision that the policy does not apply to or include:

> "Normal making good, wear, tear or the cost involved in rectifying normal wasting, wearing away, corrosion or gradual deterioration."

It is common practice for the wear and tear exclusion to include a number of other natural processes which the policy will not respond to, for example, rust, corrosion, fungus, decay, wet or dry rot and gradual deterioration. Where the exclusion refers to a number of natural processes, the exclusion will be construed noscitur a sociis.[20] The noscitur a sociis rule is used to interpret a particular word or phrase in the context of those words which appear around it, usually to impose a more precise and narrow definition upon a word that may be capable of a number of different meanings.[21] However, the noscitur a sociis maxim will not allow the courts to distort the clear meaning of the language chosen by the parties, and the precise definition ascribed to each exclusion can be modified by the choice of conjunction used to introduce it into the clause.

15-013   So, for example, where the clause refers to "wear and tear, corrosion and gradual deterioration", it can reasonably be argued that the only corrosion intended to be covered by the exclusion is gradual corrosion which is akin to gradual deterioration, i.e. corrosion is to be construed noscitur a sociis with gradual deterioration. In contrast, however, if the exclusion relating to corrosion was contained in a different exclusion clause to wear and tear or gradual deterioration or where the words "of any kind" were added following the word "corrosion", corrosion may not be limited to only gradual or natural processes, but may be construed more widely to include a chemical process which may be sudden, non-natural, unexpected or inevitable.

Three of the most common exclusions, namely wear and tear, corrosion and gradual deterioration, are considered below, but the precise interpretation of the exclusion clause will depend on its wording. It will be seen that similar principles apply to each category, so that where the insurer seeks to rely on this exclusion, the

---

[19]   *Promet Engineering v Sturge (The Nukila)* [1997] 2 Lloyd's Rep. 146; [1997] C.L.C. 966.

[20]   Latin for "it is known from its associates".

[21]   See, for example, *Tektrol Ltd* [2005] EWCA Civ 845 in which the word "loss" was construed noscitur a sociis to refer only to the "loss" caused through electronic means such as "erasure" and the "distortion or corruption of information". For more, see above, paras 13-057 to 13-058.

insured must be able to point to some abnormal circumstance, accident or casualty in order for the proximate cause of the loss to fall outside of the exclusion and for the insured to be indemnified.[22]

Wear and tear. The phrase "wear and tear" identifies a process that is sometimes **15-014** easily recognised, but often more difficult to precisely define. It directs attention towards both the cause of the damage and its manifestation, unifying both into a singular concept—the damage must be caused by the ordinary usage of the part and it must manifest gradually by degree. Breaking the phrase down into its constituent words, one can observe that "wear" is concerned with the results of usage and "tear" is concerned with the impact of ordinary natural causes, such as weather, upon a thing.[23] Together, the meaning that the words convey is "deterioration caused by ordinary use."[24] Unlike gradual deterioration or corrosion which can signify a number of different processes and causes of damage (at least in the absence of other wording or a documentary, factual or commercial context against which to be construed), there is only one type of wear and tear and that is the inevitable loss sustained by an object by action of the ordinary environmental forces and pressures exerted on it during its use. The phrase "wear and tear" has only a single meaning, and where it is included within an exclusion that is to be construed noscitur a sociis then the effect of a phrase with only one meaning is that it will restrict the possible meanings attributed to the words around it. Wear and tear therefore warrants attention before corrosion and gradual deterioration and may affect the construction of the other exclusions where all three are included in the same clause.

The meaning of wear and tear was considered by the Commercial Court in **15-015** *Prudent Tankers Ltd S.A. v Dominion Insurance Co Ltd (The Caribbean Sea).*[25] The *Caribbean Sea* had been insured with underwriters under a hull policy incorporating the American Institute Hull Clauses, including an Inchmaree clause which contained the following wording:

> "Subject to the conditions of this Policy, this insurance also covers loss of or damage to the vessel directly caused by the following ... Any latent defect in the machinery or hull".

Whilst in transit between Venezuela and the United States, the *Caribbean Sea* suffered a failure to the starboard main sea suction valve which resulted in an ingress of water into the engine room and the total loss of the ship. The exact sequence of events that had led to the fracture and resulting loss was a matter of dispute between the parties, and Goff J (as he then was) determined that the following sequence was most likely to have occurred:

1. when the vessel was built, a wedge shaped nozzle had been used to adjoin the starboard main sea suction valve with the ship's hull;
2. this nozzle had been reinforced by gusset plates which were fillet welded to both the hull and the nozzle;
3. these fillet welds would have reduced the fatigue strength of the nozzle, causing fatigue cracks to gradually develop over the 19 years of the ship's

---

[22] See above, Ch.10, where fortuity is analysed in detail.
[23] *JSM Management Pty Ltd v QBE Insurance (Aust) Ltd* [2011] VSC 339 at [25].
[24] *Black's Law Dictionary*, Bryan A. Garner (ed in chief) 8th edn, 2006.
[25] *Prudent Tankers Ltd S.A. v Dominion Insurance Co Ltd (The Caribbean Sea)* [1980] 1 Lloyd's Rep. 338.

life. These fatigue cracks would have been so small that they would not have been noticeable on a visual inspection;

4. as the fatigue cracks extended and eventually reached the area of the circumferential weld of the nozzle to the hull, the high residual stress in this area would have resulted in rapid crack growth and the sudden opening of a large, circumferential fracture in the nozzle; and

5. this fracture allowed an ingress of water into the engine room which caused the ship to sink.

The owners of the ship could only succeed against the insurers if the circumstances of the loss were such as to bring it within the Inchmaree clause, i.e. if they could establish that the loss was caused by a latent defect in the hull. However, the insurers' case was that the loss was instead ordinary wear and tear, which was excluded under s.55(2)(c) of the MIA.[26] It was impossible to distinguish between damage due to the defect and damage resulting from wear and tear simply by looking at the extent and type of damage, and so the enquiry that Goff J had to undertake was to look for the proximate cause of the loss to see whether it would fall under the exclusion:

> "In the present case, however, the casualty is not simply to be attributed to ordinary wear and tear. The defect upon which the owners rely consisted of the fatigue cracks in the wedge-shaped nozzle; and the presence of these cracks is to be attributed to two factors-the manner in which the ship was designed (viz., the welding of the gussets to the nozzle with fillet welds in proximity to the circumferential weld between the nozzle and the spool piece) and the effect upon the nozzle, in these circumstances, of the ordinary working of the ship. The result of this combination of circumstances was that the fracture opened up a significant period of time before the end of the natural life of this ship. I do not consider that recovery in respect of loss of the ship, consequent upon such a fracture, is excluded by s. 55(2)(c) of the Act. Let me take the example of a ship incorporating such a design, which results in a far swifter development of fatigue cracking, and the sinking of the ship within, say, two years of her entering service. The loss could not, in such a case, have been proximately caused by ordinary wear and tear. It is not like a case where a ship's plating simply wastes away through rust, or a ship sinks through general debility."[27]

Goff J therefore held that the damage to the nozzle could not be said to have been caused by the inevitable deterioration of the ship due to the ordinary forces and stresses exerted on it during its operation. Instead, the presence of the defect had accelerated the development of fatigue stress and caused failure well in advance of the ship's anticipated lifespan. Accordingly, the defect was the cause of the damage in this case rather than wear and tear, and so the insurers could not rely on the exclusion.

15-016   More recent authority on a wear and tear exclusion was provided by the Supreme Court of Victoria in *JSM Management PTY Ltd v QBE Insurance (Australia) Ltd*.[28] After conducting his own research into the meanings that had previously been ascribed to wear and tear, Osborn J ascertained the following definition:

> "The defendant argues that certain judicial definitions of the phrase 'wear and tear' are inapplicable here because, in the instant policy, 'wear and tear' is not modified by any adjective ... However, construing the words 'wear and tear' in their everyday common usage, we are convinced that the

---

26   Section 55(2)(c) of the MIA provides that "[u]nless the policy otherwise provides, the insurer is not liable for ordinary wear and tear, ordinary leakage and breakage, inherent vice or nature of the subject-matter insured, or for any loss proximately caused by rats or vermin, or for any injury to machinery not proximately caused by maritime perils."

27   [1980] 1 Lloyd's Rep. 338 at 247.

28   *JSM Management PTY Ltd v QBE Insurance (Australia) Ltd* [2011] VSC 339.

words "wear and tear" *mean simply and solely that ordinary and natural deterioration or abrasion which an object experiences by its expected contacts between its component parts and outside objects during the period of its natural life expectancy.*"[29]

Osborn J therefore recognised that there was a "simple and sole" definition for wear and tear in its everyday usage, and this definition incorporated a number of different elements.

First, the deterioration on the property must be ordinary or natural, so that where the property has been subject to some unusual or inappropriate use which results in damage, the damage will not be excluded. This proved to be the determinative factor in *JSM Management Pty Ltd* as the insured had made use of a container forklift on hardstanding that could not withstand the weight of the forklift, causing the hardstanding to be damaged after eight months of regular use. Although the damage was gradual and resulted from everyday use, Osborn J considered that driving a forklift over the hardstanding which bore a weight too heavy for the hardstanding to withstand was an extraordinary rather than ordinary use of the hardstanding and, therefore, the damage had not been caused by wear and tear. The phrase only applies to losses which are ordinarily the result of use or natural forces; extraordinary losses are within the scope of cover and do not fall within the exclusion. Therefore, in this case, the insurers could not rely on the wear and tear exception in respect of damage to the hardstanding.[30]

Secondly, the damage must result from "expected contacts". An example of damage resulting from "unexpected contacts" can be found in the case of *Johnson & Towers Baltimore Inc v Vessel (The Hunter)*,[31] in which engine damage was caused when the insulation surround to the exhaust was breaking up and being ingested by the engine. The Maryland District Court found that the physical abuse resulting from stepping and sitting on the insulation and lagging were not anticipated contacts and acted to reduce the life expectancy of the materials. As a result, the exception for wear and tear did not apply and the insurers were obliged to indemnify the insured. **15-017**

Thirdly, is the reference to the "natural life expectancy" of the property damaged. Where the damage occurs at the end of the natural life expectancy of the product, this may be a strong indication that the loss has resulted from wear and tear. Contrarily, the diminished life expectancy of the property will often lead to a conclusion that the cause of damage is not ordinary wear and tear. In *The Caribbean Sea*, Goff J found that the defective welding on a ship nozzle increased fatigue stress and led to the total loss of the ship well in advance of the ship's anticipated lifespan, with the result that the damage was not wear and tear.[32] **15-018**

A case in which the wear and tear exception did apply is *Midland Mainline Ltd v Eagle Star Insurance Co Ltd; WAGN Railway Ltd v St Paul International Insurance Co Ltd; sub nom. Midland Mainline Ltd v Commercial Union Assurance Co Ltd*.[33] Train operating companies sought indemnities for business interruption as a result of the imposition of speed restrictions placed on the railway network after the Hatfield rail crash, which was caused by a broken rail. The speed restrictions were **15-019**

---

[29] *JSM Management PTY Ltd v QBE Insurance (Australia) Ltd* [2011] VSC 339 at [33].
[30] The court recognised that there may be other grounds for avoiding cover, but the wear and tear exception did not apply.
[31] *Johnson & Towers Baltimore Inc v Vessel (The Hunter)* 802 F. Supp 1343. (D.Md, 1992).
[32] See above, para.15-015.
[33] *Midland Mainline Ltd v Eagle Star Insurance Co Ltd* [2004] EWCA Civ 1042; [2004] 2 Lloyd's Rep. 604; [2004] 2 C.L.C. 480; [2004] Lloyd's Rep. I.R. 739; (2004) 148 S.J.L.B. 1062.

imposed where similar damage to the network was known to exist and the areas had been identified for renewal. The insurers successfully relied on the exclusion of liability for damage caused by wear and tear. The Court of Appeal found that there were two causes of loss; the damage to the tracks caused by wear and tear and the speed restrictions, which had been imposed as a result of wear and tear damaging the tracks. Both were proximate causes and, as a result, the insurer could rely on the exclusion.

The difference between *Midland Mainline Ltd* and the other cases referred to is that the wear and tear had clearly been identified as causing a safety issue, which led to the speed restrictions causing the loss. The damage flowed from the fact that there had been natural deterioration of the track. There was no unusual contact or use of the track resulting in its damage and, in fact, it would appear that the areas of the network with speed restrictions had already been identified as requiring repair, which would suggest these parts of the track had come to the end of their natural life expectancy. Therefore, the case fell squarely within the wear and tear exception.

The following conclusions can therefore be observed about the meaning of a wear and tear exclusion within a CAR policy:

1. Unless combined with words which take it outside its ordinary usage, wear and tear has a singular and sole definition.
2. Although that definition can be formulated a number of different ways, in essence the phrase denotes deterioration caused by ordinary use.
3. Wear and tear is therefore not fortuitous, and damage caused by wear and tear would not be insured under the insuring clause in any event.
4. Consequently, wear and tear is included as an express exclusion for the insured's benefit, for the purpose of clarity.

15-020   Corrosion/erosion.   Dictionary definitions of "corrosion" typically refer to a chemical reaction which results in the breaking down or destruction of a solid material, especially metal. A typical engineering definition of corrosion is as follows:

> "[D]eterioration of a material due to interaction with its environment. It is the process in which metallic atoms leave the metal or form compounds in the presence of water and gases. Metal atoms are removed from a structural element until it fails".[34]

The essence of corrosion is, therefore, the physical alteration, removal or destruction of part of the structure by a chemical process, such that any chemical reaction which causes deterioration of a material can be construed as corrosion. "Erosion" is defined as "the process of eroding or being eroded by wind, water, or other natural agents".[35]

However, there are two possible types of corrosion that need to be distinguished as distinct causes of damage under an insurance policy. The first type of corrosion is not accidental or fortuitous because there has been no extraordinary force of nature. It is the ordinary force of nature acting on the property, atmospheric condi-

---

[34]   Engineers Edge, *"Corrosion Definition – Corrosion and Galvanic Compatibility"* (Engineers Edge, 2016) *http://www.engineersedge.com/corrosion/corrosion_1.htm* [Accessed 24 June 2016]. See also U. R. Evans, *The Corrosion and Oxidation of Metals: First Supplementary Volume* (London: Arnold, 1968), who said corrosion is "largely an electro chemical phenomenon, [which] may be defined as destruction by electrochemical or chemical agencies".

[35]   *Oxford Dictionaries*, "Erosion" (Oxford Dictionaries Online, 2016), *http://oxforddictionaries.com/definition/english/erosion* [Accessed 24 June 2016].

tions causing some deterioration, or weather. For example, given time and sufficient oxygen and water, all iron will eventually corrode into rust and disintegrate. This process is an inevitable consequence of use and therefore not a fortuitous occurrence. The second type of corrosion is that which is caused by an accidental and fortuitous event, such as a chemical being spilled onto a metal or the bursting of a pipe which floods a tunnel and causes the metal supports in that tunnel to corrode. This leads to two possible meanings of corrosion within an exclusion clause, and the clause will have to be carefully considered in order to determine which of these meanings will prevail:

1. only the corrosion that relates to the ordinary processes of nature; or
2. all types of corrosion including those resulting from accidental or fortuitous occurrences.

The difference between the two forms of corrosion was considered in *Burts &* **15-021** *Harvey Ltd and Alchemy Ltd v Vulcan Boiler & General Insurance Co Ltd; Alchemy Ltd v Vulcan Boiler and General Insurance Co Ltd*.[36] This case concerned a consequential loss (breakdown) policy, which covered "sudden and accidental damage" by any fortuitous cause, but excluded from cover loss or damage resulting from:

"wear and tear, corrosion, erosion, failure of any part or parts the nature or functions of which necessitate their regular replacement".

The policy was taken out to cover a chemical plant for the production of maleic anhydride, a substance used in the manufacture of certain plastics. As part of the manufacturing process, gaseous maleic anhydride was pumped through a set of steel tubes at very high pressures surrounded by water jackets in order to cool the gaseous substance down. It transpired that some of these tubes were defective in that they contained splits which allowed steam to escape and mix with the maleic anhydride, forming an exceedingly corrosive substance called maleic acid which was capable of "washing away" the steel around the tubes. The plant broke down and over £20,000 of damage was caused by the corrosive effects of the maleic acid. Lawton J had to determine whether this type of corrosion would be excluded under the exclusion clause (in line with meaning 2 above), or whether it constituted sudden and accidental damage to which the policy would respond (with the exclusion confined to meaning 1). In his view the losses sustained were outside of the exclusion as the clause had been intended to exclude only the corrosion caused by the ordinary operation of the plant over its lifetime:

"... on my view of the construction of the exclusion clause corrosion and erosion within the meaning of that clause were never intended (so I find as a matter of construction of this policy in the circumstances in which it was issued) to cover other than corrosion and erosion caused in use. The exclusion clause reads as follows:

(4) Wear and tear, corrosion, erosion, failure of any part or parts the nature or functions of which necessitate their regular replacement.

It seems clear to me that what the defendants had in mind was the effect of the gaseous maleic anhydride upon the tubes through which it would pass in the ordinary process of production, and they had not in mind any corrosion or erosion which was consequential upon any breakdown of the plant due to the failure of the component. It was submitted by Mr Everett that the exclusion in the policy

---

[36] *Burts & Harvey Ltd v Vulcan Boiler and General Insurance Co Ltd (No.1)* [1966] 1 Lloyd's Rep. 161; 116 N.L.J. 639.

was not really an exclusion at all, but, because of the wording of the contingency provisions; the exclusion was really nothing more than a definition of the contingency. I do not think it was ...".[37]

In other words, Lawton J considered that only damage which resulted from the natural and intended use or process of the subject matter would be excluded by the clause. Although the inclusion of other forms of gradual, non-fortuitous occurrences within the same exclusion clause may have motivated this conclusion, Lawton J's reasoning is also explicable on the basis that the insuring clause insured "sudden and accidental" damage, whereas the exclusions related to categories of damage such as "gradually developing flaws". An interpretation of the exclusion which denied indemnity for "sudden" corrosion along with gradual corrosion by the ordinary processes of nature would therefore be inconsistent with the express wording of the insuring clause.

Whilst the policy in this case was a consequential loss (breakdown) policy rather than a CAR policy, this reasoning may have direct application to CAR policies which include the word "sudden" in the insuring clause. For example, the insuring clause of the Munich Re CAR standard insurance policy (used extensively in the Pacific Rim countries) provides cover for "unforeseen and sudden" damage:

"The Insurers hereby agree with the Insured that if at any time during the period of cover the items or any part thereof entered in the Schedule shall suffer any unforeseen and sudden physical loss or damage from any cause, other than those specifically excluded, in a manner necessitating repair or replacement, the Insurers will indemnify the Insured in respect of such loss or damage as hereinafter provided by payment in cash, replacement or repair (at their own option) up to an amount not exceeding in respect of each of the items specified in the Schedule the sum set opposite thereto and not exceeding in any one event the limit of indemnity where applicable and not exceeding in all the total sum expressed in the Schedule as insured hereby."

The presence of the word "sudden" in the insuring clause supports a narrow interpretation of a corrosion exclusion and may be decisive where the other canons of construction fail to determine which meaning of corrosion is intended.

15-022   The Supreme Court of Canada has applied a similar test in *CCR Fishing Ltd v Tomenson Inc (The La Pointe)*[38]; the ship sank due to a sudden ingress of water, which flooded the engine room because the bolts and cap screws were made of carbon steel instead of brass, copper or steel. The underwriters asserted that the flange deteriorated from corrosion as a result of an accumulation of leakage in a number of areas. McLauchlin J found that there was nothing ordinary about the way in which the cap screws failed, as the trial judge had found this was due to the negligent act of the repairers who installed them. The emphasis on the "extraordinary" is similar to the view expressed in *Burts & Harvey Ltd and Alchemy Ltd* that there must be nothing external or unusual in order for the exclusion to apply.

15-023   However, the fact that there may have been something "external" does not necessarily bring the loss within the cover. In the American case of *Bettigole v American Employers Ins. Co.*,[39] damage to a parking area caused by de-icing salts brought in on car wheels caused damage to steel reinforcement bars, causing structural damage to the building. It was held that the exclusion did apply in this case, even though the corrosion was created by the action of third parties. The court in *Bettigole* stated:

---

[37]   *Burts & Harvey Ltd v Vulcan Boiler and General Insurance Co Ltd (No.1)* [1966] 1 Lloyd's Rep. 161; 116 N.L.J. 639 at 170.

[38]   *CCR Fishing v Tomenson Inc (The La Pointe)* [1991] 1 Lloyd's Rep. 89; 1990 A.M.C. 1443.

[39]   *Bettigole v American Employers Ins. Co.* 30 Mass.App.Ct. 272, 567 N.E. 2d 1259. (Mass.App.Ct, 1991).

"The defendant sees no reason—nor do we—for confining the term corrosion in the context of the policy to a wearing away by 'natural' means of weather or the like, or in consequence of conduct of the insured rather than an outsider."[40]

This makes sense, however, because the use being made of the car park was not unusual in any way and it could be anticipated that cars would drive through grit in wintery conditions and this would be brought into the car park. Therefore, although the car park users could be pointed to as being some external cause of the corrosion, there was no element of non-natural use or unusual contact. The car park was being used in the way that it was intended to be used.

Subsequently, the case of *Bettigole* was cited with approval in *Central Intern. Co. v Kemper Nat. Ins. Co.*[41] which considered the meaning of an exclusion for "discoloration and corrosion"[42] under an all risk ocean marine open cargo insurance policy. The policy in question covered all risks of "physical loss or damage [to the cargo] from any external cause"[43] but was subject to a specific exclusion: "[h]owever, as respects steel products and all metals: excluding rusting, oxidation, discoloration and corrosion".[44]   **15-024**

It was admitted by the insured that the damage was corrosion and discoloration, but it was averred by the insured that the damage had not occurred naturally, but had been primarily caused by water and the improper stowage of powder ash, which had leaked onto the steel coils during a storm. This argument was rejected by the district court, which found that the insured was not entitled to be indemnified. The appeal court upheld this decision, stating:

"Central must accept in light of its own affidavits that the harm to the steel coils manifested itself as corrosion and discoloration. Conversely, at least for purposes of this appeal, we must assume the truth of Central's claim that the anterior cause of the corrosion and discoloration was the exposure of the steel to improperly stowed powder ash as well as to sea water and that unexpected storm conditions at sea contributed to that exposure ... The case thus involves a generally covered risk (actually, two risks: sea peril and negligent stowage) resulting in excluded consequences (corrosion and discoloration).

This is a recurring issue and, under ordinary principles of contract interpretation, there is little doubt that the exclusion is presumptively a qualification on the risk coverage. Normally, specific language is treated as a limitation on general language; and in this case fixing the relationship of the clauses is made even easier because the all–risk language in Central's policy is followed by the term '[h]owever', which introduces the exclusion. In other words, facially read, there is liability for damage to cargo from all risks including storm or accident unless the damage is corrosion or discoloration.

Curiously, this straightforward approach is not always reflected in the cases. There is language, in Massachusetts decisions as elsewhere, that purports to treat a covered risk and an excluded consequence as legitimate rivals whose priorities are to be tested by asking questions about "causation"; these discussions, often in opinions with defensible results, tend not to be very illuminating ... The better explanation, where the insurer is held liable, appears to be that the court has chosen to read the exclusion *in* context more narrowly than its literal language might suggest.

But the precedent most closely in point from Massachusetts – whose law Central wants to govern this case [is *Bettigole*] ... We cite *Bettigole* primarily because its facts are apt and not because we attach conclusive weight to Massachusetts case law construing a particular policy."[45]

Drawing these cases together, it seems most likely that a corrosion exclusion   **15-025**

---

40   *Bettigole v American Employers Ins. Co.* 30 Mass.App.Ct. 272, 567 N.E. 2d 1259. (Mass.App.Ct, 1991) at 275.
41   *Central Intern. Co v Kemper Nat. Ins. Co.* 202 F.3d 372 (C.A.1 (Mass.), 2000).
42   *Central Intern. Co.* 202 F.3d 372 (C.A.1 (Mass.), 2000).
43   *Central Intern. Co.* 202 F.3d 372 at 373 (C.A.1 (Mass.), 2000).
44   *Central Intern. Co.* 202 F.3d 372 at 373 (C.A.1 (Mass.), 2000).
45   *Central Intern. Co.* 202 F.3d 372 at 374–376 (C.A.1 (Mass.), 2000).

within a CAR policy will be interpreted as only excluding the natural process of corrosion and will not exclude corrosion that results from an accidental or fortuitous occurrence. A number of principles may support this conclusion, though their application will depend on the precise wording used in the policy:

1. First, the policy must be construed as a whole with particular regard to the wording of the insuring clause. An interpretation of an exclusion clause that deprives the insured of a substantial portion of the cover under the insuring clause is unlikely to be supported unless clear words have been used.
2. Secondly, where the corrosion exclusion is contained in the same clause as wear and tear and gradual deterioration, the application of the legal maxim noscitur a sociis will support a narrow interpretation. As discussed above,[46] the phrase wear and tear is only capable of one definition when employed in its ordinary usage, and that is to exclude the deterioration of the subject matter through use. Since this is a non-fortuitous occurrence that is included expressly for the purpose of clarity, the pairing of wear and tear with corrosion suggests that corrosion is also intended to be understood as referring to a non-fortuitous occurrence that is included for the avoidance of doubt, namely corrosion caused by natural processes as distinct from corrosion resulting from accidental, fortuitous occurrences.
3. Thirdly, the application of contra proferentem rule.

15-026   It is, of course, open to insurers to include words which extend the exclusion to cover all types of corrosion, for example by the inclusion of the words "howsoever caused" or by providing a separate exclusion clause which only covers corrosion, such that the noscitur a sociis rule would not necessarily apply to narrow the interpretation applied to "corrosion". However, as can be seen from *Burts & Harvey Ltd and Alchemy Ltd*,[47] the policy will be construed as a whole in order to give effect to the express terms and purpose of the policy. In the event that there are any ambiguities in the policy, these will be strictly interpreted against the insurer pursuant to the contra proferentem rule, as discussed above in paras 13-060 to 13-061. Therefore, providing a separate or more detailed provision in relation to corrosion may be advisable in circumstances where the works include some sort of chemical plant and the insurer considers that "sudden" corrosion is a foreseeable risk and one which is not intended to be indemnified under the policy.

15-027 **Gradual deterioration.**   The meaning of gradual deterioration was considered in *AMEC Civil Engineering Limited v Norwich Union Fire Insurance Society Limited*,[48] in which the CAR policy taken out by AMEC Civil Engineering Limited ("AMEC") contained the following exclusion:

> "4. *Wear and Tear* the cost of rectifying wear, tear or gradual deterioration but this exclusion shall be limited to the part or parts immediately affected and shall not apply to loss of or damage to other Insured Property not suffering from such wear, tear or gradual deterioration as a consequence thereof."

AMEC had placed the policy to cover the construction of a sea defence wall using reinforced concrete blocks. The blocks were cast by pouring concrete over a steel cage until it set, and the contract data specified that the depth of the concrete cover-

---

[46]   See above, para.15-014.
[47]   *Burts & Harvey Ltd* [1966] 1 Lloyd's Rep. 161 at 170–171; 116 N.L.J. 639.
[48]   *AMEC Civil Engineering Limited v Norwich Union Fire Insurance Society Limited* [2003] EWHC 1341 (TCC).

ing the steel frame was required to be at least 75mm with a tolerance of plus or minus 5mm. It later transpired that the casting process utilised by AMEC was defective in that it allowed the steel cage to suffer minute rotations whilst the concrete was poured into the mould, which resulted in a number of blocks being installed into the sea wall with a depth of concrete below the 70mm minimum. After the defective blocks were discovered, AMEC was contractually required to break out and replace the blocks at the cost of £507,029, which it then claimed under the policy.

The issues for H.H. Judge Richard Seymour Q.C. to determine were, first, whether the policy would in principle respond to the losses suffered by AMEC and, second, whether the exclusion for gradual deterioration would operate to prevent cover. Whilst his determination of the first issue in the negative rendered a decision on the second both obiter and contingent, H.H. Judge Richard Seymour Q.C. did go on to consider the meaning of gradual deterioration:

> "Had I been persuaded that AMEC had sustained financial loss as a result of the rusting of reinforcement within those Blocks which showed signs of it and were required to be replaced, it would have been necessary to consider the application of Exclusion 4. I do not consider that I need explicit expert evidence to support the conclusion, based upon the common experience of mankind, that the action of water upon unprotected iron or steel produces a progressive oxidation which, unless interrupted, will lead to the eventual erosion of the iron or steel. In my judgment, the proper construction of the expression 'gradual deterioration' in the phrase 'wear, tear or gradual deterioration' in Exclusion 4 is that it means a deterioration which is progressive by degrees, as opposed to sudden and catastrophic. Mr. Mendoza submitted that 'gradual' meant 'slow', and that the speed at which signs of rust staining appeared on the Blocks affected was not slow, so that the occurrence of rust damage could not in this case be described as 'gradual deterioration'. It is implicit in that submission that the extent of the rusting at the time signs were noticed was such that there was at that point a need to replace the affected Blocks. The understanding of the word 'slow' in any particular context necessitates a comparison with that which is said in the context not to be slow. In the present context all that can be said is that in the affected Blocks the progression of rusting had been sufficient to cause manifestations upon the surface of the concrete. That does not mean that any reinforcement must have rusted through, or, indeed, that erosion must have reached any particular stage. If, contrary to my finding, a decision to replace those Blocks which showed signs of rust staining which were replaced was based upon the appearance of those signs and nothing else, then in the absence of any evidence that any reinforcement had actually failed, the decision could only have been made on the basis of the risk of failure in the future. In other words, the decision would have been an attempt to forestall the anticipated progressive effects of erosion over time, or 'gradual deterioration'."[49]

The analysis conducted by H.H. Judge Richard Seymour Q.C. focused on the word "gradual" in the exclusion in order to determine whether the erosion of the reinforced concrete would be caught. He was correct to conclude that "gradual" means "by degrees" and not simply "slow", as it is perhaps self-evident that measurement of speed is a relative assessment and that a process can be slow and gradual by degrees or fast but gradual by degrees.

However, the central question that was not considered in *AMEC* was the sort of process that was intended to be excluded by the use of the word "deterioration". The findings of fact made by H.H. Judge Richard Seymour Q.C. were consistent with accelerated rusting having occurred due to a defect, yet the point was not taken that the exclusion was only in respect of natural gradual deterioration and not gradual deterioration caused by the presence of a defect. Such an interpretation of the exclusion would have been supported by the application of the noscitur a sociis maxim as the exclusion was included within the same clause as wear and tear. This

---

49 *AMEC Civil Engineering Limited v Norwich Union Fire Insurance Society Limited* [2003] EWHC 1341 (TCC) at [75].

interpretation also finds judicial support in *JSM Management PTY Ltd v QBE Insurance (Australia) Ltd*[50]:

> "Thirdly, the specific context of cl 4(b) includes other words which are directed to other forms of gradual damage commonly generated by ordinary use and natural processes, particularly 'fading' and 'gradual deterioration or developing flaws'."[51]

15-028 Change in water table. The water table exclusion clause is a general exclusion that concerns changes in the level of the water table; whether it goes up or down. This means that damage caused to insured property as a result of a rise (e.g. water penetrating a basement) or fall (e.g. damage caused to property as a result of soil shrinkage) in the level of the water table will not be covered. The excluded event will be listed in addition to other naturally occurring excluded events such as wear and tear and gradual deterioration.[52]

15-029 Insects or vermin. A policy will exclude cover for damage to property caused by vermin or insects and also often appear in the general exclusion clause referring to wear and tear, etc. An insect is defined as "a small arthropod animal that has six legs and generally one or two pairs of wings".[53]

Vermin is defined as "wild animals which are believed to be harmful to crops, farm animals, or game, or which carry disease", such as rodents.[54] Damage caused by insects and vermin is excluded on the basis that such damage is natural and ordinary.

15-030 Summary. The result of this body of case law is that, subject to the other provisions in the policy, in order for the exclusion for wear and tear, corrosion, rust, etc. to apply, it is suggested that the insurer must demonstrate that the damage was caused by the ordinary or natural deterioration of the property insured rather than any accidental or fortuitous occurrence. Relevant to determining whether this has been demonstrated is the expected contacts of the insured property and the property's natural life expectancy.

(b) Natural events

15-031 Natural events/acts of god. An act of god is described as "an instance of uncontrollable natural forces in operation".[55] It is a natural event that occurs without human intervention, which cannot be prevented, as it is the result of natural phenomena; such as for example lightning, flood or cyclone. The act of god exclusion clause is contained in insurance policies so as to limit or exclude the insurer's

---

[50] *JSM Management PTY Ltd v QBE Insurance (Australia) Ltd* [2011] VSC 339.

[51] *JSM Management PTY Ltd v QBE Insurance (Australia) Ltd* [2011] VSC 339 at [40].

[52] See below, para.26-117 in the context of an all risks property insurance claim (ARPI).

[53] *Oxford Dictionaries* (*Oxford Dictionaries* Online, 2016), *http://oxforddictionaries.com/definition/english/insect?q=insect* [Accessed 24 June 2016].

[54] *Oxford Dictionaries*, "vermin" (*Oxford Dictionaries* Online, 2016), *http://oxforddictionaries.com/definition/english/vermin?q=vermin* [Accessed 24 June 2016].

[55] See *Oxford Dictionaries*, "Act of God" (*Oxford Dictionaries* Online, 2016) *http://oxforddictionaries.com/definition/english/act?q=act+of+god#act__37* [Accessed 24 June 2016]. In *Nugent v Smith* (1876) 1 CPD 423 at 444, Mellish LJ said "[a] common carrier is not liable for any accident as to which he can shew that it is due to natural causes directly and exclusively, without human intervention, and that it could not have been prevented by any amount of foresight and pains and care reasonably to be expected from him".

liability in respect of natural events. In recent years, there have been an unprecedented number of natural disasters resulting in property being destroyed or damaged.[56] The various natural events may be excluded from cover in a CAR policy. Commonly an exclusion clause in relation to natural events will include storm, tempest, flood, lightning, explosion and subsidence. Occasionally, a CAR policy may contain a proviso to the material damage section of the policy which lists the natural events/acts of god and may be worded as follows:

"The major perils/Acts of God claims shall mean claims arising out of

a) Earthquake – Fire & Shock
b) Landslide/Rockslide/Subsidence
c) Flood/Inundation
d) Storm/Tempest/Hurricane/Typhoon/Cyclone/Lightning or other atmospheric disturbances.
e) Collapse
f) Water damage for 'wet' risks i.e. contract involving works in rivers, canals, lakes or sea."

Item (d) listed above is likely to cover other natural events such as tsunamis, tidal waves, rain/rainstorm and storm-force winds/windstorm. Further, other natural events that may be excluded from cover are volcanism/volcanic eruption, severe ice storms, bush fire and forest fires. The meaning given to some of the natural events listed above is considered below. As explained in Ch.21, where an insurer seeks to rely on the natural events exclusion clause, the burden is on the insurer to show that it was the natural event which caused the damage. By way of example, in *S & M Hotels Ltd v Legal and General Assurance Society Ltd*,[57] Thesiger J held that it was not, in fact, the gusts of wind which had caused a wall in the hotel to collapse, but the fact that there had been inadequate support for the upper floors and the roof during the reconstruction of the property. As a result, even if the gusts of wind could amount to a storm, which Thesiger found was not the case, it was held that the cause of the damage was not the wind in any event.

Storm. *Stroud's Judicial Dictionary* provides that: 15-032

"While the word 'storm' used in the insured perils clause of an insurance policy might involve an element of violence in the sense of rapid movement of air and water, it was not to be restricted to that meaning, nor to the particular technical significance of the Beaufort Scale."[58]

Whilst the definition rightly suggests that the Beaufort Scale is not determinative, it is relevant and is sometimes treated by the English courts as the starting point when considering whether an event is a storm. This is because it assists in gaining an initial impression of the severity of the event in question.

In *Oddy v Phoenix Assurance Co Ltd*[59] Veale J defined storm in the following terms:

"Storm means storm, and to me it connotes some sort of violent wind usually accompanied by rain

---

[56] Research carried out on behalf of Lloyd's suggests that some countries such as China, Thailand and Saudi Arabia are under-insured against natural events. See J. Kollewe, "*Lloyd's Warns of £105bn deficit in insurance for natural disasters*" (November 27, 2012), *Guardian.co.uk, http://www.guardian.co.uk/business/2012/nov/27/lloyds-natural-disasters-insurance-deficit* [Accessed 24 June 2016].

[57] *S&M Hotels Ltd v Legal and General Assurance Society Ltd* [1972] 1 Lloyd's Rep. 157; (1971) 115 S.J. 888; *Times*, November 19, 1971.

[58] *Stroud's Judicial Dictionary*, 2nd edn, p.289.

[59] *Oddy v Phoenix Assurance Co Ltd* [1966] 1 Lloyd's Rep. 134; (1966) 116 N.L.J. 554.

or hail or snow. Storm does not mean persistent bad weather, nor does it mean heavy rain or persistent rain by itself."[60]

Consistent with this decision, in *S & M Hotels Ltd*[61] damage caused by wind alone was not sufficient to amount to a storm. Although not requiring violent wind, the Scottish Courts have applied a similar test and held that significant wind accompanied by very heavy snow was sufficient to constitute storm in *Glasgow Training Group (Motor Trade) Ltd v Lombard Continental Plc.*[62]

15-033 Tempest. Although there appears to be no reported case defining the term "tempest", in *Young v Sun Alliance and London Insurance Ltd*[63] Shaw LJ indicated that tempest was a more violent form of a storm, which is in line with the definition provided in the *Oxford English Dictionary* as "[a] violent windy storm".[64] Similarly, in *Oddy*, Veale J considered that a tempest might simply be a severe or exceptional storm, which accords with common sense as a reasonable, if imprecise, definition of the word.

In *Glasgow Training*,[65] the court stated:

"The word 'tempest' denotes a condition of turbulence of a degree not necessarily found in a storm. The Shorter Oxford Dictionary definition of tempest starts 'a violent storm of wind, usually accompanied by a downfall of rain, hail, or snow or by thunder'. It seems that a wind is an essential ingredient of a tempest but need not be present for there to be a storm. I do not consider that in the context of the policy 'storm' necessarily excludes wind, although wind is not a necessary ingredient."

15-034 Flood.[66] The meaning attributed to the term flood may depend on whether it appears in a standalone exclusion or within the natural events clause. Where it appears in a clause with storm and tempest, the Court of Appeal had held that "flood" was to be read in this context. In *Young v Sun Alliance and London Insurance*[67] the court found that the inclusion of flood within the natural events clause meant that the term connoted a large and elemental movement of water that was above and beyond the ordinary definition of what may be considered a flood:

"It is because the word 'flood' occurs in the context it does, that I have come to the conclusion that one must go back to first impressions, namely, that it is used there in the limited rather than the wider sense; that it means something which is a natural phenomenon which has some element of violence, suddenness or largeness about it."

60 *Oddy* [1966] 1 Lloyd's Rep. 134 at 138; (1966) 116 N.L.J. 554.
61 *S&M Hotels Ltd* [1972] 1 Lloyd's Rep. 157; (1971) 115 S.J. 888; *Times,* November 19, 1971.
62 *Glasgow Training Group (Motor Trade) Ltd v Lombard Continental Plc* 1989 S.C. 30; 1989 S.L.T. 375.
63 *Young v Sun Alliance and London Insurance Ltd* [1977] 1 W.L.R. 104; [1976] 3 All E.R. 561; [1976] 2 Lloyd's Rep. 189 at 191; (1976) 120 S.J. 469.
64 *Oxford Dictionaries,* "tempest" (Oxford Dictionaries Online, 2016), *http://oxforddictionaries.com/ definition/english/tempest* [Accessed 24 June 2016].
65 *Glasgow Training Group (Motor Trade) Ltd v Lombard Continental Plc* 1989 S.C. 30; 1989 S.L.T. 375.
66 See below, para.26-127.
67 *Young v Sun Alliance and London Insurance Ltd* [1977] 1 W.L.R. 104 at 105; [1976] 3 All E.R. 561; [1976] 2 Lloyd's Rep. 189; (1976) 120 S.J. 469.

Consistent with this, in *Rohan Investments Ltd v Cunningham and Members of Syndicate 877 at Lloyd's (t/a Criterion Insurance Services)*[68] damage to a flat caused by an ingress of water following abnormally heavy rainfall was damage which fell within the meaning of "flood" in the policy. However, unlike in *Young*, the court held that whilst categorising an event as a "flood" could depend on the volume of water, it did not believe the water needed to originate from a natural phenomenon (such as weather):

> "I think the Judge was entitled to conclude that the build-up of 4 inches of rain on the roof during a period of about a fortnight from 15th January 1995, the date of the last inspection by the Chief's handyman, was sufficiently rapid to be abnormal. I think the Judge was also entitled to infer from the extent of the damage caused that a relatively large volume of water must have found its way into the interior of the building. Its ingress must have been more than the slow seepage or percolation with which this court was concerned in *Young's* case. The precise volume of water that got in cannot in my view be decisive or even particularly important, but simple arithmetic indicates that a mere 1 centimetre of rain on a flat roof 10 metres square amounts to 1 million cubic centimetres, which is 1,000 litres or about 220 imperial gallons. That, it seems to me, is more than a sprinkling."

The meaning of the term has also been considered in a case where the flood was   **15-035**
not caused by natural phenomenon, but an employee's negligence. In *Computer & Systems Engineering Plc v John Lelliott (Ilford) Ltd*,[69] during the construction works a metal purlin was dropped onto a sprinkler system pipe, causing water to escape, which in turn caused property damage. The court considered whether this was a risk which had been assumed by the property owner pursuant to cl.22 C1 of the JCT Standard Form of Building Contract (1980 ed.),[70] which provided that the property owner would take out insurance in respect of "fire, lightning, explosion, tempest, flood, bursting or overflowing of water tanks, apparatus or pipes, earthquake, etc." As to the meaning of "flood" in the context of this clause, Bedlam LJ stated:

> "In the present case the words 'storm, tempest and flood', are followed by 'bursting or overflowing of water tanks, apparatus or pipes'. This express reference to risks associated with and emanating from an installation used for the collection, storage and distribution of water, generally located in premises, reinforces the restrictive meaning to be given to the word 'flood', for if inundation from any source or cause was encompassed by the word 'flood', no content would remain for the words which follow. As Lord Keith remarked, there have been many cases in which flooding of premises and damage originating from a natural downpour have been contributed to by a blockage of drains, downpipes or culverts due to fault on the part of the contractor. Moreover in my view since the risks associated with water tanks, apparatus or pipes are expressly confined to bursting or overflowing, any flooding of the premises from water emanating from such an installation was intended to be confined to an occurrence of that nature.
>   In the context of this contract 'flood', in my view, imports the invasion of the property, which is at the employer's risk, by a large volume of water caused by a rapid accumulation or sudden release of water from an external source, usually but not necessarily confined to the result of a natural phenomenon such as a storm, tempest or downpour."[71]

The Court of Appeal found that the employee's actions of dropping the purlin and the resulting escape of water did not constitute a flood within the meaning of the JCT Contract and so the damage was not covered by the insurance policy. Bedlam

---

[68]   *Rohan Investments Ltd v Cunningham and Members of Syndicate 877 at Lloyd's (t/a Criterion Insurance Services)* [1999] Lloyd's Rep. I.R. 190; [1998] NPC 14.
[69]   *Computer & Systems Engineering Plc v John Lelliott (Ilford) Ltd* 54 B.L.R. 1; *Times*, February 21, 1991.
[70]   Joint Contracts Tribunal. *Standard Form of Building Contract 1980 Edition: Private Without Quantities*, (London: RIBA, 1980).
[71]   *Computer & Systems Engineering Plc v John Lelliott (Ilford) Ltd* 54 B.L.R. 1 at 9–10.

LJ was reinforced in his view as to the construction of cl.22 by the fact that had the words used in the construction contract been defined in the policy, they would be afforded the same meaning.

15-036   In the more recent case of *Tate Gallery Board of Trustees v Duffy Construction Ltd*,[72] Jackson J held that the submergence of part of the Tate Gallery following the decoupling of a pipe from the water main constituted a flood and set out the following test:

> "In determining whether the unwelcome arrival of water upon property constitutes a "flood", it is relevant to consider (a) whether the source of the water was natural; (b) whether the source of the water was external or internal; (c) the quantity of water; (d) the manner of its arrival; (e) the area and character of the property upon which the water was deposited; (f) whether the arrival of that water was an abnormal event. Ultimately, it is a question of degree whether any given accumulation of water constitutes a flood."

15-037   **Lightning.**   The precise meaning of this term does not appear to have been considered by the courts. The *Oxford English Dictionary* definition is

> "the occurrence of a natural electrical discharge of very short duration and high voltage between a cloud and the ground or within a cloud, accompanied by a bright flash and typically also thunder".[73]

15-038   **Explosion.**   In *Commonwealth Smelting Ltd v Guardian Royal Exchange Assurance Ltd*,[74] the Court of Appeal upheld the trial judge's definition of explosion as

> "an event that is violent, noisy and are caused by a very rapid chemical or nuclear reaction, or the bursting out of gas or vapour under pressure".

In this case, the steel impeller attached to a shaft in a blower house, which was designed to provide air to a furnace, failed and shattered causing pieces to fly outwards as a result of the air pressure. This was not held to be an explosion within the meaning attributed to that term.

15-039   **Pollution/contamination.**   The pollution/contamination exclusion is dealt with differently in relation to the material damage section of policy to that of the third party liability section, which is discussed in Ch.17. Under the material damage section, the pollution exclusion may be worded as follows:

> "This policy does not cover loss or destruction or damage caused by pollution or contamination but this shall not exclude destruction of or damage to the Property Insured, not otherwise excluded."

The above clause makes it clear that the insurer will accept liability for any pollution/contamination damage caused to "insured property", but not for the costs of any loss or damage caused to any other property. In a construction policy, a debris removal exclusion clause will reinforce the above by stating the insurer may indemnify the insured for costs and expenses necessarily incurred by the insured in respect of the debris removal and disposal (e.g. removal of debris from property) under the material damage section of the policy but will exclude "any costs or

---

[72]   *Tate Gallery Board of Trustees v Duffy Construction Ltd* [2007] EWHC 361 (TCC) at [37]; [2007] 1 All E.R. (Comm) 1004 at 1004–1005; [2007] Lloyd's Rep. I.R. 758 at 769.

[73]   *Oxford Dictionaries*, "lightning" (Oxford Dictionaries Online, 2016), *http://oxforddictionaries.com/ definition/english/lightning* [Accessed 24 June 2016].

[74]   *Commonwealth Smelting Ltd v Guardian Royal Exchange Assurance Ltd* [1986] 1 Lloyd's Rep. 121 at 124.

expenses arising from pollution or contamination of property not insured by the policy".

If a policy covers a number of different insureds and sites, and hazardous materials are stored on site, there will be a greater risk of exposure if the materials are stored incorrectly. In order to reduce its potential for liability, insurers may make enquiries to determine how the materials are being stored on site(s) or it may on the other hand decide to adopt the pollution or contamination exclusion or limit its liability to that of "sudden identifiable unintended and unexpected" pollution in respect of the material damage section of the policy.[75]

Normal action of the sea. In relation to marine engineering and construction **15-040** works undertaken in and around harbours or at sea, insurers will seek to exclude cover for damage caused to property as a result of "normal action of the sea". The rationale for this exclusion is that the loss insured should be fortuitous, as explained at the beginning of this chapter, and, therefore, cover will not be provided for damage caused by the normal action of the sea. When construing this clause, the word "normal" is to be attached to the word "action" and not the word "sea". Accordingly, for the exclusion to operate: (i) the sea state at the time the damage occurred must be within the range which could reasonably have been anticipated[76]; and (ii) the sea must have been a cause of the damage.

Some CAR policies may define what constitutes the normal action of the sea in a particular location based on meteorological and marine data in relation to wind speed or wave action, which is likely to occur in a once in ten or twenty-five year cycle. For example, a definition of the action of the sea to a CAR policy may state that the fortuitous damage must be "consequent upon" wind speeds of Beaufort scale 7 or below as measured at the particular place concerned.

(c) Conflicts exclusions

Conflicts exclusions. The risks arising from war are of their nature very dif- **15-041** ficult to predict and quantify. They are excluded from all property insurance policies by a market agreement. The exclusion is commonly in the following form:

> "The Insurers shall not be liable in respect of any consequence of war, invasion, act of foreign enemy, hostilities (whether war be declared or not), civil war, rebellion, revolution, insurrection or military or usurped power."

Some policies include a longer form of the exclusion dealing with specific risks arising from a conflict situation, such as confiscation.

It is important when analysing the application of an exclusion relating to conflict **15-042** or some form of civil unrest to remember that the meaning of that clause in any particular circumstance is often complicated and uncertain. For example, the state of affairs said to bring a claim within the exclusion may be ongoing and unresolved. Further, as Mustill J noted in the context of a claim relating to civil unrest in Lebanon, the court is frequently being asked to determine not only what happened (which may itself be unclear) but why it happened. He said:

---

[75] As to the meaning of this phrase, see below at paras 18-130 to 18-133.
[76] *Grant, Smith & Co and McDonnell Ltd v Seattle Construction and Dry Dock Co* [1920] A.C. 162 at 171; 89 L.J.P.C. 17 at 21–22; 122 L.T. 203 at 206.

"This entails an enquiry into the motives of individuals, groups and even states, who were then active ... No such person, or member of such a group or state gave evidence at the trial, and any findings on these matters must inevitably be a matter of inference—albeit an inference guided by opinions expressed by persons having an acquaintance with Lebanese affairs of a type which the Court itself cannot possess."[77]

Each application of the exclusion clause will therefore not only turn upon its own facts but will often be less clear than is commonly the case with other exclusions. Nevertheless, the meaning of the various terms included in this exclusion has been considered in several authorities. The key principles relating to the application of each of these phrases is summarised below.

15-043 **War/civil war.** It is easy when presented with an exclusion relating to war or civil war to be diverted from the usual process of contractual interpretation into a more general enquiry as to the meaning of war and other forms of conflict in international relations or public international law. This is incorrect: it is important to interpret this type of exclusion in the same way as any other exclusion in the policy. There are, however, general principles of interpretation set out in *Spinney's (1948) Ltd v Royal Insurance Co Ltd*[78] that are particularly relevant to war exclusions:

   a. "War" does not have a fixed meaning. Methods of warfare, and of pursuing political aims by force, vary over time and develop in ways that could not be foreseen or anticipated by earlier decisions or writing. While previous authority and materials concerning public international law may be illustrative and helpful, therefore, they "cannot be relied upon as creating an exclusive list of criteria" for determining whether a particular state of affairs constituted a war.[79]

   b. The opinion of the relevant Secretary of State as to whether a particular state of affairs constituted a war or civil war will not be determinative. The court will be concerned to construe the meaning of the words used in the policy and the Secretary of State's intervention on this point is not usually helpful.[80]

   c. This will not, however, stop the court seeking the Secretary of State's view on questions of recognition by Her Majesty's Government or, occasionally, on other questions of fact.[81]

   d. A "civil war" is simply a "war which has the special characteristic of being civil – i.e. internal rather than external." It is a mistake, therefore, to apply a different test to the interpretation of an exclusion relating to civil war than would be applied to one relating to war. In particular, the application of authority concerning treason and constructive treason to exclusions relating to civil war is not helpful.[82]

Within these general principles, the courts have developed particular guidance on how to determine whether a state of affairs constitutes a war.

15-044   First, it is necessary to ask whether the conflict is between opposing "sides" to

---

[77] *Spinney's (1948) Ltd v Royal Insurance Co Ltd* [1980] 1 Lloyd's Rep. 406 at 412.
[78] *Spinney's (1948) Ltd* [1980] 1 Lloyd's Rep. 406.
[79] *Spinney's (1948) Ltd* [1980] 1 Lloyd's Rep. 406 at 429, per Mustill J.
[80] *Spinney's (1948) Ltd* [1980] 1 Lloyd's Rep. 406 at 407 and 426.
[81] *Spinney's (1948) Ltd* [1980] 1 Lloyd's Rep. 406 at 426.
[82] *Spinney's (1948) Ltd* [1980] 1 Lloyd's Rep. 406 at 428–429.

which the combatants owe allegiance.[83] This does not mean that everyone on each side must share all the same objectives but there must be some "substantial community of aim" which is being pursued by allies by force. Nor does it mean that there must only be two sides but if there are too many factions then the fighting may simply be a melee and not a war.

Secondly, the objectives of the sides must be analysed, together with their means of achieving those objectives. It was formerly thought that for a conflict to become a war, both sides must be motivated by a desire to seize or retain the control of the state. While this is one possible motivation consistent with a state of war, there could be a civil war if one side wished to force changes in the way power was exercised or was motivated by tribal or racial animosity.[84]   **15-045**

The third issue when assessing whether there is a state of war is the "character and scale of the conflict, and its effect on public order and on the life of the inhabitants."[85] This does not include a requirement that each faction holds or controls a substantial portion of territory. It does require consideration of a number of other factors including: **15-046**

1.   the number of combatants;
2.   the number of casualties;
3.   the amount and nature of the armaments employed;
4.   the relative sizes of the territories occupied by each side;
5.   whether it is possible to delineate those territories;
6.   the extent that the opposing sides purport to exercise exclusive governmental power over their controlled territories;
7.   the level of disruption to public order, public services, and private life;
8.   the duration of the conflict;
9.   the degree to which the whole population is involved in the conflict; and
10. whether there have been significant movements of people.

The issue of terrorism is presently unclear, particularly where that terrorism is sponsored, funded or supplied by a state actor. Clearly if a group within a country is sufficiently well organised and of sufficient size its activities may lead to a state of civil war.[86] It may be, however, that a series of terrorist attacks is not sufficiently coordinated by a single entity or side to amount to acts of war.[87] Some caution should be exercised before making a blanket statement, however, because the terms must be given their commercial meaning and the mere fact that an action could be classed as an act of terrorism does not prevent it also being an act of war.[88]   **15-047**

Each of the reported cases concerns physical conflict of one sort or another. It is currently unclear how the court would treat a new form of warfare such as an exchange of cyber-attacks between countries or by factions within a country. There is no reason why such a form of conflict should not satisfy the first two limbs of   **15-048**

---

[83] *Spinney's (1948) Ltd* [1980] 1 Lloyd's Rep. 406 at 429–430.

[84] *Spinney's (1948) Ltd* [1980] 1 Lloyd's Rep. 406 at 430.

[85] *Spinney's (1948) Ltd* [1980] 1 Lloyd's Rep. 406 at 430.

[86] See, for example *Curtis & Sons v Mathews* [1918] 2 K.B. 825; 17 LGR 291; 24 Com Cas 57, as interpreted in *Pesquerias y Secaderos de Bacalao de Espana SA v Beer (Pysbe)* [1949] 1 All E.R. 845n; (1948–49) 82 Ll. L. Rep. 501; 93 S.J. 371, where the 1916 Easter Rising in Ireland was assumed to amount to war.

[87] See *IF P&C Insurance Ltd (Publ) v Silversea Cruises Ltd* [2004] EWCA Civ 769 at [147]; [2004] Lloyd's Rep. I.R. 696 at 723–724, per Ward LJ; *Times,* August 13, 2004.

[88] *IF P&C Insurance Ltd (Publ)* [2004] EWCA Civ 769 at [143]; [2004] Lloyd's Rep. I.R. 696 at 723, per Rix LJ; *Times,* August 13, 2004.

Mustill J's test. Further, should such a series of attacks cause widespread disruption, it is submitted, there is no conceptual reason why damage caused by those attacks should not constitute a war or civil war. Such a result would be in keeping with Mustill J's observation that recognised methods of warfare are not closed.

15-049 **Invasion.** The exact meaning of "invasion" is presently undecided. The *Oxford Shorter Dictionary* defines it alternatively as:

(a) "an instance of invading a country or region with an armed force";

(b) "an incursion by a large number of people or things into a place or sphere of activity"; and

(c) "an unwelcome intrusion into another's domain".

All of these definitions leave open the possibility that the invading force need not come from outside a country. It may be, therefore, that the exclusion would operate where a force was raised in one region of a country and entered another, particularly where those regions were largely autonomous, as in a federal system.

15-050 A further uncertainty is whether the forces entering the region must be there with the purpose of exacting some form of political change or annexation. In *Spinney's (1948) Ltd*, Mustill J posed the question whether the entry of a foreign army into a neighbouring country as a peace-keeping force could be classed as an invasion.[89] The question was left unresolved, however, his lordship held that the presence of the foreign army could not be said to have caused the losses claimed irrespective of how it was properly characterised.

15-051 **Hostilities.** The term "hostilities" refers to "acts or operations of war committed by belligerents".[90] There are several important points that arise from this definition. The standard form of wording prevents the operation of the exclusion depending upon a formal declaration of war between two parties. Nevertheless, the operation of the clause presupposes that a state of war in fact exists at the relevant time.[91] Reference should be had in this regard to the discussion of the meaning of "war" in this context, set out above. It should be noted that the exclusion captures operations of war taking place both in a civil war and an international war.[92]

The exclusion will not capture "such operations as belligerents have recourse to in war, even though no state of war exists" so long as they were done in the context of a war.[93] Those operations were formerly captured by the use of an exclusion relating to "warlike operations". That exclusion is no longer commonly used as the war risks market felt it was unacceptable that they bear the risk of, for example, standard marine perils which occurred in the context of a war.

---

[89] *Spinney's (1948) Ltd* [1980] 1 Lloyd's Rep. 406 at 436.

[90] *Spinney's (1948) Ltd* [1980] 1 Lloyd's Rep. 406 at 437.

[91] *Spinney's (1948) Ltd* [1980] 1 Lloyd's Rep. 406; *Britain Steamship Co Ltd v The King; British India Steam Navigation Co Ltd v Liverpool & London War Risks Insurance Association Ltd; Green v British India Steam Navigation Co Ltd, sub nom. The Petersham*, [1921] 1 A.C. 99 at 114, per Lord Atkinson; at 133, per Lord Wrenbury; (1920) 4 Ll. L. Rep. 245 at 249, per Lord Atkinson; at 255–256, per Lord Wrenbury; *Board of Trade v Hain Steamship Co Ltd* [1929] A.C. 534; (1929) 34 Ll. L. Rep. 197; 98 LJKB 625.

[92] *Spinney's (1948) Ltd* [1980] 1 Lloyd's Rep. 406; *Britain Steamship Co Ltd; British India Steam Navigation Co Ltd; Green* [1921] 1 A.C. 99 at 114, per Lord Atkinson; at 133, per Lord Wrenbury; (1920) 4 Ll. L. Rep. 245 at 249, per Lord Atkinson; at 255–256, per Lord Wrenbury; *Board of Trade* [1929] A.C. 534; (1929) 34 Ll. L. Rep. 197; 98 LJKB 625.

[93] *Spinney's (1948) Ltd* [1980] 1 Lloyd's Rep. 406 at 437.

Rebellion/insurrection/revolution. The meaning of the "insurrection" and **15-052** "rebellion" exclusions has been considered in some detail both in England and Wales and abroad and the following points should be noted.

The terms "Insurrection" and "Rebellion" have "somewhat similar"[94] meanings and are often found together. Both terms mean

"an organised and violent internal uprising in a country with, as a main purpose, the object of trying to overthrow or supplant the government of that country".[95]

The difference between the terms is that insurrections are less organised and smaller than rebellions.[96]

The key issue to consider when determining if the exclusion applies is the **15-053** purpose of those involved in the activities said to constitute a rebellion or insurrection. To that end:

1. It appears that at least some of the rebels must be nationals of the state in question.[97]
2. The motivation of the rebels is irrelevant so long as their purpose is to support the government.[98]
3. It is irrelevant that the rebels are organised, equipped or even controlled from abroad or that their rebellion would fail without foreign assistance.[99]
4. Similarly it is irrelevant that the rebels have no clear idea of what they will do next.[100]
5. It is irrelevant that the rebellion or insurrection is unlikely to succeed.[101]

According to the *Oxford Shorter Dictionary* a revolution is "a forcible overthrow of a government or social order, in favour of a new system."[102] It can tentatively be suggested that a revolution is the logical conclusion of the ascending scale that begins with an insurrection and progresses through a rebellion.

The meaning of "revolution" in the conflicts exclusion does not appear to have been defined by the courts, presumably in part because it is usually relatively clear when a revolution has occurred.

It should be noted that the exceptions for damage caused by insurrection and rebellion are often associated with indirect causation clauses. The particular effect of such a causation clause is considered in this chapter below.

Military or usurped power. The wording of this exception dates back to the early **15-054**

---

94 *National Oil Co of Zimbabwe (Private) Ltd v Sturge* [1991] 2 Lloyd's Rep. 281 at 282, per Saville J.
95 *National Oil Co of Zimbabwe (Private) Ltd* [1991] 2 Lloyd's Rep. 281 at 282; *Spinney's (1948) Ltd* [1980] 1 Lloyd's Rep. 406 at 437, per Mustill J.
96 *National Oil Co of Zimbabwe (Private) Ltd* [1991] 2 Lloyd's Rep. 281 at 282; *Home Ins. Co. of New York v Davila* 212 F. 2d 731 (C.A.1, 1954).
97 *National Oil Co of Zimbabwe (Private) Ltd* [1991] 2 Lloyd's Rep. 281 at 282.
98 *National Oil Co of Zimbabwe (Private) Ltd* [1991] 2 Lloyd's Rep. 281 at 285.
99 *National Oil Co of Zimbabwe (Private) Ltd* [1991] 2 Lloyd's Rep. 281 at 284–286.
100 *National Oil Co of Zimbabwe (Private) Ltd* [1991] 2 Lloyd's Rep. 281 at 286.
101 *Tappoo Holdings Ltd v Stuchbery* [2006] FJSC 1 at [32]; [2008] Lloyd's Rep. I.R. 34 at 39; [2006] 4 L.R.C. 191 at 200 in *Home Ins. Co. of New York v Davila* 212 F. 2d 731 at 731, 736 (C.A.1, 1954), Magruder CJ said: "[a]n insurrection aimed to accomplish the overthrow of the constituted government is no less an insurrection because chances of success are forlorn"; *Pan American World Airways Inc v Aetna Casualty and Surety Co* [1975] 1 Lloyd's Rep. 77 at 96–97; 505 F.2d 989 (C.A.N.Y. 1974) at 1017–1018, per Hays J.
102 *Oxford Dictionaries*, "revolution" (Oxford Dictionaries Online, 2016), *http://oxforddictionaries.com/definition/english/revolution* [Accessed 24 June 2016].

18th century and refers back to the ancient doctrine of constructive treason. In summary it covers a situation where a mob takes to itself "a law-making and law-enforcing power which properly belongs to the sovereign".[103] This is a somewhat arcane definition. Fortunately there is further guidance upon its application in the authorities. In particular

"[u]surped power ... [is] ... more than the action of an unorganised rabble. [It can only apply to the actions of a body with some form of organisation and] ... more or less authoritative leaders".[104]

It does not include the actions of a "common mob" which is simply rioting.[105] However, it is not necessary to show that the state of affairs giving rise to the loss amounted to a rebellion or insurrection.[106]

Nor is it necessary to show that all of those involved in the violence had identical objectives. It is sufficient to show that they had purposes which lay in the public rather than the private domain.[107]

The US authorities on the meaning of "usurped power", while useful in other areas are not relevant to this question as the English and US systems have diverged.[108]

15-055   Mustill J gave a concrete example of a situation that fell either side of the line in the *Spinney's (1948) Ltd* case itself. He said:

"Applying this conclusion to the facts of the present action one must ask whether those participating in the events which occurred at the time in question had a sufficiently warlike posture, organisation and universality of purpose to constitute them an usurped power. So far as concerns casual looters, armed men settling personal scores, young people firing off guns for the sake of it, the answer is 'No'. But for the trained militia, and those armed civilians who were temporarily fighting at their side, the answer is, in my opinion, 'Yes'."[109]

15-056 Causation.   Once it has been determined whether one of the excluded conflict situations existed at the relevant time, it must be determined whether the loss or damage claimed was a "consequence" of that risk. This is not always a straightforward task. On one view, the consequences of war, for instance, are extremely wide-ranging. For example, it could be argued that, in a general sense, as a result of a state of war existing, trust between neighbours has broken down and a car is stolen. On a much narrower view, however, war itself does not cause any particular loss; instead the losses are caused by specific acts such as the firing of a torpedo that would not, taken in isolation, amount to war.

The courts resolve this issue pragmatically. A loss which arises from an act of war is proximately caused by the war.[110] For example, if a shop is looted or set fire to during fighting, or a ship is sunk by a torpedo, and it occurs in the context of an

---

103 *Spinney's (1948) Ltd* [1980] 1 Lloyd's Rep. 406 at 435.
104 *Curtis & Sons* [1919] 1 K.B. 425 at 429; 88 LJKB 529 at 534; 120 L.T. 154 at 155; *Spinney's (1948) Ltd* [1980] 1 Lloyd's Rep. 406 at 434.
105 *Drinkwater v London Assurance Corp* (1767) 2 Wils K.B. 363; Wilm 282. For the statutory definition of a riot, see s.1 of the Public Order Act 1986.
106 *Langdale v Mason* (1780) 2 Park's Marine Insce 8th edn 965; 1 Bennett's Fire Insce Cases 16; 2 Marshall on Marine Insce 3rd ed 793; *Drinkwater* (1767) 2 Wils K.B. 363; Wilm 282; *R v Lord George Gordon* (1781) 2 Doug. K.B. 590; 21 State Tr 485.
107 *Spinney's (1948) Ltd* [1980] 1 Lloyd's Rep. 406 at 436.
108 *Spinney's (1948) Ltd* [1980] 1 Lloyd's Rep. 406 at 434.
109 *Spinney's (1948) Ltd* [1980] 1 Lloyd's Rep. 406 at 435–436.
110 *Curtis & Sons* [1918] 2 K.B. 825; 17 LGR 291; 24 Com Cas 57, per Roche J. The finding was not challenged on appeal: [1919] 1 K.B. 425; 88 LJKB 529; 120 L.T. 154.

excluded conflict situation, the loss will be held to have been caused by that conflict situation.

By contrast, losses which are ancillary to the war (or conflict) itself are not caused by the war. For example, a ship which runs aground having altered its usual course in order to avoid enemy submarines will not be lost as a result of enemy peril.[111]

Further, losses which result from actions taken in anticipation of a war will not be taken to have been caused by that war.[112] Similarly, since only events occurring prior to the loss may constitute its proximate cause, the events following it may not. A loss caused by the actions of an individual hoping to prompt a war or encourage others to join him will not be taken to be caused by that war, even if it should eventually result.[113]

Indirect causation clauses. Conflict exclusions can be accompanied by clauses specifically providing that the conflict need not be the proximate cause of the damage so long as it is an indirect cause. This clause greatly increases the protection afforded to the insurer and has caused some difficulties determining exactly how far back down the chain of causation an excluded event can have occurred before it is too remote for the exclusion to operate.   **15-057**

In *Spinney's (1948) Ltd*,[114] Mustill J held that it was sufficient that the excluded events "permitted and indeed even encouraged the acts of looting and vandalism" which resulted in the damage in question.[115] This analysis was taken up by the Fijian Supreme Court in *Tappoo Holdings Ltd*, which examined Mustill J's reasoning in *Spinney's (1948) Ltd* before setting out several principles in relation to these clauses.[116] Those principles can be summarised as follows:

1.   The presence of an indirect causation clause removes the requirement that damage be proximately or directly caused by an excluded event.
2.   It is a question of fact and degree how far the chain of "indirect" causation extends in any particular case.
3.   The excluded event can still be the indirect cause of damage even if the immediate cause of that damage (in that case looting) was carried out for personal gain or did not involve any of those participating in the excluded event.

In *Tappoo Holdings Ltd*,[117] the insured's shop was damaged during rioting which followed (chronologically) immediately after an attempted coup which itself occurred during a peaceful protest march. There had been earlier peaceful marches which had not occasioned rioting or damage but it was not until the attempted coup that rioting broke out. Similarly on the day of the rioting, nothing of note happened until the coup. The court therefore concluded that the coup was an indirect   **15-058**

---

[111]   *Britain Steamship Co Ltd* [1919] 2 K.B. 670, affirmed [1921] 1 A.C. 99; (1920) 4 Ll. L. Rep. 245; *Ocean Steamship Co Ltd v Liverpool and London War Risks Association Ltd (The Priam)* [1948] A.C. 243; [1947] 2 All E.R. 586; (1947–48) 81 Ll. L. Rep. 1.

[112]   *Office Appliance Trades Association of Great Britain & Ireland v Roylance* (1940) 67 Ll. L. Rep. 86.

[113]   *Pan American World Airways Inc* [1975] 1 Lloyd's Rep. 77 at [104], per Hays CJ (Note that Hays CJ's treatment of usurped power was distinguished by Mustill J in *Spinney's (1948) Ltd* [1980] 1 Lloyd's Rep. 406).

[114]   *Spinney's (1948) Ltd* [1980] 1 Lloyd's Rep. 406.

[115]   *Spinney's (1948) Ltd* [1980] 1 Lloyd's Rep. 406 at 442.

[116]   *Tappoo Holdings Ltd* [2006] FJSC 1 at [28]; [2008] Lloyd's Rep. I.R. 34 at 38; [2006] 4 LRC 191 at 200.

[117]   *Tappoo Holdings Ltd* [2006] FJSC 1; [2008] Lloyd's Rep. I.R. 34; [2006] 4 LRC 19.

cause of the damage to the premises in question because it was caused during rioting that was itself caused or occasioned by the coup.

15-059 **Civil commotion/civil disturbance.** The meaning of the phrase "civil commotion" has not been defined but has been considered in a number of cases. In *Levy v Assicurazione Generali*,[118] it was held that

> "'civil commotion' is 'a stage between riot and civil war ... an insurrection of the people for general purposes,' but 'an organised conspiracy to commit criminal acts' does not amount to commotion."[119]

In *Pan American World Airways Inc v Aetna Casualty & Surety Co*,[120] Circuit Judge Hayes stated:

> "The district court held that 'civil commotion' is 'essentially a kind of domestic disturbance,' referring to disorders 'such as occur among fellow-citizens or within the limits of one community.' It found that 'it is not easily imaginable that any ordinary man, business or other, would have supposed a hijacking over London of an airplane that never went or was intended to go to Jordan would be deemed the result of civil commotion in Jordan."

He went on to say:

> "The district court clearly applied the correct rule of law: civil commotion does not comprehend a loss occurring in the skies over two continents. Cf. *Langdale v. Mason*, supra; *London & Manchester Plate Glass Co. v. Heath*, (1913) 3 K.B. 411 (C.A.); *Hartford Fire Insurance Co. v. War Eagle Coal Co.*, 295 F. 663 (4th Cir. 1924); *Wong Chow v. Transatlantic Fire Insurance Co.*, 13 Hawaii 160 (1900). The all risk argument that the 747 hijacking, taken together with the other September 6 hijackings to Dawson's Field constituted a single civil commotion is fanciful. For there to be a civil commotion, the agents causing the disorder must gather together and cause a disturbance and tumult. *Hartford Fire Insurance Co.*, supra, 295 F. at 665. We hold that the present loss was not caused by civil commotion for essentially the reasons set out in the district court's opinion".[121]

15-060 The general exclusions of riot, civil commotion and terrorism may be applied to overseas territories and is applicable to all sections of the policy.

(d) Nuclear material

15-061 **Nuclear material.** The risks associated with nuclear material and plant has long been excluded from all insurance policies by agreement of the market. In order to remedy this gap in 1956, Insurance Companies and Lloyd's Underwriters established the British Insurance (Atomic Energy) Committee and British Nuclear Insurers, now known as Nuclear Risk Insurers ("NRI") Ltd. NRI provides cover for all matters of nuclear insurance.[122] Similar insurance pools exist in many of the nations operating nuclear power stations.

15-062 **Sample clause.** The standard form of nuclear exclusion in England and Wales excludes losses arising from

---

[118] *Levy v Assicurazione Generali* [1940] A.C. 791; [1940] 3 All E.R. 427; (1940) 67 Ll. L. Rep. 174.
[119] *Levy* [1940] A.C. 791; [1940] 3 All E.R. 427; (1940) 67 Ll. L. Rep. 174 at 179.
[120] *Pan American World Airways Inc* 505 F.2d 989 (C.A.N.Y, 1974) at 1019–1020; [1975] 1 Lloyd's Rep. 77 at 98.
[121] *Pan American World Airways Inc* 505 F.2d 989 (C.A.N.Y, 1974) at 1020; [1975] 1 Lloyd's Rep. 77 at 98
[122] Further information about Nuclear Risk Insurers Ltd ("NRI") can be found at Nuclear Risks Insurers Ltd, "Welcome to Nuclear Risk Insurers Ltd" (Nuclear Risks Insurers Ltd, London, 2016) *http://www.nuclear-risk.com* [Accessed 24 June 2016].

"(a) ionising radiations or contamination by radioactivity from any nuclear fuel or from any nuclear waste from the combustion of nuclear fuel

(b) the radioactive toxic explosive or other hazardous properties of any explosive nuclear assembly or nuclear component thereof."[123]

In addition to the standard exclusion set out above, some insurers may require the insured to accept a clause specifically excluding work in or on any nuclear installation or installation site. The purpose of this clause is to avoid any dispute where a contractor has undertaken works on a nuclear site without first warning the insurer. If a contractor wishes to undertake such work he should procure a specific policy from NRI.

England. The operation of the nuclear exclusion in England and Wales was **15-063** considered in *Outokumpu Stainless Ltd v AXA Global Risks (UK) Ltd*.[124] In the case, the claimant insured operated a steelworks smelting scrap metal. It accidentally melted some radioactive plutonium resulting in it being left with a large amount of contaminated slag which it could not dispose of through its normal channels. The supervised disposal of the material cost money which the insured wished to recover under the policy. The policy contained the standard form exclusion but with a narrow extension bringing back into cover "loss destruction or damage due to contamination caused by the use of radioactive scrap materials utilised in the manufacturing processs".

Tomlinson J summarised the effect of the nuclear exclusion:

"Leaving aside the specialist nuclear pool, the general insurance market in London did not in 1999 offer cover against the risk of radioactive contamination. In an ordinary property damage cover written on all risks terms that exclusion would typically be brought about by two broad forms of exclusion. First, a radioactive contamination exclusion, which would be likely to relate to contamination from nuclear fuel or weapons material or from the waste produced by nuclear fission of such materials. Second, a more general pollution and/or contamination exclusion, written in terms broad enough to exclude cover for contamination caused by other radioactive sources not properly described as nuclear fuel or weapons material."[125]

Tomlinson J then found that the extension did not operate to extend the policy to purely economic loss consequent upon radioactive contamination.

Contrast with US. The extent of the English nuclear exclusion is to be contrasted **15-064** with the US standard form of nuclear exclusion. The US broad form nuclear exclusion has been a standard clause in US comprehensive general liability policies since 1958.

The US clause is over 600 words long and therefore considerably longer than the English clause. While it might be assumed that the US clause has a broadly similar effect to the English clause, in fact the US broad form of exclusion was never intended to exclude a significant number of risks associated with nuclear material and operations.[126] It is therefore extremely important, when dealing with a policy containing the US broad form nuclear exclusion, to examine the clause in detail to determine whether it responds or not.

---

[123] Item (a) is considered in *Outokumpu Stainless Ltd v AXA Global Risks (UK) Ltd* [2007] EWHC 2555 (Comm) at [11]; [2008] Lloyd's Rep. I.R. 147 at 151.

[124] *Outokumpu Stainless Ltd v AXA Global Risks (UK) Ltd* [2007] EWHC 2555 (Comm); [2008] Lloyd's Rep. I.R. 147.

[125] *Outokumpu Stainless Ltd* [2007] EWHC 2555 (Comm); [2008] Lloyd's Rep. I.R. 147 at 154–155.

[126] See Andrew M. Roman, "A New Look at the Broad Form Nuclear Exclusion" (1995) 42(4) *Risk Management*.

15-065   By way of example, in *Chemetron Investments, Inc v Fidelity & Cas. Co. of New York*,[127] the federal district court of Western Pennsylvania ruled upon the meaning and effect of the broad form nuclear exclusion in the context of the use of depleted uranium as a catalyst. The claimant had used the depleted uranium under license under the Atomic Energy Act. When Chemetron came to decommission its manufacturing site, uncontrolled contamination from depleted uranium was discovered. Chemetron was required to undertake expensive clean-up operations and tried to recover that cost from its insurer.

Had the policy contained the English form of exclusion it seems likely that the claim would have been caught by limb (a) of the English exclusion. The Pennsylvania court, however, held that the claim was not excluded. This was because the site was not a "nuclear facility", and the depleted uranium was not "spent fuel" or "waste".[128]

15-066   **Sonic bangs/sonic boom.**[129]   The sonic bang exclusion is a principal exclusion that is commonly found in the material damage section of CAR policies. The exclusion was introduced in the 1970s, when testing of supersonic aircraft first began.

15-067   **Sample clause.**   A sonic bang/boom exclusion will normally provide that the policy will not apply to, or include any

> "[l]oss destruction or damage directly occasioned by pressure waves caused by aircraft and other aerial devices travelling at sonic or supersonic speeds".[130]

The purpose of the exclusion is to exclude all damage caused by aircraft or other aerial devices travelling at sonic or supersonic speeds to property. Noise, pressure, and/or shock waves caused by overflying aircraft flying faster than the speed of sound are also referred to as sonic bangs or sonic boom. Damage to property as a result of a sonic boom includes damage to roof tiles, windows or structural damage to property.

(e)   Consequential loss

15-068   **Consequential loss.**   As a general principle the policy covers only physical damage resulting from an insured peril and not the lost profits and other pecuniary losses consequent on that physical damage.[131] There is nothing to stop a particular form of consequential loss such as, for example, loss of business or profits being brought within the policy by express provision.[132] However, without an express provision consequential losses will not be covered.

In this sense consequential losses are not, strictly viewed, excluded from cover (despite the common practice of cautious draughtsmen who purport to do just that). They are simply not included within the policy unless there is express provision for them.

The root for the principle does not appear originally to have been an issue of

---

[127] *Chemetron Investments, Inc v Fidelity & Cas. Co. of New York* 886 F. Supp. 1194 (W.D.Pa. 1994).
[128] *Chemetron Investments* 886 F. Supp. 1194 (W.D.Pa. 1994) at 1203.
[129] These are also referred to as air blasts. See further below, para.26-115.
[130] The exclusion is also discussed in the context of all risks property insurance. See below, para.26-115.
[131] See further below, para.17-048.
[132] e.g. *Barclay v Cousins* (1802) 2 East 544.

causation, despite some recent confusion on this point. Since at least 1763, consequential loss has been treated as a separate insurable interest, distinct from other types of insurable interest, and which must be specifically referred to in the policy, in order to be covered.[133]

The application of this principle is illustrated by the facts of *Wright v Pole*; sub nom. *Sun Fire Office Co and Wright, Re*.[134] The claimant in that case had insured his inn and offices against fire. The inn and offices were partly burnt and the claimant claimed both the cost of the repair of the buildings and his loss of profits during the repair works. It was held that the claimant had insured his interest in the buildings. The claimant could have insured the profits of the inn but that was not included in his buildings insurance.[135]

(f)   Reasonable precautions

Reasonable precautions.   Liability policies often contain a requirement that the   **15-069** insured must "take all reasonable precautions to prevent loss and damage" and any damage caused as a result of a failure to exercise reasonable precautions will be excluded from the indemnity. A reasonable precautions clause does not exclude cover for the insured's negligence as this would be to deprive the policy of much of its purpose. As is further set out below in this section, in order to rely on this provision, the insurer must prove that the insured was not merely negligent, but reckless. Further, the clause is personal to the insured and does not extend to the insured's servants or agents. Although, initially, there had been some divergence between the interpretation of reasonable precaution clauses found in first party policies and liability policies, in *Sofi v Prudential Assurance Co Ltd*[136] it was held that such a distinction should not be drawn. Consequently, the principles set out below apply to both first and third party policies.

The requirement rests on the insured only.   The principle that the duty to take   **15-070** reasonable precautions rests on the insured only was established in the case of *Woolfall & Rimmer Ltd v Moyle*.[137] This case concerned an employer's liability policy and a claim by the employer to recover costs incurred in paying damages for injuries sustained by employees when a plank on which workmen were standing collapsed. The insurers sought to argue that the employees were subject to the reasonable precautions clause and, as reasonable precautions had not been taken, there was no requirement for the insurers to indemnify. The Court of Appeal rejected this argument and found that to construe the policy in such a way would be a fallacy, since it would result in the policy providing an indemnity in respect of the insured's negligence only on condition that the insured was not negligent. Du Parcq LJ stated that:

"[t]he plaintiffs never warranted that everybody whom they employed would take reasonable precau-

---

[133] See for example *Glover v Black* (1763) 3 Burr. 1394 at 1401, per Lord Mansfield; *Wright v Pole*; sub nom. *Sun Fire Office Co and Wright, Re* (1834) 1 Ad & El 621 at 623; 3 Nev & MKB 819 at 819–820, per Lord Denman CJ and Taunton J.; *Cator v Great Western Insurance Co of New York*; sub nom. *Cator v Great Western Insurance Co of New York* (1872–73) LR 8 CP 552 at 559, 42 LJCP 266 at 270–271; 2 Asp MLC 90 at 93, per Bovill CJ.

[134] *Wright v Pole*; sub nom. *Sun Fire Office Co and Wright, Re* (1834) 1 Ad & El 621 at 623; 3 Nev & MKB 819.

[135] *Wright* (1834) 1 Ad & El 62 at 623; 3 Nev & MKB 819–820.

[136] *Sofi v Prudential Assurance Co Ltd* [1993] 2 Lloyd's Rep. 559.

[137] *Woolfall & Rimmer Ltd v Moyle* [1942] 1 K.B. 66; [1941] 3 All E.R. 304; (1941) 71 Ll. L. Rep. 15.

tions, or, indeed, that anybody except themselves would take reasonable precautions, and they took reasonable precautions. It is not right to say that they delegated to another the duty which they owed to the underwriters. In its nature that is a duty which they cannot delegate, and when they appointed another person to see that provision was made for the safety of their workmen they were not delegating their duty to take reasonable precautions, but were performing it".[138]

Reasonable precaution clauses, therefore, only apply to the insured and not to any servants or agents of the insured, even though the insured would be vicariously liable for the negligence of its servants or agents. This principle has been held to apply, even in circumstances where the clause provided that the insured shall take and "cause to be taken" all reasonable precautions, with the result that very clear words must be used if an insurer intends the reasonable caution clause to apply to persons other than the insured.[139]

15-071   The requirement of "reasonableness". The leading judgment as to the meaning of "reasonableness" in reasonable precautions clauses is that of Diplock LJ in *Fraser v BN Furman (Productions) Ltd (Miller Smith & Partners, third parties)*[140] which also concerned whether the claimant would have been covered under an employer's liability policy. After identifying that it was the insured personally who had to take reasonable precautions, in reliance on the decision in *Woolfall & Rimmer Ltd*, Diplock LJ went on to state:

> "'Reasonable' does not mean reasonable as between the employer and the employee. It means reasonable as between the insured and the insurer having regard to the commercial purpose of the contract, which is inter alia to indemnify the insured against liability for his (the insured's) personal negligence .... Obviously, the condition cannot mean that the insured must take measures to avert dangers which he does not himself foresee, although the hypothetical reasonably careful employer would foresee them. That would be repugnant to the commercial purpose of the contract, for failure to foresee dangers is one of the commonest grounds of liability in negligence. What, in my view, is 'reasonable' as between the insured and the insurer, without being repugnant to the commercial object of the contract, is that the insured should not deliberately court a danger, the existence of which he recognises, by refraining from taking any measures to avert it ... the insured, where he does recognise a danger should not deliberately court it by taking measures which he himself knows are inadequate to avert it. In other words, it is not enough that the employer's omission to take any particular precautions to avoid accidents should be negligent; it must be at least reckless, that is to say, made with actual recognition by the insured himself that a danger exists, and not caring whether or not it is averted. The purpose of the condition is to ensure that the insured will not, because he is covered against loss by the policy refrain from taking precautions which he knows ought to be taken."[141]

Therefore, an insurer will not necessarily be permitted to refuse to indemnify simply because the insured has acted negligently; the insurer will be required to show that the insured had acted recklessly. In order to do so, the insurer will have to show that the insured failed to take precautions in circumstances where there was a recognised risk of danger and that the insured did not care whether or not that danger was averted. There are dicta to suggest that if the insured inadvertently or accidentally

---

[138] *Woolfall & Rimmer Ltd* [1942] 1 K.B. 66; [1941] 3 All E.R. 304 at 312–313; (1941) 71 Ll. L. Rep. 15 at 20. The wording used in the last two reports is nuanced slightly differently from the passage cited, but the same point is generally made.

[139] *Tate Gallery Board of Trustees* [2007] EWHC 912 (TCC) at [11]; [2008] Lloyd's Rep. I.R. 159.

[140] *Fraser v BN Furman (Productions) Ltd* [1967] 1 W.L.R. 898; [1967] 3 All E.R. 57; [1967] 2 Lloyd's Rep. 1; 2 K.I.R. 483; (1967) 111 S.J. 471.

[141] *Fraser* [1967] 1 W.L.R. 898 at 905–906; [1967] 3 All E.R. 57 at 60–61; [1967] 2 Lloyd's Rep. 1 at 12. The passage differs slightly in the last two reports.

causes loss, such conduct may not amount to recklessness.[142]

Reasonable precautions in a CAR policy. The above cases have been fol- **15-072** lowed when interpreting the reasonable precautions clause in a CAR policy in the Scottish case of *Duncan Logan (Contractors) Ltd (In liquidation) v Royal Exchange Assurance Group*.[143] Contractors of the Tay Road Bridge sought a declaration that they were entitled to be indemnified against loss and damage sustained when the trestle of a temporary bridge, which had been holding materials used for construction, collapsed. The insurers sought to rely on the fact that the contractor's maintenance engineer was or ought to have been aware of the effect of the scouring action of the river, which ultimately caused the trestle to collapse. After referring to both *Woolfall & Rimmer Ltd*[144] and *Fraser*[145] the Outer House found that, as the insurer's case was founded solely on the employee's negligence and not that of a relevant officer of the company, the insurer had failed to prove that the reasonable precautions clause had not been complied with. The court rejected the insurer's assertion that, having averred that all reasonable precautions had not been taken, it was then for the insured to show that reasonable precautions had been taken, stating that there was nothing to take the case out of the ordinary rules applicable to the burden of proof.

Summary. In *Tate Gallery Board of Trustees v Duffy Construction Ltd*,[146] Jackson **15-073** J summarised the applicable principles as follows:

"(a) In a policy of liability or property insurance a reasonable precautions clause in the conventional form is not breached by mere negligence. Recklessness is what constitutes a breach of such a clause.

(b) The recklessness which must be established is recklessness by the insured himself, as opposed to his employees.

(c) The first two propositions are canons of construction developed by the courts, because it is improbable that the parties intend to negate a core part of the insurance cover. Nevertheless, if a reasonable precautions clause were drafted with sufficient clarity, it would be possible to achieve that harsh result."[147]

3. CONSTRUCTION EXCLUSIONS

Construction exclusions. Most CAR policies employ a mixture of exclusions and **15-074** extensions that allow them to be tailored to the specific context to which they relate.[148] The balance between construction-related exclusions and extensions will depend upon that context.

The following are particularly common issues that might be addressed by the use

---

[142] See *Devco Holder Ltd and Burrows & Paine Ltd v Legal and General Assurance Society Ltd* [1993] 2 Lloyd's Rep. 567 in which the court saw some force in the argument that had the insured inadvertently left his car keys in the ignition, as opposed to intentionally done so, such conduct would not have been reckless, as there had been no appreciation of the risk.

[143] *Duncan Logan (Contractors) Ltd (In liquidation) v Royal Exchange Assurance Group* 1973 SLT 192.

[144] *Woolfall & Rimmer Ltd* [1942] 1 K.B. 66; [1941] 3 All E.R. 304; (1941) 71 Ll. L. Rep. 15.

[145] *Fraser* [1967] 1 W.L.R. 898; [1967] 3 All E.R. 57; [1967] 2 Lloyd's Rep.1.

[146] *Tate Gallery Board of Trustees* [2007] EWHC 912 (TCC) at [26]; [2008] Lloyd's Rep. I.R. 159 at 164.

[147] In *Tate Gallery Board of Trustees* [2007] EWHC 912 (TCC) at [29]; [2008] Lloyd's Rep. I.R. 159 at 164, per Jackson J suggested that the clause could have stated "The insured shall take and shall cause all its employees and sub-contractors to take all reasonable precautions."

[148] Extensions to cover are discussed below, in Ch.17.

of an exclusion clause. It is equally possible, however, that these issues could form the basis of an extension to an otherwise narrow policy. For that reason, when dealing with the issues discussed below, particular care should be taken to ensure that the policy as a whole is construed rather than simply referring to any of the relevant exclusions.

15-075 Mechanical and electrical breakdown or derangement. Exclusion of damage to the insured property caused by its own electrical or mechanical breakdown is similar, in some respects, to exclusions for inherent vice. The clause will not operate where the cause of the mechanical breakdown was external to the machinery, but only when it results from the proper and normal operation of the thing itself.

There has been a difference in approach in Canada and the USA when it comes to whether a negligent act by the insured will prevent this exception from applying. In *Brown Fraser & Co Ltd v Indemnity Marine Assurance Co*,[149] it was held that the failure by the insured to insert a part into the machine which ought to have been inserted to make it a complete operating unit meant that the operating failure was due to negligence and not to a mechanical breakdown.

15-076 In contrast, however, in *Arawak Aviation, Inc v Indemnity Ins. Co. of North America*[150] a plane engine overheated as a result of a pilot's negligence in failing properly to apply the oil-cap. The court refused to find that this act of negligence could bring the loss back within the terms of the policy. The court relied on the judgment of the District Court of Florida in *Little Judy Industries Inc v Federal Ins. Co.*,[151] in particular that

> "the loss was due to mechanical failure of the engine. The fact that the failure thereof was traceable to negligence in its repair or to improper repair or assembly of the engine did not make it other than a mechanical failure. In a great many, if not most instances the mechanical failure of an engine could be attributed to some act of commission by improper or negligent work thereon as occurred here, or to negligent omission to inspect and repair or replace parts where needed, or other neglect in the care of the machine".

The court in *Arawak Aviation, Inc* held that if the exclusion did not apply, so long as the insured could show that upkeep of the machinery was not properly performed, this would not only defeat the exclusionary clause, but it would also encourage policy holders to forgo maintenance of the machinery to ensure maximum coverage.

This decision does not sit well with the cases on wear and tear, where if the insured could point to some external event which sped up the deterioration process, the exception will not apply and the insured will be indemnified.

15-077 An exclusion of this sort often limits the damage that it is not covered to the part of the machinery responsible, so that other parts which sustain accidental damage may be covered. As with the exclusion for defects in design and workmanship, determining the extent of cover may be complicated by trying to differentiate the part of the machinery which was responsible for the breakdown of the machinery and the parts that were damaged as a result.

15-078 Injury to machinery. This exception differs from the one discussed above, in that

---

[149] *Brown Fraser & Co Ltd v Indemnity Marine Assurance Co* (1958–59), 27 WWR 31 (BCCA); 16 DLR (2d) 263; 1958 BCJ No 145.

[150] *Arawak Aviation, Inc v Indemnity Ins. Co of North America* 285 F. 3d 954 (C.A.11 (Fla., 1973).

[151] *Little Judy Industries Inc v Federal Ins. Co.* 280 So. 2d 14 (Fla. App., 1973) cert. denied by, 284 So. 2d 220 (Fla. 1973).

injury to machinery relates to damage caused by some latent or inherent defect in the machine itself.

Existing structures, fixtures, fittings or contents.   The scheme of the 1998, 2005   **15-079** and 2011 JCT insurance provisions require an employer to take out insurance in respect of both the works and existing structures for certain projects. Two separate policies may need to be taken out where the contract provides that all contractors and subcontractors are covered by the works policy, i.e. the CAR policy, but only some contractors, for example named subcontractors, are covered by the existing structures policy. In such circumstances, it is likely that the CAR policy will provide an exclusion in respect of existing structures and contents. A typical clause may provide:

> "Property forming or which has formed part of any structure prior to the commencement of the contract or works or loss of or damage to the existing property including property being altered or repaired."

An exclusion relating to existing structures is unlikely to cause difficulties where the construction contract relates to the construction of a new building or where the employer is required under the construction contract to take out insurance in respect of both the works and existing structures and contents. However, where the contract relates to works within an existing property, for example, refurbishment works, the demarcation between what constitutes the "works" insured under the CAR policy and the "existing structures" which are either expressly excluded or are insured under a separate policy may become of crucial importance. Precisely what comprises existing structures, fixtures and fittings and what would comprise the works will be a fact sensitive matter in each case.

The meaning of "existing structures" was considered in the Scottish case of   **15-080** *Aberdeen Harbour Board v Heating Enterprises (Aberdeen) Ltd*.[152] In this case, the subcontractors (Heating Enterprises (Aberdeen) Ltd) negligently caused a fire when carrying out works for the tenant of property. The construction contract was a JCT Standard Form of Building Contract 1963 edition (July 1977 revision)[153] and cl.20C required the tenant to maintain insurance in respect of "existing structures together with the contents thereof owned by him or for which he is responsible" as well as to take out insurance in respect of the works. The subcontractor sought an indemnity from insurers of the existing structures in relation to a claim for damage to the landlord's property. The subcontractor's claim was refused, as the claim by the landlord was not in respect of property insured. Dunpack LJ stated:

> "[I]n this case the phrase 'the existing structures' must be read as qualified by 'together with the contents thereof owned by him or for which he is responsible'. ... [Heating] ... could not recover from Ferranti under cl. 20 [C] sums which they had to pay to the pursuers for damage to parts of the premises which were not occupied by Ferranti. If Heating have fulfilled cl. 4 of the subcontract, they should be able to recover the whole of their loss, if any, under their own liability insurance policy. As Heating's fourth plea for indemnity is unlimited, it was rightly repelled by the Lord Ordinary."

Consequently, "existing structures" within the meaning of the JCT Contract in this case could not relate to property which was not occupied by the employer, and, therefore, the subcontractor would not be indemnified in respect of damage to exist-

---

[152] *Aberdeen Harbour Board v Heating Enterprises (Aberdeen) Ltd* 1990 S.L.T. 416; 1989 S.C.L.R. 716.
[153] Joint Contracts Tribunal. *Standard Form of Building Contract for Use With Quantities: Private Edition 1963, July 1977 Revision* (London: RIBA, 1977).

ing structures owned by the landlord. This must be the correct analysis as the tenant, Ferranti, could only insure existing structures and contents insofar as it had an insurable interest in the same.

It is worth noting that even if there is no express exclusion in relation to existing structures and contents, it may be that the definition of insured property would act so as to exclude damage to existing structures and contents.[154]

15-081 **Hot works.**   It is becoming increasingly common for insurers to include within the policy a requirement that the insured carry out certain preventative measures in order to avoid a fire breaking out on site. Where such measures are not undertaken, the policy will not respond to damage caused by works involving heat. Such clauses have become common following a number of serious fires on construction sites. This led to the development of the *Joint Code of Practice on the Protection from Fire on Construction Sites and Buildings Undergoing Renovation* ("the Joint Code").[155] The aim of the Joint Code is to reduce the incidence of fires during construction works.

15-082   Paragraph 2.2 of the Joint Code provides that insurers will require compliance on projects with an original value of £2.5 million or above. For certain higher risk projects, the threshold may be lower. The Joint Code is applicable to building contracts, including mechanical and electrical works, and is increasingly forming part of the underlying construction contracts. It requires the contractor to appoint a person to be responsible for assessing the degree of fire risk and for creating and updating the site fire safety plan. The fire safety co-ordinator must, among other things, ensure that all procedures, precautionary measures and safety standards are clearly understood and complied with by all those on the project site and ensure that, where necessary, a system using Hot Work Permits is established and monitor compliance.

Not all policies include a specific reference to the Joint Code, but may still contain certain provisions relating to ensuring fire precautions are in place where the works involve the application of heat. The clause comes under various headings, including the "Fire Precautions Clause", the "Burning Conditions" or the "Burning and Welding Warranty". Howsoever named, what each such clause has in common is that there will be specified precautions to be taken by the insured in the event that the insured undertakes any works involving the application of heat. Compliance with the precautions is often stated to be a condition precedent to the indemnity and, therefore, the insured will have to have complied with any such provisions in order to recover under the policy. However, after the Insurance Act 2015 comes into force, s.11 will enable the insured to recover for types of losses

---

[154] See above, para.9-065.
[155] This document was first published in 1992: Building Employers Confederation, the Loss Prevention Council, and the National Contractors' Group, *Fire Prevention on Construction Sites: The Joint Code of Practice on the Protection from Fire of Construction Sites and Buildings Undergoing Renovation* (Birmingham: Building Employers Confederation, 1992). The document was produced in response to concerns raised by the insurance industry as a result of two fires that resulted in losses being sustained in excess of £150 million. The code has been updated and the most recent version of it has been produced by The Fire Protection Association, *Fire Prevention on Construction Sites: The Joint Code of Practice on the Protection from Fire on Construction Sites and Buildings Undergoing Renovation*, 9th edn (Bedford/Moreton in Marsh: Construction Industry Publications Ltd, Fire Protection Association, 2015). See further below, para.17-039 and fn.15.

other than fire even where compliance with the Joint Code is a condition precedent to liability and the insured has failed to do so.[156]

The wording of this type of clause will vary from policy to policy, with some policies referring to the entirety of the Joint Code, whilst others may set out either parts of the Joint Code or amended provisions of the Joint Code, with which the insured must comply.

Sample clause.   In relation to smaller value construction contracts, the policy may **15-083** not require compliance with the entirety of the Joint Code, but, instead, adopt certain measures contained within it. For example, the policy may adopt the measures set out para.15 of the Joint Code relating to Hot Work and provide as follows:

"It is a condition precedent to liability under this Policy that in respect of work away from the Insured's own premises involving the use or application of heat, including the use of blow torches, blow lamps and welding and flame cutting equipment, the following precautions will be complied with on each occasion.

1.   Before starting work
    a.   The Insured shall appoint an Employee on each site to be responsible for fire safety and for seeing that precautions are taken, who shall obtain from the person in charge at each site permission to start work.
    b.   All the Insured's employees on each site shall be made aware of the location of the site's fire alarms and fire fighting equipment.
    c.   The Insured's appointed person shall examine all property in the vicinity, including the area on the other side of any wall or partition, to ensure that no combustible material is in danger of ignition either directly or by conducted heat.
    d.   The area shall be cleared of all movable and/or combustible materials to a distance of not less than 15 meters from the point of application of heat. Combustible materials, which cannot be moved, must be covered and fully protected by overlapping sheets or screens of non-combustible material.
2.   During the progress of the work
    a.   The Insured shall arrange for a person to work alongside the operative(s) using the equipment to see that there is no outbreak of fire and shall have available for immediate use at least two buckets of dry sand and a hose connected to the nearest hydrant with the supply of water turned on and controlled at the nozzle of the hose. Where water would aggravate a fire or explosion or where there is not water supply there shall be available for immediate use at the site of the operations at least two suitable fully charged fire extinguishers.
    b.   The lighting of all blowlamps, blow torches and cutting equipment shall be carried out strictly in accordance with the Manufacturer's instructions and no piece of lighted equipment shall be left unattended.
    c.   Gas cylinders not required for immediate use shall be kept outside the building in which the work is taking place and in any event at least 15 meters from the point of application of heat.
3.   After ceasing work
    Upon completion of the application of heat a continuous examination for a period of one hour shall be made of:
    a.   The immediate vicinity of the work, i.e. within a radius of 15 meters.
    b.   The area on the other side of any wall or partition to ensure that there is no risk of fire."

---

[156] See above, para.5-114.

The precise terms of the clause are important to determine whether the insured must have complied with the precautions precisely or whether it simply had to arrange for such precautions to be taken, even if, as a matter of fact, the requirements of the hot works clause had not been complied with.

15-084   In *Cornhill Insurance Plc v D E Stamp Felt Roofing Contractors Ltd*,[157] the hot works clause provided that

> "[i]t is a condition precedent to any liability of Cornhill [the insurers] that the Insured shall have arranged for the following precautions to be taken whenever carrying out any work involving the application of heat."

Consequently, the Court of Appeal found that the clause only required the insured to have "arranged" that the named precautions were put in place and not that they had actually, as a matter of fact, been complied with. The Court of Appeal stated as follows:

> "It is entirely reasonable for insurers to require an arrangement that precautions be taken. That, in my view, is what this policy requires. It would be much less reasonable for insurers to require a guarantee that the arrangements should invariably be complied with, because such failure is likely to be the result of an employee's negligence for which cover is required. This policy does not, on the face of it, bear that unreasonable construction."[158]

15-085   In contrast, the Burning and Welding Warranty contained in the insurance policy in *United Marine Aggregates Ltd v GM Welding & Engineering Ltd*[159] required the insured to actually comply with the procedures set out in the policy and not simply to make arrangements for such precautions. Although no point was taken in this case that making arrangements would be sufficient, the judgment clearly indicates that the approach of the parties was correct and that actual compliance was required. Edwards-Stuart J stated:

> "It is not disputed that this warranty is a condition precedent to liability, as it states, or that it must be exactly complied with. Further, it is a warranty that precautions will actually be taken, not a warranty that arrangements will be made for precautions to be taken. It is also accepted on all sides that it is not necessary for the insurers to prove that a breach of warranty caused the loss: it is settled law that a breach by the insured of a warranty such as this discharges the insurer from any further liability under the policy from the time of the breach."[160]

In this case the contractor had failed to remove all combustible material from an area in which welding work had been conducted as required by the Burning and Welding Warranty contained in its insurance contract. Whilst the court found that the contractor did not in fact require to be indemnified under its policy, because the contractor had exercised reasonable care and skill whilst carrying out the works, the court found that had a claim for an indemnity been required, it would have failed in any event because the contractor had failed to comply with the requirements of the Burning and Welding Warranty.

15-086   Although compliance with the Joint Code does not appear to have been the subject of litigation as yet, the Joint Code sets out mandatory requirements to be

---

[157] *Cornhill Insurance Plc v DE Stamp Felt Roofing Contractors Ltd* [2002] EWCA Civ 395; [2002] Lloyd's Rep. I.R. 648 at 650.
[158] *Cornhill Insurance Plc* [2002] EWCA Civ 395 at [20]; [2002] Lloyd's Rep. I.R. 648 at 651.
[159] *United Marine Aggregates Ltd v GM Welding & Engineering Ltd* [2012] EWHC 779 (TCC).
[160] *United Marine Aggregates Ltd* [2012] EWHC 779 (TCC) at [202].

complied with and it is likely, therefore, to be afforded a similar interpretation to that indicated by Edwards-Stuart J set out above.

Hydrocarbon processing industries. Hydrocarbons are the main source of the world's electrical energy and heat sources because of the energy produced when burnt. Hydrocarbons in liquid form are referred to as petroleum and in gaseous form as natural gas. The increasing use of hydrocarbons in plant and machinery and the potential for loss or damage during the commissioning/testing phase has led to the introduction of an exclusion for damage caused by such use.　**15-087**

Sample clause.　A typical clause may provide:　**15-088**

"The insurer shall not as from the introduction of any hydrocarbons in the plant indemnify the insured in respect of loss or damage to

(a)　catalysts,
(b)　reforming units[161] as a result of overheating or cracking of tubes,
(c)　any property insured as a result of overheating or cracking following an exothermic reaction,
(d)　the insured plant as a result of the insured not complying with safety regulations or wilfully interfering with the operation of safety devices and for any liability resulting there from."

The exclusion makes plain that damage to catalysts and to reforming units caused by overheating or cracking of tubes is excluded under the policy. Reforming units are large fired heater units where the hydrocarbon (i.e. gas) or chemical product is pumped via special tubes that may be filled with a catalyst and is heated by gas burners inside the heater. The equipment is expensive, as its construction and metallurgy must be carefully designed in order to prevent overheating and cracking. If the flow rate of the chemical product increases through the tubes or the heat temperature increases beyond approved procedure during commissioning then this could result in loss of or damage to the tubes and the catalyst.

Loss and damage to any other property (that is material or components) is also excluded where the damage results from overheating or cracking as a result of an exothermic chemical reaction. The term exothermic, meaning outside heating, describes a process or reaction that releases energy from the system, usually in the form of heat, but also in the form of light (e.g. a spark, flame, or explosion), electricity (e.g. a battery), or sound (e.g. burning hydrogen). It is to be contrasted with fire, which involves combustion.　**15-089**

Consequently, the exclusion is likely to apply to unintended exothermic reactions causing unforeseen damage, i.e. to exclude the consequences of a thermal runaway. This is the meaning given to the phrase by the Health and Safety Executive ("HSE") and in the *Construction Insurance/Report of Research Study Group*

---

[161] In this context the term reforming unit concerns an arrangement of tubes, however, it can also apply to other types of process units such as fluid catalytic converters ("FCC") units, which will also be excluded. An exclusion clause may also explain what the phrase "reforming phrase" means within the body of the clause. For example, it may say that a "reforming unit" means "a steam methane, steam naphtha or any other reformer which have catalyst filled tubes in the radiant section of a furnace."

208B[162] where it says "[s]imilarly, exothermic reactions can 'run away' if not carefully controlled and lead to overheating of the vessel or cracking".

15-090   The hydrocarbons exclusion may also exclude loss of or damage to plant or machinery caused to third parties if the clause clearly states this, such as by using the words "as well as any liability resulting therefrom". The hydrocarbons exclusions is a relatively new exclusion which, as yet, does not appear to have been judicially considered.

15-091   **Refractory linings.**   Special provision either within the hydrocarbons exclusion or separate to it may apply to refractory linings, due to the special testing process they have to go through during the testing and commissioning stage. A typical standalone clause may exclude cover for the following:

> "As from the first application of heat to the refractory linings, loss of or damage to the refractory linings, unless such loss of or damage is caused by an indemnifiable loss or damage to the Insured Property (other than the refractory linings themselves)."

15-092   The above exclusion clearly limits cover only to refractory linings only when heat is applied on the first occasion. Accordingly, if the drying process is interrupted and heat has to be applied on a second occasion in order to complete the process, then any loss or damage which may arise thereafter would be excluded from cover, unless such loss or damage is caused by an indemnifiable loss. As an alternative, some policies may specify a deductible for successive losses, for example 100 per cent for the first loss, 75 per cent of the second loss and 50 per cent for the third loss, with no further losses being indemnified.

15-093   **Fines, penalties, ascertained and liquidated damages**   Fines, penalties, ascertained and liquidated damages payable under the construction contract are usually excluded from indemnity under CAR policies. However, there is a small specialist market which would provide the contractor with insurance in this regard.[163]

15-094   **Mechanically propelled vehicles.**   An exclusion in relation to mechanically propelled vehicles is aimed at excluding from the insured property mechanically propelled vehicles which travel across roads or land, including cars, lorries, dump trucks, trains and motorbikes. Such vehicles tend to be insured under specialist insurance policies, e.g. motor insurance policies and, as a result are often excluded from a CAR policy. Depending on the precise terms of the policy, the exclusion may not apply to vehicles being used as a tool of trade or whilst on site, for example, where a vehicle is used to load or unload goods.

15-095   **Aircraft/watercraft.**   Aircraft and watercraft are insured in specialist aviation and maritime markets.[164] They are almost invariably excluded from cover under standard CAR policies save in very limited cases where a construction underwriter feels able to accept the risk despite not being a specialist marine or aviation insurer. For example where the works are being carried out off the coast, the policy may

---

[162] Insurance Institute of London. *Construction Insurance/ Report of Research Study Group 208B* (London: IIL, 2010), para.8.8.4.6, p.176.
[163] See below, paras 17-012 and 17-075.
[164] See below, Chs.24 and 25.

cover small servicing craft, but such cover would have to be provided within the definition of the insured property.

Cessation/stoppage of work. CAR policies will exclude loss or damage caused **15-096** by a total or partial cessation of work by the workforce. This prevents the insurer from having to indemnify the insured in respect of direct or indirect losses caused by the works stopping as a result of late deliveries, labour disturbances or other factors leaving the site in an unattended or unsafe condition due to work stopping during construction. In some policies, the exclusion applies from the time of cessation, in others it applies after a specified period of cessation (for example the Christmas holidays and/or bank holidays).

Sample clause. A cessation of work exclusion clause may be worded as follows: **15-097**

"The Insurers shall not be liable for loss or damage due to total cessation of work and abandonment of the Insured Contract for a period exceeding 90 consecutive days."

Certain variations on the exclusion clause may restrict the scope of the clause, by providing that the exclusion will only apply if the insured did not take all reasonable precautions to prevent loss or damage during the stoppage period.

The cessation of work exclusion clause should be read with the clauses dealing **15-098** with loss or damage as a result of riot and other civil disturbances. Even where a policy does not exclude losses caused by riot or civil disturbance it may nevertheless exclude damage caused by a cessation of work such as would occur, for example, during a strike.[165]

De-watering expenses. De-watering is a specific form of water management that **15-099** is frequently excluded from CAR policies. The dictionary definition of dewatering refers to draining a waterlogged area[166] but in a construction context insurers use it to refer only to the process of lowering a water table level on a particular site or to the removal of groundwater, by pumping it out or by evaporation in order to allow works undertaken by the contractor to proceed in the dry.[167] Dewatering does not mean the removal of rainwater from a construction site or the extraction of rainwater from a hole, which has been dug as part of the construction works (e.g. to accommodate a post for the footings).

Where there is a pronounced risk of flooding on a project, for example, in tun- **15-100** nelling contracts or works which involve deep excavations, the insurer may insert an exclusion specifically dealing with the management of that water. The particular wording of the clause will depend upon the risk inherent in the particular project. The general approach of the insurer, however, is to expect the insured to have taken adequate steps to estimate the amount of water likely to be involved in the project and to have taken all necessary steps to manage that water.

---

[165] See for example *Ford Motor Co of Canada Ltd v Prudential Assurance Co Ltd* [1959] S.C.R. 539; [1959] I.L.R. 1-322; 18 D.L.R. (2d) 273 (S.C.C.).

[166] *Oxford Dictionaries*, "dewater" (Oxford Dictionaries Online, 2016), *http://oxforddictionaries.com/definition/english/dewater?q=dewatering* [Accessed 24 June 2016].

[167] See the view of the Lumley General Insurance (N.Z.) Ltd set out in A. McKay, "*Expert case. Dewatering warranties and exclusions*" (Lumley General Insurance (N.Z.) Ltd, New Zealand, June 2010) *http://www.lumley.co.nz/Libraries/Technical_Newsletter/Issue_4_-_Expertease_dewatering_article.pdf* [Accessed 24 June 2016].

The CAR policy may also contain a warranty stating that "pumps are not used for any Toxic &/or hazardous liquids &/or substances".

15-101 **Overbreak and grouting.** A CAR policy may contain special conditions concerning the construction of tunnels.[168]

Where a contractor digs a tunnel that is too large he will generate loose ground material over and above that set out in his plans which has to be removed. Further, the size of the tunnel may cause grouting or other reinforcement works to become necessary, for example to satisfy health and safety requirements. The cost of those additional works is typically excluded from indemnity under a CAR policy. It should be noted, however, that the exclusion will not prevent the policy responding should the tunnel collapse.

15-102 **Piling work.** Most construction projects involve some form of piling although the nature and extent of the piling foundations necessary will vary from site to site depending on the ground conditions. It is essential, therefore, that adequate ground investigation is carried out before a piling solution is proposed and that the piling works are then implemented and supervised properly. Insurers are frequently keen to limit their exposure to piling work undertaken without proper investigation or due care. There are a range of standard exclusions available in the market that will have the effect of limiting the coverage available in this regard and it is very important to examine the clause and determine which losses (if any) resulting from the failure of piling work are excluded.

15-103 **Sample clause.** In a CAR policy a piling exclusion may state that it does not apply to any damage or liability in respect of:

"1.   foundation piles and/or casings and/or sheet pile constructions which are:
    a)   misplaced and/or misaligned
    b)   lost or damaged during driving and/or extraction
    c)   the subject of individual or block disconnection or declutching
    for the purpose of this Policy loss or damage to foundation piles and/or casings and/or sheet pile constructions shall be deemed to have occurred during driving, extraction, disconnection or declutching unless the Insured can produce satisfactory evidence to demonstrate otherwise
2.   any leakage or infiltration of liquid or material at seams, joints, connections and/or beneath sheet pile constructions or into casings
3.   any abandoned piling work unless such abandonment is a direct consequence of other loss or damage for which indemnity is provided by this Policy
4.   piles which have failed to pass a load test or to reach the required bearing load unless such failure is a direct consequence of other loss or damage for which indemnity is provided by this Policy
5.   any dependence on revealed sub-standard installation work unless the design had been appropriately re-worked to suit."

---

[168] See The British Tunnelling Service/The Association of British Insurers, *The Joint Code of Practice for Risk Management of Tunnel Works in the UK. Prepared jointly by The Association of British Insurers The British Tunnelling Society* (London: The British Tunnelling Society, 2003) and the international version of this by The International Tunnelling Insurance Group, *A Code of Practice for Risk Management of Tunnel Works* (The International Tunnelling Insurance Group, 2012).

Alternatively, or in addition, a CAR policy may contain a clause which does not exclude cover, but limits the indemnity, for example by providing that the insurer will not indemnify the insured in respect of

"[c]osts in excess of the original pile value in place. The original pile value shall be calculated by dividing the total contract value for each particular section of piling work by the total number of piles in each section".

The piling exclusion may also be set out in some CAR policies in the special **15-104** conditions section, concerning piling in the context of foundations and "retaining wall works" or alternatively it may be listed in a separate overarching exclusion in connection with underpinning. In the former situation, the exclusion clause will differ significantly to the one set out above, and is likely to state that it does not apply to loss or damage caused by natural hazards, and that the burden of proving that such loss or damage is covered, is on the insured. The piling exclusion does not yet appear to have been litigated in the English courts.

Loss of stabilising fluid. Excavation of the ground whether by drilling (i.e. **15-105** trenchless construction) or tunnelling frequently necessitates the use of some form of stabilisation mechanism, particularly if works are taking place in soft soils (i.e. sand, fine gravel, coarse-grained stones, soil with high water content; and soft soils that expand or swell such as silt or clay) or soft rock (i.e. marl, hard clay, slate) which are unstable and less predictable than hard rock (i.e. limestone, sandstone, granite, basalt, lava, gneiss, quartzite).

Several mechanisms are available to a contractor undertaking excavation works. Historically they include using a water-based slurry or temporary casing protecting the installation of foundations, for example. The more usual modern solution, however, is to use a bentonite or synthetic polymer slurry to stabilise the ground conditions when drilling deep underground or excavating a tunnel.

The contractor will estimate the amount of the stabilisation fluid that he will require at the start of the project. The loss of stabilisation fluid exclusion will limit the insurer's liability by excluding payment for the loss of stabilising fluid even if it as a result of the contractor's underestimation of the amount of fluid needed. The exclusion may be worded to say that insurers shall not be liable to indemnify the insured

"in respect of loss of bentonite or other stabilising fluid even of the quantity of losses originally expected is exceeded".

Temporary access roads. The provision of a temporary access road into and **15-106** through the construction site is sometimes necessary in construction projects. A CAR policy will usually respond to damage caused to the road while it is under construction, but damage sustained after it has come into use will usually be excluded. The reason for this is that temporary access roads are often built to a lower standard than a permanent road and when traversed by large, heavy vehicles and construction equipment, they are more susceptible to damage. This type of damage will be excluded by the temporary access roads exclusion. The exclusion will usually be worded as follows:

"Irrespective of the periods of Insurance specified in the Policy, the Insurer will indemnify the Insured only for unforeseen accidental loss or damage to temporary access roads insured under the Policy if such loss or damage occurs prior to such roads being completed or taken into use for their purpose by the contractors, whichever takes place first."

15-107 Dredging/re-dredging and loss of fill.   There is an inherent risk in dredging and filling operations that the fill will be washed away or redistributed, resulting in more fill being necessary than was anticipated. Such a cost should be anticipated by the contractor in the contract price and, as a result, costs incurred as a result of re-dredging and loss of fill are typically excluded from cover under a CAR policy. The clause may be worded so as to exclude:

> "Damage to the works in, or around water:
>
> (i)   Loss of fill due to the normal action of the sea
> (i)   The cost of re-dredging or re-profiling of a dredged trench or area due to the normal action of the sea."

15-108 Overtopping/overflowing of coffer-dams.   Where a project is being built in a body of water, a dam or some form of temporary watertight enclosure (such as a coffer-dam) may be necessary in order to expose the ground and allow works to go ahead in a dry environment. The aim of a coffer dam is, therefore, to keep water away from the construction work area. CAR policies will generally exclude cover for damage caused by water overflowing the coffer dam. Alternatively, the exclusion may be expressly limited to damage caused by a level of flooding which could have been expected, so that damage caused by unusual or unexpected flooding is not excluded from cover.

CHAPTER 16

DEFECTS AND DEFECT EXCLUSIONS

TABLE OF CONTENTS

1. INTRODUCTION

Introduction. For the reasons discussed in Ch.14 on Loss and Damage, the **16-001** discovery that insured property is in defective condition does not trigger an indemnity for "loss of or damage to" property.[1] An all risks policy is not a guarantee of good condition or proper working order. In the context of marine hull insurance, the principle that mere defects are not covered is taken one stage further: only accidents that have a sufficient maritime connection are considered to come within the scope of "perils of the sea" cover[2]; that excludes physical damage proximately *caused by* a defect or malfunction in the hull or machinery.[3] Insurance against damage consequent on a defect must be secured by the inclusion of a provision (the Inchmaree clause)[4] to that effect. It is possible the same principle would apply to an all risks policy in the absence of a provision specifically addressing defect-caused damage, for the term "all risks" does not include damage due to the "inherent vice" of the property insured.[5]

There is a market demand for, and a willingness of insurers to provide, cover for **16-002** accidental damage that is brought about by defects in the design or build of the insured property. This is true both in relation to marine hull policies and CAR project insurance. In relation to the latter, it has been a particular concern of contractors that a relatively minor defect in some part of the works can result in a fire, explosion or collapse with catastrophic consequences. For example, a faulty piece of electrical wiring could start a fire that destroys the entire works. As regards defective workmanship, mistakes will always occur even in well-managed projects, which result in damage to the works. One might be more circumspect about extend-

---

[1] See above, para.14-014.
[2] *Thames and Mersey Marine Insurance Co Ltd v Hamilton Fraser & Co (The Inchmaree)* (1887) 12 App. Cas. 484; 56 L.J.Q.B. 626; 6 Asp. M.L.C. 200.
[3] See below, Ch.19 on causation.
[4] *The Inchmaree* (1887) 12 App. Cas. 484; 56 L.J.Q.B. 626; 6 Asp. M.L.C. 200. See below, paras 16-024 to 16-028.
[5] *Global Process Systems Inc v Syarikat Takaful Malaysia Bhd (The Cendor MOPU)* [2011] UKSC 5; [2012] 1 All E.R. (Comm) 111; [2011] 1 Lloyd's Rep. 560, see below, para.24-086.

ing that claim to inherently faulty design or specification, but contractors have been able to argue that the responsibility will usually lie with an architect or consulting engineer, against whom subrogation rights would exist. Insurers generally accept these points, and the historically common catch-all exclusion for "all loss or damage caused by a defect in design plan specification materials or workmanship" has fallen out of favour.[6] Instead, all risks project policies may provide that damage caused by a defect is covered—provided, usually, that it occurs to some other non-defective "part" of the works—whilst ensuring that costs of putting right the defect itself are excluded.[7] However, identifying property that is defective and property that is free from defective condition but has been damaged has proved to be problematic.

16-003   Since 1985 a suite of standard form defect exclusion ("DE") clauses, drafted by a committee of leading insurers, has been available to the market. The clauses, labelled "DE1" to "DE5" by the original drafting committee, provide five different levels of cover thought to adequately define the various degrees of cover that insurers were prepared to offer.[8] A similar suite of standard form defect exclusions clauses was introduced in 1996 by a consultative group of engineering insurers known as the London Engineering Group ("LEG") for engineering class risk. These clauses are labelled "LEG 1" to "LEG 3".[9]

16-004   In relation to hull insurance, cover for defect-caused damage has long been provided under the "Inchmaree clause".[10] Although the Inchmaree clause appears in policies that cover perils of the sea and other named perils (as opposed to all risks), it is considered in this chapter as it engages the same issues as the DE clauses, and it is useful to compare the two sets of drafting techniques.

2.   MEANING OF "DEFECT"; "LATENT"; "DEFECTIVELY DESIGNED"

16-005   **Use of the words "defect(s)" and "defective" in exclusion clauses.**   A defects exclusion in the DE form[11] excludes the cost of repairing or replacing property which is lost or damaged "due to defective design plan specification materials or workmanship" (DE1) or is in "defective condition due to a defect in design plan specification materials or workmanship" (DE2, DE3) or is "defective in design plan specification materials or workmanship" (DE4, DE5).[12] The various provisos or carve-outs to the exclusions use the language of "defective condition", "defective in design" and "defect". The London Engineering Group clauses adopt a similar phrase: "defects of material workmanship design plan or specification". The Inchmaree clause refers to a "latent defect".

---

6   Insurance Institute of London, *Construction Insurance—Research Study Group Report 208B* (London: IIL, 2010), para.8.8.2.1, p.158.

7   An example of such a provision can be found in the standard form defect exclusion clauses DE3 or DE4: see below, paras 16-036 to 16-049. The point remains unresolved, see below, paras 16-045 to 16-049.

8   See below, paras 16-029 to 16-030.

9   See below, paras 16-065 to 16-070.

10   See below, paras 16-024 to 16-028.

11   Note the conclusion of Myers J in *PCL Constructors Canada Inc. v Allied Global Risk US Insurance Co* [2014] ONSC 7480. See below para.16-067 which provides a useful analysis of similar clauses based on the premise that properly construed the clauses are not exclusion clauses but deeming clauses that provide special treatment for loss and damage to works containing defects.

12   The relevant phrase in each of DE2–DE5 is worded in broadly the same way, except that the wording relating to "condition" is omitted in DE4 and DE5.

In ordinary usage, a "defect" is any quality of an item which makes it less valu- **16-006** able or less fit for its purpose than is intended; a thing is in "defective condition" where it suffers from such a quality.[13] If an insurer alleges that an item unfinished at the time it was damaged was in a "defective condition" it must be shown that it ought to have been constructed to the standard contended for when the damage occurred[14]; a building is not defective simply because it is incomplete. On the other hand, if a building is constructed in the wrong order—if internal finishes were installed before the roof—this could be characterised as a defect in workmanship.[15]

In the early case of *Jackson v Mumford*[16] it was held that the phrase "latent **16-007** defect" was not appropriate to cover a non-negligent "weakness in design".[17] It is hard to understand why it was thought that this interpretation accorded with the normal meaning of the words, and indeed this dictum has not been followed. So far as design defects are concerned, it was held in *Prudent Tankers Ltd SA v The Dominion Insurance Co Ltd (The Caribbean Sea)*[18] that the fact that "the historical reason for a defect in hull or machinery is a defect in design would not preclude recovery under the Inchmaree clause"[19]; *Jackson* was sharply distinguished.[20] The standard DE wording explicitly refers, in any event, to a "defect in design" and LEG 3 refers to "defects of ... design".[21]

Repair or replacement of a defect. The discovery of a latent defect in the insured **16-008** property will not, without more, constitute "damage". However, an all risks policy may cover the cost of remedying a defect if that is the proper construction of the policy. For instance, it may be possible for a clause that excludes the cost of rectifying defects in design, materials or workmanship "unless the property insured suffers actual loss, destruction or damage as a result of such defect" to bring the costs of rectifying pre-existing defects which cause physical damage within the scope of

---

[13] The question of how one identifies the *extent* of the property affected by the "defective condition" depends on the wording of the clause in question. See below, paras 16-036 to 16-042 on DE3.

[14] In *CA Blackwell (Contractors) Ltd v Gerling Allegemeine Verischerungs-AG*; sub nom. *CA Blackwell (Contractors) Ltd v Gerling General Insurance Co* [2007] EWCA Civ 1450; [2008] 1 All E.R. (Comm) 885; [2008] Lloyd's Rep. I.R. 529, the insurers' contention that a road was defective for lacking the necessary draining channels failed because the evidence did not show "that such measures were required at this stage of the works", although the point being made there was actually the converse one: the works were not defective because it was *no longer* possible to build in protective measures without damaging the completed works: [2007] EWCA Civ 1450 at [24]; [2008] 1 All E.R. (Comm) 885 at 891; [2008] Lloyd's Rep. I.R. 529 at 534.

[15] cf. *Pentagon Construction (1969) Co Ltd v United States Fidelity and Guaranty Co* [1978] 1 Lloyd's Rep. 93; 1977 Carswell B.C. 372; [1977] 4 W.W.R 351; [1977] I.L.R 1-889, 77 DLR (3d) 189 (B.C.C.A).

[16] *Jackson v Mumford* (1902) 19 T.L.R. 18, (1902) 8 Com. Cas. 61; 51 W.R. 91.

[17] *Jackson* (1902) 19 T.L.R. 18; (1902) 8 Com. Cas. 61 at 68–69; 51 W.R. 91.

[18] *Prudent Tankers Ltd SA v The Dominion Insurance Co Ltd (The Caribbean Sea)* [1980] 1 Lloyd's Rep. 338.

[19] *The Caribbean Sea* [1980] 1 Lloyd's Rep. 338 at 347.

[20] In *Jackson* (1902) 19 T.L.R. 18; (1902) 8 Com. Cas. 61; 51 W.R. 91, an accident was caused by a breakage in a high-pressure engine mounted in a newly-designed, experimental vessel. The machinery was built to a specification that it should be as light as possible. It was held that the engineer's calculations as to the resilience of the materials were reasonably arrived at but ultimately wrong. In *The Caribbean Sea*, Goff J suggested that the result might be reinterpreted: "since the casualty occurred during the trials of a ship in whose design risks were deliberately taken, the proximate cause of the casualty was the deliberate running of the risk rather than anything that could properly be called a defect in the machinery" [1980] 1 Lloyd's Rep. 338 at 346.

[21] See the 2006 amendment to the 1996 version of LEG 3; below, para.16-036.

cover.[22] It is suggested that in "all risk of damage" insurance clear wording will be required if defects within undamaged property are to be indemnified, the usual position is for the trigger for an indemnity to be the occurrence of accidental damage to the property, including to property which is defective.[23]

Terms "defect" "defective design" and "defectively designed" do not necessarily imply negligence. As for whether a "defect" implies an element of negligence or non-compliance in the design or construction process (as the judge in *Jackson* appeared to assume),[24] it is clear following the decision of the Court of Appeal in *Hitchins (Hatfield) Ltd v Prudential Assurance Co Ltd*[25] that a defect is not necessarily something that results from negligence, although slightly different language may suggest this. In *Hitchins (Hatfield) Ltd*, the court approved a judgment of the High Court of Australia[26] in which it was held that the phrase "faulty design"[27] was descriptive of "an objective quality of a thing" connoting "a falling short; but not ... a falling short in conduct or behaviour". The judgment stated the following[28]:

> "To design something that will not work simply because at the time of its designing insufficient is known about the problems involved and their solution to achieve a successful outcome is a common enough instance of faulty design."[29]

16-010 Windeyer J thought that the result might have been different if the clause had referred to "faulty designing".[30] This point of distinction was adopted by the court in *Hitchins (Hatfield) Ltd*[31] in holding that the combination of adverb and verb in the phrase "defectively designed" in the policy pointed to "personal activity or conduct" and hence applied only in the situation where the original fault in design was negligent.[32] It is possible to follow this reasoning, but there is something to be said for the view of the judge at first instance who noted that the distinction between the words that were used and the words "defect in design" was rather small: "[i]t

---

[22] *Cementation Piling and Foundations Ltd v Commercial Union Insurance Co Plc*; sub nom. *Cementation Piling and Foundations Ltd v Aegon Insurance Ltd* [1995] 1 Lloyd's Rep. 97 at 100; 74 B.L.R. 98 at 104; (1994) 47 Con. L.R. 14 at 15.

[23] In *Cementation Piling and Foundations Ltd*, it was said not to be necessary under a defects exclusion clause in the policy to show damage to the defective property for the remedial work to be indemnified: [1995] 1 Lloyd's Rep. 97; 74 B.L.R. 98; (1994) 47 Con. L.R. 14. This may not be the case in relation to the most recent version of DE5: see below, paras 16-045 to 16-058 for a full discussion of this issue.

[24] In *Jackson* (1902) 19 T.L.R. 18; (1902) 8 Com. Cas. 61 at 68; 51 W.R. 91, Kennedy J said: "Now, I certainly am not prepared to impute negligence to the designers because it is now shown that the design was wrong."

[25] *Hitchins (Hatfield) Ltd v Prudential Assurance Co Ltd* [1991] 2 Lloyd's Rep. 580; 60 B.L.R. 51.

[26] *Queensland Government Railways and Electric Power Transmission Pty Ltd v Manufacturers' Mutual Insurance Ltd* [1969] 1 Lloyd's Rep 214; 118 C.L.R. 314.

[27] Which was treated as equivalent to "defective" design: *Queensland Government Railways and Electric Power Transmission* [1969] 1 Lloyd's Rep. 214 at 217; 118 C.L.R. 314 at 320–321.

[28] *Queensland Government Railways and Electric Power Transmission* [1969] 1 Lloyd's Rep. 214 at 218; 118 C.L.R. 314 at 322.

[29] *Queensland Government Railways and Electric Power Transmission* [1969] 1 Lloyd's Rep. 214 at 217; 118 C.L.R. 314 at 321, per Barwick, McTiernan, Kitto and Menzies LJJ.

[30] *Queensland Government Railways and Electric Power Transmission* [1969] 1 Lloyd's Rep. 214 at 219; 118 C.L.R. 314 at 323.

[31] *Hitchins (Hatfield) Ltd* [1991] 2 Lloyd's Rep. 580; 60 B.L.R. 51.

[32] *Hitchins (Hatfield) Ltd* [1991] 2 Lloyd's Rep. 580 at 585; 60 B.L.R. 51 at 62.

seems to be undesirable that the scope of a policy ... should depend upon such very fine distinctions".[33]

When a latent design flaw or latent defect constitutes damage. If a latent 16-011 design flaw[34] produces an adverse change in physical condition in the property during the period of cover it will be possible to point to "damage". The mere discovery of a defect is not without more to be treated as damage. So in a case where the repainting of a vessel revealed that its frame had been defectively cast so as to cause shrinkage cracks requiring its replacement, there was no "damage", as this was a latent defect revealing itself.[35] In some circumstances it will be difficult to distinguish a latent defect from consequential damage. In *Promet Engineering (Singapore) Pte Ltd v Sturge (The Nukila)*, Ward LJ said[36]:

"If one is considering whether there is damage to the hull and whether such damage is caused by a latent defect in the hull, it follows that the damage must be something different from ... and incrementally greater than the latent defect itself. Where the line is to be drawn is a matter of fact and degree."

Difficult issues may arise in the context of civil engineering projects where latent design flaws can result in an alteration to the size of air space within a void, as may occur when a tunnel or mine shaft floods. It is suggested that a court will apply common sense when deciding whether in this situation there has been damage. In *Merlin v British Nuclear Fuels Plc*[37] Gatehouse J said:

"'Personal injury or damage to property' is a familiar phrase and in my judgment it means, as it does in other contexts, physical (or mental) injury or physical damage to tangible property ... The Plaintiffs' argument that 'property' included the air space within the walls, ceilings and floors of [the house]; that this has been damaged by the presence of radionuclides and the house rendered less valuable as the family's home seems to me to be too far-fetched."

Under the DE wording, there is no specific requirement that the defect be latent 16-012 or undiscoverable. If the insured has actual knowledge that the property is defective that will obviously be a material matter that must be disclosed. But where the defect must be "latent" to be within the cover, as per the Inchmaree clause, does this impart a further requirement that the defect be *undetectable* before it causes damage? In *The Caribbean Sea*, Goff J held that a latent defect is one which cannot be discovered on such an examination as a reasonably careful skilled man would make[38]; although he disapproved the somewhat stricter formulation suggested in one American case that a latent defect is one which cannot be discovered by any known and customary test.[39] It would seem, then, that an insurer may be able to defeat a

---

[33] *Hitchins (Hatfield) Ltd* [1991] 2 Lloyd's Rep. 580 at 586; 60 B.L.R. 51 at 62.
[34] See below, para.16-012.
[35] *Hutchins Bros v Royal Exchange Insurance Corp* [1911] 2 K.B. 398; 80 L.J.K.B. 1169; 12 Asp. M.L.C. 21.
[36] *Promet Engineering (Singapore) Pte v Sturge (The Nukila)* [1997] 2 Lloyd's Rep. 146 at 157; [1997] C.L.C. 966 at 980. And see the discussion of *The Nukila* above in Ch.14.
[37] *Merlin v British Nuclear Fuels Plc* [1990] 2 Q.B. 557 at 570; [1990] 3 W.L.R. 383 at 394; [1990] 3 All E.R. 711 at 720.
[38] *The Caribbean Sea* [1980] 1 Lloyd's Rep. 338 at 347.
[39] *The Caribbean Sea* [1980] 1 Lloyd's Rep. 338 at 348. See *Parente v Bayville Marine Inc and General Insurance Co of America* [1975] 1 Lloyd's Rep. 333; 43 A.D.2d 956; 353 N.Y.S. 2d 24; 1974 A.M.C. 1399.

claim under a clause that indemnifies against damage caused by a "latent defect" if the insured was negligent or at fault in failing to detect the defect.

"Mere materialisation of a defect", "mere manifestation of a defect" and
16-013 **"damage".** When dealing with defects exclusions, it is important not to use the phrase "mere materialisation of a defect" or "mere manifestation of a defect" in contradistinction to "damage". This is because the line between "defect" and "damage" may be drawn in different places,[40] and the phrase "mere materialisation of a defect" has been equated with the kind of adverse physical change consequent on a defect that is regarded as damage following *The Nukila*.[41]

16-014 In *Skanska Construction Ltd v Egger (Barony) Ltd*,[42] in the context of a particular construction contract, the formation of cracks in a defective concrete floor slab was held not to be "loss or damage" under the relevant clause. Mance LJ stated that

> "[i]n this contractual scheme, the mere manifestation of a defect under ordinary usage, which the contractor is anyway obliged to make good under the contractual scheme relating to defects, cannot in my judgment constitute loss or damage to the slab."[43]

It has been suggested,[44] wrongly, in the view of the author, that this dictum casts doubt on the proposition that consequential cracking or other deterioration to a structure due to a latent defect constitutes "damage".

16-015 The issue in *Skanska Construction Ltd*[45] was whether a clause requiring the employer to obtain insurance cover for the benefit of the contractor in respect of "all loss or damage from whatever cause arising for which the Contractor is responsible under the terms of the Contract" referred: (a) only to loss and damage sustained due to mishap during the carrying out of works; or (b) extended also to loss and damage caused by the defective quality of the works.[46] The Court of Appeal held that interpretation (a) was the correct one, and accordingly that the employer was not in breach of the clause by obtaining cover under a policy with a DE3 exclusion (i.e. excluding the cost of damage to the defective part).

16-016 The matter for which the contractor sought an indemnity was the cracking of a defective floor slab. The particular interpretation of "loss and damage" articulated by Mance LJ (under "this contractual scheme" and not under the insurance policy) was clearly not intended to be of general application to all insurance which requires there to be "damage"—not least because, if it were, the contractor's complaint that a more generous defects exclusion should have been obtained would be entirely moot.[47] In any event, Latham and Aldous LJJ did not endorse the supplementary

---

40   See the discussion above in Ch.14.
41   *The Nukila* [1997] 2 Lloyd's Rep. 146; [1997] C.L.C. 966.
42   *Skanska Construction Ltd v Egger (Barony) Ltd* [2002] EWCA Civ 310; [2003] Lloyd's Rep. I.R. 479; [2002] B.L.R. 236.
43   *Skanska Construction Ltd* [2002] EWCA Civ 310 at [30]; [2003] Lloyd's Rep. I.R. 479 at 486; [2002] B.L.R. 236 at 242–243.
44   London Engineering Group, *LEG Broker Briefing Note – Defects Exclusion LEG3/96* (London: LEG, 2006).
45   *Skanska Construction Ltd* [2002] EWCA Civ 310; [2003] Lloyd's Rep. I.R. 479; [2002] B.L.R. 236.
46   *Skanska Construction Ltd* [2002] EWCA Civ 310 at [17]–[18]; [2003] Lloyd's Rep. I.R. 479 at 484; [2002] B.L.R. 236 at 241.
47   If it were otherwise, the point in issue in *Skanska Construction Ltd* [2002] EWCA Civ 310; [2003] Lloyd's Rep. I.R. 479; [2002] B.L.R. 236 —whether the employer was obliged under the contract to obtain insurance with a more generous "DE5" exclusion—would be moot. The short answer to the contractors' complaint would be that a policy with a less strict defects exclusion would have been

observations of Mance LJ and *The Nukila*[48] line of authority was not cited or referred to, so the decision is *per incuriam* to the extent that it is inconsistent with the case law on the meaning of "loss and damage" under insurance contracts.

Nevertheless there is no doubt that the cracking of the floor slab would constitute "loss and damage" for the purposes of an all risks policy, as long as the policy did not exclude damage to the defective part itself. It is suggested that the better way of expressing the relevant distinction is to contrast a latent defect becoming patent (or being "uncovered") with damage over and above the defect itself.[49] LEG 3 was amended in 2006 to clarify the meaning of defect and damage with the addition of the following words in relation to damage: "(which for the purposes of this exclusion shall include any patent detrimental change in the physical condition of the Insured Property)". It is suggested that this addition was made not only as a result of the *Skanska Construction Ltd*[50] decision but also to address concern that damage may be thought to have occurred to defective property if the existence of a defect had rendered it less useful or less valuable, with the manifestation of the physical changes drawing the parties' attention to the defect being present.

16-017

Loss of value/use of a thing does not itself constitute damage. As reflected by the amendment made to LEG 3, the mere fact that the thing is rendered less valuable or useful does not in itself constitute damage. There needs to be an adverse change in physical condition. However, as discussed in Ch.14, it appears to be a question of fact and degree, and some of the cases can be difficult to reconcile. The plugging-up of the feed-pipe of a steam engine so that it was rendered useless,[51] and the dumping of 30 lorry-loads of rubbish onto a building site have both been held to be damage.[52] Similarly, where radioactive particles intermingled with soil on the claimant's land this amounted to damage.[53] In *Hunter v Canary Wharf Ltd*,[54] it was acknowledged that whilst dust was an "inevitable incident of urban life", "excessive deposits" of dust such as would lessen the value of a carpet into which it was trodden, or would require professional cleaning, would constitute damage.[55] In *The*

16-018

---

of no benefit: the cracking of the slab could not (if the dicta of Mance LJ were of general application) constitute "loss or damage" under the insuring clause.

48 *The Nukila* [1997] 2 Lloyd's Rep. 146; [1997] C.L.C. 966.

49 *The Nukila* [1997] 2 Lloyd's Rep. 146 at 157; [1997] C.L.C. 966 at 980.

50 *Skanska Construction Ltd* [2002] EWCA Civ 310; [2003] Lloyd's Rep. I.R. 479; [2002] B.L.R. 236.

51 *R. v Fisher (William)* (1865) L.R. 1 C.C.R. 7; 29 J.P. 804; 35 L.J.M.C. 57 (criminal damage).

52 *R. v Henderson and Battley* Unreported November 29, 1984 CA (Crim Div). Although a criminal damage case, *Henderson* was cited with approval in *Losinjska Plovidba v Transco Overseas Ltd (The Orjula)* [1995] 2 Lloyd's Rep. 395 at 398–399; [1995] C.L.C. 1325 at 1328–1329, where Mance LJ held that the criminal test was relevant in a civil context.

53 *Blue Circle Industries Plc v Ministry of Defence* [1999] Ch. 289; [1999] 2 W.L.R. 295; [1998] 3 All E.R. 385 (negligence). In *Outokumpu Stainless Ltd v AXA Global Risks (UK) Ltd* [2007] EWHC 2555 (Comm); [2008] Lloyd's Rep. I.R. 147, insurers conceded that "slagpots" contaminated with radioactive waste requiring their decontamination were to be regarded as having suffered physical damage. Meanwhile, in *Field Steamship Co Ltd v Burr* [1899] 1 Q.B. 579 at 586–587, the example of a cargo of cement in bags, solidified by a sea peril so as to become stone, which might therefore cost more to discharge than if no peril had occurred was considered. If the cement became fixed to the hull, then this would be damage to the hull which would be covered; otherwise, the mere increase in the cost of removal would not be damage to the hull, and would not be covered.

54 *Hunter v Canary Wharf Ltd, Hunter v London Docklands Development Corp* [1996] 2 W.L.R. 348; [1996] 1 All E.R. 482; [1996] C.L.C. 197, reversed [1997] A.C. 655; [1997] 2 W.L.R. 684; [1997] 2 All E.R. 426 (nuisance).

55 *Hunter* [1996] 2 W.L.R. 348 at 366; [1996] 1 All E.R. 482 at 498; [1996] C.L.C. 197 at 210, per Pill

Orjula,[56] the spillage of hydrochloric acid onto a vessel, requiring decontamination, was held to be damage, even on the assumption that the cleaning operation that was carried out prevented any corrosion from occurring. However, the New South Wales Court of Appeal rejected an argument that the blockage of a grain silo by grain constituted damage.[57] Further, the mere presence of alpha-emitting radionuclides within the claimant's house where there had been no alteration in the physical fabric of the house was held not to be "damage to ... property" for the purpose of the Nuclear Installations Act 1965.[58]

16-019 **Any defect constitutes loss or damage.** It has been suggested that the wording in the DE clauses which define the meaning of a defect, in particular words

"[f]or the purpose of the Policy and not merely this Exclusion the Property insured shall not be regarded as lost or damaged solely by virtue of the existence of any defect ..."[59]

was introduced to address issues raised in *Transfield Constructions Pty Ltd*[60] and *The Orjula*[61] as to whether there had been a physical change in condition. However it is suggested that the better view is that the timing of the amendment is more consistent with its being a response to the Court of Appeal's decision in *Cementation Piling and Foundations Ltd v Commercial Union Plc*[62] which was also decided the same year and which construed an all risks of damage CAR policy containing a defects' exclusion as extending to indemnify causally connected defects.

16-020 **Incorporation of a defect does not constitute damage.** Contamination of insured subject-matter by another, unwanted, substance is capable of constituting damage. One situation, however, where the introduction of undesired material to the insured property will not apparently amount to damage is where Material A is intentionally combined with Material B to produce a finished product, and Material B is discovered to be harmful or otherwise defective, as was the case in *Bacardi-Martini Beverages Ltd v Thomas Hardy Packaging Ltd*.[63] A similar analysis was adopted by the Court of Appeal in relation to a public liability CAR policy in *Pilkington UK Ltd v CGU Insurance Plc* where Potter LJ said[64]:

"[G]enerally speaking, damage requires some altered state, the relevant alteration being harmful in the commercial context. This plainly covers a situation where there is a poisoning or contaminating effect upon the property of a third party as a result of the introduction or intermixture of the product supplied ... However, it will not extend to a position where the commodity supplied is installed in

---

LJ (point not considered on appeal: [1996] 2 W.L.R. 348; [1996] 1 All E.R. 482; [1996] C.L.C. 197) (nuisance).

[56] *The Orjula* [1995] 2 Lloyd's Rep. 395; [1995] C.L.C. 1325 (negligence).

[57] *Transfield Constructions Pty Ltd v GIO Australia Holdings Pty Ltd* (1996) 9 ANZ Ins Cas 61-336, Common Law Division, Construction List.

[58] *Merlin v British Nuclear Fuels Plc* [1990] 2 Q.B. 557; [1990] 3 W.L.R. 383; [1990] 3 All E.R. 711.

[59] This wording is found in DE2–DE5.

[60] *Transfield Constructions Pty Ltd v GIO Australia Holdings Pty Ltd* (1996) 9 ANZ Ins Cas 61-336.

[61] *The Orjula* [1995] 2 Lloyd's Rep. 395; [1995] C.L.C. 1325.

[62] *Cementation Piling and Foundations Ltd* [1995] 1 Lloyd's Rep. 97; 74 B.L.R. 98; (1994) 47 Con. L.R. 14. See discussion below, at paras 16-050 to 16-058.

[63] *Bacardi-Martini Beverages Ltd v Thomas Hardy Packaging Ltd sub nom. Messer UK Ltd v Thomas Hardy Packaging Ltd* [2002] EWCA Civ 549; [2002] 2 All E.R. (Comm) 335; [2002] 2 Lloyd's Rep. 379. This was not a property damage case, but a contract case.

[64] *Pilkington UK Ltd v CGU Insurance Plc* [2004] EWCA Civ 23; [2005] 1 All E.R. (Comm) 283; [2004] 1 C.L.C. 1059.

or juxtaposed with the property of the third party in circumstances where it does no physical harm and the harmful effect of any later defect or deterioration is contained within it."[65]

Damage need not be permanent.   The adverse change in physical condition does **16-021** not have to be permanent to constitute damage.[66] There can be damage even if the condition of the property can be restored without great cost, e.g. by the cleaning away of dust or debris.[67] So the careful dismantling of individual stones from a work of stone cladding constitutes damage to the overall stonework, notwithstanding that the stones can later be reassembled.[68]

Intended use.   If there is a change in physical condition of the subject-matter, then **16-022** in assessing whether this has rendered the property less useful or valuable, considerations extraneous to the property itself—especially the intended use— can be relevant. In one case the unwanted change of colour in uPVC products was a physical change which impaired the value of the product and was damage within the meaning of the policy.[69] Conversely, the Court of Appeal has recognised that there can theoretically be damage even without a drop in the market value of the property. In *Jan de Nul (UK) Ltd v AXA Royale Belge SA (formerly NV Royale Belge)*, Schiemann LJ said:

> "If a lump of concrete is dropped on X's car, property damage has been inflicted even if someone can persuade an *avant garde* gallery curator that the resultant object is a work of art worth more than X paid for the car."[70]

Discovery of an existing defect.   The term "damage" does not include the diminu- **16-023** tion in value represented by a pre-existing defect in the subject-matter nor the cost of remedying it.[71] This is because the terms "defect" and "damage" bear different meanings. Something will be defective if it does not function as it should.[72] The term "defect" is a static concept: to talk about the occurrence of a defect is to say that a defect exists but not that it has developed. Something can be defective from the moment it was designed and constructed—hence the term "design defect". To

---

[65] *Pilkington UK Ltd* [2004] EWCA Civ 23 at [51]; [2005] 1 All E.R. (Comm) 283 at 298; [2004] 1 C.L.C. 1059 at 1077. In *Seele Austria GmbH & Co KG v Tokio Marine Europe Insurance Ltd* [2008] EWCA Civ 441 at [51]; [2009] 1 All E.R. (Comm) 171 at 187; [2008] B.L.R. 337 at 350: defects in window panels installed in the walls of a building were "not themselves damaged and did not cause damage to other parts of the works".

[66] Note that this contrasts with the position regarding "loss", which does not embrace temporary deprivation: *Moore v Evans* [1918] A.C. 185; [2008] B.L.R. 337 at 350.

[67] *Hunter* [1996] 2 W.L.R. 348; [1996] 1 All E.R. 482; [1996] C.L.C. 197, reversed on other grounds [1997] A.C. 655; [1997] 2 W.L.R. 684; [1997] 2 All E.R. 426.

[68] *Seele Austria GmbH & Co KG* [2007] EWHC 1411 at [36]; [2007] 1 C.L.C. 972 at 984; [2007] B.L.R. 337 at 345, point affirmed on appeal: [2008] EWCA Civ 441 at [51]; [2009] 1 All E.R. (Comm) 171 at 187; [2008] B.L.R. 337 at 350. See also *The Orjula* [1995] 2 Lloyd's Rep. 395 at 399; [1995] C.L.C. 1325 at 1328–1329, where Mance J said: "[r]elevant considerations are whether there has been 'injury impairing value and usefulness' of the property in question and the need for work and the expenditure of money to restore the property to its former usable condition is material".

[69] *Tioxide Europe Ltd v CGU International Insurance Plc* [2004] EWHC 2116 (Comm); [2005] Lloyd's Rep. I.R. 114. See also *Blue Circle Industries Plc* [1999] Ch 289; [1999] 2 W.L.R. 295, [1998] 3 All E.R. 385 (contamination of land by radioactive material).

[70] *Jan De Nul (UK) Ltd v Axa Royale Belge SA (formerly NV Royale Belge)* [2002] EWCA Civ 209 at [92]; [2002] 1 All E.R. (Comm) 767 at 785; [2002] 1 Lloyd's Rep. 583 at 595.

[71] *Oceanic Steamship Co v Faber* (1906) 11 Com. Cas. 179 at 188; affirmed (1907) 13 Com. Cas. 28; (1905–1908) 10 Asp. M.L.C. 515.

[72] See above, para.16-006.

say that property has sustained "damage" is to imply that the item has suffered some event, or process, which has changed its physical condition.[73]

3. THE INCHMAREE CLAUSE

16-024 **The Inchmaree Clause.** In *The Inchmaree*,[74] the House of Lords held that the breakage of machinery on a ship was not recoverable as a peril of the sea. This decision prompted the formulation of a clause designed to provide cover for breakages and other damage caused by internal failings—including "latent defects"—in the operation of the vessel,[75] known through all its subsequent incarnations as the "Inchmaree clause". The clause is drafted so that it extends cover to embrace loss or damage caused by latent defects; the two most recent versions go on to exclude the costs of replacing the defective part itself.

16-025 **The 1983/1995 clause.** The version of the Inchmaree Clause in the 1983 Institute Time Clauses (Hulls) reads:

> "6.2 This insurance covers loss of or damage to the subject-matter insured caused by bursting of boilers breakage of shafts or any latent defect in the machinery or hull ..."

The 1995 Institute Time Clauses (Hulls) is in the same words.[76]

16-026 The decision in *The Nukila*[77] confirms that—on this wording—there is no requirement that the damage be to some other non-defective part of the installation or vessel. So long as some "damage" has been sustained, in the sense of an adverse change in the physical condition of the insured subject matter within the period of the policy, it is covered by the clause even if the part in question was originally defective. In *The Nukila*, the insured vessel was a mobile off-shore platform which stood on three retractable legs. The legs consisted of tubular steel columns which were welded to steel boxes called "spud cans", which allowed the installation to sit firmly on the seabed. Before the policy was taken out, a defect in the welding between the leg-columns and the spud cans had caused very small, undetected, fatigue cracks in the metal. During the period of the policy, these cracks developed into extensive, visible fractures in the full thickness of the tube. Hobhouse LJ held that the questions to be asked were:

(1) Was there damage to the insured property?

(2) Did that damage occur during the period of the policy?

(3) Was that damage caused by a latent defect?

---

[73] In the Insurance Institute of London *Construction Insurance – Research Study Group Report 208B* (London: IIL, 2010), para.8.8.2.1, p.158, this distinction is explained: "[b]y normal usage of the terms, 'defect' is a *condition* not an *occurrence*".

[74] *The Inchmaree* (1887) 12 App. Cas. 484; [1899] P 11156 L.J.Q.B. 626; 6 Asp. M.L.C. 200.

[75] The "1888 Clauses, As recommended by the Institute of London Underwriters": "This insurance also specially to cover loss of, or damage to the hull or machinery through the negligence of Master, Mariners, Engineers, or Pilots, or through any latent defect in the machinery or the hull, provide that such loss or damage has not resulted from want of due diligence by the owners of the vessel, or any of them, or by the manager.": set out in C. Hewer, *A Problem Shared: History of the Institute of London Underwriters, 1884–1984* (London: Witherby, 1984).

[76] Sub-clause 6.2.2 in the 1983 version is corresponds to subcl.6.2.1 in the 1995 version.

[77] *The Nukila* [1991] 2 Lloyd's Rep. 146; [1997] C.L.C. 966. See above, para.14-019.

The answer to each of those questions was in the affirmative,[78] and accordingly the insured was entitled to recover. As Ward LJ put it, the spreading and deepening of the cracks was "something different from, something over and above and incrementally greater than the latent defect itself".[79] Contrary to the view of the judge, the Court of Appeal held that there was nothing in either the concept of "damage" or the wording of the clause that required the damage to be in some other notional "part" of the structure.[80] Of interest, and probably some resonance, to practitioners struggling to interpret defects exclusion clauses which distinguish between damage to the defective "part" itself and damage to "other" insured property (DE2 to DE4), is the following observation made by Hobhouse LJ who said:

> "The submission based upon the use of the word *part* ... leads to absurd results. It provides no criterion for distinguishing between what is and what is not damage ... The word *part* is capable of being used in a variety of ways depending on the context. Its use provides no answer to any relevant question. The weld is a part just as much as is a bracket or bulkhead or plate or the totality of the leg structure."[81]

The 2002 and 2003 clauses. So under the wording of the 1983/1995 hull clauses, **16-027** the insured will effectively be able to recover the cost of putting right a defect provided it is subsumed within the cost of repairing consequential damage to the vessel. But the draftsmen of more recent versions of the Hull Clauses have sought to reverse that position. Perhaps wisely, in so doing they have eschewed the technique of attempting to distinguish between defective and non-defective parts. The 2002 International Hull Clauses cover loss of or damage to the subject-matter insured caused by:

> "2.2.2 any latent defect in the machinery or hull, *but only to the extent that the cost of repairing the loss or damage caused thereby exceeds the cost that would have been incurred to correct the latent defect.*"[82]

The wording in the 2003 version of the International Hull Clauses is slightly different. It covers loss of or damage to the insured vessel caused by:

> "2.2.2 any latent defect in the machinery or hull *but does not cover any of the costs of correcting the latent defect.*"[83]

At first sight, the two wordings appear to be to the same effect. Consider, **16-028** however, that the vessel disintegrates and sinks due to a pervasive weakness in the condition of the hull caused by poor workmanship. Had the fault been discovered before the sinking, the costs of remedial work would have been a large proportion of the replacement value of the vessel. Under the 2003 wording, an argument by the insurers that they are entitled to deduct from the indemnity the notional cost of correcting the defect would be met with the response that the insured seeks neither to incur nor claim for such costs, but simply claims an indemnity for the re-instatement of the destroyed vessel. Whether that contention will succeed depends on whether the phrase "any of the costs of correcting the latent defect" extends to

---

[78] *The Nukila* [1997] 2 Lloyd's Rep. 146 at 157; [1997] C.L.C. 966 at 979.
[79] *The Nukila* [1997] 2 Lloyd's Rep. 146 at 157; [1997] C.L.C. 966 at 980.
[80] *The Nukila* [1997] 2 Lloyd's Rep. 146 at 156; [1997] C.L.C. 966 at 978–979.
[81] *The Nukila* [1997] 2 Lloyd's Rep. 146 at 156; [1997] C.L.C. 966 at 978, Hobhouse LJ.
[82] (Emphasis added).
[83] (Emphasis added).

costs *avoided* by the complete replacement of the subject-matter (that is, the hypothetical costs of pre-damage remediation), or instead means *actual* costs *incurred* to correct the defect (that is, by improvements to the design or build). The wording is ambiguous. By contrast, under the previous year's wording, the insured would have to give credit for the remedial work made unnecessary by the total replacement of the vessel, for the 2002 clause explicitly requires the calculation of the hypothetical cost of pre-damage remedial work and its subtraction from the indemnity provided under the clause. This move from clear wording adopted in 2002 to that which is ambiguous in 2003 is noteworthy. Perhaps it was thought that the 2002 clause operated too harshly against insured parties; if so, this would lend weight to the view that the 2003 clause is not intended to require a deduction for hypothetical repair work.

4. TREATMENT OF DEFECTS UNDER CAR POLICIES: "DE" CLAUSES

16-029 **Development of the DE clauses (1985).** In 1985 a committee was formed by leading insurers in the London market to promulgate a standard set of defect exclusion clauses that would adequately define the "different levels of cover which insurers were prepared to offer".[84] Five alternative wordings, "DE1" to "DE5" were drafted, which provide in turn progressively wider forms of cover for the consequences of defects. The original 1985 wordings were as follows:

DE1: Outright defect exclusion

"This policy excludes all loss of or damage to the Property insured due to defective design, plan, specification, materials or workmanship."

DE2: Extended defective condition exclusion

"This Policy excludes the costs necessary to replace, repair or rectify any of the Property insured which is in a defective condition due to a defect in design, plan, specification, material or workmanship, or which relies for its support or stability on any of the remainder of the Property insured which is in itself in a defective condition. This Exclusion shall not apply to the remainder of the Property insured which is free of such defective condition but is damaged as a consequence of such defect."

DE3: Limited defective condition exclusion

"This Policy excludes the costs necessary to replace, repair or rectify any of the Property insured which is in a defective condition due to a defect in design, plan, specification, materials or workmanship, but this Exclusion shall not apply to the remainder of the Property insured which is free of such defective condition but is damaged as a consequence of such defect."

DE4: Defective part exclusion

"This Policy excludes the costs necessary to replace, repair or rectify any component part or individual item of the Property insured which is defective in design, plan, specification, materials or workmanship, but this Exclusion shall not apply to other parts or items of the Property insured unintentionally damaged as a consequence of such defect."

DE5: Design improvement exclusion

"This Policy excludes the costs necessary to replace, repair or rectify any defect in design, plan, specification, materials or workmanship, but should unintended damage

---

[84] Insurance Institute of London, *Construction Insurance – Research Study Group Report 208B* (London: IIL, 2010), para.8.8.2.2, p.159.

result from such a defect, this Exclusion shall be limited to the additional costs of improvements to the original design, plan or specification."

The above clauses were widely adopted in the CAR market.[85] A revised set of DE clauses were drawn up a decade later. The 1995 wordings seek to reproduce the levels of cover prescribed by the original clauses, whilst clarifying their meaning in certain respects.[86] Clauses DE2 to DE5 now include words which make it clear that the cover carved-out of the exclusion for consequential damage does not include property damaged "to enable the replacement repair or rectification of the Property insured".[87] The new clauses also contain a rider that the property

16-030

"shall not be regarded as lost or damaged solely by virtue of the existence of any defect in design plan specification materials or workmanship."

The rider confirms the underlying principle that a defect does not in itself constitute damage.[88] The 1995 clauses are set out below together with a commentary on each.

DE1 (1995): outright defect exclusion. DE1 states:

16-031

"This policy excludes loss of or damage to the Property insured due to defective design plan specification materials or workmanship."

DE1 is an outright exclusion for damage caused by a defect. To put another way, "defective design ... [etc.]" is an excluded peril. This is a very wide exclusion and probably unacceptable to many contractors. However, a number of significant limitations should be noted. Although the wording lacks clarity, the phrase "defective ... workmanship" is presumably limited to defective workmanship *built into* the insured property, as would be defective "design", "plan", "specification" or "materials", by definition. It is unlikely that the intention was to exclude damage to the building inflicted directly by some slip-up in working—e.g. the dropping of a hammer by a workman onto the works below. The thrust of the clause is to exclude damage caused through the intermediary of the defective state of the property itself.[89]

16-032

The exclusion is phrased so as to apply only where the damage is caused by ("due to") a defect. As noted below, it is anomalous that the other DE clauses contain no such requirement.[90] To rely on the exclusion under DE1, the insurer will therefore need to establish that a defect was a proximate cause of the loss. The issue of proximity will turn on the connection between the defective state of the property and the event which "triggers off" its untoward consequences.[91]

16-033

DE2 (1995): extended defective condition exclusion. DE2 states:

16-034

"This policy excludes loss of or damage to and the cost necessary to replace repair or rectify:

[85] Insurance Institute of London *Construction Insurance – Research Study Group Report 208B* (London: IIL, 2010), para.8.8.2.4, p.161.
[86] Insurance Institute of London *Construction Insurance – Research Study Group Report 208B* (London: IIL, 2010), para.8.8.2.5, p.164.
[87] That is, DE2 (iii); DE3 (ii); DE4 (ii); DE5 (ii).
[88] See above, and para.14-014.
[89] cf. DE2–DE5 where the phrases "defective condition due to a defect in ... workmanship" (DE2, DE3) and "Property insured which is defective in ... workmanship" (DE4, DE5) make this clear.
[90] See below, para.16-037.
[91] *Wayne Tank & Pump Co Ltd v Employers Liability Assurance Corp Ltd* [1974] Q.B. 57 at 74; [1973] 3 W.L.R. 483 at 495; [1973] 3 All E.R. 825 at 836, per Roskill LJ.

(i)   Property insured which is in a defective condition due to a defect in design plan specification materials or workmanship of such Property insured or any part thereof;

(ii)   Property insured which relies for its support or stability on (i) above;

(iii)   Property insured lost or damaged to enable the replacement repair or rectification of Property insured excluded by (i) and (ii) above.

Exclusions (i) and (ii) above shall not apply to other Property insured which is free of the defective condition but is damaged in consequence thereof.

For the purpose of the Policy and not merely this Exclusion the Property insured shall not be regarded as lost or damaged solely by virtue of the existence of any defect in design plan specification materials or workmanship in the Property insured or any part thereof."

This wording is designed to exclude loss or damage to: (1) any of the insured property that is in defective condition; and (2) those structures that rely for their support on (1), whilst affirming that there is cover for other parts of the insured property which are damaged as a consequence of the defect. The exclusion perhaps has the advantage over the more limited "defective part" exclusions (DE3 and DE4) of drawing a rather more expressive distinction between those parts of the property intended to be excluded, and those parts within the cover. For example, it appears to sidestep any dispute over whether the above-ground parts of a building are in "defective condition" because the building has unstable foundations: the whole building would be within (2).

16-035   DE2 wording is more common now that the JCT Standard Building Contract requires, as part of a provision detailing with some precision the minimum level of cover that the party responsible for insuring the works must obtain, an all risks policy with a defects exclusion clause.[92] Specifically, the policy must, as regards defects, exclude no more than loss of or damage to

"any work executed or any Site Materials lost or damaged as a result of its own defect in design, plan, specification, material or workmanship or any other work executed which is lost or damaged in consequence thereof where such work relied for its support or stability on such work which was defective."[93]

This formulation is potentially problematic in that it specifies a level of cover which does not fully correspond to DE2 in one important respect. Whereas this exclusion only bites where there is causal link between the defect and the excluded damage ("lost or damaged as a result of its own defect"), there is no such causal requirement in the operative exclusionary words of DE2 ("excludes ... damage to ... Property insured which is in defective condition"): see the discussion of these words in relation to DE3 below.[94] So although the JCT Standard Form requires there to be cover in the situation where a defective part, and any structure supported by it, is damaged by a peril other than the defect itself, the standard DE2 wording would exclude cover in this situation. This is a potential trap for the parties to the building contract.[95]

---

[92] See Joint Contracts Tribunal, *SBC/Q 2011 JCT Standard Building Contract With Quantities 2011* (London: Sweet & Maxwell, 2011), cl.6.7; Sch.3, pp.68, 88–92, Insurance Options A–C.

[93] Joint Contracts Tribunal, *SBC/Q 2011 JCT Standard Building Contract With Quantities 2011* (2011), cl.6.8, pp.69–70.

[94] See below, paras 16-036 to 16-042.

[95] Suppose the permanent and temporary works for the erection of a building are required to be insured by the employer under a Joint Contracts Tribunal, *SBC/Q 2011 JCT Standard Building Contract With Quantities 2011* (2011), p.90 (Schedule 3: "Insurance Option B"). The employer takes out a CAR joint names policy that contains a standard DE2 clause, believing this to correspond to the requirement in cl.6.8(b) of the JCT form. As work nears completion, it transpires that the foundations are

DE3 (1995): limited defective condition exclusion.   DE3 states: **16-036**

"This policy excludes loss of or damage to and the cost necessary to replace repair or rectify:

(i) Property insured which is in a defective condition due to a defect in design plan specification materials or workmanship of such property insured or any part thereof;

(ii) Property insured lost or damaged to enable the replacement repair or rectification of Property insured excluded by (i) above.

Exclusion (i) above shall not apply to other Property insured which is free of the defective condition but is damaged in consequence thereof.

For the purpose of the Policy and not merely this Exclusion the Property insured shall not be regarded as lost or damaged solely by virtue of the existence of any defect in design plan specification materials or workmanship in the Property insured or any part thereof."

To date DE3 has been the most widely used of the five clauses. The clause excludes loss or damage to insured "Property … which is in a defective condition", whilst affirming that there is cover for "other Property insured which is free of the defective condition" but which is damaged in consequence thereof.

The first point to note is that in order for the exclusion to apply it is not neces-   **16-037** sary to show a causal link between defect and damage, but merely that the property "is in defective condition":

"The cause of the loss or damage is irrelevant. Provided the insurer can show that the property was in a defective condition the exclusion applies. So … if the capping and sub-formation [the insured road surfaces] were in a defective condition when damaged the exclusion would apply even if the damage had been caused by a bomb falling onto it."[96]

That conclusion is inescapable on the wording, but it is anomalous, and probably unintended, that DE3 (together with DE2 to DE5, which are worded in the same way) should carve out a wider exclusion in this respect than DE1, supposedly the "outright defect exclusion", as the latter excludes only that damage that is caused by the defect. On the other hand, it is clear that the exclusion will not apply to damage inflicted directly by negligent working; so far as workmanship is concerned, it is only errors that get "built into" the works that trigger the clause. In *CA Blackwell (Contractors) Ltd*, Tuckey LJ said:

"Conversely, if it was not in a defective condition, but the damage had been caused by a failure, say, to cover some part of the road with a tarpaulin, the exclusion would not apply."[97]

The scope of this exclusion hinges on the distinction between "Property … which   **16-038** is in a defective condition" and "other Property insured which is free of the defective condition". As was noted in *CA Blackwell (Contractors) Ltd*, "[t]his suggests, and indeed requires, divisibility".[98] However, it fails to suggest very much more:

---

in a defective condition, but before remedial work is undertaken a fire (due to an unrelated cause) destroys the entire building. The insurer would be able to argue that the entire loss was excluded by the DE2 clause as the foundations were in a defective condition and the rest of the structure was reliant on them for support/stability. Yet the employer would not be able to pass on its losses to the contractor because the insurance that ought to have been taken out *would* have covered the damage (it not being *due* to the defect); a contractor's liability is excluded to the extent of the insurance required to be taken out under Option B.

[96] *CA Blackwell (Contractors) Ltd* [2007] EWCA Civ 1450 at [17]; [2008] 1 All E.R. (Comm) 885 at 890; [2008] Lloyd's Rep. I.R. 529 at 533, per Tuckey LJ.

[97] *CA Blackwell (Contractors) Ltd* [2007] EWCA Civ 1450 at [17]; [2008] 1 All E.R. (Comm) 885 at 890; [2008] Lloyd's Rep. I.R. 529 at 533.

[98] *CA Blackwell (Contractors) Ltd* [2007] EWCA Civ 1450 at [22]; [2008] 1 All E.R. (Comm) 885 at

the wording gives no clear indication as to how one should begin to distinguish between defective and non-defective parts. There are several possible tests of "property ... in a defective condition" (for example): (1) whether the material or item in question is rendered less useful or valuable by reason of the defect; (2) whether the item was likely to be damaged if the defect materialised; or (3) whether the item is distinct in "commercial" or "construction" terms from the defect. Each possibility is capable of rendering different results. The first test is very wide indeed. A fault in a connecting rod of a car engine would obviously render the whole car less useful. But the rod would be unlikely to threaten to damage the rest of the vehicle, and the engine would probably be seen by most people as a distinct unit.

16-039   The commentary to the original set of DE clauses included a worked example,[99] which was clearly intended to re-assure the reader that the clauses are straightforward to apply and unambiguous in their effect. The example reads as follows:

> "A steel frame building with roof completed, cladding partially completed, and dwarf brick wall completed. The nuts and bolts used in construction of the steel framework proved to be inadequate and the whole structure collapsed, damaging everything.
>   The various defects exclusions would limit indemnity as follows:
>
> - DE1: all the damage would be excluded;
> - DE2: all damaged items excluded except the dwarf brick wall;
> - DE3: steel framework excluded; roof, cladding and dwarf brick walls paid for;
> - DE4: only nuts and bolts excluded;
> - DE5: all damage paid for but improvement costs excluded."

No-one would dispute that DE1 would exclude all of the damage, DE2 would exclude damage to all of the work structurally supported by the nuts and bolts and DE5 would pay for the entire damage, excluding the cost of any improvements[100] (it is noted that there is also confusion between the words "betterment" and "improvement", which is considered separately in para.16-060 below). But it is hard to understand why the drafting committee were confident that DE3 and DE4 will *self-evidently* be interpreted in the way stated. Since the fault lay in the nuts and bolts, why should the steel framework be treated as being "defective"? The most intuitive reasons for bringing the steel framework within the phrase "property ... in defective condition"—is its structural dependency on the defective component, or the fact that it would be liable to be damaged by a failure of the nuts and bolts— this would also catch the wall cladding, if not also other parts of the structure. Conversely, the framework might be seen as a defective "component part or individual item", inasmuch as it is seen as suffering from a pervasive defect for never having been properly bolted together, in which case the committee's interpretation of DE4 is to be treated with caution. The worked example in the commentary is not a mirror image of the wording and suggests that the hope that the five clauses provide five logically distinct, incrementally wider levels of cover is not entirely justified.

16-040   The distinction between defective and non-defective property has been

---

891; [2008] Lloyd's Rep. I.R. 529 at 534, per Tuckey LJ.

99   Reproduced in Insurance Institute of London, *Construction Insurance – Research Study Group Report 208B* (London: IIL, 2010), para.8.8.2.3, p.160.

100   See Insurance Institute of London, *Construction Insurance – Research Study Group Report 208B* (London: IIL, 2010), para.8.8.2.5, p.164, which states that DE5 "may be misunderstood in some quarters" and that "the limitation restricts application of the exclusion to betterment."

considered in two decisions. In *CA Blackwell (Contractors) Ltd*,[101] the claimant subcontractor was responsible, as part of the construction of the M60 motorway around Manchester, for profiling earthworks (the "subformation") and for spreading "capping" materials, which formed the sub-asphalt layers of the carriageway. The claimant was insured under an all risks policy, which included a defects exclusion clause in standard DE3 terms. Before the work could be completed, rainfall caused damage to the subformation and the capping layers. The insurer contended that inadequacies in measures taken to protect the works, including the cutting of drainage channels in the capping layer, were an indivisible aspect of the damaged works: the whole road was in defective condition. As the judge recognised, applying the DE3 wording to the facts was difficult because of the "continuous, extensive, protean and eventually hidden nature of the insured property in this case".[102] Ultimately, the judge found that the exclusion did not bite, and this was upheld on appeal. Tuckey LJ drew a distinction between the carving of channels in the capping layer, and other measures such as the use of pumps and bowsers. A lack of necessary cuts and channels in the capping layer might have made the capping defective, but the evidence was that such measures were not required at this stage in the works.[103] As for a failure to adequately employ pumps and bowsers, he doubted that the works contemplated by these measures were "insured property"— they were analogous to a failure to cover the road with a tarpaulin: a deficiency in site management rather than in the physical condition of the works—but in any event such property should be distinguished from the capping and subformation, which was "other property".[104] More generally, the court was concerned that a broad interpretation of the exclusion would allow an insurer to "escape liability by finding some defect remote from the damage and entirely unconnected with its cause".[105] Yet the judgment does not articulate an answer to the underlying problem of how "property ... a in defective condition" is to be distinguished from "other property which is free of the defective condition". Tuckey LJ considered that the "property insured" excluded by the clause must be "restricted to that part of the works which has suffered damage. If that part is wholly or partly defective the exclusion applies".[106] This analysis is not considered to be helpful. That the property to which the exclusion applies must be damaged is obvious as the insured can only claim an indemnity for "loss or damage" in the first place; the real question is how the works should notionally be divided into parts for these purposes.

The Court of Appeal returned to the problem of divisibility under a DE3 clause **16-041** in *Seele Austria GmbH & Co KG*.[107] A set of "punched" windows were installed

---

[101] *CA Blackwell (Contractors) Ltd* [2007] EWCA Civ 1450; [2008] 1 All E.R. (Comm) 885; [2008] Lloyd's Rep. I.R. 529.

[102] *CA Blackwell (Contractors) Ltd* [2007] EWHC 94 (Comm) at [61]; [2007] Lloyd's Rep. I.R. 511 at 523.

[103] *CA Blackwell (Contractors) Ltd* [2007] EWCA Civ 1450 at [24]; [2008] 1 All ER (Comm) 885 at 891; [2008] Lloyd's Rep. I.R. 529 at 534.

[104] *CA Blackwell (Contractors) Ltd* [2007] EWCA Civ 1450 at [25]; [2008] 1 All E.R. (Comm) 885 at 892; [2008] Lloyd's Rep. I.R. 529 at 534.

[105] *CA Blackwell (Contractors) Ltd* [2007] EWCA Civ 1450 at [23]; [2008] 1 All ER (Comm) 885 at 891; [2008] Lloyd's Rep. I.R. 529 at 534.

[106] *CA Blackwell (Contractors) Ltd* [2007] EWCA Civ 1450 at [22]; [2008] 1 All ER (Comm) 885 at 891; [2008] Lloyd's Rep. I.R. 529 at 534.

[107] *Seele Austria GmbH & Co KG* [2008] EWCA Civ 441; [2009] 1 All E.R. (Comm) 171; [2008] B.L.R. 337. The primary dispute was over the interpretation of a bespoke additional indemnity for access damage: see below para.16-073.

during the construction of the façade of a building. Having been installed, the windows leaked during water testing and had to be replaced, which required the completed stone cladding and internal plaster finishes to be removed to gain access. The insured conceded that for the purpose of the DE3 wording, it was necessary to show damage to the works over and above damage to the window units themselves. However, it was argued that as water had penetrated onto the plasterboard ceilings there was indeed damage to non-defective property. The judge at first instance rejected this submission on the basis that there was no evidence that the water had adversely affected the state of the ceiling.[108] He held that, in any event, the ceilings were not "other Insured Property which [was] free of the defective condition", because they were in close proximity to the windows and so "vulnerable to the ingress of water by reason of the defective design and installation of the windows"; the ceilings were therefore in defective condition, as was the whole facade.[109] On appeal, Moore-Bick LJ disapproved of the judge's conclusion on the divisibility point. He considered that the clause was intended to preserve cover in respect of

"parts of the work, which in commercial terms are to be regarded as separate and distinct from that part in which the defect exists."[110]

It was wrong to treat the facade as a single item of property; in commercial terms the plasterboard ceilings and external cladding were each to be regarded as separate items.[111]

16-042   It is suggested that the view of Moore-Bick LJ in *Seele Austria GmbH & Co KG* probably represents the best attempt thus far to articulate a workable approach for distinguishing between defective and non-defective property for the purposes of DE3. He recognised that divisibility in "commercial terms" should not be equated with divisibility between subcontracts, since the test has to be able to cope with the situation "…where the work being carried out by a single subcontractor is of a complex nature".[112] It appears, then, that one asks the question: is the defect contained within an area that the project participants would treat as being a distinct package, or stage, of the works? A similar conclusion was reached by the New South Wales Court of Appeal in a case considering an exclusion limited to the "part which is defective". It was held that the word "part" was

"not a reference to a part such as a tank or a gasket; it is a reference to part of the work being carried out by the appellant."[113]

---

[108] *Seele Austria GmbH & Co KG* [2007] EWHC 1411 (Comm) at [26]; [2007] 1 C.L.C. 972 at 981–982; [2007] B.L.R. 337 at 343.

[109] *Seele Austria GmbH & Co KG* [2007] EWHC 1411 (Comm) at [27]; [2007] 1 C.L.C. 972 at 982; [2007] B.L.R. 337 at 343. The judge was applying, in effect, test (ii) set out above in para.16-038.

[110] *Seele Austria GmbH & Co KG* [2008] EWCA Civ 441 at [50]; [2009] 1 All E.R. (Comm) 171 at 187; [2008] B.L.R. 337 at 350.

[111] *Seele Austria GmbH & Co KG* [2008] EWCA Civ 441 at [50]; [2009] 1 All E.R. (Comm) 171 at 187; [2008] B.L.R. 337 at 350.

[112] *Seele Austria GmbH & Co KG* [2008] EWCA Civ 441 at [50]; [2009] 1 All E.R. (Comm) 171 at 187.

[113] *Walker Civil Engineering Pty Ltd v Sun Alliance & London Insurance Plc* (1999) 10 ANZ Insurance Cases 61-418 at [74693]. Unfortunately, the authority of *Walker* is undermined by the court's assumption (without which the claim would fail quite apart from the divisibility issue) that the all risks policy would respond even in the absence of any loss other the costs of repairing the defect: see below, fn.177. The case was distinguished in *CA Blackwell (Contractors) Ltd* as an aid to constru-

The "commercial terms" or "stage of construction" approach may also have the benefit of redeeming the drafting committee's interpretation of its example of the steel-framed building, which was criticised above, in para.16-039. The faulty nuts and bolts would have been screwed in as part of the erection of the steel framework, thus the two items could hardly be treated as distinct stages of construction work. On any other of the other tests it is impossible to see why the steelwork was in "defective condition" whilst the cladding and the roofing were not.

DE4 (1995): Defective part exclusion. DE4 states: **16-043**

"This policy excludes loss of or damage to and the cost necessary to replace, repair or rectify:

(i)   Any component part or individual item of the Property insured which is defective in design plan specification materials or workmanship;

(ii)   Property insured lost or damaged to enable the replacement repair or rectification of Property insured excluded by (i) above.

Exclusion (i) above shall not apply to other parts or items of Property insured which are free from defect but are damaged in consequence thereof.

For the purpose of the Policy and not merely this Exclusion the Property insured shall not be regarded as lost or damaged solely by virtue of the existence of any defect in design plan specification materials or workmanship in the Property insured or any part thereof."

The clause, like DE3, distinguishes between defective and non-defective parts of the insured property, but identifies the excluded property with the narrower phrase "component part or individual item".[114] In the example of the collapsing steel-frame building given by the drafting committee,[115] the exclusion is said to be limited to the faulty nuts and bolts. That may well accord with most people's interpretation of a "component part", but what about the situation where a window shatters due to pressure caused by a defective set of screws in the pre-fabricated frame: does the exclusion apply to the entire window unit or only to the screws? If the term "component part" is interpreted as an item "as delivered to site" then all damage to the window would be excluded. However, if a "component part" is something that can be replaced without requiring the replacement of the larger structure or unit of which it forms a part, only the defective screws would be excluded.

DE5 (1995): Design improvement exclusion. DE5 states: **16-044**

"This policy excludes:

(i)   The cost necessary to replace, repair or rectify any Property insured which is defective in design plan specification materials or workmanship;

(ii)   Loss or damage to the Property insured caused to enable replacement, repair or rectification of such defective Property insured.

ing DE3 on the (less compelling) basis that the wording of the exclusion in *Walker* required the defect to be the cause of the damage: *CA Blackwell (Contractors) Ltd* [2007] EWCA Civ 1450 at [21]; [2008] 1 All E.R. (Comm) 885 at 891; [2008] Lloyd's Rep. I.R. 529 at 534.

[114] The committee's designation of DE4 as a "defective part exclusion" is misleading given that it is impossible to discuss the application of DE3 without using the word "part" or a synonym. See, e.g., *CA Blackwell (Contractors) Ltd* [2007] EWCA Civ 1450 at [22]; [2008] 1 All E.R. (Comm) 885 at 891; [2008] Lloyd's Rep. I.R. 529 at 534, per Tuckey L.J.; *Seele Austria GmbH & Co KG* [2008] EWCA Civ 441 at [50]; [2009] 1 All E.R. (Comm) 171 at 187; [2008] B.L.R. 337 at 350, per Moore-Bick LJ.

[115] See above, para.16-039.

But should damage to the Property insured (other than damage as defined in (ii) above) result from such a defect, this Exclusion shall be limited to the costs of additional work resulting from and the additional costs of improvement to the original design plan specification materials or workmanship.

For the purpose of the Policy and not merely this Exclusion the Property insured shall not be regarded as lost or damaged solely by virtue of the existence of any defect in design plan specification materials or workmanship in the Property insured or any part thereof."

DE5 preserves the most generous scope of cover for consequential damage. If the defect causes damage to the property different from or incrementally greater than the defect itself, the insured is entitled to the costs of reinstating all of the damaged property, including to the defective part, less the additional costs (if any) of improving the original design, materials, etc. It is a feature of the drafting, however, that whilst the basic exclusion for the cost of remedying the defective property applies whether or not the damage is caused by the defect,[116] the write-back for loss of or damage to the defective property is limited to the situation where damage "result[s] from such a defect". Accordingly, at least if the clause is to be read literally, it has the opposite effect to DE1.[117] The policy will indemnify for damage to defective property where it is damaged as a result of the defect but not where damage to the defective property is caused by an unrelated peril. It seems unlikely that this was the effect that the drafting committee was hoping to achieve, particularly as this means that DE5 (supposedly the narrowest exclusion) will exclude cover in some situations where DE1 would preserve it. Nonetheless, it is hard to see how the plain meaning of the words can be avoided.

16-045 **DE5—is there a requirement for damage to defective property?** A contentious question under DE5 is whether the insured is indemnified for the cost of remedying defective but not damaged property that has caused damage to other insured property. One might have thought that the answer to this question was not of practical significance as the cost of remedying property that contains a defect in design but has itself suffered no damage would be excluded in any event, since remedial works to such property would always be *purely* a matter of "improvement to the original design". If property has suffered no damage, there is nothing to indemnify.[118] However, as there is an unresolved issue as to whether the exclusionary wording is to be interpreted as requiring the occurrence of damage to property containing a defect before it is indemnified, the issue is considered further.

16-046 The reasoning in support of the need for damage as a pre-condition to an indemnity for the rectification of defective property starts with consideration of the extent of the indemnity provided in the insuring clause, the scope of the DE5 exclusion and the extent of the carve-out to the exclusion. On the other hand, the argument in favour of there being no precondition for damage to defective property for there to be an indemnity is that the DE5 exclusion is an extension to the cover provided by the insuring clause. So that where damage has been caused by a defect, the cost of remedying the defect is indemnified even though the part containing the defect has not been damaged.

16-047 An example demonstrates the significance of the point: if a substantial tower

---

[116] As is the case with DE3: see above, para.16-037.

[117] See above, paras 16-031 to 16-033.

[118] See also para.16-001 above which explains an unresolved issue as to whether if there is no equivalent exclusion to DE5 in a land based policy, the operative clause indemnifies for damage caused by a defect without any additional co-operating clause.

block suffers minor cracking damage, which is caused by a defect in the founda-tions, then under DE5 the insured will be indemnified for the cost of remedying the damage. However, the real cost may be in replacing the defective but undamaged foundations, as this may require demolition and rebuilding of the tower block (including the foundations). Whilst it would appear sensible for an insurer to agree that a defect in the foundations ought to be rectified if there is damage to the founda-tions, it would be surprising if there were cover for rectification of the defect in the absence of damage to the defective part.

DE5—damage to defective property is required. The starting point to this line **16-048** of reasoning is that a CAR insuring clause provides a gateway to cover for dam-age to property to be indemnified, subject only to the other provisions and limits in the policy.[119] If a DE5 exclusion is included in the wording, then the cost of remedying *any* defective property, whether damaged or undamaged, is excluded. There is, of course, no requirement to exclude undamaged but defective property because it is not insured in the first place. The wording is to be interpreted as hav-ing been included to avoid misunderstanding as to the scope of the cover provided by an all risks policy. There is then an exception to the exclusion for damage result-ing from a defect, which is limited to the costs of remedying the defect in design but which excludes costs associated with improvements to the design. The excep-tion from the exclusion to cover is for defective property that has been damaged, but it is limited to the cost of repair and does not state that it extends to the cost of gaining access to carry out the repairs and the costs of any improvements are excluded from cover. Accordingly, cover is provided for repairing damage to defec-tive property (including the remedy of the defect), but not for the cost of remedy-ing defective undamaged property. In support of this reasoning it is suggested that to interpret DE5 as providing cover for property that is defective but not damaged would be to give an insured an unrestricted right to upgrade its property whenever damage has occurred (subject to the proviso that the damage must "result from such a defect", as required by the carve-out in DE5) and it can identify a discrepancy between the contract and other aspects of the original design plan specification materials or workmanship.

DE5—damage to defective property is not required. The contrary reasoning **16-049** does not start with the insuring clause but with a comparison between the DE clauses. The position under DE5 is contrasted with the opening words of DE3 and DE4, which provide that there is no indemnity in respect of *damage* to property insured/component parts of defective property, whereas the standard DE5 word-ing is: "The insurer shall not indemnify except as otherwise provided herein in respect of: the cost necessary to replace [etc.] defective workmanship". Therefore it is said that the DE5 exclusion does not relate to "damage" to defective property as is the case with DE3 and DE4, but that it is an exclusion for the cost of repair-ing the defective design, etc. Since there is no cover in a CAR insuring clause for the cost of remedying defective but damaged property, it is possible to characterise DE5 as an extension to cover as it does not seek to exclude something that would otherwise be covered.

---

[119] See above, para.16-001 for the position where a defect is the sole cause of the damage.

Further discussion: Cementation Piling and Foundations Ltd v Commercial
16-050 **Union Insurance Plc; and Tesco Stores Ltd v Constable.** In *Cementation Piling and Foundations Ltd*,[120] sand retained by the walls of a newly constructed dock was found to have escaped into the dock. A claim was made under the project all risks policy for the removal of the sand and the filling of the voids in the dock walls through which the sand escaped. The policy excluded the cost of remedying defects, "unless the property insured suffers actual loss, destruction or damage as a result of such defect". The clause provided that the

> "additional costs of introducing improvements, betterments or corrections in the rectification of the design, material or workmanship causing such loss or damage shall always be excluded."[121]

The insurers were prepared to pay for the sand clean-up, accepting that this constituted damage to the dock, but not for the filling of the gaps in the dock walls, which they regarded as defects in the works rather than consequential damage. The Court of Appeal held that the insured was entitled to recover the cost of repairing defects in the walls. It held that the insuring clause, which indemnified "in respect of physical damage to the property insured"[122] had to be read in the context provided by the defects exclusion clause.[123] The latter clause stated that costs of rectifying defects in design, etc., were excluded "unless" damage was suffered as a result, and this implied that if such damage did occur, the costs of remedying the defect was covered.[124] Similarly, the fact that "additional costs of introducing improvements ... in the rectification of the design materials or workmanship" was specifically excluded implied that there were "other costs of rectification" that were covered.[125] It is suggested that this reasoning is flawed in that it overlooks the possibility that the "other costs" of rectifying a defect that the clause covers are the costs of reinstating defective property *which has itself been damaged*. Instead, on the court's interpretation, the occurrence of damage was simply a trigger to recovery for the cost of putting right the defect that caused the damage, even if the defective component suffered no damage.

16-051 A feature of *Cementation Piling and Foundations Ltd*[126] is the tension between, on the one hand, the principle that "an exception clause cannot extend the cover from which the exception is made"[127] and, on the other, the need to construe the terms of an insuring clause in the light of the whole contract. In the Court of Appeal, it was held that the wide scope of the words "in respect of" in the insuring clause was sufficient to enable the court to draw inferences as to the extent of the indemnity from the wording of the exclusion clause. Sir Ralph Gibson stated that

---

[120] *Cementation Piling and Foundations Ltd* [1995] 1 Lloyd's Rep. 97; 74 B.L.R. 98; (1994) 47 Con. L.R. 14.

[121] The words "betterment and corrections" are not used in DE5.

[122] *Cementation Piling and Foundations Ltd* [1995] 1 Lloyd's Rep. 97 at 102; 74 B.L.R. 98 at 105; (1994) 47 Con. L.R. 14 at 21, per Sir Ralph Gibson.

[123] *Cementation Piling and Foundations Ltd* [1995] 1 Lloyd's Rep. 97 at 102; 74 B.L.R. 98 at 108–109; (1994) 47 Con. L.R. 14 at 22, per Sir Ralph Gibson.

[124] *Cementation Piling and Foundations Ltd* [1995] 1 Lloyd's Rep. 97 at 102–103; 74 B.L.R. 98 at 110; (1994) 47 Con. L.R. 14 at 23, per Sir Ralph Gibson.

[125] *Cementation Piling and Foundations Ltd* [1995] 1 Lloyd's Rep. 97 at 103; 74 B.L.R. 98 at 110; (1994) 47 Con. L.R. 14 at 23, per Sir Ralph Gibson.

[126] *Cementation Piling and Foundations Ltd* [1995] 1 Lloyd's Rep. 97; (1995) 74 B.L.R. 98 at 109; (1994) 47 Con. L.R. 14 at 22.

[127] *Cementation Piling and Foundations Ltd* [1995] 1 Lloyd's Rep. 97 at 102; (1994) 47 Con. L.R. 14.

"[t]he nature of the connection which is required by the words 'in respect of' is not, in my view, clear without the assistance of the context."[128]

The relevant context was the exclusion clause, which, as detailed above, excluded the cost of rectification of defects "unless the property insured suffers actual loss, destruction or damage as a result of such defect".[129] It was held that if this "trigger" operates (i.e. "actual loss [etc.]" does occur) then the clause should no longer exclude liability ("insurers shall not be liable") but positively impose it (effectively, "shall be liable"), as this is the clearest inference from the word "unless".[130] It required a strained reading of the clause, however, to overlook the fact that this led to an all risks policy responding in the absence of physical loss or damage.

It is suggested that it would require an even more strained reading to draw the **16-052** same inferences in relation to DE5 as were drawn in *Cementation Piling and Foundations Ltd*.[131] If the trigger in DE5 operates ("but should damage to the property insured ... result from such a defect"), the carve-out ("this Exclusion shall be limited to") takes effect and limits the exclusion clause.[132] It would seem counterintuitive for a clause that expressly operates within the confines of an exclusion to be construed as a standalone extension to the insuring clause. The words "in respect of", which were construed widely in *Cementation Piling and Foundations Ltd*, are not a term of art and, as Sir Ralph Gibson said in the case, they will take their meaning from the context in which they are used. For this reason it is helpful to consider interpretation of those words in a directly analogous context. In *Tesco Stores Ltd v Constable*,[133] a public liability insuring clause containing the same phrase was considered by the Court of Appeal. It concluded that the words "in respect of" in a public liability policy had a limiting effect on the scope of the indemnity. Three cases were referred to by the Court of Appeal for assistance as to the meaning of "in respect of"; these were *James Budgett Sugars Ltd v Norwich Union Insurance Ltd*,[134] *AS Screenprint Ltd v British Reserve Insurance Co Ltd*[135] and *Horbury Building Systems Ltd v Hampden Insurance NV*.[136] Each of the cases concerned product liability cover and each of them was in relation to claims for

---

[128] *Cementation Piling and Foundations Ltd* [1995] 1 Lloyd's Rep. 97 at 102; (1995) 74 B.L.R. 98 at 108–109; (1994) 47 Con. L.R. 14 at 22. This view represented a departure from the opinion of the judge at first instance, who considered that the scope of the words "in respect of" in the insuring clause was, in and of itself, sufficient to extend the indemnity so as to include the rectification of a defect which would otherwise continue to cause damage: *Cementation Piling and Foundations Ltd* [1993] 1 Lloyd's Rep. 526 at 531, 534.

[129] See above, para.16-050.

[130] *Cementation Piling and Foundations Ltd* [1995] 1 Lloyd's Rep. 97 at 103; (1995) 74 B.L.R 98 at 110; (1994) 47 Con. L.R. 14 at 23.

[131] *Cementation Piling and Foundations Ltd* [1995] 1 Lloyd's Rep. 97; (1995) 74 B.L.R 98; (1994) 47 Con. L.R. 14.

[132] Insurance Institute of London *Construction Insurance – Research Study Group Report 208B* (London: IIL, 2010), para.8.8.2.5, p.164.

[133] *Tesco Stores Ltd v Constable* [2008] EWCA Civ 362; [2008] Lloyd's Rep. I.R. 636; [2008] 1 C.L.C. 727.

[134] *James Budgett Sugars Ltd v Norwich Union Insurance Ltd* [2002] EWHC 968 (Comm); [2003] Lloyd's Rep. I.R. 110.

[135] *AS Screenprint Ltd v British Reserve Insurance Co Ltd* [1996] C.L.C. 1470; [1999] Lloyd's Rep. I.R. 430.

[136] *Horbury Building Systems Ltd v Hampden Insurance NV* [2004] EWCA Civ 418; [2007] Lloyd's Rep. I.R. 237; [2004] B.L.R. 431.

economic loss consequential upon but not directly the result of physical damage to property and each of them was rejected. In *Rexodan International Ltd v Commercial Union Assurance Co Plc*,[137] Hobhouse LJ explained the meaning of the words, "put shortly these words [in respect of] mean 'for' and not merely 'caused by', 'consequential upon' or 'in connection with'".

16-053　In the context of a public liability insuring clause, the Court of Appeal in *Tesco Stores Ltd*[138] held that the liability must be for loss or damage to material property of the person whose property it is—liability for loss suffered by someone else as a consequence of such damage is not "in respect of" it. The Court of Appeal's interpretation of the words can also be applied to the wording of a CAR contract works policy so that an operative clause would then read:

> "The Insurer will indemnify the Insured [for] physical loss or damage to insured property."

In the context of the clarification of the meaning of damage in DE5, it is suggested that it is no longer possible to "re-read" the insuring clause in the light of the defects exclusion (as the Court did in *Cementation Piling and Foundations Ltd*), as covering the rectification of undamaged property that is defective but which has not itself sustained damage. It is suggested that the Court of Appeal would construe the words in the context of the revised wording of the exclusion as limiting the indemnity to the rectification of physical damage only and not also "for" the rectification of defects that cause damage.

16-054　In *Seele Austria GmbH & Co KG*,[139] a clause similar to DE3 was construed by Waller and Moore-Bick LJJ in the context of additional wording relating to intentional damage. Waller LJ stated:

> "[Where] the accident had damaged any insured property including the defective property, the non recovery was limited to the costs of improving the design ... If thus there was damage to defective property ... the insured did recover ... replacement costs of the defective property."[140]

16-055　In the context in which the point arose it seems likely that Waller LJ considered that defective property had to be damaged in order to bring it within the write-back to the defects exclusion clause. Moore-Bick LJ on the other hand reached the opposite conclusion when he stated:

> "The effect of clause (1) is to exclude the whole of the cost of making good any original defect in the works as a whole and any damage caused to enable that defect to be made good (what for convenience I shall call 'access damage'). However, it then goes on to provide that if the defect has caused damage to the works (other than the need for access damage), the exclusion shall be limited to the cost of any additional work needed to improve the original design. In other words, if the defect has caused damage to another part of the structure, the insured can recover both the cost of making good the original defect (but not the cost of any improvement) and any necessary access damage as well as the cost of making good the consequential damage."[141]

---

137 *Rexodan International Ltd v Commercial Union Assurance Co Plc* [1999] Lloyd's Rep. I.R. 495 at 500.

138 *Tesco Stores Ltd* [2008] EWCA Civ 362; [2008] 1 C.L.C. 727; [2008] Lloyd's Rep. I.R. 636.

139 *Seele Austria GmbH & Co KG* [2008] EWCA Civ 441; [2009] 1 All E.R. (Comm) 171; [2008] B.L.R. 337.

140 *Seele Austria GmbH & Co KG* [2008] EWCA Civ 441 at [19]; [2009] 1 All E.R. (Comm) 171 at 179; [2008] B.L.R. 337.

141 *Seele Austria GmbH & Co KG* [2008] EWCA Civ 441 at [39]; [2009] 1 All E.R. (Comm) 171 at 184; [2008] B.L.R. 337.

On the basis of this paragraph Moore-Bick LJ concluded that the cost of mak- **16-056** ing good "undamaged" defective property is recoverable where there has been damage to non-defective property. The context is important for both judgments as at first instance it had been held that no damage had been caused to the defective property. For this reason it is unlikely that the point would have been the subject of detailed argument before the Court of Appeal. Furthermore, the analysis by Moore-Bick and Waller LJJ of this point was not subject to similar detailed consideration by Richards LJ, who was the third member of the Court of Appeal. This is not surprising as Waller LJ summarised the key issue in the appeal as being whether, even though no accidental damage had occurred as a result of the installation of defective windows, access costs were recoverable.[142] In the circumstances it is suggested that limited weight ought to be placed upon the obiter dicta of Moore-Bick and Waller LJJ in *Seele Austria GmbH & Co KG*.[143]

Viewpoint.   To permit payment of the cost of remedying defective property that **16-057** has not been damaged would be to construe the DE5 exclusion as an extension to cover that is unwarranted. It is suggested that the correct analysis is that the wording is more consistent with it being a deeming clause it provides cover only where defective property has been damaged. The indemnity is limited to the correction of defects when this is carried out in the course of remedying damage to property.[144]

The sharply opposed reasoning in the judgments of the Court of Appeal in *Seele* **16-058** *Austria GmbH & Co KG*.[145] as to whether the occurrence of damage is a requirement for an indemnity emphasises the difficulty that is encountered in interpreting the DE clauses generally. It is considered that it is unlikely that the DE5 wording would be construed by a court as providing for the cost of replacing defectively designed but undamaged property where the design has caused damage to other insured property, given the limited support to be found in the wording of the clause or upon a careful analysis of the facts and reasoning in the authorities. Nevertheless the point remains to be decided.

Recovery for improvements to the design.   DE5 excludes, in all cases, the "ad- **16-059** ditional work resulting from and the additional costs of improvement to the original design plan specification materials or workmanship". What this qualification does

---

[142] *Seele Austria GmbH & Co KG* [2008] EWCA Civ 441 at [4]; [2009] 1 All E.R. (Comm) 171 at 176; [2008] B.L.R. 337 at 342.

[143] *Seele Austria GmbH & Co KG* [2008] EWCA Civ 441; [2009] 1 All E.R. (Comm) 171; [2008] B.L.R. 337.

[144] See *Insurance Law for the Construction Industry*, edited by R. Hogarth, A. Anderson and S. Goldring, 2nd edn (Oxford: Oxford University Press, 2008), para.6.118. the section below would appear to support the contention that there is no cover for the defective undamaged part, it states: "DE5 is the narrowest exclusion whereby, provided there is damage to insured property (be it defective or non-defective insured property) resulting from a defect, the only costs excluded are the costs of additional work resulting from, and the additional costs of improvement to, the original design, plan, specification, materials or workmanship. Accordingly, an indemnity will be available for the cost of replacement, repair or rectification of both the defective and non-defective property and the only costs excluded will be the costs of remedying the defects in the design, plan, specification, materials, or workmanship or any betterment." When it says there is an indemnity available for the repair of defective and non-defective property, it appears to be saying that there is an indemnity available for *damaged* defective and non-defective property. Otherwise the last part of the sentence ("the only costs excluded will be the costs of remedying the defects" etc.) would be contradictory.

[145] *Seele Austria GmbH & Co KG* [2008] EWCA Civ 441; [2009] 1 All E.R. (Comm) 171; [2008] B.L.R. 337.

not do is to exclude the cost of reinstating a defective part where this is subsumed (because the defective part has itself been damaged or destroyed) in the cost of repairing the damage.[146] It is suggested that DE5 should not be interpreted as requiring more than rectification of the original defective design, which was incorporated into the "as-constructed" works. This is because there is no requirement for indemnified remedial works to satisfy a higher standard than simply to remedy the defect to its as-constructed condition. Remedying a defect in design may not require compliance with the contractual standard, or enhancement of the function or appearance to a higher standard. Neither does it subtract, as does the 2002 Inchmaree Clause,[147] the hypothetical cost of remedying the defect prior to the accident. The qualification bites only to the extent that reinstatement work costs more than did the portion of the original works that is being re-instated, as a result of a *more expensive* design, materials or workmanship being employed. As Parker LJ emphasised in *Hitchins (Hatfield) Ltd*[148]:

> "It clearly does not follow that the costs of rectifying a design defect will be increased costs. If for example damage is caused to a building by a design defect, the reinstatement of the building to a new design which contained no such defect might well be cheaper than reinstatement to the original design."[149]

16-060   The additional cost of an improvement to the design, which is more expensive to design or build, would be excluded from the indemnity by these words. In practice it is difficult to find an example of a remedy to a defect in an original as-constructed design that would not also be an improvement to the as-constructed but defective design and it is difficult to give meaning to the word "additional", which precedes "costs of improvement" within the exclusion in this situation. It would have been possible for the DE clauses drafting committee to make a distinction in DE5 between improvements to the original design of the property insured, which is carried out voluntarily and betterment that is the unavoidable consequence of carrying out remedial works.[150] For example, the fact that a design has been improved, perhaps because a particular component containing a defect in its design is no longer manufactured and the replacement component is free from defect, would not prevent deduction being made for all unavoidable improvement to the original "as-constructed" design. The distinction between "improvement" and "betterment" is not explained in the report of the Research Study Group 208B, which states only that "[t]he limitation restricts application of the exclusion to betterment."[151] The

---

146 Otherwise, DE5 would not have the effect, generally ascribed to it, of providing an indemnity "in respect of the cost of remedial work to both the defective works and the non-defective but damaged works ... [with] a further exclusion of the cost of redesign or betterment": Insurance Institute of London *Construction Insurance – Research Study Group Report 208B* (London: IIL, 2010), para.8.8.2.2, p.159.
147 See above, paras 16-027 to 16-028.
148 *Hitchins (Hatfield) Ltd* [1991] 2 Lloyd's Rep. 580; 60 B.L.R. 51.
149 *Hitchins (Hatfield) Ltd* [1991] 2 Lloyd's Rep. 580 at 584; 60 B.L.R. 51 at 59. The policy in that case indemnified against loss or damage arising out of defective design etc. subject to an exclusion for "increased costs due to redesigning the Property Insured or any part thereof which is defectively designed". The preliminary issue ordered for trial was on the meaning of the words "defectively designed" (see paras 16-009 to 16-010 above), but the court went out of its way to point out, that issue aside, that the insurers' defence was defective inasmuch as it assumed that remedial work which had the effect of correcting the defect would be "increased costs".
150 See further discussion above, at para.11-016.
151 Insurance Institute of London, *Construction Insurance – Research Study Group Report 208B*

position in relation to defective workmanship is clearer, as remedial works ought not to result in improvement to the original specification, or to the specified standard of workmanship for the works. The rectification of defective workmanship usually only arises because of non-compliance with the contractual specification.

Accordingly, the suggestion that *Cementation Piling and Foundations Ltd*[152] is authority for a conclusion that the indemnity for physical loss and damage under an all risks policy can extend to the cost of remedying defects of design represents an unjustified fundamental change in an insurer's obligations under an indemnity for physical loss and damage as compared to the interpretation set out above.[153] The reasoning relies upon a parallel being drawn between the defects exclusion in *Cementation Piling and Foundations Ltd* and the wording of DE5, so that a policy containing this exclusion provides an indemnity to the same extent. However, an important feature of the facts of *Cementation Piling and Foundations Ltd* is that the case proceeded on the basis of a concession made by insurers that there had been *no* improvement to the structure as it was originally designed and intended as a result of the repairs that had been implemented.[154] The defects were of workmanship and, in fact, Sir Godfrey Le Quesne QC at first instance held that, had improvements to the design been introduced, the additional costs attributable to them would not have been recoverable.[155] The Court of Appeal expressly approved the analysis of the judge so that, even in a case where *Cementation Piling and Foundations Ltd* applies, if improvements to the design lead to additional costs, those costs are excluded.[156]

16-061

General approach to interpretation of the DE clauses. Some general observations can be made about the way the courts have set about interpreting the clauses. First, it has been held that the report of the Insurance Institute of London,[157] which describes the background market developments and sets out the worked example discussed above at para.16-039, is

16-062

"instructive about the purpose of defect exclusion clauses and how they have evolved ... [b]ut ... cannot be used as an aid to construction of the clause in question which must be construed according to its terms."[158]

Secondly, as a consequence of this approach, the courts have not sought to construe the particular DE clause in issue in the light of the others. For example, the fact that DE4 excludes damage to the defective "component part" does not, on this view, assist in interpreting the scope of the phrase "property ... in a defective condition"

(London: IIL, 2010), para.8.8.2.5, p.164. See also, *Insurance Law for the Construction Industry*, edited by R. Hogarth, A. Anderson and S. Goldring, 2nd edn (Oxford: Oxford University Press, 2008), para.6.118.

[152] *Cementation Piling and Foundations Ltd* [1993] 1 Lloyd's Rep. 526; (1995) 74 B.L.R. 98; (1994) 47 Con. L.R. 14.

[153] See above, para.16-046, where an indemnity is characterised as the restoration of property to its condition before the occurrence of the insured peril.

[154] *Cementation Piling and Foundations Ltd* [1993] 1 Lloyd's Rep. 526 at 530.

[155] *Cementation Piling and Foundations Ltd* [1993] 1 Lloyd's Rep. 526 at 531–532.

[156] *Cementation Piling and Foundations Ltd* [1995] 1 Lloyd's Rep. 97 at 103; 74 B.L.R. 98 at 110; (1994) 47 Con. L.R. 14 at 23.

[157] Insurance Institute of London, *Construction Insurance – Research Study Group Report 208B* (London: IIL, 2010).

[158] *CA Blackwell (Contractors) Ltd* [2007] EWCA Civ 1450 at [20]; [2008] 1 All E.R. (Comm) 885 at 891; [2008] Lloyd's Rep. I.R. 529 at 533.

in DE3.[159] Nor does the fact that the "outright" exclusion in DE1 preserves cover for loss or damage to defective property caused by a peril other than the defect itself assist in determining whether DE5 excludes cover in this situation. This approach is unfortunate because the clauses were conceived, and have always been understood, as providing a spectrum of levels of cover. Considered side-by-side, the overall intention that DE1 should be a wider exclusion than DE2, DE2 wider than DE3, and so on, is clearer than the intricacies of any of the individual clauses. Arguably, despite the courts' negative stance towards taking a comparative approach to the alternative standard clauses, understood throughout the market as standing in a particular relationship to one another, it is suggested they should be considered in this way as it is relevant to the question of construction.[160] In *Acciona Infrastructure Canada Inc. v Allianz Global Risks US Insurance Co*[161] the Court of Appeal for British Columbia adopted a unified approach to interpretation, construing the meaning of LEG 2 in the context of LEG 1 and LEG 3.

16-063   Thirdly, the fact that the DE clauses are structured as exclusions from the cover subject to various "carve-outs"[162] usually means that the requirements of the insuring clause have to be met. The starting point is that an all risks policy indemnifies only against fortuitous damage to the subject matter.[163] Since the DE clauses are framed as exclusions, logic suggests that they cannot confer cover more extensive than that envisaged by the insuring clause, and indeed that is generally how they must be read.[164] However, the courts have taken the view that if the defects exclusion clause specifically indicates that non-fortuitous loss is intended to be covered, the clause will not be read-down in the light of the insuring clause. As has been seen, in *Cementation Piling and Foundations Ltd* it was held that a DE5-type clause covered the cost of replacing defective but undamaged areas of the insured property provided that some damage had been caused by the defect,[165] even though this result required a flexible reading of the words "in respect of physical loss of or damage to" in the insuring clause. More recently, in *Seele Austria GmbH & Co KG*,[166] bespoke wording, which indemnified for "intentional damage" necessarily incurred to remedy a defect, was held to be a standalone indemnity not conditional on the operation of either the rest of the wording which immediately preceded it or the

---

[159] See above, para.16-036 for the full wording of DE3.

[160] In another context, Lord Hobhouse said in *Lloyd's TSB General Insurance Holdings Ltd v Lloyds Bank Group Insurance Co Ltd; Abbey National Plc v Lee* [2003] UKHL 48 at [31]; [2003] 4 All E.R. 43 at 52; [2003] Lloyd's Rep. I.R. 623 at 631 that: "there are often well established alternatives open to the parties in the drafting of their agreement. The choice made from among these alternatives represents part of the bargain struck by the parties and must be respected by anyone ... adjudicating upon a dispute arising under the document".

[161] *Acciona Infrastructure Canada Inc. v Allianz Global Risks US Insurance Co* [2015] BCCA 347 at [74].

[162] See below para.16-067 as to whether the better views is that DE type clauses are low and damage deeming provisions where damage results from a defect.

[163] *CA Blackwell (Contractors) Ltd* [2007] EWHC 94 at [43]; [2007] Lloyd's Rep. I.R. 511 at 519–520; *Seele Austria GmbH & Co KG* [2008] EWCA Civ 441 at [35], [51] and [62]; [2009] 1 All E.R. (Comm) 171 at 183, 187 and 191; [2008] B.L.R. 337 at 347, 350 and 352.

[164] Sir Ralph Gibson makes this point in *Cementation Piling and Foundations Ltd* [1995] 1 Lloyd's Rep. 97 at 102; 74 B.L.R. 98 at 109; (1994) 47 Con. L.R. 14 at 22. He said: "It is common ground that an exception clause cannot extend the cover from which the exception is made."

[165] See above, para.16-050.

[166] *Seele Austria GmbH & Co KG* [2008] EWCA Civ 441; [2009] 1 All E.R. (Comm) 171; [2008] B.L.R. 337.

insuring clause.[167] The consequence of these decisions is that it is not safe to assume that where the opening (and seemingly controlling) words of the clause exclude loss or damage in respect of a defect or the cost of remedying a defect the rest of the clause merely defines the scope of the exclusion. In some cases, particularly where the draftsman has deviated from the standard DE wording, it is possible the clause may fall to be treated as a hybrid exclusion.

Calculation of the costs of remedying a defect in design.   The calculation of the additional costs of improvements is also not without complication. Where defective property has suffered damage, an insurer's obligation is to indemnify the insured in respect of loss. This only extends, however, to the restoration of the property to its original, "as-constructed" state.[168] Any remedial work that goes beyond this may constitute improvement and thus be excluded. It follows from this reasoning that in a case where defective property is undamaged, and is therefore already in its as-constructed state, there is unlikely to be any indemnity in respect of repairing a design. This must be the case unless DE5 is to be treated as a formula for compensation, subtracting the original cost of the works from the total cost of the remedial works.[169]   **16-064**

5.   THE LEG DEFECTS CLAUSES

LEG Defects Clauses.   The LEG has adopted an alternative set of exclusions designed to suit engineering risks.[170] There are three clauses, set out below, which provide three different levels of cover. Since first being drafted in 1996, LEG 1 and LEG 2 remain unchanged. LEG 3 was amended in 2006 in an attempt to avoid confusion over the meaning of the word "damage".[171] Like the DE clauses, the LEG clauses broadly distinguish between the costs of simply putting right a defect (excluded), and consequential damage (covered, except under LEG 1), but there are some interesting differences in the two drafting techniques. First, in all three of the LEG clauses the exclusion is defined in causal terms ("costs rendered necessary by defects"). They therefore do not replicate the oddity whereby DE2 to DE5 exclude all damage to the property "in defective condition" even where the cause is a wholly unrelated peril.[172] Secondly, the technique of dividing the property into notional parts that characterises the DE clauses has not been adopted. Instead, LEG 2 and LEG 3 exclude costs of putting right the defect, defined respectively in broad and then narrow terms.   **16-065**

LEG 1/96 model "outright" defects exclusion.   LEG 1 states: **16-066**

> "The Insurer(s) shall not be liable for Loss or Damage due to defects of material workmanship design plan or specification."

---

[167]   See below, para.16-073.
[168]   See above, para.16-059.
[169]   The principles explained in para.16-050 to 16-061 may also apply.
[170]   Insurance Institute of London, Construction Insurance - Research Study Group Report 208B (London: IIL, 2010), p.165, para.8.8.2.6.
[171]   See above, para.16-017, for discussion of the background to the amendment to LEG 3.
[172]   See above, para.16-037.

This clause has the same effect as DE1; the points made in paras 16-031 to 16-033 above apply.

16-067   LEG 2/96 model "consequences" defects exclusion. LEG 2 states:

> "The Insurer(s) shall not be liable in respect of:
> All costs rendered necessary by defects of material workmanship design plan or specification and should damage occur to any portion of the Insured Property (Contract Works) containing any of the said defects the cost of replacement or rectification which is hereby excluded is that cost which would have been incurred if replacement or rectification of the said portion of the Insured Property (Contract Works) had been put in hand immediately prior to the said damage.
> For the purpose of this policy and not merely this exclusion it is understood and agreed that any portion of the Insured Property (Contract Works) shall not be regarded as damaged solely by virtue of the existence of any defect of material workmanship design plan or specification" .

When construing an analogous "resulting loss" exclusion Myers J in *PCL Constructors Canada Inc. v Allianz Global Risks US Insurance Co*[173] considered the "exclusion" for defective workmanship not to be an exclusion at all. Rather, it is a deeming clause that provides special treatment of loss or damage to works containing defects. LEG 2 expressly preserves coverage for damage containing defects. Accordingly, despite the use of the word "exclusion" in LEG 2, defects are not excluded from cover with the effect of the wording being to protect the insurer from the moral hazard of, for example, contractors under-spending on materials and labour and then seeking to pass on the risk of their own poor performance to the insurer. Accordingly, the clause is structured so as to deduct the cost of remedying a defect, except where damage has occurred subject to an overriding "exclusion" of the

> "cost which would have been incurred if replacement or rectification of the ... [defect] ... had been put in hand immediately prior to the said damage."

Features of the clause are also the use of the colloquial words "put in hand" in preference to words such as "commenced" or "started", which are likely to be more readily understood internationally and the word "said" which appears to add little.

16-068   The clause requires a calculation of the hypothetical cost of putting right the defect, by rectification or replacement, immediately before the accident and the subtraction of this figure from the cost of reinstating the damaged works[174]; in this respect it is like the 2002 version of the Inchmaree Clause.[175] Sometimes this will produce more generous cover than DE3/DE4. Taking the example of the steel-frame building cited above at para.16-039, suppose that the nuts and bolts were defective for not having been tightened sufficiently well and were readily accessible to be tightened. The cost excluded by LEG 2 would be the nominal cost of tightening the nuts and bolts; under DE3 the cost of replacing and re-erecting the entire framework would be excluded. But in other cases, LEG 2 will operate much more harshly against the insured. Frequently, remedying defective foundations will require the demolition and rebuilding of the entire property; if the building collapses before this can be done, DE3 would cover all damage other than to the defective foundations whereas LEG 2 would be a blanket exclusion. The major advantage of LEG 2 over DE3, however, is that it defines that which is excluded with far

---

[173] *PCL Constructors Canada Inc* [2014] ONSC 7480 at [25]–[28].
[174] *Acciona Infrastructure Canada Inc. v Allianz Global Risks US Insurance Co* [2015] BCCA 347.
[175] See above, para.16-027.

greater clarity and certainty. Whereas LEG 2 requires a calculation of what a given course of remedial work would cost; it is suggested that DE3 requires a more impressionistic and inherently contentious division of the property into notional defective and non-defective parts and an apportionment of the costs of repairing damage between the two. Nevertheless both LEG 2 and DE3 require difficult assessments to be made regarding the property which is defective and not defective. It has also been suggested that LEG 2 is favoured by engineering contractors as it is symmetrical with the typical CAR insuring clause and therefore easier to understand and explain.

LEG 3/06 model "improvements" defects exclusion. LEG 3/06 states: **16-069**

"The Insurer(s) shall not be liable in respect of:
  All costs rendered necessary by defects of material workmanship design plan or specification and should damage (which for the purposes of this exclusion shall include any patent detrimental change in the physical condition of the Insured Property) occur to any portion of the Insured Property (Contract Works) containing any of the said defects the cost of replacement or rectification which is hereby excluded is that cost incurred to improve the original material workmanship design plan or specification
  For the purpose of the policy and not merely this exclusion it is understood and agreed that any portion of the Insured Property shall not be regarded as damaged solely by virtue of the existence of any defect of material workmanship design plan or specification."[176]

This clause is a close equivalent of DE5.[177] The only material difference is that, **16-070** here, the exclusion only applies where the defect has caused the damage, whereas the carve-out ("should damage occur") applies whether or not there is that causal link (the reverse is true of DE5).[178] The same points in relation to the "improvement" part of the exclusion apply here.

Two relatively short points of interpretation may be made in relation to the LEG 3 wording. First, the addition of the words "which for the purposes of this exclusion shall include any patent detrimental change in the physical condition of the Insured Property" in LEG 3 appear to be unnecessary and have the potential to cause confusion as to whether a latent physical change in condition is indemnified. Secondly, the word "and" between "specification" and "should" in LEG 2 and LEG 3 appears to make little sense. If the purpose of LEG 3 is to exclude all costs rendered necessary by defects "but" to write back into cover damage to property containing defects, then the use of conjunctive wording is inappropriate. It is understood that the use of the word "and" by LEG was intentional as it was thought to emphasise the fact that defects remain excluded from cover even though they will be indemnified if damage occurs. If this was the purpose, then it is doubted whether the drafters of LEG 3 achieved it, as the use of the word "and" implies both parts of the clause apply, when the intention is that once there has been damage, the policy also indemnifies for the rectification of defects. More persuasive is the reasoning in of Myers J in *PCL Constructors Canada Inc. v Allianz Global Risks US Insurance Company*[179] who considered a similar "exclusion" for defective workmanship not to be an exclusion at all. Rather, it is a deeming clause that

---

[176] LEG 3/96 is identical, save that it omits the wording in parentheses beginning "which for the purposes of".
[177] LEG 3/96 was drafted by the London Engineering Group from UK CAR DE5 wording.
[178] See above, para.16-044.
[179] *PCL Constructors Canada Inc. Allianz Global Risks US Insurance Co* [2014] ONSC 7480 at [25]–[28].

provides special treatment of loss or damage to contract works containing defects. The clause was also considered in *Acconia Infrastructure Canada Inc v Allianz Global Risks US Insurance*[180] where the Court of Appeal considered the operation of LEG 2 in the context of LEG 1 and LEG 3.

6.   ACCESS DAMAGE

16-071   **Intentional access damage is not within the carve-outs to DE exclusions.**   The 1995 versions of DE2 to DE5 emphasise that the write-back for consequential damage does not apply to insured property "lost or damaged to enable the replacement repair or rectification of Property insured excluded by ... [the clause]".[181] Suppose that a fault is discovered in the electrical wiring of a building and that as part of the remedial work portions of plastering and internal finishes have to be opened up and damaged. The insured cannot contend that such damage, deliberately inflicted in order to break into or gain access to the defect, is recoverable as consequential damage for the purpose of the exclusion clause. Quite apart from the wording quoted, this is clear from the fact that an all risks policy responds only to accidental loss or damage to the insured property unless there is specific wording to indicate that intentional damage is covered.[182] In other words, damage incurred in "breaking in" to a defective but undamaged part is properly regarded as part of the costs of remedying the defect and not fortuitous damage within the insuring clause. However where property that has been intentionally "damaged" to enable access to be gained for the purpose of rectifying property, which has been accidentally damaged, it will be indemnified (see below, para.16-075).

16-072   **Express indemnities for intentional access damage.**   In some cases insurers may be prepared to provide an indemnity for the costs of breaking in to repair a defect ("access damage"). The purpose of such an indemnity might be to provide, in effect, a limited form of "preventative measures" cover (see below, paras 17-013 to 17-015): some of the expenses of putting right a defect (other than replacement of the defective part itself) are paid for in order to eliminate a danger of the defect causing damage or destruction of the insured property. Where this is the intention, one would expect to see wording linking the operation of the indemnity to "actual

---

[180] [2015] BCCA 347.

[181] DE2 (iii); DE3 (ii); DE4 (ii). DE5 (ii) has the same effect, excluding: "loss or damage to the Property insured caused to enable replacement, repair or rectification of such defective Property insured".

[182] *Seele Austria GmbH & Co KG* [2008] EWCA Civ 441 at [35], [62]; [2009] 1 All E.R. (Comm) 171 at 183 and 191; [2008] B.L.R. 337 at 347 and 352. This point was missed in the decision of the Supreme Court of New South Wales in *Walker Civil Engineering Pty Ltd* (1999) 10 ANZ Insurance Cases 61–418. There, the construction of a sewerage pumping station was insured under a construction all risks policy with an exclusion for loss or damage "directly caused" by a defect, other than damage to the non-defective parts. Fibreglass tanks comprising the station were found to be leaking. Reconstruction work involved breaking up the concrete around the tanks and replacing the fibreglass walls. The judge held that the "loss or damage directly caused by the defective workmanship is the loss of the fibreglass tanks and the concrete, together with ... the necessity to replace the tanks", ((1999) 10 ANZ Insurance Cases 61–418 at [74692]), a finding that was not directly challenged on appeal, which was focused on the meaning of the word "part": see above, fn.113. Yet this treats the indemnity for "all risks of physical loss of or damage to" property as embracing deliberate access damage and the purely economic loss represented by the cost of replacing the defective tanks. Unless the law of New South Wales is radically different to English law in this respect, it is suggested that the case was decided on the wrong footing.

or imminent loss or damage" to the rest of the property. A different, but equally sensible rationale for including an indemnity for access damage would be to provide, in combination with DE3, a compromise level of cover somewhere between DE3/DE4 and DE5. The idea would be that the insured can recover *some* of the costs of repairing or reinstating damage to a defective component, limited to damage done to the property to gain access for the repair work (costs which would be covered by DE5 but excluded by DE1–DE4), but not the costs of replacing the defective part itself (which, again, would be covered by DE5, assuming that component has itself sustained damage,[183] but excluded by DE1–DE4). If that is the rationale, one would expect the indemnity to be conditional on the defect causing damage to the rest of the insured property.

On the other hand, it is highly unlikely that an insurer would be prepared to **16-073** indemnify against damage deliberately incurred as part of work to remedy a defect where there has been no accidental damage, nor is there any risk of the defect causing damage. Unfortunately, likely as a result of inept drafting, the access damage clause considered in *Seele Austria GmbH & Co KG*[184] accorded cover in precisely that situation. Memorandum 18 of the construction all risks policy was entitled "Design Workmanship and Materials". Paragraph (3) indemnified against damage "necessarily caused to the Insured Property ... to enable replacement repair or rectification of Insured Property ... which is in defective condition". It was preceded, in para.(2), by standard DE3 wording, but there was nothing that expressly stated the para.(3) indemnity to be subject to para.(2). Nor was the indemnity stated to be conditional on "actual or imminent damage" to the works. The facts were that the insured subcontractor was responsible for installing prefabricated "punched" windows, which were found to leak during post-installation testing. The leaking windows had caused no accidental damage to the rest of the works, and accordingly para.(2) (i.e. DE3) did not respond. But the insured argued that under para.(3) the insurer was liable to pay for damage to the surrounding stonework and internal finishes, which had to be dismantled in order to replace the window. At first instance, the judge rejected this claim, holding that the indemnity in para.(3) had to be read as part of the DE3 clause: fortuitous damage to another part of the property was a precondition to recovery.[185] The judge pointed to inconsistencies that would be thrown up by the insured's construction. For example, the exclusion in the defects exclusion for damage "to enable" a defect to be remedied (i.e. DE3 (ii)) was to directly the opposite effect. Moreover, the insured had to show that there had been some accidental damage; this followed

"from the fact that the policy is a ... Contractors' All Risk policy which, as such, has as its fundamental purpose the provision of cover against fortuitous damage to the contract works."[186]

By a majority, the Court of Appeal allowed an appeal by the insured on this issue, ruling that para.(3) operated as a standalone indemnity not governed by the defects exclusion clause. Moore-Bick LJ, with whom Richards LJ agreed, accepted one

---

[183] See above, paras 16-045 to 16-058 for a full discussion of this requirement.
[184] *Seele Austria GmbH & Co KG* [2008] EWCA Civ 441; [2009] 1 All E.R. (Comm) 171; [2008] B.L.R. 337.
[185] *Seele Austria GmbH & Co KG* [2007] EWHC 1411 (Comm) at [18]; [2007] 1 C.L.C. 972 at 980; [2007] B.L.R. 337 at 342.
[186] *Seele Austria GmbH & Co KG* [2007] EWHC 1411 (Comm) at [22]; [2007] 1 C.L.C. 972 at 980–981.

must start from the proposition that, this being an all risks policy, "the insurers agreed to indemnify the insured against fortuitous damage to the works",[187] but in his view "that does not prevent the insurer from providing additional cover of a different kind as an adjunct to the policy."[188] The inconsistencies detected by the judge could not be decisive inasmuch as the clause bore

"the hallmarks of a provision which has been fashioned from various different clauses rather than having been drafted as a single integral whole."[189]

That being so, Moore-Bick LJ said:

"The fact that one paragraph gives back what an earlier one has taken away ... [was not] a good reason for rejecting the plain meaning of the words used."[190]

16-074 The decision of the Court of Appeal in *Seele Austria GmbH & Co KG* caused some consternation amongst underwriters in the construction insurance market. However, the case was very much decided on the particular, confused wording of the policy in question.[191] If the intention had been to make the indemnity for damage "necessarily caused ... to enable replacement" of a defective part conditional on the occurrence of damage within DE3, this could readily have been achieved by structuring the clause so that it clearly had that effect. Nonetheless, one suspects that something had gone wrong in the drafting, not least because the syntax made no sense on any reading[192]; it could well be that the access damage indemnity was supposed to be a sub-clause of the DE3 paragraph but was automatically given its own number by the auto-numbering function of a word processor. The case is a salutary lesson in the need for care when inserting bespoke language around elements of standard policy wording, such as the DE clauses.

16-075 **Intentional damage to defective property to repair accidental damage.** There are circumstances where it may be necessary to cause damage to defective property in order to gain access to remedy accidental damage that has been caused to non-defective property. So, for example, it may be necessary for a contractor to remove defective surface layers of a road in order to gain access to the road subbase, which has been damaged by water penetration. Repairing the damaged subbase and

---

[187] *Seele Austria GmbH & Co KG* [2008] EWCA Civ 441 at [35]; [2009] 1 All E.R. (Comm) 171 at 183.
[188] *Seele Austria GmbH & Co KG* [2008] EWCA Civ 441 at [45]; [2009] 1 All E.R. (Comm) 171 at 186.
[189] *Seele Austria GmbH & Co KG* [2008] EWCA Civ 441 at [45]; [2009] 1 All E.R. (Comm) 171 at 186.
[190] *Seele Austria GmbH & Co KG* [2008] EWCA Civ 441 at [45]; [2009] 1 All E.R. (Comm) 171 at 186.
[191] Moore-Bick LJ found the clause "a difficult provision to construe" and "intricate"; Richards LJ, though agreeing with Moore-Bick LJ's judgment, thought such a description "generous": *Seele Austria GmbH & Co KG* [2008] EWCA Civ 441 at [39] and [46] (per Moore-Bick LJ), [64] (per Richards L.J.); [2009] 1 All E.R. (Comm) 171 at 184 and 186 (per Moore-Bick LJ), 191 (per Richards LJ); [2008] B.L.R. 337 at 347, 349 (per Moore-Bick LJ) and 352 (per Richards LJ).
[192] Memorandum 18 opened with "this Section includes loss or damage arising out of a defect in design plan specification workmanship or materials other than in respect of: (1) ... (2) [etc.]", which logically requires that the following numbered paragraphs will be exclusions, yet para.(3) was patently not exclusionary in effect: "The Insurers will additionally indemnify the Insured" *Seele Austria GmbH & Co KG* [2007] EWHC 1411 (Comm) at [14]; [2007] 1 C.L.C. 972 at 977–978; [2007] B.L.R. 337 at 341.

reinstating the road may also remedy the defective but undamaged surface layers of the road. Accordingly, reinstatement of the accidental damage enables the contractor to also rectify the upper defective layers, which would otherwise not be insured. The relevant part of DE3 is:

(i) Property insured which is in defective condition due to a defect in design plan specification materials or workmanship of such property insured or any part thereof;

(ii) Property insured lost or damaged to enable the replacement repair or rectification of Property insured excluded by (i) above.

It is possible to construe (ii) of DE3 as excluding from the indemnity the costs of gaining access to the subbase for the purpose of rectifying the accidental damage. However, it is suggested that the better view is that (ii) of DE3 does not exclude such costs from the indemnity. This is because the property that has been intentionally "damaged" to enable access to be gained is not for the purpose of rectifying property, which is in a defective condition due to a defect in design, but instead it is for the purpose of rectifying property that has been accidentally damaged.

Unintentional access damage. In *Seele Austria GmbH & Co KG*,[193] Moore-Bick LJ left open the question whether, under the DE3 clause, "unintentional access damage" (i.e. some slip-up that inflicts damage to the surrounding property in excess of that which would be "necessary" to break in to the defective part) is "recoverable as damage caused 'in consequence of' the original defect".[194] This, it is suggested, would be asking the wrong question, at least so far as DE3 is concerned. Inasmuch as the relevant damage affects the "property ... in defective condition", it will be excluded in all cases: see above, para.16-037. Where unintended access damage occurs to other, non-defective, property, the exclusion does not bite in the first place, whether or not the damage can be characterised as consequential on the original defect. However, the point *could* arise in relation to DE1, because this exclusion bites only if there is a causal connection between the defect and the damage. Suppose that a decorator paints a set of window frames the wrong colour, and in the course of scraping off the paintwork smashes through a window pane with his scraping tool. For the reason given above in para.16-022, whilst paintwork would be defective for being the wrong colour, the direct impact of the scraping tool on the glass is probably not a "defect" within the meaning of DE1. Nonetheless, the slip might (arguably) be seen as so closely connected with the originally defective paintwork that the exclusion for damage "due to" a defect applies. However, suppose on a different set of facts a workman manages to set a building on fire whilst using a blowtorch to correct a misalignment in a piece of metal work. It is doubtful whether the misalignment could be seen as a proximate cause of the fire inasmuch as use of a blowtorch carries the same risk of causing a fire whether it is the base works or defect-remedial work that the workman happens to be carrying out.

16-076

---

[193] *Seele Austria GmbH & Co KG* [2008] EWCA Civ 441; [2009] 1 All E.R. (Comm) 171; [2008] B.L.R. 337.
[194] *Seele Austria GmbH & Co KG* [2008] EWCA Civ 441 at [40]; [2009] 1 All E.R. (Comm) 171 at 184; [2008] B.L.R. 337 at 348.

7. DROP-DOWN ARRANGEMENTS

16-077 **Drop-down clauses.** It is common to find alternative DE3 and DE5, or LEG 2 and LEG 3 defects exclusion wording in one policy with a higher deductible for DE5 and LEG 3 exclusions in each case. These arrangements are known as drop-down clauses. The purpose of including different exclusions in one policy is to permit the insured, if it does not want to take advantage of the more limited exclusion in DE5 and LEG 3, to claim under DE3 or LEG 2 and attract a lower deductible.

EXTENSIONS TO COVER

1. INTRODUCTION

Introduction. The primary insuring clause of a CAR policy indemnifies the **17-001** insured against loss or damage to the contract works, as defined within the policy. It does not, however, cover damage to property that does not fall within the definition of the contract works, nor will it cover consequential losses caused by damage to the contract works. CAR policies therefore typically provide various extensions to cover to give the insured protection against a variety of additional costs that, but for the loss or damage to the insured property, would not have been incurred.

Extensions of cover fall into two categories. The first category contains exten- **17-002** sions to cover requiring the occurrence of damage; these can be described as "true" extensions to cover,[1] i.e. clauses that extend the scope of the cover provided by the material damage section of the policy to include various additional types of loss associated with physical damage. The second category of extensions is either for those that have no such precondition or where the loss is only consequential to such physical damage. The second category includes delay in start-up ("DSU") insurance.[2] DSU is not an extension per se, but a separate class of insurance that provides cover against the financial consequences of physical damage. It therefore concerns not the immediate impact of the physical damage on the insured (i.e. the need to repair it), but the consequential effect that the damage has upon the project as a whole. Because it is a separate class of insurance, it will be contained within its own section of the policy, with its own definitions, policy limits, and period of insurance (the latter being a crucial feature of the insurance). However, cover for this will normally be arranged by the employer in conjunction with the material damage section of the policy.

The scope of cover provided by a particular extension will depend upon its word- **17-003** ing when read in the context of the CAR policy as a whole. The aim of this chapter is therefore to explain the scope of cover provided by the various common extensions that fall within these two categories and to address issues that can commonly arise in respect of them, with the aim being to explain the meaning of the clauses and the ways in which they have been interpreted by practitioners and the courts.

---

[1] *MJ Gleeson Group Plc v AXA Corporate Solutions Assurance S.A.* [2013] Lloyd's Rep. I.R. 677.
[2] This is also known as "delay in completion insurance" or "advanced loss of profits insurance" ("ALOP"). See further below, paras 16-048 to 16-061.

2. EXTENSIONS IN RESPECT OF PHYSICAL DAMAGE

17-004   The majority of extensions to cover in CAR policies relate to costs associated with the effects of physical damage. The various extensions available have evolved over time to match the changing requirements of builders and the construction trade. Extensions to cover may require the occurrence of damage within the meaning of the insuring clause as a precondition to cover or they may provide additional cover even where physical damage has not occurred. The latter category of extension is directly analogous with subordinate insuring clauses, so for example in *Seele Austria GmbH Co KG v Tokio Marine Europe Insurance Ltd*,[3] the Court of Appeal construed an access costs extension and concluded that damage was not a necessary precondition to cover. However, the opposite conclusion was reached in *MJ Gleeson Group Plc v AXA Corporate Solutions Assurance S.A.*[4] as the extension to cover included the phrase "this Section of the Policy *extends to indemnify* the Insured" (emphasis added) rather than establishing a standalone indemnity, and so carried a requirement for the occurrence of physical damage within the meaning of the insuring clause before the extension would respond. The wording of that particular extension was contrasted with the other policy extensions which stated, more straightforwardly, that "The Company will indemnify the Insured", indicating that coverage was not predicated on the occurrence of physical damage under the primary insuring clause. In *MJ Gleeson Group Plc* the court emphasised that the language used in the policy extension would have a significant effect on the circumstances in which that extension would respond, and that the construction of the extension may be informed by the wording chosen in other parts of the policy. The main extensions of cover used in CAR policies will now be discussed in turn.

17-005   Existing structures and property.   Where the construction works involve an extension to an existing structure, it will often be advantageous for the parties to extend the policy to include coverage for any damage caused to the existing structures during the construction operations. Under the primary insuring clause of a typical CAR policy, the insured subject matter will only include the works being installed or constructed and the materials used for that construction. This will leave outside the scope of the cover provided the buildings or structures already in existence before the commencement of the works. As the employer will often be the owner of those existing structures (or will be responsible for loss or damage to them), he will be astute to mitigate that risk by passing it onto his insurers. Under the Joint Contracts Tribunal ("JCT") Contract 2011,[5] for example, Insurance Option C requires the employer to take out a joint names policy covering damage to the existing structures. If requested, insurers may decide to offer either a separate joint names policy to cover the existing structures, or, more commonly, an option to extend cover to existing structures under the CAR policy itself. If included as an extension to the CAR policy, the indemnity will be an independent provision and not subordinate to the primary insuring clause. Thus, for instance, where the new

---

[3]   *Seele Austria GmbH Co KG v Tokio Marine Europe Insurance Ltd* [2008] EWCA Civ 441; [2009] 1 All E.R. (Comm) 171; [2008] Lloyd's Rep. I.R. 739.

[4]   *MJ Gleeson Group Plc* [2013] Lloyd's Rep. I.R. 677 at [47].

[5]   Joint Contracts Tribunal, *SBC/Q 2011 JCT Standard Form of Building Contract With Quantities 2011* (London: Sweet & Maxwell, 2011), p.93. The Insurance Options can be found in Sch.3 to the JCT Standard Building Contract.

construction works remove support for the existing structure and cause subsidence or collapse, the employer will not need to prove damage to the new construction works in order for the extension to respond.

Extra or continuing interest charges and loss of use of capital. Where the **17-006** development project is to be sold on completion, delay in finishing the construction will cause a delay in receipt of the proceeds of sale. An employer can seek an extension under a CAR policy to indemnify himself against financial losses that would be suffered as a result of that delay in sale. Cover in this instance will be an agreed rate of interest on the net proceeds of sale for the period of delay, subject to a maximum indemnity period. Cover can also be provided for any additional debt servicing costs caused by the interruption, i.e. any additional interest payable to financiers of the project.

Insurance against the increased cost of constructing incomplete or unbuilt works. Delay attributable to the occurrence of an insured peril can adversely af- **17-007** fect the sequence of works and the progression of the overall project, and can lead to an increase in the cost of completing the works. External factors such as inflation in the price of materials and labour may cause the employer to incur increased costs in completing the works, which were unfinished at the date of the damage. There could also be wasted subcontractor costs, such as where a subcontractor incurs additional costs (i.e. additional labour costs) as a result of having to defer commencing its portion of the works. In these cases, the extension for the increased cost of constructing incomplete or unbuilt works provides cover for the increased costs incurred by the employer in completing the project. The extension is likely to carry its own policy sub-limit and deductible. Typically the trigger for cover under this extension will be:

"delay in completion of the Insured Operations or any part thereof due solely to loss destruction or damage to the permanent works or Temporary Works for which liability has been admitted under this Section (or would have been admitted but for the application of the Excesses)".

In such a situation, the extension will provide insurance:

"against the additional amount by which the cost of the permanent works or Temporary Works uncommenced at the date of the loss destruction or damage shall exceed the cost which would have been incurred but for the loss destruction or damage".

The extension is not intended to put the insured in a better position than he would **17-008** have been in but for the delay, and the policy will therefore make clear that it does not include:

"any amount

(a) Which would have been incurred irrespective of whether the loss or damage had occurred
(b) Solely to expedite the completion of the Insured Operations or any part thereof at an earlier date than would have been attained had the said loss or damage not occurred
(c) Incurred in redesigning altering adding to or improving the permanent and Temporary Works or rectification of defects or faults or elimination of any deficiencies carried out after the occurrence of the loss destruction or damage or any increase in costs as a result of such redesigning alteration addition or improvement. However this proviso does not apply where such redesigning is rendered necessary by the nature or extent of the loss destruction or damage
(d) Resulting from any delay due to the inability of the Insured to provide sufficient funds for the repair or replacement of the permanent or Temporary Works suffering loss or damage.

(e) In respect of any
  (i) Additional insurance premiums
  (ii) Head Office management expenses and/or overheads of any kind whatsoever
  (iii) Idle time costs incurred in respect of constructional plant and labour
  (iv) Additional financial charges or legal expenses
(f) Arising from or in respect of any other consequential losses not specifically provided for in the Policy
(g) Incurred which is indemnifiable elsewhere in the Policy."

Item (c) in the above list corresponds to DE5 wording.[6] The clause requires that certain conditions must be complied with in order to engage the indemnity. First, the insured will need to show that the increased costs were attributable to the delay, which was in turn caused solely by loss, damage or destruction to insured property. Secondly, the costs must only relate to the amount that was incurred in respect of the parts not commenced or incomplete at the date of occurrence of the insured peril.

17-009 Expediting expenses.   It will obviously be in the insured's interests to ensure that damage to insured property does not cause delay to the project as a whole. This will also be in the insurer's interest, since the financial consequences of delay are likely to fall within the scope of the insurance. An extension for expediting expenses exists to provide cover to the insured against the increased cost of expediting repairs, for example by way of overtime, express freight, etc.

A typical clause will talk of "extra charges", i.e. charges that would not usually be incurred:

> "for overtime nightwork on public holidays, express freight including liability for customs taxes excise on other duties, hire of plant or equipment, hire of labour or services, administrative and overhead expenses and the like necessarily incurred by the Insured in the reinstatement, replacement or repair of the Insured Property lost, destroyed or damage by any cause insured under this Section".

17-010   A CAR policy may also provide cover for just one of the items mentioned in the clause, e.g. extra charges for airfreight. In relation to the broadly worded clause, there is a proviso, however, to prevent the extension placing the insured in a better position, stipulating:

> "that completion of the Development is not thereby accomplished at an earlier date than if no loss destruction or damage had occurred".

Usually the extension will also have a cap in the following terms:

> "Provided that liability under this Memorandum in respect of any one occurrence or series of occurrences arising out of one event shall not exceed 20 per cent of normal repair costs."

The above clause states that the cap is a percentage of the costs of repair, but it could equally state that the cap is based on a percentage of the sum insured.

The distinction between this extension and the increased or additional cost of working is that the indemnity for expediting expenses relates only to increased costs involved in replacing, repairing or reinstating insured property. The increased cost of constructing incomplete or unbuilt works, on the other hand, covers any additional costs incurred for the purpose of avoiding delay caused by damage to

---

[6]   See above, paras 16-048 to 16-061.

insured property. Some "expediting clauses" may stipulate that the "extra cost" incurred should have been "reasonably" or "necessarily incurred".

Additional (or increased) cost of working. An extension is available to the material damage works section of the policy to indemnify the contractor in respect of additional (or increased) costs incurred in order to avoid delay to completion of the unbuilt work (in addition to the reinstatement costs incurred as a result of loss or damage to the property or works). There are a number of ways by which a contractor may try to avoid delays in order to implement the agreed programme of works: for example employing additional labour; using airfreight; paying workers to work overtime; or hiring more or specialised equipment. The extension will also specify either the sum insured, or impose a limit based on a percentage of the original contract value or the actual material damage claim that is submitted. The sum insured may also be determined by the amount of Liquidated and Ascertained Damages ("LADs") that would have been incurred if the delay had not been stopped from happening. The extension is also normally used by the employer in the context of a DSU policy where broader factors are taken into consideration: see below paras 17-066 to 17-067. **17-011**

Issues can arise where the cost of completing the works increases because a different method of working has been adopted by the contractor, which reduces its legal liability indemnified under the public liability section of the policy. In this situation such costs are usually treated as mitigation of the legal liability and will be indemnified under the public liability section of the policy and not under the works section.

Liquidated and ascertained damages. A typical CAR policy will not provide the contractor with an indemnity against its liability to pay the employer LADs. Some insurers do, however, offer such cover as an extension to the policy (though likely for a substantial premium). **17-012**

Conversely, if the employer is unable to impose LADs because it has granted the contractor an extension of time under the building contract, then any loss caused by the delay may be indemnifiable if caused by an insured peril.

Preventative measures. "Prevention is better than the cure" is a maxim that holds true for both the insured and insurers; preventative measures clauses, or "sue and labour clauses" as they are known in marine policies, therefore exist as an extension to cover the costs of mitigating the effects of threatened damage (e.g. a forecast hurricane). **17-013**

The insurance will cover:

"reasonable and necessary additional costs and/or expenses incurred by the Insured to prevent, reduce, minimise or protect any imminent threat of physical loss, destruction or damage to the Insured Property that would if it occurred be the subject of indemnity under this Section".

First, as would be expected, the costs must be reasonably and necessarily incurred: the insurance will not cover the cost of excessive preventative measures, nor measures that do not need to be carried out. Secondly, the threat of physical loss must be imminent. The policy will not therefore cover the costs of providing general protection: it must be specific protection put in place for a particular threat. **17-014**

In *Gerling General Insurance Co v Canary Wharf Group Plc*[7] Christopher Clarke J held that:

"the question of whether damage is imminent is, at any rate in the first instance, to be considered prospectively, and objectively, that is to say by considering whether on the facts available at the relevant time a reasonable man would regard the damage in question as sufficiently likely to happen sufficiently soon that it should be described as imminent. Whether that will be so is a question of fact and degree. The question has, also, to be considered in the light of the structure and provisions of the Policy to which I have referred."[8]

17-015   The insured has to establish that at the time that the decision to incur additional costs was made, there was a "serious risk, amounting to a real likelihood"[9] that physical loss to insured property would occur if the preventative measures had not been implemented.

There are usually provisos to the preventative measures clause, for example that the cost of the measures taken does not exceed the loss being prevented, and that the insured provides the insurer with prompt notification of the costs being incurred. There will also be a sub-limit of indemnity within the extension.

17-016   **Professional fees or salaries.**   As a matter of general practice, the employer is likely to have a separate contract with architects and engineers for the build and accordingly these costs will not be included as part of the overall contract price agreed between the main contractor and employer. However, the cost of engaging professionals by the main contractor and/or subcontractors, such as architects, engineers and surveyors will be included in the contract price, and thus the sum insured on the contract works. If a loss is incurred due to damage or destruction to insured property by an insured peril, the same types of people will be employed to assist with the reinstatement (as opposed to the construction) of the works. The cost of engaging such professionals for this purpose is not normally taken into account in fixing the sum insured. For this reason cover against this cost is provided by way of an extension. The cost is usually capped by reference to the scale of fees approved by the appropriate professional body of which the professional in question is a member. This can be seen in the following typical wording:

"The Insurers will in addition to the Sum Insured pay professional fees necessarily incurred in the repair reinstatement or replacement of the Insured Property consequent upon its loss, destruction or damage but not for preparing any claim. The amount payable for such fees shall not exceed those of the appropriate professional body."

---

[7]   *Gerling General Insurance Co v Canary Wharf Group Plc* [2005] EWHC 2234 (Comm); [2006] 1 Lloyd's Rep. 68. This case concerned a CAR policy providing cover for the construction of buildings at Canary Wharf. A tower crane collapsed which was "self-climbing", i.e. being used to raise itself, causing a serious accident and damaging buildings on the site. As a preventative measure, the insured changed the crane erection procedure such that the two other cranes would each be raising each other as opposed to self-climbing. This consequently caused delay and disruption in the development works because the cranes became unavailable for use in the construction and the insured sought to rely on the policy extension to cover the loss. It was held on the facts that the damage causing the loss had not been "imminent" at the material time of the policy and was not recoverable. In light of the overall circumstances, the actions taken by the employer lacked sufficient immediacy to be classified as imminent.

[8]   *Gerling General Insurance Co* [2005] EWHC 2234 (Comm) at [55]; [2006] 1 Lloyd's Rep. 68 at 80.

[9]   *Gerling General Insurance Co* [2005] EWHC 2234 (Comm) at [58]; [2006] 1 Lloyd's Rep. 68 at 81.

The extension therefore covers the insured for the cost of professional fees **17-017** incurred in the "repair reinstatement or replacement of the Insured Property". In many cases, the cost of instructing professionals for this purpose would be included in the overall indemnity for the contract works.

The extension does not provide the insured cover for preparing or challenging **17-018** claims under the policy. However, this may be included if agreed in specific circumstances, e.g. accountant's fees as a result of a delay in completing works in DSU. If an insurer requires an independent professional to inspect something, then this will normally be covered by the extension.

If certain works are excluded from cover, such as defective design or incorrect workmanship, then the fees incurred in respect of such matters will not generally be indemnified. Care should therefore be taken by the insured to ensure that professional fees that relate to the rectification of indemnified damage (and to no other purpose) are properly recorded.

Finally, legal costs are not included, nor are fees paid to a loss assessor appointed by the insured.

Debris removal. The occurrence of damage to the insured property will **17-019** frequently result in the creation of debris, which requires removal. If and insofar as the removal of such debris is a necessary part of the repair works (in that, without removing the debris, the repairs could not take place), then the cost of removing it will fall within the scope of the primary insuring clause. However, if debris does not need to be removed or the amount of debris that needs to be removed is more than is required in order to complete the repair works, then its cost will not fall within the scope of the primary insuring clause, and will only be indemnifiable under an extension to cover (known as a "debris removal clause").

The primary cover provided by the extension will typically be the cost and **17-020** expense necessarily and reasonably incurred by the insured in the removal and disposal of debris, which is the result of damage for which the insured is indemnified under the policy. The extension will also extend, however, to the costs involved in dismantling, demolishing or storing any part of the insured property if such work is necessary in order to carry out repair works. As a corollary of this, the extension will separately cover the costs of "shoring up, propping and or protecting insured property whether damaged or not".

The extension will cover separately the cost of repairing or clearing drains, sew- **17-021** ers, service mains, etc., and also of dewatering and dehumidifying the insured property. A typical policy will also include a "catch-all" clause, such as an extension for the cost of "regaining access to original working conditions".

The indemnity will be engaged only if indemnifiable damage occurs giving rise to the need for debris removal. In case of debris arriving on to the construction site before the construction work has begun (for example as a result of fly-tipping), removal of such waste will obviously fall outside the scope of the extension. Finally, the insured will only be indemnified in respect of costs that were "reasonable" and "necessary"; an insured will therefore usually only incur such expenditure after having obtained approval from insurers.

Seventy-two hours clause. A seventy-two hours clause is an aggregating provi- **17-022** sion that is commonly included in CAR policies. It may be deemed to be a condition applying to the material damage section of the policy. It provides that any loss or damage to the insured property in a given seventy-two hour period caused by storm, tempest, flood, earthquake, etc., shall be treated as a single occurrence for the purpose of the indemnity limit or excesses.

Usually the clause will make it at the option of the insured to decide when a given period of seventy-two hours begins. A clause will normally state the following:

"It is agreed that any loss of or damage to the Insured Property arising during any one period of seventy-two consecutive hours, caused by storm typhoon tempest flood or earthquake shall be deemed as single event and therefore to constitute one occurrence with regard to the excesses provided for herein. For the purpose of the foregoing the commencement of any such seventy-two hour period shall be decided at the discretion of the Insured it being understood and agreed, however, that there shall be no overlapping in any two or more such seventy-two hour periods in the event of damage occurring over a more extended period of time."

The purpose of this clause is to treat all damage caused by a natural disaster during a given seventy-two period as a single occurrence, thereby preventing the insured from having to pay a series of excesses. The corollary is that the insurer's limit of indemnity applies in respect of each (deemed) single occurrence.

17-023 Escalation clause/automatic increase. An escalation clause (also known as an automatic increase) provides for an increase in the sum insured if the actual contract price or, as the case may be, the reinstatement value of the works go above the estimated values. The increase in the sum insured will be in proportion to the increase in the contract price or reinstatement value.

The insurer may impose a cap on the increase, and an additional premium will be charged if the clause is engaged. A clause may state as follows:

"If during the Period of Insurance the actual contract price shall be in excess of the estimated project or contract price then the sum insured under section 1 shall be increased by the amount of such excess but only up to an additional 25 per cent of the Estimated Project or Contract Price."

The rationale behind such a clause is obvious. Frequently during the course of a construction project the contract price will increase, with the result that the employer will need to increase the sum insured. The clause will, however, limit the extent to which the sum insured can increase, otherwise there would be no limit to the potential exposure that insurers could face.

17-024 Offsite risks. Because the primary insuring clause covers damage only to the Insured Property, it will not cover damage to materials bought by the insured for the construction works that are stored offsite. An extension is therefore available to cover the risk of such damage. In addition to construction materials, the property insured under the extension could also include equipment, supplies, plant, and construction vehicles.

Naturally the cover will only extend to materials and other property in respect of which risk has passed to the insured.

17-025 Rewriting or re-drawing plans and documents. Plans and documents are unlikely to fall within the definition of insured property under the material damage section of the CAR policy. An extension can therefore be provided to indemnify the insured against the costs of reproducing them if damaged.

It is often a condition of an indemnity under the extension that copies of the documents in question are created and stored away from site, since otherwise the cost involved in reproducing them could be significant. A clause may be worded as follows:

"Notwithstanding anything herein contained to the contrary the insurance hereby is extended to indemnify the Insured against costs and expenses necessarily and reasonably incurred to reproduce such plans, documents and records relevant to the Project including all the information therein destroyed or damaged as a result of the insured event hereunder."

The costs and expenses incurred for reproducing plans, documents and records relevant to the project will only be recoverable if they were "necessarily and reasonably" incurred by the insured. The insured will usually only incur such expenditure after having obtained approval from insurers.

50/50 clause/undiscovered damage.   Materials which are damaged in transit will   **17-026**
in general be indemnified not under the CAR policy, but under any applicable marine insurance policy. However, there may be instances where it is impossible to ascertain whether the damage occurred in transit (in which case the marine insurance would respond) or whilst on site (in which case the CAR policy would respond). In such cases the "50/50 clause" will operate to provide that the indemnity would be shared equally by the marine insurance policy and the CAR policy.

Typically the policy will require the insured to inspect for damage to materials   **17-027**
as they are delivered to the project site, or if the materials are to remain packed until a later date, to inspect the packaging for damage (and if found, the insured must unpack the item in question). If damage is identified at this stage, then it will be the marine cargo insurer who bears responsibility, since the goods in question will have suffered damage in transit. Thus, under a typically worded clause the insured would agree to:

"examine each item of the insured property upon arrival at the project site for possible damage sustained during transit. In the case of packed items which are to be left in their packaging until a later date, the packaging is to be individually visually examined for signs of possible damage and where such damage is visible, the items are to be unpacked and inspected and any damage discovered reported to the marine cargo insurer."

If it is only at a later date that damage is discovered, but it is nevertheless pos-   **17-028**
sible to determine the cause of the damage (i.e. whether it was in transit or following delivery), then liability will fall to the marine cargo or CAR insurer as appropriate. The 50/50 clause will normally state:

"Where the packaging of an item shows no visible signs of damage to such item having been sustained during transit, any subsequent damage discovered upon unpacking will be dealt with by the marine cargo insurer or under this policy according to whether it can be clearly established that such damage was caused before or after arrival at the project site."

A 50/50 clause is needed where it is impossible to determine whether the dam-   **17-029**
age was caused during transit or subsequently. In such a scenario, the clause (which will exist in both the CAR and marine cargo policies) will apportion liability equally between the two insurers. The clause will normally be worded as follows:

"Where it is not possible to establish whether the damage to an item was caused before or after arrival at the project site it is hereby agreed that the cost of such damage shall be shared equally between the marine cargo insurer and the insurers under this policy."

In *Ace European Group Ltd v Chartis Insurance UK Ltd (formerly AIG (UK) Ltd*   **17-030**
and AIG Europe (UK) Ltd),[10] fatigue stress cracking occurred to tubes in economiser

---

[10]   *ACE European Group Ltd v Chartis Insurance UK Ltd (formerly AIG (UK) Ltd and AIG Europe*

blocks installed in a waste recycling plant. The issue was whether liability for the damage fell to the erection all risks insurer, because the damage occurred whilst the tubes were onsite, or the marine cargo insurer, because the damage occurred during transit. If it proved impossible to determine when the damage occurred, the two policies' 50/50 clauses would operate to apportion liability equally between insurers.

17-031   On the evidence, Popplewell J discounted the possibility of damage occurring onsite. However, as a matter of legal logic it did not follow that since one competing theory was impossible, the other must be correct. Despite the promotion of such reasoning by Sherlock Holmes ("When you have eliminated the impossible, whatever remains, however improbable, is the truth"), it is erroneous in law. It therefore remained to determine whether the competing theory—namely that damage occurred in transit—was proved on the balance of probabilities. Only if so would the marine cargo insurer bear full responsibility; and if neither theory was proved, then resort would be needed to the 50/50 clause.

As it happens, on the facts Popplewell J found that the damage did more likely than not occur in transit and therefore entered judgment in full against the marine cargo insurers.[11]

Finally, since each of the CAR and marine cargo policies will contain its own deductible, the 50/50 clause will provide that if it operates as a clause, the insurer in question will reduce the deductible by half, as set out below:

> "It is further agreed that in the event of the insured's retained liability under this policy being different from that under the policy of marine insurance, in settling claims as described above, each insurer shall deduct 50 per cent of the appropriate retained liability from its share of the adjusted claim."

17-032 Local authorities reinstatement.   There may be instances where as a result of legislative change the cost of reinstating damaged property is greater than it would otherwise have been. This increase can be the subject of a distinct indemnity to increase the limit of indemnity by a specified amount.

The clause will provide cover where additional costs are incurred in reinstating damaged property:

> "solely by reason of the necessity to comply with building or other regulations under or framed in pursuance of any Act of Parliament or with the by laws of any municipal or local authority or any government legislation (whether central, federal, state or local government)".

The extension will be subject to various provisos. For example, it is likely to exclude the cost incurred in complying with regulations, by-laws or legislation:

1.   under which notice has been served on the Insured prior to the loss or damage, or
2.   in respect of undamaged Insured Property other than alterations necessary as part of the reinstatement.

It will also exclude the amount of any rate, tax, duty etc. imposed as a result of capital appreciation of the Insured Property that occurs by reason of compliance with any of the relevant regulations, by-laws or legislation (for otherwise the insured would benefit from a windfall).

(UK) Ltd) [2012] EWHC 1245 (QB); [2012] 2 Lloyd's Rep. 117.

[11]   This finding was challenged, unsuccessfully, on appeal: *ACE European Group Ltd* [2013] EWCA Civ 224; [2013] Lloyd's Rep. I.R. 485.

Finally, the extension will typically contain the following proviso:

"the work of reinstatement must be commenced and carried out with reasonable despatch and may be carried out wholly or partially upon another site subject to the liability of Insurers under this extension not being increased".

This proviso means that the necessary reinstatement works caused as a result of the need to comply with the building or other regulations may be carried in whole or in part on another site (if required) but that the liability of the insurers, which will be capped for an amount not exceeding a percentage of the sum insured, will not increase.

Free issue materials. It is common in construction projects for employers or their 17-033 agents to procure certain goods, materials, equipment or services (e.g. utilities) from suppliers, and to provide them to contractors "free of charge". An employer may choose to do this in order to save time or cost (i.e. by buying materials in bulk). Thus, once the materials are provided, the contractor will typically take on responsibility for them. In order to ensure that the contractor is insured in this regard, it is crucial that the value of the goods is included in the sum insured. If the value of the goods is not included in the sum insured, then because insurers will not have received a premium that accounts for the "free issue materials" the insured will not be indemnified in the event that the materials need to be replaced or repaired. CAR policies provide an extension for such free-issue materials and a clause will typically be worded as follows:

"The Insured Property shall include all materials supplied free to the Project by the employer and/or his agents provided that the value of such items shall be included in the Limit of Indemnity and shall be declared for premium adjustment purposes."

A condition of the extension is that the insured declares the value of the materials in question. This is an obvious requirement, since it will influence both the limit of indemnity and the premium. The free issue materials will either be insured as part of the contract price or must be listed as a separate item in the schedule and priced accordingly.

A variation on the above situation is where embankments are created from mate- 17-034 rial obtained from the site (i.e. spoil) in order to plant trees along a local road, by-pass or motorway, or in and around a construction site (i.e. land near property) in order to make it more aesthetically pleasing for residents and to provide homeowners protection from the road. Obtaining material from the site in this way will be considered to be part of the works. If, however, the material is subsequently lost because it is washed away due to bad weather before it is used, then the insured can make a claim for importing replacement material to the site in order to finish off the landscaping works. In this situation the insured has not paid a premium on the material that is lost; but this does not matter because obtaining the material was included as part of the original contract value agreed between the parties.

Immobilised plant recovery. This extension provides an indemnity against the 17-035 cost of recovering and withdrawing construction equipment that has become accidentally immobilised, whether or not that would otherwise satisfy the definition of material damage under the policy. A clause will normally be worded as follows:

"In the event of construction equipment, covered under this policy, becoming accidentally immobilised in any physical situation in or about the site of any contract, the necessarily incurred cost of recovery and/or withdrawal shall be admitted by insurers as 'physical loss or damage to' within the meaning of this policy."

17-036 **Negligent breakdown of plant.** Whereas the extension for immobilised plant recovery will generally apply to plant that has become immobilised as a result of an insured peril, an additional problem is that of new plant, which forms part of the contract works, breaking down during the testing or commissioning phase of the project. The costs of remobilising or repairing such plant (but excluding the cost of hiring replacement plant) can be the subject of an extension.

The extension does not cover plant that is immobilised as a result of wilful misuse by the insured.

Ongoing hire charges from hiring construction equipment as a result of loss
17-037 **or damage.** This extension covers the insured's payment of continuing hire charges for rented construction equipment when the equipment is lost or damaged. It can also provide cover for the cost of repairing such equipment if, through the insured's fault, it is liable to pay such cost.

A typical wording is as follows:

"In respect of hired in construction equipment this policy is extended to cover the insured's liability under the terms of its hiring agreement or otherwise:

(a)   to pay continuing hire charges in consequence of loss of or damage to Construction Equipment or temporary buildings hired in by the Insured which are covered by the policy or would be but for the application of the Excess under the policy, provided that the period in respect of which payment is made hereunder in respect of any one occurrence shall be the period beginning forty-eight hours after the occurrence of the loss or damage and ending not later than three months thereafter.

(b)   to pay the necessary cost of making good damage to the Construction Equipment arising from the breakdown or of making the plant operational in the event that the breakdown of such Construction Equipment is caused by the fault error or omission of the Insured."

It will be seen from (a) above that the extension will typically contain a two-part time limit. The initial requirement that the extension is engaged only 48 hours after the relevant occurrence serves to impose a deductible. Conversely, the three-month duration sets a temporal limit to the indemnity.

A variation on the above clause is available. If the plant is over one year old the insurer can limit its liability according to the Model Conditions for the hiring of plant approved by The Construction Plant-hire Association.[12]

17-038 **New computer equipment incompatible with computer records.** If IT equipment is damaged and replaced, it may be that the new equipment is incompatible with existing computer records. This extension covers the cost of either modifying the replacement equipment, or replacing the computer records so as to render them compatible, whichever is cheapest.

A clause will normally be worded as follows:

"The Insurers will indemnify the Insured in respect of:

(a)   costs of modification of Information Technology Equipment or
(b)   costs of replacement of Computer Records together with reinstatement of programs and/or information thereon

(whichever is less) to achieve compatibility in the event that loss or destruction of Information Technology Equipment insured by this Section has resulted in undamaged Computer Records being incompatible with the replacement Information Technology Equipment.

---

[12]   Construction Plant-hire Association, *Model Conditions for the Hiring of Plant (with effect from July 2011)*, (London: Construction Plant-hire Association, 2011).

For the purposes of this Memorandum the term Computer Records shall mean all current and backup computer records (excluding fixed disks and paper records of any description) incorporating stored programs and/or information stored thereon owned by or leased hired or rented to the Insured."

It is suggested that this extension is still of some relevance (especially in the less-developed world), although it is accepted that modern computing technology is unlikely to present the same compatibility problems that may have been present in previous generations. By the same token, the inclusion of such a clause in a CAR policy is unlikely to have a significant impact upon the premium.

Best practice: Joint Code of Practice—fire prevention on construction sites.[13] Fire is perhaps the risk that first comes to mind in the context of CAR and other species of property insurance. Every year there are hundreds of fires on construction sites. It is capable of causing catastrophic damage and, therefore, imposing on insurers a substantial liability. It follows that it is in the insurers' interest that fires are not started, or, if they are, that the damage they cause is minimised. With this in mind, a typical CAR policy and (if the parties agree) JCT Forms of Building Contract will include a clause that obliges the insured to comply with a publication called *Fire Prevention on Construction Sites: The Joint Code of Practice on the Protection from Fire of Construction Sites and Buildings Undergoing Renovation.*[14] **17-039**

It will be immediately apparent that such a clause is not properly described as an extension, for the simple reason that it does not extend the scope of cover. If anything, it limits it, since it excludes from insurers' liability loss that occurs in circumstances where the insured has not fulfilled its obligations in respect of the Joint Code of Practice.

A typical wording of the clause will begin by setting out the nature of the insured's core obligation:

"The insured undertakes to comply with *Fire Prevention on Construction Sites: The Joint Code of Practice on the Protection from Fire of Construction Sites and Buildings Undergoing Renovation* (2012, 8th edition) or any subsequent amendment thereto or revised edition thereof current at the commencement of any project insured hereunder hereinafter referred to as The Joint Code."

The clause will then provide to insurers the right to inspect the contract site (exercised at reasonable times), so as to check the insured's compliance with The Joint Code:

"The appointed representative of the insurers shall have the right at all reasonable times to enter and inspect the contract site for the purpose of checking whether the conditions thereon in all respects comply with The Joint Code."

---

[13] For further discussion of this subject see above, paras 15-081 to 15-086.

[14] The latest version of the Joint Fire Code was published in October 2015. The publication produced by the Fire Prevention Authority ("FPA") Contractors Legal Group ("CLG") and the Risk Authority is called *Fire Prevention on Construction Sites: The Joint Code of Practice on the Protection from Fire of Construction Sites and Buildings Undergoing Renovation*, 9th edn (Bedford/Moreton in Marsh: Construction Industry Publications Ltd, Fire Protection Association, 2015). The Joint Code deals with, for example, emergency procedures, fire protection, temporary covering materials, site security against arson, site storage of flammable liquids, hot work, waste materials, smoking, high-rise construction sites and large timber frame structures. See also *Biffa Waste Services Ltd v Maschinenfabrik Ernst Hese Gmbh* [2008] EWCA Civ 1257; [2009] Q.B. 725; [2009] 3 W.L.R. 324, where hot works caused a fire on a construction site.

If insurers identify a breach of The Joint Code, then it is given the right: (i) to inform the insured of the breach; and (ii) to specify such remedial measures as it considers should be completed and by when they must be completed. It will, it is suggested, be an implied term that insurers may only specify such measures as are reasonably necessary. The clause will typically be worded as follows:

> "In the event of the insurers becoming aware of a breach of The Joint Code the insurers may inform the Contractor's management of the nature of the breach specifying the remedial measures required by the insurers (the Remedial Measures) and the period within which those measures must be completed.
>
> Where the insurers consider such a breach is of sufficient importance the insurers may confirm the same by notice in writing to the employer and the contractor and the first named party forming the insured when this is not the employer or contractor at their respective address nominated by the insured at the inception of cover or as subsequently amended."

If the remedial measures are not completed by the insured within the time period specified by the insurers' notice, the clause provides insurers with the right to suspend or cancel cover until such time as the remedial measures are completed. The wording makes clear, however, that the obligation of the insured to comply with the Joint Code is not a condition precedent to cover. The failure to comply with it will not, therefore, automatically render the insurers off-risk. That situation will only arise if the insured fails to comply with the procedure established by the policy.

The remainder of the clause is set out below:

> "Under the terms of this or any subsequent notice the insurers may suspend or cancel all cover under the policy from the date named in the notice not being a date earlier than the date named for completion of the Remedial Measures it being understood that upon suspension such cover shall be reinstated when the insurers are satisfied that the Remedial Measures have been completed. Such notice shall be given by registered post recorded delivery facsimile transmission or by hand.
>
> This endorsement shall not in itself be considered a condition precedent to liability but its inclusion shall not prejudice waive or remove the rights of the Insurers under the terms of the policy exclusions and conditions.
>
> In the event of cancellation only the insurers agree to return to the insured a pro rata proportion of the relevant part of the policy premium
>
> Subject otherwise to the terms conditions and exceptions of this Policy."

The Joint Fire Code applies, for the most part, to construction projects with an original contract value of £2.5 million or more, though it can also apply to lower value projects considered to be at a high risk of fire.

17-040 **Idle labour costs.** This extension covers the cost of idle labour resulting from damage to the insured property. In other words, it insures against the wasted expenditure of paying workers who, because of the damage, cannot carry out work. It will generally exclude an initial period of idle labour, and will often carry its own limit of cover for any given loss.

A clause will typically be worded as follows:

> "Notwithstanding anything contained in this section of the policy to the contrary in the event of loss or damage to the insured property insurers will also indemnify the contractor in respect of idle labour employed by the contractor or their labour only sub-contractors directly attributable thereto.
>
> Provided that the first seventy-two hours of such idle time is excluded and the insurers' liability is limited to the sum of £125,000 for any one loss."

17-041 **Construction equipment during defects liability period.** Upon completion of the construction works, the period of insurance under the CAR policy will cease. There is likely, however, to be a substantial quantity of equipment and unused materials on site, owned by the contractor, which await removal. This extension provides insurance against loss or damage to that equipment during the defects liability period or a given portion thereof.

If the extension specifies a period of cover that is less than the full defects liability period, it may also provide that the period will be extended to the full defects liability period if the insured is required to make use of the equipment or materials in question in order to fulfil its contractual obligations.

A typical wording is as follows:

"Insurers will indemnify the insured for loss or damage to Construction Equipment and other property not comprising the permanent works which was insured under this section of the policy during the initial period of insurance and where such loss or damage occurs during the first three months of the Defects Liability Period of insurance pending its removal from the site.

Insurers will also indemnify the insured for loss or damage to such property for any other period during which it may be used or reasonably required by the insured during the Defects Liability Period of insurance for the purpose of complying with his obligations under the Contracts."

Speculative building work/speculative developments awaiting sale. The 17-042 "speculative building" extension provides the insured with cover for any speculative building work that is undertaken (e.g. additional homes), which are to be sold in the future, outside the scope of the original construction contract. The clause gives a time limit for how long after the contract has expired that cover will be maintained for or will state that cover extends to the date of sale of the building, whichever occurs first. A speculative building extension clause will normally be worded as follows:

"Damage to buildings constructed by the Insured other than under Contract a) for a period not exceeding one hundred and eighty days for domestic buildings or ninety days for commercial buildings following Practical Completion or b) until the date of sale occupation or hand over whichever occurs first. Practical Completion means the completion of construction apart from decorations finishes and fitments that will be chosen by the purchaser or tenant."

Replacement of locks. The loss of keys and the need to replace locks will affect 17-043 any business. This extension clause provides the insured with cover for costs and expenses incurred as a result of having to replace locks and the loss of keys from the premises or from the homes of any principals, employers or directors. The clause will usually specify that the policy excess does not apply to the extension. The clause will also give a cap in order to limit the insurer's liability to any one occurrence.

Replacement of sanitary or other Insured Property. The material damage sec- 17-044 tion of the policy may be extended to provide the insured with cover for the replacement of sanitary or other Insured Property affected by the "outbreak of any infectious or contagious disease including but not restricted to Legionella".

A clause will normally be worded as follows:

"This insurance shall extend to indemnify the Insured in respect of the reinstatement repair or replacement of the Insured Property necessarily incurred by the Insured with the consent of the Insurers which consent shall not be unreasonably withheld as a result such Insured Property being affected by the outbreak of any infectious or contagious disease including but not restricted to Legionella and for which the Insurers will pay up to £X in respect of each Occurrence."

Loss of metered water. A common add on is where the insurer agrees to pay the 17-045 insured for costs incurred as a result of the loss of metered water from pipes or apparatus because of loss or damage caused to the Insured Property. The extension clause excludes "the cost of water lost due to a leakage from or a bursting of an underground pipe". Such a clause may be worded as follows:

"The insurance shall indemnify the Insured in respect of loss of metered water for which the Insured is charged by the water authority or utility company following loss or damage to the Insured Property which is indemnifiable hereunder but excluding the cost of water lost due to a leakage from or a bursting of an underground pipe."

17-046 Fire brigade charges.   The extension clause provides the insured cover for

"the cost of charges arising from the activities of the Fire Brigade in dealing with the consequences of Damage for which the Insurers have admitted liability. Provided that the liability of the Insurers shall not exceed £X".

A variation of the above clause is often set out below, wherein an insurer may cover the insured for the following:

"Cost of emergency services, fire fighting, fire brigade charge, fire department services charges, loss of foam or other fire extinguishing material, equipment lost, expended or destroyed in fighting fire, including loss to similar material which may be brought to the project site for the purpose of extinguishing a fire already in progress, other extinguishing expenses, and other similar costs and expenses. The maximum liability of the Insurers in respect of Emergency Services shall not exceed £X per occurrence."

17-047 Joint names/multiple insureds clause.   If the contract agreed between the parties requires insurance to be arranged in the names of the contractor and employer then this extension provides for any party named under the contract to be insured to the same manner and extent as the main insured. In other words, the same extensions, exclusions conditions, etc., will be applicable to the named insureds. The clause will therefore be worded to reflect the fact that the insurer will provide an:

"indemnity to any party that is required under the terms of the Contract to be a joint named insured to this Policy.
If there is more than one insured party each operating as a separate and distinct entity then this Policy shall apply in the same manner and to the same extent as if individual policies had been issued to each party."

The above clause is often subject to the following provisos:

"Provided that

a) the total liability of the Insurers to all of the insured parties collectively shall not exceed the Limit of Liability
b) any payment or payments by the Insurers to any one or more insured party shall reduce to the extent of that payment the Insurers liability to all parties arising from any one event giving rise to a claim under this Policy
c) the insured parties shall at all times preserve any available contractual rights agreements and remedies in the event of Damage
d) the Insurers shall be entitled to avoid liability to or claim damages from any of the insured parties in circumstances of fraud material misrepresentation material non-disclosure or breach of any Condition in this Policy each referred to in this clause as a vitiating act
e) the Contract is performed in Great Britain Northern Ireland the Isle of Man or the Channel Islands.

It is however agreed that

i) a vitiating act committed by one insured party shall not prejudice the right to indemnity of any other insured party who has an insurable interest and who has not committed a vitiating act

[494]

ii) the Insurers agree to waive all rights of subrogation which they may have or acquire against any insured party except where the rights of subrogation arise from a vitiating act

iii) any lenders to the project shall not be entitled to any indemnity under this Policy for Damage in respect of which Insurers are by reason of a vitiating act no longer liable to indemnify any one or more other insured party."

The principle behind this extension is that at the outset of a construction project the identity of particular contractor or subcontractors may not be known. The extension is intended to give a party the right to nominate a particular contractor or subcontractor to carry out the contract works and have the benefit of the CAR insurance.

The issues touched upon by the above extension, such as who the insured is under a CAR policy, fraud, material misrepresentation, non-disclosure and subrogation are all dealt with in further detail above in Chs 5, 6 and 8 and below in Ch.20.

3. DELAY IN START-UP INSURANCE AND ASSOCIATED EXTENSIONS

Consequential loss. There are many types of consequential loss, of which loss **17-048** of profits is the most common. Consequential losses and loss of profits are only insurable if an insurance policy expressly provides for this. In the context of CAR policies, loss of profit as a result of a delay to the programme of works is insurable. An insurer may grant the insured cover via an extension to the material damage section of the policy, thereby extending the scope of the indemnity beyond the cost of merely reinstating damage to the insured property. Some of the available extensions may even apply automatically, if a CAR policy is chosen by the insured.

Preliminary. As explained above in para.17-002, the "extension" for delay in **17-049** start-up insurance ("DSU") (commonly known as delay in completion insurance or advanced loss of profits ("ALOP") insurance) is in truth a separate category of insurance for the contractor or employer, and not merely an extension to the scope of the material damage cover. DSU is an all risks cover for something that has yet to be completed, and provides protection against future costs that may be incurred. It is often arranged at the same time as insurance for material damage to the construction works is placed. DSU insurance provides protection to the employer and contractor for loss of profit caused by a delay to the programme of works because of an insured peril (which insured peril will usually also trigger the material damage section of the policy). It is of particular importance to employers, and is normally taken up by them (as opposed to contractors) because the financial structuring of modern construction projects is such that any delay usually results in significant economic consequences.

The insured under DSU insurance. As stated above, it is typically the employer **17-050** who will be the insured party under DSU insurance. This is because (leaving aside the contractor's liability for breach of contract) it is the employer who will suffer from delays to the construction project. There is, however, an important exception in Private Finance Initiative ("PFI") projects, where the contractor, operator and the employer may form part of the same group of companies.

17-051   **Delay in start-up insurance.**   DSU insurance provides cover against loss of profit[15] sustained by the employer[16] as a result of delay to the commencement of commercial operations (or such other event as may be agreed, such as first production, first manufacture etc.[17]), triggered by the occurrence of indemnifiable physical damage to property. With the rapid privatisation of state-owned industries and enterprises the popularity of DSU covers gained momentum, with employers seeking to protect their interests against pecuniary losses resulting from delayed projects. Its inclusion is often demanded by lenders, whose ability to have their loans repaid is often dependent upon the project's successful completion and commencement as a profit-making enterprise. Banks require employers to take up DSU insurance in respect of project-financed transactions in order to protect the revenue stream in the event of a delay to the programme of works.

17-052   DSU is a complex category of insurance. It requires careful evaluation and consideration of the varied nature of risks involved in substantial construction projects and the corresponding impact it can have on the progress of the work. Therefore, insurers providing DSU covers often require progress reports to be made available to them so that they are aware of any deviations from the initial project plan. Due to the fact that the cause of the delay and its duration cannot be ascertained until commercial operations commence, it is unusual for insurers to make interim payments.

17-053   **Evaluation of risk.**   There are two stages to evaluating risk when underwriting a DSU policy: assessment of the events that may cause physical loss and evaluation of their potential impact on the project's scheduled business commencement date. The former will already have been carried out when writing the material damage cover. The contract-works insurers would have looked at the details of the project, including its location and duration, the type of structure being constructed, the individuals responsible for the works and their reputation in the market. In most cases, the same insurers would also be used to provide DSU cover and therefore would be fully aware of the construction risks in respect of which the material-damage cover has been provided.

17-054   The second stage involves analysis of the potential delays, which may be caused by the occurrence of an insured peril and measures that can be taken to avert any disruption to works. The following factors are likely to influence a DSU underwriter's risk assessment:

1.   The construction programme. This is one of the most important considerations as far as DSU cover is concerned. The programme contains information such as the commencement date and the duration of different phases of work, and provides a useful indication as to how realistic the project plan is in terms of being able to meet the stated deadlines. Insurers look to see

---

15   Note that it is imperative that the loss of profit should be described in the policy properly and insured as such since insurance on goods or property does not generally cover profits, see *Maurice v Goldsborough Mort & Co Ltd* [1939] A.C. 452 at 461; [1939] 3 All E.R. 63 at 67–68; (1939) 64 Ll. L. Rep. 1 at 3, per Lord Wright.

16   As set out above in para.17-049, the scope of the delay in start-up ("DSU") insurance cover does not generally extend to the contractor.

17   In this regard the words "start up" is not a term of art, and reference must always be made to the wording of the policy to determine the trigger for DSU cover (which may not involve a delay in the "start up" of anything).

whether the periods of time ensure that the critical path[18] is not influenced unduly by delay.[19] Similarly, phases in the project plan that do not contain a float[20] would have to be considered in greater detail to see how some of the factors such as late or early delivery of essential items can affect the project deadline.

2. Working patterns and methods. Some types of damage can affect the overall sequence of the work and eventually impact upon the completion date. In these cases, insurers look to see whether the project contains some built-in mechanisms such as a "slack" or "float" to deal with interruptions. The availability of skilled labour is also likely to affect an underwriter's judgement.

3. Replacement of parts and delivery periods. The replacement time schedule provides an indication of the time that would be needed to restore an item of plant by providing information regarding the availability of supplies of the original, as well as duplicates. For projects that are dependent on imported supplies or on complex machinery with which to construct the works, the likelihood of disruption to works following loss or damage is much higher. The use of second-hand machinery can also pose a similar problem and underwriters may assess the condition of items in order to evaluate the possibility of having to obtain replacements.

4. Availability and knowledge of suppliers and manufacturers. The insurers may check whether the suppliers and manufacturers are properly selected and equipped to deliver parts having regard to the magnitude of the project.

5. Contractor's reputation. It is essential that the contractor for the project is experienced and has a proven track record of completing similar projects within the designated time schedule.

6. Disruption caused by a natural disaster. The construction site itself may be affected by a natural catastrophe, with a consequent adverse impact on the overall project completion date. Territorial exposure is an equally important consideration because catastrophes such as hurricanes or floods can affect an entire locality or area. Thus, even if the construction site remains unaffected, disruption to daily life in the vicinity would cause significant delay in finishing the project works.

---

[18] The critical path relates to the longest sequence of works running throughout the construction project, for which any delay will cause the postponement of practical completion. There can be more than one critical path that runs through a project. The practice of calculating the critical path is more commonly known as the "critical path method" ("CPM") and may also be referred to as undertaking a "critical path analysis". The purpose of the CPM is to find out what has caused the delay and the duration of it. In complex projects, such as those insured by CAR insurance, the critical path cannot be determined inductively and has to be determined against the programme of works, which may be set out in a Gantt chart or in a computer programme. Delays to a critical path may be analysed by a delay analyst or a programming expert.

[19] Critical path analysis is a complex area which is discussed in detail in construction law texts. See generally, *Building Contract Disputes: Practice and Precedents* (London: Sweet & Maxwell), paras 2–150 to 2–200; K. Pickavance, *Delay and Disruption in Construction Contracts*, 4th edn (London: Sweet & Maxwell, 2010), paras 1–030 to 1–031 and *Hudson's Building and Engineering Contracts*, edited by N. Dennys and R. Clay, 13th edn (London: Sweet & Maxwell, 2015), paras 6–050 to 6–062.

[20] A float is part of the critical path analysis method. It is described in *Keating on Construction Contracts*, edited by S. Furst and V. Ramsey, 10th edn. (London: Sweet & Maxwell, 2016), at para.8–062 as being the "amount of time that non-critical activities can absorb, in excess of their original intended duration, without impacting on the critical path of the works as a whole".

7. Special projects. Some projects such as the construction of power stations and petrochemical plants are largely dependent on testing and commissioning. The risk element in these projects is higher. Hence, they are subjected to a much longer testing period, often extending beyond the normal load conditions, before they can be put to commercial use. Underwriters take into account the fact that there is usually a phased handover in these projects, which means that some parts of the project may start generating revenue before the entire works are complete.

8. Extension to cover in respect of premises other than the project site. Customers and Suppliers may be included as extensions to interruption policies. DSU cover may be extended to include these risks, where an employer wants to indemnify himself against loss of revenue, which he may incur as a result of damage caused, e.g. a customer's premises who can no longer accept the insured product. Similarly, a supplier's premises may be destroyed by fire and consequently can no longer provide supply of raw materials and essential plants, which were stored on the site, causing acute disruption to works. These additional risks require careful individual evaluation. For instance, underwriters would need to assess the safety standards exercised or in place at the supplier's premises and availability of supplies from another source in such a situation.

9. Seasonal effects on business. A cover may take into account the fact that there may be seasonal variations in the financial loss. For example the roads may be busier in the summer months and power generation plants may produce a higher output in winter months.

10. Liquidated damages and penalty clauses. Compensation from liquidated damages and penalty clauses are often excluded from cover. Where cover is provided, care must be taken to ensure that the terms of the insurance are integrated with the terms of the underlying construction contract. If an employer is named as an insured, it may suffer no loss if delays occur but damages have been ascertained and are payable by the contractor. It is usual to include within the terms of cover a waiver of the liquidated damages payable under the construction contract.

11. The selected indemnity period and the deductible period.[21]

17-055 Apart from considering the factors listed above in para.17-054, an interruption study can also be used by underwriters to assess the impact of the occurrence of a particular event at the construction site. This is used most often in case of machinery installation contracts. It will consider the lead-in times for replacement plant following loss or damage along with the anticipated revenue and operational cost of machineries. Where DSU extends to cover the contractor's plant, an interruption study can be used to consider the effect of loss or damage of a key item such as heavy uplifting plant on the overall project.

Finally, contingency plans may also be useful to show the extent to which losses may be minimised and cost-effective action taken.

17-056 **The cover.** DSU cover is generally contained in a separate section of the material damage policy. A typical DSU wording is as follows:

"If at any time during the Period of Insurance as stated in the Schedule or any extension thereof any

---

[21] See below, para.17-061.

of the Insured Property suffers Damage as defined herein and in consequence thereof the Insurers will indemnify the Insured for the amount of loss resulting from such Delay in Completion or Business Interruption in accordance with provisions of the Policy. The amount payable as indemnity hereunder shall be:

(i) The amount of the Insured Rent due during the Indemnity Period which shall in consequence of the Damage fall below the Anticipated Insured Rent; or

(ii) The amount of the Increased Cost of Working incurred by the Insured during the Indemnity Period in consequence of Damage

(iii) Additional expenditure necessarily and reasonably incurred for the sole purpose of avoiding or diminishing the reduction in the Insured Rent or avoiding the Increased Cost of Working which, without such expenditure, would have taken place during the Indemnity Period, but not exceeding the amount of reduction in Insured Rent thereby avoided or diminished or the amount of Increased Cost of Working thereby avoided

Less any sum saved during the Indemnity Period as may cease or be reduced in consequence of Damage."

Nature of the cover.   The precursor to a DSU claim is usually the occurrence of **17-057** an insured peril under the construction policy, which subsequently causes delay or interruption in the completion of the project works. As the wording of the clause set out above shows, a hallmark of DSU cover is usually that the insured peril corresponds with that in the material damage section of the policy. DSU cover will usually also be subject to the same exclusions. However, it is open to insurers to omit from the scope of the DSU cover any extensions provided under the material damage policy, such as damage to plant and machinery or to pre-existing property. On the other hand, DSU will not provide the insured (in contrast to the material damage section of the policy) with an extension to cover the costs of mitigating the effects of threatened damage.

Features of the cover.   DSU cover will specify the employer as the insured party, **17-058** details of the project completion date, a date for commencement of business operations, provisions for occurrence of a delay and the sum of indemnity under the policy. If an indemnifiable event occurs and the completion of the project is delayed beyond the scheduled commencement date, the insured is indemnified against the actual loss of gross profit sustained. This will ordinarily be defined as the projected revenue less any savings in operational costs. The sum insured can, however, be limited to fixed costs incurred during the period of delay (e.g. wages, essential services etc.), without the addition of loss of profit.

Furthermore, it is becoming increasingly common for DSU policies to define the loss in advance, rather than calculating it at the time of the claim. For example, in relation to DSU cover for an oil refinery, the parties can agree within the policy a defined price for a barrel of oil. This provides certainty for insurers, since the only variable is the period of delay, and not extraneous market conditions (in this example the price of oil).

Most DSU wording will contain a claims-handling provision that provides a procedure for the investigation of claims. Where delay is caused by a combination of insured and uninsured events, the claims condition will usually state how delay is to be treated and how the sum indemnified is calculated.

Time periods.   The time periods relevant to a DSU policy include the period of **17-059** insurance, the indemnity period and the deductible period.

The period of insurance is the time during which the insurer is at risk, i.e. when material damage must occur to insured property in order for the insured to bring a claim. It commences at the same time as the CAR policy and ends on the date specified in the policy schedule as the scheduled business-commencement date.

17-060   The indemnity period (which is chosen by the insured) is the period between the identified business commencement date and the end date of DSU. The period will usually be calculated to ensure it is of sufficient duration to allow repairs to or replacement of damaged property to be effected in respect of any reasonably foreseeable damage. If repairs are completed and business commences before the end of the period specified in the policy, the indemnity will cease to apply.

17-061   The deductible period, or time excess, is the period specified in the policy during which the insured must bear the loss of profit. Some insurers[22] consider that because time excess is triggered only once, i.e. when an insured event causes a failure to meet the scheduled business commencement date, it is contrary to principle to have multiple deductibles. In other words, under DSU insurance a number of insurable events can cause only one delay to the project, and the insured can only make one claim, meaning that only one excess applies to that claim. It is suggested that this approach is, however, problematic because each delay will erode the indemnity period. Thus a series of delays of 12 hours duration may each come within the retained liability and at the same time cumulatively erode the period of indemnity. Moreover, the insurers would have to undertake the potentially arduous and costly task of having carefully to investigate each incident to ascertain whether it is indemnifiable. This would involve having to carry out a detailed analysis of the programme of works to establish the real effects of each event on delay. Where the interruption may be caused by multiple incidents, the works programme would have to be evaluated to distinguish between concurrent and cumulative delays.

One solution is for the policy to stipulate that for the purposes of a DSU claim, it is only delays beyond a certain period (e.g. one week) caused by the occurrence of any given insured event that qualify for an indemnity. In this way, the deductible period will be not eroded by the occurrence of a series of minor events. Alternatively, the policy may simply impose a separate deductible period of delay in respect of each insured event. This view may not find favour with the insured.

If, however, a single policy covers a number of independent facilities (e.g. as part of a private finance initiative—for example a number of prisons built at different times and on different sites), then each facility will be insured for a specific sum and have its own indemnity period.

17-062   **Special conditions relevant to DSU cover.**   Owing to the nature of the risk indemnified under DSU cover, the insured is usually required to adhere to special conditions in order to claim an indemnity under the policy. One of these requirements includes furnishing progress reports to the insurers at regular intervals in order to assist them in the evaluation of any subsequent claim. This ensures that the insurers are aware of the manner in which the works are progressing and puts them in the best position to identify and determine whether the delay was caused by an insured or an uninsured event. In most cases, once the progress reports are provided, insurers will in turn instruct independent consultants or claim adjusters to monitor the progress of the works. It is also important that reports provided subsequent to

---

[22]   See, e.g., M. Bommeli, *Delay in start-up insurance* (Zurich: Swiss Reinsurance Company, 2003), p.16.

the occurrence of an indemnifiable event suggest measures that can be adopted to avoid business interruption. The employer is expected to take reasonable steps to ensure that the project completion dates are adhered to and regulations imposed by authorised bodies are complied with.

Notification is an important requirement in DSU covers. The employer is usually required to notify the insurers immediately of any change in the original risk and in the insured's business status. Such terms are fundamental to the formation of the insurance contract and therefore any change or amendment would require consent from the insurers. Apart from these, an employer must also urgently notify the insurers of the occurrence of an event that is likely to give rise to a claim under the policy.

Finally, once there has been an interruption to project operations, the employer is required to permit insurers to have immediate access to plants and personnel so that they can properly investigate the situation and take control of remedial measures. Problems arise where delay has occurred and there is a dispute between the employer and contractor as to the cause of the delay and its duration. In this situation, which is common, the contractor may be unwilling to provide the insurer with access to contemporaneous information for fear of prejudicing its position with the employer.

Causes of delay: concurrent causes. The most likely cause of disagreement **17-063** between the insured and the insurer in relation to a DSU policy is where both insured and uninsured events (e.g. strikes, slow progress or late supply of materials) cause delay. In many cases, it is often difficult to state with certainty whether the proximate cause of the loss is an indemnifiable peril.[23]

In *Orient-Express Hotels Ltd v Assicurazioni Generali SpA (UK) (t/a Generali Global Risk)*,[24] the claimant owned a hotel in New Orleans that was damaged by Hurricanes Katrina and Rita in 2005. The hotel closed for two months and suffered significant business interruption losses.[25] At the same time, the surrounding area of New Orleans was also devastated by the hurricanes, causing a mandatory evacuation of the city. The issue was whether the claimant was entitled to an indemnity under a business interruption policy in respect of loss that was concurrently caused by damage to the hotel (an insured event) and damage to the vicinity (an uninsured event). On the facts, Hamblen J held that the tribunal had not erred in applying the "but for" test of causation; and because it could not be shown that "but for" the insured event taking place the loss would not have occurred, the insurers were not liable.

However, he then went on to make the broader point that the "but for" test cannot be mechanically applied to every situation. He said that:

"As a general rule the 'but for' test is a necessary condition for establishing causation in fact. However, there may be cases in which fairness and reasonableness require that it should not be a necessary condition ... I would also accept that a case in which there are two concurrent independent causes of a loss, with the consequence that the application of the 'but for' test would mean that there is no cause of the loss, is potentially an example of a case in which fairness and reasonableness would require that the 'but for' test should not be a necessary condition of causation, particularly

---

[23] For a more comprehensive discussion on issues of causation in CAR insurance see below, Ch.19.
[24] *Orient-Express Hotels Ltd v Assicurazioni Generali SpA (UK) (t/a Generali Global Risk)* [2010] EWHC 1186 (Comm); [2010] 1 C.L.C. 847; [2010] Lloyd's Rep. I.R. 531.
[25] Business interruption insurance ("BII") is discussed below in Ch.26.

where two wrongdoers are involved. However, whether or not that is so will depend on all the circumstances of the particular case".[26]

Therefore, in cases where there are two concurrent independent causes, each of which is sufficient to bring out the resultant loss, departure from the test was permissible to reach a fair and reasonable decision since the application of the "but for" test would result in the insured having no recoverable loss.[27]

17-064   In general, therefore, a DSU insurer will not be liable for delay caused by the occurrence of an insured event if it can show that the same delay would have occurred as a result of an uninsured event (i.e. general project delays). Where both insured and uninsured events contribute to delay, much would depend on whether the case concerned two concurrent "interdependent" or "independent" causes. Finally, if an insured event occurs and causes delay, but that delay is prolonged by the occurrence of an uninsured event, the indemnity will not cover the period of prolonged delay.

17-065   **Sequential events.**   In the context of DSU, delays must be sequential and aggregated in order to qualify for a DSU loss. For example, if a delay occurs to the installation of a rooflight because of a delay to installing a roof stand, then these will be deemed to be sequential events that will qualify for a single aggregated DSU loss. In contrast, concurrent events, such as a delay to the installation of windows in one part of the building and a delay to the installation of glass splashbacks in a bathroom in another part of the building will not be aggregated to form part of a DSU claim because they will be deemed to be two independent events; and as such only the longer of the two delays would be included as part of a DSU claim.

17-066   **Additional (or increased) cost of working.**   As the clause set out above in para.17-056 demonstrates, in addition to providing cover for loss of profits, DSU policies also indemnify the employer against the increased and additional cost of working. In many projects, delay in completion can be avoided by the employer making increased payments to the contractor, e.g. by paying overtime to workers, hiring additional plant or by increasing the workforce. Renting out alternative premises or purchasing partially manufactured goods can also ensure that the business continues to operate during the time period required for reinstatement.[28] In such cases, so long as the increased payments do not exceed what would otherwise have been lost by reason of the delay, it obviously makes economic sense for the insurer to encourage the insured to incur that additional cost.

17-067   In order to engage this indemnity, the insured will need to show that the mate-

---

[26]   *Orient-Express Hotels Ltd* [2010] EWHC 1186 (Comm) at [33]; [2010] 1 C.L.C. 847 at 861; [2010] Lloyd's Rep. I.R. 531 at 538.

[27]   *MacGillivray on Insurance Law*, edited by J. Birds, B. Lynch and S. Milnes, 13th edn (London: Sweet & Maxwell, 2015), para.21-001, fn.1 and para.21-005, fn.27. Note that, in this case, Hamblen J held that the "but for" test of causation applied because it was an express term of the policy that the test would be applied to the assessment of loss of revenue. Moreover, the judge felt that the question of whether "fairness and reasonableness" required departure from the "but for" test was a question of fact and one the present court could not comment on. Finally, this was not a case where the application of the test left the insured with no recoverable loss. While the "but for" test meant that the insured could not formulate a claim under the main insuring clause, it was able to recover under the "Prevention of Access" or "Loss of Attraction" policies, albeit the amount recoverable was more limited.

[28]   *Henry Booth & Sons v Commercial Union Assurance Co Ltd* (1923) 14 Ll. L. Rep. 114.

rial damage in question would, but for the increased costs, affect the project's critical path. In other words, it is necessary to show that the sole purpose of the expenditure was to prevent or minimise business interruption without which the project's completion date would have been affected. Furthermore, the additional expenditure must have been both "necessary" (i.e. there must have been no other choice) and "reasonable". The indemnity will be limited to the loss avoided by the incurring of additional costs.

Liquidated damages for delay during the indemnity period. The amount pay-   **17-068**
able by the insurer to the insured for the loss resulting from a delay to the programme of works, will exclude "any sum saved during the Indemnity Period as may cease or be reduced in consequence of Damage". In addition to this, however:

> "[i]f any amount is received by the Insured in respect of liquidated damages for delay during the Indemnity Period it is understood and agreed that such amount of liquidated damages shall be applied to reduce the Insured's overall loss attributable to the circumstances leading to the payment of such liquidated damages even if the amount of such loss is greater than the sum insured hereunder.
>
> Any amount of liquidated damages received subsequent to a loss settlement under this Policy shall be applied as if recovered or received prior to such settlement and all necessary adjustments shall then be made between the Insured and the Insurer, provided always that nothing in this Policy shall be construed to mean that losses under this Policy are not payable until the Insured's ultimate net loss has been finally ascertained.
>
> In addition to the foregoing the Insured shall be entitled to retain the amount of any liquidated damages for delay it shall receive from any contractor, subcontractor or supplier equivalent to the amount of the Time Excess application to this Section 2.
>
> In the event of loss indemnifiable under this section of the policy, the Sum Insured hereunder shall notwithstanding be automatically reinstated and maintained in force during the period of insurance."

Offsite delays. It is possible to obtain an extension to DSU cover that indemni-   **17-069**
fies against the loss of profit caused by offsite delays, such as utility failure (water, gas, electricity) and delay in the production of components for the project. For example, it may be discovered during the course of construction that the measurements of steel connection details are wrong, and so there may be a delay caused to the works whilst new ones are produced by fabricators.

Calculating delay in DSU insurance. In order to assess the employer's entitle-   **17-070**
ment to DSU cover, the task of the claims handler or (as the case may be) loss adjuster or programmer is to determine whether the cause of the delay was an indemnifiable event.[29]

The most effective way of performing this task is by analysis of the project schedule. The most important objective is to assess whether the indemnifiable event altered the schedule's critical path—that is, the sequence of activities whose completion is necessary before the next activity can begin. If an indemnifiable event does not affect the schedule's critical path (because it affects an activity that is either not on the path, or which has a sufficient degree of float[30] that the critical path is not affected), then it should not cause any delay to the completion of the project. If, for example, damage is caused only to a site's car park, then, subject to the scheduling of the project, it is unlikely to prevent works being done elsewhere.

---

[29] For a discussion about the principles at play where delay is caused concurrently by insured and uninsured causes see above, para.17-063.

[30] That is the period of time by which a task can be delayed without having a knock-on effect on other tasks.

The insured's task will be to demonstrate by reference to the project schedule that the indemnifiable event in question caused delay to the commencement of commercial operations (or whatever other trigger may be set out in the DSU policy), and if so to what extent.

Claims handlers have two choices when it comes to monitoring a DSU policy. They can either take a post-loss approach, which means that the involvement of the adjustment team takes place only after a claim is made; or a pre-loss approach, which involves monitoring the programme and sequence of works through the construction phase. The advantage of a post-loss approach is that, if no claim is made under the policy, insurers do not have to incur the cost of any monitoring at all. If a claim is made, particularly at a late stage of the works, the task of calculating the delay without the benefit of prior monitoring can prove extremely complex and therefore expensive. However, a post-loss approach may be cost effective if the loss is substantial. A pre-loss approach incurs the cost of monitoring whether or not a claim is actually made, but has the advantage of avoiding a surge in expenditure. In practice, under a post-loss approach insurers will often seek to reach a commercial settlement with the insured, rather than incur unnecessary costs of carrying out a detailed assessment of the claim.

17-071 Loss of income. Since DSU insurance covers the employer's loss of profit, it is axiomatic that the insured must give credit for any savings in operational costs that have been made by reason of the delay.

17-072 Loss of additional and/or prolonged interest. If a project involves the construction of a building that is intended to be sold on completion, DSU insurance can be obtained to pay an agreed rate of interest on the deferred net proceeds of sale for the period of delay. Alternatively insurance can be obtained to pay the interest under the loan used to fund the development, which is paid for the prolonged periods. In each case the payments will be subject to a maximum indemnity period.

17-073 Increased cost of finishing uncompleted building works. This extension is discussed in the context of the material-damage section of the policy at para.17-007 above. It is also possible to obtain it as an extension to DSU cover, in which case it should carry its own indemnity limit. Although there may be instances where the insured can seek to rely upon the extension under both sections of the policy, equally there will be occasions where it is only within the DSU section that the extension will be engaged because of the nature of the trigger for the insurance.

17-074 Increased and additional increased costs of working. This extension is discussed at para.17-011 above. As with the extension for the increased cost of finishing uncompleted building works, if separately obtained within a DSU policy it should carry its own indemnity limit.

17-075 Liquidated damages. As discussed at para.17-012 above in the context of the material-damage section of the policy, it is possible (if rare) to obtain insurance within a DSU policy against the contractor's liability to pay liquidated damages as a result of delay.

Delay or loss of income incurred by the employer as a result of damage to its existing property. It is possible to extend the scope of DSU insurance to cover **17-076** loss of profit caused by damage to the employer's existing property, which can, of course, cause the loss or delay of income whether or not the construction works in question are completed in time.

Waiver of subrogation rights. If an insurer indemnifies the insured against the **17-077** consequences of delay that are caused by the default of the contractor, then the insurer has a prima facie right to bring a subrogated claim against the contractor in the name of the insured. It is common, however, for insurers expressly to waive such rights of subrogation, especially where the contractor and employer are co-assureds or when the contractor and the owner are in effect the one and the same, such as in a PFI project.[31] The effect of this is to place on the insurer the ultimate risk of insured delay and the consequences thereof regardless of whether the contractor is liable, because the insurer has included an express waiver of subrogation clause in the contractor's insurance contract. There may also be a waiver of liquidated damages for the purposes of insurance, as without such waiver the employer would not be able to point to a loss capable of being indemnified.

---

[31] Insurers are unable to bring a subrogated claim against a co-insured, subject to exceptions, whether or not there is an express waiver. See further the discussion below at paras 20-040 to 20-041.

CHAPTER 18

PUBLIC LIABILITY

TABLE OF CONTENTS

1. INTRODUCTION

Introduction. The two main types of construction liability insurance are employ- **18-001** ers' and public liability insurance (the latter of which is also often called "third party liability" insurance).[1] The former concerns the legal liability owed by employers for injury caused to employees, whilst the latter (which is the focus of this chapter) concerns personal injury suffered, or the loss of or damage to property incurred by a third party.

A CAR insurance policy normally comprises public liability, delay or conse- **18-002** quential loss and construction works insurance (including perhaps plant, machinery and other equipment). A CAR policy may be either for a single project or in respect of all of the projects that a single party decides to undertake during the year when the insurance is in force; this type of policy is known as an annual/open cover or floater policy. Public liability insurance cover may also be provided by a separate policy to either of these two types of CAR policy (rather than being contained in a section of it).

Public liability is one of the three key risks against which the insured will usu- **18-003** ally be covered by a CAR policy; the other two are damage to the insured's property (see Ch.9) and consequential losses incurred as a result of delay in completion or business interruption (see Ch.17).

Public liability policies are important because during the course of construction **18-004** an insured party may be liable to a number of different categories of third party (including the general public); it is therefore important from both the insured's and the third parties' perspective that sufficient insurance is in place to cover any eventualities that may arise. The purpose of a public liability policy is, however, clear: to indemnify third parties in respect of legal liabilities of the insured, as a consequence of any personal injury suffered or loss of or damage to property incurred by them during the period of insurance.

Coverage. A CAR policy, despite what its name suggests, will not cover a **18-005** contractor against "all risks" in respect of any public liability incurred by it as a

---

[1] The terms "public liability" and "third party liability" are used interchangeably in this chapter.

result of construction activities. The scope of the public liability section of a CAR policy will normally be restricted and this may be achieved in a number of ways, such as by, for example, limiting it to liability imposed on the insured by law, or as a result of the contract or by reference to the type of *business* carried on by the insured under the wording of the policy (in an annual/open/floater policy) in contrast to the *project* (which will be specified in a project policy).

18-006   In terms of the scope of public liability cover provided in a CAR policy (including a project policy), there is no standard level of cover. A typical clause in a CAR policy covering personal injury (including death) and loss of or damage to property to a third party may be worded as follows:

> "The Insurers will indemnity the Insured except as hereinafter provided in respect of all sums which the Insured shall become legally or contractually liable to pay consequent upon:
>
> (a)   personal Injury suffered by any person
> (b)   loss of or damage to property
>
>   occurring during the Period of Insurance anywhere within the Territorial Limits in connection with the [Business or the] Project [or the execution of the Contract]."

18-007   Public liability cover may be extended to "indemnify the Insured against all sums which the Insured shall become legally liable to pay consequent upon obstruction" nuisance, etc. This particular extension will normally be found in the extension clauses section, which is applicable to the third party liability section.[2]

18-008   **Third party cover for liability in tort and/or contract.**   A public liability policy provides cover for liability to third parties (such as members of the public and owners of property, real and personal, who are not parties to a relevant contract). A public liability policy normally provides cover for claims in tort or the effect of this liability (i.e. interference with third parties and the type of harm that results as protected by the law of tort), or cover for liability in contract that is co-extensive with duties that arise in tort, but does not afford (if the words "legally liable" are used) the insured with cover against liability in contract for pure economic loss.[3] It is now generally accepted that public liability policies are not designed to provide the insured with cover for liability in contract, but to provide cover against liability in tort.

18-009   **The CAR policy.**   The beginning of a CAR policy will usually expressly state that under the Contract (Rights of Third Parties) Act 1999 the contract does not "confer or create any right enforceable ... by any person who is not a party to the contract". In other words, a third party who is not named in the contract as a party or by category as an insured does not have any contractual rights. Normally, following this, a schedule will appear, which will set out key information, explaining how the policy is to operate (i.e. stating the identity of the insured, the scope of the building contract, the period of insurance, financial information and how the sum insured in respect of delay(s) in completion and the limit of indemnity and the deposit premium to be paid (omitting the last item) will be calculated).[4]

---

[2]   See below, para.18-056.
[3]   *Tesco Stores Ltd v Constable* [2008] EWCA Civ 362; [2008] 1 C.L.C. 727; [2008] Lloyd's Rep. I.R. 636.
[4]   See below, paras 18-020 to 18-026.

2. GENERAL DEFINITIONS

The general definitions. The general definitions section in the policy will either   **18-010**
form part of the schedule or will be set out in a separate section following it, some
of which relate to the third party liability section. The general definitions apply to
the whole of the insurance policy.

Occurrence. The term "occurrence" in a public liability section of a CAR policy   **18-011**
is most often defined as meaning "each and every occurrence or series of occurrences consequent upon or attributable to one source or original cause".[5] An occurrence is an event that arises during the period of insurance, which causes a third
party personal injury or damage to its property located in and around a construction site. Each occurrence or series of occurrences will be attributable to one source
or original cause, so as to determine any one occurrence and the same approach is
applicable, when the limit of indemnity set out in the schedule is applied regarding third party liability.[6] In conjunction with the financial limits relevant to the
public liability section of the policy, the effect is to limit the amount an insurer will
be required to pay under the policy.

Definition of terms. A CAR policy may import definitions that are contained in   **18-012**
the contract that has been signed by the parties. The terms that will be defined in

---

[5]   Aggregation under a CAR works policy came before the Court of Appeal in *Seele Austria GmbH
& Co KG v Tokio Marine Europe Insurance Ltd* [2008] EWCA Civ 441; [2009] 1 All E.R. (Comm)
171; [2008] B.L.R. 337. The Court of Appeal considered and applied the case of *Kuwait Airways
Corp v Kuwait Insurance Co SAK* [1996] 1 Lloyd's Rep 664. *Kuwait Airways* concerned a claim
under a war risks cover for the loss of 15 aircraft belonging to Kuwait Airways which were seized
by the Iraqi armed forces at Kuwait airport during the invasion of Kuwait. The Court of Appeal
concluded: (a) an "occurrence" is not materially different from an event or happening "unless
perchance the contractual context requires some distinction to be made", (b) however, an "occurrence" is not the same as a loss because one occurrence can embrace a plurality of losses, (c) the
issue is to examine whether the circumstances of the loss involve such a degree of unity so as to
justify their being described as, or as arising out of, one occurrence, (d) in assessing the degree of
unity, regard may be had to factors as cause, locality, time and the intentions of the human agent (i.e.
the unity of cause, location, time and intent). The case of *Seele Austria GmbH* [2008] EWCA Civ
441; [2009] 1 All E.R. (Comm) 171; [2008] B.L.R. 337 concerned the installation of a number of
defective windows and whether the cost of each defective window could be aggregated under the
wording "each and every occurrence or series of occurrences arising out of any one event". The court
proceeded by identifying the occurrences of damage and asking whether there was one event that
can properly be regarded as the cause of all the damage. This was because the aggregation wording
required the separate instances of damage should arise out of (in the sense of being caused by) one
event. The defects were found to be the result of poor workmanship repeated over and over again.
Although the workmanship deficiencies to each window constituted an occurrence, and there was a
series of occurrences, they did not arise out of one event. Compare this with the analysis of Sir
Thomas Bingham MR in *Mitsubishi Electric UK Ltd v Royal London Insurance (UK) Ltd* [1994] 2
Lloyd's Rep. 249; 74 B.L.R. 87; [1994] C.L.C. 367.

[6]   In *M J Gleeson Group Plc v AXA Corporate Solutions Assurance S.A.* [2013] Lloyd's Rep I.R. 677
(TCC), before HHJ Raynor QC, counsel for the insurer relied on Staughton LJ's dictum in *Robert
Irving & Burns v Stone* [1997] C.L.C. 1593 at 1595; [1998] Lloyd's Rep. I.R. 258 at 261; [2003]
Lloyd's Rep. P.N. 46 at 48, and counsel for the contractor relied on McLachlin J in *Reid Crowther
and Partners Ltd v Simcoe & Erie General Insurance Co* [1993] S.C.J. No 10; (1993) D.L.R. (4th)
741; [1993] 1 S.C.R. 252. HHJ Raynor QC, when concluding that a request for comments on apparent deficiencies does not amount to an assertion of a right to relief, followed Steyn LJ in *Thorman v New Hampshire Insurance Co (UK) Ltd*; sub nom. *Home Insurance Co v New Hampshire
Insurance Co (UK) Ltd* [1988] 1 Lloyd's Rep. 7 at 11; 39 B.L.R. 41 at 51; [1988] 1 F.T.L.R. 30 at
35.

the contract, and imported into the policy will normally include the following phases of the works: the works; and practical completion. In this instance therefore, the insurance and building contract documents interlink with one another. The contract terms, as incorporated, will apply to aspects of the third party liability section and assist in establishing for instance, property which is insured under the construction works.

18-013 Information technology equipment. The term information technology equipment ("IT equipment") will normally be defined as follows:

> "Computer equipment (including interconnecting wiring and fixed discs) used for the storage and communication of electronically processed data, ancillary equipment solely for the use with computer equipment comprising air conditioning equipment, generating equipment, voltage regulating equipment, temperature humidity recording equipment, electronic access equipment, heat and smoke detection equipment, gas flooding cylinders and pipework, telecommunication and information systems, all current and backup computer records (excluding fixed discs and paper records of any description) incorporating stored programs and/or information thereon.
>
> Information Technology Equipment shall also include but not be limited to all vertical and other infrastructural cabling, all horizontal data/voice distribution, cabling, connection, patching labelling and documentation thereof, PABX and handsets, dealerboard switch and dealerboards, LAN and Comms data switches routers, firewalls, external data feed termination equipment, video distribution video broadcast and TV headend equipment, frames, patch panels, active hubs and the building, erection, installation, testing and commissioning thereof."

The definition includes computer equipment and ancillary equipment (excluding fixed discs and any paper records) solely for the use of it; vertical and other infrastructural cabling, telephonic and video distribution equipment. In terms of the policy, it is clear that IT equipment usually covers a broad range of IT equipment and not just one specific type.

18-014 Construction equipment. The term construction equipment will normally be defined in the general definitions section of the policy as follows:

> "All appliances or things of whatsoever nature required for the performance of the Works and the remedying of any defects for the performance of the Works and the remedying of any defects therein but not including plant and materials or other things intended to form or forming part of the Works and the remedying of any defects therein but not including plant and materials or other things intended to form or forming part of the Works as defined in the Contract. For the avoidance of doubt Construction Equipment shall include but not be limited to tunnelling shields, compressed air locks and compressors, reusable pile casings, cutting tools, drilling, lifting and excavation equipment generally, batching plant, power cables and transformers associated therewith surveying instruments and other fixed or mobile constructional plant tools and equipment plant tools and equipment on land or afloat, not being part of the permanent or Temporary Works."

18-015   The degree to which the term construction equipment is defined in a policy will vary. The definition will normally include "all appliances or things of whatsoever nature required for the performance of the Works and the remedying of any defects therein" but not "plant and materials or other things intended to form or forming part of the Works as defined in the Contract" which the insured will be responsible for. The definition may list some of the plant and equipment for the performance of the works. The list of items will not be exhaustive. Sometimes it may be difficult to ascertain whether an item, such as scaffolding, falls within the definition of the term construction equipment or not. In terms of the items that come within the definition, it does not matter if the insured owns or hires the equipment in order to do the works. Substantial loss, damage and personal injury can be caused by construction equipment, especially where over-sailing cranes, conveyors and tunnel-boring machines ("TBMs") are used. It is therefore important to identify precisely the site and the construction equipment that is insured.

Temporary buildings. In a CAR policy the words "temporary buildings" may be defined to mean: **18-016**

> "Offices, workshops; warehouses, accommodation, campsites and any other buildings situated on or about or in the vicinity of the Site and which are to be used in connection with the Project [or Business]."

The temporary buildings definition may be combined with the construction equipment definition or set out separate to it. The definition cited above, will cover items such as porta-cabins and porta-loos and other similar structures. The importance of the definition is that it includes buildings used temporarily which are "off-site" for the purpose of storage and accommodation.

Temporary works. In the general definitions section, "temporary works" will typically be defined as follows: **18-017**

> "All temporary works of every kind required in or about the execution or maintenance of the Works but does not include materials or other things intended to form or forming part of the permanent Works as defined in the Contract. For the avoidance of doubt Temporary Works shall include but not be limited to all shuttering, formwork, falsework, scaffolding, temporary conveyor systems, sheet steel piling, temporary bridges, tunnel supports and the like."

The site. Under a CAR policy a site will normally be defined as follows: **18-018**

> "The actual place or places to which the Insured Property is to be delivered or where work is to be done by the Insured together with so much of the area surrounding the said place or places as the Insured shall actually use in connection with the Contract or Project [or Business] or sub-contracts and shall include offsite storage. This definition shall also include any place or places defined as the Site or Sites in the Contract or any building or premises used by the Insured in connection with the Project [or Business]."

The site location and extent will usually be identified in the contract (although the definition of the construction works contained in the policy is also important). A site may be construed to be the site where works are to be undertaken, the site environs as well as any other sites identified that are used by the insured in connection with the construction project, and/or defined as being part of the site in the contract. In terms of third party liability, the insured may be liable to third parties who suffer personal injury or damage to their property in and around a site, and not just in relation to one specific place.

The insured business. If a CAR policy indemnifies the insured for the amount of loss incurred as a result of the insured property suffering damage (as defined) and, consequently, incurring delay in completion and/or business interruption; then the insured's business will be defined in the general definition section of the policy. The definition of the insured's business will clearly vary according to the business concerned. In one policy for example, an insured's business was defined in the following way: **18-019**

> "The business to be undertaken by at or in connection with the Development and all ancillary and incidental facilities and operations thereto or anything forming part of the Project or the Business and shall include the provision of canteen, sports, social and welfare organisations and fire, first aid and ambulance services and the medical services."

Under an annual policy, cover will be provided to the insured for liability "in connection with" the insured business rather than "the Project" (the latter concerns a project policy).

3. The schedule

18-020 **The schedule.** The schedule is an important section of a CAR policy and will normally appear after the first page and will typically run to some 8–9 pages.[7] The schedule will cover a number of key areas, as its main purpose is to explain how the insurance policy is to be operated. First, the policy will state who the insured is in respect of each section of the CAR policy, Secondly, it will state who the parties are to the building contract in terms of carrying out the works (and in doing so, will refer back to the works defined in the contract); and will also give a brief description of the business/project proposed. Thirdly, a section called the leases may follow which states that any existing lease or agreement to leases or future lease entered into by the employer for the lease of the property will form part of the business/project.

18-021 Fourthly, the schedule will specify the duration of the policy regarding the building project, and also give the defects liability period. Fifthly, the schedule will under a heading called "interest" specify under which specific sections of the policy the insured have cover, with reference to the three main heads of cover, namely: insured property, consequential loss and delay in completion and business interruption and third party liability.

18-022 Sixthly, the schedule will set out the sum insured for each section under which cover is provided to the insured. In relation to the public liability section, it will specify the limit of indemnity that applies to any one occurrence or confirm that it is unlimited during the period of insurance.

18-023 Seventhly, the schedule will have a section that specifies the territorial limits that apply to each section of cover. In respect of third party liability the territorial limit may be defined or it may be stated as being worldwide; in the former situation the insurers will still face risks from public liability claims being made outside of the defined area.

18-024 Eighthly, if there are several subscribing insurers or underwriters to the insurance policy, then the schedule will include a clause called "several liability notice". This means that each and every subscribing insurer "are severable and not jointly liable and are limited solely to the extent of their individual subscriptions." In other words, the subscribing insurer is not responsible for any other insurer if they do not meet all or part of their obligations.

18-025 Ninthly, the schedule will specify the maximum indemnity periods that will apply to the sections for which the insured is covered. The penultimate section of the schedule will list the excesses (also known as deductibles) that the insured will have to pay in respect of each section of cover before it applies. In respect of third party liability, the excess will usually state an amount that the insured would have to pay in respect of each and every loss incurred by a third party regarding property damage.

---

[7] In a more complex project policy the schedule may be longer and may be broken up according to each section concerned; with the definitions, exclusions, extensions and conditions regarding that section following thereafter. The last section of the policy may then set out the general policy definitions, policy exclusions, policy extensions and general policy conditions that apply to the policy as a whole.

The final section of the schedule is called "deposit premium" (sometimes called **18-026** "provisional premium") and it explains the premium the insured is required to pay; when and in relation to which item of each section for which the insured is covered (including third party liability). The premium is normally paid in full at the start of the policy, however, if the project is to go on for several years it may be paid in instalments. If the instalments are paid late then the insurer can increase the premium to compensate for this. In calculating the deposit premium to be paid by the insured, for a single project policy (as opposed to an annual policy) the insurer will take into account information provided by the insured and calculate at a percentage rate as applied to the estimated contract value, which will vary according to each item listed in each section. For an annual policy, however, in relation to building and civil engineering works, the premium will be based on rates that apply to turnover (which is not normally stated in the schedule); that will be set out in attached contracts (and any other information underwriters may use to arrive at their calculation). The insured is required to provide the insurer with the relevant information in accordance with the doctrine of the utmost good faith. In either case it will be possible, depending on the performance of the contract, to adjust the initial sum and the deposit premium by declaring the actual "out-turn value" or turnover. The insurer will either increase or return the premium to the insured (subject to retaining the minimum premium that will have been agreed between the parties) if: (1) one of the parties to the policy decides to cancel or terminate the policy; (2) the policy extends beyond the expected date; (3) there is a material change in the risk; or (4) for some other reason(s) depending on the performance of the contract.

4. THE PUBLIC LIABILITY SECTION OF A CAR POLICY

Public liability. A CAR policy will normally compose of three sections under **18-027** which the insured is usually covered; that is construction all risks and property all risks; consequential loss (delay in completion and business interruption) and third party liability, with additional sections following each section that set out the specific definitions that apply to a particular section and the exclusions and/or extensions for cover regarding each one.

Insuring or "Operative" clause. In a CAR policy, the public liability section **18-028** provides the insured with protection against liabilities incurred to third parties (i.e. the public at large and owners of property [real and personal]) as a result of carrying out the construction works. The core insuring clause that deals with this, which will be set out in the public liability section of a CAR policy, will normally be worded as follows:

> "The Insurers will indemnify the Insured except as hereinafter provided in respect of all sums which the Insured shall become legally or contractually liable to pay consequent upon:
>
> (a) personal Injury suffered by any person
> (b) loss of or damage to property
>
> occurring during the Period of Insurance anywhere within the Territorial Limits in connection with the Project [or the Business] or the execution of the Contract."

The above clause (if not generally provided) may be extended to provide cover **18-029** to the insured against claims made by third parties as a result of suffering personal injury or loss or damage to its property as a result of obstruction, nuisance, etc. This extension of cover is discussed in greater detail below.[8]

18-030 **Personal injury (including death and bodily injury).** The term bodily injury falls under the ambit of the term personal injury. The words "personal injury" in the context of the insuring clause, will be deemed to mean (as defined in the extensions section applicable to third party liability) all of the following:

> "Bodily injury, death, disease, illness, disability, mental injury, shock, false arrest, discrimination, invasion of rights of privacy, detention, false imprisonment, false eviction, malicious prosecution, libel, slander and defamation of character, unintentional breach or infringement or unauthorised use of Intellectual Property Rights and Advertising Injury."

18-031 Further, under the Fatal Accidents Act 1976, dependants of the deceased, if they come within the definition in the 1976 Act, can claim damages against the insured for financial and other dependency. Claims can also be made by the estate of a deceased under the Law Reform (Miscellaneous Provisions) Act 1934. This includes claims such as funeral expenses as well as claims which a deceased could have made had he not died (and which vest in the estate), for example general damages for injuries sustained and pre-death suffering.

18-032 **Loss of or damage to property.** The second aspect of the insuring clause concerns the loss of or damage to third parties' property. In this context, the loss suffered by a third party must occur during the period of insurance within the territorial limit (as defined) as a result of construction works undertaken by the insured, in connection with the insured's business (project or the execution of the contract). Further, the damage or loss to a third party's property would have to be accidental in order to be covered by the public liability section of a CAR policy, as insurers will not indemnify the insured for loss of or damage to property that is foreseeable as being inevitable. If the word accidental (as in the above example in para.18-028) is not used (in the insuring clause) then the policy will normally contain an exclusion clause to this effect, in the third party liability section, which states that insurers are not liable

> "[f]or loss of or damage to property which is foreseeable as being inevitable[9] having regard to the nature of work undertaken or operations bringing it about."

This particular exclusion clause is considered in more detail below.[10]

18-033 The word "damage" is not defined in the policy, and the meaning of it will vary according to the situation concerned. Indeed, in the above situation, the word "damage" is deemed to exclude injuries suffered by persons and to loss of life, but to cover damage done to a third party's property during the course of a construction project. In *Hunter v Canary Wharf Ltd*; sub nom. *Hunter v London Docklands Development Corp*,[11] the residents (not all of whom were householders) brought two actions in private nuisance. In the first of the two actions they argued that there was interference with television reception as a result of the presence of a building. In

---

8 See below, para.18-056.
9 If the loss of or damage to property is foreseeable as inevitable it is not fortuitous.
10 See below, para.18-081.
11 *Hunter v Canary Wharf Ltd*; sub nom. *Hunter v London Docklands Development Corp* [1997] A.C. 655; [1997] 2 W.L.R. 684; [1997] 2 All E.R. 426.

the second action, the claimants argued that their properties had been damaged by excessive dust that had been released into the air, due to road construction work that was taking place nearby. Initially on

"preliminary issues, the judge ruled ... that interference with television reception was capable of constituting an actionable private nuisance but that to claim in private nuisance it was necessary to have a right to exclusive possession of the property."[12]

The plaintiffs in the dust action appealed. The Court of Appeal reversed the judge's decision and held

"that it was established law that an action in private nuisance was brought in respect of acts directed against the plaintiff's enjoyment of his rights over the land, so that, generally, only a person with an interest in the land could sue; and that there was no good reason to depart from the law as established."[13]

In other words, an occupier of a property (not necessarily a householder) did have **18-034** a sufficiently substantial link to allow him to bring a claim in private nuisance. In respect of the question of whether the dust deposits could damage property it was unanimously held that they could and that the plaintiffs could bring an action in negligence. Similarly, in *Blue Circle Industries Plc v Ministry of Defence*,[14] the question of damage to property was considered. In this case, an owner of a large property that adjoined the Atomic Weapons Establishment ("AWE") site argued that the property had been damaged as a result of a storm, which caused a pond on the AWE site to overflow, and radioactive material to escape and contaminate the marshland surrounding the property. At first instance, the judge held in favour of the claimant finding that the property had been damaged as a result of a nuclear occurrence, however the defendant, the Ministry of Defence ("MoD") appealed, contending that no damage to property had occurred as a result of nuclear properties. On appeal it was held that the physical properties of the marshland around the property had changed as a result of the "intermingling of plutonium with the topsoil"[15] and that the land had become "physically damaged"[16] even though the "consequence was economic".[17] In other words there had been damage to the property. To be indemnified under a public liability policy a claimant will usually need to establish the existence of a legal liability to a third party in tort. Such liability will normally be for physical damage or personal injury.[18]

---

12 *Hunter* [1997] A.C. 655; [1997] 2 W.L.R. 684-685; [1997] 2 All E.R. 426.
13 *Hunter* [1997] A.C. 655 at 656; [1997] 2 W.L.R. 684; [1997] 2 All E.R. 426.
14 *Blue Circle Industries Plc v Ministry of Defence* [1999] Ch. 289; [1999] 2 W.L.R. 295; [1998] 3 All E.R. 385.
15 *Blue Circle Industries Plc* [1999] Ch. 289 at 299; [1999] 2 W.L.R. 295; [1998] 3 All E.R. 385.
16 *Blue Circle Industries Plc* [1999] Ch. 289 at 299; [1999] 2 W.L.R. 295; [1998] 3 All E.R. 385 at 300.
17 *Blue Circle Industries Plc* [1999] Ch. 289; [1999] 2 W.L.R. 295; [1998] 3 All E.R. 385 at 386.
18 In *Horbury Building Systems Ltd v Hampden Insurance NV* [2004] EWCA Civ 418 at [13]; [2004] 2 C.L.C. 453 at 460; [2004] B.L.R. 431 at 435 Keene LJ said: "It will at once be observed that the claimant does not seek to identify the basis upon which it would be liable to a third party, whether contractual or tortious, nor even to whom it would be so liable. I am bound to say that, while I appreciate the value to the claimant and perhaps to others of obtaining a decision on the construction of the policy, to seek a declaration in circumstances such as those just described leaves a great deal to be desired from the point of view of the court. To be asked to determine whether liability for certain losses would fall within the terms of the policy without knowing on what legal basis the insured would be liable for those losses is unsatisfactory, both because one is having to proceed to arrive at an interpretation in the abstract and because these present proceedings may be unneces-

18-035 The question of damage to property was also considered in *Mills (John) v Smith (Robert)*.[19] In this case, the claimant, Mills, argued that the foundations of his house had been damaged as a result of an oak tree that was growing in his neighbour's garden some 25 feet away, penetrating the soil, extracting water which in turn led to movement to his house. The insured's (Smith's) policy indemnified him for "damage to property ... caused ... by accident".[20] Smith argued that these words covered him for encroachment of tree roots that stemmed from his garden onto neighbouring land and damaging property on the site as a result of extracting water by "accident". It was held that the insurers were liable to indemnify, and that the settlement damage to Mill's property's foundations was caused by "accident"; the test applied being "whether there had been at any particular moment, or moments, of time some unexpected event or events which led to damage".[21] The reasoning adopted in this case is ambiguous in that the behaviour of the tree would seem to be natural rather than being caused by "accident". CAR insurance policies now rarely use the word "accident" in this context.

18-036 **Property.** The word "property" (which is used in the insuring clause) is normally restricted to mean material; in other words physical property rather than other forms of property such as intellectual property rights or electronic data, which will be excluded.

18-037 The next part of the insuring clause specifies that any personal injury or loss of or damage incurred by a third party must occur during the period of insurance anywhere within the territorial limits in connection with the business or project or the execution of the contract. The territorial limits applicable to the third party liability section of the policy will be set out in the schedule.

18-038 In terms of liability under the third party liability section, insurers will not be liable for a claim exceeding the limit of indemnity set out in the schedule. However, that said, insurers may agree to extend the insuring clause, so as to pay in addition to the limit of indemnity set out in the schedule, the legal costs and expenses of the insured.

18-039 **"Legally liable to pay".** The words "[l]egally liable to pay" indemnify the insured against being liable for negligence, breach of statutory and other torts it may commit during the lifetime of the policy as a result of the agreed works. In *Tesco Stores Ltd*,[22] it was held that in the absence of clear express words in a public liability policy (or a section contained in a CAR policy), the insured is only afforded cover for liability in contract that is co-extensive with duties that arise in tort (and is not afforded cover for liability in contract for pure economic loss).

18-040 In respect of large construction projects an extension may be provided so as to provide cover against claims based on contractual liability[23] or those assumed under agreement between the insured and the insurer, for which the insured otherwise would not have been indemnified. There is nothing to preclude extending a policy

---

sary if the claimant is not liable in law for those losses."

[19] *Mills (John) v Smith (Robert)* [1964] 1 Q.B. 30; [1963] 3 W.L.R. 367; [1963] 2 All E.R. 1078.
[20] *Mills (John)* [1964] 1 Q.B. 30 at 34; [1963] 3 W.L.R. 367; [1963] 2 All E.R. 1078.
[21] *Mills (John)* [1964] 1 Q.B. 30 at 31; [1963] 3 W.L.R. 367 at 368; [1963] 2 All E.R. 1078.
[22] *Tesco Stores Ltd* [2008] EWCA Civ 362; [2008] 1 C.L.C. 727; [2008] Lloyd's Rep. I.R. 636.
[23] *M/S Aswan Engineering Establishment Co v Iron Trades Mutual Insurance Co* [1989] 1 Lloyd's Rep. 289; *Times,* July 28, 1988.

to cover contractual liability including for pure economic loss, provided the extension clause clearly confirms this to be the case. In *Tesco Stores Ltd* Tuckey J said[24]:

"A public liability policy provides cover against liability to the public at large. By contrast private liability arises from contracts entered into between individuals. Public liability in this sense arises in tort; it does not and cannot arise in contract...Of course it is not conclusive: The wording may extend cover to third party claims in contract even for pure economic loss although one would expect it to say so clearly and for such insurance to be described as contract liability, financial or consequential cover."

In *Tesco Stores Ltd*,[25] there was an extension to cover for contractual liability in the following terms:

"Contractual Liability
Other than as may be stated or implied in the Contract, liability assumed by the Insured under contract or agreement and which would not have attached in the absence of such contract or agreement shall be the subject of indemnity under this section only if the conduct and control of any claim so relating is vested in the Insurers and subject to the Exceptions and Extensions of this section."

Tuckey LJ considered the extension concluding that it did not assist *Tesco Stores Ltd*[26]:

"I think the simple answer to this question is that it does not apply because any loss which Chiltern suffer is not in respect of physical impact on its property or property rights. Its loss is only the consequences of such impact on the property and property rights of others. In other words, Chiltern's claim under the contract extension runs into precisely the same difficulties as its claim in tort. Mr Fenwick sought to get around this by suggesting that Tesco had a contractual claim from obstruction, loss of amenity or even nuisance which would not encounter such difficulties. But this reintroduces his argument, which I have already rejected, that the words in class c) should be given a non-technical meaning. If, as I think, the words define the insured's liability in terms of the law of tort the fact that the third party claims in contract can make no difference. So for these reasons I do not think the contractual liability extension assists Tesco ...
    [I]t adds some weight to the conclusion that the insuring clause was intended to cover coextensive contractual liability but goes no further than that. On any view it cannot transform of [sic] this policy into one which covers contractual liability for pure economic loss."

"In respect of ... or consequent upon".   The meaning of the wording "in respect **18-041** of ... or consequent upon" was also considered by the Court of Appeal in *Tesco Stores Ltd*,[27] where, following the case of *Horbury Building Systems Ltd*,[28] it was held that it refers to sums which the insured is legally liable to pay for damage to third party property and not merely "caused by", "consequent upon" or "in connection with" third party property. Accordingly the wording "in respect of" does not provide cover for all the consequences of damage to property; it has a limiting effect on cover and does not merely identify the causal event i.e. damage to property.[29]

---

24 *Tesco Stores Ltd* [2008] EWCA Civ 362 at [14]; [2008] 1 C.L.C. 727 at 733; [2008] Lloyd's Rep. I.R. 636 at 639.
25 *Tesco Stores Ltd* [2008] EWCA Civ 362 at [7]; [2008] 1 C.L.C. 727 at 731; [2008] Lloyd's Rep. I.R. 636 at 638.
26 *Tesco Stores Ltd* [2008] EWCA Civ 362 at [27]–[28]; [2008] 1 C.L.C. 727 at 736; [2008] Lloyd's Rep. I.R. 636 at 641.
27 *Tesco Stores Ltd* [2008] EWCA Civ 362 at [7]; [2008] 1 C.L.C. 727 at 730; [2008] Lloyd's Rep. I.R. 636 at 638.
28 *Horbury Building Systems Ltd* [2004] 2 C.L.C. 453 at 464; [2004] B.L.R. 431 at 438.
29 *Horbury Building Systems Ltd* [2004] 2 C.L.C. 453 at 464; [2004] B.L.R. 431 at 438; *Rodan International Ltd v Commercial Union Assurance Plc* [1999] Lloyd's Rep. I.R. 495; *AS Screenprinting Ltd v British Reserve Insurance Co Ltd* [1996] C.L.C. 1470 at 1474–1475; [1999] Lloyd's Rep.

The meaning of the words "in respect of" was considered in *Rodan International Ltd*,[30] where Hobhouse LJ held that the direct or proximate consequences of damage are "in respect of" damage to property but that secondary, indirect or remoter consequences are not:

> "A products liability policy in which the cover is defined in words such as those used in the present policy is confined to liability for physical consequences caused by the commodity or article supplied. The liability of the assured in damages will have to be expressed in terms of money but that liability must be in respect of the consequences of the physical loss or damage to physical property … Provided that the commodity or article supplied has caused the physical consequence, the compensation payable by the assured to the third party will include, and the liability of the insurer to indemnify the assured will extend to the totality of the loss which the third party is entitled to recover from the assured by way of damages in respect of that physical consequence. Thus if a defective article supplied by the assured causes bodily injury to the third party disabling him or, for example, causes his premises to be destroyed by fire, the third party will be entitled to recover from the assured the full value of what he has lost which will, in the two examples I have given, include compensation for future loss of earnings. They are part of what the third party has lost as a consequence of the physical loss or injury and they are accordingly part of the liability of the assured in respect of that physical consequence."

Rodan International Ltd[31] was a case involving liability for defective soap powder that caused damage to another product. If there had not been an exclusion, the insured supplier would have been entitled to be indemnified in respect of its contractual liability for the diminution in value of the defective powder and for the costs incurred in handling defective powder. It would not have been entitled to an indemnity for other wasted costs or lost profits. *Rodan International Ltd* was followed in *Horbury Building Systems Ltd*,[32] in which the insured was entitled to be indemnified for his liability for a defective cinema ceiling that collapsed and loss of profit, but not for losses arising from the closure of other cinemas as a precaution. Despite the Court of Appeal's consideration of the words "in respect of" in *Tesco Stores Ltd*, there remains some doubt as to their meaning, principally because the Court of Appeal case of *Cementation Piling and Foundations Ltd v Commercial Union Insurance Co Plc*; sub nom. *Cementation Piling and Foundations Ltd v Aegon Insurance Ltd*[33] was not drawn to the court's attention in *Tesco Stores Ltd*. The Court of Appeal in *Cementation Piling and Foundations Ltd* interpreted the words "in respect of" more widely when holding that the insured was entitled to recover the cost of repairing defects because the words "in respect of" in the insuring clause had to be read in the context provided by the defects exclusion clause. The latter clause stated that the costs of rectifying defects in design, etc., were excluded "unless" damage was suffered as a result, and this implied that if such damage did occur, the costs of remedying the defect were also covered.

I.R. 430 at 434 and *James Budgett Sugars Ltd v Norwich Union Insurance Ltd* [2002] EWHC 968 (Comm); [2003] Lloyd's Rep. I.R. 110.

30 *Rodan International Ltd* [1999] Lloyd's Rep. I.R. 495 at 500. Hobhouse LJ said in this case that: "[i]t is not sufficient that it should simply have had some connection with the Occurrence": [1999] Lloyd's Rep. I.R. 495 at 500.

31 *Rodan International Ltd* [1999] Lloyd's Rep. I.R. 495 at 500.

32 *Horbury Building Systems Ltd* [2004] EWCA Civ 418; [2004] 2 C.L.C. 453; [2004] B.L.R. 431.

33 *Cementation Piling and Foundations Ltd v Commercial Union Insurance Co Plc*; sub nom. *Cementation Piling and Foundations Ltd v Aegon Insurance Ltd* [1995] 1 Lloyd's Rep. 97; 74 B.L.R. 98; 47 Con. L.R. 14.

Application to construction projects. One surprising result of the combined ef- **18-042** fect of the *Tesco Stores Ltd* principle and the standard form exclusion arises when dealing with damage to structures that have been handed over at the completion of a project. Once handover has taken place the building is in the possession and control of the employer and not under the contractor's control. There is nothing that the contractor can do at that point to prevent damage to property or bodily injury occurring as a result of the condition of the building. Nevertheless, many construction contracts continue to make the contractor liable to the employer not only for the condition of the building itself but also for losses flowing from that condition. In a normal case this poses few problems for the public liability section of the policy. If the building is defective and causes physical injury to the employer, or even damages other property belonging to the employer, then the contractor will be liable to the employer in tort. He will also have a co-extensive contractual liability. It does not matter which claim is in fact brought by the employer since the public liability section of the policy responds to both claims. However, if one assumes that the building is structurally defective but only damages itself and that the whole building was erected by a single contractor then the building is one structure.[34] A defect in the structural elements of the building is a defect in the whole. The most significant consequence of this is that as soon as the defect in the building is discovered, any further damage caused to the remainder of that building will be pure economic loss and therefore irrecoverable in tort,[35] since no other property will have been damaged. Even if the building suffers severe damage as a result of the defect, therefore, there is normally no claim against the contractor in tort.[36] In this situation the contractor does not face a claim in tort. He will, however, face a large claim under the building contract. The contractor may be surprised to discover that his liability will not be indemnified under the public liability section of the policy since it arises under a claim in contract in respect of pure economic loss and not in tort in respect of property damage. The answer to the contractor's problem may be to try and claim under the other sections of the policy, unless such a claim is excluded or the issue does not come to light until after handover and the expiry of the defects liability period.

Legal costs and expenses. As previously noted, the insuring clause may be **18-043** extended, so that insurers will agree to pay for, in addition to the limit of indemnity stated in the schedule: "[a]ll legal costs and expenses recovered by any claimant from the Insured", other legal costs and fees, for which the insurers have given written consent (which may of course be quite considerable), and in respect of costs incurred by the insured as a result of providing it with legal representation at the Coroner's Court (in England); the Fatal Accident Enquiry (in Scotland) or "in a Court of Summary Jurisdiction in request of proceedings arising out of an alleged breach of statutory duty".

However, in respect of the above extension, if the insurer pays the insured up to **18-044** the limit of indemnity (taking into account the deduction of any damages) or an

---

[34] *Murphy v Brentwood DC* [1991] 1 A.C. 398 at 470; [1990] 3 W.L.R. 414 at 431; [1990] 2 All E.R. 908 at 922.
[35] *Murphy* [1991] 1 A.C. 398 at 478; [1990] 3 W.L.R. 414 at 438–439; [1990] 2 All E.R. 908 at 927, per Lord Bridge.
[36] *Murphy* [1991] 1 A.C. 398 at 469, 479 and 497; [1990] 3 W.L.R. 414 at 430, 439 and 456; [1990] 2 All E.R. 908 at 921, 927 and 941.

amount that has been agreed that can be settled upon between the parties concerned, then the insurer will not be liable further. If however, a claim for legal costs and expenses "[e]xceeds the Limit of Indemnity shown in the Schedule" then the liability of the insurer

> "[i]n respect of additional legal costs and expenses shall be limited in the same proportion that the Limit of Indemnity ... bears to the total claim against the Insured."

This means that the insurer will only pay the insured's legal costs and expenses up to the limit of indemnity set out in the schedule, hence if there is a shortfall then the insured will have to pay the difference. The potential costs liability will always form part of an insurer's assessment of risk and commercial viability before a case goes to trial, not least as the costs will be substantial and can of course, on occasions, exceed the damages.

18-045 **Territorial limits.** The territorial limits will be defined in the schedule for each section of the policy (and as such may vary according to each section concerned). The cover provided may be restricted according to a specific geographical area or be worldwide. The third party liability section will normally state that the insurer will indemnify the insured if any third party person suffers personal injury, or loss of or damage to property, if it occurs anywhere within the territorial limit (as defined in the schedule) in connection with the business (as in an annual policy) or project if it concerns a project policy or in the execution of the contract. The insurer will not be liable for overseas losses, for instance, if a business uses manufacturers abroad and incurs a loss. In order to cover itself for this eventuality, the insured must seek an extension for coverage abroad. The territorial limits set out in the third party section will not prevent a claim being made by a third party in a jurisdiction outside for the area in which cover is provided.

18-046 **Damages.** The public liability section will normally state whether a third party claimant will receive damages or compensation, or may refer to the word "damages" in the context of the limit of indemnity that insurers will pay up to (after the deduction of sum or sums that may be paid as damages are taken into account) in respect of the legal costs and expenses that may be incurred by the insured. The only difference between the terms "compensation" and "damages", which can usually be used interchangeably, is that compensation does not include "punitive damages" which are levied against the defendant so as to punish it for wronging the claimant. Indeed, in contrast to compensatory damages, the aim of punitive damages is not as an award of compensation, but to deter or prevent the defendant from doing something similar in the future. In order to avoid any confusion, the exclusions applicable to the third party liability section may contain a clause which excludes punitive damages.

18-047 In terms of the common structure of a CAR policy, exclusions applicable to the third party liability section of a CAR policy will normally be listed immediately after it, with the commonly encountered extensions to cover applicable to it being listed thereafter, followed by the general exclusions and general memoranda applicable to all sections of the policy.

5. EXTENSIONS TO COVER APPLICABLE TO PUBLIC LIABILITY

Extensions to cover applicable to third party liability. A CAR policy will often **18-048** have a section that lists a number of extensions that are applicable specifically to the third party liability section, thus extending the coverage offered by the insurer beyond that set out in the core insuring clause. The extensions will (as per the insuring clause) be subject to the same terms, conditions and exclusions applicable to the third party liability section. Any money that is paid by the insurer as a result of any one of the extensions of cover will reduce the limit of indemnity unless the contrary is stated.

"This Section of the Policy extends to indemnify"—"The Company will indemnify". In *M J Gleeson Group Plc v AXA Corporate Solutions Assurance* **18-049** *S.A.*,[37] the court had to consider whether an extension to a public liability policy was self-standing in that it did not require the occurrence of physical damage within the meaning of the insuring clause or whether the extension, which was unusual in that it permitted recovery in respect of defective workmanship by sub-contractors, also required physical damage. In *M J Gleeson*, the court considered there was a distinction to be made between the expressions: "[t]his Section of the Policy extends to indemnify" and "[t]he Company will indemnify"; the former expression indicates that the extension was not intended to be a self-standing insuring clause but was to be governed by the insuring clause and the requirement for physical damage, whereas the latter expression indicates that the extension was intended to be self-standing.

Cross liability clause. If a claim is made by a third party arising out of personal **18-050** injury or of loss or damage to its property, the cross liability extension clause (which will be listed as one of the extensions to the third party liability section) will typically state that if there is more than one party that is insured, then the insurer will indemnify "[e]ach of the parties comprising the Insured who will be considered as a separate and distinct party" to the extent that

> "[t]he Insured shall be considered as applying to each party in the same manner as if a separate Policy had been issued to each of the said parties."

Further, insurers will

> "[a]gree to waive all rights of subrogation or action which they may have or acquire against any of the aforesaid parties [the Insured's] arising out of any Occurrence in respect of which any claim is made ... provided nevertheless that nothing in [the] Memorandum shall be deemed to increase the Limit of Indemnity in respect of any one Occurrence or series of Occurrences as stated in the Schedule."

Therefore, the above extension clause allows insurers to indemnify each insured **18-051** party against a third party claim, as if a separate policy had been issued to each party; but they will only do so to the extent that the total liability of the insurer does not exceed the defined limit of indemnity as a result of one occurrence or series of occurrences. One of the effects of the clause is that it extends coverage between insureds under the policy; for example, if one insured suffers personal injury or loss of or damage to property because of another insured, then the insurer will indemnify

---

[37] *M J Gleeson Group Plc* [2013] Lloyd's Rep I.R. 677 (TCC).

the insured against liability for any costs and damages incurred. However, because the insurer will have waived all rights of subrogation, they will then be prevented from bringing an action against the indemnified insured in the name of the other insured in order to recover their initial outlay (which would in any event appear to be effectively a claim by the insurer against itself).

18-052 Territorial limits.   The term "territorial limits" will normally be referred to in the insuring clause or the third party liability section. An extension to the territorial limits of the third party liability section may be found in the extensions section if agreed with the insured. The extension may allow the insured (and certain persons, such as directors, partners or employees of the insured if identified) to be covered beyond the defined territorial limits "[i]n respect of business visits inspections, training or similar activities which do not involve manual work anywhere in the World", made by any of them in connection with the business/project. Accordingly if applicable, the insured and other persons will be insured in respect of any legal liability that may arise from making a business trip in connection with the business/project anywhere in the world. However, that said, the extension of cover may be restricted, so that the insured and named persons are not indemnified in respect of any legal liability that arises in respect of land or buildings that may be owned or occupied by them, or if legal liability arises under any other insurance policy.

18-053 Personal injury.   The words "personal injury" will be referred to in the insuring clause contained in the third party liability section. An extension of cover will normally be provided to the third party section, in order to explain what the words "personal injury" actually include. The extension may define the words personal injury to include:

> "Bodily injury, death, disease, illness, disability, mental injury, mental anguish, shock, false, arrest, discrimination, invasion of rights of privacy, detention, false imprisonment, false eviction, malicious prosecution, libel, slander and defamation of character, unintentional breach or infringement or unauthorised use of Intellectual Property Rights and Advertising Injury."

Some of the terms listed in the above extract will be easier to interpret than others in the context of a construction enterprise. For instance the term death is easier to understand in a construction case, than disease and illness the boundaries of which may be more problematic.

18-054 Advertising injury.   The purpose of the advertising injury clause is to indemnify the insured from third party claims brought against it arising out of "[a]dvertising or broadcasting or publishing undertaken [by it] in connection with the Project" or the business, due to:

> "(a) written or spoken material made public which belittles the products or services of others
> (b) written or spoken material made public which violates an individual's right to privacy
> (c) unauthorised taking of advertising ideas or style of business
> (d) negligent misstatement
> (e) errors or omissions arising out of publishing or exhibiting of advertising materials."

The advertising injury extension clause to the third party liability section of a CAR policy has yet to be litigated to a reported judgment between parties involved in construction.

Intellectual property rights.   An extension is normally provided to the third party   **18-055**
liability section so as to provide the insured with cover against claims from third
parties in the event that intellectual property rights that they acquired before or during the course of construction works are affected. The intellectual property rights
should be clearly identified. A typical extension will refer to intellectual property
rights as including all of the following:

> "Confidential information, trade secrets, trademarks (including trademarks protected by common law
> rights or passing off), patent rights, copyrights, design rights (registered or unregistered) moral rights,
> database rights, copyright title or slogan and/or as defined in the Construction Contract."

The above extension interconnects with the construction contract, in that if intellectual property rights are defined, then these may be incorporated into the policy
and as such will need to be taken into consideration by all those involved with the
implementation of the policy.

Obstruction, nuisance, etc.   As previously noted above, the cover provided by   **18-056**
the third party liability section will be (if not generally provided) extended in order
to indemnify the insured against claims made by third parties as a result of suffering personal injury or incurring loss or damage to its property due, for example, to

> "[o]bstruction, loss of amenities, trespass nuisance or interference with any right of way light air or
> water or any like cause which results in the interference with any property of third parties or their
> employment or use or the value thereof other than that which is reasonably foreseeable as being
> inevitable having regard to the nature of work undertaken."

The important wording is the proviso "other than that which is reasonably foreseeable as being inevitable" as it makes clear that, objectively considered, the loss or
damage must be accidental.

Site visitors.   An extension of cover will normally be provided to the third party   **18-057**
liability section so as to indemnify the insured against legal liability incurred as a
result of visitors attending the site as part of the contract or to do works or

> "[o]ther premises of the Insured in connection with ground breaking, topping out or other similar
> ceremonies and other invited visitors not directly involved in the execution or the performance of
> the contracts or works"

in connection with the insured's business or project. In practical terms, the extension is important because the insured could face claims from site visitors or, if visit-
ing the premises of the insured, by other visitors not directly involved in implementing the contract or works. which gives significant potential for claims.

Joint Contracts Tribunal (JCT) Standard Form of Building Contract (SBC)
2011 clause 6.5 coverage (derived from JCT 1980 clause 21.2.1).   Clause 6.5.1   **18-058**
of the SBC 2011[38] replaced SBC 2005[39] cl.6.5.1 and its predecessor cl.21.2.1 of the
1988 JCT,[40] which are similar in terms. Clause 6.5.1 is applicable if a JCT SBC
agreed between the employer and the contractor specifies that the contractor must

---

[38]   JCT Contracts, *SBC/Q 2011 JCT Standard Form of Building Contract With Quantities 2011* (London:
Sweet & Maxwell, 2011), pp.68–69.
[39]   Joint Contracts Tribunal, *SBC/Q Standard Building Contract With Quantities (2005 Edition)*
(London: Sweet & Maxwell, 2005).
[40]   Joint Contracts Tribunal, *JCT Standard Form of Building Contract 1998 Edition Private with Quantities* (London: RIBA, 1999).

take out a joint names insurance policy (in the names of the contractor and employer)[41] so as to indemnify the employer against

> "any expense, liability, loss, claim or proceedings which the Employer may incur or sustain [due to a third party] by reason of injury or damage to any property [but not including the Contract Works or the site materials] caused by collapse, subsidence, heave, vibration, weakening or removal of support or lowering of ground water arising out of or in the course of or by reason of the carrying out of the Works."[42]

18-059   The perils listed in the clause above, such as collapse, subsidence, heave etc. are discussed further in detail below. However, for the clause to take effect, it is important to note that the contract must also state the minimum amount of indemnity[43] for any one occurrence or series of occurrences arising out of one event, which (if stated) then provides the architect/contract administrator with the power to instruct[44] the contractor to take out a joint names policy,[45] so as to cover the employer's liability. If the architect/contract administrator decides to instruct the contractor to take out a joint names policy, then the request will usually be made by him before the works commence, so as not to involve or make the employer liable in any way.

18-060   The joint names policy must be provided by insurers "approved by the Employer"[46] and the contractor must send the "Architect/Contract Administrator for deposit with the Employer the policy or policies and related premium receipts."[47] The amount spent by the contractor to "take out and maintain the insurance"[48] policy will be added to the contract sum.[49] Under the 1998 JCT, if the contractor did not buy and maintain the insurance policy required then the employer had the opportunity to insure against any risk "in respect of ... the default"[50] that occurred (by taking out an initial policy against the risk rather than a joint names liability policy). This option is however, no longer available in SBC 2011.

18-061   JCT cl.6.5.1 (which covers perils such as collapse, subsidence, heave etc.) to SBC 2011 is subject to a number of perils/exceptions (cll.6.5.1.1—6.5.1.9), which the contractor need not insure against for injury or damage caused to property belonging to third party persons. In brief the exceptions include the following:

---

41   In JCT Contracts, *JCT Standard Form of Building Contract With Quantities 2011* (2011) a joint names policy is defined as: "[a] policy of insurance which includes the Employer and Contractor as composite insured under which the insurers have no right of recourse against any person having an interest in the policy as an insured, or, pursuant to clause 6.9, recognised as an insured thereunder", cl.6.8.

42   SBC 2011 cl.6.5.1; SBC 2005 cl.6.5.1; JCT 1988 cl.21.2.1 "Subsidence" means sinking or movement in the vertical direction as opposed to "settlement" which is movement in a lateral direction. "Collapse" means a falling (or shrinking together) or breaking down or giving way through external pressure or loss of support, but not intentional demolition. "Landslip" has been defined as "[a] rapid downward movement under the influence of gravity of a mass of rock or earth on a slope": *Oddy v Phoenix Assurance Co* [1966] 1 Lloyd's Rep. 134 at 139, per Veale J.

43   SBC 2011 cl.6.5.1; SBC 2005 cl.6.5.1; JCT 1988 cl.21.2.1.

44   SBC 2011 cl.6.5.1; SBC 2005 cl.6.5.1; JCT 1988 cl.21.2.1. Under JCT 1980 the architect does not have the power to give this instruction.

45   SBC 2011 cl.6.5.1; SBC 2005 cl.6.5.1; JCT 1988 cl.21.2.1. Up until 1996 the contractor had to take out and maintain the insurance policy.

46   SBC 2011 cl.6.5.2; SBC 2005 cl.6.5.2; JCT 1988 cl.21.2.2. Under the JCT 1980 the architect had to approve the insurer on behalf of the employer.

47   SBC 2011 cl.6.5.2; SBC 2005 cl.6.5.2; JCT 1988 cl.21.2.2.

48   SBC 2011 cl.6.5.3; SBC 2005 cl.6.5.3; JCT 1988 cl.21.2.3.

49   SBC 2011 cl.6.5.3; SBC 2005 cl.6.5.3; JCT 1988 cl.21.2.3.

50   JCT 1998 cl.21.2.4.

"6.5.1.1. for which the Contractor is liable under clause 6.2[51]; or

6.5.1.2. which is attributable to errors or omissions in the designing of the Works[52]; or

6.5.1.3. which can reasonably be foreseen to be inevitable having regard to the nature of the work to be executed and the manner of its execution[53]; or

6.5.1.4. (if Insurance Option C applies) which it is the responsibility of the Employer to insure under paragraph C.1 of Schedule 3[54]; or

6.5.1.5. to the Works and Site materials except where the Practical Completion Certificate has been issued or in so far as any Section is the subject of a Section Completion Certificate[55]; or...."

The "insured perils" (such as collapse, subsidence and heave etc.) listed in **18-062** cl.6.5.1 are also subject to the following other risks:

"6.5.1.6. which arises from any consequence of war, invasion, act of foreign enemy, hostilities (whether war is declared or not), civil war, rebellion or revolution, insurrection or military or usurped power[56]; or

6.5.1.7. which is directly or indirectly caused by or contributed to by or arises from the Excepted Risks[57]; or

6.5.1.8. which is directly or indirectly caused by or arises out of pollution or contamination of buildings or other structures or of water or land or the atmosphere happening during the period of insurance, save that this exception shall not apply in respect of pollution or contamination caused by a sudden identifiable, unintended and unexpected incident which takes place in its entirety at a specific moment in time and place during the period of insurance (all pollution or contamination which arises out of one incident being considered for the purpose of this insurance to have occurred at the time such incident takes place)[58]; or

6.5.1.9. which results in any costs or expenses being incurred by the Employer or in any other sums being payable by the Employer in respect of damages for breach of contract, except to the extent that such costs or expenses or damages would have attached in the absence of any contract."[59]

The contractor need not take out insurance for any losses incurred by an **18-063** employer, in relation to the "insured perils" (such as collapse, subsidence, heave etc.) due to war risks, the excepted risks, pollution or contamination or costs or expenses incurred or other sums payable by an employer, which would not have been incurred if it were not contractually liable. There now follows a consideration of some of the perils/exceptions listed above. Clause 6.5.1.1 to SBC 2011 confirms that if the contractor is liable under cl.6.2 for injury or loss of or damage caused to a third party then the contractor need not take out insurance against this. The next provision, cl.6.5.1.2 states that if an error or omission in a design produced by an architect causes personal injury or loss of or damage to a third party, then the architect or his insurer will pay the claim, and so the contractor need not insure against this risk. The next exception, cl.6.5.1.3 confirms that anything that can reasonably be foreseeable to be inevitable having regard to the nature of the work

---

[51] SBC 2005 cl.6.5.1.1; JCT 1988 cl.21.2.1.1.
[52] SBC 2005 cl.6.5.1.2; JCT 1988 cl.21.2.1.2.
[53] SBC 2005 cl.6.5.1.3; JCT 1988 cl.21.2.1.3.
[54] SBC 2005 cl.6.5.1.4; JCT 1988 cl.21.2.1.4.
[55] SBC 2005 cl.6.5.1.5; JCT 1988 cl.21.2.1.5.
[56] SBC 2005 cl.6.5.1.6; JCT 1988 cl.21.2.1.6.
[57] SBC 2005 cl.6.5.1.7; JCT 1988 cl.21.2.1.7.
[58] SBC 2005 cl.6.5.1.8; JCT 1988 cl.21.2.1.8.
[59] SBC 2005 cl.6.5.1.9; JCT 1988 cl.21.2.1.9.

cannot be insured against. In relation to this clause however, there clearly may be situations which could not have been foreseen; that leaves the employer exposed to claims for which no insurance cover exists. The next clause, cl.6.5.1.4 confirms that if an employer is responsible for taking out joint names insurance for specified perils against existing structures and contents, then the contractor need not insure against this risk as this is the employer's responsibility.

18-064 The purpose of cl.6.5 is thus to provide the employer with cover against claims arising in nuisance or specifically strict liability claims (e.g. *Rylands v Fletcher*).[60] However, it is difficult to see exactly what the clause covers in practice, after the risks identified by the exceptions are taken into consideration. That said, however, cl.6.5 gives an employer the opportunity to request that a contractor provide an indemnity for it in respect of a situation where neither the employer nor the contractor is liable for personal injury or damage to property caused to a third party because of nuisance or the rule under *Rylands* (i.e. strict liability).[61] The origins of cl.6.5 to SBC 2011 can be found in the case of *Gold v Patman & Fotheringham*.[62]

18-065 The implementation of cl.6.5 SBC 2011 (and its predecessors) regarding what the contractor's indemnity extends to on behalf of the employer in respect of third party claims concerning the insured perils (i.e. collapse, subsidence) is complicated in that the case law touches upon some conceptually difficult terrain. It is important to note that, when seeking to interpret the meaning of the insured perils, the case law that concerns the original wording of the 1963 and the 1980 JCT clauses is not applicable to versions of these clauses that came into operation post 1 January 1987; and as such the earlier decisions must (it is contended) be viewed with some caution. Heave was added to the JCT cl.21.2.1 as an insured peril in 1986.[63]

18-066 In terms of the practicalities of arranging the cover, the actual cover provided by the contractor on behalf of the employer may be arranged by either party; but it is likely to be undertaken by the party that has the strongest insurance bargaining power. The cover under cl.6.5 may be set out in a separate insurance policy for the contract period or by extending an annual insurance policy, however this would only apply to the contracts attached to it, and only up until the point when practical completion is granted by the architect/contract administrator.

---

[60] *Rylands v Fletcher* (1868) L.R. 3 H.L. 330; 33 JP 70; 37 LJ Ex 161. Following on from this, in *Cambridge Water Co Ltd v Eastern Counties Leather Plc; Cambridge Water Co Ltd v Hutchings & Harding Ltd* [1994] 2 A.C. 264; [1994] 2 W.L.R. 53 at 54; 1 All E.R. 53 it was held that "[f]oreseeability of harm of the relevant type by the defendants was a prerequisite of the recovery of damages both in nuisance and under the rule in *Rylands v. Fletcher*". The principle of *Rylands* was applied in *Ellison v Ministry of Defence* [1996] 81 B.L.R. 101 at 107, which concluded that "...the defendants escaped liability for the damage which was caused by their building works primarily because that damage was found by the judge not to be foreseeable." Further, *Gore v Stannard (t/a Wyvern Tyres)* [2013] W.L.R. 623 supports the view that cases of fire damage are likely to be very difficult to bring within the rule because the exceptionally dangerous "thing" brought onto the land (which escapes onto the property of another) must be the fire rather than something which starts or increases the fire (in this case tyres).

[61] *Rylands* (1868) L.R. 3 H.L. 330; 33 JP 70; 37 LJ Ex 161.

[62] *Gold v Patman & Fotheringham* [1958] 1 W.L.R. 697; [1958] 2 All E.R. 497; [1958] 1 Lloyd's Rep. 587.

[63] See *Kelly v Norwich Union Fire Insurance Ltd* [1990] 1 W.L.R. 139; [1989] 2 All E.R. 888; [1989] 2 Lloyd's Rep. 333. Heave is distinguishable from subsidence in that the former is concerned with "bulging".

Criminal proceedings brought under the Health and Safety at Work Act 1974/ Consumer Protection Act 1987/ Food Safety Act 1990 (prosecution and defence costs). The purpose of this extension is to indemnify the insured: **18-067**

"And if the Insured so requests any director, officer or employee of the Insured in respect of legal costs and expenses incurred with the Insurers written consent in the defence of any criminal proceedings brought for a breach of:

a) the Health and Safety at Work etc. Act 1974 or any similar UK Health & Safety legislation
b) the Consumer Protection Act 1987 or
c) the Food Safety Act 1990 "Committed or alleged to have been committed during the Period of Insurance in the course of or in connection with the Project or the business or "The Contract(s)". The insurance will normally cover:

'Such costs and expenses incurred in an appeal against conviction or any improvement or prohibition notice or prosecution costs awarded against the Insured arising from or in connection with the said proceedings.'"

Apart from paying for defence costs against prosecution, insurers may therefore **18-068** also agree to pay the prosecution costs awarded against the insured, arising or in connection with the business/project concerned. Insurers will not however indemnify the insured regarding proceedings if the insured or those acting on the insured's behalf deliberately act or omit to do something,

"[t]he result thereof could reasonably have been expected by the Insured having regard to the nature and circumstances of such act or omission."

Moreover, insurers will not extend the cover if the insured or those acting on its behalf are covered by another insurance policy or pay for any fines or penalties that are imposed, which will be expressly excluded.

Data Protection Act 1984. The public liability section may contain an exten- **18-069** sion that indemnifies the insured (and at the request of the insured, any director, officer or employee of the insured):

"Against all sums which the Insured becomes legally liable to pay in respect of compensation for damage or distress under Sections 22 and 23 of the Data Protection Act 1984 and Section 13 of the Data Protection Act 1998 for the failure to comply with any requirement of the Act including defence costs and expenses in relation to a claim made by any person."

For example, the insured could be found liable as a result of misuse of informa- **18-070** tion retained about individuals on computer systems. The cover provided for an insured is normally subject to the following exclusions:

"(i) [T]he payment of fines or penalties
(ii) the cost of amending any processing or personal data including replacing, reinstating rectifying, blocking or erasing any personal data
(iii) liability caused by or arising from a deliberate or intentional act by or omission of the Insured or any other party entitled to an indemnity by this insurance the effect of which will knowingly result in liability under the Data Protection Act 1984
(iv) claims which arrive out of circumstances notified to previous insurers or are known to the Insured at inception of this insurance."

Defective Premises Act 1972. An extension will normally be provided in order **18-071** to indemnify the insured against liability arising under s.3 to the Defective Premises Act 1972 in respect of third party personal injury or loss of or damage to property following the disposal of property previously owned by the insured. Insurers will however be excluded from the costs of having to remedy any defect or alleged defect found in such premises and any that are covered by any other insurance policy.

18-072 **Motor contingent liability.**   Even though an exclusion clause to third party liability in respect of mechanically propelled vehicles exists, an extension of cover to third party liability may be provided by an insurer for:

> "Personal Injury or loss of or damage to property arising out of the use of any motor vehicle:
>
> (a) not owned or leased by the Insured being used in connection with the Project [or business];
> (b) owned or leased by the Insured being used by any person in circumstances unauthorised by the Insured."

The above cover will however be subject to the following exclusions:

> "(a) if, loss or damage occurs to any such vehicle;
> (b) if, the vehicle is driven by the insured or someone else (whom the insured does not know holds a licence) not unless the person concerned has held and is not disqualified and will be able to hold or obtain a licence
> (c) if the insured is entitled to be indemnified under any other insurance policy ... Except in respect of any amounts in excess of the limits applying under such insurance."

If any of the above exclusions apply, then the insured will not be covered.

18-073   The purpose of the motor contingent liability extension is to cover the insured if its employees drive their own motor vehicles negligently, in connection with the business or project and cause personal injury or loss of or damage to property belonging to a third party as the insured may be vicariously liable. Indeed, whilst employees will be insured by their own motor vehicle policy, their policy will not indemnify the insured against vicarious liability (as their employer), and so the extension of cover deals with this particular situation. If, however, an employee's motor vehicle policy does cover third party liability then the extension of cover is unlikely to answer. It covers the situation where the employee is not insured or there are coverage issues relating to the employee's motor policy when the employee causes personal injury or loss of or damage to property belonging to a third party.

18-074 **United States and Canada jurisdiction.**   If the territorial limits (as defined in the schedule) regarding the third party liability section of the policy do not indemnify the insured against legal proceedings instituted in the United States and Canada, then an extension will normally be included in the extensions to cover section regarding third party liability. The extension will in essence seek to do the following: first, to confirm that the provision of the policy does not cover the insured for any liability incurred for punitive and exemplary damages or for that caused by industries, seepage, pollution and contamination that results in:

> "(i)   [I]njury (including death or illness) to any person or loss of or damage to or loss of use of property directly or indirectly caused by seepage, pollution or contamination;
> (ii)   the cost of removing, nullifying or cleaning-up seeping, polluting or contaminating substances;
> (iii)   fines, penalties, punitive or exemplary damages."

18-075   Secondly, it will confirm that if any proceedings are started within the United

States or Canada or any territories falling within either of these jurisdictions and a dispute emerges over the interpretation of any of the "[t]erms, conditions, limitations and/or exclusions contained…" then it will (as the parties will have agreed) be subject to the law of England and Wales. Thirdly, the provision will confirm that the insurer will pay for: (i) legal costs and expenses recoverable by any claimant from the insured; (ii) costs and expenses incurred in the defence of any claim for the insured, both subject to the limits of indemnity stated in the schedule and (iii) fees for legal representation provided for the insured at a

> "Coroner's Court, Fatal Accident Enquiry or in a Court of Summary Jurisdiction in respect of proceedings arising out of an alleged breach of statutory duty subject to the Limits of Indemnity"

that were agreed between the parties when the insurance policy was taken out.

6. EXCLUSIONS TO PUBLIC LIABILITY

Exclusions to third party liability.   There are a number of exclusions that will **18-076** specifically apply to the third party liability section of the CAR policy only. The exclusions to the third party liability section are included in this section because they will either concern risks that will either be covered by other policies, are unknown, or could potentially be catastrophic and will thus be uninsurable. As is explained above, a CAR policy will commonly insure not only the works being performed by the contractor but will also provide all the named parties with public liability cover in a separate section. That section will usually contain several standard exclusion clauses that are common to liability policies generally. Those clauses are considered individually below.

In order properly to apply the standard form public liability exclusions it is neces- **18-077** sary to consider the purpose of public liability in the context of construction works. A public liability policy is designed to indemnify the contractor for damage he has caused to third parties and their property. This is particularly significant for construction as it is not uncommon for construction accidents to result in damage to property other than the works themselves. The contractor wishes to re-allocate this risk to the insurer and so he purchases the coverage recorded in the public liability section of a CAR policy.[64]

The public liability section is not designed to indemnify the contractor for the **18-078** quality of the works, or to provide discounted insurance for activities that are covered by other properly priced products available on the market. The premiums paid by the contractor have not usually been designed to encompass these additional risks. Should the contractor want those risks to be covered he should purchase further cover from the insurer.

The key feature common to each of the standard public liability exclusions **18-079** considered below is that they prevent the risk being assumed by the insurer moving beyond that which would ordinarily be encompassed in a public liability policy. For example, they prevent the contractor claiming that the insurer is liable for the quality of work he is carrying out, or "contracting in" risks that would not otherwise be covered.

---

[64] For an illuminating discussion of the allocation of risk see J. Mustachio, "Manufacturers' and Contractors' Liability Insurance Policy: The Care, Custody, or Control Exclusion Clause" (1968) 6 Hous. L. Rev. 359.

18-080 **Liability, death, illness, disease or bodily injury sustained by any person under a contract of employment or apprenticeship with the insured directly.** The indemnity provided to the insured regarding third party liability will exclude:

> "Liability, death, illness, disease or bodily injury sustained by any person under a contract of employment or apprenticeship with the Insured directly arising out of or in the course of employment of such person in the service of the Insured."

The above exclusion is provided because any injury caused to an employee of the insured during the course of employment should be covered by an employer's liability insurance policy. The exclusion does not however extend to:

> "Any liability which may attach to any Insured under the Policy in respect of Personal Injury suffered by a person employed by any other Insured."

18-081 **Liability for loss of or damage to property which is foreseeable.** The insured will not be covered for loss of or damage to property belonging to a third party which is "[f]oreseeable as being inevitable" regarding the construction works or operations that are undertaken in order to implement the employer's vision. Plainly if damage is foreseeable as being "inevitable", then when damage occurs it will not be accidental or fortuitous and will not be covered.

18-082 **Liability resulting from, attributable to or caused by the ownership of possession of or the use by or on behalf of the insured of any aircraft or the navigation of any waterborne vessel or craft.** An exclusion will normally be contained in the exclusions to the third party liability section, which confirms that there will be no cover for injury or loss or damage occurring to property as a result of the insured or someone on its behalf using, owning or possessing "[a]ny aircraft or the navigation of any waterborne vessel or craft, [as well as a hovercraft]". The exclusion does not however apply to smaller vessels such as "[w]ork boats, safety boats or non-power driven vessels or craft not exceeding 12 metres in length".

18-083 **Mechanically propelled vehicles and excesses above level of insurance excluded.** The insured will not be indemnified against liability to a third party for personal injury or loss or damage to property arising from the use by the insured or anyone on its behalf of mechanically propelled vehicles that are compulsorily insured under the relevant legislation. However, the exclusion will not apply to "[v]ehicles ... being used as a tool of trade or whilst on the Site". Thus, if for example, a tradesperson drives a vehicle onto the insured's site and either loads or unloads goods, then the insured will be indemnified against any injury or loss or damage to property that occurs to a third party. In addition to this, via this exclusion clause, there will be no cover for any liability above the limit of indemnity in a specific motor policy insurance policy or the respective motor vehicle legislation. The exclusion in respect of compulsorily insured motor vehicles will not however prevent the insured from being indemnified against:

> "Legal liability for damage caused by mechanically propelled vehicles to the surface of roads, bridges or viaducts or to anything beneath them caused by the weight or vibration of such vehicles or their loads or by vibration from such vehicles to adjacent building or property."

18-084 **Liability in respect of pre-determined penalties or liquidated damages.** The insured will be indemnified from having to pay a third party damages if found liable for causing personal injury or loss or damage to property incurred by a third

[530]

party. However, an exclusion clause to the third party liability section usually confirms that the insured will be excluded from being liable for having to pay a third party in respect of pre-determined penalties or liquidated damages incurred as a result of breach of contract, in respect of any contract that has been entered into by the parties in connection with the project or business "[e]xcept to the extent that liability would have attached even in the absence of such contractual penalties or liquidated damages". The exclusion is logical as an insurer will only be able to assess the risk of the insured's liability for damages based upon known legal principles, but not where the amount of any loss has by agreement been pre-determined between the parties to the construction contract. The same reasoning applies in respect of penalties, principally because they are punitive and are not compensatory. Confusion can occur where the exclusion includes wording such as

"the Insurer shall nevertheless indemnify the Insured for their liability under such clauses to the extent that the Insured would have been liable for general damages if such clauses had not been agreed to."

The word "general" is sometimes attributed to death or personal injury only, the suggestion being that all other damages are excluded. It is suggested that the more natural interpretation is that the word "general" in this context is a counterpoint to the use of the word "liquidated" before damages.

Fines incurred by the insured.   An exclusion will also be contained to the public **18-085** liability section, which states that the insurer will not indemnify the insured for fines the insured is ordered to pay as part of any criminal proceedings or indeed any aggravated, punitive or exemplary damages it is required to pay, as a result of a third party suffering injury or incurring loss of or damage to property. This is because it reflects the fact that the insured is being punished, as opposed to compensating the third party who will have suffered injury or loss or damage to property. Arguably any order to pay prosecution costs is part of the financial penalty imposed in criminal proceedings (against which a party cannot insure), although some insurance policies provide cover for these prosecution costs.

Loss of or damage to property belonging to or in the care custody or control of the insured or leased let rented or loaned to the insured.   An exclusion **18-086** clause to third party liability will preclude cover for the loss of or damage to property belonging to the insured (whether it is in the "[c]are custody or control of the Insured or leased let rented or loaned to the Insured").

The exclusion clause will not however, exclude: **18-087**

"(a)   Premises or contents thereof or any other property of whatsoever nature or description at or on which the Insured is undertaking work or utilising or occupying in connection with the Project [or business];

(b)   property not being hired leased rented by or loaned to the Insured which is on the Site of the Contract or the Project [or business] and which does not form part of the Insured's permanent Works or Temporary Works;

(c)   those premises (or fixtures or fittings thereof) leased or rented to the Insured. Provided always that this shall not apply to any physical loss or damage caused by Fire or any other Peril against which the Lease or Tenancy Agreement stipulates that insurance shall be effected by the Insured;

(d)   the property of employees or visitors or customers including vehicles and/or their contents or property deposited in any cloakroom."

Property in the "custody or control" of the contractor.   It has been pointed out **18-088** that in the United States at one time "every insurance policy which has an insuring liability for property damage contains some form of an exclusion ... commonly known as the 'care, custody, or control' exclusion."[65]

Such clauses are also commonplace in the United Kingdom and international markets[66] particularly in respect of construction works, as control over property is more naturally to be insured under the insurance of the construction works. Given the widespread use of such exclusions it is perhaps surprising that they have received comparatively little attention in English reported decisions. This may indicate that the clause is well understood and easily applied. However, the rare decisions where care, custody or control clauses have been in issue are not easy to follow and would suggest that this is not necessarily the case. Care, custody or control exclusions have been dealt with extensively in various Commonwealth jurisdictions as well as receiving detailed attention in the United States.

18-089 Sample clauses. As is explained above, the usual wording of this exclusion contains one or more of the terms "custody", "care", or "control". Not every clause has every one of these qualifying words. Each policy must be construed on its own terms and with regard to its own language. However, the particular combination of those words does not seem to have affected the application of the exclusion in many of the decided cases. It is safe, therefore, to analyse the "custody, care or control" clause as a single object subject to the *caveat* that in any particular case its meaning will necessarily depend upon the wording of the particular policy in issue. For ease of reference, the versions of the exclusion that are referred to in the leading cases discussed below are:

a. "damage to property held in trust by or in the custody or control of the Insured or any member of his family or servants"[67];

b. "loss or damage, while in Supplier's custody and care"[68];

c. "damage to property belonging to or held in trust by or in the custody or control of the Insured or any person indemnified by this Section"[69]; and

d. "[property] in the care custody or control of the Insured."[70]

18-090 Purpose of clause. The purpose underpinning the exclusion has been explained in several of the overseas judgments considering the clause. The leading expositions of its purpose and rationale are set out in the Australian case of *Botany Fork*

---

[65] F.D. Cooke, "Care, Custody or Control Exclusions" (1959) Ins. L. J. 7.

[66] "The Insurer shall not be liable for any claim in respect of loss or damage to Material Property belonging to hired by or in the custody or control of the Insured or an Employee other than:

buildings, constructions, premises or places occupied by the Insured or an Employee for the purpose of the Project including the contents or other Material Property in, on or about the buildings, constructions, premises, sites or places whether or not such Material Property is being worked upon.
Any premises leased, hired or rented to the Insured provided that the Insurers shall not be liable for any liability which attaches to the Insured by reason of an express term of any contract unless such liability would have attached to the insured notwithstanding the existence of such term."

[67] *Oei v Foster (formerly Crawford) and Eagle Star Insurance Co Ltd* [1982] 2 Lloyd's Rep. 170.

[68] *Acergy Shipping Ltd v Societe Bretonne de Reparation Navale SAS (The Acergy Falcon)* [2011] EWHC 2490 (Comm); [2012] 1 All E.R. (Comm) 369.

[69] *Botany Fork & Crane Hire Pty Ltd v The New Zealand Insurance Co* (1993) 116 ALR 473.

[70] *Bolanowski v McKinney* 220 Ill. App. 3d 910; 581 N.E. 2d 345 (1991).

& *Crane Hire Pty Ltd v The New Zealand Insurance Co*[71] and the US case of
Stewart Warner Corp v Burns International Security Services Inc.[72]

In the *Botany Fork & Crane Hire Pty Ltd* case the Federal Court of Australia was
considering the liability of Botany Fork's insurer for damage negligently caused by
one of Botany Fork's forklift truck drivers when handling a gondola. The joint judgment of the court considered the purpose of the "custody, care or control" exclusion.
After considering both the Australian and Canadian authorities the court explained:

> "Consistent with the policy not directly covering loss or damage to the property of the insured (other
> than the vehicle insured), the exclusion to Section 2 of the policy precludes claims being brought
> under the policy for damage to property which, while not belonging to the insured, nevertheless had
> some connection with the insured which otherwise could make the insured responsible for the loss
> or damage of the item in question. That idea is expressed through the concepts of custody or
> control."[73]

This view is consistent with the classic US exposition of the rationale underpinning the exclusion, set out by the US Court of Appeals, Seventh Circuit in *Stewart
Warner Corp*.[74] In that case Burns was retained to provide security for a warehouse
owned by Stewart Warner. It therefore employed a watchman. Instead of protecting the warehouse, however, the watchman set fire to it. Burns had to pay Stewart
Warner damages for the loss of the warehouse and sought to recover from its
insurer. The claim failed as the warehouse was held to be within Burns' "care,
custody or control" at the time of the fire. In the course of the leading judgment,
Fairchild CJ discussed the rationale for the "custody, care or control" exclusion. He
said:

> "One purpose is to prevent the general liability insurer from becoming a guarantor of the insured's
> workmanship in his ordinary operations. Failures of workmanship are a normal business risk which
> the insured is in the best position to prevent. If such risk be transferred to the insurer via general li-
> ability provisions, the cost of general liability coverage will be greater. The 'care, custody or control'
> exclusion is designed to avoid such a result."[75]

It will be suggested below that these twin rationales of limiting the insurer's liability for property for which the contractor is responsible and preventing the
insurer becoming a guarantor of the contractor's workmanship lie at the root of
many of the decided cases and can be used as a guide for application of the clause
in the future.

English cases. Clauses regulating a party's liability for damage to property in the   **18-091**
"custody or control" of another have been considered in two English cases, neither
of which involved construction contractors. The absence of extensive judicial
discussion of the meaning of custody or control clauses means that it is important
to consider those two authorities in detail.

Oei v Foster (formerly Crawford) and Eagle Star Insurance Co Ltd. The   **18-092**
leading English authority is *Oei v Foster (formerly Crawford) and Eagle Star Insur-*

---

[71] *Botany Fork & Crane Hire Pty Ltd* (1993) 116 ALR 473.
[72] *Stewart Warner Corp v Burns International Security Services Inc.* 527 F. 2d 1025 (C.A. Ill. 1975).
[73] *Botany Fork & Crane Hire Pty Ltd* (1993) 116 ALR 473 at [478].
[74] *Stewart Warner Corp* 527 F. 2d 1025 (C.A. Ill. 1975).
[75] *Stewart Warner Corp* 527 F. 2d 1025 at 1030 (C.A. Ill. 1975).

ance Co Ltd.[76] In that case the claimant was insured under a householder's and owner's "all-in" policy. The policy covered damage to property caused by the members of his family and servants residing with him, wherever that damage was caused. However, the policy excluded liability for damage to property "held in trust by or in the custody or control of" the insured, his family or domestic servants.

18-093 The claimant and his wife moved into their neighbour's house for a few days to look after his children. Unfortunately a fire broke out during that period as a result, it was alleged, of the claimant's wife heating a pan of oil and then leaving it unattended. The insurer relied upon the "custody or control" exclusion in addition to other exclusions.

18-094 Glidewell J analysed the meaning of both "custody" and "control". As regards "custody", Glidewell J placed his greatest emphasis on the purpose for which the claimant and his wife were present in the property. He said:

> "As to custody, I accept from [Mrs Foster] that they were not asked to enter the house and live there to look after the house, they were there to look after the children. No doubt incidentally they would look after the house; if their presence prevented some risk to the house then they were fulfilling that role, but it was still incidental to the reason why they were there."[77]

18-095 Glidewell J indicated that "control" refers to legal control and not physical control. In other words it is possible to have complete physical control of property but in the absence of the right to take decisions on behalf of the owner regarding that property it will not be considered within the control of the insured.[78] While physical control may be a necessary condition for the exclusion to operate (although this is not made clear by Glidewell J), it is not a sufficient condition.

18-096 Glidewell J's reliance upon the purpose for which Mr and Mrs Foster were looking after their neighbour's house is particularly noteworthy. It is to be contrasted with *Samuelson v National Insurance and Guarantee Corp Ltd*[79] in which Goff LJ specifically denied the purpose for which a car was being used was irrelevant to the discrete issue of whether it was "in the charge of" a particular individual.[80] The difference between "custody, care and control" and "in the charge of" is not obvious, although the judge's decision may have been influenced by the wording of the particular policy before him.[81]

Acergy Shipping Ltd v Societe Bretonne de Reparation Navale SAS (The
18-097 **Acergy Falcon).** The second English case considering the meaning of a "custody or control" exclusion is *Acergy Shipping Ltd v Societe Bretonne de Reparation Navale SAS (The Acergy Falcon)*.[82] In that case David Steel J was required to interpret a contract for the provision of dry-dock services.

18-098 The claimant's ship was being repaired in the defendant's dock. The defendant was cutting out and replacing a part of the main deck above the hold. That work

---

76 *Oei* [1982] 2 Lloyd's Rep. 170.
77 *Oei* [1982] 2 Lloyd's Rep. 170 at 177.
78 *Oei* [1982] 2 Lloyd's Rep. 170 at 177.
79 *Samuelson v National Insurance and Guarantee Corp Ltd* [1986] 3 All E.R. 417; [1985] 2 Lloyd's Rep. 541; [1987] R.T.R. 94.
80 *Samuelson* [1986] 3 All E.R. 417 at 421–422; [1985] 2 Lloyd's Rep. 541 at 544–545; [1987] R.T.R. 94 at 102.
81 Cf. *Stewart Warner Corp* 527 F.2d 1025 at 1029, Fairchild CJ where the US Court of Appeals (7th Circuit) commented that "there is little distinction between" and "in charge of" exclusion in an automobile policy, and a "care, custody and control" exclusion in a general liability policy.
82 *Acergy Shipping Ltd* [2011] EWHC 2490 (Comm); [2012] 1 All E.R. (Comm) 369.

required the erection of scaffolding in the hold to give access to the deck. Fire then broke out in the combustible material in the bottom of the hold, causing damage to the hold and to some surrounding spaces including to the deck plating above the hold and to pipework already installed by the defendant. It was unclear who caused the fire but the contract contained a system of indemnities that applied irrespective of fault. In particular the defendant would be liable if the property damaged was within its "custody and care" at the time of the fire.

David Steel J considered the meaning of "custody and care". The judge first **18-099** found that, by reason of other provisions of the policy, the exclusion could not be taken to apply to the ship itself.[83] In case he was wrong the judge then considered whether the ship, and the hold in particular, was in the custody and control of the defendant. As regards the ship, David Steel J held that the defendant had enough physical control of the vessel to exercise a lien over it but that this was not enough to bring it within the defendant's "custody and care".[84] The judge's reasoning was threefold: (1) there was no contract deeming the ship to be the defendant's worksite[85]; (2) the ship was crewed throughout and the master of the ship retained authority to exclude the defendant from parts of the ship[86]; and (3) the claimant's crew continued to maintain fire watches while the defendant was working.

Similarly, the judge considered that the hold was not within the defendant's custody and care. This was because access to the hold was available to the claimant throughout the works and the claimant's crew made use of that access.[87]

It is interesting to note that David Steel J did not separate out the terms "custody" and "care" but treated the clause as a whole. Further, it does not appear from the reports of the case that either party relied upon Glidewell J's comments in *Oei* or the foreign decisions considered below. It will be suggested, however, that David Steel J's decision is consistent with the framework established in both the United States and Australia.

Commonwealth cases. "Custody or control" clauses have received much more **18-100** extensive judicial consideration in other commonwealth jurisdictions and, in particular, in Australia and Canada. The long line of authorities upon the meaning of these clauses has given the Australian and Canadian courts the opportunity to set out a more explicit framework for their interpretation.

Australia and New Zealand. The leading Australian authority on "custody or **18-101** control" clauses is *Botany Fork & Crane Hire Pty Ltd*.[88] In that case the claimant stored a gondola for a third party. The gondola was damaged while being moved on a fork lift truck driven by the claimant's employee and Botany Fork was liable to compensate the gondola owner. It then sought an indemnity from the defendant who was its insurer.

The Federal Court of Australia considered whether the defendant was entitled to rely upon an exclusion clause of "damage to property ... in the custody or control of the insured".

---

[83] See *Acergy Shipping Ltd* [2011] EWHC 2490 (Comm) at [29]–[31]; [2012] 1 All E.R. (Comm) 369 at 377. This is a good illustration of the importance of examining the policy as a whole rather than turning straight to authority concerning any particular provision.

[84] *Acergy Shipping Ltd* [2011] EWHC 2490 (Comm) at [34]; [2012] 1 All E.R. (Comm) 369 at 378.

[85] *Acergy Shipping Ltd* [2011] EWHC 2490 (Comm) at [35]–[37]; [2012] 1 All E.R. (Comm) 369 at 378.

[86] *Acergy Shipping Ltd* [2011] EWHC 2490 (Comm) at [38]; [2012] 1 All E.R. (Comm) 369 at 378.

[87] *Acergy Shipping Ltd* [2011] EWHC 2490 (Comm) at [41]; [2012] 1 All E.R. (Comm) 369 at 379.

[88] *Botany Fork & Crane Hire Pty Ltd* (1993) 116 ALR 473.

18-102   The court emphasised that the meaning of "custody" and "control" depends upon the factual context and as such that one cannot import cases wholesale from one factual context to another.[89] The court stated "the issue in the present case is whether the gondola was in the possession or power of Botany at the time of the accident" and went on to distil principles for the interpretation of the clauses in the future. In summary, the court stated that:

1.   Custody and control "refer not only to legal custody and control but also to actual or de facto custody or control".

2.   Custody or control "need not be exclusive of some other person, that is to say, that more than one person may have, at any given point of time, custody or control of the item in question."

3.   Control "clearly relates to dominion or power over the item ultimately damaged".

4.   The exclusion clause would not apply "where the control is merely in relation to [the item damaged] but not over it. Nor will the exclusion clause be attracted if the control is of a part only but not the whole of the item."[90]

18-103   These principles are illustrated by two authorities from the Australian and New Zealand courts. In *Gray Brothers Engineering Ltd v New Zealand Insurance Co Ltd*, the boom of an excavator repaired in situ at a mining site was not "in the charge or under the control of ... the Insured" as: (i) the insured had control over some part of the goods but not over the goods themselves; and (ii) the insured had no authority to move the vehicle, to alter it structurally, or to make decisions about the vehicle's future.[91] In *Commercial Union Insurance Co Ltd v Willetts Radio & TV Ltd*, a vendor of video recorders remained in legal control (as bailee) of a faulty recorder returned to him and then sent by him for repairs even though he no longer had physical control of it. This case would suggest that in New Zealand at least it does not matter if the property is not in the contractor's physical control or custody, so long as it continues to be under his legal control.[92]

18-104   Canada.   The Canadian authorities have taken a slightly different line to that set out in *Botany Fork & Crane Hire Pty Ltd*. The classic Canadian authority is *Indemnity Insurance Co of North America v Excel Cleaning Service*.[93] In that case the insured was a cleaning contractor employed to clean a rug in a customer's house. The rug was tacked to the floor. Unfortunately the cleaning process went wrong and the contractor was liable to compensate the owner of the rug. He then claimed upon his insurance. The policy contained an exclusion in respect of property damaged while in the "care, custody or control" of the contractor.

18-105   The Canadian Supreme Court held that the rug was not in the care, custody or control of the contractor. The members of the court each gave their own judgment. However, certain common principles can be discerned:

1.   "custody" requires the transfer of responsibility for the property from the owner to the contractor, potentially including the creation of some form of proprietary relationship between the contractor and the property;

---

[89]   *Botany Fork & Crane Hire Pty Ltd* (1993) 116 ALR 473 at [477].

[90]   *Botany Fork & Crane Hire Pty Ltd* (1993) 116 ALR 473 at [480].

[91]   *Gray Brothers Engineering Ltd v New Zealand Insurance Co Ltd* (1992) 7 ANZ Ins Cas 61-124.

[92]   *Commercial Union Insurance Co Ltd v Willetts Radio & TV Ltd* (1985) 3 ANZ Ins Cas 60-677.

[93]   *Indemnity Insurance Co of North America v Excel Cleaning Service* (1954) S.C.R. 169; [1954] 2 D.L.R. 721; 1954 CarswellOnt 132.

2. "care" and "control" require the assumption by the contractor of some form of responsibility over and above the provision of the contracted services (in this case cleaning)[94];
3. generally speaking "care, custody and control" require the assumption of responsibility by the contractor "in respect to preservation, safekeeping, protection, direction or domination".[95]

It appears, therefore, that for the Canadian Supreme Court, the phrase "care, **18-106** custody and control" was not primarily a question of de facto possession or control but rather the responsibility assumed by the contractor and his legal rights over the property. This has subsequently been confirmed by the Supreme Courts of Alberta and Newfoundland and Labrador.[96]

It should be noted that the Canadian approach is to analyse the meaning of each **18-107** word of the clause individually, and not collectively. This is particularly the case where the precise wording of the clause is "care, custody *or* control" of the insured[97] but also appears to be the accepted approach where property is excluded where it was in the "care, custody *and* control" of the insured.[98]

The *Indemnity Insurance of North America* case has since been followed in **18-108** Canada. The scope and application of its principles can be illustrated by several of the authorities following it:

1. an oil storage tank damaged in the course of cleaning was not in the care, custody or control of the insured because while the contractor may have had some control in relation to the pipe it did not have control of the pipe itself[99];
2. two cranes supplied by third parties for the insured's construction works but operated by drivers also supplied by the crane company were not in the control or custody of the insured but were in fact in the care, custody and control of the supplier of the crane[100];
3. a house being shown by an estate agent was in his "custody, care or control" at the time he was showing it to potential purchasers because he had a "greater level of dominion over the house" than anyone else and the owners had entrusted the care of the house to him and left him in control[101]; and
4. a digger which, together with its driver (who kept control of the key), had been provided by the insured to a third party had not left the custody of the insured. This was because, following *Indemnity Insurance Co of North America*, the term "custody" meant "having possession of, authority over and responsibility for the safekeeping of the property in question".[102]

---

[94] See *Indemnity Insurance Co of North America* (1954) S.C.R. 169 at 175; [1954] 2 D.L.R. 721 at 726, per Rand J.
[95] *Indemnity Insurance Co of North America* (1954) S.C.R. 169 at 179; [1954] 2 D.L.R. 721 at 729, per Estey J.
[96] See *Fialkow v The Personal Insurance Co* (2006) ABCA 383 at [10]; *Newfoundland Power Inc v Insurance Corp of Newfoundland Ltd* 202 Nfld & P.E.I.R. 26 at [33], per Dunn J.
[97] As in *Fialkow* (2006) ABCA 383 at [7].
[98] As in *Indemnity Insurance Co of North America* (1954) S.C.R. 169 at 174-175; [1954] 2 D.L.R. at 726, per Rand J.
[99] *Interprovincial Pipe Line Co v Seller's Oil Field Ltd; Lloyd's of London et al* 66 D.L.R. (3d) 360; 3 W.W.R. 31; (1976) I.L.R. 172.
[100] *Acadia Road Contractors Ltd v Canadian Surety Co* 81 D.L.R. (3d) 169; 27 NSR (Zd) 608; 3 B.L.R. 33.
[101] *Fialkow* (2006) ABCA 383 at [10].
[102] *Chief and Council of Paul First Nation v Zurich Insurance Co et al* [2010] ABQB 473 at [18], per

It also appears to be the case that in Canada more than one person can simultaneously have custody of a piece of property and that "custody can be exclusive or nonexclusive".[103]

18-109 **US cases principles.** The common law jurisdiction that has evolved the most clearly considered and defined mechanism for interpreting "custody, care or control" clauses is the United States. The US authorities must be treated with some care as there are differences in interpretative approach between the United States and England.[104] Further, the law on the application of particular clauses is not always consistent between individual states within the United States. However, it is suggested that the approach of the US courts is well enough established to consider it at a generalised level.

18-110   The general approach of the US courts when interpreting a "custody, care or control" clause was set out most clearly by the Illinois Court of Appeals in *Bolanowski v McKinney*.[105] In that case the insured owned and operated a bar which staged live music. Musicians were allowed to leave their instruments in the bar while not playing during their weekend engagements. Unfortunately the bar was destroyed by fire, also destroying the musicians' instruments. The insured tried to claim under their policy. The insurer relied upon an exclusion relating to property in the "care, custody and control" of the insured.

18-111   The court reviewed the leading authorities and textbooks and explained that the US courts had devised a two-part test to determine whether property was within the care, custody or control of the insured:

"1.   whether the property was in the possessory control of the insured at the time of the loss; and

2.   whether the property was a necessary element of the work."[106]

18-112 **A framework for analysis.** The large number of US cases considering the operation of the "care, custody, or control" exclusion (or one of its variants) has enabled writers within that jurisdiction to develop a framework for analysing the operation of the clause in any particular context. It will be suggested below that this framework can provide a useful guide to interpreting and applying the exclusion in England and Wales.

18-113   In order properly to analyse the operation of the exclusion, it is necessary to assess: the nature of the property damaged; the extent of any limits upon the insured's control of that property; and, where that control is limited, the nature of that limit.[107]

18-114   It is necessary to consider the nature of the property damaged and, in particular, whether the property is real or personal. Where the property is real property the court will be reluctant to find that it was within the "care, custody, or control" of the insured save for the actual part of the property upon which the insured is

---

Burrows J.

[103]   *Chief and Council of Paul First Nation* [2010] ABQB 473 at [19].

[104]   Consider, for example, the heavy emphasis placed on a purposive construction of the policy by the Georgia Court of Appeals in *Royal Indemnity Co v T.B Smith* 121 Ga App 272 at 276; 173 S.E. 2d 738 at 740–741 (1970), per Hall J.

[105]   *Bolanowski* 220 Ill. App. 3d 910; 581 NE 2d 345 (1991).

[106]   *Bolanowski* 220 Ill. App. 3d 910 at 914; 581 NE 2d 345 (1991) at 348, per McMorrow J.

[107]   The framework set out below was originally developed by F.D. Cooke Jr and set out in detail in "Care, Custody or Control Exclusions" (1959) Ins. L. J. 7, and cited with approval in *Stewart Warner Corp* 527 F. 2d 1025 (C.A. Ill. 1975).

working. By contrast the court will be more willing to find that personal property was within the "custody, care or control" of the insured.[108]

As to the nature and extent of the insured's physical possession of the property, **18-115** at one extreme, where an insured has complete and unlimited physical control of the property, it is likely to be within the exclusion. Similarly, where the insured's possessory control is unlimited but joint the object is also likely be within the exclusion.[109] However:

1. the control exercised by the insured must be exclusive[110];
2. the insured's control need not be continuous[111];
3. temporary or incidental access to the property is not enough to bring the property under the insured's custody, care or control[112];
4. the fact that the owner of the property also has some access will not preclude a finding that the property was within the insured's care, custody or control[113]; and
5. the insured need not be able physically to handle the property in an intimate way.[114]

Notwithstanding the insured's complete physical possession of the object, there **18-116** may have been limits placed on his control over that object. A limit might arise by agreement, by operation of law (as in the case of a trespasser on a plane),[115] or as a result of the physical nature of the property. Where the insured's control of the property was limited in this way, it is less likely to fall within the exclusion. In determining whether the insured was in possession of the property it is worth noting: (i) possession incorporates the legal right to interfere with the property rather than simply the factual ability to do so[116]; and that (ii) the exclusion applies to property held by the insured in some form of legally recognised proprietary relationship such as bailment.[117]

Illustrations. The application of these principles is illustrated by the facts of **18-117** several cases from across the United States:

1. an oil tank was not in the care, custody or control of an insured who was laying flow lines to connect the tank to a well and a gathering pipeline. This was both because it was "merely necessary or incidental to" the laying of the pipe (which may no longer be a good reason) and was a part of the real

---

[108] See for example, *Leiter Electric Co v Bituminous Casualty Corp* 99 Ill App. 2d 386 at 389; 241 N.E. 2d 325 at 327 (1968); F.D. Cooke, "Care, Custody or Control Exclusions" (1959) Ins. L. J. 7, 11.

[109] See F.D. Cooke, "Care, Custody or Control Exclusions" (1959) Ins LJ 7, 13–14 and the cases therein.

[110] *McCreary Roofing Co, Inc v The Nothern Insurance Co of New York* 218 Pa. Super 193 at 195; 275 A. 2d 388 at 389 (1971), per Montgomery J; *Country Mutual Insurance v Waldman Mercantile Co, Inc.* 103 Ill. App. 3d 39 at 42–43; 430 N.E. 2d 606 at 606–610; 58 I.11. Dec. 574 at 577–578 (1981), per Kasserman J.

[111] *McCreary Roofing Co, Inc* 218 Pa. Super 193 at 195; 275 A.2d 388 at 389 (1971), per Montgomery J; *Country Mutual Insurance* 103 Ill. App. 3d 39 at 42–43; 430 N.E. 2d 606 at 609–610; 58 I.ll Dec. 574 at 577–578 (1981), per Kasserman J.

[112] *Leiter Electric Co* 99 Ill App. 2d 386 at 389; 241 N.E. 2d 325 at 327 (1968), per Stouder J.

[113] *Essex Insurance Co v Soy City Sock Co* 503 F. Supp 2d 1068 (2007).

[114] *Stewart Warner Corp* 527 F. 2d 1025 at 1030 (C.A. Ill. 1975), per Fairchild C.J.

[115] *Great American Indem. Co of New York v Saltzman* 213 F. 2d 743 (1954).

[116] *Bolanowski* 220 Ill. App. 3d 910 at 915-916; 581 NE 2d 345 at 349 (1991).

[117] *Leiter Electric Co* 99 Ill. App. 2d 386 at 388; 241 N.E. 2d 325 at 327 (1968).

estate which was intended to remain in the care, custody and control of the owners (which probably still is a good reason)[118];

2. a steel deck structure which was damaged by construction traffic from an insured who was installing roofing material on it was not within the "care, custody or control" of the insured. This was because the insured's presence on the roof was incidental to the work involved and was not exclusive of the control of anyone else[119];

3. a warehouse and its contents were within the "care, custody and control" of a security guard and, vicariously, his employer.[120] This was because the security guard's possession of the warehouse and its contents was, while intermittent, exclusive. It did not matter that he rarely had intimate physical contact with the property;

4. a dockyard operator who dropped a pleasure boat while he was lifting it from the water with a crane had care, custody or control of the boat during the process despite the owner of the boat being present at the time[121];

5. a third party's goods being stored and sold from space leased within the insured's store were within the custody, care or control of the insured. The insured retained possession by keeping the keys to the building, providing security, and limiting the access of the third party's employees. The property was a necessary part of the work performed by the insured as the insured was required to sell the third party's merchandise[122];

6. installation of a cylindrical plug within an oil well bore was not sufficient to bring the well itself within the insured's "care, custody or control" as the insured had done nothing except manipulate the plug within the well bore which was not sufficient[123]; and

7. musical equipment locked in the insured's bar between shows was not within the insured's custody, care or control because the insured had no right to interfere with the equipment.[124]

18-118 Two approaches.   From the analysis of the treatment of "care, custody and control" clauses in the Commonwealth and the United States set out above, it is suggested that there are several principles that apply to the treatment of "care, custody and control" clauses in every jurisdiction. In particular, in order for the exclusion to operate:

1. the property must usually be within the physical control of the insured unless it is deemed to be within his possession by operation of bailment or some other similar rule;

2. that control must be exclusive (in the sense of encompassing the right to exclude others), although it may be shared with another person; and

3. the insured's control must not be limited so that, for example, he no longer has authority to take key actions in relation to the property.

There are, however, key differences between jurisdictions. For example, it ap-

---

[118] *Maryland Casualty Co v Hopper* 237 S.W. 2d 411 (1950).
[119] *McCreary Roofing Co, Inc* 218 Pa. Super. 193; 275 A. 2d 388 (1971).
[120] *Stewart Warner Corp* 527 F. 2d 1025 (C.A. Ill. 1975).
[121] *Monari v Surfside Boat Club, Inc* 469 F. 2d 9 (1972).
[122] *Country Mutual Insurance Co* 103 Ill. App. 3d 39; 430 N.E. 2d 606; 58 I.ll. Dec. (1981).
[123] *Bituminous Casualty Corp v Fulkerson* 212 Ill. App. 3d 556; 571 NE. 2d 256; 156 Ill. Dec. 669 (1991).
[124] *Bolanowski* 220 Ill. App. 3d 910; 581 NE 2d 345 349 (1991).

pears that in Canada there is an additional requirement that the insured has assumed a particular form of responsibility for the safekeeping and preservation of the property over and above his factual and legal possession of it. By contrast, in the United States it is sufficient that the property is within the physical and legal control of the insured and is necessary for his work.

It is not clear where the Australian authorities stand on these two issues. It is sug-**18-119** gested that they are closer to the US approach than the focus on "assumption of responsibility" found in the Canadian authorities. Further, in *Botany Fork* itself it is difficult to see how the contractor was performing any service other than that for which he was contracted. Nevertheless, the Australian court does cite the Canadian authorities with apparent approval.

Application to the English cases. As has been explained the English authori-**18-120** ties concerning the interpretation of care, custody and control clauses do not consider the foreign cases discussed above. Nor do they attempt to provide a systematic guide to the interpretation of care, custody or control clauses. Despite this absence of a systematic approach to the clause, it is possible to analyse the courts' reasoning and see which system fits most closely the approach of the English courts.

In *Oei*[125] the following points would suggest that the exclusion should have **18-121** operated:

1.   the defendants had physical control of the house;
2.   the defendants had authority to control the house while they were in occupation (i.e. they could come, go, lock the door, cook etc.); and
3.   their physical control was necessary for the work being undertaken by them.

Nevertheless, the house was held not to involve the defendants' control because **18-122** the care of the house was not the purpose for which they were in possession. In other words, they had not assumed responsibility for the house. This line of reasoning strongly suggests that Glidewell J's approach in *Oei*[126] was closest to the Canadian analysis, set out above.

It should be noted that Glidewell J also found that the defendants only had author-**18-123** ity to use and take decisions over

"such parts of the house as they required to use and to use so much of the equipment in the house as in ordinary life they required to use."[127]

Glidewell J felt this took the house out of the defendants' control. It is suggested that this is best understood as an alternative way of expressing Glidewell J's purposive analysis as it is difficult to see how the defendants' rights were in fact limited if they could use the whole house and its contents as they wished and needed within the performance of their task. They were not excluded, for example, from any particular room.

Glidewell J's findings could be a manifestation of the view, found in the US **18-124** authorities, that it is hard for real property to be within the control of the insured. This would not explain Glidewell J's emphasis on the purpose for which the defendants were in occupation of the house, however, or the easy way that he moves between consideration of the house and "the knives, forks and spoons" within it.

---

[125]   *Oei* [1982] 2 Lloyd's Rep. 170.
[126]   *Oei* [1982] 2 Lloyd's Rep. 170.
[127]   *Oei* [1982] 2 Lloyd's Rep. 170 at 177.

18-125   In *Acergy Shipping Ltd*,[128] David Steel J ruled that the exclusion did operate. In doing so it is submitted that the judge's approach followed much more closely the US reasoning. The judge focused on the insured's physical control over the ship and its hold. It was also of significance that the owner of the ship continued to have access to it and protected it. These two points fit in with the US authorities analysed above. Further, the judge did not analyse the question from the perspective of whether the insured had assumed a responsibility over the ship in excess of its contractual obligations or whether he had gone beyond the services for which it was employed. It would seem, therefore, that David Steel J was not necessarily following the same approach as had been set out by Glidewell J.

18-126   Conclusions.   Accordingly, the two English authorities appear to be within different lines of reasoning on the proper interpretation of the "custody, care and control" exclusion. Further, since neither authority refers to the other or to the consideration of these clauses in other jurisdictions, it is difficult to set out clear guidance upon how the exclusions are to be treated in the future. It is suggested, however, that the following principles are a helpful starting point:

1.   real property is unlikely to be within an insured's care, custody or control. This is consistent with Glidewell J's ruling in *Oei* and with the US approach to these clauses;

2.   in order to fall within an insured's "care, custody or control" property must be within his exclusive possession. If the employer or any other person retains and exercises a right to access or use the property then it will not be within the insured's "care, custody or control". This is consistent with each of the other jurisdictions and with David Steel J's reasoning in *Acergy Shipping Ltd*;

3.   the fact that the insured's right to take decisions about property is limited in some way will suggest that it is not within his "care, custody and control". This is consistent with *Oei* and with each of the other jurisdictions;

4.   following *Oei* it is likely that the purpose of the insured's possession of the property must include its protection or preservation.[129] However, this principle must be treated with some care as it does not feature in the court's reasoning in *Acergy Shipping Ltd*,[130] which is inconsistent with the thorough and well tested US authorities, and is not supported by the leading Australian case.

Cost of repairing or replacing loss of or damage to the permanent works or
18-127   temporary works.   An exclusion clause to the third party liability section of the policy will normally state that the insured will not be indemnified against loss of or damage to the insured property for

> "[t]he cost of repairing or replacing loss of or damage to the permanent Works or Temporary Works which is indemnifiable under' the first section of the policy, namely the 'construction all risks and property all risks' section."

Liability arising out of the failure of work done products supplied or services
18-128   provided by the insured to perform as intended.   In relation to the third party liability section, there will be no cover for a failure to perform or complete the

---

[128] *Acergy Shipping Ltd* [2011] EWHC 2490 (Comm); [2012] 1 All E.R. (Comm) 369.
[129] See *Oei* [1982] 2 Lloyd's Rep. 170 at 177.
[130] *Acergy Shipping Ltd* [2011] EWHC 2490 (Comm); [2012] 1 All E.R. (Comm) 369.

contract works. This is because an insurer will not usually warrant the performance of work done, products supplied or services provided. However, it is important to note that the "[e]xception does not apply to Personal Injury or to loss of or damage to property caused to a third party from such failure".

Pollution exclusion. An exclusion will be contained in the exclusions section to **18-129** the third party liability section, which confirms that the insured will not be covered for personal injury or loss or damage to property caused to a third party arising from pollution, unless the "[s]eepage, pollution is caused by a sudden unintended and unexpected happening during the Period of Insurance". However, notwithstanding this, the pollution exclusion clause will normally exclude cover in respect of:

"(a) Liability directly or indirectly caused by seepage, pollution or contamination, provided always that this paragraph (a) shall not [as noted above] apply to liability for personal injury or bodily injury or loss of or physical damage to or destruction of tangible property, or loss of use of such property damaged or destroyed where such seepage, pollution contamination is caused by a sudden unintended and unexpected happening during the Period of Insurance.

(b) The cost of removing, nullifying or cleaning-up seeping, polluting or contaminating substances unless the seepage, pollution or contamination is caused by a sudden unintended and unexpected happening during the Period of Insurance.

(c) Fines, penalties, punitive or exemplary damages."

In addition, the pollution clause will not

"[e]xtend the Policy to cover any liability which would not have been covered under the Policy had the Exclusion not been included"

or apply to

"[s]eepage, pollution or contamination in respect of ionising radiation or contamination by radioactivity arising from the use of testing, inspection and diagnostic equipment."

Although many CAR policies provide an indemnity for the costs of removing **18-130** debris caused by loss or damage which would otherwise be covered under the contract works section of the policy, following the decision of the Court of Appeal in *King v Brandywine Reinsurance Co (UK) Ltd (formerly Cigna RE Co (UK) Ltd)*,[131] such a provision is unlikely to provide cover for the clean-up costs resulting from pollution or contamination. Consequently, some liability policies provide an exclusion in respect of pollution and contamination. A typical exclusion may provide as follows:

"[T]he Insurers shall not be liable for any claim in respect of liability arising directly or indirectly out of pollution or contamination unless cause by a sudden identifiable unintended and unexpected incident which occurred in its entirety at a specific time and place during the period of insurance."

Similar language is used in the insuring provisions in the JCT Standard Form of Building Contract (2011 edn).[132] The exclusion makes plain that all pollution or contamination is excluded, save for where it is caused by a sudden identifiable unintended *and* unexpected incident which occurred at a specific time. Therefore, the circumstances are very limited. The burden of proof is likely to be on the insured

---

[131] *King v Brandywine Reinsurance Co (UK) Ltd (formerly Cigna RE Co (UK) Ltd)* [2005] EWCA Civ 235; [2005] 1 Lloyd's Rep. 655.

[132] JCT Contracts, SBC/Q 2011 JCT Standard Form of Building Contract with Quantities 2011 (2011).

to prove that the pollution or contamination happened as a result of a sudden, unintended and unexpected incident. If the insured fails to discharge the burden then it will be uninsured for any pollution/contamination claims it receives from third party persons. On the other hand, if it receives claims from employees then these will be covered by the insured's employer's liability insurance. However, that said, an insurer may decide to not insure someone, if the pollution or contamination is a by-product of its business (e.g. coal combustion residue).

18-131   The pollution exclusion has been extensively litigated in the US courts, resulting in case law which is not easy to reconcile, particularly as to the meaning of the word "sudden". Whilst it is accepted that the exclusion removed all pollution from coverage, save in limited circumstances, the interpretation of the exclusion has differed. Some decisions have held that the reference to "sudden" requires a temporal limitation, such that gradual or sustained releases are not within the exclusion,[133] for example seepage of polluted groundwater, whereas others have allowed the insured to recover even where the pollution has occurred over an extended period, so long as the insured is unaware of the pollution and the release was unexpected.[134]

18-132   The precise meaning of the pollution and contamination exclusion does not appear to have been litigated in England and Wales as yet, so it is not clear which line of reasoning the English courts will follow.[135] The terms of the exclusion set out above arguably import a temporal limit to the instance of pollution or contamination by reference to the event occurring in its entirety at a specific time and this may act so as to allow insurers to argue that it is only where there is some non-gradual form of pollution or contamination that the policy will respond. However, the reference in the provision set out above is to the "event" giving rise to the pollution and not to the release of the pollutant or contaminant itself, which arguably may still be gradual. If an insured is successful in arguing that the above provision is ambiguous, in particular by relying on the conflicting authorities in the United States, the exclusion may be construed against the insurer,[136] with the result that the insured may be permitted to recover.

18-133   The potential clean-up costs resulting from contamination or pollution may be extensive where hazardous materials are present or where works are carried out on potentially contaminated land. The particular features of the project and the likelihood exposure to hazardous materials will be a matter both the contractor and insurer will need to consider when determining whether an exclusion clause relat-

---

[133] See for example *Upjohn Co v New Hampshire Ins Co* , 438 Mich. 197 at 207; 476 N.W. 2d 392 at 397 (Mich., 1991) in which the court stated "[w]e conclude that when considered in its plain and easily understood sense, 'sudden' is defined with a 'temporal element that joins together conceptually the immediate and the unexpected'" and *ACL Technologies, Inc v Northbrook Property & Casualty Ins Co* , 17 Cal. App. 4th 1773; 22 Cal. Rptr. 2d 206 (Cal.App.4.Dist., 1993) in which the conflicting authorities are identified and the court expressly states: "Whatever 'sudden' means, it does not mean gradual and the ordinary person would never think that something which happens gradually also happened suddenly."

[134] See for example *Hecla Min. Co. v New Hampshire Ins. Co* , 811 P. 2d 1083 at 1092 (Colo. 1991) in which the Supreme Court of Colorado stated: "Since the term 'sudden' is susceptible to more than one reasonable definition, the term is ambiguous, and we therefore construe the phrase against the insurer to mean unexpected and unintended."

[135] However, a recent case in which Stuart-Smith J construed "pollution and contamination" in contract and warranties (as opposed to in an insurance policy) may shed some light on the likely approach: see *Persimmon Homes Ltd v Ove Arup Partners Ltd* [2015] EWHC 3573 (TCC).

[136] See above, paras 13-060 to 13-061.

ing to pollution or contamination is suitable for the policy either in the terms set out above or at all.

Loss or damage to property arising from professional advice rendered for a fee by consultancy or engineer (including the employers' professional team). An **18-134** exclusion clause will normally be contained in the public liability section, which confirms that the insured will not be indemnified in respect of

"any consultant or engineer including the Employer's professional team consequent upon physical loss or damage to property arising from professional advice rendered for a fee by that consultant or engineer."

In this situation therefore, the insured will not be covered for injury suffered or loss or damage to property incurred by a third party as a result of advice given by a consultant or engineer for a fee. Use of the words "for a fee" distinguishes the exclusion clause from the insured's professional indemnity insurance, which concerns the situation when advice is given in a professional capacity for a fee.

Damage to contract works. A public liability policy may contain an exclusion **18-135** for the contract works:

"The Insurer shall not be liable under this Policy for any claim in respect of the loss or damage to or the cost incurred by anyone in recalling removing repairing rectifying replacing or reapplying any contract works provided that after handover of any part of the contract works this exclusion shall only apply to the part of the contract works which is defective."

The purpose of the exclusion is to exclude the construction works from cover on the basis that it is or should be insured under all risks construction works insurance. There are three limbs to the exclusion: (a) "loss of" the contract works; (b) "damage to" the contract works; and (c) the costs incurred in recalling removing replacing or reapplying any contract works. In relation to the third limb it is important to note that there is no requirement for loss or damage to the contract works. This might apply in two situations: first, where contract works have to be removed or replaced to access damaged property (access costs), and secondly, where costs are incurred in replacing contract works etc. which are defective but not damaged. However as the insuring clause will operate only where there has been physical damage to property and the exclusion ought not to be construed as an extension to cover after handover; the exclusion is limited to that part of the contract works which is both damaged and defective. Nevertheless it is arguable that financial losses incurred after handover are not excluded; this is because the exclusion may be taken to read "after handover insurers are not liable for the cost incurred by anyone in rectifying damage to defective contract works".

Damage before practical completion. Circumstances can arise where construc- **18-136** tion works may be covered under the construction works and the public liability sections of the same CAR policy. This situation occurs most commonly in private finance initiative (PFI) arrangements where a property holding company owns the land upon which the building is constructed and the building contractor, who may be a subsidiary of the property holding company, are both insured under the same (composite)[137] CAR policy. If the contract does not transfer possession of the land

---

[137] The distinction between joint and composite policies is considered in para.20-030 below.

to the contractor, then the works may become part of the land[138]; the most obvious example of this are concrete piles placed in the ground, where the property holding company may seek to bring a claim against the contractor for damage caused to the land. The damage may be the ground beneath end bearing piles having been compressed beyond the amount that had expressly or impliedly been consented to, or a more tangible form of damage. The building contractor will then claim to be indemnified under the public liability section of the policy in respect of the holding company's claim against it that its land has been damaged and also under the works section of the policy on the basis that the piles and the ground form part of the works. The reasoning for this is that both the pile and the ground are required for the piles to operate effectively. The advantages for the contractor in making a claim under the public liability section of the policy are that the level of cover may be higher and consequential financial loss may also be indemnified (e.g. see para.18-135 above). However, it will not be possible to obtain payment under the public liability section of the CAR policy where the ground is considered to be part of the construction works only, where there has been no material change to the value and usefulness of the compressed ground, or where, either expressly or impliedly, the alleged damage had been consented to by the owner of the land.

18-137   **Damage during the defects liability period.**   Once practical completion is achieved, there will typically be a defects liability/rectification period expiring six months to a year later. During this period possession of the site will usually have reverted to the employer notwithstanding that, if properly notified of defects, the main contractor will be obliged to return to site (now under the possession of the owner) and carry out remedial works. This marks a shift in the contractor's interest in that the site is no longer under his control and, depending on the size and nature of the project, may no longer be covered under his CAR policy for the works.

The defects liability period will usually last for six to twelve months after practical completion of the construction works has been achieved. Accordingly, there is a not insubstantial risk that damage to the completed works will be suffered. The owner of the property may seek to bring a claim against the contractor for causing physical damage to its property, for example where a water leak causes physical damage to the other parts of the property. In turn the contractor may seek to bring a claim for an indemnity under the public liability section of the policy. In this situation if the claim is to be successful it will be necessary to ascertain whether there has been damage capable of giving rise to a claim in tort against the contractor, or whether the loss is purely economic (see para.18-042 above).

---

[138] This is expressed in the Latin maxim *quicquid plantatur solo, solo credit* (whatever is attached to the soil becomes part of it): *Elitestone Ltd v Morris* [1997] 1 W.L.R. 687.

CHAPTER 19

CAUSATION

1. PROXIMATE CAUSE: NATURE OF THE INQUIRY

Introduction. An insurer is liable only for loss proximately caused by an insured **19-001**
peril[1] and is not liable for any loss that is proximately caused by an excluded peril.
Whilst recovery in tort or for breach of contract excludes losses that are merely a
remote consequence of the breach of duty, there is no recovery under a policy of
insurance for any "but for" cause of the insured event unless that is the proximate
cause of the loss. Equally, a policy exclusion can avail the insurer only if the
excluded peril is the proximate cause of the loss. The principle is based on the
presumed intentions of the parties: since the chain of causation can potentially be
traced back infinitely, common sense suggests that a line has to be drawn
somewhere.[2] The flapping of a butterfly's wings in Brazil is theoretically capable
of bringing about—to the extent of being a "but for" cause of—a hurricane in the
United Kingdom[3]; but even if science could trace back weather patterns to that level
of precision, the wing flaps would not engage an insurance policy clause that
excludes damage "due to the action of insects".

In the law of insurance, causation issues may arise in two ways: first, there can **19-002**
be a question as to whether the proximate cause of the loss was an insured peril,
as opposed to an uninsured peril (that is, something outside of the risks covered by
the insuring clause); secondly, there may be an issue as to whether the proximate
cause of the loss was an event within a specific policy exemption. In the context
of all risks insurance, however, the first type of inquiry does not really arise since

---

[1] The Marine Insurance Act 1906 s.55(1) reflects the common law rule, providing that: "unless the
policy otherwise provides, the insurer is liable for any loss proximately caused by a peril insured
against, but ... he is not liable for any loss which is not proximately caused by a peril insured
against."

[2] Maxim I said: "It were infinite for the law to judge the causes of causes, and their impulsions one
of another; therefore it contenteth itself with the immediate cause and judgeth of acts by that, without
looking to any further degree." in F. Bacon, *The Elements of the Common Lawes of England
Branched into a Double Tract: the One Containing a Collection of Some Principall Rules and
Maximes of the Common Law, with their Latitude and Extent. Explicated for the More Facile
Introduction of such as are Studiously Addicted to that Noble Profession. The Other The use of the
Common Law, for Preservation of our Persons, Goods, and Good Names. According to the Lawes
and Customes of this Land* (London: J More, 1636).

[3] The "butterfly effect" or sensitive dependence on initial conditions: see J. Gleick, *Chaos: Making
a New Science* (Heinemann: London, 1988), p.320, fn.20.

all risks are insured unless expressly or impliedly exempted[4]; there is simply no "uninsured peril" for the insurer to point to as the more proximate cause of the loss. To put it another way, having determined that the damage was fortuitous, one can then proceed to consider whether any express exclusions apply. It is in the context of the policy exclusions that the problem of "competition between causes"[5] can occur: the situation where the loss arises from a series of events, some of which are, and some of which are not, excluded perils.

19-003 **Framework rules.** The immediate purpose of the task of distinguishing proximate from remote causes in a given case is to apply the following set of rules:

1. To qualify as a "cause" in the first place the event under consideration must be a "but for" cause of the loss—it must be the case that the loss would not have been suffered had the event not happened.

2. If the event is a merely remote or insufficiently proximate (even if a "but for") cause of the loss, it must be excluded from consideration. It cannot be identified as something that will bring the loss within the insuring clause or as an event triggering a policy exclusion.

3. The remaining cause or set of causes are proximate and if any fall within the insuring clause they will, subject to exclusions, be covered[6]: if one of two proximate causes is an insured peril and one is an uninsured peril there will be cover.[7]

4. If one of the proximate causes is an excluded peril, however, the insured cannot recover, whether or not another proximate cause is an insured peril.[8]

---

[4]   In other words, the insured peril is "damage" by any cause unless expressly or impliedly exempted.
[5]   *Leyland Shipping Co Ltd v Norwich Union Fire Insurance Society Ltd* [1918] A.C. 350 at 363; 14 Asp M.L.C. 258 at 262; [1918–1919] All E.R. Rep 443 at 450 HL.
[6]   *Wayne Tank & Pump Co Ltd v Employers Liability Assurance Corp Ltd* [1974] Q.B. 57 at 68–69; [1973] 3 W.L.R. 483 at 490; [1973] 3 All E.R. 825 at 831 CA, per Cairns LJ. But see paras 19-004 to 19-006 below for the opposing view (and criticism of that view) that a single dominant cause must be identified.
[7]   *JJ Lloyd Instruments Ltd v Northern Star Insurance Co Ltd (The Miss Jay Jay)* [1987] 1 Lloyd's Rep. 32; [1987] F.T.L.R. 14 CA; *Standard Life Assurance Ltd v Ace European Group*; sub nom. *Ace European Group v Standard Life Assurance Ltd* [2012] EWHC 104 (Comm); [2012] Lloyd's Rep. I.R. 655. For the reason indicated above in para.19-002, this stage of the inquiry can be skipped over in the context of all risks policies since, where cover is open-ended, there is no such thing as an uninsured (as opposed to an excluded) risk.
[8]   *P Samuel & Co Ltd v Dumas* [1924] A.C. 431 at 467; (1924) 18 Ll. L. Rep. 211 at 222; [1924] All E.R. Rep. 66 at 86 HL; *Wayne Tank & Pump Co Ltd* [1974] Q.B. 57 at 67, 69 and 74; [1973] 3 W.L.R. 483 at 488, 490 and 495; [1973] 3 All E.R. 825 at 830–832 and 836 CA. Parties often seek to write-back cover in relation to ensuing loss otherwise caused by an excluded peril through wording such as the following: "This policy does not insure loss or damage caused directly or indirectly by an Peril excluded ... unless loss or damage from an insured Peril ensues and then only for such ensuing loss or damage." The effect of such wording is discussed below in para.26-107. Equally, where damage results from wear and tear that is the consequence of a defect, the question whether the loss is excluded by virtue of a 'wear and tear' exclusion becomes a difficult one: see paras 15-014 to 15-019. The better view is that such loss is proximately caused by a defect, thereby bringing any damage within the ambit of the policy rather than being caught by the "wear and tear" exclusion (see *JSM Management PTY Ltd v QBE Insurance (Australia) Ltd* [2011] VSC 339 and *AWH Pty Ltd v Impact Fertilisers Australia Pty Ltd* [2015] VCC 346).

The search for the proximate cause. Many of the authorities suggest that the 19-004 proper approach is to look for a single, dominant or *the* proximate cause[9] and that only if it is impossible to identify which of two causes is the proximate cause will they both be regarded as concurrent proximate causes. However, the better view, it is suggested, is that one must start with the policy's description of the peril or the exclusion in question and then ask whether the occurrence of this risk on the facts was *a* (not necessarily *the*) proximate cause of the loss. On this view, the principle of proximity is concerned not so much with a choice between competing causes as with excluding causes that are too remote. There are a number of dicta which concur with this approach. For example, in the leading case on proximity, *Leyland Shipping Co Ltd v Norwich Union Fire Insurance Society Ltd*,[10] Lord Atkinson referred to the rule that "the proximate, not the remote, causes are to be regarded".[11]

The point was considered in *Wayne Tank & Pump Co Ltd v Employers Liability* 19-005 *Assurance Corp Ltd*.[12] The insured had been found liable for a factory fire caused by its installation of equipment for storing and conveying liquid wax. It was found that the insured had been negligent in two respects: (i) in using unsuitable plastic material in conjunction with a defective thermometer when installing the equipment; and (ii) in leaving the equipment switched on in the factory and unattended before being properly tested. The latter act of negligence would be within the insured's liability policy, but there was an express exclusion for "damage caused by the nature or conditions of any goods ... sold or supplied by or on behalf of the assured".[13] The majority held that the single proximate cause of the damage was the installation of a defective product and on that basis the insurers could avail themselves of the exclusion.[14] Cairns LJ agreed with the conclusion that the exclusion was effective but expressed the view that:

---

[9] *Reischer v Borwick* [1894] 2 Q.B. 548 at 552; [1891-4] All E.R. Rep. 531 at 534; 63 L.J.Q.B. 753 at 756 CA, per Lopes LJ: "it is well-settled law that it is only the proximate cause that is to be regarded and all others rejected". *Leyland Shipping Co Ltd* [1918] A.C. 350 at 363; 14 Asp M.L.C. 258 at 262; [1918-19] All E.R. Rep. 443 at 450, per Lord Dunedin: "[t]he solution will always lie in settling as a question of fact which of the two causes was what I will venture to call ... the dominant cause of the two." In the same case [1918] A.C. 350 at 369; 14 Asp M.L.C. 258 at 262; [1918-19] All E.R. Rep. 443 at 453, per Lord Shaw of Dunfermline: "[t]he cause which is truly proximate is that which is proximate in efficiency." *P Samuel & Co Ltd v Dumas* [1924] A.C. 431 at 446; (1924) 18 Ll. L. Rep. 211 at 214; [1924] All E.R. Rep. 66 at 76 HL, per Viscount Cave: "the question is whether the proximate cause of her sinking was the act of letting the water into the vessel, or the actual inrush of the water." *Handelsbanken ASA v Dandridge (The Aliza Glacial)* [2002] EWCA Civ 577 at [48]; [2002] 2 All E.R. (Comm) 39 at 53; [2002] 2 Lloyd's Rep. 421 at 431, per Potter LJ: "the first task of the court is to look to see whether one of the causes is plainly the proximate cause of the loss."

[10] *Leyland Shipping Co Ltd* [1918] A.C. 350; 14 Asp M.L.C. 258; [1918-19] All E.R. Rep. 443.

[11] *Leyland Shipping Co Ltd* [1918] A.C. 350 at 365; 14 Asp M.L.C. 258 at 262; [1918-19] All E.R. Rep. 443 at 451. Similarly, in *Reischer* [1894] 2 Q.B. 548 at 550; 63 L.J.Q.B. 753 at 754; [1891-4] All E.R. Rep. 531 at 533, Lindley LJ said: "it is a cardinal rule to regard proximate, and not remote, causes of loss." In *JJ Lloyd Instruments Ltd* [1987] 1 Lloyd's Rep. 32 at 37; [1987] F.T.L.R. 14 at 17, per Lawton LJ considered that the judge had properly "directed himself as to whether what happened was *a* proximate cause of the loss. As there were no relevant exclusions or warranties in the policy the fact that there may have been another proximate cause of the loss did not call for specific mention since proof of *a* peril within the policy was enough to entitle the plaintiffs to judgment."

[12] *Wayne Tank & Pump Co Ltd* [1974] Q.B. 57; [1973] 3 W.L.R. 483; [1973] 3 All E.R. 825.

[13] *Wayne Tank & Pump Co Ltd* [1974] Q.B. 57 at 65; [1973] 3 W.L.R. 483 at 486-487; [1973] 3 All E.R. 825 at 828.

[14] Lord Denning MR thought that one should "approach this case by asking which of the two causes was the effective or dominant cause": *Wayne Tank & Pump Co Ltd* [1974] Q.B. 57 at 66; [1973] 3 W.L.R. 483 at 488; [1973] 3 All E.R. 825 at 829. Roskill LJ considered that "the court must, if it

"I do not consider that the court should strain to find a dominant cause if, as here, there are two causes both of which can properly be described as effective causes of the loss ... I should prefer to say that unless one cause is clearly more decisive than the other, it should be accepted that there are two causes of the loss and no attempt should be made to give one of them the quality of dominance. On this approach if one cause is within the words of the policy and the other comes within an exception in the policy, it must be taken that the loss cannot be recovered under the policy."[15]

19-006 It is suggested that the approach of Cairns LJ should be followed in preference to the views of the majority.[16] So long as the event said to be within the exclusion clause is not merely a remote, trivial or coincidental cause, it is difficult to see why a requirement that it be a more dominant cause than any other should enter into the matter unless the wording of the exclusion expressly requires. As one commentator suggests:

"In principle, there is no reason why a court should approach a question of causation predisposed to arriving at the conclusion that one event or circumstance is the sole proximate cause of the loss."[17]

19-007 Moreover, a rule that requires only that the event be *a*, rather than *the*, proximate cause has a much better fit with the actual outcomes of the reported cases and makes sense of decisions that are otherwise hard to reconcile. In *Leyland Shipping Co Ltd*,[18] Lord Dunedin, after stating that one must identify "the dominant cause of the two",[19] immediately went on to give an analysis of an earlier case that could only be consistent with a rule that does not require the identification of a single proximate cause. In that earlier case,[20] damage to cargo, which occurred after a rat had gnawed through a pipe causing seawater to enter the vessel, was held to be proximately caused by the "perils of the sea".[21] Lord Dunedin, in *Leyland Shipping Co Ltd*,[22] commented on that decision, saying:

---

can, determine the proximate cause of the loss": [1974] Q.B. 57 at 72; [1973] 3 W.L.R. 483 at 493; [1973] 3 All E.R. 825 at 834.

15 *Wayne Tank & Pump Co Ltd* [1974] Q.B. 57 at 68–69; [1973] 3 W.L.R. 483 at 490; [1973] 3 All E.R. 825 at 831.

16 It can be argued that all three members of the court (Lord Denning M.R., Cairns and Roskill LJJ) were speaking obiter inasmuch as having decided that the defective condition of the thing supplied was a sufficiently proximate cause of the loss and that this was enough to bring the exception into play, it was unnecessary to consider whether the other candidate cause was or was not also sufficiently proximate. The same can be said about the dicta on this point in *Handelsbanken ASA* [2002] EWCA Civ 577; [2002] 2 All E.R. (Comm) 39; [2002] 2 Lloyd's Rep. 421, where the issue was whether the detention of a vessel by the Australian Navy (covered) was effectively superseded by detention due to "ordinary judicial process" (excepted) at the point when foreclosure proceedings were brought against the vessel. The ruling that "[h]ad the claimants not invoked the court process, there is no reason to suppose that the detention of the vessel would not have continued indefinitely" ([2002] EWCA Civ 577 at [46]; [2002] 2 All E.R. (Comm) 39 at 53; [2002] 2 Lloyd's Rep. 421 at 431) means that the excepted peril was not even a "but for" cause of the loss. Therefore the view that the court must try to identify the one dominant cause (as expressed in the case cited above at [2002] EWCA Civ 577 at [48]; [2002] 2 All E.R. (Comm) 39 at 53; [2002] 2 Lloyd's Rep. 421 at 431) was, it is suggested, off-point: proximity only needs to be considered if the candidate cause passes the threshold "but for" test.

17 H. Bennett, *The Law of Marine Insurance*, 2nd edn (Oxford: OUP, 2006), para.9.21.

18 *Leyland Shipping Co Ltd* [1918] A.C. 350; 14 Asp M.L.C. 258; [1918-19] All E.R. Rep. 443.

19 *Leyland Shipping Co Ltd* [1918] A.C. 350 at 363; [1918-19] All E.R. Rep. 443 at 450, per Lord Dunedin.

20 *Hamilton, Fraser & Co v Pandorf & Co* (1887) 12 App. Cas. 518; [1886-90] All E.R. Rep 220.

21 If the House of Lords in *Hamilton, Fraser & Co v Pandorf & Co* (1887) 12 App. Cas. 518; (1888) 52 J.P. 196; [1886-1890] All E.R. Rep. 220 HL really did decide (as the way the decision is expressed does, unfortunately, tend to suggest) that the only proximate cause of the loss was the perils of the sea via the ingress of seawater, to the exclusion of the action of the rats in making a hole in the pipe, the case would be impossible to reconcile with other decisions: this was the conclusion of Scrutton

"If in that case there had been an exception of all dangers brought about by rats, then the decision, I take it, would have been different."[23]

This is surely correct: neither the gnawing of the pipe nor the ingress of the seawater were remote nor trivial causes of the loss; liability could be excluded by a clause speaking to either of these co-effective[24] causes.

2. PROXIMITY

Guideline principles.   A proximate cause is one that is substantial and effective. **19-008** Descriptions include something that can be "justly described as the cause of the ultimate damage",[25] or a situation where there is a "direct relation between the cause and its effect".[26] It is probably impossible to lay down a set of categorical propositions as to what will satisfy the test of proximity that holds up in every factual situation.[27] Instead, a number of guiding principles can be suggested.

Proximate does not simply mean last in time.   In *Leyland Shipping Co Ltd*,[28] the **19-009** House of Lords held that "proximate" does not mean simply closest in time to the accident. Lord Shaw noted that to identify proximity with nearness in time would make it impossible for any excluded peril to apply in the case of insurance for perils of the sea, since the ingress of water that attends accidents at sea is usually the last significant event between the ship sinking or the cargo getting wet.[29] Accordingly, the existence of other subsequent events, which are also "but for" causes of the

---

LJ in *Leyland Shipping Co Ltd* [1917] 1 K.B. 873 at 899; 86 L.J.K.B. 905; 14 Asp M.L.C. 4, affirmed [1918] A.C. 350; 14 Asp M.L.C. 258; [1918-1919] All E.R. Rep. 443. In *Reischer* [1894] 2 Q.B. 548; 63 L.J.Q.B. 753; [1891–1894] All E.R. Rep. 531, where, through a collision, a ship sustained a leak which was repaired but later opened up by the effect of motion through the water, the collision was held to be the proximate cause of the loss. In *P Samuel & Co Ltd v Dumas* [1924] A.C. 431 at 446–447; (1924) 18 Ll. L. Rep. 211 at 214; [1924] All E.R. Rep. 66 at 76, Viscount Cave said "[t]here appears to me something absurd in saying that, when a ship is scuttled by her crew, her loss is not caused by the act of scuttling, but by the incursion of water which results from it."

22 *Leyland Shipping Co Ltd* [1918] A.C. 350; 14 Asp M.L.C. 258; [1918–1919] All E.R. Rep. 443.

23 *Leyland Shipping Co Ltd* [1918] A.C. 350 at 364; 14 Asp M.L.C. 258 at 262; [1918-1919] All E.R. Rep. 443 at 450, per Lord Dunedin.

24 Some commentators describe two effective proximate causes as "concurrent" causes; this language is potentially misleading since the issue usually arises in relation to successive events.

25 *Reischer* [1894] 2 Q.B. 548 at 553; 63 L.J.Q.B. 753; [1891-4] All E.R. Rep. 531 at 534, per Davey LJ.

26 *Leyland Shipping Co Ltd* [1918] A.C. 350 at 362; 14 Asp M.L.C. 258 at 261; [1918-1919] All E.R. Rep. 443 at 449, per Viscount Haldane.

27 For example, one commentary states that "[i]t is not, however, sufficient for the peril insured against to have facilitated the loss; it must have caused the loss" (*MacGillivray on Insurance Law*, edited by J. Birds, B. Lynch and S. Milnes, 13th edn (London: Sweet & Maxwell, 2015), para.21-002). It gives the example of the case where goods were stolen from a building during an air-raid, in which the court held that it was the theft and not the air-raid that caused the loss (*Winicofsky v Army and Navy General Insurance* (1919) 88 L.J.K.B. 1111; (1919) 35 T.L.R. 283). The air-raid in that case undoubtedly did cause the loss in a "but for" sense; if merely "facilitating" the loss means causing the loss in a way which the law regards as too remote, it adds nothing to the idea of proximity. If, instead, a "facilitating cause" is a cause that sets the backdrop to the immediate accident, the proposition is too wide to be a correct statement of law; where the two causes of an accident were supplying a defective piping system and leaving the system on all night before testing, the supplying of the defective product was held to be the proximate cause (*Wayne Tank & Pump Co Ltd* [1974] Q.B. 57; [1973] 3 W.L.R. 483; [1973] 3 All E.R. 825).

28 *Leyland Shipping Co Ltd* [1918] A.C. 350; 14 Asp M.L.C. 258; [1918-19] All E.R. Rep 443.

29 *Leyland Shipping Co Ltd* [1918] A.C. 350 at 369–370; 14 Asp M.L.C. 258 at 264; [1918-19] All E.R. Rep. 443 at 453–454. However, this problem is premised on the questionable assumption (see above,

damage, will not necessarily relegate the earlier incident to a merely remote cause. For example, in *Wayne Tank & Pump Co Ltd*,[30] there were two causes of damage: the defective design and installation of equipment and, subsequently, leaving on the equipment unsupervised overnight. The former cause, which was covered by a policy exception, was held to be a proximate cause of the loss, and accordingly the insured could not recover.

19-010   Nonetheless it is reasonable to suggest that an event that happens immediately before the casualty is much more likely to be treated as a proximate cause than something that happened many weeks previously. Indeed, if the event in question occurred mere seconds before the accident it is very difficult to argue that it was not a proximate cause of the loss for the purpose of applying a policy exception, which speaks to such an event. So, in the case of rats gnawing a hole in a pipe, which allowed the ingress of water that damaged the insured cargo, although the damage was clearly the inevitable consequence of the activities of the rats, the loss was held to be within an exclusion for "accidents of the sea".[31] Whilst the rats would undoubtedly have also been a proximate cause and could have been caught by an appropriately worded exclusion,[32] "the sea was in such a case not the less the immediate cause of the damage".[33]

19-011   Inevitability of damage points towards proximity.   Despite the foregoing, ordinarily if the ultimate damage is a natural consequence of the incident in question—to a greater extent if it is the *inevitable* consequence—that event is likely to be a proximate cause.[34] In *Leyland Shipping Co Ltd*,[35] the torpedoed vessel was said to be a "doomed ship" unless she could be moved into a place of safety (which she never quite reached). The ultimate sinking was held to be "the natural sequel to the injury by the torpedo"[36] and so the torpedo was the proximate cause of the loss, rather than the grounding of the vessel in the outer harbour of a port, which finally smashed the hull. Similarly, in the context of fire insurance, any loss that immediately results from an "apparently necessary and bona fide effort to put out a fire", such as damage by water thrown on the property, will nevertheless be treated as proximately caused by the fire.[37]

19-012   Coincidental causes are too remote.   The corollary of the principle that proximity is generally established where the loss is an ordinary or likely consequence of the event in question is that where damage is a quite unexpected result of the event, the connection between cause and loss is likely to be treated as too remote. At the extreme end of the scale, if the event could not be said even to increase the

---

paras 19-004 to 19-007) that there must be a single proximate cause.

[30] *Wayne Tank & Pump Co Ltd* [1974] Q.B. 57; [1973] 3 W.L.R. 483; [1973] 3 All E.R. 825.
[31] *Hamilton, Fraser & Co* (1887) 12 App. Cas. 518; (1888) 52 J.P. 196; [1886-90] All E.R. Rep. 220 HL.
[32] See above, para.19-007.
[33] Viscount Haldane, commenting on *Hamilton, Fraser & Co* (1887) 12 App. Cas. 518; (1888) 52 J.P. 196; [1886-90] All E.R. Rep. 220 HL, in *Leyland Shipping Co Ltd* [1918] A.C. 350 at 362; 14 Asp M.L.C. 258 at 261; [1918-19] All E.R. Rep. 443 at 449.
[34] M. Clarke, *The Law of Insurance Contracts*, (London: Informa), Vol.2, para.25-4; *Re Arbitration Etherington and Lancashire & Yorkshire Accident Insurance Co* [1909] 1 K.B. 591 at 598; 78 L.J.K.B. 684 at 687–688; [1908-10] All E.R. Rep. 581 at 585, per Vaughan Williams LJ.
[35] *Leyland Shipping Co Ltd* [1918] A.C. 350; [1918-19] All E.R. Rep. 443.
[36] *Leyland Shipping Co Ltd* [1918] A.C. 350 at 364; 14 Asp M.L.C. 258 at 262; [1918-19] All E.R. Rep. 443 at 450, per Lord Dunedin.
[37] *Stanley v The Western Insurance Co* (1867–1868) L.R. 3 Ex. 71 at 74; 37 L.J. Ex. 73 at 75.

background danger of the kind of accident that ultimately occurred (despite being, in the events which occurred, a "but for" cause of it) we would regard the causal connection as "trivial" or "coincidental".[38] An example was given in one case of a person suffering from a fit whilst playing sports, retiring to one side of the field to recover, and then being accidentally shot by another sportsman: it would be absurd if the seizure was treated as the cause of the accident.[39] If an event is a cause only inasmuch as it caused the accident to happen by causing the relevant actors to be in the wrong place at the wrong time the event is not a proximate cause of the loss.[40] We tend only to regard causes as significant, and hence non-trivial, if they are events that create a special risk, or increase the pre-existing danger, of the kind of outcome that actually occurred. So where a vessel was stranded, without being damaged, on an enemy coast and there captured, the loss was by capture and not perils of the sea

"for had the ship been driven on any other coast but that of an enemy, she would have been in perfect safety."[41]

Consequences of negligence and defective design tend to be proximate. Where 19-013 the relevant exclusion to cover is for the consequences of some form of negligence or for defects, provided that "but for" causation is established it is much harder to argue that this was not a proximate cause of the damage.[42] This is because negligence and defective design will, almost by definition, tend to increase the background risk of damage. In those circumstances it is not natural to perceive the connection between the negligence or the defect and the damage as being merely coincidental.

Subsequent wrongful conduct likely to break the chain of causation. Where 19-014 a fire encouraged a mob to plunder and insured glass was broken as a result, it was the violent lawlessness of the mob that was the proximate cause and the fire was too remote a cause to engage a policy exclusion.[43] Similarly, where the temporary absence of the occupier of premises during an air raid facilitated the stealing of goods, the theft and not the air raid was the proximate cause of their loss.[44] These decisions appear to stand for the proposition that the law is instinctively reluctant to allow the causal inquiry to be pushed back beyond deliberate and wrongful actions, which brought about the loss or damage. In the context of all risks cover, this

---

[38] A completely coincidental connection—that is where the insured peril does not even increase the background danger of the risk which ultimately occurs—would not even satisfy a clause that requires the loss to be "directly or indirectly caused by" the peril: *Coxe v Employers' Liability Assurance Corp Ltd* [1916] 2 K.B. 629 at 634 KB; 85 L.J.K.B. 1557 at 1559–1560; 114 L.T. 1180 at 1181.

[39] *Lawrence v Accidental Insurance Co Ltd* (1881) 7 Q.B.D. 216; 45 J.P. 781; 50 JLQB 522. The actual use of the example as an analogy in that case is questionable. The facts were that the insured, whilst standing at a railway station platform, was seized by a fit and fell onto the tracks where he was promptly killed by a passing train. This sequence of events was held not to be caught by exception for death "arising from fits" and accordingly the insured could recover. Yet the insured, being hit by the train, was hardly a coincidental consequence of the fit: having a seizure on a station platform creates an obvious and immediate danger of the very kind of accident that occurred. That was hardly a case of someone wandering into an unrelated danger as a result of their epilepsy.

[40] *Coxe* [1916] 2 K.B. 629 at 634; 85 L.J.K.B. 1557 at 1559 1560; 114 L.T. 1180 at 1181.

[41] *Green v Elmslie* 170 E.R. 156; (1794) Peake 278 at 279.

[42] See the discussion in *Wayne Tank & Pump Co Ltd* [1974] Q.B. 57 at 73–74; [1973] 3 W.L.R. 483 at 494–495; [1973] 3 All E.R. 825 at 836, per Roskill LJ.

[43] *Marsden v City and County Assurance Co* (1865–1866) L.R. 1 C.P. 232; (1865) 12 Jur. N.S. 76; (1865) 35 L.J.C.P. 60.

[44] *Winicofsky* (1919) 88 L.J.K.B. 1111; (1919) 35 TLR 283.

principle is, on balance, helpful to insured parties since the wilful misconduct of third parties is, prima facie, covered; where such misconduct is an operative cause of the loss it will tend to eclipse the range of previous causes, some of which might have otherwise brought policy exclusions into play.[45]

3.   EFFECT OF EXPRESS WORDING

19-015   The requirement of proximate cause is based on the presumed intentions of the parties. A policy covering, for example, "all risks ... except fire..." clearly only makes sense if that exclusion for fire risk is read as requiring a causal link between the damage and the fire. The principles of proximity outlined above are essentially the default approach to the question of how close that connection between cause and loss need be. A "proximate cause" is required inasmuch as it is assumed that the parties envisage a reasonably direct connection between the excluded event and the damage. But the parties are free to recalibrate the closeness of connection required between cause and loss by using appropriately limited or expansive wording. As such, the precise form of wording used by the parties will determine the nature of the causal enquiry that a court must undertake.

19-016   **"Directly or indirectly caused by".**   So if the policy excludes loss that is "directly or indirectly caused by" the specified peril, this exclusion can be engaged even if the peril played only an indirect role in bringing about the loss. In *Coxe*,[46] the insurers successfully defeated a claim under a life policy excluding death "directly or indirectly caused" by war risks where the insured was killed by a train whilst performing military sentry duties along a railway line, which was subject to a war-time blackout. Scrutton J held that the usual proximate cause rule was inconsistent with the words "directly or indirectly": it would be nonsensical to talk about an "indirect proximate cause".[47] It was still necessary on such wording, however, to demonstrate a more than wholly coincidental connection between the excluded peril and the accident. Scrutton J said:

> "If war had merely placed Captain Ewing in a position not specially exposed to any danger, and in that position a particular incident not connected with war caused his death, I think that most probably in that case the matter would not come within the condition."[48]

So if the insured had been sent to a military camp and struck by lightning there, the war would be so remote from the death that it could not be said that the death was indirectly caused by it. On the facts, however, the insured had been placed in a position of heightened danger by his military duties and had been killed by reason of that danger. That was enough to establish that his death was "indirectly traceable" to the war.[49]

19-017   In *Oei v Foster (formerly Crawford) and Eagle Star Insurance Co Ltd*,[50] the insured and his wife were covered by a householder's public liability policy, which excluded "damage arising directly or indirectly from ... ownership or occupation

---

[45]   *Marsden v City and County Assurance Co* (1865-66) L.R. 1 C.P. 232; (1865) 12 Jur. N.S. 76; (1865) 35 L.J.C.P. 60 was a case of all risks cover: the actions of the mob were not excluded, whereas loss originating from the cause of fire was specifically excluded.

[46]   *Coxe* [1916] 2 K.B. 629; 85 L.J.K.B. 1557; 114 L.T. 1180.

[47]   *Coxe* [1916] 2 K.B. 629 at 634; 85 L.J.K.B. 1557 at 1559–1560; 114 L.T. 1180 at 1181.

[48]   *Coxe* [1916] 2 K.B. 629 at 634–635.

[49]   *Coxe* [1916] 2 K.B. 629 at 635.

[50]   *Oei v Foster (formerly Crawford) and Eagle Star Insurance Co Ltd* [1982] 2 Lloyd's Rep. 170.

of any land or building".[51] Whilst staying in a neighbour's house, the insured's wife left some fat heating on an electric cooker, which caught fire while she went out. The insurers conceded that the occupation of the property was not the proximate cause of the damage—the proximate causes were turning on the heat on the cooker, putting a pan of fat on the cooker and failing to turn it off—but contended that the word "indirectly" brought the occupation within the exclusion. The judge agreed with that analysis: the occupation was an indirect cause because cooking meals was a necessary incident of the insured's occupation of the house.

In 2005, the Court of Appeal considered an exclusion for "disablement directly **19-018** or indirectly consequent upon" arthritic or other degenerative conditions in the context of an exclusion to an accidental injury policy taken out by a football club in respect of its players.[52] The court stressed that with such wording it was still necessary for the insurer to show that the pre-existing condition was a "but for" cause of the disablement, and not just the extent of the player's disability. However, the extended wording, "directly or indirectly", would reverse the usual rule that where a disease of the insured leads to an accident, that accident and not the disease is the proximate cause of the injury[53]: in the present case, if the pre-existing degeneration of the player's disc was the proximate cause of his sustaining injury to it, the exclusion applied.[54]

"Arising out of" and "arising from".   There is no difference between "arising   **19-019** out of" and "arising from."[55] In *Coxe*,[56] the judge suggested that the words "arising from" do not depart from the concept of proximate cause.[57] However, the better view is that these words do allow for a more relaxed connection between cause

---

[51]   *Oei* [1982] 2 Lloyd's Rep. 170 at 173.

[52]   *Blackburn Rovers Football & Athletic Club Plc v Avon Insurance Plc* [2005] EWCA Civ 423; [2005] 1 C.L.C. 554; [2005] Lloyd's Rep. I.R. 447.

[53]   The court stated that the usual rule was derived from two cases in which the insured's epileptic fit caused him to fall to a hazard: *Winspear v Accident Insurance Co Ltd* (1880) 6 Q.B.D. 42 (drowning in a river); and *Lawrence v Accidental Insurance Co Ltd* (1881) 7 Q.B.D. 216 (falling in front of a moving railway train). In both cases it was held that the immediate accident and not the epilepsy was the proximate cause of the loss and so the relevant exclusion was not engaged: *Blackburn Rovers Football & Athletic Club Plc* [2005] EWCA Civ 423 at [11]–[12]; [2005] 1 C.L.C. 554 at 562; [2005] Lloyd's Rep. I.R. 447 at 451–452. However, the court went on to state that the usual rule was, in this case, reversed (at [2005] EWCA Civ 423 at [13]; [2005] 1 C.L.C. 554 at 562; [2005] Lloyd's Rep. I.R. 447 at 452).

[54]   *Blackburn Rovers Football & Athletic Club Plc* [2005] EWCA Civ 423 at [18]; [2005] 1 C.L.C. 554 at 563; [2005] Lloyd's Rep. I.R. 447 at 452.

[55]   The effect of the wording "in respect of" is considered in the context of public liability policies at paras 18-040–18.041. As set out in *Tesco Stores Ltd v Constable* [2008] EWCA Civ 362; [2008] 1 C.L.C. 727; [2008] Lloyd's Rep. I.R. 636, in this context such wording means "for" and not merely caused by or in connection with. This wording identifies the causal event for the liability to a third party in respect of which the policy provides cover and may demarcate the limit on the extent of the cover provided by a public liability policy. In a different context it is possible for the wording "in respect of" to have a wider meaning, for example "in relation to". Ultimately, it is a question of construction.

[56]   *Coxe* [1916] 2 K.B. 629; 85 L.J.K.B. 1557; 114 L.T. 1180.

[57]   *Coxe* [1916] 2 K.B. 629 at 634; 85 L.J.K.B. 1557 at 1559-1560; 114 L.T. 1180 at 1181. Similarly, and though the point was not considered on appeal, in *Lloyds TSB General Insurance Holdings v Lloyds Bank Group Insurance Co Ltd; Abbey National Plc v Lee* [2001] EWCA Civ 1643 at [42]; [2002] 1 All E.R. (Comm) 42 at 54; [2002] Lloyd's Rep. I.R. 113 at 123, Potter LJ expressed the view, that the words "resulting from" did not weaken the causal connection required and were consistent with a search for a proximate cause. Although, see the broader view of such wording in *Cementation Piling and Foundations Ltd v Commercial Union Plc* [1995] 1 Lloyd's Rep 97; 74 B.L.R. 98; (1994) 47 Con. L.R. 14 in the context of write-back wording in a policy exclusion, which

and loss. In *Dunthorne v Bentley*,[58] a motorist's liability insurance covered accidents "caused by, or arising out of" the use of her car. The Court of Appeal held that this covered her liability for an accident in which she was struck by a passing vehicle as she ran across the road to get help after running out of petrol. This result seems to test the outer bounds of proximity; it is not easy to conceive of the use of the car as being itself a proximate cause of the loss. If the liability cover had been expressed in terms of accidents "caused by the use of your car" or "involving the insured car", would the decision have been the same?

19-020 In the same vein, more recent cases have suggested that "arising from" or "arising out of" denotes a weaker causal connection than a search for a proximate cause. In *Kajima UK Engineering Ltd v The Underwriter Insurance Co Ltd*, Akenhead J referred to the:

> "... relatively obvious proposition that where an insurance clause relates to cover for something 'arising out of' a particular contingency that expression may well be wider than an expression such as 'caused by'."[59]

19-021 **"Sole cause".** The doctrine of proximity can be restricted by a policy term that stipulates that the loss must be "solely caused by" the peril in question.[60] This wording could in theory be used to limit the scope of an exclusion to all risks cover, but in practice it is seen only in the context of defining the limits of primary cover under named perils, and, in particular, personal injury policies. The concept of exclusive causation is problematic, at least if taken literally, since every event must have an infinite (or, at least, uncountable) number of causes,[61] albeit that most (such as the fact that the insured was born) will be too remote to merit consideration. To give such words independent force, the phrase "solely" must be interpreted as meaning "not by any other proximate cause". In the context of a personal injury policy which responds only to injury that occasions disablement "solely and independently of any other cause", the insured will not recover where the injury has aggravated a pre-

---

is discussed above in Ch.16.

[58] *Dunthorne v Bentley* [1996] R.T.R. 428; [1996] P.I.Q.R. P323; 1999 Lloyd's Rep. I.R. 560. Also see *Government Insurance Office of New South Wales v RJ Green and Lloyd Pty Ltd* [1966] 114 CLR 437.

[59] *Kajima UK Engineering Ltd v The Underwriter Insurance Co Ltd* [2008] EWHC 83 (TCC) at [97]; [2008] 1 All E.R. (Comm) 855 at 879; [2008] Lloyd's Rep. I.R. 391 at 408. Equally, in *Beazley Underwriting Ltd v The Travelers Companies Inc.* [2011] EWHC 1520 (Comm); [2012] 1 All E.R. (Comm) 1241; [2012] Lloyd's Rep. I.R. 78, Christopher Clarke J., as he then was, stated that he was prepared to accept that "arising out of" denoted a weaker causal connection. However, in *British Waterways v Royal & Sun Alliance Insurance Plc* [2012] EWHC 460 (Comm) at [42]–[45]; [2012] Lloyd's Rep. I.R. 562 at 574 and 575 Burton J discussed the authorities on "arising out of" at [42]–[45], and stated, obiter, that he had "... the inevitable feeling that a court may in fact have a different approach to concluding whether there is cover for an event from where the court is being asked to conclude that an insurer can exclude cover, even though the words the court is considering may be identical." Indeed, the weaker causal connection denoted by such words does, to a certain extent, depend on context. For example, the test may be different in relation to the words "arising out of" in the context of aggregation clauses, which are dealt with in Ch.11. See Rix LJ's discussion in *Scott v Copenhagen Reinsurance Co (UK) Ltd* [2003] EWCA Civ 688 at [67]–[68]; [2003] 2 All E.R. (Comm) 190 at 211–212; [2003] Lloyd's Rep. I.R. 696 at 713–714 or *Lloyds TSB General Insurance Holdings Ltd v Lloyds Bank Group Insurance Co Ltd; Abbey National Plc v Lee* [2003] UKHL 48 at [15]–[16]; [2003] 2 All E.R. (Comm) 665 at 670–671; [2003] Lloyd's Rep. I.R. 623 at 629, per Lord Hoffmann, in relation to the wording "attributable to".

[60] *Mardorf v Accident Insurance Co* [1903] 1 K.B. 584; 72 L.J.Q.B. 362; [1900–1903] All E.R. Rep. 310 ("direct and sole cause"); *Fidelity & Casualty Co of New York v Mitchell* [1917] A.C. 592; 86 L.J.P.C. 204; 117 L.T. 494 ("independently and exclusively of all other causes").

[61] See above, para.19-001.

existing arthritic condition—a scenario which has played out in relation to professional footballers.[62] By contrast, if the injury reactivates a latent and previously symptomless medical condition, which then hampers the recovery process, the insured may be entitled to recover despite wording requiring the injury to have been caused "exclusively" by accidental means.[63]

Redefining the peril.   The more straightforward way of expanding or limiting the   **19-022** reach of a peril is simply to define that peril in wider or narrower terms. This technique can be less hit-and-miss than the often impressionistic exercise of identifying causes as "proximate", "indirect", "sole" and so on. For example, if insurers wish to exclude, as well as the risk of direct fire damage, the risk of looting encouraged or facilitated by civil commotion[64] they could choose to express this simply by excluding "fire and any theft or looting during the course of a fire at the insured property".[65]

---

[62] *Southampton Leisure Holdings Plc v Avon Insurance Plc* [2004] EWHC 571 (QB); *Blackburn Rovers Football and Athletic Club Plc* [2005] EWCA Civ 423; [2005] 1 C.L.C. 554; [2005] Lloyd's Rep. I.R. 447.

[63] *Fidelity & Casualty Co of New York v Mitchell* [1917] 1 A.C. 592; 86 LJPC 204; 117 L.T. 494. It appears that the accident was considered the sole proximate cause of injury because the existing condition would have remained harmless had the accident not occurred.

[64] See above, para.19-014.

[65] That particular wording would remove any causal requirement in relation to the looting: if it could be determined that a burglary had by coincidence been planned in advance the burglary would nonetheless be caught by the exclusion. This may seem like a crude way of identifying looting connected with the fire, but it does have the significant advantage that it is dispute-resistant: it avoids argument as to the motives of unknown thieves and hooligans, which would probably have to be anyway resolved with the inference that the theft, from its timing, was encouraged by the fire. Looking at the matter from another perspective, an insurer may be keen to limit cover by reference to the time and place of some event, without being interested in a causal link between that event and damage, because it is associated with unacceptably high levels of risk: see M. Clarke, *The Law of Insurance Contracts*, (London: Informa), Vol.2, para.25-9C1(b).

CHAPTER 20

CO-INSURANCE

1. INTRODUCTION

Outline. Multi-party insurance is especially common in the context of construc- **20-001**
tion projects, in that policies against all risks of loss of damage to the works are usu-

ally taken out in the "joint names"[1] of the employer and the contractor. This chapter considers the issues that arise from such policies in three key areas. First, it deals with whether a person named or identified as an insured person in the policy is a party to it, or can otherwise take the benefit of the insurance. Secondly, it addresses whether the rights of the co-insureds are "joint" or "composite", an issue that determines whether one co-insured is affected by the misconduct or fraud of another. Thirdly, it considers the circumstances in which a co-insured party is protected from a subrogated claim brought by the insurer in the name of another co-insured.

2. Identifying the co-insureds

(a) Background

20-002 **No intention to insure by named insureds.** Where the person or persons in whose name the policy is made insure on behalf of themselves and on behalf of other persons identified in the policy—typically under the heading "Other Assureds" or "Additional Assureds"—either by name or by description, the question arises as to whether those other persons can take the benefit of the insurance. The mere fact that a policy states that it covers the interests of both the contracting insured as well as named or identifiable third parties does not, in itself, permit those third parties the right to rely upon the terms of the policy. In the *Boston Fruit Co* case,[2] owners of a vessel arranged insurance that was stated to be

> "as well in their own name as ... in the name ... [of] ... every other person ... to whom the subject-matter of this policy does may or shall appertain".[3]

The charterers, who were undoubtedly included within the description, argued that the provision "must be taken to mean what it says"[4] and sought an indemnity under the policy. The House of Lords upheld the judgment for the insurers, holding that where the person claiming the benefit was not intended to be insured by those who effected the policy, his claim will fail "though he might be within the description".[5]

20-003 **Additional insureds enforcing the insurance policy: the options available.** There are two routes by which a party identified as an additional insured in the policy may be entitled to enforce the insurance:

---

[1] It is important not to be misled by this terminology. "Joint names policy" is a convenient term for a policy that names more than one person as a co-insured—it does not indicate that the rights of the parties are "joint" rather than "composite" (see below, paras 20-030 to 20-031 of this chapter). This point is made clear under the revised Joint Contracts Tribunal (JCT); e.g. SBC/Q 2011 *JCT Standard Building Contract With Quantities 2011* (London: Sweet & Maxwell, 2011), pp.69–70, cl.6.8, which defines a "joint names policy" as "a policy of insurance which includes the Employer and the Contractor as composite insured".

[2] *Boston Fruit Co v British and Foreign Marine Insurance Co Ltd* [1905] 1 K.B. 637.

[3] *Boston Fruit Co* [1905] 1 K.B. 637 at 638.

[4] *Boston Fruit Co v British and Foreign Marine Insurance Co Ltd* [1906] A.C. 336 at 338; 75 L.J.K.B. 537 at 539; 10 Asp. M.L.C. 260 at 261.

[5] *Boston Fruit Co* [1906] 1 A.C. 336 at 339; 75 L.J.K.B. 537 at 540; 10 Asp. M.L.C. 260 at 261, per Lord Loreburn L.C. It is quite possible that this case, and others discussed in the context of the agency rules, would have been decided differently under the Contracts (Rights of Third Parties) Act 1999. See further below, paras 20-003, 20-018 to 20-023.

1.   by way of an agency relationship. If the person in whose name the policy
      was placed was authorised to insure the additional insured and intended to
      do so (or if his act can be ratified),[6] the third party may become a party to
      the contract in his own right at common law; or
2.   under the Contracts (Rights of Third Parties) Act 1999 (the "1999 Act"). A
      person named or otherwise identified in the policy as an additional insured
      may, provided the conditions in the 1999 Act are satisfied, have a right to
      enforce the policy on the basis that it was made for his benefit.

Prior to the 1999 Act.   In the past third party insureds had no choice but to rely   **20-004**
upon the rules of agency. Under these rules, the question of whether and to what
extent they may enforce the policy is not straightforward.[7] The inquiry does not stop
with the wording of the policy terms said to bring the third party within the
insurance. In the case of CAR insurance, it is also necessary to consider the insurance obligations in the original building contract. Moreover, the oral and written
communications between the primary insured and the third party may become
relevant as evidence of the subjective intentions of the former to act on behalf of
the latter.

In contrast, under the 1999 Act the question is whether, on a proper interpreta-   **20-005**
tion of the insurance contract, the third party is sufficiently identified and intended
to benefit. However, the courts have yet to consider the application of the 1999 Act
to multi-party insurance contracts, and it is suggested that there is a question mark
as to its effect in certain situations. Accordingly, it is necessary to consider the
agency rules as they apply in this context.

(b)   Enforcing insurance by a third party according to the rules of agency

Third party establishing an agency relationship.   If "A" (the insurer) insures   **20-006**
"B" (the primary insured) under a policy that names or refers to "C" (the third party)
as an additional insured, C may be able to establish an agency relationship, and so
enforce the insurance as a party, in one of three ways:

(i)   Rule (1): disclosed principal (B authorised to insure C; policy identifies C)

Three elements to the rule.   There are three requirements under this rule. First,   **20-007**
C must be identified by the insurance policy by name or as a member of a described
class. Secondly and thirdly, C will only be covered to the extent that B had the
authority and the intention to contract on behalf of C at the time the insurance was
taken out.[8]

Named or described.   First, the policy must be expressed to extend cover to C   **20-008**
either by name or by C fitting into a generic class stated to be insured under the
policy. If the policy is not so worded, C will be left to rely, if he can, on the rules

---

[6]   See below, para.20-017.
[7]   See below, paras 20-006 to 20-017.
[8]   *National Oilwell (UK) Ltd v Davy Offshore Ltd* [1993] 2 Lloyd's Rep. 582; [1994] C.L.Y. 4086 QB.

governing the ability of an undisclosed principal to enforce a contract.[9] A description of insureds commonly included in CAR policies is "subcontractors". In *Hopewell Project Management Ltd and Hopewell Energy (Philippines) Corp v Ewbank Preece Ltd*, a firm engaged by a project developer to provide engineering consultancy contended that it was covered by a clause in a CAR policy that defined the insured as, inter alia, "all contractors and subcontractors".[10] The judge held that this phrase was limited to those carrying out "physical works of construction" and accordingly did not cover a firm providing only professional (i.e. consultancy) services.[11] On the other hand, a sub-subcontractor has been held to be within the meaning of the term "subcontractor".[12] It is suggested that in the same way that the phrase "subcontractor" is implicitly limited to those carrying out on-site construction works, a "supplier" in this context is someone who has produced or delivered up products for the specific project in question.[13] Thus an insured "supplier" does not refer to all suppliers of every tier. A supplier with no knowledge of the relevant project nor any contractual link to any of the parties working on site—for example, the manufacturer of a pre-installed screw in a manufactured window unit—is unlikely to have the benefit of project insurance that names "suppliers" as additional insureds even if there is an agency relationship.[14]

20-009   In *O'Kane v Jones (The Martin P)*, it was held that a shipowner qualified as an "affiliated and/or associated company"[15] of the ship's managers, given the "close relationship"[16] between the two parties, despite the fact that the two companies were not part of the same corporate group. That decision was distinguished in another case in which it was held that a company the insured shipowner had engaged to outfit the vessel was not within the phrase "and/or Subsidiary, Affiliates, Associated and Joint Ventures".[17] The judge considered that the adjectives used suggested a familial relationship or the sharing of a common enterprise; and that an outfitting or building contract concerning the outfitting company was an arm's-length commercial contract and, as such, did not give rise to the necessary type of relationship required by the clause.[18]

---

[9]   *Talbot Underwriting Ltd v Nausch, Hogan & Murray Inc (The Jascon 5)* [2006] EWCA Civ 889; [2006] 2 All E.R. (Comm) 75; [2006] 2 Lloyd's Rep. 195. See below paras 20-014 to 20-016.

[10]   *Hopewell Project Management Ltd and Hopewell Energy (Philippines) Corp v Ewbank Preece Ltd* [1998] 1 Lloyd's Rep. 448.

[11]   *Hopewell* [1998] 1 Lloyd's Rep. 448 at 455–456. See above paras 8-011 to 8-014.

[12]   *Petrofina (UK) Ltd v Magnaload Ltd* [1984] Q.B. 127; [1983] 3 W.L.R. 805; [1983] 3 All E.R. 35. The judge in *Hopewell* [1998] 1 Lloyd's Rep. 448 at 449 approved that view, subject to the point that the contractor, of whatever tier, must be carrying out physical works of construction to fall within the term.

[13]   Even if the policy adopts the phrase "suppliers of every tier", there surely must still be some implicit requirement of proximity. The phrase is arguably limited to suppliers who have, at the very least, been given notice of the particular project in which the component is being used. Alternatively, it may mean those with a direct-supply contract with any contractor or subcontractor (of any tier) working on site.

[14]   See above, paras 8-026 to 8-027.

[15]   *O'Kane v Jones (The Martin P)* [2003] EWHC 3470 (Comm) at [127]; [2004] 1 Lloyd's Rep. 389 at 415; [2005] Lloyd's Rep. I.R. 174 at 201.

[16]   *O'Kane* [2003] EWHC 3470 (Comm) at [127]; [2004] 1 Lloyd's Rep. 389 at 415; [2005] Lloyd's Rep. I.R. 174 at 201.

[17]   *Talbot Underwriting Ltd v Nausch, Hogan & Murray* [2005] EWHC 2359 (Comm); [2005] 2 C.L.C. 868; [2005] All E.R. (D) 95 (Nov). The decision on this point was not challenged on appeal: [2006] EWCA Civ 889; [2006] 2 All E.R. (Comm) 751; [2006] 2 Lloyd's Rep. 195.

[18]   *Talbot Underwriting Ltd* [2006] EWCA Civ 889 at [31]–[35]; [2006] 2 All E.R. (Comm) 751 at 763–

There is an analogous requirement that the third party be expressly identified **20-010** either by name or as answering to a particular description under the 1999 Act.[19]

Authority. Secondly, B must have had authority to take out insurance on C's **20-011** behalf. The most likely source for this authorisation is an obligation in an agreement between B and C to the effect that B will obtain insurance for C.[20] So in the context of CAR insurance, the building contract to which B and C are parties (the main contract or subcontract as the case may be) should be considered if the CAR policy does not indicate whether B had authority to take out insurance on C's behalf. If the building contract obliges B to take out CAR insurance on behalf of C, B's authorisation extends to taking out insurance meeting that description.[21] If, conversely, there was no contractual obligation on the part of B to procure the benefit of cover for C, there is no reason to suppose that B had authority to contract on C's behalf,[22] unless C had specifically requested (for example, in a letter) that B arrange cover.[23]

If B's authority to insure is limited to particular risks, yet B procures wider cover, **20-012** C will become a party to the policy but will be a co-insured only in respect of those particular risks. This is the effect of the decision in *National Oilwell (UK) Ltd v Davy Offshore Ltd*.[24] Davy Offshore Ltd ("DOL"), as main contractor for the construction of a floating oil-production facility in the North Sea, entered into a contract with National Oilwell (UK) Ltd ("NOW") under which NOW was to supply a wellhead completion system to form part of the installation. DOL obtained insurance, which was expressed to include subcontractors as "Other Assureds".[25] The subcontract provided that DOL should insure on behalf of the subcontractors work and materials "in the course of manufacture up until the time of delivery" (clearly a specified risk).[26] NOW sought to defend a subrogated claim by DOL's insurers on the basis that NOW was jointly insured in respect of the loss.[27] DOL conceded that NOW was co-insured but only to the extent envisaged in the subcontract and therefore not in respect of the post-delivery damage in respect of which it was claiming. The judge held that the obligation to procure insurance was confined to cover only up to the time of delivery of each item by NOW, as required by the subcontract.[28] There was nothing elsewhere in the agreement that gave any wider authority to DOL to secure cover, nor did anything pass in between the par-

---

765; [2006] 2 Lloyd's Rep. 195 at 207, per Cooke J.

[19] Section 1(3) of the 1999 Act provides: "The third party must be expressly identified in the contract by name, as a member of a class or as answering a particular description but need not be in existence when the contract is entered into."

[20] *National Oilwell (UK) Ltd* [1993] 2 Lloyd's Rep. 582 at 597; [1994] C.L.Y. 4086.

[21] *National Oilwell (UK) Ltd* [1993] 2 Lloyd's Rep. 582 at 598; [1994] C.L.Y. 4086; applied in *BP Exploration Operating Co Ltd v Kvaerner Oilfield Properties Ltd* [2004] EWHC 999 (Comm) at [12] and [16]; [2004] 2 All E.R. (Comm) 266 at 270; [2005] 1 Lloyd's Rep. 307 at 310 and 311.

[22] *Boston Fruit Co* [1906] 1 A.C. 336; 75 L.J.K.B. 537; 10 Asp. M.L.C. 260; *Stone Vickers Ltd v Appledore Ferguson Shipbuilders Ltd* [1992] 2 Lloyd's Rep. 578.

[23] As was the case in *O'Kane* [2003] EWHC 3470 (Comm) at 106–123; [2004] 1 Lloyd's Rep. 389 at 411–414; [2005] Lloyd's Rep. I.R. 174 at 198–201.

[24] *National Oilwell (UK) Ltd* [1993] 2 Lloyd's Rep. 582; [1994] C.L.Y. 4086.

[25] *National Oilwell (UK) Ltd* [1993] 2 Lloyd's Rep. 582 at 588; [1994] C.L.Y. 4086 at [1099–1100].

[26] *National Oilwell (UK) Ltd* [1993] 2 Lloyd's Rep. 582 at 592; [1994] C.L.Y. 4086.

[27] The issue of co-insurance as a defence to subrogation is discussed further below at paras 20-040 to 20-052.

[28] *National Oilwell (UK) Ltd* [1993] 2 Lloyd's Rep. 582 at 597–598; [1994] C.L.Y. 4086 at [1099–1100].

ties in the course of pre-contractual negotiations to that effect.[29] Accordingly, NOW was only co-insured to the limited extent envisaged by the subcontract agreed with DOL. It is important to note that in the context of CAR insurance, it is ordinarily the case that the insurance policy is incepted before any subcontract has come into existence, or even prior to all subcontractors being selected. Indeed, a CAR policy will typically name the employer and main contractor, but state that the policy is to cover "subcontractors of any tier" or use similar wording. Therefore the approach adopted in *National Oilwell (UK) Ltd*,[30] whereby the terms of the subcontract between B and C were used to establish B's authority and intention to contract on behalf of C in respect of the policy, is of limited application. .

20-013 **Intention.** Thirdly, B must intend, at the time the policy was taken out, to insure on behalf of C. In practice, the issue of intention will usually be controlled by the issue of authority. Absent evidence to the contrary, it can be assumed that B, when taking out insurance, intends to act in accordance with his instructions.[31] Conversely, if B was not contractually obliged or otherwise requested to arrange insurance for C, the courts will assume (unless there is evidence of specific intention to the contrary) that B intended to insure purely for its own benefit.[32]

(ii)   Rule (2): undisclosed principal (B authorised to insure C; policy does not expressly cover C)

20-014 **Undisclosed principal.** If C does not fall within the description of the insureds specified in the policy, C cannot enforce the insurance unless the doctrine of undisclosed principal applies. In order for C to sue as an undisclosed principal, B must have had actual authority and an intention to contract on C's behalf when taking out the insurance, as discussed above under Rule 1. However, A (the insurer) must also have been willing or ostensibly willing to treat as a principal anyone on whose behalf the agent may have been authorised to contract.[33] A further issue that makes establishing agency under this rule difficult is that the right of an undisclosed principal to sue on the contract will be excluded if the terms of the policy, expressly or by implication, indicate that the person in whose name the policy is taken out is the true and only principal, or if the circumstances surrounding the contract point to that conclusion.[34] Moreover, it has been held that for this rule to work C's identity must be a matter of indifference to the insurer—otherwise failure to disclose C's

---

[29]   *National Oilwell (UK) Ltd* [1993] 2 Lloyd's Rep. 582 at 598; [1994] C.L.Y. 4086 at [1099–1100].

[30]   *National Oilwell (UK) Ltd* [1993] 2 Lloyd's Rep. 582; [1994] C.L.Y. 4086.

[31]   See *Talbot Underwriting Ltd* [2006] EWCA Civ 889 at [23]; [2006] 2 All E.R. (Comm) 751 at 761; [2006] 2 Lloyd's Rep. 195 at 227. Indeed, if B intends not to cover C despite being obliged to do so, this is likely to be a breach of contract. Further, an obligation to insure C may be in itself an answer to a subrogated claim brought by the insurer in the name of B against C: *Co-operative Retail Services Ltd v Taylor Young Partnership Ltd* [2002] UKHL 17; [2002] 1 W.L.R. 1419; [2002] 1 All E.R. (Comm) 918.

[32]   *Boston Fruit Co* [1906] 1 A.C. 336; 75 L.J.K.B. 537; 10 Asp. M.L.C. 260; *National Oilwell (UK) Ltd* [1993] 2 Lloyd's Rep. 582; [1994] C.L.Y. 4086.

[33]   *Teheran-Europe Co Ltd v ST Belton (Tractors) Ltd (No.1)* [1968] 2 Q.B. 545 at 555; [1968] 3 W.L.R. 205 at 211–212; [1968] 2 All E.R. 886 at 890 CA, per Diplock LJ (on the undisclosed principal doctrine generally). Lord Diplock added: "in the case of an ordinary commercial contract such willingness of the other party may be assumed by the agent unless either the other party manifests his unwillingness or there are other circumstances which should lead the agent to realise that the other party was not so willing".

[34]   *Siu Yin Kwan v Eastern Insurance Co Ltd* [1994] 2 A.C. 199 at 207; [1994] 2 W.L.R. 370 at 376–

identity may entitle the insurer to avoid the policy for breach of the insured's disclosure duties.[35]

Despite these hurdles, the undisclosed principal doctrine was relied upon successfully in *Siu Yin Kwan*.[36] An employers' liability policy was taken out by shipping agents, who were described in the policy as the insured, on behalf of shipowners, who employed the crew covered by the policy. The insurers denied that the shipowners had any right to claim under the policy as they were not named or identified as an insured. The Privy Council, overturning the decisions of the Hong Kong courts,[37] held that the shipowners/employers were entitled to sue under the policy. There was nothing in the terms of the proposal form, or the policy, which expressly or by implication excluded the shipowners' right to sue as undisclosed principal. Indeed, there were obvious clues in the proposal form that the shipping agents were not in fact the employers of the crew, and in those circumstances the insurers were not entitled to assume that the shipping agents were the true employers.[38] Whilst the issue of material non-disclosure was not apparently considered, the Privy Council stressed that the actual identity of the employer was a matter of indifference to the insurer: it was not material to the risk because the insurer would have been prepared to insure the employer of the crew of the vessel, whoever that might be. **20-015**

Application to CAR policies. It is hard to imagine a CAR policy where the existence of additional co-insureds could be said to be a matter of indifference to the insurer. In a typical case, the right of a subcontractor to be treated as a co-insured would be likely to affect the insurer's ability to pursue a claim against it in the name of the insured main contractor or developer.[39] **20-016**

(iii) Rule (3): ratification (B not initially authorised to insure C; policy identifies C)

Ratification. If B takes out insurance on behalf of C without proper authority to do so, C will still be able to take advantage of the insurance by ratifying B's act provided at least three requirements are met. First, since ratification is a matter of retrospectively conferring authority on an agent acting without authority, B must have specifically intended to insure on C's behalf when entering into the contract. For this reason, ratification will rarely avail third parties in this context: if B was **20-017**

377; [1994] 1 All E.R. 213 at 220–221. It was said in this case at [1994] 2 A.C. 199 at 208–209; [1994] 2 W.L.R. 370 at 378; [1994] 1 All E.R. 213 at 222 that courts should not be "too ready to construe written contracts as contradicting the right of an undisclosed principal to intervene" because this would be inconsistent with the presumption that commercial parties are willing to treat as principal anyone on whose behalf the agent may have been authorised to contract. However, the practical effect of this dictum is diminished by the decision in *Talbot Underwriting Ltd* [2006] EWCA Civ 889; [2006] 2 All E.R. (Comm) 751; [2006] 2 Lloyd's Rep. 195 that the undisclosed principal doctrine is subject to the duty of utmost good faith. To defeat such a claim an insurer does not have to contest the existence of an agency relationship, but merely establish that the identity of the insured would have been a material matter.

[35] *Talbot Underwriting Ltd* [2006] EWCA Civ 889; [2006] 2 All E.R. (Comm) 751; [2006] 2 Lloyd's Rep. 195. See above, Ch.6 for further discussion of an insured's disclosure duties.
[36] *Siu Yin Kwan* [1994] 2 A.C. 199; [1994] 2 W.L.R. 370; [1994] 1 All E.R. 213.
[37] *Siu Yin Kwan* [1992] HKCA 316; [1993] HKLR 101 and [1992] HKCFI 104.
[38] *Siu Yin Kwan* [1994] 2 A.C. 199 at 208; [1994] 2 W.L.R. 370 at 378; [1994] 1 All E.R. 213 at 221.
[39] *Talbot Underwriting Ltd* [2006] EWCA Civ 889 at [41]; [2006] 2 All E.R. (Comm) 751 at 766; [2006] 2 Lloyd's Rep. 195 at 230–231.

not required or authorised to insure C's interests, the courts will not presume B had the intention to do so.[40] Secondly, it follows from the fact that ratification relates back to the act of the purported agent that C must have been of full capacity and legally competent to enter the contract as principal at the date of the contract.[41] Thirdly, the policy must expressly cover C as a co-insured either by name or as a member of a class of co-insureds; the undisclosed principal doctrine[42] cannot be relied upon in conjunction with ratification, in that the principal's identity must be disclosed in circumstances where the person purporting to act on his behalf (i.e. B on behalf of C) is not authorised to do so.[43] Finally, it may be that in the context of non-marine insurance[44] ratification must take place before the principal became aware of the loss. There is, however, a conflict of authority on this point.[45]

(c)   Enforcement under the Contracts (Rights of Third Parties) Act 1999

(i)   Acquiring rights under the 1999 Act

20-018   **Conditions.**   A third party derives a right to enforce contract terms under the 1999 Act if two conditions are satisfied. First, the third party must be identified by name, or identifiable by description or by membership of a class.[46] Secondly, the contract must indicate that the third party can enforce the relevant term, either (a) by expressly providing that the third party may do so (s.1(1)(a) of the 1999 Act); or (b) it is clear the term in question "purports to confer a benefit on him" (s.1(1)(b) of the 1991 Act), but this will not be the case if "on a proper construction of the contract it appears that the parties did not intend the term to be enforceable by the third party" (s.1(2) of the 1999 Act).

20-019   A policy which, for example, provides that "subcontractors" are "insured" or "additionally insured" or identifies subcontractors as an insured class and as such purports to confer on them the status of being insured under the policy, would plainly satisfy the requirement in s.1(1)(b) of the 1999 Act. Accordingly, anyone answering to the description of a subcontractor would be entitled to rely on the identification-of-insureds clause and claim the benefit of the insurance unless and to the extent that the terms of the policy indicate otherwise. The interpretation of definitional terms such as "subcontractor" or "affiliated company" have been

---

[40]   See above, para.20-013.
[41]   So a company cannot ratify a contract made on its behalf before the company was formed: *Natal Land and Colonization Co Ltd v Pauline Colliery and Development Syndicate Ltd* [1904] A.C. 120; 73 L.J.P.C 22; 11 Mans 29.
[42]   See above, para.20-014.
[43]   *Keighley, Maxsted & Co v Durant (t/a Byran Durant & Co)*; sub nom. *Durant & Co v Roberts* [1901] A.C. 240; 70 L.J.K.B. 662; [1900–3] All E.R. Rep 40.
[44]   In marine insurance, s.86 of the Marine Insurance Act 1906 however, provides that "[w]here a contract of marine insurance is in good faith effected by one person on behalf of another, the person on whose behalf it is effected may ratify the contract even after he is aware of a loss."
[45]   See discussion of Colman J in *National Oilwell (UK) Ltd* [1993] 2 Lloyd's Rep. 582 at 607–608. Colman J notes that there is little authority on this point. He establishes that what English authority there is suggests that the party seeking to rely on a policy cannot ratify it after he becomes aware of his loss. But he also said that he could see no legal principle or commercial reason why the English courts should hold that a party's ability to ratify should depend on his state of mind. He also stated that it was undesirable for marine insurance and general insurance to be treated differently.
[46]   Section 1(3) of the 1999 Act.

considered above in connection with the rules of agency and there is no reason to suppose their interpretation under the 1999 Act will be any different.[47]

The position may be more difficult where the party intending to enforce a right **20-020** under the 1999 Act is not identified by name or by class on the policy, but may instead have an interest in the insured subject matter and may seek to bring a claim on that basis. The wording of s.1(3) of the 1999 Act does not appear to allow such a party to bring a claim, as it provides that a third party "must be *expressly* identified in the contract by name, as a member of a class or as answering a particular description". However, it is possible to envisage circumstances in which the surrounding factual matrix against which the policy was incepted would indicate that a third party was intended to receive the benefit of the policy, despite not being named in the policy documents. In such circumstances, the courts would have to determine whether the proper interpretation of s.1(3) of the 1999 Act would incorporate the usual canons of contractual construction to permit reliance on the factual matrix as an aid to the interpretation of the policy, or whether the wording of the 1999 Act is sufficiently clear to preclude this possibility. To date, there has been no authority on the point. The closest the English courts have come to dealing with this issue was in *Petromec Inc v Petroleo Brasiliero SA Petrobas*,[48] a case in which the court was considering an analogous provision in Brazilian law. Whilst the court determined that the third party's retained interest in the insured property was not sufficient to allow the third party to bring the claim, what is notable about the decision is that the court took account of the surrounding factual matrix in order to reach this decision. It is suggested that similar reasoning could be applied to a claim brought under the 1999 Act.[49]

Acquiring rights under the 1999 Act and the rules of agency compared. The **20-021** manner of acquiring rights under the 1999 Act does differ significantly from the position under the rules of agency. First, the third party's rights will be determined purely by the expressed intentions of the parties, as discerned by ordinary principles of contractual construction.[50] A term that purports to confer a benefit on a third party will create an enforceable right unless on "a proper construction of the contract"[51] it is not intended to do so. There is no need to show a subjective intention to confer rights on a particular third party any more than it is necessary to show, on the ordinary principles for interpreting a written agreement, that either party consciously intended to subscribe, for example, to the retained liability limit specified in the written agreement.

Secondly, it is not necessary, as it would be under the rules of agency, for the par- **20-022** ties to the insurance contract to have had in their specific contemplation the third party now seeking to enforce the policy. Such a requirement would be contrary to the provision in s.1(3) of the 1999 Act that the third party, if sufficiently identified by the contract, need not be in existence when the contract is entered into.

Thirdly, it follows that it is unnecessary to show that the primary insured had any **20-023**

---

[47] See above, paras 20-008 to 20-009.
[48] *Petromec Inc v Petroleo Brasiliero SA Petrobas* [2004] EWHC 1180 (Comm) at [40]–[43]; [2005] 1 Lloyd's Rep. 219 at 227–229.
[49] A similar view is expressed in *Chitty on Contracts*, edited by H.G. Beale, A.S. Burrows et al, 32nd edn (London: Sweet & Maxwell, 2015), Vol.1, para.18–093.
[50] *Nisshin Shipping Co Ltd v Cleaves & Co Ltd* [2003] EWHC 2602 (Comm) at [23]; [2004] 1 All E.R. (Comm) 481 at 487; [2004] 1 Lloyd's Rep. 38 at 42. For a full discussion about the principles of contractual construction and interpretation; see above, Ch.13.
[51] Section 1(2) of the 1999 Act.

particular reason—such as a prior contractual obligation—to insure the third party. It will only be necessary to refer to extraneous contractual arrangements if there is a term in the policy itself that expressly indicates that the scope of cover should be limited to what was envisaged in a prior contract,[52] or because the description of the class of insureds (e.g. "contractors") by its very nature has to be interpreted by reference to some other agreement.[53]

(ii)   Nature of rights derived under the 1999 Act

20-024   Limitations on a third party's rights.   The third party's right to enforce the term that confers cover (that is, the insuring clause) will be subject to the various exclusions, retained liability provisions, etc., that appear in the rest of the policy,[54] as well as the policy's notification requirements or any other pre-condition to making a claim.[55]

20-025   Act of misconduct or material non-disclosure by the primary insured.   If the primary insured defaults on the insurance policy—for example, through his wilful misconduct or material non-disclosure[56]—s.3(2) of the 1999 Act provides that:

"The promisor shall have available to him by way of defence or set-off any matter that—

(a)   arises from or in connection with the contract and is relevant to the term, and
(b)   would have been available to him by way of defence or set-off if the proceedings had been brought by the promisee."

20-026   The question arises as to whether, an insurer could defeat a claim by a third party (who is otherwise entitled to an indemnity by virtue of s.1 of the 1999 Act) by relying on a default of the primary insured in circumstances where the insurer would not have been able to avoid liability had the claimant been a party to the insurance contract. Where a mortgagor and mortgagee together insure a property, their policy is a treated as composite insurance.[57] Where they are both parties to the insurance policy, a material non-disclosure on the part of the mortgagor does not affect the

---

52   In *National Oilwell (UK) Ltd* [1993] 2 Lloyd's Rep. 582 at 588 and 601 there was precisely such a term: the policy stated that "[t]he interests of the 'Other Assured(s)' shall be covered ... unless specific contract(s) contain provisions to the contrary". Colman J held that this clause as a matter of contract—even apart from the limited extent of the main contractor's authority and intention to insure—cut down the scope of cover provided to the subcontractor to the cover which had to be procured under the subcontract. For this reason, it is suggested that the actual decision in *National Oilwell (UK) Ltd* would be the same if it had been decided under the 1999 Act.

53   But in the latter case, the purpose of referring to the contract would be simply to determine whether the third party seeking to enforce the insurance was indeed a subcontractor, and not to determine whether the contract conferred authority on the main contractor to procure insurance.

54   Further, ss.3(1)–(4) of the 1999 Act have the effect that, inter alia, the insurer can raise any defence that would have been available to it had the third party been a party to the contract or that is relevant to the term sought to be enforced and would have been available had proceedings been brought by the promisee.

55   Indeed, s.3(6) of the 1999 Act provides that: "Where in any proceedings brought against him a third party seeks in reliance on section 1 to enforce a term of a contract (including, in particular, a term purporting to exclude or limit liability), he may not do so if he could not have done so (whether by reason of any particular circumstances relating to him or otherwise) had he been a party to the contract."

56   See above, Ch.6 for the remedies available for material non-disclosure.

57   *Woolcott v Sun Alliance and London Insurance Ltd* [1978] 1 W.L.R. 493; [1978] 1 All E.R. 1253; [1978] 1 Lloyd's Rep. 629. See below, para.20-030.

rights of the mortgagee.[58] However, where the mortgagee is *not* a party to the policy—although he is named as an additional insured—it is possible that a claim by the mortgagee could be defeated under s.3 of the 1999 Act.

Where the mortgagee is not a party to the insurance policy, s.3(2)(b) of the 1999 **20-027** Act is satisfied: a claim brought by the property owner would have been prevented by his non-disclosure. There are two views regarding s.3(2)(a). Under one interpretation, the phrase "term" refers not to a discrete clause, but rather the particular right or obligation sought to be enforced: in this context the (prima facie) right under the insuring clause of the third party to be indemnified. If that is correct, it could be said that, this being a composite policy, the matter of the mortgagor's non-disclosure is "not relevant" to the term allowing the mortgagee to have the benefit of the insurance. However, the alternative view is that, the "term" sought to be enforced is the insuring clause of the policy; the mortgagor's non-disclosure or other default is then plainly "relevant to" that term as well as being something that "arises from or in connection with the contract". Accordingly, the insurer would have a defence to the mortgagee's claim under the 1999 Act. There may be some cases, therefore, where an additional insured may have a more secure entitlement if he can establish privity of contract via the rules of agency.

Effect on third party of subrogated claim brought by co-insured. A further is- **20-028** sue is whether a party that is named as an additional insured and has derivative rights under the 1999 Act is immune from a subrogated claim brought by a co-insured. Undoubtedly a third party could take the benefit of any waiver-of-subrogation clause that would apply to it. However, without an express clause it is unclear whether a third party would have a defence to subrogation as a co-insured in respect of the loss under the *Petrofina*[59] line of authority.[60] Inasmuch as the cover granted to the third party by the policy extends to the loss that forms the basis of the subrogated claim, the logic of the co-insurance defence does seem to apply. However, there is a potential problem: it is suggested that the *Petrofina*[61] defence is based on an implied term in the insurance contract,[62] yet it is not at all clear that the 1999 Act applies to anything other than express terms. The wording "purports to confer a benefit" in s.1(1)(b) of the 1999 Act is arguably inapt to apply to an implied term. The point is yet to be decided.

(iii) Summary

The 1999 Act and rules of agency compared. Under the 1999 Act it is gener- **20-029** ally simpler than under the rules of agency for a person identified as an additional insured to enforce the cover that the policy expresses to confer on him. However, there are four situations where an additional insured person will still need to establish that he is a party to the contract via the agency of the primary insured. First, there could be difficulties in enforcement under the 1999 Act where the

---

[58] *Woolcott v Sun Alliance and London Insurance Ltd* [1978] 1 W.L.R. 493; [1978] 1 All E.R. 1253; [1978] 1 Lloyd's Rep. 629.

[59] *Petrofina (UK) Ltd v Magnaload Ltd* [1984] Q.B. 127; [1983] 3 W.L.R. 805; [1983] 3 All E.R. 35.

[60] See below, paras 20-040 to 20-052.

[61] *Petrofina (UK) Ltd* [1984] Q.B. 127; [1983] 3 W.L.R. 805; [1983] 3 All E.R. 35.

[62] *Co-operative Retail Services Ltd v Taylor Young Partnership Ltd* [2002] UKHL 17 at [63]–[65]; [2002] 1 W.L.R. 1419 at 1438; [2002] 1 All E.R. (Comm) 918 at 936–937. See below, paras 20-045 to 20-052.

primary insured has committed a default, such as wilful misconduct or material non-disclosure. Secondly, there is also a question mark over the capacity of derivative rights under the 1999 Act to confer immunity from a subrogated action in the name of a co-insured under the *Petrofina (UK) Ltd*[63] doctrine. Thirdly, there is no scope for acquiring rights under the 1999 Act where the third party is not named or identified in the policy.[64] Fourthly, construction project insurances very commonly include a term excluding the effect of the 1999 Act. To that extent the undisclosed principal doctrine is wider in scope. However, there is probably no circumstance in which a person could claim on a typical CAR policy as an undisclosed principal.

3. JOINT AND COMPOSITE POLICIES

(a) Distinguishing between joint and composite insurance

20-030 **Joint or composite insured.** A policy that insures the interests of two or more persons will be either "joint" or "composite" in nature. A joint policy is regarded as a single contract of insurance with the result that the rights of the co-insureds stand or fall together. A composite policy, by contrast, is treated as a bundle of contracts "in one piece of paper" covering:

> "[A] number of persons whose connection with the subject matter of the insurance makes it natural and reasonable that the whole matter should be dealt with in one policy."[65]

The result is that the misconduct of one co-insured does not (unless there is a term to the contrary) prejudice the other's right of recovery.

20-031   The label given to the co-insureds in the policy may also be a relevant matter to take into account, but it is not determinative of the question whether a policy is joint or composite.[66] Which category a particular policy will fall into depends on the nature of the interests of the co-insureds in the insured subject matter. If the insureds share a common or joint interest in the subject matter and are subject to the same risk, as will be the case if they are joint tenants of property or partners, then the policy is joint. If the parties have different interests in the subject matter, as where a mortgagor and mortgagee are co-insureds,[67] the policy is composite.[68] Most policies (including CAR ones) will thus usually be construed as composite.[69]

20-032 **Construction insurance.** Where CAR insurance is taken out in the joint names

---

[63] *Petrofina (UK) Ltd* [1984] Q.B. 127; [1983] 3 W.L.R. 805; [1983] 3 All E.R. 35.

[64] Section 1 (3) of the 1991 Act.

[65] *General Accident Fire and Life Assurance Corp Ltd v Midland Bank Ltd* [1940] 2 K.B. 388 at 405; [1940] 3 All E.R. 252 at 258; (1940) 67 Ll. L. Rep. 218 at 235.

[66] *Parker v National Farmers Union Mutual Insurance Society Ltd* [2012] EWHC 2156 (Comm) at [165]; [2013] Lloyd's Rep. I.R. 253, at 274, per Teare J.

[67] *P Samuel & Co Ltd v Dumas*; sub nom.*P Samuel & Co Ltd v Motor Union Insurance Co Ltd* [1924] 1 A.C. 431; (1924) 18 Ll. L. Rep. 211; 93 L.J.K.B. 415.

[68] The following forms of co-insurance have been held to be composite in nature: landlord and tenant (*General Accident Fire and Life Assurance Corp Ltd* [1940] 2 K.B. 388; [1940] 3 All E.R. 252; 67 Ll. L. Rep. 218); mortgagor and mortgagee (*Woolcott* [1978] 1 W.L.R. 493; [1978] 1 All E.R. 1253; [1978] 1 Lloyd's Rep. 629); companies in the same group (*New Hampshire Insurance Co Ltd v MGN Ltd; Maxwell Communication Corp Plc (In Administration) v New Hampshire Insurance Co Ltd* [1997] L.R.L.R. 24; [1996] C.L.C. 1728) and directors of a company (*Arab Bank Plc v Zurich Insurance Co; Banque Bruxelles Lambert SA v Zurich Insurance Co* [1999] 1 Lloyd's Rep. 262; [1998] C.L.C. 1351; [1998] All E.R. (D) 273).

[69] *Arnould Law of Marine Insurance and Average*, edited by J. Gilman et al., 18th edn (London: Sweet & Maxwell, 2013), para.11–31.

of contractors and subcontractors, the policy will be regarded as composite.[70] In *Netherlands v Youell; Netherlands v Hayward*; sub nom. *State of the Netherlands v Youell and Hayward*,[71] the fact that several co-insureds each had a "pervasive interest" in the insured property (that is, an interest more extensive than their limited proprietary or possessory rights to the property),[72] which allowed them to claim in respect of the entire property was not held to prevent the policy being regarded as composite.[73] This is clearly correct: where various contractors each have a pervasive interest in the entire works, the interest of each "relates to the entire property" but relates to it "from different angles".[74] The mere fact that two parties are both insured in respect of the same building site or vessel does not mean that their interests are identical: hence the treatment of mortgage/mortgagor and lessor/lessee policies as composite rather than joint.

Express wording in an insurance policy may affect whether it is treated as joint or composite. It is possible for express wording in a policy to alter how it is viewed, so that a policy that insures different interests and is by nature composite is instead treated as a joint policy and vice versa. In the *New Hampshire Insurance Co Ltd* case,[75] a policy covering a number of companies in a corporate group against fraudulent acts of employees was held to be composite, with each company insured separately because each company had a separate interest to insure. That construction was not altered by the fact that the words "joint insured" appeared in the policy.[76] The Court of Appeal noted that

20-033

> "the content of the clause does not go as far as to say that all those insured have joint interests or are joint contractors".[77]

In doing so, it appeared to accept that it would have been possible, using appropriate language, for the parties to contract for joint insurance, despite the lack of any jointly held interest in the subject matter. From the perspective of practical policy drafting, the point is probably an academic one: if an insurer is concerned to reserve a right to avoid liability where any one of the co-insureds commits wilful misconduct or breaches their disclosure duties,[78] the safest course is to include a term specifically to that effect; such a provision will be effective regardless of whether the policy falls to be treated as joint or composite. Alternatively, but to the

---

[70] In *Netherlands v Youell; Netherlands v Hayward*; sub nom. *State of the Netherlands v Youell and Hayward* [1997] 2 Lloyd's Rep. 440 at 451; [1997] C.L.C. 938 at 953 Rix J decided that the marine construction all risks policy before him was composite in nature. Several of his reasons for so finding apply generally to any construction joint names policy: the works might be destroyed in circumstances which would frustrate the building contract in which case any insurance would be for the benefit of the owner and not the contractor; or the works might be damaged in circumstances where there was a dispute as to whether the contractor was liable. More simply, it could be argued that such a policy is composite inasmuch as the owner and the various contractors have different proprietary and possessory rights in the contract works.

[71] *Netherlands v Youell* [1997] 2 Lloyd's Rep. 440; [1997] C.L.C. 938.

[72] See below, para.20-053.

[73] *Netherlands v Youell* [1997] 2 Lloyd's Rep. 440 at 451; [1997] C.L.C. 938 at 953.

[74] *Commonwealth Construction Co Ltd v Imperial Oil Ltd* (1976) 69 D.L.R. (3d) 558 at 561; [1976] 6 W.W.R. 219 at 222 (Can SC); cited by Lloyd J in *Petrofina (UK) Ltd v Magnaload Ltd* [1984] Q.B. 127 at 139; [1983] 3 W.L.R. 805 at 815–816; [1983] 3 All E.R. 35 at 44.

[75] *New Hampshire Insurance Co Ltd v MGN Ltd* [1997] L.R.L.R. 24; [1996] C.L.C. 1728.

[76] *New Hampshire Insurance Co Ltd v MGN Ltd* [1997] L.R.L.R. 24 at 57; [1996] C.L.C. 1728 at 1737.

[77] *New Hampshire Insurance Co Ltd v MGN Ltd* [1997] L.R.L.R. 24 at 57; [1996] C.L.C. 1728 at 1737.

[78] See above, Ch.6 for a further discussion of an insured's disclosure duties.

same end, the policy may be worded so that on a proper construction the cover provided to one co-insured (X) is dependent on another co-insured (Y) being covered and able to bring a claim. In those circumstances material non-disclosure by Y will deprive X of cover.[79]

(b) Consequences of the distinction

20-034 **Rights of the co-insured.** The most significant consequence of the distinction between joint and composite insurance policies concerns the rights of the co-insured. Under a composite policy to which the co-insureds are parties, the insurer has a defence to liability based on the conduct of one of the co-insureds against that co-insured. The rights of an innocent co-insured to recover his loss will not be prejudiced by the fraud or wilful misconduct of another co-insured unless there is express wording to achieve that result.[80] However a co-insured employer cannot rely upon its pervasive insurable interest to recover the full amount under a CAR policy and then pay the contractor sums in excess of the employer's own insurable interest as this will amount to indirect enforcement of the policy.[81] In contrast, under a joint policy, the rights of all of the co-insured stand or fall together. Where a husband and wife are jointly insured in respect of their home and money is paid out pursuant to the husband's fraudulent claim, the wife cannot escape liability to repay insurance monies.[82]

20-035 **Composite policy and effect of non-disclosure by one co-insured.** The principle mentioned above in para.20-034 has been applied under the provisions of the MIA to a breach of the duty of utmost good faith by one co-insured under a composite policy, perhaps surprisingly given that non-disclosure may have affected the insurer's decision to provide cover in the first place. In *Woolcott*,[83] a property was insured under a policy, which covered the respective interests of the mortgagor property owner and the mortgagee building society. The insurer sought to avoid liability following damage to the property on the basis that the mortgagor had failed to disclose his criminal record. It was held that although the insurer was permitted to set aside the policy as regards the mortgagor, the building society's interest was unaffected.

This position may be different under the 2015 Act. Although the basic principle holds true that a material non-disclosure by a co-insured will not affect the rights of the other co-insureds under a composite policy, the 2015 Act provides for a

---

[79] *Brit Syndicates Ltd v Grant Thornton International*; sub nom. *Brit Syndicates Ltd v Italaudit SpA (In Liquidation) (formerly Grant Thornton SpA)* [2006] EWCA Civ 1661 at [17]–[19]; [2007] 1 All E.R. (Comm) 785 at 780–781; [2007] 1 Lloyd's Rep. 329 at 331–332. The policy was undoubtedly composite in nature; that fact did not affect the issue of whether as a matter of construction the cover granted to X depended on Y being covered.

[80] *P Samuel & Co Ltd v Dumas* [1924] 1 A.C. 431; (1924) 18 Ll. L. Rep. 211; 93 L.J.K.B. 415; *Netherlands v Youell* [1997] 2 Lloyd's Rep. 440; [1997] C.L.C. 938. For the issue of whether there is fortuity in the event of deliberate destruction of the insured property by one co-insured, see above, para.10-026.

[81] *Netherlands v Youell* [1997] 2 Lloyd's Rep. 440; [1997] C.L.C. 938.

[82] *Direct Line Insurance Plc v Khan* [2002] Lloyd's Rep. I.R. 364; per Jackson J at first instance. The Court of Appeal found, in any event, that as the husband made the claim as agent for his wife as well as on his own behalf, the wife was fixed with the consequences of his actions: [2001] EWCA Civ 1794; [2002] Lloyd's Rep. I.R. 364; [2001] All E.R. (D) 476 (Oct). By way of comparison, see further below, para.26-007 and in particular fn.17.

[83] *Woolcott* [1978] 1 W.L.R. 493; [1978] 1 All E.R. 1253; [1978] 1 Lloyd's Rep. 629.

number of mechanisms through which the knowledge held by one co-insured can be imputed to another co-insured. Once the non-disclosed information has been imputed, it will form part of that co-insured's own disclosure duties and entitle the insurer to the same remedy against that co-insured as against the original co-insured in breach of their pre-contractual disclosure duties. This possibility is discussed in relation to CAR insurance above, at para.5-049.

Composite policy: fraudulent claim made by one co-insured acting on behalf of another co-insured. Under the provisions of the MIA, the principle that the **20-036** rights of an innocent co-insured under a composite policy were divisible for the purposes of fraud was subject to an important limitation: if the defaulting party had authority to act as an agent on behalf of another co-insured when communicating with the insurer, that other co-insured may have been bound by the consequences of the defaulting party's actions. Thus where a husband made a fraudulent claim on a home insurance policy, which was held in the joint names of him and his wife, the Court of Appeal held that, regardless of whether the policy was joint or composite, the wife was bound by the fraud of her husband since the claim was made partly on her behalf.[84] In the context of CAR insurance, which will invariably be composite in nature, this point could arise where the main named insured makes a claim on behalf of itself and the other contractors.

The 2015 Act introduced a default statutory remedy for fraudulent claims made under the policy that will apply in lieu of any bespoke arrangements. The new provisions do not disturb the treatment of a fraudulent claim by one co-insured under a composite policy, though s.13 of the 2015 Act provides that a fraudulent claim made under a group insurance scheme will be treated in the same way as composite insurance in that it will only entitle the insurer to a remedy against the fraudster, without affecting the cover held by other members of the group.[85] For CAR insurance and other composite policies, it is therefore considered likely that the courts will apply the pre-existing case law under the MIA in circumstances where one co-insured can be found to be acting as an agent for the benefit of another co-insured.

Parties can contract out of the default position that a composite policy is divisible for the purposes of misconduct and good faith by including wording in the policy to the contrary effect. Contracting out is permitted under the provisions of the 2015 Act provided that any term purporting to impose a more onerous obligation on the insured than that imposed by an equivalent provision under the 2015 Act must comply with the transparency requirements.[86] Since there are no provisions under the 2015 Act that regulate the obligations owed by parties under composite insurance, it is unlikely that any such term purporting to preclude the divisibility

---

[84] *Direct Line Insurance Plc v Khan* [2001] EWCA Civ 1794 at [31]–[32], [41], [44]; [2002] Lloyd's Rep. I.R. 364 at 371–372; [2001] All E.R. (D) 476 (Oct). However, a different rule would appear to apply where one co-assured is guilty of fraud or non-disclosure in making the insurance proposal (as opposed to making a claim on the policy): *Arab Bank Plc* [1999] 1 Lloyd's Rep. 262 at 278–283; [1998] C.L.C. 1351 at 1370–1376; [1998] All E.R. (D) 273. Rix J held at [1999] 1 Lloyd's Rep. 262 at 280; [1998] C.L.C. 1351 at 1373; [1998] All E.R. (D) 273 at 23; that the "common sense" exception or "rule of attribution" in *Re Hampshire Land Co* [1896] 2 Ch. 743; 65 L.J. Ch 860; 3 Mans 269; that it is inherently unlikely—and therefore should not be presumed—that any agent would communicate fraud or any other wrong-doing to his principal should be applied with regards to the making of the insurance proposal.

[85] Section 13(2) of the 2015 Act. For further analysis of this provision, see above, para.5-131 above.

[86] See above, para.5-135.

of the composite policy would be subjected to the transparency requirements. However, there may be some scope to argue that the provisions of the 2015 Act would not entitle an insurer to a remedy against an innocent insured in respect of fraudulent claims made by another co-insured, and to that extent a term purporting to prevent the divisibility of the composite policy may place a co-insured in a worse position than they would have been under the 2015 Act. This position is strengthened by the pre-existing law on the matter, under which it was held that a policy that simply reserves the insurer's right to avoid for fraud does not have the effect of contracting out of the divisibility of composite insurance because clear wording had not been used to that effect; it was necessary for the policy to go further and state that the insurers could have avoided in the case of fraud *by any assured*.[87]

20-037 **Payment mechanism.** The composite or joint nature of the policy, as the case may be, may also have an impact on termination[88] and on the mechanism for payment under the policy.[89] As far as payment is concerned, under a joint policy the insurer may meet his obligations by paying out the sum due to any of the joint policyholders.[90] Under a composite policy, a clause dealing with payment is likely to be construed as providing for payment to the particular insured or insureds who have suffered loss, rather to all of the co-insureds.[91] If, on the other hand, the contract provides that the insurer must make payment jointly to all of the insureds, those recipients who are not entitled to be indemnified must pass on the money to those who have suffered the loss.[92]

4. TERMINATION OF CO-INSURANCE

(a) Termination

20-038 **Termination by joint or composite insured.** In the case of joint insurance, the exercise of a right of termination probably requires the agreement of all of the joint insureds to be effective except where the policy wording provides otherwise or unless the party seeking to terminate ostensibly does so on behalf of the other insureds.[93] The nature of a composite policy would, by contrast, suggest that one

---

[87] *Arab Bank Plc* [1999] 1 Lloyd's Rep. 262 at 273; [1998] C.L.C. 1351 at 1365; [1998] All E.R. (D) 273, per Rix J.

[88] See below, para.20-038.

[89] See below, Ch.23.

[90] This follows the principle at common law that a debt owed to joint creditors may be discharged by payment to one of them: *Powell v Brodhurst* [1901] 2 Ch. 160; 70 L.J. Ch 587; 49 W.R. 532; see *Colinvaux's Law of Insurance* edited by R. Merkin, 10th edn (London: Sweet & Maxwell, 2014), para.14–033.

[91] *General Accident Fire and Life Assurance Corp Ltd* [1940] 2 K.B. 388 at 407–408, [1940] 3 All E.R. 252 at 259–260; 67 Ll. L. Rep 218 at 235–236, per Sir Wilfred Greene M.R.

[92] *General Accident Fire and Life Assurance Corp Ltd* [1940] 2 K.B. 388 at 415; [1940] 3 All E.R. 252 at 262–263; 67 Ll. L. Rep. 218 at 237–238.

[93] This conclusion is reached by analogy with the rule for joint tenancies whereby all positive dealing with the tenancy requires the concurrence of all joint tenants to be effective (see *Hammersmith and Fulham London Borough Council v Monk*; sub nom. *Hammersmith and Fulham LBC v Monk Barnet LBC v Smith* [1992] 1 A.C. 478 at 490–491; [1991] 3 W.L.R. 1144 at 1153–1154; [1992] 1 All E.R. 1 at 9–10, per Lord Bridge).

co-insured should be able to terminate in respect of his own interest,[94] although in principle one co-insured should not be able to terminate the cover of another co-insured, again unless the policy expressly provides that he may or unless he has actual or ostensible authority to act on the other's behalf. If the policy is terminated, avoided or there is a material breach, the implied term that a claim cannot be brought against a co-insured no longer operates.[95]

(b) Effect on third-party insureds

Additional insureds. The parties to the insurance contract may not be able to terminate the insurance if the policy provides for third parties to have the benefit of the insurance (i.e. under an "additional assureds" clause). Whether or not the third party seeks to enforce the cover under the Contracts (Rights of Third Parties) Act 1999 depends on the application of s.2 of the 1999 Act. It provides that the parties to the contract may not vary or rescind so as to extinguish the third party's rights in circumstances where the third party has either communicated assent to the term to the promisor (i.e. the insurer) or has actually relied on it and the promisor is aware of, or could be expected to have foreseen, reliance by the third party. Accordingly, where the named insured has communicated a desire to terminate the insurance, it may be open to a person falling within the description of other or additional insureds to argue that this termination is ineffective against him because he has relied on the cover (e.g. by not taking out alternative insurance) and that the insurer should have foreseen that outcome. **20-039**

5.   CO-INSURANCE AS A DEFENCE TO A SUBROGATED ACTION IN THE NAME OF A CO-INSURED

(a)   The rule

Joint names insurance: insurer cannot exercise subrogation rights against a co-insured.   In insurance law, under a joint names policy an insurer may not exercise rights of subrogation to bring an action in the name of one co-insured against a second co-insured in respect of loss or damage to property for which the latter is insured. In *Petrofina (UK) Ltd v Magnaload Ltd*,[96] subcontractors were alleged to have negligently caused damage to an oil refinery in an action brought by the insurers in the name of the primary insured owners of the refinery.[97] Having decided that the subcontractors were co-insureds under the policy,[98] and co-insured to the extent **20-040**

---

[94]   In *Federation Insurance Ltd v Wasson* [1987] H.C.A. 34 at [20]; (1987) 72 A.L.R. 567 at 575–576; (1987) 163 C.L.R. 303 (HCA) at 315 the Australian High Court held that a clause in a composite policy allowing termination of "the Policy ... at the request of the Insured" required the participation of all of the insured in that request. A purported unilateral termination by one co-assured was simply ineffective; that party could still maintain a claim. The court suggested that a clause which referred to the termination of "the insurance of the respective rights and interests" of the insureds might have been construed differently.

[95]   *Matalan Discount Club (Cash & Carry) Ltd v Tokenspire Properties (North Western) Ltd; Richmond Cladding Systems Ltd v Parmenter* [2001] All E.R. (D) 260 (May); *Tate Gallery Board of Trustees v Duffy Construction Ltd* [2007] EWHC 361 (TCC); [2007] 1 All E.R. (Comm) 1004; [2007] Lloyd's Rep. I.R. 758.

[96]   *Petrofina (UK) Ltd* [1984] Q.B. 127; [1983] 3 W.L.R. 805; [1983] 3 All E.R. 35.

[97]   *Petrofina (UK) Ltd* [1984] 1 Q.B. 127; [1983] 3 W.L.R. 805; [1983] 3 All E.R. 35.

[98]   Applying the agency principles set out above in paras 20-003 to 20-017 of this chapter.

of the damage in question,[99] Lloyd J held that the subcontractors were immune from a subrogated action in the name of the owner. He considered that as a matter of principle an insurer should not be able to sue one co-insured in the name of another so as to recoup a loss for which the defendant is insured.[100] This decision has been upheld in subsequent authority.[101]

20-041 **Limits to the principle.** There are several limits to the principle, however, all of which stem from the requirement that the defendant must be insured in respect of the particular loss that forms the basis of the subrogated claim. Thus, the defendant must: (a) have an insurable interest, which extends to the damage in question; (b) be covered by the policy in respect of the damage; and (c) not be guilty of any default which would deprive him of the benefit of cover.

20-042 **Effect of no joint names insurance being purchased under the contract.** Even if there is no joint-names insurance in place, a defendant contractor facing a claim by an employer may be exempted from liability where the building contract required one party to procure insurance that would have covered the defendant.[102] Whether a requirement to procure insurance in the building contract has this effect depends, in the first place, on whether the contract can be properly construed as excluding the defendant contractor's tortuous and contractual liability within the scope of the contemplated insurance.[103] If it can be so construed, the defence depends on whether the specified insurance would have covered the defendant contractor in respect of the damage in question. The extent of this notional cover depends on the same considerations that apply in the context of the defence based on co-insurance, and hence it is convenient to consider these related principles side by side (as a number of decisions have done).[104]

20-043 However, before considering these principles, it is important to note that a party who fails to procure joint-names insurance in circumstances where they were contractually obliged to do so, has acted in breach of contract.[105] In principle, this would entitle the party who would have been indemnified by an insurer in the case

---

99 See further the discussion below, at para.20-053.

100 *Petrofina (UK) Ltd* [1984] 1 Q.B. 127 at 139; [1983] 3 W.L.R. 805 at 815–816; [1983] 3 All E.R. 35 at 44.

101 *National Oilwell (UK) Ltd* [1993] 2 Lloyd's Rep. 582; [1994] C.L.Y. 4086; *Stone Vickers Ltd* [1991] 2 Lloyd's Rep. 288; *Times*, January 30, 1991 reversed ([1992] 2 Lloyd's Rep. 578) on the different ground that the defendant was not in fact a co-insured under the policy; *Co-operative Retail Services Ltd* [2002] UKHL 17; [2002] 1 W.L.R. 1419; [2002] 1 All E.R. (Comm) 918; *BP Exploration Operating Co Ltd v Kvaerner Oilfield Properties Ltd*; sub nom. *BP Exploration Operating Co Ltd v Kvaerner Oilfield Products Ltd (Cooper Cameron (UK) Ltd, Pt 20 defendant)* [2004] EWHC 999; [2004] 2 All E.R. (Comm) 266; [2005] 1 Lloyd's Rep. 307.

102 *Co-operative Retail Services Ltd* [2002] UKHL 17 at [46]–[51]; [2002] 1 W.L.R. 1419 at 1433–1435; [2002] 1 All E.R. (Comm) 918 at 932–933. Such a term shows that the parties have entered into a contractual arrangement whereby they will look to the joint insurance policy to pay the cost of repairing the damage and that they would therefore not attempt to pass on their losses by bringing litigation against each other.

103 See further the discussion below, at paras 20-064 to 20-071.

104 See in particular *Co-operative Retail Services Ltd* [2002] UKHL 17; [2002] 1 W.L.R. 1419; [2002] 1 All E.R. (Comm) 918 and *Tyco Fire & Integrated Solutions (UK) Ltd v Rolls Royce Motor Cars Ltd*; sub nom. *Tyco Fire & Integrated Solutions (UK) Ltd (formerly Wormald Ansul (UK) Ltd) v Rolls Royce Motor Ltd (formerly Hireus Ltd)* [2008] EWCA Civ 286; [2008] 2 All E.R. (Comm) 584; [2008] Lloyd's Rep. I.R. 617.

105 *Gard Marine & Energy Ltd v China National Chartering Co Ltd; China National Chartering Co Ltd v Daiichii Chuo Kisen Kaisha* [2015] EWCA Civ 16 at [91]; [2015] 2 All E.R. (Comm) 894 at

of loss, to recover from the party who should have taken out a joint-names insurance policy. The damages recoverable by the innocent party will reflect the sums which would have been recoverable under the policy.

(b) Nature of the rule

Purpose of the rule. Whatever the theoretical basis of the rule against subrogation against a co-insured, its purpose is to avoid the inconsistency of an insurer recovering a loss from a person whom he has agreed to indemnify in respect of that same loss.   **20-044**

Basis of the rule. While the policy behind the rule may be clear, it has historically proved difficult for the courts to settle on any single legal basis for the rule's imposition. The courts have at various points formulated different reasons behind the rule, though it appears that each basis advanced by the courts has encountered difficulties in its application.[106] Given the previous conflicting authority on the point, it is suggested that the basis of the rule may not yet be fully settled and there may be scope to advance a different basis to that identified in recent Court of Appeal authority[107] if such an alternative basis would to be less problematic in its application.   **20-045**

The original basis advanced for the rule was that an attempt to recover a loss by an insurer from a co-insured who is himself covered by the same insurer for the same loss or damage would give rise to a plea of circuity of action.[108] This justification recognised that damages recovered by the insurer bringing a subrogated action against a co-insured would be the same damages recoverable by that co-insured from the insurer under the policy, and for that reason the subrogated action should be barred to prevent the circuity arising. The problem with this analysis was identified by Brooke LJ in *Co-operative Retail Services Ltd*,[109] inasmuch as the insurer has discharged its liability under the policy by paying out to the first co-insured, the other co-insured cannot look to the insurer to pay him those losses a second time.

Recent authority has therefore moved on from this position and held that the rule against subrogation against a co-insured should be seen as being based on an   **20-046**

938; [[2015] Lloyd's Rep. I.R. 295 at 324 per Longmore LJ delivering the judgment of the court. On 20 May 2015 permission to appeal was granted to Daiichi Chuo Kisen Kaisha (the charterers) to the Supreme Court in respect of this decision, which permitted an appeal on the following ground that "... the conditions which affected Kashima on the 24 October 2006 were an abnormal occurrence, that there was no breach by the charterers of the safe port obligation ...". See *Gard Marine & Energy Ltd* [2015] EWCA Civ 16 at [64]; [2015] 2 All E.R. (Comm) 894 at 927; [2015] Lloyd's Rep. I.R. 295 at 317. At the time of writing, the appeal is still outstanding.

[106] However, it may be suggested that this confusion could have been avoided if the courts had instead adopted the approach that where a composite policy is taken out between the parties, as a matter of public policy there is no right of subrogation.

[107] *Gard Marine & Energy Ltd* [2015] EWCA Civ 16; [2015] 2 All E.R. (Comm) 894; [2015] Lloyd's Rep. I.R. 295.

[108] *Petrofina (UK) Ltd* [1984] Q.B. 127 at 140; [1983] 3 W.L.R. 805 at 816; [1983] 3 All E.R. 35 at 44–45, per Lloyd J.

[109] *Co-operative Retail Services Ltd v Taylor Young Partnership Ltd and another (Tarmac Construction (Contracts) Ltd (formerly Wimpey Construction UK Ltd) and another, third parties) (Genergy Plc (formerly Dale Power Systems Plc), fourth party) (Flue-Stox Engineering Ltd, fifth party)* [2000] EWCA Civ 207 at [72]; [2000] 2 All E.R. (Comm) 865 at 885; 74 Con. L.R. 12 at 49.

implied term.[110] In *Co-operative Retail Services Ltd*, Brooke LJ's support for this theory was linked to his finding that the building contract before him should be construed as exempting the contractor's liability for damage insurable under the relevant provisions of that contract.[111] This was affirmed by the Court of Appeal in *Gard Marine & Energy Ltd v China National Chartering Co Ltd; China National Chartering Co Ltd v Daiichii Chuo Kisen Kaisha*,[112] where they considered that it was now clear that the basis of the principle:

"... ultimately depends on the underlying contract of the parties rather than on the terms of the insurance policy made pursuant to that contract."[113]

20-047   However, basing the rule on the existence of an implied term in the building contract between the parties is also not without its difficulties. The implied term will be most problematic where, as is commonly the case in relation to CAR insurance, the policy is taken out by the employer long before the building contract has even come into existence. In such circumstances, it is undesirable and legally unsound for the rights and obligations owed under one contract to be determined or modified by the terms of a second contract that is not entered into until after the original contract has been finalised. Equally, it is a mistake to conflate the position between the parties to the building contract with the position between the insurer and the insureds. Focusing only on the building contract, there would be nothing to prevent an insurer from bringing a claim against one co-insured in the name of another in circumstances where there is no contract between the two co-insureds, as where a sub-subcontractor is sued in the name of a main contractor.[114] It must be borne in mind that the basis of the doctrine is thought to be that the exercise of rights of subrogation by an insurer to recover for a loss in respect of which a co-insured is indemnified would be "inconsistent with the insurer's obligation to the co-assured".[115] There must be an implied waiver of subrogation co-extensive with the co-insured's cover under the policy, regardless of what the building contract may provide as regards the parties' liabilities to one another. Once one recognises that there does not even have to be a contractual relationship between the two co-insureds for the rule against subrogation to apply, it is difficult to argue that the rule depends on there being an implied exclusion of liability in such a contract as there might be between the parties.

20-048   Another difficulty created by the implied term basis for the rule against subrogation was recognised in *Tyco Fire & Integrated Solutions (UK) Ltd v Rolls Royce Motor Cars Ltd*; sub nom.*Tyco Fire & Integrated Solutions (UK) Ltd (formerly*

---

[110] See the decisions of *Co-operative Retail Services Ltd* [2000] EWCA Civ 207 at [72]; [2000] 2 All E.R. (Comm) 865 at 885; 74 Con. L.R. 12 at 49 and [2002] UKHL 17 at [65]; [2002] 1 W.L.R. 1419 at 1438; [2002] 1 All E.R. (Comm) 918 at 937.

[111] *Co-operative Retail Services Ltd* [2000] EWCA Civ 207 at [72]–[73]; [2000] 2 All E.R. (Comm) 865 at 885; 74 Con. L.R. 12 at 49–50.

[112] *Gard Marine & Energy Ltd* [2015] EWCA Civ 16; [2015] 2 All E.R. (Comm) 894; [2015] Lloyd's Rep. I.R. 295.

[113] *Gard Marine & Energy Ltd* [2015] EWCA Civ 16 at [79]; [2015] 2 All E.R. (Comm) 894 at 935; [2015] Lloyd's Rep. I.R. 295 at 322, per Longmore LJ delivering the judgment of the court.

[114] Otherwise, the decision in *Petrofina (UK) Ltd* [1984] Q.B. 127; [1983] 3 W.L.R. 805; [1983] 3 All E.R. 35 itself could not have been reached, because the defendant sub-subcontractors had no contractual relationship with the claimant employer in whose name the claim was being brought.

[115] *Stone Vickers Ltd* [1991] 2 Lloyd's Rep. 288 at 302; *Times,* January 30, 1991, per Lloyd J.

Wormald Ansul (UK) Ltd) v Rolls Royce Motor Cars Ltd (formerly Hireus Ltd).[116] Rix LJ considered, obiter, that a building contract may permit the co-insureds to claim against one another even in respect of insured risks. He said:

"... I can well see that a provision for joint names insurance may influence, perhaps even strongly, the construction of the contract in which it appears. It may lead to the carving out of an exception from the underlying regime so far as specified perils are concerned. But an implied term cannot withstand express language to the contrary. Moreover, if the underlying contract envisages that one co-assured may be liable to another for negligence even within the sphere of the cover provided by the policy, I am inclined to think that there is nothing in the doctrine of subrogation to prevent the insurer suing in the name of the employer to recover the insurance proceeds which the insurer has paid in the absence of any express ouster of the right of subrogation, either generally or at least in cases where the joint names insurance is really a bundle of composite insurance policies which insure each insured for his respective interest."[117]

What Rix LJ had recognised was that basing the rule against subrogation on an implied term in the building contract limited that rule to having the legal potency of an implied term, which could not, therefore, override the express terms of the context if they appeared to contradict that rule. This may be considered undesirable in relation to CAR insurance where it is axiomatic that the risks jointly insured against are ones for which none of the parties would expect to be found liable without very clear wording in the building contract to provide otherwise. However, one qualification does need to be made on this point, which is that the Court of Appeal in *Gard Marine & Energy Ltd*, while not disagreeing with Rix LJ's obiter comments, emphasised that:

"... the prima facie position where a contract requires a party to that contract to insure should be that the parties have agreed to look to the insurers for indemnification rather than to each other."[118]

Nevertheless, the issue arose in the case of *SSE Generation Ltd v Hochtief Solu-* **20-049** *tions AG,*[119] a decision of the Scottish Outer House Court of Session. In *SSE Generation Ltd*, the implied term was applied in relation to the provisions of a new engineering contract ("NEC2") of which cl.83.1 stated: "Each Party indemnifies the other against claims, proceedings, compensation and costs due to an event which is at his risk."[120] Lord Woolman considered that this term was inconsistent with and therefore overrode the implied term preventing the employer from bringing an action against the main contractor in respect of losses insured under the CAR policy:

"If Hochtief's submission is correct, it renders clause 83.1 redundant. There is no need for a liability provision if SSE has no right to sue in the first place. A similar point can be made about the limitation provision in option Z11. Why have the parties sought to limit liability to the total tender price? The inference is that they have done so because they recognise that each is obliged to the other in respect of loss and did not intend the CAR policy to supplant liability. Hochtief has pleaded the

---

[116] *Tyco Fire & Integrated Solutions (UK) Ltd* [2008] EWCA Civ 286; [2008] 2 All E.R. (Comm) 584; [2008] Lloyd's Rep. I.R. 617.
[117] *Tyco Fire & Integrated Solutions (UK) Ltd* [2008] EWCA Civ 286 at [77]; [2008] 2 All E.R. (Comm) 584 at 610; [2008] Lloyd's Rep. I.R. 617 at 634.
[118] *Gard Marine & Energy Ltd* [2015] EWCA Civ 16 at [83]; [2015] 2 All E.R. (Comm) 894 at 936; [2015] Lloyd's Rep. I.R. 295 at 323, per Longmore LJ delivering the judgment of the court.
[119] *SSE Generation Ltd v Hochtief Solutions AG* [2015] CSOH 92; [2015] B.L.R. 774; [2016] P.N.L.R. 6.
[120] Institution of Civil Engineers. The Engineering and Construction Contract: A New Engineering Contract (NEC) Document Second Edition (London: Thomas Telford Ltd, 1995), p.20.

limitation provision in the defences. In consequence, SSE has restricted the sum it claims to reflect the limitation provision."[121]

Whilst Lord Woolman referenced the decision in *Gard Marine & Energy Ltd* and purported to rely on it as the basis for his own decision, it is suggested that his application of the point failed to take into account the Court of Appeal's reasoning and give adequate weight to the implied term in the contract. Clause 83.1 of the NEC2 contract was noticeably far from a term that explicitly permitted one party to bring an action against a co-insured in respect of the insured risks. The effect of Lord Woolman's decision was to deprive the parties of the protection of the implied term on the basis of only minor inconsistencies with a different contract term, in circumstances where that term could reasonably have been interpreted as applying to different contractual obligations to the insured risks.

20-050   An alternative justification for the rule against bringing a subrogated action against a co-insured that might therefore be preferred is that there is an implied term in the *insurance policy* that the insurer waives the right to bring any such action. If this basis were to be adopted, inconsistencies within the building contract could not have the effect of depriving the implied term of its legal force and the difficulties encountered in circumstances where the CAR policy pre-dates the building contract would not arise. One possible difficulty with this analysis is that if the basis of the rule rests on the existence of an implied term in the insurance policy, the following scenario could potentially arise: an implied term in the insurance policy could prevent the insurer from exercising a right of subrogation against a co-insured, while concurrently, the building contract could allow one co-insured to sue the other co-insured in respect of the same insured risk (thus shortcutting the need to recover from the insurer). This scenario would entitle a co-insured (who has perhaps lost the benefit of the insurance policy) to recover its loss from the other co-insured under the building contract.

20-051   This problem has been addressed by Elias LJ in *Rathbone Brothers Plc v Novae Corporate Underwriting*.[122] Elias LJ doubted whether the above scenario could arise as he considered that where a building contract permitted the co-insureds to sue each other in respect of an insured risk, "… it is difficult to see why, absent an express term, the insurer should be taken to have waived the right of subrogation."[123] To put this point differently, Elias LJ's view is that where the building contract permits the co-insureds to sue each other, there will be no implied term in the insurance policy ousting the insurer's right to subrogate against a co-insured, and so no inconsistency between the insurance policy and the building contract would arise. It is therefore suggested that an implied term in the insurance policy would lead to fewer difficulties in practice than have been encountered implying a term into the building contract, and that this basis for the rule may be preferred.

20-052   Whether the term containing the bar on subrogation is implied into the building contract between the parties or the insurance policy between insurer and the co-insured, certain factors limit the extent to which a co-insurance defence can succeed.

---

[121] *SSE Generation Ltd v Hochtief Solutions AG* [2015] CSOH 92; [2015] B.L.R. 774; [2016] P.N.L.R. 6 at [82].
[122] *Rathbone Brothers Plc* [2014] EWCA Civ 1464; [2014] 2 C.L.C. 818; [2015] Lloyd's Rep. I.R. 95.
[123] *Rathbone Brothers Plc* [2014] EWCA Civ 1464 at [83]; [2014] 2 C.L.C. 818 at 841; [2015] Lloyd's Rep. I.R. 95 at 109, per Elias LJ.

(c) Limits to co-insurance defence

(i) Insurable interest

Extent of cover. Typically, a joint-names CAR policy will extend to various   **20-053**
contractors and subcontractors involved in the project and the insured property will
be defined as the permanent and temporary works (that is, the construction site).
Given that all risks insurance is an indemnity against damage to property, a
subcontractor defending a subrogated action on the basis that he is co-insured in
respect of the loss faces the apparent difficulty of having no relevant insurable interest unless the damaged part of the works belongs to him. He will not, apparently,
have suffered loss of a type (property loss or damage) indemnified by the policy.[124]
Yet in the *Petrofina (UK) Ltd*[125] case, Lloyd J held that a subcontractor is entitled
to insure the entire contract works and recover the whole of the loss insured despite
having only limited proprietary and possessory rights in the works, holding the
excess over his own interest on trust for the others.[126] Accordingly, the defendants
in that case, who were responsible for a heavy lifting system, which collapsed causing extensive damage to the rest of the works, were held to be co-insureds in respect
of the damage. In reaching this conclusion, the judge relied on a Canadian authority, in which it was held on a similar set of facts that the subcontractors had a
"pervasive interest" in the contract works,[127] on the basis that they had "such a
relationship with the entire works that their potential liability therefore constituted
an insurable interest in the whole".[128]

Limits to the doctrine of "pervasive interest". Significant limitations have been   **20-054**
imposed on the idea that a subcontractor may have a pervasive interest in the
contract works. In *Deepak Fertilisers and Petrochemical Co v Davy Mckee
(London) Ltd*,[129] the defendant contractor was responsible for the designing and
supervising the construction of a power plant, which exploded after it began
operating. An action was brought in the name of the employers against the defendant for negligence. It was argued that the claimant employers were contractually
obliged to procure joint insurance naming the defendants and thus an action brought
in the name of the employers was excluded. The claimants accepted that the claim
would fail inasmuch as they were obliged to procure insurance that would cover the
loss, but denied that the defendants had any relevant insurable interest *at the time*
of the explosion. Overruling the decision of the judge on this point, the Court of

---

[124] See above, further discussion on insurable interest in Ch.9.
[125] *Petrofina (UK) Ltd* [1984] Q.B. 127; [1983] 3 W.L.R. 805; [1983] 3 All E.R. 35.
[126] *Petrofina (UK) Ltd* [1984] Q.B. 127 at 136; [1983] 3 W.L.R. 805 at 813; [1983] 3 All E.R. 35 at 42.
[127] *Commonwealth Construction Co Ltd v Imperial Oil Ltd* (1976) 69 D.L.R. (3d) 558 at 560–565;
[1976] 6 W.W.R. 219 (Can SC) at 222–226. See also above, paras 9-043 to 9-048.
[128] *Commonwealth Construction Co Ltd* (1976) 69 D.L.R. (3d) 558 at 562; [1976] 6 W.W.R. 219 (Can
SC) at 223–224. See also *National Oilwell (UK) Ltd* [1993] 2 Lloyd's Rep. 582 at 611; [1994] C.L.Y
4086, per Colman J who said: "the suggestion that there cannot as a matter of law be an insurable
interest based merely on potential liability arising from the existence of a contract between the assured and the owner of property or from the assured's proximate physical relationship to the property
in question, is in my judgement, to confine far too narrowly the requirements of insurable interest".
[129] *Deepak Fertilisers and Petrochemical Co* [1998] EWCA Civ 1753; [1999] 1 All E.R. (Comm) 69;
[1999] 1 Lloyd's Rep. 387.

Appeal held that the defendant would have had no insurable interest *after* the works were completed[130]:

> "In our judgment Davy undoubtedly had an insurable interest in the plant under construction and on which they were working because they might lose the opportunity to do the work and to be remunerated for it if the property or structure were damaged or destroyed by any of the 'all risks', such as fire or flood. Thereafter Davy would only suffer disadvantage if the damage to or destruction of the property or structure was the result of their breach of contract or duty of care. In order to protect the contractor and subcontractors against the risk of disadvantage by reason of damage or destruction of the property or structure resulting from their breach of contract or duty they would, in accordance with normal practice, take out liability insurance, or, in the case of architects, professional indemnity insurance."

20-055 **Deepak compared with Petrofina and National Oilwell cases.** The above analysis of what constitutes an insurable interest for the purpose of joint-names insurance is plainly at odds with the reasoning in *Petrofina (UK) Ltd*[131] and *National Oilwell (UK) Ltd* cases.[132] In the earlier cases, the pervasive interest of the subcontractor was justified on the basis of the subcontractors' "potential liability" for damaging the works, not merely that they might lose the opportunity to complete the contract if the subject matter were destroyed. Indeed, in *National Oilwell (UK) Ltd*,[133] the losses were sustained after delivery by the subcontractor of the items it had contracted to supply and yet the judge found that the subcontractor had an insurable interest.[134] It is unfortunate that the Court of Appeal in *Deepak Fertilisers and Petrochemical Co*[135] did not, apparently, notice this marked departure from the earlier authorities.

20-056 However, the inconsistency was noted by the Court of Appeal in *Feasey v Sun Life Assurance Co of Canada; Steamship Mutual Underwriting Association (Bermuda) Ltd v Feasey*,[136] where there was a difference of opinion as to the proper approach. Ward LJ approved the approach in *Deepak Fertilisers and Petrochemical Co*.[137] His view was that

> "there has to be some legal or equitable interest between the insured and the subject matter of the insurance, expectation of harm or benefit not being enough".[138]

---

[130] *Deepak Fertilisers and Petrochemical Co* [1998] EWCA Civ 1753 at [65]; [1999] 1 All E.R. (Comm) 69 at 85; [1999] 1 Lloyd's Rep. 387 at 399.
[131] *Petrofina (UK) Ltd* [1984] 1 Q.B. 127; [1983] 3 W.L.R. 805; [1983] 3 All E.R. 35.
[132] *National Oilwell (UK) Ltd* [1993] 2 Lloyd's Rep. 582; [1994] C.L.Y. 4086.
[133] *National Oilwell (UK) Ltd* [1993] 2 Lloyd's Rep. 582; [1994] C.L.Y. 4086.
[134] *National Oilwell (UK) Ltd* [1993] 2 Lloyd's Rep. 582 at 608–612; [1994] C.L.Y. 4086.
[135] *Deepak Fertilisers and Petrochemical Co* [1998] EWCA Civ 1753; [1999] 1 All E.R. (Comm) 69; [1999] 1 Lloyd's Rep. 387.
[136] *Feasey v Sun Life Assurance Co of Canada* [2003] EWCA Civ 885; [2003] 2 All E.R. (Comm) 587; [2004] 1 C.L.C. 237. The court's observations on the pervasive interest doctrine in CAR insurance were obiter inasmuch as the case was concerned with insurable interest in the very different context of a quasi-reinsurance policy which paid fixed benefits to a professional and indemnity ("P&I") insurance insurer, triggered by the occurrence of personal injuries to the employees of its members. The majority in the Court of Appeal considered that a subcontractor may have an insurable interest in works based on the fact that he may suffer loss of employment.
[137] *Deepak Fertilisers and Petrochemical Co* [1998] EWCA Civ 1753; [1999] 1 All E.R. (Comm) 69; [1999] 1 Lloyd's Rep. 387.
[138] *Feasey v Sun Life Assurance Co of Canada* [2003] EWCA Civ 885 at [188]; [2003] 2 All E.R. (Comm) 587 at 638; [2004] 1 C.L.C. 237 at 298.

Nevertheless, that is hard to reconcile with the suggestion in the *Deepak Fertilisers and Petrochemical Co*[139] case that a subcontractor has an interest in the pre-completion works based on his expectation of remuneration for the job.[140] Dyson LJ, on the other hand, sharply criticised the distinction drawn in *Deepak*[141] between a contractor's interest pre- and post-completion. He considered that

> "the subcontractor's commercial interest in the plant as a whole during the construction and commissioning stage lies at least as much in his potential liability for damage caused to the plant by his breach of contract and duty as in his interest in not losing the opportunity to do the work and be remunerated for it if the plant is damaged or destroyed by any of the risks covered by an all risks policy".[142]

There is force in this point. Surely a view must be taken that an insured under a **20-057** property policy suffers no relevant loss unless he has a proprietary interest in the thing that has been damaged. Otherwise it must be accepted that a person can have a pervasive interest entitling him to the benefit of insurance on property based on potential detriment to him or loss of benefit if the property is harmed. Either way, there seems to be no reason for drawing the line at the subcontractor's interest in the opportunity of completing the works. In that regard it proves too much to say, as the court did in *Deepak*, that an interest in avoiding liability in respect of the property should be insured via liability insurance.[143] By the same logic, the subcontractor's economic interest in protecting his remuneration should the works be destroyed must be protected by insurance that responds to loss of profit. At any rate, the scope of the pervasive interest doctrine remains in need of clarification.[144]

(ii) Defendant's policy cover must extend to the loss in question.

Defendant's cover must extend to the loss. To take advantage of the co- **20-058** insurance defence to subrogation the defendant must be covered by the policy in respect of the loss that is the subject of the claim.[145] As discussed above at para.20-003, a person identified as an additional insured may have to rely on the rules of agency to participate in the policy and hence limitations on the primary insured's authority to contract on the other's behalf may cut down the scope of cover to which the additional insured becomes party.[146]

The policy wording itself may also provide for differential coverage as between **20-059** the co-insureds. In *National Oilwell (UK) Ltd*, the policy provided that

---

[139] *Deepak Fertilisers and Petrochemical Co* [1998] EWCA Civ 1753; [1999] 1 All E.R. (Comm) 69; [1999] 1 Lloyd's Rep. 387.

[140] *Deepak Fertilisers and Petrochemical Co* [1998] EWCA Civ 1753 at [65]; [1999] 1 All E.R. (Comm) 69 at 85; [1999] 1 Lloyd's Rep. 387 at 399.

[141] *Deepak Fertilisers and Petrochemical Co* [1998] EWCA Civ 1753, [1999] 1 All E.R. (Comm) 69, [1999] 1 Lloyd's Rep. 387.

[142] *Feasey v Sun Life Assurance Co of Canada* [2003] EWCA Civ 885 at [122]; [2003] 2 All E.R. (Comm) 587 at 619; [2004] 1 C.L.C. 237 at 276.

[143] *Deepak Fertilisers and Petrochemical Co* [1998] EWCA Civ 1753 at [67]; [1999] 1 All E.R. (Comm) 69 at 86; [1999] 1 Lloyd's Rep. 387 at 400.

[144] The pervasive interest doctrine is also discussed above at paras 9-043 to 9-048.

[145] Where a contract does not require the employer to insure against consequential losses, the employer can prepare that part of the claim against a contractor *Kruger Tissue (Industrial) Ltd (formerly Industrial Cleaning Papers Ltd) v Frank Galliers Ltd* 57 Con. L.R. 1; (1998) 14 Const. L.J. 437. See also *Barking and Dagenham London Borough Council v Stamford Asphalt Co Ltd* [1997] C.L.C. 929; 82 B.L.R. 25; (1997) 54 Con. L.R. 1 in relation to contractors' liability for damage which is excluded from the policy.

[146] *National Oilwell (UK) Ltd* [1993] 2 Lloyd's Rep. 582; [1994] C.L.Y. 4086.

"[t]he interests of the "Other Assured(s)" shall be covered throughout the entire policy period ... subject to full coverage as herein, unless specific contract(s) contain provisions to the contrary".[147]

The judge held that this clause meant that if the subcontract contained terms the effect of which was to define the insurance cover to be procured by the contractor for the subcontractor more restrictively than that actually provided by the policy, the subcontractor will be entitled to the reduced scope of insurance as defined by the provisions in the subcontract.[148] Since the subcontract in that case provided for the procurement of insurance of the work and materials "in the course of manufacture until the time of delivery",[149] the subcontractor was not covered (quite apart from the problems of agency addressed earlier in the judgment) for losses after that time.[150]

20-060   In the same way, where the defendant seeks to rely on a contractual duty of one of the parties to procure insurance as excluding his liability, the damage that forms the basis of the claim must be within the notional scope of the required cover.[151]

(iii)   Defendant must not be guilty of default that would deprive him of policy cover

20-061   **Guilty party's conduct is a bar to the subrogation defence.**   It was decided in *National Oilwell (UK) Ltd*[152] that if the defendant is guilty of conduct that would bar him from making a claim under the policy this deprives him of the status of being "co-insured". In the case, the judge rejected a suggestion that the incidence of wilful misconduct was irrelevant to the availability of the subrogation defence.[153]

(iv)   Express waiver of subrogation

20-062   **Co-insured with limited insurable interest or cover under the policy.**   Joint-names policies commonly include a waiver of subrogation clause, by which the insurer expressly agrees to not to exercise rights of subrogation against other co-insureds. Where a co-insured has only a limited insurable interest in the subject matter, or for some other reason has only limited cover under the policy, whether a waiver of subrogation clause provides protection as wide as the full scope of the policy is a question that has been considered. In *National Oilwell (UK) Ltd*,[154] the judge held that a clause which read "[u]nderwriters agree to waive rights of subrogation against any Assured and any person ... whose interests are covered by this policy" was confined to claims for losses in respect of which the defendant was insured under the policy.[155] A person did not qualify for the benefit of waiver clause merely by being a party to the contract of insurance—that person had to be covered

---

147   *National Oilwell (UK) Ltd* [1993] 2 Lloyd's Rep. 582 at 588; [1994] C.L.Y. 4086.
148   *National Oilwell (UK) Ltd* [1993] 2 Lloyd's Rep. 582 at 601; [1994] C.L.Y. 4086.
149   *National Oilwell (UK) Ltd* [1993] 2 Lloyd's Rep. 582 at 592; [1994] C.L.Y. 4086.
150   *National Oilwell (UK) Ltd* [1993] 2 Lloyd's Rep. 582 at 602; [1994] C.L.Y. 4086.
151   See below, paras 20-069 to 20-070.
152   *National Oilwell (UK) Ltd* [1993] 2 Lloyd's Rep. 582; [1994] C.L.Y. 4086.
153   *National Oilwell (UK) Ltd* [1993] 2 Lloyd's Rep. 582 at 615–616; [1994] C.L.Y. 4086 at [1099–1100]. See also *Tate Gallery Board of Trustees* [2007] EWHC 361 (TCC); [2007] 1 All E.R. (Comm) 1004; [2007] B.L.R. 216; *P Samuel & Co Ltd v Dumas* [1924] 1 A.C. 431; (1924) 18 Ll. L. Rep. 211; 93 L.J.K.B. 415 and *Netherlands v Youell* [1997] 2 Lloyd's Rep. 440; [1997] C.L.C. 938.
154   *National Oilwell (UK) Ltd* [1993] 2 Lloyd's Rep. 582; [1994] C.L.Y. 4086.
155   *National Oilwell (UK) Ltd* [1993] 2 Lloyd's Rep. 582 at 591, 603; [1994] C.L.Y. 4086. The intention is not to supplant and exclude the liability of the contractor towards the employer altogether,

in respect of the particular loss that formed the basis of the claim to have the benefit of the clause. As the judge recognised, this interpretation meant that the clause simply confirmed what was held in *Petrofina (UK) Ltd*[156] to be the automatic consequence of the subcontractor being co-insured in respect of losses on the basis of which the insurers attempt a subrogated claim.

Waiver of subrogation benefit extended. If the parties wish to include a waiver **20-063** with any wider effect, clear wording must be used. For example, the insurer might agree

> "to waive rights of subrogation against any Assured, whether or not entitled to an indemnity under this policy in respect of the particular loss which would be recovered in a subrogated claim, provided that the Assured who has incurred liability to the other Assured(s) is not guilty of wilful misconduct or conduct which would entitle the Insurer to avoid the policy as against that Assured".

Such wording would, it is suggested, extend the benefit of the waiver to a co-insured who would not actually be able to sustain a claim under the policy in respect of the loss that the insurer has paid—for example, a subcontractor with no insurable interest in that part of the works. But in order to reflect the likely insistence of insurers that parties who are guilty of misconduct or breach of their disclosure duties should not derive any benefit under the policy, the suggested wording includes a carve-out to the extension with that effect.

(v)   Obligations to take out joint-names insurance

Joint insurance: no automatic limit to joint insured's liability arising in tort or contract.   As has been noted, a provision in a building contract that one party **20-064** procure joint-names insurance on behalf of itself and another party will sometimes be construed as an agreement that the two parties will not bring claims against each other in respect of damage, which would be covered by the contemplated insurance. This issue is particularly relevant where no joint-names insurance has, in fact, been taken out.[157] However, an obligation to procure joint-names insurance does not automatically exclude or curtail the primary contractual or tortuous liability of contractors or subcontractors[158] —whether it will have this effect is a matter of construction.[159] Here, "(even small) differences in wording can make all the differ-

---

but only to the extent recovery is obtained from the insurer *Tyco Fire & Integrated Solutions (UK) Ltd* [2008] EWCA Civ 286 at [79]; [2008] 2 All E.R. (Comm) 584 at 610, [2008] Lloyd's Rep. I.R. 617 at 635.

[156] *Petrofina (UK) Ltd* [1984] Q.B. 127; [1983] 3 W.L.R. 805; [1983] 3 All E.R. 35.

[157] As was the case in *Scottish & Newcastle Plc v GD Construction (St Albans) Ltd*; sub nom. *GD Construction (St Albans) Ltd v Scottish & Newcastle Plc* [2003] EWCA Civ 16; [2006] B.L.R. 131; 86 Con. L.R. 1 and *Tyco Fire & Integrated Solutions (UK) Ltd* [2008] EWCA Civ 286; [2008] 2 All E.R. (Comm) 584; [2008] Lloyd's Rep. I.R. 617.

[158] It was held in *Barking and Dagenham London Borough Council* [1997] C.L.C. 929; 82 B.L.R. 25; (1997) 54 Con. L.R. 1 that in the absence of clear words the obligation to take out joint names insurance does not displace an express indemnity clause.

[159] *Surrey Heath Borough Council v Lovell Construction Ltd and Haden Young (third party)* [1990] 48 B.L.R. 108; (1990) 24 Con. L.R. 1; (1990) 6 Const. L.J. 179; *Co-operative Retail Services Ltd* [2002] UKHL 17 at [39]–[49]; [2002] 1 W.L.R. 1419 at 1431–1434; [2002] 1 All E.R. (Comm) 918 at 930–933; *Tyco Fire & Integrated Solutions (UK) Ltd* [2008] EWCA Civ 286; [2008] 2 All E.R. (Comm) 584; [2008] Lloyd's Rep. I.R. 617.

ence",[160] and accordingly it is not easy to extract general principles from the sizeable case law on this matter.

20-065 **Principles.** Some principles do emerge and these may be summarised as follows:

1. If the contractor is expressly required to indemnify the employer for damage that has occurred due to his negligence or breach, the obligation to insure will be read as subject to the contractor's indemnity—unless there is some proviso to the contrary in the indemnity clause.[161] Effectively, the contractor's indemnity is presumed to have priority over the insurance requirement.[162] However, if the insuring clause to which the indemnity clause is subject provides that some peril, loss or damage is at the sole risk of the employer, who has the obligation to insure, that provision will act as a carve-out, which excludes the contractor's liability to the extent that the employer is required to insure some risks on his own.[163]

2. If the insurance is required to include a "without recourse" (waiver of subrogation) clause,[164] this is an indication that the insurance is intended to cover damage caused by the default of the contractor, and that the contractor is intended to be immune to claims within the scope of the contemplated cover.[165]

3. The contractor's liability will be excluded within the contemplated cover if the contract contains a detailed procedure for the carrying out of reinstatement works in the event of damage occasioned by a risk required to be

---

[160] *Tyco Fire & Integrated Solutions (UK) Ltd* [2008] EWCA Civ 286 at [42]; [2008] 2 All E.R. (Comm) 584 at 599; [2008] Lloyd's Rep. I.R. 617 at 627–628.

[161] *Surrey Heath Borough Council* [1990] 48 B.L.R 108 at 119–121; (1990) 24 Con. L.R. 1 at 9–11; (1990) 6 Const. L.J. 179 at 183–185; *Barking and Dagenham London Borough Council* [1997] C.L.C. 929; (1997) 82 B.L.R. 25; (1997) 54 Con. L.R. 1 as interpreted in *Scottish & Newcastle Plc* [2003] EWCA Civ 16 at [36]–[39]; 86 Con. L.R. 1 at 16–18; [2003] Lloyd's Rep. I.R. 809 at 820; *Tyco Fire & Integrated Solutions (UK) Ltd* [2008] EWCA Civ 286; [2008] 2 All E.R. (Comm) 584; [2008] Lloyd's Rep. I.R. 617. The indemnity clause or the insuring clause must be able to be read together to have this effect. See *The National Trust for Places of Historic Interest or Natural Beauty v Haden Young Ltd* (1994) 72 B.L.R. 1; [1994] B.L.M. (September) 1; *Times,* August 11, 1994; *James Archdale & Co Ltd v Comservices Ltd* [1954] 1 W.L.R. 459; [1954] 1 All E.R. 210; (1954) 98 SJ 143 and *Scottish Special Housing Association v Wimpey Construction UK Ltd* [1986] 1 W.L.R. 995; [1986] 2 All E.R. 957; 1986 S.C. (H.L.) 57.

[162] To say that the contractors' indemnity has priority over the insurance obligation clearly entails that the insurance obligation cannot be relied on as a defence by the contractor. However, it is unclear whether this also means that the employer is obliged only to take out insurance which covers damage caused without the contractor's default, even if the description of the perils required to be insured would normally include negligently caused loss (e.g. "fire" or "all risks"). In *Barking and Dagenham London Borough Council* [1997] C.L.C. 929; (1997) 82 B.L.R. 25; (1997) 54 Con. L.R. 1, per Auld LJ thought that the employer's insurance obligation was so limited, but this was doubted by Aitkens J sitting in the Court of Appeal in *Scottish & Newcastle Plc* [2003] EWCA Civ 16 at [39]; 86 Con. L.R. 1 at 17–18; [2003] Lloyd's Rep. I.R. 809 at 820.

[163] *James Archdale & Co Ltd* [1954] 1 W.L.R. 459; [1954] 1 All E.R. 210; (1954) 98 SJ 143; *Scottish Special Housing Association* [1986] 1 W.L.R. 995 at 998; [1986] 2 All E.R. 957 at 959; 1986 SC (HL) 57 at 58–59; *Scottish & Newcastle Plc* [2003] EWCA Civ 16; 86 Con. L.R. 1; [2003] Lloyd's Rep. I.R. 809.

[164] Waiver of subrogation clauses are enforceable by their parties pursuant to the Contracts (Rights of Third Parties) Act 1999. In *Woodside Petroleum Development Pty Ltd v H & R—E & W Pty Ltd* [1999] W.A.S.C.A. 1024 the absence of privity of contract has not considered a bar to their enforceability.

[165] *Scottish & Newcastle Plc* [2003] EWCA Civ 16 at [54] and [57]; 86 Con. L.R. 1 at 22–24; [2003] Lloyd's Rep. I.R. 809 at 823.

insured against. Under this arrangement, the employer's right to deduct anything from the monies falling due to the contractor in respect of the loss is excluded, while the contractor's right to payment for the reinstatement works is confined to the insurance proceeds.[166] In those circumstances, it was found in *Co-operative Retail Services Ltd* that the parties:

> "had entered into contractual arrangements which meant that if a fire occurred, they should look to the joint insurance policy to provide the fund for the cost of restoring and repairing the fire damage ... and that they would bear other losses themselves ... rather than indulge in litigation with each other".[167]

JCT Standard Form of Building Contract options. The current (2011) JCT Standard Form of Building Contract presents a selection of three "Insurance Options" for the parties to choose from[168]:

20-066

1. Under Option A, the contractor is obliged to take out a joint-names[169] all risks policy for the works, with cover no less than that specified in cl.6.8,[170] to be maintained up until the date of practical completion or, if earlier, the termination of the contractor's employment.[171] Option A includes the same procedure for making insurance claims and carrying out reinstatement work,

---

[166] That is the scheme set out in the Joint Contracts Tribunal. *SBC/Q 2011 JCT Standard Building Contract With Quantities 2011* (London: Sweet & Maxwell, 2011), pp.89–90, at Sch.3, paras A.4.1–A.4.6 and B.3.1–B.3.3 (previously known as cl.22A.4.1–22A.4.5 of the 1980 and 1998 forms; Joint Contracts Tribunal, *The JCT Standard Form of Building Contract 1980 Edition Local Authorities, With Approximate Quantities* (RIBA Publications, 1980), p.24; Joint Contracts Tribunal, *JCT Standard Form of Building Contract 1998 Edition Private With Quantities*, (RIBA Publications, 1999), p.40.

[167] *Co-operative Retail Services Ltd* [2000] EWCA Civ 207 at [73]; [2000] 2 All E.R. (Comm) 865 at 885; 74 Con. L.R. 12 at 49–50; *Co-operative Retail Services Ltd* [2002] UKHL 17 at [43] and [48]; [2002] 1 W.L.R. 1419 at 1432 and 1434; [2002] 1 All E.R. (Comm) 918 at 931–933; *John F Hunt Demolition Ltd v ASME Engineering Ltd* [2007] EWHC 1507 (TCC) at [38]; [2008] 1 All E.R. (Comm) 473 at 486; [2008] Bus. L.R. 558 at 572 and *Ossory Road (Skelmersdale) Ltd v Balfour Beatty Building Ltd* [1993] C.I.L.L. 882.

[168] Joint Contracts Tribunal (JCT), *SBC/Q 2011 JCT Standard Building Contract With Quantities 2011* (London: Sweet & Maxwell, 2011), pp.69–71, see cll.6.7–6.9 and Sch.3. See *Keating on Construction Contracts*, S. Furst, Sir V. Ramsey, S. Hannaford, A. Williamson, J. Uff, 10th edn (London: Sweet & Maxwell, 2016) paras 20–394 and 20–437 to 20–444.

[169] Defined as a policy which includes the employer and contractor as composite insured and under which the insurers have no right of recourse: cl.6.8. It is to be noted that the employer is not obliged to include the interest of subcontractors in the policy. The requirement that there be "no right of recourse" (i.e. either implied or express waiver of subrogation) lends weight to the conclusion that the contractor's liability is intended to be curtailed by the insurance provision: *Scottish & Newcastle Plc* [2003] EWCA Civ 16 at [54], [56] and [57]; 86 Con. L.R. 1 at 22–24; [2003] Lloyd's Rep. I.R. 809 at 823.

[170] That provision defines "all risks insurance" as cover against physical loss or damage to the site and materials, extending also to consequential costs of debris removal and any shoring or propping of the works. Such insurance may exclude a number of specified excepted perils (cl.6.8(c)(i)). As for defects liability, the policy may exclude any work or site materials damaged as a result of "its own" defect in design, workmanship etc or any other work which is lost or damaged in consequence thereof "where such work relied for its support or stability on such work which was defective" (cl.6.8(b), in Joint Contracts Tribunal (JCT) *SBC/Q 2011 JCT Standard Building Contract With Quantities 2011* (London: Sweet & Maxwell, 2011). This is essentially DE2 wording: see above, paras 16-034 to 16-035.

[171] So under this wording the contractor is not required to be covered in respect of losses which occur after his involvement in the works has come to an end, and accordingly would not be immunised by the building contract in respect of damage to the completed works, quite apart from the issue of whether a contractor has an insurable interest post-completion: cf. *Deepak Fertilisers and*

which was considered (in the guise of an earlier version of the form) in *Co-operative Retail Services Ltd*[172] and held to prevent the employer claiming damages from the contractor in respect of loss to be insured (see above para.20-064).[173]

2. Option B is essentially the same as Option A, but the obligation to procure joint-names insurance is placed on the employer. The same insurance claims and reinstatement mechanism applies, and this again will exempt the contractor from liability in respect of the loss that is required to be insured.

3. Option C is designed for works in or extensions to existing structures. Under this provision, the employer is obliged to take out joint-names policies both in respect of the existing structures (Sch.3 para.C.1) and in respect of the works (Sch.3 para.C.2).[174] Where Option C insurance is selected, the contractor's liability under cl.6.2 to indemnify the employer against loss or damage to property other than the works is expressly excluded to the extent of any loss or damage that is required to be insured under Sch.3 para.C.1—so again, the contractor is exempted from liability in respect of loss required to be insured.[175]

20-067 **Infrastructure Conditions of Contract Measurement form.** Under the Infrastructure Conditions of Contract Measurement form,[176] the position is different. The contractor is obliged under cl.21[177] to procure insurance of the works in the joint names of the contractor and the employer to cover all risks of loss or damage other

---

Petrochemical Co [1998] EWCA Civ 1753; [1999] 1 All E.R. (Comm) 69; [1999] 1 Lloyd's Rep. 387.

[172] *Co-operative Retail Services Ltd* [2000] EWCA Civ 207; [2000] 2 All E.R. (Comm) 865; 74 Con. L.R. 12; *Co-operative Retail Services Ltd* [2002] UKHL 17; [2002] 1 W.L.R. 1419; [2002] 1 All E.R. (Comm) 918.

[173] See also, Sch.3, paras A.4.1–A.4.6 in the Joint Contracts Tribunal (JCT) *SBC/Q 2011 JCT Standard Building Contract With Quantities 2011* (London: Sweet & Maxwell, 2011), p.89 and paras 22A.4.1–22A.4.5 of the 1980 and 1998 forms; i.e. Joint Contracts Tribunal, *The JCT Standard Form of Building Contract 1980 Edition Local Authorities, With Approximate Quantities* (London: RIBA Publications, 1980), p.24; Joint Contracts Tribunal, *JCT Standard Form of Building Contract 1998 Edition Private With Quantities*, (London: RIBA Publications, 1980), p.40.

[174] The Sch.3, C.2 obligation is again subject to the claims and reinstatement mechanism discussed in relation to Option A and Option B (Sch.3, paras C.4.1–C.4.5) of the Joint Contracts Tribunal (JCT) *SBC/Q 2011 JCT Standard Building Contract With Quantities 2011* (London: Sweet & Maxwell, 2011), pp.91–92.

[175] *Scottish & Newcastle Plc* [2003] EWCA Civ 16; 86 Con. L.R. 1; [2003] Lloyd's Rep. I.R. 809 (concerning the equivalent cll 6.2.1 and 6.3C.1 of the JCT, Joint Contracts Tribunal For the Standard Form of Building Contract. *Intermediate Form of Building Contract for Works of Simple Content*, 1984 Edition: IFC 84 (London: RIBA, c.1984). The contractor would be exempt from liability for losses falling within Option 3 insurance additionally by reason of Sch.3 paras C.4.1–C.4.5, which like paras A.4.1–A.4.6 and B.3.1–B.3.3 applies a version of the claims and reinstatement scheme considered in *Co-operative Retail Services Ltd* [2000] EWCA Civ 207; [2000] 2 All E.R. (Comm) 865; 74 Con. L.R. 12. See above, para.20-065.

[176] Association for Consultancy and Engineering and Civil Engineering Contractors Association. *Infrastructure Conditions of Contract: Measurement Version August 2011 Based on the ICE Conditions of Contract*, 1st edn (London: Association for Consultancy and Engineering, 2011). See above, para.3-005.

[177] Association for Consultancy and Engineering and Civil Engineering Contractors Association. *Infrastructure Conditions of Contract: Measurement Version August 2011 Based on the ICE Conditions of Contract*, 1st edn (London: Association for Consultancy and Engineering, 2011), pp.13–14.

than those for which the contractor is exempted from liability in cl.20(2).[178] In other words, the contractor is required to fully insure his potential liability to the employer. It is clear, however, that the fact that joint-names insurance is required does not absolve the contractor of any of his liability: cl.21(1) provides that the contractor shall insure "without limiting his ... obligations and responsibilities under Clause 20".[179] Clause 20 places the works at the risk of the contractor until substantial completion.[180] There is no mechanism for the funding of reinstatement works out of the insurance proceeds of the type considered in *Co-operative Retail Services Ltd*,[181] nor is there any requirement that the joint-names policy is "without recourse".[182]

However, it is suggested that if the contractor does take out joint-names insur- **20-068** ance, despite the liability inter partes under the building contract, the insurer will be barred from making subrogated claims in respect of losses for which the contractor is in fact covered. That proposition is dependent on the correctness of the view expressed above that the exclusion of liability by the insurance provisions of the building contract and the rule against subrogation in the name of one co-insured in respect of another are separate and not necessarily co-extensive defences.

Cover must still be established. The conclusion that a particular set of provi- **20-069** sions for joint-names insurance in the building contract curtails the contractor's liability in respect of losses required to be insured does not necessarily mean that the contractor has a defence: the defendant contractor must still establish that he would be covered by the policy envisaged by the contract. It is not too difficult to determine whether there would be cover in respect of the loss that has occurred if the building contract includes, as the 2011 JCT Standard Form does at cl.6.7, a detailed set of specifications for the type of policy that must be taken out.[183] There is more difficulty where the contract is rather more vague.[184] For example, whereas the 2011 JCT Standard Form makes it clear that the works policy should include a

---

[178] Association for Consultancy and Engineering and Civil Engineering Contractors Association. *Infrastructure Conditions of Contract: Measurement Version August 2011 Based on the ICE Conditions of Contract*, 1st edn (London: Association for Consultancy and Engineering, 2011), p.13.

[179] Association for Consultancy and Engineering and Civil Engineering Contractors Association. *Infrastructure Conditions of Contract: Measurement Version August 2011 Based on the ICE Conditions of Contract*, 1st edn (London: Association for Consultancy and Engineering, 2011), p.13. See below fn.180.

[180] Association for Consultancy and Engineering and Civil Engineering Contractors Association. *Infrastructure Conditions of Contract: Measurement Version August 2011 Based on the ICE Conditions of Contract*, 1st edn (London: Association for Consultancy and Engineering, 2011), pp.12–13.

[181] *Co-operative Retail Services Ltd* [2000] EWCA Civ 207; [2000] 2 All E.R. (Comm) 865; 74 Con. L.R. 12. See above, para.20-065.

[182] See above, para.20-065.

[183] Joint Contracts Tribunal, *JCT Standard Building Contract With Quantities 2011* (London: Sweet & Maxwell, 2011), p.69.

[184] In *Deepak Fertilisers and Petrochemical Co* [1998] EWCA Civ 1753 at [68]; [1999] 1 All E.R. (Comm) 69 at 86; [1999] 1 Lloyd's Rep. 387 at 400 the building contract simply required the contractor "to be named as co-insured in all policies of insurance effected in respect of the Plant". The judge held this wording imposed no obligation for the employer to insure the plant, only to include the contractor in any insurance that was taken out (see [1998] EWCA Civ 1753 at [69]; [1999] 1 All E.R. (Comm) 69 at 86; [1999] 1 Lloyd's Rep. 387 at 400). If the provision had imposed a positive duty to procure insurance, it would have been impossible to determine what degree of cover was required.

defects exclusion at least as generous (from the insured's point of view)[185] as the DE2 clause (that is, excluding loss or damage, due to a defect, to the defective part itself or property that is structurally dependent on it),[186] other draftsmen may not address the extent of coverage for defects so carefully.

20-070   In *Skanska Construction UK Ltd (formerly Kvaerner Construction Ltd)*,[187] the contract required the employer to procure insurance to cover

> "loss or damage arising during the Defects Liability Period from such cause occurring prior to the commencement of the Defects Liability Period".[188]

The issue was whether this language required the employer to take out a policy covering the cost of repairing any damage due to a defect, including damage to the defective part itself (i.e. DE5 cover)[189] or whether, instead, damage had to be to another distinct part of the works to fall within the insurance requirement (DE3 or DE4 cover).[190] Despite the wide wording of the insurance provision, the Court of Appeal considered that in the context of the wider contract and given the contractor's obligations to make good defective work, it was unlikely that the mere manifestation of a defect causing damage to the defective part of the works was intended to be insured.[191] This interpretation may well have made for the best fit with the contract as a whole, but it is fair to say the particular words that the contract used to define the required cover, quoted above, are obscure. Given the importance of provision for the procurement of joint-names insurance—and the potential for disputes over their interpretation—it might be suggested that it is unwise to draft such clauses with any less clarity than insurance policies themselves.

Contract wording silent on the duration of the joint-names insurance
20-071 **obligation.**   Problems also arise where the form of wording is silent as to the duration of the insurance obligation, as was the case with older versions of the JCT forms. The 1993 revision of the *JCT Agreement for Minor Building Works*[192] required the employer to procure joint-names insurance of the works. In a case on this provision, a contractor facing a claim for damage to the building, which was

---

[185] In Joint Contracts Tribunal, *JCT Standard Building Contract With Quantities 2011* (London: Sweet & Maxwell, 2011), p.88–92. Sch.3 paras A.1, B.1 and C.2 (insurance of the works) require insurance "with cover no less than that specified in clause 6.8". So the person required to procure the insurance would be perfectly able to take out a policy with a narrower defects exclusion.

[186] See further above, Ch.16.

[187] *Skanska Construction UK Ltd (formerly Kvaerner Construction Ltd) v Egger (Barony) Ltd*; sub nom.*Skanska Construction Ltd v Egger (Barony) Ltd* [2002] EWCA Civ 310 at [6]; 83 Con. L.R. 132 at 135–137; [2003] Lloyd's Rep. I.R. 479 at 482.

[188] This wording originates from the *ICE Conditions of Contract* (see 7th edn, 1999, at cl.21(2)(b)) revised 2011 and now set out in the document produced by the Association for Consultancy and Engineering and Civil Engineering Contractors Association called the *Infrastructure Conditions of Contract: Measurement Version August 2011 Based on the ICE Conditions of Contract*, 1st edn (London: Association for Consultancy and Engineering, 2011). However, since the current form places the obligation to insure the works on the contractor rather than the employer it would not have been open for the contractor, had the standard form been used, to argue that the employer was in breach for failing to obtain sufficient cover.

[189] See above, paras 16-044 to 16-061.

[190] See above, paras 16-036 to 16-043.

[191] *Skanska Construction UK Ltd (formerly Kvaerner Construction Ltd) v Egger (Barony) Ltd* [2002] EWCA Civ 310 at [18]–[19], [30]; 83 Con. L.R. 132 at 140–143; [2003] Lloyd's Rep. I.R. 479 at 484–486.

[192] Joint Contracts Tribunal, *JCT Agreement for Minor Building Works* (London: RIBA Publications Ltd, 1993).

sustained after completion, contended that the obligation to insure continued until the end of the defects liability period.[193] The Court of Appeal held, however, that there was no requirement to insure past the completion date because, inter alia, the finished state of the building was not within the meaning of the phrase "the Works".[194] The issue is now dealt with expressly in the current *JCT Standard Form of Contract* (2011 edn), Sch.3 para.B.1.[195] This states that the obligation to maintain insurance on the works subsists:

> "up to and including the date of issue of the Practical Completion Certificate or, if earlier, the date of termination of the Contractor's employment".[196]

---

[193] *TFW Printers Ltd v Interserve Project Services Ltd* [2006] EWCA Civ 875; [2006] 2 C.L.C. 106; [2006] B.L.R. 299.

[194] *TFW Printers Ltd* [2006] EWCA Civ 875 at [27]–[30]; [2006] 2 C.L.C. 106 at 115–116; 109 Con. L.R. 1 at 9–10.

[195] Joint Contracts Tribunal, *JCT Standard Building Contract With Quantities 2011* (London: Sweet & Maxwell, 2011), p.90.

[196] Joint Contracts Tribunal, *JCT Standard Building Contract With Quantities 2011* (London: Sweet & Maxwell, 2011), p.90.

CHAPTER 21

CLAIMS PROCEDURE

1. INTRODUCTION

Introduction. The manner in which the word "claim" is used in insurance is **21-001** largely dependent upon the type of policy in question. There are three ways in which a "claim" may arise in the context of a CAR policy:

1. a claim submitted by the insured to the insurer for an indemnity under the policy;
2. a claim made against the insured by a third party; and
3. a claim that the insured may have against a third party to recover loss covered under the policy.

This chapter deals with the most common procedural aspects and obligations that **21-002** arise as between the insurer and the insured at the various stages of the claims process; issues relating to aggregation, proof and payment are dealt with in detail elsewhere in this text.[1] The law on claims procedure governs the content of the claim, the manner in which the claim is presented to or brought to the attention of the insurer by the insured, the manner in which the claim is addressed and handled by the insurer and any subsequent negotiation and settlement of a claim. These are all subject to stipulations agreed between the parties, which are contained within the contract of insurance, to statutes, and to common law rules.

Nature of claims conditions. The different ways in which terms in insurance **21-003** contracts can be classified is dealt with in Ch.12. Under the law as enacted under the Marine Insurance Act 1906 ("MIA"), the position was that those terms, commonly called "claims conditions", for example those relating to notification, the duty to provide particulars, claims control and claims co-operation were not conditions in the normal contractual sense. In other words, they were not terms that by their mere nature go to the root of the contract, breach of which would entitle the insurer to repudiate liability. Instead, they have often been held to be terms that are ancillary, breach of which will only sound in damages or, to the extent they have been considered by the courts to be innominate terms, as discussed at para.12-010

---

[1] See above, Ch.11 (The Indemnity) and below, Chs 22 (Proof) and 23 (Payment).

above, the authorities are clear that breach is extremely unlikely ever to permit repudiation of the contract.[2]

21-004   Depending on the wording employed in the policy, however, it is possible for a claims condition to be construed as a condition precedent to the insurer's liability in respect of a particular claim or claims in general. As summarised in *Cox v Bankside Members Agency Ltd*[3]:

> "It is not always easy to decide whether clauses requiring notice of a claim are conditions precedent to the liability of the insurer under the policy, or merely terms of the policy for breach of which the insurer's only remedy is to claim damages for the extra expense flowing from the insured's failure to give notice within the proper time. Little more can be said than that it is a matter of construing the policy as a whole."

The enactment of the Insurance Act 2015 ("the 2015 Act") has effected widespread reforms to the remedies available to an insurer for the breach of particular policy terms. Where a claims condition is construed as an ancillary or innominate term, the effect of an insured's breach will be no different under the 2015 Act as the previous position under the MIA. However, where the term purports to entitle the insurer to suspend or deny liability following an insured's breach, the new controls enacted under the 2015 Act may be applied to limit or restrict an insurer's ability to do so. Under s.10 of the 2015 Act, any term that is classified as a warranty is only capable of suspending an insurer's liability until remedied rather than discharging an insurer's liability entirely as from the date of breach. Because there is some suggestion that the courts will apply the provisions of s.10 to terms other than warranties including conditions precedent to liability, it is possible that the new provisions could apply to claims conditions with the effect that an insured may be able to revive a claim even after it has failed to comply with the claims condition if it is able to remedy the breach. This possibility is discussed in greater detail above at para.5-102, with more general attention given to the classification of terms under the policy in Ch.12.

21-005   Limitation.   Section 5 of the Limitation Act 1980 provides a six-year period within which the insured must bring any claim against the insurer. The point at which limitation starts to run is the moment of the occurrence of the insured peril.[4] Where the policy is a liability policy, under which the insurer is under an obligation to indemnify the insured for its third party liability, the six-year period starts to run from the date on which the third party formally establishes and quantifies the insured's liability under the policy by way of judgment, arbitral award or adjudication.[5] The parties to the insurance contract may agree to vary the limitation period under the terms of the contract, by expressly shortening or lengthening the period for bringing a claim. Indeed, it is common for an insurer to restrict the period of time the insured has in which to bring a claim against it to a period much shorter than six years.

---

[2]   See for instance Mance LJ in *Friends Provident Life & Pensions Ltd v Sirius International Insurance Corp* [2005] EWCA Civ 601 at [31]; [2005] 2 All E.R. (Comm) 145 at 161–162; [2005] 2 Lloyd's Rep. 517 at 530.

[3]   *Cox v Bankside Members Agency Ltd* [1995] 2 Lloyd's Rep. 437 at 453; [1995] C.L.C. 671.

[4]   *Seele Austria GmbH & Co KG v Tokio Marine Europe Insurance Ltd* [2008] EWCA Civ 441; [2009] 1 All E.R. (Comm) 171; [2008] B.L.R. 337.

[5]   *London Steamship Owners Mutual Insurance Association Ltd v Bombay Trading Co Ltd (The Felicie)* [1990] 2 Lloyd's Rep. 21 (Note).

2. NOTIFICATION CLAUSES

Purpose of notification clauses. One of the main provisions of the claims **21-006** procedure in any insurance policy is that relating to notification. The notification clause or clauses set out the circumstances and manner in which an insured must notify the insurer if it wishes to claim under the policy.[6] There is a broad spectrum of such clauses ranging from those that set out with a great deal of specificity the steps that an insured must take to those which are less demanding or less prescriptive. The purpose behind any notification was well summarised by Potter LJ in *George Hunt Cranes Ltd v Scottish Boiler and General Insurance Co Ltd*[7] who stated:

> "[T]he insurer should be properly placed in possession of a notification, with accompanying information, in sufficient time for him to make a reasoned decision, (a) in relation to the existence of cover under the terms of the policy; (b) as to the prima facie amount of the loss; (c), and most important, as to the investigations necessary or advisable to be made while the incident is fresh and evidence still available, whether in the form of an investigation at the accident scene or the availability and memory of potential witnesses."

The insurer will be concerned to know exactly how much exposure it may face **21-007** and the chances of that exposure becoming a reality. The insurer will wish to assume control of investigation and settlement in order for it to minimise its loss, to ensure it has sufficient funds to meet its liability and to preserve as much evidence as possible in order to enhance its chances of success in recovering damages from a third party. In order to press upon the insured the importance to the insurer of notification, compliance with the notification clause by the insured may be stated as a condition precedent to liability.

Matters to be notified: event. A CAR policy is an occurrence-based rather than **21-008** claims-made policy, meaning that the insurer will cover the occurrence of an event that arises during the period of insurance, as opposed to simply covering claims made during the period of insurance. This distinction is significant because there will often be a time lag between the occurrence that gives rise to the insurer's liability and the making of the claim, and the occurrence policy leaves the insurer exposed to claims made after the end of the insurance period. As such, the usual term in such a policy requires the insured to notify the insurer of the occurrence of any event that may or is likely to give rise or has given rise to a claim under the policy or similar such wording. A claim under the policy in this sense means a request by the insured for the insurer to confirm that it is liable to indemnify the insured under the terms of the policy.

Matters to be notified: physical damage. Where physical damage is the subject **21-009** of the cover, the event of which the insurer must be notified is likely to be

---

[6] The position where there is no express obligation to notify in the policy is not resolved. It is suggested by the editors of *MacGillivray on Insurance Law*, 13th edn, para.21-036 that "the insured should give notice of his loss within a reasonable time as part of his general obligation to act with good faith towards his insurer." However, M. Clarke, *The Law of Insurance Contracts*, Vol.2, para.26-2A suggests that the insured is under no such duty to notify in the absence of an express obligation as such a term is not necessary to give the contract business efficacy. There is no direct authority on the point, however it would be unusual for a modern CAR policy not to contain an express notification provision.

[7] *George Hunt Cranes Ltd v Scottish Boiler and General Insurance Co Ltd* [2001] EWCA Civ 1964 at [14]; [2002] 1 All E.R. (Comm) 366 at 370; [2003] 1 C.L.C. 1 at 7.

contemporaneous with the physical damage to the contract works or other insured property. In such circumstances, there will be little difficulty in identifying the relevant event. A simple example is the occurrence of an earthquake or other natural peril that results in damage to the construction works. Another example might be the occurrence of "bottom heave" during an excavation, which may cause physical damage to foundations already laid.

21-010   **Matters to be notified: latent damage.**   An insured can only notify of events, or circumstances, of which it is aware. Issues can also arise where damage does not immediately or obviously result from those events or circumstances that arise. In particular, a claims-made policy may preclude the insured from recovering when knowledge of latent damage emerges after the policy has ended. As a result, the insurance industry provides the option of taking out separate latent damage/defects insurance. The benefit of an occurrence-based policy is that it will provide cover for latent damage; that is, damage that only becomes apparent some time after the event occurs. It has been held that the court is entitled to review subjectively what the insured was aware of in relation to the notified circumstances at the time notification was given, since only those circumstances that are the subject matter of a notification can be those that the insured can recover for. For example, where a notification is made that identifies the circumstances causing damage and states that investigations are ongoing, the discovery of further latent damage unrelated to the circumstances cannot be attributed to the initial notification and will need to be the subject of a fresh notification, even where the further investigation was related to those circumstances initially notified.[8]

21-011   **Matters to be notified: claims by third parties.**   A CAR policy may expressly provide for the insurer to be notified of and provided with relevant documents if there is any claim or potential claim against the insured by a third party. This is essential where the policy includes third party/public liability cover. Even if the contract does not specify that a potential claim by a third party should be notified it will invariably be implicit from the wording of the notification clause that the insured should be notified of such a claim. Further, an insured is likely to be obliged to provide notice of receipt of any Notice of Adjudication under the Housing Grants Construction and Regeneration Act 1996 or the Local Democracy, Economic Development and Construction Act 2009.

21-012   **Claims by third parties: when to notify.**   There are a number of different ways in which the obligation to notify of a claim could be phrased. For example, the obligation may arise where a third-party claim "may", "might", "could" or "is likely to" give rise to a claim under the policy, rather than when a claim is in fact made. Further difficulty arises as to what constitutes a notifiable circumstance in relation to a third-party claim, for it may be more difficult to determine whether a third party may have a claim than it would be to determine whether the insured itself may have a claim. In all cases, it must be determined whether there is sufficient possibility or probability of such circumstances giving rise to a claim by the insured under the policy to fall within the notification obligation.

21-013   **What is a claim?**   The courts have grappled with this predominantly in the context

---

[8]   Akenhead J in *Kajima (UK) Engineering Ltd v The Underwriter Insurance Co Ltd* [2008] EWHC 83 (TCC); [2008] 1 All E.R. (Comm) 855; 122 Con. L.R. 123—in the context of a contractor's claims-made professional indemnity policy.

of claims-made or liability policies. For instance, Devlin J stated in *West Wake Price & Co v Ching*[9]:

> "[T]he primary meaning of the word 'claim'—whether used in a popular sense or in a strict legal sense—is such as to attach it to the object that is claimed; and is not the same thing as the cause of action by which the claim may be supported or as the grounds on which it may be based."

West Wake Price & Co was followed by the Court of Appeal in *Thorman v New Hampshire Insurance Co (UK) Ltd and Home Insurance; sub nom. Home Insurance Co v New Hampshire Insurance Co (UK) Ltd*,[10] where Stocker LJ said that "the cause of action is not, itself, a claim but the necessary vehicle for its legal enforcement."[11] The courts have therefore stressed that they are concerned with the underlying facts and substance rather than the form of the claim. For instance, Thomas J stated in the Privy Council case of *Haydon v Lo & Lo*,[12] applying *West Wake Price & Co* and which was itself applied in *Citibank NA v Excess Insurance Co Ltd (t/a ITT London and Edinburgh)*,[13] that:

> "[i]t is clear from [Haydon] that it is the underlying facts that are determinative of the question whether there is one claim and not the formulation of the claim by the claimant, but that it does not follow that there is a separate claim for each separate cause of action. The way the demand is made initially is a useful starting point, but what is paramount is the reality of the position."

Both *Haydon* and *Citibank NA* were referred to in *Mabey & Johnson Ltd v Ecclesiastical Insurance Office Plc*[14] where Morrison J stated:

> "As is so often the case when the court is engaged on an issue of construction, the word concerned, in this case 'claim', is one in normal use and does not take on any new meaning when it appears in the contractual document, the policy. The process of reasoning which leads the court to a conclusion will involve an examination of the underlying facts so that it can assess whether the characteristics of a claim suggest that there is one or perhaps two claims."

Matters to be notified: degree of likelihood of claim and objective test. Regardless of whether the obligation is to notify of an event or a claim, the policy may provide that notification is only necessary if there is a certain degree of possibility or probability of the event giving rise to a claim under the policy or a claim being made against the insured. The current law is set out by Teare J in *Aspen Insurance UK Ltd v Pectel Ltd*[15] when recording the common ground between the parties that an obligation to notify of "any occurrence which may give rise to indemnity under this insurance":   **21-014**

> "meant that there must be a real as opposed to a fanciful risk of the underwriters having to indemnify the assured and that in determining whether there was such a risk the court applied an objective test,

---

[9] *West Wake Price & Co v Ching* [1957] 1 W.L.R. 45 at 55; [1956] 3 All E.R. 821 at 829; [1956] 2 Lloyd's Rep. 618 at 627.
[10] *Home Insurance Co v New Hampshire Insurance Co (UK) Ltd* [1988] 1 Lloyd's Rep. 7; 39 B.L.R. 41; [1988] 1 F.T.L.R. 30.
[11] *Home Insurance Co* [1988] 1 Lloyd's Rep. 7 at 16; 39 B.L.R. 41 at 59; [1988] 1 F.T.L.R. 30 at 39.
[12] *Haydon v Lo & Lo* [1997] 1 W.L.R. 198; [1997] 1 Lloyd's Rep. 336; [1997] C.L.C. 626.
[13] *Citibank NA v Excess Insurance Co Ltd (t/a ITT London and Edinburgh)* [1999] C.L.C. 120 at 126; [1999] Lloyd's Rep. I.R. 122 at 127–128.
[14] *Mabey & Johnson Ltd v Ecclesiastical Insurance Office Plc* [2003] EWHC 1523 (Comm) at [13]; [2004] Lloyd's Rep. I.R. 10 at 14. This case is dealt with in the context of aggregation above, at para.11-028.
[15] *Aspen Insurance UK Ltd v Pectel Ltd* [2008] EWHC 2804 (Comm); [2009] 2 All E.R. (Comm) 873; [2009] Lloyd's Rep. I.R. 440.

taking into account the knowledge that the assured possessed in order to determine the extent to which the assured was aware of, and hence capable of notifying, occurrences which may give rise to an indemnity; see *Rothschild v Collyear* [1999] 1 Lloyd's [I] R ... 6 at p 22 (per Rix J) and *HLB Kidsons v Lloyds Underwriters* [2008] 1 Lloyd's Reports I.R. 237 at paras 72 and 73 (per Gloster J) and [2008] EWCA 1206 at paras 72 and 141-142 (per Rix and Toulson LJJ)."[16]

The fact that the test is objective and not subjective was confirmed by Aikens LJ in *Laker Vent Engineering Ltd v Templeton Insurance Co Ltd*,[17] cited with approval in *Loyaltrend Ltd v Creechurch Dedicated Ltd*.[18] Where the obligation is to notify of any occurrence that is "likely" to give rise to indemnity, this equates to "probable" or "more likely than not".[19]

21-015   Form and contents of notice.   The policy may provide for the specific form and contents of the notice required; the most common provision is that on notification the insured must provide such particulars and proofs of claims as may reasonably be required by the insurer. Alternatively, the policy may provide for notification followed shortly thereafter by further necessary particulars and proofs.[20] The policy ought to provide for whatever is required to permit the insured sufficient information to investigate the claim and assess its liability under the policy.[21]

21-016   Communication of notice.   The mode of communication of notice and person(s) to whom it should be given will usually be outlined in the policy. For instance, the policy may specify whether notice must be written and to whom such notice must be addressed; obvious examples being to a particular branch or office of the insurer or to a designated employee or agent. When considering whether a communication constitutes a valid notification, the courts will adopt an objective approach and "subjective intentions and understandings of the party sending the notice [are] irrelevant".[22]

21-017   Timing of notice: no time stipulated.   Notification clauses can range from the unusual position where no reference is made to when notice must be given through to setting out stringent conditions requiring notice to be given immediately. Where no time limit is given within which the insured must notify the insurer,

---

[16]   *Aspen Insurance UK Ltd* [2008] EWHC 2804 (Comm) at [9]; [2009] 2 All E.R. (Comm) 873 at 877; [2009] Lloyd's Rep. I.R. 440 at 444.

[17]   *Laker Vent Engineering Ltd v Templeton Insurance Co Ltd* [2009] EWCA Civ 62; [2009] 2 All E.R. (Comm) 755; [2009] Lloyd's Rep. I.R. 704.

[18]   *Loyaltrend Ltd v Creechurch Dedicated Ltd* [2010] EWHC 425 (Comm); [2010] Lloyd's Rep. I.R. 466.

[19]   This was agreed as common ground between the parties in *Laker Vent Engineering Ltd*; see [2008] EWHC B6 (QB) at [149] and [2009] EWCA Civ 62 at [18]; [2009] 2 All E.R. (Comm) 755 at 761; [2009] Lloyd's Rep. I.R. 704 at 708.

[20]   See below, Ch.22, for a detailed discussion of issues of proof.

[21]   See *Rendal A/S v Arcos Ltd* [1937] 3 All E.R. 577 at 580; (1937) 58 Ll. L. Rep. 287 at 292 (1937) 43 Com. Cas. 1 at 4 where it was held that a notice did not need to be presented as a fully fledged claim as long as the notice enabled "the party to whom it is given to take steps to meet the claim, by preparing and obtaining appropriate evidence for that purpose".

[22]   *HLB Kidsons (a firm) v Lloyd's Underwriters subscribing to Lloyd's Policy No. 621/PKID00101* [2007] EWHC 1951 (Comm) at [72]; [2008] 1 All E.R. (Comm) 769 at 799; [2008] Lloyd's Rep. I.R. 237 at 263, per Gloster J referring to *Rennie v Westbury Homes (Holdings) Ltd* [2007] EWHC 164 (Ch) at [38]; [2007] 2 P. & C.R. 239 at 249; [2007] 2 E.G.L.R. 95 at 98. See also above, para.21-014.

"there must ... be a term, implied in order to give business efficacy to the policy, that the insured will do the things required of it by way of notification and co-operation within a reasonable time."[23]

The Court of Appeal held in *Shinedean Ltd v Alldown Demolition (London) Ltd (in Liquidation)*[24] that what constitutes a reasonable time will depend on the particular facts of each case and there is no absolute principle that eventual prejudice to the insurer should be included or excluded when assessing what that period should be. The Court of Appeal considered that, in the circumstances, the insurer was entitled to receive the information in good time to be able to assess its potential liability and to take appropriate action, whether or not it was ultimately prejudiced by the failure to provide the information.

Timing of notice: immediate/forthwith. A policy may provide that notice is to   **21-018** be given to the insurer of a specified occurrence or claim immediately or forthwith. The meaning of immediate in this sense was determined by Fletcher Moulton LJ in *Re Coleman's Depositories Ltd and Life & Health Assurance Association's Arbitration*,[25] where he stated that it meant "with all reasonable speed considering the circumstances of the case". In CAR policies notice may have to be given immediately or forthwith of the insured's receipt of any notice to refer a matter to adjudication because of the tight statutory time-limits involved in the determination of adjudications.

Timing of notice: within specified time. Some policies may require notifica-   **21-019** tion and/or particulars of the claim within a specified time from the loss arising or circumstances being known. Such time limits must be strictly complied with.[26] In *Nasser Diab v Regent Insurance Co Ltd*,[27] the Privy Council had to consider a condition in a fire-insurance policy, which provided that:

"[o]n the happening of any loss or damage the Insured shall forthwith give notice thereof to the Company, and shall within 15 days after the loss or damage, or such further time as the Company may in writing allow in that behalf, deliver to the Company: (a) a claim in writing for the loss or damage containing as particular an account as may be reasonably practicable of all the several articles of property damages or destroyed, and of the amount of the loss or damage thereto respectively, having regard to their value at the time of the loss or damage, not including profit of any kind; (b) particulars of all other insurances if any ... No claim under this Policy shall be payable unless the terms of this condition have been complied with."

The first part of this clause was complied with in that Regent was informed of the fire forthwith but no claim in writing was delivered until after the expiry of the 15-day period and the requisite particulars were never delivered. Lord Scott made the point that since s.25 of the Supreme Court of Judicature Act 1873 came into force "time [was] not to be deemed to be or to become of the essence of the contract

---

[23] *Shinedean Ltd v Alldown Demolition (London) Ltd (In Liquidation)* [2005] EWHC 2319 (TCC) at [28]; [2006] 1 All E.R. (Comm) 224 at 232; [2005] 2 C.L.C. 1159 at 1169. This point was not challenged on appeal: *Shinedean Ltd v Alldown Demolition (London) Ltd (In Liquidation)* [2006] EWCA Civ 939; [2006] 1 W.L.R. 2696; [2006] 2 All E.R. (Comm) 982.

[24] *Shinedean Ltd* [2006] EWCA Civ 939; [2006] 1 W.L.R. 2696; [2006] 2 All E.R. (Comm) 982.

[25] *Re Coleman's Depositories Ltd and Life & Health Assurance Association's Arbitration* [1907] 2 K.B. 798 at 807; 76 L.J.K.B. 865 at 870; [1904-7] All E.R. Rep 383 at 387.

[26] See *Ralston v Bignold* (1853) 22 L.T.O.S. 106; and *Roper v Lendon* 120 E.R. 1120; (1859) 1 El. & El. 825; 28 L.J.Q.B. 260; 5 Jur. N.S. 491.

[27] *Nasser Diab v Regent Insurance Co Ltd* [2006] UKPC 29 at [13]; [2007] 1W.L.R. 797 at 801–802; [2006] 2 All E.R. (Comm) 704 at 709.

unless they would be so treated in equity."[28] He went on to state that:

"[i]n a case where notice of a claim has been given forthwith to the insurer and where a claim in writing with the requisite particulars of the loss and damage has followed sufficiently promptly to enable the insurer to verify that the claim is a good one, it is not obvious that a failure to deliver the claim in writing and the particulars within the specified period should be treated as relieving the insurer of any liability in respect of the claim. Perhaps the specified time should, as Lord Salmon suggested (at 951) [in *United Scientific Holdings Ltd v Burnley Borough Council* [1978] A.C. 904] be treated as directory, not mandatory. Perhaps the insurer's consent to an extension of the time should be subject to a proviso that it be not unreasonably withheld. But no argument on these points has been addressed to their Lordships and no conclusion on them can be reached on this appeal."[29]

As matters therefore stand, the law appears to remain that time limits should be strictly complied with both in terms of the provision of notice and any accompanying particulars, later particulars or more detailed claim.[30]

21-020 **Timing of notice: as soon as possible/practicable.** The leading case as to what will satisfy an obligation to notify as soon as possible or reasonably practicable is *Verelst's Administratrix v Motor Union Insurance Co Ltd*; sub nom. *Administratrix of Mary Madge Verelst v Motor Union Insurance Co Ltd*.[31] In that case Roche J had to consider a clause in a policy, which stated that:

"In case of any accident, injury, damage or loss ... the insured or the insured's representative for the time being shall give notice ... in writing to the head office of the company of such accident, injury, damage or loss as soon as possible after it has come to the knowledge of the insured or of the insured's representative for the time being."

The judge held that "as soon as possible" meant "as soon as possible in the circumstances which prevail and apply"[32] to the insured. Consequently, all of the existing circumstances had to be taken into account including, in that case, the means of the administratrix's knowledge of the policy and of the identity of the insurance company upon whom the claim was to be made. More recently in *HLB Kidsons (a firm) v Lloyd's Underwriters subscribing to Lloyd's policy No. 621/ PK1D00*,[33] it was held that notice that was to be given "as soon as practicable" required notice to be given as soon as reasonably possible after becoming aware of the relevant circumstances. A useful example of the application of this principle to a construction project is the case of *Kier Construction Ltd v Royal Insurance UK Ltd*,[34] which concerned damage to piles arising out of ground conditions. Bowsher Q.C. held that notice was not given as soon as possible within the meaning of the notification condition, because four weeks had elapsed between the occurrence and

---

28 *Nasser Diab* [2006] UKPC 29 at [15]; [2007] 1 W.L.R. 797 at 802; [2006] 2 All E.R. (Comm) 704 at 709.

29 *Nasser Diab* [2006] UKPC 29 at [16]; [2007] 1W.L.R. 797 at 802–803; [2006] 2 All E.R. (Comm) 704 at 710.

30 *Ralston* (1853) 22 L.T.O.S. 106; and *Roper* 120 E.R. 1120; (1859) 1 El. & El. 825; 28 L.J.Q.B. 260; 5 Jur. N.S. 491.

31 *Verelst's Administratrix v Motor Union Insurance Co Ltd*; sub nom. *Administratrix of Mary Madge Verelst v Motor Union Insurance Co Ltd* [1925] 2 K.B. 137; 94 L.J.K.B. 659 at 660; 30 Com. Cas. 256 at 257.

32 *Verelst's Administratrix* [1925] 2 K.B. 137 at 142; 94 L.J.K.B. 659 at 661; 30 Com. Cas. 256 at 261.

33 *HLB Kidsons (a firm) v Lloyd's Underwriters subscribing to Lloyd's policy No. 621/PK1D00* [2008] EWCA Civ 1206; [2009] 2 All E.R. (Comm) 81; [2009] Bus. L.R. 759.

34 *Kier Construction Ltd v Royal Insurance (UK) Ltd* 30 Con. L.R. 45.

the giving of the notice, although on the facts it was found that the insurer had waived its right to rely upon the notification condition.

3. OBLIGATIONS OF THE INSURER IN INVESTIGATING THE CLAIM

The continuing duty of good faith. The origin and nature of the duty of good **21-021** faith as enacted under the MIA has been dealt with in detail above in Ch.6 in the context of misrepresentation and the post-contractual duty of good faith. The remedy of avoidance for breach of the duty has now been repealed by the 2015 Act, leaving the duty to persist as an interpretive principle, discussed above at para.05-142. This position leaves the application of the duty of good faith to the post contractual relationship between the parties somewhat uncertain. Under the MIA, the continuing duty was of particular importance in the context of the claims procedure because it was clear that the insurer had continuing duties to act with good faith towards the insured in the investigation, defence or settlement of any claim, though the precise scope of the duty was uncertain. Similarly, the insured had to act with good faith in the presentation of the claim and where the policy provided that the insurer had a right to further information during the currency of the policy.[35]

The position under the 2015 Act is likely to be different. Part of the insurer's duty of good faith in the post contractual relationship has now been codified by the Enterprise Act 2016 which inserts into the 2015 Act a new duty for the insurer to pay claims within a reasonable time, discussed further in Ch.23. Similarly, the 2015 Act has introduced a new default remedy for an insured's fraudulent claims under the policy that will apply in lieu of any bespoke arrangements, discussed above from paras 5-116 to 5-132 and below at paras 21-037 to 21-047.

Investigation of claim by insurer. Once the insurer has received the necessary **21-022** notification and any further particulars and proofs as may be required under the policy, it has an obligation to investigate the claim. As stated in *Gan Insurance Co Ltd v Tai Ping Insurance Co Ltd*[36]:

"The ordinary course of claims handling would include considering not merely the nature, scope and quantum of any loss, and the application of the policy cover to such a loss, but also whether the loss involved any breach of any policy term or warranty."

The insurer is under a duty to investigate the claim properly by seeking professional and expert assistance wherever necessary. While technically the insurer's liability crystalises as soon as the insured liability occurs and a sum will become due under a policy at that time, as a general rule an insurer is permitted a period of time to assess the claim. As stated in *Quorum A/S v Schramm (Costs)*,[37] the time allowed

"varies accordingly to the nature of the loss, the way the claim is presented and the circumstances that require investigation. In many cases the time may be quite short. The court will always have regard to the particular circumstances specific to that claim."

---

[35] *K/S Merc-Scandia XXXXII v Certain Lloyd's Underwriters (The Mercandian Continent)* [2001] EWCA Civ 1275 at [22]; [2001] 2 Lloyd's Rep. 563 at 571–572; [2001] C.L.C. 1836 at 1844–1845, per Longmore LJ.

[36] *Gan Insurance Co Ltd v Tai Ping Insurance Co Ltd* [2002] EWCA Civ 248 at [37]; [2002] C.L.C. 870 at 881; [2002] Lloyd's Rep. I.R. 612 at 615.

[37] *Quorum A/S v Schramm (Costs)* [2002] 2 All E.R. (Comm) 179 at [8]; [2002] 2 Lloyd's Rep. 72 at 75; [2002] C.L.C. 77 at 106.

21-023 **Obligation to pay within a reasonable time.** A longstanding incongruity in insurance law is the fact that insurers were not under any duty to pay claims within a reasonable time.[38] This was confirmed by the Court of Appeal in the case of *Sprung v Royal Insurance (UK) Ltd*.[39] This incongruity is to be corrected by the Enterprise Act 2016. From its coming into force on 4 May 2017, the Act inserts a new s.13A into the Insurance Act 2015. The section provides:

> **"Implied term about payment of claims**
>
> **13A.**(1)   It is an implied term of every contract of insurance that if the insured makes a claim under the contract, the insurer must pay any sums due in respect of the claim within a reasonable time.
>
> (2)   A reasonable time includes a reasonable time to investigate and assess the claim.
>
> (3)   What is reasonable will depend on all the relevant circumstances, but the following are examples of things which may need to be taken into account-
>
> (a)   the type of insurance,
>
> (b)   the size and complexity of the claim,
>
> (c)   compliance with any relevant statutory or regulatory rules or guidance,
>
> (d)   factors outside the insurer's control.
>
> (4)   If the insurer shows that there were reasonable grounds for disputing the claim (whether as to the amount of any sum payable, or as to whether anything at all is payable)-
>
> (a)   the insurer does not breach the term implied by subsection (1) merely by failing to pay the claim (or the affected part of it) while the dispute is continuing, but
>
> (b)   the conduct of the insurer in handling the claim may be a relevant factor in deciding whether that term was breached and, if so, when.
>
> (5)   Remedies (for example, damages) available for breach of the term implied by subsection (1) are in addition to and distinct from-
>
> (a)   any right to enforce payment of the sums due, and
>
> (b)   any right to interest on those sums (whether under the contract, under another enactment, at the court's discretion or otherwise)."

21-024   The new s.13A will avoid the issue which arose in *Sprung*. An insured is able to recover damages in respect of foreseeable losses which are caused by an insurer's failure to pay sums due within a reasonable time. Until there is case law decided under the Act, it is not clear to what extent the scope of a reasonable time will be affected by the examples set out in s.13A(3). It seems likely, however, that the approach set out above derived from *Gan Insurance Co Ltd v Tai Ping Insurance Co Ltd* and *Quorum A/S v Schramm (Costs)*[40] will continue to be good law.

21-025 **Use of loss adjuster.** A loss adjuster is commonly used in the construction industry to handle claims made by insured parties. With large construction projects, there may be a higher frequency of individual losses and therefore a continuous stream of claims made by the insured and payments made by the insurer. The loss adjuster will be appointed by the insurer to administrate and investigate those claims by gathering evidence and negotiating settlement or at least advising the insurer as to a reasonable level of settlement. The loss adjuster will either be an employee of the insurer or an independent appointment who holds himself out as having expert construction experience. The legal relationship between the loss adjuster and the

---

[38]   See above, para.11-022, and below, Ch.23.

[39]   *Sprung v Royal Insurance (UK) Ltd* [1997] C.L.C. 70; [1999] 1 Lloyd's Rep. I.R. 111.

[40]   See above, para.21-022.

insurer will be defined by the policy or the contract of appointment but as regards its interaction with the insured it will be agent of the insurer and may, therefore, have the authority to bind the insurer to a settlement of the claim.

Impact of the Insurance Act 2015. From the date of the coming into force of the **21-026** 2015 Act, 12 August 2016 in respect of the majority of its provisions, an insured faces a significantly different landscape with regard to the presentation of its claim. For these purposes, the principal changes relate to fraudulent claims. Part 4 of the Act sets out and clarifies the remedies available to an insurer which has received a fraudulent claim. The changes are dealt with in detail below. For a full explanation of the impact of the Act, see Ch.5 above.

Presentation of the claim. The insured is under an obligation to act honestly **21-027** when presenting a claim to the insurer. It is widely recognised that insurers face the difficulty of being susceptible to inflated or fabricated claims and other deceitful action by insured parties in order that those parties can maximise their own recovery under a policy. The courts have therefore set their face firmly against such practices by an insured and the consequences of being found to have wilfully presented a false or misleading claim to the insurer are severe.

The test for fraud. In the context of insurance, a claim made by an insured for **21-028** payment of insurance monies will be fraudulent when the claim is "wilfully false in any substantial respect".[41] An accurate definition of what amounts to a fraudulent claim was given by Evans J in *Continental Illinois National Bank and Trust Co of Chicago and Xenofon Maritime SA v Alliance Assurance Co Ltd (The Captain Panagos DP)*,[42] where he stated that it is a claim that

> "is made on the basis that facts exist which constitute a loss by an insured peril, when to the knowledge of the assured those alleged facts are untrue."

There are numerous ways that a fraud may be committed. For instance, the total loss may be fabricated or an actual loss may be caused purposefully, the cause of the loss may be falsely explained or the value or amount of loss may be exaggerated. There is no difficulty in showing that a claim was wilfully false where it can be shown that the loss was entirely fabricated or caused purposefully. However, in relation to an exaggeration the distinction between innocently or negligently overstating the value of a claim and wilfully or recklessly doing so is significant, since only wilful or reckless overstatements will constitute fraud and entitle the insurer to repudiate liability.[43] Thus the court has to consider the degree of exaggeration involved in order to determine whether fraud has been committed.

Culpable or unconscionable conduct. There was an attempt in *Manifest Ship-* **21-029** *ping & Co Ltd v Uni-Polaris Insurance Co Ltd and La Reunion Europeenne (The Star Sea)*[44] to extend the scope of the fraudulent claim to encompass those made

---

[41] *Goulstone v Royal Insurance Co* 175 E.R. 725; (1858) 1 F. & F. 276 at 279, Pollock C.B. Sections 2, 3 and 4 of the Fraud Act 2006 set out the various ways in which a fraud may be committed.

[42] *Continental Illinois National Bank and Trust Co of Chicago and Xenofon Maritime SA v Alliance Assurance Co Ltd ("The Captain Panagos DP")* [1986] 2 Lloyd's Rep. 470 at 511.

[43] *Lek v Mathews* (1927) 29 Ll. L. Rep. 141 at 145, per Viscount Sumner.

[44] *Manifest Shipping & Co Ltd v Uni-Polaris Insurance Co Ltd and La Reunion Europeenne ("The Star*

"culpably", i.e. claims submitted that had been negligently overstated. However, this was rejected by the Court of Appeal on the basis that there was:

"no warrant for any widening of the duty so as to embrace 'culpable' non-disclosure. Either it does not enlarge the scope of fraud, in which case it is not needed, or it does, in which case the extent of the enlargement is unclear and the concept should be rejected."[45]

21-030 Exaggeration of claim. It is accepted as a:

"commercial reality that people will often put forward a claim that is more than they believe they will recover ... because they expect to engage in some form of 'horse-trading' or other negotiation."[46]

Not every claim put forward that has been exaggerated will be held to be fraudulent. For the claim to constitute a fraud the exaggeration must be more than de minimis but also, as expressed by H.H. Judge Coulson Q.C. (as he then was) in *Danepoint Ltd v Allied Underwriting Insurance Ltd*[47]

"mere exaggeration of an insurance claim will not of *itself* be fraud. On the other hand, exaggeration which is wilful, or which is allied to misrepresentation or concealment will, in all probability, be fraudulent. In addition, I consider that exaggeration is more likely and more excusable where the value of the particular claim or head of loss in question is unclear or a matter of opinion; where, as Lord Hoffman put it [in *Orakpo v Barclays Insurance Services Co Ltd* [1995] LRLR 443; [1994] CLC 373],[48] the insurer's loss adjuster is in as good a position to value the claim as the insured. Conversely, where the value of the claim is or should be clear-cut, and the information on which it is based is wholly within the control of the insured, exaggeration is much less easy to excuse and thus much more likely to be fraudulent."

21-031 De minimis or substantial fraud/exaggeration of claim. Although nothing less than fraud will suffice, as discussed above, at para.21-028, the fraud must be substantial and not de minimis. For example, in *Galloway v Guardian Royal Exchange (UK) Ltd*,[49] the Court of Appeal unanimously decided that where a claim for £18,143 contained an obviously fraudulent claim for £2,000[50] the whole claim would be tainted by the fraud. Lord Woolf M.R. stated:

"In determining whether or not the fraud is material so that it has that effect, one of course has, in my judgment, to look at the whole of the claim ... [I]f you have a claim (which admittedly there is for a much more substantial sum than the part which is fraudulent) where the part which is fraudulent is ... £2,000 (which amounts to about 10 per cent of the whole) that is an amount which is substantial and therefore an amount which taints the whole."[51]

Sea") [1997] 1 Lloyd's Rep. 360; [1997] C.L.C. 481; [1997] 6 Re. L.R. 175.

45 *Manifest Shipping & Co Ltd* [1997] 1 Lloyd's Rep. 360 at 361; [1997] C.L.C. 481 at 496.
46 Thomas J (as he then was) in *Nsubuga v Commercial Union Assurance Co Plc* [1998] 2 Lloyd's Rep. 682 at 686.
47 *Danepoint Ltd v Allied Underwriting Insurance Ltd* [2005] EWHC 2318 (TCC) at [56]; [2006] Lloyd's Rep. I.R. 429 at 430.
48 This case must be treated with caution as it used the language of contractual analysis and it is now clear since *Banque Keyser Ullmann SA v Skandia (UK) Insurance Co Ltd* [1990] 1 Q.B. 665; [1989] 3 W.L.R. 25 as affirmed by the House of Lords at [1991] 2 A.C. 249 at 280; [1990] 3 W.L.R. 364 that the duty not to present a fraudulent claim does not arise by reason of an implication of a contractual term but as an incident of the nature of the insurance contract.
49 *Galloway v Guardian Royal Exchange (UK) Ltd* [1999] Lloyd's Rep. I.R. 209.
50 The £2,000 represented a computer that the insured had never bought. He had faked an invoice to support that claim. By the time the civil court heard the matter the insured had already been convicted by a criminal court of attempting to obtain property by deception via his insurance claim.
51 *Galloway* [1999] Lloyd's Rep. I.R. 209 at 213–214.

Millett LJ, while agreeing in full with Lord Woolf M.R. as to the outcome, appeared to take a different approach. He emphasised that whether the fraud is "substantial" should not be tested by reference to the entire claim because, in his view, such an approach would lead to:

"the absurd conclusion that the greater the genuine loss, the larger the fraudulent claim which may be made at the same time without penalty."[52]

He stated that the right approach in such a case was to consider the fraudulent claim as if it were the only claim and then consider whether, taken in isolation, the making of that claim by the insured was "sufficiently serious to justify stigmatising it".[53]

To date, the courts have not enunciated a precise rule or established a correct test as to what will constitute a fraudulent exaggeration. Lord Woolf's view appears to have been favoured in *Tonkin v UK Insurance Ltd*,[54] whilst Lord Millett's appears to have been followed in *Agapitos v Agnew (The Aegeon) (No.1)*.[55] In *Tonkin* it was held that a falsely inflated claim will not necessarily be treated as amounting to a fraudulent claim in circumstances where the inflated part is insignificant compared with the valid portion of the claim. In that case the inflated portion amounted to 0.3 per cent of the total claim and this was held not to be fraudulent.[56] This decision appears to place insufficient emphasis on the possibility that a small portion of the claim could in fact be a significant amount (in the case in question 0.3 per cent amounted to £2,000). It also fails to place sufficient emphasis on the fact that the claim remains dishonest, even if the amount was small.

The courts' use of the word "substantial" to describe what will amount to a **21-032** fraudulent claim creates a level of ambiguity, which is undesirable. It is suggested that "substantial" should be read to include "deliberate" so that where the fraudulent claim is deliberate it will be substantial, regardless of its size relative to the genuine claim. Further, in light of the observations of Lord Millett in *Galloway*,[57] in particular where he maintained that the rule against fraudulent claims should not be diluted,[58] it is suggested that the courts will be inclined, as a point of policy, to treat any material amount of exaggeration, with the exception of inconsequential amounts, to be fraudulent if made deliberately.

Negotiation of claim. There are dicta to support the view that the insured may **21-033** submit an optimistic claim with the understanding that there will be a period of negotiation to determine the value to be paid under the policy.[59] It has been recognised by the higher courts that where the insurer is in as good a position as the insured to judge the real value of the claim then exaggeration by the latter may

---

52 *Galloway* [1999] Lloyd's Rep. I.R. 209 at 214.
53 *Galloway* [1999] Lloyd's Rep. I.R. 209 at 214.
54 *Tonkin v UK Insurance Ltd* [2006] EWHC 1120 (TCC); [2006] 2 All E.R. (Comm) 550; [2007] 1 Lloyd's Rep. I.R. 283.
55 *Agapitos v Agnew ("The Aegeon") (No.1)* [2002] EWCA Civ 247; [2003] QB 556; [2002] 3 W.L.R. 616.
56 *Tonkin* [2006] EWHC 1120 (TCC) at [189]; [2006] 2 All E.R. (Comm) 550 at 592; [2007] 1 Lloyd's Rep. I.R. 283 at 312.
57 *Galloway* [1999] Lloyd's Rep. I.R. 209.
58 *Galloway* [1999] Lloyd's Rep. I.R. 209 at 214, per Millett LJ.
59 See Hoffmann LJ in *Orakpo v Barclays Insurance Services Co Ltd* [1995] L.R.L.R. 443 at 451; [1994] C.L.C. 373 at 383 and Thomas J in *Nsubuga* [1998] 2 Lloyd's Rep. 682 at 686.

be acceptable and it may also be said that the insurer will be in such a position when it appoints a loss adjuster. For example, in *Orakpo v Barclays Insurance Services Co Ltd*, Hoffmann LJ stated that:

> "[i]n cases where nothing is misrepresented or concealed, and the loss adjuster is in as good a position to form a view of the validity or value of the claim as the insured, it will be a legitimate reason that the assured was merely putting forward a start[ing] figure for negotiation."[60]

It has been suggested that it may not amount to fraud to seek to recover for the value of the replacement cost of an item where the value of the item lost would have depreciated, with the expectation that a loss adjuster would form its own view.[61] However, where the depreciation in value of the item renders it worthless then a claim for the replacement cost of the item is likely to amount to fraud.[62] In large construction-insurance claims, there may be considerable scope for negotiation between the parties for the value of a claim, which will be subject to the opinions of both the insured and the insurer as to the nature, scope and cost of remedial works and of indemnified consequential losses. For example, cl.6.7, which concerns three options set out in the Joint Contracts Tribunal (JCT) standard term building contract,[63] provides that the contract works are to be insured for their full reinstatement value. While this gives a basis of valuation, the parties may have very different views as to the cost of full reinstatement in relation to cost of materials, the length of time required for the works and the effect of inflation and other economic factors. Therefore, much will depend on the nature of damage and the remedial works as well as the relationship between the parties when settling claims, for if it can be shown from a course of dealing that the type of negotiation is standard practice then submitting an overly optimistic claim may be acceptable. Nevertheless, there may be a fine line between a fraudulently inflated claim and a claim that seeks to maximise recovery optimistically. Any deliberate attempt to deceive an insurer is likely to be treated as fraudulent.

21-034   **Materiality and inducement.**   There is a lack of clarity in the case law as to whether the fraud or fraudulent device (discussed below at para.21-045) must be material in the sense of being causative of the insurer's willingness to pay. Having been referred to *Agapitos*,[64] H.H. Judge Coulson QC (as he then was) in *Danepoint Ltd*[65] stated that "[t]he fraud must be material in that it must have a decisive effect on the readiness of the insurer to pay."[66] However, in *Agapitos*[67] Mance LJ (as he then was) considered it sufficient for the fraudulent claim rule to apply that the fraud occur in making a claim and relate to part of the claim which, when viewed discretely, was not itself immaterial or unsubstantial. In his view, nothing further was necessary. This recognises the departure of the fraudulent claim rule from the

---

60   See Hoffmann LJ in *Orakpo* [1995] L.R.L.R. 433 at 451; [1994] C.L.C. 373 at 383.

61   *Orakpo* [1995] L.R.L.R. 443 at 450; [1994] C.L.C. 373 at 382, per Staughton LJ.

62   *Transthene Packaging Co Ltd v Royal Insurance (UK) Ltd* [1996] L.R.L.R. 32 at 44, per H.H. Judge Kershaw Q.C.

63   See Sch.3 in Joint Contracts Tribunal. SBC/Q 2011 *JCT Standard Building Contract With Quantities* 2011 (London: Sweet & Maxwell, 2011), pp.88–92, which sets out the three options in detail.

64   *The Aegeon* [2002] EWCA Civ 247; [2003] Q.B. 556; [2002] 3 W.L.R. 616.

65   *Danepoint Ltd* [2005] EWHC 2318 (TCC); [2006] Lloyd's Rep. I.R. 429.

66   *Danepoint Ltd* [2005] EWHC 2318 (TCC) at [51]; [2006] Lloyd's Rep. I.R. 429 at 437.

67   *The Aegeon* [2002] EWCA Civ 247 at [33] and [36]; [2003] Q.B. 556 at 570–571; [2002] 3 W.L.R. 616 at 629–630.

duty of utmost good faith under which there is a requirement that the breach induced the insurer to make the payment.[68]

The landmark Supreme Court decision in *Versloot Dredging BV v HDI Gerling Industrie Versicherung AG*[69] considered the application of the fraudulent claim rule to fraudulent devices. It was decided by a 4–1 majority that the rule should not apply to fraudulent devices. As a result, Lord Sumption JSC held that the materiality test suggested in previous cases, as outlined above, did not apply in the context of fraudulent devices.[70] Lord Mance JSC, dissenting, revised his earlier views on materiality and suggested that what was required was "a significant improvement of the insured's prospects, before a claim is barred."[71]

Contracting out of the Insurance Act 2015.   In non-consumer contracts, which all CAR insurance will be, parties are free to contract out of the provisions of the 2015 Act in relation to fraudulent claims. To the extent that an insured is put in a worse position by any term in such a situation, that term must comply with the transparency requirements set out in s.17 of the Act. In consumer contracts, any attempt to contract out of the Act and put the insured in a worse position than it would be under the Act has no effect.   **21-035**

Contract clauses dealing with fraudulent claims.   Often the policy will set out in express terms the effect on the policy or claim of the making of a fraudulent claim or the use of fraudulent devices or means. Both insurers and insureds may prefer the certainty of retaining such wording, at least for a period while the industry adjusts to the impact of the 2015 Act. Many such clauses may already provide for remedies in line with those set out in the Act. The terms may be simple and provide only for the fraudulent claim to be rejected or may go further and provide for forfeiture of all benefits under the policy. However, it has been held that the term "forfeiture" does not imply avoidance ab initio but rather a right to reject the claim. For instance in *Direct Line Insurance Plc v Fox*,[72] there was a contract clause, which provided that, in the event of fraud "the policy shall become void and all benefit under this policy will be forfeited". The court held that such a clause should be construed in light of the common law position. Since the common law position, as discussed below at para.21-040, does not allow for ab initio avoidance of the contract the clause only operated to deny the fraudulent claim, and possibly future claims. However, in *Joseph Fielding Properties (Blackpool) Ltd v Aviva Insurance Ltd*[73] a clause stating that in the event of a fraudulent claim the insurer "may avoid the policy from inception" was upheld by the court to the same effect as ab initio avoidance and entitled the insurer to recoup money it had paid out on previous claims. The differing interpretation of these contractual clauses might be explained by the fact that the former case concerned a consumer contract and the latter a commercial contract where there is generally perceived to be greater equal-   **21-036**

---

68   Section 17 of the Marine Insurance Act 1906 requires there to be materiality and inducement in the sense of causation in relation to breaches of the duty of utmost good faith.

69   *Versloot Dredging BV v HDI Gerling Versicherung AG* [2016] UKSC 45; [2016] 3 W.L.R. 543.

70   *Versloot Dredging BV v HDI Gerling Versicherung AG* [2016] UKSC 45 at [31].

71   *Versloot Dredging BV v HDI Gerling Versicherung AG* [2016] UKSC 45 at [113].

72   *Direct Line Insurance Plc v Fox* [2009] EWHC 386 (QB) at [5]; [2009] 1 All E.R. (Comm) 1017 at 1019; [2010] Lloyd's Rep. I.R. 324 at 326.

73   *Joseph Fielding Properties (Blackpool) Ltd v Aviva Insurance Ltd* [2010] EWHC 2192 (QB) at [96]–[99]; [2011] Lloyd's Rep. I.R. 238 at 253–254.

ity of bargaining power between the parties. In commercial insurance contracts, express terms setting out the available remedies to the insurer following an insured's fraud are likely to be valid, provided they are not ambiguous. This line of case law would likely remain good authority following the coming into force of the 2015 Act, given that the Act also does not provide for ab initio avoidance of the contract.

21-037 **Effect of fraud: Insurance Act 2015.** If there is no term in the policy contracting out of the statutory provisions relating to fraud, the Act will apply. The relevant provisions of Part 4 of the Act set out the remedies available to an insurer: forfeiture of the claim and the option to terminate the policy. These remedies are broadly in line with the common law position prior to the coming into force of the Act. In providing for forfeiture of a fraudulent claim, for example, the Act largely reflects the "fraudulent claim rule" which existed at common law.[74]

Section 12(1) of the Act provides:

"(1) If the insured makes a fraudulent claim under a contract of insurance—
    (a)   the insurer is not liable to pay the claim,
    (b)   the insurer may recover from the insured any sums paid by the insurer to the insured in respect of the claim, and
    (c)   in addition, the insurer may by notice to the insured treat the contract as having been terminated with effect from the time of the fraudulent act."

Under s.12(1)(a), the fraudulent claim is forfeited in its entirety. As a corollary of this, under s.12(1)(b) the insurer is also able to recover any sums paid out to the insured in respect of the fraudulent claim. There is a deliberately punitive effect to the legislation as drafted. This accords with the common law position that an unsuccessful fraudster cannot be permitted to recover the true value of its claim once discovered.[75]

21-038 Section 12(1)(c) of the Act gives the option of a further remedy to the insurer by entitling it to treat the contract as having been terminated with effect from the time of the fraudulent act. The statute provides for the issues arising from such a termination in the following subsections:

"(2) If the insurer does treat the contract as having been terminated—
    (a)   it may refuse all liability to the insured under the contract in respect of a relevant event occurring after the time of the fraudulent act, and
    (b)   it need not return any of the premiums paid under the contract.
(3)   Treating a contract as having been terminated under this section does not affect the rights and obligations of the parties to the contract with respect to a relevant event occurring before the time of the fraudulent act.
(4)   In subsections (2)(a) and (3), "relevant event" refers to whatever gives rise to the insurer's liability under the contract (and includes, for example, the occurrence of a loss, the making of a claim, or the notification of a potential claim, depending on how the contract is written)."

As set out in the paragraphs below, if an insurer elects to terminate the contract, it will have no liability in respect of genuine claims which were submitted after the fraudulent act. That does not affect its obligations, however, in respect of claims that have already accrued. Despite this, the insurer is not under any obligation to return

---

[74] See below, para.21-039.
[75] *Britton v Royal Insurance Co* 176 E.R. 843 at 909; (1886) 4 F. & F. 905 at 909; 15 L.T. 72 at 73.

premiums paid to it after the fraudulent act, even though it was not liable to pay out under the policy for that period.

Effect of fraud: general common law rule. Prior to the coming into force of the **21-039**
Act, the common law applied to contracts which did not have express terms relating to fraudulent claims. The Act applies to all contracts concluded after 12 August 2016, including variations to contracts after this date. As a result, the common law will be of diminishing relevance as time passes. The common law rule for fraudulent claims was set out in the often quoted direction of Willes J to the jury in the case of *Britton v Royal Insurance Co*,[76] namely that:

> "[t]he law upon such a case is in accordance with justice, and also with sound policy. The law, is that a person who has made such a fraudulent claim could not be permitted to recover at all. The contract of insurance is one of perfect good faith on both sides, and it is most important that such good faith should be maintained. It is the common practice to insert in fire-policies conditions that they shall be void in the event of a fraudulent claim; and there was such a condition in the present case. Such a condition is only in accord with legal principle and sound policy. It would be most dangerous to permit parties to practise such frauds, and then, notwithstanding their falsehood and fraud, to recover the real value of the goods consumed. And if there is wilful falsehood and fraud in the claim, the insured forfeits all claim whatever upon the policy."

In *Manifest Shipping Co Ltd*,[77] the above direction of Willes J was considered together with the cases of *Goulstone v Royal Insurance Co*[78] and *Beresford v Royal Insurance Co Ltd*[79] and Lord Hobhouse succinctly summarised the position:

> "The law is that the insured who has made a fraudulent claim may not recover the claim which could have been honestly made ... This result is not dependent upon the inclusion in the contract of a term having that effect or the type of insurance; it is the consequence of a rule of law. Just as the law will not allow an insured to commit a crime and then use it as a basis for recovering an indemnity (*Beresford v Royal Insurance Co Ltd* [1937] 2 K.B. 197) so it will not allow an insured who has made a fraudulent claim to recover. The logic is simple. The fraudulent insured must not be allowed to think: if the fraud is successful, then I will gain; if it is unsuccessful, I will lose nothing."

The principle applied was that if a substantial part of the claim, that is a non de minimis part of the claim, was fraudulent then an insured lost all right to recover for that claim.[80] This is often referred to as "the fraudulent claim rule". As set out above, this accords with the position as it now stands under the 2015 Act.

Effect of fraud: void ab initio? Prior to the coming into force of the 2015 Act, **21-040**
the question arose as to whether the fraudulent claim rule entitled an insurer to avoid the contract ab initio. This is not provided for as a remedy in the Act and, in s.12(1)(c), the date from which a contract is terminated is clearly that of the fraudulent act. It is clear from the drafting that ab initio avoidance is not available as a remedy to an insurer. From the case law, it can be seen that the statute accords with the position as it stood at common law.

---

[76] *Britton v Royal Insurance Co* 176 E.R. 843 at 909; (1886) 4 F. & F. 905 at 909; 15 L.T. 72 at 73.
[77] *Manifest Shipping Co Ltd* [2001] UKHL 1 at [62]; [2003] 1 A.C. 469 at 499; [2001] 2 W.L.R. 170 at 191.
[78] *Goulstone* (1858) 1 F. & F. 276; 175 E.R. 725.
[79] *Beresford v Royal Insurance Co Ltd* [1937] 2 K.B. 197; [1937] 2 All E.R. 243 affirmed by the House of Lords at [1938] A.C. 586; [1938] 2 All E.R. 602; 107 L.J.K.B. 464.
[80] *Galloway* [1999] Lloyd's Rep. 209 applied in *Direct Line Insurance Plc v Khan* [2001] EWCA Civ 1794; [2002] Lloyd's Rep. I.R. 364.

At common law, the question was academic in *Orakpo*[81] and not in issue in *Manifest Shipping Co Ltd*[82] and has been confused by the application of s.17 of the Marine Insurance Act 1906 ("MIA") in certain cases. As stated, obiter, by Lord Scott in *Manifest Shipping Co Ltd*[83]:

> "The presentation of a dishonest or fraudulent claim constitutes a breach of duty that entitles the insurer to repudiate any liability for the claim and, prospectively at least, to avoid any liability under the policy. Whether the presentation of such a claim should be regarded as a breach of continuing duty under section 17 that entitles the insurer to avoid the policy with retrospective effect, enabling any payments made in satisfaction of previous unimpeachable claims to be recovered by the insurer, is more debatable."

In *The Aegeon*,[84] Mance LJ favoured the view that the fraudulent claim rule was not governed by or analogous with s.17 of the MIA. He therefore considered that no question of ab initio avoidance would arise.[85] He had cause to reconsider the position in *AXA General Insurance Ltd v Gottlieb*,[86] where one of the issues for determination was whether a fraudulent claim had any effect on interim payments made prior to any fraud in respect of genuine loss insured on the claim to which the subsequent fraud related. The court concluded that:

> "the proper scope of the common law relating to fraudulent insurance claims is to forfeit the whole of the claim to which the fraud relates, with the effect that the consideration for any interim payments made on that claim fails and they are recoverable."[87]

However, where genuine separate claims to which the subsequent fraud did not relate were settled the settlement payments were held not to be recoverable. The question was expressly left open by the court as to the common law position relating to separate claims, which are still unpaid at the time of the fraud, though Mance LJ went on to state that in his view there was:

> "some force in the argument that the common law rule relating to fraudulent claims should be confined to the particular claim to which any fraud relates, while the potential scope and operation of more general contractual principles might in some circumstances also require consideration."[88]

In light of these judgments, it is clear that a fraudulent claim would automatically forfeit the entire claim, thus preventing recovery of any amount by the insured. It would not, however, allow the contract to be void ab initio.

Effect of fraud under the Insurance Act 2015: claims already
21-041 **accrued.** Section 12(3) of the Act makes clear that an insurer is still liable to pay out in respect of claims which had already accrued at the time of the fraudulent act.

---

[81] *Orakpo* [1995] L.R.L.R. 443; [1994] C.L.C. 373.
[82] *Manifest Shipping Co Ltd* [2001] UKHL 1; [2003] 1 A.C. 469; [2001] 2 W.L.R. 170.
[83] *Manifest Shipping Co Ltd* [2001] UKHL 1 at [110]; [2003] 1 A.C. 469 at 514–515; [2001] 2 W.L.R. 170 at 207.
[84] *The Aegeon* [2002] EWCA Civ 247; [2003] Q.B. 556; [2002] 3 W.L.R. 616.
[85] *The Aegeon* [2002] EWCA Civ 247 at [45]; [2003] Q.B. 556 at 574–575; [2002] 3 W.L.R. 616 at 633–634.
[86] *Gottleib v AXA General Insurance Ltd* [2005] EWCA Civ 112; [2005] 1 All E.R. (Comm) 445; [2005] Lloyd's Rep. I.R. 369.
[87] *Gottleib* [2005] EWCA Civ 112 at [32]; [2005] 1 All E.R. (Comm) 445 at 459; [2005] Lloyd's Rep. I.R. 369 at 378, per Mance LJ with which Keene LJ and Pill LJ agreed.
[88] *Gottleib* [2005] EWCA Civ 112 at [22]; [2005] 1 All E.R. (Comm) 445 at 454; [2005] Lloyd's Rep. I.R. 369 at 375.

For a claim to have accrued, a "relevant event" must have occurred prior to the fraudulent act. Section 12(4) of the Act provides that a relevant event is "whatever gives rise to the insurer's liability under the contract". This will vary depending on the type of insurance policy in question, as reflected in the examples given in this subsection of the Act: "the occurrence of a loss, the making of a claim, or the notification of a potential claim, depending on how the contract is written". In a typical CAR policy, an insurer's liability arises on the occurrence of damage, sometimes with a requirement to first notify the insurer. Accordingly, if this has happened prior to the fraudulent act, the claim will be deemed to have accrued and will be recoverable.

The statute is silent as to the definition of the fraudulent act. Accordingly, the common law will remain relevant on this issue. At common law, the date from which the insurer was entitled to terminate the policy was the date on which the fraud is committed, and not the date of the loss that gave rise to the fraudulent claim. This remains the case and remains relevant in the situation where, for example, an insured does suffer a true loss but, at a later date, fraudulently exaggerates it.

Effect of fraud at common law: claims already accrued. As under the Act, at common law the insured's right to recover under the policy arose at the moment an occurrence of an insured peril caused a loss and not at the moment the claim was made.[89] General contractual principles provide that rights acquired before the time of a repudiatory breach are not discharged by reason of the repudiatory breach.[90] It was therefore possible for the insured to recover for losses which had accrued prior to the date of the fraud, but which had not yet been claimed for. Unlike the ordinary position in relation to repudiatory breach, the law ensured that the fraud retrospectively attached to the claim to which it related even though the right of the insured to recover was acquired at an earlier date. This accords with the position under the Act.   **21-042**

Effect of fraud under the Insurance Act 2015: future claims. One area that was unclear at common law was the effect of fraud upon future, legitimate claims under a policy. This has now been clarified by s.12(2)(a) of the Act. This provision makes clear that the insurer may refuse all liability for future claims which arise after the time of the fraudulent act. The Act brings much-needed clarification to an area which was previously unclear but could lead to potentially harsh results. This is particularly true when, under s.12(2)(b), the insurer is under no obligation to return premiums paid by the insured. In a situation where a fraudulent act goes undetected for a prolonged period, the insured will effectively be left without cover and will only discover this retrospectively once the fraud has been detected.   **21-043**

A more difficult question arises in respect of future claims which post-date the fraudulent act but which have been paid before the fraud is detected. It appears that there is no statutory right for an insurer to recover such sums. However, the Act does remove liability for the insurer from the date of the fraudulent act. Given that these provisions of the Act are intended to have retrospective effect, it appears that a claim

---

[89] *Gottleib* [2005] EWCA Civ 112 at [26]; [2005] 1 All E.R. (Comm) 445 at 456; [2005] Lloyd's Rep. I.R. 369 at 376–377.

[90] *Collidge v Freeport Plc* [2007] EWHC 1216 (QB) at [9] (affirmed by the Court of Appeal at [2008] EWCA Civ 485; [2008] I.R.L.R 697). See also *Chitty on Contracts*, edited by H.G. Beale, A.S. Burrows et al, 31st edn (London: Sweet & Maxwell, 2012), Vol.1, para.24–053.

could be brought on the basis of unjust enrichment to recover sums paid out. A fuller discussion of this point is set out above at para.5-130.

21-044   Effect of fraud at common law: future claims.   At common law, it was not certain what the correct position was regarding future claims where a previous fraudulent claim had been made under a policy. There was support for the view that fraud amounted to a repudiatory breach of contract and until the time the repudiatory breach was accepted by the insurer any claims that arose that proved to be valid should be paid.[91] It had been suggested that the theory that the policy could survive following a fraud was a logical conclusion,[92] but the point was not conclusively decided. Since the insurer had the right to elect to continue with the policy or to terminate it, it seemed likely that future claims could be accepted. However, it was also likely that there would be a period of time between the date the fraud was perpetrated and its detection by the insurer, during which other losses may occur. The insurer would inevitably wish to exercise its right to repudiate the policy from the date of the fraud thereby escaping liability for losses arising between that date and the date of the detection of the fraud. This position has now been made explicit in the drafting of the Act.

21-045   Fraudulent devices or means.   As a result of the enactment of the Insurance Act, the law around fraudulent claims is now significantly clearer. One question left open by the Act was the extent to which the fraudulent claim rule extended beyond claims which are themselves fraudulent. Until recently, an insured which sought to bolster a valid claim through the use of a lie would be caught by the fraudulent claim rule. Such a lie was described as the use of 'fraudulent devices' or 'means', this archaic terminology being derived from early insurance contracts. The law on fraudulent devices was controversial due to the harsh outcome that it could lead to; an insured with a valid claim could be refused cover on the basis that it told a lie in relation to an irrelevant matter. The recent Supreme Court decision in *Versloot Dredging BV v HDI Gerling Industrie Versicherung AG*[93] has altered the landscape in this area and effectively eliminated the doctrine of fraudulent devices and means. The Supreme Court, using the preferred term "collateral lies", held that the fraudulent claim rule does not apply to a lie which is immaterial to the insured's right to recover.

To fully understand the law in this area, it is necessary to consider the case law that led up to the decision in *Versloot*. Originally, the issue was considered in detail by the Court of Appeal in *The Aegeon*.[94] The court considered the applicability of the fraudulent claim rule where a fraudulent device was used,[95] noting the distinction between a fraudulent claim and the use of a fraudulent device. As stated by Mance LJ in *The Aegeon*:

---

[91] *Gottleib* [2005] EWCA Civ 112 at [22]; [2005] 1 All E.R. (Comm) 445 at 454; [2005] Lloyd's Rep. I.R. 369 at 375.

[92] See *Arnould's Law of Marine Insurance and Average*, edited by J. Gilman and R. Merkin, 18th edn (London: Sweet & Maxwell: 2013), para.18–54.

[93] *Versloot Dredging BV v HDI Gerling Versicherung AG* [2016] UKSC 45; [2016] 3 W.L.R. 543

[94] *The Aegeon* [2002] Lloyd's Rep. I.R. 191. Followed in *Sharon's Bakery (Europe) Ltd v AXA Insurance UK Plc* [2011] EWHC 210 (Comm); [2012] Lloyd's Rep. I.R. 164.

[95] The court thought that there should be no distinction drawn between whether the device was used before or after the initial making of any claim.

> "A fraudulent claim exists where the insured claims, knowing that he has suffered no loss, or only a lesser loss than that which he claims (or is reckless as to whether this is the case). A fraudulent device is used if the insured believes that he has suffered the loss claimed, but seeks to improve or embellish the facts surrounding the claim, by some lie. There may however be intermediate factual situations, where the lies become so significant, that they may be viewed as changing the nature of the claim being advanced."[96]

Thus, a fraudulent device was a term used to describe a lie or other ploy, which an insured used in order to advance its chances of securing payment or settlement of a claim or to advance its chances of winning a trial of a disputed claim. A fraudulent device could be distinguished from a fraudulent claim on the basis that the insured already had a genuinely valid claim, which had not been exaggerated, but lied about the circumstances surrounding the claim. The facts of *The Aegeon*[97] are instructive. In that case, owners of a vessel secured slip insurance with an endorsed warranty that no hot works be commenced until the vessel had received a London Salvage Association (LSA) certificate. On 19 February 1996 the vessel caught fire due to hot works being carried out. The owners first stated that hot works had not begun until 12 February 1996, after the certificate had been received. Then in 2001 the owners inadvertently disclosed documents including sworn affidavits of two workmen, which attested that the hot works had commenced by 1 February 1996. It was held that the date given in the first statement must have been a lie, and that the lie was deliberately given in order to avert the consequences of breaching the hot works warranty that would have provided the insurer with a defence to the claim.

Mance LJ held that:

> "[T]he fraudulent claim rule ... in my view ... either applies, or should be matched by an equivalent rule, in the case of use of a fraudulent device to promote a claim—even though at the end of a trial it may be shown that the claim was all along in other respects valid."[98]

There were two caveats to this principle. First, the fraud had to be directly related to and intended to promote the claim. Secondly, it was tentatively suggested by Mance LJ that the fraudulent claim rule should only be applied if the fraudulent device or means

> "would, if believed, have tended objectively but prior to any final determination at trial of the parties' rights, to yield a not insignificant improvement in the insured's prospects—whether they be prospects of obtaining a settlement, or a better settlement, or of winning at trial."[99]

This was considered to be equivalent to the requirement that any non-existent or exaggerated element of loss had to be more than de minimis when a fraud claim was being considered for the fraudulent claim rule to apply.

The court's reasoning on fraudulent devices in *The Aegeon* was then followed by the lower courts in *Versloot Dredging*.[100] In *Versloot*, the insured was the owner of a dredging vessel which suffered significant damage to its engine as a result of water ingress, causing a loss of over €3m. The cause of the loss was, as found by Popplewell J at first instance, an insured peril. However, in making its claim, the general

---

[96] *The Aegeon* [2002] EWCA Civ 247 at [30]; [2003] Q.B. 556 at 569; [2002] 3 W.L.R. 616 at 628.
[97] *The Aegeon* [2002] EWCA Civ 247; [2003] Q.B. 556 at 569; [2002] 3 W.L.R. 616.
[98] *The Aegeon* [2002] EWCA Civ 247 at [37]; [2003] Q.B. 556 at 572; [2002] 3 W.L.R. 616 at 631.
[99] *The Aegeon* [2002] EWCA Civ 247 at [38]; [2003] Q.B. 556 at 572; [2002] 3 W.L.R. 616 at 631.
[100] *Versloot Dredging BV v HDI Gerling Versicherung AG* [2013] EWHC 1666 (Comm); CA: [2014] EWCA Civ 1349.

manager of the insured's vessel had made allegedly false statements to the underwriters. The statements were to the effect that he had been informed by the vessel's master and crew that the bilge alarm had gone off but had been ignored because its sounding was attributed to the rolling of the vessel in heavy weather. It was argued by the insurer that these statements constituted a fraudulent device and that the principles of The Aegeon should be applied, leading to the forfeit of the insured's claim. This was accepted, with a degree of reluctance, by Popplewell J at first instance. The decision was upheld on appeal. Christopher Clarke LJ, giving the lead judgment of the Court of Appeal, made clear that:

> "For all these reasons I would hold (i) that the principles of *The Aegeon* were applicable to the Owners' claim, subject to the qualification in the previous paragraph; (ii) that the fraudulent devices doctrine as there expounded should in this case be applied by way of ratio; (iii) that the judge was right to hold that the Owners made a claim which was fraudulent by reason of a fraudulent device consisting of the recklessly false representation which he found to have been made; and (iv) that the claim was forfeit on that account."[101]

Ultimately, the potential harshness of the fraudulent claim rule in the case of a fraudulent device was justified on the basis of it being a proportionate deterrence. Christopher Clarke LJ stated that:

> "Once it is accepted that deterrence is itself a legitimate aim, the fact that forfeiture is a harsh, in some circumstances very harsh, sanction does not mean that it is disproportionate to that aim. The rule is only applicable in the case of fraud, from which no insured should have any difficulty in abstaining. The careless or forgetful insured is not affected, nor is the insured who tells some irrelevant lie or whose lie is not told in order to induce payment. These limitations on the scope of the rule render it a proportionate response to the aim of deterrence of fraud, which crosses a moral red line, and has, as Lord Hobhouse put it 'a fundamental impact upon the parties' relationships', and may be difficult to detect."[102]

The Court of Appeal's decision was then reversed in the Supreme Court by a majority of 4 to 1. The majority—Lords Sumption, Clarke, Hughes and Toulson JJSC—were in agreement on the overall principles in the case despite different emphases in the judgments from each judge. The overarching point decided by the Court was that the fraudulent claim rule does not apply to fraudulent devices or, to use Lord Sumption JSC's preferred term, to collateral lies. This point was made clearly by Lord Sumption JSC in stating that[103]:

> "...the fraudulent claims rule applies to a wholly fabricated claim. It applies to an exaggerated claim. It applies even to the genuine part of an exaggerated claim if the whole is to be regarded as a single claim, as it must be. But it does not apply to a lie which the true facts, once admitted or ascertained, show to have been immaterial to the insured's right to recover."

The judges were in agreement on this critical point. Lord Clarke JSC noted that the difference between a fraudulent claim and a collateral lie was that the latter did not affect the insured's entitlement to an indemnity. On the subject of a collateral lie, he explained that[104]:

> "...the insured is trying to obtain no more than the law regards as his entitlement and the lie is irrelevant to the existence or amount of that entitlement. Such a lie is thus immaterial to the claim."

---

[101] *Versloot Dredging BV v HDI Gerling Versicherung AG* [2014] EWCA Civ 1349 at [166].
[102] *Versloot Dredging BV v HDI Gerling Versicherung AG* [2014] EWCA Civ 1349 at [166].
[103] *Versloot Dredging BV v HDI Gerling Versicherung AG* [2016] UKSC 45 at [36].
[104] *Versloot Dredging BV v HDI Gerling Versicherung AG* [2016] UKSC 45 at [40].

In his judgment, Lord Sumption JSC similarly distinguished a collateral lie from a fraudulent claim. He summarised this distinction as follows[105]:

"The position is different where the insured is trying to obtain no more than the law regards as his entitlement and the lie is irrelevant to the existence or amount of that entitlement. In this case the lie is dishonest, but the claim is not. The immateriality of the lie to the claim makes it not just possible but appropriate to distinguish between them."

From the Supreme Court decision in *Versloot*, the relevant question is thus whether the lie told by an insured is relevant to the existence or amount of its entitlement. If it is irrelevant to these issues, it is a collateral lie and does not entitle the insurer to avoid the claim.

Whereas the law on fraudulent devices had previously been justified on the basis that it was a proportionate deterrence, the majority in the Supreme Court dismissed this view. Regarding proportionality, Lord Hughes considered the application of the law "simply too large a sledgehammer for the nut involved".[106] The arguments offered previously in support of the fraudulent devices rule were rejected. Lord Toulson JSC stated that it is not "risk free" for an insured to lie in support of a valid claim. As he outlined, the potential negative consequences of such a lie could include damage to an insured's credibility or being penalised in costs.[107]

Fraudulent claims by co-insureds. As discussed above in Ch.8, there may be a number of insured parties under a CAR policy. The question of whether a fraudulent claim of one insured binds the others to the consequences of the fraud will depend on a number of factors, in particular whether the insurable interest is a joint or severable interest. If the interest is a joint interest, the question arises whether the claiming party has the authority to bind the other insured(s) as their agent. If an innocent co-insured can demonstrate that the party claiming is acting beyond its actual or apparent authority, then the innocent co-insured's rights under the policy will not be affected.[108] If the co-insured is a party to the fraud or has knowledge of the occurrence of fraud, then it will be bound by that fraud.[109] Often a CAR policy will contain a non-invalidation clause or a multiple insureds' clause, which will negate the effect of one insured's fraud as against the co-insured(s) by preventing the insurer from avoiding the entire policy. **21-046**

Section 13 of the Insurance Act 2015 provides for the impact of fraudulent claims upon group insurance policies. Such policies are commonly taken out by an employer on behalf of a group of employees. A CAR policy is not a group insurance policy and so this provision will not apply in the context of CAR insurance.

Retraction of fraud. The case law suggests that where an insured voluntarily retracts a fraudulent claim prior to its detection by the insurer this will not prevent the fraudulent claim rule applying. In particular, in *Fox*,[110] the court was satisfied **21-047**

---

[105] *Versloot Dredging BV v HDI Gerling Versicherung AG* [2016] UKSC 45 at [26].
[106] *Versloot Dredging BV v HDI Gerling Versicherung AG* [2016] UKSC 45 at [100].
[107] *Versloot Dredging BV v HDI Gerling Versicherung AG* [2016] UKSC 45 at [108].
[108] *Direct Line Insurance Plc v Khan* [2001] EWCA Civ 1794 at [41]; [2002] Lloyd's Rep. I.R. 364 at 372.
[109] *Khan* [2001] EWCA Civ 1794; [2002] Lloyd's Rep. I.R. 364.
[110] *Fox* [2009] EWHC 386 (QB); [2009] 1 All E.R. (Comm) 1017; [2010] Lloyd's Rep. I.R. 324.

that there was no authority to support retraction as a defence. H.H. Judge Seymour Q.C. was referred to a number of authorities[111] but concluded that:

"The whole tenor of the authorities to which my attention has been drawn, the most material passages in [sic] which I have quoted, in my judgment leads to the conclusion that it is no part of English law that the consequences of the rule concerning fraudulent claims can be mitigated in the case of retraction. However, if, contrary to my view, retraction could be material in any case, such a case, on principle, could only be one in which the fraudulent insured retracted voluntarily, and at a point at which the insurer had not raised any suggestion that he was suspicious about the claim or the relevant element in it. [Counsel for the insured] submitted that retraction should be possible at any stage prior to the insurer declining the relevant claim. On any view that must, I think, be too wide a formulation. If it were the true principle, it would set a premium on a fraudulent insured guessing how long it would take the insurer to assemble evidence which would justify declining cover, so as to be able to retract, if necessary, before the insurer had assembled the necessary evidence."[112]

5. CLAIMS BY AND AGAINST THIRD PARTIES

21-048   Claims against third parties: insurer's rights of subrogation. It is a fundamental principle of indemnity insurance that once the insurer has indemnified the insured under the policy, it is entitled to "the advantages of every right of action of the assured, whether in contract or in tort, which may go in diminution of the loss".[113] It follows that the insurer can have no greater rights than those of the insured.[114] These rights of subrogation are often expressly set out in the policy of insurance but even in the absence of an express term, such a term arises as a matter of equity.[115]

The rights of subrogation do not entitle the insurer to sue a third party in the insurer's own name[116]; that can only be the case where there has been a valid assignment of the insured's cause of action to the insurer.[117] Any proceedings must be issued in the name of the insured, although it has always been the case that equity will step in to compel the insured to allow his name to be used on terms that are just and equitable.[118] However, in the absence of any express term to the contrary in the policy, an insured cannot be prevented from bringing proceedings of its own against a third party and the court will not interfere with the insured's conduct of

---

[111] *The Aegeon* [2002] EWCA Civ 247; [2003] QB 556; [2002] 3 W.L.R. 616; *Stemson v AMP General Insurance (NZ) Ltd* [2006] UKPC 30; [2006] Lloyd's Rep. I.R. 852; [2007] 1 L.R.C. 531; and *Gottlieb* [2005] EWCA Civ 112; [2005] 1 All E.R. (Comm) 445; [2005] Lloyd's Rep. I.R. 369.

[112] *Direct Line Insurance Plc v Fox* [2009] EWHC 386 (QB) at [43] and [44]; [2009] 1 All E.R. (Comm) 1017 at 1032; [2010] Lloyd's Rep. I.R. 324 at 334.

[113] Denning LJ in *Morris v Ford Motor Co Ltd* [1973] Q.B. 792 at 800; [1973] 2 W.L.R. 843 at 848; [1973] 2 All E.R. 1084 at 1089 citing the leading authority for this proposition of *Castellain v Preston* (1883) 11 Q.B.D. 380; 52 L.J.Q.B. 366; 31 W.R. 557.

[114] See Griffiths LJ in *Buckland v Palmer* [1984] 1 W.L.R. 1109 at 1116; [1984] 3 All E.R. 554 at 560; [1985] R.T.R. 5 at 11.

[115] *Castellain* (1883) 11 Q.B.D. 380; 52 L.J.Q.B. 366; 31 W.R. 557.

[116] *London Assurance Co v Sainsbury* (1783) 3 Doug. K.B. 245; *Simpson & Co v Thomson; Simpson & Co v Burrell* (1877) 3 App. Cas. 279; 3 Asp MLC 567; 38 LT 1 and *Central Insurance Co Ltd v Seacalf Shipping Corp ("The Aiolis")* [1983] 2 Lloyd's Rep. 25 at 33.

[117] *Compania Colombiana de Seguros v Pacific Steam Navigation Co ("The Colombiana"); Empressa de Telefona de Bogota v Pacific Steam Navigation Co ("The Colombiana")* [1965] 1 Q.B. 101; [1964] 2 W.L.R. 484; [1964] 1 All E.R. 216.

[118] *Yorkshire Insurance Co Ltd v Nisbet Shipping Co Ltd* [1962] 2 Q.B. 330; [1961] 2 W.L.R. 1043; [1961] 2 All E.R. 487. For an example of a case where it has been held not to be just and equitable because the claim was against the insured's servant see the majority judgment in *Morris* [1973] Q.B. 792; [1973] 2 W.L.R. 843; [1973] 2 All E.R. 1084.

such an action, although it must conduct the litigation with proper regard for the insurer's interests and will be liable in damages to the insurer for any misconduct or abandonment of rights.[119] The practice has therefore developed of including claims co-operation clauses and/or claims-control clauses in indemnity policies and these are often found within the terms of CAR policies. Such clauses do not confer more exclusive rights of subrogation than those enjoyed under the general law but ensure the full enjoyment of those rights by the insurer.

Claims co-operation and control clauses. A claims co-operation clause normally **21-049** requires the insured to do such acts and things as may be necessary or reasonably required by the insurer for the purposes of obtaining relief or indemnity from others. They can take a number of different express forms but common obligations include an obligation to furnish all information available and to permit insurers to take all necessary steps to enforce their rights of subrogation including, for example:

1. preserving any damaged or defective insured property for inspection by the insurer or its agents;
2. taking all practicable steps (including giving notice to the police) to discover the guilty party where the insured property has been lost, stolen or wilfully damaged and to trace and recover that property; and
3. not accepting payment, incurring expenses, admitting liability, promising payment or making any arrangement concerning settlement of a third party claim without the written consent of the insurer.

These terms are normally broken down into: (a) prohibitions on the insured not to compromise or settle any claim or admit liability; and (b) permissions for the insurer to have conduct and control of all proceedings in relation to any claims for which the insurer may be liable under the policy and to use the insured's name to do so for its own benefit. There will then be co-extensive duties on the insured to co-operate in those proceedings. The insurer's conduct in exercising that exclusive control must be exercised by the insurer "in what they bona fide consider to be the common interest of themselves and their assured."[120]

A claims control condition was considered by the courts in a products liability insurance policy in *Horwood v Land of Leather Ltd*,[121] where the relevant clause stated:

> "The Insured shall not, except at his own cost, take any steps to compromise or settle any claim or admit liability, without specific instructions in writing from the Insurer nor give any information or assistance to any person claiming against him, but the Insurer shall for so long as they shall so desire *have* the absolute conduct and control of all proceedings (including arbitrations) in respect of any claims for which the Insurer may be liable under this policy, and may use the name of the Insured to enforce for the benefit of the Insurer any order made for costs or otherwise or to make or defend any claim for indemnity or damages against any third party or for any other purpose connected with this policy."

Teare J construed the prohibitions and permissions contained in the clause and stated that it was:

> "clear from the content of the condition that its object is to grant control of claims to the Insurer. That

---

[119] *Arthur Barnett Ltd v National Insurance Co of NZ Ltd* [1965] N.Z.L.R. 874.
[120] *Beacon Insurance Co Ltd v Langdale* [1939] 4 All E.R. 204 at 206; (1939) 65 Ll. L. Rep. 57, 58.
[121] *Horwood v Land of Leather Ltd (In Administration)* [2010] EWHC 546 (Comm) at [2]; [2010] 1 C.L.C. 423 at 427; [2010] Lloyd's Rep. I.R. 453.

is achieved by the positive grant of permission to the Insurer and the imposition of prohibitions on the Insured. The latter enable the former to be effective."[122]

He held that the wording of the clause was such that the control of claims conferred on the insurer extended not only to claims against the insured but also to claims by the insured against others. He therefore went on to say:

"[t]hat being so one would expect that the prohibitions on the Insured, which are part and parcel of the mechanism by which the Insurer has control of 'all proceedings', would also extend both to claims against the Insured and to claims by the Insured. It would be absurd if the Insurer had control of proceedings commenced in the name of the Insured against others but yet the Insured was under no prohibition not to settle such claims."[123]

Having construed the clause in this way Teare J did not need to determine whether there was any implied term that would assist the insurer in the absence of the claims control clause. However, he made certain obiter comments on that issue. The insurer argued that it was an implied term of the policy that the insured would act reasonably and in good faith with due regard to the insurer's interests and rights of subrogation under the policy. It was accepted on behalf of the third-party claimant that there was an implied term but they contended that such a term was that the insured would not deal with any claim that it possessed against a third party in such a manner as to prejudice the insurer's rights of subrogation in relation to that claim. Teare J stated that had it been necessary to decide the issue he would have preferred the insurer's formulation of the implied term because:

"[t]he implied term arises because the insurer has a right to be subrogated to the rights of the insured when he indemnifies him pursuant to the policy of insurance. If the insured acts without regard to that contingent right he may harm the value of that right to the insurer. The most obvious harm occurs where the insured settles a claim he may have against a third party for an indemnity and so deprives the insurer of its benefit in whole or in part. But in principle harm may be caused to the insurer's rights of subrogation where the claim against the third party is not lost or reduced in value by settlement. For example, the documents necessary to establish such claim may be destroyed. I therefore consider that the implied duty must be one which obliges the insured to act in good faith and reasonably with regard to the interests of the insurer. [The Claimant] accepts that if the insured does so act he will not incur any liability to the insurer even if he has settled a claim and so deprived the insurer of the benefit of that claim. I do not understand why the insured should only be liable, subject to that defence, for one type of damage to the insurer's contingent rights of subrogation and not for other types of damage to such rights."[124]

The position remains to be resolved by the courts as to the precise scope of this implied term but there is an attractive logic to the obiter comments of Teare J set out above.

21-050 **Settlement of claims by third parties.** Subject to policy terms and conditions, an insured is, in principle, entitled to an indemnity from the insurer in respect of loss crystallised by a settlement with a third party claimant. The case of *AstraZeneca Insurance Co Ltd v XL Insurance (Bermuda) Ltd*[125] makes clear that any loss must take the form of actual legal liability, as opposed to merely alleged liability.

---

[122] *Horwood* [2010] EWHC 546 (Comm) at [44]; [2010] 1 C.L.C. 423 at 437–438; [2010] Lloyd's Rep. I.R. 453 at 461.

[123] *Horwood* [2010] EWHC 546 (Comm) at [46]; [2010] 1 C.L.C. 423 at 438; [2010] Lloyd's Rep. I.R. 453 at 462.

[124] *Horwood* [2010] EWHC 546 (Comm) at [67]; [2010] 1 C.L.C. 423 at 443; [2010] Lloyd's Rep. I.R. 453 at 464.

[125] *AstraZeneca Insurance Co Ltd v XL Insurance (Bermuda) Ltd* [2013] EWHC 349 (Comm); ap-

A judgment will provide strong evidence of such an actual liability and an agreed settlement can provide the same. However, from the perspective of the insurer, neither a judgment nor an agreement is determinative of the question of whether the insured is entitled to an indemnity. If the insurer was not party to the proceedings or to the agreement, it is not thereby bound and is entitled to dispute that the insured was in fact subject to a legal liability.[126]

Global settlements of claims by third parties. A particular difficulty in claim- **21-051** ing an indemnity in respect of a settlement with a third party claimant arises in the case of a global settlement. It is common practice for an insured to settle a number of claims by means of a single settlement. The settlement may, for example, encompass claims separate to the insured liability or a counterclaim by the insured. If such a settlement does not specify the sum paid in respect of the insured liability, it is arguable that the insured is unable to recover the sum from the insurer. The case law on the issue sets out two contrasting conclusions to the argument.

In the case of *Lumbermens Mutual Casualty Co v Bovis Lend Lease Ltd*,[127] Colman J held that the insured was required to show that its liability had been specifically ascertained in order to recover from its insurer. In his view, the global settlement that the insured entered into did not specifically ascertain its loss. In the absence of an identifiable loss arising from an identifiable insured eventuality, the insured had no cause of action against the insurer in order to recover its loss.

By contrast, in the case of *Enterprise Oil Ltd v Strand Insurance Co Ltd*,[128] Aikens J held that an insured which entered into a global settlement was entitled to rely on extrinsic evidence in order to prove that it was liable for a particular sum under a global settlement and that that sum was recoverable under the policy. His comments were obiter dicta as a result of his previous findings which meant that the issue did not arise for decision in the case. Accordingly, notwithstanding thorough consideration of the issue by Aikens J the decision is technically, only persuasive authority on the point. This has been recognised in the later case of *AIG Europe (Ireland) Ltd v Faraday Capital Ltd*.[129] In that case, Morison J stated that, if required to decide, he would follow *Enterprise Oil* over the decision in *Lumbermens*. Again, Morison J's comments were obiter dicta and there is no conclusive authority on the point. Accordingly, the issue could still be considered arguable either way.

Claims by third parties against insurers. The issue of claims by third parties **21-052** against insurers directly is a topic of particular importance in the field of indemnity insurance. Accordingly, it is only of secondary importance in this text and will be dealt with briefly. The basis for a third party's claim against an insurer is the Third Parties (Rights Against Insurers) Act 1930. The Act applies only to liability policies. At common law, there is no right for a third party to bring a claim directly against an insurer.

The Act provides for a statutory assignment of the rights of the insured to the

---

proved on appeal in *AstraZeneca Insurance Co Ltd v XL Insurance (Bermuda) Ltd* [2013] EWCA Civ 1660.

126 *Omega Proteins Ltd v Aspen Insurance UK Ltd* [2010] EWHC 2280 (Comm).
127 *Lumbermens Mutual Casualty Co v Bovis Lend Lease Ltd* [2004] EWHC 2197 (Comm).
128 *Enterprise Oil Ltd v Strand Insurance Co Ltd* [2006] EWHC 58 (Comm).
129 *AIG Europe (Ireland) Ltd v Faraday Capital Ltd* [2006] 2 C.L.C 770 reversed on appeal on different grounds: [2007]2 C.L.C 844.

third party in certain conditions.[130] Principally, the Act operates where the insured becomes insolvent and provides machinery for the third party to recover its loss despite the insolvency. It is necessary for the third party to first establish liability on the part of the insured. As a result of the insolvency of the insured, this may lead to procedural hurdles which the third party must overcome. This shortcoming is addressed in the Third Parties (Rights against Insurers) Act 2010 which, at the time of writing, will soon come into force.[131] As with general principles of assignment, the third party cannot be put in a better position than the insured as a result of the operation of the Act.

Claims by third parties: Third Parties (Rights Against Insurers) Act
21-053 **2010.** The coming into force of the Third Parties (Rights Against Insurers) Act 2010 on 1 August 2016 will have an impact on the construction industry. Principally, the Act will provide a more streamlined method by which a third party is able to make a claim against the liability insurer of an insolvent company. Currently, a claimant is required to apply to restore a dissolved company to the register in order to establish liability on the part of the company. Under the Act, a claimant can instead bring a claim directly against the insurer without needing to restore the company.[132]

Prior to 1 August 2016, this area was covered by the Third Parties (Rights Against Insurers) Act 1930. In order to understand which act applies, the relevant dates are the date the company incurred a liability and the date that the insolvency started. If one of those dates is after 1 August 2016, the 2010 Act will apply. If both dates were before 1 August 2016, the 1930 Act will apply.

---

[130] Section 1 of the 1930 Act.
[131] See below, para.21-053.
[132] Section 1(2) of the 2010 Act.

CHAPTER 22

PROOF

1. INTRODUCTION

Introduction. The burden of proving the occurrence of the loss or damage that **22-001** is the subject of the claim under the policy and the extent of that loss lies with the insured. There is a slightly more complex set of rules as to who bears the burden of proving that the loss or damage in question is covered by the policy. The general approach is essentially an application of the principle that the person who alleges some matter bears the burden of proving it[1]: the insured is responsible for showing that the loss falls within the definition of an insured peril and the insurer must prove an allegation that the loss falls within an exception to the policy. Under an all risks policy, however, the open-ended nature of the cover relaxes the insured's burden of proof in certain respects and can justify the making of inferences favourable to the insured.[2]

It should be borne in mind that the rules on evidential burdens are decisive only **22-002** where the tribunal lacks the information to come to a definite view: "the prime duty of a court is to make up its mind how the loss occurred".[3] In *Cooper v General Accident Fire and Life Assurance Corp Ltd*,[4] Sir John Ross said:

"[W]here the facts are not in dispute, and where everything depends on the inferences to be drawn from the facts, there is little advantage in discussing the question of onus. The judicial mind derives a certain amount of comfort and satisfaction in arriving at a doubtful conclusion by throwing the onus argument into the scale. The truth is that the facts will support either of the two antagonistic conclusions. If to an equal degree, the question of onus is all-important."[5]

---

[1] *The Glendarroch* [1894] P. 226; 7 Asp. M.L.C. 420; 63 L.J.P. 89.
[2] *British & Foreign Marine Insurance Co Ltd v Gaunt (No. 3)* [1921] 2 A.C. 41; 7 Ll. L. Rep. 62; 90 L.J.K.B. 801, see below, paras 22-003 to 22-005.
[3] *MacGillivray on Insurance Law*, edited by J. Birds, B. Lynch and S. Milnes, 13th edn (London: Sweet & Maxwell, 2015), para.21-008.
[4] *Cooper v General Accident Fire and Life Assurance Corp Ltd* [1922] 2 I.R. 38, affirmed [1922] 2 I.R. 214.
[5] *Cooper* [1922] 2 I.R. 38 at 48.

2. THE INSURED'S BURDEN OF PROOF

22-003 **Insured must prove accidental loss—no need to prove the exact cause.** The starting point is that the burden of proof is upon the insured to show that the loss was caused by a peril insured against.[6] Thus, if the evidence leaves the court in doubt as to whether the cause of the loss was within or outside of the policy, the claim will fail.[7] However, the general rule is modified to an extent in the context of an all risks policy. In *British & Foreign Marine Insurance Co Ltd v Gaunt (No.3)*,[8] it was held that in view of the open-ended nature of such insurance,

> "the plaintiff discharges his special onus when he has proved that the loss was caused by some event covered by the general expression, and he is not bound to go further and prove the exact nature of the accident or casualty which, in fact, occasioned his loss."[9]

In *Gaunt*,[10] the insured was the purchaser of a consignment of Patagonian wool, which was covered by an all risks policy during transit from the sheep's back to the port of shipment. The wool was found to have suffered water damage occurring at some point in the period covered by the policy, but the evidence did not establish with any certainty how the damage occurred. The House of Lords held that this was not fatal to the insured's claim. Lord Sumner explained:

> "[T]he quasi-universality of the description does affect the onus of proof in one way. The claimant insured against and averring a loss by fire must prove loss by fire, which involves proving that it is not by something else. When he avers loss by some risk coming within 'all risks', as used in this policy, he need only give evidence reasonably showing that the loss was due to a casualty, not to a certainty or to inherent vice or to wear and tear. That is easily done. I do not think he has to go further and pick out one of the multitude of risks covered, so as to show exactly how his loss was caused."[11]

Hence, the insured will discharge his burden of proof under an all risks policy if he can show that the loss occurred accidentally, but does not need to show precisely how the loss was brought about.

22-004 **Presumption of accidental loss.** It was also held in *Gaunt*[12] that a fortuitous event could be inferred from the fact that there had been damage and that this could not

---

6   *Munro Brice & Co v War Risks Association Ltd*; sub nom. *Munro, Brice* [1918] 2 K.B. 78 at 88; 88 L.J.K.B. 509 at 515; 14 Asp. M.L.C. 312 at 315, per Bailhache J: "[t]he plaintiff must prove such facts as bring him prima facie within the terms of the promise" (reversed on other grounds [1920] 3 K.B. 94; 2 Ll. L. Rep. 2; 89 L.J.K.B. 1009); *Compania Martiartu v Royal Exchange Assurance Corp* [1923] 1 K.B. 650 at 656; 92 L.J.K.B. 546 at 548, per Bankes LJ: the claimants must establish "that the loss of the vessel was due to a peril covered by the policy" (affirmed [1924] A.C. 850; 19 Ll. L. Rep. 95; 93 L.J.K.B. 1007); *Rhesa Shipping Co SA v Edmunds (The Popi M); Rhesa Shipping Co SA v Fenton Insurance Co Ltd* [1985] 1 W.L.R. 948 at 951; [1985] 2 All E.R. 712 at 714; [1985] 2 Lloyd's Rep. 1 at 2–3, per Lord Brandon of Oarbrook: "the burden of proving, on a balance of probabilities, that the ship was lost by perils of the sea, is and remains throughout on the shipowners."
7   *Compania Martiartu* [1923] 1 K.B. 650 at 657; 92 L.J.K.B. 546 at 552, per Scrutton LJ; *NE Neter & Co Ltd v Licenses and General Insurance Co Ltd* [1944] 1 All E.R. 341 at 343; 77 Ll. L. Rep. 202 at 205; 170 L.T. 165 at 166, per Tucker J.
8   *Gaunt* [1921] 2 A.C. 41; 7 Ll. L. Rep. 62; 90 L.J.K.B. 801.
9   *Gaunt* [1921] 2 A.C. 41 at 47; 7 Ll. L. Rep. 62 at 63; 90 L.J.K.B. 801 at 804, per Lord Birkenhead L.C.
10   *Gaunt* [1921] 2 A.C. 41; 7 Ll. L. Rep. 62; 90 L.J.K.B. 801.
11   *Gaunt* [1921] 2 A.C. 41 at 57–58; 90 L.J.K.B. 801 at 807–808.
12   *Gaunt* [1921] 2 A.C. 41; 7 Ll. L. Rep. 62; 90 L.J.K.B. 801.

be expected to occur in the normal course of the insured adventure.[13] This might appear to create significant problems for insurers in defending claims inasmuch as it appears to place upon them the entire burden of disproving a claim once loss has been established.[14] However, there are two significant limits on the principle that an accidental cause can be inferred from unexpected loss or damage. First, unless the cause is a complete mystery, it is not sufficient for the insured to state that loss has occurred in respect of the insured property but decline to give any information as to the circumstances[15]: the insured is expected to give the best information that he can as to how the loss occurred. Secondly, where the evidence *is* sufficiently complete for the claimant to advance an explanation of how the loss or damage occurred, that explanation must be proved on a balance of probabilities. In that case, the claimant cannot fall back on any presumption that the unexplained loss is due to an accident,[16] so that if the judge is persuaded neither by the explanation of the claimant nor that put forward by the defendant, the claim will fail.[17] In *Regina Fur Co Ltd v Bossom*,[18] the judge found that the claimants had failed to prove that the insured goods had been stolen by persons unknown in a burglary between 08.50 and 09.20 as alleged, and accordingly gave judgment to the defendant insurers. On appeal, the claimants argued that even if the evidence did not support a finding that there was a burglary at this time it ultimately did not matter when the goods were taken, or by whom, as this was an all risks policy. This argument was rejected because the claim had never been made in that way.[19] Having advanced a particular case as to how the loss occurred, the insured must make good that case: he cannot backtrack by pointing to the presumption that unexplained loss is within the phrase "all risks".

---

[13] *Gaunt* [1921] 2 A.C. 41 at 47; 7 Ll. L. Rep. 62 at 63; 90 L.J.K.B. 801 at 803–804, per Lord Birkenhead L.C.; [1921] 2 A.C. 41 at 51–52; 90 L.J.K.B. 801 at 805, per Viscount Finlay.

[14] Spencer Bell J said "it would appear that all risk insurance arose for the very purpose of protecting the insured in those cases where difficulties of logical explanation or some mystery surrounded the disappearance of property": *Betty v Liverpool & London & Globe Insurance Co Ltd* 310 F.2d 308 at 311 (4th Cir. 1962), quoted in *Aquarius Financial Enterprises Inc v Certain Underwriters at Lloyd's (The Delphine)* [2001] 2 Lloyd's Rep. 542 at 543–544; [2001] All E.R. (D) 222 (Apr) at [11].

[15] *The Delphine* [2001] 2 Lloyd's Rep. 542 at 543; [2001] All E.R. (D) 222 (Apr) at [11].

[16] It is an old rule of marine insurance that if a seaworthy ship disappears in unexplained circumstances there is a presumption—analogous to the inference of accidental loss drawn in *Gaunt*) [1921] 2 A.C. 41; 7 Ll. L. Rep. 62; 90 L.J.K.B. 801—that the loss is due to a peril of the sea: *Green v Brown* 93 E.R. 1126 (1743) 2 Str. 1199. That presumption has no application, however, where there is some evidence as to the cause of the admission of seawater: *Compania Martiartu* [1923] 1 K.B. 650; 18 Ll. L. Rep. 247; 92 L.J.K.B. 546; *Compania Naviera Santi SA v Indemnity Marine Assurance Co Ltd (The Tropaioforos)* [1960] 2 Lloyd's Rep. 469; *The Popi M* [1985] 1 W.L.R. 948; [1985] 2 All E.R. 712; [1985] 2 Lloyd's Rep. 1. In *The Popi M*, the claimant's vessel sank in calm waters. The crew survived and were able to give evidence about the entry of water through a hole in the vessel's plating, but the cause of the hole was a matter of conjecture. The claimants contended it was caused by an undetected submerged submarine; the defendants suggested wear and tear. Bingham J found that the submarine hypothesis was inherently improbable but still more likely than the defendant's explanation, and held that the claimants' case was proved on the balance of probabilities. The House of Lords allowed an appeal on the basis that inasmuch as the claimants' explanation was improbable they had failed to establish their case. The presumption of loss due to a peril of the sea did not apply since (i) there was no finding that the vessel was seaworthy and (ii) the sinking was not wholly unexplained: [1985] 1 W.L.R. 948 at 953; [1985] 2 All E.R. 712 at 716; [1985] 2 Lloyd's Rep. 1 at 4, per Lord Brandon of Oarbrook.

[17] *The Popi M* [1985] 1 W.L.R. 948; [1985] 2 All E.R. 712; [1985] 2 Lloyd's Rep. 1.

[18] *Regina Fur Co Ltd v Bossom* [1958] 2 Lloyd's Rep. 425.

[19] *Regina Fur Co Ltd* [1958] 2 Lloyd's Rep. 425 at 428.

22-005   The result is that the more removed in space and time the insured is from the scene of the loss or damage, the less that is required of him in discharging his burden of proof.[20] Thus, a cargo owner insured under an all risks policy will generally be able to rely on the inference applied in *Gaunt*[21] that unexplained loss or damage to the goods during shipment is fortuitous, requiring the insurer to counter this presumption. However, if the insured property is alleged to have been stolen from the person or the premises of the insured, there will usually be no room for such an inference: the court will expect the insured to give an account of the circumstances of the alleged theft, and the veracity of that account will have to be proved on the balance of probabilities. The interrelationship of these principles can be seen as creating a sensible balance between, on the one hand, ensuring that it is not made too easy for those who fraudulently dispose of the insured property to hide behind a presumption of accidental loss, and on the other, affording protection for the insured in cases where it is not practicable to prove the precise cause of the loss.

3.   PROOF OF EXCEPTIONS TO COVER

Burden is on the insurer of proving matters relieving him/her of
22-006   liability.   Once the insured has discharged the burden of proving that the loss occurred fortuitously in accordance with the principles discussed above, it is for the insurer to bring himself within any exception in the policy on which he relies.[22] In one case a consignment of goods insured under an all risks policy was lost in unknown circumstances during the turmoil of the Russian Civil War; it was held not to be necessary for the claimant to prove that the goods were not lost due to an excepted peril.[23] However, it was suggested in one first instance decision, *Hurst v Evans*,[24] that the burden of proving exceptions is reversed under all risks insurance. In that case, jewellery was insured against loss or damage

> "arising from any cause whatsoever ... save and except loss by theft or dishonesty committed by any servant ... of the assured."[25]

It was established that the jewellery had been stolen; the insurers contended that a servant of the claimants was implicated. Lush J held that the onus was on the insured to prove that the theft was not committed by the servant:

---

[20]   Where a shipowner is accused of scuttling the ship "[n]o doubt one reason for placing the burden of proof on the shipowners in such a case as this is that they are likely to have all, or almost all, the relevant information, and the insurers are likely to have virtually no information initially": *Compania Naviera Santi SA v Indemnity Marine Assurance Co Ltd (The Tropaioforos)* [1960] 2 Lloyd's Rep. 469 at 473, per Pearson J.

[21]   *Gaunt* [1921] 2 A.C. 41; 7 Ll. L. Rep. 62; 90 L.J.K.B. 801.

[22]   *Gorman v Hand-in-Hand Insurance Co* (1877) I.R. 11 C.L. 224 at 230; *Munro Brice & Co* [1918] 2 K.B. 78; 88 L.J.K.B. 509; 14 Asp. M.L.C. 312 (reversed on other grounds [1920] 3 K.B. 94; 2 Ll. L. Rep. 2; 89 L.J.K.B. 1009); *Gaunt* [1920] 1 K.B. 903 at 910; *Re National Benefit Assurance Co Ltd (Application of Sthyr)* (1933) 45 Ll. L. Rep. 147; *Greaves v Drysdale* (1935) 53 Ll. L. Rep. 16 at 17 (reversed on other grounds [1936] 2 All E.R. 470; (1936) 55 Ll. L. Rep. 95; 80 S.J. 464); *Bond Air Services Ltd v Hill* [1955] 2 Q.B. 417; [1955] 2 W.L.R. 1194; [1955] 2 All E.R. 476. See also *Green v Brown* (1743) 2 Str. 1199 at 1200, for which the report records that the underwriters argued, unsuccessfully, that "as captures and seizures were excepted, it lay upon the insured to prove the loss happened in the particular manner [perils of the sea] declared on".

[23]   *Re National Benefit Assurance Co Ltd (Application of Sthyr)* (1933) 45 Ll. L. Rep. 147 at 151.

[24]   *Hurst v Evans* [1917] 1 K.B. 352; 86 L.J.K.B. 305.

[25]   *Hurst* [1917] 1 K.B. 352; 86 L.J.K.B. 305.

"[T]he plaintiff must allege facts to show that the lost goods were covered by the policy, that the loss was one against which the defendant had agreed to indemnify the plaintiff."[26]

This reasoning has been strongly criticised and has not been followed in later cases[27]; it is suggested the decision can no longer be considered good law.

The burden of proof is also on an insurer to prove breach of any condition which he alleges relieves him of liability.[28] This remains so where the policy expressly provides that the observance of the condition is a pre-condition to the insured's right of recovery.[29]

22-007

Distinguishing terms that define the scope of cover from exceptions. How does one distinguish between wording that forms an integral part of the definition of the cover and words that carve out an exception from the cover?[30] In *Munro Brice & Co*,[31] Bailhache J attempted to answer that question by drawing a distinction between: (1) wording which is "as wide as the promise, and thus qualifies the whole of the promise",[32] in which case the claimant must prove that the qualification does not apply; and (2) wording that

22-008

"excludes from the operation of the promise particular classes of cases which but for the exception would fall within it, leaving some part of the general scope of the promise unqualified",[33]

---

26 *Hurst* [1917] 1 K.B. 352 at 357; 86 L.J.K.B. 305 at 308. The words used in the last report differ slightly to the quote but the same point is made. Lush J considered that the all risks nature of the policy compelled this conclusion: "[t]his is not a case of an insurance against loss caused by some specified reason, such as fire or theft. It is an insurance against loss due to any cause except the two specified … If the contention of the plaintiff is right, he need only aver a loss of jewellery": [1917] 1 K.B. 352 at 357; 86 L.J.K.B. 305 at 307–308.

27 *Munro Brice & Co* [1918] 2 K.B. 78 at 87–88; 88 L.J.K.B. 509 at 515; 14 Asp. M.L.C. 312 at 315, Bailhache J The view of Bailhache J was applied in *Re National Benefit Assurance Co Ltd (Application of Sthyr)* (1933) 45 Ll. L. Rep. 147 at 151 and *Greaves* (1935) 53 Ll. L. Rep. 16 at 17 (on very similar facts to *Hurst* [1917] 1 K.B. 352; 86 L.J.K.B. 305). Indeed, there was no suggestion in *Gaunt* ([1921] 2 A.C. 41; 7 Ll. L. Rep. 62; 90 L.J.K.B. 801) that the insured, as part of his burden of showing that the loss occurred fortuitously within the meaning of an all risks policy, had additionally to negative the possibility that one of the policy exceptions might apply. MacGillivray suggests that the case of *Hurst* can be defended ("if at all") only on the basis that the exception could be viewed as part of the very definition of the insured peril because in that case the description of cover and the exception were part of the same clause: *MacGillivray on Insurance Law*, edited by Birds, Lynch and Milnes, (2015), para.21-007. However, such a distinction was deprecated in *Munro Brice & Co* [1918] 2 K.B. 78 at 83–84, 87–88; 88 L.J.K.B. 509 at 513, 515; 14 Asp. M.L.C. 312 at 314, 315. In any event, it does not seem to have been part of the judge's actual reasoning in *Hurst*.

28 *Bond Air Services Ltd* [1955] 2 Q.B. 417; [1955] 2 W.L.R. 1194; [1955] 2 All E.R. 476; *Fraser v BN Furman (Productions) Ltd (Miller Smith & Partners, third parties)* [1967] 1 W.L.R. 898 at 905; [1967] 3 All E.R. 57 at 60; [1967] 2 Lloyd's Rep. 1 at 12, per Diplock LJ; *Sofi v Prudential Assurance Co Ltd* [1993] 2 Lloyd's Rep. 559 at 564.

29 *Bond Air Services Ltd* [1955] 2 Q.B. 417; [1955] 2 W.L.R. 1194; [1955] 2 All E.R. 476.

30 The problem of distinguishing an exception from the definition of the promise itself has been discussed in the general law of contract where, quite apart from the onus of proof, the applicability of the Unfair Contract Terms Act 1977 (UCTA, 1977) jurisdiction (to which insurance contracts are exempt: Sch.1 para.1(a) of the 1977 Act) depends on the clause under attack being an exclusion of liability: B. Coote, "The Unfair Contract Terms Act 1977" (1978) 41 M.L.R. 312; J. Adams, "An Optimistic Look at the Contract Provisions of Unfair Contract Terms Act 1977" (1978) 41 MLR 703; *Chitty on Contracts*, edited by H.G. Beale, A.S. Burrows et al, 32nd edn (London: Sweet & Maxwell, 2015), Vol.1, para.15-070.

31 *Munro Brice & Co* [1918] 2 K.B. 78; 88 L.J.K.B. 509; 14 Asp. M.L.C. 312, reversed on other grounds [1920] 3 K.B. 94; 2 Ll. L. Rep. 2; 89 L.J.K.B. 1009.

32 *Munro Brice & Co* [1918] 2 K.B. 78 at 88; 88 L.J.K.B. 509 at 515; 14 Asp. M.L.C. 312 at 315.

33 *Munro Brice & Co* [1918] 2 K.B. 78 at 88; 88 L.J.K.B. 509 at 515; 14 Asp. M.L.C. 312 at 315.

in which case, it would be for the insurer to prove that the exception applied.[34] As to case (1), he gave an example of a marine policy with a particular average 3 per cent franchise; it would be for the claimant to prove a particular average loss of over 3 per cent. On the other hand, a "free of capture and seizure" exception was an example of (2)—a true exception because it excluded particular classes of cases, which would otherwise be within the policy cover; he held that the burden was on the insurer to prove that the vessel had been captured. This method of identifying exclusions is open to criticism, however. The concept of wording which "qualifies the whole promise" is vague, unless it is taken to mean a provision that applies in every case. Even that formulation is problematic. If it means that the provision must apply and actually restrict the insured's recovery in every case then the 3 per cent franchise example would, contrary to the judge's view, be an exception and not a qualified promise, since under a franchise provision there is no deductible whenever the particular average loss exceeds the stated minimum. If, instead, a qualified promise is wording which is potentially applicable in every case, this could apply to almost anything usually thought of as an exception or a condition. Perhaps the better view is that it is simply a matter of impression whether a clause is to be treated as an exception or as a part of the definition of cover. In *Munro Brice & Co*, Bailhache J accepted that an alteration in the phraseology of the contract could turn an exception into a qualified promise.[35] However, he did not think that the relative positions in the policy of the words defining cover and the exception (e.g. if the description of the insured peril and the exception were found in the same clause) should affect matters.[36]

22-009   A further issue that arises in relation to all risks policies is whether the insured is required to prove, beyond showing that the loss was probably accidental, that none of the implied exceptions associated with the concept of fortuity apply. As noted above in para.10-013, damage due to inherent vice in the insured subject matter is impliedly excluded from the scope of all risks cover and yet damage by inherent vice can still be fortuitous in the sense of it being non-inevitable.[37] It could be argued, therefore, that the burden is on the insurer to prove that damage is due to inherent vice.[38] On the other hand, it is undoubtedly for the insured to show (subject to the court being prepared to draw the type of inferences that were drawn in *Gaunt*)[39] that the damage was not inevitable, nor due to ordinary wear and tear.

---

[34]   *Munro Brice & Co* [1918] 2 K.B. 78 at 88; 88 L.J.K.B. 509 at 515; 14 Asp. M.L.C. 312 at 315.

[35]   *Munro Brice & Co* [1918] 2 K.B. 78 at 89; 88 L.J.K.B. 509 at 516; 14 Asp. M.L.C. 312 at 316.

[36]   *Munro Brice & Co* [1918] 2 K.B. 78 at 83; 88 L.J.K.B. 509 at 513; 14 Asp. M.L.C. 312 at 314.

[37]   See above, para.10-014.

[38]   The contrary view was given in *M Golodetz & Co Inc v Czarnikow-Rionda Co Inc (The Galatia)* [1980] 1 W.L.R. 495 at 514; [1979] 2 All E.R. 726 at 742; [1979] 2 Lloyd's Rep. 450 at 458; affirmed [1980] 1 W.L.R. 495; [1980] 1 All E.R. 501; [1980] 1 Lloyd's Rep. 453, inasmuch as Donaldson J considered that, if the insured fails to show that the damage to the subject matter was not due to the natural behaviour of the subject matter, "he will be unable to prove the essentially accidental nature of the broad cover provided". However, he went on to make the interesting suggestion that given that an all risks policy takes effect as if all insurable risks were separately enumerated (*Gaunt* [1921] 2 A.C. 41 at 57–58; 90 L.J.K.B. 801 at 807–808, per Lord Sumner) so long as the insured can show that the damage occurred due to a specific peril which does not as a matter of definition implicitly exclude loss caused by an inherent vice (e.g. fire), the question of inherent vice can be treated as an exception to cover and therefore a matter which it is for the insurer to prove: *M Golodetz & Co Inc* [1980] 1 W.L.R. 495 at 513–515; [1979] 2 All E.R. 726 at 742–743; [1979] 2 Lloyd's Rep. 450 at 458–459.

[39]   *Gaunt* [1921] 2 A.C. 41; 7 Ll. L. Rep. 62; 90 L.J.K.B. 801.

4. Proof of misconduct

The question of whether the burden of proving wilful misconduct under an all **22-010** risks policy should, as a matter of principle, lie with the insured or the insurer is not an easy one to resolve. On the one hand, in the case of "perils of the sea", it was held in *Compania Naviera Santi SA v Indemnity Marine Assurance Co Ltd (The Tropaioforos)*[40] that where the insurer (on reasonable grounds)[41] raises the possibility that the insured himself wilfully caused the loss the insured has to prove that he was not responsible. On the other hand, in *Slattery v Mance*,[42] it was held that in a claim on a fire policy it is for the defendant to prove that the fire was caused or connived at by the claimant. Salmon J considered that the onus of proof under a fire policy was different to that under a policy against perils of the sea. Whereas the phrase "perils of the sea" does not cover the deliberate scuttling of the ship even without the involvement of the claimant insured,[43] by contrast,

> "[t]he risk of fire insured against is quite obviously not confined to an accidental fire. If the ship had been set alight by some mischievous person but without the plaintiff's connivance, there can be no doubt but that the plaintiff would be entitled to recover. Of course the plaintiff cannot recover if he was the person who fired the ship ... This result, however, does not depend upon the construction of the word 'fire' in the policy but on the well-known principle of insurance law that no man can recover for a loss which he himself has deliberately and fraudulently caused."[44]

By the same reasoning, since an all risks policy *does* respond to loss or damage caused by the deliberate acts of third parties,[45] it can be argued that the implied exclusion for wilful misconduct by the insured is a discrete exception and so a matter to be proved by the insurer.[46] At any rate, as a matter of practice, in cases where wilful misconduct is raised against a person insured under an all risks policy, the

---

[40] *Compania Naviera Santi SA* [1960] 2 Lloyd's Rep. 469.

[41] Which must be properly particularised so that the insured is informed of the case against him: *Astrovlanis Compania Naviera SA v Linard (The Gold Sky)* [1972] 2 Q.B. 611; [1972] 2 W.L.R. 1414; [1972] 2 All E.R. 647; *Palamisto General Enterprises SA v Ocean Marine Insurance Co Ltd (The Dias)* [1972] 2 Q.B. 625; [1972] 2 W.L.R. 1425; [1972] 2 All E.R. 1112.

[42] *Slattery v Mance* [1962] 1 Q.B. 676; [1962] 2 W.L.R. 569; [1962] 1 All E.R. 525; approved in *Schiffshypothekenbank ZU Luebeck AG v Norman Philip Compton (The Alexion Hope)* [1988] 1 Lloyd's Rep. 311; [1988] FTLR 270; [1988] Fin. L.R. 131.

[43] *P Samuel & Co Ltd v Dumas (The Grigorios)*; sub nom. *P Samuel & Co Ltd v Motor Union Insurance Co Ltd* [1924] A.C. 431; (1924) 18 Ll. L. Rep. 211; 93 L.J.K.B. 415.

[44] *Slattery* [1962] 1 Q.B. 676 at 680-681; [1962] 2 W.L.R. 569 at 571–572; [1962] 1 All E.R. 525 at 526.

[45] See above, Ch.17.

[46] Compare H. Bennett, *The Law of Marine Insurance*, 2nd edn (Oxford: OUP, 2006), para.7.56 where the proposition that under an all risks policy wilful misconduct has to be proved by the insurer is criticised; *Slattery* [1962] 1 Q.B. 676; [1962] 2 W.L.R. 569; [1962] 1 All E.R. 525 is not there cited. It is true that loss must be fortuitous to be within all risks cover, but not in the "perils of the sea" sense of being independent of any deliberate human agency. Rather it must be fortuitous in the sense of being accidental from the point of view of the insured—a basic requirement which is surely also implicit in the notion of fire cover, and indeed any form of "insurance". Moreover, since all risks insurance takes effect as if all risks were separately enumerated (*Gaunt* [1921] 2 A.C. 41 at 57; 90 L.J.K.B. 801 at 807, per Lord Sumner), the insured could arguably circumvent the (supposed) need to disprove wilful misconduct by pleading loss due to a specific peril, so long as that peril is of a type which includes non-accidental loss, at least following the analysis of Donaldson J in *M Golodetz & Co Inc* [1980] 1 W.L.R. 495 at 513–514; [1979] 2 All E.R. 726 at 742; [1979] 2 Lloyd's Rep. 450 at 458.

court will look to the insurer to provide convincing evidence for the allegation rather than to the insured to negative it.[47]

22-011   There is a line of authority to the effect that the court must be satisfied to a high degree of probability that the insured set fire to the insured property before making a finding that he did so, on the principle that the degree of proof required of an allegation of criminal conduct must be commensurate with the gravity of the charge.[48] However, there is some tension between the effects of that rule and the rule that the burden remains on the insured to prove his account of how the loss occurred even if disbelieving that account effectively stigmatises him as having made a fraudulent claim.[49]

5.   EFFECT OF EXPRESS WORDING

22-012   **Reverse burden provisions.**   The normal rules on the burden of proof may be displaced by express words of the policy. In particular, an excluded peril may be subject to a provision that places the burden on the insured of proving that the loss or damage is not within the exclusion.[50] However, in *Spinney's (1948) Ltd, Spinney's Centres SAL and Michel Doumet, Joseph Doumet and Distributors and Agencies SAL v Royal Insurance Co Ltd*,[51] Mustill J suggested that a reverse burden clause "should not be construed in such a sense as to make the policy unworkable."[52] He considered that

> "the insurers cannot bring the clause into play simply by asserting that the loss was excluded by a particular exception, and challenging the insured to prove the contrary. They must produce evidence from which it can reasonably be argued that: (a) a state of affairs existed or an event occurred falling within an exception; and (b) the excepted peril directly or indirectly caused the loss. It is only when an arguable case of this nature is made out that the insured is required to disprove it."[53]

22-013   **Mysterious disappearance exclusions.**   Policies on stock in trade or other personal property sometimes include a clause exempting loss due to the "mysterious disappearance" of the insured property, e.g. "unexplained loss, mysterious disappearance or loss or shortage disclosed on taking inventory". Under an all risks policy the effect of such a clause is to reverse the rule in *Gaunt*[54] that the insured does not have to prove the specific manner in which the loss occurred. However, the insertion of a mysterious disappearance exclusion in an all risks policy has been criticised as:

---

[47]   *The Delphine* [2001] 2 Lloyd's Rep. 542 at 544; [2001] All E.R. (D) 222 (Apr) at [15]; *CA Blackwell (Contractors) Ltd v Gerling Allegemeine Verischerungs-AG* [2007] EWHC 94 (Comm) at [52]; [2007] Lloyd's Rep. I.R. 511 at 521.

[48]   *S & M Carpets (London) Ltd v Cornhill Insurance Co Ltd* [1981] 1 Lloyd's Rep. 667, affirmed [1982] 1 Lloyd's Rep. 423; *Watkins & Davis Ltd v Legal & General Assurance Co Ltd* [1981] 1 Lloyd's Rep. 674; *Polivitte Ltd v Commercial Union Assurance Co Plc* [1987] 1 Lloyd's Rep. 379.

[49]   *Regina Fur Co Ltd* [1958] 2 Lloyd's Rep. 425.

[50]   *Levy v Assicurazioni Generali* [1940] A.C. 791; [1940] 3 All E.R. 427; (1940) 67 Ll. L. Rep. 174; *Spinney's (1948) Ltd, Spinney's Centres SAL and Michel Doumet, Joseph Doumet and Distributors and Agencies SAL v Royal Insurance Co Ltd* [1980] 1 Lloyd's Rep. 406.

[51]   *Spinney's (1948) Ltd* [1980] 1 Lloyd's Rep. 406.

[52]   *Spinney's (1948) Ltd* [1980] 1 Lloyd's Rep. 406 at 426.

[53]   *Spinney's (1948) Ltd* [1980] 1 Lloyd's Rep. 406 at 426.

[54]   *Gaunt* [1921] 2 A.C. 41; 7 Ll. L. Rep. 62; 90 L.J.K.B. 801.

"...potentially inconsistent with the basic cover of the policy itself, because the very essence of all-risks cover is that the assured is entitled to succeed if he shows fortuitous loss and not how and why that loss occurred."[55]

On that basis US courts have given a restricted effect to such clauses.[56] Such hostility is hard to understand: there is no reason why the parties should not be able to contract for cover against the wide range of perils represented by all risks insurance whilst at the same time agreeing that it will be for the insured to prove how the loss occurred.

---

[55] *Colinvaux's Law of Insurance*, edited by R. Merkin, 10th edn (London: Sweet & Maxwell, 2014), para.19-100.

[56] *Betty* 310 F.2d 308 (4th Cir. 1962); *HCA Inc v American Protection Insurance Co* 174 S.W.3d 184 (Tenn. Ct. App. 2005).

CHAPTER 23

PAYMENT

1. INTRODUCTION

Payment: premiums and issues arising from payments made by insurers. A **23-001** number of issues may arise in relation to payment under an insurance policy. First is the payment of premiums under the policy by the insured, and this chapter considers the particular factors that may influence the level at which the premium is set by insurers under a CAR policy, together with the legal implications for non-payment by the insured. Secondly, the enactment of the Enterprise Act 2016 ("the 2016 Act") will impose new obligations on insurers to pay a policyholder's claim within a reasonable time of the claim being made, with damages available to the insured for the insurer's breach of this requirement. Thirdly, a number of disputes may also arise under a CAR policy regarding the correct use to which funds are put following payment by the insurer.

2. PAYMENT OF THE PREMIUM BY THE INSURED

Premium. Subject to inconsistent definition in the policy, the word "premium" **23-002** in the context of CAR policies shares the common meaning of the word in other policies of insurance. The definition, "the consideration required of the insured in return for which the insurer undertakes his obligations under the contract of insurance" has been repeatedly cited with approval.[1]

A CAR policy will usually set out key information such as whether a single premium is payable for the policy (or if further premiums are payable in subsequent years); when, where and how[2] premiums are to be paid, including whether or not

---

[1] The definition, is set out in *MacGillivray on Insurance Law*, edited by J. Birds, B. Lynch and S. Milnes, 13th edn (London: Sweet & Maxwell, 2015), para.7-002, and is drawn from *Lewis Ltd v Norwich Fire Insurance Co* [1916] A.C. 509 at 519 and was cited with approval in *Re Claims Direct Test Cases* [2003] EWCA Civ 136 at [25]; [2003] 4 All E.R. 508 at 516; [2003] Lloyd's Rep. I.R. 677 at 685.

[2] If an insured makes payment to a duly authorised agent of an insurer, absent any complicating factor, the premium will be deemed to have been received by the insurer. As a broker is typically employed by the insured, payment to a broker usually does not constitute payment to the insurer. Specific provision should be made in the drafting of the policy if the parties wish to achieve a different result.

payments are to be made by instalments; and whether there is a right of renewal and upon what terms.

23-003 Payment and cover. In common with most contracts of insurance, while the premium is commonly stated to be payable as soon as the risk arises,[3] subject to the terms of a particular policy, payment of the premium is not generally a condition precedent to the provision of cover under a CAR policy.

23-004 Formulation of policy premium. A large number of factors will have been taken into account in formulating the premium appropriate to a CAR policy. Given the range of factors considered and the fact that insurers will often apply their own historical data when assessing aspects of the same risk, quotes for premiums for the same project are likely to vary considerably across the market. In general, insurers will consider the property damage rates and third party liability rates separately.

23-005 Property damage rates. A common approach to the formulation of premium is as follows. Property damage rates typically take into account: (i) risk associated with the construction project in question; (ii) risk factors connected with the time over which risk will endure (e.g. the duration of the works, fire risk at particular points in construction and natural hazards); and (iii) the level of cover that is sought.

Insurers will often break the works up into discrete sections (such as into permanent and temporary works, which are likely to be subdivided further; and the replacement value of plant) with rates for each section adjusted to take into account matters such as time sensitive perils (both environmental and those that are inherent in the works, such as testing and commissioning phases). The premiums calculated for each section are added together to identify a total premium, which is then divided by the estimated contract price to obtain a provisional rate.

23-006 Third party liability rates. Premiums for any third party liability cover[4] offered under a policy tend to be calculated separately but are often included in the final premium for the policy. In setting the third party premium, insurers will usually take into account risks to neighbouring property and persons; the value of property, both that under construction and that surrounding the site; the proposed insureds' claims history; and potential consequential loss for surrounding property owners.

The final rates provide a useful benchmark for comparison across the market and can be employed usefully to re-fix premium rates where the contract price changes, if the policy so provides. This is dealt with in more detail below.[5]

23-007 Other forms of premium calculation. Other less common forms of premium calculation include an object/time method and the breakdown procedure. The former involves identifying rates appropriate to the nature of the project e.g. airport or office block and applying to that additional period related rates that reflect perils that could affect the works. The latter looks to break the works into phases, with rates apportioned to the phases according to the risks involved.

3　See, for example, the policy considered in *Swiss Reinsurance Co v United India Insurance Co Ltd* [2005] EWHC 237 (Comm); [2005] 2 All E.R. (Comm) 367; [2005] 1 C.L.C. 203.
4　See generally above, Ch.18.
5　See below, para.23-007.

Where a premium is calculated by reference to estimates provided at the inception of the policy, as is typically the case with project policies, it will commonly require the insured to provide the insurer with reasonable information, to enable the premium charged to be adjusted. Such a provision might provide for a premium to be adjustable on (or shortly prior to) the expiry of the period of cover, to take into account factors that increased the size of the risk, such as additional works or variations that occurred in the lifetime of the project.

Premiums in respect of annual policies will often be shaped by the contract value of the works, as declared by the insured to the insurer. As a result, the policy premium can be adjusted in subsequent years by reference to updated information as to the value of further contract works.

Policy renewal.   CAR policies typically provide cover up to the practical completion of works. As construction projects frequently call for additional work to be carried out after that date (due, for example, to variations to works that have been agreed) policies often make provision for cover to be extended on the payment of additional payments and acknowledgement by the insurer. Usually, the policy and/or any renewal notice that might be sent will state when, where and how any renewal premium is to be paid.   **23-008**

"Days of grace".   Typically, the policy will include "days of grace" provisions, which serve to extend the period over which payment can be made. Where used, the provisions usually provide that policy renewal is conditional on the payment of a premium within a particular time frame of the date on which it is stated to be due. Days of grace provisions are particularly useful in the context of CAR insurance, as they provide the insured parties with the opportunity to seek alternative coverage while retaining the option of continuing their existing cover; and by providing a degree of leeway, reduces the risk the insureds will be left without cover if a specific renewal date is overlooked in the short term.   **23-009**

To minimise disputes as to when the premium for any renewal period is to be paid, questions of cover in the grace period, and any rights of the insurer to refuse cover or amend cover, will be dealt with by well drafted policies expressly.

Failures to make payment.   Subject to the policy terms, a failure by the insured to pay premiums when they fall due may entitle the insurer to initiate proceedings for payment, to reject any claims raised until payment is made and/or forfeit or determine the policy of insurance.   **23-010**

Generally, an insurer will have a cause of action for the payment of premium when it falls due for payment. Whether or not an insurer is entitled to reject claims made pending the payment of premium will turn on the wording of the policy: the starting point is that the payment of the premium and payment of loss are not interdependent. An insurer will have a right to set-off unpaid premium against amounts claimed under the policy.[6] A CAR policy may adopt the following policy wording:

---

[6]   *Lake NNO v Reinsurance Corp Ltd* 1967 (3) S.A. 124 (W). See further *Accident Compensation Commission v CE Heath Underwriting and Insurance (Aust) Pty Ltd* [1990] Vic. Rp 21; [1990] V.R. 224.

"Insurers may, at their discretion, deduct overdue unpaid premium from claims settlements but shall not set off or deduct premium that is not overdue or any other amounts payable by [X] under or in relation to the Policy."

An insurer's rights where premiums are not paid (or paid late) will turn on the terms of the policy and standard contract principles. The policy wording may dictate that the conclusion of the policy and/or the initiation of the risk does not occur until payment has been received. Alternatively, the policy may stipulate the time for payment of the premium and any instalment. Provided the policy states explicitly that the payment provisions must be complied with, or that "time is to be of the essence" for payment (or clear words to the same effect), then, without more, late payment will constitute a repudiatory breach of contract entitling the insurer to terminate the policy. Where clear words are not employed, it is open to the insurer to make time of the essence by giving notice to the insured requiring payment within a reasonable time (and on a failure to make payment, equivalent principles are likely to apply). If no such notice is given then usual contractual rules are to be applied to determine whether the insured's conduct should be regarded as repudiatory breach of contract, entitling the insurer to bring the contract to an end.[7]

23-011   **The return of premium.** A CAR Policy may provide that in certain circumstances part or all of any premium paid by an insured will be repaid by the insurer. Commonly used clauses include "cancellation provisions". Allowing an insurer to cancel the policy on written notice, such clauses usually provide that where the premium has been paid in full the insured will be entitled to a rebate of a proportion of the premium to reflect the unexpired period of insurance. Other provisions include a right to a return of a proportionate part of premium paid where there is a reduction in the insured risk.

In general terms, if the insurer has never been on risk, any premium paid has not been earned and the insured is entitled to recover it.[8] However, CAR policies have historically provided that no premium will be returned where the insured stands in breach of his duty of utmost good faith. Indeed post the introduction of the Insurance Act 2015 ("the 2015 Act"), this position has not changed in that where the insured has committed a deliberate or reckless breach of the duty of fair presentation, the insurer will be entitled to the retention of the premium.[9] Further, subject to agreement to the contrary, once an insurer has been at risk under a policy, no premium is recoverable.[10] Questions may arise as to whether or not the risk is "apportionable" (in essence, whether the risks under the policy in question can be apportioned to parts of the premium paid) and whether the insured can recover part of the premium paid if the policy were brought to a premature end before some risk began. Ultimately, that is a matter of construction of the policy of insurance.[11]

---

[7]   For a useful discussion of key principles see *Figre Ltd v Mander* [1999] Lloyd's Rep. I.R. 193, per Cresswell J.

[8]   See *Stevenson v Snow* (1761) 3 Burr. 1237, per Lord Mansfield as discussed in *Clydesdale Financial Services Ltd v Smailes* [2009] EWHC 3190 (Ch) at [29]; [2011] 2 B.C.L.C. 405 at 427; [2010] Lloyd's Rep. I.R. 577 at 583.

[9]   See above, paras 5-075 and 5-078.

[10]   See *Swiss Reinsurance Co* [2005] EWHC 237 (Comm) at [22], [64]–[65]; [2005] 2 All E.R. (Comm) 367 at 373, 384–385; [2005] 1 C.L.C. 203 at 212 and 226.

[11]   For a useful application of the principles in the context of a CAR Policy, see *Swiss Reinsurance Co* [2005] EWHC 237 (Comm); [2005] 2 All E.R. (Comm) 367; [2005] 1 C.L.C. 203. See also above, Ch.13.

While the matter has yet to be dealt with directly in modern cases,[12] it is likely that in keeping with the prevailing position in maritime insurance that the courts would find that an insurer will not be required to return premiums in the case of fraud on the part of the insured.[13]

Circumstances in which an insured might look to recover premium(s) paid **23-012** include the following. First, (subject to any rights of rectification that the insured may have) the insured may seek to recover premium where the policy of insurance issued was not on the terms of the application made, or is otherwise void. Secondly, pre the introduction of the 2015 Act the insured may have been entitled to the return of the premium where the policy of insurance was avoided by the insurer ab initio on grounds of innocent misrepresentation or non-fraudulent non-disclosure.[14] Similar principles apply where a policy is avoided by the insured on account of misrepresentation or failure to disclose material facts by the insurer.[15] However, now under the 2015 Act, it is important to note the insured has the right to recover the premium where a non-deliberate and non-reckless breach of the duty of fair presentation entitles the insurer to the remedy of avoidance.[16] Thirdly, where the insured stands in breach of a condition precedent to the inception of the risk, he is entitled to recover the premium(s) paid on the basis that the risk had not begun to run.[17]

3. DAMAGES FOR LATE PAYMENT OF CLAIMS BY THE INSURER

The hold harmless principle. A legal fiction in the law of insurance is that an **23-013** insurer's primary obligation under the policy is to prevent the insured losses from materialising in the first place, rather than the insurer having a contractual duty to compensate the insured for its losses. This fiction is known as the "hold harmless" principle, and in exchange for the payment of the premium the insured enjoys the benefit of being "held harmless" by the insurer against any of the insured losses. Thus, for example, an insurer would be in breach of its primary obligation under a fire policy as soon as a fire occurred on the insured premises, and would have to pay *damages* to the insured for the losses occasioned by that fire. Were the hold harmless principle to be absent from the law, the insurer's contractual obligations would instead relate only to the *reimbursement* of the actual loss suffered by the insured, and the insurer would owe *damages* in the event of any failure to pay. This legal fiction is absent from many other major common law jurisdictions and carries a number of significant implications for both parties to an insurance policy.

The first consequence of the "hold harmless" principle is that, for the majority

---

[12] See *MacGillivray on Insurance Law*, edited by Birds, Lynch and Milnes, 13th edn (2015), paras 8-028 to 8-030 and in *Colinvaux's Law of Insurance*, edited by R. Merkin, 10th edn (London: Sweet & Maxwell, 2014), para.8-029 for a discussion of the earlier case law.

[13] See further *MacGillivray on Insurance Law*, edited by Birds, Lynch and Milnes, 13th edn (2015), paras 8-028 to 8-030.

[14] *Anderson v Fitzgerald* (1853) 4 H.L. Cas. 484; 10 E.R. 551. See further the discussion of the case in *Pan Atlantic Insurance Co Ltd v Pine Top Insurance Co Ltd* [1995] 1 A.C. 501 at 508.

[15] *Carter v Boehm* (1766) 3 Burr. 1905; 97 E.R. 1162. See further discussion of the case in *Drake Insurance Plc (In Provisional Liquidation) v Provident Insurance Plc* [2003] EWCA Civ 1834 at 166; [2004] Q.B. 601 at 646–647; [2004] 2 W.L.R. 530 at 575–576.

[16] See above, para.5-073.

[17] Where the term in question was a condition subsequent to the commencement of the policy, the insured is generally not entitled to recover premiums paid.

of cases, the date of the insurer's breach of duty is affixed onto the date of the loss. This has the result that both limitation and interest are calculated as from the date that the loss occurred rather than at the later date of, for example, the insurer being notified of the claim or the insurer's failure to pay the claim within a reasonable time.

A second consequence of this legal fiction was recognised by the Court of Appeal in *Sprung v Royal Insurance (UK) Ltd*.[18] Mr Sprung had owned a business involved with the collection, processing and redistribution of animal waste products and had taken out a theft policy with Royal Insurance (UK) Ltd to cover plant and machinery held and operated in one of his abattoirs. On 5 April 1986 the premises were broken into by vandals and the machinery was damaged, causing losses to Mr Sprung of around £30,000. Royal Insurance (UK) Ltd denied liability for the majority of the damage and refused to make payment under the policy until March 1990, by which point Mr Sprung's business had collapsed without the financial resources necessary to carry out repairs. The trial judge found that the insurers should have paid the claim by the end of October 1986, and because of their failure to do so Mr Sprung had also lost out on the opportunity to sell the business to a competitor that year. This loss was calculated at £75,000, and the Court of Appeal had to determine whether this was an additional loss that was recoverable from the insurers separate and in addition to the £30,000 for the indemnity. Delivering the leading judgment of the Court, Evans LJ found that the claim was not recoverable as it would amount to a claim for damages on damages. He said:

"As a matter of law, it seems to me that the decisions already referred to show that there cannot be a claim for damages of this sort where the breach of contract relied upon is the late payment or non-payment of a sum of money by way of damages."[19]

Although the decision was reached "[w]ith undisguised reluctance",[20] Evans LJ found himself compelled to reach the conclusion that an insured was only entitled to interest for the late payment of insurance claims rather than being able to claim separately for damages. This position holds true under the law as currently enacted.

23-014   Statutory reform. The prohibition against damages for the late payment of insurance claims has attracted substantial and compelling criticism as lacking in principle, being biased against the interests of the insured, failing to reflect commercial reality and being out of step with general contractual principles and expectations.[21] The prejudice suffered in Mr Sprung's case heralded a clear warning of the injustice that could result from insurers refusing to pay claims on time and taking every available avenue to delay payment with legal impunity, though such fears would have been allayed to some extent by the detriment suffered to an insurer's international reputation if it adopted such tactics as a matter of routine. Late payment has attracted yet more significance in the wake of the 2007–2008 financial crisis, as the retreat of many bank lenders from financing construction

---

18   *Sprung v Royal Insurance (UK) Ltd* [1997] C.L.C. 70; [1999] Lloyd's Rep. I.R. 111.
19   *Sprung v Royal Insurance (UK) Ltd* [1997] C.L.C. 70 at 76; [1999] Lloyd's Rep. I.R. 111 at 116.
20   *Sprung v Royal Insurance (UK) Ltd* [1997] C.L.C. 70 at 79; [1999] Lloyd's Rep. I.R. 111 at 118.
21   Law Commission and the Scottish Law Commission "Insurance Contract Law: Business Disclosure; Warranties; Insurers' Remedies for Fraudulent Claims; and Late Payment" (HMSO, 2014). *http://www.lawcom.gov.uk/wp-content/uploads/2015/03/lc353_insurance-contract-law.pdf* [Accessed 24 June 2016], ch.26.

projects has required more businesses to become dependent on insurance to survive after a substantial loss event and the timely payment of any insurance claims will therefore be crucial to avoid escalating losses.[22]

Statutory reform in this area was proposed by the Law Commission and the Scottish Law Commission in their July 2014 report on insurance contract law,[23] though the proposed reforms were ultimately omitted from the 2015 Act as they were deemed too contentious to be included given the opposing views of many stakeholders. The proposals were reconsidered and incorporated into the 2016 Act, which received royal assent on 4 May 2016.

The Enterprise Act 2016. Part 5 of the 2016 Act inserts a new s.13A into the **23-015** 2015 Act which introduces an implied term into every contract of insurance that the insurer will pay the insured's claim within a reasonable time. The new provisions come into force on 4 May 2017[24] and the implied term will be incorporated into all insurance policies incepted after that date, but will not apply to policies entered into before 4 May 2017 and subsequently varied after the provisions come into force.[25]

Reasonable time. Section 13A(1) of the new provisions establishes the implied **23-016** term, and provides as follows:

> "It is an implied term of every contract of insurance that if the insured makes a claim under the contract, the insurer must pay any sums due in respect of the claim within a reasonable time."

A breach of this implied term by the insurer will allow the insured to claim for separate and additional losses to those claimed for the underlying indemnity, provided such losses were caused by the insurer's unreasonable refusal to pay the insurance claim on time. Because the new provisions introduce an implied contractual term into insurance policies rather than creating a standalone statutory duty, the term will be subject to the normal contractual principles of factual causation, remoteness and mitigation which the courts will use to contain the new obligations within a balanced remit. The concept of "reasonableness" is defined in ss.(2) and (3) of s.13A (which is to be inserted into the 2015 Act), together offer guidance as to how the courts will assess whether an insurer has complied with this new obligation. The provisions state:

> "(2) A reasonable time includes a reasonable time to investigate and assess the claim.

---

22 Law Commission and the Scottish Law Commission "Insurance Contract Law: Business Disclosure; Warranties; Insurers' Remedies for Fraudulent Claims; and Late Payment" (HMSO, 2014). *http:// www.lawcom.gov.uk/wp-content/uploads/2015/03/lc353_insurance-contract-law.pdf* [Accessed 24 June 2016], ch.26 at para.26.9.

23 Law Commission and the Scottish Law Commission "Insurance Contract Law: Business Disclosure; Warranties; Insurers' Remedies for Fraudulent Claims; and Late Payment" (HMSO, 2014). *http:// www.lawcom.gov.uk/wp-content/uploads/2015/03/lc353_insurance-contract-law.pdf* [Accessed 24 June 2016], ch.26 at para.26.9.

24 Section 44(3) of the Enterprise Act 2016 (the "2016 Act") provides that "[s]ections 28 to 30 (late payment of insurance claims) come into force at the end of the period of one year beginning with the day on which this Act is passed (and section 23(2) of the Insurance Act 2015 (which provides for the coming into force of provisions of that Act) does not apply to the provisions inserted into that Act by those sections)."

25 Section 28(2) of the 2016 Act provides "[i]n section 22 of that Act (application etc of Parts 2 to 5), after subsection (3) insert— "(3A) Part 4A applies only in relation to contracts of insurance entered into after that Part has come into force, and variations to such contracts."

(3)　What is reasonable will depend on all the relevant circumstances, but the following are examples of things which may need to be taken into account—

    (a)　the type of insurance,

    (b)　the size and complexity of the claim,

    (c)　compliance with any relevant statutory or regulatory rules or guidance,

    (d)　factors outside the insurer's control."

Though the provisions identify a non-exhaustive list of the factors that the courts may take into account in their assessment, what amounts to "a reasonable time" will ultimately depend on the facts of any particular case. Challenges under the new provisions are likely to be invoked by policyholders in circumstances where there has been a clear and substantial time lag between the notification of the claim and the eventual pay out, and although the burden of proof will rest on the insured to substantiate its claim for breach of the implied term, it is likely that in such circumstances the practical effect will be that the insurer must justify the length of time taken to investigate the claim. Whilst the type of insurance and the size and complexity of the claim can be established without recourse to the details of an insurer's investigation into the claim, it may benefit the insurer to adduce documentation or other evidence of its claims process in order to demonstrate where each portion of the time was spent and, accordingly, which portions of the total investigative time are attributable to reasonable time taken to investigate the claim. Particularly where any factors are outside of the insurer's control, such as a surge in claims resulting from a natural disaster or a failure by the insured to respond timeously to an insurer's request for information, the courts are likely to extend the allotted reasonable time for payment to incorporate those delays. Finally, it may benefit the insurer to establish that a later date for payment than the date proposed by the insured would have been reasonable even where there is clear evidence that the claim should have been paid earlier than it was, as a finding on those terms may make it more difficult for the insured to establish that the shorter delay was the proximate cause of any losses sustained.

In relation to CAR insurance, the assessment of a reasonable time for payment may prove to be more complex than in other areas of insurance. A typical CAR policy will provide for the amount of the indemnity to be calculated as the cost of reinstatement following loss or damage to the building works, and such costs may be difficult for the insurer to assess in advance. In such circumstances it may be reasonable for an insurer to wait until the costs of reinstatement have been determined before making any payment under the policy, and circumstances (a) and (b) permit the courts to take such factors into account when assessing the length of time that is reasonable. However, that is not to say that it will be reasonable for the insurer to make no payment under the policy at all until the ultimate net cost of reinstatement has been ascertained; the statutory provisions are intended to balance the insured's interest in prompt payment against the capacity of the insurer to fully investigate a claim before making payment, and it would frustrate this balance if the insurer had no obligation to pay the claim until the very last. The insurer is entitled to enough time to make a detailed assessment of the claim, which must include time to ascertain the cause of damage and the approximate value of any losses. Although such measures are not envisaged by the explicit wording of the statute, there may also arise circumstances in which it would be reasonable for the insurer to make payment of a definite portion of the losses by way of interim payment if such losses can be clearly distinguished from other losses which will require further investigation. Whether the courts take a wholesale approach to the allotted time for investigating the claim or whether they are amenable to arguments that the lion's share of the losses should clearly have been paid within a particular timeframe is likely to be debated and elucidated in the case law which follows after the provisions come into force.

The assessment of a "reasonable time" for payment may be particularly difficult to apply in relation to delay in start up ("DSU") insurance claims.[26] A detailed assessment of a DSU claim will often be a complex and substantial undertaking, and the full measure of the delays caused by a particular indemnifiable event will frequently not be known until the project is completed. There may be substantial factual disputes concerning the cause of any delays or whether a period of delay relates to an insured or uninsured event, which may require a complex critical path analysis to be conducted before the extent of the insured delay can be ascertained. In some cases, the legal cause of different periods of delay may not be established until a decision is reached in court years after the project is completed. In such circumstances, it may not be reasonable to require the insurer to pay the claim before the measure of losses attributable to an insured event becomes fully apparent.

More general guidance on the impact of market practice on the assessment of a "reasonable time" was provided by the 2014 Law Commission and the Scottish Law Commission report on insurance contract law.[27] Following consultation on whether "market practice" should be included within the statute as a further distinct category of circumstances that the courts may take into account when assessing the reasonable time for payment of a claim, the Law Commissions decided against the inclusion of such a category and instead endorsed the viewpoint of K&L Gates LLP and Covington & Burling LLP that market practice should not be accepted by the courts at face value to relieve an insurer of liability. The report quotes K&L Gates LLP who said:

> "We are concerned at the suggestion that a concept as nebulous as 'market practice' should be included within any definition of 'reasonable time' as it might be used as a basis for insurers to justify delay. There may well be divergences of opinion as to what is market practice, and just because a practice has grown up in the insurance market does not necessarily mean it is right."[28]

Whilst voluntary protocols and accepted industry practice may provide the context against which the courts will assess the reasonableness of the time taken by an insurer to make a payment for a claim, the reasonableness of that time will ultimately remain a question concerning the facts of the particular case and the circumstances of the particular claim. Where there is any doubt about the correct application of the test of reasonableness to a set of facts, the objective of the courts will remain to provide an appropriate balance between allowing the insurer to undertake a detailed assessment of the claim and allowing the insured to receive payment reasonably promptly; where the guidance provided by the statute is insuf-

---

[26] Delay in start up ("DSU") insurance is considered in greater detail above in Ch.17.

[27] Law Commission and the Scottish Law Commission "Insurance Contract Law: Business Disclosure; Warranties; Insurers' Remedies for Fraudulent Claims; and Late Payment" (HMSO, 2014). http://www.lawcom.gov.uk/wp-content/uploads/2015/03/lc353_insurance-contract-law.pdf [Accessed 24 June 2016].

[28] Law Commission and the Scottish Law Commission "Insurance Contract Law: Business Disclosure; Warranties; Insurers' Remedies for Fraudulent Claims; and Late Payment" (HMSO, 2014). http://www.lawcom.gov.uk/wp-content/uploads/2015/03/lc353_insurance-contract-law.pdf [Accessed 24 June 2016] at para.28.39.

ficient to determine whether the length of time taken was reasonable, such considerations may prove to be the decisive factor.

23-017 **Reasonable grounds for disputing the claim.** Under s.13A(4) (which is to be inserted into the 2015 Act), an insurer will have a defence to any claim for late payment where it can show that it had reasonable grounds for disputing the claim:

> "(4) If the insurer shows that there were reasonable grounds for disputing the claim (whether as to the amount of any sum payable, or as to whether anything at all is payable)—
>
> (a) the insurer does not breach the term implied by subsection (1) merely by failing to pay the claim (or the affected part of it) while the dispute is continuing, but
>
> (b) the conduct of the insurer in handling the claim may be a relevant factor in deciding whether that term was breached and, if so, when."

To avail of this defence, the insurer must adduce sufficient evidence to substantiate that a dispute was ongoing through any period in which it failed to pay the claim. Such evidence may take the form of communications with the insured, instructions to loss adjusters or more general insurers' criteria for claims management. However, an internal criteria document is unlikely to be taken at face value as establishing those matters which constitute "reasonable grounds" for disputing a claim. The purpose of the provision is to allow an insurer to dispute a claim all the way to the courtroom without being at risk of becoming liable for consequential losses in the event that it loses the substantive dispute on the indemnity, and it is axiomatic that an insurer must be free to do so where there are grounds for suspecting that the claim may be fraudulent or the insurer might otherwise not be liable for the damage.

The insurer's conduct under s.14(A)(b) may be sufficient to establish the liability of the insurer for breach of the implied term even where there was a dispute between the parties and the insurer had reasonable grounds for continuing that dispute. An insurer may suspect that a claim was fraudulent on the basis of a single piece of evidence, and that evidence will remain a reasonable ground for disputing the claim up to and until further evidence is discovered which renders the chance of fraud unlikely or remote. In such circumstances, the conduct of the insurer will become relevant to determine whether it acted in breach of the implied term, and the continued existence of a reasonable ground for disputing the claim will not entitle the insurer to disregard its duty to continue investigating the claim with reasonable expedience.

23-018 **Remedies.** Damages will be available to the insured for a breach of the implied term to pay the claim within a reasonable time, and such damages will be in addition to and distinct from any right to enforce payment of the underlying claim and any interest on that payment.[29] The obligation takes effect as an implied contractual term in the underlying policy and so the usual rules concerning causation, remote-

---

29 Section 13A(5) which is to be inserted into the Insurance Act 2015 (the "2015 Act") provides that "[r]emedies (for example, damages) available for breach of the term implied by subsection (1) are in addition to and distinct from— (a) any right to enforce payment of the sums due, and (b) any right to interest on those sums (whether under the contract, under another enactment, at the court's discretion or otherwise)."

ness and mitigation that limit claims for breach of contract will apply to claims for breach of the implied term.

Causation, remoteness, mitigation. In accordance with ordinary contractual **23-019** principles, there are three principal limits on the ability of an insured to recover for a breach of the implied term: the insurer's failure to pay within a reasonable time must be the proximate cause of the loss, the losses sustained must not be too remote and the insured is under a duty to mitigate its losses.

Issues of causation may pose unusual difficulties for the insured in relation to the late payment of insurance claims. The insured must establish that the delay in payment between what would have been the last reasonable date for payment and the actual date at which the insurer paid the claim was the proximate cause of the consequential losses suffered. Where such losses would have been sustained in any event had the insurer paid the claim at the last date which would have been reasonable, those losses will not be recoverable by the insured. Similarly, where the unavailability of funds was contributed to or caused by a number of different debts or other losses, it may be difficult for the insured to establish "but for" causation if it would have remained impecunious regardless of whether the insurer had paid a particular claim on time or not.

For a claim made under a CAR policy, the most likely causal burden on the insured will be to establish that a late payment by the insurer delayed the reinstatement of the works and caused a knock-on delay to the entire project and a number of associated losses. A number of different factors may be relevant to this assessment: a critical path analysis may be required to establish the delay attributable to the lapse in payment; consideration may be given to any funding available to the employer (including alternative financing options) to begin reinstatement before the insurer's payment; a court may also consider whether an employer should have given an instruction to accelerate construction to the contractor, though such a concern is more likely to fall under the head of mitigation.

The insured will only be entitled to recover those losses which were within the reasonable contemplation of the parties at the time the policy was concluded, in accordance with the classic statement of the test for remoteness in *Hadley v Baxendale*[30] which states:

> "Where two parties have made a contract which one of them has broken, the damages which the other party ought to receive in respect of such breach of contract should be such as may fairly and reasonably be considered either [1] arising naturally, i.e. according to the usual course of things, from such breach of contract itself, or [2] such as may reasonably be supposed to have been in the contemplation of both parties, at the time they made the contract, as the probable result of the breach of it. Now, if the special circumstances under which the contract was actually made were communicated by the plaintiffs to the defendants, and thus known to both parties, the damages resulting from the breach of such a contract, which they would reasonably contemplate, would be the amount of injury which would ordinarily follow from a breach of contract under these special circumstances so known and communicated."[31]

An insurer will be liable under the first limb for any losses that arise naturally out of a delay to a construction project, and may additionally be liable under the second limb for special circumstances which had been communicated to it from the insured during the underwriting process. Where the building project is procured under a

---

[30] *Hadley v Baxendale* 156 E.R. 145; (1854) 9 Ex. 341.
[31] *Hadley v Baxendale* 156 E.R. 145 at 151; (1854) 9 Ex. 341 at 355–356.

financing agreement with a third party lender, there may be special or unusual losses for delay if the lender becomes entitled to pursue remedies against the employer under the terms of the financing agreement for a failure to complete on time. In the usual course of things, an insurer will request copies of any financing agreements before concluding the CAR policy with the insured, and in such circumstances those losses would be recoverable under the second limb of *Hadley v Baxendale*. However, there may still be some scope for an insured to assert that such losses should be recoverable under the first limb of *Hadley v Baxendale* where the insurer was not made aware of the precise terms of the financing agreement. Those losses which arise according to the usual course of things must be considered against the commercial context in which the policy was entered into, and it is a matter of common knowledge that many projects are financed by a number of third parties under agreements which may impose severe consequences for the employer upon a failure to complete the project on time. Accordingly, the courts may be tempted to find that such losses fall under the first limb of *Hadley v Baxendale* and are therefore, in principle, recoverable even if the insurer had no actual knowledge of the terms or even existence of any financing agreements.

An insured's duty to mitigate its losses may also limit the amount recoverable on any claim for late payment. However, such a limit is unlikely to play a significant role under the new reforms as the losses occasioned by late payment will generally result from the insured's impecuniosity, and an insured would not be in breach of its duty to mitigate for failing to do that which it cannot afford. Accordingly, an insurer would have greater prospects of limiting the recovery of consequential losses on the basis of a failure to mitigate if the alleged failures occurred after the insurance claim was in fact paid, such as a failure by the employer to issue instructions to accelerate the project.

23-020   **Limitation.**   Section 30 of the 2016 Act introduces a new s.5A into the Limitation Act 1980 (the "1980 Act") which establishes the time limit for an insured to bring any action for the late payment of insurance claims. Section 5A(1) provides that time starts to run as soon as the insurer pays the underlying indemnity claim, and the insured will have a year after which to bring any claim for late payment. It states:

> "An action in respect of breach of the term implied into a contract of insurance by section 13A of the Insurance Act 2015 (late payment of claims) may not be brought after the expiration of one year from the date on which the insurer has paid all the sums referred to in subsection (1) of that section."

Section 5A(2) of the new provisions to be inserted into the 1980 Act covers those circumstances in which an insurance claim is resolved by way of a settlement agreement rather than the insurer paying the full claim. The wording of the provision provides that limitation will begin to run on the payment of any sums which extinguish an insurer's liability for a claim. It states:

> "Any payment which extinguishes an insurer's liability to pay a sum referred to in section 13A of the Insurance Act 2015 is to be treated for the purposes of this section as payment of that sum."

23-021   **Contracting out.**   In accordance with the other provisions contained within the 2015 Act, the parties are free to contract out of the provisions for late payment provided any changes are made in accordance with the transparency requirements.[32] Section 29 of the 2016 Act introduces a new s.16A into the 2015 Act which regulates the extent to which the late payment provisions may be contracted out of. Section 16A(4) provides:

> "A term of a non-consumer insurance contract, or of any other contract, which would put the insured in a worse position as respects any of the other matters provided for in section 13A than the insured would be in by virtue of the provisions of that section (so far as relating to non-consumer insurance contracts) is to that extent of no effect, unless the requirements of section 17 have been satisfied in relation to the term."

A term which contracts out of the effects of s.13A (to be inserted into the 2015 Act) is defined as any term which places the insured in a worse position than they would otherwise have been in under the statutory provisions. Thus a contractual term purporting to allow an insurer additional time to investigate a claim on the occurrence of various circumstances will be contracting out of s.13A if its practical effect is to allow the insurer more than a "reasonable" time to investigate a claim, and such a term must therefore meet the transparency requirements if it is to have contractual effect. The transparency requirements are contained in s.17 of the 2015 Act and impose procedural hurdles that the insurer must satisfy in order to impose terms which have the effect of placing the insured in a worse position than they would be under statute, and are discussed above in more detail above at para.5-135.

Section 16A(2) which is to be inserted into the 2015 Act introduces a limit on an insurer's capacity to contract out of the new obligation to pay claims within a reasonable time where the insurer's breach of that term is deliberate or reckless. It states:

> "A term of a non-consumer insurance contract, or of any other contract, which would put the insured in a worse position as respects deliberate or reckless breaches of the term implied by section 13A than the insured would be in by virtue of that section is to that extent of no effect."

Following usual legal principles, the burden of proof will be on the insured to establish that a breach of the implied term was committed deliberately or recklessly by the insurer. Deliberate or reckless breaches are defined under s.16A(3) which is to be inserted into the 2015 Act in the following manner:

> "(3) For the purposes of subsection (2) a breach is deliberate or reckless if the insurer—
> (a) knew that it was in breach, or
> (b) did not care whether or not it was in breach."

Accordingly, the provisions incorporate the same test used under the 2015 Act to determine whether an insured's breach of the duty of fair presentation was committed intentionally or recklessly, discussed above at paras 5-075 to 5-076. Incorporating a blanket ban on an insurer's capacity to contract out of the implied term as regards deliberate or reckless breaches will allow an insured to claim damages for an insurer's late payment even where the policy specifically provides that no such damages will be available in any event, subject to the insured being able to establish a deliberate or reckless breach.

Finally, s.16A(6) which is to be inserted into the 2015 Act provides that the contracting out provisions do not apply to any settlement agreements. The parties

---

[32] See above, para.5-135.

are therefore able to reach a settlement of any claims under an insurance policy which precludes the rights of an insured to bring any future late payment claims.

4. SUMS PAID BY THE INSURER UNDER A CAR POLICY

23-022 **Treatment of sums paid by the insurer in the context of joint names insurance.** Joint names policies[33] will typically dictate the mode in which payment for claims will be made. They may state that the payment (or payments under or over a certain amount) are to be made to a particular insured, but may also state that payment is to be made to a third party, such as a loss payee. That loss payee may be a project funder, lending or a holding bank. Such policy wording may be akin to the following:

> "In respect of payment under this Policy:
>
> a.   All claim payments over [x] shall be paid into [bank account held in the names of the joint insured] or to such other account as the [loss payee] may specify in writing.
> b.   All claim payments less than [x] shall be paid into [an account held in the name of a particular insured] or to such other account as the [loss payee] may specify in writing."

It is not uncommon for the designated loss payee to be one of the insureds. Conflicts of interest can arise where, for example, the joint insureds under a policy are the employer and a contractor of a particular project. In the event the contractor carried out works which caused damage, triggering a payment out by the insurer to the employer (as loss payee), questions can arise as to what the employer is required and/or entitled to do with those funds together with what rights (if any) the contractor has to those funds. Absent specific wording in the CAR policy and/or the contract(s) of works dealing with those issues, the questions are essentially at large.

Similar issues can arise in the context of public liability and loss of revenue cover. In respect of public liability cover, policy wording might be drafted along the lines of:

> "In respect of payment under this Policy of public liability risks only all claims payments in respect of a third party liability shall be paid to person(s) whose claim(s) constitute the risk or liability insured against except in the case where the Insured has properly discharged its liability to such person(s), in which case the claim payment shall be made to the [account held in the name of a particular insured] or such account as the [loss payee] directs in writing."

The scope for controversy is reduced by the fact that, in the first instance, the insurer will make payment to a qualifying third party claimant. However, the operation of such a clause may give rise to circumstances where an insurer is, again, obliged to make a payment out to the employer (as loss payee) with the scope for questions to arise as to what the employer is required/entitled to do with the funds (and what rights, if any, the contractor could have to those funds).

In a similar vein, the same lacuna could exist in the context of loss of revenue cover, where wording to the effect that "all claim payments or return premiums shall be paid to the [account held in the name of a particular party] or such other account as the [loss payee] directs in writing", could generate a similar situation.

In general, on one view it is certainly arguable that, by parity of reasoning with *Lonsdale & Thompson Ltd v Black Arrow Group Plc*; sub nom. *Lonsdale &*

---

[33] See generally above, Ch.20.

Thompson Ltd v Black Arrow Group Plc and American International Underwriters UK Ltd[34] and *Talbot Underwriting Ltd v Nausch Hogan & Murray Inc (The Jascon 5)*[35]; that the employer might be said to hold a proportion of the sums on trust for its co-insured, the contractor.[36] In practice, further issues can arise including the extent to which an employer should be entitled to set-off against those sums claims for damages under the works contract. It is clearly arguable that to adopt such an approach would be inconsistent with both the foregoing, and the non-fault regime established by most CAR policies. The issue can be, and under some policies usefully is, avoided through the use of language that provides specifically that a joint insured is not permitted to set-off in that manner.

Interim payment of indemnified sums.   CAR policies will frequently provide **23-023** that sums paid under the indemnity will be made by way of instalments or stage payments. By way of example, insurers often engage the services of loss adjusters who will examine the claims presented and it may be agreed with the contractor that stage payments to cover reinstatement costs will be made at regular intervals (or, potentially, when those works have been completed).

Where liability is in dispute, and proceedings have been issued, an insured may be in a position to apply to the court under CPR Pt 25 for an interim payment in respect of sums claimed from the insurer. It should be noted that CPR Pt 25 sets out strict criteria limiting the circumstances in which an interim payment will be made.

---

[34] *Lonsdale & Thompson Ltd v Black Arrow Group Plc* [1993] Ch. 361; [1993] 2 W.L.R. 815; [1993] 3 All E.R. 648.

[35] *Talbot Underwriting Ltd v Nausch Hogan & Murray Inc (The Jascon 5)* [2006] EWCA Civ 889; [2006] 2 All E.R. (Comm) 75; [2006] 2 Lloyd's Rep. 195.

[36] A further point of dispute could well be what proportion of those sums the employer should hold on trust for the contractor.

MARINE ALL RISKS

1. INTRODUCTION

Marine and land-based CAR. Much of modern insurance law has maritime **24-001**
roots; land-based CAR is no exception. The terms of CAR policies for land-based
construction works are often similar to those found in marine policies, and may be
interpreted by reference to decided cases on the latter. However, contractors who
work mainly in marine construction should understand the special risks involved,
and the need to obtain specialised CAR insurance for this type of work. This chapter
discusses a number of specialised all risks policies frequently encountered in the
marine construction field.

Marine construction works and risks. The marine construction industry **24-002**
employs large numbers of specialists, including marine and subsurface contractors, marine surveyors, specialist architects and engineers, shipyards and heavy lift
transporters, etc, some or all of whom may be involved, at different stages, in a
project. Marine construction works[1] may be undertaken onshore (in docks and
harbours), inshore (such as coastal-protection works), and offshore (e.g. offshore

---

[1] Sometimes referred to as "wet risks".

operating structures and ancillary structures, such as living quarters, which are designed and constructed onshore and then positioned far out at sea).

Marine construction often carries special, substantial risks. For example, in constructing an offshore platform the components are typically fabricated in a yard or dock, loaded out onto a vessel or floated, and then carried or towed to their intended final offshore location. Once arrived they must be positioned and then, depending on the nature of the component, submerged and fixed with piles or by permanent moorings, or "mated" atop a previously installed structure or "jacket". The platform will then need to be connected and tied-in, e.g. to various risers or pipes, fitted-out, tested and commissioned, before it can begin to operate. In carrying out these steps in the project there will, clearly, be many different risks—some of them specific to work in a marine environment—to which the project works will be exposed and that a marine policy should cover.

The types of property with which marine contractors and specialists may be involved as part of a marine-construction project can vary enormously depending on the nature of the project. If contractors are working at a shipyard, port, or in and around the waterfront, they may need to, for example, obtain cover against physical loss or damage to slipways, piers, jetties, berths, wharves, port craft (such as tugs and floating cranes) and specialist equipment. Inshore and offshore, given the increasing demands for energy, marine contractors working in the energy field are now involved with more innovative and challenging projects, requiring them to bring together a wide range of skills in order to deliver a project. Specialist marine contractors may install wave- or tidal-energy machines or wind turbines, fix or moor structures and units to the seabed, carry out dredging, trenching and cable burial. In relation to offshore oil and gas, they also install, inspect and repair structures, pipelines, and other property, undertaking underwater welding and cutting, drilling and piling, and demolition or decommissioning work. Contractors involved in non-energy-related work may construct coastal protection or defences, carry out underwater blasting and dredging, install sheet piles, undertake concrete work both above and below water, repair and maintain existing structures, or build ships or ship-like structures.

Frequently, important financial losses to the parties interested in marine construction projects will result from the wind, waves and action of the sea increasing the costs of construction. Delays due to bad weather and to difficulties in working in the marine environment are also important considerations. Some marine policies can cover such exposures.

24-003 **Marine insurance and marine "all risks" insurance.** Marine insurance typically provides those with an interest in a vessel or cargo with protection against loss, damage or liability that may be incurred as a result of the "maritime perils".[2] Of the

---

[2] The Marine Insurance Act 1906 ("MIA"), ss.1 and 3, codified the common law's notions of "marine insurance" and "maritime perils" as they stood at that time:

"1. A contract of marine insurance is a contract whereby the insurer undertakes to indemnify the assured ... against marine losses, that is to say, the losses incident to marine adventure."

"3.(1) Subject to the provisions of this Act, every lawful marine adventure may be the subject of a contract of marine insurance. (2) In particular, there is a marine adventure where—(a) Any ship goods or other moveables are exposed to maritime perils ...; (b) The earning or acquisition of any freight, passage money, commission, profit, or other pecuniary benefit, or the security for any advances, loan, or disbursements, is endangered by the exposure of insurable property to maritime perils; (c) Any liability to a third party may be incurred by the owner of, or other person

[648]

broad categories of marine insurance,[3] those most obviously relevant to marine construction are first-party property insurance on hull[4] and cargo,[5] and insurance against third-party marine liability.[6]

This chapter is focused primarily on three standard "all risks" policy wordings, that are commonly encountered in the context of marine construction.[7] These are:

---

    interested in or responsible for, insurable property, by reason of maritime perils. 'Maritime perils' means the perils consequent on, or incidental to, the navigation of the sea, that is to say, perils of the seas, fire, war perils, pirates, rovers, thieves, captures, seisures, restraints, and detainments of princes and peoples, jettisons, barratry, and any other perils, either of the like kind or which may be designated by the policy."

[3] There are other, important categories of marine insurance, covering other, particularly financial, interests, e.g. insurance against loss of freight, loss of hire or loss of earnings, and mortgagee's interest insurance ("MII"). These are not considered further here. Further, it is worth noting that until 1982, the standard form of marine insurance policy in London was the "Lloyd's S.G. policy". Created 12 January 1799, it is thought that the letter "S" stands for ship and the letter "G" for goods. The S.G. form's former ubiquity is demonstrated by its inclusion in the Sch.1 to the MIA. In 1982 and 1983, the London market introduced a number of new standard policy wordings, to be used with a new policy form (the "MAR" or, later, "MAR 91" form). In October 2010, the English and Scottish Law Commissions consulted on whether the S.G. form appended to the MIA should be retained, since it was considered to be archaic and, by then, hardly ever used. Responses were mixed and the Lloyd's S.G. policy has survived the changes introduced, inter alia, by the Insurance Act 2015. See: *Arnould: Law of Marine Insurance and Average*, edited by J. Gilman et al, 18th edn (London: Sweet & Maxwell, 2013) ("Arnould"), paras 2–21 to 2–38; Law Commission and Scottish Law Commission "*Reforming Insurance Contract Law, Issues Paper 9, The Requirement for Formal Marine Policy: Should Section 22 Be Repealed?*" (Law Commission and Scottish Law Commission, 2010) *http://www.lawcom.gov.uk/wp-content/uploads/2015/06/ICL9_Requirement_for_Formal_Marine_Policy.pdf* [Accessed 8 August 2016], "*The Law Commission Consultation Paper No 201 and The Scottish Law Commission Discussion Paper No 152 Insurance Contract Law: Post Contract Duties and Other Issues A Joint Consultation Paper*" (Law Commission and Scottish Law Commission, 2011), *http://lawcommission.justice.gov.uk/docs/cp201_ICL_post_contract_duties.pdf* [Accessed 24 September 2013], paras 16-25 to 16-31, and "*Insurance Contract Law, Summary of Responses to Issues Paper 9, The Requirement for a Formal Marine Policy: Should Section 22 be Repealed?*" (Law Commission and Scottish Law Commission, April 2011), *http://www.lawcom.gov.uk/wp-content/uploads/2015/06/ICL9_Section-22.pdf* [Accessed 16 May 2016], paras 2.23 to 2.25.

[4] Insurance of vessels against physical loss or damage is known as "hull", "hull & machinery" or "H&M" insurance. It provides cover for loss or damage to the hull (the structure of the vessel etc) and the machinery with which the vessel is equipped. Such cover is usually against "named perils", rather than all risks. The named perils typically include standard marine perils (e.g. perils of the seas, etc), as well as the additional perils that originally would have been included in an "Inchmaree Clause" (e.g. International Hull Clauses (01/11/03) cl.2.2). See further discussion of additional perils above, at paras 16-024 to 16-028. In addition to insurance against marine perils, including additional perils, cover is often sought against war and political risks: the latter are mentioned, but not considered in detail, in this chapter.

[5] Marine cargo insurance provides cover for goods and/or merchandise that are lost, stolen or damaged whilst transported by sea.

[6] This line of insurance business is diverse: of particular relevance to marine construction, cover can generally be obtained against liability for loss or damage to third party property, for injury to or death of persons, and for regulatory liabilities such as in respect of pollution, wreck removal, etc., arising in the context of marine-related works or operations.

[7] There have been and are other types of marine all risks clauses: e.g. the Institute Flour "All Risks" Clauses (1/11/25) agreed between the Institute of London Underwriters ("ILU") and various trade organisations for use with the S.G Form (see above, fn.3). The Flour All Risks Clauses were withdrawn at the end of 1983 and no new clauses were drafted for use. See V. Dover, *Students Reference Book of Marine Insurance Clauses Including an Analysis of Clauses*; also the *York-Antwerp Rules, 1890 and 1924, and a Table of Stamp Duties*, 3rd edn (London: Witherby & Co, 1926), pp.14 and 228–229. Standard form shipbuilders' all risks policies existed at least as early as 1903: see below, fn.732. More recently, see the Institute Additional Perils Clauses, Hulls (1/11/95), an extension to Institute Time Clauses-Hulls (1/11/95), which covers, inter alia, "loss of or damage to the

Wellington Syndicate 2020's Offshore Construction Project Policy, which first appeared in 2001 ("WELCAR")[8]; the Institute Cargo Clauses ("ICC"), particularly ICC (A); and the Institute Clauses for Builders' Risks (1/6/88) ("ICBR"). These three London market wordings are expressly governed by English law and practice.[9] Brief reference is also made to a newer shipbuilder's risks wording, called the London Marine Construction All Risks ("MARCAR") form.[10] It should also be noted that contractors undertaking occasional marine construction projects sometimes prefer to use a modified land-based CAR policy, given their greater familiarity with onshore wordings, rather than go to a specialist marine underwriter to obtain a marine-specific policy.

A number of other types of coverage are available to contractors: these can be specifically tailored towards a marine construction programme, sometimes combining marine and non-marine products. Such coverage may include (amongst others types): (i) marine general liability insurance, which is a broad form of liability cover that can be specifically tailored towards the needs of, for example, marine contractors, vessel operators, marina operators, charterers, terminal operators, etc.; (ii) marine contractors' liability insurance, which provides contractors with protection against the risks associated with construction in and around the waterfront, such as damage to marine structures that are being constructed whilst in the care, custody or control of the contractor; (iii) bumbershoot or umbrella marine liability insurance, which is an excess marine liability policy for boatyards and shipyards that is designed to provide excess liability coverage over and above primary marine insurance and may also include non-marine insurance, such as automotive and employer's liability; (iv) commercial hull insurance[11]; (v) protection and indemnity ("P&I") insurance, which provides parties interested in a vessel with protection against liabilities arising from its operation (including for personal injury and cargo damage); and (vi) contractor's equipment insurance, covering specialist marine contractors for equipment used by them in working both onshore and offshore, including, for example, remotely operated underwater vehicles ("ROV") and subsea equipment. Insurers may also cover insureds in respect of delays, joint ventures, discontinued operations, business interruption, and for their independent (sub)contractors (i.e. in the form of owners and contractors protective liability insur-

---

Vessel caused by any accident…": discussed in N. Hudson et al, *Marine Insurance Clauses*, 5th edn (London: Informa, 2012), pp.176–178.

8   The wording was developed by the Wellington Syndicate 2020 at Lloyd's, as reflected by its name. The Wellington syndicate's business was largely absorbed by the Catlin Group Ltd, which was acquired by XL Group in 2015.

9   *Evialis SA v SIAT* [2003] EWHC 863 (Comm); [2003] 2 Lloyd's Rep. 377; *Shamil Bank of Bahrain EC v Beximo Pharmaceuticals Ltd (No.1)* [2004] EWCA Civ 19; [2004] 1 W.L.R. 1784; [2004] 4 All E.R. 1072. See also *Thor Navigation Inc v Ingosstrakh Insurance Co Ltd (The Thor 11)* [2005] EWHC 19 (Comm); [2005] 1 Lloyd's Rep. 547; [2005] 1 C.L.C. 12, which confirmed that if the contract was not (strictly speaking) governed by English law it should nevertheless be interpreted in accordance with English marine insurance principles, practices and understanding. However, Gloster J stated that such practices if the express terms of the policy in question so required: *The Thor II* [2005] EWHC 19 (Comm) at [30]–[31] and [34]; [2005] 1 Lloyd's Rep. 547 at 556–557; [2005] 1 C.L.C. 12 at 26–28. In practice, policies written on these standard forms are often amended to provide for the application of legal systems other than English law. In such circumstances, English-law rules and precedents, and English-market practices and understandings, may be taken as providing persuasive, if not authoritative, guidance as to the effect to be given to the forms. The discussion in this chapter assumes the application of English law.

10   CL 371 MARCAR (01/09/07). See below para.24-104.

11   Mentioned above at fn.4.

ance, which provides the insured with protection against losses flowing from contractors' or subcontractors' negligence).

2. OFFSHORE CONSTRUCTION INSURANCE

(a) WELCAR 2001 Offshore Construction Project Policy: introduction

WELCAR: introduction. WELCAR[12] is an all risks insurance policy form, introduced in 2001, which was drafted specifically for insuring offshore construction projects. It provides cover for all aspects of the project from procurement to completion (including the maintenance and discovery period, which may last for 12 months or more).   **24-004**

The policy was devised in response to the increasing losses that were being faced by the insurance industry, particularly as a result of faulty design and latent defects (e.g. faulty welding, which resulted in submarine pipeline leaks, amongst other issues)[13] for which contractors were blamed.[14] CAR policies in common use in relation to offshore projects, such as WELCAR, now exclude the cost of repairing faulty welds.

The WELCAR wording is the standard policy wording in the energy market for offshore construction projects.[15] The policy is designed to be taken out by the company—i.e. generally the field operating company and its co-venturers—as the principal insureds. The policy then protects the contractor and subcontractors as additional insureds, but mandates that any claims made by any of the latter be pursued by the principal insureds. However, in some cases a contractor may purchase the policy under an Engineering Procurement and Construction ("EPC") contract. In 2009 the International Underwriting Association's and Lloyd's Market Association's Joint Rig Committee started work on a revised policy form, with the intention to publish in 2010. As at the date of writing a revised WELCAR remains a work in progress.

International Marine Contractors Association. The International Marine Contractors Association ("IMCA") is the organisation that represents marine, underwater and offshore engineering companies undertaking marine construction work. It provides technical guidance and information to its members, including their clients and subcontractors in order to support them in their work. The IMCA has produced a standard contract called the IMCA Marine Construction Contract (revised December 2015)[16] which may be used by contractors and other parties as   **24-005**

---

[12] On offshore construction generally, and WELCAR in particular, see also the standard reference work from a broking and technical expert's perspective: D.W. Sharp, *Upstream and Offshore Energy Insurance* (Livingston Witherbys Insurance, 2009) ("Sharp"), Chs 5 to 9.

[13] See Sharp, paras 5.2.8 and 7.1.0.

[14] Regarding pre-WELCAR wordings, see Sharp, paras 7.1.0 to 7.1.9.

[15] Sharp, p.214, refers to WELCAR as "an established market wording ... which is consistently used on a global basis for offshore CAR insurance ...".

[16] International Marine Contractors Association. IMCA Contracts & Insurance Workgroup, *IMCA Marine Construction Contract* Rev.2, December 2015 (London: IMCA, 2015). The IMCA contract is based on a document produced by an organisation called the "Leading Oil and Gas Industry Competitiveness", otherwise known as LOGIC: *General Conditions of Contact (including Guidance Notes) for Marine Construction*, 2nd edn, October (LOGIC: Aberdeen, 2004). This document

they deem fit, without its use being compulsory for IMCA members. Clauses 23.5–23.7 set out the insurance obligations imposed on the company if it decides to arrange or provide CAR cover. Clause 23.8 states that if the company decides to be self-insured and not obtain CAR cover, it should inform the contractor at its "earliest convenience".

24-006 Offshore CAR as marine insurance. An offshore construction project may be regarded as a marine adventure, or analogous thereto.[17] Being situated in the marine environment, the insured property will be exposed to maritime perils. It must be conceded that, apart from cases as where materials are being transported to or from the construction site, their exposure to such perils will not be "consequent on, or incidental to, the navigation of the sea."[18] However, even offshore structures intended to be permanently positioned, such as platforms, which will not be capable of being "navigated" after installation, are constructed in yards or docks onshore, then "launched" and towed, "wet" or "dry", or carried as cargo, to their final position. The analogy with a "ship in the course of building, or the launch of a ship"[19] is arguably close, and is clearly one that the drafters of WELCAR intended to apply.[20] Moreover, marine CAR forms, such as WELCAR, may be based on or incorporate other standard marine policy wordings (e.g. standard shipbuilders' risks and cargo insurance wordings),[21] which provide cover for losses specific to marine insurance, such as constructive total loss, sue and labour, general average, salvage, removal of wreckage, etc,[22] or expressly provide for matters addressed only in the context of marine insurance, such as the calculation of indemnity on a "new for old" basis.[23] Factors such as these indicate an intention that the MIA should apply to marine CAR wordings such as WELCAR, and suggest that such wordings should be treated as policies "in the form of a marine policy".[24] Accordingly, it is suggested that insurance on an offshore construction project written on the WELCAR form should be treated as marine insurance, to which the MIA should apply.

24-007 General scheme of the WELCAR policy form. The WELCAR wording provides two types of insurance: (i) cover against physical loss of or physical dam-

---

is part of a suite of standard contracts produced by LOGIC for the UK offshore oil and gas industry. LOGIC was initially set up in 1999 as part of an initiative started by the UK Oil and Gas Industry Task Force ("OCITF"). The LOGIC contract can be used for a variety of offshore activities, such as the installation of pipes, platforms, or other subsea construction, inspecting repairing and maintaining structures using diving professionals and other vessels in support, etc.

[17] See discussion of Colman J in *National Oilwell (UK) Ltd v Davy Offshore Ltd* [1993] 2 Lloyd's Rep. 582, at 606–607 (CAR insurance covering subsea wellhead completion system, part of a floating oil production facility). See also Sharp, paras 1.7.0 to 1.7.7 (inter alia, expressing some doubts on this issues, and emphasising in particular the insurance market's treatment of fixed offshore installations in a manner akin to non-marine property, as regards the availability of war risks insurance).

[18] MIA s.3.

[19] MIA s.2(2).

[20] See, e.g., WELCAR, Section I, Definitions, cll. 1 and 2, substituting in incorporated clauses (e.g. ICBR 1/6/1988), where appropriate, the phrase "the property insured hereunder" for the word "vessel", and adapting the word "launch" to include "skidding onto and off launch barge/vessel and/or mating and/or floating in dry dock and/or flooding thereof and/or transfer of the property insured into water and/or emplacement and/or positioning in water at site."

[21] E.g. WELCAR, Section I, Terms and Conditions, cl.2.

[22] E.g. WELCAR, Section I, Terms and Conditions, cll.1(c)(i), 8, 9, and 11.

[23] See below, para.24-033 (Basis of Recovery clause).

[24] MIA s 2(2).

age to insured property, under Section I; and (ii) cover against certain third-party liabilities, under Section II. The two sections are said to be "distinct": they are intended to be interpreted and applied separately, subject to general provisions, included under the headings "Scope of Insurance" and "General Terms and Conditions", that apply to both Sections.[25] In practice, it is not unheard of for cover to be written under only one of the two Sections.[26]

The policy wording is accompanied by a standard form for Declarations, for the purpose of identifying, inter alia, the insured (or "Assured"), the Project, the Policy Period, various limits and deductibles, the Premium, and the Initial Estimated Final Contract Value.[27] The policy form is also intended to be accompanied by declared project values in two schedules: Schedule A and Schedule B.

Some additional coverages may appear in endorsements to the WELCAR form: the London market has developed quasi-standard wordings for some such endorsements. The policy form is typically used with a Marine Warranty Surveyor endorsement.

As previously mentioned, the unamended WELCAR policy form provides that it should be governed by English law and practice: in addition, it provides for the submission of "any dispute, controversy or claim arising out of or relating to" the policy to the exclusive jurisdiction of the courts of England and Wales.[28]

The various elements of the WELCAR scheme are discussed in detail below.

(b) WELCAR: general provisions

Scope of Insurance: insured activities and the Project. A logical starting point **24-008** for considering the scope of cover under WELCAR is the definition of the project to be insured. As will be seen, a wide range of insureds and insured property can be encompassed under WELCAR. WELCAR defines the potential scope of the Project by reference to insured activities, in correspondingly broad terms:

> "Subject to the insuring agreements, applicable terms, conditions and exclusions, this insurance covers the following activities undertaken in the course of the project identified in Item 2 of the Declarations (hereinafter, the 'Project'), provided such activities are within the insured values. Covered activities include: procurement, construction, fabrication, load out, loading/unloading, transportation by land, sea or air (including call(s) at port(s) or place(s) as may be required), storage, towage, mating, installation, burying, hook-up, connection and/or tie-in operations, testing and commissioning, existence, initial operations and maintenance, project studies, engineering, design, project management, testing, trials, pipelaying, trenching, and commissioning. Covered activities may also include direct consequences from drilling operations, but only where declared to and agreed by Underwriters."[29]

---

[25] WELCAR, Heading. See also Sharp, para.7.2.0.

[26] E.g. *Houston Exploration Co and Offshore Specialty Fabricators Inc v Wellington Underwriting Agencies Ltd*, 352 S.W. 3d 462; 54 Tex.Sup.Ct.J. 1683 (Sup. Ct. Tex. 2011) (Section I only, Section II being "lined through" in that case).

[27] Where capitalised expressions—such as "Assured", "Project", "Project Period", "Occurrence", etc—appear in this section, they are generally used in the same manner as the WELCAR policy form. WELCAR itself is sometimes inconsistent in its employment of both capitalised or lower-case expressions: e.g. "the Project" and "the project" are both employed.

[28] WELCAR, General Terms and Conditions, cl.6.

[29] WELCAR, Scope of Insurance, para.1. See also Sharp, para.7.3.0: the list of insured activities is intended to be "comprehensive … the intent is that continuous coverage is given through the life of the construction programme".

The expression "Project" intervenes at various points in the WELCAR scheme to delimit the scope of cover. For example, the notion is invoked in the identification of the property insured against physical loss or damage under Section I,[30] and in defining the scope of the liability cover under Section II.[31] Ultimately, declarations regarding the Project, and in particular the scope of the activities included within the declared project values, play the definitive role in delimiting insured activities.[32]

The WELCAR form does not prescribe any particular manner in which the specification of the Project should be identified. In practice, the Declarations may simply include the name and a description of the project, and then refer to the relevant construction contract or contracts which will have been provided to the insurers by the brokers during placement, though in other cases fuller information is included in the form.[33]

Finally, it should be noted that the covered activities will only include "direct consequences from drilling operations" if such operations are, additionally, expressly declared and agreed to by insurers.[34]

24-009 **Project Alterations and Amendments clause.** In the event of a "material and/or significant" change to the Project specification, WELCAR provides that such changes are held covered under the Policy for sixty days from the date of the relevant amendments or alterations.[35] This is subject to the (named) Principal Assured giving notice to insurers "promptly within the 60-day period." Cover for such Project changes beyond the 60-day period must be agreed.

The provision's reference to "material and/or significant" amendments or alterations to the Project specification, would likely be approached in a manner analogous to clauses addressing material changes in risk, given the similar concerns that underlie both.[36] Indeed, the "held covered" provision was presumably intended to soften the impact of the common law rules relating to material changes in the risk insured, which might otherwise operate to discharge insurers from liability. Accordingly, a "material" or "significant" change to the Project would be one not contemplated by the parties as being within the Project specification when the policy was concluded. "Promptly" probably bears a meaning similar to "immediately", or "without delay", implying a quicker response than "within a reasonable time"[37]: the intention being that the parties should have as much of the held-

---

30   WELCAR, Section I, cl.2. See below para.24-025.
31   WELCAR, Section II, Insuring Agreement, cl.1. See below para.24-056.
32   See below, para.24-027, regarding declarations of values under WELCAR.
33   Where no formal policy is drawn up, such details may also be included in an "Information" section in the slip. In any event, detailed information regarding the project will normally be provided to, and required by, insurers during placement: this will include full written disclosure, and may involve an engineering presentation to insurers. See Sharp, para.9.6.1.
34   The commercial justification for requiring specific declaration and agreement in relation to drilling has been questioned, while at the same time it has been noted that "the drilling operation, in the perception of insurers, represents a different category of risk to any other": Sharp, paras 7.3.0, 7.4.1.
35   WELCAR, Section I, Terms and Conditions, cl.5. Despite the initial reference to "all amendments and alterations", the clause would seem effectively only to apply to "material" changes that, at common law, would release insurers from liability (in the absence of an express "held covered" provision). On this clause, see Sharp, para.8.4.0, noting: "The clause could be described as maladroit ..." On "held covered" clauses, see also above para.6-045, and see Arnould, paras 14-93 to 14-99.
36   See above, paras 3-066, 9-073 to 9-075 and below, paras 26-147 to 26-148.
37   See above, para.21-018; see also *MacGillivray on Insurance Law*, edited by J. Birds et al, 13th edn,

covered period as possible to negotiate continued cover. It would seem arguable that a loss occurring following a change to the Project specification, and after the time when the Principal Assured, acting promptly, could have notified the insurers, would not be covered: the holding of cover following the change to the Project is "subject to" notice.[38]

The word "specification" is not defined, but probably refers to the information about the project disclosed during placement.[39]

The provision regarding amendments or alterations to the Project specification is directly applicable to Section I only. An agreed change to the Project specification may indirectly have an effect on cover under Section II, in particular if it extends or modifies the scope of "the Assured's operations as declared" under the policy.[40] There is no equivalent "held covered" provision under Section II, so arguably there can be a mismatch in cover between Section I and Section II during the held covered period, until the changes to the Project specification are agreed.

Scope of Insurance: the Assureds. In offshore construction, the CAR policy is **24-010** normally, though not always, underwritten for the operator as principal insured[41]: this is so even though the works may often be the entire responsibility of the main contractor, subcontractors, and others during the currency of the policy. But, as with terrestrial CAR, offshore CAR insurance is generally intended to cover all of the parties interested in works.[42] Waiver of subrogation is, accordingly, an important feature of offshore CAR policies.[43] The number of potential insureds—and thus, claimants—under an offshore CAR insurance also explains those provisions channelling the exercise of all insureds' rights through the Principal Assureds,[44] and the payment of any insurance indemnities to an identified loss payee.[45] The issues arising in relation to terrestrial CAR regarding the identification of the insureds are equally present in the offshore context.[46]

WELCAR identifies and classifies the insureds as follows[47]:

"1. ASSUREDS
Principal Assureds

(i) [*Name of the named principal insured, e.g. the field operating company and/or main contractor*]

Company and/or joint venturers as they may now or subsequently exist.

(ii) Parent and/or subsidiary and/or affiliated and/or associated and/or inter-related companies of the above as they are now or may hereafter be constituted and their directors, officers and employees, while acting in their capacities as such.

Other Assureds

(London: Sweet & Maxwell, 2015) ("MacGillivray"), para.21–041.
[38] A suggestion discussed in Arnould, para.14-97.
[39] This is Sharp's view: see his para.8.4.0.
[40] See definitions of "Bodily Injury" and "Property Damage" under Section II, discussed below, at para.24-056.
[41] See Sharp, paras 6.2.0, 7.3.1.
[42] See above, para.8-001.
[43] See above, paras 20-062 to 20-063.
[44] WELCAR, Scope of Insurance, cl.2, para.2. See below, para 24-011.
[45] E.g. WELCAR, Scope of Insurance, cl.3. See also above, para.23-022.
[46] See above, paras 8-004 to 8-029, 20-002.
[47] WELCAR, Scope of Insurance, cl.1.

(iii)   Project managers.
(iv)   Any other company, firm, person or party (including contractors and/or subcontractors and/or manufacturers and/or suppliers) with whom the Assured(s) named in i, ii, iii and iv have entered into written contract(s) directly in connection with the Project."[48]

This clause merits further comment:

1.   Insofar as there has been judicial consideration of expressions such as "joint venturers", "parent", "subsidiary", "affiliated and/or associated company", and "inter-related company" in sub-clauses (i) and (ii),[49] and "contractors", "subcontractors", "manufacturers" and "suppliers" in sub-clause (iv),[50] this is discussed elsewhere in this work.

2.   The words "as they may now or subsequently exist" and "as they are now or may hereafter be constituted" in sub-clauses (i) and (ii), reflect the possibility that the composition of the group of Principal Assureds may change during the currency of the policy. In the event that a Principal Assured divests itself of some or all of its interest in the project, however, subject to notice being given to the insurers, cover under the policy is extended to the new owners in respect of the divested interest for fourteen days following the divestment: continuation of cover thereafter is subject to agreement between insurers and the new owner.[51]

3.   The named Principal Assured may include the main contractor, e.g. in a case where the main contractor procures the policy. In other cases the project manager may be named as a Principal Assured. In such cases, the operating company and its co-venturers, etc will typically also be included as co-venturers. Including the main contractor or project manager as a Principal Assured will have knock-on consequences, which the drafters of WELCAR presumably did not intend: in particular the special conditions and provisions applicable to Other Assureds, discussed below,[52] will not apply to such parties.

4.   Contractors under sub-clause (iv) must have "entered into written contract(s) directly in connection with the Project." A contract "entered into ... directly in connection with the Project" is not defined, but it is suggested that the conclusion of such contracts must have been caused by the Project. The types of contracts in contemplation are almost certainly those referred to elsewhere in the policy form, variously, as "specific contracts" or "written contracts awarded within the scope of insured works as scheduled under the Policy",[53] "contracts relating to the Project" under which insured works are executed,[54] and "individual" or "specific contracts" under which maintenance or warranty periods are specified.[55]

---

[48]   In the remainder of this section, it will sometimes be convenient to refer generically to the Other Assureds referred to under (iv) of this provision as "Contractor(s)".
[49]   See above para.20-009.
[50]   See above paras 8-008 to 8-021, 8-026 to 8-027 and para.20-008.
[51]   WELCAR, General Terms and Conditions, cl.9. See also Sharp, paras 7.3.1, 7.4.4.
[52]   Below, at para.24-011.
[53]   WELCAR, Scope of Insurance, cll.2, 3.
[54]   WELCAR, Section I, cl.2.
[55]   WELCAR, Section I, Terms and Conditions, cl.19; and Declarations, item 3.

Finally, in this context, WELCAR expressly provides that "... this insurance shall not inure to the benefit of any carrier, warehousemen or bailee."[56] This may be effective to exclude the Contracts (Rights of Third Parties) Act 1999, in relation to such parties.[57]

Scope of Insurance: special considerations relating to Other Assureds. A **24-011** number of special conditions apply only to "Other Assureds" under WELCAR, i.e. project managers and Contractors (as previously defined)[58]:

1. It is expressed to be a "condition precedent for any ... Other Assureds ... to benefit from [their] ... status under the Policy", that they must "perform their operations" in accordance with "Quality Assurance/Quality Control system(s)" that comply with whatever "Quality Assurance/Quality Control provisions" required by the Principal Assureds to be present in "each and every written contract awarded within the scope of the insured works".[59] Given its language, it is possible that the provision was intended to take effect as a condition precedent to the inception or continuation of cover vis-à-vis any party in breach of their contractual QA/QC obligations: a project manager or Contractor in breach of such obligations is, apparently, not to benefit from Assured status under the policy.[60] However, as with any such clause, there is a real possibility that a court might construe it in a less draconian manner, e.g. as a suspensory condition.[61] The presumption underlying this condition is, clearly, that relevant contract(s) between the named Principal Assured and the main Contractor(s) will contain QA/QC procedures and standards, and will stipulate that compliance with such procedures and standards shall be required, in turn, of Contractors of other tiers. In a particular case, there clearly may be scope for disputes as to, inter alia, whether a Contractor's QA/QC systems comply with the applicable contractual standards, and (if so) whether that Contractor has performed its operations in accordance with its systems. Though there is no authority on the question, it would seem reasonable to construe the condition in a manner analogous to "reasonable precautions" clauses, given the similar purposes of the two clauses.[62] Accordingly, the obligation to "perform their operations" in accordance with compliant QA/QC systems would be binding on the relevant Other Assureds personally, but not on their agents or employees generally; that is, in considering whether or not there had been a breach of the condition, the question would be whether the breach was that of personnel of such seniority within the Other Assured (if a company) that their failure to "perform ... operations according to Quality Assurance/

---

56 WELCAR, General Terms and Conditions, cl.12.
57 See Arnould, para.8-18.
58 See above, fn.48.
59 WELCAR, Scope of Insurance, cl.2, para.1. For the background to this clause, see Sharp, para. 7.1.4: "It is fair to say that this stipulation has been the subject of more debate and scrutiny than any other in the WELCAR form with a number of observers expressing the view that it might be impractical to apply, depending on the way contracts between the Principal and 'other Assureds' are structured."
60 See above, para.12-004. See Sharp, para.7.3.2.
61 See above, para.12-014.
62 See paras 15-069 to 15-073.

Quality Control system(s)" should be attributed to the company.[63] Such persons are likely to be the senior management or employee(s) ultimately charged with establishing and directing compliance with the Other Assured's QA/QC system.[64]

2. The aforementioned condition precedent is connected to another relating to waiver of subrogation. As "a condition precedent to their benefiting from the automatic waiver of subrogation" accorded to Assureds under WELCAR, Other Assureds must comply with the same Quality Assurance/ Quality Control obligations.[65] If they do not so comply, the intention is that they be both stripped of coverage and exposed to subrogated claims from insurers (though they would, in many cases, still be protected against such claims by any contractual indemnities and releases in their contracts with other insureds).[66]

3. It is suggested that these conditions precedent should be treated as terms defining the risk as a whole, and in any event are not specific to the risks of losses of any particular kind, or at any particular time or location. Accordingly, they should not fall within s.11 of the Insurance Act 2015.[67]

4. Other Assureds are to be covered during the entire Policy Period, "for their direct participation in the venture", subject to any provisions in "specific contract(s)" to the contrary.[68] The Declarations further specify that Other Assureds are included "for the[ir] Respective Rights and interests as per wording."[69] These provisions reflect the position of co-insureds at common law: the existence and extent of the cover extended to other insureds is governed by the extent of their insurable interest, and by the scope of the cover their contractual counterparty intends or is obliged to procure for them.[70] A similar position is expressed to apply in the case where the "benefits" of the policy "have been passed to an Assured by contract", in which case the insured can receive only such rights under the policy "as such contract allows" (and, of course, no greater benefits than the policy itself provides).[71]

5. The rights of any Assured—and thus, of the Other Assureds—are only to be "exercised through" the Principal Assureds. In practice, it has been noted that, "[w]here the contractual responsibility for damage to the works is passed to the contractor, the Principal [Assured] acts in an agency capacity on behalf of the contractor for the recovery of any such claims monies due

---

[63] See *Tate Gallery Board of Trustees v Duffy Construction Ltd (No.2)* [2007] EWHC 912 (TCC), [2008] 1 Lloyd's Rep. I.R. 159 at paras 26, 31.

[64] See, by analogy, the discussion of attribution of knowledge to an insured company, above at para.6-023.

[65] WELCAR, General Terms and Conditions, cl.3. This reflects the construction given to other express waiver of subrogation clauses, in cases of co-insurance: see above para.20-062.

[66] See above, paras 2-030 to 2-031, and 2-067 to 2-68 on "knock-for-knock" contracting practices. See also, Sharp, paras 6.7.0 and 7.4.1, on this point.

[67] See above, paras 5-103 to 5-104, 5-110 to 5-114.

[68] WELCAR, Scope of Insurance, cl.2, para.2. The wording is substantially the same as that considered in *National Oilwell* [1993] 2 Lloyd's Rep. 582 QBD. See also Sharp, paras 7.3.2 and 8.7.0. This provision is of potential relevance to the date of commencement of the Maintenance Period(s), as discussed below at para.24-018.

[69] WELCAR, Declarations, item 1.

[70] See above, paras 8-022 to 8-025, 8-030 to 8-039, 20-007 to 20-013.

[71] WELCAR, Scope of Insurance, cl.2, para.2.

to the contractor."[72] Equally, it has been suggested that the Principal Assureds may, if so advised, delegate the task of claiming under the policy to an Other Assured.[73]

Finally, it is expressly provided that there is deemed to be a separate insurance under WELCAR in respect of each *Principal Assured* (without thereby increasing the limits of liability under the policy).[74] No such provision is made regarding *Other Assureds*, presumably because it would be redundant: Other Assureds will generally all have different interests in the insured works and thus are, at common law, co-insureds under a composite policy, each treated as having a separate, bi-lateral contract with the insurers.[75] On the other hand, there clearly may be a danger that the Principal Assureds, or some of them, would be treated as co-insureds under a joint insurance, in that the named Principal Assured and its joint venturers (and other companies in their respective groups) may have the same (or shares in the same) indivisible interest in the insured works. It was presumably to avoid the potential consequences of such joint insurance—e.g. the risk that one Principal Assured's misconduct may vitiate cover for the others[76]—that the relevant provision was included.[77]

Loss payee and claims representative. Provision is made in the policy form for **24-012** the designation of a loss payee, to receive payment of indemnities and returns of premiums.[78] Issues arising in relation to loss payees are discussed elsewhere in this work.[79]

In practice, the loss payee may, or may not, be the same person referred to elsewhere in the wording as the Assureds' "Claims Representative".[80]

Assignment or Modification of the Policy clause, and "entire contract" wording. Another general provision relevant, to the identity of the insureds under **24-013** the policy, provides as follows:

> "17. *ASSIGNMENT OR MODIFICATION OF POLICY* This Policy is made and accepted subject to the conditions, limitations, agreements and declarations and all endorsements signed by Underwriters, and shall constitute the entire contract between the Underwriters and the Assured(s). No notice or assignment of any right under the Policy nor any change, waiver or extension of its terms shall be valid unless endorsed hereon and signed by Underwriters.
>
>   In the event of the death, bankruptcy or receivership of an Assured within the Policy Period, the Policy shall, except in the event of cancellation, cover the legal representative of the Assured, provided that notice in writing is given to the Underwriters through [*blank*] within thirty days after the date of such death, insolvency, bankruptcy or receivership."[81]

---

[72] Sharp, para.6.2.0.
[73] Sharp, para.7.3.2.
[74] WELCAR, Scope of Insurance, para.2.
[75] See above, paras 20-030 to 20-032. See also Arnould, para 8-13.
[76] See above, paras 20-030 and 20-034.
[77] See above, para.20-033.
[78] WELCAR, Scope of Insurance, cl.3.
[79] See above, para.23-022.
[80] WELCAR, Declarations, item 8; Section I, Terms and Conditions, cl.18, "Payment of Claims". As discussed above, at para.24-011, the Assureds' rights under the policy are only to be exercised through the Principal Assureds.
[81] WELCAR, General Terms and Conditions, cl.17.

The first sentence of the first paragraph defines the "Policy" as including a range of documents "signed by Underwriters", including, notably, "agreements and declarations and all endorsements". The Policy, thus defined, is stated to be the "entire contract" between the insurers and the Assureds (though this must be read subject to the Acceptance clause, discussed below)[82]: such provisions generally have the effect of preventing statements made during negotiations from becoming actionable, e.g. as binding collateral contracts,[83] and may also prevent the implication of terms from usage or custom.[84] The purpose of this sentence, in formally identifying the contract, is presumably to ensure contract certainty, the need for which is heightened in the context of WELCAR given the potentially large number of insureds. The second sentence reinforces this in declaring that no changes, waivers or extensions of the Policy's terms are to "be valid" unless insurers agree to the same in a signed endorsement.

The second sentence of this clause's first paragraph declares that no "notice or assignment of any right under the Policy" is to be valid—i.e. to bind insurers—unless agreed in a signed endorsement. This should probably not be read as requiring that parties who qualify as Assureds, within the meaning of that term,[85] be endorsed to the Policy as such before they may benefit from that status, as this would generally prove to be highly impractical. Instead, the provision was almost certainly aimed at parties such as lenders, who will normally not be Assureds, but to whom an assignment of the Policy may be effected, resulting in a notice of the assignment or of the assignee's interest to insurers.[86]

24-014 **Acceptance clause.** This provides as follows:

> "18. *ACCEPTANCE* By accepting the Policy, each Assured declares that the several statements in the application, schedules and proposal are true and are hereby made a part of the Policy. Each Assured recognises that the Policy is issued by the Underwriters in reliance upon such statements and in consideration of the premium to be paid by the Assured."[87]

This provision serves to address uncertainties as to whether various Assureds will be bound by statements made by or on behalf of the named Principal Assured during placement of the policy. Such uncertainties might arise, e.g. as regards Other Assureds, from the composite nature of insurance on WELCAR terms.[88] The clause purports to fix each Assured who "accepts" the policy with a contractual promise as to truth of such statements made in certain named writings: "the application, schedules and proposal".

Such statements are "made part of the Policy", and each Assured "recognises"

---

[82] See below, para.24-014.

[83] *Chitty on Contracts*, edited by H.G. Beale, 32nd edn (London: Sweet & Maxwell, 2015), Vol.1, paras 2–174 and 13–107.

[84] *Chitty on Contracts* (2015), para 14–021, fn.156. It seems doubtful that the exclusion of usages and customs was intended: certain customs are implicitly assumed to apply to WELCAR, e.g. provision for indemnity on a "new for old" basis, in the Basis of Recovery clause, discussed below at para.24-033.

[85] See above, para.24-010.

[86] See above, paras 8-028 and 8-029, regarding funders. See also Sharp, para.7.4.7.

[87] WELCAR, General Terms and Conditions, cl.18. See also Sharp, para.7.4.8.

[88] E.g. material misrepresentations made by the named Principal Assured during placement of the policy may not give insurers a remedy against innocent Other Assureds. See above, para.20-035,; *Arab Bank Plc v Zurich Insurance Co* [1998] C.L.C. 1351 at 1367–1370; [1999] 1 Lloyd's Rep. 262 at 276–278 QBD. See also Arnould, paras 8–14, 16–49, 19–13 fn.74.

that insurers have relied upon the same in concluding the insurance. This provision is arguably meant to treat each Assured as having warranted the truth of the relevant statements. Whether it achieves this may depend on whether the wording is treated as equivalent to a "basis of contract clause", or alternatively whether the particular statements are deemed to be sufficiently material to the risk to constitute warranties.[89] The effect of this provision will thus be significantly altered by ss.9 and 10 of the Insurance Act 2015, in policies concluded after its coming into force.[90]

"Accepting the Policy" probably refers generically to the receipt and adoption by the relevant insured of the policy documents issued, without objection, formal execution of the documents by the insured not being required to indicate their agreement to the terms contained therein.[91] These words would also seem apt to cover ratification of the insurance contract by an Other Assured whose involvement in the project post-dates the policy,[92] and perhaps also the "assent" of a relevant party under the Contracts (Rights of Third Parties) Act 1999 s.2 (which predates the WELCAR policy form).[93]

The clause also declares that each Assured recognises that the "consideration" for the Policy is "the premium to be paid by the Assured." This would probably not exclude MIA s.53(1), according to which the broker is directly responsible for the payment of premium to the insurers, with the insured's liability for premium being owed to the broker.[94]

Subrogation and waiver of subrogation. As with CAR generally, subrogation **24-015** is an important consideration under WELCAR, given the potentially large number of contractors involved in insured projects.[95]

The principle of subrogation applies to insurance written in the WELCAR form by reason of its nature as a contract of indemnity.[96] WELCAR expressly provides for insurers to be subrogated to the rights of any of the Assureds against any third person or entity, in respect of "any claim or payment" under Section I or Section

---

[89] See above, paras 4-024 to 4-026, 12-015 to 12-018, and 12-027. Otherwise, the Acceptance clause would provide insurers with a potential cross-claim in damages for breach of contract, if any relevant statements prove to be untrue. The inclusion in WELCAR of the Errors and Omissions clause lends support to the proposition that statements covered by the Acceptance clause are to take effect as warranties: see below, para.24-026.

[90] i.e. after 12 August 2016. Under s.9 of the 2015 Act, "basis of contract" clauses and other contractual provisions are prevented from converting pre-contractual representations into warranties. Section 10 modifies the consequences of breaching a warranty and, by virtue of this, may influence the courts in their categorisation of policy terms as warranties, suspensory conditions, conditions precedent, etc. See above, paras 5–090 to 5–102.

[91] *Macdonald v The Law Union Fire and Life Insurance Co* (1873–74) L.R. 9 Q.B. 328, at 329–330 and 332; *Universo Insurance Company of Milan v Merchants Marine Insurance Co Ltd* [1897] 2 Q.B. 93 CA, 100. See also *John Scott v Scottish Accident Insurance Co Ltd* (1889) 16 R. 630 Ct of Session, 631 fn. *James Muirhead v Forth and North Sea Steamboat Mutual Insurance Association* (1893) 20 R. 442 Ct of Session.

[92] See discussion above, at para.20-017. Cf. *Boston Fruit Co v British and Foreign Marine Insurance Co Ltd* [1905] 1 K.B. 637, the evidence was that owners, who procured the policy, intended to insure their own interest and no other.

[93] See above, para 20-039

[94] See Arnould, paras 6–05 to 6–07, 6–11, and 6–24; *Universo Insurance Company of Milan v Merchants Marine Insurance Co Ltd* [1897] 2 QB 93 CA; *JA Chapman & Co Ltd v Kadirga Denizcilik ve Ticaret AS* [1998] C.L.C. 860, at 865; [1998] Lloyd's Rep. I.R. 377 CA.

[95] See discussion and references above, at para.24-010.

[96] On subrogation, generally, see above, at para.21-048; and see also Arnould, Ch.31, regarding subrogation under the MIA, s.79.

II.[97] At common law, the exercise of a right of subrogation is contingent on indemnification by the insurer of all claims under the relevant insurance arising from the relevant casualty[98]: if an insured has received less than a full indemnity from insurers, e.g. because their claim has been settled at a discount, this may prevent insurers' right of subrogation from being exercised.[99] The reference in WELCAR to "any claim or payment made" may have been intended to afford insurers' the right to bring a subrogative action even where a full indemnity has not been provided.[100]

The Assureds are, themselves, under a duty to "execute all papers required" by insurers and to "co-operate with the Underwriters to secure their subrogation rights."[101] This obligation may need to be read in conjunction with the Forfeiture clause, discussed below.[102]

Insurers' right to subrogate is expressly stated to relate to the Assureds' rights "against any person or entity, other than Principal Assureds or Other Assureds".[103] WELCAR provides expressly that insurers waive their rights of subrogation "against any Principal Assured(s) and/or Other Assured(s)."[104] This waiver of subrogation is subject to two conditions, in the case of Other Assureds:

1.   The "condition precedent" requiring compliance by Other Assureds with Quality Assurance/Quality Control provisions in their contracts, has already been discussed.[105]

2.   As regards drilling contractors and their sub-contractors, the Assureds are not to grant any waiver of subrogation to the same without obtaining the prior agreement of insurers in an endorsement to the policy. This complements the need for insurers' agreement to include drilling-related activities within the definition of the Project.[106] Again, the Forfeiture clause may be relevant to this obligation.[107]

Finally, Assureds are expressly permitted to waive or limit their rights against carriers, warehousemen and other bailees.[108]

24-016   Percentage Interest clause.   This clause provides:

> "4.   *PERCENTAGE INTEREST CLAUSE* All values, limits, deductibles and premiums contained in the Policy are in respect of a 100% interest and shall be reduced in

---

97   WELCAR, General Terms and Conditions, cl.2.

98   See Arnould, at para.31–12.

99   See Arnould, at para.31–13.

100   A very similar clause was included in an early US aviation casualty policy form: see W.P. Comstock, *"Aviation Casualty Insurance" in Proceedings of the Casualty Actuarial Society, 1932–1933* (New York: The Casualty Actuarial Society, 1933) Vol.19, Nos.39 & 40, 265. A somewhat different clause appears in the AIMU's Landing Dock Bailee Liability policy form, cl.11: "in respect of any claim or payment made under this policy, *to the extent of such payment* ..." (emphasis added).

101   See above, para.21-049; and see also Arnould, para.31-31.

102   See below, para.24-021.

103   WELCAR, General Terms and Conditions, cl.2.

104   WELCAR, General Terms and Conditions, cl.3. See above, paras 20-062 to 20-063. See also Sharp, para.7.4.1.

105   See above, para.24-011.

106   Discussed above, at para.24-008. See also Sharp, para.7.4.1.

107   See below, para.24-021.

108   WELCAR, General Terms and Conditions, cl.12.

proportion to the individual Principal Assured(s) interest as declared or as may be subsequently declared and agreed by Underwriters."[109]

The Policy contemplates that the Principal Assureds may include a number of entities participating, to varying extents, in the Project, often as joint venturers.[110] It is not unusual for various quantities in energy market policies—such as insured values and limits, deductibles and premiums—to be accompanied by the notation "(100%)". This has an established meaning in the energy insurance market, to the effect that the relevant values are to be scaled down proportionately to the relevant insured's interest in the insured project. Conversely, where the relevant quantity is accompanied by notation such as "for assured's interest", the stated quantity is treated as already reflecting that interest, and is not to be scaled down further.[111] The Percentage Interest clause treats all relevant quantities in the Policy as if they were accompanied by "(100%)" notation.[112] This must be borne in mind when considering, in particular, the application of (sub-)limits and deductibles to claims by those Principal Assureds only partially interested in the project.

Policy Period: the Project Period. The insured property under WELCAR will **24-017** generally include all materials and components intended to be integrated in the works, from the earliest procurement phase.[113] Accordingly, the period of cover should be agreed to commence correspondingly early. The period of cover commences with the "Project Period." Normally, Project Period cover is intended to continue until completion of the project, to be followed by a period of maintenance cover.[114]

The final stages of constructing an offshore energy project, such as a platform, typically involve testing and commissioning: the latter generally requires that some hydrocarbons be pumped through the platform.[115] Reflecting this reality, WELCAR envisages that covered activities should include, after "testing and commissioning", "existence" (e.g. while initial wells are being drilled),[116] followed by "initial operations".[117] While the latter is probably not intended to refer to full production operation, the WELCAR wording provides no guidance as to how or where the line is to be drawn. But if properly declared, it is envisaged that the wording should cover some "subsequent [viz to completion] operational risks."[118] In practice, some policies are amended to provide expressly for cover to run until the commencement of an operating insurance policy (though always subject to the long-stop "expiry" date discussed below).[119]

The WELCAR wording provides that the Project Period of cover is to end fol-

---

[109] WELCAR, General Terms and Conditions, cl.4.

[110] See above, paras 24-010 and 24-011.

[111] *Gard Marine & Energy Ltd v Lloyd Tunnicliffe* [2011] EWHC 1658 (Comm), [35]–[52].

[112] In this regard, WELCAR, Declarations, item 9, actually states: "Initial Estimated Final Contract Value (100%)".

[113] E.g. WELCAR, Scope of Insurance: "Covered activities include: procurement, construction, fabrication, load out, loading/unloading, transportation by land, sea or air ..." See also Sharp, paras 6.3.0, 7.3.0.

[114] E.g. WELCAR, Section I, Terms and Conditions, cl.19. See also above, paras 4-011 to 4-013.

[115] Sharp, para.6.3.3.

[116] Sharp, para.5.2.6.

[117] WELCAR, Scope of Insurance.

[118] WELCAR, Section I, cl.2 (in the context of defining the property insured).

[119] Sharp, para. 6.3.4. See *Mopani Copper Mines Plc v Millennium Underwriting Ltd* [2008] EWHC 1331 (Comm); [2008] 2 All E.R. (Comm) 976; [2009] Lloyd's Rep. I.R. 158, discussing the pos-

lowing "completion of the last part, item or portion of the property insured."[120] It is expressly provided, however, that, subject to prior notification to insurers and any appropriate adjustments to the premium, "any portion or portions" of the insured property may be occupied and operated (e.g. for purposes such as "initial operations"), without this constituting "acceptance of the property insured".[121] Implicitly, this provision contemplates that the Project Period may be lengthened by a period of occupation and operation.

Finally, WELCAR assumes that an expected long-stop completion date will be stipulated: this "expiry" date provides a temporal basis for setting the premium, with extensions to the Project Period thereafter to be at terms and premium to be agreed.[122]

Under Section II, cover is for relevant liabilities only if caused by an "Occurrence" taking place during the Project Period.[123]

24-018 **Policy Period: Maintenance and Discovery Periods.** With the expiry of the Project Period, the Maintenance Period and Discovery Period begin: these periods then run concurrently, for up to 12 months.[124]

The Maintenance Period is relevant to Section I of WELCAR. During the Maintenance Period, coverage is more limited under Section I than during the Project Period, as discussed below.[125] The Maintenance Period runs for the duration of the maintenance or warranty periods stipulated in "specific" or "individual" contracts,[126] for a maximum duration of twelve months.[127] It has been suggested that, while the Maintenance Period for the Principal Assureds will commence with the expiry of the Project Period, there may be different Maintenance Periods commencing earlier, for different Contractors, depending on when the maintenance or warranty periods under their individual contracts begins.[128] However, while not all of the relevant provisions are entirely clear on this issue, it seems more likely that, for all Assureds, the Maintenance Period(s) under the policy should all begin upon the expiry of the Project Period.[129]

The Discovery Period also begins upon expiry of the Project Period, and is prob-

---

sibility of cover for operational risks under a CAR policy.
[120] WELCAR, Declarations, item 3.
[121] WELCAR, General Terms and Conditions, cl.11 "Permission to Occupy and Operate".
[122] WELCAR, Declarations, item 3. See above, para.4-012.
[123] WELCAR, Section II, Insuring Agreement, cl.1.
[124] WELCAR, Declarations, item 3.
[125] WELCAR, Section I, Terms and Conditions, cl.19. See below, para.24-032.
[126] WELCAR, Section I, Terms and Conditions, cl.19, and Declarations, item 3. "[I]ndividual contracts" almost certainly those referred to as written contract(s) entered into "directly in connection with" the project and/or "awarded within the scope of insured works as scheduled under the Policy": WELCAR, Scope of Insurance, cll.1(iv) and 2, 3. Theoretically, one can envisage a case where there will be *no* Maintenance Period, because the relevant contracts contain no post-completion warranties. See Sharp, para. 6.3.5.
[127] WELCAR, Section I, Terms and Conditions, cl.19, and Declarations, item 3. See also Sharp, para.8.7.0.
[128] Sharp, para.8.7.0: the basis for Sharp's assertion that "a strict interpretation of the [Maintenance] clause, suggests that *Principal Assureds* should enjoy the full benefit of cover" is unclear. See below, fn.129.
[129] WELCAR's Declarations, item 3, provides that the Project Period is to extend until "completion of the last part, item or portion of the property insured". The "Maintenance Period" (expressed in the singular) is then said to be a period during which cover under Section I is to "*continue* during the maintenance period(s) of specific contracts" (emphasis added): the provision does not state that the Maintenance Periods are to *commence with* those provided for under specific contracts. The

[664]

ably intended to run for a fixed period[130]: the generic WELCAR form provides for 12 months. The Discovery Period is relevant to both Section I and Section II of WELCAR.

Under Section I, the primary cover is against physical loss or damage caused by an "Occurrence" (as defined in Section I) occurring during the Policy Period: which, in the context of Section I, means that the Occurrence must intervene during the Project Period or the subsequent Maintenance Period (when more limited cover is applicable).[131] The fixed Discovery Period acts as a long-stop date for the discovery and reporting of loss, damage or Occurrences following the completion of the project: a "loss, damage or Occurrence" reported to insurers after expiry of the Discovery Period is not recoverable.[132] This ensures that a policy on WELCAR terms will not generate a "tail" of claims under Section I.[133]

Under Section II, cover is against liability caused by an "Occurrence" (as defined in Section II) occurring during the Project Period, i.e. prior to completion of the works.[134] The Discovery Period, again, serves to truncate the "tail" of claims under Section II: if an Occurrence is not reported to insurers by the expiry of the Discovery Period, insurers will not be obliged to indemnify liabilities caused by that Occurrence.

Attachment of cover. WELCAR's Section I cover attaches when an item of **24-019** insured property first becomes "at the risk" of an Assured.[135] The time at which this occurs will often depend on the Assureds' contractual arrangements with others (e.g. sellers/suppliers, transporters, etc, not being Insureds under the CAR policy). If and

---

Maintenance clause in Section I of WELCAR (Terms and Conditions, cl.19) is similarly expressed as the *continuation* of cover under Section I following expiry of the Project Period. The second paragraph of the Special Conditions for Other Assureds clause, discussed above at para.24-011, also points to this construction (as noted by Sharp, para.8.7.0). Further, construing the relevant provisions so that various "Maintenance Periods" commence earlier than the end of the Project Period would lead to an unreasonable result. In particular, there is only limited cover provided during the Maintenance Period, and as no distinction is drawn between Principal Assureds and Other Assureds in this regard, the Principal Assureds would also find themselves with only the very limited Maintenance Period cover (e.g. excluding purely external fortuitous occurrences, such as bad weather) in relation to elements of the insured project completed early relative to the whole, which is unlikely to have been intended. Moreover, such a construction would give rise to an argument as to whether various Discovery Periods were also intended to commence on different days: whereas, instead, the Discovery clause (General Terms and Conditions, cl.20) and in particular item 3 of the Declarations indicate that the "Discovery Period" (expressed in the singular) is to commence "on *the same date* as and run concurrently with *the* 12 month Maintenance Period." (Emphasis added, again to highlight the singular form.) See also Sharp, para.10.5.1, on the transition, in practice, between construction and operational insurance policies.

[130] WELCAR, General Terms and Conditions, cl.20; Declarations, item 3. These clauses could be more clearly drafted. It would seem that the Discovery Period, and any Maintenance Period, are intended to *commence* together—see above fn.129—and to run *concurrently*, it being then possible for the Maintenance Period to expire before or at the same time as the fixed-length Discovery Period (depending on the length of the warranty periods in the relevant contracts). There would seem to be no logical reason for the Discovery Period, applicable to *both Section I and Section II*, to vary depending on the length of the warranty periods in contracts dictating the length (and, indeed, the existence) of any Maintenance Period(s). See also Sharp, para.7.4.10.

[131] WELCAR, Section I, cl.1; Terms and Conditions, cl.19; Definitions, cl.3. See below, para.24-032.

[132] WELCAR, General Terms and Conditions, cl.20.

[133] See Sharp, paras 6.3.6 and 7.4.10: "The *Discovery* clause effectively makes the policy a Claims Made form …"

[134] WELCAR, Section II, Insuring Agreement, cl.1.

[135] WELCAR, Declarations, item 3. See above at paras 8-032, 9-005 to 9-020, 9-041 to 9-055. See also Sharp, para.6.3.2.

to the extent that subcontractors, manufacturers and suppliers are included as Other Assureds under the policy, cover may attach in relation to relevant items of property at relatively early dates.

Cover under Section II attaches "from commencement of signing individual contracts."[136] It has thus been commented that, "theoretically", subject to the limited terms of cover provided under Section II, the WELCAR policy form can respond to third party liability for injury or damage caused at Contractors' premises, at places potentially far distant from the project site, and at times prior to the commencement of any actual work.[137]

24-020   Due Diligence clause.   WELCAR's Due Diligence clause provides as follows:

> "10. *DUE DILIGENCE* It is a condition of the Policy that the Assureds shall exercise due care and diligence in the conduct of all operations covered under the Policy, utilising all safety practices and equipment generally considered prudent for such operations. In the event any hazardous condition develops, including with respect to any well from which consequential damages covered by the Policy may arise, the Assureds shall at their expense make all reasonable efforts to prevent the occurrence of a loss insured against under the Policy."[138]

Similar clauses in CAR policies, referred to as "reasonable precautions" clauses, have been discussed elsewhere in this work.[139] In the context of WELCAR, the similarity has been noted between such clauses and the Quality Assurance / Quality Control requirements imposed on Other Assureds.[140] The Due Diligence clause, on the other hand, applies to all Assureds. It seems likely that the first sentence of the Due Diligence clause would be treated in a manner analogous to a "reasonable precautions" clause:

1.   The obligation to exercise "due care and diligence", etc. should rest upon the Assureds only—in the case of a corporate insured, on persons of such seniority within the company that their conduct will be attributed to the company itself—, not on their servants or agents.[141]

2.   Breach of the "due care and diligence" standard may require advertent recklessness, rather than mere negligence. The words requiring in addition that the Assured should employ "all safety practices and equipment generally considered prudent for such operations" may have been intended to increase the obligation on the Assured, but if so it is an open question whether this has been achieved. It is suggested that, if possible, the provision should not be read as excluding cover for losses arising negligently. Accordingly, the words "utilising all safety practices and equipment generally considered prudent" could be construed as informing the phrase "exercise due care and diligence": this would make clear that the Assureds' obligation not to act with advertent recklessness requires the employment of safety practices and equipment generally considered prudent, but only in relation to potential dangers *actually recognised by the Assureds*.

---

[136] WELCAR, Declarations, item 3. On the meaning of "individual contracts", see above, para.24-010.

[137] Sharp, para.6.3.2.

[138] WELCAR, General Terms and conditions, cl.10. See also Sharp, para.7.4.5.

[139] Above at paras 15-069 to 15-073; see also below, A–092.

[140] See above, at para.24-011.

[141] *Tate Gallery Board of Trustees* [2007] EWHC 912 (TCC) at [26], [31]; [2008] Lloyd's Rep. I.R. 159.

The first sentence of the Due Diligence clause is said to be a "condition of the Policy", but the intended consequence of any breach is not explained. The proper approach may be to construe it as a condition precedent to liability, breach of which would prevent a claim or claims under the policy in relation to any relevant loss.[142] If so, then the provision, construed in the restricted manner suggested above, might be seen to complement the Quality Assurance/Quality Control obligations imposed on the Other Assureds, without producing an un-commercial result. The Forfeiture clause, discussed below, would tend to support this construction, if it applies.[143]

The second sentence of the Due Diligence clause is suggestive of the requirement in English law that an insured under a policy of marine insurance must "sue and labour", acting as a reasonable, prudent uninsured in taking measures to avert or minimise a loss.[144] The common law duty arises after the occurrence of a casualty has created a potential loss that would be covered by the policy if it is not avoided or minimised. If the proximate cause of a loss (or part thereof) is the negligence of the Assured in responding to the casualty—i.e. to "any hazardous condition [which] develops"—the Assured's claim under the policy in respect of that loss will fail. It seems likely that the second sentence would be construed as declaratory of the English common law position, as is the case for sue and labour provisions in a number of standard marine insurance policy forms. The second sentence does so in neutral terms applicable to both Section I and Section II. It makes explicit reference to hazards with respect to "any well" (which normally would not be insured under WELCAR, but which might result in insured damage to property under Section I, or an insured liability under Section II). Additional, limited, cover for suing and labouring is provided under Section I, though not under Section II.[145]

Forfeiture and fraudulent claims. The Forfeiture clause in WELCAR provides **24-021** as follows:

> "19. *FORFEITURE* If an Assured shall breach any provision of the Policy, there shall be no coverage for that Assured as to the particular claim in connection with which the breach occurred, provided that there is no statute to the contrary in the country or state in which the insurance was made.
>
> If any Assured shall make any demand for indemnity under this Policy that is false or fraudulent, as regards amount or otherwise, this Policy shall become null and void, and all coverage hereunder shall be forfeited."[146]

The first sentence of the Forfeiture clause appears to have been intended to take effect as a "due observance" clause, of the kind discussed earlier in this work[147]: it purports to make compliance with "any provision" of the policy a condition precedent to insurers' liability; a claim "in connection with which" the breach of any provision of the policy occurs, is not covered. The potential scope of this provision merits further discussion:

1.   The words "any provision of the Policy" are, clearly, wide. WELCAR provisions imposing duties on the Assureds, to which the first sentence of the

---

[142] See above, para.12-005. As in the case of the QA/QC obligations, discussed above (at para.24-011), it is suggested that the first sentence of the Due Diligence clause should not be subject to the Insurance Act 2015, s.11. See above, paras 5-103 to 5-104, 5-110 to 5-114.

[143] See below, para.24-021.

[144] MIA, s.78(4). See Arnould, paras 22-09, 22-13.

[145] See below, para.24-042 (Sue and Labour).

[146] WELCAR, General Terms and Conditions, cl.19.

[147] See above, para.12-007.

Forfeiture clause could potentially apply, might include: the obligation under the Subrogation clause, requiring the Assureds' co-operation in securing insurers' subrogation rights[148]; the Waiver of Subrogation clause, prohibiting the Assureds from granting waivers of subrogation to drilling contractors without insurers' agreement[149]; the first sentence of the Due Diligence clause, discussed above[150]; the Loss Notification clause in Section I[151]; the Defence and Settlement clause in Section II, in respect of insurers' right to associate with, and have the co-operation of, the Assureds in the defence of claims[152]; and the Notice to Underwriters and Admission of Liability clauses in Section II.[153] Also potentially affected by the Forfeiture clause are the Warranty clause and the Marine Warranty Surveyor ("MWS") provisions in the JR 2010/010 MWS endorsement, discussed below.[154]

2. However, it is not clear that the Forfeiture clause would be construed as applying to all of the above-mentioned clauses and duties. The MWS provisions in JR 2010/010, mentioned above, are the most obvious exception. They will normally be contained in an endorsement, rather than in the main body of the Policy.[155] Moreover, that endorsement contains its own express statements as to the consequences of breach (in terms which are similar, but not identical, to the Forfeiture clause). The same might arguably be said of the first sentence of the Due Diligence clause, which is expressed to be a "condition of the Policy" and, as noted above, may have been intended to be a condition precedent to liability. It might be argued that obligations of the Assureds such as these, expressed in the form of conditions, containing their own bespoke provisions regarding the effect of breach, and in substance concerned with the conduct of the insured activities and operations—rather than claims-related matters such as waivers of subrogation or notice to insurers—fall outside of the Forfeiture clause.

3. Provisions imposing claims-related obligations on Assureds, on the other hand, which generally are not expressed to be "conditions" and do not expressly provide for the consequences of their breach, might be said to more naturally fall within the scope of the Forfeiture clause's first sentence.[156] Limiting the first sentence of the clause to claims-related obligations would make it a more natural complement to the second sentence of the clause (discussed further below), which also relates to claims under the policy (i.e. provides for the invalidity of the policy in the event of a false or fraudulent claim).

4. The words "claim in connection with which the breach occurred", if ap-

---

[148] WELCAR, General Terms and Conditions, cl.2. See above, para.24-015.
[149] WELCAR, General Terms and Conditions, cl.3. See above, para.24-015.
[150] WELCAR, General Terms and Conditions, cl.10. See above, para.24-020. See also Sharp, para.7.4.5.
[151] WELCAR, Section I, Terms and Conditions, cl.3. See below, para.24-054.
[152] WELCAR, Section II, Insuring Agreement, cl.4. See below, para.24-060.
[153] WELCAR, Section II, Terms and Conditions, cll.1 and 2. See below, paras 24-059 and 24-060.
[154] See below, paras 24-036 to 24-038.
[155] Though elsewhere, the Policy is expressly stated to be "made and accepted subject to the conditions, limitations, agreements and declarations and all endorsements signed by Underwriters, and shall constitute the entire contract between the Underwriters and the Assured(s)." See WELCAR, General Terms and Conditions, cl.17, discussed above at para.24-013.
[156] The "commercial purpose" underlying claims notification clauses has been held to justify construing them as conditions precedent to liability: see *Aspen Insurance UK Ltd v Pectel Ltd* [2008] EWHC 2804 (Comm) at [64]–[65]; [2009] 2 All E.R. (Comm) 873; [2009] Lloyd's Rep. I.R. 440. See above, paras 21-006 to 21-007.

plied to all provisions in WELCAR that the Assureds might breach, may need to be construed differently depending on the particular provision breached. Where a provision imposes an obligation regarding the conduct of the Assureds' activities or operations, then arguably the "connection" required would be that the breach should be a cause of the claim under the policy.[157] It is suggested that clearer words would be required to achieve alternative constructions, whereby breaches constituting only remote causes of the underlying loss, damage or liability, would bar the Assured's claim.[158] On the other hand, where the provision breached is claims-related, e.g. imposes an obligation on the Assureds to secure insurers' subrogation rights, or to respond in a certain way to a loss or potential liability, the words "claim in connection with which the breach occurred" would seem to refer to a relationship of relevance between the breach and the "claim"—either an Assured's claim under the policy, or by a third party claim against the Assured which results in such a claim—which will not normally be a causal relationship. This need to construe the words "in connection" differently, depending on the nature of the provision breached by the Assured, may lend support to the suggestion that it is only the second, claims-related type of provision to which the first sentence of the Forfeiture clause should apply.

The second sentence of the Forfeiture clause should probably be construed as encompassing such fraudulent claims as would fall within the scope of the common law rule.[159] In the event of such a claim, it is provided that "this Policy shall become null and void, and all coverage hereunder shall be forfeited."[160] Similar clauses, though generally referring to the forfeiting of "all *claims* hereunder", rather than "all *coverage* hereunder", have long been in use: they have been held to reflect the common law rule against fraudulent claims.[161] In the event of a fraudulent claim, the second sentence of the Forfeiture clause probably acts automatically to discharge insurers from liability under the whole policy—i.e. from "all coverage"—, though probably only (save as regards the fraudulent claim itself) prospectively.[162]

The reference to a fraudulent claim being made by "any Assured" suggests it is arguable that *all* Assureds would lose cover where the provision applies, should *any*

---

[157] Arguably, a proximate cause: see, by analogy, obiter comments in *Aspen Insurance UK Ltd v Adana Construction Ltd* [2015] EWCA Civ 176 at [51]–[58]; [2015] 1 C.L.C. 270; [2015] Lloyd's Rep. I.R. 511 (exception in contractor's liability policy for liability "arising in connection with the failure of any product to fulfil its intended function"). Cf. *Khanty-Mansiysk Recoveries Ltd v Forsters LLP* [2016] EWHC 522 (Comm), at [39]–[40], dealing with a settlement agreement including the expression "arising out of or in connection with", where it was noted that "as a matter of language, the words 'in connection with' are plainly of wider scope than the words 'arising out of'". Eder J also observed: "In my view, reference to earlier authorities as to the meaning of a particular word or phrase is often unhelpful and sometimes dangerous particularly where the context in which that word or phrase may have been used is different from the instant case or wording."

[158] See above, paras 19-016 to 19-018.

[159] See discussion above, at paras 21-027 to 21-047.

[160] In relation to such clauses, see para.3-072. See also Sharp, para.7.4.9.

[161] See MacGillivray, paras 21-062 to 21-063. See also *K/S Merc-Scandia XXXXII v Certain Lloyd's Underwriters (The "Mercandian Continent")* [2001] EWCA Civ 1275 at [10]; [2001] 2 Lloyd's Rep. 563; [2001] C.L.C. 1836 (per Longmore LJ): "It is well recognised that, even if the policy did not have such an express term, the term expresses what would, in any event, be the law."

[162] See *Insurance Corporation of the Channel Islands Ltd v McHugh* [1997] L.R.L.R 94 QBD at 133–135 (clause provided that "all benefit under this policy shall be forfeited"); see also MacGillivray, para.21-066.

Assured make a fraudulent claim under the policy[163]: this result might be considered un-commercial, and the better view is probably that only the insured advancing a fraudulent claim should be affected.

For policies to which the Insurance Act 2015 applies, the second sentence of the Forfeiture clause may be construed as an attempt to contract out of the provisions of Part 4: if so, it will have to satisfy the "transparency requirements" in ss.17 and 18.[164]

24-022   **Cancellation.**   A right to cancel the Policy, on behalf of all Assureds, is vested in the "first named Principal Assured":

> "15. *CANCELLATION* The first named Principal Assured set out in Item 1 of the Declarations may cancel the Policy on behalf of all Assureds at any time prior to the first Occurrence that gives rise or may give rise to a covered loss. Notice of cancellation shall be sent to Underwriters through the party identified in Item 7 of the Declarations. Such notice shall be sent by registered mail, facsimile, e-mail or hand-delivery, and shall state when, not less than thirty (30) days thereafter, cancellation shall be effective. Notice of cancellation shall not be effective on the date specified in the notice unless the party identified in Item 7 of the Declarations forwards the notice to Underwriters within 72 hours after receiving it. A notice of cancellation complying with the requirements of this clause shall terminate the coverage of all Assureds under this Policy on the effective date stated in the notice. The first named Principal Assured shall be responsible for notifying all Assureds that the Policy has been cancelled.
>
> If the first named Principal Assured cancels the Policy, Underwriters shall calculate the return premium in accordance with the level of exposure on the date of cancellation. In any event, Underwriters shall retain at least the short rate proportion of the premium for the period the Policy has been in force, in accordance with the attached table."[165]

Termination of composite insurance has been discussed earlier in this work.[166] The Cancellation clause provides that notice of termination must be transmitted through the person designated in the Declarations for this purpose, within 72 hours of receipt of the notice by that designated person. The termination date stated in the notice must be no earlier than thirty days after the date of the notice. Such notice can only be given "at any time prior to the first Occurrence that gives rise or may give rise to a covered loss." No express provision is made for the case where the "first Occurrence" intervenes without the knowledge of the first named Principal Assured, prior to the date of notice or to the effective date of cancellation. It is suggested that, in such a case, notice of cancellation should be ineffective. This would be in keeping with the usual common law rule, which should apply to Section I, that an insured's cause of action under a contract of property insurance accrues upon the occurrence of the insured peril.[167] It would also accord with the provisions of Section II, which responds to liabilities caused by Occurrences "which may result" in "damages" taking place during the Project Period and notified within the Policy Period.[168] The alternative construction seems un-businesslike, as it would permit the first named Principal Assured to give notice of cancellation in ignorance of a previ-

---

163 See above, para.20–034; *Arab Bank Plc v Zurich Insurance Co* [1998] C.L.C. 1351, at 1363–1364; [1999] 1 Lloyd's Rep. 262.
164 See above, paras 5-116 to 5-137.
165 WELCAR, General Terms and Conditions, cl.15. See also Sharp, para.7.4.6.
166 See above, paras 20-038 to 20-039.
167 See above, para.21-005.
168 See WELCAR, Section II, Terms and Conditions, cl.1 para.2, and discussion above, at paras 24-

ous Occurrence, and then upon learning of the Occurrence before the effective cancellation date, to bring a claim under Section I or to notify the Occurrence under Section II, while remaining entitled to a return of premium.

Upon cancellation, the insurers must make a return of premium but are entitled to retain "at least the short rate proportion of the premium for the period the Policy has been in force." The "short rate premium" will normally be more than a pro-rata share of the full agreed premium for the Policy Period: the wording suggests that the insurers' short rate premium calculation table should be annexed to the policy documents. But insurers may be entitled to retain a larger part of the premium "in accordance with the level of exposure on the date of cancellation", which presumably would take into account the effective limits of indemnity to which insurers were exposed under Section I and Section II at the relevant date.

Conflicting Statutes clause. WELCAR's Conflicting Statutes clause provides: **24-023**

> "Any and all provisions of this insurance that conflict with the statutes of the state or country wherein this insurance is issued are understood, declared and acknowledged by Underwriters and the As-sured(s) to be amended to conform to such statutes."[169]

This clause acknowledges the international nature of the offshore construction business. The un-amended WELCAR form provides for English law to apply[170]: at the time WELCAR first appeared, conflicts between the form and English law, lead-ing to the application of the Conflicting Statutes clause, would have been expected to be rare. In many jurisdictions, however, direct insurance covering an offshore project is required to be governed by local law, in accordance with local domestic insurance regulation. Further, it is often the case that there is insufficient underwrit-ing capacity in the local market to write large offshore construction risks. Accord-ingly, the insurance of the offshore project depends on reinsuring the local, direct insurers in a foreign market with adequate capacity, e.g. London. The reinsurance, though written in London on WELCAR terms, is often amended to be governed by the same legal system as the direct insurance, so that cover can be effectively "back-to-back". The Conflicting Statutes clause attempts to anticipate at least some of the potential difficulties that can arise in circumstances where policies written on the WELCAR form are issued in jurisdictions far from London and are thus subject to conflicting local laws.'

It is suggested, speculatively, that the English courts might be reluctant to "rewrite" the insurance contract if it conflicted with an applicable non-English statute, without clear guidance from the relevant statute regarding the manner in which the contract should be amended: otherwise, the courts might only be will-ing to run a "blue pencil" through conflicting parts of the wording judged to be severable without affecting the meaning of the remainder.[171] This may also prove to be the approach adopted where the Conflicting Statutes clause comes into play in the event of conflict between an English-law policy and the Insurance Act 2015.

Other general provisions. Other clauses included in WELCAR's General Terms **24-024**
and Conditions include the following:

---

017 and 24-018 and below at para.24-059.
[169] WELCAR, General Terms and Conditions, cl.16. In this regard, see also Sharp, para.7.4.3.
[170] See above, para.24-007.
[171] In a manner analogous to severance of terms which are illegal or contrary to public policy, at com-mon law: see discussion in *Chitty on Contracts* (2015), Vol.1, paras 16–211 to 16–220.

1. A Claims Currency clause[172] gives the Assureds the option to have payment of any claim accepted by insurers made in either US dollars or British pounds sterling.

2. Held Covered clause[173] addresses the risk of expropriation of the insured property (which, in respect of energy projects, must in many cases continue to be a serious possibility[174]). WELCAR provides that, in the event of an expropriation, the policy continues for a further fourteen days to cover the "contingent liability of the Assured". The meaning of "contingent liability" in this context is obscure. It has been noted that such a clause "presumably recognises that, following an event of expropriation, the insureds may not immediately know with any certainty whether or to what extent they will be compensated by the expropriating state."[175] The liabilities held covered may be those an Assured may incur for damage to another Assured's property or for injury to their personnel: the first-mentioned Assured may not have the reciprocal indemnities and releases in place with the last-mentioned Assured to ensure that the loss is allocated to the latter, consistently with "knock-for-knock" contracting practices.[176] Further, or alternatively, the "contingent liabilities" envisaged may be those of the Principal Assured who incurs liability to a third party jointly with, and by reason of the fault of, an Other Assured (such as a Contractor): in practice, such a liability might rest finally with the Principal Assured if the Other Assured's own insurances did not respond. Both types of liabilities discussed here have been referred to as "contingent liabilities", in the offshore construction context.[177]

3. An Insolvency clause[178] makes clear that, even in the event of the "insolvency, bankruptcy, receivership or any refusal or inability to pay of the Assured and/or any other insurer", each subscribing (re)insurer's liability under the policy is several, limited to their proportion of the risks written, and subject to the policy deductibles. This provision may clarify the position in cases, potentially being decided before non-English courts or tribunals, involving inter-insurer claims for contribution, or direct actions by third parties against insurers (where legislation allows such actions).

4. Finally, there is an Inspection and Audit clause,[179] under which insurers are permitted to inspect an Assured's property and operations at any time, and examine and audit and Assured's relevant "books and records" at any time during the Policy Period or any extensions thereof, and within three years following "final termination of the Policy".[180]

---

172 WELCAR, General Terms and Conditions, cl.7.
173 WELCAR, General Terms and Conditions, cl.8.
174 The expropriation of Spanish controlled Yacimientos Petroliferos Fiscales ("YPF") by Argentina in 2012 is a relatively recent example.
175 Sharp, para.17.4.3.
176 See above, fn.66.
177 See Sharp, paras 9.1.1 and 9.5.2, where he also sets out the wording of a Contingent Liabilities endorsement (similar to that referred to in *BP Plc v GE Frankona Reinsurance Ltd* [2003] EWHC 344 (Comm) at [25]; [2003] 1 Lloyd's Rep. 537).
178 WELCAR, General Terms and Conditions, cl.13.
179 WELCAR, General Terms and Conditions, cl.14.
180 See above, paras 3-077.

(c)   WELCAR, Section 1—Physical Damage

Insured property under WELCAR Section I.   Broadly, WELCAR Section I can   **24-025**
cover any property or works relating to the project, whether destined to become
permanent parts of the works, temporary works, or other equipment and property
"not for incorporation" being used for the project (including during removal from,
but not during carriage to, the project sites), and whether in the nature of site
preparatory works or equipment used during initial operation at, near or after
completion.

> *"2. COVERED PROPERTY*
>
> This insurance covers works executed anywhere in the world in the performance of
> all contracts relating to the Project including (provided they are included in the
> contract values declared to Underwriters and insured herein) materials, components,
> parts, machinery, fixtures, equipment and any other property destined to become a
> part of the completed project, or used up or consumed in the completion of the
> project. This insurance shall also cover (provided they are declared to and agreed
> by Underwriters) all temporary works, plant, equipment, machinery, materials,
> outfits and all property associated therewith, whether such items are intended to form
> a permanent part of the works or not, including site preparatory work and subsequent
> operational risks.
>
> It is understood and agreed that any insured equipment and/or property that is not for
> incorporation into the contract works shall be covered whilst it is being utilised in the Project
> and whilst in transit from the Project site(s) until the earlier of the date of arrival at its final
> destination or the 30th day after its removal from the Project site(s)."[181]

Within this broad definition, the Assureds' declarations of project values and
specific items of property or "works" committed to the performance of contracts
relating to the Project play the key role in resolving any uncertainty as to the identity
of the insured property.[182] Thus, for example, non-material or "soft" costs, such as
project management or design costs, or taxes and duties, can and often are declared,
if the Insured believes they may need to be incurred again in the event of a loss.[183]

The reference in the Covered Property clause to "works ... and any other
property destined to become a part of the completed project, or used up and
consumed in the completion of the project" would seem unlikely to raise any
problems of construction. The same may be said of "[S]ite preparatory work". A
number of terms in the phrase "temporary works, plant, equipment, machinery,
materials, outfits and all property associated therewith" are discussed elsewhere in
this work.[184] "[S]ubsequent operational risks" is an expression that calls for some
comment[185]: it is suggested that this expression encompasses property employed,
after completion of the Project, for whatever initial operations may be covered by
the Policy, which might not otherwise fall within the definition of the insured
property.[186]

The definition of insured property distinguishes between property intended for

---

[181] WELCAR, Section I, cl.2.
[182] See Sharp, paras 6.4.0 and 7.5.2, where he notes that the insured property is "defined in expansive
terms and it is safe to say that the scope of the works insured by the policy meets the criteria appropriate for industry needs".
[183] See Sharp, para.6.5.2.
[184] See above, paras 3-006 to 3-008, 9-061 to 9-069.
[185] See Sharp, para.7.5.2.
[186] See above, paras 24-008 and 24-017, regarding cover for initial operations.

inclusion in or to be used up in the completion of the Project, which is insured "anywhere in the world" (including, implicitly, while in transit), and property "not for incorporation" which is covered "whilst it is being utilised in the Project and whilst in transit from the Project site(s)". The WELCAR policy form does not define "site(s)", though elsewhere in the wording are references to "offshore site(s)" and to the "final offshore site".[187] Nevertheless, it is suggested that there is no reason to restrict the meaning of the expression "Project site(s)" to the final offshore site(s), particularly in circumstances where significant aspects of an offshore project are normally executed onshore, before being moved to the final offshore location. Accordingly, property "not for incorporation" should be covered when it is being utilised for the Project, regardless of its location. Logically, "utilisation" of such property should include transit to any place where contract works are to be executed. Cover is continued for property "not for incorporation", while in transit away from such Project site(s) and no longer being "utilised": though only for a limited time.[188]

24-026 **Errors and Omissions clause.**   This clause provides:

> *"4. ERRORS AND OMISSIONS*
>
>> Any unintentional or inadvertent error or omission in name or description under Section I shall not operate to the prejudice of the Assured, provided that the error or omission is corrected when discovered by the Assured and advised to Underwriters prior to any Occurrence giving rise to a claim hereunder."[189]

An error in name or description, particularly in relation to the project, the subject matter insured, clearly has the potential to prejudice the Assureds' cover under Section I. A policy covers only the risks described therein.[190] The clause is meant to allow the Assureds to rectify any such errors or omissions that are unintentional or inadvertent by advising insurers upon discovery. Implicitly, it would seem, insurers would then be obliged to accept the Assureds' corrections. There is no provision in the clause for the payment of additional premium, which may indicate that the errors contemplated really are limited to those in the nature of "mis-labelling". More fundamental changes to the nature of, or operations involved in, the project, may instead fall under provisions such as the Project Alterations and Amendments clause, under which additional premium is contemplated.[191]

24-027 **Insured values declared: Policy Limit clause, and Schedules A and B.**   Declared values play a number of roles under WELCAR. For example: they serve to identify the insured property, activities, and costs; they form the basis of the calculation of indemnities payable in the event of loss, under Section I; they form the threshold for the recognition of a constructive total loss in respect of the various parts of the insured property; they act as limits on indemnities payable; and form the basis for the calculation of premium.[192] Declared values for the project will

---

[187] E.g. WELCAR, Section I, Terms and Conditions, cl.15; Declarations, item 5.

[188] Restrictions of coverage by location are discussed above, at para.9-070.

[189] WELCAR, Section I, Terms and Conditions, cl.4. See also Sharp, para.8.8.2.

[190] See above, paras 12-012 to 12-013. See also Arnould, paras 19–06 and 19–07.

[191] See discussion above, at para.24-009.

[192] See Sharp, para.7.3.0: the need for activities to be included within declared insured project values "is a clear hint that insurers are only seeking to reimburse expenditures that have actually been

normally be informed by and closely dependent on the project specification, and seek to represent a reliable estimate of the project costs incurred and projected.[193]

WELCAR anticipates that the parties will have agreed the following types of declared values:

1. The Schedule A valuation is intended to act as an aggregate limit to insurers' exposure, based on a multiple ("ideally" 150%, but in practice often 125%)[194] of the estimated completed value of the project.

2. The Schedule B values are meant to represent completed construction costs corresponding to the "milestone stages" of the project. The policy form anticipates that these may be subject to agreed revisions from time to time over the course of the project.[195]

The Policy Limit closure then provides for the use of Schedules A and B as limits of indemnity, as follows:

"3. POLICY LIMIT

Underwriters' total liability under Section I for all claims arising out of any one Occurrence shall not exceed 125% of the latest agreed Schedule 'B' values, including payments made under the sue and labour clause, the additional work clause and the removal of wreckage and/or debris clause (each of which is separately limited under the appropriate coverage clauses).

In the event of escalation as provided under clause 5 of Section I, Underwriters' total liability under Section I for all claims arising out of any one Occurrence shall not exceed 150% of the initial Schedule 'B' values, including payments made under the sue and labour clause, the additional work clause and the removal of wreckage and/or debris clause, and the Escalation Clause (each of which is separately limited under the appropriate coverage clauses).

Notwithstanding anything contained herein, Underwriters' maximum limit of liability in respect of Section I shall not exceed the Schedule 'A' value in the aggregate."[196]

A number of observations can be made regarding the Policy Limit clause:

1. A first limit, set out in the first sentence of the Policy Limit clause, is applicable to all claims under Section I arising out of any one Occurrence, including claims under extensions to or additional covers under Sue and Labour, Additional Work and Removal of Wreckage and/or Debris clauses.[197] This limit is set at 125% of the *latest agreed* Schedule B values. Notably, though the clause refers to "total liability under Section I for all claims", only certain extensions to and additional coverage clauses are expressly mentioned. Nevertheless, other additional covers, such as under the Stand-by Charges and Forwarding Charges clauses, though unmentioned are arguably also caught by this first limit, as the Policy Limit clause refers to "all claims" under Section I.

2. This first limit is intended to allow for a hypothetical worst case scenario, where a total loss of insured property is accompanied by costs and expenses

---

included within the declared estimated completed value (ECV). This aligns with the principle of indemnity, i.e. that Assureds are entitled to be put in the same position as before the loss, but only with respect to those costs which have been declared and on which premium has been paid." See also Sharp, paras 9.6.2 and 9.6.6.

[193] See Sharp, paras 6.5.4 and 7.1.6.
[194] Sharp, para.7.5.3.
[195] See Sharp, para.7.5.3.
[196] WELCAR, Section I, cl.3. Virtually the same wording appears in the Declarations, item 4.
[197] Additional covers and extensions to cover are discussed below, at paras 24-040 to 24-050.

falling within the mentioned additional covers. However, reinstating lost or damaged works can be more costly than their initial construction costs: e.g. retrieving, rectifying and reinstalling a damaged component may require removing other property to gain access, additional costs for transportation or for performing work afloat that was initially performed ashore, etc.[198] It has been suggested that, where there are no claims under additional covers, "it must be inferred ... that a claim for repair or replacement for a complete *Schedule B* listed item is payable up to 125% of the applicable limit".[199] While this is a possible reading of the Policy Limit clause, taken alone, it seems more likely, on balance, that by virtue of the Basis of Recovery clause, repair and replacement costs as such are limited to 100% of the relevant Schedule B values. Accordingly, the "additional" 25% of the 125% limit is available only for costs and expenses under the aforementioned additional covers.[200]

3. A second, *maximum* per Occurrence limit, is provided for under the second sentence of the Policy Limit clause. It applies in the event of "escalation"— i.e. of actual costs overrunning the budgeted costs declared in Schedule B— under the Escalation clause.[201] In theory, the WELCAR form does not limit the amount by which insured values may escalate above initial Schedule B values. However, with any escalation the per Occurrence limit under the first sentence of the Policy Limit clause, which is based on the *latest agreed* Schedule B values, will also increase. The second sentence of the Policy Limit clause (and the last sentence of the Escalation clause) ensures that the maximum per Occurrence limit for which insurers may be liable will be 150% of *initial* Schedule B values (i.e. representing 100% of initial Schedule B values, a further 25% of such values to cover additional covers such as sue and labour, etc, and an additional 25% of initial Schedule B values to reflect cost escalation).[202]

4. In many places, Section I suggests that the values declared in Schedule B are to be set out in a number of listed "items". As discussed further below, the indemnity for loss or damage to property payable under Section I is based on identifying lost or damaged items[203]; and the Sue and Labour, Additional Work, and Removal of Wreckage clauses equally require identification of the item or items in relation to which the relevant expenses or costs were incurred.[204] Further, cover under the Sue and Labour and Additional Work clauses is subject to a sub-limit (or two inter-related sub-limits[205]) of 25% of the value of the relevant items in the latest agreed Schedule B; and

---

[198] See Sharp, para.6.5.4.
[199] Sharp, para.7.5.3.
[200] See discussion below, at para.24-033.
[201] Discussed below, at para.24-028.
[202] In practice, the apparent result is that no escalation in costs beyond 20% of initial Schedule B values will affect the per Occurrence limit. E.g. given initial Schedule B values of £100, and latest agreed Schedule B values of £120 (following 20% escalation), then applying the first sentence of the Policy Limit clause gives a per Occurrence limit of 125% x £120 = £150. Sharp, para.7.5.3, notes that it may have been "quite deliberate on the part of insurers" to insist on "an overall Schedule B limit fixed from the outset for reasons of their own capacity considerations." The result is that while declared costs under Schedule B may escalate above 125% and even 150% of initial values, the per Occurrence limit is "locked" at 150% of initial Schedule B values.
[203] See below, para.24-033.
[204] WELCAR, Section I, Terms and Conditions, cll.9–11.
[205] See discussion of Sue and Labour and Additional Work clauses, below at paras 24-042 to 24-043.

cover under the Removal of Wreckage clause is subject to a separate sub-limit of 25% of the value of the relevant Schedule B items. The Policy Limit clause does not employ the word "item", imposing limits instead by reference to Schedule B "values". But it seems likely that the "values" forming the basis for the limits in the first two sentences of the clause, were also intended to be only those corresponding to the relevant Schedule B items. This construction is consistent with the clauses just mentioned. It is also in keeping with the Escalation clause,[206] and makes sense of the scheme of limits in the Policy Limit clause: the Escalation clause recites that the "values stated in the Declaration [viz in Schedule B] at the time the risk was bound represent the Estimated Completed Value"; as noted above, in practice the Schedule A limit has tended to be set at 125% or 150% of this estimated completed value; and as the Schedule A limit in the third sentence of the Policy Limit clause is a maximum aggregate limit of liability under Section I, the "per Occurrence" limits under the first two sentences of the clause would be redundant if, in all cases, they were to be based on 125% or 150% of the *total* Schedule B values (i.e. even in cases where only a limited number of Schedule B items were damaged or lost).

5. The above-mentioned limits employ aggregation language: all claims "arising out of"—i.e. having a significant causal connection with[207]—the same "Occurrence" (a term which, as discussed below, is itself defined using aggregation language)[208] are subject to the same per Occurrence limits.

6. There is a potential mismatch between the applicable Schedule B values at the time damage or loss occurs—which might be onshore, early in the course of the project—and the date when the damage or loss is discovered—which might be offshore, after installation, when rectification would be very costly. It has been noted that, prior to WELCAR, insurers were willing to compensate for this mismatch, but that the practice has been abandoned.[209] Accordingly, insureds must take special care to check regularly and often for damage and defects.

7. The third limit, under the third sentence of the Policy Limit clause, is a maximum aggregate limit of liability under Section I. There is no provision for it to vary in the event of any escalation in costs.

Escalation clause. This provision,[210] which has already been mentioned,[211] begins **24-028** by reciting that the Schedule B values initially declared at the time of conclusion of the policy represent only a provisional estimated completion value. Construction costs, over the course of construction during the Project Period, may or may not exceed these provisional estimates.[212] The "insured value" is agreed to be the "final completed value of the property insured". (In practice, however, it seems to

---

[206] WELCAR, Section I, cl.5.

[207] See above, paras 11-029, 11-031, 18-011 fn.5, and 19-019. Note, however, that in the context of limitation of liability, it may be arguable that arising out of should be construed, as it would be in an exclusion, as meaning "proximately caused by": see MacGillivray, para.21-004 fn.24.

[208] See below, at para.24-029

[209] Sharp, paras 6.5.4 and 7.5.3: Sharp notes that, from the insurer's point of view, this result may be considered fair, as the premium will have been calculated based on the construction cost of the relevant property at around the time the damage occurred.

[210] WELCAR, Section I, cl.5. See also above, para.17-023.

[211] See discussion above, at para.24-027.

[212] See Sharp, para.7.5.4.

be generally presumed that WELCAR policies are to be treated as unvalued or "open" policies, not valued policies).[213]

Accordingly, the Assureds are bound to declare to insurers any excess in the final completed value above the provisional values initially declared, and "pay premium as agreed". In turn, insurers are bound to "accept their proportionate share of the increase", though it is expressly provided that this will not increase the maximum per Occurrence limit of indemnity beyond 125% of initial Schedule B values, and their liability is "always subject to the limits of recovery as provided for elsewhere in the Policy".[214] This wording appears at first to be inconsistent with the second sentence of the Policy Limit clause, but it is suggested that the Escalation clause should be understood as reiterating the maximum possible effect of *escalation* on the per Occurrence limits under the Policy Limit clause—i.e. the maximum increase in the per Occurrence limit, due to escalation alone, is 25%—, without contradicting that clause's maximum per Occurrence limit of *150%* of initial Schedule B values in the event of escalation (i.e. thus allowing a further 25% for additional covers such as sue and labour, etc, as discussed above at para.24-027).

If the final completed value is less than the initial Schedule B values, the insured value is correspondingly less and insurers are required to make proportionate return of premium "as agreed".[215]

24-029   **Covered Perils clause: all risks of physical loss or damage.**   Offshore construction cover has traditionally always been of the "all risks", rather than "named perils", type.[216] WELCAR reflects this, under Section I, in providing as follows:

> "*1. COVERED PERILS*
>
> Subject to the terms, conditions and exclusions herein, Section I insures against all risks of physical loss of and/or physical damage to the property covered hereunder, provided such loss or damage arises from an Occurrence within the Policy Period set out in Item 3 of the Declarations."[217]

> "3.   The term 'Occurrence,' wherever used in Section I of the Policy, shall mean one loss, accident, disaster or casualty or series of losses, accidents, disasters or casualties arising out of one event; (i) as respects windstorm, all tornadoes, cyclones, hurricanes, similar storms and systems of winds of a violent and destructive nature, arising out of the same atmospheric disturbance within any period of seventy-two consecutive hours commencing during the period of this insurance, shall be considered one event; (ii) each earthquake, shock or volcanic eruption, shall constitute one event hereunder, provided that if more than one earthquake, shock or volcanic eruption shall occur within any period of seventy-two consecutive hours commencing dur-

---

[213] See discussion of the Basis of Recovery clause, below at para.24-033. See also above, paras 11-004 to 11-006; Arnould, paras 2–20, 12–06 to 12–07.

[214] See Sharp, paras 6.5.1 and 7.5.4, describing: an "automatic increase in cover up to an agreed percentage of the provisionally estimated value. Typically this escalation factor is 25% of the initially estimated comp[l]eted value". Further: "where the 'final completed value' (FCV), exceeds 125% of the ECV, the premium is adjustable on this higher value even though the maximum recovery is limited to 125%, these limits themselves being subject to the [initial] Schedule B values."

[215] The practicalities are discussed in Sharp, para.9.6.3.

[216] See Sharp, para.6.6.1.

[217] WELCAR, Section I, cl.1. Sharp, para.7.5.0, refers to this clause as "[t]he core element of coverage, the nucleus of Section I …".

ing the period of this insurance, such earthquake, shocks or volcanic eruptions shall be deemed to be one event within the meaning hereof."[218]

Accordingly, the basic insured peril under Section I is "all risks of physical loss and/or damage"[219] to the insured property, arising from "one loss, accident, disaster or casualty" (or from a "series" of these "arising out of one event").[220] Broadly put, the insurance can be said to respond to physical losses or damage proximately caused by: (i) a fortuitous occurrence; or (ii) several losses or occurrences each having a significant causal link with a fortuitous occurrence.[221]

The special aggregation wordings regarding violent storms and geological events are similar to those discussed elsewhere in this work.[222]

Defective Parts clause. As has been discussed in the terrestrial context, CAR **24-030** policies may adopt one of a variety of possible approaches to the issue of defective or faulty design, workmanship, or materials.[223]

WELCAR, Section I, provides as follows[224]:

"7. DEFECTIVE PARTS

The insurance afforded by Section I covers physical loss and/or physical damage to the property insured herein occurring during the Policy Period and resulting from a Defective Part, faulty design, faulty materials, faulty or defective workmanship or latent defect even though the fault in design may have occurred prior to the attachment date of the Policy.

Section I, however, *does not provide coverage* for loss or damage to (including the cost of modifying, replacing or repairing) any Defective Part itself, unless all of the following are satisfied: (a) such Defective Part has suffered physical loss or physical damage during the Policy Period; (b) such physical loss or physical damage was caused by an insured peril external to that part; and (c) the defect did not cause or contribute to the physical loss or physical damage.

In no case shall Section I provide coverage for any cost or expense incurred by reason of betterment or alterations in design.

In the event of the total physical loss or total physical destruction of one or more of the items listed in the Schedule 'B' attached to the Policy, then this exclusion shall only apply to an identifiable part or parts of such scheduled item or items.

For the purposes of this clause a 'Defective Part' shall mean any part of the subject matter insured which is or becomes defective and/or unfit or unsuitable for its actual or intended purpose, whether by reason of faulty design, faulty materials, faulty workmanship, a combination of one or more thereof or any other reason whatsoever. The term 'Defective Part' shall also include such ancillary components, which are not themselves faulty, but which would normally be removed and replaced by new components when the component that is faulty is rectified.

This clause shall prevail in the event of any conflict or inconsistency with any other clause

---

[218] WELCAR, Section I, Definitions, cl.3. See also Sharp, para.8.9.2.

[219] Regarding: physical loss, see above, para.14-003; for physical damage, see above paras 14-007 to 14-023. See also Sharp, para.6.6.2.

[220] In relation to "loss", "accident", "event", "casualty" and "series", see above, paras 10-004 to 10-015 and 15-005 to 15-013 (discussing inevitable losses and "non risk" events), 11-027 to 11-033, and 18-035.

[221] In relation to the expressions "arising from" and "arising out of", see references above, at fn.207.

[222] See above, discussion of: storms, etc, at paras 15-031 to 15-033; "72-hours" provisions, at para.2-086 (in context of policy excess), and para.17-022 (in context of extensions of cover).

[223] See also Sharp, paras 6.6.3, and 8.5.0, where he notes that the Defective Parts clause is "one of the most contentious areas of the WELCAR policy, not so much from the construction of the clause, since the intent is expressed with clarity, but from the viewpoint that an element of coverage previously available is withdrawn; i.e. damage to the faulty part itself."

[224] Regarding the history of this provision, and of the related buy-back discussed below at para.24-031, see Sharp, para.7.1.5.

forming part of the Policy. The terms of this clause are not intended and shall not be construed as providing coverage not otherwise provided under the Policy."[225]

In respect of the above provision a number of observations can be made:

1. The provision is intended to clarify and direct the interpretation of, and to limit, the scope of cover under Section I. It is suggested that it is not intended to function as an extension of cover. The wording of the clause— and in particular its final sentence—supports this construction.[226]

2. The relevant "defects" and "faults" are defined broadly.[227] Cover under Section I is provided for loss or damage resulting from "a Defective Part, faulty design, faulty materials, faulty or defective workmanship or latent defect".

3. The clause provides that Section I covers physical loss or damage occurring *during the Policy Period*: this should be construed as meaning during the Project Period or the Maintenance Period.[228] The loss or damage must be "resulting from"—which would probably be construed as meaning "proximately caused by"[229]—a "Defective Part", etc. Generally, where insurance covers damage caused by defects, the relevant defects can be insured perils even if they pre-date inception of the policy or attachment of the risk.[230] Only in the case of loss or damage caused by a "fault in design", however, does WELCAR state expressly that it is permissible for that fault to have "occurred prior to the attachment date of the Policy." This limited clarification may be explicable as, in practice, some design work in relation to components, which later prove to have been "faulty", is likely to have been undertaken prior to inception of the policy or attachment of the risk in relation to the particular components.[231] It is suggested, however, that loss or damage caused by defects pre-dating inception or attachment of risk arising from factors other than faults in design (e.g. from faulty materials) would, in the usual way, also be covered by Section I, despite the absence of an express indication in this regard.

4. The Defective Parts clause clarifies that Section I covers physical loss or physical damage to insured property *other than* the "Defective Part" itself: it is expressly provided that the loss of, damage to, or the cost of modifying, replacing or repairing, a "Defective Part", is generally not covered. It

---

225 WELCAR, Section I, Terms and Conditions, cl.7.

226 See discussion of cover for physical damage caused by defects, etc, generally, above at paras 16-001 to 16-002. See also Sharp, para.6.6.3: "Physical loss or physical damage resulting from defects in design, workmanship and materials may be considered as 'risks' within the ambit of an 'all risks' coverage, yet there always exists the possibility of an argument being raised that the loss is inevitable if the defect is discovered and not corrected. In other words insurers could have a defence to the claim on the grounds that the loss did not result from a 'risk' and could have been avoided. To avoid this situation it is common in construction insurance to include a specific clause that makes it absolutely clear that consequential damage from these causes is covered." WELCAR, Section I, Terms and Conditions, cl.7 is just such a clause.

227 See discussion of terms such as "defect", etc, above, at paras 16-005 to 16-007, 16-009 to 16-010.

228 See above, paras 24-017 and 24-018.

229 See generally Ch.19 above: in particular para.19-019 ("arising from").

230 See discussion above, of latent defect cover at para.16-026; and see also Arnould, paras 22–02, 23–55 to 23–58.

231 On inception of the policy period, and attachment of risk, see above, paras 24-017 to 24-019. Compare "faulty materials" and "faulty or defective workmanship", which may be more likely to intervene (i) after the design stage, during the procurement stage of the project at the earliest, when in the normal case the WELCAR cover would be in place, and (ii) generally, in the course of performance of a project-related contract. See also Sharp, para.6.6.3.

follows that WELCAR distinguishes between that part of the insured property which is defective, and other parts which are not defective but which have been damaged, etc by the defective part.[232] As with other defects provisions, dividing up the insured property in this way is an evaluative exercise, in relation to which the wording offers little assistance.[233] The definition of "Defective Part" is circular, being "*any part* of the subject matter insured ..." (emphasis added). Little guidance is to be obtained from the indication that a "part" is a "Defective Part" if it "is or becomes defective and/or unfit or unsuitable for its actual or intended purpose ... for any ... reason whatsoever": these words could, for example, apply to either very simple or complex components. Again, little help is to be derived from the recognition that the "Defective Part" may have "ancillary components". The wording goes on to point out that, in the event of a total loss of a Schedule B item, the excluded "part" shall be limited to "an identifiable part or parts of such scheduled item".[234] Thus, a "part" may in theory be a smaller element of a listed Schedule B item: but this observation will, again, assist little in typical cases where the Schedule B items represent substantial, aggregate stages of the overall project, with little breakdown provided. Accordingly, it is suggested that the defective "part" should be delineated in a "natural", "ordinary", "common sense"[235] or "commercial"[236] way, with the objective of identifying some element of the insured property which the project participants would reasonably treat as having a distinct purpose. The "part" thus identified may represent a distinct package or stage in the works, though in a normal case it is likely to constitute only an element in a more compendious Schedule B item.

5.   The expression "Defective Part" is defined as including "such ancillary components, which are not themselves faulty" but which would be replaced in the normal course of rectifying the defect. This is not, it is suggested, equivalent to saying that every element of the insured property which needs to be removed and replaced in order to rectify the defect is automatically to be assimilated to the "Defective Part". Instead, the meaning seems narrower, referring to components "ancillary" to the defective part (i.e. supporting the carrying out of its normal function), that are normally not reused once disconnected from the defective part or otherwise removed (e.g. seals or gaskets, fluids, etc).

6.   As an exception to the exclusion, loss or damage to the defective part itself is covered if (i) occurring during the currency of the policy (i.e. during the Project Period or Maintenance Period), and (ii) caused by "an insured peril external to that part" without the defect having caused or contributed to the loss or damage. Thus, if a defective part is dropped by a workman,[237]

---

[232] Compare the Inchmaree Clause, discussed at paras 16-024 to 16-026. See Sharp, paras 8.5.2 to 8.5.2(d).

[233] See discussion in the context of DE3 and DE4 (1995), above at paras 16-038 to 16-043.

[234] See Sharp, para.8.5.2; and above, para.24-027 (discussion of Schedule B "items"). Total loss is discussed below, at para.24-033.

[235] *Mitsubishi Electric UK Ltd v Royal London Insurance (UK) Ltd* [1994] 2 Lloyd's Rep. 249 at 253; [1994] C.L.C. 367 at 371; 74 B.L.R. 87 at 89 CA (Civ Div).

[236] See above, para.16-042.

[237] The dropping not constituting faulty or defective workmanship, for present purposes: because it is not built into the defective part (see above, paras 16-032, fn.87, and 16-037); and, in any event,

thereby sustaining damage for reasons unrelated to the defective condition of that part, this is covered by Section I.[238]

7.   Finally, costs and expenses incurred by reason of betterment or alterations in design are excluded.[239]

24-031   **Defective Part Exclusion Buy-back endorsement.**   A standard endorsement to WELCAR will operate, where agreed,[240] to cover or "buy-back" the cost of repair or replacement of defective parts that have suffered physical loss or damage during the Policy Period or Maintenance Period[241]:

> "Notwithstanding the provisions of the Defective Part Clause in Section I of the attached Policy, this insurance will pay for the cost of repair or replacement of defective parts which have suffered physical loss and or physical damage during the Policy Period, but the recovery of such costs is subject to:
>
> (a)   deductible [*blank*] each part, each accident or Occurrence; and
> (b)   a total aggregate limit of [*blank*] for all losses during the Policy Period, including the Maintenance Period; and
> (c)   the provisions of the Basis of Recovery Clauses in Section I of the Policy; and
> (d)   an additional premium [*blank*] being paid in full.
>
> However, it is specifically understood and agreed that this endorsement will not provide recovery for cancellation charges, stand-by costs or consequential costs or expenses that would not be recoverable under the terms and conditions of the Policy in the absence of this clause."

Cover under the endorsement is thus subject to the application of a per/part, per Occurrence deductible, an aggregate sub-limit, and payment of additional premium. The application of the deductible means that the endorsement does not obviate the need to identify the Defective Part.[242] While it has been suggested that where cover under the Defective Part Exclusion Buy-back applies, its particular deductible is solely applicable, and not additional to any other deductible applicable under Section I,[243] there is no clear support for this construction in the wording itself. The better view may be that the normal Section I deductibles apply in the usual way, to "each and every Occurrence", while the endorsement's "each part, each ... Occurrence" deductible applies to such additional losses arising from the same Occurrence as are covered by the endorsement.

In practice the endorsement will be called upon where a Defective Part suffers damage caused by or contributed to by the relevant defect in that Part. The indemnity is limited to amounts derived by applying the Basis of Recovery clause.[244] The final words of the endorsement expressly provide that the extension of cover it operates does not extend to "consequential costs or expenses", such as cancellation charges incurred by reason of delays arising from damage to Defective Parts (even if such damage is, itself, covered under the endorsement).[245]

---

because the defective workmanship is not, by hypothesis in this example, related to the pre-existing defect already affecting the part.

[238]   Compare DE3 (1995), discussed above at paras 16-036 to 16-037. See Sharp, para.8.5.1.

[239]   See discussion, in the context of DE5 (1995), above at paras 16-059 to 16-061 and 16-064.

[240]   It has been noted that insurers are not all willing to underwrite cover under this endorsement, at least not for all insureds or projects: Sharp, para.8.5.3.

[241]   See also above, para.16-008.

[242]   See discussion in context of the Defective Parts clause, above at para.24-030.

[243]   Sharp, para.8.5.3. See discussion of Section I's Deductibles clause, below at para.24-053.

[244]   Discussed below, at para.24-033.

[245]   Extensions to Section I are discussed below, at paras 24-040 to 24-050.

Limited cover under Section I during Maintenance Period. Following comple- 24-032
tion of the project there will normally ensue a period during which, under project-
related contracts, contractors and suppliers will remain liable under provisions such
as warranties and guarantees to rectify any defects or performance problems
exhibited by the works they carried out.[246] This may entail further attendance on site
by the relevant contractors, for further work, and the transportation of particular
items to the site (e.g. replacement parts) and from the site (e.g. parts destined to be
repaired).

A risk to such contractors, in carrying out such maintenance duties, is that they
may cause damage to the project works without being covered under the operator's
operating insurance policy. A further concern is that the manifestation of defects
after the Project Period may be accompanied by physical loss or damage to the
project works.

To address these issues, WELCAR Section I provides for a limited extension of
cover under Section I during the Maintenance Period:

> "*19. MAINTENANCE*
>
> The cover provided hereunder shall be no wider than that contained elsewhere in the
> Policy. Coverage under Section I only shall continue during the maintenance
> period(s) specified in individual contracts but not exceeding a further 12 months
> from expiry date of the Project Period as set out in Item 3 of the Declarations. Dur-
> ing such maintenance period(s), coverage is limited to physical loss or physical dam-
> age resulting from or attributable to:
> (a) faulty or defective workmanship, construction, material or design arising from
>   a cause occurring prior to the commencement of the maintenance period; and
> (b) operations carried out by Other Assureds during the maintenance period(s) for
>   the purpose of complying with their obligations in respect of maintenance or
>   the making good of defects as may be referred to in the conditions of contract,
>   or by any other visits to the site necessarily incurred to comply with qualifica-
>   tions to the acceptance certificate."[247]

The duration of cover under this provision has already been discussed.[248] The cover
provided is no wider than that otherwise provided for physical loss or damage under
Section I, and moreover is further limited to two instances:

1. First, there is cover for physical loss or damage caused by faulty or defective workmanship, etc.,[249] on condition that the fault or defect itself arises
   from "a cause"[250] that occurred prior to expiry of the Project Period.[251] The
   policy is not intended to cover faults or defects introduced to the insured
   property after completion of the works.
2. Secondly, physical loss or damage to the insured property caused by

---

[246] See Sharp, paras 6.3.5 and 8.7.0. On maintenance periods in CAR more generally, see above, paras
3-039, 4-011, and 9-077.
[247] WELCAR, Section I, Terms and Conditions, cl.19.
[248] See above, at para.24-018.
[249] See discussion of Defective Parts clause, and its "Buy-back", above at paras 24-030 and 24-031.
[250] See discussion of "originating cause" above, at para.11-033.
[251] This construction results from that concerning the commencement of the Maintenance Period,
discussed above (see above, fn.129). Accordingly, the references to "maintenance period(s)" in the
third sentence of the Maintenance clause and in sub-clause 19(b), and to "the maintenance period"
in sub-clause 19(a), should be taken to refer to the Maintenance Period under the policy, i.e. such
parts of the maintenance period(s) specified in individual contracts during which coverage continues
following "the expiry date of the Project Period".

contractors, carrying out maintenance obligations under their contracts, is covered.

24-033 Basis of Recovery clause: partial and total loss. This long clause provides for the measures of indemnity applicable, in various circumstances, following an insured peril under Section I (e.g. under the Covered Perils clause or the Defective Parts clause):

"1. BASIS OF RECOVERY

In the event of an Occurrence covered under Section I of the Policy, Underwriters agree to indemnify the Assured on the following basis:

(a) *items repaired or replaced* – 'New for Old' plus towage, installation and all other costs necessarily incurred and duly justified in repair or replacement – as per latest agreed Schedule B.

(b) *replacement with items which are redesigned or of new design* – provided such replacement is actually commenced and no repairs or replacements are carried out on the item which sustained physical loss or physical damage, indemnification hereunder shall be on the basis of reasonably estimated figures in accordance with paragraph 1a. above.

(c) *items not repaired or replaced*:
  (i) for items which are a total and/or constructive total loss, the actual items costs incurred up to time of loss as per latest agreed Schedule B.
  (ii) for partial physical loss of or physical damage to an insured item, the reasonable depreciation arising from the unrepaired damage, deemed to be the reasonable cost of repairing such damage on a new for old basis plus (in the event repairs are not undertaken for reasons entirely outside the control of the Assured) towage, installation and other similar costs directly incurred in respect of the item lost or damaged, up to the point of loss and, to the extent that such costs have been prepaid or the Assured is committed to paying and is unable to revoke, but not to exceed amounts as per the latest agreed Schedule B.

(d) *use of prehired vessels/equipment* – It is understood and agreed that if, in the event of physical loss and/or physical damage to the property insured which is covered by Section I, repairs and/or reinstatement and/or replacement and/or salvage are carried out by vessels and/or craft and/or equipment and/or labour which the Assured have on charter, hire or contracted to them, the cost or the proportion thereof shall be based on the pre-agreed hire or contract rates for such employment when used in or about the repair, reinstatement, replacement, or salvage of losses covered by Section I and shall be so recoverable as a claim hereon. In the event that the Assured utilises its own vessels, craft, equipment, material or labour for any repair, reinstatement, replacement or other work in respect of physical loss and/or physical damage covered by Section I, then, subject otherwise to the terms and conditions of the Policy, a reasonable charge in respect of such work shall be recoverable as a claim hereon. Provided always that the recoverable costs referred to in this paragraph shall not exceed the costs of employing approved vessels and/or craft and/or equipment and/or materials and/or labour from other available sources.

In respect of paragraphs a. and b. above, in no event shall Underwriters be liable for any increased cost or expense of repair or construction by reason of law, ordinance, regulation, permit or licence regulating construction or repair or any increased cost or expense incurred by reason of betterment or alteration in design.

Additional insurance costs and (re)certification costs attaching to damage repair or replacement work are covered hereunder as part of the values insured subject to inclusion of the original insurance costs in the initial Estimated Final Completed Value of the works.

Provided always that where any of the aforesaid costs relate to retrieval of a damaged item and/or subsequent (re)installation of that repaired item or a replacement, and such costs or part thereof would in any event have been incurred by the Assured irrespective of the insured physical damage, or otherwise benefit the Assured in respect of uninsured matters, then such costs shall be apportioned in a fair and reasonable manner between the Assured and Underwriters."[252]

As with hull insurance on a vessel, WELCAR assumes that a lost or damaged vessel will be repaired or replaced: the usual measure of indemnity is thus based on the cost of repair or replacement. This is because, as with a vessel, a project insured under WELCAR is not usually intended for sale (unlike cargo): it is presumed that the owner may reasonably elect to repair or replace.[253]

Where damaged or lost "items"[254] *of insured property are repaired or replaced*, sub-clause 1(a) of the Basis of Recovery clause provides an indemnity for the item itself, as well for all costs "necessarily incurred ... in repair or replacement". The item itself is indemnified on a "new for old" basis: the "customary allowance" of one-third applicable in the context of marine insurance is excluded.[255]

Regarding the somewhat cryptic reference in the final words of sub-clause 1(a) to "—as per latest agreed Schedule B", it has been suggested that this is intended to function as a limit of indemnity.[256] This is probably correct. There is no actual inconsistency between this construction of sub-clause 1(a) and the Policy Limit clause, discussed above (though, admittedly, the wording of the Policy Limit clause could engender a false expectation that the full per Occurrence limit of 125% of the relevant Schedule B values could be available for repairs or replacement).[257] It is difficult to imagine what purpose the words "as per latest agreed Schedule B" are to serve, in this context, other than as a limit of indemnity. Further, other provisions in the policy form support this construction. In particular: this is suggested by the final words of the Escalation clause[258]; it is consistent with the General Aver-

---

[252] WELCAR, Section I, Terms and Conditions, cl.1. See also Sharp, para.8.2.0.

[253] See above, para.11-013. See also Arnould, para.27–14; *Lohre v Aitchison* (1877) 2 Q.B.D. 501, at 506–508, where Lush J stated: "If ships were kept merely for sale, it might reasonably be contended that the same principle should be applied which is applied to damaged goods. But a ship is intended to be used for profit. The owner is in many contingencies bound to repair. He has always the right to repair, and it is in the contemplation of both parties that if damage happens the ship will be repaired if it is worth the cost. If, instead of repairing, the owner chooses to sell the ship in her damaged condition, he fixes his loss at the difference between what she was worth at the commencement of the risk and what she sold for. But if he elects to repair, the loss is ascertained by the cost of the repairs, less a proper deduction on account of having new timber for old. Nothing short of this, would be an indemnity."

In the WELCAR context, Sharp, para.8.2.5, notes: "[I]t is difficult to envisage a position where the loss is not repaired or replaced, given that the revenue earning potential of the site, being the oil or gas within the reservoir, remains to be exploited. On field developments that consist of interdependent structures, such as platforms, pipelines and subsea wells, much of this infrastructure may have been ordered and possibly installed and it is inconceivable to consider that the owners would, in effect, abandon any such undamaged property."

[254] See discussion above, at para.24-027.

[255] See: para.11-016, at fn.13, above; MIA, s.69(1); Arnould, paras 27–14 and 27–18.

[256] Sharp, para 8.2.1: "The reference to *Schedule B* should be noted. Costs incurred *new for old* may be somewhat higher than the costs originally incurred because it may not be possible to replicate the costs or the installation methodology. *Schedule B* costs will comprise the historic original costs. It must therefore be assumed that the reference to *Schedule B* is the means by which insurers are applying a limit to their liability."

[257] See discussion above, at para.24-027.

[258] Discussed above, at para.24-028: "should the insured value exceed 125% of the initial declared value as per Schedule B, then *the limits of indemnity under Section I* shall be 125% of the initial schedule values, any one Occurrence, but *always subject to the limits of recovery as provided for elsewhere in the Policy and in accordance with the agreed 'B' scheduled amounts as per the Declarations at the time of loss.*" (Emphasis added.)

age and Salvage Charges clause, which also purports to limit the indemnity for partial losses (which should include, inter alia, particular average losses) "arising from any one casualty" to "the value applicable to the item"[259]; it is consistent with the Additional Work clause, which refers specifically to the Policy Limit being "exhausted by a claim under the sue and labour clause", but does not recognise the possibility of the Policy Limit being "exhausted" by repair or replacement costs alone[260]; and finally it would be consistent with sub-clause 1(c) of the Basis of Recovery Clause.[261]

If this construction is correct, then (subject to there being any other partial losses, such as general average losses or salvage charges)[262] the whole of the latest agreed Schedule B amount corresponding to the relevant item should be available for repair or replacement costs. This should be so, even if the item were only partly constructed at the time of loss or damage, such that the Schedule B amount were to be provisional and includes an estimated element of the completed value of the item. This would be consistent with the calculation of the premium on the basis of such provisional values and, ultimately, on the basis of the final completed value of the item.[263] Thus, so long as the Assureds remain committed to repairing or replacing (and thus, to completing) the relevant item, the whole provisional "insured value" for that item should be available under the policy.[264]

Sub-clause 1(b) addresses the case where items lost or damaged are replaced with items which are "redesigned or of new design". Such costs will not always be excluded under the Defective Parts clause: e.g. the damaged or lost item requiring replacement, though redesigned, may not have been defective.[265] In such a case the sub-clause requires an estimate of the cost of repair or replacement of the original item, as if, counter-factually, the item were being repaired or replaced as originally designed. Thus, the measure of indemnity provided for under sub-clause 1(a) is applied. Sub-clause 1(b) applies only in circumstances where replacement of the lost or damaged item with a redesigned item has "actually commenced", and where

---

[259] See discussion of General Average and Salvage Charges clause, below, at para.24-041.

[260] See discussion of Additional Work clause, below at para.24-043. Admittedly, the Additional Work clause does not refer to "exhaustion" of the Policy Limit by a claim under the Removal of Wreckage and/or Debris clause (discussed below, at para.24-044), either, though clearly this might occur.

[261] Note in particular sub-clause 1(c)(ii): where items are partially lost or damaged, and neither repaired nor replaced due to reasons outside the Assureds' control, the Assured can recover reasonable depreciation—"deemed to be the reasonable cost of repairing such damage on a new for old basis", and is thus based on an estimate of the actual repair or replacement costs—plus "towage, installation and other similar costs directly incurred in respect of the item lost or damaged" already incurred or irrevocably committed to at the point of loss; but the whole is capped, "*not to exceed amounts as per the latest agreed Schedule B.*" (Emphasis added.) Against this, might be argued that the indemnity was intended to be more generous under sub-clause 1(a), where items are actually repaired or replaced, than where they are not (even where the Assureds wish to repair but are prevented from doing so by reasons outwith their control). But the policy contains no clear suggestion of any intention to discriminate in this way in favour of sub-clause 1(a).

[262] Which would erode this limit: see discussion of the General Average and Salvage Charges clause, below, at para.24-041.

[263] The practicalities regarding the calculation of the premium are discussed in Sharp, para.9.6.2.

[264] In practice, the indemnity under s.1(a) is not treated as being subject to the rules determining the measure of indemnity under simple valued policies: see discussion of the Escalation clause, above at para.24-028. Allowing repair costs up to the latest agreed provisional value in Schedule B should, in many cases, allow some margin for repair costs indemnified to be "higher than the costs originally incurred because it may not be possible to replicate the costs or the installation methodology": Sharp, para.8.2.1.

[265] See above, para.24-030; and Sharp, para.8.2.2.

"no repairs or replacements are carried out on the item which sustained physical loss or physical damage". The effect of these provisos is, thus, to apply sub-clauses 1(a) or 1(c) in preference to sub-clause 1(b), wherever possible.

The second, or ante-penultimate, paragraph of the Basis of Recovery clause, which applies in conjunction with sub-clauses 1(a) or 1(b), states that insurers should not be liable for any "increased cost or expense of repair or construction" incurred by reason of legal norms or permits or licences regulating construction or repair—it would seem, in anticipation of potential changes in such legal norms as compared to those applicable when the property lost or damaged was originally constructed—,[266] or for any increased cost or expense incurred by reason of "betterment or alteration in design".[267] Where repair or replacement is undertaken, the third, or penultimate, paragraph of the clause provides cover for additional insurance and (re)certification costs associated with the repair or replacement work, provided the original insurance costs were included in the initially declared Schedule B values.[268]

Sub-clause 1(d) makes special provision for the use of vessels, craft, equipment or labour, owned or already contracted for by the Assureds, in carrying out repairs, reinstatement, replacement, salvage or other work in respect of physical loss or damage covered by Section I. In practice, it will be expedient to use such resources, which may already be in the field at the time the reinstatement of damage needs to be undertaken.[269] Use of resources owned by the Assureds, subject to the terms of the policy, attracts an indemnity for "a reasonable charge". Use of pre-contracted resources is indemnified at the pre-agreed contract rates. In both cases, costs are not recoverable if they exceed the cost of employing resources from other available sources.[270]

The final proviso to the Basis of Recovery clause stipulates that where costs (or parts thereof) relating to retrieving a damaged item, or (re)installing a repaired item or a replacement, either would have been incurred by the Assureds irrespective of the insured loss or damage, or benefit the Assureds in relation to uninsured matters, then "such costs shall be apportioned in a fair and reasonable manner" between the Assureds and insurers. In some cases, actions undertaken to retrieve or (re)install an item might serve both to respond to insured damage and also to serve the Assureds' other interests, such as ensuring employee safety, avoiding a pollution risk, retrieving an uninsured vessel, etc.[271] In the context of sue and labour, the difficulties of making a "fair and reasonable" apportionment of interests which are not arithmetically comparable has led to the rejection of apportionment (e.g. between insured vessel, on the one hand, and the owner's crew, on the other) as unsound in principle: indeed, apportionment has been said to apply only to marine property

---

[266] See above, para.17–032, discussing extensions to non-marine CAR to cover some such matters. See also Sharp, para.8.2.1, noting that in practice this "makes it necessary to deduct an appropriate allowance from the claim".

[267] See para.11–016, fn.13; and references given above at para.24–030, fn.239 regarding similar provisions in the Defective Parts clause.

[268] Sharp, para.8.2.3, comments that similar costs, "such as owner's and contractor's project management costs", should also be recoverable if they were included amongst the initially declared values.

[269] See Sharp, para.8.2.4.

[270] Sharp notes, at para.8.2.4, that employing vessels from other sources will rarely be less expensive, as generally there will be mobilisation and demobilisation charges involved.

[271] Sharp, para.8.2.3, gives the example of items due to be sent back to their manufacturers for maintenance in any event.

insurance, and then only in the narrow case where the separate interests of insurer and insured arise purely due to underinsurance.[272] Nevertheless, the wording of the clause in this case clearly requires that there be an apportionment, taking into account the Assureds' interests considered more broadly.[273]

Where the items lost or damaged are neither repaired nor replaced, sub-clause 1(c) applies:

1. Sub-clause 1(c)(i) addresses the situation where there is an "[actual] total and/or constructive total loss" of an item or items.[274] This is the only mention of constructive total loss in the WELCAR form. The language of the sub-clause suggests, employing the language of the MIA, s.76(1), that the policy's Schedule B items are intended to be treated as "apportionable part[s]" of the subject-matter insured, with the "contract contained in the policy" being itself "apportionable". Accordingly, "the assured may recover for a total loss of any apportionable part."[275] In the event of an actual or constructive total loss of a Schedule B item, the measure of indemnity is the *"actual items['] costs incurred up to time of loss* as per latest agreed Schedule B" (emphasis added). It is thus anticipated that it will be possible to identify such actual costs incurred in the latest agreed Schedule B, in addition to the latest agreed estimated completed values.[276] As sub-clause 1(c)(i) deals with the total loss and non-replacement of an insured item, it is appropriate to fix the indemnity at the level of actual construction costs incurred, rather than on the basis of an estimated final completed value which, on this hypothesis, will never be reached.[277] The sub-clause, in effect, treats the policy as a valued policy in the event of total loss of an item

---

[272] See *Royal Boskalis Westminster NV v Mountain* [1999] Q.B. 674 at 738–739, per Phillips LJ (obiter). See also *Ace European Group v Standard Life Assurance Ltd* [2012] EWCA Civ 1713, at [30]–[49]; [2013] 1 All E.R. (Comm) 1371; [2013] Lloyd's Rep. I.R. 415; and *Atlasnavios–Navegação LDA v Navigators Insurance Co Ltd (The B Atlantic)* [2014] EWHC 4133 (Comm), at [346]; [2015] 1 All E.R (Comm) 439; [2015] 1 Lloyd's Rep. 117; [2015] Lloyd's Rep. I.R. 151.

[273] Where the costs would have been incurred by the Assureds in any event, arguably the fair and reasonable apportionment would often be 50:50. But where the costs merely "benefit the Assured in respect of uninsured matters", but the benefit would not have been sufficient to induce the Assured to incur the costs in any event, then presumably the Assureds' apportioned share should be significantly less than 50%. Sharp, para.8.2.3, suggests that the "benefit" to the Assureds may include reductions in delays. Expediting expenses can be covered by an appropriate extension to cover.

[274] See above, paras 11–012, and 14-003 to 14-005. See also Sharp, para.8.2.5. The MIA, s.57(1), notes that "there is an actual total loss" where "the subject-matter insured is destroyed, or so damaged as to cease to be a thing of the kind insured, or where the assured is irretrievably deprived thereof".

[275] See Arnould, paras 28–21, and 28–24 to 28–25. Amendments to WELCAR policies sometimes specify that only a constructive total loss of the whole project shall be possible.

[276] As Sharp notes, "*Schedule B* costs will comprise the historic original costs" (para.8.2.1). WELCAR Section I, Terms and Conditions, cl.12, the Tests, Leak and/or Damage Search Costs clause, is comparable in providing: "never to exceed original expenditure as identified in the latest agreed Schedule B." Other WELCAR Section I clauses referring to Schedule B values do not expressly refer to actual costs incurred (and references to 'initial' Schedule B values demonstrate that estimated completed values should also be included in Schedule B): Policy Limit clause ("shall not exceed [X]% of the [latest agreed/initial] Schedule 'B' values"); Escalation clause ("in accordance with the agreed 'B' scheduled amounts as per the Declarations at the time of loss"); Basis of Recovery clause, sub-clause 1(a) ("as per latest agreed Schedule B"), and sub-clause 1(c)(ii) ("not to exceed amounts as per the latest agreed Schedule B"); Sue and Labour clause and Removal of Wreckage clause ("the scheduled value contained in the latest agreed Schedule B at the time of loss"). See also Declarations, cl.4: "shall not exceed 125% of the latest agreed Schedule 'B' values".

[277] By virtue of the Escalation clause, discussed above at para.24–028, the premium can be adjusted downward upon completion of the project, to take account of the abandonment of an item lost in

not repaired or replaced.[278] The latest agreed declaration of costs actually incurred thus fixes the measure of indemnity in the case of the total loss of an item. Further, it would seem reasonably arguable that by incorporating the ICBR, cl.12, into Section I of WELCAR,[279] the latest agreed costs actually incurred are to be taken as the item's repaired value for the purpose of determining whether there has been a constructive total loss.[280] Marine insurance rules relating to the conditions for the existence and timing of an actual or constructive total loss, to the giving of notice of abandonment, and to abandonment itself as an incident of a total loss, should apply to WELCAR.[281]

2. Sub-clause 1(c)(ii) is concerned with cases of partial loss or damage to an insured item. In a manner not wholly different from the MIA's treatment,[282] the measure of indemnity is stated to be the reasonable depreciation arising from the unrepaired damage. This is "deemed to be the reasonable cost of repairing such damage on a new for old basis".[283] But in cases where repairs are not undertaken by the Assureds "for reasons entirely outside [of their] control", the indemnity also covers costs, like towage, "directly incurred in respect of the item lost or damaged", which the Assureds had already paid or were irrevocably committed to paying at the time of the loss. "Reasons entirely outside the control of the Assured" should exclude commercial reasons, even if well-founded, and more generally circumstances where the Assureds have by express choice or deliberate conduct—e.g. in allocating their resources—not undertaken repairs.[284] But "reasons" arising from the negligence of the Assureds should not be excluded.[285] It is suggested that "directly incurred in respect of the item" probably refers to costs incurred exclusively for the purpose of constructing the relevant item. This would sensibly give effect to the phrase, indemnifying those costs which in effect become totally lost by reason of

---

the course of construction and not replaced. Cf. Sharp, para.8.2.5, who suggests that the reference in sub-clause 1(c)(i), to "as per latest agreed Schedule B", "infers that the *Schedule B* amount would be paid, irrespective of having to prove that all such costs had actually been incurred." It is suggested that the construction favoured in the main text is to be preferred.

[278] See para.11–004, above; see also Arnould, paras 12–13 to 12–15, and 12–33.

[279] See discussion of Incorporated Clauses, below at para.24–034. The ICBR were mentioned above, at para.24-003, and are also discussed below, at paras 24-093 to 24-103.

[280] MIA ss.27(3) and (4), and 68(1). Standing back, if the notion of constructive total loss is to apply to property under construction, then in practice the value of the works in the state of completion they were in at the time of loss (represented by the actual construction costs incurred up to that time) must be the relevant benchmark. In practice, an item's actual construction costs may be a reasonable estimate of its "market value". Cf. Hudson et al, *Marine Insurance Clauses* (2012), pp.291–292 (commenting on cll.11 and 12 of ICBR).

[281] Further discussion of these matters is beyond the scope of this work: see Arnould, Chs 28 to 30, in this regard.

[282] MIA s.69(3).

[283] See also *Pitman v The Universal Marine Insurance Co* (1882) 9 Q.B.D. 192, at 216–217, per Cotton L.J (adopting similar reasoning, in a hull insurance context, in estimating depreciation by reference to the cost of repair).

[284] E.g. *Safadi v Western Assurance Co* (1933) 46 Ll. L. Rep. 140, at 142–143 (held covered provision in cargo insurance). See also *Chitty on Contracts* (2015), at paras 15–153 (discussing force majeure clauses), and 23–061 to 23–065 (discussing self-induced frustration).

[285] Given the normal position that cover is presumed to encompass the negligence of the insured: see above, paras 10–020 to 10–021, above. However, see reasoning in e.g. *J Lauritzen AS v Wijsmuller BV (The Super Servant Two)* [1990] 1 Lloyd's Rep. 1, at 5–8 (force majeure clause in a charterparty), and references to *Chitty on Contracts* (2015), above at fn.284.

the Assureds' inability to repair the damaged item.[286] It is suggested that the final words of the sub-clause, "as per the latest agreed Schedule B", apply the same limit of indemnity as is applicable under sub-clause 1(a).[287]

3. It is to be implied, presumably, that where an insured item suffers partial loss or damage, which is only *partially* repaired or replaced, sub-clauses 1(a) (or 1(b), if appropriate) and 1(c)(ii) must be applied to the repaired and unrepaired damage, respectively.[288]

24-034 Incorporated Clauses and Order of Precedence clause. Section I incorporates a number of standard marine insurance policy wordings, most notably ICBR and ICC (A) (1/1/82). Also incorporated are various other standard wordings, some of which are concerned with insuring against war and political risks.[289]

The potential confusion that could result from the incorporation of these other wordings into WELCAR, is partly addressed by the Order of Precedence clause, which provides:

> *"5. ORDER OF PRECEDENCE*
>
> All clauses incorporated into the Policy by reference (hereinafter the "Incorporated Clauses") apply insofar as they do not conflict with the wording of the Policy. In the event that the Incorporated Clauses conflict with this Policy wording, this wording shall take precedence."[290]

In many situations arising under WELCAR, the provisions of the Incorporated Clauses will conflict with, and thus be overridden by, WELCAR's own wording.[291] In other cases, the incorporated wordings may provide additional cover, or clarify issues not addressed by the main WELCAR wording.[292] Nevertheless, the technique of incorporating entire standard wordings such as ICBR into the WELCAR form is a potential source of uncertainty as to the ultimately intended scope of cover.[293]

ICBR and ICC (A) (1/1/82) are discussed in greater detail later in this chapter: some general comments regarding the manner of their incorporation into WELCAR are made here. It is beyond the scope of this work to comment on the remaining Incorporated Clauses.[294]

ICBR are incorporated into WELCAR subject to certain amendments. These

---

[286] See also discussion of "in respect of", in the public liability context, above, at para.18–041.

[287] Discussed in this paragraph, above.

[288] I.e. in a manner analogous to MIA s.69(2).

[289] WELCAR, Section I, Terms and Conditions, cl.2. The other incorporated wordings are (or in some cases, would appear to be): to complement ICBR, the Institute War Clauses Builders Risks (1/6/88) and Institute Strikes Clauses – Builders Risks (1/6/88); to complement the ICC (A) (1/1/82), the Institute Classification Clause (13/4/92), the Institute War Clauses (Cargo) (1/1/82), the Institute War Clauses (Air Cargo) (1/1/82), the Institute War Clauses (sendings by Post) (1/1/82), the Institute Strikes Clauses (Cargo) (1/1/82), the Institute Strikes Clauses (Air Cargo) (1/1/82), and the MAR 91 Form.

[290] WELCAR, General Terms and Conditions, cl.5.

[291] See also Sharp, paras 7.4.2 and 8.3.0: Sharp notes a previous practice, no longer common, for conflicting provisions in Incorporated Clauses to be deleted from the policy prior to signing.

[292] See, e.g. the potential relevance of ICBR cl.12 in relation to constructive total loss, above at para.24–033.

[293] E.g. ICBR, incorporated into Section I (which mainly covers physical damage), includes collision liability and protection and indemnity cover: the Assureds' under WELCAR were probably intended to benefit from these, though operating such a significant extension of cover in this manner may seem surprising.

[294] It is suggested that the reader consult: Arnould; J. Dunt, *Marine Cargo Insurance*, 2nd edn

include the deletion of the earthquake and volcanic eruption exclusion, and the express inclusion within the scope of the subject-matter insured under ICBR of the "cost of site preparatory work lost or expended as a result of insured perils".[295] The first part of the Perils clause in ICBR—cl.5.1—is then modified, so as to omit ICBR's defective parts wording, while adding emphasis to the exclusion relating to faulty welds. The amended ICBR cl.5.1 is as follows:

> "*5. PERILS*
>
> 5.1 SUBJECT ALWAYS TO ITS TERMS, CONDITIONS AND EXCLUSIONS this insurance covers all risks of physical loss of or physical damage to the subject matter insured caused and discovered during the period of the insurance.
> *AS SET FORTH IN EXCLUSION 1.1. HEREIN, IN NO CASE SHALL THIS POLICY COVER THE COST OF RENEWING FAULTY WELDS.*"[296]

The Definitions to Section I of WELCAR contain two elements of particular relevance in adapting ICBR to the particular nature of construction projects insured under WELCAR:

> "1. The phrase '*the property insured hereunder*' shall be substituted for the word '*vessel*,' as used in the Incorporated Clauses, where the context of Section I of the Policy allows.
> 2. The word '*launch*' shall be deemed to include skidding onto and off launch barge/vessel and/or mating and/or floating in dry dock and/or flooding thereof and/or transfer of the property insured into water and/or emplacement and/or positioning in water at site."[297]

By incorporating ICBR, the drafters of WELCAR may have intended them to take effect primarily in relation to the construction of parts of the insured property ashore, at the premises of sub-contractors or builders, until "delivery" to a means of transit to the offshore site. But the extended definition of "launch" set out above suggests that "delivery" to the Assureds may not take place until the relevant insured item arrives at the final offshore site and is skidded off the launch barge or vessel, mated with other elements of the works, or transferred into the water and finally positioned. Accordingly, prior to "delivery" under ICBR, both the ICBR and WELCAR wordings may apply simultaneously, with precedence given to WELCAR's provisions in the event of any conflict.

WELCAR's extended definition of "launch" has further importance because ICBR cl.5.2 is incorporated, providing: "In case of failure of launch, the Underwriters to bear all subsequent expenses incurred in completing launch." The insured peril, in this case, is simply the failure of "launching": though implicitly, this must

---

(Abingdon: Routledge, 2015); Hudson et al, *Marine Insurance Clauses* (2012); M.M. Miller, *Marine War Risks*, 3rd edn (London: Informa Law, 2005). For the clauses themselves, see *Reference Book of Marine Insurance Clauses*, various edns (latest is the 78th) (Witherby: London, various dates (the latest is 2015)).

[295] WELCAR, Section I, Terms and Conditions, cl.2(a). the inclusion of site preparatory work is consistent with the redefinition of the subject-matter insured under ICBR as "the property insured hereunder" (i.e. insured under the WELCAR policy into which ICBR is incorporated), as noted later in this paragraph.

[296] WELCAR, Section I, Terms and Conditions, cl.2(a). See also Sharp, para.8.3.1. ICBR cl.5 is discussed at para.24-098, below.

[297] WELCAR, Section I, Definitions, cll.1 and 2.

be the result of some fortuitous accident or occurrence, not otherwise excluded.[298] The per Occurrence limits in WELCAR's Policy Limits clause should apply to the indemnity for failure of launch. There is clearly an overlap between the cover provided here and that provided under WELCAR's Additional Work clause, discussed below.[299] Cover under the Additional Work clause is subject to a sub-limit, and it would seem sensible for insurers also to insist on a sub-limit in relation to ICRB cl.5.2 (if they are prepared to leave it in).[300]

The incorporation of the cargo insurance wordings—of which the principal is ICC (A) (1/1/82)—is addressed in sub-clause (b) of the Incorporated Clauses clause[301]:

> "b)   The following conditions shall apply to any parts of the property insured herein that are in storage (ashore or afloat), loading, unloading and in transit other than by means of their own buoyancy or by means of floatation tanks. These conditions shall continue until midnight on the day on which off-loading at final offshore site is completed and shall include the Collision Clause provisions of the Institute Clauses for Builders Risks (1st June 1988).
> > Subject as applicable to:
> > Institute Cargo Clauses (A) 1st January 1982 ..."[302]

In this regard:

1.   ICC (A) (1/1/82), the MAR Form, and the other named cargo clauses, are said to apply to parts of the property insured that are in storage, loading, unloading or in transit "other than by means of their own buoyancy or by means of floatation tanks." But each of these named activities is also within the definition of the insured Project under WELCAR.[303] Accordingly, the WELCAR wording applies simultaneously with the cargo wordings (and, in some cases and for some periods, also simultaneously with ICBR), to insured property in storage, in transit (other than "wet" transit), etc., up until midnight on the day of off-loading at the offshore site. By virtue of the Order of Precedence clause the WELCAR wording applies alone in the event of a conflict.

2.   The incorporation of the "Collision Clause provisions" from ICBR[304] into the incorporated cargo clauses, must be accompanied by the substitution of the phrase "the property insured hereunder" for the word "vessel" (meaning the vessel insured), as appropriate. This express incorporation of collision liability cover into the incorporated cargo clauses is significant. It tends to confirm that collision liability and protection and indemnity covers in ICBR were intended to apply under WELCAR. More generally, it indicates

---

298   Indeed, this would seem to be the effect of the exclusions. See in particular WELCAR, Section I, Exclusions, sub-clauses 1(e) and (j): placement of "platforms and/or structures" in the "wrong locations" is excluded "unless caused by an Occurrence which is covered by the terms of Section I", and dumping of rocks or other similar materials in the wrong place is excluded. See Sharp, para.8.9.1. See also above, paras 10–001 to 10–003.

299   See below, para.24–043.

300   A default sub-limit of 10% of the sum insured is stipulated in respect of failure to launch in MARCAR CL 371 (1/9/2007), cl.45.1.8.

301   See Sharp, paras 8.3.0 to 8.3.1, and 8.3.3.

302   WELCAR, Section I, Terms and Conditions, cl.2(b). The full list of incorporated cargo clauses is set out in fn.289, above.

303   See discussion above, at para.24–008.

304   Which expression certainly encompasses ICBR cl.17 ("Collision Liability"), but arguably may also encompass cl.18 ("Sistership").

that elements of the Incorporated Clauses are not to be treated as "conflict-ing" with WELCAR simply because they extend cover beyond that which WELCAR's main provisions would otherwise provide.

Pollution Hazard clause.   This clause reads as follows: **24-035**

"6. POLLUTION HAZARD CLAUSE

Subject to the terms and conditions of the Policy, this insurance covers physical loss of or physical damage to the property insured hereunder directly caused by any governmental authority acting under the powers vested in them to prevent or mitigate a pollution hazard, or threat thereof, provided such act of governmental authority must not have arisen from a want of due diligence by the operator for the Principal Assureds to prevent or mitigate such hazard or threat.

Coverage provided by the above paragraph shall also extend to cover any other physical loss or physical damage caused or inflicted by order of any governmental body or agency after consultation with officials and engineers of the Assured relating to the insured project but only in respect of interests covered by Section I, and always subsequent to physical loss and physi-cal damage resulting from a peril insured against."[305]

Clauses similar to the first paragraph of this clause were introduced into marine hull policies following the grounding of the tanker *Torrey Canyon* in 1967: that incident, involving the spilling of thousands of tons of oil into the English Channel, culminated in the decision of the British Government to destroy the tanker by bomb-ing in an attempt to burn off the cargo remaining onboard.[306] The cover provided is against physical loss of or damage to the insured property "directly caused by any governmental authority acting under the powers vested in them to prevent or mitigate a pollution hazard, or threat thereof".

The version included in WELCAR does not expressly require that the pollution hazard must have arisen from damage to the insured property for which insurers are liable under the Policy.[307] But, as the cover under Section I is all risks, and as the cover under the Pollution Hazard clause applies "[s]ubject to the terms and condi-tions of the Policy", the same outcome is probably achieved.[308]

The cover extended by the first paragraph of the Pollution Hazard clause is subject to a proviso that the "act of governmental authority has not resulted from want of due diligence by the operator for the Principal Assureds to prevent or mitigate such hazard or threat [viz of pollution]." It has been suggested, in the context of clauses which expressly state that the pollution hazard must have resulted from insured property damage, that the proviso probably mandates the exercise of due diligence in response to the casualty which caused the pollution hazard, but not in operations prior to the occurrence of any casualty.[309] The same suggestion may be made regarding WELCAR's Pollution Hazard clause, despite its different wording. A further point relates to the co-existence of the Due Diligence clause and the Pollution Hazard clause in the WELCAR form. It is suggested that, in order for

---

[305] WELCAR, Section I, Terms and Conditions, cl.6.
[306] See: Sharp, paras 8.3.5 and 15.1.1; Hudson et al, *Marine Insurance Clauses* (2012), pp.122–123; Arnould, para.23–27
[307] Cf ICBR cl.7; Institute Time Clauses Hulls (1/11/95) cl.7 (which additionally refers to action to prevent "damage to the environment").
[308] Note also that the wording at the end of the clause's second paragraph (which is expressed to be an extension of the cover provided under the first paragraph) ends with: "…and always subsequent to physical loss and physical damage resulting from a peril insured against."
[309] Arnould, para.23–27; see also Hudson et al, *Marine Insurance Clauses* (2012), p.123.

the two clauses to operate consistently, the obligation of "due diligence" imposed under the Pollution Hazard clause should only be breached in the event of advertent recklessness, rather than mere negligence, on the part of persons whose conduct is to be attributed to the "operator for the Principal Assureds".[310]

The second paragraph of the Pollution Hazard clause is thought to be original to WELCAR. It purports to extend the cover provided by the first paragraph to "any other physical loss or physical damage caused or inflicted by order of any governmental body or agency" to "interests covered by Section I"—i.e. to property insured under Section I—, if the governmental order intervenes "after consultation with officials and engineers of the Assured relating to the insured project", and "always subsequent to physical loss and physical damage resulting from a peril insured against [viz under Section I]." It has been suggested that this paragraph may have been introduced to address the deliberate destruction by the Assureds of a platform in an unsafe state due to previously suffered, "catastrophic" damage that could not be safely rectified.[311] But the width of the cover under the second paragraph should not be exaggerated: it is an extension to the cover provided under the first paragraph, and accordingly the relevant "governmental order" should be directed at the prevention or mitigation of a pollution hazard, and the due diligence proviso from the first paragraph should probably also apply.

24-036 **The marine warranty surveyor.** The WELCAR form assumes that a MWS will be involved in the construction project.[312] An MWS is an independent expert—in practice, generally a named marine surveying practice—employed by the insureds or on the insureds' behalf, to fulfil verification, approval and certification requirements imposed on them by the insurers.[313]

The MWS is appointed pursuant to an express "warranty" in the policy. WELCAR contains an "exemplar" of such a provision[314]: in practice a more detailed MWS provision is often agreed. A scope of works detailing the construction activities to be assessed by the MWS is generally contained in an endorsement to a WELCAR policy.

24-037 **Is the Warranty clause a warranty?** Unamended, the Warranty clause in the WELCAR form begins as follows:

> "*15. WARRANTY (EXEMPLAR—FINAL VERSION TO BE AGREED)*
>
> Warranted London Offshore Consultants and/or Global Maritime and/or Noble Denton Associates and/or London Salvage Association approve and issue as applicable certificates on the project as follows ..."[315]

---

[310] See discussion of the Due Diligence clause above, at para.24–020.

[311] Sharp, para.8.3.5.

[312] See Sharp, paras 5.3.0 to 5.3.3, and 8.8.1.

[313] For a further, non-legal, overview of the role of the offshore MWS, see A.R. Harrison, "Marine warranty surveying for offshore projects and issues faced in the current market" (2009) 23 A & NZ Mar LJ 122–142.

[314] WELCAR, Section I, Terms and Conditions, cl.15.

[315] WELCAR, Section I, Terms and Conditions, cl.15,

On its face, the clause might thus have been construed as a promissory warranty, as understood by English law under s.33 of the MIA, prior to the Insurance Act 2015.[316] But the effect of construing the Warranty clause in this way would have been to discharge insurers from all liability under the policy from the date of a breach, regardless of whether the breach was relatively trivial or pertained only to an isolated aspect of the project: e.g. where an MWS approved a particular procedure or operation prior to its being undertaken, but issued their formal certificate of approval only afterwards. As the use of the word "warranty" is not conclusive,[317] and to avoid such an unreasonably severe and un-commercial outcome, it is suggested that the Warranty clause would probably have been construed as a suspensory condition under the pre-2015 Act law.[318]

Further, and alternatively, the first paragraph of WELCAR's Forfeiture clause,[319] which is triggered by "breach [of] any provision of the Policy", would arguably displace the normal consequences of breaching a promissory warranty.[320] The consequence of breaching the Warranty clause would then be loss of coverage only as to "the particular claim in connection with which the breach occurred", i.e. for claims caused by a failure to obtain MWS approval or certification for a particular procedure or operation.

There are at least two reasons why it will not usuallybe necessary to understand the intended effect of WELCAR's Warranty clause. First, under the Insurance Act 2015, it is clearly no longer arguable that the Warranty clause should take effect as a traditional promissory warranty[321]: instead, it should take effect as a suspensory condition,[322] under which only breaches that cause the risk to become essentially different from that originally contemplated by the parties would afford insurers with a defence to claims.[323] Further, a breach of the Warranty clause may not provide the insurers with a defence unless it increases the risk of the loss that actually occurs in the circumstances in which it occurs.[324]

Secondly, in any event, the Warranty clause is often replaced by alternative provisions, such as those contained in the standard MWS endorsement discussed in the following paragraph.

JR 2010/10: MWS endorsement, code of practice and scope of works. In   24-038

---

[316] Unamended, WELCAR is governed by English law and practice: General Terms and Conditions, cl.6. The construction and effect of insurance law "promissory warranties" under English law are discussed above, at paras 12–015 to 12–028. The position has been modified dramatically for policies concluded after the coming into force of the Insurance Act 2015: see discussion below, and see above, paras 5-090 to 5-104, 5-110 to 5-115. See also Sharp, paras 8.8.1 and 9.6.8.

[317] See above, at para.12–018.

[318] Discussed above, at para.12-014. See *Pratt v Aigaion Insurance Co SA (The Resolute)* [2008] EWCA Civ 1314; [2009] 2 All E.R. (Comm) 387; [2009] 1 Lloyd's Rep. 225 (where it was common ground that the warranty was of the "delimiting" kind). Cf. *J Kirkaldy & Sons v Walker* [1999] C.L.C. 722 at 735; [1999] 1 All E.R. (Comm) 334 at 349; [1999] Lloyd's Rep. I.R 410 at 421; where it was common ground that a towage and conditions survey provision was a promissory warranty under MIA s.33, (a condition precedent to insurers' liability); however, in that case the failure to obtain the required surveys was never rectified, so the possibility that the provision might have been qualified as a suspensory condition was moot.

[319] That is, if the Forfeiture clause applies to breaches of the Warranty clause: see discussion above, at para.24–021.

[320] Per MIA s.33(3).

[321] Insurance Act 2015, s.10(1).

[322] Insurance Act 2015, s.10(2).

[323] Insurance Act 2015, ss.10(5) and (6).

[324] Insurance Act 2015, s.11.

2010, the Joint Rig Committee of the International Underwriting Association and Lloyd's Market Association issued JR 2010/010, containing a generic MWS endorsement, accompanied by and incorporating a revised Marine Warranty Surveyors Code of Practice and Generic Scope of Works.[325] These have proved popular with the energy (re)insurance market, being frequently employed—often with amendments—in relation to offshore construction projects insured on WELCAR.[326]

The generic endorsement begins with the following principal provisions:

"1)   Coverage under this Policy for project activities is conditional upon: a) A Marine Warranty Surveyor being appointed by the Assured from the following panel ... [*blank*] on or before [*date*] ...; and b) Issuance of the Certificates of Approval (C of A's) by the Marine Warranty Surveyor for each operation as specified in the Generic Scope of Work (GSOW) contained herein or the Project Specific Scope of Work (PSOW) explicitly agreed by Underwriters. ...

2)   It is the duty of the Assured to procure the compliance with all recommendations, requirements or restrictions of the Marine Warranty Surveyor within the specified timescales. In the event of a breach of this duty, Underwriters will not be liable for any loss, damage, liability or expense arising from or contributed to by such breach.

3)   The Marine Warranty Survey shall be conducted in accordance with the Marine Warranty Surveyor Code of Practice (CoP) and the GSOW contained herein (or the Project specific Scope of Work (PSOW) as agreed by the Contract leader(s)). A material change to the project will require a review of the Scope of Work."[327]

The way in which the MWS scheme is intended to operate is relatively clear.[328] The appointment of an MWS from the panel, and issuance of certificates of approval for each operation for which this is stipulated, is a condition of coverage. The MWS is expected to provide insurers with a schedule of certificates of approval to be issued,[329] and to advise insurers if any certificate is withheld or a "Non Conformance Certificate issued".[330] Breach by the insureds of their obligations to appoint an MWS from the panel, or to ensure that the latter issues certificates of approval as required by the MWS scope of works, is intended to relieve insurers from liability under the policy. A total failure to appoint an MWS was probably intended to affect coverage under the policy generally,[331] whereas only the specific, relevant activity should be affected where the default consists in a failure to obtain a required approval or certificate. In either case, it would seem reasonable to construe these aspects of the endorsement as suspensory conditions.[332]

Thereafter, it is the duty of the insureds to comply with the MWS's recommenda-

---

[325] JR 2010/010, 23 July 2010.

[326] The incorporation of an MWS endorsement may be accompanied by the express deletion of WELCAR, Section I, cl.15: where this is not the case, it may be necessary to consider whether that clause is still intended to apply.

[327] JR 2010/010, Endorsement, cll.1–3.

[328] Insurance Act 2015 s.16, allows the parties to non-consumer insurance contracts to contract out of its Part 3 (including ss.10 and 11), subject to satisfying the "transparency requirements" in s.17. It seems likely that, in most cases, a WELCAR policy incorporating JR 2010/10 by endorsement will satisfy these requirements.

[329] JR 2010/010, MWS Code of Practice, para.1.4.

[330] JR 2010/010, MWS Code of Practice, para.1.9.

[331] Under the Insurance Act 2015, s.11(1), the condition that a MWS be appointed per se by a particular date should be construed as a term defining the risk as a whole, and does not relate to risks of loss of any particular type, or at any particular location or time: accordingly, s.11 of the 2015 Act should not apply. See above, para.5-112.

[332] See discussion above, at para.24–037.

tions, etc. Such recommendations are to be issued by the MWS to the insureds, to be implemented or complied with prior to or during the course of proposed operations.[333] Recommendations to be satisfied during the course of the proposed operation are generally incorporated in or endorsed on the relevant certificate of approval (or, in practice, sometimes included in a report from the MWS which is incorporated into the certificate by reference).[334] Instances of non-compliance with the MWS' recommendations are to be advised by the MWS to the insurers.[335] It is expressly provided in the generic MWS endorsement (cl.2) that it is only the loss, damage, liability or expense suffered by the insureds, which arises from or is contributed to by that breach, which is excluded from cover.[336]

As exemplified by the Generic Scope of Works in JR 2010/010, an MWS scope of works used with WELCAR is frequently in tabular form, containing a list of the items and activities to be assessed by the MWS. These items are generally grouped under appropriate construction phases, and listed in the intended order of completion. Additional columns allow the parties to stipulate the extent of the MWS' duties with regards to those items or activities: i.e. whether the MWS is to review the insured's procedures, drawings, design calculations and analysis, to be in attendance during the proposed activity, and/or to issue a formal certificate of approval (with the potential consequences discussed above). An extract from the Generic Scope of Works may serve to illustrate:

"*GENERIC SCOPE OF WORK (GSOW) ...*

Project Activity	Review and approve: 1 Procedures 2 Dwgs 3 Design Calcs 4 Analysis	Attend	Issue Certificate of Approval
VESSEL ACTIVITY DURING CONSTRUCTION PERIOD ...			
b) Jack-Up Rigs			
Sufficiency of Soil Analysis for Jack-Up Rig punch through assessment. Independent punch through risk assessment and mitigation measures.	X		

---

[333] JR 2010/010, MWS Code of Practice, paras 1.6 and 1.7.
[334] JR 2010/010, MWS Code of Practice, para.1.7.
[335] JR 2010/010, MWS Code of Practice, para.1.9.
[336] Accordingly, this aspect of the endorsement is expressly not a promissory warranty as defined in the MIA s.33. See above, para.12–028, for a discussion of a similar type of clause. In this context, the words "arising from" suggests that the breach should be a proximate or dominant cause of the relevant loss: see above, para.19–019. The phrase "contributed to" (in the generic MWS endorsement, cl.2) is not known to have been considered in the insurance context. It may be construed as referring to breaches that, in combination with other factors, have been a partial (and not insubstantial) cause of an indivisible loss: see *Williams v The Bermuda Hospitals Board* [2016] UKPC 4 at [26]–[47]; [2016] A.C. 888; [2016] 2 W.L.R. 774 (considering "material contribution" in a negligence claim).

Project Activity	Review and approve: 1 Procedures 2 Dwgs 3 Design Calcs 4 Analysis	Attend	Issue Certificate of Approval
Risk Reduction measures (well shut-in, blowdown, pipeline depressurisation etc.) for Jack-up move onto/off location.	X		
Rig Move – Jack Up/Jack Down Operations	X	X	X

Key
    X Denotes activity to be performed ..."

24-039 **Role and authority of MWS.** The involvement of an MWS is intended to provide the insurers with some independent assurance that, from an engineering perspective, phases of the construction project perceived to be hazardous will be designed and executed in a reasonably safe and sensible manner.[337] Thus, while the MWS is appointed and employed by the Insured or on their behalf,[338] the principal intended beneficiaries of the MWS' services are the insurers.[339] The MWS is typically expected to provide information and reports to, and consult with, insurers without restriction.[340] Failure to comply with an MWS provision in the policy is intended to have significant adverse consequences for the insureds' coverage. Other factors which can contribute to a blurred picture regarding the MWS's role, include the restriction of the insureds' choice of MWS to a limited panel of surveying practices put forward by insurers (in some cases, a single firm is imposed), and terms in the policy providing for payment of the MWS's fees, directly or indirectly (e.g. through deductions from premium), by the insurers.

Accordingly, there can be genuine uncertainty regarding whether an MWS has authority to act on behalf of, and to bind, insurers. This can arise, notably, in circumstances where it might be argued that the MWS, by words or conduct, had implicitly approved a step in the project, or waived a requirement under the MWS provision (e.g. where the MWS has indicated their approval informally, but failed to issue a formal certificate; or where the insureds fail to obtain approval from the MWS for a vessel's route, but then subsequently the MWS is present onboard during and approves the vessel's actual departure).

There is little authority on the role of the MWS. In *J Kirkaldy & Sons Ltd v Walker*,[341] insurers argued that the MWS had failed to carry out the condition and towage approval surveys required for a floating dry-dock, prior to an insured tow across the North Sea to be followed by a period of operation in port. It was argued

---

[337] E.g. JR 2010/010, MWS Code of Practice, paras 1.1–1.11, 2.1 and 2.7.
[338] E.g. JR 2010/010, Endorsement, cll.4–5.
[339] A situation which has been referred to as "a somewhat curious arrangement": Sharp, p.170. See also *Amoco (UK) Exploration Co v British American Offshore Ltd*, Unreported November 16, 2001, Q.B.D. Commercial Court, per Langley J, at [334].
[340] E.g. JR 2010/010, Endorsement, cll.6–7; MWS Code of Practice, paras 1.9–1.10.
[341] *Kirkaldy & Sons* [1999] 1 All E.R. (Comm) 334; [1999] Lloyd's Rep. I.R. 410; [1999] C.L.C. 722.

on behalf of the insureds that the MWS had had authority to interpret his instructions and decide what he was required to do in carrying out the surveys. In the alternative, it was argued that "as a matter of market practice", the surveyor was acting on behalf of insurers and accordingly, if the MWS failed to carry out the required survey, insurers could not complain.[342] The first argument failed. Had the surveyor purported to carry out the condition survey for the purposes of both the tow and the ensuing period of operation, his decision as to what was required—even if erroneous—would have been unimpeachable: but the MWS had failed to carry out a condition survey for the purpose of the intended post-towing operation at all, so had failed to perform the task assigned to him.[343]

The second argument also failed. Regarding the plea that it was

"usual or customary underwriting practice to regard surveyors, nominated in the insurance contract to carry out towage approval, condition or other surveys, as acting on behalf of and with the authority of underwriters" ,

having heard evidence from underwriting experts the judge was not able to conclude that there was any such practice.[344] The judge observed:

"Of course, in one sense a nominated surveyor, although paid by the vessel's owners (as he was in this case), is looking after underwriters' interests, because the underwriters do not wish to insure a vessel which has not passed whatever type of survey it is that the underwriters require; but it is a far cry from that to say that underwriters accept responsibility for anything and everything done by the surveyor named in the insurance contract. Mr Outhwaite [viz the insureds' underwriting expert] did not suggest in his oral evidence that underwriters would be liable if the nominated surveyor damaged the ship and he was quite clear that, if no condition survey of the kind required by the contract was done, the terms of the insurance were not complied with. It would be odd indeed if the surveyor were to have authority to vary the contract of insurance."[345]

Accordingly, as a general proposition insurers will be bound by the MWS's conduct in purporting to issue such approvals and certificates, and to take such other steps, as are required under the applicable MWS scope of works. This will be because of the terms of the MWS provisions in the policy, however, not due to a relationship of agency between insurers and the MWS. The expectation in the London market is understood to be that, typically, an MWS is engaged by the insureds in order to act independently in providing advice to insurers and in carrying out the MWS scope of works. But in every case, whether the MWS has in fact been clothed with authority to bind insurers will depend on the application of the normal rules of the law of agency to the particular circumstances.

Additional coverages and extensions to cover: introduction. Additional costs **24-040** and expenses may arise as a result of an insured peril under Section 1, which may

---

[342] *Kirkaldy & Sons* [1999] 1 All E.R. (Comm) 334 at 347; [1999] Lloyd's Rep. I.R. 410 at 420; [1999] C.L.C. 722 at 733–734.

[343] *Kirkaldy & Sons* [1999] 1 All E.R. (Comm) 334 at 347–348; [1999] Lloyd's Rep. I.R. 410 at 420–421; [1999] C.L.C. 722 at 734–735. Accordingly, as the MWS had purported to carry out a towage approval survey, it was not open to the insurers to argue that in fact he had failed to do so because an essential element of any towage approval survey had been omitted. see *Kirkaldy & Sons* [1999] 1 All E.R. (Comm) 334 at 350–351; [1999] Lloyd's Rep. I.R. 410 at 421–422; [1999] C.L.C. 722 at 736–737.

[344] At least as regards non-Salvage Association surveyors: *Kirkaldy & Sons* [1999] 1 All E.R. (Comm) 334 at 349; [1999] Lloyd's Rep. I.R. 410 at 421; [1999] C.L.C. 722 at 735.

[345] *Kirkaldy & Sons v Walker* [1999] 1 All E.R. (Comm) 334 at 349; [1999] Lloyd's Rep. I.R. 410 at 421; [1999] C.L.C. 722 at 735.

not be covered by the provisions discussed above. Additional coverages and extensions to WELCAR cover may address:

1. general average and salvage;
2. sue and labour;
3. additional work;
4. removal of wreckage and/or debris
5. tests, leak and/or damage search costs;
6. stand-by charges;
7. forwarding charges;
8. war and political risks;
9. cancellation costs and charges; and
10. expediting expenses.

Further comments on each of these are set out below.[346] In order to control insurers' exposure, WELCAR policies generally provide for sub-limits in relation to each such extension.[347]

24-041 **General Average and Salvage Charges clause.** In maritime law, "general average" refers to a sacrifice or expenditure, in the nature of an extraordinary and voluntary act or sacrifice, reasonably made under pressure of a real danger, for the common benefit of a marine adventure. A general average act or expenditure by one participant in a common marine adventure imposes an obligation on other participants, who will have benefitted from the sacrifice, to make a general average contribution, which will generally be adjusted according to international rules.[348]

"Salvage", broadly put, can occur where a vessel is in danger and in need of assistance: according to maritime law, salvors who attend and provide effective assistance are generally entitled to be remunerated, with the remuneration adjusted according to applicable law or international conventions. "Salvage charges" refers to this remuneration, due to salvors under maritime law, rather than to payment under a contract with the insureds.[349] Often, where professional salvors are involved, standard form contracts (such as the various revisions of the Lloyd's Open Form) will be employed, regulating how the salvage remuneration due is to be determined, in which case their remuneration is properly treated as "particular charges" or as a general average loss, as the case may be.[350]

WELCAR provides cover for both general average and salvage charges as follows[351]:

"8. GENERAL AVERAGE AND SALVAGE CHARGES

General Average and Salvage charges are payable as provided in the contract of af-

---

[346] A further endorsement to WELCAR policies sometimes seen extends cover under Section I to include the reasonable costs of evacuating personnel from the insured property and/or from contractors' property, where necessary for the purpose of preserving life. Such extensions are not discussed here.

[347] On the history of sub-limits on additional coverages, see Sharp, para.7.1.6.

[348] See MIA ss.66(2) and 66(3). A detailed discussion regarding general average and salvage is beyond the scope of this work: see further Arnould, Ch.26.

[349] MIA s.65(2).

[350] See MIA s.65(2). See: Arnould, paras 26–56 to 26–57; F. Rose, *Marine Insurance: Law and Practice*, 2nd edn (London: Informa Law, 2012), para.20.8. Contractual salvage remuneration may be covered under the Sue and Labour clause, discussed below at para.24–042.

[351] See Sharp, paras 6.6.4(c), and 8.6.1.

freightment, or if there be no contract of affreightment according to York/Antwerp Rules 1990 amended. In the event the contributory value for the purpose of contribution to General Average or Salvage charges exceed the insured value, it is agreed that such General Average or Salvage charges shall nevertheless be paid in full by Underwriters hereon, provided always that the amount recoverable under Section I in respect of partial loss arising from any one casualty shall not exceed the value applicable to the item.

General Average deposits are payable on production of General Average Deposit receipts.
Underwriters agree, if required, to provide General Average guarantees or Salvage security in respect of property insured by the Policy."[352]

The particular phrasing of this clause is thought to be original to WELCAR. Only the second sentence of the clause calls for particular comment. It recognises that the adjusted value of the property saved—the contributory value[353]—may exceed the insured value under the WELCAR policy, in which case insurers are nevertheless to pay any general average contributions or salvage charges owed by the Assureds in full (i.e. without averaging down to reflect the proportion the insured value bears to the contributory value).[354] There is then a proviso at the end of the second sentence, whose meaning may appear, at first glance, unclear. It has been suggested that it is intended to limit the indemnity for general average contributions to the value—presumably, the latest agreed value—of the relevant item in Schedule B.[355] But there would seem to be no reason to restrict the phrase "partial loss" to general average contributions only. Under the MIA, the phrase "partial loss" means "[a]ny loss other than a total loss",[356] and includes particular average losses (i.e. actual loss or damage to the subject-matter insured) and particular charges,[357] salvage charges (under maritime law, as explained above),[358] and general average losses (including general average sacrifices and expenditures) and contributions.[359] Accordingly, the restriction of recoveries under Section I for "partial loss arising from any one casualty" should impose an aggregate limit of liability—probably in the amount of the latest agreed Schedule B value for the relevant item[360]—on all types of partial loss proximately caused by any one fortuitous occurrence (i.e. "casualty").[361]

The General Average and Salvage Charges clause does not expressly provide that

---

[352] WELCAR, Section I, Terms and Conditions, cl.8.

[353] See Arnould, paras 26–05, 26–80.

[354] See Arnould, paras 26–100 to 26–101.

[355] Sharp, para.8.6.1.

[356] MIA s.56(1).

[357] MIA s 64. "Particular charges" are defined in MIA s.64(2) as "[e]xpenses incurred by or on behalf of the assured for the safety or preservation of the subject-matter insured, other than general average and salvage charges", and are stated to be excluded from particular average. See Arnould, at paras 25–26 and 27–34, regarding the recoverability of particular charges as partial losses. Where particular charges are not so recoverable, they may be recoverable under the Sue and Labour clause: see below, para.24–042.

[358] See MIA s.65 ("salvage charges incurred in preventing a loss by perils insured against may be recovered as a loss by those perils").

[359] See MIA s.66(1). Note also the heading to ss.64–66: "Partial Losses (Including Salvage and General Average and Particular Charges)." See also Arnould, at para.25-01.

[360] This would be consistent with provisions of the Basis of Recovery clause, such as sub-clause 1(a): see discussion, above, at para.24-033.

[361] There is a logic to bundling all types of partial losses under the same per Occurrence sub-limit as particular average. General average losses and contributions, salvage charges (under maritime law, not under contract), and (arguably, some) particular charges, are all recoverable under the main insuring provision in a marine insurance policy, even in the absence of a sue and labour clause: MIA

the general average losses, contributions, and salvage charges must have been incurred in relation to preventing a loss by perils insured against[362]: but this condition should apply from the definitions of those terms in the MIA.[363]

24-042 **Sue and Labour clause.** Provisions known as "sue and labour" clauses have featured in English marine insurance policies since at least as early as the sixteenth century.[364] For example, the Lloyd's S.G. Policy provided:

> "And in case of any loss or misfortune it shall be lawful to the assured, their factors, servants and assigns, to sue, labour, and travel for, in and about the defence, safeguards, and recovery of the said goods and merchandises, and ship, &c., or any part thereof, without prejudice to this insurance; to the charges whereof we, the assurers, will contribute ..."[365]

Such clauses generally cover unusual or extraordinary expenses or acts, reasonably incurred or undertaken by the assured, their servants or agents, for the purpose of averting or minimising an imminent loss which otherwise would be covered by the insurance.[366]

WELCAR's Sue and Labour clause is as follows[367]:

> "9. SUE AND LABOUR CLAUSE
>
>> It is further agreed that in the case of any imminent physical loss or physical damage to the property insured hereunder, which is the direct result of a peril insured against, the Assureds, their servants and their agents may sue, labour and travel for, in and about the defence, safeguard and recovery of the subject matters insured without prejudice to this insurance and may incur reasonable expenses in efforts to avert or minimise a loss which may fall under Section I.
>>
>> The expense so incurred shall be borne by the Assureds and Underwriters proportionately to the extent of their respective interests. No acts of Underwriters or the Assureds in recovering, saving or preserving the property insured shall be considered as a waiver or acceptance of abandonment.
>>
>> Underwriters limit of liability under this clause shall be 25% of the scheduled value contained in the latest agreed Schedule B at time of loss of the item or items that are the subject of such sue and labour."[368]

The following particular comments can be made about this clause:

1. The clause covers the expense of efforts by the assured, their servants and agents, to avert or minimise a loss "which may fall under Section I."[369] This phrase begs the question as to the degree of likelihood of a threatened

---

ss.64–66, 73, discussed above at fnn.357 to 359; Rose, *Marine Insurance: Law and Practice* (2012), paras 20.7, 20.8 and 20.11 to 20.13. Salvage and general average expenses are allowed to rank in determining whether there has been a constructive total loss: Arnould, para.29–33. Other expenses incurred in seeking to avert or minimise an insured loss—e.g. particular charges such as contractual salvage remuneration—may be covered under the Sue and Labour clause—a supplementary engagement, with its own separate sub-limit—, discussed below at para.24–042.

[362] Cf. other standard policy forms, such as ITC Hulls (1/10/83) cl.11.4, and ICBR cl.13.4.

[363] MIA ss.65(1) and 66(6).

[364] See translation of policy dated 8 January 1565, in *De Moucheron c Sadler* (1565) in R. Marsden, *Select Pleas in the Court of Admiralty*, Vol. II (London: Bernard Quaritch, 1897), Selden Society Vol.11, p.54, at p.56.

[365] MIA Sch.1.

[366] See further Arnould, Ch.25: a full discussion of the law of sue and labour is beyond the scope of this work.

[367] See Sharp, para.8.6.2. See also above at paras 17–013 to 17–015.

[368] WELCAR, Section I, Terms and Conditions, cl.9.

[369] General average losses and contributions, and salvage charges (under maritime law) are not recover-

insured loss required before the insureds are entitled to recover sue and labour expenses. Under earlier sue and labour clauses, courts have opined diversely that it was necessary that the loss "would" be, or "probably" or "very probably" would be, indemnified by the policy if the assured did not take unusual or extraordinary steps,[370] or alternatively that there would have to be "a risk" of an insured loss sufficient to prompt a reasonable insured to take such unusual steps.[371] Further, it has been suggested that hindsight should be used in considering whether the threatened loss would, or would probably, have been recoverable under the policy.[372] But the Sue and Labour clause in WELCAR differs from those considered in previous cases by its use of the phrase "a loss which *may* fall under Section I." (emphasis added). This suggests that all that is required is a real, as opposed to fanciful, risk of insurers being liable to indemnify the insureds under Section I.[373] If this is correct, in some cases expenses may be covered under the clause in relation to threatened losses which, with the benefit of hindsight and full information, would not in fact be covered by Section I.[374]

2. The trigger to the insureds' right to sue and labour and incur reasonable expenses is "imminent" physical loss or damage to the insured property that is a "direct result" of one of Section I's insured perils. "Imminent", in this context, generally refers to a situation where the insured peril is actually in operation or obviously threatens to operate, such that a reasonable insured would take extraordinary steps.[375] "[T]he direct result of" should mean "proximately caused by".[376] It is suggested that whether there has been imminent physical loss or damage as a direct result of an insured peril is to be judged against the standard mentioned above, i.e. a real risk or possibility.[377]

3. The expense incurred must be "reasonable". The MIA, ss.65(2) and 78(1) provide that such expenses must be "properly incurred", which means inter alia that such expenses must have been reasonably necessary, in order to be covered by the clause.[378] It must have been reasonably necessary to incur

---

able under the Sue and Labour clause. See: para.24–041, above; MIA s.78(2).

[370] The requirement that expenses be unusual or extraordinary in nature in order to be indemnified, is not expressly stated in the Sue and Labour clause: however, such a requirement has been held to be implicit in sue and labour clauses which are, in all respects material to this issue, identical, such as that in the Lloyd's S.G. Policy quoted above. See Arnould, para.25–22.

[371] See: *Lohre v Aitchison* (1878) 3 Q.B.D. 558, 566, per Brett LJ (reversed in *Aitchison v Lohre* (1879) 4 App. Cas. 755, without approving or disapproving of this aspect of Brett LJ's judgment); *Integrated Container Service Inc v British Traders Insurance Co Ltd* [1984] 1 Lloyd's Rep. 154, 158–159 (Eveleigh LJ) and 162 (Dillon LJ); Arnould, paras 25–08, at fn.39, 25–12.

[372] Arnould, para.25–12.

[373] See above, paras 21–012, 21–014, discussing obligations to notify events or claims. In the context of the Sue and Labour clause, the assessment is probably objective, being that of the reasonable person in the position of the insureds. Quære, whether the reasonable person should additionally be reasonably informed, imbued with knowledge of the actual facts as they were at the time (rather than only possessing the insureds' actual knowledge), as suggested in Arnould, para.25–12.

[374] To this extent, the clause purports to derogate from MIA s.78(3).

[375] Arnould, paras 25–10 and 25–11, discussing, inter alia, *National Oilwell (UK) Ltd v Davy Offshore Ltd* [1993] 2 Lloyd's Rep. 582, 618, per Colman J, and *Royal Boskalis Westminster NV v Mountain* [1997] L.R.L.R. 523, 606–608, per Rix J.

[376] See above, paras 19–008 and 19–016; *The Miss Jay Jay* [1987] 1 Lloyd's Rep. 32, CA, at 39; Arnould, para.22–20, fn.239.

[377] See discussion earlier in this paragraph.

[378] See Arnould, paras 25–05, 25–07 and 25–18.

the expenses for the relevant purpose, and the expenses must also be reasonable in amount.

4. Sue and labour cover is to some extent an additional engagement, supplementary to the main insuring provisions: it has been noted that the word "further" in the clause's initial sentence reflects this[379]; and this is also the effect of s.78(1) of the MIA. Accordingly, sue and labour expenses can be recovered under the clause even if they have been unsuccessful: such that, for example, insurers can be liable to indemnify an insured for sue and labour as well as for a total loss in respect of the relevant item.[380]

5. A limit of liability is imposed on the indemnity recoverable under the Sue and Labour clause, set at 25% of latest agreed Schedule B value, at the time of loss (viz at the time of the sue and labour effort), of the item or items for which the insured has sued and laboured. This was discussed earlier in this section, in considering the Policy Limit clause, Schedule B and its "items".[381] Though it is not stated expressly, the limit should apply to each Occurrence.

6. The second paragraph of the clause provides for the apportionment of sue and labour expenses incurred, "proportionately to the extent of their [viz the insurers' and the insureds'] respective interests".[382] The basis for apportionment is not fully explained: in particular, the clause does not specify which interests of insurers and insureds are to be taken into account. A narrow reading of the provision, consistent with the common law position, would restrict its effect to cases of suing and labouring for the preservation of under-insurance, by reason of which both insureds and insurers would have clearly apportionable interests in the insured proper. It might also be permissible to extend the provision for apportionment to analogous cases where un-insured property, of a kind that could have been insured under a marine property policy like WELCAR, was also targeted by sue and labour efforts.[383] Wider interests of the parties, not easily comparable for the purpose of apportionment, probably should not be considered.[384]

---

[379] See Sharp, para.8.6.2.

[380] Arnould, para.25–14.

[381] See above, para.24–027.

[382] A somewhat different apportionment provision appears in the final paragraph of the Basis of Recovery clause, discussed above at para.24–033.

[383] See text and cases referred to above, at fn.272. A similar apportionment issue can arise where the insureds' expenditure targets more than one *purpose* (but concerns the same insured property). For example, where an expenditure contains a component which would have been incurred in any event, in the ordinary course of the insured's business, but also contains an additional, extraordinary component for the purpose of averting an insured loss. In such cases, where these components can be distinguished, then the costs should be apportioned, with only the latter falling within the sue and labour cover. But where the expenditure cannot be divided between separate purposes in this manner, then arguably apportionment is not legitimate. See Arnould, para.25–18. Sed quære whether express wording is required, in any event, for there to be an apportionment where appropriate: other features of sue and labour cover—e.g. that the efforts need to target insured property, or that the expenditure or efforts needs to be unusual or extraordinary—tend to achieve the same result.

[384] Cf. Sharp, para.8.6.2, arguing that the "interests" taken into consideration should broadly include matters such as avoiding potential control of well losses and redrilling expenses, avoiding delays to the construction programme, and noting that "the underlying intent of the clause is to ensure that an equitable apportionment is agreed between the parties." But the clause refers neither to any such agreement between insurers and insureds, nor to an equitable or fair apportionment (cf. the Basis of Recovery clause, discussed above at para.23–033). Accordingly, it is suggested that the narrow

Additional Work clause.   This clause provides as follows[385]:   **24-043**

> *"10. ADDITIONAL WORK*
>
> In the event that the structure or insured property is set down or wrongly positioned, which is the direct result of a peril insured against, Underwriters shall indemnify the Assureds for the cost of additional work that is required in respect of positioning or repositioning, sinking, submerging and stabilising the property insured herein insofar as such cost does not fall within the cover afforded by the sue and labour clause. However Underwriters' liability under this clause shall not exceed the percentage amount that would be recoverable under the sue and labour clause and then only to the extent that the Policy Limit is not exhausted by a claim under the sue and labour clause."[386]

The additional cover provided under this clause has been described as "valuable"[387]: it extends beyond physical loss or damage to the insured property to cover certain additional work directly resulting from (i.e. proximately caused by) an insured peril.

The similarity of its language with that of, and its express references to, the Sue and Labour clause, indicate an intention to link the cover under this clause to that provided under the Sue and Labour clause.[388] The drafters did not, however, carry through from the Sue and Labour clause the wording of that clause's "trigger", i.e. "*imminent* physical loss or physical damage" (emphasis added). But the clause appears intended to complement the Sue and Labour clause, covering works undertaken to reposition insured property which had been set down by reason of an insured peril (e.g. a fortuitous occurrence or event).[389] Accordingly, while the Additional Work clause would certainly cover work arising from the setting down or wrong positioning of insured property proximately caused by a fortuitous occurrence of physical loss or damage, it is suggested that actual physical loss or damage is not required.[390] Instead, so long as the setting down or wrong positioning was proximately caused by a fortuitous occurrence,[391] or other insured peril, acting immediately on the insured property—i.e. by an imminent and *certain* danger of physical loss or damage from the insured peril, rather than by voluntary action taken in response to the apprehension or the strong probability of the same—then the Additional Work clause should respond.[392]

The remainder of the clause further explains the relationship between the Ad-

---

construction advanced here is to be preferred.

[385]   See also Sharp, paras 6.6.4(a) and 8.6.3. See also above, at para.17–011.

[386]   WELCAR, Section I, Terms and Conditions, cl.10.

[387]   Sharp, para.8.6.3.

[388]   Discussed above, at para.24–042.

[389]   See discussion of the Covered Perils clause, above at para.24–029. The restriction of cover under the Additional Work clause for repositioning costs that are "the direct result of a peril insured against" is consistent with the exclusion in WELCAR, Section I, Exclusions, sub-clause 1(e), which removes from Section I "any claim by reason of the platforms and/or structures being placed in the wrong locations *unless caused by an Occurrence which is covered by the terms of Section I*" (emphasis added).

[390]   This is also the view taken by Sharp, para.8.6.3.

[391]   E.g. a storm.

[392]   See, in this regard, Arnould, paras 22-09 to 22-12. The suggestion in Sharp, para.8.6.3, that the clause might cover wrong positioning caused by faulty design or workmanship in the form of a mere error in the planned positioning of the property, or in the execution of the positioning of the property, seems open to question. The cover under WELCAR in respect of faulty design, etc, under the Defective Parts clause (discussed above, at para.24-030), is cover against *physical loss or damage* resulting from faulty design, etc; if the faulty design or workmanship did not cause actual loss or damage, it would then at least have to be operating upon the insured property, creating an immediate and

ditional Work clause and the Sue and Labour clause. Any cost indemnifiable under the Sue and Labour clause is excluded from cover under the Additional Work clause. As to the limits of liability under the Additional Work clause, the effect of the wording would appear to be as follows. First, insurers' liability under the Additional Work clause is limited to "the percentage amount that would be recoverable under the sue and labour clause", which probably refers to 25% of the latest agreed Schedule B value, at the time of "loss" (i.e. of the setting down or wrong positioning), of the relevant item or items. Second, it is further limited to the extent that the relevant "Policy Limit"—set out in the Policy Limit clause and declaration[393]—has not already been reached due to "a claim under the sue and labour clause." Accordingly, it is not simply the case that the Sue and Labour and Additional Work clauses share a common sub-limit of 25% of the relevant Schedule B values. Instead, there is an inter-relationship between the sub-limits applicable to those clauses: depending on the amounts claimed for costs of repair or replacement, sue and labour, additional work and removal of wreckage or debris, the aggregate amount recoverable under the Sue and Labour and Additional Work clauses could range up to a maximum of 50% of the relevant Schedule B values.[394]

24-044   **Removal of Wreck, Wreckage and/or Debris clause.**   WELCAR's Removal of Wreckage clause provides as follows[395]:

> *"11. REMOVAL OF WRECK, WRECKAGE AND/OR DEBRIS*
>
> Following an Occurrence covered by Section I, Underwriters shall indemnify the Assureds for all costs of or incidental to the actual or attempted raising, removal or destruction of the wreckage and/or debris of the insured property, or the provision and maintenance of lights, markings, audible warnings for such wreckage and/or debris when the incurring of such costs is compulsory by any law, ordinance or regulation or when the Assured hereunder is liable for such costs under written contract or when such wreckage and/or debris interferes with the Assured's normal operations.
>
> Underwriters' limit of liability under this clause shall be 25% of the scheduled value contained in the latest agreed Schedule B at time of loss of the item or items which are the subject of such removal of wreckage and/or debris."[396]

The change in the wording of the "trigger" under this clause, as compared to the additional and extended coverage clauses discussed above, has been recognised[397]: removal of wreckage and debris is covered "[f]ollowing an Occurrence covered by

---

certain danger of physical loss or damage, for there to be cover for the correction of any setting down or wrong positioning caused thereby.

[393] See discussion above, at para.24-027.

[394] E.g. assume that: the latest agreed Schedule B value for the relevant item is £100; and the relevant Policy Limit "any one Occurrence", representing 125% of the latest agreed Schedule B value, is £125. Assume also, for simplicity, that there is no claim for wreck removal. In such a case, the sub-limit under the Sue and Labour clause is £25; and the limit applicable under the Additional Work clause is whatever remains of the Policy Limit of £125, after damage repair or loss replacement and sue and labour have been indemnified, subject to a maximum of £25. Thus: if damage repair costs are £100, and sue and labour costs are £25, then there is no cover for additional work; if damage repair costs are £100, and sue and labour costs are £10, then there is £15 available for additional work; if damage repair costs are £60, and sue and labour costs are £25, there is the maximum possible £25 available for additional work.

[395] See above, paras 3-048, 15-039, and 17-019 to 17-021. See also Sharp, para.8.6.4.

[396] WELCAR, Section I, Terms and Conditions, cl.11.

[397] Sharp, para.8.6.4.

Section I".[398] The change is probably of little practical significance: the words "[f]ollowing an Occurrence", while they refer to a temporal sequence, do not of themselves require a causal link; but references in other parts of the clause strongly suggest that the "wreckage and/or debris of the insured property" referred to is that which has suffered physical loss or damage caused by an Occurrence.[399]

Removal of wreckage or debris can, in some circumstances, fall to be indemnified as costs of repairing or replacing lost or damaged property. Where this is not the case, the costs of compulsory wreck removal are typically covered by protection and indemnity insurance.[400] WELCAR's Removal of Wreckage clause covers the relevant costs, not only where the incurring of the same is compulsory for the Assureds, but also when the wreckage or debris "interferes with the Assured's normal operations." "[N]ormal operations" could, prima facie, encompass construction and non-construction related operations affected by the presence of the wreckage or debris. It is suggested that whether there has been an interference with an Assured's "normal operations" might be determined by considering whether the operations of the Assureds would be carried out in a substantially different manner in the absence of the wreckage or debris.

The meaning of "wreckage" has not been authoritatively considered.[401] "Debris" probably does not include spilled liquids, such as oil, or pollution from the same.[402]

The second paragraph of the clause provides for a sub-limit of liability in the amount of 25% of the latest agreed Schedule B values of the relevant items. Construed in the context of the clause as a whole, and against the background of the Policy Limit provisions,[403] this sub-limit should apply to all removal costs arising from any one Occurrence.

Excess wreck removal cover can be obtained, and is generally written as an endorsement to Section II: this is discussed below.[404]

Tests, Leak and/or Damage Search Costs clause. This additional coverage **24-045** clause provides:

"12. TESTS, LEAK AND/OR DAMAGE SEARCH COSTS

If it becomes necessary to repeat any test(s) and/or trial(s) or to carry out subsequent test(s) and/or trial(s) as a result of a physical loss or physical damage to the insured property arising from an Occurrence covered under Section I, Underwriters will bear the cost of any such repeated and/or subsequent test(s) and/or trial(s) subject to a

---

[398] Rather than "which is the direct result of a peril insured against".
[399] E.g. the words "at the time of loss of the item or items which are the subject of such removal ..." at the end of the clause. Further, as Sharp notes (para.8.6.4), the removal of wreckage or debris of contractors' property, or "pure" third parties' property, is not covered.
[400] See S. Hazelwood and D. Semark, *P. & I. Clubs Law and Practice*, 4th edn (London: Informa Law, 2010), paras 10.212 to 10.215.
[401] *OED Online* (OUP: September 2016) *http://www.oed.com/view/Entry/230601?redirectedFrom =wreckage* [Accessed 8 September 2016] defines "wreckage, n." as follows: "2.a. Fragments or remains of a shattered or wrecked vessel; wreck. ... 3.a. Material of or from a wrecked or shattered structure; a ruined fabric, building, etc." Hazelwood and Semark, *P. & I. Clubs Law and Practice* (2010), para.10.212, fn.212, refer to London Arbitration n° 4/88, LMLN 227, in which it was held that the word "wreck", in the relevant P&I club rules, simply referred to any ship "in a damaged, grounded or sunken condition which required her removal".
[402] See *King v Brandywine Reinsurance Co* [2005] EWCA Civ 235, at [117]; [2005] 2 All E.R. (Comm) 1; [2005] 1 Lloyd's Rep. 655; [2005] Lloyd's Rep. I.R. 509.
[403] Discussed above, at para.24-027.
[404] See below, para.24-064.

sub-limit of [*blank*] (100%) any one Occurrence, but never to exceed original expenditure as identified in the latest agreed Schedule B."[405]

This clause, as its title suggests, is intended to indemnify the cost of tests and trials where an occurrence of physical loss or damage indemnified under Section I causes a need for the same. As the repeating of tests of trials whose costs are included in the latest agreed Schedule B would in principle be covered under the main insuring provisions of Section I, the particular concern of this Tests, Leak and/or Damage Search Costs extension must be subsequent tests or trials not undertaken at the time of the original installation, but required following the Occurrence.[406] In particular, the drafters must have been concerned at the prospect of carrying out testing or trials—in some cases, repeatedly—in order to detect leaks or other damage following an insured Occurrence.

The final words of the clause provide for a per Occurrence sub-limit, to be agreed as an absolute quantity, in the appropriate currency denomination.[407] It is further provided that insurers' liability is "never to exceed original expenditure as identified in the latest agreed Schedule B." This cryptic phrase is sometimes removed or replaced by amendment, in practice. It is tentatively suggested that it refers to the amount originally expended on initial testing and trialling of the relevant insured property, imposing this amount as a further per Occurrence sub-limit on testing and trialling costs—including both "repeated" and "subsequent" tests and trials—in relation to such property.[408]

24-046   Stand-by Charges clause.

"13. STAND-BY CHARGES

Subject to a sub-limit of [*blank*] any one Occurrence aggregated at [*blank*] over the Policy Period, Underwriters shall indemnify the Assureds for the cost of stand-by time on vessels and/or craft and/or equipment actively engaged in the course of repair following an Occurrence covered under Section I, where the Assureds are prevented from working in, around or about the damaged property by bad weather, including named hurricanes."[409]

This clause provides an extension of cover for the cost of stand-by time for vessels and equipment being utilised in repairing loss or damage caused by an Occurrence covered under Section I.[410] The cover is narrow, in that the insured "stand-by time" only runs when the Assureds are prevented from working "in, around or about the damaged property"—i.e. prevented from working on the relevant repairs—by bad weather. It is suggested that vessels, etc, are "activity engaged in the course of repair" only if they are waiting, idle, for an appropriate weather window in which to undertake repairs, and are not engaged in other productive work: otherwise, there would be no loss to indemnify.

The clause does not specify whether the costs indemnified must relate to ves-

---

[405] WELCAR, Section I, Terms and Conditions, cl.12.
[406] As Sharp argues, at para.8.6.5.
[407] For an explanation of the expression "(100%)", see discussion of Percentage Interest clause, above at para.24-016.
[408] This would seem consistent with WELCAR's preference, as illustrated by the Policy Limit and Basis of Recovery clauses (discussed above at paras 24-027 and 24-033), to limit insurers' per occurrence exposure to the latest agreed Schedule B values.
[409] WELCAR, Section I, Terms and Conditions, cl.13.
[410] See Sharp, para.8.6.6.

sels, etc contracted from third parties only, or whether the cost of the Assureds' own vessels are also covered. Elsewhere, the WELCAR form provides for recovery of both types of costs,[411] which suggests that both should also be recoverable here.

The Stand-by Charges clause envisages that figures for per Occurrence and total aggregate sub-limits will be agreed. The cover provided under this clause is limited in two further ways. First, the definition of "Occurrence",[412] in the case of serious bad weather (i.e. "of a violent and destructive nature"), includes all such weather "arising out of the same atmospheric disturbance within any period of seventy-two consecutive hours". This clearly has the potential to make the per Occurrence sub-limit applicable more frequently. Secondly, the WELCAR form provides for a deductible of "48 hours each and every Occurrence in respect of stand-by charges."[413]

It has been suggested that stand-by costs covered by this clause would normally be indemnified as costs of repair under the main insuring provisions in Section I.[414] This may be correct, but the clause may be construed as providing additional cover for such costs, not limited by the Basis of Recovery clause (though arguably still caught by the limits in the Policy Limit clause).[415] Such additional cover would be valuable in circumstances where repair costs may easily exceed initial installation costs.

Forwarding Charges clause. This provision has been transposed, with appropri- **24-047** ate modifications, from cargo policies such as ICC (A).[416] In the context of an all risks cargo policy covering particular average (which WELCAR is, inter alia because it incorporates ICC (A)),[417] it has been described as:

> "largely declaratory, and its chief virtue [lying] ... in drawing attention to the fact that in the event of the voyage being abandoned by the carrier, it is the duty of the assured as well as being in his own interest to forward the goods to destination if possible."[418]

This view is explicable because cargo insurance generally covers both the physical safety of the property insured and the insured voyage or transit specified in the policy. Even in the absence of a clause such as this, where the cost of forwarding cargo to its intended destination, from an unintended place of termination, would exceed its value on arrival, or where to do so would otherwise be practically impossible, there is a constructive total loss. But where forwarding the cargo to its intended destination is neither impossible nor unreasonably costly, the "extra charges properly and reasonably incurred in unloading, storing and forwarding the property insured"[419] constitute a partial loss which may be recovered under a sue and labour clause.[420] Accordingly, the Forwarding Charges clause is in the nature of a special sue and labour provision, providing further, supplementary cover for such costs (though arguably, still within the limits imposed by the Policy Limit

---

[411] See, e.g., the Basis of Recovery clause, sub-clause 1(d), discussed above at para.24-033.
[412] See discussion above, at para.24-029.
[413] WELCAR, Declarations, item 5(vi).
[414] Sharp, para.8.6.6.
[415] See above, paras 24-033 and 24-027, respectively.
[416] I.e. ICC (A) (1/1/82), cl.12. See Sharp, paras 6.6.4(c) and 8.6.7.
[417] See discussion of Incorporated Clauses, above at para.24-034.
[418] Hudson et al, *Marine Insurance Clauses* (2012), pp.32–33.
[419] WELCAR, Section I, Terms and Conditions, cl.17.
[420] MIA s.60(2)(iii); Hudson et al, *Marine Insurance Clauses* (2012), pp.32–33.

clause),[421] subject to special sub-limits.

The Forwarding Charges clause applies in the event of early termination of the insured cargo voyage at an unintended port or place, caused by "an Occurrence covered by the terms of Section I". The WELCAR form contemplates that such additional cover will be sub-limited to an agreed figure in relation to "any one Occurrence."[422]

It should also be noted that special deductibles apply in relation to, "each and every Occurrence", to "all cargo sendings", "tows within waters to final offshore site" and "transocean tows or heavy lift movements to final offshore site".[423] Depending on the circumstances in which forwarding charges are claimed, one of more of these may apply.

War and political risks: exclusion, Terrorist "Buy-back" clause, and JR 2015/
24-048 003. It is beyond the scope of this work to consider WELCAR's war and political risks provisions in detail.[424] A brief summary is nevertheless provided:

1.   Exclusion 2 to Section I provides:

> "2.   The following clauses (i) and (ii) are only to apply to property on land and/or installed at the offshore location, but they shall not be construed to exclude physical loss or physical damage caused by mines, bombs, torpedoes, missiles or other weaponry remaining from previous hostilities or military exercises.
>
>   (i)   Notwithstanding anything to the contrary contained herein, this section does not cover loss or damage directly or indirectly occasioned by, happening through, or in consequence of war (whether war be declared or not), invasion, acts of foreign enemies, hostilities, civil war, rebellion, revolution, insurrection, military or usurped power or confiscation or nationalisation or requisition or destruction of or damage to property by or under the order of any government or public or local authority except as otherwise provided in Section I of the Policy.
>
>   (ii)   There shall be no liability whatsoever for any claim caused by or resulting from, or incurred as a consequence of:
>
>   (a)   1.   The detonation of an explosive.
>
>   2.   Any weapon of war and caused by any person acting maliciously or from a political motive.[[425]]
>
>   (b)   Any act for political or terrorist purposes of any persons, whether or not agents of a Sovereign Power, and whether the loss, damage or expense resulting therefrom is accidental or intentional.
>
> However, Exclusion 2(ii) above is subject to Terrorist Buyback Clause 16 herein."[426]

2.   This Exclusion, it may be noted, does not apply to insured property in transit

---

[421] See above, para.24-027.

[422] For the meaning of "(100%)", see discussion of the Percentage Interest clause, above at para.24-016.

[423] WELCAR, Declarations, items 5(i) and (iii).

[424] See Sharp, para.6.6.4(d). See also general more general works, such as Arnould, Ch.24; and Miller, *Marine War Risks* (2005).

[425] The Terrorist "Buy-back" clause (WELCAR, Section I, Terms and Conditions, cl.16) sets out a different version of sub-clause 2(ii)(a): "(a) (i) the detonation of an explosive *and/or* (ii) any weapon of war *[line break] and* is caused by any person acting maliciously or from a political motive". (emphasis added.) This is probably closer to what was intended for the Exclusion, as it seems unlikely that the drafters of WELCAR meant to exclude any claim whatsoever arising from the detonation of any explosive (as this would potentially encompass trenching work requiring blasting, etc).

[426] WELCAR, Section I, Exclusions, cl.2.

by air or when water-borne: it applies only to property on land or following installation offshore. Even then, damage from derelict weapons is covered.

3. Where sub-clause 2(i) applies, it should exclude any loss or damage that is at least a remote consequence of any one of a number of a range of named political risks. These risks are generally concerned with large-scale conflicts, and with acts by governments or public authorities.[427] There is a general carve-out: "except as otherwise provided in Section I of the Policy." This may have been intended to avoid compromising the cover provided by the Pollution Hazard clause, discussed above.[428]

4. Where it applies, sub-clause 2(ii) should exclude claims proximately caused by a person or persons maliciously detonating an explosive or using a weapon of war, or more generally acting ("whether or not as agents of a Sovereign Power") for political or terrorist purposes. It is this sub-clause 2(ii) of the Exclusion that the Terrorist "Buy-back" clause in effect removes.[429] There is clearly some potential for overlapping between sub-clause 2(i)—which excludes e.g. "acts of foreign enemies", "insurrection", "destruction or damage to property by or under the order of any government", etc—and sub-clause 2(ii).[430] Accordingly, any cover provided or restored by virtue of the Terrorist "Buy-back" clause may be substantially limited where it overlaps with sub-clause 2(i) of Exclusion 2 to Section 1.[431]

5. The political risks cover restored by the Terrorist "Buy-back" clause is subject to provisions for cancellation on notice, automatic termination (in the event of war between various named States or the hostile detonation of a nuclear weapon), and suspension upon expropriation by the government of the state in which the insured property is owned or registered.[432] Further, in the event of expropriation of the insured property, coverage restored by the clause is "held" in respect of "the contingent liability of the Assured" for a period of fourteen days.[433]

The Joint Rig Committee issued JR 2015/003 in July 2015, including a new Offshore Terrorism Buy-back clause. This reflects the common use in the offshore energy insurance market of new forms of terrorism exclusions clauses,[434] which have largely replaced the "Addendum 42B" that first appeared in the 1970s. The newer exclusions reflect a broader conception of terrorism, which may be motivated by ideological or religious convictions instead of by "political" convictions, and

---

[427] See discussion above, at paras 15-041 to 15-060. WELCAR, Section I, Exclusions, sub-clauses 2(i), and Terrorist "Buy-back" clause sub-clauses (ii) and (iii) are amended versions of the war exclusion, cancellation and held covered provisions appearing in the Offshore Facilities Limited Terrorist Cover, Form 2 (1/1/1978): see Sharp, paras 17.4.3, 17.4.6, and Appendix H.

[428] See above, at para.24-035.

[429] WELCAR, Section I, Terms and Conditions, cl.16(i). WELCAR, Section I, Exclusions, sub-clause 2(ii) is a somewhat amended version of the exclusion in Addendum 42b to the Drilling Risk Memorandum: the Terrorist "Buy-back" clause, sub-clause (i), replicates the coverage provision in the Offshore Facilities Limited Terrorist Cover, Form 2 (1/1/1978): see Sharp, paras 17.4.2 to 17.4.3.

[430] The wording of the carve-out at the end of WELCAR, Section I, Exclusions, sub-clause (2)(i) is not apt to resolve such conflicts.

[431] This overlap between terrorist acts and acts of war reflects the limited nature of the terrorism cover intended: see discussion in Sharp, para.17.4.6.

[432] WELCAR, Terms and Conditions, cl.16(ii).

[433] WELCAR, Terms and Conditions, cl.16(iii). See discussion of Held Covered clause, above at para.24-024.

[434] E.g. NMA2920, which appeared in late 2001.

which should encompass acts not involving the use of explosives or weapons of war.[435] Despite these developments, until it is revised, WELCAR's standard wording will remain that which it has borrowed from Addendum 42B and the Offshore Facilities Limited Terrorist Cover, Form 2.[436]

24-049 **Cancellation charges.** The occurrence of loss or damage to the offshore project under construction may lead to delays to the construction programme, which may make it necessary to re-schedule the attendance of vessels or equipment. This may involve the cancelling of contracts with third parties, under which the vessels and equipment were to be supplied, and the incurring of cancellation fees or penalties. It may also involve the incurring of further expense in re-contracting with third parties for the supply of such vessels and equipment at later dates, in accordance with the revised programme.

The WELCAR policy form per se contains no cover for consequential losses in the form of cancellation fees or penalties, or the extra expense of re-contracting for vessels etc, even if the proximate cause of such losses and expenses were loss or damage to the insured property covered under Section I. But such cover is sometimes added by an endorsement, the wording of which has become more or less standard.[437] Such an endorsement may be worded as follows:

> "*OFFSHORE CANCELLATION COSTS CLAUSE*
> This Insurance shall also indemnify the Principal Assured(s) in respect of cancellation costs on offshore vessels and construction equipment under contract in relation to the project (including but not limited to, heavy lift vessels, derrick barges, tugs, barges and supply vessels), and/or extra expense to hire offshore vessels and construction equipment to complete the project and/or operation(s) in respect of which such costs are incurred, arising directly from a peril insured against giving rise to a claim under this policy, deductible application notwithstanding.
> It is further understood and agreed that Insurers shall not be liable for additional costs and/or expenses of alterations in procedures, which may be employed following such loss or damage.
> Coverage under this clause is subject to a sub-limit of [*blank*] any one accident and in the aggregate.
> All other insuring agreements, terms, conditions, definitions, exclusions, notice requirements, schedules and endorsements of the policy remain unchanged."[438]

The cover extended by such endorsements typically benefits only the Principal Assureds. The reference to "such loss or damage", in the second paragraph of the example above, indicates that the cover is intended to be additional to Section I, responding to cancellation costs and extra expenses proximately caused by an insured peril under that Section.[439] To be indemnified, the extra expense of hiring vessels and equipment to complete the project must relate to vessels and equipment "in respect of which such [cancellation] costs are incurred": this may indicate that cover for such extra hiring expenses is limited to the cost of re-hiring such vessels and equipment as were originally contracted but then cancelled. Accordingly,

---

[435] E.g. the attack on the World Trade Center in New York in September 2011.

[436] See above, in fnn.427 and 429.

[437] See Sharp, paras 6.6.4(b) and 8.6.8. See also below, para.26-081, discussing a similar additional cover in the context of business interruption insurance.

[438] "Offshore Construction Project Policy" (undated), *http://www.hi-ins.com.cn/ebusiness/cms/upload/ insuranceCatalogue/hullInsurance/11_hullInsurance03.pdf*, [Accessed 28 April 2016], p.32. See also A. Kelly, "CAR Optional Coverages Explored" (Braemar Adjusting presentation slides, 5 November 2015), *http://braemaradjusting.com/files/WELCAR-Sub-limits-Explored-5-November-2015.pdf* [Accessed 28 April 2016], pp.14 and 19 (including a variant endorsement wording which also covers extra stand-by costs incurred).

[439] A view shared by Sharp: see para.8.6.8.

other extra expenses, incurred in order to expedite the completion of the project, i.e. to reverse some of the impact on the programme of the loss or damage to the insured property, should not be covered by endorsements such as this one.[440] The second paragraph of the endorsement makes clear, similarly, that additional costs or expenses incurred in changing "procedures" following loss or damage, are not covered. Finally, cancellation costs endorsements generally provide for sub-limits, as in the example given.

Expediting expenses.   Additional costs of repair or replacement incurred in order   **24-050** to avoid delays to the construction project—with which, normally, property insurers would not be concerned—are sometimes insured under a further endorsement to WELCAR as an extension to Section I. Commonly, such endorsements cover additional costs and expenses "necessarily and reasonably incurred" or "reasonably incurred and duly justified" by the Assureds, in "expediting the commencement, carrying out or the completion of the repair, reinstatement or replacement of the interest [insured]", arising from loss or damage caused by a peril insured against under Section I.[441] Expediting expenses endorsements typically also specify that the cover they provide shall not cover losses insured by other provisions of the policy, or which would be recoverable from any other policy in the absence of the endorsement. As with cancellation costs endorsements, expediting expenses endorsements usually make clear that additional costs and expenses incurred in changing "procedures" following loss or damage are not covered, and are usually subject to their own, specific sub-limit.

Sub-limits on "marine spreads".   In an attempt to control their exposures, insur-   **24-051** ers sometimes contract for a further sub-limit in relation to "marine spreads", generally contained in an endorsement to the policy. There are various wordings for such endorsements. Some in common use provide that the part of any recoverable claim under Section I relating to "marine spreads, mobilisation and demobilisation costs (or equivalent)" should be sub-limited to a certain amount per Occurrence and in aggregate. Sometimes such costs are additionally limited to the original contracted amounts declared in relation to each vessel or unit. "Marine spreads" probably refers to vessels and associated equipment contracted from third parties,[442] though in particular cases the precise delimitation of the phrase could give rise to differences of opinion. A per Occurrence sub-limit thus set can tend to cut across several different project items in Schedule B, while an aggregate sub-limit in relation to marine spread costs can be eroded by numerous claims. Accordingly, sub-limits on marine spreads can give rise to disputes both as to their construction, and in relation to loss adjusting.

Section 1 exclusions.   Given the wide potential scope of the "all risks" cover   **24-052** under Section 1, exclusions are employed to give effect to the scope of cover actu-

---

[440] Expediting expenses incurred in accelerating repairs or replacement, to minimise disruption to the programme, can be insured under a separate endorsement. See below at para.24-050.

[441] See Sharp, para.8.2.3, and e.g. "Offshore Construction Project Policy" (undated), *http://www.hi-ins.com.cn/ebusiness/cms/upload/insuranceCatalogue/hullInsurance/11_hullInsurance03.pdf* [Accessed 28 April 2016], p.31.

[442] On "spread costs", though in a different context, see *Transocean Drilling UK Ltd v Providence Resources Plc* [2016] EWCA Civ 372 at [10].

ally intended.[443] Exclusions relating to war and political risks were addressed above.[444] The other express exclusions in Section I can be summarised as follows[445]:

1. "[V]essels or other watercraft" and "aircraft and/or helicopters" are excluded from Section I (sub-clauses 1(a) and (b)): they are intended to be insured separately.

2. "[F]loating materials that are destined to become a permanent part of the completed Project" are excluded unless declared and accepted by insurers prior to loss (sub-clause 1(a)).

3. "[T]emporary works", "site preparatory works", and "property and/or equipment that are not owner by the Principal Assureds and are not for incorporation in the contract work" are excluded unless separately scheduled to the policy, with additional premium agreed, prior to loss (sub-clause 1(c)).

4. Generally, any operations, works, assets or equipment, "for which budgeted costs are not included within the latest agreed Schedule B" are excluded (sub-clause 1(k)).

5. Excluded are "any claim(s) by reason of the platforms and/or structures being placed in the wrong locations unless caused by an Occurrence which is covered by the terms of Section I" (sub-clause 1(e)).[446] Further,

    > "any claim arising from or in connection with the dumping of rocks and/or similar materials, where such rocks and/or similar materials have been placed in the wrong position or location"

    is excluded (sub-clause 1(j)).

6. Financial and consequential losses, such as contractual penalties for non-completion or delay in completion or other instances of non-compliance under contract, loss of use or delay in start-up of the insured property ("howsoever caused"), and any liability for performance guarantees given by suppliers, are excluded, as is infidelity of or known to a Principal Assured (sub-clauses 1(d), (f), (g) and (h)). Some of these matters can be insured separately.[447]

7. As has been mentioned, the "costs or expenses of repairing, renewing or replacing faulty welds" are excluded (sub-clause 1(l)).[448] It has been noted that there may be "differing interpretations as to as to what precisely constitutes the weld": some consider the heat affected zone (between weld metal and "parent" metal) to form part of the weld.[449] The wording of the sub-clause purports to exclude absolutely the costs of rectifying faulty welds, regardless as to whether an insured peril has intervened and caused damage to such welds, or to property adjacent to or incorporating them (such that the welds would need to be replaced in any event). In this way,

---

[443] See Sharp, paras 6.6.1 and 8.10.0. Ch.10, above, and paras 24-081, 24-083, 24-084, 24-086 and 24-087, below, discuss general limitations applicable to all risks insurance, including WELCAR.
[444] See above, para.24-048.
[445] I.e. summarising WELCAR, Section I, Exclusions, cl.1, sub-clauses (a) to (m).
[446] This exclusion is clearly linked to incorporated ICBR cl.5.2, and to the Additional Work clause, discussed at paras 24-034 and 24-043, respectively.
[447] See, e.g.: above, para.17-012, regarding insurance against LADs; above, paras 17-048 to 17-077, regarding DSU cover. Regarding credit insurance and fidelity policies, see *MacGillivray*, paras 33-016 to 33-039.
[448] See above, para.24-004.
[449] Sharp, para.8.3.1.

it goes beyond the exclusion in the Defective Parts clause.[450] However, sub-clause 1(i) should not apply where the defective condition of the welds is itself simply the result of an insured peril. To qualify as "faulty", the relevant defect should be present in the weld at the time it is made, or when the policy attaches (if later).[451]

8. Also excluded are the "costs of repairing, correcting or rectifying wear and tear, rust and oxidisation and fluctuations in temperature" (sub-clause 1(i)). Exclusions relating to wear and tear, corrosion and rust have been discussed elsewhere in this work.[452] As discussed in those parts, where several natural processes are listed in an exclusion, the terms are normally construed ejusdem generis. However, it is not immediately apparent what common genus would naturally encompass "fluctuations in temperature" along with the other processes named in sub-clause 1. Nevertheless, if "fluctuations in temperature" is treated analogously to the other named processes—e.g. to wear and tear—, then it could be argued that the temperature variations excluded should be limited to those which are natural and ordinary, i.e. those to which the property would be exposed at the locations and in the environments where the insured property would ordinarily be present during construction. There may be large variations in the temperatures encountered between onshore assembly locations, the final offshore location, and during transit in between, and the insured property should be designed and built to withstand the same[453]: loss or damage arising from such changes in temperature should be caught by the exclusion. On the other hand, if unnatural or extraordinary temperature variations are encountered, arising from sources of heat[454] or cold[455] that would not ordinarily have been expected, this could constitute a fortuitous occurrence taking the resulting loss or damage outwith sub-clause 1(i).

9. Finally, excluded are "loss, damage, liability or expense directly or indirectly caused by or contributed to by or arising from": radiation from, contamination by, or toxic, explosive, or other contaminating or hazardous properties of, nuclear sources; atomic, nuclear or similar weapons of war; and radioactive contamination "however caused whenever or wherever happening" (sub-clause 1(i) 1(m)). The causal language used could hardly be more inclusive: even losses to which the named risks make only a remote contribution will be caught.[456] Exclusions covering nuclear material have been discussed elsewhere in this work.[457]

---

[450] Discussed above, at para.24-030.

[451] See above, paras 14-007 to 14-022.

[452] See above, paras 15-012 to 15-030. See also below, paras 24-084 and 24-086 (discussing the approach to limitations to cover relating to wear and tear and inherent vice).

[453] See Sharp, para.8.10.0. For example, consider the gloves in *TM Noten BV v Harding* [1989] 2 Lloyd's Rep. 527, QBD; [1990] 2 Lloyd's Rep. 283, CA: because they were shipped in warm conditions at Calcutta, they were vulnerable to evaporation of their absorbed moisture and condensation within their container during transit to Rotterdam. It was held that the damage to the gloves was simply caused by their own natural behaviour, without the intervention of any fortuitous occurrence. Had there been an exclusion against "fluctuations in temperature" in the policy in that case, it probably would have applied.

[454] E.g. from fire, welding.

[455] E.g. from transit through colder climates due to not taking the ordinary, intended route.

[456] See above, paras 19-016 to 19-020.

[457] See above, paras 15-061 to 15-065.

24-053 **Section I deductibles.** Section I states: "Underwriters' liability under Section I of the Policy shall be subject to the Deductibles set out in Item 5 of the Declarations."[458] The Declarations then provide:

> "5. DEDUCTIBLES:
> SECTION I
>
> (i) US$ [blank] each and every Occurrence in respect of all cargo sendings.
> (ii) US$ [blank] each and every Occurrence in respect of Onshore Fabrication Risks.
> (iii) US$ [blank] each and every Occurrence in respect of tows within waters to final offshore site
>
> or
>
> US$ [blank] each and every Occurrence in respect of transocean tows or heavy lift movements to final offshore site.
>
> (iv) US$ [blank] each and every Occurrence in respect of offshore works and associated subsequent maintenance; but
> (v) US$ [blank] for up to 24" diameter pipes or US$ [blank] for over 24" diameter pipes each and every Occurrence in respect of installation of pipelines, cables, tie-ins, risers, spool, pieces and any other subsea, and associated subsequent maintenance.
> (vi) 48 hours each and every Occurrence in respect of stand-by charges.
> (vii) US$ [blank] each and every Occurrence in respect of all non-specified hereunder."[459]

The various deductibles are generally distinguished according to the type of activity or operation in the context of which a relevant Occurrence intervenes and causes loss or damage. This, in addition to the provision of a final, catch-all deductible, indicates that the deductibles were not intended to be applied cumulatively.[460]

Most of the phrases and expressions used in these deductibles are undefined by WELCAR. The distinction in deductible (iii) between a tow "within waters" and a "transocean tow" is not explained, but it may reflect the distinction drawn in international guidance on ocean towing, between operations where the distance between designated ports of refuge or safe anchoring along the route is more than twenty-four hours, taking weather conditions into account, and other operations where the route of the tow stays within closer proximity of places of safety.[461]

Deductibles, and associated aggregation wording,[462] are discussed in detail in an earlier part of this work.[463]

24-054 **Section I: other clauses.** Other provisions set out in Section I of WELCAR include:

1. An Other Insurance clause,[464] which, unusually, declares that the cover provided under Section I "shall be primary to, and receive no contribution from, any other insurance maintained by or for" any of the Assureds.

---

[458] WELCAR, Section I, cl.4.
[459] WELCAR, Declarations, item 5.
[460] See Sharp, para.9.6.4. He suggests further, however, that different losses (he employs the phrase "heads of claims") arising out of the same Occurrence may attract different deductibles, depending (presumably) on the activity or operation to which they relate.
[461] See "Guidelines for safe ocean towing", IMO MSC/Circ.884 (December 21, 1998), Annex, p.2.
[462] Such as that included in the definition of "Occurrence", discussed above at para.24-029.
[463] See above, paras 11-025 to 11-035. See also R. Merkin, *Colinvaux's Law of Insurance*, 10th edn (London: Sweet & Maxwell, 2014), paras 10-150 to 10-171.
[464] WELCAR, Section I, Terms and Conditions, cl.20. See also Sharp, para.8.8.3.

2. A Loss Notification clause,[465] under which the Assureds are, as soon as reasonably practicable after an Occurrence, to provide various particulars regarding the loss in a "signed and sworn proof of loss". The potential relationship between this clause and the Forfeiture clause has been discussed above.[466]

3. A Claims Surveys/Adjusting clause,[467] which empowers the Assureds to instruct a loss adjuster, chosen from a list of firms, to carry out a damage survey on behalf of insurers, in the event of physical loss or damage covered under Section I, but only where there is an emergency or "over weekends". In other circumstances, the adjusters are to be appointed by insurers upon receipt of a notification under the Loss Notification clause mentioned above.

4. Finally, a Payment of Claims clause obliges insurers to pay claims under Section I to the Assureds' representative, identified in the Declarations,[468] within thirty days "after presentation and acceptance of proofs of loss by Underwriters or their approved representatives."[469]

(d) WELCAR Section II—Liability

WELCAR public liability cover: introduction. The public liability insurance **24-055** aspect of the WELCAR policy form is, for various reasons, given less prominence than the physical loss and damage cover provided under Section I. It has been observed that, in practice:

"[e]xposure to third party risks in offshore construction insurance is generally considered as comparatively low, particularly if the field development is taking place at a Greenfield site with no third party property in the vicinity."[470] As has been mentioned,[471] between the many entities involved at the project site, mutual contractual releases and indemnities will generally be employed wherever possible so that each entity assumes sole responsibility for damage to its own property and for injury to its own personnel. Any residual liabilities between separate contractors, not mutually bound by the relevant contractual protections, are generally intended to be addressed by ensuring that each has its own appropriate liability cover. Such insurance is intended to be primary to the liability cover provided under WELCAR's Section II.[472]

As regards the Principal Assureds, the important risks sought to be addressed under Section II include the following:

1. the risks of liability to third-party owners of property already in the field, arising particularly in the context of tie-ins or crossings (e.g. pipelines, submarine cables)[473];

2. the exposure to the Principal Assureds' own, existing property, e.g. in respect of any intended tying-in of the new project. This is generally insured

---

465 WELCAR, Section I, Terms and Conditions, cl.3.
466 See above, at para.24-021.
467 WELCAR, Section I, Terms and Condtiions, cl.14.
468 WELCAR, Declarations, item 8.
469 WELCAR, Section I, Terms and Conditions, cl.18. On the potential authority of loss adjusters to act for insurers, in this regard, see above, paras 11-015 and 21-025. Regarding damages for late payment of claims, see paras 11-021 to 11-024 and 21-023 to 21-024, and 23-013 to 23-021.
470 Sharp, para.6.7.0.
471 See above, fn.66. See also Sharp, para.9.1.1.
472 See discussion of Section II's Other Insurance clause, below at para.24-062.
473 See Sharp, para.9.6.7.

under Section II, because the structure of ownership of existing property may not exactly match that of the new project[474];

3.   pollution liability from the project during testing, commissioning, and initial operations.

In considering WELCAR, this work's primary focus has been on Section I: for the reasons outlined above, it is called upon far more frequently in practice than Section II. Further, in its wording Section II is relatively less original than Section I.[475] Nevertheless, some commentary on Section II is set out below.[476]

24-056 **Insuring agreement: Coverage clause and Section II Definitions.** Section II provides cover to the Assureds against[477]:

(i)   the obligation to pay "Ultimate Net Loss";

(ii)   by reason of either legal liability "imposed upon the Assured(s)",[478] or an "Express Contractual Liability"[479];

(iii)   for "Bodily Injury" or "Property Damage"[480];

(iv)   subject to the Bodily Injury or Property Damage being caused by an "Occurrence" (as defined in Section II) that takes place during the Project Period,[481] and that arises out of activities described in the Scope of Insurance section of the policy.[482]

A number of these phrases and expressions set out above are further defined in Section II:

1.   "Ultimate Net Loss" means the total sum the claimant-Assured is obligated to pay as "Damages", and is to include "Claims Expenses in respect of claims covered under this Policy."[483] "Damages" include only compensatory damages, money judgments, arbitral awards, and settlement agreements (though, importantly, only if "entered [into] with Underwriters' consent"); they exclude fines, penalties, punitive or exemplary damages, multiple damages, and equitable or injunctive relief (e.g. orders for specific

---

[474] E.g. even if the same joint venturers are involved, there may be variation in their proportionate shareholdings in the companies owning the existing property and the new project, respectively. See below, at para.24-063.

[475] Sharp notes, at para.9.1.0, that compared to legal and contractual liability coverage previously offered, in the offshore construction context, Section II is "far more akin to the traditional energy market liability wordings."

[476] Public liability insurance is discussed in more detail above, in Ch.18. See also generally: *MacGillivray*, Ch.30; M. Clarke, *Law of Liability Insurance*, (Informa: London, 2013).

[477] WELCAR, Section II, Insuring Agreement, cl.1.

[478] See above, para.18-039 discussing the words "legally liable to pay".

[479] "By reason of" has been construed, in a similar context, as indicating the need for a "clear causal link between what is paid and an actual legal liability: so a settlement agreement which the insured concludes with a third party where, in truth, the insured was under no obligation to indemnify the third party, would not be covered. See *AstraZeneca Insurance Co Ltd v XL Insurance (Bermuda) Ltd* [2013] EWHC 349 (Comm) at [98]–[102].

[480] Sharp, para.9.2.1, refers to Section II cover against legal liability to third parties for "defined losses".

[481] See discussion of the Project Period above, at para.24-017.

[482] See discussion of the scope of the insured activities, above, at para.24-008. A phrase similar to "arising out of activities" was construed in *King v Brandywine Reinsurance Co (UK) Ltd* [2004] EWHC 1033 (Comm) at [231]–[236] (liability cover for pollution "arising out of the operations of the Insured.") See further below, fnn.491 and 493.

[483] WELCAR, Section II, Definitions, cl.7.

performance).[484] "Claims Expenses" means "reasonable legal costs and other expenses incurred by or on behalf of the Assured(s) in the defence of any covered claim ...".[485] Because it applies only to costs incurred "in defence of any covered claim", the Assureds' costs of meeting a claim falling outwith the scope of the Section II cover, or which is unsuccessful, are probably not covered.[486]

2. "Express Contractual Liability" means liability "expressly assumed", in a written contract, or in an oral contract "reduced to writing within 7 days after the contract is orally agreed", "prior to any Occurrence covered by this Policy".[487] As "Occurrence" in Section II is defined differently from Section I, and Sections I and II are intended to be "distinct",[488] "any Occurrence covered by this Policy" should be taken to mean any Occurrence covered by Section II.

3. "Bodily Injury" means "bodily injury, sickness or disease, including death resulting therefrom (and including damages allowed for loss of services) and mental anguish", with the proviso that these injuries be "accidentally sustained by any person by reason of the Assured's operations as declared..."[489] The inclusion of "damages for loss of services", in the case of death, relates to damages for loss of services rendered by the deceased person to the third-party claimant (where these is a right to claim these).[490] The proviso states that the Bodily Injury must be sustained "by reason of the Assured's operations as declared". "[B]y reason of" probably requires a causal connection between the injury and the relevant operations, though not necessarily a relationship of proximate cause.[491] "[O]perations as declared" must refer to the operations undertaken in the course of the Project described in the Declarations, and probably encompasses any details provided in the Assureds' proposal during placement,[492] provided that such

---

[484] WELCAR, Section II, Definitions, cl.3. See also above, para.18-046.

[485] WELCAR, Section II, Definitions, cl.2: "*including* attorney's fees and disbursements, investigation, adjustment, appraisal, appeal costs and expenses and pre- and post-judgment interest, *excluding* salaries, wages and benefits of the Assured's employees and the Assured's administrative expenses." (Emphasis added.)

[486] See *Thornton Springer v NEM Insurance Co Ltd* [2000] 1 Lloyd's Rep. I.R. 590 at [47]; *Poole Harbour Yacht Club Marine Ltd v Excess Insurance Co Ltd* [2001] Lloyd's Rep. 580 at 583–584; *MacGillivray*, para.30-051. Cf. discussion of "Insured claims" in R. Merkin, *Colinvaux & Merkin's Insurance Contract Law*, (London: Sweet & Maxwell) Vol.2, para.B–0925, and in R. Merkin, *Colinvaux's Law of Insurance* (2014), para.20-086.

[487] WELCAR, Section II, Definitions, cl.4. See also Sharp, para.9.2.5.

[488] See above, para.24-007.

[489] WELCAR, Section II, Definitions, cl.1. Further discussion of "personal injury", see above at para.18-030. See also Sharp, para.9.2.3.

[490] The tortious action for loss of services was abolished in English law by the Administration of Justice Act 1982, s.2.

[491] This construction would be consistent with the requirement in the Coverage clause (WELCAR, Section II, Insuring Agreement, cl.1) that the Occurrence "arises out of the activities described in the Scope of Insurance section herein." See: *King v Brandywine Reinsurance Co (UK) Ltd* [2004] EWHC 1033 (Comm) at [231]–[236] (liability cover for pollution "arising out of the operations of the Insured."); *AstraZeneca Insurance Co Ltd v XL Insurance (Bermuda) Ltd* [2013] EWHC 349 (Comm) at [98]–[102].

[492] i.e the "application, schedules and proposal" referred to in the Acceptance clause, discussed above at para.24-014.

operations fall within the activities set out in the Scope of Insurance provision and within the insured values in Schedule B.[493]

4. "Property Damage" means physical loss or destruction of, or damage to, tangible property[494];; it includes loss of use of such property that is not accompanied by physical damage or destruction, provided that the loss of use is caused by an Occurrence during the Policy Period[495] (in practice, the Occurrence will have to have occurred during the Project Period).[496] Again, as with Bodily Injury, to qualify as "Property Damage" the relevant losses must be "accidentally sustained by reason of the Assured's operations as declared ...".

5. Finally, an "Occurrence" in the context of Section II is defined as:

> "an accident, including continuous or repeated exposure to conditions, which results in Bodily Injury or Property Damage neither expected nor intended from the standpoint of the Assured."[497]

24-057 **Section II exclusions.** In light of the above, the coverage provided under the Coverage clause is, broadly stated, against all risks of legal liability for injury, death, or loss of or damage to material property. But the wide cover thus provided is significantly cut down by a list of exclusions. In summary, the exclusions cover actual or alleged liability[498]:

1. (*Intentional violation of law*) "arising out of operations in intentional violation of any national, international, federal or state statute or law" (Exclusions, cl.1). Presumably, the "operations", and the "intentional[ity]" must be those of the relevant Assured. A similarly-worded condition appears in the carve out to Exclusions, cl.1, relating to seepage, pollution and contamination liability (discussed below);

2. (*Employees*) to an Assured's employees, whether the liability accrues to the Assured in their capacity as employer or otherwise (Exclusions, cl.6). Also excluded is actual or alleged liability: to surviving relatives or dependants of the Assureds' employees, or to their estates, arising out of injury, illness or death of such employees (Exclusions, cl.7); or arising out of Bodily Injury to any Assured's employees, including liability to indemnify or contribute towards losses of other parties arising out of the same (Exclusions, cl.8).[499] Vicarious liability of the Assureds for Bodily Injury caused by one employee to another is also excluded (Exclusions, cl.9), as is any li-

---

[493] Again, this construction seems correct as it maintains consistency between the definition of Bodily Injury and the requirement in Coverage clause that the Occurrence "arises out of the activities described in the Scope of Insurance section herein." See also the discussion of the Scope of Insurance provision, above at para.24-008.

[494] See above, paras 18-032 to 18-036, for further discussion of damage to material property.

[495] WELCAR, Section II, Definitions, cl.6. See also Sharp, para.9.2.2.

[496] See Section II, Insuring Agreement, cl.1, and para.24-018, above.

[497] WELCAR, Section II, Definitions, cl.5. See also Sharp, para.9.2.2.

[498] WELCAR, Section II, Exclusions begins: "The insurance afforded by Section II does not apply to actual or alleged liability:..." See also Sharp, para.9.4.0. Many of the exclusions in Section II are similar or identical to those in other standard policy forms, in particular the London Standard Wordings entitled "Excess Liability Claims Made Policy—LSW 244" and "Endorsement Containing Energy Exclusions (LSW 244)—LSW 245". The causal phrases employed in some of the provisions discussed below—"arising out of", "arising from", "directly or indirectly caused by", caused or arising "solely" by or from, etc—are considered above in paras 19-015 to 19-021.

[499] "Bodily Injury" is discussed above, at para.24-056.

ability which the Assureds directors, officers, partners, principals, employees or stockholders may have "to any employee or any Assured" (Exclusions, cl.10). By these sometimes overlapping provisions, Section II excludes risks to the Assureds' personnel normally covered by employer's liability insurance, in particular[500];

3. (*Vehicles and watercraft*) "caused by" automobiles or other types of vehicles or things drawn by the same, animal teams, or aircraft (Exclusions, cl.2). Exception is made for equipment in the nature of "crawler type" tractors, cranes, shovels, etc., which are "not subject to motor vehicle registration". Likewise, actual or alleged liability "arising out of the use or operation of watercraft ... other than as declared" is excluded (Exclusions, cl.5)[501];

4. (*War and political risks*) "directly or indirectly occasioned by, happening through or in consequence of" various war, expropriation, political and terrorist risks (Exclusions, cl.3: the perils listed being the same as those in Section I, Exclusions, sub-clauses 2(i) and (ii)(b), which are set out above)[502];

5. (*Nuclear and radioactivity*) "directly or indirectly caused by or contributed to by or arising from" risks from radioactivity, nuclear or atomic sources (Exclusions, cl.25: the perils listed being the same as those excluded under Section I, discussed above)[503];

6. (*Health hazards*) "directly or indirectly arising out of" a list of named substances, emanations, items and conditions, including: (potentially) harmful or toxic substances asbestos, coal dust, PCBs, MTBE, silica, benzene, lead, talc, and dioxins; "electromagnetic fields"; "carpal tunnel" (presumably a reference to an injury to this part of the human body); and "pharmaceutical or medical drugs/products/substances/devices" (Exclusions, cl.24). The elements in this somewhat incoherent list are linked chiefly by their perceived potential to generate "mass tort" litigation. The exclusion ends with a catch-all phrase—"or any substance containing such material or any derivative thereof"—which is clearly not well-suited to all items in the preceding list[504];

7. (*Products*) "arising out of" goods or products (including containers of the same), "manufactured, sold, handled or distributed" by either the Assureds or by "others trading under [the Assureds'] name" (Exclusions, cl.20); or "for the costs of removal, recovery, repair, alteration or replacement of any product (or any part thereof)" which fails to perform the function for which it was "manufactured, designed, sold, supplied, installed, repaired or altered by or on behalf of the Assured in the normal course of the Assured's operations" (Exclusions, cl.23)[505];

8. (*Warranties of fitness and quality*) "assumed under a warranty", either relating to "the fitness or quality of the Assured's products", or to the performance of the Assureds' work "in a workmanlike manner" (Exclusions, cl.26);

9. (*Professional services*) "arising from any negligence, error or omission,

---

500 See Sharp, paras 6.7.1 and 14.4.4(a).
501 See above, paras 18-082 and 18-083, discussing similar exclusions in relation to vessels and "mechanically propelled vehicles". See also discussion in Sharp, para.9.4.1.
502 See the discussion and references above, at para.24-048.
503 WELCAR, Section I, Exclusions, cl.1(m), discussed above at para.24-052.
504 E.g. "carpal tunnel", "electromagnetic fields".
505 See also the exclusion discussed above at para.18-128.

malpractice or mistake in providing or failing to provide professional services", by or on behalf of the Assureds "in the conduct of any of the Assured[s'] business activities" (Exclusions, cl.22).[506] Without limitation, it is provided that this exclusion covers "the preparation or approval of maps, plans, opinions, reports, surveys, designs [and] specifications", and supervisory, inspection, engineering, and data processing services;

10. *(Tools, materials and equipment of "any persons")* for damage to or loss of any persons' tools, materials or equipment while performing operations for any Assured (Exclusions, cl.4)[507];

11. *(Property in Assureds' ownership, occupation, use, care, custody or control)* for damage to, loss or loss of use of property "owned or occupied by or rented or leased to", "used by", "in the care, custody or control of" an Assured, "or over which the Assured is for any purpose exercising physical control" (Exclusions, cl.21).[508] Again, these exclusions reflect the expectation that such property will be covered by the Assureds' other property insurances. However, coverage against liability in relation to the Assureds' own "existing property" can be subject to a "buy-back"[509];

12. *(Wells and holes, underground equipment and control of well)*[510] for loss of or damage to any well or hole, whether being drilled or "worked over" by or on behalf of the Assureds, in the care, custody or control of the Assureds, or in connection with which the Assured has provided services, equipment or materials (Exclusions, cl.11), or for loss of or damage to any equipment while below the surface of the earth in any such well or hole (Exclusions, cl.13). Also excluded are liabilities for any cost or expense incurred in redrilling or restoring "any such" well or hole or any substitute (Exclusions, cl.12), for controlling or bringing under control any well or hole, extinguishing fire in or from any such wells or holes, or drilling relief wells or holes (whether or not successful) (Exclusions, cl.14). It seems likely that where the phrase "such well or hole" is employed in Exclusions, cl.12, it was intended to refer to wells and holes falling within the scope of Exclusions, cll.11 and 13[511];

13. *(Subsidence caused by sub-surface operations)* "for loss of, damage to, or loss of use of property directly or indirectly resulting from subsidence caused by sub-surface operations of the Assured" (Exclusions, cl.17)[512];

14. *(Seepage, pollution and contamination)* "directly or indirectly caused by or arising out of seepage, pollution or contamination however caused whenever or wherever happening" (Exclusions, cl.15):
   (a) This exclusion is qualified by a carve-out, where: (i) the seepage, pol-

---

[506] See also the exclusion discussed above at para.18-134.

[507] Sharp, para.9.4.0, describes this exclusion as "somewhat illogical": liability for damage to an independent worker's tools is excluded, but liability for loss or damage to the same worker's personal effects, or for their injury or death, is not.

[508] See also the extensive discussion of "care, custody and control" exclusions above at paras 18-086 to 18-126.

[509] See below at para.24-063.

[510] See discussion of these exclusions in Sharp, paras 14.5.0(a) to (c).

[511] It may be arguable, though it is not clearly the case, that the same should be said in relation to the "wells and holes" referred to in Exclusions, cl.14.

[512] Sharp notes, para.14.5.0(e), that the exclusion "contemplates that the drilling of a well may result in cratering causing loss or damage to a drilling rig, or that the exhaustion of the reservoir may result in subsidence."

lution or contamination "was caused by an event"; (ii) the event "commenced" on a specific, identified date during the Policy Period; (iii) the event was discovered by the Assureds within fourteen days of such commencement, and (iv) notified in writing to insurers within sixty days of that discovery[513]; and (v) the event did not "result from the Assured's intentional violation of any statute, rule, ordinance or regulation." In effect, broadly put, these conditions allow cover under Section II to apply, subject to its terms, if the Assured can establish by evidence that the seepage, pollution or contamination, causing Bodily Injury or Property Damage, was caused by a discrete, identified fortuitous occurrence on a specific date: incidents of gradual seepage of unknown or only approximately known origins are to be excluded.

(b)   Even if the carve-out applies, Section II will "*not*"[514] cover certain liabilities in relation to seepage, pollution or contamination, viz: (i) liability, arising "solely" from an obligation under statute or imposed by contract, to "evaluate, monitor, control, remove, nullify or clean up seeping, polluting or contaminating substances"; (ii) liability "to abate or investigate any threat" of seepage, pollution or contamination onto or of a third party's property; (iii) liability for seepage, pollution or contamination of property—including "soil, minerals, water or any other substance on, in or under such ... property"—"which is or was, at any time," owned, leased, rented, occupied, or in the care, custody or control, by or of any Assured; (iv) liability "arising directly" out of the Assureds' carriage of oil or similar substances (other than substances, such as fuel, "used in furtherance of the Assured's operations") "by watercraft"; and (v) liability arising "directly or indirectly" from seepage, pollution or contamination "intended from the standpoint of the Assured or any other person or organisation acting for or on behalf of the Assured"[515];

15. (*Waste materials*) "for or arising out of "the handling, processing, treatment, storage, disposal, dumping, monitoring, controlling, removing or cleaning-up of any waste materials or substances", or arising out of such materials during transportation (Exclusions, cl.16).[516] "[W]aste materials or substances" is not defined, but should probably be distinguished from wreckage and debris, liability for the removal of which is covered under Section I and can also be covered under Section II.[517] Subject to this, the phrase may refer to any matter generated or acquired by the Assureds in the

---

[513] Notice to insurers needs to include the matters set out in the Notice to Underwriters clause, discussed below at para.24-059.

[514] Emphasis in original.

[515] See also: discussion of pollution exclusions above, at paras 18-129 to 18-133; and Sharp's discussion of this exclusion, at paras 9.4.2 and 14.4.4(f) (the latter discussing the similar exclusion in LSW 244).

[516] Sharp comments, para.14.4.4(e), that this exclusion arose from "claims faced by oil companies, among other entities, resulting from pollution caused by deliberate dumping of waste, even though at the time the activity may have been legitimate." The exclusion, however, is not limited to deliberate acts of pollution.

[517] See discussion of excess wreckage removal, below at para.24-064.

ordinary course of their insured activities,[518] which the Assureds discard, or
intend or are required to discard.[519]

16. (*Sub-surface oil, gas, water, and other substances or materials*)

"for loss of or damage to sub-surface oil, gas, water, or other substance or material, or for the cost or expense of reducing to physical possession above the
surface of the earth any oil, gas, water, or other substance or material, or for the
cost or expense incurred or rendered necessary to prevent or minimise such loss
or damage"(Exclusions, cl.18)[520];

17. (*Fines and penalties, and exemplary damages*) for fines and penalties, and
for "punitive or exemplary damages" including multiple damages (Exclusions, cl.19).[521]

24-058 Deductible and Limit of Liability clauses. Cover under Section II is subject to
a "per Occurrence" deductible to be agreed and set out in the Declarations.[522] It is
provided that a single deductible is to be applied "in respect of each and every Occurrence", to the Ultimate Net Loss from the aggregate of all claims or suits caused
thereby, against any and all relevant Assureds, brought by any and all third-party
claimants, "including expenses, liability, debris removal,[523] uncollected accrued
charges and legal fees, and/or defence charges, or all combined."[524]

The cover under Section II is also subject to a "per Occurrence" limit of
liability.[525] This is intended to be an aggregate limit for "all Ultimate Net Loss by
reason of any one Occurrence without regard to the number of Assureds, claims or
claimants." It is specifically provided that "Ultimate Net Loss payments" made by
insurers, or the depositing of amounts in "a court of competent jurisdiction", up to

---

[518] *Bennett (t/a Soho Pizzeria) v AXA Insurance Plc* [2003] EWHC 86 (Comm) at [15]–[17] (considering the meaning of "trade waste" in a warranty).

[519] See the *Shorter OED*, 6th edn (OUP: 2007), Tit. "waste [noun and adjective]": item A. noun, III.10,
"Waste matter, refuse; unusable material left over from a process of manufacture, the use of consumer
goods, etc.: the useless by-products of a process; material or manufactured articles so damaged as
to be useless or unsaleable..."; item B. adjective, 7., "Of a material, a by-product, etc.: eliminated
or thrown aside as worthless after the completion of a process; refuse. ... b. Of a manufactured
article: rejected as defective. Also, (e.g. of sheets of a printed book) produced in excess of what can
be used." In the regulatory context, Directive 2008/98/EC (The Waste Framework Directive),
art.3(1), defines "waste" as "any substance or object which the holder discards or intends or is
required to discard"; and art.5, distinguishes a "by-product" from "waste", the former being a
substance produced as an integral part of the production process, which is certain to be re-used, and
can lawfully and directly be re-used without any further processing (other than normal industrial
practice): see R. Burnett-Hall and B. Jones, *Burnett-Hall on Environmental Law*, 3rd edn (London:
Sweet & Maxwell, 2012), at paras 14-069 to 14-089.

[520] Sharp, para.14.5.0(f), commenting on a similar exclusion in LSW 245, notes: "The exclusion is
aimed at drilling contractors, who are invariably relieved of this responsibility by oil companies
under the drilling contract. It can also apply to oil companies in respect of operations being conducted
in lease blocks adjoining others owned by third parties."

[521] This reflects the definition of "Damages", discussed above at para.24-056. See further, the discussion of exclusions regarding fines and penalties, above, at paras 18-084 to 18-085.

[522] WELCAR, Section II, Insuring Agreement, cl.2, and Declarations, item 5. The meaning of "Occurrence" under Section II is discussed above, at para.24-056.

[523] The appearance of "debris removal" in Section II is explained below, at para.24-064.

[524] See also Sharp, para.9.2.8.

[525] WELCAR, Section II, Insuring Agreement, cl.3, and Declarations, item 4. The "per Occurrence"
nature of the limit is clear from the wording. As to the suggestion that the Ultimate Net Loss was
also intended to function as an "aggregate limit over the policy" (Sharp, para.9.2.7), the wording of
the Limit of Liability clause would appear to provide little support for this.

any remaining limit of liability, will reduce and eventually exhaust the per Occurrence limit. This may have been intended to provide explicit protection for insurers even in circumstances where, for example, the sum of all payments to third party claimants has reached the per Occurrence limit of liability, but other claimants nevertheless seek to bring direct actions against insurers (e.g. under legislation allowing such direct claims in the event of the Assureds' insolvency).[526]

The deductible should be subtracted from the amount payable under Section II, following application of the limit of liability: that is, insurers maximum exposure per Occurrence should be the difference between the limit and the deductible.[527]

Notice to Underwriters clause.   It will be noted from the matters discussed above **24-059** that the liability cover provided by Section II is "occurrence-based", rather than "claims-made".[528] However, the Assureds are required to provide written notice to insurers following an Occurrence, specifying the Occurrence, stating "the damages which may result or [have already] resulted from the Occurrence", and "the circumstance by which the Assured(s) first became aware of the Occurrence."[529] Such notice is to be given "as soon as is practicable" from the time when the relevant Assured first became aware of the Occurrence.[530] (Different time limits for giving notice apply to claims by reason of seepage, pollution or contamination, under the carve out to Section II's Exclusion 15.)[531]

No sanction is specified in the event the clause is breached: breach may give rise only to a claim for damages. It is uncertain whether, considered alone, the clause would be construed as a condition precedent to liability.[532] The first sentence of the Forfeiture clause, however, would probably apply to the Notice to Underwriters clause.[533] Accordingly, breach of the notice provision by an Assured would result in there being "no coverage for that Assured as to the particular claim in connection with which the breach occurred". In the longer term, a failure to notify insurers of Occurrences within the Discovery Period will result in insurers bearing no liability for claims caused by such Occurrences.[534]

Claims handling provisions: Defence and Settlement and Admission of Liability clauses.   Section II's Defence and Settlement and Admission of Liability **24-060** clauses provide as follows:

"*4. DEFENCE AND SETTLEMENT*

Underwriters shall not be called upon to assume charge of the settlement or defence of any claim or suit brought or proceeding instituted against the Assured(s), but Underwriters shall have the right and shall be given the opportunity to associate with

---

[526] If this is correct, the provisions address the same concerns discussed in relation to the Insolvency clause, discussed above at para.24-024.

[527] See R. Merkin, *Colinvaux & Merkin's Insurance Contract Law*, Vol.2, para.C–0156. There is no apparent basis for the suggestion (Sharp, para.9.2.8) that "the limit is available in full, rather than being partially eroded by a deductible." In particular, this would appear contrary to the wording of the Deductible clause, which states that insurers "shall only be liable for Ultimate Net Loss exceeding the Deductible ...".

[528] See above, para.21-008.

[529] WELCAR, Section II, Terms and Conditions, cl.1.

[530] WELCAR, Section II, Terms and Conditions, cl.1(3). See also above, para.21-020.

[531] Discussed above, at para.24-057.

[532] See above, paras 12-005 and 12-009.

[533] The Forfeiture clause is discussed above, at para.24-021.

[534] See discussion of the Discovery clause above, at para.24-018.

the Assured(s) in the defence and control of any claim, suit or proceeding relative to an Occurrence where the claim or suit involves, or appears reasonably likely to involve amounts payable by Underwriters, in which event the Assured(s) and Underwriters shall co-operate in all things in the defence of such claim, suit or proceeding."[535]

"2. ADMISSION OF LIABILITY

The Assured(s) shall not in any way acknowledge or admit any liability on account of any Occurrence nor settle nor negotiate the settlement of any claim or suit resulting therefrom, nor without the consent of Underwriters, incur any expense other than such immediate medical or surgical aid as is imperative at the time of the accident."[536]

The effect of the Defence and Settlement clause would appear to be as follows. Insurers are not obliged to take conduct of the settlement or defence of any third party claim against the Assureds. However, if any such claim "involves, or appears reasonably likely to involve" the payment of an indemnity by insurers, then insurers have the right, and the Assureds must give them the opportunity, to "associate" with the Assureds in the defence and control of any such claim. In the event that insurers exercise this right to "associate" in the defence and control of a claim, then insurers and Assureds are mutually obliged to co-operate in all things in the defence of the claim. In this context, the expression "appears reasonably likely" probably requires an objective assessment, based on the circumstances known to insurers and Assureds at the time they become aware of the third party claim, as to whether it is probable that the claim will require insurers to make payments.[537] Claims co-operation obligations are discussed earlier in this work.[538]

The effect of the Admission of Liability clause is to prohibit the Assureds from admitting liability in relation to any Occurrence, or seeking to settle or settling any third party claim resulting from the same. The Assureds are also prohibited from incurring any expenses, other than urgent medical expenses immediately necessary at the time of the Occurrence, without insurers' consent. The practical effect of this clause is that the Assureds are effectively required to act on their own initiative to deny (or at least not to admit) any third party claim, unless and until insurers agree otherwise. Further, the Assureds are in practice obliged to keep insurers informed as to the course they intend to take in defending the claim and to obtain insurers' permission in incurring costs in this regard. These consequences flow from the Admission of Liability clause, even where insurers are not entitled or choose not to "associate" in the defence and control of the claim under the Defence and Settlement clause.

No sanction is specified in the event that either of these clauses is breached by the Assureds.[539] As in the case of the Notice to Underwriters clause, it seems uncertain whether either clause would be construed as a condition precedent to li-

---

[535] WELCAR, Section II, Insuring Agreement, cl.4.

[536] WELCAR, Section II, Terms and Conditions, cl.2.

[537] See: *Jacobs v Coster and Avon Insurance* [2000] Lloyd's Rep. I.R. 506 at [16]–[22]; *Laker Vent Engineering Ltd v Templeton Insurance Co Ltd* [2009] EWCA Civ 62, at [18]–[19], [72]–[83]. See also discussion above, at paras 21-012 to 21-014.

[538] See above, at para.21-049.

[539] In practice, breach by *insurers* of their obligation to co-operate in the defence of a claim will not impede the Assureds in defending or settling it: further, such a breach would give the Assureds a claim for any damages they suffered (e.g. increased costs) as a result, in accordance with normal rules of contract law.

ability, if read alone, but in both cases the first sentence of the Forfeiture clause should probably apply.[540]

Cross Liabilities clause. Cross liabilities clauses have been discussed in an earlier **24-061** part of this work.[541] Section II's Cross Liabilities clause provides that where one Assured incurs liability to another, which is covered under Section II, the defendant–Assured will be covered "as if separate policies had been issued to each Assured."[542] "However," the clause continues, "the inclusion of more than one Assured hereunder shall not operate to increase the Limit of Liability"—a reference to the per Occurrence limit under Section II.[543]

It is not intended that Section II, by virtue of the Cross Liabilities clause, should provide further cover for property insured under Section I: this issue might arise, for example, if one Assured became liable to another for causing loss of or damage to some element of the insured property. Accordingly, it is expressly provided that: "In no case shall this Section II ... provide coverage for any physical loss of or physical damage to or defects discovered in the property insured under Section I."[544]

Notably, it is further provided that Other Assureds are not covered under Section II for "actual or alleged liability" to "other contractors and/or vendors and/or suppliers"[545] for "consequential loss, loss of profit or business interruption."[546]

Other insurance clause. As mentioned above,[547] Section II is intended to provide **24-062** secondary insurance against third party liability, ranking behind the Assureds' own liability insurances. Accordingly, Section II's Other Insurance clause provides as follows:

"3. OTHER INSURANCE

If other valid and collectible insurance with any other insurer is available to the Assured(s) covering a loss also covered by this Section II of the Policy, other than insurance that is specifically stated to be excess of the Policy, the insurance afforded by Section II shall be in excess of and shall not contribute with such other insurance. Nothing herein shall be construed to make the Policy subject to the terms, conditions and limitations of other insurance."[548]

Existing property exclusion and buy-back endorsement. Section I of **24-063** WELCAR covers the insured project works against physical loss or damage.[549] Other property in which the Assureds have an interest—"existing property"—,

---

[540] See commentary and references in relation to the Notice to Underwriters clause, above at para.24-059. There may also be a claim for damages caused by breaches of either of the two clauses discussed in this paragraph: *Milton Keynes BC v Nulty* [2011] EWHC 2847 (TCC).

[541] See above, para.18-050.

[542] WELCAR, Section II, Terms and Conditions, cl.4.

[543] See above, at para.24-058.

[544] See above, paras 18-127 and 18-135, discuss similar exclusions.

[545] Such parties may, or may not, also be Other Assureds.

[546] See Sharp, para.9.3.2; para.9.2.2, he notes that "in most offshore construction contracts, the contracting parties tend to be responsible for their own consequential losses, providing each other with an appropriate indemnity."

[547] See above at para.24-055.

[548] WELCAR, Section II, Terms and Conditions, cl.3. See further: above, para.3-075; Sharp, para.9.3.1. See also *MacGillivray*, para.25-022; R. Merkin, *Colinvaux' Law of Insurance* (2014), paras 11-088 et seq.

[549] As has been seen, the Cross Liabilities clause, discussed above at para.24-061, provides no cover

which may include previously constructed facilities such as platforms, pipelines, etc, may lie in the vicinity of the project works. If such existing property suffers accidental damage during the course of the construction project, it should normally be covered against physical loss or damage under its own, separate insurance.

However, where accidental damage is caused to an Assured's existing property by another Assured, then by virtue of the Cross Liabilities clause, and despite Section II's "care, custody or control" exclusion,[550] in some cases there may be cover for any resulting liability under Section II of WELCAR. In particular, even where each and every one of a number of parties are interested in the damaged existing property, and those same parties are all Principal Assureds under the WELCAR policy, such parties may not hold the same proportionate interests in the existing property as they do in the new project: accordingly, a third party liability situation may arise.[551]

In order to clarify their exposure in relation to the existing property of the Principal Assureds (and in order to price it, by way of additional premium), insurers may stipulate for an exclusion and buy-back endorsement, in terms such as the following[552]:

"*Existing Property Contractual Exclusion*
The coverage provided under Section II of this policy shall not apply to any claim for damage to or loss of use of any property for which the Principal Assured:

1) owns that is not otherwise provided for in this policy;
2) has use of, custody, physical control, access, right of way or an easement to by operation of a contract or agreement, or
3) is liable or claimed to be liable by operation of any indemnification, hold harmless or similar provision contained within any contract or agreement.

All other insuring agreements, terms, conditions, definitions, exclusions, notice requirements, schedules and endorsements of the policy remain unchanged.

Existing Property Contractual Exclusion Buyback
Notwithstanding the Existing Property Contractual Exclusion above, it shall not apply to any claim for:
Physical loss of and/or physical damage to existing property as per Schedule of Existing Property. Cover as above is subject to: Sub-limit: US$ [*blank*] (100%) any one Occurrence.
All other insuring agreements, terms, conditions, definitions, exclusions, notice requirements, schedules and endorsements of the policy remain unchanged."[553]

The above-quoted example exclusion is limited to the existing property of the Principal Assureds because, in practice, insurers will normally have little if any such exposure in relation to Other Assureds.[554] The scope of the exclusion set out above is potentially broad. It encompasses not only existing property that the Principal Assured owns, uses, has custody of, or controls, but also existing property in relation to which the Principal Assured has access, a right of way or an easement, "by operation of a contract or agreement". Further, the exclusion extends to any existing property in relation to which the Principal Assured has agreed to an "indemnifica-

---

for the same under Section II.
[550] I.e. Section II's Exclusions, cl.21, relating to property in Assureds' ownership, occupation, use, care, custody or control, discussed above at para.24-057.
[551] As highlighted by Sharp, para.6.7.0.
[552] See Sharp, paras 9.4.3 to 9.5.1.
[553] "Offshore Construction Project Policy" (undated), *http://www.hi-ins.com.cn/ebusiness/cms/upload/insuranceCatalogue/hullInsurance/11_hullInsurance03.pdf*, [Accessed 28 April 2016], p.34.
[554] Contractors will typically be indemnified by the Principal Assureds in relation to damage to existing property: see Sharp, paras 9.1.4 and 9.5.1.

tion, hold harmless or similar provision", as might be entered into with "true" third parties in relation to substantial installations that the insured project is intended to tie into or cross. Accordingly, an existing property exclusion often extends far beyond the scope of Section II's "care, custody or control" exclusion (Exclusions, cl.21), covering property in which the Principal Assureds have less immediate interests, and even some "genuine third party exposures".[555]

Where an existing property exclusion is applied, the insureds typically have the option of re-balancing the cover provided under Section II by "buying back" specifically identified items of existing property (as in the example set out above). Note, however, that the cover thus "bought back" is normally provided under the terms, conditions and exclusions of Section II: it thus remains limited, inter alia, by Section II's Exclusions cl.21.[556]

Excess removal of wreckage and debris endorsements. Costs relating to the removal of wreckage and debris following an Occurrence are generally covered under Section I of WELCAR.[557] Such costs are often, but not always, incurred as a result of the Assureds' obligation to undertake the removal of their property under local laws or orders from competent local authorities. As discussed above, where wreckage and debris interferes with the Assureds' "normal operations", there is also cover for removal costs under Section I. **24-064**

Depending on the extent of the Assureds' losses for repair or replacement, sue and labour, additional work, etc., the relevant per Occurrence limit of liability under Section I may prove inadequate to cover all of the Assureds' exposure in relation to removal of wreckage and debris.[558] Yet the Assureds' liability for the costs of removing wreckage and debris following a casualty can be very extensive.

Accordingly, insurers sometimes agree by endorsement, against payment of additional premium, to cover removal of wreckage or debris costs, in excess of those indemnified under Section I, under Section II (up to the limit of liability applicable to that Section).[559] The wording of Section II's Deductible clause anticipates that cover under Section II may be extended in this way: the deductible applies to Ultimate Net Loss from the aggregate of all claims or suits by third-party claimants caused by an Occurrence, including "debris removal".[560] This suggests WELCAR's drafters intended that the extension under Section II should normally only cover wreckage and debris removal costs for which the Assureds are legally liable: that is, excess costs for removal of wreckage and debris which merely interferes with the Assureds' operations were probably not intended to be covered under an endorsement to Section II.[561]

3. CARGO INSURANCE

Introduction. Marine "cargo" has been defined as: **24-065**

---

[555] Sharp, para.9.4.4.
[556] See above, para.24-057.
[557] See discussion of Section I's Removal of Wreck, Wreckage and/or Debris clause, above at para.24-044.
[558] See discussion of Section I's Policy Limit clause, above at para.24-027.
[559] See Sharp, para.9.5.3.
[560] See discussion of Section II's Deductible clause, above at para.24-058.
[561] Though, in practice, excess removal of wreckage endorsements sometimes expressly cover the full scope of costs indemnified under Section I.

"Goods and/or merchandise carried on a ship, vessel, craft, lighter, barge, raft, or other means of carriage by water. The term is applied, also to goods in transit overland or in temporary storage, during the ordinary course of transit, when they are intended to be carried by a ship or vessel or have been discharged from a ship or vessel following carriage by water."[562]

Cargo all risks insurance will often be one of the first types of cover to become relevant in a marine construction project, as materials destined for incorporation into a ship or offshore structure are dispatched towards the building yard or site. For this reason, as discussed above, WELCAR incorporates standard cargo all risks policy forms and makes them applicable to materials in transit.[563] Cargo insurance is, accordingly, an important form of cover for marine construction projects, and merits some discussion in the present work.

The treatment of marine cargo insurance in this section comprises an introductory presentation of the insured risks and exclusions conditioning the first-party property damage cover provided under the most recently issued London-market marine risks cargo forms. Many important topics in relation to cargo insurance—such as general average cover, collision liability cover, forwarding charges cover, sue and labour, constructive total loss, the commencement and termination of cover, deviation and change of voyage, the assignment of policies, etc—are not addressed here.[564]

The development of the law and practice relating to cargo insurance occurred relatively early. Marine cargo insurance is common, and disputes under such policies have been litigated relatively often. Accordingly, the principles applicable to cargo insurance have been worked out in relatively greater detail than is the case for some other types of marine insurance. By comparison, there is little judicial authority directly addressing shipbuilding insurance: and English court judgments concerned with WELCAR are nearly non-existent. Thus, marine construction insurance often looks to all risks cargo insurance for answers to legal issues.

(a)   The Institute Cargo Clauses: a short history

24-066   Origins of the Institute Cargo Clauses.   The ICC have been worked out and refined by the London marine market for over a century.[565] Most cargo risks are today written on an all-risks basis, but it was not always so. Cargo risks were, in the days of sail, underwritten on the standard marine Lloyd's S.G. policy"[566]—

---

[562]   R.H. Brown, *Witherby's Encyclopaedic Dictionary of Marine Insurance: Incorporating Dictionary of Marine Insurance Terms and Clauses*, 6th edn (London: Witherby & Co Ltd, 2005), p.81.

[563]   See above, para.24-034.

[564]   For a more complete exposition, than could reasonably be included in a specialist book on construction insurance, see: J. Dunt, *Marine Cargo Insurance*, 2nd edn (London: Informa, 2015); Hudson et al, *Marine Insurance Clauses* (2012), Part II; and relevant sections in Arnould.

[565]   The term "Institute Cargo Clauses" was adopted by practitioners when the first cargo-specific conditions were produced by the London insurance market on 1 August 1912. These comprised a "neutral" form, for writing "with average" cover, and the ICC (F.P.A.) ("free from particular average") conditions: both intended to be used with the Lloyd's S.G. form of policy (a standard named perils policy form, discussed above at fn.3). See L.R. Phillips et al, *Report H.R.5 of The Historic Records Committee by the Working Party on Institute Cargo Clauses* (London: The Insurance Institute of London, 1963), pp.5–7. In fact, the origins of the F.P.A. Clauses go back to 17 July 1883: an explanation of their historical development is in W. Gow, *Marine Insurance*, 1st edn (London: Macmillan and Co Ltd, 1896), pp.183–187).

[566]   See above, fn.3.

often accompanied by the complex scheme of the "Common Memorandum"[567]—, so in general cover was by definition offered only against the standard named perils.

The earliest versions of the ICC were produced by the ILU, in co-operation with Lloyd's underwriters and London brokers, inter alia to address the lack of any standard clauses.[568] Cargo cover was then underwritten by amending the S.G. policy through the incorporation of the new ICC conditions. The resulting insurance was, accordingly, against named perils. In the event of inconsistency, the ICC conditions took precedence over the S.G. policy.

By 1951, the London market responded to cargo interests' changing needs by also providing a set of standard "all risks" conditions, the ICC (All Risks).[569] The all risks version of the ICC adopted a fundamentally different approach to the standard hull and machinery policies that, almost without exception, provided—and, still today, provide—cover in respect of named perils only.

ICC (F.P.A.) ("free from particular average"), ICC (W.A.) ("with average") and ICC (All Risks). Throughout much of the twentieth century, prior to the **24-067** emergence of new ICC forms in 1982,[570] the London market had three alternative sets of standard clauses from which to choose when underwriting cargo risks[571]:

1. ICC (F.P.A.) conditions were used with, and thus insured against, marine risks identified in the S.G. policy form. The F.P.A. clause in ICC (F.P.A.) stated that the cover was:

    "Warranted free from Particular Average unless the vessel or craft be stranded sunk or burnt, but the Assurers are to pay the insured value of any package or packages which may be totally lost in loading transhipment or discharge, also any loss of or damage to the interest insured which may reasonably be attributed to fire, collision or contact of the vessel and/or craft and/or conveyance with any external substance (ice included) other than water, or to discharge of cargo at a

---

[567] The Common Memorandum was first adopted in Lloyd's policies in May 1794. See further: *Arnould: Law of Marine Insurance and Average*, edited by M.J. Mustill and J.C.B Gilman, 16th edn (London: Stevens & Sons, 1981), Vol.2, paras 839–850; W. Gow, *Marine Insurance*, 3rd edn (London: Macmillan and Co Ltd, 1903), pp.171–183.

[568] L.R. Phillips et al, *Report H.R.5 of The Historic Records Committee by the Working Party on Institute Cargo Clauses* (1963), pp.5–24.

[569] The ILU introduced the ICC (All Risks) conditions on 1 January 1951, the third and final member of the original set of Institute Cargo Clauses. The practice of insuring against all risks was, at that time, not a new one, and pre-1951 case law on all risks insurance remains useful in interpreting the modern ICC clauses. See L.R. Phillips et al, *Report H.R.5 of The Historic Records Committee by the Working Party on Institute Cargo Clauses* (1963), pp.91–93. A copy of the 1951 All Risks conditions can also be found in an Appendix to a conference paper delivered by C.H. Johnson: see Institute of Bankers (Great Britain) *Banking and Foreign Trade. Being the Lectures Delivered at the Fifth International Banking Summer School, Christ Church, Oxford, July 1952* (London: Europa Publications, 1952), appendix called "Appendix to Paper Delivered to the Fifth International Banking Summer School, Christchurch, Oxford on 'Some Practice Points Regarding Documents and Clauses in Relation to Overseas Trade'".

[570] Namely, CL 252 ICC (A) (1/1/82), CL 253 ICC (B) (1/1/82), and CL 254 ICC (C) (1/1/82).

[571] ICC (F.P.A.) (1/7/12), ICC (W.A.) (7/6/21), and ICC All Risks conditions (1/1/51). A detailed consideration of these old clauses falls outside the scope of this work. For further discussion see: *Arnould: Law of Marine Insurance and Average*, 16th edn (1981), Vol.2, pp.405–409; and Brown, *Witherby's Encyclopaedic Dictionary of Marine Insurance incorporating Dictionary of Marine Insurance Terms and Clauses* (2005), p.328.

> port of distress, also to pay landing warehousing forwarding and special charges if incurred."[572]

ICC (F.P.A.) also incorporated the Free of Capture & Seizure ("F.C. & S.") clause and the Strikes, Riots and Civil Commotions clause, with the intention of excluding a range of war and political risks.[573]

2.   ICC (W.A.) conditions were the same as ICC (F.P.A.), with the F.P.A. clause (quoted above) at first omitted, and then later included but expressed to apply only in relation to losses below an agreed percentage franchise.[574]
3.   ICC (All Risks) conditions provided for an extension to the S.G. form's named perils cover, by stipulating that:

> "This insurance is against all risks of loss of or damage to the subject-matter insured but shall in no case be deemed to extend to cover loss damage or expense proximately caused by delay or inherent vice or nature of the subject-matter insured."[575]

These clauses remained largely unaltered through various revisions, with the last major revision prior to 1982 taking place in 1963.[576] Again, the three ICC forms produced in 1963 were largely the same, save for the clauses that qualified (or, in the case of the All Risks form, extended) the cover provided by the S.G. form. ICC (All Risks)[577] was the widest standard form of cover available on the London market. ICC (W.A.)[578] and ICC (F.P.A.)[579] were more restrictive, and more complex in structure, language and operation.[580]

The various ICC were, prior to 1982, intended to supplement and modify the S.G. form: but the use of S.G. form and ICC, together, resulted in a contract of not inconsiderable complexity, which needed to be interpreted as a whole. Given that the wording of these standards forms, of itself, could be archaic and difficult to interpret and understand, London-market contracting practices attracted criticism.[581]

In response to this situation, the London market resolved to stop using the SG

---

[572]   L.R. Phillips et al, *Report H.R.5 of The Historic Records Committee by the Working Party on Institute Cargo Clauses* (1963), p.7.

[573]   See L.R. Phillips et al, *Report H.R.5 of The Historic Records Committee by the Working Party on Institute Cargo Clauses* (1963), pp.6–7. F.C. & S. clauses first appeared around 1739: they remained in use until the 1980s. The precise wording of the F.C. & S. clause varied, as did its effect. Owen comments that the clause is "[s]ometimes inaccurately referred to as the 'War' Clause". A number of examples of the F.C.& S clause are set out in D. Owen *Marine Insurance Notes and Clauses*, 3rd edn (London: Sampson Low, Marson, Searle & Rivington, 1890), pp.28–31.

[574]   See L.R. Phillips et al, *Report H.R.5 of The Historic Records Committee by the Working Party on Institute Cargo Clauses* (1963), pp.6–7, 19–24. The ICC (W.A.) ("with average") conditions were introduced by the ILU on 7 June 1921. A copy of the ICC (W.A.) conditions (7/6/21) is in *Marine Insurance Clauses A Reference Book Containing all Institute of London Underwriters', a selection of Lloyd's, and of General Clauses and Warranties*, 4th and revised edition (London: Witherby & Co, 1921), p.10.

[575]   L.R. Phillips et al, *Report H.R.5 of The Historic Records Committee by the Working Party on Institute Cargo Clauses* (1963), p.93.

[576]   Copies of ICC (F.P.A.) (1/6/63), ICC (W.A.) (1/6/63) and ICC (All Risks) (1/6/63) are in E.R. Hardy Ivamy, *Marine Insurance*, 3rd edn (London: Butterworths, 1979), pp.550–553.

[577]   ICC (All Risks) (1/6/63).

[578]   ICC (W.A.) (1/6/63).

[579]   ICC (F.P.A.) (1/6/63).

[580]   ICC (F.P.A.) (1/1/63) are the same as ICC (W.A.) (1/1/63), save for cl.5: see further Brown, *Witherby's Encyclopaedic Dictionary of Marine Insurance Incorporating Dictionary of Marine Insurance Terms and Clauses*, 6th edn (2005), pp.255 and 333.

[581]   As discussed in: W. Gow, *Marine Insurance: A Handbook*, 4th edn with additions (London: Macmil-

form of policy after 31 March 1983. At the same time, instead of merely amending the existing ICC (1963 versions), the opportunity was taken to rewrite them entirely. The F.P.A.[582] and W.A.[583] forms of cover were withdrawn by the ILU and replaced on the 1 January 1982 with the completely new ICC (B)[584] and (C),[585] while the All Risks form was substantially reproduced in ICC (A).[586] These new ICC were expressly intended to be used with the "New Marine Policy Form" (later designated "MAR 91"), which contains very few substantive provisions.[587]

The latest revision of the ICC took place in 2009: the changes made were (for the purposes of this presentation) relatively minor. Nevertheless, policies are still written on the basis of previous versions of the ICC.

The revision of the ICC in 1982 resulted in a far simpler, clearer contractual document. However, there are still necessary traces of the S.G. policy to be found in the 1982 and 2009 clauses, particularly as regards the insured named perils, the sue and labour and waiver clauses.

(b)   The Institute Cargo Clauses (1/1/09)

(i)   Risks covered by the Institute Cargo Clauses (1/1/09)

The Risks clauses.   As with the 1982 versions, the 2009 ICC are presented in   **24-068** three alternative forms: (A), (B) and (C). Their characteristic Risks clauses, which set out the insured perils they cover, are as follows:

"INSTITUTE CARGO CLAUSES (A)
RISKS COVERED
   Risks

1.   This insurance covers all risks of loss of or damage to the subject matter insured except as excluded by the provisions of Clauses 4, 5, 6 and 7 below".[588]

"INSTITUTE CARGO CLAUSES (B)

RISKS COVERED
   Risks

1.   This insurance covers, except as excluded by the provisions of Clauses 4, 5, 6 and 7 below,
    1.1   loss of or damage to the subject matter insured reasonably attributable to
        1.1.1   fire or explosion
        1.1.2   vessel or craft being stranded grounded sunk or capsized
        1.1.3   overturning or derailment of land conveyance
        1.1.4   collision or contact of vessel craft or conveyance with any external object other than water
        1.1.5   discharge of cargo at a port of distress
        1.1.6   earthquake volcanic eruption or lightning,
    1.2   loss of or damage to the subject matter insured caused by

---

lan & Co, 1917), pp.28, 130; Arnould, at paras 2–21 to 2–26; Dunt, *Marine Cargo Insurance* (2015), para.1.8.

[582]   ICC (F.P.A.) (1/6/63).
[583]   ICC (W A) (1/6/63).
[584]   CL 253 ICC (B) (1/1/82).
[585]   CL 254 ICC (C) (1/1/82).
[586]   CL 252 ICC (A) (1/1/82).
[587]   The MAR 91 form stipulates only: that each insurer's liability is to be several, proportionate to its written line; and that the insurance is to be subject to English jurisdiction.
[588]   CL 383 ICC (A) (1/1/09), cl.1.

          1.2.1   general average sacrifice
          1.2.2   jettison or washing overboard
          1.2.3   entry of sea lake or river water into vessel craft hold conveyance container
                   or place of storage,
     1.3   total loss of any package lost overboard or dropped whilst loading on to, or unload-
         ing from, vessel or craft." [589]

"INSTITUTE CARGO CLAUSES (C)
RISKS COVERED
   Risks

    1.   This insurance covers, except as excluded by the provision of Clauses 4, 5, 6 and 7 below,
        1.1   loss of or damage to the subject matter insured reasonably attributable to
              1.1.1   fire or explosion
              1.1.2   vessel or craft being stranded grounded sunk or capsized
              1.1.3   overturning or derailment of land conveyance
              1.1.4   collision or contact of vessel craft or conveyance with any external object
                    other than water
              1.1.5   discharge of cargo at a port of distress,
        1.2   loss of or damage to the subject matter insured caused by
              1.2.1   general average sacrifice
              1.2.2   jettison." [590]

24-069   The cover provided by ICC (A) is clearly what would be recognised as "all risks": it covers all damage caused by any fortuitous occurrence,[591] unless an exclusion applies. The exclusions applicable to all of the 2009 ICC, discussed further below, are in summary: wilful misconduct of the insured[592]; ordinary leakage, loss in weight or volume, or wear and tear[593]; insufficiency or unsuitability of packing or preparation[594]; inherent vice or nature of the cargo[595]; delay[596]; insolvency or financial default of the owners, managers, charterers or operators of the carrying vessel[597]; nuclear weapons[598]; unseaworthiness or "un-cargoworthiness"[599]; war, conflict, and detention[600]; terrorism, strikes or political risks.[601] ICC (B) and (C) additionally exclude deliberate damage or destruction by the wrongful act of any person(s)[602]: this exclusion is not present in ICC (A).

Whether a loss is prima facie covered under ICC (B) or (C) is a question of construction of their respective named perils. In summary, the (B) and (C) clauses cover loss of or damage to the cargo:

    (1)   *reasonably attributable to* any of the perils enumerated in their respective cll.1.1, viz: fire or explosion; stranding, grounding, sink or capsizing of the carrying vessel; overturning or derailing of a land conveyance; collision or contact by the conveyance with any object (other than water); or the

---

[589] CL 383 ICC (B) (1/1/09), cl.1.
[590] CL 384 ICC (C) (1/1/09), cl.1.
[591] See above, Ch.10, and below para.24-081.
[592] See below para.24-083, and above para.10-016.
[593] See below para.24-084, and above paras 10-012 and 15-014 to 15-019.
[594] See below para.24-085.
[595] See below para.24-086, and above, paras 10-013 to 10-015 and paras 15-006 to 15-010.
[596] See below para.24-087.
[597] See below para.24-088.
[598] See below para.24-090, and above paras 15-061 to 15-065.
[599] See below para.24-091.
[600] See below para.24-092, and above paras 15-041 to 15-060.
[601] See below para.24-092.
[602] See below para.24-089.

discharging of the cargo at a port of distress. To this common list, ICC (B) adds the following perils beyond those covered by ICC (C): earthquake, volcanic eruption and lighting;

(2) *caused by* any of the perils in their respective cll.1.2, viz[603]: general average sacrifice or jettison of cargo, in both ICC (B) and (C); additionally, in the case of ICC (B) only, the washing overboard of cargo, and the ingress of "sea lake or river water" into the vessel, craft, hold, conveyance, container, or place of storage where the cargo is to be found; or

(3) in the case of ICC (B) only, in the nature of the total loss of "any package" by losing it overboard or dropping during loading onto or unloading from a vessel.

The phrase "reasonably attributable", in cl.1.1, is arguably satisfied by proof of a causal link of somewhat lesser efficiency than "proximate cause": a concurrent cause that is an effective, though not the (or a) dominant cause, may suffice.[604] Clause 1.2 clearly requires that the loss or damage be proximately caused by the insured peril.[605] In the case of cl.1.3 of ICC (B), which is worded differently, cover is probably against the total loss of the cargo proximately caused by its being lost overboard or dropped during loading or unloading.[606]

From the preceding discussion, it can be seen that ICC (B) and (C) differ in the number of insured perils they cover, and not, as was the case with the ICC (W.A.) and ICC (F.P.A.), in whether particular average or only total loss are covered. Further, a useful characteristic of all risks cover is highlighted: under ICC (A), the insured claimant has a comparatively easier task, needing only to show a loss caused by a non-excluded fortuity, whereas under ICC (B) and (C), the loss must be shown to have been caused by, or reasonably attributable to, one of the named perils discussed further below.

(ii) *Institute Cargo Clauses (B) and (C): named perils*

Fire or explosion.[607]   Loss or damage "reasonably attributable to fire or explo-   **24-070** sion" is covered, so long as the said fire or explosion was not itself caused by an excluded peril (the obvious examples being war risks, arson by the insured, or inherent vice in the cargo). Damage from heating by a fire or explosion would be covered by this sub-clause,[608] provided it could be said to be "reasonably attributable" to the fire or explosion. Again, subject to the same proviso, cover should extend to water

---

[603] CL 383 ICC (B) (1/1/09) and CL 384 ICC (C) (1/1/09) cll.1.2.1 and 1.2.2.

[604] See: *Global Process Systems Inc v Syarikat Takaful Malaysia Bhd (The Cendor MOPU)* [2011] UKSC 5 at [57]; Arnould, para.23–74; Hudson et al, *Marine Insurance Clauses* (2012), pp.40; and especially the full discussion in Dunt, *Marine Cargo Insurance* (2015), paras 7.43–7.51. See also D. O'May and J. Hill, (editor and co-author) *Marine Insurance: Law and Policy* (London: Sweet & Maxwell Ltd, 1993), p.174, who opine that the word "reasonable" in this phrase is "no more than the addition of a mellifluous epithet and does not affect the principle of causation."

[605] See, in this regard, Dunt, *Marine Cargo Insurance* (2015), paras 7.32–7.33.

[606] MIA s.55(1): "... unless the policy otherwise provides, the insurer is liable for any loss proximately caused by a peril insured against ..." Cf. Dunt, *Marine Cargo Insurance* (2015), paras 9.9 and 9.36, considers that such "sling losses" are covered without the need for any "causation requirement", under cl.1.3. But some causation requirement must be implicit in cl.1.3. Otherwise, in the case of a package that was "dropped" but not thereby damaged, cl.1.3 might be construed as a guarantee against all risks of subsequent total loss (even if not caused by loss overboard or dropping): which, it is suggested, cannot have been intended.

[607] CL 383 ICC (B) (1/1/09) and CL 384 ICC (C) (1/1/09), cl.1.1.1.

[608] See R.H. Brown, *Analysis of Marine Insurance Clauses. Book 1: The Institute Cargo Clauses*, 2nd

damage suffered as a result of fire-fighting activity. It has been suggested that the word "explosion", when used as an insured peril, designates an "event that is violent, noisy and ... caused by a very rapid chemical or nuclear reaction, or the bursting out of gas or vapour under pressure", including "explosion of air from ... confinement".[609]

24-071 **Stranded, grounded, sunk or capsized.**[610] "Stranding" or "grounding" occurs, in this context, where the carrying vessel takes the ground accidentally.[611] Being "sunk", it has been suggested, "implies an element of finality", referring to cases where "a vessel can sink no more, is not navigable and is unable to complete the voyage."[612] There has been disagreement regarding the degree of inclination a vessel must undergo before it has "capsized"[613]: but the natural meaning of the word, it is suggested, connotes the overturning or upsetting of the vessel.[614] Again, the insured's task is probably limited to showing that the cargo damage is "reasonably attributable" to one of these perils: thus, they may not need to establish that the particular peril was the proximate, rather than merely an efficient cause of the loss.[615] Interestingly, as R.H. Brown[616] points out, an insured could recover for seawater damage as a result of the vessel or craft sinking/capsizing under ICC (C), even though there is otherwise no cover for seawater ingress.

24-072 **Overturning or derailment of land conveyance.**[617] Multimodal transport was not intended to be covered by the S.G. policy and the earlier attempts to extend cover during the 1912 to 1963 revisions of the ICC were unsatisfactory.[618] The issue is now partly addressed by this named peril, which is in some ways analogous to the capsizing, stranding or grounding of a sea vessel.[619] Insurers are liable if the damage is "reasonably attributable" to the overturning or derailment. "[L]and conveyance" should, it is submitted, be construed broadly. "Overturning" probably requires that the conveyance be fully upset or tipped over.

24-073 **Collision or contact of vessel craft or conveyance with any external object.**[620] This sub-clause is largely self-explanatory, making clear that loss or damage reasonably attributable to the vessel coming into contact with any external object ("other than water") will be covered.[621] The reference to "conveyances" brings land-based conveyances into the scope of cover: damage through shifting of

---

edn (London: Witherby, 1983), p.8.
[609] *Commonwealth Smelting Ltd v Guardian Royal Exchange Assurance Ltd* [1986] 1 Lloyd's Rep., at pp.124–126; *Aegis Electrical & Gas International Services Ltd v Continental Casualty Co* [2007] EWHC 1762 (Comm) at [79]–[81] ("the word connotes violence and manifest violence ... and it connotes a shattering destruction"). See above, para.15-038.
[610] CL 383 ICC (B) (1/1/09) and CL 384 ICC (C) (1/1/09), cl.1.1.2.
[611] Or, it has been suggested, deliberately, if a normal, deliberate grounding resulted in accidental damage to cargo: Dunt, *Marine Cargo Insurance* (2015), para.9.18.
[612] Dunt, *Marine Cargo Insurance* (2015), para.9.19.
[613] The debate is summarised in Dunt, *Marine Cargo Insurance* (2015), para.20.
[614] *Shorter OED*, 6th edn (OUP: 2007), "capsize".
[615] See above, fn.604.
[616] See Brown, *Analysis of Marine Insurance Clauses. Book 1: The Institute Cargo Clauses*, (1983), p.8.
[617] CL 383 ICC (B) (1/1/09) and CL 384 ICC (C) (1/1/09), cl.1.1.3.
[618] See ICC (F.P.A.) (1/7/12), ICC (F.P.A) (1/6/63), ICC (W.A.) (1/6/63) and ICC (All Risks) (1/6/63).
[619] See also below, para.24-073.
[620] CL 383 ICC (B) (1/1/09) and CL 384 ICC (C) (1/1/09), cl.1.1.4.
[621] Both collisions and allisions are covered.

cargo during carriage in a land-based vehicle due, for example, to travel over bad roads or ground,[622] would arguably be covered if the relevant "contact" has the nature of a fortuitous accident or casualty.[623]

Discharge at a port of distress.[624]   This named peril addresses the situation where   **24-074** a vessel encounters troubles during a voyage, such that it is unable to continue with the carriage of the insured cargo[625] and must discharge it at a place other than the contractual discharge port. As a practical matter, it will frequently be difficult to establish whether or not the damage exhibited by cargo upon arrival at its final destination was "proximately caused" by an earlier forced discharge. This may not be necessary, however, as the damage need only be "reasonably attributable" to the forced discharge. The cover provided under this peril is separate from, and may overlap with, cover for loss or damage to cargo as general average.[626]

Earthquake, volcanic eruption and lightning.[627]   When cargo risks were insured   **24-075** under the S.G. policy, earthquakes[628] and volcanic eruptions were not covered because they are not "perils of the sea" (save, of course, if they are accompanied by adverse seas). When the ICC first extended cover to losses suffered during land transit, it made no express provision for these risks; but since 1982, ICC (B) does so. Lightning, on the other hand, was always covered as either heavy weather at sea or fire on land.[629]

General average sacrifice.[630]   Insurers must pay the insured upon the insured   **24-076** cargo suffering loss or damage "caused by [a] general average sacrifice".[631] General average was discussed earlier in this Chapter.[632] Upon indemnifying the insured, insurers are subrogated to the insured's right to claim general average contributions (e.g. from owners of other cargo and of the carrying vessel).

---

[622] Arguably, if a pier qualifies as an "external object", vis-à-vis a waterborne conveyance, then features of the road or ground should qualify as such, vis-à-vis a land conveyance.

[623] Cf. Dunt, *Marine Cargo Insurance* (2015), para.9.24.

[624] CL 383 ICC (B) (1/1/09) and CL 384 ICC (C) (1/1/09), cl.1.1.5.

[625] Although it is not expressly stated in the wording of this peril, Brown, *Analysis of Marine Insurance Clauses. Book 1: The Institute Cargo Clauses*, (1983), at p.9, expresses the view that the word "cargo" means the "insured cargo": this must be correct.

[626] Under cll.2 of the 2009 ICC: see discussion in Dunt, *Marine Cargo Insurance* (2015), para.9.25.

[627] CL. 383 (B) (1/1/09)), cl.1.1.6.

[628] Cf. tsunamis.

[629] See above, para.15-037.

[630] CL 383 ICC (B) (1/1/09) and CL 384 ICC (C) (1/1/09), cl.1.2.1.

[631] Dunt, *Marine Cargo Insurance* (2015), para.9.28, notes inter alia that cover is in any event provided for general average under cll.2 of the 2009 ICC; and he and Hudson et al, *Marine Insurance Clauses* (2012), p.43, referring to MIA s.66(4), describe cl.1.2.1 as "merely declaratory" of the common law. However, cover under cll.2 responds to "general average ... incurred to avoid or in connection with the avoidance of loss from *any cause*..." (emphasis added), subject to the policies' exclusions. This appears to go beyond the common law, in that it purports to cover general average losses unconnected with the insured named perils: see MIA s.66(6); Arnould, para.26–103, fn.444. Similarly, cll.1.2.1 could be argued to extend cover to general average sacrifices generally, whether or not connected with another insured peril.

[632] See above, para.24-041.

24-077 Jettison.[633] This peril concerns the throwing overboard of cargo in order to save the carrying vessel or other cargo.[634] In circumstances where the cargo and the carrying vessel are owned by different entities, the jettison of cargo in order to safeguard the common marine adventure would be a general average sacrifice. This clause, however, makes clear that the jettison is an insured peril even if it does not constitute general average.

24-078 Washing overboard.[635] This peril is only insured under ICC (B). It is to be noted that the loss must be proximately caused by "washing" overboard and not merely by falling overboard when the carrying vessel pitches and rolls in heavy weather. Under the old ICC (W.A.) clauses,[636] falling overboard (and other damage due to heavy weather) would have been covered as a peril of the seas (which ICC (B) does not cover per se). If the insured requires cover for losses caused by falling overboard or other perils of the seas, then ICC (A) is the appropriate standard form.

24-079 Ingress of water.[637] Loss or damage "caused by entry of sea lake or river water into vessel craft hold conveyance container or place of storage" is only insured under ICC (B). ICC (C) provides cover for ingress of water only indirectly, where the damage is due to another insured peril, e.g. where the carrying vessel is stranded, grounded, sunk or capsized, or suffers a collision, or where there is a jettison or general average sacrifice. Under ICC (B), cover is provided where damage is proximately caused by the entry of water (whether sea, lake or river water) into the carrying vessel, craft, conveyance or container. Such ingress of water could occur for any fortuitous reason,[638] and should cover the entry into the hold of ballast water or the flooding of warehouses (so long as the flood water originates from sea, lake or river). It has been suggested that this peril is in some ways narrower than the more traditional "peril of the seas".[639]

24-080 Total loss of any package lost overboard or dropped during loading or unloading.[640] Although the wording of the peril does not say so expressly, the most logical view is that it will cover transhipment,[641] and not just cargo operations at the initial load port and the port of final discharge. It would not, however, cover loss or damage in the course of shifting cargo onboard or cargo operations in connection with land conveyances, unless such operations were undertaken during "loading on to, or unloading from, [a] vessel or craft".[642] It should be noted, however, that the clause covers only the *total* loss of an insured package.

---

[633] CL 383 ICC (B) (1/1/09) and CL 384 ICC (C) (1/1/09), cl.1.2.2.

[634] See Dunt, *Marine Cargo Insurance* (2015), para.9.30; Hudson et al, *Marine Insurance Clauses* (2012), pp.42–43.

[635] CL 383 ICC (B) (1/1/09), cl.1.2.2.

[636] E.g. ICC (W.A.) (1/6/63).

[637] CL 383 ICC (B) (1/1/09), cl.1.2.3.

[638] See Brown, *Analysis of Marine Insurance Clauses. Book 1: The Institute Cargo Clauses*, (1983), p.10; Dunt, *Marine Cargo Insurance* (2015), paras 9.32–9.34.

[639] As would have been covered under e.g. ICC (W.A.) (1/6/63). See Dunt, *Marine Cargo Insurance* (2015), para.9.35, suggesting that sea water damage from condensation is not covered by ICC (B).

[640] CL 383 ICC (B) (1/1/09), cl.1.3. See also above, fn.606.

[641] See Brown, *Analysis of Marine Insurance Clauses. Book 1: The Institute Cargo Clauses*, (1983), p.10.

[642] Hudson et al, *Marine Insurance Clauses* (2012), p.43.

(iii)   Limits to and exclusions from cover under the Institute Cargo Clauses (1/1/09)

ICC (A): limits to and extent of all risks cover.   The extent of cover under the   **24-081**
ICC (A) clauses is broadly the same as under earlier "all risks" clauses. The name
"All Risks" was withdrawn in 1981 because the ICC drafting committee considered
it could give the impression that the cover provided was wider than it is. Despite
this, in contrast with the "named perils" clauses, the cover provided under ICC (A)
is very wide indeed.[643]

While ICC (A) covers "all risks", this does not mean that the insured can claim
for *every* loss no matter how caused. As the contract is one of insurance, loss by a
fortuitous accident or casualty must be established; even all risks cover will not
indemnify losses that are inevitable or caused by wilful misconduct. Subject to this,
where sound goods are damaged in transit in circumstances that on the face of it
are consistent with the occurrence of a marine peril, the insured's burden in proving their claim under the policy will be light. On this point, Arnould helpfully sum-
marises the position in stating:

> "A policy against all risks does not absolve the assured from the need to prove that he has suffered
> loss from an insured peril; he must, as it is sometimes expressed, prove a casualty; but the class of
> insured perils is so wide that he may be able to do this by necessary inference. If the goods are shipped
> sound and arrive damaged, and the damage is of such a kind as to raise a presumption of some
> external cause, there is prime facie evidence of loss by an insured peril, and the burden is on the
> underwriter to prove that the loss in fact occurred in some way for which he is not liable."[644]

In the leading case on all risks insurance, *British and Foreign Marine Insurance Co
Ltd v Gaunt*,[645] it was confirmed that the "quasi-universal" nature of such cover
reduced the onus on an insured making a claim. In this regard, Lord Sumner said:

> "[T]he quasi-universality of the description [i.e. 'all risks'] does affect the onus of proof in one way.
> The claimant insured against and averring a loss by fire must prove loss by fire, which involves prov-
> ing that it is not by something else. When he avers loss by some risk coming within 'all risks' as used
> in this policy, he need only give evidence reasonably showing that the loss was due to a casualty, not
> to a certainty or to inherent vice or to wear and tear. That is easily done. I do not think he has to go
> further and pick out one of the multitude of risks covered, so as to show exactly how his loss was
> caused."[646]

Lord Birkenhead L.C. put it thus:

> "[W]here all risks are covered by the policy and not merely risks of a specified class or classes, the
> plaintiff discharges his special onus when he has proved that the loss was caused by some event
> covered by the general expression and he is not bound to go further and prove the exact nature of
> the accident of casualty which, in fact, occasioned the loss."[647]

---

[643]   i.e. it is of the "all risks" type, and accordingly not subject to being narrowed by application of the
ejusdem generis principle of interpretation, as befell the General Clause in the S.G. policy form: see
Arnould, para.2 32.

[644]   Arnould, para.23–72.

[645]   *British and Foreign Marine Insurance Co Ltd v Gaunt* [1921] 2 A.C. 41; (1921) 7 Ll. L. Rep. 62;
90 L.J.K.B. 801.

[646]   *Gaunt* [1921] 2 A.C. 41 at 57–58; 90 L.J.K.B. 801 at 807–808.

[647]   *Gaunt* [1921] 2 A.C. 41 at 47; (1921) 7 Ll. L. Rep. 62 at 63; 90 L.J.K.B. 801 at 803–804. See also
the discussion in Dunt, *Marine Cargo Insurance* (2015), paras 8.7–8.9.

Despite its "quasi-universality", all risks marine insurance is, nevertheless, subject to limitations and exclusions:

1. In the absence of contrary provision in the policy, MIA s.55[648] provides that there is no cover, inter alia, where the loss is caused by wilful misconduct, was inevitable or for any other reason was not caused by an insured fortuity.

2. In the *Gaunt* case,[649] Lord Sumner described these and some further of the limits to all risks cover stating:

> "There are, of course, limits to 'all risks'. They are risks, and risks insured against. Accordingly, the expression does not cover inherent vice or mere wear and tear ... It covers a risk, not a certainty; it is something, which happens to the subject matter from without, not the natural behaviour of the subject matter, being what it is, in the circumstances under which it is carried. Nor is it a loss which the assured brings about by his own act, for then he has not merely exposed the goods to the chance of injury, he has injured them himself."[650]

3. Finally, most policy forms, like the ICC, contain express policy exclusions, of which a number will often reflect the inherent limitations to all risks cover just discussed.

24-082 **Exclusions under the Institute Cargo Clauses (1/1/09).** As with the 1982 ICC, cll.4–7 of the 2009 ICC are presented under the heading "Exclusions". Some of these clauses correspond to exclusions or limitations contained in MIA s.55,[651] which sought to codify the common law. Others represent additional, express exclusions developed in cargo insurance practice over the years. The full set of 2009 ICC Exclusions, as contained in ICC (B) and (C), are as follows[652]:

"*EXCLUSIONS*

4. In no case shall this insurance cover
   4.1 loss damage or expense attributable to wilful misconduct of the Assured
   4.2 ordinary leakage, ordinary loss in weight or volume, or ordinary wear and tear of the subject matter insured
   4.3 loss damage or expense caused by insufficiency or unsuitability of packing or

---

[648] MIA s.55 provides: "55.—(1) Subject to the provisions of this Act, and unless the policy otherwise provides, the insurer is liable for any loss proximately caused by a peril insured against, but, subject as aforesaid, he is not liable for any loss which is not proximately caused by a peril insured against. (2) In particular—(a) The insurer is not liable for any loss attributable to the wilful misconduct of the assured, but, unless the policy otherwise provides, he is liable for any loss proximately caused by a peril insured against, even though the loss would not have happened but for the misconduct or negligence of the master or crew; (b) Unless the policy otherwise provides, the insurer on ship or goods is not liable for any loss proximately caused by delay, although the delay be caused by a peril insured against; (c) Unless the policy otherwise provides, the insurer is not liable for ordinary wear and tear, ordinary leakage and breakage, inherent vice or nature of the subject matter insured, or for any loss proximately caused by rats or vermin, or for any injury to machinery not proximately caused by maritime perils." The meaning of "rats or vermin" is discussed above, at para.15-029.

[649] *Gaunt* [1921] 2 A.C. 41; (1921) 7 Ll. L. Rep. 62; 90 L.J.K.B. 801.

[650] *Gaunt* [1921] 2 A.C. 41 at 57; 90 L.J.K.B. 801 at 807.

[651] MIA s.55 is quoted above, at fn.648.

[652] Regarding ICC (A), as indicated above at para.24-069, and in the quoted text below: cl.4 of ICC (A) (1/1/09) differs from the corresponding clauses from ICC (B) and (C), quoted below, in that it does not contain an exclusion relating to "deliberate damage to or deliberate destruction ... by the wrongful act of any person or persons"; and further cl.6.2 of ICC (A) differs from the provision quoted below in that the exclusion covering "capture seizure arrest restraint or detainment" is subject to a carve-out for piracy (which ICC (A) thus covers).

preparation of the subject matter insured to withstand the ordinary incidents of the insured transit where such packing or preparation is carried out by the Assured or their employees or prior to the attachment of this insurance (for the purpose of these Clauses 'packing' shall be deemed to include stowage in a container and 'employees' shall not include independent contractors)

4.4 loss damage or expense caused by inherent vice or nature of the subject matter insured

4.5 loss damage or expense caused by delay, even though the delay be caused by a risk insured against (except expenses payable under Clause 2 above)

4.6 loss damage or expense caused by insolvency or financial default of the owners managers charterers or operators of the vessel where, at the time of loading of the subject matter insured on board the vessel, the Assured are aware, or in the ordinary course of business should be aware, that such insolvency or financial default could prevent the normal prosecution of the voyage. This exclusion shall not apply where the contract of insurance has been assigned to the party claiming hereunder who has bought or agreed to buy the subject matter insured in good faith under a binding contract

4.7 deliberate damage to or deliberate destruction of the subject matter insured or any part thereof by the wrongful act of any person or persons[653]

4.8 loss damage or expense directly or indirectly caused by or arising from the use of any weapon or device employing atomic or nuclear fission and/or fusion or other like reaction or radioactive force or matter.[654]

5.

5.1 In no case shall this insurance cover loss damage or expense arising from

5.1.1 unseaworthiness of vessel or craft or unfitness of vessel or craft for the safe carriage of the subject matter insured, where the Assured are privy to such unseaworthiness or unfitness, at the time the subject matter insured is loaded therein

5.1.2 unfitness of container or conveyance for the safe carriage of the subject matter insured, where loading therein or thereon is carried out prior to attachment of this insurance or by the Assured or their employees and they are privy to such unfitness at the time of loading.

5.2 Exclusion 5.1.1 above shall not apply where the contract of insurance has been assigned to the party claiming hereunder who has bought or agreed to buy the subject matter insured in good faith under a binding contract.

5.3 The Insurers waive any breach of the implied warranties of seaworthiness of the ship and fitness of the ship to carry the subject matter insured to destination.

6. In no case shall this insurance cover loss damage or expense caused by

6.1 war civil war revolution rebellion insurrection, or civil strife arising therefrom, or any hostile act by or against a belligerent power

6.2 capture seizure arrest restraint or detainment[655], and the consequences thereof or any attempt thereat

6.3 derelict mines, torpedoes, bombs or other derelict weapons of war.

7. In no case shall this insurance cover loss damage or expense

7.1 caused by strikers, locked-out workmen, or persons taking part in labour disturbances, riots or civil commotions

7.2 resulting from strikes, lock-outs, labour disturbances, riots or civil commotions

7.3 caused by any act of terrorism being an act of any person acting on behalf of, or in connection with, any organisation which carries out activities directed

---

653 Sub-clause 4.7 is not present in CL 382 ICC (A) (1/1/09): see above, fn.652.
654 This clause is numbered cl.4.7 in CL 382 ICC (A) (1/1/09).
655 Note that in CL 382 ICC (A) (1/1/09), the word "detainment" is followed by "(piracy excepted)": see above, fn.652.

towards the overthrowing or influencing, by force or violence, of any government whether or not legally constituted

7.4 caused by any person acting from a political, ideological or religious motive."

Each of these provisions is introduced, in turn, below.

24-083 **Loss damage or expense attributable to wilful misconduct of the Assured.**[656] This exclusion reflects the initial words of MIA s.55(2)(a).[657] Unlike the rest of s.55, that part of s.55(2)(a) concerned with wilful misconduct is not preceded by the words: "Unless the policy otherwise provides". Arnould takes the view that the relevant part of s.55(2)(a) "cannot be ousted by agreement", as this would be contrary to the general rule of public policy that a person may not profit from their own wrongdoing.[658]

Even in the absence of the exclusion, an insured's claim for property lost or damaged by their own wilful conduct should normally fail. Wilful loss or damage would lack the necessary element of fortuity (from the insured's point of view), the claim would in many cases constitute a fraud on insurers, and, moreover, the insured's act—and not any insured peril—would in many cases be retained as the proximate cause of the loss.[659]

The word "attributable" in this exclusion, and in MIA s.55(2)(a), may connote a looser causal requirement than proximate cause.[660] The meaning of the expression "wilful misconduct of the insured" has been discussed earlier in this work.[661] It has also been usefully considered in the context of the Warsaw Convention,[662] where it has been held to require something, beyond gross negligence, in the nature of either intentional misconduct or advertent recklessness. In *Thomas Cook Group Ltd v Air Malta Co Ltd (t/a Air Malta)*, Cresswell J said[663]:

"What does amount to wilful misconduct? A person wilfully misconducts himself if he knows and appreciates that it is misconduct on his part in the circumstances to do or fail to do something yet (a) intentionally does or fails or omits to do it or (b) persists in the act, failure or omission regardless of the consequences or (c) acts with reckless carelessness, not caring what the result of his carelessness may be. (A person acts with reckless carelessness if, aware of a risk that goods in his care may be lost or damaged, he deliberately goes ahead and takes the risk, when it is unreasonable in all the circumstances for him to do so.)"

24-084 **Ordinary leakage, ordinary loss in weight or volume, or ordinary wear and tear.**[664] Ordinary leakage and loss in weight or volume also covers evaporation, shrinkage and ullage. It is common for viscose liquid cargoes in bulk to stick to tanks, pipes and manifolds with an inevitable small loss of out-turned volume as a

---

[656] CL 382 ICC (A) (1/1/09), CL 383 ICC (B) (1/1/09) and CL 384 ICC (C) (1/1/09), cl.4.1.

[657] Quoted above, at fn.648.

[658] Arnould, paras 22–36.

[659] See Dunt, *Marine Cargo Insurance* (2015), paras 8.4, 8.48 and 8.54. See also: above para.10-018(regarding intentional damage); paras 19-009 and 19-010 (proximate cause); and paras 21-037 to 21-039 (fraudulent claims).

[660] See discussion above, at fn.604.

[661] See above paras 10-016 to 10-026. See also Dunt, *Marine Cargo Insurance* (2015), paras 8.48 to 8.54.

[662] Convention for the unification of certain rules relating to international carriage by air (1929) ("Warsaw Convention"), T.S. 11 (1933), Cmd. 4284; P. (1932-3) XXVIII 63; 134 B.S.P. 406; 137 L.N.T.S. 11.

[663] *Thomas Cook Group Ltd v Air Malta Co Ltd (t/a Air Malta)* [1997] 2 Lloyd's Rep. 399 at 408.

[664] CL 382 ICC (A) (1/1/09), CL 383 ICC (B) (1/1/09) and CL 384 ICC (C) (1/1/09), cl.4.2.

result. Policies can be amended as appropriate so that this exclusion provides cover for leakage, etc. over an agreed percentage regarded as "ordinary": this can make this exclusion's effect more certain.

Ordinary wear and tear and similar, gradually occurring conditions were considered earlier in this work.[665] Wear and tear, by its very nature, is most likely to occur in the property which has been in service for some time, but there is no reason in principle why, in a very special case, this exclusion should not apply to newly manufactured but insufficiently durable cargo (or indeed raw materials).[666]

This exclusion, as regards "ordinary wear and tear" and "ordinary leakage", reflects MIA s.55(2)(c).[667] Following *The Cendor MOPU*,[668] the intervention of any fortuitous external accident or casualty in a loss should render this exclusion or limitation inapplicable. It is submitted that, as a matter of natural construction, and by virtue of its inclusion in this exclusion alongside "ordinary wear and tear" and "ordinary leakage", "ordinary loss in weight or volume" stands to be treated similarly: only "uneventful" loss in weight or volume should be excluded.

Insufficiency or unsuitability of packing or preparation.[669] This exclusion applies if the loss damage or expense is shown to be proximately caused by "insufficiently of packing[670] or preparation of the subject-matter insured to withstand the ordinary incidents of the insured transit", subject to the packing or preparation being "carried out" by the insured, by the insured's employees, or prior to attachment of the insurance.[671] This is a change from the 1982 ICC,[672] which provided simply that loss damage or expense caused by any insufficiency of packing or preparation would trigger the exclusion.[673]   **24-085**

As packing materials are often themselves part of the insured property, the question has been posed whether insufficiency or unsuitability of packing to withstand an otherwise uneventful transit would constitute an inherent vice under MIA s.55(2)(c).[674] An obvious observation in this regard is that packing and containers are not always insured property. Another is that the drafters of the ICC have provided for separate exclusions, covering inherent vice on the one hand, and insufficiency of packing on the other. Moreover, cargo that is unfit for the insured voy-

---

[665] See above, paras 15-012 to 15-027.
[666] Though see Dunt, *Marine Cargo Insurance* (2015), para.8.17, commenting on the decision not to transpose the exclusion in MIA s.55(2)(c) regarding "ordinary breakage" into cl.4.2: he suggests this indicates that "ordinary breakage" is not excluded per se, insurers instead being expected to rely on the exclusion relating to insufficiency of packing.
[667] Quoted above, at fn.648.
[668] *The Cendor MOPU* [2011] UKSC 5 at [81]: discussed below at para.24-086.
[669] CL 382 ICC (A) (1/1/09), CL 383 ICC (B) (1/1/09) and CL 384 ICC (C) (1/1/09), cl.4.3.
[670] The text of the exclusion states that this includes "stowage in a container".
[671] The insurance "attaches" when the particular insured item or package is first moved in the warehouse or place of storage at the place of departure named in the contract of insurance for the purpose of "immediate loading into or onto the carrying vehicle or other conveyance for the commencement of [the insured] transit": CL 382 ICC (A) (1/1/09), CL 383 ICC (B) (1/1/09) and CL 384 ICC (C) (1/1/09), cl.8.1.
[672] CL 252 ICC (A) (1/1/82), CL 253 ICC (B) (1/1/82) and CL 254 ICC (C) (1/1/82) cl.4.3.
[673] Though "packing" included stowage in a container only if carried out by the insureds "or their servants" or if carried out prior to attachment: see, e.g. CL 252 ICC (A) (1/1/82), cl.4.3.
[674] Dunt, *Marine Cargo Insurance* (2015), paras 8.35-8.37. For the position in the Hague/Hague-Visby Rules context, see J.Cooke et al, *Voyage Charters*, 4th edn (London: Informa, 2014), paras 85.333 and 85.337.

age is not, for that reason per se, considered to be affected by an inherent vice.[675] Further, the 2009 revision also introduced an express statement that the packaging and preparation must be sufficient "to withstand the ordinary incidents of the insured transit". Accordingly, the present exclusion should be construed as an additional, express exclusion, in some senses broader than and not simply a reflection of the inherent vice limitation in s.55(2)(c).[676] As a result—unlike MIA s.55(2)(c) limitations like inherent vice, ordinary leakage or wear and tear—the intervention of a fortuitous external accident or casualty should not prevent a loss being attributed to insufficiency of packing or preparation.[677]

"Packing" and "preparation" within the meaning of the exclusion probably refers to steps carried out prior to the commencement of loading: taken together, the two expressions cover a range of matters, including the stowing of the cargo in a box or container, the use of braces or other means of securing the cargo to prevent (parts of) it from moving, the application of protective coverings, and the employment of suitable materials—including desiccants—to ensure that the cargo is able to withstand the "ordinary incidents" of the insured voyage.[678]

24-086 **Inherent vice or nature of the subject-matter insured.**[679] This exclusion is derived from and is declaratory of the corresponding limitation in MIA s.55(2)(c): thus, like ordinary leakage and wear and tear, discussed above,[680] it should not be treated as a "true" exclusion.[681]

The meaning of the phrase "inherent vice" was defined by Lord Diplock in *Soya GmbH Mainz KG v White*[682]:

> "It means the risk of deterioration of the goods shipped as a result of their natural behaviour in the ordinary course of the contemplated voyage without the intervention of any fortuitous external accident or casualty."

The exclusion applies only where the loss damage or expense is proximately caused by inherent vice or nature of the insured cargo itself, but not where damage is caused by an inherent vice of neighbouring cargo. It applies, inter alia, to rotting or deterioration of the cargo proximately caused by its inherent nature, for example,

---

675 *The Cendor MOPU* [2011] UKSC 5 at [78]; discussed below, at para.24-086.

676 See Dunt, *Marine Cargo Insurance* (2015), paras 8.37 and 8.44.

677 A point made by Dunt, *Marine Cargo Insurance* (2015), at para.8.44.

678 See Dunt, *Marine Cargo Insurance* (2015), paras 8.42-8.43, and cases cited therein.

679 CL 382 ICC (A) (1/1/09), CL 383 ICC (B) (1/1/09) and CL 384 ICC (C) (1/1/09), cl.4.4. Inherent vice is also discussed above, at paras 10-013 to 10-015, 15-006 to 15-010.

680 See above, para.24-084.

681 Section 55(2)(c) is set out above, at fn.648. In *The Cendor MOPU*, the exclusion in ICC (A) covering "loss, damage or expense *caused by* inherent vice or nature of the subject matter insured" (emphasis added) was taken to have the same effect as s.55(2)(c). See [2011] UKSC 5, at [22]; [24], quoting Lord Diplock in *Soya GmbH Mainz KG v White* [1983] 1 Lloyd's Rep. 122, 126 ("This phrase (generally shortened to 'inherent vice') where it is used in section 55(2)(c) refers to a peril by which a loss is proximately caused; it is not descriptive of the loss itself."); [81], discussing s.55(2)(c) ("inherent vice [in that section] would cover inherent characteristics of or defects in a hull or cargo leading to it causing loss or damage to itself..."); [88], noting that "clause 4.4 on the face of it simply makes clear the continuing relevance in the context of all risks cover of the limitation on cover against perils of the sea provided by section 55(2)(c). There seems to me some oddity in treating clause 4.4 as leading to a fundamentally different result from that which would have applied had section 55(2)(c) alone been in question"; [99]; and [105]. See also Dunt, *Marine Cargo Insurance* (2015), para.8.24.

682 *Soya GmbH Mainz KG v White* [1983] 1 Lloyd's Rep. 122 at 126; [1983] Com. L.R. 46.

during a delay at the discharge port (which would also be excluded under cl.4.5[683] and MIA s.55(2)(b),[684] in any event). It can apply to exclude damage caused by moisture from within the cargo condensing on the inside of its container and then, from there, falling or running back onto the cargo.[685]

The relationship between this exclusion and that relating to insufficiency of packing or preparation has been discussed above.[686]

The Supreme Court considered and clarified the scope of the inherent vice exclusion, or limitation, in *The Cendor MOPU*.[687] The claimants owned a mobile offshore unit—a "jack-up rig"—that was to be carried on a barge from Galveston, Texas to Lumut, Malaysia, via the Cape of Good Hope. The rig was loaded with its three legs raised, extending some 300ft up into the air. The legs were tubular structures and the jacking mechanism by which the legs were raised and lowered worked by engaging steel pins into apertures some 16in wide and 10in high; each leg had 45 apertures (known as "pinholes") at 6ft intervals. Cargo insurance covering the rig was on the terms of ICC (A) (1/1/1982), covering "all risks of loss of or damage",[688] subject to the standard exclusion of "loss, damage or expense caused by inherent vice or nature of the subject matter insured".[689] The voyage commenced on 23 August 2005 but was interrupted at Saldanha Bay near Cape Town for repairs to be carried out to the rig's legs. The voyage recommenced on 28 October 2005 but, on 4 November, the rig's starboard leg broke off 30ft along its length and fell overboard. The next day, the forward and port legs also broke off at the 30ft and 18ft levels, respectively, and fell overboard. The loss resulted from a form of metal fatigue, namely a progressive cracking mechanism; this was, in turn, caused by repeated stresses on the legs, during pitching and rolling of the carrying vessel, which were intensified around the pinholes. The weather encountered during the voyage was within the range of what reasonably could have been contemplated for the voyage. Nevertheless, eventually, the legs were weakened sufficiently that a "leg breaking wave" caused the starboard leg to break entirely: the loss of the starboard leg, in turn, increased the stresses on the remaining two legs.

Insurers declined the insureds' claim, inter alia, on the basis that the cause of the loss was inherent vice in the legs, i.e. that the legs were not capable of withstanding the normal incidents of the insured voyage, including the weather reasonably to be expected. The Supreme Court ruled in favour of the insureds. It held that there was one, and only one, proximate cause of the loss: neither inherent vice, nor the "ordinary action of the wind and waves", but the pitching and rolling of the vessel as a result of "leg breaking waves"—fortuitous external occurrences—acting in just the right way and at just the right time to produce sufficient stress on the rig's legs to break them, each in turn.[690]

In reaching this conclusion, Lord Mance[691] tentatively suggested meanings of

---

[683] Discussed below, at para.24-087.
[684] Quoted above, at fn.648.
[685] E.g. *TM Noten BV v Harding* [1990] 2 Lloyd's Rep. 283, discussed in Dunt, *Marine Cargo Insurance* (2015), paras 8.32–8.34.
[686] See above, para.24-085.
[687] *The Cendor MOPU* [2011] UKSC 5; [2011] 1 All E.R. 869; [2011] Bus. L.R. 537.
[688] CL 252 ICC (A) (1/1/82), cl.1.
[689] CL 252 ICC (A) (1/1/82), cl.4.4.
[690] *The Cendor MOPU* [2011] UKSC 5 at [82]–[87].
[691] With whom Lords Collins, Clarke and Dyson agreed. Lord Saville's concurring opinion was to similar effect: see *The Cendor MOPU* [2011] UKSC 5 at [31], and [45]–[46].

both "ordinary wear and tear" and "inherent vice". He stated:

> "While not myself attempting any exact definition, ordinary wear and tear and ordinary leakage and breakage would thus cover loss or damage resulting from the normal vicissitudes of use in the case of a vessel, or of handling and carriage in the case of cargo, while inherent vice would cover inherent characteristics of or defects in a hull or cargo leading to it causing loss or damage to itself—in each case without any fortuitous external accident or casualty."[692]

What is the position if there are two concurrent causes of the loss, the alleged inherent vice and the sea state? According to the Supreme Court in *The Cendor MOPU*,[693] the question does not arise if the sea conditions are such as to constitute a fortuitous external accident or casualty: in such a case, the loss cannot be attributed to inherent vice, so there cannot be "multiple proximate clauses" to consider. Inherent vice can only be retained as a proximate cause where it is the *only* proximate cause.[694]

24-087 **Delay.**[695] This exclusion expressly applies to loss damage or expense proximately caused by delay, even if the delay is caused by an insured peril.[696] It reflects the limitation in MIA s.55(2)(b). For example, if the carrying vessel were detained by reason of a grounding, there would be no cover for losses caused by the resulting delay, such as might result from loss of market for the cargo at the port of destination.

In the context of this exclusion, it has been suggested, judicially, that the burden is on the insured to show that the damage claimed was not caused by delay.[697] This view is based on the historical provenance of the exclusion, i.e. it was formerly part of the definition of the insured peril that delay should not have caused the loss, and this was thus an element for the insured to prove. That reasoning is firmly rejected by Professor Bennett,[698] who would treat the exclusion as such, irrespective of its historical antecedents, thus placing the burden on insurers to prove that the damage comes within the exception.

24-088 **Insolvency or financial default of owners managers charterers or operators of the vessel.**[699] This exclusion is reduced in scope in the 2009 revision, as compared to the 1982 ICC.[700] The 1982 clauses simply provided that the insured had no cover

---

[692] *The Cendor MOPU* [2011] UKSC 5 at [81]; [2011] 1 All E.R. 869 at 894; [2011] Bus. L.R. 537 at 561.

[693] *The Cendor MOPU* [2011] UKSC 5; [2011] 1 All E.R. 869; [2011] Bus. L.R. 537. See also: *European Group Ltd v Chartis Insurance UK Ltd* [2012] EWHC 1245 (Comm) at [138]; Dunt, *Marine Cargo Insurance* (2015), para.8.24.

[694] Following Lord Diplock's definition of "inherent vice" in *Soya v White* [1983] 1 Lloyd's Rep. 122 at 126; [1983] Com. L.R. 46 at 46–47, which assumes the absence of any external intervention, and which was expressly approved by Lord Mance in *The Cendor MOPU* [2011] UKSC 5 at [80]–[81]; [2011] 1 All E.R. at 894; [2011] Bus. L.R. 537 at 560–561. See, in this regard, the discussion in Dunt, *Marine Cargo Insurance* (2015), paras 8.27–8.31.

[695] CL 382 ICC (A) (1/1/09), CL 383 ICC (B) (1/1/09) and CL 384 ICC (C) (1/1/09), cl.4.5. Consequential loss is discussed above, at para.15-068.

[696] Expenses in the nature of general average and salvage charges covered by the policies are excepted.

[697] E.g. *Ikerigi Compania Naviera SA v Palmer (The Wondrous); Global Transeas Corp v Palmer (The Wondrous)* [1992] 2 Lloyd's Rep. 566 at 572.

[698] H. Bennett, *The Law of Marine Insurance*, 2nd edn (Oxford: OUP, 2006), p.260.

[699] CL 382 ICC (A) (1/1/09), CL 383 ICC (B) (1/1/09) and CL 384 ICC (C) (1/1/09), cl.4.6.

[700] The background to the changes is set out in Dunt, *Marine Cargo Insurance* (2015), paras 8.65–8.68.

for any loss damage or expense arising from the insolvency or financial default of the vessel's owners, charterers, managers or operators.[701] The provision had been introduced in order to protect insurers from exposure to conversion of the cargo, and to sue and labour and forwarding expenses incurred, where a voyage had been abandoned by an insolvent carrier.[702] An express forwarding expenses cover was introduced at the same time, which must be read alongside this exclusion.[703]

Under the 2009 ICC, the exclusion covers loss damage or expense proximately caused by the insolvency or financial default of the vessel's owners, managers, charterers or operators "prevent[ing] the normal prosecution of the voyage". However, the exclusion applies only if, at the time the insured cargo was loaded, the insured knew, or in the ordinary course of business should have known, that such insolvency or financial default "could" so interrupt the voyage.[704] Further, the exclusion does not apply where the claimant under the policy is a buyer[705] of the cargo in good faith to whom the policy has been assigned.[706] Finally, the insolvency must relate to vessel interests: insolvency of land-based carriers or warehousing contractors is not excluded. Accordingly, this narrowly framed exclusion applies only to the insured who, with actual or imputed knowledge, ships the cargo on a vessel whose owners, managers, etc. are in a financially precarious situation, or who later purchases the cargo (and the policy) in bad faith.

Deliberate damage or destruction by the wrongful act of any person(s).[707] This exclusion does not appear in ICC (A), the all risks cargo form. It results in a significant narrowing of the cover provided under ICC (B) and (C), e.g. in relation to fire, sinking, etc: accordingly, insureds under those forms are frequently led to seek additional cover for malicious damage.[708]   **24-089**

Nuclear or similar weapon or device.[709] This exclusion covers "loss damage or expense directly or indirectly caused by or arising from" the use of a nuclear or similar weapon or device. Such exclusions have been discussed elsewhere in this work.[710] It might have been thought that the war and conflicts exclusion would suffice, but this exclusion is needed to make clear that damage caused from the peacetime use of nuclear weapons, for example during testing, is also excluded from cover.   **24-090**

Unseaworthiness or unfitness for safe carriage of cargo.[711] Cargo policies are generally voyage policies. Into voyage policies, MIA s.39 implies a warranty that   **24-091**

---

[701] CL 252 ICC (A) (1/1/82), CL 253 ICC (B) (1/1/82) and CL 254 ICC (C) (1/1/82), cl.4.6.

[702] See Dunt, *Marine Cargo Insurance* (2015), paras 8.61–8.63.

[703] CL 252 ICC (A) (1/1/82), CL 253 ICC (B) (1/1/82) and CL 254 ICC (C) (1/1/82), cl.12, discussed in Dunt, *Marine Cargo Insurance* (2015), at para.8.64. See also above, at para.24-047.

[704] It is suggested that "could" means the same as "may", i.e. in this context, it relates to a real possibility, not merely fanciful, of the insured voyage being interrupted by insolvency or financial difficulties: see above, paras 21-012, 21-014.

[705] "[U]nder a binding contract" of sale: see discussion in Dunt, *Marine Cargo Insurance* (2015), para 8.60 and 8.79.

[706] Such purchasers, it is assumed, will generally have had no control over the choice of carrier.

[707] CL 383 ICC (B) (1/1/09) and CL 384 ICC (C) (1/1/09), cl.4.7.

[708] See discussion in Dunt, *Marine Cargo Insurance* (2015), paras 9.41–9.48.

[709] CL 383 ICC (B) (1/1/09) and CL 384 ICC (C) (1/1/09), cl.4.8; CL 382 ICC (A) (1/1/09), cl.4.7.

[710] See paras 15-061 to 15-065, and above, para.24-052.

[711] CL 382 ICC (A) (1/1/09), CL 383 ICC (B) (1/1/09), and CL 384 ICC (C) (1/1/09), cl.5.

the carrying vessel is seaworthy at the commencement of the voyage (and, where relevant, of each stage thereof). A vessel is "seaworthy", for these purposes, when "reasonably fit in all respects to encounter the ordinary perils of the seas of the adventure insured."[712]

As regards policies on "goods or other moveables", specifically, there is no corresponding implied warranty regarding the seaworthiness of the cargo.[713] However, where the voyage policy is on cargo there is an implied warranty

"that at the commencement of the voyage *the ship* is not only seaworthy as a ship, but also that she is reasonably fit to carry the goods or other moveables to the destination contemplated by the policy."[714]

Application of these warranties would mean that if a cargo-carrying vessel sailed on an insured voyage in an unseaworthy or "unfit" condition, insurers would be automatically discharged from liability under the policy by reason of the breach of warranty (whether or not any subsequent loss related to the breach).

The (2009) ICC forms expressly modify the position just described.[715] By cl.5.3 of the forms, insurers expressly waive "any breach" of the aforementioned implied warranties. In their place, cl.5.1 substitutes exclusions (not warranties) covering loss damage or expense "arising from"[716]:

1. unseaworthiness of vessel or craft or unfitness of the same to carry the insured cargo safely, where the insured is "privy to" unseaworthiness or unfitness at the time of loading.[717] Clause 5.2 expressly exempts from this exclusion any innocent purchasers[718] of the cargo who have had the policy assigned to them in good faith. Such purchasers will generally have no control over or knowledge of the suitability of the vessel, conveyance or container;

2. unfitness of any container or conveyance (which must be taken to include land conveyances) for the safe carriage of the insured cargo, provided the loading of the cargo into the container or onto the conveyance was carried out either: (i) prior to attachment of the insurance; or (ii) by the insureds or their employees, being "privy to" the unfitness at the time of such loading).[719]

---

712 MIA s.39(4).

713 MIA s.40(1).

714 MIA s.40(2), emphasis added.

715 The history of the relevant provisions is discussed in Dunt, *Marine Cargo Insurance* (2015), paras 8.73–8.74.

716 It is suggested that this means simply "proximately caused by".

717 Cl.5.1.1: this is similar to the implied warranty in time policies, under MIA s.39(5). "Privity" under that provision requires actual knowledge (including "blind eye" knowledge) of the relevant condition, by the insured (personally) or by their alter ego or directing mind: *Manifest Shipping & Co Ltd v Uni-Polaris Shipping Co Ltd (The Star Sea)* [2001] Lloyd's Rep. 389. See Dunt, *Marine Cargo Insurance* (2015), para.8.78.

718 "[U]nder a binding contract" of sale: see above, fn.705.

719 Cl.5.1.2: there is a clear parallel between this sub-clause of the exclusion and cl.4.3 (exclusion relating to insufficiency or unsuitability of packing or preparation). See discussion above, at para.24-085.

War and conflict; capture and detention; derelict weapons; strikes, terror-   **24-092**
ism, and political risks.[720]   In summary, cll.6 and 7 of the 2009 ICC forms exclude
loss damage or expense proximately caused by: war or conflict[721]; "capture seizure
arrest restraint or detainment"—in the case of ICC (A), piracy being excepted (and,
thus, insured)—, or the consequences thereof or any attempt[722]; derelict weapons
of war[723]; strikes or strikers, lock-outs or locked-out workers, labour disturbances
and their participants, riots or civil commotions[724]; acts of terrorism[725]; or any person
"acting from a political, ideological or religious motive."[726]

In the absence of these exclusions, ICC (A) would cover many war and strikes
risks; and the fire, explosion and contact clauses in ICC (B)[727] and (C), for example,
could be read as covering damage caused by missiles, torpedoes or mines. Marine
insurance market practice, however, is to exclude such risks from "marine perils"
policies (including all risks policies such as ICC (A)), so as to price and insure them
under separate terms.[728]

As compared to the 1982 ICC, the terrorism exclusions in the 2009 ICC have
been expanded in light of the perceived increase and changed nature of the threat
of terrorism in recent years.[729] Commentary relating to some of the exclusions in
cll.6 and 7 is contained elsewhere in this work.[730] Subject to this, it is beyond the
scope of this chapter to consider war and strikes risks in detail.[731]

4.   Shipbuilders' risks

(a)   Introduction

Shipbuilders' risks insurance.   The purpose of shipbuilders' risks insurance is to   **24-093**
cover the shipyard against physical loss of or damage to a vessel during her
construction, before risk is transferred to the buyer. Standard forms of builders' risks
insurance provide all risks cover during the building process in respect of the hull,
machinery and fittings.

Until relatively recently, the only standard London market policy form for builders' risks was the ILU's Institute Clauses for Builders' Risks (1/6/88) ("ICBR").[732]
ICBR were the basis for many of the provisions later to appear in WELCAR,

---

[720] CL 382 ICC (A) (1/1/09), CL 383 ICC (B) (1/1/09) and CL 384 ICC (C) (1/1/09), cll.6 and 7.
[721] Cl.6.1.
[722] Cl.6.2.
[723] Cl.6.3.
[724] Cll.7.1 and 7.2.
[725] Cl.7.3.
[726] Cl.7.4.
[727] CL 382 ICC (B) (1/1/09) cll.1.1.1 and 1.1.4.
[728] See CL 385 Institute War Clauses (Cargo) (1/1/09) and CL 386 the Institute Strike Clauses (Cargo)
(1/1/09). See discussion in Dunt, *Marine Cargo Insurance* (2015), paras 10.1 to 10.4.
[729] Compare, e.g. CL 252 ICC (A) (1/1/82) cl.7.3 and CL 382 ICC (A) (1/1/09) cll.7.3 and 7.4.
[730] See above, paras: 15-041 to 15-058 (war, conflict, etc); and 15-059 (civil commotion).
[731] See the full discussion of war and strikes cargo cover in Dunt, *Marine Cargo Insurance* (2015),
Ch.10. See also: Arnould, paras 23-32 to 23-34 (piracy) and Ch.24 ("War Risks"); and Miller, *Marine
War Risks* (2005).
[732] CL 351 Institute Clauses for Builders' Risks (1/6/88). An early form of institute builders' risks clauses
can be found in W. Gow, *Marine Insurance: A Handbook*, 3rd edn (London: Macmillan & Co Ltd,
1903), pp.365–368. It was intended to be used with the S.G. policy form (discussed above at fn.3),
and provided:

discussed above.[733] Indeed, WELCAR expressly incorporates the ICBR form (subject to amendments).[734] In 2007, the Joint Hull Committee of the International Underwriting Association and Lloyd's Market Association ("JHC") issued London Marine Construction All Risks Wording (1/9/07) ("MARCAR").[735] To date, it appears that ICBR are still being widely used by the insurance market, and the take up of MARCAR has been slow.[736]

This Section contains an introductory presentation of the ICBR.[737] The differences between ICBR and MARCAR are summarised at the end.[738]

24-094 **Shipbuilders' risks insurance as marine insurance.** The MIA not only governs what can most readily be described as "marine adventures" but extends up the slipway and into the shipyards. Section 2(2) to the MIA provides:

> "2. Mixed sea and land risks
> (2) Where a ship in course of building, or the launch of a ship, or any adventure analogous to a marine adventure, is covered by a policy in the form of a marine policy, the provisions of this Act, in so far as applicable, shall apply thereto".[739]

Accordingly, insurance on ships under construction will generally be treated as contracts of marine insurance, to which the MIA will apply.[740] A rare judicial decision dealing with shipbuilders' risks policies confirms the point.[741]

(b) Institute Clauses for Builders' Risks (1/6/88)

24-095 **The vessel and the insureds.** ICBR begins with a heading containing blank spaces for the identification of the insured vessel, by name or, for a newbuilding,

---

> "This insurance is also to cover all risks, including fire, while under construction and/or fitting out, except in buildings or workshops, but including materials in yards and docks of the assured, or on quays, pontoons, craft, etc., and all risk while in transit to and from the works and/or the vessel wherever she may be lying, also all risks of loss or damage through collapse of supports or ways from any cause whatever, and all risks of launching and breakage of the ways. This insurance is also to cover all risks of trial trips, loaded or otherwise, as often as required, and all risks whilst proceeding to and returning from the trial course. ... In case of failure to launch, underwriters to bear all subsequent expenses incurred in completing launch."

The policy contained, inter alia, collision and protection & indemnity liability cover. A later version was introduced on 11 November 1918, which can be found in *Marine Insurance Clauses A Reference Book Containing all Institute of London Underwriters', a selection of Lloyd's, and of General Clauses and Warranties*, 4th and revised edition (London: Witherby & Co, 1921), p.7.

[733] See above, section 2 of this chapter.
[734] See above, para.24-034.
[735] CL 371 London Marine Construction All Risks (1/9/07).
[736] Though one commentator has noted that MARCAR has gained "a significant measure of industry support": S. Curtis, *The Law of Shipbuilding Contracts*, 4th edn (London: Informa, 2012), Part 3, Art XII, "The London Insurance Clauses".
[737] Commentary on the ICBR can also be found in Hudson et al, *Marine Insurance Clauses* (2012), pp.284–296. Curtis, *The Law of Shipbuilding Contracts* (2012), Part 3, Art XII, "The London Insurance Clauses", contains brief commentary on the ICBR and on MARCAR.
[738] Below at para.24-104.
[739] MIA s.2(2).
[740] See also the discussion of the applicability of the MIA to offshore construction, above at para.24-006.
[741] *James Yachts Ltd v Thames and Mersey Marine Insurance Co* [1977] 1 Lloyd's Rep. 206, BC Sup. Ct., at 207–208 (a case decided under British Columbian legislation analogous to the MIA).

more typically by yard or hull number. Blanks are also included for the identification of the insured "Builders"—generally, the main building contractors[742]—and of the "Yards" where they are to construct the hull and the other components of the vessel.

Subject of insurance: insured "parts", periods of cover and places insured. Following the initial heading, ICBR sets out various provisions under the heading "Subject of Insurance". Broadly, the purpose of these provisions is to identify the insured property, and to establish the periods during which, and places where, ICBR's cover will apply to that property. **24-096**

The somewhat complex provisions described below, establishing different coverage "Sections", different (generally, overlapping)[743] provisional periods of cover, and varying categorisation of the insured "parts" depending on whether they are being worked on by the Builders or by their Sub-Contractors, reflect the critical importance of sub-contracting in shipbuilding,[744] and the potential differences in the risks (and in the levels of premium) associated with the Builders' operations and premises as compared with those of the various Sub-Contractors.[745]

ICBR's cover is divided into two periods of time, corresponding to two Sections: "Section I" and "Section II". As to these:

1. A provisional period of cover is to be agreed for *Section I*, to run for a fixed period from a set inception date. During this provisional period, cover is further divided up between Section I(A) and Section I(B), depending on whether the Builders or one of their Sub-Contractors are engaged in the construction of the particular part.

    (a) *Section I(A)* applies to parts of the hull, the machinery, and of any other property under construction, being procured, built or allocated to the vessel under construction, *by the Builders themselves*. ICBR contemplates that such parts are to be described, identified, and provisionally valued in the form, in each case with an indication as to where and by whom each part is to be constructed. Section I(A) covers such parts whilst at the Builders' named Yard and other premises elsewhere within the same port or place of construction as the Yard, and while in transit between such locations. Insurers' liability "attaches" to each part described: from the date of inception under Section I, if the items to

---

[742] It has been noted, however, that it is "the most common practice" for Owners, Builders and all Sub-Contractors (whether or not named) to be co-insureds under the ICBR policy: Hudson et al, *Marine Insurance Clauses* (2012), p.293.

[743] C. Gasparotti, "Shipbuilding process from project management perspective", in *Proceedings of the 15th International Conference on Manufacturing Systems* (Editura Academiei Romane, January 2006), 539–542. ResearchGate, *https://www.researchgate.net/publication/260085588* [Accessed May 21, 2016], describes the stages of an efficiently run shipbuilding project, including how the procurement of units and components from sub-contractors (e.g. for prefabricated units including pumps, filters, heat exchangers, valves, electricals, etc) must proceed in parallel with construction work carried out by the yard, so that delivery of sub-contracted works to the yard can occur at the appropriate points in the programme.

[744] For example, J. Schank et al, *Outsourcing and Outfitting Practices: Implications for the Ministry of Defence Shipbuilding Programmes* (Santa Monica, CA: Rand Corporation, 2005). *http://www.rand.org/content/dam/rand/pubs/monographs/2005/RAND_MG198.pdf* [Accessed 21 May 2016], shows that all UK- and EU-based shipyards—including yards producing significant numbers of large, commercial vessels—outsource major components of shipbuilding projects (e.g. machinery such as engines and generators) to subcontractors.

[745] Hudson et al, *Marine Insurance Clauses* (2012), p.286.

be insured have already been allocated to the vessel by that date; from the time of delivery to the Builders, if already allocated to the vessel but delivered after inception; or upon allocation to the vessel if this occurs after inception. It is contemplated that cover under Section I(A) will attach to the different identified parts at different times, depending on when the conditions for attachment are satisfied in relation to each part.[746]

(b) *Section I(B)* applies to parts of the machinery and of any other property under construction, being procured, built or allocated to the vessel, *by the Builders' Sub-Contractors*. Again, such parts are to be described, identified, and provisionally valued in the form, in each case with an indication as to where and by whom each part is to be constructed. Section I(B) covers such parts whilst at the Sub-Contractors' premises or elsewhere within the same port or place of construction as those premises, as well as in transit between such locations. In addition, the relevant parts are covered when in transit to the Builders, if the transit is within the same port or place of construction as the Builders' Yard, and they are further covered at the Builders' Yard or premises elsewhere within the same port or place of construction (and whilst in transit between such locations). The cover under Section I(B) "attaches" to relevant parts in the same way as the cover under Section I(A) (discussed above), though with the trigger being delivery to or allocation by Sub-Contractors (rather than Builders). Again, the cover under Section I(B) is expected to attach to different parts at different times.[747]

2. A separate provisional period of cover is then to be agreed for *Section II*, to run for a separate fixed period from a separate inception date. Section II provides cover for machinery and any other property *from the time of delivery to the Builders*. The parts to be covered under Section II are, again, to be described, identified, and provisionally valued in the ICBR form, with an indication as to where and by whom each part is to be constructed. Section II covers such parts while at the Builders' Yard or at their other premises within the same port or place of construction, and while in transit between such locations. The cover under section II attaches to each relevant part from the time of delivery to the Builders, which again may be at different times for different parts.[748]

3. Cover under both Section I and Section II is to terminate upon the first occurrence of one of two events: (i) expiry of the relevant provisional period; or (ii) delivery of the relevant insured part to "Owners" (the persons for whom the vessel is being constructed).[749] The provisional periods may be extended under ICBR cl.3,[750] which provides that the insurance is "held covered" if delivery to Owners is delayed beyond the end of either of the

---

[746] The Subject of Insurance provision begins with a parenthetical comment that makes this clear: "(Where more than one part of the subject-matter insured is described in Section I(A), Section I(B) or Section II below, then the respective wording of Section I(A), Section I(B) or Section II shall be applied to each part separately.)"

[747] See above, fn.746.

[748] See above, fn.746.

[749] Again, the result of the provision quoted at fn.746 is that delivery of any part to Owners terminates cover for that part under ICBR.

[750] CL 351 ICBR (1/6/88) cl.3.

[752]

provisional periods (subject to any additional premium being agreed with insurers). This extended cover is limited to a period of up to thirty days from completion of the Builders' trials (discussed further below[751]).

Finally, under ICBR cl.2, cover is also "held" in respect of any transit not already covered under Sections I or II, subject to additional premium being agreed.

Navigation, deviation or change of voyage. Once the vessel is at a point where she can properly go to sea for trials, cover for the same is subject to ICBR cl.9. The vessel may proceed to and from both wet and dry docks, harbours, pontoons and cradles, within the port or place of construction, under her own power, as often as need be, for fitting out, docking, trials or delivery. In doing so, it is provided that the vessel must remain within 250nm of the place of construction: but a vessel going beyond the 250nm limit is held covered "at a premium to be arranged". Movement under tow outside the port of construction is also held covered, subject to prior notice being given to insurers, again "at a premium to be arranged".

Under ICBR cl.4, the insured is also "held covered" despite a deviation or change of voyage,[752] subject to: immediate notice being given to insurers upon receipt by the insured of "advices" (regarding the deviation or change of voyage); and agreement of any amended terms of cover and additional premium required by insurers. This provision was presumably intended to apply, as appropriate, to the only "voyages" expressly contemplated by ICBR, i.e. those referred to in cl.9 for the purpose of fitting out, docking, trials or delivery.[753]

Insured perils: all risks, faulty design and pollution hazard. ICBR cl.5 provides:

"PERILS

5.1 SUBJECT ALWAYS TO ITS TERMS, CONDITION AND EXCLUSIONS this insurance is against all risks of loss of or damage to the subject matter insured caused and discovered during the period of this insurance including the cost of repairing replacing or renewing any defective part condemned solely in consequence of the discovery therein during the period of this insurance of a latent defect. In no case shall this insurance cover the cost of renewing faulty welds.

5.2 In case of failure of launch, the Underwriters to bear all subsequent expenses incurred in completing launch."[754]

It is to be noted that the indemnity applies only to loss or damage both "caused" and "discovered" during the period of insurance: insurers are to have no liability for a "tail" of later-discovered losses after the expiry of the policy. Cover comes to an end upon delivery of the vessel to Owners: the policy is not intended to cover Builders' "guarantee risks".

Subject to this, the breadth of the coverage is striking. Generally, the limitations

24-097

24-098

---

[751] At para.24-097.

[752] See Arnould, Ch.14. In practice, it may be difficult to apply the doctrines of deviation and change of voyage to voyages under ICBR, such as trials voyages, in that it may be difficult to identify the voyage's usual course, etc.

[753] Hudson et al, *Marine Insurance Clauses* (2012), p.288. Cover for "transits"—presumably, referring to parts of the vessel not yet capable of being "navigated"—is addressed in the Subject of Insurance provision and in ICBR cl.2: see above, para.24-096.

[754] See also commentary in Hudson et al, *Marine Insurance Clauses* (2012), pp.288–289.

to cover—including all risks cover—set out in MIA s.55(2) will apply.[755] However, ICBR cl.5 expressly extends cover to include the cost of repairing, replacing or renewing any part—arguably, even if otherwise undamaged[756]—condemned solely by reason of a latent defect.[757] This is subject (again) to that latent defect being discovered within the currency of the policy; and to the clearly stated exclusion of the costs of "renewing faulty welds".

The aforementioned provisions regarding latent defects must be read subject to ICBR cl.8, which provides:

> "*FAULTY DESIGN*
> Notwithstanding anything to the contrary which may be contained in the policy or the clauses attached thereto, this insurance includes loss of or damage to the subject-matter insured caused and discovered during the period of this insurance arising from faulty design of any part or parts thereof but in no case shall this insurance extend to cover the cost or expense of repairing, modifying, replacing or renewing such part or parts, nor any cost or expense incurred by reason of betterment or alteration in design."

Accordingly, it can be seen that where faulty design[758] of any "part or parts" is in issue,[759] loss or damage to other insured property caused by the faulty part(s) is covered (if caused and discovered during the currency of the policy). But the rectification of the part(s) affected by faulty design themselves is not covered, nor is any cost or expense incurred in improving or altering the design.[760] The treatment of defects arising from faulty design is thus significantly different from the treatment of latent defects arising from defective materials, faulty workmanship, etc.

ICBR cl.7 provides "Pollution Hazard" cover for loss of or damage to the vessel caused by governmental authorities acting within their powers to prevent or mitigate a pollution hazard resulting from damage to the vessel for which underwriters would be liable under the policy, unless the government's action is the result of want of due diligence by the insured Builders, the Owners, or the managers of the vessel.[761]

24-099   Exclusions.   In brief summary, ICBR specifically excludes loss, damage, liability or expense[762]:

---

[755] MIA s.55 is quoted above at fn.648. See discussion of the limitations to "all risks" cover under ICC (A), above at para.24-081; see also above at paras 24-083 (wilful misconduct), 24-084 (wear and tear), 24-086 (inherent vice), and 24-087 (delay).

[756] Cf. C. Zavos, *"Builders' Risks—Proposed Changes"*, Presentation at International Marine Claims Conference, Dublin, on 26 October 2005 (17 October 2005). *http://www.marine claimsconference.com/2005/docs/Chris%20Zavos%20paper.pdf* [Accessed 22 May 2016], paras 5(a)(iii) and (iv), and 8(s) and (t) referring to "uncertainty" regarding whether, under ICBR cl.5, "simple discovery of a latent defect", without other damage, is sufficient to "trigger cover", and concluding that such cover was "probably only [given] where other damage is caused".

[757] See above, paras 16-008, 16-011 and 16-012, regarding "latent" defects. The "inherent vice" limitation in MIA s.55(2)(c) clearly ought to be excluded where this latent defect cover applies: *Promet Engineering (Singapore) Ltd v Sturge (The Nukila)* [1997] 2 Lloyd's Rep. 146 at 150–151.

[758] See above, para.16-009.

[759] See above, discussion of meaning of "part" in the context of DE3 and DE4 (1995), at paras 16-038 to 16-043, and in the context of WELCAR at para.24-030.

[760] See discussion, in the context of DE5 (1995), above at paras 16-059 to 16-061 and 16-064.

[761] See discussion of the very similar provision in the first paragraph of WELCAR's Pollution Hazard clause, above at para.24-035.

[762] In relation to these exclusions, generally, see: Hudson et al, *Marine Insurance Clauses* (2012), pp.160–161, 215–216, 289, 296–297; Dunt, *Marine Cargo Insurance* (2015), Ch.10; Arnould, Ch.24 ("War Risks"); Miller, *Marine War Risks* (2005).

1. caused by earthquake or volcanic eruption[763];
2. caused by war or various kinds of civil strife, by "capture seizure arrest restraint or detainment (barratry and piracy excepted)", or derelict weapons of war[764];
3. caused by strikers, locked-out workers, labour disturbances, riots or civil commotions, or acts of terrorists or those acting for political motives[765];
4. arising from detonation of explosives or weapons of war done maliciously or from a political motive[766]; or
5. directly or indirectly caused or contributed to or arising from radiation from, contamination by, or toxic, explosive, or other contaminating or hazardous properties of, nuclear sources, or atomic, nuclear or similar weapons of war.[767]

Insured value and maximum limit of indemnity. As discussed above at **24-100** para.24-096, the Scope of Insurance clause contemplates that "provisional values" will be inserted in the ICBR form in relation to each insured part to be constructed. ICBR cl.1.1 then provides a formula for calculating the "insured value" under the policy, namely the greater of: (i) the total building cost plus a set percentage; and (ii) the final contract price as between Builders and Owners.

If the insured value, thus determined, exceeds the provisional value, then under ICBR cl.1.2 the insured is required to declare the same to insurers and to pay an additional premium, while insurers are bound to accept their proportionate shares of the increased sum insured. If, instead, the insured value is lower than the provisional value, then insurers' respective several liabilities and the premium are reduced proportionately. Where the insured value exceeds the provisional value, ICBR cl.1.3 limits the available uplifted cover. For insured values in excess of 125% of the provisional value, the "limits of indemnity under [ICBR] shall be 125% of the provisional value, any one accident or series of accidents arising out of the same event."[768]

A distinction is drawn between increases or decreases of insured values above or below provisional values due to estimation errors, on the one hand, and variations in the build cost or purchase prices due to "material alterations" in the plans or fittings or to a change in type of the vessel, on the other. In the latter case, ICBR cl.1.4 provides that there is to be no automatic, proportionate variation in the insured value: insurers' specific agreement is required.[769]

Measure of indemnity. Where damage arising from an insured casualty is **24-101** repaired, under MIA s.69(1) the measure of indemnity is the reasonable cost of repairs, less customary deductions, but not exceeding the sum insured. Where damage is not repaired, however, ICBR cl.11 provides that the measure of indemnity

---

[763] CL 351 ICBR (1/6/88), cl.6 ("Earthquake and Volcanic Eruption Exclusion"); see also, above, para.24-075.

[764] CL 351 ICBR (1/6/88), cl.21 ("War Exclusion"); see also, above, at para.24-092.

[765] CL 351 ICBR (1/6/88), cl.22 ("Strikes Exclusion"), see also, above, para.24-092.

[766] CL 351 ICBR (1/6/88), cl.23 ("Malicious Acts Exclusion"); see also, above, para.24-092.

[767] CL 351 ICBR (1/6/88), cl.24 ("Nuclear Exclusion"); see also, above, paras 15-061 to 15-065, and 24-090.

[768] This is similar to the Escalation Clause in WELCAR, discussed above, at para.24-028.

[769] See also the discussion of "material alterations" in the context of WELCAR's Project Alterations and Amendments clause, above at para.24-009.

is to be the reasonable depreciation in the vessel's "market value" at the time of termination of the policy, but not exceeding the reasonable cost of repairs.[770]

As usual, underwriters are not liable in respect of a partial loss where it is followed by an actual or constructive total loss.[771] In determining whether there has been a constructive total loss, ICBR cl.12 provides that the insured value is to stand as the point of reference, with any damaged or break-up value of the vessel disregarded from the assessment.[772]

24-102 Deductible.[773] ICBR cl.10.1 provides that the insured is to bear an agreed amount by way of deductible in relation to the aggregate of all claims (including claims for general average, collision liability, protection & indemnity liability, and sue and labour) arising out of any one accident or occurrence, save in claims for an actual or constructive total loss.

Under ICBR cl.10.2, claims for damage by heavy weather (including contact with floating ice) during one "sea passage" are deemed to arise out of one accident, unless the damaging conditions continue beyond the currency of the policy, in which case the deductible is apportioned according to the number of days of heavy weather within the policy period as a proportion of the total number of days of heavy weather during the sea passage.

ICBR cll.10.3 and 10.4 provide for subrogated recoveries from third parties to be allocated to insurers, first, before being allocated to the insured in relation to the "self-insured" deductible, but for the interest component in any such recovery to be apportioned between insurers and insureds.

24-103 General average and salvage, collision liability, protection & indemnity, and duty of assured (sue & labour). In brief summary, ICBR also covers:

1. the vessel's proportion of salvage, salvage charges and general average, where the relevant loss or expense was incurred in connection with an insured peril[774];
2. legal liability of the Builder for collisions with other vessels, subject to usual exclusions[775]; and
3. some protection & indemnity-type liabilities.[776]

---

[770] Or the Insured Value: CL 351 ICBR (1/6/88), cl.11.3. See discussion in Hudson et al, *Marine Insurance Clauses* (2012), pp.150–153.

[771] CL 351 ICBR (1/6/88), cl.11.2.

[772] Zavos, *"Builders' Risks—Proposed Changes"* (2005), para.5(a)(v), notes that the CTL provision "has limited application in the context of a construction project. Only at or close to the end of a project is the cost of recovery and repair likely to exceed the insured value, which is generally the anticipated value of the project as a whole." See also Hudson et al, *Marine Insurance Clauses* (2012), pp.153–154, 291–292. (The criticisms levelled at ICBR cl.11 in the latter work, at pp.291–292, seem questionable. A "market value" for a vessel under construction could be estimated by a competent expert, based on what a hypothetical buyer would reasonably pay, even though in reality there might be no liquid market for such a vessel. And the constructive total loss of a partly-built vessel, assessed by reference to the (provisional) insured value, seems a readily comprehensible notion.)

[773] See Hudson et al, *Marine Insurance Clauses* (2012), pp.139–145.

[774] CL 351 ICBR (1/6/88), cl.13: see Hudson et al, *Marine Insurance Clauses* (2012), pp.130–135, 292; see also Arnould, Ch.26.

[775] CL 351 ICBR (1/6/88), cll.17 and 18: see Hudson et al, *Marine Insurance Clauses* (2012), pp.123–130, 216, 293–294; see also Arnould, paras 23–22 to 23–26.

[776] CL 351 ICBR (1/6/88). cl.19: see Hudson et al, *Marine Insurance Clauses* (2012), pp.139–145, 217–218, 272–278, 294–295.

ICBR's Duty of Assured (Sue and Labour) clause places on the insured the familiar duty to: "take such measures as may be reasonable for the purpose of averting or minimising a loss which would be recoverable under this insurance", whilst indemnifying the insured for the necessary and reasonable costs of complying with that duty.[777]

(c)   London Marine Construction All Risks Wording (1/9/2007)

London Marine Construction All Risks Wording (1/9/07) ("MARCAR").   In   **24-104** 2005, the JHC decided to revise the ICBR clauses, discussed above,[778] so that they could better address the increased exposures that insurers were facing from the shipbuilding industry.[779] The JHC working group decided it was desirable to completely rewrite the policy form instead, as "[i]t was felt that amendments would not be sufficient to introduce the level of clarity desired by Underwriters and Assureds alike."[780]

Accordingly, the JHC issued MARCAR in 2007. The policy wording may be used to provide specialist marine construction contractors with coverage suited to a broader range of types of insurable property, such as platforms, rigs, pipelines, boatyards, and vessels, etc, and a broader range of operations, including repairing, converting and lengthening a ship, than had been envisaged in relation to ICBR. MARCAR also updates elements of the old policy wording that were perceived to have shortcomings.

MARCAR is divided into the following five parts: (i) coverage; (ii) exclusions to coverage; (iii) claims conditions; (iv) general provisions and definitions; and (v) optional buy-back clauses. Significant differences between the old ICBR and the new policy wording, briefly, include the following:

1.   While it remains possible to set fixed inception and termination dates, in default of so doing cover runs from the commencement of construction (or, in relation to war risks, from the launching date) until delivery of the vessel or earlier termination (cl.56.16).

2.   ICBR's "Sections" are abandoned. Instead, the subject matter insured under MARCAR is identified as the Vessel, and any Items allocated to the Vessel, and cover for these is generally restricted to the Vessel and Items while at the Builder's Yard (cll.50, 56.11, 56.16, 56.19 and 56.21).

3.   MARCAR contemplates cover being procured on behalf of the Assured— meaning the Builder, the Buyer, or both—and Additional Assureds— meaning those Builder's Contractors and Contractors' Sub-contractors afforded the benefit of the policy under written contracts relating to the construction of the vessel (cll.56.2, 56.4–56.7, 56.18). Additional Assureds are covered to the extent of their respective interests, within the limits of cover to be procured under their written contracts (cl.42). Express provisions relate, inter alia, to subrogation, including against Additional Assureds (cl.38), to making insurers' defences against the Builder binding against the Buyer, and vice versa (cl.41), and also to making any of the

---

[777]   CL 351 ICBR (1/6/88), cl.20. See also Arnould, Ch.25.

[778]   See above, paras 24-095 to 24-103.

[779]   See Zavos, *"Builders' Risks—Proposed Changes"* (2005), para.2, referring to "a horrendous run of losses between October 2002 and January 2004", and between then and October 2005, adding up to over US$1 billion.

[780]   Zavos, *"Builders' Risks—Proposed Changes"* (2005), para.4(b).

insurers' defences against or agreements with the Assured valid against Additional Assureds (cl.42).

4. As with ICBR, the basic construction insurance is against all risks of physical loss of or damage to the property insured caused and discovered during the currency of the policy (cl.2). However, it is made clear that the costs of rectifying defects, including defects in design, workmanship, materials, and latent defects, are excluded, though damage or loss caused by defects is covered (cl.3).[781] Cover for rectifying defects in workmanship, material or latent defects can be bought back, along with some cover for rectification of defects in design, plan or specification (cl.57).

5. Earthquakes and volcanic eruptions are no longer excluded.

6. Protection & indemnity liability cover has been extended to include some cover for pollution liability (cl.7).

7. War risks cover is incorporated into the policy form, attaching from the date the vessel is launched (cll.9–15). Cover is also incorporated against strikes, terrorism, political and malicious acts (cll.16–20).

8. The treatment of total loss is much altered. The measure of indemnity in the case of actual total loss is based on the Works Value—a measure of the total construction costs incurred, a figure which will increase as the project progresses, but which in no case can exceed the sum insured—plus a Profit Percentage (10% by default) (cll.29, 56.17, 56.29 and 56.22). In the case of constructive total loss, the measure of indemnity is to be the sum insured (cl.28). However, provision is also made for "Abandonment", a notion akin to constructive total loss: where the cost of recovering or repairing damage to the vessel does not exceed the sum insured, but exceeds the Works Value at the time of loss, the Builder and Buyer can agree, with the insurers' consent, to abandon the works (i.e by "an agreement … that the Builder is relieved of the obligation to build or deliver the Vessel to the Buyer, by reason of physical loss of or physical damage to the Vessel": cll.31 and 56.1). In such a case, the measure of indemnity is the Works Value plus the Profit Percentage thereon at the time of loss.

9. For claims in respect of unrepaired damage, the measure of indemnity is the reasonable cost of repairs, but not to exceed the "Contract Deduction", which is the amount by which the sum payable by Buyers to Builders is agreed to be reduced, with insurers' prior consent, by reason of the unrepaired damage (cll.30 and 56.9).

10. Breach of the Navigation clause suspends cover: prior written consent from insurers to breach the condition is required, subject to agreement of amended terms of cover and additional premium (cl.49).

11. A due diligence clause is imposed on the Assured, providing insurers with a potential defence against claims linked to breaches of the same (cl.48).

12. Various limits of liability are made applicable to extended coverages under the policy.

13. Finally, while the policy remains subject to the jurisdiction of the English courts (cl.1.4), various clauses provide for arbitration, under the rules of the London Maritime Arbitrators Association, in order to resolve disputes on certain discrete, identified issues (e.g. cll.4.7, 6.5, 30.4, 31.2, and 37).

---

[781] See above, fn.754, and Zavos, *"Builders' Risks—Proposed Changes"* (2005), para.8(u).

AVIATION ALL RISKS

1. INTRODUCTION

Introduction. Aviation insurance is unique. Whilst the underlying principle of **25-001** traditional insurance markets is that the premiums of the many pay for the losses of the few, the aviation insurance market is different. Both the premium base and the customer base are very narrow, with a small number of insured parties. The International Air Travel Association ("IATA") has just over 260 airline members (as at 2016), representing approximately 83 per cent of global air traffic.[1] But concurrently, the potential exposure of each aircraft operator and each airline is huge. This is why it is vanishingly rare for any single insurer to underwrite the entire amount of an operator's/airline's overall risk. A number of insurers will each underwrite a small percentage of that exposure, thus keeping the exposure for any one insurer within acceptable limits.

The cover provided by a construction policy does not normally include that provided by a marine,[2] professional indemnity, employer's liability, motor or indeed an aviation policy. Although significant aviation accidents happen relatively infrequently, they have the potential to cause enormous (and sometimes catastrophic) damage to property and loss of human life, both within the aircraft and without. No automotive accident will equal the risk of loss posed by an aircraft crash, where the damages could run into hundreds of millions of pounds (if not considerably more). Unlike more static insured risks, aircraft fly to destinations over which the carrier has little or no control, to countries where the risks are often unforeseeable and in circumstances where the preparation of the aircraft is in the hands of a multiplicity of third parties. An aviation "all risks" policy (which is a bespoke policy) will reflect those unique risks and usually provide cover for aviation risks faced by an airline (or carrier) for the loss or damage to aircraft, coupled

---

[1] International Air Travel Association *"About IATA and what it does for the Air Transport Industry"* (2016). See *http://www.iata.org/Pages/faq.aspx* [Accessed 5 May 2016].

[2] See above, Ch.24.

with legal liability owed to passengers and third parties arising out of the use of aircraft, and also for loss or damage caused to cargo carried on board.

To put the risks in some perspective: the Air Transport Action Group ("ATAG") reported in 2016 that 32.8 million flights took place in 2014 (in 2015, there were 34.8 million flights). This averages out at 102,465 flights per day. Set against this, the number of commercial aviation deaths in 2014 was 761.[3] Down from a peak of 2,429 in 1972; and 2014's figure which was almost three times the death rate in 2013.[4] The number of aircraft crashes per year is fairly steady, although declining slightly. There were 122 aircraft crashes in 2015 and the same in 2014, 139 in 2013, and 156 in 2012; according to data from the Bureau of Aircraft Accidents Archives ("BEA").[5]

25-002   The focus of this chapter is to discuss aviation all risks insurance, which is also known as airlines' insurance or all risks hull and liability insurance,[6] the latter of which may provide cover for third party, passenger and cargo all risks insurance. All risks, hull and/or liability insurance cover may be extended by aircraft operators to include loss or damage to aircraft and liabilities insured as a result of war and war-like situations (such as strikes, riots, civil commotions, sabotage and hijacking). Thus the standard hull policy will become the "all risks aircraft hull and liability policy", and as such obviously provides more comprehensive cover. Aviation insurance has grown out of marine insurance and it is no accident that the terminology relating to marine insurance, such as "hull", has become absorbed into aviation. The meaning of the word "hull" in the context of aviation actually refers to the entire aircraft including instruments, radios, autopilots, wings, engines and other equipment attached to or carried on the aircraft as described in the policy.

25-003 Aviation and construction.   The construction and aviation sectors are significantly intertwined and therefore often interact in a number of ways. Aviation requires a substantial construction infrastructure, not only the major engineering project of the building of the aircraft itself. Commercial aircraft require substantial facilities, including airports and airport-related facilities (e.g. maintenance hangars, fuel facilities, baggage-screening and handling facilities, construction and parking garages etc.). Airports themselves are some of the largest land-based infrastructure projects. As such, construction works at airports are common and indeed routine. Airports constantly require maintenance, re-modelling, extensions and refurbishment to the buildings, perimeter, aprons and runways. This is due to the heavy traffic loads they bear, the very high standard of maintenance required at such facilities by national authorities and the changing needs of the industry.

Aviation operation works ("airside") pose risks to aircraft movement and aircraft operations. The degree of risk varies with time and progress of the project. Like with many construction projects, the creation of new airport facilities and/or remodel-

---

[3]   Air Transport Action Group, "Aviation Benefits Beyond Borders Global Summary" (Switzerland: Air Transport Action Group, 2016) *http://www.atag.org/our-publications/latest.html* [Accessed 28 September 2016].

[4]   In 2013 there were 265 aviation deaths. C. Tolan et al, "Is 2014 the deadliest year for flights? Not even close" (28 July 2015) *http://edition.cnn.com/interactive/2014/07/travel/aviation-data/* [Accessed 28 September 2016].

[5]   Bureau of Aircraft Accidents Archives, "Crashes from 2010 to 2019" (2016) *http://www.baaa-acro.com/result-histogram-crash-page/?from=2010&to=2019&type=9* [Accessed 2 August 2016].

[6]   An aviation all risks policy (howsoever labelled) is distinct from a conventional/general aviation or hull insurance policy.

ling works means that the degree of risk requires continuous re-evaluation. But the increasing value, complexity and capacity of modern aircraft (and their support facilities) means that the premiums are likely to exceed those of a standard construction all-risks policy, and cover is likely to be provided by more specialist aviation insurers.

The interaction between construction and aviation can also arise in tragic circumstances, such as those of 11 September 2001[7] and more recently in January 2013 when a helicopter struck a construction crane in Central London.[8]   **25-004**

Aviation also assists in construction projects directly and indirectly. Helicopters are extensively used in off-shore construction and maintenance. Specialist construction helicopters assist in construction projects in remote and inaccessible areas, to take part in marine salvage operations etc. The huge variety of uses to which aircraft are put, whether to carry passengers, cargo, assisting in construction, rescue or salvage, places heavy logistical and drafting demands on those insurers providing cover.

The aviation sector. The aviation sector itself is multifaceted, divided between airlines, general aviation,[9] space[10] and aerospace.[11] These divisions are themselves sub-divided, airlines for example are divided into majors, nationals, regionals, cargo and banks. Aviation is, of course, larger than those who own or operate aircraft. The global airline industry comprises air transport service providers of both passenger and cargo. The sector services international, domestic, and regional individuals and business and governments across the globe. Although the industry has many suppliers and buyers, the industry is currently led by North America followed by Europe and Asia.[12] But times are changing. By 2020 it is anticipated that China will be the second largest aviation market (behind the USA) and India will be third by 2020.[13] The sector includes aviation manufactures (from the large commercial to   **25-005**

---

[7] Which itself gave rise to insurance litigation, e.g.: *Aioi Nissay Dowa Insurance Co Ltd (formerly Chiyoda Fire and Marine Insurance Co Ltd) v (1) Heraldglen Ltd (2) Advent Capital (no.3) Ltd* [2013] EWHC 154 (Comm); [2013] 2 All E.R. (Comm) 231: [2013] Lloyd's Rep. I.R. 281.

[8] A. Topping et al, "*Vauxhall helicopter crash: two die after aircraft hits crane*" (16 January 2013), *theguardian.com/uk, http://www.theguardian.com/uk/2013/jan/16/london-helicopter-crash-two-die* [Accessed 5 May 2016].

[9] For this, hull and liability cover is provided for a wide portfolio of general aviation risks, from a single aircraft to helicopters, private/business jets, commercial aircraft and fleets, clubs and flying schools, airfields and fixed base operators and ground service providers.

[10] See *Margo on Aviation Insurance: the law and practice of aviation insurance, including space and hovercraft insurance*, edited by K.B. Posner, T. Marland and P. Chrystal, 4th edn (London: LexisNexis Butterworths, 2014), paras 21–10 to 21–11 for a discussion about pre-launch insurance available for spacecraft and the insurance policy for this, which will insure against all risks of physical loss and/or damage to the aircraft subject to the terms, conditions and exclusions incorporated into the policy.

[11] Aerospace insurance is of crucial importance to the whole aviation industry and provides physical damage and liability cover for manufacturers and suppliers of component parts, airports, airfields, airport authorities, airport service providers, airport navigation service providers, refuellers and oil companies and maintenance repair and overhaul providers.

[12] Research and Markets, PR Newswire, "*Global Airline Industry 2013–2020: Airlines Industry Expected to Reach an Estimated $832.8 Billion in 2020*" (2013) *http://www.prnewswire.com/news-releases/global-airline-industry-2013-2020-airlines-industry-expected-to-reach-an-estimated-8328-billion-in-2020-210801541.html* [Accessed 5 May 5, 2016].

[13] KPMG, "India on way to become the third largest aviation market by 2020" (17 March 2016) *https://home.kpmg.com/in/en/home/media/press-releases/2016/03/aviation-report-march.html* [Accessed 28 September 2016].

the smallest private aircraft), the providers of airports and airport services, air traffic control and those tangentially involved in the sector such as banks and leasing companies. The airline industry alone is behemoth and continues to grow. Growth of the North American market is driven by growing demand in long-haul international services. The size of the global airlines industry is expected to reach an estimated $832.8 billion in 2020 with a compound annual growth rate of 3.7 per cent between 2013 and 2020.[14] Increasing demand from emerging economies, continuous demand for new low-cost carriers, deregulation, and rising personal incomes are factors driving growth in markets such as Asia and the Middle East.[15]

25-006   **Aviation all risks insurance.**   Although the aviation industry is large, even in global terms aviation insurance is relatively small compared to, for example, motor or household insurance. The insurance industry provides cover for a broad range of aircraft including commercial airlines, general aviation and industrial aircrafts as well as for aviation manufacturers, airport services, specialist aircraft lenders and leasing companies. This chapter concerns the all risks cover specifically provided by the insurance industry to commercial airlines and the aircraft they operate to carry people and cargo from one destination to another.

The legal systems of countries across the globe require aircraft operators to provide aviation insurance. Any aircraft operator must insure its commercial airline. Aviation all risks insurance is a type of insurance policy that has adapted over time to meet the needs of commercial airlines.

25-007   Within the EU, there are strict regulatory requirements concerning aviation insurance. Regulation (EC) No.785/2004 (as amended by Regulation (EU) No.285/2010)[16] applies to all air carriers and to all aircraft operators flying within, into, out of or over the territory of an EC Member State to which the Treaty (establishing the European Community) applies.[17] Its objective is to establish minimum insurance requirements for air carriers and aircraft operators in respect of passengers, baggage, cargo and third parties including cover for risks of war and terrorism. This EC Regulation was implemented in the United Kingdom by the Civil Aviation (Insurance) Regulations 2005 (SI 1089/2005), which came into force on April 30, 2005. Carriers and operators are thereby obligated to carry relevant insurance in respect of passengers, baggage, cargo and third parties including cover for risks of war and terrorism.

The scope of the all risks hull liability insurance policy (initially covered loss or damage for the use of aircraft) was extended at or around 2001 to provide airline operators for cover against legal liability incurred as a result of operating an aircraft to passengers and non-passengers. Aircraft themselves are continually increasing in size and the demand for international air travel shows no sign of abating. Boeing's Airbus A380 is approximately 50 per cent larger in terms of floor space

---

14   See above, fn.12.
15   See above, fn.12.
16   Regulation (EU) No.285/2010 of April 6, 2010 amending Regulation (EC) No.785/2004 of the European Parliament and of the Council on insurance requirements for air carriers and aircraft operators [2010] OJ L87/19.
17   Treaty establishing the European Economic Community 1957 (pre-Union Treaty) (as amended), Miscellaneous Series 005 (1972) Cmnd. 4864; 298 UNTS 11. See also the Consolidated versions of the Treaty on the European Union and the Treaty on the Functioning of the European Union, [2016] OJ C202, 7.6.2016, pp.1-388.

than the next largest airliner, also made by Boeing. The Airbus can carry over 850 passengers.

The minimum levels of insurance cover by regulatory requirement is dependent upon the number of passengers carried and in relation to third party cover the Maximum Take Off Mass ("MTOM") of the aircraft concerned. Regulation 785/2004 identifies the minimum level of cover required depending on the category of aircraft (of which there are currently ten).[18] There is also a regulatory requirement for cover in respect of baggage and cargo and, in certain cases, to insure against war and terrorism.

The term "all risks" can be misleading in the context of aviation insurance. The policies cover many standard risks but, save for specific instances, exclude many risks associated with the operation of an aircraft. Cargo all risks insurance has its origins in the London insurance market, which is one of the pre-eminent aviation insurance markets. Although much of the market is now outside the United Kingdom (especially in the United States with a large percentage of the world's aviation fleet), the London insurance market is still the largest single centre for aviation insurance. A number of institutions support the London market including the Aviation Insurance Clauses Group ("AICG"), the International Underwriting Association of London ("IUA"), the Lloyd's Market Association ("LMA"), the London & International Brokers Association and the London Market Group. In 2014 (almost two years ago), the London market had a premium income of just under £23 billion (GPB) of which aviation premiums accounted for around 7 per cent of total business for that year.[19] **25-008**

Aviation risks. In contrast to the other types of insurance, in aviation insurance there are a limited number of risks to insure. All insurance is a means of risk management and aviation insurance is no different. The airline transfers the risk of loss or liability to the insurers. Aviation insurance includes risks associated with the manufacture, ownership and operation of the aircraft, and the operation of aviation facilities. The insurer, as with all types of insurance, wishes to identify the possible hazards, analyse the risks associated with those hazards and determine whether the risk is acceptable. Aviation risk arises in a number of ways: mechanical failure, human error, communication and/or navigation error, hijacking and those risks associated with terrorism and war. Airlines and aircraft are uniquely vulnerable to exogenous events that happen with regularity, such as security concerns, volcanic eruptions (such as those in 2014 in Papua New Guinea and Iceland),[20] and infectious diseases (Ebola in 2014 and Zika in 2016).[21] **25-009**

---

[18] The 10 categories are set out in Regulation (EC) No.785/2004 of the European Parliament and of the Council of April 21, 2004 on insurance requirements for air carriers and aircraft operators [2004] OJ L138/1, art.7.

[19] International Underwriting Association of London, "*London Company Market Statistics Report*" (International Underwriting Association Ltd: London, 2015) *http://www.iua.co.uk/IUA_Member/ Publications/London_Company_Market_Statistics_Report/IUA_Member/Publications/London_ Company_Market_Statistics_Report.aspx?hkey=5b5ed373-25ee-40a3-8b82-3630dd78899d* [Accessed 5 May 2016].

[20] S. Calder, "Air travel disrupted by fresh volcano threats in Iceland and Papua New Guinea" (29 August 2014) *http://www.independent.co.uk/travel/news-and-advice/air-travel-disrupted-by-fresh-volcano-threats-in-iceland-and-papua-new-guinea-9700353.html* [Accessed 28 September 2016].

[21] J. Dastin, "U.S. airline stocks fall on renewed fears of Ebola effect on travel" (15 October 2014) *http://www.reuters.com/article/us-usa-airlines-stocks-idUSKCN0I429U20141015* [Accessed 28

Perhaps uniquely in aviation insurance, the risks to the insured can vary by country and continent. This is reflected in this quote by an insurer who states:

"... [K]nowing the different conditions and circumstances under which aircraft operate in Africa, enables an accurate identification of the real risks that each individual aircraft faces."[22]

The range of hazards faced by an aircraft has, if anything, grown in recent years—drones being a case in point. Drones weighing 20kg or less are defined[23] as "small unmanned aircraft" and regulated by the Civil Aviation Authority. The UK Airprox Board ("UKAB") found[24] there were 23 cases of drones coming into conflict with aircraft in the six months between April and October 2015. A suspected drone/ aircraft impact at London Heathrow was reported and investigated in April 2016 but the results were inconclusive as to cause.[25] Drones are not currently formally regulated at the date of writing although the UK Government is considering a formal register. The Civil Aviation Authority advises that drone operators must be able to see the craft at all times and must not fly above 400ft (122 metres). Drones fitted with cameras must not be flown within 50 metres (164ft) of a person, vehicle or structure or over congested areas or large gatherings such as concerts and sports events.[26]

Regulation 785/2004 on insurance requirements for air carrier and aircraft operators,[27] provides for minimum insurance requirements by reference to the weight of the aircraft. Article 2(b) states that the regulation does not apply to model aircraft weighing less than 20kg (the vast majority of "recreational" drones). The consequence is that there is no legal minimum insurance requirement in respect of small unmanned aircraft in the UK.

In addition to the above, it has been predicted that climate change and its effects on meteorological characteristics may pose an increasing hazard to aircraft. Climate scientists—while identifying the airline sector as a major contribution to the phenomenon—have predicted[28] that turbulence on the North Atlantic flight corridor alone could dramatically increase by 40% to 170%[29] if—as the International Energy Agency ("IEA") forecasts, carbon dioxide emissions double by 2050.[30] Moreover, it is well recognised that climate change increases the likelihood and frequency of severe weather events globally, most of which pose a hazard to aircraft.

September 2016].

[22] H. Wilmot, *"Insurance and risk: An overview of aviation in Africa"* (Norton Rose South Africa: 8 March 2012) *http://www.nortonrosefulbright.com/files/insurance-and-risk-65123.pdf* [Accessed 5 May 2016].

[23] Part 33 art.255(1) of the Air Navigation Order 2009 (SI 2009/3015).

[24] See Airport Watch "BALPA wants DfT and CAA to fund drone strike research – fears of cockpit hit or engine fire" (March 2, 2016) *http://www.airportwatch.org.uk/2016/03/balpa-wants-dft-and-caa-to-fund-drone-strike-research-fears-of-cockpit-hit-or-engine-fire/* [Accessed 2 August 2016].

[25] The Guardian "Heathrow plane strike 'not a drone incident'" (28 April 2016) *https://www.theguardian.com/technology/2016/apr/28/heathrow-ba-plane-strike-not-a-drone-incident* [Accessed 28 September 2016].

[26] Articles 166(4)(c) and 167(2)(c) of the Air Navigation Order 2009 (SI 2009/3015).

[27] See above fn.16.

[28] P.D. Williams, "Transatlantic Flight Times and Climate Change" (2016) *Environ. Res. Lett.* 11 (2)

[29] J. Amos "Transatlantic flights 'to get more turbulent'" (8 April 2013) *http://www.bbc.co.uk/news/science-environment-22063340* [Accessed 5 August 2016].

[30] A. Stangeland "Scenarios for Global CO2 Emissions" (2007) *Bellona Paper http://bellona.org/assets/sites/3/2015/06/fil_Bellona_Paper_-_Scenarios_for_global_CO2_emissions-29May071.pdf* [Accessed 28 September 2016].

Aircraft hulls are considered to be vulnerable to increased hailstorm and lightning strike losses.[31]

There is also the potential in the future that climate change litigation may be an existential risk to the aviation sector in the period of ten to twenty years hence; and something that insurers will wish to consider within their premiums. The nature and extent of that hazard is outside the scope of this text, but has been considered in some detail by the Bank of England Prudential Regulation Authority.[32]

Whilst there is no standard aviation policy, underwriters have developed standard **25-010** clauses over time covering basic coverage and main categories. These standard clauses can be altered or supplemented by class specific wording. Approved clauses were once allocated a unique reference and published by the Lloyd's Aviation Underwriter Association in the "Blue Book". Since 2005 the AICG has published non-binding standard wording, clauses and variants for use in aviation policies. These are the subject of user consultation and are published on the AICG website.[33] The published clauses are expressly non-binding and no recommendations are made as to the wording used or any variant. They are, however, commonly used with minimal variation.

London aircraft insurance policy (AVN 1C).[34] The standard text for a policy is **25-011** the London aircraft insurance policy (AVN 1C), first published in 1998.[35] This type of policy is issued by underwriters and sometimes brokers when the risks are much smaller. The standard AVN 1C is divided into four sections.

Section I. Section I concerns loss or damage to the aircraft with exclusions for **25-012** wear and tear, deterioration and breakdown.

Section II. Section II deals with legal liability to third parties (other than pas- **25-013** sengers) of accidental bodily injury (fatal or otherwise) and accidental damage to property caused by the aircraft or by any person,[36] or object[37] falling from the

---

[31] N. Bruce et al, "The Impact of Climate Change on Non-Life Insurance" Climate Change Working Party – GIRO (2007).

[32] *"The impact of climate change on the UK insurance sector"* Prudential Regulation Authority (September 2015).

[33] Bank of England Prudential Regulation Authority "The Impact of Climate Change on the UK Insurance Sector: A Climate Change Adaptation Report by the Prudential Regulation Authority" (2015) *http://www.bankofengland.co.uk/pra/Documents/supervision/activities/pradefra0915.pdf* [Accessed 3 August 2016].

[34] AVN 1C (21/12/98).

[35] See Lloyd's Aviation Underwriters Association *"Lloyd's Aviation Underwriters Association Standard Policy Forms, Proposal Forms and Clauses, Etc. Part 1"* (London Aviation Underwriters Association, 2010), *http://www.raaks.ru/docs/sb1.doc* [Accessed 5 May 2016].

[36] Sadly, such events are not unheard of—in September 2012 a stowaway fell from an aircraft onto a suburban street in West London having fallen from the undercarriage as it was lowered on the approach to Heathrow Airport. See P. Walker, *"Man found dead on London street 'was probably stowaway who fell from plane'"* (25 April 2013), *theguardian.com/uk, http://www.theguardian.com/uk/2013/apr/25/man-street-stowaway-fell-plane* [Accessed 5 May 2016].

[37] Ice forming on plane wings is a more common hazard. In 2009 a man in Bristol, England was struck by a lump of ice which it was believed fell from a plane. See BBC *"Ice falls from plane and hits man"* (8 July 2009), *http://news.bbc.co.uk/1/hi/england/bristol/8139714.stm* [Accessed 5 May 2016]. In 2007, an ice boulder punched a hole through the wall of a recreation centre in California, which the local airport said may have fallen from planes overhead. In 2003 a car in Manitoba, Canada, was struck by a basketball-sized chunk of ice believed to have come from a passing plane. See BBC News Magazine "What happens to ice falling from planes?" (9 July 2009), *http://news.bbc.co.uk/*

aircraft. Section II contains a number of exclusions, including employees engaged in the operation of the aircraft and injuries to passengers whilst entering, on board or alighting from the aircraft; liability for such injuries ordinarily come within the Montreal Convention[38] and the Warsaw Convention.[39]

25-014   **Section III.**   Section III of standard AVN 1C covers legal liability to passengers including personal injury claims which would ordinarily be brought under the Montreal Convention[40] and loss and damage to baggage. The same exclusions apply as under s.II.

Section IV contains general exclusions applicable to the preceding three sections including for example, exclusions for illegal use of the aircraft, transport of the plane by conveyance (such as by road), landing or take-off from a place outwith the manufacturers recommendations.[41] Section IV also contains a list of conditions precedent, most of which are within the "officious bystander" realms of obvious. These include the obligation of the insured to act with due diligence, to comply with air navigation and air worthiness orders and compliance with the laid down claims procedure. Commonly attached to the standard wording are a series of additional mandatory standard clauses (and exclusion clauses), identified by their respective international reference codes.

In 2012 the AICG agreed to review the wording of AVN 1C with a view to updating it but retaining the structure whilst allowing the addition of new clauses where appropriate. In March 2014 the AICG concluded its work and published AVN 1D,[42] following which it had to be slightly amended (as an error was found in the policy wording) on its website on 5 August 2014.[43] It seems likely, therefore, that AVN 1C (as amended) will be the default policy wording and structure that is used by underwriters for the foreseeable future. It is noteworthy to point out that on 8 December 2015 the AICG stated that it would commence a review of the Insurance Act 2015 ("the 2015 Act") and the potential impact of it on AVN wordings.[44] Subsequently AICG Consultation Draft 45 was published in May 2016 with comments open for one month.[45] On 26 July 2016, having considered the comments

---

1/hi/magazine/8141195.stm [Accessed 5 May 2016].

[38] Convention for the Unification of Certain Rules for International Carriage by Air ("Montreal Convention") T.S. 44 (2004) Cmnd.6369; 2242 UNTS 309.

[39] Convention for the Unification of Certain Rules relating to International Carriage by Air 1929 ("Warsaw Convention") T.S. 11 (1933) Cmnd.4284; P. (1932-1933) XXVIII 63; 134 B.S.P. 406; 137 L.N.T.S. 11.

[40] See above, fn.38.

[41] Exclusion clauses in CAR policies are dealt with in greater detail above, in Ch.15.

[42] AVN 1D (12/09/14).

[43] See AICG "Aviation Insurance Clauses Group (AICG) 31 October 2014 Annex 1 Ninth Statement of Activities October 2013 — September 2014 (inclusive)" (AICG, 2014). *http://www.aicg.co.uk/AICG_Web/Activity/AICG_Web/Activity.aspx?hkey=cf3af5e0-9f49-4aad-8c57-aef24e597eaf* [Accessed 6 May 2016] and AICG *"AVNID Redraft 050814: Aircraft Insurance Policy: Policy Schedule"* (AICG, 2014). *http://www.aicg.co.uk/AICG_Web/Clauses/AVN1D_Redraft_050814.aspx* [Accessed 6 May 2016].

[44] See AICG *"Aviation Insurance Clauses Group (AICG) 31 October 2015 Annex 1 Tenth Statement of Activities October 2014 — September 2015 (inclusive)"* (AICG, 2015). *http://www.aicg.co.uk/AICG_Web/Activity/AICG_Web/Activity.aspx?hkey=cf3af5e0-9f49-4aad-8c57-aef24e597eaf* [Accessed 10 May 2016].

[45] Aviation Insurance Clauses Group "AICG Consultation Draft No. 45 UK Insurance Act 2015 – Review of AVN Clauses and Wordings" (2016) *http://www.aicg.co.uk/AICG_Web/work_in_progress.aspx* [Accessed 28 September 2016].

regarding the proposed AVN policy wording and clauses produced in the light of the 2015 Act, some of them were approved and adopted.[46]

Changes have been made to AVN 1C,[47] AVN 37B,[48] AVN 47,[49] AVN 104,[50] AVN 105[51] and AVN 113[52] with key changes relating to:

1. Conditions Precedent;
2. Warranties;
3. Material Change;
4. False and Fraudulent Claims (the change herein is a correction to AVN 100, now AVN 100A (26/07/16)).

In addition changes have been made to AVN 66[53] and AVN 98[54] relating to:

1. Misrepresentation;
2. Compliance by the Insured with all conditions (a condition precedent to Insurers' liability).

Finally, changes have been made to AVN 21,[55] AVN 25,[56] AVN 34A,[57] AVN 41A[58] and AVN 89[59] (some of which are reinsurance clauses) concerning:

1. Warranties;
2. Conditions Precedent.

A new aircraft insurance proposal form (AVN 2C)[60] and AVN 36[61] on passenger settlement has also been produced. The endorsements to existing AVN wordings and amended AVN provisions (where changes relate to the specific) are to be used where the 2015 Act applies. But notwithstanding this, it is to be noted that the AVN policy clauses will still continue to form the foundation of aviation all risks insurance policies and will be amended as required to produce a bespoke aviation all risks policy.

Aviation all risks insurance policy. All risks is, of course, a misnomer. No insurance policy provides cover for literally every eventuality and aviation all risks is no exception.[62] Policies of insurance are as much defined by what they exclude as what they cover, and the key wording in any aviation policy usually follows the phrase "except as may be hereinafter excluded". The policy will include, for

25-015

---

[46] 16. See Aviation Insurance Clauses Group "AICG Consultation Draft No.45: Publication of New Clauses Per CD45 (Insurance Act 2015)" (2016) *http://www.aicg.co.uk/AICG_Web/work_in_progress.aspx* [Accessed 28 September 2016] and Aviation Insurance Clauses Group which lists all of the clauses that have been approved at *http://www.aicg.co.uk/AICG_Web/Product/AICG_Web/AICG_clauses.aspx?hkey=50cc4f72-2cb0-4bb7-9603-163752b22aa5* [Accessed 28 September 2016].
[47] AVN 1C Endorsement (26/07/16).
[48] AVN 37B Endorsement (26/07/16).
[49] AVN 47 Endorsement (26/07/16).
[50] AVN 104 Endorsement (26/07/16).
[51] AVN 105 Endorsement (26/07/16).
[52] AVN 113 Endorsement (26/07/16).
[53] AVN 66 Endorsement (26/07/16).
[54] AVN 98 Endorsement (26/07/16).
[55] AVN 21A (26/07/16).
[56] Now AVN 25A (26/07/16).
[57] Now AVN 34B (26/07/16).
[58] Now AVN 41B (26/07/16).
[59] Now AVN 89A (26/07/16).
[60] AVN 2C (26/07/16).
[61] Now AVN 36A (26/07/16).
[62] See above, paras 1-012 to 1-014.

example, risks of physical loss or damage.[63] The word "physical" is no drafting afterthought. The operator of an aircraft may lose the use of an aircraft without any physical damage at all. A (relatively) common instance is the grounding of a class or type of aircraft following one or more accidents or incidents which may suggest some inherent defect. A hitherto unprecedented example was the grounding of all aircraft within US airspace by the Federal Aviation Administration ("FAA") in the hours following the 9/11 attacks.[64] The aircraft in either instance were "lost" to the owners and operators for a considerable period, yet it is improbable—save for a tiny number which may have had very specific additional clauses—that the all risks policies in force paid out to any of the operators affected.

25-016   All risks itself may be sub-divided into all risks and all risks—while not in flight. Statistically aircraft are much more likely to be damaged, and to cause loss and damage, whilst on the ground. All risks—while not in flight will also cover damage whilst being taxied. A standard "aviation all-risks" policy will fall into essentially three categories of cover:

   (i)   aircraft hull and components; this covers physical loss or damage to the aircraft itself (subject to a variety of exclusions, such as mechanical wear and tear);

   (ii)   passengers, baggage (both registered baggage in the hold and unregistered baggage carried by passengers), cargo and mail carried on the aircraft; this will ordinarily be limited to passengers and items in transit, although both types of loss will normally be subject to exclusions and limitations under their respective conditions of carriage. A passenger will generally be defined as a person boarding, occupying or leaving an insured aircraft. The payment of a fare is not normally a pre-requisite; and

   (iii) third party liability for loss or damage to people and property outside the aircraft. This will include loss or damage to structures or items with which the aircraft accidently comes into contact with and physical injury to those outside the aircraft injured by the operation of the aircraft itself.

25-017   **Extensions to cover.**   In addition, the policyholder can take out additional cover to insure against perils normally excluded under an all risks policy. These are multitudinous but can include: (i) liability for defective product manufacture of the hull or components; (ii) war and associated perils; (iii) contingent liability for banks and financing organisations; (iv) liability cover for airport and airport operators and air traffic controllers; (v) maintenance, ground handling and refuelling liability; and (vi) extra expense protection—mitigating additional business cost following a catastrophic aviation event. For large risks, a specially tailored policy, such as an aviation all risks insurance policy will be drafted by an insurance broker, subject to the approval of underwriters and the lead underwriter who will decide whether or not to incorporate the wording into the policy document.

---

63   The requirement under an aviation all risks policy (and in the context of some general aviation policies) that the risks of physical loss or damage must result from an accident or occurrence may depending on the way the policy is worded be dispensed with by instead relying on the requirement of fortuity as imposed by law. See *Coven SpA v Hong Kong Chinese Insurance Co* [1999] Lloyd's Rep. I.R. 565 at 568; [1996] C.L.C. 223 at 226, per Clarke, LJ and above, Ch.10.

64   See A. Levin, M. Adams and B Morrison *"Part 1: Terror attacks brought drastic decision: Clear the skies"* (2008), *usatoday.com/, http://usatoday30.usatoday.com/news/sept11/2002-08-12-clearskies_ x.htm* [Accessed 6 May 2016].

2. ALL RISKS AIRCRAFT HULL AND LIABILITY INSURANCE

(a) Aircraft hull all risks insurance

Insured property. The term "aircraft" in a hull all risks policy is taken to mean **25-018** the aircraft itself, and can include for example all of the following:

> "Aircraft spare engines, spare parts, components and equipment (including equipment to aircraft and employees' tools), ground support equipment, medical equipment and all other equipment used in connection with the Insured's aviation operations related to the Services."

An aircraft hull all risks policy is normally taken out taken out by the owner of the aircraft to protect the aircraft against loss or damage to the aircraft itself. The responsibility is normally that of the owner and premiums will normally be included within any lease or charter price. This can be on a "total loss" basis or an "all risks" basis. If the hull policy is placed on an "insured" basis then the parties agree on the maximum sum for which the aircraft is insured. In the event of total loss, then the insured is therefore entitled to recover only the market value of the aircraft at the date (and if relevant, the place) of loss up to the agreed value insured under the policy. In respect of an "agreed value" policy, the parties pre-agree on the value of the aircraft to be paid in the event of total loss. The insurers then pay the agreed value of the aircraft, assuming it is destroyed and irreparable, irrespective of the market value at the date of loss. This type of policy is most commonly used when the aircraft is financed so that the parties know with certainty the sum to be paid out in the event of total loss of the aircraft.

Coverage. As noted above at para.25-008 a hull all risks policy does not provide **25-019** the insured cover for every eventuality or risk. The policy is subject to a number of standard exclusions, and normally excludes for example, mechanical (or machinery) breakdown. Separate insurance is available to cover mechanical breakdown, but it is not commonly purchased. A policy will normally simply say that cover is provided for "all risks of physical loss or, or damage to the Insured Property from any cause not excluded".

There are particular policy considerations regarding damage to aircraft engines. **25-020** Although plainly an integral part of the aircraft, unsurprisingly the aircraft engines are the component most likely to fail. Therefore, the policy normally limits coverage to ingestion of an object or objects which cause engine damage or engine failure, subject to those exclusions set out below.[65] The policy is likely to require strict conditions to be met regarding any claim for engine damage before cover is confirmed. These include: a provision that an object or material entered the engine from a region external to the actual engine itself[66]; that a log or record is made at the time of the occurrence or damage, and the notification was made to the insurers within a specified period (usually 30 days) of the log being made; that the engine was not run at any point after detection of the damage; and that the engine was dispatched for repair at the earliest available opportunity.

An all risks policy will indemnify the insured against liability and damage result- **25-021** ing from a specified event or an "occurrence". As with many similar policies, an occurrence is essentially an accident or unexpected or unintended event from the

---

[65] See below, para.25-038.
[66] That is, it was not an internal defect within the engine itself.

standpoint of the insured.[67] The primary difference being that the "accident" refers to an event causing injury or loss to an individual whereas an "occurrence" refers to the cause of the damage and not to the number of injuries or claims.[68] Thereby, in the event of a passenger aircraft accident, there is one occurrence, but several accidents.

25-022 The distinction may be of considerable importance. Following the invasion of Kuwait by Iraq in 1990, Iraqi forces seized a number of civilian aircraft from Kuwait airport, and flew them back to Iraq before the Gulf War broke out. The remaining aircraft (which belonged to a major UK carrier) at the airport were later destroyed by bombing during the ensuing war. In terms of determining the excess, it was necessary to determine whether the aircraft seized and taken back to Iraq were lost in the same event as the remaining aircraft destroyed at the airport. It was determined that the two events were distinct and there was no significant causal link.[69]

25-023 As with automotive cover, if the insurers are indemnifiable they will arrange (at their option) for the aircraft to be repaired or reinstated to its pre-accident condition, assuming the repairs can be safely undertaken and at a proportionate cost. The insurer will either directly commission the repairs to be undertaken, or agree to discharge the fees for repairs to be undertaken elsewhere. If the damage is irreparable, or can only be undertaken at a cost disproportionate to the value of the aircraft, then the policy conditions will determine the form of settlement.

25-024 Of course, unlike structures and buildings, aircraft are sometimes declared "lost" in that they do occasionally disappear, sometimes without leaving any trace.[70] The standard policy will consider an aircraft to have disappeared if it is unreported for a specific period (usually between 15 and 60 days) after the commencement of flight. This provision came under scrutiny following the loss of Malaysia Airlines MH370 in March 2016 where it was unclear for a considerable period what had happened to the aircraft or how it was lost. The situation was also repeated recently in May 2016 with the unexplained loss of EgyptAir flight MS804 over the Mediterranean.

In accordance with the 50/50 Provisional Claims Settlement clause, AVS 103,[71] in such circumstances the airline will still receive compensation timeously, with the underwriters of the "all risk" and "war risk" policies each agreeing to cover half the costs and the balance reimbursed if or when the cause of the loss is ascertained. Whereas premiums across the industry are not anticipated to be affected by such incidents, premiums for certain airlines and certain routes may well rise steeply.

25-025 **The insured.** The insured may be the owner or operator of the aircraft alongside any additional insured. The insured will be identified within the policy as set out in the schedule.

25-026 **The certificate of insurance.** A typical aviation certificate of insurance will identify the insured and any additional insured. This may include a charter or hirer

---

67 *CPC International Inc v Northbrook Excess & Surplus Insurance Co* (1992) 962 F.2d 77 at 87.
68 *South Staffordshire Tramways Co Ltd v Sickness & Accident Assurance Association Ltd* [1891] 1 Q.B. 402 at 407; 55 J.P. 372 at 372–373; 60 L.J.Q.B. 260 at 260–261.
69 *Scott v Copenhagen Reinsurance Co (UK) Ltd* [2003] EWCA Civ 688; [2003] 2 All E.R. (Comm) 190; [2003] Lloyd's Rep. I.R. 696.
70 *Scott* [2003] EWCA Civ 688; [2003] 2 All E.R. (Comm) 190; [2003] Lloyd's Rep. I.R. 696.
71 AVS 103 (12/10/83).

or individual owners for their respective rights and interest. The policy will identify the period of insurance (commencement and expiry dates) and the descriptor of the aircraft including its unique registration and its cargo and/or passenger capacity. The certificate will identify the combined single liability maximum (for any one occurrence) and the cargo legal liability. The certificate may go on to identify the minimum flying hours requirement of the captain/pilots and the uses to which the aircraft may be put under the terms of the policy. The certificate will also contain territorial exclusions which reflect the geo-political period in which the insurance is taken out. Typical exclusions include Iraq, Afghanistan, Libya, Rwanda, Sierra Leone, Sudan and Yemen as well as a number of other specified countries where specific risks are perceived to arise. The certificate will normally specify that in respect of an excluded country, coverage is granted for flight within an internationally recognised air corridor.

The insurance anatomy of a plane crash. In the event of (for example) a **25-027** catastrophic plane crash, many aspects of the insurance coverage will come into operation. The aircraft owner/operator will claim and receive indemnity payment from the insurer with whom the aircraft was insured. The insurance company (or more probably, companies) will provide a sum of money as per the sum insured, less the applicable deductible. Or the insurer will replace the aircraft entirely. Assuming a total loss crash, the family of the flight crew will receive death in service compensation under the terms of the crew personal accident insurance. The family members of the passengers will receive compensation as a result of the passenger liability insurance. The multiple owners of cargo and mail on board the aircraft will require compensation. Any property damaged or persons injured on the ground will be entitled to compensation. The insurer may also be required to pay for the recovery of the aircraft and associated debris. It is no small wonder that a single aircraft may have many insurers to spread the risk.

Sums insured. The insurer will commonly provide the insured with cover for loss **25-028** or damage to aircraft on an "agreed value" basis. This means that if the aircraft is destroyed that insurers will pay the agreed value in full. Such a clause may state the

> "[a]greed value of the Insured Property as per the schedule of aircraft subject to a maximum agreed value of [£] [in respect of] any one aircraft,"

subject to any deductible.

Maximum deductible. The policy will set maximum deductibles in relation to **25-029** each of the sums insured. A deductible is an uninsured amount that the insured must pay in respect of each loss insured. The deductible applicable to the policy is determined by reference to the MTOM of the aircraft concerned and the category within which the aircraft falls. Within the context of a hull all risks policy the deductible is defined as the amount or proportion to be deducted from claims in accordance with the hull policy, whether as a deductible of excess and applied in relation to each claim, or to each aircraft, or to each engine.

As with any other type of loss excluded under the hull all risks policy, the main **25-030** policy may be supplemented by a separate all risks deductible insurance policy. The purpose of this deductible insurance policy is to cover the aircraft for the amounts to be deducted from each and every claim by way of deductibles applicable in respect of loss or damage. The policy therefore pays up to the difference between the deductibles under the hull all risks insurance policy for each loss and the excess under the policy for each loss.

The deductible insurance policy will itself contain exclusions such as loss and damage confined to wear and tear, deterioration, freezing, mechanical, structural and electrical breakdown or failure.

25-031 **Territorial limits.** Aircraft are at least risk of damage whilst stationary. But that is not what aircraft are for. Whilst the insurers cannot determine where an aircraft will fly to, they can identify those areas where cover will be provided, and where it will not. An all risks policy will therefore contain a clause which will define the geographical scope of the cover. This may provide "worldwide" cover (for larger aircraft with a global reach) or be limited geographically to a defined area. Coverage for search and rescue helicopters, for example, is normally limited to the United Kingdom and its territorial waters. Territorial limits are normally defined by reference to political, rather than physical boundaries. Typical wording within a North American policy might be:

"... within the political boundaries of the United States of America, Mexico, Central America, Canada, the islands of the West Indies (excluding Cuba) and while enroute between places therein."

This wording may change to reflect the restoration of scheduled flights between North America and Cuba from February 2016.

25-032 Some policies will define the territorial limit as being "the Western Hemisphere" or, as indicated above "anywhere in the world". However, most polices have restrictions as to certain geographical locations, even those offering global coverage. Extension of territorial limits may be allowed to coincide with the particular needs of the policyholder and as indicated above,[72] flights over countries excluded under the terms of the policy may be permitted if an internationally recognised air corridor or if so directed by a national aviation body, such as the FAA (US) or Civil Aviation Authority ("CAA") (UK).

25-033 **Period of insurance.** As with almost any policy of insurance, the cover provided by the insurer will commence on a specific date identified within the policy, or on a date which is referable to a specific event. For example:

"From the date upon which the relevant Aircraft Hull 'all risks' Insurance risk commences which shall be no later than the Operational Delivery Date and renewable on an annual basis unless agreed otherwise by the Parties."

The insurer is not liable for an occurrence giving rise to losses which occurs outside the period of insurance and would ordinarily not be liable for those losses which may arise before the commencement of the period of insurance but continue once the period of insurance commences.

25-034 **Cover features and extensions—supplementary payments clause.** A supplementary payments clause (AVN 76)[73] extends coverage for specific accident-related costs and expenses which may arise following an insured incident. This will typically include:

(a) reasonable expenses incurred for the search and rescue of an insured Aircraft;

---

[72] See above, para.25-026.
[73] AVN 76 (09/02/01).

(b) expenses incurred at an airport to prevent or mitigate loss of an insured Aircraft (i.e. runway foaming to prevent or suppress fire);

(c) raising, removal disposal and destruction of the Aircraft itself (save when arising when the aircraft has reached the end of its serviceable life) including salvage expenses; and

(d) costs arising out of a consequential CAA inquiry (in the United Kingdom) or similar authority.

Because of the potential scope of such expenses, the insurers liability under the terms of the clause will be limited to a percentage (typically 10 per cent) of the aircraft agreed value.

(b) Exclusions

Principal exclusions. A more detailed section on exclusions standard to all poli-   **25-035**
cies of insurance can be found above in Ch.15 but there are those elements unique to aviation. In aircraft policies, specific exceptions, conditions and provisions are deemed to override general conditions, conditions and provisions.

Mechanical breakdown. The mechanical breakdown of an aircraft is normally   **25-036**
excluded in an aviation hull all risks insurance policy.[74] Mechanical breakdown is treated by insurers under a standard all risks policy as an operating expense, arising out of maintenance. But insurance coverage as against mechanical breakdown is available; although given the high degree of exposure the policy is accordingly relatively expensive. Accordingly many airlines choose not to carry insurance for mechanical breakdown.

Wear and tear, corrosion or erosion and gradual deterioration. This is   **25-037**
impliedly excluded from cover absent provisions to the contrary. Where wear and tear is insured the repair may result in betterment, in which the condition of the aircraft following repair is superior to that beforehand. In such circumstances, the policyholder insured may be required to contribute to the repair cost to reflect the "betterment".

Ingestion damage. Ingestion is the entry into the engine of items which may   **25-038**
cause damage to the engine or even stop it entirely. A single catastrophic ingestion incident, such as by a flock of birds, would ordinarily be covered by the policy. But aircraft engine indigestion also occurs daily with dust, grit, stones, ice and airborne material thrown up by the process of taking off and landing. This form of ingestion will rarely cause the engine to shut down, but does cause progressive deterioration within the engine and would therefore ordinarily fall within the gradual wear and tear exclusion.

Date recognition exclusion. The genus of this exclusion arose from the concern   **25-039**
that computer software may malfunction with the switch after 31 December 1999 to 1 January 2000. The "Millennium Bug" failed to materialise, but the exclusion clause lives on. As with all policies, once such exclusions become incorporated into the standard policy, they are easier to retain, and no-one wishes to take responsibility for their deletion. Such a clause will normally read as follows:

---

[74] The mechanical breakdown exclusion is also discussed in the context of construction above at para.15-075.

> "Date recognition exclusion in accordance with prevailing aviation insurance market practice AVN2000A[75] subject to AVN2001A".[76]

25-040 **Pressure waves caused by aircraft (or other aerial devices) travelling at sonic or supersonic speeds.** Although a common exclusion, there are as at date of writing no civilian supersonic aircraft in commercials service. Since the cessation of Concorde in 2003, only military jets reach supersonic speeds.[77]

25-041 **Contracts (Rights of Third Parties) Act 1999.** Typically, the provisions of the Contracts (Rights of Third Parties) Act 1999 are excluded under the standard wording in accordance with prevailing aviation insurance market practice AVN 72.[78] This clause will normally say:

> "The rights of a person who is not a party to this insurance or reinsurance to enforce a term of this insurance or reinsurance and/or not to have this insurance or reinsurance rescinded, varied or altered without his consent by virtue of the provisions of the Contracts (Rights of Third Parties) Act 1999 are excluded from this insurance or reinsurance."

Broadly, the 1999 Act permits third parties to enforce terms of contracts that provide them with a benefit, or which the contract allows them to enforce. It also grants the third party access to a range of remedies if the terms of the contract are breached. In addition, the 1999 Act limits the ways in which a contract can be altered without the permission of a third party who is a beneficiary under the contract. The 1999 Act also allows parties to a contract to specifically exclude the protection afforded by it, if they want to limit the involvement of third parties. AVN 72[79] provides for this exclusion.

25-042 **Nuclear risk exclusion.** The all risks policy explicitly excludes liability for "nuclear risks" by reference to standard policy terms contained within AVN 38B.[80] This would ordinarily be incorporated by the following standard wording:

> "Nuclear risks exclusion in accordance with prevailing aviation insurance market practice AVN38B."

AVN 38B excludes liability for loss or damage and the insurers legal liability for the radioactive, toxic, explosive or other hazardous properties of an explosive nuclear device or component of the same. It excludes liability for the radioactive properties of radioactive material whilst in cargo, or whilst being handled or in storage. It also excludes liability for contamination of any radioactive source whatsoever. Whilst the prospects of an airline storing or carrying a nuclear device or radioactive material inadvertently or unknowingly must be small, the risk of radioactive contamination of an aircraft by other sources must have seemed fairly theoretical, at least until the 2011 Japanese tsunami and the consequential damage to the Fukushima nuclear plant released unknown quantities of radioactive material into the environment.

25-043 **War and allied perils.** The war risks exclusion is usually incorporated via standard policy wording, such as: "[w]ar, hijacking and other perils exclusion clause

---

[75] AVN 2000A (03/14/01).
[76] AVN 2001A (03/21/01).
[77] However, see further above, para.15-066 and below, para.26-112.
[78] AVN 72 (02/09/00).
[79] AVN 72 (02/09/00).
[80] AVN 38B (10/10/02).

in accordance with prevailing aviation insurance market practice AVN48B",[81] which was published in 1996 and continues in general usage notwithstanding a review following the unprecedented multiple hijack incidents on 11 September 2001. A review of AVN 48B and AVN 51 (hulls)[82] and AVN 52 (liability)[83] write backs was undertaken because it was considered that these clauses were inadequate as they did not deal with the threat of weapons of mass destruction ("WMD") and terrorism sufficiently. However, since then similar versions of the AVN 48B clause, namely AVN 48C[84] and AVN 48D[85] (which deal with terrorism and WMD, e.g. chemical or biological attacks), have received regulatory approval. Following the events of 11 September 2001, insurers have generally restricted the level of primary third party liability cover for war, terrorism and other perils within the main liability policy to between \$150m (USD) and \$250m in the aggregate. A few governments still offer additional cover above this limit, but the majority of air carriers must obtain excess cover from specialist markets.

AVN 48B.[86] AVN 48B lists and defines what are terms "war and allied perils"; **25-044** which extends well beyond any common definition of war. The war need not in fact be a war, and "allied perils" encompass a wide range of acts by individuals and governments. These include:

(a) war—this includes civil war and war where there is no formal declaration;
(b) the detonation of a weapon of war employing nuclear fission or fusion;
(c) strikes, riots, civil commotions and labour disturbances;
(d) political or terrorist acts;
(e) malicious acts or acts of sabotage;
(f) confiscation, nationalization, requisition and the like by any government; and
(g) hijacking or any unlawful seizure or exercise of control of the aircraft or crew in flight.

In addition, the exclusion applies to any loss or damage occurring whilst the **25-045** aircraft is outside the control of the operator by reason of any of these "war and allied perils". AVN 48B plainly extends the exclusion beyond what may be considered as "war and invasion" perils. It excludes any hostile detonation of a weapon, strikes, riots, civil commotions, malicious acts or acts of sabotage, confiscation, nationalisation, seizure by any government or local authority and hijacking without the consent of the insured.

But aircraft operate in the practical world where wars break out, hostilities flare **25-046** and hijacking sometime occurs. Aircraft still have to fly and accordingly carriers and operators seek to expressly include cover for the various elements comprising "war and allied perils". These risks are covered by way of a separate policy.

---

[81] AVN 48B (10/01/96). In the London aircraft insurance policy AVN 1C the general exclusion covering war, hijacking and other perils is set out in s.IV, General exclusion 10(a).
[82] AVN 51 (10/01/96).
[83] AVN 52 (08/26/71).
[84] AVN 48C (04/08/06).
[85] AVN 48D (04/08/06).
[86] AVN 48B (10/01/96).

(i)   Aircraft hull war risks insurance

25-047   **Extended coverage endorsement (war risks).**   Although war "and associated perils" are ordinarily excluded in an all risks policy, commercial and civilian aircraft often operate in war-zones and areas of unrest, often precisely because they are the only relatively safe means of transport. After the invasion of Iraq for example, flying to or from Baghdad Airport was certainly risky, but travelling to and from the airport was considered to be much more risky. In the case of the aircraft hull, coverage is provided as required by a separate "war and allied perils" policy.

25-048   The insured may extend coverage endorsement under the terms of AVN 48B (war and associated perils)[87] in accordance with prevailing aviation insurance market practice. One of the reasons as to why insurers permit the write back of war risks in an aviation all risks insurance policy is because the insured has greater security as they are able to hold one set of insurers to account if a claim is made. Excluded war risks may be covered under LSW555 clauses (which are generally used for major airlines)[88] or by using either AVN 51 (hull)[89] or AVN 52 (liability)[90] clauses. AVN51, has a specified claim limit. Operators commonly "buy-back" the majority of these exclusions in respect of both hull and liability coverage. Operators can purchase a liability "write back" endorsement which provides liability coverage for the majority of the excluded perils contained in AVN 48B. AVN 52 is regularly amended and updated.[91]

25-049   Policies may therefore expressly include coverage for all acts of war, hostilities, actions for individuals whether acting as agents of a state or otherwise and hijacking. The extent of the exclusions to such polices can be of considerable importance. In the early 1970s, a hijacked aircraft was diverted to Cairo by a Palestinian armed group and later destroyed. The insured claimed under the all-risks policy which excluded liability for: (i) destruction by any military or usurped power; (ii) war, usurpation or revolution; and (iii) riots or civil commotions. It was determined that none of the exclusions applied and the all-risk insurer was accordingly liable for the loss of the aircraft.[92]

25-050   **LSW 555D.**   Hull war coverage can also be purchased independently, known as LSW 555D (also regularly updated and revised).[93] The coverage provided mirrors that excluded by AVN 48B[94] in respect of hull coverage and covers claims for physical loss and damage to the aircraft arising from:

    (a)   war, invasion, acts of foreign enemies, civil war, war where there is no formal declaration insurrection, revolution and usurpation (or attempted usurpation) of power;

---

87   AVN 48B (10/01/96).
88   LSW 555B (11/94); LSW 555C (06/05) and LSW 555D (04/06).
89   AVN 51 (10/01/96). In respect of AVN 51 the risks excluded by paras (c), (e) and (g) of AVN 48B may be written back into the policy.
90   AVN 52 (08/26/71). In respect of AVN 52 all of the risks excluded by paragraph AVN 48B except those set out in paragraph (b) may be written back into the policy.
91   See AVN 52C (01/10/96); AVN 52D (12/12/01); AVN 52E (12/12/01); AVN 52F (17/10/01); AVN 52G (17/10/01); AVN 52H (04/8/06); AVN 52J (04/8/06); AVN 52K (04/08/06).
92   *Pan American World Airways Inc v The Aetna Casualty & Surety Co* (1974) 505 F. 2d 989 (C.A.N.Y.); [1975] 1 Lloyd's Rep. 77 (US). In this case an aviation all risks and a separate war risk policy was effected.
93   See LSW 555B (11/94); LSW 555C (06/05) and LSW 555D (04/06).
94   AVN 48B (10/01/96).

(b) strikes, riots, civil commotions and labour disturbances;

(c) acts by one or more persons for political or terrorist purposes, whether the damage was deliberate or accidental;

(d) malicious acts or acts of sabotage;

(e) confiscation, nationalization, requisition and the like by any government or public body;

(f) hijacking or any unlawful seizure or exercise of control of the aircraft or crew in flight (defined as any time after the external doors are closed);

(g) ninety per cent of payment made by the insured as a result of threats or extortion in respect of threats against any Aircraft or its passengers or crew made during the currency of the Policy; and

(h) extra expenses necessarily incurred following confiscation or hijacking of the Aircraft stated in the Schedule.

Such policies whereby, for example, ransom demands are paid by insurers are not **25-051** lawful in every country and therefore the policy excludes such "unlawful" payments from the terms of the policy cover. It also has a safeguard in that any such payments made—in order to fall within the policy—must be permitted by the proper authorities. Insurers are only prepared to write back certain of the risk included in AVN 48B[95] in relation to aircraft hulls, and therefore if additional war risks are required these will be insured in the specialist war insurance market (part of the marine insurance market) for war risk insurance. Full war risk insurance cover remains available for hulls and passenger liabilities and options are available to purchase separate policies to increase the standard third party limit. The extended coverage provided by the war risks clause will only be provided by the insurer if the insured has paid or has agreed to pay the additional premium required by the insurers in respect of the extension. Substantial changes in security procedures since 2001 have resulted in much reduced premiums.

Where war risk coverage is expressly included, it has traditionally contained a **25-052** seven day notice clause which allowed insurers to review and reassess the risk and, if necessary, amend or cancel the cover in the event of a radical and adverse change in conditions or circumstances, such as occurred on September 11, 2001. In the immediate aftermath of this unprecedented event, the risk of loss from terrorism and hijacking could not be accurately assessed or priced. Thereby insurers invoked the only worldwide cancellation provision for all war risk cover on September 17, 2001, to take effect seven days later. Coverage was later reinstated for airlines following a global review on different terms than before.

Sum insured. The aircraft will, as under the hull policy, be insured at an agreed **25-053** level although any extortion, hijack or confiscation expense is likely to be limited at a sum far below the value of the aircraft. Such claims can be significant. In 2014, notable losses came from MH370, MH17, the attacks at Karachi Airport and the Tripoli Airport. The net hull reserve for Malaysia Airlines (MH370 — aircraft type B777-200) was $52,598,685 (USD); the loss of Malaysian Airlines (MH17) involved a net hull reserve of $97,335,000. The Tripoli Airport attack which involved a variety of aircraft the net hull reserve was $450,000,000. Airline Hull War losses in 2015 were $89,370,765 compared to $615,933,685 in 2014.[96]

Maximum deductible. As with the hull policy the deductible will be determined **25-054**

---

[95] AVN 48B (10/01/96).

[96] Jardine Lloyd Thompson Group "Technical Review of Aviation Insurance" (2016) *https://*

by the size of the aircraft, although special provisions may apply depending on the perceived risk within the territory where the aircraft is expected to fly or land. The deductible for payment of what are euphemistically-termed extortion and hijack "expenses" will be predetermined at a percentage of the sum paid.

25-055 Territorial limits. The standard hull policy excludes those parts of the world where there is unrest, has been unrest or there is a perception of unrest. The territorial restrictions within a policy explicitly taken out to cover war risks and allied perils is likely therefore to be more limited, it presumably being improbable that war or civil insurrection will imminently break out in the country concerned.

25-056 Period of insurance. This may mirror the hull policy or it may be shorter depending on the nature of the flights anticipated. In an area where the political climate is uncertain or volatile, the policy may be much shorter to enable the insurer to monitor the level of risk and review the premium and/or scope of cover (or whether cover is offered at all) more readily.

25-057 Aviation spares. The means by which spares may be covered for war and allied perils will depend on the structure of the policy concerned. This is discussed further below at para.25-058. If spares are covered under the standard hull policy, it is probable they will also be covered under an extension to that policy to cover war risks. Before considering whether spares are in fact covered, one must first determine what a spare (or spare part) actually is.

Under the terms of a hull all risks insurance policy, the "aircraft" consists of the hull, machinery, instruments and the entire equipment and components[97] of the aircraft. A part which is removed is treated as part of the aircraft. The status of the part is defined within the policy. "Parts being removed" is defined as until the moment such part is safely in contact with the ground or the trolley/stand on which it is to be located when the process of removing it from the aircraft is completed and it is totally disconnected from the aircraft. Once a part is replaced it is no longer, from an insurance perspective, part of the aircraft. Therefore in when determining what is a "spare", one uncomplicated answer might be: when it is not attached to the aircraft. The definition of "parts being attached" is from the moment that such part ceases to be in contact with the ground or the trolley/stand on which it is located when the process of fitting it to the aircraft is commenced. Once a spare part is attached to an aircraft, as an integral part of that aircraft (not carried in the hold as cargo), it is no longer a "spare". An extra pod carried on the wing, rather than in the hold, is not treated as being part of the aircraft.

25-058 Therefore, once the item concerned is classified as a spare, it requires insurance coverage. That can be achieved by either coverage within the "spares" section of a hull policy; or by a separate spares policy. Whichever it is, the scope of cover is likely to be broadly the same. Typical wording of spares insurance may be:

"Subject to the terms, conditions and exclusions hereinafter contained this Policy insures Property being only Engines, Spare Parts and Equipment destined to be fitted to or to form part of an aircraft and being the property of the Assured or the property of others for which the Assured is responsible, while such property is in the care, custody or control of the Assured on the ground, or is being carried as cargo in transit, by air (including Assured's aircraft) and/or steamers (approved or held covered at a premium to be arranged) and/or road and/or rail and/or conveyance."

---

www.jltspecialty.com/~/media/files/sites/specialty/events/jlt-aerospace/day-2/technical_review_aviation_coverage_2016.pdf?la=en-gb [Accessed 28 September 2016].

[97] e.g. Components of an aircraft may include for example, the airframe, engines and spares.

The care custody and control (known as CCC) provision has been determined to entail physical possession of the property; in others, any party with a legal obligation to exercise care with respect to property has been deemed to have that property in its CCC. The spares insurance, like all such policies, contains a number of internal exclusions. In addition to the standard exclusions for war, nuclear risks etc. the policy will also exclude liability for loss of or damage occurring at any time after the commencement of the operation of fitting it to or placing it on board the aircraft to which it is destined—at that point the spare becomes part of the aircraft itself. The policy also excludes those parts which have been temporarily removed for later refitting, those parts which are carried as a spare parts kit in the aircraft, or damages through deterioration and wear and tear and, perhaps most intriguingly; typical exclusion clause wording may include "[m]ysterious disappearance or unexplained loss or shortage disclosed upon taking inventory".

Principal exclusions.   Although virtually every exclusion under AVN 48B[98] can **25-059** be covered by either writeback or a separate specialist war policy, there is one overarching exception which cannot be covered. The rather apocalyptic exception to this availability of coverage is the detonation of a nuclear weapon and a war between the Great Powers (which within the aviation insurance sector are defined as the five permanent members of the Security Council—the United States, the Russian Federation, China, France and the United Kingdom). In such circumstances, it may be considered unlikely that insurance coverage issues would be the primary area of concern for the insured.

(b)   Aviation liability insurance

Third party liability.   The purpose of third party liability cover is to indemnify **25-060** the insured in respect of the sums that they may become legally liable to pay as a consequence of:

(a)   death, bodily injury, illness or disease contracted by any person; or
(b)   loss of damage to property,

which occurs during the period of the insurance. Invariably, such liability will be limited for each separate occurrence, but will commonly include liability to pay by way of contract, damages for tort, as well as the claimant's costs and expenses. Invariably, the potential damages liability if an aircraft crashes (for example) is somewhere between very significant and extremely large, and is almost entirely out of the hands of the insurer and the insured, hence the limitation of liability clause.

Bodily injury.   This is generally defined within the policy and is the phrase used **25-061** within the terms of the Montreal Convention[99] to define what is more generally known as personal injury. Personal injury within an aviation context is covered by AVN 60A[100] and is dealt with below at para.25-070. It is more akin to "offences against the person". Bodily injury is actual injury, sickness, death shock and (in some polices) psychiatric injury. Bodily injury is governed by initially by the

---

[98]   AVN 48B (10/01/96).
[99]   See above fn.22.
[100]   AVN 60A (12/24/04).

Warsaw Convention[101] and latterly the Montreal Convention[102] which determine the circumstances in which passengers on board an aircraft can claim and the maximum sums permitted. Under the Montreal Convention, the passenger need not establish any negligence. Article 17(1) of the Convention imposes liability on air carriers for bodily injury where injury is caused by an accident "on board the aircraft or in the course of any of the operation of embarking or disembarking …". An accident within the meaning of the Convention is an event which is unusual or unexpected and external to the passenger; the accident is not the fact of the injury.[103] Bearing in mind the predicted significant rise in air turbulence as a consequence of climate change (see above para.24-009) the potential for a rise in consequential passenger injury[104] and claims under the Convention is a real one.

25-062 Loss or damage to property. Cargo and mail are carried subject to conditions of carriage. The rules and regulations for the carriage of cargo were established by the Warsaw Convention in 1929.[105] The 1929 Convention (as updated by the Montreal Convention)[106] determines the sums that are payable under any claim. Such clauses are subject to exceptions, which are detailed below at paras 25-075 to 25-079.

25-063 Non-aviation liability. This is incorporated into aviation policies under AVN 59,[107] created in 1996, and excludes general third party liability save in four specified circumstances:

> "The Policy does not cover the Insured's liability unless it arises from one or more of the following:
>
> (a) Occurrences involving aircraft or parts or equipment relating thereto.
> (b) Occurrences arising at airport locations.
> (c) Occurrences arising at any other location in connection with the Insured's business of transporting passengers or goods by air.
> (d) Occurrences arising out of the supply of goods or services to others (i) in connection with the use and/or operation of aircraft; and (ii) involved in the air transport industry."

25-064 Aviation general third party liability. This covers liability for damage to property or persons arising out of the activities of the insured, but not directly as a result of use of the aircraft. This may include liability arising out of the use or occupancy of premises, liability arising when the insured has responsibility for aircraft or aircraft equipment on the ground ("hangarkeepers liability"); and liability for products sold or distributed by a party. The products concerned may be intangible (e.g. software) or may in fact be services (e.g. cleaning). Such policies are inevitably subject to a limit and a deductible.

25-065 Maximum deductible. As with the all-risks hull policy, the third party liability

---

[101] See above, fn.23.
[102] See above, fn.22.
[103] *Deep Vein Thrombosis and Air Travel Group Litigation* [2005] UKHL 72; [2006[1 A.C. 495; [2005] 3 W.L.R. 1320.
[104] In 2016, 30 passengers were injured following severe and unexpected turbulence on flight EY474 Abu Dhabi to Jakarta. Associated Press and Agence France-Presse "More than 30 injured as turbulence hits Etihad Airways flight to Indonesia" (5 May 2016) *https://www.theguardian.com/world/2016/may/05/injured-turbulence-etihad-airways-flight-indonesia* [Accessed 4 August 2016].
[105] See above, fn.39.
[106] See above, fn.38.
[107] AVN 59 (10/01/96).

policy will set maximum deductibles in relation to each of the sums insured. The approach is the same—and as may be seen above, the deductible is defined within the policy or policy extension: e.g. the deductible in respect of payment made in respect of a hijack or extortion is 10 per cent of the sum properly paid. Apart from that particular unusual set of circumstances, deductibles can represent significant sums to smaller airlines. Insurance policies are available to reduce the deductible exposure per event or within the course of one year.

Territorial limits.   The territorial limits under the third party liability policy will   **25-066**
mirror those under the all-risk hull cover. The territorial restrictions mirror the political climate of the date the policy is underwritten, although presumably once a territory finds its way onto the general exclusion list, it is rather difficult to get off it again. In 2012, the countries and regions whose geographical limits were generally excluded (under standard aviation practice LSW 617G,[108] subject to any writeback) were: Algeria, Burundi, Cabinda, Central African Republic, Congo, Democratic Republic of Congo, Eritrea, Ethiopia, Ivory Coast, Liberia, Mauritania, Nigeria, Somalia, The Republic of Sudan, South Sudan, Colombia, Ecuador, Peru, Afghanistan, Jammu & Kashmir, Myanmar, North Korea, Pakistan, Georgia, Nagorno-Karabakh, North Caucasian Federal District, Iran, Iraq, Libya, Syria, Yemen and any country where operation of the aircraft would be in breach of United Nations sanctions. Plainly, many of these countries have international airports and major airlines operate flights to and from most Western countries. Therefore it may be presumed that many were covered by extensions to policies almost as a matter of course.

LSW 617G was replaced with LSW 617H with effect from July 2015.[109] In contrast to LSW 617G it also excludes loss, damage or expense howsoever occurring within the geographical limits of the following countries and regions: the Far North Region of Cameroon, Abkhazia, Donetsk & Lugansk regions of Ukraine, South Ossetia and Lebanon. It does not however, include the following countries or regions, namely Cabinda, Congo, Eritrea, Ivory Coast, Liberia, Ecuador, Myanmar and Georgia.

Limit of indemnity.   As with any policy of insurance, the cover under a hull all   **25-067**
risks policy in respect of the third party liability section is subject to limits of indemnity within the terms of the policy, by standard wording such as:

> "Not less than a combined single limit for bodily injury and property damage, two hundred million pounds Sterling (£200,000,000) any one occurrence the number of occurrences being unlimited but in the annual aggregate in respect of aviation product liability."

The limits of liability will differ depending on the risk insured. The limit for grounding liability (i.e. the aircraft or fleet being grounded as a result of external forces) will be less than, for example, third party or product liability. It is for the insured to buy such cover as they consider they are reasonably likely to require. However, unexpected eventualities can and do arise. In January 2013, the FAA in the USA grounded Boeing's entire 787 Dreamliner fleet (approximately 50 aircraft) over battery-related problems.[110]

---

[108] LSW 617G (03/08/11).
[109] LSW 617H (09/07/15).
[110] See B. Jansen, *"FAA grounds Boeing Dreamliner jets"* (17 January 2013) *usatoday.com/*, *http://*

25-068 Choice of law in relation to policy interpretation. The policy, in accordance with similar insurance policies and other contracts, will have a standard choice of law clause, e.g. "[t]he insurance shall be governed and construed in accordance with the laws of England and Wales". The choice of law clause may indicate the appropriate legal jurisdiction for the resolution of any dispute. Such issues give rise to conflict of laws arguments as well as to *forum conveniens* arguments which are outside the scope of this chapter.

25-069 Period of insurance. The policy will contain a date (and usually a time) from which coverage is provided, either by reference to a defined date or specific event. The policy will also indicate the date on which coverage will expire, or be automatically renewed as applicable. Typical wording may say:

> "From the date upon which the relevant Aviation Liability Insurance risk commences, which shall be no later than the Operational Delivery Date and renewable on an annual basis unless agreed otherwise by the Parties."

(i)   Policy extensions

25-070 Personal injury extension. Whilst personal injury claims are covered under the terms of the standard policy and under the terms of the Montreal Convention 1999,[111] the insured can opt for a personal injury extension clause in accordance with prevailing aviation insurance market practice AVN 6OA.[112] This provides cover to indemnify the insured for legal liability for damages awarded to any person arising out of one or more of a number of specified offences committed during the policy period, but only where such offences are committed in connection with that part of the insured's aviation operations or interests for which other coverage is granted by the policy. These include:

(a)   False arrest, restraint, detention or imprisonment.
(b)   Malicious prosecution.
(c)   Wrongful entry, eviction or other invasion of the right of private occupancy.
(d)   Inadvertent discrimination with respect to withholding or refusal of transportation except with respect to overbooking.
(e)   The publication or utterance of a libel or slander or of other defamatory or disparaging material in violation of an individual's right of privacy except publication or utterance in the course of or related to advertising, broadcasting or telecasting activities conducted by or on behalf of the Insured.
(f)   Incidental medical malpractice, error or mistake by a physician, surgeon, nurse, medical technician or other person performing medical services but only for or on behalf of the Insured in the provision of emergency medical relief.

---

www.usatoday.com/story/travel/flights/2013/01/15/boeing-dreamliner-787-emergency-landing/1837943/ [Accessed 9 May 2016] (and similar global news outlets).
[111]   See above, fn.38.
[112]   AVN 60A (24/12/04).

Liability is limited to the specific figure stated in the policy.

Extended coverage endorsement (aviation liabilities). This is available under **25-071**
standard aviation practice AVN 52E[113] whereby the insured obtains cover for those
perils excluded under AVN 48D (war and associated perils)[114] and will identify those
clauses and sub-clauses within AVN48D which are to be treated as deleted.

Other liability extensions. Common extensions can be added for personal ac- **25-072**
cident insurance and illness or injury to the pilots resulting in loss of flying licenses.

Airside third party motor liability. If a vehicle travels airside (beyond the point **25-073**
where members of the public without boarding cards are generally not permitted)
for the purposes of collecting, dispatching or other business, it is likely that the
vehicles standard policy will not cover that vehicle in the event of an accident.
Airside liability insurance will provide specific cover for such eventualities for third
party vehicle and vehicle loss and damage (including personal injury). The standard
exclusions apply to such policies as apply to hull all risks including war, asbestos,
UK Road Traffic Act claims, radioactive contamination etc. and any claims covered
under other policies such as employers liability.

Supplementary payments clause. A supplementary payments clause (AVN **25-074**
76)[115] may be required for an aviation liability policy unless already covered within
the hull all risks policy.

(ii) Exclusions

Principal exclusions. Aviation liability insurance contains broadly the same **25-075**
principal exclusions in common with a hull policy, including the nuclear risk exclusion in accordance with insurance market practice AVN 38B,[116] war and associated perils (AVN 48B),[117] data recognition exclusion (AVN 2000A[118] subject to AVN
2001A),[119] and the Contracts (Rights of Third Parties) 1999 exclusion (AVN 72).[120]

Aggravation of existing injury. The policy excludes liability and expenses aris- **25-076**
ing from the aggravation of an existing illness or injury to an insured person
"howsoever caused", including consequential loss arising out of the carriage of
blood, plasma or human organs. The policy also excludes malpractice by a medical professional which causes an injury, loss or expense. The conduct concerned
need not amount to negligence but can simply be an omission, or mistake.

Noise and pollution and other perils. The policy will contain a noise and pol- **25-077**
lution and other perils exclusion clause, in accordance with prevailing aviation

---

113 AVN 52E (12/12/01).
114 AVN 48D (08/04/06).
115 AVN 76 (02/09/01).
116 AVN 38B (22/07/96).
117 AVN 48B (10/01/96).
118 AVN 2000 (14/03/01).
119 AVN 2001A (21/03/01).
120 AVN 72 (09/02/00).

insurance market practice AVN 46B.[121] This excludes liability for loss and damage caused (directly or indirectly) by noise whether audible or inaudible (to the human ear), or vibration or sonic boom. Pollution and contamination are also excluded (in conjunction with AVN 38B concerning nuclear risk)[122] as well as electrical and electromagnetic interference and interference with the use of property unless caused by or resulting in a crash fire explosion or collision or a recorded in-flight emergency causing abnormal aircraft operation.

25-078   Asbestos.   Loss or damage arising from asbestos is excluded in accordance with prevailing aviation insurance market practice LSW 2488 AGM 00003.[123] This exclusion is unusual in that it not only deals with the actual presence of asbestos but the *alleged* or *threatened* presence of asbestos, presumably even where none is actually present. The clause excludes liability for claims of any kind, arising out of or in consequence of:

(a)   the actual, alleged or threatened presence of asbestos in any form whatsoever; or

(b)   any request or obligation upon the Insured or others test for or remove or treat the actual, alleged or threatened presence of asbestos.

The exclusion does not apply to any claim caused by or resulting in a crash, fire, explosion or collision or a recorded in-flight emergency causing abnormal aircraft operation.

25-079   Other exclusions.   Whilst the precise wording of individual clauses will vary from policy to policy, there will too be consistency in the areas excluded. These areas are extensive and in addition to those set out above include exclusions of liability for loss or damage arising out of:

(a)   liability assumed by the insured under a contract or agreement unless pre-agreed by the insurer;

(b)   vehicles owned or operated by the insured in the public highway;

(c)   bodily injury or sickness or death of an employee—although this may be the subject of an extension to the policy;

(d)   claims arising out of employment or dismissal;

(e)   unlawful activities or liabilities arising out of fiduciary duties;

(f)   costs arising out of the repair or replacement of defective goods or products;

(g)   ownership or operation of non-aviation-related property such as hotels;

(h)   shops restaurants save for those operated by the insured at airport premises; or

(i)   advertising and promotional activities.

(c)   Cargo all risks insurance

25-080   Cargo all risks.   Cargo is the term used to identify goods (excluding passenger baggage) carried onto an aircraft. Such carriage is usually subject to an airway bill or consignment note that sets out the conditions and limitations applicable to their carriage. Such goods are sometimes described as "freight", although freight (or freightage) actually describes the fees paid to the carrier for carriage of cargo.

---

[121]   AVN 46B (01/10/96).
[122]   AVN 38B (22/07/96).
[123]   LSW 2488 AGM 00003 (10/08/12).

There are, in the London market at least, two types of cargo insurance. Cargo legal liability insurance offers protection to the carrier for legal liability resulting from the loss or damage to goods whilst in the care, custody or control of the carrier.[124] Cargo all risks insurance is affected by the consignor or consignee against loss or damage of the cargo during shipment by air.

LPO 359B.[125]   Loss or damage to cargo or mail[126] is not ordinarily covered by a   **25-081** standard hull all risks policy and therefore such cover is affected by a separate policy or endorsement to an existing policy. Standard wording within the London market (LPO 359B)[127] provides both types of cargo insurance, typical wording of which will read:

"(a) to indemnify the Assured for all sums up to any one aircraft or location, which the Assured becomes legally liable to pay for physical loss of or damage to cargo under the Warsaw Convention or under other Conditions of Carriage agreed by Underwriters hereon including cargo in respect of which a Special Declaration of Value for Carriage in excess of the normal limit of liability provided for by the Warsaw Convention is made by the Consignor prior to or at the time of the issue of the Air Waybill or other Contract of Carriage.

(b) coverage with respect to such Cargo shall commence from the time of issue of the Air Waybill or other Contract of Carriage by the Assured or their Agent for carriage by aircraft and connecting land and water conveyances and shall terminate upon delivery by the Assured or their Agent at final warehouse or upon handing over to the succeeding Carriers or their Agent or if Through Air Waybill or Contract of Carriage be issued and any succeeding Carriers are unwilling to accept the Special Declaration of Value then this Policy will cover interest to destination named in the Air Waybill or Contract of Carriage."

As indicated, the consignor or consignee will frequently take out all risks cover   **25-082** in respect of cargo shipped by air. This may be done is various ways. It can be effected via the insurance held by the air carrier and under the terms of their policy (such as LPO 359B above)[128] or taken out under a separate policy of insurance. The airline may be authorised under the terms of their all risks policy to bind the insurer in respect of cargo and baggage in respect of the consignee's request for insurance. This is envisaged under, for example, LPO 359B[129]:

"The Assured and their Agents are authorised to bind and issue on behalf of the Underwriters Certificates of Insurance with respect to Cargo, including Baggage carried as Cargo, in response to a Consignor's request for insurance thereof against ALL RISKS OF PHYSICAL LOSS OR DAMAGE in accordance with:

INSTITUTE CARGO CLAUSES (AIR);
INSTITUTE WAR CLAUSES (AIR CARGO);
INSTITUTE STRIKES CLAUSES (AIR CARGO)."

The policy will ordinarily cover loss and damage whilst being carried in the aircraft itself, including the loading and unloading of the cargo. The policy may also

---

[124] See above para.25-058 regarding the "care, custody and control" provision.
[125] LPO 359B (01/07/96).
[126] Mail is ordinarily carried under the terms of a separate contract between the national postal authority, or private courier, and the airline.
[127] LPO 359B (01/07/96).
[128] LPO 359B (01/07/96).
[129] LPO 359B (01/07/96).

cover the cargo when in transit between its departure location and the aircraft, and from the aircraft to its next destination. These locations will be defined within the policy itself. As well as physical damage to cargo when in transit by air, a policy will also cover the cargo for a specified period (e.g. up to 60 days) whilst in storage after flight or while awaiting flight transport.

25-083 **Constructive total loss.** Where the policy contains a constructive total loss provision regarding cargo, the clause will provide that no claim shall be recoverable unless the subject matter insured is reasonably abandoned on account of its total loss being unavoidable or because the costs of recovering, repairing/reconditioning and forwarding the cargo concerned to its (insured) destination would exceed the likely value upon arrival.

25-084 **Exclusions.** Airlines have limited control over what they carry and such policies obviously include a range of standard exclusions to reflect the fact that the cargo may be carried by the insured's aircraft, but has been packed by a third party. Therefore the insured excludes liability for including consequential loss howsoever arising, for leakage or breakage of the cargo not caused by an accident (e.g. inappropriate packaging) or contamination by leakage from other cargo, even where the cargo is the property of the insured.

25-085 The policy will also contain a wide range of exclusions for loss or damage to cargo, many of which are similar if not identical to marine insurance, this includes loss arising from:

    (a)   wilful misconduct[130] or negligence of the insured or his employees or agents;

    (b)   delays to delivery[131] to the destination(s) identified within the policy;

    (c)   wear and tear, depreciation or gradual deterioration of the cargo;

    (d)   matters which are outside the scope of transit of the cargo are also excluded such as:

        (i)   the adverse actions of insects or vermin;

        (ii) any process or cleaning or restoring or repairing;

    (e)   explicitly, defective packaging of the cargo itself—or other cargo in proximity which results in damage to the insured cargo;

    (f)   any loss arising from the inherent "vice or nature" of the cargo itself, such as a latent defect;

    (g)   losses arising from strike or civil commotion, revolution and the like;

    (h)   losses arising from the unfitness of the aircraft carrying the cargo;

    (i)   insolvency of those responsible for the aircraft; and (j) war and allied perils.

25-086 The policy will also exclude payment by the insured when the same cargo is covered under any other insurance. Such issues can obviously arise when cargo is damaged as a result of a third party who carries its own third party liability insurance. The policy may also entitle the insurer, much as with the hull policy, to replace the cargo or make good the loss and damage, rather than make payment. A like-for-like replacement is not necessary under the policy, and the common phrase used is as found in insurance policies worldwide arising out of replacement in lieu

---

[130] A phrase, in this context, taken from art.25 of the Warsaw Convention. See above, fn.39.

[131] Regarding mail, most national postal services do not accept any liability to delays to delivery in any event.

of loss and damage, that of: "substantially as nearly circumstances permit, and in a reasonably sufficient manner".

In November 2008, the Joint Cargo Committee ("JCC") released a series of **25-087** Institute Cargo Clauses[132] concerning cargo liability[133] and specimen exclusionary clauses concerning war[134] and strikes.[135] In July 2013, the JCC released a series of supplementary[136] and specimen[137] clauses concerning the transport of cargo which was primarily commodities (cocoa, coffee, cotton, hides, sugar etc). In respect of standard exclusions for war and strikes, these can be written back utilising the Institute War Clauses (Air Cargo)[138] in respect of loss or damage occasioned by war and allied perils; and the Institute Strikes Clauses (Air Cargo)[139] in respect of war, civil war, insurrection and similar. Following the revision of the ICC, the Commodity and Ancillary Cargo Clauses were updated after a lengthy consultation process took place. The final clauses were published by the LMA on 3 May 2016.[140]

---

[132] See "*JCC Cargo Clauses*" (24 November 2008) *http://www.lmalloyds.com/lma/underwriting/marine/ JCC/JCC_Clauses_Project/Cargo_Clauses.aspx* [Accessed 11 May 2016].

[133] For goods carried by ship CL.382 ICC (A) (01/01/09); CL.383 ICC (B) (01/01/09); CL.384 ICC (C) (01/01/09) and by air CL.387 ICC (Air) (01/01/09).

[134] CL.388 ICC (Air Cargo) (01/01/09) SPECIMEN.

[135] CL.389 ICC (Air Cargo) (01/01/09) SPECIMEN.

[136] CL.418 (01/06/13); CL.419 (01/06/13); CL.420 (01/06/13); CL.421 (01/06/13).

[137] CL.410 (01/06/13); CL.411 (01/06/13); CL.412 (01/06/13); CL.413 (01/06/13) DRAFT; CL.414 (01/ 06/13); CL.415 (01/06/13); CL.416 (01/06/13); CL.417 (01/06/13).

[138] CL.388 ICC (Air Cargo) (01/01/09).

[139] CL.389 ICC (Air Cargo) (01/01/09).

[140] 1CL. 391 (03/05/16); CL. 392 (03/05/16); CL. 393 (03/05/16); CL. 394 (03/05/16); CL. 395 (03/ 05/16); CL. 396 (03/05/16); CL. 397 (03/05/16); CL. 398 (03/05/16); CL. 399 (03/05/16); CL. 401 (03/05/16); CL. 402 (03/05/16); CL. 403 (03/05/16); CL. 404 (03/05/16); CL. 405 (03/05/16) and CL. 406 (03/05/16).

PROPERTY ALL RISKS

1. INTRODUCTION

(a) Property insurance

Property insurance. When the construction works are complete and the defects **26-001** liability period (if applicable) has ended, property needs to be insured. The property insurance industry has grown significantly since the first commercial fire-insurance policies became available shortly after the Great Fire of London in 1666. In 2014, 1.56 million claims were made on household insurance with a total value of £2.9 billion or £8.2 million per day. During this period, a further £4.7 million per day was paid to businesses on property damage, or in total 1.7 billion.[1]

Property insurance at its most basic provides cover from either specified risks or all risks for damage to a building (house, factory, office block) and its contents (personal possessions, stock, business assets). Property insurance is very competitive. Businesses in particular want to maximise their cover and will look to insurers to cover them for all risks and a wider scope of losses including consequential losses, such as "business interruption", which may be combined with or separate to an all risks property insurance ("ARPI") policy. In contrast to a CAR policy, which provides cover against loss or damage to works during construction, this chapter focuses on the broadest type of cover provided by the insurance industry for property after it has been built, namely ARPI for commercial property[2] to cover the physical assets of the completed project, combined with business interruption insurance ("BII") to cover for loss of profits arising from physical damage.[3]

(b)   All risks property insurance

26-002   **ARPI.**   ARPI is a policy which insures against all risks as opposed to specified perils (e.g. flood, fire, earthquake, terrorism, etc.). As with CAR insurance, all risks property policies can be a misnomer as the policies are subject to a number of exceptions and will, for example, not cover loss caused by wear and tear or inherent vice. The real effect of the term "all risks" is that the insured is only required to prove that there has been a loss and that loss was fortuitous. The burden of proof then shifts to the insurer to show that the loss was caused by one of the excluded perils. If the insurer cannot do so then the insured is entitled to recover. ARPI is becoming increasingly popular in the property insurance market because it is seen as being a more attractive option for the insured. It is generally thought that the substance of the coverage on all risks insurance is actually quite similar to that under "specified risks" due to the use of exclusions, but all risks cover is preferred by policyholders because it removes doubts over non-specific contingencies and puts the onus on the insurer to show that the exclusion applies.

(c)   Contractors' all risks insurance and all risks property insurance

26-003   **From construction insurance to property insurance.**   CAR insurance generally runs to the certified date of practical completion of the works, but may be extended to include the defects liability period, if a defects liability clause[4] in the construction contract requires the contractor to obtain such cover for latent defects.

---

1   Association of British Insurers ("ABI"), *"UK Insurance and Long Term Savings Key Facts 2015"*, (September 2015) *https://www.abi.org.uk/~/media/Files/Documents/Publications/Public/2015/Statistics/Key%20Facts%202015.pdf* [Accessed 12 May 2016].

2   There are three main types of commercial property: industrial, such as: warehouses, industrial estates, studio units; retail such as: shopping centres, supermarkets, shops, convenience stores; and offices, such as: ordinary offices, serviced offices and business parks.

3   In the past it has been referred to as "consequential loss insurance". See below, paras 26-053 to 26-105.

4   See, for example JCT Contracts, *SBC/Q 2011 JCT Standard Form of Building Contract With Quantities* 2011 (London: Sweet & Maxwell, 2011), p.68 cl.6.5.1 states that if damage to property occurs through no fault of the contractor, then subject to the exclusions mentioned, the contractor is required to obtain insurance to be maintained for this until the expiry of the defects liability period. See also above, para.2-084.

The defects liability period normally runs for 6 or 12 months following practical completion of the works. The CAR insurance ceases to attach following the expiry of the defects liability period. After this point, the employer will need to obtain adequate property insurance in order to insure that the completed property is covered for property damage. If this was not the position, then the contractor would be liable for damage to the property for an indefinite period.

Contractors' all risks and all risks property insurance compared. In *Swiss* **26-004** *Reinsurance Co v United India Insurance Co Ltd*[5] Morison J succinctly set out the differences in risk between an "active" construction site and a "passive" property site. Where a building project has been abandoned, he said:

> "Instead of there being risks associated with a building project with a contractors' all risks cover, the emphasis is now on the dangers of fire, deterioration owing to climate and damage due to inclement weather. The site is passive and not active. What was insurance in relation to a substantial building project has become an insurance resembling property insurance; CAR policies are essentially different from property insurance, although some of the risks may be the same in each."

As the above quote highlights, the risks faced by an insured during an abandoned construction project, under a CAR policy will nearly be the same as those faced in respect of a completed building project, which is covered by a property insurance policy (e.g. storm, tempest, flood, subsidence, fire, lightning and explosion). However, in contrast to a CAR policy, property insurance policies will also provide coverage for escape of liquid and loss or damage caused to a building as a result of an impact (such as by a vehicle, train, animal or aircraft). CAR policies are however, fundamentally quite different to ARPI policies. First, in terms of structure, although the headings in each policy will be similar (such as the insuring clause, extensions and exclusions), the substantive content will differ according to the project, property or business concerned.[6] Secondly, coverage under a CAR policy will be for works during a construction project, whereas under a property insurance policy it will be for a completed building. Other notable differences between the two types of insurance cover are the indemnity period, that is to say the fact that property insurance is only annual, whereas under CAR insurance both annual and project-based cover is available and finally the types of consequential loss cover provided by insurers. For example, under a CAR policy, delay in start-up ("DSU") insurance[7] may be provided whereas under an ARPI policy BII may be provided.

2. THE INSURED AND INSURED PROPERTY

(a) General considerations

The insured. As with construction insurance there are often multiple parties seek- **26-005** ing insurance cover with different interests in the insured property.[8] For property insurance, as compared to construction insurance, it is usually easier to identify the party's legal or equitable interest in the property. There may be one insured who owns the freehold unencumbered and occupies the building. However, it is more

---

[5] *Swiss Reinsurance Co v United India Insurance Co Ltd* [2005] EWHC 237 (Comm) at [32]; [2005] 2 All E.R. (Comm) 367 at 376; [2005] 1 C.L.C. 203 at 216.
[6] See below, para.26-019.
[7] See further above, paras 17-048 to 17-077.
[8] See above, para.20-030.

likely the premises will be let, sub-let and/or charged to one or various lenders. The most typical interests are the freeholder, landlord, tenant, mortgagor and mortgagee and it is likely that all the parties will want their respective interests to be protected by insurance.

26-006 **An insurable interest and the indemnity principle.** As discussed in detail above in Ch.9, the requirement of an insurable interest under the common law is in an unsatisfactory state.[9] In the context of property insurance, the prevailing view is that statute does not require an insurable interest in the property as a precondition to recovery under an insurance policy.[10]

Difficulties with an "insurable interest" are largely avoided in practice due to the fundamental principle of indemnity in insurance law, which requires that a party can only recover that which it has lost and no more, which will often lead to the same result as would the requirement to show an insurable interest.

The indemnity principle can be easily misunderstood. A valued policy is sometimes viewed as an exception to the indemnity principle, because the insured may recover more than he has lost, but actually this is a means by which the parties can agree the level of indemnity in advance. So it is not against the indemnity principle, but rather a contractual variation of the same. Further, where a party has a limited interest in a property (e.g. tenant or mortgagee) they can often insure more than the actuarial value of their interest as a marketable asset. This, again, does not violate the indemnity principle because the appropriate indemnity depends on what the party's legal obligations are as to the use of the insurance proceeds when he has got them. If he is accountable for the proceeds to the owners of the other interests, then he will not be receiving more than an indemnity if the insurer pays the full amount for which the property was insured. This will be so, whether the insured is accountable to the owners of the other interests as a trustee of the proceeds of the insurance or simply on the basis that he owes them a contractual obligation to pay those proceeds over to them or to employ them in the reinstatement of a building.[11]

For example, in *Lonsdale & Thompson Ltd v Black Arrow Group Plc*; sub nom. *Lonsdale & Thompson Ltd v Black Arrow Group Plc and American International Underwriters UK Ltd*,[12] the insured landlord seemed to suffer no financial loss where the property was damaged after a sale had been agreed by him and the purchasers still paid the insured the full purchase price. The court held that the landlord had insured the whole of his interest in the property for full reinstatement value against specified perils and that it expressly said in the lease that he had a liability to the tenant to reinstate the premises, which was unaffected by the subsequent receipt of the purchase price. The payment of that money had thus not diminished the loss and the insurers were held to be liable for the cost of full reinstatement of the property. Therefore a party's obligations need to be considered as well as the value of his proprietary interest to determine the appropriate

---

[9] See above, para.9-040.
[10] *Mark Rowlands Ltd v Berni Inns Ltd* [1986] Q.B. 211 at 227–228; [1985] 3 W.L.R. 964 at 975; [1985] 3 All E.R. 473 at 481, per Kerr LJ approved by the Privy Council (Hong Kong) in *Siu Yin Kwan v Eastern Insurance Co Ltd* [1994] 2 A.C. 199; [1994] 2 W.L.R. 370; [1994] 1 All E.R. 213.
[11] See below, para.26-047 to 26-048.
[12] *Lonsdale & Thompson Ltd v Black Arrow Group Plc* [1993] Ch. 361; [1993] 2 W.L.R. 815; [1993] 3 All E.R. 648.

indemnity and his insurable interest. This point is discussed in more detail below at para.26-018.

Joint or composite insurance. Where two or more interests are insured under a **26-007** single policy the insurance will be either "joint" or "composite". There can only be joint insurance where the interests in the subject-matter are joint interests, exposed to the same risks and will suffer a joint loss by the occurrence of an insured peril, for example joint owners of property.[13]

Where the interest of each insured is different and the amount of each party's loss, if the subject-matter of the insurance is destroyed or damaged, depends on the nature of his interest, then the insurance must be composite rather than joint. A composite policy comprises in one policy the interests of a number of persons whose connection with the subject-matter of the insurance makes it natural and reasonable that the whole matter should be dealt with in one policy.[14] The significance of this distinction is that where parties are jointly insured a non-disclosure, misrepresentation or wilful misconduct on the part of one insured will affect the rights of the co-insured to recover on the policy.[15] In contrast, where the insurance is composite, the wilful misconduct or fraud of one party will not prevent an innocent co-insured from recovering in respect of his loss.[16]

Fires Prevention (Metropolis) Act 1774. Section 83 of the Fires Prevention **26-008** (Metropolis) Act 1774 gives "interested persons" the right to demand that insurance money is used to reinstate the property after damage by fire, rather than being paid to the policyholder. This provides a way for persons who are not insured but have an interest in the property to call for reinstatement.

Originally s.83 of the 1774 Act was enacted as a way of preventing arson or fraud. Now it is more useful in cases where landlords have either not pursued claims or have been intransigent or slow in dealing with a claim, or where the insured is

---

[13] See above paras 20-030 to 20-031.

[14] *General Accident Fire and Life Assurance Corp Ltd v Midland Bank Ltd* [1940] 2 K.B. 388 at 404–405; [1940] 3 All E.R. 252 at 257–258; (1940) 67 Ll. L. Rep. 218 at 234–235, per Sir Wilfrid Greene MR. This part of the judgment has been described as "the classic statement of the difference between a joint and a composite insurance" in *Netherlands v Youell* [1997] 2 Lloyd's Rep. 440 at 447; [1997] C.L.C. 938 at 947, per Rix J.

[15] *P Samuel & Co Ltd v Dumas (The Grigorios)*, sub nom. *P Samuel & Co Ltd v Motor Union Insurance Co Ltd* [1924] A.C. 431; (1924) 18 Ll. L. Rep. 211; 93 L.J.K.B. cited in *Netherlands* [1997] 2 Lloyd's Rep. 440 at 446–447; [1997] C.L.C. 938 at 946. But in *Netherlands*, Rix J makes the point that the concept of separate interests under a composite insurance is to be distinguished from the concept of a "pervasive interest" where the owner of one such separate interest may have to claim in respect of the loss suffered by all separately interested co-insureds under a single policy on property. A claim upon a pervasive interest by an entirely innocent insured may well be affected by defences available to insurers by reason of the wilful misconduct of a co-insured; *Netherlands* [1997] 2 Lloyd's Rep. 440 at 450; [1997] C.L.C. 938 at 949.

[16] See above para.20-034 and *Parker v National Farmers Union Mutual Insurance Society Ltd* [2012] EWHC 2156 (Comm); [2013] Lloyd's Rep. I.R. 253 where the insurer was not able to avoid the policy as against a wife who owned the relevant property, in circumstances where she was not aware of her husband's (a named insured) previous fraudulent claim, and nor was she a party to a conspiracy to set fire to the relevant property. Her right to claim was not affected by her husband's misconduct because the nature of their interests was different (with the wife as legal and equitable owner of the property and her husband had at best an equitable interest); it was therefore a composite policy.

insolvent, to prevent the insurance monies being paid to the insured's creditors.[17] Although it is still of some relevance it is little used, due to: (i) commercial preferences of insurers to reinstate rather than pay money over; (ii) tenant's interests being noted on policies; and (iii) the modern convention of leases incorporating a covenant to reinstate.[18]

(b) Specific interested parties in insured property

26-009 **Vendor and purchaser of land.** Difficulties can arise due to the staged process of exchange and completion for the sale of buildings in England and Wales. Under the common law, the risk immediately passes to the purchaser once a valid contract for sale of land has been entered into, unless the contract expressly states otherwise. The legal title does not pass until completion but when any loss or damage arises in the intervening period between exchange of contracts and completion this loss falls upon the purchaser who must accept a conveyance of the damaged property and pay the full contract price. The purchaser's insurable interest arises at the signing of the contract as at that point he has an equitable interest as he is entitled to specific performance of the contract. Further, the property is at his risk and any loss or damage to the property would diminish the value of his contractual right and therefore he has an insurable interest in the loss he may suffer.

26-010   An unpaid vendor in possession after exchange of contracts maintains an insurable interest to the full value as he has right to possession of the premises and a lien for the purchase money. If it were otherwise he would suffer great inconvenience and would have to rely on the solvency of the purchaser of his property.[19] The solution adopted in practice is by standard terms of sale which are different for residential and commercial property.

The current 5th edition of the Law Society, *Standard Conditions of Sale* ("SCS")[20] for residential sales took effect on 1 April 2011, and provides that the purchaser is to assume the risk from the date of exchange (reversing the position from in the 4th edition of the SCS).[21] The terms do not oblige the purchaser to insure the property, but any purchaser would be well advised to do so, since they will be obliged to complete the purchase even if the property is destroyed. The vendor may still have an obligation to insure the property between exchange and completion by virtue of condition 5.1.2 of the SCS.[22] Under this condition the vendor is obliged

---

[17] Law Commission, "*Law Commission: Review of Insurance Contract Law. Section 83 Summary of Responses*" (February 2010), *http://www.lawcom.gov.uk/wp-content/uploads/2015/03/ICL_s83_Fires_Prevention_Act_responses.pdf* [Accessed 17 May 2016].

[18] Law Commission, "*Law Commission: Review of Insurance Contract Law. Section 83 Summary of Responses* (February 2010), *http://www.lawcom.gov.uk/wp-content/uploads/2015/03/ICL_s83_Fires_Prevention_Act_responses.pdf* at [1.16] citing unpublished academic research [Accessed 17 May 2016].

[19] *Collingridge v Royal Exchange Assurance Corp* (1877) 3 Q.B.D. 173 at 177; 42 J.P. 118 at 119; 47 L.J.Q.B. 32 at 34, per Mellor J.

[20] Law Society, *Standard Conditions of Sale*, 5th edn (London: Law Society, 2011). Available at: *https://www.lawsociety.org.uk/support-services/advice/articles/standard-conditions-of-sale/* [Accessed 17 May 2016].

[21] Law Society, *Standard Conditions of Sale*, 4th edn (London: Law Society, 2003).

[22] Law Society, *Standard Conditions of Sale*, 5th edn (London: Law Society, 2011). Available at: *https://www.lawsociety.org.uk/support-services/advice/articles/standard-conditions-of-sale/* [Accessed 17 May 2016].

to insure if the contract so provides, or if the property is leasehold and the vendor (whether as tenant or landlord) is obliged to do so under the terms of the lease.[23]

The Law Society *Standard Commercial Property Conditions* ("SCPC")[24] provide alternatives for responsibility for insuring the property between the purchaser and the vendor. There is no purchaser's right to rescind under the SCPC if the property burns down between exchange and completion so the risk passes to the purchaser on exchange. The SCS have now been brought in line with the SCPC in this regard.

Landlord and tenant.   Where a property is tenanted, insurance can be taken out **26-011** by either the landlord or the tenant or both. The nature of a landlord or tenant's insurable interest depends on the terms of the lease. A landlord has an insurable interest as a reversioner. In addition, he may be obliged under the lease to undertake repairs[25] and can therefore insure to the extent to which he may become liable under covenant to repair (usually the full reinstatement value) and is not limited to the value of the reversion. A tenant, on the other hand, has an insurable interest due to their right to possession, their liability to pay rent and any liability to repair.[26]

Most leases will contain a covenant to insure, which is in itself an insurable interest, as a failure to obtain insurance will lead to liability for loss suffered as damages for breach of covenant. The obligation to insure can be either on the landlord or the tenant, as directed by the lease, to insure for specified "insured risks" or "all risks". Damage from an uninsured risk will be the responsibility of the tenant unless the lease states otherwise, as landlord's reinstatement obligations are usually limited to damage caused by insured risks. For this reason an all risks policy may be better for both landlord (who is more likely to be able to recover from the insurer) and tenant (who is less likely to be liable if the damage falls outside the insured risks).

Landlord's covenant to insure.   The terms of the lease may require the landlord **26-012** to obtain insurance on behalf of himself and the tenant. This is usual on a multi-occupied site, such as a shopping centre or an office block. The tenant will be required to contribute to the insurance premium by an additional element in the rent or service charge. The insurance will then have been obtained on the tenant's behalf and the policy is composite[27] and accordingly each party, as an independent insured, has independent rights against the insurer.[28]

---

[23] Further conditions relating to insurance are set out at 5.1.3 to 5.1.5 of the Law Society, *Standard Conditions of Sale*, 5th edn (London: Law Society, 2011).

[24] See conditions 7.1.2 (for the seller) and 7.1.3 (for the buyer) of the Law *Society Standard Commercial Property Conditions*, 2nd edn (London: Law Society, 2004), pp.3–4. Prior to this condition 7.1.1 states that the seller is required to insure the property "… if: (a) the contract provides that the policy effected by or for the seller and insuring the property or any part of it against loss or damage should continue in force after the exchange of contracts, or (b) the property or any part of it is let on terms under which the seller (whether as landlord or as tenant) is obliged to insure against loss or damage."

[25] Where the property is let as a dwelling-house for less than seven years the landlord will have repairing obligations under statute: Landlord and Tenant Act 1985 s.11.

[26] *MacGillivray on Insurance Law*, edited by J. Birds, B. Lynch and S. Milnes, 13th edn (London: Sweet & Maxwell, 2015), paras 1-151 to 1-152.

[27] See above, paras 20-030 to 20-031.

[28] The insurer could then seek to be subrogated to the rights of the landlord against the tenant or vice versa if the damage was caused by their actionable fault; see below for limits to such subrogation at para.26-150.

Where a tenant is liable to pay insurance premiums to the landlord in respect of residential property, the tenant has various protections under the Landlord and Tenant Act 1985. The tenant has rights to obtain a summary of insurance cover, to notify the landlord's insurer of a possible claim, and to challenge unsatisfactory insurance.[29] In contrast, no similar statutory protections exist for tenants of commercial premises. To try and avoid the need for such similar legislation, a voluntary code, produced by the Joint Working Group on Commercial Leases called *Code for Leasing Business Premises in England and Wales 2007*,[30] has been published as a result of collaboration between commercial property professionals and industry bodies representing both owners and occupiers. The Code sets out best practice in relation to lease negotiations and lease renewal, which includes, where the landlord is arranging insurance, for it to be fair and on reasonable terms and to disclose any commission they will receive.

If a tenant wants to be certain that the landlord will have to use the insurance monies for reinstatement works, then the lease should expressly put the landlord under an obligation to do so. Although, in *Mumford Hotels Ltd v Wheeler*,[31] the landlord only covenanted to insure (through payment of premiums by the commercial tenant) and not to reinstate but the court held that the landlord was obliged to use the insurance monies for reinstatement if called upon to do so because the landlord's obligation to insure at the tenant's expense was intended to have effect for the benefit of both the landlord and tenant.

26-013 **Tenant's covenant to insure.** If the tenant is under an obligation to insure, and he insures for his benefit only, then he can recover no more than he has personally lost, unless he is obliged, e.g. by a covenant to repair or reinstate in the lease, in which case he is liable to his landlord in respect of the whole value of the loss.

A lease may also include: (i) a rent abatement/suspension clause whereby the tenant has no liability to repair damage caused by an insured risk and the rent is abated or suspended for an agreed period when damage by an insured risk occurs[32]; (ii) requirement for rent to be insured; (iii) requirement for engineering insurance; (iv) choice of insurer; (v) subrogation rights under policies in landlord's name[33]; (vi) covenants for lessee to carry out requirements of insurer e.g. upkeep of fire prevention equipment and notification of material changes in risk.[34]

26-014 **Commonhold land.** Commonhold land is a relatively new way of owning freehold properties that are divided into separate units with some communal facilities. It is a creature of statute and governed by extensive regulations[35]; although it has proved less popular than anticipated.

---

29 Landlord and Tenant Act 1985 s.30A and Schedule (on the Rights of Tenants With Respect to Insurance) to the 1985 Act.
30 The Joint Working Group on Commercial Leases, "*The Code for Leasing Business Premises in England and Wales 2007*" (2009) *Leasingbusinesspremises.co.uk*; *http:// www.leasingbusinesspremises.co.uk/index.html* [Accessed 19 May 2016].
31 *Mumford Hotels Ltd v Wheeler* [1964] Ch. 117; [1963] 3 W.L.R. 735; [1963] 3 All E.R. 250.
32 See below, para.26-031.
33 See below, para.26-150.
34 See below, paras 26-128 to 26-138.
35 Part 1 of the Commonhold and Leasehold Reform Act 2002 came into force on 27 September 2004 together with the Commonhold Regulations 2004 (SI 2004/1829) as amended by the Commonhold (Amendment) Regulations 2009 (SI 2009/2363) and the Commonhold (Land Registration) Rules 2004 (SI 2004/1830).

Under the commonhold scheme, individuals own the freehold of a unit (e.g. flat or shop), and the freehold of the common parts are owned and managed by a commonhold association whose members are the unit holders. Thus the unit holders have the security of a freehold but the common parts will be managed for the benefit of all the unit holders. The rules are set out in a commonhold community statement ("CCS"); a copy of a model CCS is set out in Sch.3 to the Commonhold Regulations 2004 (SI 2004/1829). The CCS must make provision for and impose duties in respect of the insurance, repair and maintenance of each commonhold unit.

Generally, therefore, the individuals arrange insurance of their freehold unit, and the commonhold association is responsible not only for the insurance of all common parts (against fire and other specified risks) but also for any units for which the CCS puts an onus on the association. Further it is usual for the commonhold association to be required to use the proceeds of any insurance for the purpose of rebuilding or reinstating the common parts.[36]

Mortgagor and mortgagee. A mortgagor of land, as the owner of the equity of redemption, has an insurable interest to the full value, notwithstanding the mortgage. He may be impecunious but so long as he has the equity of redemption, the loss of the property means a reduction in his assets to the full value of the property, and therefore he has an interest to that extent.[37]   **26-015**

Mortgagees, both legal and equitable, have an insurable interest in the mortgaged property to the amount of the debt secured, and if a mortgagee has covenanted to insure he has an interest to the full amount in respect of that liability. A mortgagee to whom a title to any property has been conveyed will have an insurable interest to the full value of the property; though he will hold on trust any indemnity owed to the mortgagor.[38]

Although mortgagees have a power under s.101(1)(ii) of the Law of Property Act 1925 to insure where a mortgage is made by deed, there are limits to this statutorily conferred power, which mean that it is usual for the mortgage deed to include a covenant by the mortgagor to insure the security for a specified amount, or for the full value of the property. Further, there may be an express covenant that the mortgagee may require the proceeds of the policy to be used to reinstate the premises or to pay off the mortgage debt.

If the policy is in the name of the mortgagor pursuant to a covenant to insure, the mortgagor is entitled to the proceeds in law and the mortgagee has an interest by way of a charge on the proceeds in order to secure the mortgage debt.[39]

---

[36] This stipulation is set out at para.4.4.2 of the example commonhold community statement ("CCS") contained in a document published by the Department for Constitutional Affairs called *Commonhold Guidance on the Drafting of a Commonhold Community Statement Including Specimen Local Rules* (London: Department for Constitutional Affairs, 2005). See *http://webarchive.nationalarchives.gov.uk/+/http://www.dca.gov.uk/legist/commholdone.htm* [Accessed 19 May 2016].

[37] *MacGillivray on Insurance Law*, edited by J. Birds, B. Lynch and S. Milnes (2015), para.1-154.

[38] *Hepburn v A. Tomlinson (Hauliers) Ltd* [1966] A.C. 451 at 469–470, 478–482; [1966] 2 W.L.R. 453 at 459, 466–470; [1966] 1 All E.R. 418 at 423–424, 428 431. Hepburn holds that the mortgagee can recover for his own and a mortgagor's interest without needing to prove an intention to recover. In *Hepburn*, the House of Lords discussed *Irving v Richardson* (1831) 2 B. & Ad. 193; 9; (1831) 1 Mood. & R. 153. *Irving* previously held that the mortgagee could recover above his own interest, if he could prove an intention to insure for the mortgagor.

[39] *Colonial Mutual General Insurance Co Ltd v ANZ Banking Group (New Zealand) Ltd* [1995] 1 W.L.R. 1140; [1995] 3 All E.R. 987; [1995] 2 Lloyd's Rep. 433.

26-016 Trustee and beneficiary. A trustee holds legal title and may therefore insure the subject-matter of the trust to its full value,[40] he would then be accountable to the beneficiaries for such insurance proceeds as he may receive. A beneficiary under a trust can insure his equitable interest in the property independently.

26-017 Personal representatives. As with trustees, executors and administrators have an insurable interest in the deceased's estate.[41] Money paid under a policy effected or renewed by an executor is payable to the parties interested in the property insured. It cannot be considered as part of the testator's general personal estate.[42]

26-018 Bailor and bailee. Where premises are insured that contain goods in which the insured has no proprietary or equitable interest commonly the insured will be a bailee of these goods, if they are held voluntarily in possession and he has assumed responsibility for their safe keeping (e.g. car in a garage, or storage of goods). It depends on the wording of the policy as to whether and to what extent those goods are covered by the insurance. Generally, although a bailee's interest is limited to the extent of his liability to the bailor, he will also generally be able to insure to the full value of the goods.

It became customary for insurers to use the words "for which the insured is responsible", in order to restrict liability for damage to goods held by a bailee to circumstances when the insured bailee was liable for the damage. This line of authority was carefully examined and upheld in *Ramco (UK) Ltd v International Insurance Co of Hanover*.[43] If however, the insurer agrees to insure the goods and does not clearly make such an exception then the insured bailee will commonly recover the full value regardless of whether they are legally liable, although they would be liable to the owners of the goods (or other persons bearing the loss) for the excess.[44]

Where both bailor and bailee have insured the same goods, the contracts of insurance are entirely independent and so the position is as follows[45]:

1. The bailor has a right directly against the bailee in respect of the goods consumed by the fire as "the primary liability";
2. If the bailor's insurers pay the amount of the insurance before the primary liability has been fulfilled, the bailor's insurers can bring a subrogated claim against the bailee and their insurers;
3. If the bailee or their insurers fulfil the primary liability and pay the value of the goods destroyed before the bailor's insurers have paid under their policy, the bailor has no claim upon its own insurers.

---

[40] *Yallop, Ex Parte* (1808) 15 Ves. Jr. 60 at 67; 33 E.R. 677 at 680, per Lord Eldon. Trustees also have various statutory powers under which insurance can be effected, see s.19 Trustee Act 1925; s.8(3) Trustee Act 2000 and s.6(1) Trusts of Land and Appointment of Trustees Act 1996. For the application of insurance monies see s.20 Trustee Act 1925.

[41] See *Re Betty* [1899] 1 Ch. 821 and statutory powers under the Trusts of Land and Appointment of Trustees Act 1996 by virtue of the Administration of Estates Act 1925 s.39(1)(ii).

[42] *Parry v Ashley* (1829) 3 Sim. 97 at 100.

[43] *Ramco (UK) Ltd v International Insurance Co of Hanover* [2004] EWCA Civ 675; [2004] 2 All E.R. (Comm); [2004] 2 Lloyd's Rep. 595.

[44] *Hepburn* [1966] A.C. 451; [1966] 2 W.L.R. 453; [1966] 1 All E.R. 418.

[45] *North British & Mercantile Insurance Co v London Liverpool & Globe Insurance Co* (1877) 5 Ch. D. 569 applied in *Darrell v Tibbitts* (1880) 5 Q.B.D. 560 at 565–566; 44 J.P. 695 at 696; 50 L.J.Q.B. 33 at 37, per Thesiger LJ.

In terms of the policy proceeds, unless the owners specify in the contract of bailment that the insured would insure the goods, the owners would only have an action in contract against the bailee for surplus funds. If the requirement for insurance was incorporated into the contract of bailment then the insured would hold the surplus funds on trust.[46] This is an important distinction if the insured were ever to become insolvent.

3.   THE ALL RISKS PROPERTY INSURANCE POLICY

(a)   Overview

All risks property insurance policy structure.   A skeletal structure of a typical **26-019** ARPI policy, combined with BII, is set out below. An ARPI policy will normally be accompanied by a schedule and also a specification. The schedule will set out the key policy details such as the insured property, period of insurance, sum insured and details of premium.

Property (All Risks) Insurance Policy
Contents
1.   Our agreement in general
2.   Insured section A – Property
3.   Insured section B – Business interruption
4.   Insured section A and B exclusions
5.   Duties in the event of a claim or potential claim
6.   General terms and conditions
7.   General definitions and interpretation
8.   Complaints

The insured property section of the policy (s.A) listed above is also called the "Material Damage" section of a policy. It contains all the provisions relevant to buildings and contents insurance, as well as the extensions, exclusions and terms and conditions that are relevant to the policy. The BII section of the policy (s.B) again sets out the extensions including cover to be provided at and away from premises, the limitations and exclusions, terms and conditions applicable to the policy. The policy will also set out the exclusions, duties in the event of a claim and general terms and conditions applicable to both sections of the policy. A variation of the ARPI is that of commercial combined policies or a "Commercial All Risks" policy, which may contain other separate extensions in appendices in addition to the business interruption section, such as public liability,[47] mechanical failure[48] and terrorism.[49] This wider type of policy is not discussed in this work.

The schedule contains important information relevant to both the material dam- **26-020**

---

[46]   *Re E Dibbens & Sons Ltd (In Liquidation)* [1990] B.C.L.C. 577.
[47]   See above, Ch.18 for a discussion about public liability in general.
[48]   Mechanical failure is both an extension and an exclusion in commercial all risks policies. See further above, at paras 15-075 to 15-077 for a discussion about this clause in the context of construction all risks insurance ("CAR").
[49]   Terrorism is both an extension and an exclusion in commercial all risks policies. See generally above, para.15-047 which, mentions terrorism in the context of CAR and also para. 25-043.

age and the business interruption sections of the policy. An example of an ARPI policy schedule is set out below.[50]

Policy No:
The Schedule
THE INSURER
THE INSURED
THE BUSINESS
THE PREMISES

THE PROPERTY IN-SURED	As detailed in Section 1	)
		)
		) of the attached Specification
ITEMS (Business Interruption)	As detailed in Section 2	)

	Section 1 Material Damage	Section 2 Business Interruption
TOTAL SPECIFICATION SUM INSURED AND/OR ESTIMATED GROSS PROFIT	£	£
LIMIT OF LIABILITY AND DEDUCTIBLES	LIMIT OF LIABILITY DEDUCTIBLE	LIMIT OF LIABILITY DEDUCTIBLE
In respect of: (i) Loss destruction or Damage by fire lightning Explosion aircraft or Other aerial devices or Articles dropped Therefrom riot civil Commotion strikers Locked-out workers Persons taking part in Labour disturbances Malicious persons or Earthquake	The sum the first Insured £	The sum the first Insured or £ as detailed in the Specification
(ii) Loss destruction or Damage by storm flood Escape of water from Any tank apparatus or Pipe or impact by any	£ the first £	£ the first £

---

[50] This working example is set out in a policy produced by the Association of British Insurers called "Standard All Risk Policy (Material Damage and Business Interruption)" which is contained in Section 2 Appendix 8 of a publication produced by the Association of British Insurers called the "Blue Book".

Road vehicle or animal

(iii) other insured loss ££   ££

Destruction or damage

THE SUM INSURED ££ being [ ]% of the respective total Specification AND / OR ESTIMATED sums insured and/or estimated gross profit GROSS PROFIT BY THIS POLICY

INSURER'S LIABILITY   The insurer's liability under this policy is limited to [ ]% of the Amounts otherwise payable under the provisions of the Specification and this Schedule

                                            THE SCHEDULE

PERIOD OF INSURANCE   From

RENEWAL DATE   to

FIRST PREMIUM   Section 1

                                      Section 2

                                      Sub Total

                                      Insurance premium tax

                                      Total

ANNUAL PREMIUM   Section 1

                                      Section 2

                                      Sub Total

                                      Insurance premium tax

                                      Total

AGENCY

Note: For insurance solely on a Sum Insured basis references to Estimated Gross Profit should be deleted.

The ARPI policy structure is broadly the same as that of the CAR policy. Both **26-021** will have a recital or "principal operative clause" at the start, signed by the parties, setting out the agreement in the broadest terms, usually including a statement of the applicable jurisdiction. Both policies will contain schedules describing the insured, the property, locations, the sums insured under each section, and the payable premiums. The most obvious similarity is that both policies set out the distinct types of cover provided in separate sections, each section having its own definitions, clauses and supplemental conditions (sometimes known as memoranda). Both forms of policy will have general exclusions, terms, conditions, conditions precedent and claims conditions applicable to the policy generally. In terms of the structure of both these policies the main difference is the type of cover under each section and that the CAR policy will usually contain a section on third-party liability/ public liability, which is not applicable to an ARPI policy.

4. THE INSURED PROPERTY

(a) The insuring provision (material damage)

The insuring provision (material damage). A typical ARPI indemnity clause **26-022** will read as follows:

"In the event of the Insured Property described in the Schedule being accidentally lost destroyed or damaged during the Period of Insurance the Insurer will pay to the Insured the value of the property at the time of loss, damage or destruction or the cost of repair or at the Insurer's option reinstate or replace such property or any part of it provided that the liability of the Insurer shall not exceed the Sum Insured or any other limit of liability stated in the Schedule."

The insuring provision must be read together with any terms in the policy as to the basis of settlement. These will generally set out that in the event of damage the basis on which the insurer's liability is to be calculated is on the cost of reinstatement of the property.[51] This is subject to certain exceptions, for example, reinstatement costs will not be paid where the repairs are not undertaken. Insurers can reinstate at their option but if they take on responsibility for reinstatement they will be liable for the reinstatement cost even if it exceeds the sum insured. Understandably, insurers will rarely want to take on this liability.

26-023 **Insured property.** The property insured will be defined in the schedule to the policy. A simple definition adopted in the policy might describe the premises as "[b]uildings including landlord's fixtures and fittings therein". Modern commercial insurance policies tend to include wider and more detailed definitions such as the one set out in the following extract:

"Buildings shall mean buildings (including foundations); landlord's fixtures and fittings (including all machinery, plant and consumables used in connection with the premises), and tenant's improvements for which the landlord is responsible, on or around the buildings; building management and security systems; furnishings and other contents of common parts of the buildings; gangways, pedestrian malls and pedestrian access bridges; walls, gates, fences and services (defined elsewhere); roads, pavements, car parks and street furniture; landscaping and recreational features, including garden furniture and statutes."[52]

The precise wording of each policy will vary and the exercise of determining whether a particular property is covered by the definition is a question of contractual interpretation.[53] The schedule should be clear if the policy covers contents including stock and/or money. The premises must be sufficiently described for the insured to be able to demonstrate that the damaged property is covered by the insurance policy. If the building has not been correctly described to the insurers then this will be a bar to an action.[54]

26-024 **Damage.** Loss or damage must be physical loss or damage as detailed in Ch.14 above.

26-025 **Fortuity.** Property insurance, as with insurance generally, provides cover for accidental events. It does not cover, for example, deliberate harm or inevitable occurrences. These principles of fortuity are discussed in detail above in Ch.10.

---

[51] See below, paras 26-047 to 26-048.
[52] Royal Institute of Chartered Surveyors. (2010) *RICS Practice Standards UK, Insurance for Commercial Property Managers*, 1st edition, Guidance Note (GN 62/2010), s.3.1.2, p.10.
[53] See above Ch.9, especially paras 9-056 to 9-058.
[54] *Dobson v Sotheby* (1827) Mood. & M. 90; 173 E.R. 1091.

The period of insurance.   Most property policies are for a fixed period of one   **26-026**
year and are renewed by payment of premium. This differs to CAR policies, which
often last for the length of the construction project.[55]

Sum insured.   The sum insured should usually be the reinstatement cost.[56] It must   **26-027**
be sufficient to represent the cost of reinstating any building insured should it be
destroyed. It will generally be calculated for commercial properties on a day one
reinstatement basis.[57] A party insuring a commercial property should use a surveyor
to calculate the reinstatement value at least every few years.[58]

(b)   Property extensions

Capital additions.   For an additional premium a capital additions clause will   **26-028**
cover the insured for changes in value or additions to the property over the period
of insurance up to a specified limit. The limit may be expressed as a percentage of
the sum insured or an additional insured value. The advantage of such a clause is
that it cuts down on the administrative inconvenience of notifying the insurer of
changes on a regular basis.

Glass, glass surrounds and washroom facilities.   The insurer may require an   **26-029**
increase in the premium to cover glass and items used in bathrooms and the like,
which are highly susceptible to damage. Such items include glass cabinets, mirrors, shelves, bespoke shower doors and windows but also ceramics like cisterns,
wash basins and baths.

Metered water.   Under this extension the insurer will cover any charges the   **26-030**
insured is responsible for and unable to recover from any other party in respect of
loss of metered water or gas, provided that such loss is due to damage at the
premises covered by the policy.

Loss of rent.   Most leases will contain a rent suspension or abatement clause   **26-031**
whereupon a tenant is not liable to pay the rent while the property is unavailable
and/or inaccessible to the tenant. The precise length of abatement will be prescribed
by the wording of the lease. A landlord can obtain an extension for loss of rent insurance to cover this period.

This type of clause will be more complex in multi-tenanted properties and when
there is a degree of inter-reliance, e.g. shopping centre. A landlord would need to
consider obtaining cover not just for loss of rent and service charge but also secondary sources of rent such as advertising space and car parks, together with post-loss
expenditure (re-letting, business rates, professional fees), as well as any new rental
income lost from premises not yet leased and rent increases that would have arisen
during indemnity period.

The indemnity period should be the longer of either: (i) the rent abatement period
in the lease; or (ii) the expected period for rebuilding and finding a new tenant. The
standard period is three years but different periods are not unusual.

---

[55]   See above, paras 4-008 to 4-013.
[56]   See below, para.26-047.
[57]   See below, para.26-048.
[58]   For a discussion about the sum insured and reinstatement in a CAR context, see above paras 3-031
to 3-032.

26-032   Valuables.   A valuables clause will usually place a cap on the valuables insured (e.g. works of art and jewellery). If the insured is aware of valuable items stored at the property, then these should be specifically identified in the schedule to ensure that the items are insured for an appropriate sum.

26-033   Professional fees.   In common with the standard CAR extensions considered above,[59] it is usual for this type of clause to be included, limiting the fees to those necessarily incurred in the reinstatement of loss in the event of damage (i.e. architects, surveyors, engineers and others). This will specifically exclude professional fees incurred in the preparation and negotiation of claims settlements.[60]

26-034   Debris removal.   This will usually provide cover for the costs and expenses incurred by the insured in removing from the property (or in and around the adjacent area, within a specified distance) debris from or clearing drains, sewers and/or gutters of, or dismantling or demolishing the insured property that has been damaged. It may also include removal of extraneous material and can extend so far as to make the building secure and safe for others who may decide to use or trespass on it, as well as clearing up any pollution or contamination (but not in respect of property that is not insured by the policy). The costs (and therefore the premium) will be much higher if access to the site is restricted and/or if the building is not able to be dismantled easily.[61]

26-035   European Union and public authorities.   This extension clause provides that insurers will pay the insured the additional costs incurred for reinstatement to meet modifications required by building or other regulations or any statute or bye-laws. In practice this relates to legislative requirements such as providing disabled access for the building and improved fire protection, such as fire doors, fire compartments and enclosed staircases. Other requirements can relate to green issues and making buildings more energy efficient. It will usually exclude any costs incurred where compliance was sought prior to the damage happening.[62]

26-036   Trace and access.   Without this extension an ARPI policy would only cover the cost of reinstating damage caused to the insured property by a burst pipe. The "trace and access" extension provides certainty for the insured in that they are also covered for tracing, accessing and repairing the leak, and making good any damage caused.

26-037   Landscaping/trees/shrubs.   Insurance cover may also be provided to a property owner for trees, landscaping, plants and lawns by way of an extension to the policy. The trees, landscaping, plants and lawns extension may be especially important in and around a building to a property owner in an urban area for a number of reasons. Trees for example, provide shade, shelter, fruit, attract wildlife, habitats for animals, reduce noise, hide unsightly features and enhance the appearance of an area. An ARPI policy will normally exclude cover for trees and other vegetation, including lawns and shrubs. However, an extension to the policy may be obtained to provide insurance cover for direct physical loss or damage to trees, shrubs, plants and lawns at an insured location caused by or resulting from named perils (such as, for

---

[59]   Above, paras 17-004 to 17-046.
[60]   See also above, in a CAR context paras 17-016 to 17-018.
[61]   For discussion on this in the context of CAR, see above, paras 17-019 to 17-021.
[62]   For discussion on this in the context of CAR, see above para.17-032.

example by fire, lightning, explosion and smoke). When it comes to the reinstatement of such items, the general conditions of an ARPI policy may state items such as trees, shrubs, plants and lawns will be valued at the time of loss limited to "standard local nursery stock". This means therefore that if a mature oak tree is destroyed or damaged, then it would be replaced by a tree from stock available at a standard local nursery. It will of course take many years for an old oak tree to grow back to a similar size. Alternatively, the insurer may agree to pay costs and expenses to the insured to "make good" the destruction of or damage to landscaped gardens at the premises caused by damage as insured; but in doing so exclude the following:

"1. the cost of movement of soil other than as necessary for surface preparation
2. the failure of trees, shrubs or turf to become established following replanting
3. the failure of seeds to germinate."

Further, an insurer will state that it is not liable for an amount in respect of each and every loss:

"[A]rising from damage caused by storm, flood or malicious persons (other than by fire or explosion) not acting on behalf of or in connection with any political organisation or all other damage."

The insurer will also impose a cap on its liability, specifying that its liability for any one occurrence will not extend beyond a set figure or a percentage of the sum insured regarding the item insured, whichever is the less.

Other extensions. Other property extensions may include: (i) lock replacement; **26-038** (ii) machinery re-erection; (iii) fire extinguishment expenses and emergency services damage; and (iv) temporary repairs following damage.

(c)   Property extensions—off site

Off-site extensions. Coverage is usually available for documents removed off **26-039** site, exhibitions and trade fairs, temporary removal of goods (whether for cleaning, renovation, repair, etc.) and goods in transit. There may be a separate limit on the sum insured for off-site losses and this will require an additional premium. "Goods in transit" is often treated as a wholly separate extension as it usually requires specific exclusions.

(d)   Property exclusions

Property exclusions. Exclusions are the most important part of an ARPI policy **26-040** because they define the scope of coverage. This section deals with exclusions specific to material damage, the remainder of the exclusions that apply to both property and BII are dealt with under the section titled "General exclusions" below at paras 26-106 to 26-127. The factors taken into account when interpreting exclusions in an all risks policy are considered in detail above.[63]

Consequential loss. Damage under an ARPI is limited to physical loss and dam- **26-041** age and does not include consequential loss such as loss of profits, increasing work-

---

[63]   See above, para.15-002.

ing costs and standard charges.[64] In any event, a standard ARPI policy will expressly exclude consequential loss except where specifically insured by extensions, e.g. loss of rent and business interruption.[65]

26-042 **Dishonesty.** In relation to property damage the insurer may exclude loss, destruction or damage which is caused or facilitated by the dishonesty of employees, directors or partners or any person in the service of the insured. It has been held that such a clause relates to acts of fraud or dishonesty but not to theft, when there is a separate theft exclusion clause in place.[66] A dishonesty clause may apply where property is deliberately or maliciously damaged with the intention to make a fraudulent claim or intending to conceal unrelated criminal activity. It may apply where property is sabotaged by an employee, or following collusion of an employee with others unrelated to the business. The policy may also contain a separate fidelity exclusion that excludes damage or loss ordinarily covered by fidelity guarantee insurance. This form of insurance provides cover against financial fraud, dishonesty and theft by a business's employees.

Dishonesty clauses can be very broadly expressed, causing an ambiguity that leads the court to construe the clause against the insurer.[67] However, in two High Court cases the court upheld a wide interpretation of dishonesty clauses.[68]

26-043 **Glass, glass surrounds and washroom facilities.** Where property damage extends to cover these items, insurers will limit liability for chipping and scratching, damage caused by repairs to the building and glass defective or broken at the time of insurance, since these items can be delicate and highly susceptible to sustaining damage easily.

26-044 **Interest.** An interest exclusion may exclude the insured's right to recover interest to which they would otherwise be entitled. For example: "interest on any claim payment or compensation benefit for any reason whatsoever".[69]

26-045 **Damage insured elsewhere.** The insurer may exclude liability where the damage in respect of any property that is more specifically insured elsewhere by or on

---

[64] *AS Screenprint v British Reserve Insurance Co Ltd* [1999] Lloyd's Rep. I.R. 430; [1996] C.L.C. 1470.

[65] See above, para.15-068 in respect of CAR and below, paras 26-073 to 26-079.

[66] See *Ted Baker Plc v AXA Insurance UK Plc* [2012] EWHC 1406 (Comm); [2013] 1 All E.R. (Comm) 129; [2013] Lloyd's Rep. I.R. 174, though Eder J did indicate that whether a dishonesty exclusion could relate to theft would depend on whether there were separate theft extension or exclusion clauses in the policy, and this was a matter of fact in an instant case: *Ted Baker Plc* [2012] EWHC 1406 (Comm) at [113]; [2013] 1 All E.R. (Comm) 129 at 172; [2013] Lloyd's Rep. I.R. 174 at 202.

[67] *Ted Baker Plc* [2012] EWHC 1406 (Comm) at [113]; [2013] 1 All E.R. (Comm) 129 at 172; [2013] Lloyd's Rep. I.R. 174 at 202.

[68] *Zurich Professional Ltd v Karim* [2006] EWHC 3355 (QB); *Goldsmith Williams (A Firm) v Travelers Insurance Co Ltd* [2010] EWHC 26 (QB); [2010] Lloyd's Rep. I.R. 309. Both of these cases concerned dishonesty clauses in relation to solicitors' professional indemnity insurance, and provide guidance on how the court might apply a dishonesty clause.

[69] On a related point, presently an insurer's failure to pay a claim promptly does not give rise to a separate cause of action as this amounts to a claim for damages for the failure to pay damages: *Sprung v Royal Insurance (UK) Ltd* [1997] C.L.C. 70; [1999] 1 Lloyd's Rep. I.R. 111. However, post the enactment of the Enterprise Act 2016 (EA 2016) this situation will change. Sections 28, 29 and 30 of the EA 2016 which concern the late payment of insurance claims will come into force on 4 May 2017. For further details about the changes that are going to be coming into force see above, paras 11-021 to 11-024 and paras 23-013 to 23-021.

behalf of the insured. This is likely to cover motor vehicles and perhaps equipment. The insured may also specifically exclude damage covered by fidelity guarantee insurance; that is, coverage against any direct pecuniary loss sustained through acts of fraud or dishonesty committed by employees.

(e) Property terms and conditions

Other parties. Most ARPI policies contain a general "other parties" or "other interests" clause, whereby the insurer acknowledges other parties (e.g. tenants, mortgagee) have an interest in the insured property. It may provide for the interests to be specified in the schedule or in writing to the insurer from time to time and they will be considered as "noted" on the insurance. In the event of a claim the insured should provide the names of the interested parties and the insurer will consult with those interested parties as to the manner and method of indemnity.   **26-046**

The noting in an insurance policy of an interest in a property by a lessee means no more than the recording of the existence of the interest and does not mean that the policy was concluded for the benefit of the lessee.[70]

Reinstatement of property. Reinstatement is the usual starting point for quantification of loss or damage to property (excluding stock and materials which are dealt with separately). In *Vural Ltd v Security Archives Ltd*[71] Knox J made clear that "reinstatement" does not require slavish reconstruction of what was previously in existence. He discussed at length the unreported decision in *Camden Theatre Ltd v London Scottish Properties Ltd*,[72] which held that restoration is not required to be exact where it would obviously be pointless and serve no useful purpose for anyone. For example, replacement by gold paint for what was previously gold leaf might be acceptable in a warehouse, but not in a place where the aesthetic qualities were of considerable importance. Knox J held that for a substitute material to be acceptable it has, in relation to such a utilitarian object as a factory floor, to produce as effective a result as the original. If the original material is appreciably more efficient, a substitute will not in general constitute reinstatement even though it may be that the substitute is better value for money. Modern policies will deal with this difficulty by defining "reinstatement" as replacement or restoration "to a condition substantially the same as but not better or more extensive than its condition when new".   **26-047**

In terms of practicalities, some useful guidance is set out in the case of *Tonkin v UK Insurance Ltd*[73] where Coulson P held that an insured should set out the reinstatement options to the insurer and advise which option is to be taken. In *Tonkin*, these options were: (1) a like-for-like replacement so far as possible; (2) minor changes; and (3) significant changes. The insured should then discuss the appropriate contribution for reinstatement value with the insurer. In *Tonkin*, the insured sought to make changes (in some instances, major changes) without telling the insurer. They opted for a scheme that was largely a mixture of options (2) and (3) but were found to have sought at all times to pass it off as a reinstatement scheme under option (1). In that situation the insured is at risk of leading insurers to suspect fraud. The insured must be open and direct with insurers.

---

[70] *Eurocrest Ventures Ltd v Zurich Insurance Plc* Unreported April 25, 2012 Ch. D.
[71] *Vural Ltd v Security Archives Ltd* (1990) 60 P. & C.R. 258 at 274.
[72] *Camden Theatre Ltd v London Scottish Properties Ltd* Unreported November 30, 1984.
[73] *Tonkin v UK Insurance Ltd* [2006] EWHC 1120 (TCC); [2006] 2 All E.R. (Comm) 550; [2007] Lloyd's Rep. I.R. 283.

26-048 Reinstatement day one basis. This is the calculation behind the sum insured where the property is insured on a reinstatement basis. It derives from two elements, a "Declared Value" multiplied by an "Inflation Provision". The Declared Value is the cost of rebuilding the insured property on the first day of each period of insurance. The "Inflation Provision" is an allowance for inflation.

26-049 Other bases of indemnity. Reinstatement is not always the appropriate assessment of the insured's actual loss. The actual value of the loss must be ascertained from the facts of the case. Where, for example, the insured was ready and willing to sell a property for a certain sale price and it was then destroyed by fire, his actual loss was the sale price (i.e. loss of market value) not the reinstatement cost.[74] Another basis of indemnity might be reinstatement less wear and tear, particularly suitable for a building that is very old or not in a good state of repair.

26-050 Reinstatement of sum insured. The sum insured reduces each time the insurer pays under the policy in respect of an indemnifiable event.[75] The sum insured will reduce by the amount of the indemnity required to be paid out by the insurer. To prevent this reduction from causing the insured to be underinsured for the remainder of the duration of the policy, a clause providing for the reinstatement of the sum insured following each claim indemnified allows the insured to pay an additional premium in consideration of the insurer not reducing the sum insured by the amount of any loss. Some policies provide for "automatic" reinstatement without payment of further premium, though it is important to note when the automatic reinstatement occurs, whether immediately after the event, or after repairs are completed; the latter leaves a period without reinstatement whilst the repairs are carried out.

26-051 Stock declaration/valuing stock. Stock and materials in trade require special treatment in order to ensure that they are adequately covered. Stock and materials in trade encompasses raw materials used in production, work in progress and finished units and is subject to fluctuation in quantity and value throughout the period of insurance. To obtain appropriate cover the insured will first state a sum to be insured for stock and materials prior to commencement/renewal of insurance. The premium for this will be provisional and subject to adjustment. The insured will periodically declare the value of the stock and materials (usually at the end of the month or quarter). At the end of the period of insurance the premium is adjusted to reflect any over/under valuation of stock made at the outset. Accordingly, the insurer will either return a portion of the premium paid or demand that additional premium is paid. A loss adjuster will value raw materials at the cost of replacement. Work in progress and finished units will be valued at their net manufacturing cost including factory overheads (standing charges).[76]

26-052 Condition of average (under-insurance) clause. This clause will penalise insured parties that do not insure for adequate amounts by reducing the claims pay-

---

[74] *Leppard v Excess Insurance Co Ltd* [1979] 1 W.L.R. 512; [1979] 2 All E.R. 668; [1979] 2 Lloyd's Rep. 91.

[75] For an example reinstatement clause, see annex 1 to *IF P&C Insurance Ltd (Publ) v Silversea Cruises Ltd* [2004] EWCA Civ 769; [2004] Lloyd's Rep. I.R. 696.

[76] Standing charges are a business' fixed costs or overheads, such as rent and rates, utilities costs, fixed salaries, depreciation and finance costs.

ment in proportion to the degree of underinsurance.[77] This is known as the average principle and follows this simple formula: the indemnity = the value of the claim × (the sum insured ÷ the value the policy should have been insured for).[78]

5. BUSINESS INTERRUPTION INSURANCE

(a) Introduction

Business interruption insurance. An insured will not be covered for business interruption insurance ("BII") unless he or she specifically requests such an extension to the material damage section of the policy. BII provides cover for the loss of profits consequent upon or caused by a business interruption resulting from the occurrence of an insured peril. The insured will be covered for business-interruption loss caused by any damage, destruction or loss to property at its premises that is used for the purpose of the business. This form of cover can be important to a business because it will cover the loss of income during the interruption, thus enabling the business to meet its fixed costs and still record a profit, which would not otherwise be possible during the interruption. BII will normally form part of an ARPI policy,[79] or it may be secured under a standalone all risks BII policy. **26-053**

In contrast, in CAR policies a form of consequential-loss cover provided is that of DSU insurance.[80] BII and DSU are distinct in the sense that DSU cover relates to the indemnity period prior to practical completion of a construction project, whereas BII covers the loss of profits that can be achieved once the business activity has commenced.

(b) Structure

Structure of the BII section in an ARPI policy. As noted above, at para.26-019 the structure of the BII section of the policy in the main reflects the property damage section of a policy. The BII section will first set out the insuring provision, which states what the insurer agrees to provide cover for and describes the basic circumstance that will give rise to a claim in favour of the insured. The policy will then go on to set out additional business-interruption cover, known as the policy extensions,[81] which can also be obtained in respect of property away from the premises. This will then be followed by the limitations and exclusions, setting the limits to recovery under the policy.[82] After this, the contractual terms and conditions that specifically relate to the BII section will be set out.[83] The BII section will then be followed by general policy exclusions, conditions precedent and claims **26-054**

---

[77] See above, paras 11-019 to 11-020.

[78] An illustration of how the average clause works is given below, at para.26-084.

[79] These composite policies are sometimes referred to as "commercial combined" policies. These are different from and should not be confused with "commercial all risks" policies. See above para.26-019.

[80] See above, paras 17-048 to 17-077.

[81] See below, paras 26-073 to 26-079.

[82] See below, paras 26-080 to 26-092. A standalone BII policy may include the limitations within the specification.

[83] See below, paras 26-093 to 26-105.

conditions, which are applicable to both the material damage section and the BII section of the policy.[84]

26-055 **The schedule.**[85] The schedule that accompanies the policy identifies the insured(s), the business to be insured, the premises on which the business to be insured is based and other premises that are to be covered by the insurance. It also lists the "items" to be insured under the policy, the total sum insured, the insurer's liability and the maximum indemnity period.

Defining the business to be insured is important particularly where the insured operates many businesses from the same premises. The business may be defined in the schedule as "all operations and activities now or hereinafter carried on by the insured", which provides no qualification or limitation in terms of scope or time.[86] This definition recognises the fact that a business's activities can change between the time of securing the insurance and the time of an interruption.

The items referred to in the schedule are the separate heads of loss recoverable under the policy. The main head of loss is gross profit and the increased cost of working. Other heads of loss include fines and penalties, research and development, rent receivable, and book debts. The schedule will then list the limit of liability of the insurer for consequential loss in respect of each item before arriving at an "Estimated Gross Profit" or "Sum Insured" covered by the policy.[87]

26-056 **The specification.** The specification is appended to the schedule and is integral to the policy because it will contain the accounting definitions of gross profit and turnover for the purpose of the calculation of loss.[88]

(c) The insuring provision for BII

26-057 **The insuring provision for BII.** A typical insuring provision for business interruption cover in an ARPI policy will provide that:

> "In the event that any building or other property used by the Insured at the premises for the purpose of the business is damaged by an insured peril during the period of insurance and in consequence the business carried on by the insured at the premises is interrupted or interfered with then the insurer will pay in respect of each item of Business interruption insurance stated in the schedule the amount of loss resulting from such interruption or interference."

In order to trigger the cover, the interruption to the business must be caused by damage to property used "at the premises" for "the purpose of the business". This is a more restrictive insuring provision than may at first appear, since, in addition to any issues relating to causation of loss, there may be difficulty in establishing that the damaged property causing the interruption was "used for the purpose of the business". For example, if the property damaged was an unfinished extension to the property or a vacant building not in use, it will not be considered to have been used "for the purpose of" the business within the terms of the policy.

The property damaged must be "at the premises" and it is possible that the interruption is caused by damage to property based at the premises of another business

---

[84] See below, paras 26-106 to 26-157.
[85] An example of an ARPI policy schedule is set out above, at para.26-020.
[86] *Coromin Ltd v AXA Re* [2007] EWHC 2818 (Comm) at [89]; [2008] Lloyd's Rep. I.R. 467 at 486.
[87] The relevance of the difference in wording between "Estimated Gross Profit" and "Sum insured" is explained below at para.26-065.
[88] The calculation of loss is explained in further detail below at paras 26-066 to 26-070.

within the chain of production, such as a supplier's premises. In order to cover for such eventualities, an extension can be included in the policy to provide cover to the insured in respect of additional premises.

The "business" must be the same business for which the policy was secured. It is possible that the insured is engaged in a number of different businesses, which will create uncertainty over whether the property used was damaged for that "business" which has been interrupted. That is why it is important for the description of "the business" contained in the policy schedule to include the distinct business activities carried out by the insured.

Material damage proviso. Insurers are minded to insist that the insured will be **26-058** in a position to reinstate the damaged property in order to restore the business. As such, the insuring provision contains a material damage proviso, requiring not only that the property damaged was subject to property insurance but also that the insurer has agreed to accept liability for a claim brought under the property policy. Such a clause may be worded as follows:

> "[T]he insurer will pay in respect of each item of Business interruption insurance stated in the schedule the amount of loss resulting from such interruption or interference provided that at the time the damage occurs:
>
> (a) there is in force an insurance policy covering the interest of the Insured in the property at the Premises against such damage;
> (b) The Insured has claimed under the policy referred to in clause (a), and the relevant insurer has paid such claim in full or admitted liability for such claim, or would have done so but for the operation of a proviso in such insurance policy excluding liability for losses below a specified amount."

In theory, such a clause should ensure that funds will be available to correct the damage and bring an end to the business interruption promptly. However, there is no guarantee that monies paid out under the material damage section of the ARPI policy will be sufficient to reinstate the property. For example, a fluctuation in exchange rates may mean that imported property required to be reinstated is no longer affordable.

Ownership requirement. The wording of the initial insuring provision does not **26-059** require that the insured party is the owner of the property insured in that it refers to "any building or other property used by the Insured". This means that "use" by the insured of the property for the purpose of the business as opposed to ownership will be sufficient to trigger the business interruption policy. For example, it has been held in *Glengate-KG Properties Ltd v Norwich Union Fire Insurance Society Ltd*[89] that a property development company's use of architect's drawings to build a property, constituted use of property and was sufficient to trigger the insuring clause of a business interruption policy, even where the drawings were owned by the architect.[90]

The material damage proviso requires that there is insurance covering the interest of the insured in the property at the premises against such damage. In

---

[89] *Glengate-KG Properties Ltd v Norwich Union Fire Insurance Society Ltd* [1996] 2 All E.R. 487; [1996] 1 Lloyd's Rep. 614; [1996] C.L.C. 676.
[90] *Glengate-KG Properties Ltd* [1996] 2 All E.R. 487 at 495 and 503; [1996] 1 Lloyd's Rep. 614 at 620 and 625; [1996] C.L.C. 676 at 683 and 689.

Glengate-KG Properties Ltd,[91] it was held that an "interest" for the purpose of the material damage proviso is to be interpreted in a narrow sense: a "personal property interest" that the insured could reasonably be expected to insure.[92] In that case, it was decided that architects drawings, not owned by the insured but owned by the architect, would not fall within the definition of insurable interest for the purpose of the material damage proviso. Therefore, the insured was not obliged to insure the drawings and as such the proviso would not prevent the insured from recovering under the BII policy.[93] The decision appears to be based on policy considerations; namely that it would be onerous for the business to insure all items of property it used in the course of business. The decision in *Glengate-KG Properties Ltd*[94] does create uncertainty in the law when determining whether a policyholder has an insurable interest in the property for the purpose of the material damage proviso. There is little English authority on BII and this point has yet to be clarified by the courts. On the other hand, it is argued that it will be rare for this issue to arise in practice, since businesses tend either to own property or lease it and invariably will secure property insurance in respect of it. In relation to hired machinery, property and equipment, there is very often a requirement in the lease agreement that the lessee obtains property insurance to cover any damage or loss.

In the context of insurable interests in leasehold property, it has been held that a leasehold tenant does acquire an insurable interest in the property.[95] Therefore rented property will be covered by BII, provided that the insured has insurance in place in respect of the rented or leased property.

26-060 **Conditions for a valid claim.** When the insuring provision and the material damage proviso are considered together, in order for the insured to establish a valid claim under the policy, the following five circumstances set out below must exist:

1. there must be damage at the premises to property used by the insured for the purpose of business;
2. the damage must result from an insured peril;
3. the business must be interrupted as a result of the damage;
4. a loss must result from the interruption; and
5. the property damaged must be insured against material damage and the insurer of the property must have accepted liability for the damage to property.

---

91 *Glengate-KG Properties Ltd* [1996] 2 All E.R. 487; [1996] 1 Lloyd's Rep. 614; [1996] C.L.C. 676.
92 *Glengate-KG Properties Ltd* [1996] 2 All E.R. 487 at 498–499; [1996] 1 Lloyd's Rep. 614 at 622; [1996] C.L.C. 676 at 686. See above, paras 9-035 to 9-036 which discusses in detail the different views on what falls within the scope of the insured's insurable interest.
93 *Glengate-KG Properties Ltd* [1996] 2 All E.R. 487 at 497–499, [1996] 1 Lloyd's Rep. 614 at 622–623; [1996] C.L.C. 676 at 686–687, per Neill LJ. See also the judgment of Auld LJ where he states that the requirement for the policyholder to insure against material damage only extends to the policyholders own property or that in respect of which the cost of repair or replacement would fall on the policyholder. But see the dissenting judgment of Sir Iain Glidewell where he found the material damage proviso applied since *Glengate-KG Properties Ltd* had an interest in the continued existence of the architects drawings and could either have insured them or requested the architects to insure them: [1996] 2 All E.R. 487 at 497–499; [1996] 1 Lloyd's Rep. 614 at 625–626; [1996] C.L.C. 676 at 690–691.
94 *Glengate-KG Properties Ltd* [1996] 2 All E.R. 487; [1996] 1 Lloyd's Rep. 614; [1996] C.L.C. 676.
95 *Mark Rowlands Ltd* [1986] Q.B. 211; [1985] 3 W.L.R. 964; [1985] 3 All E.R. 473.

(d)   Calculating the amount of cover

Gross profit as a measure of loss.   The most effective way of protecting the busi-   **26-061**
ness against business interruption loss is to insure against the loss of gross profit
because gross profit is the most appropriate measure to reflect the loss caused by a
business interruption. Insurance covering the loss of net profit will not be sufficient to indemnify the loss to the business. This is because standing charges (fixed
costs) will remain payable after business has been interrupted and given that net
profit reflects gross profit less standing charges, then an indemnity for loss of net
profit may not be sufficient to pay outstanding standing charges. Put another way,
an indemnity based on gross profit will provide enough money for the business to
cover its standing charges and still retain a net profit, despite the business
interruption.

Estimating gross profit: the sum insured.   The policy schedule will set out the   **26-062**
figure for the total sum insured for loss of gross profit. It is important for the insured
to insure the correct amount so as to avoid the possibility of being underinsured.[96]
In order to do this the insured needs to establish the expected future gross profit of
the business and decide on the required indemnity period. The indemnity period is
the maximum period for which loss of profit will be indemnified for under the
policy. If the insured believes a worst-case scenario would lead to an interruption
period of 12 months then he may wish to obtain insurance for a maximum
indemnity period of 12 months.

Basis of insurance.   There are two methods of insuring the gross profit: the sum   **26-063**
insured basis and the declaration linked basis. The difference between these two
methods was explained by Neuberger LJ in *Kyle Bay Ltd (t/a Astons Nightclub) v
Underwriters subscribing to policy no 019057/08/01*; sub nom. *Kyle Bay Ltd (t/a
Astons Nightclub) v Underwriters*,[97] which was a claim to set aside the settlement
of an insurance claim on the basis of mistake; the alleged mistake being that the
policy was not declaration linked (which it was) but was on the gross profits basis,
and as such was subject to average. The two methods mentioned are now discussed
in turn below.

Sum insured (or average) basis.   The insured should insure a sum based on its   **26-064**
estimate of future gross profit. The insured should review its gross profit annually.
The insured may also add an annual uplift for growth in turnover and inflation. As
Neuberger LJ explained in *Kyle Bay Ltd (t/a Astons Nightclub)*,[98] where the actual
profit lost is greater than the profit sum insured, the insurer's liability will be
proportionately reduced. This reflects the fact that the insured underinsured the risk
to the business and the insurer has taken on a greater risk than it agreed to. Provision is made, however, for this by way of the average proviso clause, which can be

---

[96]   See further below, para.26-064.
[97]   *Kyle Bay Ltd (t/a Astons Nightclub) v Underwriters* [2007] EWCA Civ 57 at [3]–[4]; [2007] 1 C.L.C.
164 at 166; [2007] Lloyd's Rep. I.R. 460 at 462–463.
[98]   *Kyle Bay Ltd (t/a Astons Nightclub)* [2007] EWCA Civ 57 at [3]–[4]; [2007] 1 C.L.C. 164; [2007]
Lloyd's Rep. I.R. 460 at 463–463.

found set out in the limitation to the gross profit clause contained in the limitations and exclusions section of the policy.[99]

26-065 Declaration linked basis. The declaration-based policy will pay out on the actual gross profit lost, and not on the sum insured. It does this by allowing the insured to pay a retrospective increase in the premium to reflect that the actual loss (and risk to the insurer) was greater than originally estimated. This alleviates the problem of underinsurance that can arise with sum insured policies. As Neuberger LJ stated in *Kyle Bay Ltd (t/a Astons Nightclub)*,[100] the increase in liability to the insurer will be capped, usually to 133.3 per cent of the declared gross profit. The sum to be insured is called the "estimated gross profit" as opposed to the "sum insured", though it represents the same figure.

(e) Calculating the recoverable loss for gross profit

26-066 Gross profit derived from turnover: "the difference basis". Standard accounting practice provides that turnover less variable costs equals gross profit. BII will usually adopt this accounting principle to calculate gross profit.[101] It is known as the difference basis. The specification to the policy will include the calculation to reflect the difference basis, which will precisely reflect accounting standards, by making provision for depreciation and uninsured working expenses such as discounts allowed and bad debts.

26-067 Gross profit. The loss to be indemnified under BII cover will be the gross profit that would have been earned on turnover lost during the interruption to the business. The calculation is usually expressed in the following way:

> "The insurance is limited to loss of Gross Profit due to (a) Reduction in Turnover and the amount payable as indemnity thereunder shall be:—
>
> (a) In respect of Reduction in Turnover: the sum produced by applying the Rate of Gross Profit to the amount by which Turnover during the Indemnity Period shall fall short of Standard Turnover in consequence of the incident."

26-068 Standard turnover. Standard turnover is the recorded turnover for the period of 12 months immediately prior to the date of the interruption, which corresponds with the indemnity period. If, for example, the interruption occurs between June and August, then the turnover used for comparison will be taken from the June to August period in the year prior to interruption, to accurately reflect seasonal changes. The standard turnover can be adjusted by applying the "other circumstances clause" to reflect growth or decline in turnover that would have been achieved but for the interruption.[102]

26-069 Rate of gross profit. The rate of gross profit represents the gross profit as a percentage of turnover achieved in the 12-month accounting period immediately

---

[99] The average proviso may also be set out in the specification. See, further below, at para.26-084.

[100] *Kyle Bay Ltd (t/a Astons Nightclub)* [2007] EWCA Civ 57 at [3]–[4]; [2007] 1 C.L.C. 164; [2007] Lloyd's Rep. I.R. 460 at 463–463.

[101] An alternative calculation of gross profit is to apply the "additions basis", which entails adding net profit to the insured standing charges. This method is now not standard practice owing to the onerous requirement to list all the insured standing charges.

[102] See further below, para.26-088.

prior to the interruption and the latest annual accounting statements will be used to identify the rate. If turnover during that accounting period was £1 million and gross profit was £700,000, then the rate of gross profit would be 70 per cent.

The calculation.   The actual turnover achieved during the interrupted period is   **26-070** subtracted from the standard turnover, giving a figure for turnover lost due to the interruption. The turnover lost is then multiplied by the rate of gross profit percentage and this will give the actual gross profit loss caused by the interruption. For example:

Turnover during interruption = £100,000
Standard turnover = £500,000
Turnover lost due to interruption is £500,000 less £100,000 = £400,000
The rate of gross profit = 70%
The gross profit lost due to the interruption is £400,000 ×70% = £280,000

The indemnity will be £280,000. Of course, the "other circumstances clause" can be used to adjust the standard turnover or rate of gross profit to reflect a trend towards growth or decline in profits and the indemnity can be amended accordingly.

Other items of loss.   If the insured has obtained cover for the other "items" of loss   **26-071** such as the increase in cost of working, the additional increase in cost of working, rent receivable, fines and penalties, research and development and book debts, then recoverable amounts for these items will be added to the total indemnity to be paid under the policy. Each of these items of loss will be subject to clauses that limit recovery.[103]

Business operating at a loss.   Recovery for business interruption is possible   **26-072** where the business is making a net loss. In applying the "difference basis", the calculation will be turnover less variable costs and this will still produce a positive figure, which will contribute to paying the standing charges. It may be said, therefore, that BII is even more important when the business is vulnerable due to weak financial performance.

(f)   Business interruption extensions: off site

Extensions.   Extensions can be included in the policy to adequately cover the   **26-073** insured against business interruption loss caused by loss or damage to property belonging to other businesses or property at other locations, which the insured's business relies upon in some way. These are often termed dependency extensions.

Damage to property at contract sites.   This extension provides cover for busi-   **26-074** nesses that are contracted to carry out work at premises belonging to other businesses. Loss or damage to the contract site may prevent the contractor from fulfilling the contract, and this can cause interruption to the business. A business that sends its employees and/or subcontractors to off-site locations to perform their business activity would require this extension. Such businesses include building contractors, electrical engineers, fire-alarm installers, glaziers and IT-support contractors. The extension will normally limit cover to loss and damage caused by

---

[103]   See below, paras 26-083 to 26-092.

an insured peril under the material damage section of the ARPI policy and that the insurer's liability for such loss will be limited to a specified sum for any one claim.

26-075 **Denial of access.** This extension provides cover for business-interruption loss caused by damage to other property in the vicinity that "prevents or hinders" customers and staff from using or accessing the business (e.g. a car park that forms part of a shopping complex, which is closed because it is structurally unsafe). The extension requires that the damage must be caused by an insured peril, but expressly states that the insured's property or premises need not be damaged for the extension to apply. The use of the word "hinders" in the extension is pertinent because in reality there will rarely be a complete denial of access to the premises, as there will normally be alternative means of access, albeit restricted.

26-076 **Damage to supply utilities.** The inclusion of a utilities dependency clause will be important for businesses heavily reliant on the utilities: electricity, gas, water and telecommunications. Two forms of insurance are available: "supplier extension" and "terminal end cover". The supplier extension provides cover for "damage or loss" of property at the generating station or substation of the supplier. The terminal end cover provides insurance for any "failures" to terminal points which feed the various utilities to the business.

The premium for terminal end cover will be higher than for the supplier extension because "failures" can occur at any point between the generating station and the end user and therefore the insurer is exposed to losses from a wider variety of causes. The clause will normally limit recovery to a specified sum for any one claim.

26-077 **Loss of attraction.** A business may suffer loss or damage due to business interruption caused by a loss of attraction of customers to the surrounding areas (e.g. the impact of oil pollution to the tourist industry in the Gulf of Mexico following the Deepwater Horizon disaster in 2010). A "loss of attraction" clause can be included to extend cover to such losses. In *Orient-Express Hotels Ltd v Assicurazioni General SpA (UK) (t/a Generali Global Risk)*[104] the "loss of attraction" clause read as follows:

> "This Policy extends to indemnify the Insured in respect of a reduction in Revenue resulting directly from loss destruction or damage to property or land in the vicinity of any premises owned and/or managed by the Insured and insured under this Policy."

As such, the clause made no reference to a requirement that the damage or loss of property in the vicinity cause a loss of attraction. A variation on the above clause might read as follows:

> "The insurance is extended to include loss in consequence of damage to property in the vicinity of the premises which causes a fall in the number of customers attracted to the vicinity of the premises whether the property used by the insured for the purpose of the Business shall be damaged or not."

---

[104] *Orient-Express Hotels Ltd v Assicurazioni General SpA (UK Branch) (t/a Generali Global Risk)* [2010] EWHC 1186 (Comm) at [15]; [2010] 1 C.L.C. 847 at 853; [2010] Lloyd's Rep. I.R. 531 at 534.

The second clause is narrower than the first clause in the sense that the insured must establish that damage to property in the vicinity reduced the number of customers attracted to the vicinity. This clause expressly provides that the premises used by the insured need not be damaged. The word "vicinity" is also open to interpretation.

Suppliers, customers and related businesses.   An extension is available to cover   **26-078** the business interruption loss caused by damage or loss to property of a supplier, or customer or related business. The clause requires that the property and situations (i.e. locations) to be covered must be listed in a memorandum to the policy; then any damage or loss to that property caused by an insured peril will be "deemed" to have occurred to the business's property at its premises. The sum insured for such business-interruption loss will be either recorded in the memorandum or will be the sum insured in the schedule in respect of BII loss caused by damage to the insured's own property, though in reality recovery under the clause is typically capped at around 10 per cent of the gross profit recoverable under the BII policy. The material damage proviso does not apply in respect of this clause. Thus, the fact that the insured does not have insurance in place for property damage in respect of other locations or property, will not preclude the insured from recovering under the policy.

Other extensions.   There are various other extensions that can be included in the   **26-079** BII cover. For example, property of the insured in transit, motor vehicles and documents belonging to or held on trust by professionals can be insured under BII cover.

(g)   Business interruption limitations and exclusions

BII limitations and exclusions.   BII limitation clauses limit the amount of money   **26-080** the insured can recover for each item of loss under the policy. BII exclusions operate to exclude the insured from recovering for certain types of loss. The main limitations and exclusions that are normally found in the BII section of an ARPI policy will be considered in detail below.

Fines and penalties.   BII cover may expressly exclude the insured from recover-   **26-081** ing any "fines or damages" for breach of contract as a result of late or noncompletion of orders or any penalties imposed for whatever reason that were incurred due to business interruption. If, however, a business recognises its own potential exposure to incurring significant fines and penalties as a result of an interruption to the business, then it can insure this cost as a separate item of loss. Recovery for this item of loss will be limited to cancellation charges, fines or damages for breach of contract incurred by the insured in relation to contracts it entered into for the purchase of goods and services.

Supply utilities.   The BII section may include a clause excluding recovery for   **26-082** damage or loss resulting from certain incidents involving the cessation of supply of utilities, which result in an interruption to the business. The clause will provide that the insurer is not liable for business-interruption loss caused by damage resulting from the utilities supplier withholding supply, strikes or any labour dispute, drought, atmospheric or weather conditions or interruptions to supply of less than 24 hours, even if the insured has a separate supply utilities extension clause in place.

Accidental failure due to damage to supply utility equipment caused by atmospheric or weather conditions is not excluded.

26-083 **Limit of liability clause.** The insurer's liability under the BII section of the policy will be limited for any one claim, and will not exceed the lesser of:

"(a) In the whole the total sum insured, or

(b) in respect of any item of settlement specification, its sum insured at the time of damage; or

(c) any other limit of liability stated in the schedule at the time of damage; or

(d) the sum insured (or limit of liability) remaining after deduction for any other interruption consequent on upon damage occurring during the same period of insurance, unless the insurer has agreed to reinstate any such sum insured."

In relation to sub-clause (b) listed above, where the insured is covered for a number of items of loss and where the insured makes a claim under only one item of loss, then the sum insured for that item will be the limit of liability. In relation to sub-clause (d) it provides that the limit of liability will be reduced after a previous successful claim, unless there is a reinstatement clause in place.[105] The insurer's liability can also be expressed as a percentage of the amount payable under the policy.

26-084 **Gross profit/estimated gross profit clause.** This clause sets out the calculation of gross profit[106] and also contains a limiting clause called the "average proviso". The insurer's liability will be limited to the sum insured, however, if as the clause states:

"the sum insured in respect of schedule item 1 (gross profit) is less than the sum produced by applying the Rate of Gross Profit to Annual Turnover (or to a proportionately increased multiple thereof where the maximum indemnity period exceeds 12 months) the amount payable shall be proportionately reduced."

The average proviso seeks to reduce the liability of the insurer where the insured has not obtained enough cover at the commencement of the policy. For example, if cover is obtained for £500,000 and the actual loss is £1 million, then the risk to the insurer would be twice as much as it originally anticipated. The cover would be proportionately reduced by half and the insurer's liability would be £250,000 thereby reflecting the actual risk it agreed to take on.

26-085 **Increase in cost of working clause.**[107] Cover provided by the insurer for the increase in cost of working incurred as a result of a business interruption, such as labour costs, will normally be limited to:

"(a) the additional expenditure (subject to the provisions of the Uninsured Standard Charges Clause) necessarily and reasonably incurred for the sole purpose of avoiding or diminishing the reduction in Turnover which but for the expenditure would have taken place during the Indemnity Period in consequence of the Incident, but not exceeding the sum produced by applying the Rate of Gross Profit to the amount of the reduction thereby avoided."

---

[105] See below, para.26-096.
[106] See above, para.26-067.
[107] For a discussion on increased cost of working in a CAR context. See above, para.17-011.

The clause limits the recovery of the increase in cost of working to the amount of gross profit preserved as a result of incurring the cost. Where the increase in cost of working exceeds the gross profit that is saved, the excess cost is not ordinarily recoverable, unless the policy includes another clause allowing for recovery of the additional increase in cost of working.

Additional increase in cost of working clause.[108]   The purpose of this clause is   **26-086**
to provide the insured with cover for the additional cost of restoring the gross profit to the level that would have been achieved but for the interruption, even where the additional cost is greater than the profit restored (e.g. there may be an urgent need to continue operating due to concerns that competitors will absorb the business's market share). If the insured obtains cover for the additional increase in cost of working, then recovery will be limited to "additional expenditure necessarily and reasonably incurred" by the insured to prevent or minimise a reduction in turnover or to resume/maintain the business operations "for an amount that does not exceed" the sum insured under this item of loss.

Uninsured standing charges clause.   This clause applies standard accounting   **26-087**
practise to ensure the insured does not over recover for the increase in cost of working. If certain standing charges are not insured under the policy, the turnover preserved by the increase in cost of working will help to pay for those uninsured standing charges. Therefore the insured will have to pay a portion of the increase in cost of working to reflect the proportion of uninsured standing charges to gross profit recovered.

Other circumstances (or trends) clause.   This provision enables the insured to   **26-088**
recover a figure for gross profit that reflects increased business growth that would have been achieved but for the interruption to the business. The insurer can also rely on this clause to reduce its liability under the policy where it can produce empirical evidence to show that the turnover or gross profit would have fallen in the indemnity period.

Alternative-trading clause.   The alternative-trading clause expressly provides for   **26-089**
the insurer to account for profits earned by the insured through alternative means of trading and thereby reduce its own liability under the claim. The inclusion of this clause is important to the insurer because the court may not be willing to imply a term into the policy that profits earned from temporary premises during the interruption will be brought into account in diminution of the loss payable by the insurer.[109] Any additional cost to the insured in making alternative trading arrangements can be recovered under the "increase in cost of working" item of loss.

Research and development clause.   Where interruption to research and develop-   **26-090**
ment is a specified item of loss in the schedule, the insured will insure a sum to be paid in weekly instalments for the duration of the interruption to the research and development program. The sum insured will be an arbitrary figure arrived at by the insured. The clause will permit recovery of increase in cost of working associated with restoring the research and development program but will limit recovery to the

---

[108] Additional increase in cost of working is also considered in the context of CAR. See above, para.17-011.
[109] *City Tailors Ltd v Evans* (1921) 9 Ll. L. Rep. 394; (1921) 91 L.J.K.B. 379.

amount saved by avoiding or diminishing the weekly instalments as a result of incurring the additional cost. The clause will also contain an average proviso, which would reduce the insurer's liability if the insured had underinsured the risk and provide for recovery to be adjusted down for any savings in costs in research and development following the interruption.

26-091 **Rent receivable.** Where rent receivable is an item of loss under the policy, the limitation section will contain a rent-receivable clause. The loss will be limited to the amount by which the rent receivable during the indemnity period falls short of the standard rent receivable, including additional expenditure incurred for the purpose of avoiding that loss, but less any sum saved in respect of the expenses and charges payable out of the rent receivable.

26-092 **Book debts.** When accounting records are destroyed, it may be difficult to trace outstanding book debts (known as accounts receivable for the purpose of accounting standards) and so the loss of book debts is an insurable head of loss. Such loss will be limited to the outstanding debt balances less the total of amounts received/traced plus the additional cost of tracing the accounts receivable with the prior consent of the insurer.

(h) Business interruption terms and conditions

26-093 **BII terms and conditions.** Terms and conditions that are specific to BII will be discussed below at paras 26-094 to 26-105.

26-094 **Alteration clause.** This clause relates only to BII cover and provides that the policy shall be void if, after the commencement of the insurance, the business is wound up, carried on by a liquidator or receiver, the business is permanently discontinued or if an alteration to the business or premises increases the risk of damage.[110]

26-095 **Declaration-linked condition.** Where sums insured under the policy are declaration linked, a clause is included to set out the steps the insured is required to take in order to adjust the premium. Prior to renewal the insured must provide an estimate of gross profit to be insured based on the latest annual financial statements of the business. The premium will be based on these figures. Then, within six months after the end of the period of insurance, the insured must submit the latest annual financial statements certified by a professional accountant. Any amount of loss of gross profit during the insurance period will be added by the insurer to the figure for gross profit in the certified statement, which gives a "deemed" gross profit figure. If the deemed figure is less than the original estimate supplied by the insured, then the insurer will return up to 50 per cent of the premium paid. If the deemed figure is greater than the original estimate, then the insured will have to pay an additional premium. The insurer's additional liability for loss of gross profit will be capped at 133.3 per cent of the original estimated figure given by the insured. Finally, the declaration-linked clause will provide for automatic reinstatement of cover.

26-096 **Automatic reinstatement.** A reinstatement clause has the effect of reinstating the

---

[110] The standard material alteration clause for ARPI policies and BII is discussed below at paras 26-147 to 26-148.

full liability of the insurer following a claim under the policy, on the condition that the insured undertakes to pay an additional premium. This is an important inclusion, for otherwise the insured may be underinsured for the remainder of the period of insurance.

Delayed loss.   The insured cannot delay in claiming under the business-   **26-097** interruption cover following material damage to the property. There is little authority on this point, however, this issue did arise in a case involving subsidence to a building.[111] In the case, initial subsidence occurred in November 2003, which the claimant noticed, but which did not cause an interruption. In October 2004 the subsidence worsened, and it was in 2005 that the interruption became prevalent prompting a claim by the insured. The case was decided on the basis that a clause in the insurance policy required immediate notice of the damage or loss for which a claim was brought or to be brought and that this had not been given. The judge made obiter comments indicating that the date of the incident had to refer to the material damage causing the interruption and not the interruption itself.[112]

A policy can make provision for a delayed loss in circumstances where the business is able to continue trading following an interruption because it has reserves of stock. Sales revenue may not be affected for a considerable time following a business interruption where the business is able to sell reserves of stock. This provision is often called an "accumulated stocks clause" and allows for a time delay in the interruption to turnover.

Department gross profit; gross revenue "departmental clause".   In circum-   **26-098** stances where a business has two or more revenue earning departments, which may produce different products or services each earning different rates of gross profit, a policy condition may provide for the ratio of gross profit to be averaged between them to avoid the consequence that the insured would be otherwise over or under indemnified for its loss.

Salvage sale.   A salvage sale helps the business maintain much needed cash flow   **26-099** during the period of interruption. A salvage sale sees goods being sold at below their usual price and hence the gross profit margin per sale is lower. Turnover in the immediate period after a loss may increase, albeit that the gross profit margin will reduce. The effect of the salvage sale clause is that the insurer agrees to disregard the turnover from the salvage sale in the calculation of loss of turnover caused by the interruption except that the gross profit figure will be adjusted by subtracting any gross profit made on the salvage sale. The result will be that the insured will not have suffered as a result of having to sell the goods at below the usual profit margin.

Premium-adjustment clause.   Such a clause will allow for the return of premium   **26-100** to the insured after the expiry of the indemnity period, where it becomes apparent that the insured sum (or estimated gross profit for declaration linked policies) exceeded the actual amount of profit generated (or would have been generated but for the loss). The return of premium will be capped at 50 per cent of the premium

---

[111] *Loyaltrend Ltd v Creechurch Dedicated Ltd (Sued on behalf of itself and on behalf of all other underwriting names of syndicate 962, 2002 Underwriting Year)* [2010] EWHC 425 (Comm); [2010] Lloyd's Rep. I.R. 466.

[112] *Loyaltrend Ltd* [2010] EWHC 425 (Comm) at [32]–[33]; [2010] Lloyd's Rep. I.R. 466 at 476.

paid. The insured will need to provide evidence of the difference in profit within a set period of time and the insurer may reserve the right to examine an auditor's certificate attesting to the accuracy of the accounts.

26-101 **Payments on account.** A clause will provide for interim payments on account to be made to the business during the indemnity period to avoid the problem caused by having no cash flow during an interruption to a business. Historically, English insurance policies have contained a payment on account clause stating "[i]n the event of a loss the insurers will make interim payments to the insured if desired/ appropriate". This is vague in the extreme, for it does not state the amount to be paid, or how promptly the payment will be made. It does not state whether the payment will be made before liability is admitted, or make provision for reimbursement if the claim turns out not to be valid. It is suggested that a clause should make provision for the insured to submit a schedule of loss and a cash flow projection with a claim for payment on account.

26-102 **Reimbursement of amounts recovered.** Where the BII section provides for the recovery of accounts receivable following the destruction of all accounting records, a clause will be included requiring the insured to reimburse any accounts receivable subsequently paid to the business by trade debtors.

26-103 **Inspection of records.** An inspection of records clause is included to permit the insurer to inspect the premises and the records of accounts receivable, kept by the insured and to examine and audit them during the period of insurance and a period of time afterwards (i.e. perhaps a number of years).

26-104 **Professional-accountants clause.** A professional-accountants clause gives the insurer the ability to have professional accountants produce the insured's financial statements, and other business books and documents that may be required by the insurer to investigate or verify a claim made under the policy. Usually the insurer will pay the insured reasonable charges of producing the accounts. The clause enables the insurer to assess the claim and rely on the accuracy of the accountants' work.

26-105 **Conditions precedent for business interruption insurance.** The conditions precedent in an ARPI policy which relate to the property damage section are deemed to also apply to the business interruption section, in order to avoid unnecessary duplication they will be discussed below at paras 26-129 to 26-151.

6. GENERAL EXCLUSIONS

26-106 **General exclusions.** An ARPI policy will contain a section called "general exclusions", which applies to both the material damage and BII sections. Some or all of the exclusions may contain a rider stating: "this shall not exclude subsequent damage or business interruption resulting from a cause not otherwise excluded." The general view is that this does not add much to the common law position in that the court will need to investigate the proximate cause in any event.

26-107 **Ensuing loss.** An "ensuing loss" or "subsequent damage" clause limits the effect of other exclusions to provide cover where the loss was, in part at least, caused by an excluded cause.

Some examples of policy wording which follow the listing of an exclusion, or multiple exclusions, are:

"But this shall not exclude subsequent Damage which itself results from a cause not otherwise excluded.

None of the above Perils Excluded shall exclude any Damage (or consequential loss insofar as it is covered by Section [x]) arising therefrom if resulting from a cause which is not otherwise excluded, nor subsequent Damage (or consequential loss arising therefrom insofar as it is covered by Section [x]) resulting from an ensuing cause which is not otherwise excluded.

Unless loss or damage from an insured Peril ensues and then only for such ensuing loss or damage.

except for loss caused by ... [excluded causes of loss] any ensuing loss from items [...] not excluded is covered.

We will not pay for loss or damage caused by, resulting from, or arising out of any acts, errors, or omissions by you or others in any of the following activities, regardless of any other cause or event that contributes concurrently, or in any sequence to the loss or damage: [...]

However if physical loss or damage by a covered cause of action ensues, we will pay for such ensuing loss or damage."

There is relatively little guidance about how the English courts would approach these types of clauses. There is a plethora of English law on the question or damage or defect which plays a part in these decisions.[113]

In the Queensland Court of Appeal decision of *Prime Infrastructure (DBCT) Management P/L v Vero Insurance Ltd*[114] the Court had to consider an ensuing loss provision which provided that the exclusions:

"... shall not apply to subsequent loss, destruction of or damage to the Property Insured occasioned by a peril (not otherwise excluded) resulting from any event or peril referred to in this exclusion."

The case concerned a claim for $8m in respect of a machine which collapsed onto two conveyor belts as a result of the final severing of an internal fatigue crack in a defective weld which was a workmanship defect at the time of construction. The crack had grown progressively over time. As a result of the collapse the machine and the conveyor belts were extensively damaged. The major damage was caused by the collapse which occurred after the failure of the weld. The failure of the weld was itself caused by faulty workmanship and therefore the damage would be excluded unless it came within the "subsequent loss" write back.

The Court of Appeal (by a majority) allowed the claim on the basis that the failure of the weld amounted to "initial damage" and the collapse of the machine was "subsequent damage" and therefore fell within the write back. "Subsequent damage" was damage *after* the "initial damage", and did not need to be distinct, independent or separate from the initial damage.

It must be noted that two other courts have reached different conclusions on similar clauses,[115] holding that such subsequent or ensuing loss must be caused by a non-excluded peril separate and independent but resulting from the original excluded peril. This interpretation has been subject to academic criticism.[116]

---

[113] See further above, Chs 14 and 16.
[114] [2005] QCA 369 at [11].
[115] See *Acme Galvanizing Co Inc v Fireman's Fund Insurance Co* 221 Cal.App.3d 170 at 179 to 180; 270 Cal. Rptr. 405 at 411 (1990) and *Weeks v Co-Operative Insurance Cos* 149 N.H. 174 at 177; 817 A.2d 292 at 296 (2003).
[116] C.C. French, "The 'Ensuing Loss' Clause in Insurance Policies: The Forgotten and Misunderstood Antidote to Anti-Concurrent Causation Exclusions" (2012) 13 Nev. L.J. 215 at p.246.

In the context of the Insurance Act 2015 (the "2015 Act")[117] and the introduction of principles of causation and proportionate remedies it is likely that the English courts will adopt a pro-cover approach and favour the majority decision in *Prime*.[118]

26-108 **Excess/deductible.**   The ARPI policy will exclude recovery of the excess that the insured is required to pay. In relation to ARPI policies it is unusual to find large excesses or deductibles in the leasehold market because there is no incentive for a landlord to carry an increased risk where he is passing on the cost of the premium to the tenants.

26-109 **Wear and tear, inherent vice and gradual deterioration.**   Insurance only acts to indemnify the insured for fortuitous happenings and for that reason damage caused by wear and tear, inherent vice and gradual change will be excluded from the ARPI policy.[119] In relation to inherent vice, goods—particularly food stuffs, textiles and forms of furniture—these can be vulnerable to inherent changes in quality, for example, by developing mould or mildew.

26-110 **Defective design.**   Faulty design and workmanship is commonly excluded from ARPI policies. The form of such a clause might exclude damage caused by "faulty or defective workmanship, design or materials".[120]

26-111 **Electrical or mechanical breakdown.**   The reasoning behind this exclusion is to encourage the insured to properly maintain their equipment and not to provide an additional warranty for equipment that has been purchased.[121] Coverage for electrical or mechanical breakdown can be purchased as a separate engineering extension.

26-112 **Boiler explosion, failure and collapse.**   As with the exclusion for machinery breakdown, boiler explosion, failure and collapse can be covered under a separate engineering extension. However, it is normally excluded from ARPI policies together with the "joint leakage" exclusion set out below at para.26-114. A boiler-exclusion clause will normally exclude:

> "Explosion, failure or collapse of a boiler (but not a boiler used for domestic purposes only) economiser or other vessel, machine, apparatus or pipework at the premises in which internal pressure is due to steam only belonging to or under the control of the insured."

"Explosion" has been defined as "violent, noisy and are … caused by a very rapid chemical or nuclear reaction or the bursting out of gas or vapour under pressure".[122]

26-113 **Joint leakage.**   In conjunction with the boiler exclusion a standard joint-leakage clause will usually exclude

---

[117] See further above, Ch.5.
[118] *Infrastructure (DBCT) Management P/L v Vero Insurance Ltd* [2005] QCA 369.
[119] There can often be difficulties in determining whether damage was caused by an accidental event or an inevitable event. This is considered in detail above at para.3-061 and paras 15-006 to 15-010; 15-012 to 15-019 and para.15-027, and in the context of "fortuity" at paras 10-012 to 10-015.
[120] See further above, Ch.16.
[121] See above, paras 15-075 to 15-077.
[122] *Commonwealth Smelting Ltd v Guardian Royal Exchange Assurance Ltd* [1984] 2 Lloyd's Rep. 608 at 612; (1984) 134 N.L.J. 1018. The decision was upheld by the Court of Appeal although the definition was not expressly upheld: [1986] 1 Lloyd's Rep. 121. Cited in *Aegis Electrical and Gas International Services Co Ltd v Continental Casualty Co* [2007] EWHC 1762 (Comm) at [80]; [2008] Lloyd's Rep. I.R. 17 at 28.

"joint leakage failure of welds cracking fracturing collapse or overheating of boiler economisers superheaters pressure vessels of any range of steam and feed piping in connection therewith."

Processing. As with mechanical breakdown it is not the purpose of property **26-114** insurance to cover a manufacturer for loss occasioned by its own commercial activities. A common exclusion will therefore exclude "[d]amage resulting from stock or materials undergoing any process of production, packing treatment, commissioning or testing". "Stock" and "materials" are distinct and it is important to cover both. Insurers may additionally exclude damage resulting from "heating process or any process involving the application of heat".

Aircraft travelling at supersonic speeds. When aircraft travel at supersonic **26-115** speed they will produce pressure waves known as "sonic booms", which can cause property damage, in particular smashing windows.[123] The exclusion will not provide cover for damage caused by debris falling from passenger aircraft, which may be of concern if the insured property is located near an airport or under a flight path.

Theft. A standard theft exclusion in an ARPI will exclude **26-116**

"[d]amage resulting from theft or attempted theft unless involving forcible and violent entry to or exit from buildings at the premises."

The phrase "forcible and violent" was considered by the Court of Appeal in *Nash (t/a Dino Services Ltd) v Prudential Assurance Co Ltd*,[124] where the keys to the insured premises were stolen from a vehicle and used to gain access. The insurers agreed that, under the authorities in criminal law, the opening of various doors by means of the stolen keys satisfied the word "forcible" since "force" in this context means the application of energy to an obstacle with a view to its removal. The court further held that "violent" should be given its ordinary meaning, that is, the use of some force to effect entry, which may be minimal, such as the turning of a key in a lock or the turning of a door handle, is accentuated or accompanied by some physical act that can properly be described as violent in its nature or character. As a result the court held that it was not sufficient that the keys were stolen "violently" from the vehicle as the violence must be directed to the insured property. The requirement for "forcible and violent" entry or exit will often mean that employee theft is not covered. This can also be expressly excluded as "any loss by theft or dishonesty of the insured's directors, officers, employees or servants" as considered above at para.26-042. For protection against this loss the insured can obtain separate fidelity cover.

Water table level. Damage caused by changes to the water table is frequently **26-117** excluded in ARPI policies.[125] Only where damage is caused solely by an increase in the water table level (and not by flooding) will recovery be excluded for property damage and business interruption.

Disused, unoccupied or vacant buildings. A standard clause may exclude: **26-118**

"Damage resulting from:

---

[123] See above, para.15-095 and para.25-040.
[124] *Nash (t/a Dino Services Ltd) v Prudential Assurance Co Ltd* [1989] 1 All E.R. 422; [1989] 1 Lloyd's Rep. 379; [1989] Fin. L.R. 316.
[125] See also above, in the context of CAR, para.15-028.

(a)   escaping water from any pipe, tank, water system or automatic sprinkler installation;
(b)   riot, civil commotion or malicious damage;
(c)   theft or theft damage;

in respect of any building which is unoccupied, vacant or disused for a period for 30 or more consecutive days."

The reason for the inclusion of such a clause is, because the risk to insurers is generally higher when a building is unoccupied, especially from escape of water, malicious damage and theft. Also, from a business-interruption perspective, buildings that are empty and unused should have no impact on the continuation of business after sustaining damage because no business activity is taking place there. Of course, if an adjacent building happens to collapse then there may be genuine interruption to buildings and property being used for business purposes and as such the option to buy back BII cover for this will normally be available to the insured.

26-119   **Electronic risks.**   A standard clause may exclude: "damage caused by virus or similar mechanism of hacking, or denial of service attacks"; or, a wider clause may exclude "distortion, erasure, corruption or alteration of electronic data from any cause whatsoever".[126] To cover these risks a separate computer policy cover can be obtained—similar to machinery breakdown cover—which may also cover expenditure necessarily and reasonably incurred to prevent or minimise interruption or interference with computer equipment.

An ARPI policy will respond to damage caused by "any risk" subject to the exclusions that are contained within it. While ARPI policies are not designed to cater for cyber-risks, it has now become clear that cyber-attacks can cause substantial physical damage to property, either directly or where the cyber event is one of the causes of the damage as part of a chain of events (which is clearly relevant when BII is included as part of a property policy). For example, in 2010 the release of the Stuxnet "worm" against an Iranian nuclear facility caused the mechanisms of the centrifuges to malfunction, resulting in physical damage. In December 2014 hackers managed to penetrate the control systems of a German steelworks, and were able to shut down one of its blast furnaces, which resulted in extensive physical damage. If a business does not obtain a stand-alone computer/cyber liability policy (for first and/or third parties) for losses relating to damage, or loss of information from its IT systems and networks, then it will inevitably turn to its existing insurance policy to see if it can claim for the damage or loss it has incurred. If there is no effective exclusion in place, and the cyber-risk is deemed to be the proximate cause of the loss then it is likely the loss will be covered by the policy.

26-120   **Excluded property.**   Most ARPI policies will include a list of excluded property. This will commonly include: animals; land, property underground and offshore; trees and other vegetation; valuables; electronic data; overhead electrical and telecommunication transmission; money; vehicles required to be licensed for road use; property in transit; property or structures in the course of demolition, construc-

---

[126] In *Tektrol Ltd (formerly Atto Power Controls Ltd) v International Insurance Co of Hanover Ltd* [2005] EWCA Civ 845 at [19]; [2006] 1 All E.R. (Comm) 780 at 786; [2006] Lloyd's Rep. I.R. 38 at 43 the court held that the exclusion clauses relied upon by the insurers in the "All Risks" business loss policy issued by them could not be relied upon by them to exclude liability for the losses incurred by the insured for the virus or the theft.

tion, erection or installation. It will usually also include "moveable property in the open" qualified so that only damage caused by natural elements is excluded i.e. "in respect of damage caused by wind, rain, hail, sleet, snow or dust" and it will still be covered for damage from other causes such as fire, lightening, aircraft, explosion, riot, civil commotion, malicious persons, impact or earthquake.

Ionising radiation.   This is usually excluded in substantially similar terms as   **26-121**
under CAR policies.[127]

Non-specific loss or damage.   This exclusion may also be known as a "mysteri-   **26-122**
ous loss" provision and excludes unexplained losses. A particular form of the exclusion may exclude

> "[p]roperty Insured found to be missing at stocktaking where the Insured is unable to prove the date and circumstances of any loss."

This provision was considered in *Widefree Ltd (t/a Abrahams & Ballard) v Brit Insurance Ltd*,[128] where the court held that "stocktaking" is not something that takes place every time property is searched for, but rather the process of making an examination and inventory of the stock in a shop or warehouse. This interpretation naturally limits when the exclusion will be engaged to a formal stocktake rather than in respect of any search. Notwithstanding this, the court decided the case on the basis that the insured had sufficiently proved the date and circumstances of the loss.

Pollution.   Insurers frequently exclude loss or damage caused by or resulting from   **26-123**
"pollution" or "contamination" from ARPI policies.[129]

Subsidence or collapse.   An ARPI policy will normally exclude subsidence and   **26-124**
collapse in respect of buildings. A typical clause will exclude "[s]ubsidence, ground heave or landslip; normal settlement and bedding down of new structures; or collapse".

   Most subsidence happens very slowly with foundation movement occurring over months or years. It is possible for subsidence damage to occur rapidly as a result of previous mining or the collapse of an underground void. The insured will usually be able to determine if property is at risk from a geographical survey. If an extension is obtained to cover subsidence there can be difficulties where the subsidence damage has resulted from a long-standing problem that has existed for longer than the particular insurer has been on risk for the insured building. The insured needs to ensure they bring a claim against the correct insurer for the relevant policy year.

---

[127] See above, paras 15-061 to 15-065.
[128] *Widefree Ltd (t/a Abrahams & Ballard) v Brit Insurance Ltd* [2009] EWHC 3671 (QB); [2010] 2 All E.R. (Comm) 477; [2011] Lloyd's Rep. I.R. 63.
[129] In the context of CAR, first party and third party liability claims see above, para.15-039 and paras 18-129 to 18-133.

26-125 War and terrorism. The various "war" exclusions are considered above in Ch.15.[130] Terrorism is mentioned above at para.15-047 and briefly touched upon in Ch.25.[131]

26-126 Frost or freezing/extremes of temperature. Damage from frost or freezing can take on many forms. Repetition of frost or freezing can cause wear and tear leading to gradual deterioration to buildings and windows and therefore insurers seek to exclude damage caused by it. Also, buildings that are empty are susceptible to damage from freezing because often the heating system is turned off when a building is empty. Freezing can cause pipes to crack and lead to water damage. Frost damage can also cause severe losses to farm crops. In addition to damage caused to property by frost/freezing or that interrupts business "extremes of temperature" causing such damage or interruption will also be excluded.

26-127 Flooding. Flooding[132] is usually covered by ARPI policies but if the property is located in a region that is particularly susceptible to flooding it can be excluded or is only insurable on payment of an additional premium. There has been some concern in the industry for a while that as the frequency and severity of flood event rises in the United Kingdom, flooding may become an uninsurable risk without government intervention. Insurers had to pay nearly £5 billion to households and businesses affected by flooding between 2000 and 2010.[133] More recently between 3 December 2015 and 3 January 2016, as a result of the bad weather (as at 3 February 2016) 22,000 claims for property damaged as a result of flooding of which more than 5,600 came from businesses were made. During that period the insurance industry also spent £21 million on emergency payments to homeowners and £49 million to businesses, with the average cost of a domestic property claim costing it £50,000. It is estimated that the total spend on customers for this period alone affected by flood damage will be around £1.3 billion.[134]

Up until 31 July 2013, there had been an official agreement between the Government and the insurance industry called the *Revised Statement of Principles on the Provision of Flood Insurance*,[135] which safeguarded flood cover in most cases, though not the cost of the premiums. The existing agreement expired but prior to this the Association of British Insurers ("ABI") proposed a new scheme to deal with flood insurance for properties at risk called the Flood Reinsurance Scheme ("Flood

---

[130] See above, paras 15-041 to 15-060.

[131] See above, para.25-043 and para. 25-052.

[132] For definition of "flood" see the propositions derived from authorities in *Tate Gallery Board of Trustees v Duffy Construction Ltd* [2007] EWHC 361 (TCC) at [37]; [2007] 1 All E.R. (Comm) 1004 at 1019; [2007] Lloyd's Rep. I.R. 758 at 769.

[133] Association of British Insurers, News Release "*Massive rise in Britain's flood damage bill highlights the need for more help for flood vulnerable communities says the ABI*" (February 2013) https://www.abi.org.uk/News/News-releases/2010/11/Massive-rise-in-Britains-flood-damage-bill-highlights-the-need-for-more-help-for-flood-vulnerable-communities-says-the-ABI [Accessed 3 June 2016].

[134] Association of British Insurers, ABI News Updates "*Winter Flooding 2015/16: The Story So Far*" (January 2011) https://www.abi.org.uk/News/News-updates/2016/01/Winter-flooding-2015-16-the-story-so-far [Accessed 20 May 2016].

[135] Department for Environment, Food and Rural Affairs "*Revised Statement of Principles on the Provision of Flood Insurance*" (Defra, July 2008). http://webarchive.nationalarchives.gov.uk/20130402151656/http://archive.defra.gov.uk/environment/flooding/documents/interim2/sop-insurance-agreement-080709.pdf [Accessed 3 June 2016]. There are separate Statements of Principles agreements for England, Wales, Scotland and Northern Ireland.

Re"). On 27 June 2013, the government and ABI agreed a memorandum of understanding on how the Flood Re scheme was going to be implemented.[136] The main purpose behind the scheme is to continue to make sure that flood insurance is affordable and available to all those that need it. Flood Re is a reinsurance company, and it allows insurers to insure themselves against losses incurred as a result of flooding. In order for this not-for-profit fund scheme, which is run by the insurance industry to be implemented it required government legislation.[137] On 4 April 2016 the new Flood Re scheme received regulatory approval from Prudential Regulation Authority and the Financial Conduct Authority following negotiations that took place between the insurance industry and government. The Flood Re scheme replaces the *Statement of Principles*[138] agreed in 2002 (later revised) to provide affordable flood insurance for people that own and live in properties located in flood risk areas. The scheme, which works with existing insurance companies, allows people to shop around for buildings and contents insurance, in the normal way so that they can find policies with more affordable premiums and excesses. When the flood risk part of the insurance policies climbs above a certain level, then the insurer places this part of the policy with Flood Re. A property built after 1 January 2009 or flats in leasehold blocks of more than four homes are not eligible for the scheme. When a customer makes a claim as a result of flooding, it is managed by the insurer in the normal way, except for the fact that, that insurer will then be able to recover those costs from Flood Re. The scheme does not apply to businesses.

7. GENERAL CONDITIONS

(a) Conditions precedent

In general. This section will consider common conditions precedent found in ARPI policies, which apply to both the property damage and BII sections of the policy. These are significant because what can seem to be a minor breach on the part of the insured can allow the insurer to escape liability.[139] The insurer does not have to show they have been prejudiced by the breach to rely upon the condition precedent. For policies governed by the 2015 Act an insurer will be unable to rely on conditions precedent to deny liability where breach is immaterial to loss suffered.[140] The various conditions precedent and terms and conditions are discussed below at paras 26-129 to 26-138 and 26-139 to 26-151 respectively.   **26-128**

Automatic-sprinkler installations. Where the insured property is protected by an automatic-sprinkler installation, it will likely be a condition precedent to the   **26-129**

---

[136] Association of British Insurers, *"ABI and Government agree Memorandum of Understanding on scheme to safeguard UK flood insurance"* (ABI, 27 June 2013). *https://www.abi.org.uk/News/News-releases/2013/06/ABI-and-Government-agree-Memorandum-of-Understanding-on-scheme-to-safeguard-UK-flood-insurance* [Accessed 3 June 2016].

[137] Flood Reinsurance (Scheme and Scheme Administrator Designation) Regulations (SI 2015/1875); Flood Reinsurance (Scheme Funding and Administration) Regulations (SI 2015/1902).

[138] See T. Edmonds, "Briefing Paper Number 06613, 4 April 2016 Household Flood Insurance" (House of Commons Library, 2014) pp.6–7. *http://researchbriefings.files.parliament.uk/documents/SN06613/SN06613.pdf.* [Accessed 3 June 2016].

[139] See above, paras 12-003 to 12-006 where the effect of a breach of a condition precedent is compared to warranties.

[140] For a fuller analysis see, paras 5-103 to 5-115.

insurer's liability that the insured has maintained the installation and tested the same at prescribed intervals. The insured will usually benefit from a premium discount if such a system has been installed.

26-130 **Sprinkler leakage.** The insured may be required to take additional precautions such as regular inspections before the insurer will be liable for damage caused by sprinkler leakage.

26-131 **Fire-extinguishing appliances.** As with an automatic-sprinkler installation, for fire-extinguishing appliances there will likely be a condition precedent that the insured properly maintains the appliances. The condition could simply read "the insured shall keep the fire-extinguishing appliances in working order during the period of insurance" or it may be more complex, setting out requirements for regular inspections, a written maintenance record, a training programme for the operation of the appliances and a documented register of all such training.

26-132 **Maintenance agreements.** Insurers may require the insured to warrant that the maintenance of any sprinkler systems, fire alarms and fire extinguishers is placed with an approved specialist contractor. It may further provide that any defect with the system will not invalidate the insurance, provided that the maintenance contract is in place. This condition is therefore in the interests of both the insurer and the insured, with the only disadvantage being the additional cost to the insured. Moreover, it gives the insurer a right of subrogated recovery if the contractor can be shown to be in breach of its maintenance contract.

26-133 **Hot works.** The insurer may include a requirement that certain precautions are to be taken during any hot work to lessen the risk of combustible materials being ignited.[141]

26-134 **Unoccupied or vacant premises.** The insured will usually be required to take additional precautions if any buildings within the insured property become unoccupied, vacant or disused for a period of 30 or more consecutive days. Such precautions may include turning off the mains services, removing all combustible materials not forming part of the fittings, securely boarding over any ground-floor windows and taking reasonable precautions to secure the buildings against unauthorised entry. It seems onerous but it is probably better to have such express conditions, as it makes clear the action required by the insured. Otherwise, the insurer may seek to rely on the "reasonable precautions" condition precedent discussed below at para.26-137 where neither party will have certainty over what precautions are "reasonable".

26-135 **Waste.** Trade refuse can pose a fire hazard. For this reason insurers may require as a condition precedent to its liability that waste and other trade refuse is kept in closed metal receptacles during work hours and removed from the premises daily. A standard condition may read:

"It is a condition precedent to liability that:

---

[141] Hot works is both an exclusion (i.e. no hot working allowed) and an extension (i.e. permitted but subject to an extension). See further above, paras 15-081 to 15-086 and para.17-039.

(a) all greasy cloths will be placed in lidded metal bins
(b) all trade waste be swept up and bagged daily following or by the end of the day's trading and removed to a secure waste disposal area or designated storage building pending removal from the premises."

In *Bennett (t/a Soho Pizzeria) v Axa Insurance Plc*,[142] Axa successfully relied on such a condition where a fire started in a waste bin at a pizza restaurant. Tomlinson J accepted a wide definition of trade waste as being "waste which has been generated in the ordinary course of trading from trade premises" and this could be just "one or more paper napkins".[143] There was an inescapable finding that the bin had within it a source of ignition and combustible material. The insured was in breach of the condition, the breach had increased the risk of fire and therefore the insured could not recover.

Intruder and fire alarm. A typical condition precedent may state: **26-136**

"It is a condition precedent to liability of the insurer that the insured will:

(a) Ensure the intruder and or fire alarm system is installed in accordance with the specification approved by the insurer and no alteration of variation or structural alteration of the premises which would affect the system will be made without the written consent of the insurer;
(b) Ensure that any system is inspected and maintained under the manufacturer's maintenance contract or otherwise approved by the insurer;
(c) Ensure that any system is in full and efficient working order;
(d) Ensure that the intruder alarm is fully set whenever the alarmed portion of the premises is closed for business or left unattended;
(e) Ensure that any alarm system is tested at least weekly;
(f) Ensure that all the available keyholders are notified to all the appropriate services."

The insurer may specify that the installer must be from official list of recognised firms of the National Approval Council for Security Systems ("NACOSS"). Furthermore, the insurer may state that the insurer will not be liable if the insured has received notice from his intruder or fire alarm company that maintenance is suspended or from a relevant authority that alarm signals will no longer be answered. The phrases "kept in efficient working order" and "kept in full operation" were examined by Woolf J in *Melik & Co v Norwich Union Fire Insurance Society*.[144] He held that the insertion of the word "kept" in both phrases implied within it a requirement that before there could be a breach of that condition by the insured they had to be aware of the facts, which gave rise to the alarm not being in efficient order or in full operation and had to be given the opportunity to have the alarm restored to efficient working order or full operation.

Reasonable precautions. ARPI policies will normally include a condition   **26-137**
precedent that the insured shall exercise reasonable care to protect the property from loss or damage.[145] In a property context, a failure to take reasonable precautions was upheld where an insured failed to activate his burglar alarm and use locks at the back for the property when going away for the weekend when he believed he was

---

[142] *Bennett (t/a Soho Pizzeria) v Axa Insurance Plc* [2003] EWHC 86 (Comm); [2004] Lloyd's Rep. I.R. 615.
[143] *Bennett* [2003] EWHC 86 (Comm) at [16]; [2004] Lloyd's Rep. I.R. 615 at 619.
[144] *Melik & Co v Norwich Union Fire Insurance Society* [1980] 1 Lloyd's Rep. 523.
[145] For a discussion about this clause in a CAR context, see above, paras 15-069 to 15-073.

being followed and the contents of the house were of high value,[146] or where a tenant had habitually stored large quantities of combustible materials and lit bonfires in close proximity to a property, where warnings had been given as to the obvious danger.[147]

26-138 **Maintenance.** The insurer will wish the insured to engage in maintenance of its property as a condition precedent to liability under the policy. As with regular checks of fire-hazard equipment, regular checks should be carried out on refrigeration where refrigeration is essential for storing materials and stock. It may be a condition precedent to a claim for loss of property from theft that intruder-alarm systems were sufficiently maintained.

Maintenance clauses are particularly useful to the insurer when it agrees to an insured buying back cover of an excluded peril. For instance, as a condition of allowing a manufacturer to buy back cover for breakdown or failure of electrical or mechanical equipment, the insurer will wish to insist on including a maintenance condition precedent that thorough maintenance checks are carried out, in order to reduce its own exposure to risk particularly under an ARPI policy that provides cover for both material damage and BII. The insurer will also require the insured to keep a proper record of the maintenance checks carried out in order to show that the maintenance procedure has been followed.

(b) Other terms and conditions

26-139 **Adjustment of premium.** Where the premium is provisionally based in whole or part on estimates provided by the insured, the insured is then obliged to keep accurate records and declare information required by the insurer such that the premium can be adjusted and any difference paid.

26-140 **Assignment.** An assignment of interest under the policy will not bind the insurer without their written consent.

26-141 **Cancellation.** Insurers will seek to reserve the right to serve written notice to cancel insurance at any time during the period of insurance. The notice period can be as short as 30 days. This could lead to difficulties for a landlord, who could quickly find himself in breach of an obligation to insure the property contained in a lease.

26-142 **Voidable.** Traditionally in ARPI policies there was often an express clause providing that the policy will be voidable in the event of misrepresentation, misdescription or non-disclosure of any material fact. It is likely that this would be interpreted as doing no more than stating the insurer's rights under ss.17–20 Marine Insurance Act 1906 ("MIA"), which codified the common law on duties of truthful representation and disclosure imposed on the insured.[148] The position has now changed for policies incepted after 12 August 2016 which will now be governed by

---

[146] *Gunns v Par Insurance Brokers* [1997] 1 Lloyd's Rep. 173.
[147] *Lambert v Keymood Ltd* [1999] Lloyd's Rep. I.R. 80 at 91–92; [1997] 2 E.G.L.R. 70 at 78; [1997] 43 E.G. 131 at 139.
[148] See further above, Ch.5.

the provisions of the 2015 Act, and any such terms may not be effective if they fail to meet the transparency requirement.[149]

Contribution.   A contribution provision will commonly set out that the insurer's   **26-143**
liability will be limited where there is other insurance covering the same risk or any part thereof. The insurer will not be liable for more than its rateable proportion. In the absence of such a clause the insured would be able to claim 100 per cent of the loss from the insurer, even if the same loss was insured with a second insurer, leaving the first insurer to seek a contribution from the second. The effect of this clause is, therefore, to place the burden of contribution on the insured, who can only seek a rateable proportion (i.e. no more than that insurer would be liable if all the other insurers were contributing to the insured at that time). It also puts the risk of insolvency of any of the co-insurers onto the insured.

Dispute resolution.   A dispute resolution clause may oblige the parties to medi-   **26-144**
ate or arbitrate a dispute before bringing a claim in the civil courts. If the parties are obliged to mediate, the clause should set out the procedure by which the parties are to enter into that mediation to avoid any uncertainty.

Fraud.   A standard clause may read: **26-145**

> "If the claim is in any respect fraudulent or if any fraudulent means or devices are used by the insured or anyone acting on their behalf to obtain any benefit under this policy or if any liability, loss, destruction or damage is occasioned by wilful act or with the connivance of the insured there will be no rights to any form of payment or indemnity under this policy."

This covers both fraudulent claims or devices and self-induced loss.[150]

Inspection and audit.   The insured may be required to allow the insurer to inspect   **26-146**
the property and operations at any time.

Material alteration.   This clause will usually state that the insurance will be void   **26-147**
or voidable if, after the commencement of the insurance, the risk of damage or interruption is increased by any act or omission of the insured, unless such change of circumstances has been expressly acknowledged and accepted in writing on behalf of the insurer. This has been considered above in the context of CAR,[151] where suspension of work may amount to a material alteration in the risk and thus ending the policy cover.

Even without such a clause, under the common law a contract of insurance is confined to particular risk insured and if the risk in respect of which a claim is made differs from that insured, the other party is not liable to make good that claim. An alteration would only be sufficient to void the policy if it is one that was not in contemplation of the parties at the time of the contract.[152] It needs to have changed

---

[149] See above Ch.5 generally and in particular para.5-135.
[150] The latter is dealt with above, at paras 10-016 to 10-026. For discussion on fraud, see generally above, Ch.6 and also para.21-045 (fraudulent claims. For the position under the Insurance Act (the "2015 Act") see above, paras 5-116 to 5-132.
[151] See above, paras 9-073 to 9-075.
[152] *Law Guarantee Trust & Accident Society v Munich Reinsurance Co* [1912] 1 Ch. 138 at 153–154, per Warrington J; 81 L.J. Ch. 188 at 197; 56 Sol Jo 108. An example of the application of this principle can be found in *Sillem v Thornton*; sub nom. *Augustus Sillem, Dredrich Heinrich*

the subject-matter, not just increased the danger. It is a matter of degree but insurers are generally not satisfied with this common law protection and instead prefer to insert a specific material alteration clause.

26-148 The wording of material alteration clauses has developed over time. Two cases in the 1970s and 1980s considered the following provision:

> "[T]his policy shall be avoided with respect to any item thereof in regard to which there be any alteration after the commencement of this insurance ... whereby the risk of destruction or damage is increased."

In *Farnham v Royal Insurance Co Ltd*[153] the court held that where the risk had been classified as "carriers and transit warehousing" and actually the insured was using the warehouse to repair metal containers with welding equipment, that there was an alteration, which increased the risk of damage. Whereas in *Exchange Theatre Ltd v Iron Trades Mutual Insurance Co Ltd*,[154] the court held that the policy was not avoided by virtue of the insured bringing onto the premises a petrol generator and a quantity of petrol in a plastic container, as the condition concerned the alteration of the subject matter and although an added hazard had been introduced this did not take away or alter the subject-matter of the insurance (i.e. the buildings). This in line with common law rules; whereby in *Farnham* the subject matter had changed, whereas in *Exchange Theatre Ltd* it was an increase in the risk of damage. The reflection of the common law position can also be seen in *Kausar v Eagle Star Insurance Co Ltd*,[155] where the relevant provision read:

> "You must tell us of any change of circumstances after the start of the insurance which increases the risk of injury or damage. You will not be insured under the policy until we have agreed in writing to accept the increased risk."

The court held that all this condition did was

> "to state the position as it would exist anyway as a matter of common law, namely that without the further agreement of the insurer, there would be no cover where the circumstances had so changed that it could properly be said by the insurers that the new situation was something which, on the true construction of the policy, they had not agreed to cover."[156]

But this interpretation depends on the construction of the clause. In *Ansari v New India Assurance Ltd*,[157] the condition stated:

> "This insurance shall cease to be in force if there is any material alteration to the Premises or Business or any material change in the facts stated in the Proposal Form or other facts supplied to the Insurer unless the Insurer agrees in writing to continue the insurance."

Gadechens, and Frederick Doenig v Richard Thornton (1854) 3 El. & Bl. 868; 23; L.J.Q.B 362; 18 Jur 748, where it was held that structurally increasing the insured building from two storeys to three after the commencement of the insurance did increase the risk and liability of the insurer, and thus breached the implied warranty.

[153] *Farnham v Royal Insurance Co Ltd* [1976] 2 Lloyd's Rep. 437.

[154] *Exchange Theatre Ltd v Iron Trades Mutual Insurance Co Ltd* [1984] 1 Lloyd's Rep. 149.

[155] *Kausar v Eagle Star Insurance Co Ltd* [1997] C.L.C. 129; [2000] Lloyd's Rep. I.R. 154; [1996] 5 Re. L.R. 191.

[156] *Kausar* [1997] C.L.C. 129 at 131; [2000] Lloyd's Rep. I.R. 154 at 156.

[157] *Ansari v New India Assurance Ltd* [2009] EWCA Civ 93 at [6]; [2009] 2 All E.R. (Comm) 926 at 928; [2009] Lloyd's Rep. I.R. 562 at 564–565. In this case the court held on the facts that the permanent disabling of the sprinkler system was a material change.

The condition was construed as concerning a change in facts *as referable to the proposal form* and in this regard it differed to the common law rule. But the Court of Appeal held that the materiality of that change had to be interpreted in line with the common law, that is, whether it is an alteration or change that takes the risk outside that which was in the reasonable contemplation of the parties at the time the policy was issued.

Representation.   The policy may provide that the insured is to act on behalf of all other insured parties. This is for the insurer's administrative convenience.   **26-149**

Subrogation waiver.   It is common for an ARPI to include subrogation waivers. These are discussed above in the context of CAR Policies at paras 20-062 to 20-063. In property insurance the common waivers sought are for: (i) associated companies; (ii) lender; and (iii) tenants. In respect of associate companies an insurer may agree to waive their rights, to which they might become entitled by subrogation, against, a parent, subsidiary or group company of the insured. Lenders will tend to request subrogation waivers in their favour but these are unnecessary if they are co-insured, as the insurer cannot exercise subrogation rights against a co-insured.[158] In relation to tenants, the position is slightly more complicated, as often they are not named as a co-insured and there is a reasonable risk that damage may be caused by their negligence. The ARPI may include an express waiver, whereby an insurer agrees to waive their rights against a tenant or lessee in respect of damage in their demise, or damage to common parts, usually subject to that damage arising out of criminal, fraudulent or malicious acts of the lessee or tenant. Under this clause a tenant would still be liable for damage to other tenants' portions of the property. Landlords may be obliged under the terms of the lease to negotiate specific wording of the subrogation waiver.   **26-150**

Even in the absence of an express waiver, the insurer may be prevented from pursing a subrogated action if the insured landlord is prevented from bringing an action against the tenant by the terms of the lease. The Court of Appeal in *Mark Rowlands Ltd v Berni Inns Ltd*[159] followed authority from the Supreme Court of Canada[160] and from the United States[161] and held that there can be a common intention under the terms of the lease that the insurance was to enure for the benefit of both the landlord and the tenant without recourse to the tenant, and therefore the landlord (and their insurers by subrogation) cannot maintain an action against the tenant in the event of damage caused by the tenant's negligence.

In the later case of *Lambert*,[162] Laws J held that the common intention does not arise on a bare covenant to insure and the circumstances that gave rise to the com-

---

[158] See *Petrofina (UK) Ltd v Magnaload Ltd* [1984] Q.B. 127 at 139–140; [1983] 3 W.L.R. 805 at 816; [1983] 3 All E.R. 35 at 44–45 and the position with co-insured sub-contractors above, at para.20-040.

[159] *Mark Rowlands Ltd* [1986] Q.B. 211; [1985] 3 W.L.R. 964; [1985] 3 All E.R. 473.

[160] *Greenwood Shopping Plaza Ltd v Neil J Buchanan Ltd* (1979) 31 N.S.R. (2d) 168; 52 A.P.R. 168; (1980) 99 D.L.R. (3d) 289.

[161] *General Mills Inc. v Goldman (Ind. Lubermans Mut. Ins. Co of Indianapolis, Ind., Intervener)* (1950) 184 F. 2d 359; *Fred A. Chapin Lumber Co v Lumber Bargains Inc.* 189 Cal.App.2d 613; 11 Cal.Rptr.634 (1961); *General Accident Fire & Life Assurance Corp. Ltd v Traders Furniture Co* Ariz.App.203; 401 P.2d 157 (1965); *New Hampshire Insurance Co v Fox Midwest Theatres Inc.* 203 Kan.720; 457 P.2d 133 (1969).

[162] *Lambert* [1999] Lloyd's Rep. I.R. 80; [1997] 2 E.G.L.R. 70; [1997] 43 E.G. 131.

mon intention in *Mark Rowlands Ltd* were: (i) an obligation for tenant to contribute to cost of insurance; (ii) a provision relieving the tenant from repairing obligations in the event of damage by an insured risk; and (iii) an obligation on the part of the landlord to reinstate in the event of such damage.

Even though tenants may fall within the scope of the *Mark Rowlands Ltd* case, express waivers are still important, particularly where a landlord is obliged under the lease to obtain one and it also creates certainty for the tenant. However, an insurer cannot assume they will be able to proceed with subrogated action against a tenant in the absence of an express subrogation waiver.

26-151   **Non-invalidation.**   A non-invalidation clause protects an insured or interested party against a breach of policy conditions of which they are unaware.[163] They are particularly useful for multi-let buildings. Mortgagees' or freeholders' protection clauses are variations of non-invalidation clauses, and may say the following:

> "[T]he interest of the freeholder lessor or mortgagee in this insurance shall not be prejudiced by any act or neglect whereby the risk of destruction or damage is increased without the authority or knowledge of the freeholder lessor or mortgagee provided they shall immediately on becoming aware thereof give notice in writing to the insurer and on demand pay such reasonable additional premium as the insurer may require."

The wording should reflect the appropriate parties covered. A multiple insured should protect all co-insured against a breach of condition by stating that the "any other party named" section in the schedule is applicable. It is important to examine the wording carefully to determine who is protected and against what, as it may not always include all breaches of warranty/condition precedent.

A non-invalidation clause will often increase the cost of a policy but it is usually worth the additional cost. The clause ensures that no act or omission that increases the risk of damage will invalidate the policy as long as that act of omission is unknown to the insured and the insured gives notice of it to the insurance company as soon as it becomes aware of it.

8.   CLAIMS HANDLING AND PROCEDURE

26-152   **Claims handling and procedure.**   Substantive discussion regarding claims handling and procedure and the law on this area generally can be found above in Ch.21. The points especially relevant to both the material damage and BII sections of the ARPI policy will now be discussed below in paras 26-153 to 26-155.

26-153   **Claim notification.**[164]   Notification of damage to property caused by an insured peril is usually required either immediately, within 7 days of the damage, or as soon as practical but in any event within 30 days of the damage. Usually, immediate notification is required to be given for damage or loss that has been caused by malicious persons, theft or attempted theft.

In respect of business interruption, the requirement is to notify whether there is or may be a claim, since it might not immediately be apparent whether the busi-

---

[163] For discussion in the context of CAR, see further above, para.12-033.
[164] This is discussed in the context of CAR. See above, paras 21-006 to 21-020.

ness will be interrupted.[165] Although policy stipulations may vary, the same time proviso may apply.

Insured's duties.[166] The insured may be required to take reasonably practicable **26-154** steps or measures to prevent further damage and minimise interruption to the business and to avoid or diminish loss. The insured will also be under other duties, for example, to act honestly in making a claim, to provide the insurer with assistance and documentation to enable the insurer to deal with the claim appropriately,[167] to preserve all evidence and not to offer payment or indemnity without the consent of the insurer. Breach of the various duties can lead to different consequences. If the insured fails to take reasonably practicable steps to minimise losses then they will not be able to recover such losses as could have been avoided had the steps been taken. In contrast, if an insured fails to act honestly in making the claim they risk forfeiting the right to recover in that claim. For a more detailed exposition of the insured's duties in relation to claims under CAR policies see Ch.21 above.

Burden of proof.   As with a claim under a CAR policy,[168] the burden of proof is **26-155** on the insured to prove their claim, and on the insurer to establish that an exclusion (if any) applies.

Claims procedure.   Claims will be overseen by the insurer. In relation to dam- **26-156** age to the property, the insured will be required to provide the insurer with full details in writing of the damage and the amount of damage together with details of any other insurance cover. This will usually have to be provided within 30 days after the damage is sustained.

In the context of the business interruption, written particulars of the consequential loss resulting from the damage will have to be given to the insurer within 30 days after the end of the indemnity period; that is, considered to be the end of the interruption. Information may already have been provided during the interruption for the purpose of obtaining the insurers consent to spend money to mitigate the interruption, and to request interim payments on account during the interruption. The insured will also have to deliver financial statements and other documents, proofs and information as may reasonably be required by the insurer for the purpose

---

[165] In *Loyaltrend Ltd* [2010] EWHC 425 (Comm) at [32]–[33]; [2010] Lloyd's Rep. I.R. 466 at 476 it was held that because the insurer (the defendant) had not been notified in a timely manner by the claimant as per the condition precedent on notice, the insured was therefore not entitled to claim on the policy. See above para.26-097.

[166] For discussion about the insured's duties in the context of CAR. See above, paras 21-027 to 21-047.

[167] In *Ted Baker Plc v Axa Insurance UK Plc* [2014] EWHC 3548 (Comm) at [27]; [2015] Lloyd's Rep. I.R. 325 at 333 (case under appeal) the court had to decide whether the clothing retailer had breached condition precedent 2(b)(i) by (i) failing to provide particulars of claim in writing within the time required; or (ii) in respect of condition precedent 2(b)(ii) by failing to provide information reasonably required by the insurer for the purpose of investigating or verifying the claim. The court concluded that the insured did not breach condition 2(b)(i) but that it was in breach of the claims cooperation condition 2(b) (ii) because it had failed to provide some additional financial information that the insurer reasonably required, in order to assess the claim. The decision confirms that an insured must supply the insurer with the requisite information at an early enough stage in order that it can investigate the claim properly and so that it can in turn set a reserve and notify its reinsurers if required.

[168] This is discussed in the context of CAR. See above, para.1-013 and paras 22-003 to 22-005.

of investigating and verifying the claim, and, if demanded, a statutory declaration of truth, confirming the insured's understanding of the facts.

26-157   **Claims conditions precedent.**   There will usually be a condition precedent stating that due compliance with all the terms of the claims conditions section of the policy will be condition precedent to the insurer's liability for a claim.

PRECEDENTS

1. CAR PROJECT POLICY WORDING ILLUSTRATION

A sample CAR project policy is provided in this appendix so as to give an il- **A-001**
lustration of the standard clauses used in CAR policies. The policy is not designed
to be a policy to meet all needs, being instead intended to demonstrate the types of
clauses that are in common use in insurance policies. Parties should obtain advice
to ensure that any policy reflects the intention of the parties. The sample policy is
divided into the following sections:

- The preamble
- The schedule
- General definitions
- Section 1: Construction "All Risks"
- Section 2: public liability
- Section 3: consequential loss
- General exclusions
- General conditions

2. THE PREAMBLE

Preamble

WHEREAS the Insured has applied to the Insurers for the insurance hereinafter **A-002**
contained and has paid or agreed to pay premium as consideration for such
insurance.

NOW THIS POLICY WITNESSETH that in respect of events occurring during
the Period of insurance and subject to the terms and exceptions and conditions
herein or endorsed hereon the Insurers will provide Insurance in the manner and to
the extent specified hereinafter.

3. THE SCHEDULE[1]

(a) Sample schedule

Schedule

INSURERS:	[..........]	**A-003**
POLICY NUMBER:	[..........]	
THE INSURED:	[..........]	
THE BUSINESS:	[..........]	
THE BUILDING CONTRACT:	[..........]	
THE PERIOD OF INSURANCE:	*[Initial Period of Insurance*	

---

[1]   See Ch.3.

From [insert date] until the Implementation Date [insert date] followed by the whole period of the Project, estimated to be [X months] with effect from the Implementation Date or other date to be agreed by Leading Underwriter only, until the date of taking over stated in the Statement of Practical Completion of the last phase or section of the Works to be undertaken in connection with the Project, and automatically held covered for further periods if required at additional premium to be agreed by Leading Insurer only (but not exceeding pro rata) followed by:

Defects Liability Period of Insurance

The period commencing from the date of expiry of the Initial Period of Insurance and expiring in respect of each phase or section of the Works to be undertaken in connection with the Project [X] months from the date of its taking over as stated in its Statement of Practical Completion.]

INTEREST: *[Section 1: ALL RISKS*

Item 1—The Contract Works

Works, temporary works, materials, plant, machinery, spares, and all other property or equipment of whatsoever nature or description (but excluding Construction, Equipment and Temporary Buildings as defined in the policy wording) the property of the Insured or for which they may be responsible at the site of The Project or elsewhere in the territorial limits whilst in off-site storage and in transit between the sites of the off-site storage and the site of the Project all in connection with the Project.

Estimated Contract Value £[X]

Item 2—Existing Properties and Contents

Any existing structures and/or contents retained on site by the Insured that are to be worked upon, and/or that are to be retained on the site of the Project during any part of the Period of Insurance, and for which the Employer is responsible or has agreed or is required to insure, including but not limited to the properties listed in Schedule 1 hereof.

Item 3— Completed Properties and Contents

Any property or properties (including their contents) that have been completed under The Construction Contract during the Period of Insurance, and for which the Employer is responsible or has agreed or is required to insure including but not limited to the properties listed in Schedule 1 hereof.

Item 4—Construction Equipment and Temporary Buildings and Contents

Construction Equipment and Temporary Buildings and contents thereof owned or hired in by [The Contractor] or loaned to them or for which they are responsible.

Section 2: PUBLIC LIABILITY

Section 3: *CONSEQUENTIAL LOSS (DELAY IN COMPLE-
TION AND BUSINESS INTERRUPTION)*
Loss of Anticipated Insured Rent and/or Loss of Insured
Rent.]

SUMS INSURED: *[Section 1: £X*

Section 2: £X

Section 3: £X]

LIMITS   OF *[Section 1: ALL RISKS*
INDEMNITY:

    (a) £X any one loss any one contract or development site
on contract works temporary works materials plant and
equipment for incorporation therein (including free issue materials).

    (b) £X any one site on constructional plant, equipment,
hired in plant, temporary building and contents and all
other things brought onto site for purposes of the
contract.

    (c) £X any one employee in respect of tools and personal
effects.

Section 2: PUBLIC LIABILITY

£X

Section 3: CONSEQUENTIAL LOSS

£X]

THE TERRITO- [Are as follows:
RIAL LIMITS

    (a) In respect of Sections 1 and 2: Anywhere in Europe

    (b) In respect of Section 2: Anywhere in the World in
respect of commercial visits by Directors or Employees
normally resident in the Territories stated in 1 above.

    (c) In respect of Section 3: Great Britain.

PROVIDED THAT the action for damages is brought
against the Insured in a Court of Law within the European
Economic Area.]

EXCESSES: *[Section 1: ALL RISKS*

    •   in respect of Employees personal effects and tools

    •   each and every loss in respect of DE4

    •   each and every loss

Section 2: PUBLIC LIABILITY

    •   each and every claim in respect of third party
property damage.

Section 3: CONSEQUENTIAL LOSS

    •   days in all in respect of Delay in Completion in respect
of each

THE   [...............]
PREMIUM:

DATED in   [...............]   the [..........] day..........].
                                                   of[...............

4. GENERAL DEFINITIONS

Occurrence

A-004   Wherever the word Occurrence appears in the Policy it shall mean each and every occurrence or series of occurrences consequent upon or attributable to one source or original cause.

The Insured Property

A-005   All permanent and temporary works, preliminary works (including associated works and project site mobilisation) executed or in the course of execution, including materials, goods, parts, excavations, spare parts, inventory, consumables and all other things, equipment of whatsoever nature used for or intended to be used in the Project, and including electricity, gas and water connections, all designs, drawings, specifications and plans to be provided, together with computer and building services equipment, all other parts or units or equipment, plant and machinery of whatever nature the property of the Insured or for which they are responsible (other than contractor's or subcontractor's constructional plant and equipment except plant and equipment forming part of or intended to form part of the temporary and/or permanent works) while on or adjacent to the Project Site or elsewhere within the Territorial Limits, and all associated and ancillary works connected therewith built, constructed, erected, supplied, installed, repaired, revised or otherwise, tested, commissioned and brought into full operation, and including project management and other similar costs of the insured or others.

   Materials shall include all raw and shaped materials, including catalysts, as well as finished parts, units, installations, machinery, constructions and/or property of every kind and description and/or parts, units installations, machinery. Constructions and/or other property of every kind and description in the course of construction and/or whilst being otherwise worked upon.

Definition of Terms

A-006   For the purpose of this insurance each of the following terms shall have the meaning defined in the Building Contract:—
   Practical Completion, Phase 1 Works, Main Works, Works.

Construction Equipment

A-007   Construction Equipment shall mean all appliances or things of whatsoever nature required for the performance of the Works and the remedying of any defects therein but not including plant and materials or other things intended to form or forming part of the Works as defined in the Contract. For the avoidance of doubt Construction Equipment shall include but not be limited to [insert description], not being part of the permanent or Temporary Works.

Temporary Buildings

A-008   Temporary Buildings shall mean offices, workshops, warehouses, accommodation, campsites and any other buildings situated on or about or in the vicinity of the Site and which are to be used in connection with the Project.

Temporary Works

Temporary Works shall mean all temporary works of every kind required in or about the execution of maintenance of the Works but does not include materials or other things intended to form or forming part of the permanent Works as defined in the Contract.

A-009

Site

The actual place or places to which the Insured Property is to be delivered or where work is to be done by the Insured together with so much of the area surrounding the said places or places as the Insured shall actually use in connection with the Contract or Project or subcontracts and shall include offsite storage. This definition shall also include any place or places defined as the Site or Sites in the Contract or any building or premises used by the Insured in connection with the Project.

A-010

Construction and/or Erection Period

The Construction and/or Erection Period shall mean and be limited to that period from commencement of work at the site or any operation provided for under The Contract whichever shall first occur and terminating with the completion of all construction and/or assembly and/or erection work and all mechanical electrical hydrostatic and/or pneumatic testing incidental thereto or expiry of the period of time specified in the Schedule or the commencement of Operational Testing whichever shall first occur.

A-011

Employee

Employee shall mean
(a) Any person under a contract of service or apprenticeship with the Insured.
(b) In connection with the Business while working for the Insured any:
    (i) Person under a contract of service or apprenticeship with some other employer and who is hired to or borrowed by the Insured.
    (ii) Labour master or person supplied by him.
    (iii) Labour only subcontractor or person engaged by him.
    (iv) Self-employed person performing work under a similar degree of control and direction by the Insured as a person under a contract of service or apprenticeship with the Insured.
    (v) Driver or operator of hired-in-plant.
    (vi) Person engaged under the Manpower Commission Schemes or any similar Government sponsored agency.

A-012

Damage

Damage means loss, destruction or damage.

A-013

Personal Injury

Personal Injury shall mean bodily injury, death, disease, illness, disability, mental injury, mental anguish, shock, false arrest, discrimination, invasion of rights of privacy, detention, false imprisonment, false eviction, malicious prosecution, libel, slander and defamation of character, unintentional breach or infringement or unauthorised use of Intellectual Property Rights.

A-014

Operational Testing Period

The Operational Testing Period shall mean and be limited to that period beginning either with the introduction into the Insured Property of feedstock or other

A-015

materials for processing or handling or the commencement of supply to a system and terminating on expiry of the period of time specified in the Schedule or when the property is taken over or taken into use by the Purchaser or Principal whichever shall first occur.

Pollution and Contamination

A-016   For the purposes of this policy, Pollution or Contamination shall be deemed to mean:

    (a) All Pollution or Contamination of buildings or other structures or of water or land or the atmosphere; and

    (b) All loss or damage or injury directly or indirectly caused by such Pollution or Contamination.

Territorial Limits

A-017   Territorial Limits shall mean the Contract Site and elsewhere in [name of country] for the purposes of the Contract.

Great Britain

A-018   Means England and Wales and Scotland but not the territorial seas adjacent thereto (as defined by the Territorial Sea Act 1987) nor the Isle of Man nor the Channel Islands.

Terrorism

A-019   Terrorism shall mean:

    (a) Any action or threat of action of any person acting on behalf of or in connection with any organisation with activities directed towards the overthrowing or influencing of any government de jure or de facto of any nation or any political division thereof, or in pursuit of political, religious, ideological, or similar purposes to intimidate the public or a section of the public of any nation by any person or group(s) of persons whether acting alone or on behalf of or in connection with any organisation(s) or government(s) de jure or de facto, and which:

       (i) involves violence against one or more persons; or

       (ii) involves Damage; or

       (iii) endangers life other than that of the person committing the action; or

       (iv) creates a risk to health or safety of the public or a section of the public; or

       (v) is designed to interfere with or to disrupt an electronic system.

    (b) Any action in controlling, preventing, suppressing, retaliating against or responding to any act, or preparation in respect of any action, or threat of action described in (a) above.

Limits of Indemnity

A-020   The total liability of the Insurers shall not exceed the Limits of Indemnity shown in the Schedule and any payment or payments by Insurers to any one or more of the insured parties shall reduce to the extent of that payment the liability of the Insurers to all such parties.

5.   SECTION 1: CONSTRUCTION "ALL RISKS"[2]

Section 1

"The Insurers will, subject to the conditions and exclusions hereinafter   **A-021**
contained, indemnify the Insured against:"

SECTION 1—"ALL RISKS"
RISKS COVERED
Physical loss of and/or damage of whatsoever nature sustained during the Period
of Insurance to:

(a)   The works, whether permanent or temporary, materials incorporated or for
incorporation therein (including free issue materials) and any other property
of whatsoever nature other than property insured by item (b) below, the
property of the Insured or for which the Insured are responsible whilst
anywhere within the Territorial Limits, including all transits therein (other
than transits by sea or air) in respect of any contract or work undertaken
whether such contract or work was commenced during the Period of Insurance or otherwise, including liability arising under any maintenance or
defects liability provisions of such contract or work.

(b)   Contractors plant tools and equipment, demountable and temporary buildings and/or caravans, and/or other items of a like nature and materials and/or
stores and/or any other property of whatsoever nature, other than property
insured by item (a) above, for use in connection therewith the property of
the Insured or for which the Insured are responsible whilst anywhere within
the Territorial Limits including all transits therein (other than transits by sea
or air) and at any of the Insured's own premises.

The Insurers' liability under this Section in respect of each and every loss any
one contract or development site shall not exceed the Limit of Indemnity stated in
the Schedule.

The Insurers shall not be liable for the amount of the Excess as stated in the
Schedule.

(a)   Exclusions to Section 1[3]

Exclusions to Section 1

No indemnity is provided hereunder in respect of: **A-022**

1.   Consequential loss, loss of use, liquidated damages, penalties for delay or
non-completion.

2.   Loss of or damage to:
  (a)   Aircraft
  (b)   Waterborne craft other than safety boats, non-self-propelled craft or
    other craft up to 20 feet in length whilst on or about the contract site.

3.   Loss of or damage to any vehicle constructed for the carriage of persons or
goods unless on or about the site of a contract insured.

4.   Loss of or damage to and the cost necessary to replace, repair or rectify:
  (a)   any component part or individual item of the Property Insured,
    which is defective in design plan specification materials or
    workmanship;

---

[2]   See Ch.3.
[3]   See Chs 15 and 16.

[845]

     (b)   property insured lost or damaged to enable the replacement repair or rectification of Property insured excluded by (a) above.

Exclusion (a) above shall not apply to other parts or items of Property Insured which are free from defect but are damaged in consequence thereof;

     (c)   any part of any item of contractor's plant or vehicle due to its own breakdown or derangement but this exclusion shall not be deemed to apply in respect of damage to other parts of such item arising as a consequence of such breakdown or derangement.

For the purposes of the Policy and not merely this Exclusion the Property Insured shall not be regarded as lost or damaged solely by virtue of the existence of any defect in design plan specification materials or workmanship in the Property Insured or any part thereof.

5.   Stock and materials in trade (except as provided under Risks Covered) whilst at any premises owned, leased or rented by the Insured other than property allocated for incorporation in specific works being or to be carried out by the Insured away from such premises.

6.   Loss of or damage to cash, notes, postal and/or money orders, cheques, stamps or negotiable instruments of whatsoever nature or other securities for money.

7.   Loss of any property by disappearance or by shortage if such disappearance or shortage is revealed only after the making of a periodic inventory.

8.   Normal upkeep or making good.

9.   Wasting, wearing away or wearing out or gradual deterioration but this exclusion shall not apply to damage to any part of Insured Property free of such defect.

10.   Loss or damage consisting of or caused by any form of corrosion or erosion howsoever the same may arise but this exclusion shall not apply to damage to any other part of the Insured Property free from any corrosion or erosion which is otherwise insured by this Policy.

11.   Loss of or damage to any part of the Insured Property under item 1

     (a)   After such part has been taken into use or occupation other than in performance of the contract by the Purchaser, Principal, Owner, Tenant or occupier; or

     (b)   For which a certificate of completion has been issued.

         Other than

         (i)   Arising during the Maintenance Period from a cause which occurred on site during the Construction Erection/Testing Period

        (ii)   Where loss or damage is caused by the Contractor whilst complying with the terms of any Maintenance Period or Defects Liability Period clause incorporated into the Contract.

(b) Memoranda to Section 1[4]

Defects Liability

A-023   Subject otherwise to the terms, exclusions and conditions contained herein or endorsed hereon, this Policy extends to the Defects Liability Period specified in the Schedule to cover Damage:

    (a) Caused by the contractor(s) in the course of the operations carried out for

---

4   See Ch.17.

the purpose of complying with their obligations under the defects liability and warranty provisions of the [X] Contract.

(b) Occurring during the Defects Liability Period provided that such Damage was caused at the Project Site during the Period of Insurance and prior to the Provisional Acceptance Date as defined in the [X] Contract.

Marine/Non-marine Loss Sharing (also known as a 50/50 clause)

Where separate marine insurance has been effected by the Insured it is agreed **A-024** that in the event of loss of or damage to the Insured Property due to a peril insured against being discovered after the risk has terminated under the marine insurance and, if, after proper investigation, it is not possible to ascertain whether the cause of such loss or damage happened prior to the termination of the marine venture or subsequently, it is understood and agreed that the Insurers hereon shall contribute 50 per cent of the properly adjusted claim, such contribution to be without prejudice to subsequent final appointment of the claim as may be agreed between the Insurers hereon and the marine insurers in the light of the terms and conditions of the respective policies.

Hired-in Constructional Plant

Section 1 of this Policy is extended to indemnify the Insured in respect of their **A-025** legal liability for the payment of hiring charges in respect of Plant hired in by the Insured whilst such Plant is out of use following loss or damage for which an indemnity is provided by Section 1 of this Policy (or which would be provided thereunder but for the application of the Policy Excess).

The indemnity provided by this Memorandum will:

(a) be limited to:
  (i) hiring charges incurred during the period of [X] months following such loss or damage; or
  (ii) GPB [X];
  whichever is the less;
(b) exclude the first [X] days following loss or damage;
(c) be provided notwithstanding that the hiring of plant may be between two parties included in "the Insured" under this Policy.

Professional Fees

The insurance by this Section shall indemnify the Insured in addition to the Sum **A-026** Insured stated in the Schedule for an amount not exceeding [X per cent] of the Sum Insured stated in the Schedule in respect of professional fees necessarily incurred in the reinstatement of the Insured Property consequent upon its loss or damage.

Expediting Expenses

The insurance by this Section of the Policy extends to include an amount not **A-027** exceeding £[X] any one Occurrence in addition to the Sum Insured in respect of such extra charges as overtime work, night work on public holidays, costs incurred in the provision of extra plant test equipment and the like and express freight, including air freight, provided that such extra charges are incurred in connection with any loss of or damage to the Insured Property for which indemnity is granted under this Policy.

Debris Removal

The indemnity by this Section includes in addition to the Sum Insured stated in **A-028** the Schedule an amount not exceeding £[X] in respect of costs and expenses necessarily incurred by the Insured with the consent of the Insurers for:

(a) removal and disposal of debris;

(b) dismantling or demolishing of any part of the Insured Property;

(c) shoring, propping or protecting the Insured Property whether damaged or not;

(d) clearing or repairing drains or service mains insofar as such drains or mains form part of the Insured Property;

(e) Dewatering and dehumidifying the Insured Property;

(f) The removal and/or clearing up of mud, silt and materials foreign to the Insured Property introduced to the site of the Insured Property as a result of an insured peril.

Seventy-two Hour Clause

A-029 It is agreed that any loss or damage to the Insured Property arising during any one period of seventy-two consecutive hours, caused by storm, typhoon, tempest, flood or earthquake, shall be deemed a single event and therefore to constitute one occurrence with regard to the Excesses provided herein. For the purposes of the foregoing the commencement of any such seventy-two hour period shall be decided at the discretion of Insured it being understood and agreed, however, that there shall be no overlapping in any two or more such seventy-two hour periods in the event of damage occurring over a more extended period of time.

Series Losses

A-030 If the development or discovery of a defect in the contract works shall indicate or suggest that a similar defect shall exist in other parts of such property the Insured shall as soon as reasonably practicable investigate and if necessary rectify the defect in such property at his own expense or alternatively bear all losses arising out of such defect.

Automatic Reinstatement

A-031 In the event of loss or damage in respect of which payment is made by the Insurers the insurance hereunder shall be maintained in force for the Limit of Indemnity in consideration of the Insured having agreed to pay an appropriate reinstatement premium on the amount of the loss which premium shall be disregarded for the purpose of any adjustment of premium under Condition [X] of this Policy. Furthermore it is understood and agreed such additional premium is not recoverable as indemnity under any Section of this Policy.

Contract Price Increase

A-032 If the final price of the contract exceeds the Sum Insured the amount stated in the Schedule then the Sum Insured shall be increased proportionately to a figure not exceeding 125 per cent of the Sum Insured.

Cost Escalation

A-033 If during the Period of Insurance the actual reinstatement value of the Insured Property under item 1 of the Contract Works of the Schedule shall be in excess of the original Limit of Indemnity in this respect then this limit shall be deemed to be increased by the amount of such excess but not exceeding in all [X] per cent of the Limit of Indemnity stated in the Schedule.

[848]

Immobilisation of Plant and Equipment

In the event of constructional plant and/or equipment which is not more specifi- **A-034** cally insured becoming unintentionally immobilised in any physical situation on or about the site of any insured contract the necessarily incurred cost of recovery and/or withdrawal shall be deemed to be "damage" within the meaning of Section 1 of this Policy.

No indemnity shall be provided hereunder in these circumstances in respect of the cost of rectifying electrical and/or mechanical breakdown or derangement where such is the sole requirement necessary to effect the said recovery or withdrawal.

Construction Equipment during Defects Liability Period

Insurers will indemnify the Insured for loss or damage to Construction Equip- **A-035** ment and other property not comprising the permanent works which was insured under this Section of the Policy during the Initial Period of Insurance and where such loss or damage occurs during the first three months of the Defects Liability Period of Insurance pending its removal from the Site.

Insurers will also indemnify the Insured for loss or damage to such property for any other period during which it may be used or reasonably required by the Insured during the Defects Liability Period of Insurance for the purpose of complying with his obligations under the Contract(s).

Principals and Other Interests

This Policy extends to include: **A-036**

(a) The interest of any Principal or Contractor or Subcontractor in respect of any contract to which this Policy applies but only to the extent to which that interest is required to be insured jointly with that of the Insured by the terms of any contract entered into between the Principal or Contractor and the Insured.

(b) The interest of any Funder or Financier of the Insured is noted under this Policy and/or added under this Policy as a named insured if required.

(c) The interest of any landlord from whom the Insured is renting or leasing property is noted under this Policy

(d) The interest of any tenant, subtenant or occupier of any Insured Property, and/or their mortgagees or lenders, but only to the extent that such interest is required to be included under the terms of any of the Leases in connection with the Project or in connection with any mortgage or loan entered into by such tenant, subtenant or occupier.

Provided always that any party mentioned in (a), (b), (c) and (d) above shall act as though they were the Insured observe fulfil and be subject to the terms conditions exceptions and endorsements of the Policy.

European Community Local Authorities Reinstatement

The cover provided by Section 1 of this Policy is extended to include such ad- **A-037** ditional costs of reinstatement of the property insured lost or damaged as may be incurred solely by reason of the necessity to comply with European Union Legislation Statutory Building and/or other Building and/or other Regulations under or framed in pursuance of any Act of Parliament or with Bye-Laws of any Municipal or Local Authority or any change by the Secretary of State to regulations with or without an Act of Parliament or the Insurers requirements to replace the automatic sprinkler installation in accordance with the current LPC Sprinkler Rules or any change in interpretation of existing regulations provided that:

a) The amount recoverable under this Memorandum shall not include:

    1. the cost incurred in complying with any of the aforesaid Regulations or Bye-Laws

        (i) in respect of loss or damage not insured by this Policy;

        (ii) under which notice has been served on the Insured prior to the occurrence of the loss or damage;

        (iii) in respect of undamaged property or undamaged portions of property other than foundations of the portion of the property lost or damaged.

    2. the amount of any rate, tax, duty, development or other charge or assessment arising out of capital appreciation which may be payable in respect of the property by the owner thereof by reason of compliance with any of the aforesaid Regulations or Bye-Laws.

(b) The work or reinstatement must be commenced and carried out with reasonable despatch and may be carried out wholly or partially upon another site subject to the liability of the Insurers under this Memorandum not being thereby increased.

(c) The total amount recoverable hereunder shall not exceed the Sum Insured shown in the Schedule.

Free Issue Materials

A-038   The Insured Property shall include all materials supplied free to the Project by any Principal and/or his agents provided that the value of such items shall be included within the declaration of Estimated Value of Construction Contract(s) for the purposes of adjustment of the premium.

Plans, Specifications, etc

A-039   Notwithstanding anything herein contained to the contrary the insurance hereby is extended to indemnify the Insured against costs and expenses necessarily and reasonably incurred to reproduce such plans, documents and records relevant to the Project including all the information therein destroyed or damaged as a result of an insured event hereunder.

Employees' Personal Effects and Tools

A-040   At the request of the Insured the Insurers will indemnify under Section 1 any:

(a) Employee of the Insured;

(b) Clerk of Works, Resident Engineer or his employee;

as if he were the Insured in respect of loss of or damage to tools, clothing and personal effects whilst on or about any contract site or the Insured's premises or elsewhere in the Territorial Limits subject to Insurers' liability being limited to the sum of £[X] any one person.

Increased or Additional Cost of Working

A-041   Subject to Policy conditions Exceptions and limitations the Insurers shall indemnify the Insured in respect of the additional costs necessarily and reasonably incurred for the sole purpose of preventing or minimising the interruption of or the interference with the carrying out of the contract in the event of delay in completion of the contract due solely to loss or damage to any of the Insured Property for which liability has been admitted under this Section or would have been admitted but for the contracted responsibility of the Principal or the application of the deductible.

Provided that the liability of the Insurers under this extension shall not exceed £[X] However the Insurers shall not be liable for the first [X] per cent of each and every claim (subject to a minimum of £[X]).

This extension does not include any amount:

(a) Which would have been incurred irrespective of whether the loss destruction or damage had occurred;

(b) Solely to expedite the completion of the contract or any part thereof at an earlier date than would have been attained had the said loss or damage not occurred.

Increased Cost of Constructing Incomplete or Unbuilt Works (inflation)

The Insurers shall indemnify the Insured in the event of delay in completion of **A-042** the Contract or any part thereof due solely to loss or damage to the permanent or temporary works for which liability has been admitted under Section 1 of the Policy (or would have been admitted but for the application of the deductible) against the additional amount by which the cost of the permanent or temporary works uncommenced at the date of the loss or damage shall exceed the cost which would have been incurred but for the loss or damage.

Provided that such additional amount shall solely relate to the effect of inflation on the cost of materials usage of plant and labour and shall not exceed £[X] however the Insurers shall not be liable for the first 10 per cent of each and every claim (subject to a minimum of £X).

This Extension does not include any amount:

(a) Which would have been incurred irrespective of whether the loss or damage had occurred;

(b) Solely to expedite the completion of the contract or any part thereof at an earlier date than would have been attained had the said loss and damage not occurred;

(c) Incurred in redesigning altering adding to or improving permanent or temporary works of rectification of defects or faults or elimination of any deficiencies carried out after the occurrence or any increase in costs as a result of such redesigning alteration addition or improvement;

(d) Resulting from any delay due to the inability of the Insured to provide sufficient funds for the repair or replacement of the permanent or temporary works suffering loss or damage;

(e) In respect of any:

   (i) Additional insurance premiums;

   (ii) Head office management expenses and/or overheads of any kind whatsoever;

   (iii) Constructional plant and equipment and labour idle time costs;

   (iv) Additional finance charges or legal expenses;

   (v) Any change from the works programme which would otherwise have occurred had it not been for the loss or damage.

(f) Arising from or in respect of any other consequential losses not specifically provided for herein;

(g) Incurred which is specified elsewhere in this Policy,

All subject otherwise to the terms, conditions and exceptions of this Policy.

Joint Code of Practice

In respect of all contracts or work whose estimated value (including free issue **A-043** materials) exceeds £[X] the Insured undertakes to comply with the Joint Code of

Practice on the Protection from Fire of Construction Sites and Buildings Undergoing Renovation Fifth Edition dated January 2006 ("the Joint Code") or any subsequent edition thereof.

The appointed representative of Insurers shall have the right at all reasonable times to enter and inspect any such contract sites for the purpose of ensuring that the conditions of such sites or work in all respects comply with the Joint Code.

For the purpose of paragraph 6.3 of the Joint Code any building site including those where demolition, alterations, fitting out, renovations, refurbishment or repair work is carried out whose estimated value (including free issue materials) exceeds £[X] shall be deemed to be a "Large Project".

In the event of a breach of the Joint Code the Insurers may inform the Employer and the Insured's site management of the nature of the breach and may specify the required remedial measures (the Remedial Measures) and the reasonable period of time in which such Remedial Measures are to be completed. If the Insured should fail to complete such Remedial Measures within the specified time the Insurers may confirm the same by notice in writing given by actual delivery or by registered post or by recorded delivery to both the Employer and the Insured at their respective addresses nominated by the Insured at the inception of cover or as otherwise subsequently amended.

Such notice shall at the discretion of the Insurers either suspend or cancel the Insurance under Section 1 of this Policy from the date named in the notice which shall not be less than 30 days from the date of delivery of such notice it being understood the Insurance may be reinstated with effect from the date on which the Insurers are satisfied that the Remedial Measures have been completed.

This Memorandum shall not in itself be considered a condition precedent to liability but its inclusion shall not prejudice waive or remove the rights of the Insurer or Insured under the terms, exceptions and conditions of Section 1 of this Policy.

6.   SECTION 2: PUBLIC LIABILITY[5]

Section 2

SECTION 2—PUBLIC LIABILITY
RISKS COVERED

A-044   All sums of which the Insured may become legally liable to pay (including claimant's costs and expenses) in respect of:
   (a)   Accidental death of or bodily injury to or disease contracted by any person;
   (b)   Accidental loss of or damage to material property;
   (c)   Accidental obstruction or trespass, loss of amenities or nuisance, stoppage of or interference with road, rail, air or waterborne traffic;
occurring during the Period of Insurance within the Territorial Limits in connection with any contract or work undertaken by the Insured or otherwise in connection with the Insured's Business (including such liability assumed under contract or agreement).

---

[5]   See Ch.18.

Insurers' liability under this Section shall not exceed the Limit of Indemnity stated in the schedule in respect of each and every occurrence and/or series of occurrences arising out of any one event.

Other Costs and Expenses

In addition Insurers will pay all costs, charges and expenses incurred with their consent: **A-045**
(a)   In the defence and settlement of any claim;
(b)   For representation of the Insured at any Coroner's Inquest or Fatal Accident Enquiry or for the defence in any Court of Summary Jurisdiction of any proceedings arising out of any event which may become the subject of a claim under this Policy.

The Insurers will not be liable for the amount of the Excess as stated in the Schedule.

Indemnity to Other Persons

The indemnity provided by this section will also apply: **A-046**
(a)   At the request of the Insured:
    (i)   To any owner from whom the Insured have hired contractor's plant or equipment;
    (ii)   To any director or partner of the Insured or any Employee in respect of liability for which the Insured would have been entitled to indemnify under this Section if the claim had been made against the Insured; and
    (iii)   To any officer or member of the Insured's canteen, social, sports or welfare organisations or ambulance, first aid, fire, medical or security services in his/her respective capacity as such.
(b)   In the event of the death of the Insured, to any personal representative in respect of liability incurred by the Insured.

Provided that such parties will observe, fulfil and be subject to the terms, provisions, exceptions, and conditions of this Policy so far as they can apply.

(a)   Exclusions to Section 2

Employees

No indemnity is provided hereunder for liability: **A-047**
In respect of death, bodily injury, illness or disease sustained by any Employee as defined in the Policy arising out of and in the course of their employment or engagement by the Insured in the Business.

Property in Charge or in Control

No indemnity is provided hereunder for liability: For loss of or damage to   **A-048**
property in the care, custody or control of the Insured (or liability to the owner or user thereof in consequence of such loss or damage) other than:
(a)   Land, buildings or other structures (and the fixtures, fittings and contents thereof and appertaining thereto) in the Insured's care, custody or control for the purpose of carrying out any contract or work therein or thereupon;
(b)   Premises leased or rented by or loaned to the Insured but the Insurers shall not be liable in respect of liability attaching by virtue of any agreement which would not have attached in the absence of such agreement;
(c)   Parked motor vehicles of the Insured's employees or of subcontractor's employees or of visitors; or

[853]

(d) Any goods being lifted or lowered by any crane or other lifting apparatus used by the insured not being property for which the Insurance is provided under Section 1 but Insurers' liability shall not exceed £[X] in respect of each and every occurrence.

Vehicles, Vessel or Craft

A-049 No indemnity is provided hereunder for liability
(a) Arising out of the ownership, possession or use under the control of the Insured of:
    (i) Aircraft; or
    (ii) Waterborne craft other than safety boats, non-self propelled craft or other craft up to 7 metres in length on or about the contract site.
(b) Arising out of the ownership possession or use under the control of the Insured or any mechanically propelled vehicle whilst such vehicle is subject to the provisions of any Road Traffic Act.
Provided that nothing in this exclusion shall be deemed to exclude liability:
(a) For damage to any bridge and/or weighbridge and/or viaduct and/or road and/or other property and/or anything beneath by vibration and/or by the weight of such vehicle.
(b) Arising out of the use of any such vehicle as a tool of trade or whilst such vehicle is in or on that part of any commercial or military airport or airfield provided for:
    (i) The take off or landing of aircraft or the movement of aircraft on the ground;
    (ii) Aircraft parking, including any associated service roads, refuelling areas, ground equipment parking areas, aprons, maintenance areas and hangers.
(c) Arising out of the condition of any road or highway brought about by the use of such vehicle.
But nonetheless, the Insurers shall not be liable for liability compulsorily insurable under the provisions of the Road Traffic Act.

Contract Works

A-050 For loss or damage to Insured Property which forms or has formed any part of or is to be incorporated into permanent or temporary works executed in performance of the Contract occurring:
(a) Before the date of issue of a form of certificate of completion in accordance the terms of the contract or agreement.
(b) After the date of issue of a form of certificate of completion in accordance with the terms of the contract or agreement and in respect of which the Contractor is expressly responsible under the terms of the Contract or agreement.

JCT cl.6.5 (formerly JCT cl.21.2.1)

A-051 For loss or damage to property to the extent that the Contractor is required to effect insurance under the terms of clause 6.5 (2011 Edition) of the Standard Form of Building Contract issued by the Joint Contracts Tribunal or of any other contract condition incorporating a similar requirement.

Advice/Design

No indemnity is provided hereunder for liability:

For professional advice design or specification given by the Insured for a separate fee however, this exclusion shall not apply to bodily injury.

A-052

Defective Work and Costs of Repair

No indemnity is provided hereunder for liability: For the cost of making good faulty or defective design workmanship or materials but this exclusion shall be limited to the faulty or defective part and shall not apply to loss or damage arising in consequence thereof.

A-053

Fines/Liquidated Damages

(a) Liability in respect of pre-determined penalties or liquidated damages imposed under any contract entered into by the Insured for the performance of the Project except to the extent that liability would have attached even in the absence of such contractual penalties or liquidated damages;

(b) Fines incurred by the insured.

A-054

Non-Performance and Non-Completion

For the non-performance, non-completion or delay in completion of any contract.

A-055

Inevitable Loss or Damage

Liability for loss of or damage to property which is foreseeable as being inevitable having regard to the nature of the work undertaken or operations bringing it about.

A-056

Pollution or Contamination

No indemnity is provided hereunder for liability.

Which arises directly or indirectly from Pollution or Contamination unless such Pollution or Contamination is caused by a sudden identifiable unintended and unexpected incident which takes place in its entirety at a specific time and place during the Period of Insurance.

All Pollution or Contamination which arises out of one incident shall be deemed to have occurred at the time such incident takes place.

The liability of the Insurers for all incidents of Pollution or Contamination which occur during the Period of Insurance shall not exceed in the aggregate the Limit of Indemnity specified in the Schedule.

A-057

Libel or Slander

In respect of libel, slander, defamation of character, slander of title to goods or other injurious falsehood.

A-058

Intellectual Property Rights

For the purpose of this Section of the policy, Intellectual Property Rights shall mean confidential information, trade secrets, trademarks (including trademarks protected by common law rights or passing off), patent rights, copyrights, design rights (registered or unregistered) moral rights, data base rights, copyright title or slogan and/or as defined in the Construction Contract.

A-059

(b)   Memoranda to Section 2

Cross-Liability Clause

A-060   Each of the parties comprising the Insured shall for the purpose of this Section be considered as a separate and distinct party and the words "the Insured" shall be considered as applying to each party in the same manner as if a separate Policy had been issued to each of the said parties and the Insurers hereby agree to waive all rights of subrogation or action which they may have or acquire against any of the aforesaid parties arising out of any Occurrence in respect of which any claim is made hereunder provided nevertheless that nothing in this Section shall be deemed to increase the Limit of Indemnity in respect of any one Occurrence or series of Occurrences as stated in the Schedule.

Health and Safety at Work

A-061   Under Section 2 of this Policy the Insurers shall indemnify the Insured and at the request of the Insured any Director or Employee of the Insured against:

(a)   The legal fees or expenses incurred with the Insurers written consent in defending any such party;

(b)   Prosecution costs which such party may be ordered to pay by a Court;

(c)   Compensation awards arising out of Health and Safety Executive prosecutions;

In respect of a prosecution for manslaughter and/or under the Health and Safety at Work etc. Act 1974 or any amending or subsequent legislation or any other Health and Safety legislation or regulations including, inter alia, the CDM Regulations for an offence committed during the Period of Insurance arising in the course of the Business irrespective of whether death, bodily injury, illness or disease or loss of or damage to property has been caused.

Provided that:

(i)   the indemnity shall not apply in respect of any fines or penalties;

(ii)   the conduct and control of the defence is vested in the Insurers;

(iii)   the director or Employee shall—as though he were the Insured—observe, fulfil and be subject to the terms exclusions conditions and endorsements of this Policy so far as they can apply;

(iv)   the director or Employee shall advise the Insurers immediately of any summons or other process served upon him and of any impending prosecution of which he has knowledge;

(v)   in the event of any dispute arising between the Insured or a director or Employee and the Insurers as to whether a prosecution should be defended or an appeal made such dispute shall be referred to a Queen's Counsel as arbitrator to be mutually agreed between the Insured, the director or Employee and the Insurers (or failing agreement to be nominated by the President of the Law Society) whose decision shall be final.

Consumer Protection and Food Safety Acts

A-062   The Insurers will indemnify the Insured and at the Insured's request, any director or partner of the Insured any Employee against legal costs and expenses incurred, with the Insurers consent, in the defence of any proceedings brought for a breach of:

(a)   Part II of the Consumer Protection Act 1987; or

(b)   Part II of the Food Safety Act 1990;

committed or alleged to have been committed in the course of the Insured's business during the Period of Insurance, including legal costs and expenses incurred in an appeal against conviction arising from such proceedings.

This extension does not cover:

(i) Legal costs and expenses where an indemnity is provided by any other insurance;

(ii) Proceedings arising out of any deliberate act or omission by the Insured; or

(iii) The payment of fines or penalties.

Defective Premises Act 1972

The indemnity provided by this Section shall extend to include liability arising   **A-063**
under Section 3 of the Defective Premises Act 1972 in respect of the disposal of any premises which were occupied or owned by the Insured as a place of business.

Provided that the Insurers shall not be liable for the cost of remedying any defect or alleged defect in such premises.

Motor Contingent Liability

The Insurers will indemnify the Insured in respect of Personal Injury or loss of   **A-064**
or damage to property arising out of the use of any motor vehicle:

a) not owned or leased by the Insured being used in connection with the Project;

(b) owned or leased by the Insured being used by any person in circumstances unauthorised by the Insured.

Provided that the Insurers will not be liable:

(i) in respect of loss of or damage to any such vehicle;

(ii) if the Insured is entitled to indemnify under any other insurance except in respect of any amounts in excess of the limits applying under such insurance.

Data Protection Act

This policy shall indemnify the Insured (and at the request of the Insured any   **A-065**
director or Employee of the Insured) against all sums which the Insured becomes legally liable to pay in respect of:

(a) compensation for damage or distress under Section 13 of the Data protection Act 1998 or any amendment thereto including defence costs and expenses;

(b) defence costs relating to a prosecution brought under Section 60 of that Act or any amendment thereto in relation to a claim made by any person.

Provided that:

1. the claim is first made against the Insured during the Period of Insurance;
2. the Insured having registered in accordance with the terms of the Act;
3. this Memorandum shall not apply in respect of:
   (i) the payment of fines or penalties;
   (ii) the cost of replacing reinstating rectifying or erasing any personal data;
   (iii) liability caused by or arising from a deliberate or intentional act by of the Insured or any other party entitled to an indemnity by this Insurance the effect of which will knowingly result in liability under the Data Protection Act 1998 or any amendment thereto;
   (iv) claims which arise out of circumstances notified to previous Insurers or are known to the Insured at inception of this Insurance; or

(v) liability for which indemnity is provided under any other Insurance;

4. the insurers shall not be liable for 10 per cent of each and every claim subject to a minimum contribution of £[X] each and every claim; and

5. the Insurers' liability in respect of any one claim and in the aggregate in respect of any one period of Insurance shall not exceed £[X].

7. SECTION 3: CONSEQUENTIAL LOSS[6]

Section 3: Delay in Completion Insurance and Business Interruption

A-066   If at any time during the Period Insurance as stated in the Schedule or any extension thereof any of the Insured Property suffers Damage as defined herein and in consequence thereof:

1. its Insured Rent Date is delayed beyond its Scheduled Insured Rent Date (hereinafter referred to as Delay in Completion); or

2. in respect of Damage to Existing Property where such Damage causes the Insured Business to be interrupted or interfered with (hereinafter referred to as Business Interruption); or

3. in respect of Damage to Completed Property occurring after its Insured Rent Date where such Damage causes the Insured Business to be interrupted or interfered with (hereinafter referred to as Business Interruption);

the insurers will indemnify the Insured for the amount of loss resulting from such Delay in Completion or Business Interruption in accordance with the provisions of the Policy. The amount payable as indemnity hereunder shall be:

(i) The amount of the Insured Rent due during the Indemnity Period which shall in consequence of the Damage fall below the Anticipated Insured Rent; or

(ii) The amount of the Increased Cost of Working incurred by the Insured during the Indemnity Period in consequence of Damage; and

(iii) Additional expenditure necessarily and reasonably incurred for the sole purpose of avoiding or diminishing the reduction in the Insured Rent or avoiding the Increased Cost of Working which, without such expenditure, would have taken place during the Indemnity Period, but not exceeding the amount of the reduction in Insured Rent thereby avoided or diminished or the amount of Increased Cost of Working thereby avoided,

less any sum saved during the Indemnity Period as may cease or be reduced in consequence of Damage.

If any amount is received by the Insured in respect of liquidated damages for delay during the Indemnity Period it is understood and agreed that such amount of liquidated damages shall be applied to reduce the Insured's overall loss attributable to the circumstances leading to the payment of such liquidated damages even if the amount of such loss is greater than the sum insured hereunder.

Any amount of liquidated damages received subsequent to a loss settlement under this Policy shall be applied as if recovered or received prior to such settlement and all necessary adjustments shall then be made between the Insured and the Insurer, provided always that nothing in this Policy shall be construed to mean that losses under this Policy are not payable until the Insured's ultimate net loss has been finally ascertained.

---

[6]   See Chs 17 and 26.

In addition to the foregoing the Insured shall be entitled to retain the amount of any liquidated damages for delay it shall receive from any contractor, subcontractor or supplier equivalent to the amount of the Time Excess applicable to this Section 2.

In the event of loss indemnifiable under this Section of the policy, the Sum Insured hereunder shall notwithstanding be automatically reinstated and maintained in force during the period of insurance.

(a) Definitions applicable to Section 3

Indemnity Period

In the case of Delay in completion to any Unit forming part of the Project that **A-067** has not achieved its Scheduled Insured Rent Date the period commencing on the date of its Scheduled Insured Rent Date and ending when the Insured Business ceases to be affected in consequence of the Damage but not exceeding the Indemnity Period Limit stated in the Schedule herein in respect of any one occurrence (and subject always to exhaustion of the Sum Insured stated in the Schedule).

In the case of Business Interruption to the Insured Business the period commencing on the date of the Damage and ending when the Insured Business ceases to be interrupted or interfered with but not exceeding the Indemnity Period Limit stated in the Schedule herein in respect of any one occurrence (and subject always to exhaustion of the Sum Insured stated in the Schedule).

Insured Rent

Insured Rent shall mean: **A-068**
- In respect of Delay in Completion—the Initial Rent and/or the Basic Rent as defined in the various Agreements to Lease and Leases.
- In respect of Business Interruption—the Initial Rent and/or the Basic Rent and/or the Insurance Rent and/or the Service Charge all as defined in the various Agreements to Lease and the Leases all derived from the Insured Business.

Anticipated Insured Rent

Anticipated Insured Rent shall mean the Insured Rent expected to be paid or **A-069** expected to be payable to the Insured derived from the Insured Business as specified in the Section 3 Sums Insured Schedule.

Increased Cost of Working

Increased Cost of Working shall mean all costs and expenses of whatsoever **A-070** nature or description which the Insured shall incur in connection with the Insured Business, consequent upon Delay in Completion or Business Interruption arising as a result of Damage and which the Insured would not have incurred or would not have incurred to the same extent had no such Delay in Completion or Business Interruption occurred.

8.   GENERAL EXCLUSIONS[7]

General Exclusions

A-071   The Indemnity provided by this policy shall not apply to or include:

Radioactivity

A-072   Loss or destruction of or damage to any property or any loss or expense whatsoever resulting or arising therefrom or any consequential loss or legal liability of whatsoever nature arising directly or indirectly caused by or contributed to by or arising from:

(a)   Ionising radiations or contamination by radioactivity from any nuclear fuel or from any nuclear waste from the combustion of nuclear fuel;

(b)   The radioactive toxic explosive or other hazardous properties of any explosive nuclear assembly or nuclear component thereof.

War

A-073   Loss, damage or liability directly or indirectly occasioned by happening through or in consequence of war, invasion, acts of foreign enemies, hostilities (whether war be declared or not), civil war, rebellion, revolution, insurrection, military or usurped power or confiscation, commandeering, requisition or destruction or damage by order of any Government de jure or de facto or by any public authority.

Notwithstanding this war exclusion clause, this Insurance shall cover loss or damage:

(a)   caused by missiles and/or mines and/or bombs and/or other explosives not discovered at the moment of commencement of the work on any part of the project insured hereunder, so long as no state of war exists in the country where the subject matter will be erected is involved;

(b)   caused by strikes, locked-out workmen or persons taking part in labour disturbances, riots or civil commotion or persons acting maliciously.

Terrorism

A-074   Notwithstanding anything contained in this Policy to the contrary, this Policy does not cover loss or destruction of or damage to:

(a)   any property in Great Britain by fire or explosion occasioned by or happening through or in consequence directly or indirectly of Terrorism except to the extent stated below in the Special Provision (Terrorism);

(b)   any property in Northern Ireland or loss resulting therefrom occasioned by or happening through or in consequence directly or indirectly of:

(i)   civil commotion;

(ii)   Terrorism.

In any action, suit or other proceedings where the Insurers allege that by reason of this definition any Damage is not covered by this Policy (or is covered only up to a specified limit of liability or sum insured) the burden of proving such Damage is covered (or is covered beyond that specified limit of liability or sum insured) shall be upon the Insured.

Special Provision (Terrorism)

A-075   Subject otherwise to the terms, definitions, exclusions, provisions and conditions of the Policy, this insurance includes Damage in England and Wales and

---

[7]   See Ch.15.

Scotland but not the territorial waters adjacent thereto as defined by the Territorial Sea Act 1987 by fire or explosion occasioned by or happening through or in consequence of Terrorism as defined in this Exclusion.

Provided that the liability of the Insurers in respect of such Damage shall not exceed in respect of any one occurrence:

[insert limits]

Any provision in this policy which provides for any sum insured or limit of liability to be automatically reinstated following a loss shall not apply to losses covered under this Special Provision.

Sonic Bangs

Loss destruction or damage directly occasioned by pressure waves caused by aircraft and other aerial devices travelling at sonic or supersonic speeds.   **A-076**

Nuclear Risks

Performance of any contract in or on any nuclear installation or any nuclear installation site.   **A-077**

Contract Conditions

This provision would only apply to a policy arranged for a contractor for his own benefit.   **A-078**

Any loss or damage which under the terms and conditions of contract is the responsibility of the Purchaser of Principal or any party to a contract other than the Contractor.

Computer Data Recognition

Loss or damage directly or indirectly caused by or consisting of or arising from the failure of any computer or other equipment or system for processing storing or retrieving data whether the property of the Insured or not.   **A-079**

9. GENERAL CONDITIONS[8]

General Conditions

The General Conditions incorporated into this policy are as follows: **A-080**

Interpretation

This Policy and Schedule shall be read together as one contract. Any word or expression to which a specific meaning has been attached in any part of this Policy or of the Schedule shall bear such meaning wherever it may appear.   **A-081**

Observation of Policy Terms

The Liability of the Insurers shall be conditional on the due observance and fulfilment by the Insured of the terms, provisions, conditions and endorsements of this Policy and the truth of the statements and answers in the information provided shall be conditions precedent to any liability of the Insurers to make any payment under this policy.   **A-082**

---

[8]   See Ch.21.

Policy Voidable

A-083   This Policy shall be voidable in the event of misrepresentation, misdescription or non-disclosure in any material particular.

Termination

A-084   Termination:
In the event of:
(a)   Termination of the Contract by the Purchaser or Principal or the contractor;
(b)   Withdrawal from the Contract by the Insured Contractor; or
(c)   Total cessation of work occasioned by any cause other than (a) and (b) above for a period of three consecutive months;
cover provided by this Policy shall be terminated unless its continuance be admitted by endorsement signed by the Insurers.

This condition shall not affect settlement of any claim or claims which occurred before the date of termination.

Claims Procedure

A-085   Claim Procedure:
The Insured shall upon becoming aware of any circumstances giving rise or likely to give rise to a claim under this Policy:
(a)   Give notice to Insurers through the Brokers as soon as possible and at their own expense supply full particulars and information and afford such assistance as Insurers may reasonably require;
(b)   Give notice to in the case of theft or wilful damage to the Police and render to them all reasonable assistance;
(c)   Send to Insurers immediately on receipt any writ summons or other proceedings which may be commenced against the Insured.
In the event of a claim being made against the Insured for which the Insured may seek indemnity under this Policy the Insured shall not negotiate pay settle admit or repudiate such claims without the written consent of the Insurers.

Insurers' Rights in the Event of a Claim

A-086   Insurers' Rights in the Event of a Claim.
In the event of a claim arising for which the Insurers shall be liable under this Policy Insurers shall be entitled:
(a)   To undertake in the name of and on behalf of the Insured the absolute conduct and control of any proceedings and the settlement of the same;
(b)   To take proceedings at their own expense and for their own benefit but in the name of the Insured to recover compensation or secure any indemnity from any Third Party in respect of anything covered by this Policy;
(c)   To pay to the Insured in respect of any claim or claims the maximum liability of the Insurers as stated in the applicable Schedule of this Policy or such lesser sum for which the said claim or claims can be settled (subject to deduction in either case of any such sum or sums already paid on account of such claim or claims) and thereafter the Insurers shall be under no further liability in respect of said claim or claims except for the payment of costs and expenses incurred prior to the date of such payment and for which the Insurers may be liable hereunder.

Basis of Claims Settlement

Basis of Claims Settlement.   **A-087**
In settlement of claims under Section 1 of this Policy Insurers shall, subject to
the terms and conditions of the Policy, indemnify the Insured on the basis of the full
cost of repairing, reinstating or replacing property lost or damaged even though such
costs may vary from the original construction costs and shall include all taxes and
import duties even if they have been varied or imposed subsequent to the inception of the Policy.

In the calculation of the costs of restoration or replacement of the Works or the
existing structures, those elements of cost for which provision is made in the
computation of the Sum Insured and such other costs and expenses for which
specific provision is made in this Policy will be taken into account and in the case
of repairs or replacement made by the Insured, the Insured shall be entitled to charge
an amount for overheads and profit equivalent to that included in the original
contract price.

The cost of restoration or replacement of Construction Equipment shall not
exceed fair market value except in the case of hired in plant where the Insured shall
be indemnified for the amount which they are contractually liable for under the
terms of the hire agreement.

Fraudulent Claims

If the Insured shall make any claim knowing the same to be false or fraudulent   **A-088**
as regards amount or otherwise this Policy shall become void and all claims
hereunder shall be forfeited.

Other Insurance

The Insurers shall not be liable for loss or damage which is or would but for the   **A-089**
existence of this Policy be insured by any other policy, except in respect of any
excess beyond that amount that would have been payable under such policy or policies had this insurance not been effected.

If such other insurance be subject to any contribution condition of advantage to
such other insurers this Policy shall be subject to such condition in a like manner
and in no case shall the Insurers be liable for more than their rateable proportion
of any loss or damage covered by such other insurance.

Other non-contribution or primary insurance clauses may also be encountered in
a policy.

Primary Insurance

It is expressly agreed that this insurance provides the primary cover for risks   **A-090**
insured hereunder and in the event that any such risk which is insured hereunder
is also insured under any other Policy of insurance effected by the Insured or any
party comprising the Insured, the Insurers agree to indemnify the Insured as if such
other Policy of insurance did not exist.

Access and Inspection

The Insurers or their representatives shall have the right at all reasonable times   **A-091**
to visit the Contract Site and to Inspect and examine the Insured Property.

Precautions

The Insured shall take and cause to be taken all reasonable precautions for the   **A-092**
safety of persons and property at to prevent injury or loss or damage. In the event

of an occurrence giving rise or which may give rise to a claim under this Policy, the Insured shall at their own expense take such immediate action as is necessary to minimise any loss and prevent repetition.

Alternatively, the clause may be drafted in the following way:

It shall be a condition precedent to any liability of the Insurers to make any payment under this Policy that the Insured shall at their own expense take reasonable precautions:

    (a)   For the safety of the Property Insured;

    (b)   To prevent accidents and shall take reasonable steps to comply with all statutory obligations bearing upon this insurance and to maintain their ways works machinery plant and Premises in good order and repair;

    (c)   In the selection of employees;

    (d)   To remedy any defect or danger upon discovery thereof and take such additional precautions as the circumstances may require; and

    (e)   To prevent any circumstances arising or to cease any activity which may give rise to liability under this Policy.

Change in Circumstances

A-093   If any change shall occur materially varying any of the circumstances disclosed to or known to the Insurers the Insured shall as soon as reasonably practical be given notice of such change with full particulars thereof and the Insurers shall have the right to vary the terms of the Policy.

Discharge of Liability

A-094   The Insurers may in the event of any occurrence resulting in any claim(s) under the Public Liability Section of this Policy pay to the Insured the Limit of Indemnity for such occurrence (but deducting such sum or sums already paid as damages in respect of such occurrence) or any lesser amount for which the claim(s) can be settled and the Insurers shall thereafter be under no further liability in respect of such occurrence except for costs and expenses incurred prior to the date of the payment.

Contractual Liability

A-095   In respect of liability assumed by the Insured by agreement and which would not have attached in the absence of such agreement the indemnity provided by Section 2 of the Policy is subject to:

    (a)   the conduct and control of the claims being invested in the Insurers; and

    (b)   the terms, exclusions, conditions and limits of Section 2.

Premium Adjustment

A-096   If the premium for this Policy is based wholly or in part on estimates furnished by the Insured then the Insured shall as soon as possible after the expiration of the Period of Insurance furnish such information as the Insurers may reasonably require to adjust the premium accordingly.

Arbitration

A-097   If any difference shall arise as to the amount to be paid under Section 1 of this Policy (liability being otherwise admitted), such difference shall be referred to an Arbitrator to be appointed by the parties in accordance with the statutory provision in that behalf for the time being in force. Where any difference is by this condition to be referred to arbitration the making of an award shall be a condition precedent to any right of action against the Insurers.

Disputes

The Insured and the Insurers agree that this Policy shall be solely governed and construed in accordance with English Law. Each party agrees to submit to the jurisdiction of a court of competent jurisdiction within England. **A-098**

Contracts (Rights of Third Parties) Act 1999

This contract does not, and is not intended to, confer or create any right enforceable under the Contracts (Rights of Third Parties) Act 1999 by any person who is not a party to the contract; and the parties to this contract reserve the right to amend or rescind the contract without giving notice to, or requiring the consent of, any third party. **A-099**

INDEX